THE FUTURE OF BUSINESS

> Millennium Edition <

> **Larry J. Gitman**
San Diego State University

> **Carl McDaniel**
University of Texas, Arlington

South-Western College Publishing
Thomson Learning™

Australia • Canada • Denmark • Japan • Mexico • New Zealand • Philippines
Puerto Rico • Singapore • South Africa • Spain • United Kingdom • United States

The Future of Business, Millennium Edition by Larry J. Gitman &
Carl McDaniel

Acquisitions Editor: Dave Shaut
Developmental Editor: Mary Draper, Draper Development
Executive Marketing Director: Steve Scoble
Production Editor: Kara ZumBahlen
Manufacturing Coordinator: Sandee Milewski
Internal Design: Michael H. Stratton
Internal Icons: Lewis Agrell
Cover Design: Michael H. Stratton
Cover Photographs: Photonica/Ron Rovtar; Photo Disk, Inc.; and Joe Higgins
Photo Research: Feldman & Associates, Inc.
Photo Manager: Cary Benbow
Production House: Pre-Press Company, Inc. Compositor: Pre-Press Company, Inc.
Printer: Courier Kendallville INC.

Printed in the United States of America
1   2   3   4   5   05   04   03   02   01

For more information contact South-Western College Publishing,
5101 Madison Road, Cincinnati, Ohio, 45227 or find us on the Internet at
http://www.swcollege.com

For permission to use material from this text or product, contact us by
• **telephone: 1-800-730-2214**
• **fax: 1-800-730-2215**
• **web:** http://www.thomsonrights.com

Library of Congress Cataloging-in-Publication Data
Gitman, Lawrence J.
    The future of business/Larry J. Gitman, Carl McDaniel.—3rd ed.
        p. cm.
    Rev. ed. of: The world of business. 2nd ed. ©1995.
    Includes bibliographical references and index.
    ISBN 0-324-01571-2 (hc : alk. paper)
      1. Management—United States. 2. Marketing—United States. 3. Business
enterprises—United States—Finance. 4. Accounting—United States. 5.
Business—Data processing. I. McDaniel, Carl D. II. Gitman, Lawrence J. World
of business III. Title.

HD70.U5 G53 2000
650—dc21
Soft Cover Edition ISBN 0-324-15490-9   99-048395

This book is printed on acid-free paper.

>PART 1   THE BUSINESS ENVIRONMENT

>**1**   Your Future in Business Begins Now   1
APPENDIX: Getting Your Career Off on the Right Track   26
>**2**   Understanding Evolving Economic Systems and Competition   34
>**3**   Competing in the Global Marketplace   64
>**4**   Making Ethical Decisions and Managing a Socially Responsible Business   98
APPENDIX: Understanding the Legal and Tax Environment   125

>PART 2   BUSINESS OWNERSHIP

>**5**   Forms of Business Ownership   136
>**6**   Entrepreneurship: Starting and Managing Your Own Business   168
Careers in Small Business   200

>PART 3   BUSINESS MANAGEMENT

>**7**   Management and Leadership in Today's Organization   202
>**8**   Designing Organizational Structures   228
>**9**   Managing Human Resources   259
>**10**   Motivating Employees and Creating Self-managed Teams   286
>**11**   Understanding Labor-Management Relations   314
>**12**   Achieving World-class Operations Management   344
Careers in Management   376

>PART 4   MARKETING MANAGEMENT

>**13**   Understanding the Customer and Creating Goods and Services that Satisfy   380
>**14**   Developing Quality Products at the Right Price   410
>**15**   Distributing Products in a Timely and Efficient Manner   442
>**16**   Using Integrated Marketing Communications to Promote Products   470
Careers in Marketing   497

>PART 5   TECHNOLOGY AND INFORMATION

>**17**   Using Technology to Manage Information   500
>**18**   Using the Internet for Business Success   532
>**19**   Using Financial Information and Accounting   566
Careers in Technology and Managing Information   595

>PART 6   FINANCE

>**20**   Understanding Money and Financial Institutions   600
>**21**   Financial Management   620
>**22**   Understanding Securities and Securities Markets   646
>**23**   Managing Your Personal Finances   678
APPENDIX: Managing Risk and Insurance   708
Careers in Finance   714

iii

34

contents

PREFACE xxiii

>PART 1 THE BUSINESS ENVIRONMENT

>1 YOUR FUTURE IN BUSINESS BEGINS NOW 1

Section 1
Business in the 21st Century 2
THE NATURE OF BUSINESS 2
Not-for-Profit Organizations 3 Factors
of Production: The Building Blocks of
Business 3

Section 2
Capitalizing on Trends in Business 6
SOCIAL TRENDS 7
The Growth of Component Lifestyles 7
The Changing Role of Families and
Working Women 8
DEMOGRAPHIC TRENDS 8
Generation Y—Born to Shop 8
Generation X—Savvy and Cynical 9
Baby Boomers—America's Mass Market 9
Older Consumers—Not Just Grand-
parents 10 Americans on the Move 10
Growing Ethnic Markets 11
EVOLVING GLOBAL ECONOMIC
SYSTEMS 11
Capitalism 11 The Command
Economy 12 Socialism 13 Mixed
Economic Systems 13
TECHNOLOGICAL TRENDS 13
TRENDS IN GLOBAL COMPETITION 15
Technology and Communications 15
Improvements in Productivity 17
Global Quality Standards 18

Section 3
Applying This Chapter's Topics 19
THE TALENT WAR AMONG
EMPLOYERS 19
Choosing the Right Job for You 20

SUMMARY OF LEARNING GOALS 21
PREPARING FOR TOMORROW'S
WORKPLACE 23
WORKING THE NET 23
CREATIVE THINKING CASE 24
VIDEO CASE 24
APPENDIX 1: GETTING YOUR CAREER
OFF ON THE RIGHT TRACK 26

>2 UNDERSTANDING EVOLVING ECONOMIC
SYSTEMS AND COMPETITION 34

Section 1
Business in the 21st Century 36
HOW BUSINESSES AND ECONOMIES
WORK 36

Macroeconomics and Microeconomics 37
Economics as a Circular Flow 37
MACROECONOMICS: THE BIG
PICTURE 38
Striving for Economic Growth 39
Keeping People on the Job 40 Keeping
Prices Steady 41
ACHIEVING MACROECONOMIC
GOALS 42
Monetary Policy 42 Fiscal Policy 43
MICROECONOMICS: ZEROING IN ON
BUSINESSES AND CONSUMERS 46
The Nature of Demand 46 The Nature
of Supply 47 How Demand and Supply
Interact to Determine Prices 47
COMPETING IN A FREE MARKET 49
Perfect Competition 50 Pure
Monopoly 50 Monopolistic
Competition 51 Oligopoly 52

Section 2
Capitalizing on Trends in Business 52
Delivering Value and Quality 52
Creating Long-Term Relation-
ships 54 Creating a Competitive
Workforce 55 Entrepreneurial Spirit in
Former Command Economies 55

Section 3
Applying This Chapter's Topics 57
SUMMARY OF LEARNING GOALS 58
PREPARING FOR TOMORROW'S
WORKPLACE 60
WORKING THE NET 60
CREATIVE THINKING CASE 61
VIDEO CASE 62

>3 COMPETING IN THE GLOBAL
MARKETPLACE 64

Section 1
Business in the 21st Century 66
AMERICA GOES GLOBAL 66
The Importance of Global Business to the
United States 67
MEASURING TRADE BETWEEN
NATIONS 67
Exports and Imports 67 Balance of
Trade 68 Balance of Payments 68
The Changing Value of Currencies 69
WHY NATIONS TRADE 70
Absolute Advantage 70 Comparative
Advantage 70
BARRIERS TO TRADE 70
Natural Barriers 71 Tariff Barriers 72
Nontariff Barriers 73
FOSTERING GLOBAL TRADE 74
Antidumping Laws 74 The Uruguay
Round and the World Trade Organi-
zation 74 The World Bank and
International Monetary Fund 76

INTERNATIONAL ECONOMIC COMMUNITIES 77

North American Free Trade Agreement (NAFTA) 77   The European Union 78 The Euro 80

PARTICIPATING IN THE GLOBAL MARKETPLACE 80

Exporting 81   Licensing 81 Contract Manufacturing 83   Joint Ventures 83   Direct Foreign Investment 83   Countertrade 84

THREATS AND OPPORTUNITIES IN THE GLOBAL MARKETPLACE 84

Political Considerations 84   Cultural Differences 85   Economic Environment 85

THE IMPACT OF MULTINATIONAL CORPORATIONS 87

The Multinational Advantage 88

Capitalizing on Trends in Business 89

Section 2

Market Expansion 89   Resource Acquisition 90   Competition 90 Technological Change 90   Government Actions 90

Applying This Chapter's Topics 91

Section 3

Continue Your Education 91   Study the Role of a Global Manager 91

SUMMARY OF LEARNING GOALS 92 PREPARING FOR TOMORROW'S WORKPLACE 94 WORKING THE NET 95 CREATIVE THINKING CASE 95 VIDEO CASE 96

>4   MAKING ETHICAL DECISIONS AND MANAGING A SOCIALLY RESPONSIBLE BUSINESS 98

Business in the 21st Century 100

Section 1

INDIVIDUAL BUSINESS ETHICS 100

Utilitarianism 100   Individual Rights 101   Justice—The Question of Fairness 101   Stages of Ethical Development 101

HOW ORGANIZATIONS INFLUENCE ETHICAL CONDUCT 102

Recognizing Unethical Business Actions 103   Resolving Ethical Problems

in Business 104   Leading by Example 105   Ethics Training 106 Establishing a Formal Code of Ethics 107

MANAGING TO BE SOCIALLY RESPONSIBLE 107

Understanding Social Responsibility 110

RESPONSIBILITIES TO STAKEHOLDERS 112

Responsibility to Employees 112 Responsibility to Customers 113 Responsibility to the General Public 115 Responsibilities to Investors 116

Capitalizing on Trends in Business 116

Section 2

Trends in Corporate Philanthropy 116 A New Social Contract Trend between Employer and Employee 117   Trends in Global Ethics and Social Responsibility 118

Applying This Chapter's Topics 118

Section 3

Ethics are Part of Everyday Life 119   Work for a Firm That Cares about Its Social Responsibilities 120

SUMMARY OF LEARNING GOALS 120 PREPARING FOR TOMORROW'S WORKPLACE 122 WORKING THE NET 122 CREATIVE THINKING CASE 123 VIDEO CASE 124 **APPENDIX 4: UNDERSTANDING THE LEGAL AND TAX ENVIRONMENT 125**

>PART 2   BUSINESS OWNERSHIP

>5   FORMS OF BUSINESS OWNERSHIP 136

Business in the 21st Century 138

Section 1

TYPES OF BUSINESS ORGANIZATION 139

SOLE PROPRIETORSHIPS 139

Advantages of Sole Proprietorships 140 Disadvantages of Sole Proprietorships 140

PARTNERSHIPS 141

Advantages of Partnerships 142 Disadvantages of Partnerships 142

CORPORATIONS 144

The Incorporation Process 145   The Corporate Structure 146   Advantages of Corporations 147   Disadvantages of Corporations 148   Types of Corporations 148

SPECIALIZED FORMS OF BUSINESS ORGANIZATION 150

Cooperatives 150   Joint Ventures 151

98

168

FRANCHISING   151
    Advantages of Franchises   152
    Disadvantages of Franchises   153
    Franchise Growth   154   International
    Franchising   155
**CORPORATE GROWTH THROUGH
MERGERS AND ACQUISITIONS   155**
    Merger Motives   156   Types of
    Mergers   157

Section 2
Capitalizing on Trends in Business   158
    Niche Markets   158   New Twists for
    Existing Franchises   158   The Big Get
    Bigger   159   Hands across the Sea   159

Section 3
Applying This Chapter's Topics   160
    Is Franchising in Your Future?   160
    Mergers and You   162

SUMMARY OF LEARNING GOALS   162
PREPARING FOR TOMORROW'S
WORKPLACE   164
WORKING THE NET   165
CREATIVE THINKING CASE   166
VIDEO CASE   166

**>6   ENTREPRENEURSHIP: STARTING AND
         MANAGING YOUR OWN BUSINESS   168**

Section 1
Business in the 21st Century   170
ENTREPRENEURSHIP TODAY   171
    Entrepreneur or Small Business
    Owner?   171   Types of Entrepre-
    neurs   171   Why Become an
    Entrepreneur?   173
**CHARACTERISTICS OF SUCCESSFUL
ENTREPRENEURS   173**
    The Entrepreneurial Personality   174
    Managerial Ability and Technical
    Knowledge   174
SMALL BUSINESS   175
    What Is a Small Business?   176
    Advantages of Small Business   177
    Disadvantages of Small Business   178
    The Small Business Administration   179
STARTING YOUR OWN BUSINESS   180
    Getting Started   180   Developing the
    Business Plan   181   Financing the
    Business   183   Buying a Small

Business   184   Risks of Small Business
Ownership   184
MANAGING A SMALL BUSINESS   185
    Using Outside Consultants   186   Hiring
    and Retaining Employees   186   Operating
    Internationally   187

Section 2
Capitalizing on Trends in Business   187
    Home is Where the Office Is   188
    Ownership Trends   188   The Internet
    Explosion   191

Section 3
Applying This Chapter's Topics   192
    Taking the First Steps   192   Working at
    a Small Business   193

SUMMARY OF LEARNING GOALS   194
PREPARING FOR TOMORROW'S
WORKPLACE   196
WORKING THE NET   197
CREATIVE THINKING CASE   197
VIDEO CASE   198
your career   YOUR CAREER AS AN
ENTREPRENEUR   200

>PART 3   BUSINESS MANAGEMENT

**>7   MANAGEMENT AND LEADERSHIP
         IN TODAY'S ORGANIZATION   202**

Section 1
Business in the 21st Century   204
THE ROLE OF MANAGEMENT   204
PLANNING   204
ORGANIZING   208
LEADING   209
    Leadership Styles   210   Employee
    Empowerment   211   Corporate
    Culture   212
CONTROLLING   213
MANAGERIAL ROLES   215
    Managerial Decision Making   215
MANAGERIAL SKILLS   217
    Technical Skills   217   Human Relations
    Skills   219   Conceptual Skills   219
    Global Management Skills   220

Section 2
Capitalizing on Trends in Business   220
    Managers Empowering Employees   220
    Managers and Information Technology   221
    Managing in a Global Marketplace   221

Section 3
Applying This Chapter's Topics   221
    Effective Time Management   222
    Decision-Making Skills   222

SUMMARY OF LEARNING GOALS   223
PREPARING FOR TOMORROW'S
WORKPLACE   225
WORKING THE NET   225
CREATIVE THINKING CASE   226
VIDEO CASE   227

>8 DESIGNING ORGANIZATIONAL STRUCTURES 228

Section 1 Business in the 21st Century 230
STRUCTURAL BUILDING BLOCKS 230
Division of Labor 230
Departmentalization 231   Managerial
Hierarchy 232   Span of Control 234
Centralization of Decision Making 235
MECHANISTIC VERSUS ORGANIC STRUCTURES 237
COMMON ORGANIZATIONAL STRUCTURES 238
Line Organization 239   Line-and-Staff
Organization 239   Committee
Structure 239   Matrix Structure 240
REENGINEERING ORGANIZATIONAL STRUCTURE 242
THE INFORMAL ORGANIZATION 244
Functions of the Informal
Organization 244

Section 2 Capitalizing on Trends in Business 246
The Virtual Corporation 246
Structuring for Global Mergers 247

Section 3 Applying This Chapter's Topics 247
SUMMARY OF LEARNING GOALS 249
PREPARING FOR TOMORROW'S
WORKPLACE 250
WORKING THE NET 251
CREATIVE THINKING CASE 251
VIDEO CASE 252

>9 MANAGING HUMAN RESOURCES 254

Section 1 Business in the 21st Century 256
DEVELOPING PEOPLE TO HELP REACH ORGANIZATIONAL GOALS 256
HUMAN RESOURCE PLANNING 257
Job Analysis and Design 258   Human
Resource Planning and Forecasting 259
EMPLOYEE RECRUITMENT 260
EMPLOYEE SELECTION 262
EMPLOYEE TRAINING AND DEVELOPMENT 264
On-the-Job Training 265   Off-the-Job
Training 265

PERFORMANCE PLANNING AND EVALUATION 266
EMPLOYEE COMPENSATION AND BENEFITS 267
Types of Compensation or Pay 268
ORGANIZATIONAL CAREER MANAGEMENT 269
Job Changes within the Organization 269
Separations 270
LAWS AFFECTING HUMAN RESOURCE MANAGEMENT 271
The Role of Government Agencies in
Human Resource Management 274
Making Affirmative Action Work in the
New Millennium 274

Section 2 Capitalizing on Trends in Business 275
Social Change 275   Demographics 275
Advancing Technology 276   Global
Competition 277

Section 3 Applying This Chapter's Topics 278
You Will Be Involved in Human Resources
Decision Making 279

SUMMARY OF LEARNING GOALS 279
PREPARING FOR TOMORROW'S
WORKPLACE 281
WORKING THE NET 282
CREATIVE THINKING CASE 283
VIDEO CASE 283

>10 MOTIVATING EMPLOYEES AND CREATING SELF-MANAGED TEAMS 286

Section 1 Business in the 21st Century 288
THE EVOLUTION OF MOTIVATION THEORY 288
Frederick Taylor's Scientific Manage-
ment 288   The Hawthorne Studies 289
Maslow's Hierarchy of Needs 290
McGregor's Theories X and Y 292
Herzberg's Motivator-Hygiene Theory 293
CONTEMPORARY VIEWS ON MOTIVATION 294
Expectancy Theory 294   Equity
Theory 295   Goal-Setting Theory 295
FROM MOTIVATION THEORY TO APPLICATION 297
Motivational Job Design 297   Work
Scheduling Options 298   Recognition,
Empowerment, and Economic
Incentives 298

228

344

USING TEAMS TO ENHANCE MOTIVATION AND PERFORMANCE 299
Understanding Group Behavior 300
Work Groups versus Work Teams 301
Types of Teams 301   Building High-Performance Teams 303

Section 2
Capitalizing on Trends in Business 304
Education and Training 304   Employee Ownership 305   Work-Life Benefits 305

Section 3
Applying This Chapter's Topics 304
SUMMARY OF LEARNING GOALS 306
PREPARING FOR TOMORROW'S WORKPLACE 309
WORKING THE NET 310
CREATIVE THINKING CASE 311
VIDEO CASE 312

>11 UNDERSTANDING LABOR-MANAGEMENT RELATIONS 314

Section 1
Business in the 21st Century 316
THE EMERGENCE OF UNIONS AND COLLECTIVE BARGAINING 316
American Federation of Labor 316
Congress of Industrial Organizations 317
The AFL and CIO: Rivalry and Merger 317
The Labor Movement Today 318
THE LEGAL ENVIRONMENT OF UNIONS 320
Norris-La Guardia Act (Anti-Injunction Act) 320   Wagner Act (National Labor Relations Act) 320   Taft-Hartley Act (Labor-Management Relations Act) 321
Landrum-Griffin Act (Labor-Management Reporting and Disclosure Act) 321
UNION ORGANIZING 322
NEGOTIATING UNION CONTRACTS 324
Union Security 326   Management Rights 327   Wages 328   Benefits 329   Job Security and Seniority 330
GRIEVANCE AND ARBITRATION 330
MANAGING LABOR-MANAGEMENT CONFLICT 331
Union Strategies 332   Employer Strategies 333

Section 2
Capitalizing on Trends in Business 334
Union Organizing and Membership 334
Shortages of Skilled Labor 335

Section 3
Applying This Chapter's Topics 336
SUMMARY OF LEARNING GOALS 337
PREPARING FOR TOMORROW'S WORKPLACE 339
WORKING THE NET 340
CREATIVE THINKING 341
VIDEO CASE 342

>12 ACHIEVING WORLD-CLASS OPERATIONS MANAGEMENT 344

Section 1
Business in the 21st Century 346
PRODUCTION AND OPERATIONS MANAGEMENT—AN OVERVIEW 347
PRODUCTION PLANNING 348
Production Process 349   Site Selection 351   Facility Layout 354
Resource Planning 354   Supply Chain Management 359
PRODUCTION AND OPERATIONS CONTROL 360
Routing Production 360
Scheduling 360
IMPROVING PRODUCTION AND OPERATIONS 363
Total Quality Management 363   The Move toward Lean Manufacturing 363
Automation in Productions and Operations Management 364   Technology and Automation in Nonmanufacturing Operations 366

Section 2
Capitalizing on Trends in Business 367
Modular Production 367   Agile Manufacturing 368   Trends in Facility Layout 368

Section 3
Applying This Chapter's Topics 368
SUMMARY OF LEARNING GOALS 369
PREPARING FOR TOMORROW'S WORKPLACE 372
WORKING THE NET 373
CREATIVE THINKING CASE 373
VIDEO CASE 374
your career YOUR CAREER IN MANAGEMENT 376

>PART 4 MARKETING MANAGEMENT

>13 UNDERSTANDING THE CUSTOMER AND CREATING GOODS AND SERVICES THAT SATISFY 380

Section 1
Business in the 21st Century 382
THE MARKETING CONCEPT 382
Customer Value 383   Customer Satisfaction 383   Building Relationships 385

CREATING A MARKETING STRATEGY 386

Understanding the External Environment 386   Defining the Target Market 387   Creating a Competitive Advantage 387

DEVELOPING A MARKETING MIX 389

Product Strategy 390   Pricing Strategy 390   Distribution Strategy 390   Promotion Strategy 390   Not-for-Profit Marketing 391

BUYER BEHAVIOR 392

Influences on Consumer Decision Making 392   Business-to-Business Purchase Decision Making 393

MARKET SEGMENTATION 394

Demographic Segmentation 395   Geographic Segmentation 396   Psychographic Segmentation 397   Benefit Segmentation 397   Volume Segmentation 397

USING MARKETING RESEARCH TO SERVE EXISTING CUSTOMERS AND FIND NEW CUSTOMERS 397

Define the Marketing Problem 399   Choose a Method of Research 399   Collect the Data 400   Analyze the Data 401   Make Recommendations to Management 401

Section 2 —Capitalizing on Trends in Business 401

Advanced Observation Research Methods 401   Decision Support Systems 402   Using Databases for Micromarketing 402

Section 3 —Applying This Chapter's Topics 403

Participate in Marketing Research Surveys 403   Understand Cognitive Dissonance 403

SUMMARY OF LEARNING GOALS 404
PREPARING FOR TOMORROW'S WORKPLACE 406
WORKING THE NET 406
CREATIVE THINKING CASE 407
VIDEO CASE 408

>14 DEVELOPING QUALITY PRODUCTS AT THE RIGHT PRICE 410

Section 1 —Business in the 21st Century 412

WHAT IS A PRODUCT? 412

Classifying Consumer Products 413   Classifying Business Products 414

BUILDING BRAND EQUITY AND MASTER BRANDS 415

Benefits of Branding 416   Building Repeat Sales with Brand Loyalty 417   Facilitating New Product Sales 418   Types of Brands 418

THE IMPORTANCE OF PACKAGING IN A SELF-SERVICE ECONOMY 419

The Functions of a Package 419   Adding Value through Warranties 420

CREATING PRODUCTS THAT DELIVER VALUE 421

Organizing the New Product Effort 421   How New Products Are Developed 422   The Role of the Product Manager 424

THE PRODUCT LIFE CYCLE 424

Stages of the Life Cycle 424   The Product Life Cycle as a Management Tool 425

PRICING PRODUCTS RIGHT 425

Pricing Objectives 426   Maximizing Profits 426   Achieving a Target Return on Investment 427   Value Pricing 428

HOW MANAGERS SET PRICES 429

Markup Pricing 429   Breakeven Analysis 430

PRODUCT PRICING 430

Price Skimming 431   Penetration Pricing 431   Leader Pricing 431   Bundling 431   Odd-Even Pricing 432   Prestige Pricing 432

Section 2 —Capitalizing on Trends in Business 432

Building Immediate Brand Recognition 432   Mass Customization 434   The Growth of Internet Auctions 434

Section 3 —Applying This Chapter's Topics 434

Custom Products and Services 435   Using the Internet to Find Product Information 436

SUMMARY OF LEARNING GOALS 436
PREPARING FOR TOMORROW'S WORKPLACE 437
WORKING THE NET 438
CREATIVE THINKING CASE 439
VIDEO CASE 440

470

>15 DISTRIBUTING PRODUCTS IN A TIMELY AND EFFICIENT MANNER 442

Business in the 21st Century 444

Section 1
THE ROLE OF DISTRIBUTION 444
THE NATURE AND FUNCTIONS OF DISTRIBUTION CHANNELS 445
Marketing Intermediaries in the Distribution Channel 445 The Functions of Distribution Channels 447
HOW CHANNELS ORGANIZE AND COVER MARKETS 448
Vertical Marketing Systems 449 The Intensity of Market Coverage 450
WHOLESALING 451
Types of Wholesalers 452
THE COMPETITIVE WORLD OF RETAILING 454
Types of Retail Operations 454 Components of a Successful Retailing Strategy 456
USING PHYSICAL DISTRIBUTION TO INCREASE EFFICIENCY AND CUSTOMER SATISFACTION 460
Choosing a Warehouse Location and Type 460 Setting Up a Materials-Handling System 460 Making Transportation Decisions 460

Section 2
Capitalizing on Trends in Business 461
The Rough and Tumble Practice of Stocklifting 462 Services and Physical Distribution 462

Section 3
Applying This Chapter's Topics 463
The Internet Makes Shopping a Breeze 464 The Web Is Changing Your Life 464

SUMMARY OF LEARNING GOALS 465
PREPARING FOR TOMORROW'S WORKPLACE 466
WORKING THE NET 467
CREATIVE THINKING CASE 467
VIDEO CASE 468

>16 USING INTEGRATED MARKETING COMMUNICATIONS TO PROMOTE PRODUCTS 470

Business in the 21st Century 472

Section 1
PROMOTIONAL GOALS 472
The Promotional Mix 473

ADVERTISING BUILDS BRAND RECOGNITION 474
Types of Advertising 474 Choosing Advertising Media 475 Advertising Agencies 478 Advertising Regulation 479
THE IMPORTANCE OF PERSONAL SELLING 480
The Professional Salesperson 480 Sales Positions 481 The Selling Process 481
SALES PROMOTION 483
PUBLIC RELATIONS HELPS BUILD GOODWILL 486
New Product Publicity 486 Event Sponsorship 487
FACTORS THAT AFFECT THE PROMOTIONAL MIX 487
The Nature of the Product 487 Market Characteristics 487 Available Funds 488 Push and Pull Strategies 488

Section 2
Capitalizing on Trends in Business 489
Integrated Marketing Communications 489 The Growth of Web Advertising 490 The Impact of Digital VCRs on Television 490

Section 3
Applying This Chapter's Topics 491
Advertising Will Be More Beneficial to You 491 Always Sell Yourself 492

SUMMARY OF LEARNING GOALS 493
PREPARING FOR TOMORROW'S WORKPLACE 494
WORKING THE NET 494
CREATIVE THINKING CASE 495
VIDEO CASE 495
your career YOUR CAREER IN MARKETING 497

>PART 5 TECHNOLOGY AND INFORMATION

>17 USING TECHNOLOGY TO MANAGE INFORMATION 500

Business in the 21st Century 502

Section 1
USING INFORMATION FOR DECISION MAKING 503
COMPUTER HARDWARE 504
Components of a Computer 505 Types of Computers 506
COMPUTER SOFTWARE 508
Word Processing 508 Spreadsheets 509 Database Management 510 Graphics 510 Desktop Publishing 510 Communications 511 Integrated Software 511
COMPUTER NETWORKS 512
Local Area Networks 512 Wide Area Networks 512 Intranets 513

BUSINESS INFORMATION SYSTEMS   513
  Transaction Processing Systems   514
  Management Support Systems   515
  Office Automation Systems   517
**MANAGING INFORMATION
TECHNOLOGY**   517
  Technology Planning   518   Protecting
  Computers and Information   518

Section 2
  Capitalizing on Trends in Business   523
  Managing Knowledge Resources   523
  End of the Personal Computer Era?   524
  Searching for Information Technology
  Talent   524

Section 3
  Applying This Chapter's Topics   525
  Preparation Pays Off   525   Keeping
  Secrets   526

  SUMMARY OF LEARNING GOALS   526
  PREPARING FOR TOMORROW'S
  WORKPLACE   528
  WORKING THE NET   528
  CREATIVE THINKING CASE   529
  VIDEO CASE   530

>18   USING THE INTERNET FOR BUSINESS
      SUCCESS   532

Section 1
  Business in the 21st Century   534
  THE INTERNET   535
  How the Internet Works   536   The Who,
  What, and Where of the Internet   537
  THE NEW INTERNET ECONOMY   539
  The New Face of Competition   539
  Going Direct   539   Power to the
  Consumer   541   Capitilizing on
  E-Commerce   542   New E-Commerce
  Business Models Emerge   543
  The Business-to-Business Boom   543
  E-Tailing Hits Its Stride   545   Where's
  the Profit?   546   Benefiting from
  E-Commerce   548   Roadblocks on the
  E-Commerce Highway   549
  **LAUNCHING A SUCCESSFUL
  E-BUSINESS**   550
  Merchandising   551   Site Costs and
  Design   552   Marketing   552

  Customer Service and Order Fulfillment   554   Web Site Operations and
  Infrastructure   554

Section 2
  Capitalizing on Trends in Business   555
  Let's Get Personal   555   Privacy Policies
  Go Public   556   Trying to Catch
  Amazon   556

Section 3
  Applying This Chapter's Topics   558
  Creating a Successful Web Site   558
  Gearing up for E-Commerce   559

  SUMMARY OF LEARNING GOALS   560
  PREPARING FOR TOMORROW'S
  WORKPLACE   561
  WORKING THE NET   562
  CREATIVE THINKING CASE   000
  VIDEO CASE   564

>19   USING FINANCIAL INFORMATION AND
      ACCOUNTING   566

Section 1
  Business in the 21st Century   568
  THE PURPOSE OF ACCOUNTING   568
  Who Uses Financial Reports?   569   The
  Accounting Profession   570
  BASIC ACCOUNTING PROCEDURES   571
  The Accounting Equation   572   The
  Accounting Cycle   572   Computers in
  Accounting   573
  THE BALANCE SHEET   574
  Assets   575   Liabilities   575   Owners'
  Equity   577
  THE INCOME STATEMENT   577
  Revenues   577   Expenses   578   Net
  Profit or Loss   579
  THE STATEMENT OF CASH FLOWS   579
  **ANALYZING FINANCIAL
  STATEMENTS**   581
  Liquidity Ratios   582   Profitability
  Ratios   584   Activity Ratios   584   Debt
  Ratios   584

Section 2
  Capitalizing on Trends in Business   585
  Accountants Expand Their Role   585
  Valuing Knowledge Assets   586
  Tightening the GAAP   586

532

620

Applying This Chapter's Topics   587

Section 3
SUMMARY OF LEARNING GOALS   588
PREPARING FOR TOMORROW'S
WORKPLACE   590
WORKING THE NET   592
CREATIVE THINKING CASE   592
VIDEO CASE   593

your career
YOUR CAREER IN MANAGING
INFORMATION   595

>PART 6 FINANCE

>20 UNDERSTANDING MONEY AND FINANCIAL INSTITUTIONS 598

Section 1
Business in the 21st Century   600
MONEY   600
Characteristics of Money   600   Functions
of Money   601   The U.S. Money
Supply   601
THE FEDERAL RESERVE SYSTEM   602
Carrying Out Monetary Policy   602
Setting Rules on Credit   603
Distributing Currency   603   Making
Check Clearing Easier   603
THE U.S. FINANCIAL SYSTEM   604
Depository Financial Institutions   606
Nondepository Financial Institutions   608
INSURING BANK DEPOSITS   609
Role of the FDIC   610   Enforcement by
the FDIC   610
INTERNATIONAL BANKING   610

Section 2
Capitalizing on Trends in Business   611
Online Banking   612   Consoli-
dation   612   The Integration of Banking,
Brokerage, and Insurance Services   000

Section 3
Applying This Chapter's Topics   614
Getting Connected   615   Finding
Financing   615

SUMMARY OF LEARNING GOALS   615
PREPARING FOR TOMORROW'S
WORKPLACE   616
WORKING THE NET   617
CREATIVE THINKING CASE   617
VIDEO CASE   618

>21 FINANCIAL MANAGEMENT 620

Section 1
Business in the 21st Century   620
THE ROLE OF FINANCE   620
The Financial Manager's Responsibilities
and Activities   623   The Goal of the
Financial Manager   624
FINANCIAL PLANNING   624
Forecasts   625   Budgets   626
HOW ORGANIZATIONS USE FUNDS   626
Short-Term Expenses   626   Long-Term
Expenditures   628
**OBTAINING SHORT-TERM
FINANCING   628**
Unsecured Short-Term Loans   629
Secured Short-Term Loans   631
RAISING LONG-TERM FINANCING   632
Debt versus Equity Financing   632   Debt
Financing   633   Equity Financing   634

Section 2
Capitalizing on Trends in Business   637
Finance Goes Global   637   Risk
Management   638

Section 3
Applying This Chapter's Topics   639
SUMMARY OF LEARNING GOALS   640
PREPARING FOR TOMORROW'S
WORKPLACE   642
WORKING THE NET   643
CREATIVE THINKING CASE   644
VIDEO CASE   644

>22 UNDERSTANDING SECURITIES AND SECURITIES MARKETS 647

Section 1
Business in the 21st Century   648
SECURITIES MARKETS   649
Types of Markets   649   The Role of
Investment Bankers and Stockbrokers   650
STOCK: EQUITY FINANCING   650
Common Stock   650   Preferred
Stock   651
BONDS: DEBT FINANCING   652
Corporate Bonds   652   U.S. Government
Securities   653   Municipal Bonds   653
Bond Ratings   654
OTHER POPULAR SECURITIES   654
Mutual Funds   654   Futures
Contracts   655   Options   656
SECURITIES EXCHANGES   656
U.S. Stock Exchanges   657   Global
Trading and Foreign Exchanges   657
The Over-the-Counter Market   657
Market Conditions: Bull Market or Bear
Market?   657   Regulation of Securities
Markets   657

HOW TO BUY AND SELL SECURITIES   660
Securities Transaction Basics   660
Online Investing   660
POPULAR SOURCES OF INVESTMENT INFORMATION   661
Economic and Financial Publications   661
Online Information Resources   661
Security Price Quotations   662   Market Averages and Indexes   667

Section 2
Capitalizing on Trends in Business   668
Market Competition Heats Up   668   Rise of the Individual Investor   669

Section 3
Applying This Chapter's Topics   671
The Time Is Now   671   Tips for Online Investing   671

SUMMARY OF LEARNING GOALS   672
PREPARING FOR TOMORROW'S WORKPLACE   674
WORKING THE NET   675
CREATIVE THINKING CASE   676
VIDEO CASE   676

>23   MANAGING YOUR PERSONAL FINANCES   678

Section 1
Business in the 21st Century   680
FINANCIAL PLANNING AND CASH MANAGEMENT   680
The Cash Flow Plan   681   The Net Worth Statement   682   Checking Accounts   682   Savings Instruments   684
USING CONSUMER CREDIT   686
The Pros and Cons of Using Credit   686
Credit Cards   687   Loans   688   Credit History and Credit Ratings   690

MANAGING TAXES   691
Income Taxes   691   Social Security and Medicare Taxes   692   Sales and Property Taxes   693
SELECTING INSURANCE   693
Prioritizing Insurance Needs   693
Property and Liability Insurance   694
Health Insurance   695   Disability Income Insurance   696   Life Insurance   696
MAKING INVESTMENT DECISIONS   697
Investment Goals   697   Developing an Investment Strategy   698

Section 2
Capitalizing on Trends in Business   700
Cafeteria Benefit Plans   700   Self-Directed Retirement Accounts   701

Section 3
Applying This Chapter's Topics   701
SUMMARY OF LEARNING GOALS   703
PREPARING FOR TOMORROW'S WORKPLACE   704
WORKING THE NET   705
CREATIVE THINKING CASE   706
VIDEO CASE   706
APPENDIX 23: MANAGING RISK AND INSURANCE   708
your career   YOUR CAREER IN FINANCE   714

GLOSSARY   717

END NOTES   734

SUBJECT INDEX   747

COMPANY INDEX   761

PHOTO CREDITS   766

Dedicated to the memory of my mother,
Dr. Edith Gitman, who instilled in me the
importance of education and hard work.

To my brother and his wife,
Maxwell and Dawn McDaniel.

Are You Ready...For the Future of Business?

Workplace 2000

>millennium edition<

SPECIAL FEATURES

SAMPLER

Understand. Anticipate. Prepare.

The world of business is yours to explore today, tomorrow, and beyond. Gitman/McDaniel's unique three-part approach to chapter organization will help you to better understand business trends and anticipate future conditions as you prepare for a successful business career.

 BUSINESS IN THE 21ST CENTURY
At the beginning of each chapter, you'll find comprehensive coverage of current business principles and practices that provides you a complete framework for understanding business today.

 CAPITALIZING ON TRENDS IN BUSINESS
In the second section of every chapter, you'll explore new business trends and examine how they are re-shaping today's business landscape and altering tomorrow's competitive environment.

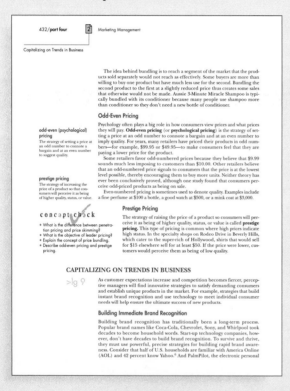

 APPLYING THIS CHAPTER'S TOPICS
Here's where you put what you've learned to work! The final section of each chapter gives you practical suggestions on preparing yourself for a successful career in the business world.

Technology. Ethics. Entrepreneurship.

The study of business would not be complete without focusing on these important concepts. With the help of the following features, you'll closely examine how they relate to business and your future success.

APPLYING TECHNOLOGY

The Web. Telecommuting. E-commerce. There is no question that the future of business centers on technology. **Applying Technology** boxes in every chapter explore and describe the technological developments critical to each functional area of business and how they will affect the way you work.

MAKING ETHICAL CHOICES

Today's diverse workplace can create increasingly complex issues. With the help of **Making Ethical Choices** boxes in each chapter, you'll have the opportunity to explore ethical conduct in the workplace and consider how you might react to ethical dilemmas.

FOCUSING ON SMALL BUSINESS

The foundation of business was built on entrepreneurship, but what does the next millennium hold? The new boxed feature **Focusing on Small Business** highlights entrepreneurship and offers suggestions for starting and managing your own business.

Real Companies. Real Issues.

OPENING VIGNETTES

What better way to understand current business topics than to go right to the source? Real situations facing companies are explored in opening vignettes that feature current business practices and preview the material you are about to read. Each vignette also includes a series of questions that anticipate key issues in the chapter.

eToys Doesn't Play Around

>c18

The concept seems simple: set up an online store that just sells toys, take orders, and ship customers the merchandise. Edward "Toby" Lenk, founder and CEO of eToys, will tell you otherwise: "I can't tell you how amazingly complex this business is. To be really good at this is really hard."

Just two years after starting the company, Lenk succeeded in being "really good." eToys (www.etoys.com) is the leading Web toy retailer. In 1998 it sold $23 million in toys, video games, software, and music in the three months before Christmas, up from $500,000 a year earlier. Ranked number 5 on MediaMetrix's list of December's top shopping Web sites, eToys was also named most customer-focused online merchant of the 1998 holiday season by Patricia Seybold, technology consultant and author of a best-seller on Internet retailing.

Lenk got the idea for eToys while buying his niece a Christmas gift. Like most adults, he found the toy-buying experience unpleasant: long lines, noisy kids, poor service, and insufficient supplies of popular toys. The former Disney executive didn't know much about toys, but he saw an opportunity to use the Internet to give consumers what they wanted most: convenience, selection, and service.

Convenience was easy. Web stores are open 24 hours a day. The site's search engine quickly provides recommendations in categories like Picks of the Month, Toybox Essentials, and Favorites by Age. Shoppers click for detailed product information.

Selection proved harder. Book, music, and computer products e-tailers can buy from large distributors with a wide product range. The toy industry has no consolidated distributors, so eToys must deal with over 500 manufacturers. Today eToys features a much larger selection than any land-based store—10,000 products, both well-known brands and specialty brands that toy superstores don't carry—and keeps large inventories in its own warehouse.

Superior service won eToys rave reviews in the busy 1998 holiday season. Many Web merchants ran out of products, but Lenk was ready for the onslaught of cybershoppers. eToys shipped 95 percent of its orders within 24 hours, providing free shipping upgrades to deliver on time and $5 coupons if toys were out of stock. This focus on customer satisfaction paid off in customer retention and referrals. According to one study, satisfied Web customers bring six new customers to the site.

Critical Thinking Questions
As you read this chapter, consider the following questions as they relate to eToys:

- What advantages does an online merchant like eToys have compared to traditional retailers? Disadvantages?
- Identify the reasons why eToys has jumped ahead of the well-known Toys "R" Us brand.
- Are toys well-suited for Web sales? Why or why not?

LOOKING AHEAD

At the end of each chapter, we'll go back to take a closer look at the issues presented in the Opening Vignette. Our Looking Ahead feature will also give you updates on the status of the company profiled and offer suggestions on how it may need to refocus its business to compete in the future.

You can also use similar questions to evaluate the success of an existing operation. In addition, you would determine the number of visitors, the percentage who buy, how well the order fulfillment and customer service procedures work, and what improvements and upgrades are necessary.

>looking ahead
at eToys

In the fast-paced world of Web retailing, a company cannot rest on its laurels. eToys is working hard to hold onto its lead as the Web's top toy retailer. The company raised additional capital to support expansion by going public in May 1999. A second warehouse on the East Coast will improve customer service. Lenk is adding more categories, including kids' sporting goods and maternity and baby products, to tap the larger children's products market—and its relatively high profit margins and attractive demographics. "Our anchor category is toys, but the vision for the company is to be the preeminent kids' retailing name for the 21st century," says eToys chief financial officer Steven Schoch.

Although eToys is well positioned in an industry tailor-made for the Net, it faces plenty of competition. Major retailers like Toys "R" Us are investing heavily in their sites. They also have the clout to put pressure on manufacturers. The manufacturers themselves could decide to sell directly to consumers from their own Web sites instead of selling to eToys. But perhaps the biggest threat comes from Amazon.com. In mid-1999 the online retailer everyone wants to copy announced that it, too, was opening an online toy store.[37]

SUMMARY OF LEARNING GOALS

>lg 1 What is the Internet, and how does it work?
The Internet is a global "network of networks" that is revolutionizing how businesses operate. It combines high-speed communications and computing power to transmit information immediately. All networks in the Internet use TCP/IP, a special language that allows different types of computers to communicate. In addition to the resources of the World Wide Web, the Internet provides file transfer capabilities, e-mail, chat sessions, and newsgroups. Data travel from the user's access point to the Internet service provider and then through a series of interlinked national backbones to the recipient's ISP.

>lg 2 Who uses the Internet, and for what?
About 170 million people worldwide use the Internet. About 64 million adults in the United States are regular users. Although adopters of the technology were younger, more affluent, and better educated than the general population, the profile of the Net user is moving closer to the national averages in these areas. Among the most popular Web sites are those with company and product information, news, reference materials, periodicals, financial quotes, and entertainment. Businesses use the Internet to research economic trends; gather industry information; learn about competitors; provide customer service; communicate with employees; vendors; and customers; market and sell products; and purchase supplies.

>lg 3 How has the Internet economy changed the business environment?
New types of companies provide enabling technology and services. The competitive arena is expanding as the Internet eliminates barriers of time and place and reduces barriers to entry. Channel relationships are changing as well. The Internet allows companies to sell directly to consumers without using distributors. Some distributors are finding new roles by providing services to online merchants who want to outsource order fulfillment. The Internet also em-

Lights. Camera. Action!

VIDEO CASES

Actual companies are the stars of our end-of-chapter video cases that bring chapter concepts to life. These interesting videos present the very real world experiences and challenges of innovative organizations like Ben & Jerry's, Burton Snowboards, Vermont Teddy Bear Company, and the Toronto Blue Jays.

VIDEO CASE

The Internet and Burton Snowboards' Distribution System: Reaching Out to Newbies

The Internet is rapidly becoming an important element in the distribution system of many companies. Burton Snowboards (**www.burton.com/main.asp**), a manufacturer of snowboards and outerwear for snowboard riders, is no exception. Located in Burlington, Vermont, Burton Snowboards uses its Web site to promote the sport of snowboarding as well as to market its products to professionals and amateurs alike.

Part of Burton Snowboards' Web site caters to "newbies"—people who are new to the sport of snowboarding. Burton's Newbie Guide takes the novice through seven steps to a "great day on the hill." First, the new snowboarder decides what type of snowboard to ride. The newbie can choose from freestyle, freeride, and carving snowboards. Second, the newbie is asked about performance requirements. At the third step, the newbie is linked to the "hardgoods" page of Burton's online catalog and asked to select from a specific board series in the product line and to choose a board length in light of the rider's weight. Next, the new rider chooses a boot/binding combination—known as an interface—from three options: FreeSole, Soft SI, and Direct Drive. At the fifth step, the Newbie Guide asks the novice what type of clothing she or he would like to wear when snowboarding. The newbie is then linked to the "softgoods" or outerwear page of Burton's online catalog. At the sixth step, the newbie is asked to head to a local retailer or to an on-snow demonstration. A link to a list of dealer locations is provided, and a demo calendar is installed on the Web site for the fall and winter months. Finally, the newbie is asked to take a snowboarding lesson.

Selected retailers sell Burton Snowboards' products to newbies as well as to those with more snowboarding experience. The products are intended to appeal to the discriminating buyer regardless of experience or ability level. Burton's snowboards are premium products—"equipment that starts where

Building Your Future

Workplace 2000 will no doubt demand a distinctly qualified worker. You'll find the following activities in each chapter to help you apply critical concepts, build skills, and ensure your competency for the workplace of the future.

HOT LINKS

Hot Links are short, simple activities highlighted in the margins that help you explore how actual businesses are using the Web. Hot Links frequently guide you to sites that offer career guidance.

For tips on how to start, grow, or manage your business, check out *Entrepreneur* magazine's "Smart Tip of the Day" at

www.entrepreneurmag.com/ smarttip.hts.

WORKING THE NET

Each chapter will include **Working the Net** projects that will help you to build online skills while exploring information relevant to the issues you're studying.

WORKING THE NET

1. Visit the JobDirect Web site at **www.jobdirect.com.** Click on "JobDirect Guide" to read a brief company profile, and then follow links to get more details about the company's founders and team and the story of how they developed their idea. What qualifications did Rachel Bell and Sara Sutton bring to the venture? How did they compensate for resources they lacked? What were some of the lessons they learned about organizing a company?

2. Consult *Entrepreneur* magazine's guide to business start-ups, "One Step at a Time," at **www.entrepreneurmag.com/startup/52steps/** and link to the articles at Step 12 on choosing a form of business organization. Summarize for the class the reasons that the entrepreneurs profiled chose a particular structure. Do you agree with their choices?

3. Research how to form a corporation and an LLC in your state using a search engine to find relevant sites. Here are two to get you started: **www. corporate.com** and **www.incorporate-usa.com.** What steps are necessary to set up a corporation in your state? How do the fees compare to other states? If you were incorporating a business, what state would you choose and why?

4. Select three franchises that interest you. Research them at sites such as the Franchise Handbook Online (**www.franchise1.com/directory.html**), *Entrepreneur* magazine's Franchise 500 (**www.entrepreneurmag.com/ franchise500/**), and Be the Boss (**www.betheboss.com**). Prepare a chart comparing them, including history, number and location of units, financial requirements (initial franchise fee, other start-up costs, royalty and advertising fees), and any other information that would help you evaluate the franchise.

5. Check out the latest merger trends at Industry Week (**www.industryweek.com**). Find examples of a horizontal merger and a merger that failed.

PREPARING FOR TOMORROW'S WORKPLACE

Preparing for Tomorrow's Workplace activities will assist you in developing career skills such as communication, writing, negotiating, teamwork, global thinking, and research that every business values.

372/**part three**   Business Management

product (or assembly-line) layout 354
production 347
production planning 348
production process 349
program evaluation and review technique (PERT) 362
purchasing 356
quality control 363
robotics 365
routing 360
scheduling 360
supply chain 359
supply chain management 359
total quality management (TQM) 363

PREPARING FOR TOMORROW'S WORKPLACE

1. Reliance Systems, headquartered in Oklahoma City, is a manufacturer of computer keyboards. The company plans to build a second factory and hopes to find a location with access to low-cost but skilled workers, national and international transportation, and favorable government incentives. The company has zeroed in on three possible states for the site: Connecticut, Kentucky, and Louisiana. Divide the class into four groups. Assign one state to each of three groups, while the fourth group will represent the company's board of directors. The state groups should read information about their state, available at **www.corporatelocation.com,** and develop a case for that state. The board group should read about all three states. Each group will make a brief presentation to the board on behalf of their state. The board will choose the new site. After the presentations, have a general discussion about the board's decision: whether you agree with it, the factors the board used to support the decision, and other factors Reliance should consider in the site selection process.

2. Tom Lawrence and Sally Zickle are co-owners of L-Z Marketing, an advertising agency. Last week, they landed a major aerospace manufacturer as a client. The company wants the agency to create its annual report. Tom, who develops the art for the agency, needs about a week to develop the preliminary report design, another two weeks to set the type, and three weeks to get the report printed. Sally writes the material for the report and doesn't need as much time: two days to meet with the client to review the company's financial information and about three weeks to write the report copy. Of course, Tom can't set type until Sally has finished writing the report. The client will also need two days between each step to review and approve Tom and Sally's work. Sally will also need three days to proofread the report before it goes to the printer. Divide the class into three or four groups. Each team should develop either a Gantt chart or a critical path diagram for Tom and Sally to use in scheduling the project. Explain why you chose the method you did. How long will it take Tom and Sally to finish the project if there are no unforeseen delays? Compare the groups' answers and discuss any variations.

3. Look for ways that technology and automation are used at your school, in the local supermarket, at your doctor's office. As a class, discuss how automation affects the service you receive from each of these organizations. Does one organization use any types of automation that might be effectively used by one of the others? Explain.

4. Pick a small business in your community. Make a list of the resources critical to the firm's production and operations. What would happen if the business suddenly couldn't acquire any of these resources? Divide the class into small groups and discuss strategies that small businesses can use to manage their supply chain.

5. Pretend the class has been assigned the task of making sandwiches for the annual school homecoming party. The homecoming committee wants 120 peanut butter and jelly sandwiches, 179 ham and cheese sandwiches, 87 cheese sandwiches, and 99 turkey sandwiches. All of the peanut butter and jelly sandwiches must be on white bread. Half of the remaining sandwiches should be on white, a quarter on whole wheat, and the rest on rye bread. All of the ham and cheese sandwiches should have pickles and mustard. Half of the cheese and turkey sandwiches should have mayonnaise only and the other half both mayo and mustard. As a class, decide which production layout and processes will be most effective for producing the sandwich order.

CREATIVE THINKING CASE

Creative Thinking Cases in each chapter put you in the role of decision maker, challenging you to apply what you've learned to real business situations.

166/**part two**   Business Ownership

CREATIVE THINKING CASE

Should Jason take the subway?

Jason Braden's dream of starting and running a business in his hometown became reality when he inherited $35,000 from his grandfather. Jason, who wanted a low-risk venture that provided a decent income, decided that his town needed a sandwich store near two large office parks. Jason had worked during college at a Subway Sandwich store and knew that designing the store, rent, and equipment and supply costs would quickly eat up his $35,000, leaving little for advertising or promotion. Jason also didn't know much about finding suppliers, setting up an accounting system, and hiring employees.

Jason contacted his former boss José Gonzalez, who owned five Subway franchises. Mr. Gonzalez was very positive about his experiences, telling Jason that Subway was one of the lowest cost food franchises to start and pointing to his late-model sports car and house in an affluent neighborhood as proof of the income potential.

Jason requested information about becoming a franchisee from Subway's corporate offices. He learned that his total initial investment could range from $60,000 to $103,000, depending on store size and location. The company could help with financing for most of the costs and provide training to help him set up an efficient operation. The only cash down payment was the $10,000 franchise fee. After the store opened, out of weekly gross sales Jason would pay 8 percent royalties and 3.5 percent to Subway's fund for national advertising.

Before he submitted his application, however, Jason searched the Internet for more information. He discovered that many Subway franchisees had filed lawsuits against the company for reasons such as not completely explaining their rights and obligations as franchisees or opening too many franchises in their neighborhoods. "Subway is the biggest problem in franchising," said one congressional economist. "If anyone in my family ever asked whether they should buy a Subway franchise, I would say absolutely not, no way."

Jason spoke again to Mr. Gonzalez, who assured him that many of the lawsuits had been filed by unsuccessful franchisees who had not followed Subway's operating procedures. Also, the company had resolved some issues raised by the disgruntled franchisees.

The Student Web Site

The Student Web Site provides content that maximizes student learning and builds online skills. Access the site at **http://gitman.swcollege.com**.

INTERNET EXERCISES

Internet Exercises demonstrate how actual companies are applying key chapter concepts. These exercises are organized by chapter and include discussion questions and links to related Web sites.

ONLINE QUIZZES

Online Quizzes test student understanding of business terminology and offer customized feedback for incorrect answers. Each chapter is supported by two online quizzes.

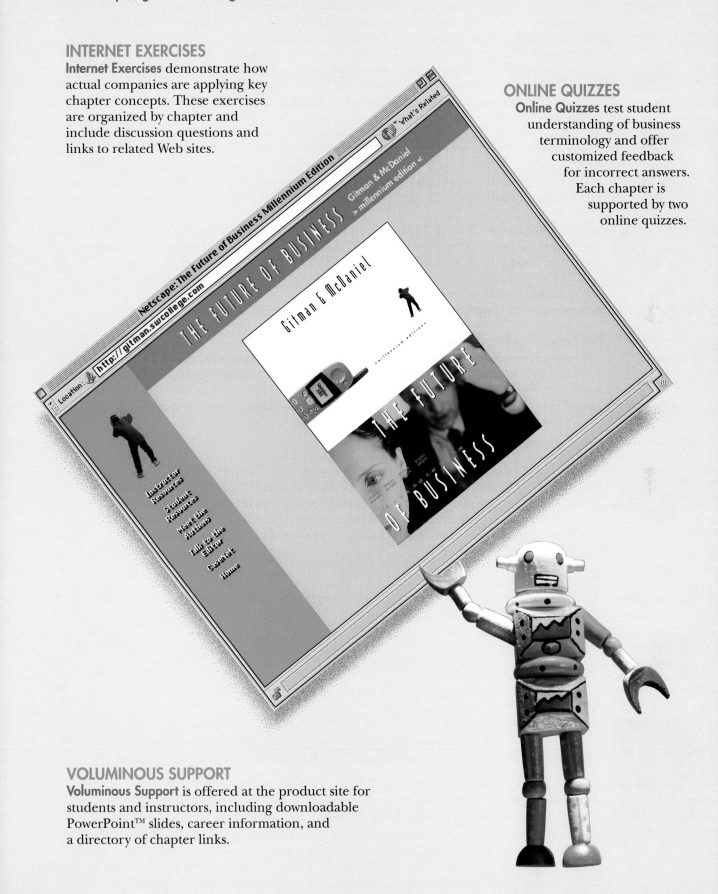

VOLUMINOUS SUPPORT

Voluminous Support is offered at the product site for students and instructors, including downloadable PowerPoint™ slides, career information, and a directory of chapter links.

Instructors:
Complete the Future…with these Outstanding Supplements.

Comprehensive Instructor's Manual with Transparency Masters & Video Guide (ISBN 0-324-017200). At the core of the integrated learning system for **THE FUTURE OF BUSINESS** is the Instructor's Manual. Developed in response to numerous suggestions from instructors teaching this course, each chapter is designed to provide maximum guidance on delivering the content in an interesting and dynamic manner. A comprehensive Video Guide includes the running time of each video, concepts illustrated in the video, teaching objectives for the case, and solutions for case study questions. A complete set of Transparency Masters is available to create overhead transparencies.

PowerPoint™ Lecture System (ISBN 0-324-017227).
Over 300 slides of key chapter concepts and actual business examples not included in the text are available in PowerPoint™ presentation software to improve lecture organization and reduce preparation time.

Instructor's Resource CD (ISBN 0-324-017219).
For maximum convenience, the Instructor's Manual, PowerPoint™ slides, and Thomson Learning Testing Tools™ are all available on CD.

Color Acetate Transparencies (ISBN 0-324-017235).
Color acetate transparencies feature key concepts and exhibits from the text.

Test Bank (ISBN 0-324-020481).
The comprehensive test bank is organized by learning objective to support the integrated learning system. With over 2000 true/false, multiple-choice, fill-in-the-blank, and short-answer questions, tests can be customized to support a variety of course objectives. The test bank is available in print and new Windows software formats – **Thomson Learning Testing Tools™** (ISBN 0-324-017189).

Comprehensive BusinessLink Video Package (ISBN: 0-034-022697, 0-324-022700, 0-324-022719).
Designed by business professors, the BusinessLink videos reinforce chapter concepts by allowing students to step into actual business situations and develop appropriate responses to a variety of business issues. Each chapter is supported by a video and video case.

JIAN MarketingBuilder Express
An "express" version of JIAN's popular *MarketingBuilder* software, this tool contains everything students need to develop a marketing plan.

Inc. Booklets
This popular series provides an extensive resource on business topics including guidance for creating a successful business plan and *301 Great Ideas for Using Technology*.

Web Tutor on WebCT
Go beyond the classroom with Web Tutor. It offers in-depth content with concept presentations, flashcards, audio clips, Internet links, discussion questions, and tutorials. An internal e-mail system, chat and discussion areas, search capabilities, calendars, custom printing features, and instructor customization options provide an unparalleled level of functionality. Visit http://www.swcollege.com/elearning.html for more information.

A few years ago, running a business was far simpler than it is today. Managers were concerned with producing a competitive product or service, keeping workers motivated, holding down costs, and keeping prices in line. For organizations to truly excel in the future, today's business managers must manage these same issues and many more.

In this new century, the primary competitive tool of many organizations is knowledge. Organizations that obtain it, harness it, and apply it faster than competitors will reap extraordinary results. Technology is another tool organizations use to create a competitive advantage. Yesterday's companies competed locally, statewide, and sometimes nationally. In the blink of an eye, the Internet has enabled even the smallest entrepreneur to produce and sell in the global marketplace. Moreover, domestic markets that once had relatively little contact with the outside world now are utilized and served by giant global corporations.

To succeed in a rapidly changing, complex business environment, a successful organization—now more than ever—requires fast and accurate knowledge. To help prepare students for their futures in business, *The Future of Business, Millennium Edition,* showcases the dramatic changes occurring in the business environment.

A TEXT THAT DELIVERS VALUE TO THE STUDENT AND PROFESSOR LIKE NO OTHER

The guiding principle of business today is building relationships. We seek to build long-term relationships with our customers (both professors and students) that result in trust and confidence in our product. The key to our creating these long-term relationships is to deliver value to you. We and the South-Western College Publishing Company team have designed and developed a text that provides extraordinary value to professors and students.

To deliver exceptional and unmatched student value, we broke the mold of traditional introduction to business texts. We started with a clean slate and cast aside the traditional formula for introduction to business texts. We asked, "How can we maximize the value of this text for both professors and students?" Marketing research with professors and students, along with long nights of brainstorming and hard work, has led to a totally new text.

SETTING THE STAGE FOR A FUTURE IN BUSINESS

Chapter 1 (Your Future in Business Begins Now) lays the foundation for this exciting new text. Any businessperson knows that the only thing certain about the business environment is that it always changes. With this in mind, Chapter 1 describes the business trends altering the business landscape. The value for students is not only learning "what" trends influence business, but "how" these trends will influence business.

The appendix to Chapter 1 (Getting Your Career Off on the Right Track) also delivers value by describing the steps students need to take to find their first professional job. We describe how to use the Internet to jump-start a job search and how to prepare a cyber résumé. We explain how to use the Internet to research potential new employers and offer tips on what to say to get an interviewer's attention. For those lucky enough to receive several job offers, we explain how the Internet can be used to make the right employment choice. We show students how to discover economic, demographic, and climatic information about cities in which they might work. We also help them calculate the cost of living in various cities and how to get details on crime rates. We close the appendix with tips on winning that first promotion.

THREE VALUE-DRIVEN THEMES

Each chapter in *The Future of Business, Millennium Edition* is organized to support three themes:

1 BUSINESS IN THE 21ST CENTURY. Each chapter begins with a comprehensive overview of current business principles and practices. Students will learn what is happening in today's businesses with examples from the largest global corporate giants, such as Ford and Airbus Industries, to the smallest Internet start-ups.

2 CAPITALIZING ON TRENDS IN BUSINESS. The second part of each chapter explores new business trends and how they are reshaping today's business and altering tomorrow's competitive environment. Technology and the global economy are covered extensively in every trends section. We deliver value to students by explaining the factors that are reshaping the business world in which they will soon begin professional careers. With a glimpse into the future, students will have a keen advantage when entering the workplace.

3 APPLYING THIS CHAPTER'S TOPICS. A unique feature, found only in *The Future of Business, Millennium Edition,* brings the chapter topics to life for students with relevant and interesting tips for making the most of a professional career or becoming a smart consumer. These suggestions can be used by students immediately after reading the chapter. In Chapter 5 (Forms of Business Ownership), students explore their readiness for starting a franchise or learn how to protect their jobs during a merger. In Chapter 18 (Using the Internet for Business Success), students learn how to design a winning Web site.

COVERAGE OF CURRENT ISSUES

Today's most fundamental business trends and topics are thoroughly covered—this means more value added for students. Topics shaping the future of business that are covered in this edition include the following:

- Customer value
- Knowledge management
- Relationship management
- Euro and the European Union
- New Internet economy
- Launching an e-business
- Global mergers
- Entrepreneurs/intrapreneurs
- Database marketing
- Mass customization
- Web advertising
- Global management skills
- Motivational job design
- Virtual corporations
- Online trading
- Online banking
- Integration of banking, brokerage, and insurance services
- Risk management

- Agile manufacturing
- Intranets and extranets

Technology and E-Commerce

Technology touches all areas of business. Chapter 18 (Using the Internet for Business Success) looks at the impact of the Internet on business operations and describes the growth of e-commerce in both consumer and business-to-business markets. This chapter also explores the process for launching an e-business and looks ahead to the future of the Internet in business. No other introduction to business textbook offers such comprehensive coverage of the profound impact of the Internet on business.

In addition, each chapter addresses how businesses are applying technology to improve processes and maximize value to the customer. Technology issues are integrated throughout the chapters, where appropriate, and featured in Applying Technology boxes. For example, the Applying Technology box in Chapter 22 (Understanding Securities and Securities Markets) explains why investment companies with effective Internet strategies, like Charles Schwab, are outperforming traditional investment companies.

Global Business Economy

Chapter 3 (Competing in the Global Marketplace) offers a complete and exciting picture of competition in the global marketplace. We discuss why global trade is important to the United States, why nations trade, barriers to international trade, how companies enter the global marketplace, and a host of other international concepts and topics.

The trends section found in each chapter explains how globalization will affect specific business activities. For example, the trends section in Chapter 13 (Understanding the Customer and Creating Goods and Services That Satisfy) examines the unique problems faced by human resource managers as more and more companies "go global."

Entrepreneurship and Small Business Management

Because many students will either open their own businesses or go to work for small organizations, entrepreneurship and small business principles are presented throughout the text. Chapter 6 (Entrepreneurship: Starting and Managing Your Own Business) delivers insightful discussions on issues related to starting and managing a small business including the advantages and disadvantages of small business ownership. In addition, each chapter contains a feature called Focusing on Small Business that offers practical insights into the challenges and rewards of actually owning and managing a small business. In Chapter 13, for example, the Focusing on Small Business box explains how Michael Bracken's small landscape nursery took on Wal-Mart and Home Depot and survived. In Chapter 10 (Motivating Employees and Creating Self-Managed Teams), students see how a small technology start-up business motivates employees to perform their best.

Ethics and Social Responsibility

A paramount theme of this text is that business must be conducted in an ethical and socially responsible manner. Chapter 4 (Making Ethical Decisions and Managing a Socially Responsible Business) is completely devoted to business ethics and social responsibility. We discuss techniques for setting personal ethical standards and the stages of ethical development. Also presented are ways managers influence organizational ethics, tools for creating employee ethical awareness, and the concept of social responsibility.

Each chapter drives this theme home with a Making Ethical Choices box. Each box presents sticky ethical issues, taken from actual business situations, and poses provocative questions about right and wrong. For example, the Making Ethical Choices box in Chapter 17 (Using Technology to Manage Information) tests students' reactions to false and misleading information on the Internet.

Careers

The Future of Business is a rich source of career guidance for students. As already mentioned, the appendix to Chapter 1 (Getting Your Career Off on the Right Track) helps students use the Internet to find their first professional job. In addition, each of the six parts of the text has an appendix on careers that describes employment opportunities in a different area of business.

Students will find excellent career information in the Hot Links activities and in the last part of each chapter, Applying This Chapter's Topics. For example, in Chapter 3 (Competing in the Global Marketplace), students are given insights into the importance of developing global management skills. Try It Now! boxes also emphasize career development. The Try It Now! box in Chapter 11 (Understanding Labor-Management Relations) explains how to negotiate for compensation and benefits. The Try It Now! in Chapter 17 (Using Technology to Manage Information), tells students how to stay tuned to the latest information technology developments to enhance employment opportunities.

STUDENT-ORIENTED PEDAGOGY DELIVERS VALUE LIKE NO OTHER

The Future of Business, Millennium Edition, is designed to engage students and arouse interest in all facets of business. Delivered in a precise, crisp writing style, each chapter includes various applications to strengthen students' understanding and involve them in actual business practices.

Integrated Learning System

To anchor key concepts and provide a framework for study, an integrated learning system links all major concepts with the chapter, end-of-chapter, and supplements package. Learning goals at the beginning of each chapter outline the goals for study. Major headings in the chapter are identified with an icon and supported by concept checks and a chapter summary. In addition, the study guide, instructor's manual, and test bank are all framed around the integrated learning system. Each piece of the system reinforces the others to help students learn quickly and to ease lecture preparation.

Hundreds of Actual Business Applications Hold Student Interest and Clarify Concepts

We focused this book on the needs, abilities, and experience of the typical student. We drew on our experiences inside and outside the classroom to create the most readable and enjoyable textbook in business administration. We believe that the actual business applications that are interspersed throughout the chapters set the standard for readability and lucid explanation of key concepts.

>lg 1 ### Opening Vignettes Don't Leave You Hanging

Many texts use short stories to open the chapters. We deliver extra value to you by beginning each chapter with a vignette about a prominent, student-friendly company that previews that chapter's content. We then provide several questions to prompt critical thinking about the chapter. At the end of the chapter, we provide an update on the company featured in the opening vignette and offer suggestions on how it may have to adapt to meet emerging trends.

Videos Introduce Actual Businesses to the Classroom

Developed by business professors, in conjunction with a professional video studio, 23 videos reinforce chapter concepts. These videos feature companies such as Yahoo! and Valassis Communications and bring chapter topics to life.

Tools to Help You Master Business Vocabulary

Every key business term is carefully defined within the text. Terms are in bold type throughout the chapter to make them easier to identify. Terms are also defined in the margin where first introduced. We also include a complete glossary of all key terms at the end of the book. We deliver extra value by featuring two online quizzes for each chapter that test student comprehension of chapter terminology along with customized feedback to guide students in strengthening their business vocabularies.

Skills Development to Prepare Students for the Workplace 2000

Professors have told us that one of their course goals is to strengthen research, communication, business writing, presentation, and teamwork skills. To aid in skills development, *The Future of Business, Millennium Edition,* integrates the following features in each chapter:

1. *Preparing for Tomorrow's Workplace.* This section, found at the end of each chapter, includes five or six activities designed to help students build their business skills. These exercises deliver value to students by giving them an advantage over fellow graduates in the workplace.

2. *Internet Activities.* Hot Links in each chapter guide students to check out the Web sites of companies and products that reinforce chapter concepts. Students will learn how actual companies use the Internet to find new customers and earn a profit. At the end of each chapter, Working the Net projects make it easy to get students online and strengthen their research skills. As noted later in the preface, over 80 Internet exercises are provided at the Gitman/McDaniel Web site to offer additional research opportunities.

3. *Critical Thinking Activities.* Each boxed feature has two purposes—to amplify and reinforce concepts presented in the chapter and to challenge students to think in-depth about chapter concepts. Critical thinking questions can be used to generate class discussion or prompt further student analysis. In addition, each chapter contains a Creative Thinking Case that features interesting organizations such as the New England Aquarium, the Internet Monster Board, Girl Scouts of America, Ford's Acquisition of Volvo, and the American Automobile Association.

A FULLY INTEGRATED TEACHING/LEARNING SYSTEM DELIVERS EXCEPTIONAL INSTRUCTOR VALUE

The text and all major supplements are organized around the learning goals that appear at the beginning of each chapter to provide professors and students with an easy-to-use teaching/learning system. A numbered icon like the one shown in the margin identifies each chapter goal and appears next to its related material in the text and in all key supplements. The system is illustrated on the inside front cover of the text.

The comprehensive support package helps professors prepare lectures and offers teaching aids in a variety of print and electronic formats to fit various teaching styles. Each component of the comprehensive supplements package has been carefully crafted by outstanding teachers to ensure that the introduction to business course is a rewarding experience for both professors and students. The supplements package includes time-tested teaching tools as well as new supplements designed for the electronic classroom.

Innovative Instructor's Supplements

- **Comprehensive Instructor's Manual with Transparency Masters and Video Guide (ISBN: 0-324-017200).** At the core of the integrated learning system for *The Future of Business* is the Instructor's Manual prepared by Gene Hastings, Portland Community College. Developed in response to numerous suggestions from instructors teaching this course, each chapter is designed to provide maximum guidance for delivering the content in an interesting and dynamic manner. Each chapter begins with learning goals that anchor the integrated learning system. A lecture outline guides professors through key terminology and concepts. Lecture enhancers provide additional information and examples from actual businesses to illustrate key chapter concepts. Each chapter includes guidance for integrating PowerPoint™ slides and other visuals that illustrate and reinforce the lecture. A comprehensive Video Guide includes the running time of each video, concepts illustrated in the video, teaching objectives for the case, and solutions for video case study questions. A complete set of transparency masters is available to create overhead acetates. The transparency masters include exhibits from the text and additional teaching notes designed to add fresh examples to your lectures.

- **PowerPoint™ Lecture System (ISBN: 0-324-017227).** Over 300 slides of key chapter concepts and actual business examples not included in the text are available in PowerPoint™ presentation software to improve lecture organization and reduce preparation time. The PowerPoint™ slides were prepared by Carol Luce, Arizona State University.

- **Instructor's Resource CD (ISBN: 0-324-017219).** For maximum convenience, the Instructor's Manual, the PowerPoint™ slides, and the Thomson Learning Testing Tools are all available on a CD.

- **Color Acetate Transparencies (ISBN: 0-324-017235).** Color acetate transparencies feature key concepts, exhibits from the text, and additional examples and exhibits not found in the text.

- **Test Bank (ISBN: 0-324-020481).** The comprehensive Test Bank, written by Tom and Betty Pritchett, Kennesaw State University, is organized by learning goal to support the integrated learning system. With over 2,000 true/false, multiple-choice, fill-in-the-blank, and short-answer questions, tests can be customized to support a variety of course objectives. The Test Bank is available in print and new Windows software formats (Thomson Learning Testing Tool™) (ISBN: 0-324-017189).

- **Complete Video Package and Video Guide (ISBN: 0-034-022697, 0-324-022700, and 0-324-022719).** Designed to enrich and support chapter concepts, each of the 23 videos presents real business issues faced by a variety of service and manufacturing organizations. The video cases challenge students to study business issues and develop solutions to business problems. The instructor's video guide, included in the Instructor's Manual and written by Michael McCuddy, Valparaiso University, outlines the key teaching objectives of each video case and suggests answers to the critical thinking questions.

- *The Future of Business* **Web Site (http://gitman.swcollege.com).** Designed to support your course objectives, the text Web site is a source of downloadable supplements and over 80 Internet exercises organized by chapter. Two on-line quizzes per chapter are designed to test student comprehension and provide customized feedback.

INNOVATIVE STUDENT SUPPLEMENTS

The Future of Business, Millennium Edition, provides several tools to help students learn fundamental business terminology and key business concepts.

- **Student Study Guide (ISBN: 0-324-017243).** Designed using the integrated learning system, the Student Study Guide, written by Jonas Falik and Brenda Hersch of Queensborough Community College, tests student comprehension of concepts through the use of multiple-choice questions, matching exercises, and a vocabulary builder that reinforces both terms from the text and other non-business terms used within the text.
- *The Future of Business* **Student Web Site (http://gitman.swcollege.com).** *The Future of Business* Web site provides rich content to maximize student learning and build online skills. Each text chapter is supported by two online quizzes, written by Ron Weidenfeller of Grand Rapids Community College, that test student understanding and offer customized feedback for incorrect answers. In addition, the Web site provides over 80 Internet exercises that demonstrate how actual companies are applying concepts from the text chapters. These Internet exercises are organized by chapter and include discussion questions and links to related Web sites. The Web site also offers voluminous support for students including Power-Point™ slides that emphasize key concepts, career information, and a directory of chapter links.

- **MarketingBuilder Express.** An "express" version of JIAN's popular *Marketing Builder* software, this tool contains everything students need to develop a marketing plan.
- **Inc. Booklets.** This popular series provides extensive resources on business topics including guidance for creating a successful business plan and 301 Great Ideas for Using Technology.

ACKNOWLEDGMENTS

This book could not have been written and published without the generous expert assistance of many people. First, we wish to thank Marlene Bellamy, Writeline Associates, for her major and outstanding contributions to numerous aspects of this text. Thanks is also extended to Nancy Moudry, Vickie Hampton, Texas Tech University, and Carolyn Lawrence for their work on a number of chapters. A special thanks is also extended to Rosemary Wild of San Diego State for her guidance on the computer chapter. Paula Daly, James Madison University, prepared excellent first drafts for Chapters 7, 8, and 10. Also, David Gray, The University of Texas at Arlington, made excellent contributions to Chapters 9 and 11. A special thanks is extended to Michael McCuddy, Valparaiso University, for his creativity in developing the Making Ethical Choices boxes and video cases. We wish to thank Gene Hastings, Portland Community College, for his comprehensive and creative work on the Instructor's Manual and Carol Luce, Arizona State University, for developing the PowerPoint™ lecture system. We also extend a special thanks to Tom and Betty Pritchett, Kennesaw State University, for their conscientious development of the Test Bank. In addition, we appreciate the creative energy of Jonas Falik and

Brenda Hersch, Queensborough Community College, who wrote the Student Study Guide. Because of the efforts of Ron Weidenfeller, Grand Rapids Community College, *The Future of Business* Web site offers compelling and up-to-date quizzes that build understanding of today's business terminology. We would also like to thank RoseAnn Reddick, who typed a significant part of the manuscript.

A special word of appreciation goes to Mary Draper, our developmental editor. Her insights and vision not only kept this mammoth project on track, but made it a far better product in the end. It is truly an honor to work with the very best. Also, our deepest gratitude goes to Dave Shaut, Vice President of South-Western Publishing Company, for believing in us. Dave made this text a reality. Thanks also goes to Steve Scoble for managing the marketing and sales efforts, Kara ZumBahlen for organizing the multitude of production issues, Kevin von Gillern for implementing a creative video and Web plan, and Cary Benbow for researching and managing the photo selection process. We also appreciate the keen design efforts of Michael Stratton who designed the cover and internal pages.

We have benefited from the detailed and constructive reviews provided by many individuals. In particular, we wish to thank the following educators who have served as reviewers:

Joseph H. Atallah
Devry Institute of Technology

Herm Baine
Broward Community College

Harvey Bronstein
Oakland Community College

Bonnie R. Chavez
Santa Barbara City College

M. Bixby Cooper
Michigan State University

Jonas Falik
Queensborough Community College

Janice M. Feldbauer
Austin Community College—Northridge

Dennis Foster
Northern Arizona University

James Giles
Bergen Community College

Carnella Hardin
Glendale College

Frederic H. Hawkins
Westchester Business Institute

Connie Johnson
Tampa College

Jerry Kinskey
Sinclair Community College

Raymond T. Lamanna
Berkeley College

Carol Luce
Arizona State University

Carl Meskimen
Sinclair Community College

Andrew Miller
Hudson Valley Community College

H. Lynn Moretz
Central Piedmont Community College

Joseph Newton
Bakersfield College

Teresa Palmer
Illinois State University

Robert F. Reck
Western Michigan University

Ann Squire
Blackhawk Technical College

Ron Weidenfeller
Grand Rapids Community College

Lawrence J. Gitman

Lawrence J. Gitman is a professor of finance at San Diego State University. He received his Bachelor's Degree from Purdue University, his M.B.A. from the University of Dayton, and his Ph.D. from the University of Cincinnati. Professor Gitman is a prolific textbook author and has over 45 articles appearing in *Financial Management, Financial Review, Journal of Financial Planning, Journal of Risk and Insurance, Journal of Financial Research, Financial Practice and Education, Journal of Financial Education*, and other publications. He currently serves as an associate editor of *Journal of Financial Planning*, and *Financial Practice and Education*.

His singly authored major textbooks include *Principles of Managerial Finance: Brief*, Second Edition, *Principles of Managerial Finance*, Ninth Edition, and *Foundations of Managerial Finance*, Fourth Edition. Other major textbooks include *Personal Financial Planning*, Eighth Edition, and *Fundamentals of Investing*, Seventh Edition, both co-authored with Michael D. Joehnk. Gitman and Joehnk also wrote *Investment Fundamentals: A Guide to Becoming a Knowledgeable Investor*, which was selected as one of 1988's ten best personal finance books by *Money* magazine.

An active member of numerous professional organizations, Professor Gitman is past president of the Academy of Financial Services, the San Diego Chapter of the Financial Executives Institute, the Midwest Finance Association, and the FMA National Honor Society. In addition he is a Certified Financial Planner (CFP) and a Certified Cash Manager (CCM). Gitman recently served as Vice-President, Financial Education for the Financial Management Association and as a Director of the San Diego MIT Enterprise Forum. He currently serves on the CFP Board of Standards. He lives with his wife and two children in La Jolla, California, where he is an avid bicyclist.

Carl McDaniel

Carl McDaniel is a professor of marketing at the University of Texas—Arlington, where he is Chairman of the Marketing Department. He has been an instructor for more than 20 years and is the recipient of several awards for outstanding teaching. McDaniel has also been a District Sales Manager for Southwestern Bell Telephone Company. Currently, he serves as a board member of the North Texas Higher Education Authority, a $300 million financial institution.

In addition to this text, McDaniel also has co-authored a number of textbooks in marketing. McDaniel's research has appeared in such publications as *Journal of Marketing Research, Journal of Marketing, Journal of Business Research, Journal of the Academy of Marketing Science*, and *California Management Review*.

McDaniel is a member of the American Marketing Association, Academy of Marketing Science, Southern Marketing Association, Southwestern Marketing Association, and Western Marketing Association.

Besides his academic experience, McDaniel has business experience as the co-owner of a marketing research firm. Recently, McDaniel served as senior consultant to the International Trade Centre (ITC), Geneva, Switzerland. The ITC's mission is to help developing nations increase their exports. McDaniel also teaches international business each year in France. He has a Bachelor's Degree from the University of Arkansas and his Master's Degree and Doctorate from Arizona State University.

1-800-342-5437

chapter one

Your Future in Business Begins Now

learning goals

>lg 1   How do businesses and not-for-profit organizations help create our standard of living?

>lg 2   How are social trends, such as more women entering the workforce, affecting business?

>lg 3   How are demographic trends creating new opportunities for business?

>lg 4   What are the primary features of the

>lg 6   What are the trends in global competition?

Appendix:

>lg 7   What are the first steps toward finding your first professional job?

>lg 8   How can the Internet be a valuable tool in your job search?

>lg 9   How can you start off on the right track in your new job and, then later, move up to

Entering New Worlds of Fashion

A few years ago, executives at Fort Worth–based work-apparel maker Williamson-Dickie (**www.dickies.com/**) noticed a phenomenon on the West Coast. For an unknown reason, its twill pants were becoming hugely popular with teens and young adults who are traditionally attracted to designer brands. They were buying Dickies clothes for everyday wear, and buying them in larger sizes for a baggy look.

Company executives dubbed it an "anti-fashion fashion," says Jon Ragsdale, Williamson-Dickie's marketing director. "We did absolutely nothing about it," he says. "Our theory at the time was, 'We make the best workwear in the world and we make more of it than anybody else. This is a trend. It will probably be gone next year.' " But the trend didn't go away. Instead, it expanded nationwide and onto the streets of Europe.

As Dickies found itself caught up in a grassroots fashion movement, it was also in the midst of rolling out a new line of women's workwear, a huge undertaking for a company that had been making men's workwear for more than 75 years. The marketing team was called on to address both new markets with campaigns to strengthen brand awareness and broaden market appeal.

One new marketing initiative was to add mainstream magazines to the company's advertising mix. *Spin*, *Details*, and *Transworld Skateboarding* magazines featured ads encouraging readers to "Discover Dickies Streetwear." The women's line was touted in *Good Housekeeping* and *First For Women*. The ability to create brand awareness in a variety of magazines has helped Dickies reach new markets, says Elena Romero, market editor with *Daily News Record*, a men's fashion trade publication.

Although Dickies is focusing on reaching the new markets, Ragsdale says, it is not overlooking its core business of men's workwear, where sales increase steadily each year. The company attributes those increases to the growth of the economy and the diversification of industry. In addition, Ragsdale says, more new industries are using uniforms and allowing employees more choice of styles.[1]

Dickies benefited from a surprising trend in teen fashions. But it also anticipated and reacted to the trend of more women in the workforce.

Critical Thinking Questions

As you read this chapter, consider the following questions as they relate to Willliamson-Dickie:

- What other emerging trends might offer opportunities for Dickies?
- What business trends could pose threats for the firm?
- How can Dickies position itself so that it can respond rapidly to changing trends?

BUSINESS IN THE 21ST CENTURY

Each day in America thousands of new businesses are born and a rare few will become the next General Electric or Amazon.com. Unfortunately, many others will never see their first anniversary. The survivors are those that understand the trends that affect all businesses and then successfully adapt to those trends. Williamson-Dickies survives and prospers because it capitalizes on evolving trends. We begin our study of business by explaining what a business does and how it is created. Next, you will discover the key trends of the 21st century that will have an impact on all business organizations. The appendix offers you a road map to successfully finding your first professional job in business.

THE NATURE OF BUSINESS

business

An organization that strives for a profit by providing goods and services desired by its customers.

goods

Tangible items manufactured by businesses.

services

Intangible offerings of businesses that can't be held, touched, or stored.

standard of living

A country's output of goods and services that people can buy with the money they have.

quality of life

The general level of human happiness based on such things as life expectancy, educational standards, health, sanitation, and leisure time.

risk

The potential to lose time and money or otherwise not be able to accomplish an organization's goals.

revenue

The money a company earns from providing services or selling goods to customers.

costs

Expenses incurred in creating and selling goods and services.

profit

The money left over after all expenses are paid.

A **business** is an organization that strives for a profit by providing goods and services desired by its customers. Businesses meet the needs of consumers by providing movies, medical care, autos, and countless other goods and services. **Goods** are tangible items manufactured by businesses, such as desks. **Services** are intangible offerings of businesses that can't be held, touched, or stored. Physicians, lawyers, restaurants, car washes, and airlines all provide services. Businesses also serve other organizations, such as hospitals, retailers, and governments, by providing machinery, goods for resale, computers, and thousands of other items.

Thus, businesses create the goods and services that are the basis of our standard of living. The **standard of living** of any country is measured by the output of goods and services people can buy with the money they have. The United States has one of the highest standards of living in the world. Several countries such as Switzerland and Germany have higher wages than the United States, but their standard of living isn't higher. The reason is that prices are so much higher in those countries that people are able to purchase less than people in the United States with the same amount of money. For example, a "Real Meal Deal" at McDonald's in Geneva, Switzerland, costs about $9 compared to less than $4 in the United States.

Businesses play a key role in determining our quality of life by providing jobs and goods and services to society. **Quality of life** refers to the general level of human happiness based on such things as life expectancy, educational standards, health, sanitation, and leisure time. Countries with the highest quality of life are Canada, the United States, Japan, the Netherlands, and Norway. In a list of 174 countries, Russia ranks 57th, China 108th, and India 135th.[2] Building a high quality of life is a combined effort of businesses, government, and not-for-profit organizations.

Creating a quality of life is not without risks. **Risk** is the potential to lose time and money or otherwise not be able to accomplish an organization's goals. The Boy Scouts of America, for example, face the risk of not recruiting enough new scouts each year, while Compaq Computer risks not reaching its revenue goals. **Revenue** is the money a company earns from providing services or selling goods to customers. **Costs** are expenses for rent, salaries, supplies, transportation, and many other items that a company incurs from creating and selling goods and services. Some of the costs incurred by Williamson-Dickie (featured in our opening story) include expenses for cloth, pattern designers, cutting machines, workers, managers, building rental or purchase, advertising, and transportation. **Profit** is the money left over after all expenses are paid.

When a company like Dickies uses its resources intelligently, it can often increase sales, hold costs down, and earn a profit. Not all companies earn profit, but that is the risk of being in business. In American business today, there is generally a direct relationship between risks and profit: the greater the risks, the greater the potential profit (or loss). ZymeTX is an Oklahoma-based biotechnology company that is trying to create vaccines for viruses. So far, the company has not earned a profit, but if it develops a vaccine for AIDS, the rewards will be huge.

Is ZymeTX still losing money? Find out how ZymeTX and other businesses are doing at **www.hoovers.com**

Not-for-Profit Organizations

not-for-profit organization

An organization that exists to achieve some goal other than the usual business goal of profit.

Not all organizations strive to make a profit. A **not-for-profit organization** is an organization that exists to achieve some goal other than the usual business goal of profit. The United Way, Keep America Beautiful, the American Cancer Society, Greenpeace, and the Sierra Club are all not-for-profit organizations. Most hospitals, zoos, museums, and charities are also not-for-profit organizations. Government is our largest and most pervasive not-for-profit group. Not-for-profit organizations (not including government expenditures) now account for over 28 percent of the economic activity in the United States.

Successful not-for-profit organizations follow sound business principles. These groups have goals they hope to accomplish, but the goals are not focused on profits. For example, a not-for-profit organization's goal might be feeding the poor, stopping destruction of the environment, increasing attendance at the ballet, or preventing drunk driving. Reaching such goals takes good planning, management, and control. Not-for-profit organizations do not compete directly with each other as, for example, American and United Airlines do, but they do compete for people's scarce volunteer time and donations.

Factors of Production: The Building Blocks of Business

factors of production

The resources used to create goods and services.

Factors of production are the resources used to create goods and services. By using the factors of production efficiently, a company can produce more output with the same resources. Four traditional factors of production are common to all productive activity: natural resources, labor, capital, and entrepreneurship. A fifth factor, knowledge, is gaining in importance.

Commodities that are useful inputs in their natural state are known as natural resources. They include farmland, forests, mineral and oil deposits, and water. Sometimes natural resources are simply called *land*, although, as you can see, the term means more than just land. Today, urban sprawl, pollution, and limited resources have raised questions about resource use. Conservationists, ecologists, and government bodies are proposing laws to require land-use planning and resource conservation.

The economic contributions of people working with their minds and muscles are called labor. This input includes the talents of everyone—from a restaurant cook to a nuclear physicist—who performs the many tasks of manufacturing and selling goods and services.

capital

The inputs, such as tools, machinery, equipment, and buildings, used to produce goods and services and get them to the customer.

The tools, machinery, equipment, and buildings used to produce goods and services and get them to the consumer are known as **capital.** Sometimes the term *capital* is also used to mean the money that buys machinery, factories, and other production and distribution facilities. However, because money itself produces nothing, it is *not* one of the basic inputs. Instead, it is a means of acquiring the inputs. Therefore, in this context, capital does not include money.

TO FIND HIP, YOUNG SMOKERS— HAVE A BALL

At the Hammerstein Ballroom in midtown Manhattan, go-go dancers gyrate energetically to pounding electronic music, as a stilt-walker dressed like a fairy blows bubbles over guests' heads. Psychedelic colors swirl on five large screens.

But this ain't no disco. The revelers at this party are hundreds of Manhattan bartenders frolicking at the annual Bartender's Ball, in a sybaritic pleasure palace created specially for them by cigarette conglomerate RJR Nabisco Holdings Corp. Above the entrance, a wall is festooned, tongue-in-cheek, with a supersize copy of the Surgeon General's familiar warning: "Quitting smoking now greatly reduces serious risk to your health."

Meanwhile, cigarette girls, clad in low-cut zebra-striped shirts and white hip-huggers, work the crowd with trays overflowing with candies and free packs of RJR's Camel cigarettes.

Late in the evening, guest host Rocco Primavera, decked out in a wide-collared shirt and an enormous red Afro, assumes the stage. "Thank Camel for footing the bill for this shindig and supplying the booze for this party!" he cries out. "God bless you! Camel loves you!"

With their traditional marketing techniques under siege—tobacco ads have been kicked off billboards and shut out of sports stadiums—cigarette makers are building a new arsenal of selling strategies. Among their hottest prospects: bars that attract young, hip drinkers, and the army of bartenders who interact with them. With vending machines disappearing in many cities, bartenders are now the vital link in selling smokes directly to their customers.

Although bar promotions have always been part of the tobacco industry, cigarette makers are now burrowing into urban night life like never before. Deploying their massive marketing budgets, the biggest U.S. tobacco firms are pounding on the doors of bar owners, offering them thousands of dollars in exclusive deals. While Reynolds pays for parties and ads, Philip Morris simply cuts a check. In exchange, bar owners promise to use bar supplies plastered with the sponsoring company's brand names. More importantly, the bars often pledge not to sell or promote a rival behind their counters. (Philip Morris says it doesn't require bars to sell its brands only.)

"We've had everybody in here pitching to us—Camel, Marlboro, Lucky Strike," says Patrick Evangelista, owner of an uptown bar called Who's On First. "I've heard they're paying anywhere from $2,000 to $50,000 annually."

Critical Thinking Questions

1. Is RJR Nabisco simply trying to protect its market from the competition?
2. Is it ethical for tobacco companies to target young smokers? Young nonsmokers?
3. Is it unethical for a manufacturer to pay a retailer (like a bar or any other retail business) to stock its products and not the competition's?

entrepreneurs

People who combine the inputs of natural resources, labor, and capital to produce goods or services with the intention of making a profit or accomplishing a not-for-profit goal.

Entrepreneurs are people who combine the inputs of natural resources, labor, and capital to produce goods or services with the intention of making a profit. These people make all the decisions that set the course for their firms; they create products and production processes. Because they are not guaranteed a profit in return for their time and effort, they must be risk takers. Of course, if their firms succeed, the rewards may be great.

Today, Americans between the ages of 14 and 34 are creating almost half of the new businesses in the country.[3] One study found that 87 percent of young people ages 16 to 25 want to own a business.[4] They are attracted by the opportunity to be their own boss and reap the financial rewards of a successful business. Many start

FINDING GOLD IN VINTAGE SNEAKERS

It takes Tace Chalfa just a moment to identify the blue-and-yellow Nike sneakers that the paunchy man across the counter pulls from a crumpled paper bag. "Oregon waffle trainers, 1975, made in Japan," says Chalfa. "I'll give you $80 for them. You won't be able to sell them for more." The man pauses for an instant, grabs the bills, and runs out the door. "I'll sell these for $160," Chalfa predicts, flipping the Nikes into a heap of colorful shoes in a bin. Chalfa's keen eye and eclectic supply line have made her one of the world's best-known dealers in vintage sneakers—used or in mint condition.

A slight 26-year-old with a penchant for 1950s dresses, Chalfa didn't go to college and didn't do very well in high school. She tried waitressing, telemarketing, and panhandling but didn't excel at any of them. Then she got married and became co-owner of her husband's musty secondhand store, the Red Light, near the University of Washington campus.

One day about three years ago, a teenage collector from Japan came into the store and plunked down $1,000 for a size 13 pair of 1978 Nike Stings,

orange-suede and green-nylon trainers with gum soles that Chalfa had picked up for $50. "I said to myself, 'I'm in the shoe business now,' " she recalls.

According to Chalfa, Red Light grossed about $1 million in 1998, with a $400,000 boost from selling old sneakers. Demand has been fueled by growing cadres of Asian and American teenagers who are into (mostly) 1970s styles and by sports collectors. Red Light's customers, its publicists confirm, include Courtney Love, members of the band Alice in Chains, and others from the Seattle rock scene.

Critical Thinking Questions

1. Tace Chalfa started her new business almost by chance. Would detailed planning have been a better approach?
2. What do you see as the rewards for someone like Chalfa?
3. What are the potential risks?

their first business from their dorm rooms or while living at home, so their cost is almost zero.

Entrepreneurs include people like Bill Gates, the founder of Microsoft, who is now one of the richest people in the world. The list of entrepreneurs also includes countless thousands of individuals who have started small companies that, while remaining small, still contribute to America's economic well-being. One such entrepreneur is Tace Chalfa of Seattle, Washington. Her story unfolds in the Focusing on Small Business box.

A number of outstanding managers and noted academics are beginning to emphasize a fifth factor of production—knowledge. **Knowledge** is the combined talents and skills of the workforce. As the world becomes ever more uncertain, the very nature of work, organizations, and management is changing. The new competitive environment places a premium on knowledge and learning. Lester Thurow, a leading world expert on economic issues, says that "the dominant competitive weapon of the twenty-first century will be the

knowledge
The combined talents and skills of the workforce.

Knowledge gives businesses a competitive edge. For insight into how companies are turning themselves into learning-based organizations, go to
www.brint.com

Capitalizing on Trends in Business

concəpt chəck

- Explain the difference between a business and a not-for-profit organization.
- Explain the concepts of revenue, costs, and profit.
- What are the five factors of production?
- What is the role of an entrepreneur in society?

knowledge of the work force."[5] The companies that will become and remain successful will be the ones that can learn fast, assimilate this learning, and develop new insights. General Electric and Coca Cola are two firms often cited as learning-based organizations because they utilize their human resources so effectively.

CAPITALIZING ON TRENDS IN BUSINESS

Business owners and managers use their skills and resources to create goods and services that will satisfy customers and prospective customers. Owners and managers have a wide latitude of control over day-to-day business decisions such as which supplies are purchased, which employees are hired, what products are sold, and where they are sold. However, certain environmental conditions that affect a business cannot be controlled. These conditions are constantly changing and include social change, demographics, economic conditions, technology, and global competition, as shown in Exhibit 1-1. Successful owners and managers must continuously study these conditions and adapt their businesses, or they will lose their ability to compete.

> e x h i b i t   1 - 1 <

The Environment of Business

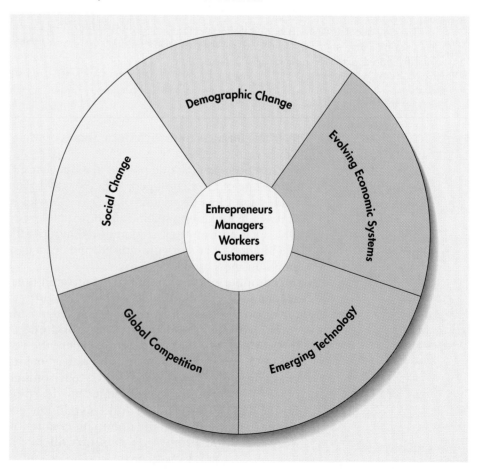

Consider two examples of how companies have responded to changes in the business environment:

- The average age of the traditional buyer of some Cadillac models is approaching 70. An aging target market means big problems for the company. Cadillac's share of the roughly 1.2 million-unit luxury market is now 15 percent, down from 24 percent in the early 1990s. To offset this trend, Cadillac created the Catera. Its target market is entry-level luxury car buyers, such as buyers of the BMW 3 series or the Lexus ES300. The car has been modestly successful and is scheduled to be produced at least through 2002.[6]

What else is Cadillac doing to respond to a changing business environment? Take a look at the company's plans and new car models at **www.cadillac.com**

- The social trend toward casualness has finally reached the office. Many firms now have a "dress-down" day on Fridays, when coats and ties aren't required. When Charles Schwab, the discount stockbroker, considered offering a "dress-down" day, it called Levi Strauss and Co., the blue jeans and casual wear manufacturer, for a little fashion advice. Recognizing the significance of this trend, Levi Strauss responded with more than advice. It provided brochures showing how dress could be casual without being sloppy, names of other companies that had successfully shed traditional attire, and studies that showed how the apparel shift had improved workers' productivity and morale. By capitalizing on a new social trend, Levi's Dockers now capture one-third of all department store pants sales.[7]

No one business is large or powerful enough to create major changes in the external environment. Thus, managers are basically adapters to rather than agents of change. For example, despite the huge size of General Motors, Ford, and DaimlerChrysler, these companies have only recently been able to stem the competitive push by the Japanese for an ever growing share of the U.S. automobile market. Global competition is basically an uncontrollable element in the external environment. This section examines trends in the business environment that are reshaping today's business landscape.

SOCIAL TRENDS

>lg 2

Social change is perhaps the most difficult environmental factor for owners and managers to forecast, influence, or integrate into business plans. Social factors include our attitudes, values, and lifestyles. Social factors influence the products people buy, the prices paid for products, the effectiveness of specific promotions, and how, where, and when people expect to purchase products.

The Growth of Component Lifestyles

component lifestyle

A lifestyle made up of a complex set of interests and choices.

People in the United States today are piecing together component lifestyles. A lifestyle is a mode of living; it is the way people decide to live their lives. A **component lifestyle** is a lifestyle made up of a complex set of interests and choices. In other words, people are choosing products and services that meet diverse needs and interests rather than conforming to traditional stereotypes.

In the past, a person's profession—for instance, banker—defined that person's lifestyle. Today a person can be a banker, gourmet, fitness enthusiast, dedicated single parent, and conservationist—all at once. Each of these lifestyles is associated with different goods and services and represents a unique market.

For example, businesses advertise cooking utensils, wines, and exotic foods through magazines like *Bon Appetit* and *Gourmet* for the gourmets. The fitness enthusiast buys Adidas equipment and special jogging outfits and reads *Runner's World* magazine. Component lifestyles increase the complexity of consumers' buying habits. The banker may own a BMW but change the oil herself. She may buy fast food for lunch but French wine for dinner, own sophisticated photographic equipment and a low-priced home stereo, and shop for stockings at Kmart or Wal-Mart and suits at Brooks Brothers.

The Changing Role of Families and Working Women

Component lifestyles have evolved because consumers can choose from a growing number of goods and services, and most have the money to exercise more options. Increased purchasing power is largely a result of the growth of dual-income families. Wives' incomes amounted to only 26.6 percent of their families' household incomes in 1970, but make up over 42 percent today. Now more than 72 percent of women with children under 18 are working in the paid labor force, compared with 47 percent in 1970. The increase is even sharper for women with children younger than three, from 34 percent to 62 percent.[8] The phenomenon of working women has had a greater effect on business than any other social change.

As women's earnings grow, so do their levels of expertise, experience, and authority. The word *handyman* may no longer be politically correct—or correct at all—as women become a more potent force in buying tools and hardware for both inside and outside the home. From simply using more "feminine" colors to designing tools especially for women do-it-yourselfers, companies are responding by creating products with women in mind. "Our research shows more females are the primary decision-makers and buyers of home items," says Lorrie Crum, a spokeswoman for Rubbermaid, Inc.[9]

Other hardware companies have assembled "kits" for customers tackling a specific home project for the first time. The Miracle Restoration Kit includes a Miracle Eraser pumice stone sander and rejuvenation oil for refinishing furniture. "The stores say that women are the people who refinish furniture, and we came up with a product that doesn't take any pressure at all and doesn't get clogged up like sandpaper," said Hank Greenfield, who makes the kit.[10]

concept check

- Why are social changes the most difficult environmental factor to predict?
- How do component lifestyles make it more difficult to predict a consumer's buying habits?
- What social change has had the greatest impact on business?

DEMOGRAPHIC TRENDS

>lg 3

demography
The study of people's vital statistics, such as their age, race and ethnicity, and location.

Demographic trends—another uncontrollable factor in the business environment—are also extremely important to managers. **Demography** is the study of people's vital statistics, such as their age, race and ethnicity, and location. Demographics are significant because the basis for any market is people. Demographics also determine the size and composition of the workforce. Let's begin by taking a closer look at key age groups.

Generation Y—Born to Shop

Generation Y
Americans born after 1982.

Today there are about 58 million Americans age 16 and under. These people—those born after 1982—make up **Generation Y.** And though Generation Y is much smaller than the baby boom, which lasted nearly 20 years and produced 78 million children, its members are plentiful enough to put their own footprints on society.

Members of Generation Y love to shop. Born into a world of technology, they're big consumers of high-tech products like cellular phones.

The marketing impact of Generation Y has been immense. Companies that sell toys, videos, software, and clothing to kids have boomed in recent years. Nine of the 10 best-selling videos of all time are animated films from Walt Disney Co. Club Med, the French vacation company, now earns half its U.S. revenues from family resorts. The members of Generation Y were born into a world vastly different from the one their parents entered. The changes in families, the workforce, technology, and demographics in recent decades will no doubt affect their attitudes, but in unpredictable ways. Among those changes:

- Some 61 percent of U.S. children aged three to five are attending preschool, compared with 38 percent in 1970.

- Nearly 60 percent of households with children aged seven or younger have personal computers, according to IDC/LINK Resources Corp., a market research firm in New York.

- Approximately 15 percent of U.S. births in recent years were to foreign-born mothers, with origins so diverse that more than 100 different languages are spoken in the school systems of New York City, Chicago, Los Angeles, and Fairfax County, Virginia.[11]

Generation Y is also driving the educational software industry, which has grown to a $600 million business from practically nothing in 1990. Titles like Baby-ROM from Byron Preiss Multimedia Co. are designed to help infants as young as six months learn to identify numbers, shapes, colors, and body parts.

Generation X—Savvy and Cynical

Generation X

Americans born between 1968 and 1979.

There are approximately 47 million people between the ages of 20 and 31. These people—those born between 1968 and 1979—have been labeled **Generation X.** They are the first generation of latchkey children—products of dual-career households or, in roughly half the cases, of divorced or separated parents. The members of Generation X began entering the workforce in the era of downsizing, so they are likelier than the previous generation to be unemployed, underemployed, and living at home with mom and dad. Still, 18 million are married and not living at home, and 8 million are full-time college students. As a generation that's been bombarded by multiple media since their cradle days, they're savvy and cynical consumers.

For decades, Ford marketed its light-duty pickups by emphasizing their roughness and toughness. Advertisements featured trucks climbing rugged mountains or four-wheeling through mud. But Ford quickly realized that this approach was not going to work with Generation Xers. Instead, Ford chose to lead with a new product. The company created a new version of its popular Ranger pickup, giving it flares on the fenders, jazzy graphics, and a youthful new name—Splash. The promotion campaign attempted to infuse the vehicle with personality by combining the truck with adventuresome sports.

Baby Boomers—America's Mass Market

baby boomers

Americans born between 1946 and 1964.

People born between 1946 and 1964 are called **baby boomers.** Many baby boomers are now over 50, but they still cling to their youth. Most continue to live a very active life. This group cherishes convenience, which has resulted in a growing demand for home delivery of large appliances, furniture, groceries, and other items. In addition, the spreading culture of convenience explains the tremendous appeal of prepared take-out foods, VCRs, portable telephones, and the Internet.

Baby boomers' parents raised their children to think for and of themselves. Studies of child-rearing practices show that parents of the 1950s and 1960s consistently ranked "to think for themselves" as the number-one trait they wanted to nurture in their children. Postwar affluence also enabled parents to indulge their children as never before. They invested in their children's skills by sending them to college. They encouraged their children to succeed in a job market that rewarded competitive drive more than cooperative spirit and individual skills more than teamwork.

In turn, the sheer size of the generation encouraged businesses to play to the emerging individuality of baby boomers. Even before the oldest baby boomers started earning a living more than two decades ago, astute business-people anticipated the profits that could come from giving millions of young people what they wanted. Businesses offered individualistic baby boomers a growing array of customized products and services—houses, cars, furniture, appliances, clothes, vacations, jobs, leisure time, and even beliefs.

Older Consumers—Not Just Grandparents

The oldest baby boomers have already crossed the 50-year threshold that many demographers use to define the "mature market." Yet today's mature consumers are wealthier, healthier, and better educated than those of earlier generations.[12] Although they make up only 26 percent of the population, 50-plus consumers buy half of all domestic cars, half of all silverware, and nearly half of all home remodeling. By 2020, over a third of the population will be age 50 or older.

Businesspeople who want to actively pursue the mature market must understand it. Aging consumers create some obvious opportunities. JC Penney's Easy Dressing clothes feature Velcro-fasteners for women with arthritis or other ailments who may have difficulty with zippers or buttons. Sales from the first Easy Dressing catalog were three times higher than expected. Chicago-based Cadaco offers a line of games with easy-to-read big print and larger game pieces. The series focuses on nostalgia by including Michigan rummy, hearts, poker, and bingo. Trivia buffs more familiar with Mitch Miller than Guns 'n' Roses can play Parker Brothers' "The Vintage Years" edition of Trivial Pursuit.

Firms like Ford Motor Company market their products to the growing number of Spanish-speaking immigrants, whose buying power boosts the U.S. economy.

Americans on the Move

The average U.S. citizen moves every six years. This trend has implications for business. A large influx of new people into an area creates many new opportunities for all types of businesses. Conversely, significant out-migration from a city or town may force many of its businesses to move or close down because they can't find qualified employees. The cities with the greatest projected population growth from 1995 to 2005 are Houston, Washington D.C., Atlanta, San Diego, Phoenix, Orlando, and Dallas.

The United States experiences both immigration from other countries and migration within its borders. In the 1990s, the six states with the highest levels of immigration from abroad were California, New York, New Jersey, Illinois, Texas, and Massachusetts. The six states with the greatest population increases due to in-

Boeing is one of many U.S. companies that benefit from global competition. While the Boeing 777 may be assembled in the U.S., the actual parts of this airplane come from both U.S. and international suppliers.

in revenue. And in Europe, it will soon move up from a seasonal flavor to year-round status.[16]

Other companies are hoping for similar outcomes. Levi Strauss, famous for exporting the all-American look of blue jeans to the world, is hoping to bring an offshore trend to U.S. consumers. For three years, a dark version of Levi's denim has been the hot seller in Japan. Now Levi's is launching an offshoot to U.S. customers; called "hard jeans," it will be darker and stiffer than typical denim. Levi's has told its U.S. managers that looking abroad for ideas is part of their job.[17]

Improvements in Productivity

Good planning and efficient use of resources have made American companies world-class competitors. American businesses are now the most productive in the world. During the 1990s American businesses downsized to become more efficient. Downsizing means terminating employees, or laying off workers, to reduce costs and become more efficient. The goal is to produce as many or more goods and services with fewer employees. Many companies including AT&T, Boeing, and General Motors laid off tens of thousands of workers to become more competitive.

Often downsizing has been coupled with a greater use of technology, thereby greatly increasing productivity. Today, for example, there are about 65 personal computers per 100 workers in the United States. In Japan there are 20 personal computers per 100 workers. Contrary to popular belief, American businesses are much more productive than the Japanese. American manufacturers are 20 percent more productive than Japanese manufacturers, and American

service providers are 50 percent more productive than Japan's service sector.

The relentless drive for efficiency has made many American firms leaders around the globe. Coca Cola, Microsoft, Wal-Mart, McDonald's, Ford, and Exxon are truly world leaders in their fields. Other, less well known American firms are just as effective in their markets against global competitors. Though American companies have led the way into the world marketplace of the 21st century, one thing is certain—competition from domestic and foreign competitors is only going to get tougher.

Global Quality Standards

American goods and services have a reputation for quality around the globe. **Quality** goods and services offer customer value and satisfaction. **Customer value** is the ratio of benefits to the sacrifices necessary to obtain those benefits. Customers receive value in the form of well-known brand names, durability, design, ease of use, and customer service. To receive those benefits, they give up money, time, and effort.

A popular technique for increasing quality is continuous improvement. **Continuous improvement** is a commitment to constantly seek better ways of doing things so as to maintain and improve quality. Companywide teams try to prevent problems and systematically improve key processes instead of troubleshooting problems as they arise. Continuous improvement also means looking for ways to apply new technology in innovative production methods, shortening product-development time, and continually measuring performance using statistical methods. Ford Motor Co. has used continuous improvement successfully for several years. It is now more efficient than General Motors or DaimlerChrysler.

The Malcolm Baldrige National Quality Award   The **Malcolm Baldrige National Quality Award**, named for a former secretary of commerce, was established by the U.S. Congress in 1987 to recognize U.S. companies that offer goods and services of world-class quality. The award also promotes awareness of quality and transfers information about quality to others in the business community.

The Baldrige Award is administered by the U.S. Departmentof Commerce's National Institute of Standards and Technology. The most important criterion of the Baldrige Award is whether the firm meets customer expectations. The firm must also demonstrate that it offers quality goods and services. To qualify for the award, a company must also show continuous improvement in internal operations.Company leaders and employees must participate actively, and they must respond quickly to data and analysis.

ISO 9000 and ISO 14000 Standards   Competition in the global marketplace now requires more and more companies to meet ISO standards. **ISO 9000** (pronounced "ice-o-nine thousand") is a standard of quality management, hugely popular in Europe, that is rapidly taking hold in the United States and around the globe.

quality

Goods and services that offer customer value and satisfaction.

customer value

The ratio of benefits to the sacrifices necessary to obtain those benefits.

continuous improvement

A commitment to constantly seek better ways of doing things so as to maintain and increase quality.

Malcolm Baldrige National Quality Award

An award bestowed on U.S. companies whose goods and services offer world-class quality; established by Congress in 1987 and named for a former secretary of commerce.

ISO 9000

A set of five technical standards of quality management that were created in the late 1980s by the International Organization for Standardization to provide a uniform way of determining whether manufacturing plants and service organizations have sound quality procedures.

The ISO 9000 series was created in the late 1980s by the International Organization for Standardization. The set of five technical standards, known collectively as ISO 9000, was designed to offer a uniform way of determining whether manufacturing plants and service organizations have sound quality procedures. To register, a company must undergo an audit of its manufacturing and customer-service processes, covering everything from how it designs, produces, and installs its goods to how it inspects, packages, and markets them. Worldwide, more than 50,000 certificates have been issued to document compliance with the standards. Caterpillar's engine division in Mossville, Illinois, was among the first U.S. diesel engine factories to win the certificate. Richard Thompson, vice president and general manager of the plant, says, "Today, having ISO 9000 is a competitive advantage. Tomorrow, it will be the ante to the global poker game."[18]

DuPont, General Electric, Eastman Kodak, British Telecom, and Philips Electronics are among the big-name companies that are urging—or even coercing—suppliers to adopt ISO 9000. GE's plastics business, for instance, commanded 340 vendors to meet the standard. Declares John Yates, general manager of global sourcing for the company: "There is absolutely no negotiation. If you want to work with us, you have to get it."[19]

The latest standards are **ISO 14000**, which are designed to help ensure clean production processes to reduce growing environmental problems such as global warming, depletion of the ozone layer, and water pollution. To meet ISO 14000 standards, the executive of a firm must commit to (1) continue to improve environmental management, (2) prevent pollution, (3) obey the laws of the particular country and be a good citizen, (4) manage activities with serious consideration of their effect on the environment, and (5) announce to employees and the public the firm's environmental protection policy.[20] IBM has met the ISO 14000 worldwide.

ISO 14000
A set of technical standards designed by the International Organization for Standardization to help ensure clean production processes to protect the environment.

concept check

- How have U.S. companies improved productivity?
- How can the Malcolm Baldrige Award stimulate quality business practices?
- What are the ISO standards?

APPLYING THIS CHAPTER'S TOPICS

The trends that are reshaping the domestic and global business community are also creating abundant job opportunities. Those seeking jobs will be able to choose from a variety of career paths and job options. Businesses, however, will be competing with each other to attract skilled employees from a shrinking talent pool.

THE TALENT WAR AMONG EMPLOYERS

A survey of 77 large companies and almost 6,000 managers found that they believe the most important resource over the next 20 years will be talent. And even as the demand for talent goes up, the supply will be going down. In a report entitled "The War for Talent," McKinsey Consulting predicts that the search for the best and the brightest will become a constant, costly battle, a fight with no final victory. Not only will companies have to devise more imaginative hiring practices, but they will also have to work harder to keep their best people. In the new economy, competition is global, money is abundant, ideas are developed quickly and cheaply, and people are willing to change jobs often. In that kind of environment, says Ed Michaels, a McKinsey director who helped manage the study, "all that matters is talent. Talent wins."[21]

A lot of the talent war has to do with demographics. In 15 years, there will be 15 percent fewer Americans aged 35 to 45 than there are now. At the same time, the U.S. economy is likely to grow at a rate of 3 to 4 percent per year. So, over that period, the demand for bright, talented 35- to 45-year-olds will increase by 25 percent, but the supply will be declining by 15 percent. That sets the stage for a talent war.

Only 60 percent of the corporate officers at the companies in the McKinsey report said that they were able to pursue most of their growth opportunities. They have good ideas, they have money—they just don't have enough talented people to pursue those ideas. They are "talent-constrained." The leaders at Johnson & Johnson, a world-class firm, said that they never used to go outside the company to recruit top-level managers. Now they have to go outside as often as 25 percent of the time—because they are talent-constrained.

Choosing the Right Job for You

The typical American holds 8.6 different jobs between the ages of 18 and 32, with most of the changes coming before age 27.[22] Felix Batcup, age 26, associate art director at *Women's Sports and Fitness* magazine in New York, has had five jobs in five years. He now earns nearly three times the $26,000 he received when he entered the job market. Since earning a B.A. in political science in 1995, Heather Dahl has had seven jobs, working for three TV broadcasters and as deputy press secretary for a U.S. senator. Her six-month contract as an editorial assistant at National Public Radio in Washington ended in November 1999. "I never stop job hunting," she says.[23]

Job hopping can often lead to a promotion and a raise in salary. It can also take a lot of energy, require a continual relearning of a corporate culture, and may lead to jobs that turn out to be less than you expected. Many traditional industries such as banking and heavy equipment manufacturing still put a premium on company loyalty. High-tech firms, in contrast, don't expect a long-term commitment.

> t r y   i t   n o w !   <

1. **Start a Business** It's never too early to start your own business. People as young as 14 have become successful entrepreneurs. Each year two million businesses are started by people under 35 years old. The average young entrepreneur now employs 18 people with sales of approximately $1 million.[24] You can be next! For start-up help, check out the Young Americans Business Network at **www.ybiz.com** and the Young Entrepreneurs Network at **www.idye.com.**

2. **Assess Your Skills** The earlier you choose a major field, the more efficiently you can plan your college coursework. Make sure you don't end up taking a lot of courses that won't count toward your degree. Do a self-assessment and skills assessment right now. Next, go to the Career Mosaic at **www.careermosaic.com**. This site offers thousands of job postings as well as information about companies. Use this information to help you decide on a career field and major. Do you want to stay in your home state? This site will break down job postings by city and even zip code, so you can find a job in any part of town, like the north side of St. Louis.

>looking ahead
At Williamson-Dickie

Look back at the story about Williamson-Dickie at the beginning of the chapter. Dickies capitalized on two social trends: (1) changing ideas about what's fashionable, and (2) the continuing entry of women into the workforce. As America becomes more multicultural, Dickies might consider clothing aimed at specific ethnic markets. As incomes continue to rise, Dickies might consider higher priced "fashionable" work clothes. The company may even look toward export markets for growth.

As the marketplace continues to evolve, certain trends may pose a threat to Dickies. Fashion trends and fads may quickly erode demand for some of Dickies's product lines. Competition will become even more intense as global competitors attack Dickies's markets. If the firm doesn't keep abreast of the latest manufacturing technology, it could find itself at a cost disadvantage. Also, changing labor laws might raise the costs of production.

A corporate recruiter for one of America's largest and most dynamic high-tech firms recently said, "If you stay with us longer than three years, we begin to wonder what's wrong with you." Was this said in jest? Probably, but there may be an element of truth in her statement. Learn more about finding the right job for you in the appendix to this chapter.

SUMMARY OF LEARNING GOALS

>lg 1 **How do businesses and not-for-profit organizations help create our standard of living?**
Businesses attempt to earn a profit by providing goods and services desired by their customers. Not-for-profit organizations, though not striving for a profit, still deliver many needed services for our society. Our standard of living is measured by the output of goods and services. Thus, businesses and not-for-profit organizations help create our standard of living. Our quality of life is not simply the amount of goods and services available for consumers but rather the society's general level of happiness.

Economists refer to the building blocks of a business as the factors of production. To produce anything, one must have natural resources, labor, capital, and entrepreneurship to assemble the resources and manage the business. The competitive environment of our new millennium is based upon knowledge and learning. The companies that will succeed in this new era will be those that learn fast, use knowledge effectively, and develop new insights.

>lg 2 **How are social trends, such as more women entering the workforce, affecting business?**
The business environment consists of social, demographic, economic, technological, and competitive trends. Managers cannot control environmental trends. Instead, they must understand how the environment is changing and the impact of those changes on the business. Several social trends are currently influencing businesses. First, people of all ages have a broader range of interests, defying traditional consumer profiles. Second, changing gender roles are bringing more women into the workforce. This trend is increasing family incomes, heightening demand for time-saving goods and services, and changing family shopping patterns.

>lg 3 **How are demographic trends creating new opportunities for business?**
Businesses today must deal with the unique shopping preferences of Generations X and Y and the baby boomers. Each must be appealed to in a different way with different goods and services. Generation Y, for example, is the most computer literate and the most interested in computers and accessories. And because the population is growing older, businesses are offering more products that appeal to middle-aged and elderly markets. As we continue to become a multicultural marketplace, new opportunities for business are being created.

>lg 4   **What are the primary features of the world's economic systems?**
Today there is a global trend toward capitalism. Capitalism, also known as the
private enterprise system, is based upon marketplace competition and private
ownership of the factors of production. Competition leads to more diverse
goods and services, keeps prices stable, and pushes businesses to become more
efficient.

    In a command economy, or communism, the government owns virtually all
resources, and economic decision making is done by central government planning. Governments have generally moved away from command economies because they are inefficient and deliver a low standard of living. Socialism is an
economic system in which the basic industries are owned by the government or
by the private sector under strong government control. The state is also somewhat influential in determining the goals of business, the prices and selection
of products, and the rights of workers. Most economies are a mix of socialism
and capitalism.

>lg 5   **How can technological effectiveness help a firm reach its goals?**
The application of technology by a firm can increase efficiency, lower costs, and
help the firm grow by producing higher quality goods and services. New technologies such as miniaturization and microelectromechanical systems are
changing the world as we know it. The Internet is changing how companies sell
and communicate. It is also changing how and what consumers buy. Technology
enables continuous improvement.

>lg 6   **What are the trends in global competition?**
The world is becoming more competitive. Exports continue to rise as a percentage of world gross domestic product. As countries open their markets, U.S.
firms are finding greater opportunities abroad, but free trade also means that
U.S. firms will face tougher competition at home. Nevertheless, efficient U.S.
companies are meeting the global challenge.

    Appendix:

>lg 7   **What are the first steps toward finding your first professional job?**
Opportunities are greater than ever for bright, creative, hard-working, well-ed-
ucated people like you. In fact, employers are engaging in a talent war to hire
the best and brightest. To begin your career search, you should first do a self-
assessment and then a skills assessment. Then begin to look at employment
opportunities.

>lg 8   **How can the Internet be a valuable tool in your job search?**
The Internet can help you create a résumé, which you can then send out to
sites with thousands of job openings. A few of the best job sites include the
MonsterBoard, America's Job Bank, Careerpath.com, HotJobs.com, Online
Career Center, NationJob Network, 4Work, and E.Span. After you are
invited for a job interview, you can go to **www.hovers.com** or **www.experi-
enceonline.com** to learn more about your potential employer. The Homefair site will tell you all about the geographic area and the cost of living
there.

>lg 9   **How can you start off on the right track in your new job and, then later, move up
to the next level?**
When you start a new job, you should (1) listen and learn, (2) be nice to others, (3) not try to change the world immediately, and (4) find a great mentor. A quick way to get promoted is to (1) love what you do, (2) never stop
learning, (3) be an internal entrepreneur, and (4) be really good at what
you do.

KEY TERMS

baby boomers 9
business 2
capital 3
capitalism 11
command economy
  12
component lifestyle
  7
continuous
  improvement 18
costs 2
customer value 18
demography 8
entrepreneurs 4
exports 15
factors of
  production 3
Generation X 9
Generation Y 8
goods 2
gross domestic
  product (GDP) 15
ISO 14000 19
ISO 9000 18
knowledge 5
Malcolm Baldrige
  National Quality
  Award 18
mixed economies
  13
multiculturalism 11
not-for-profit
  organization 3
productivity 13
profit 2
quality 18
quality of life 2
revenue 2
risk 2
services 2
socialism 13
standard of living
  2
technology 13

PREPARING FOR TOMORROW'S WORKPLACE

1. Your company president has heard a speech at the Rotary Club that stressed the importance of knowledge as a key to beating the competition. The president tells you, "I think we already know how to produce a good product so this knowledge stuff is overblown. The Rotary Club speaker, though, thinks it's pretty important. Write me a memo and explain why we should become a learning-based organization."

2. Form small groups with three or four members each. Each group should then go to a small business that has opened in the past two years. Ask the owner to describe (1) the most important lesson learned since opening the business, (2) unexpected pitfalls the business encountered, and (3) the information that helped the most prior to opening the business.

3. Every country has its own customs, beliefs, and social trends. Talk to several international students at your college. Ask them to identify five customs that make doing business in their country different from the United States.

4. Create two teams of four people each. Have one side choose a command economy and the other capitalism. Debate the proposition that "capitalism/a command economy is good for developing nations."

5. You have been asked to address the local Chamber of Commerce on the impact of the growing number of women in the workforce. Write an outline for your speech.

6. Give three examples of how technology has benefited business in the last five years. Also, give at least one example of a company that has been hurt by failing to keep up with technological change.

7. Form five teams. Each team is responsible for one of the five major types of trends in business discussed in the chapter (social, demographic, evolving economic systems, technology, and global competition). Your boss, the company president, has asked each team to provide a forecast of how the trend you have chosen will affect the firm over the next five years. The firm is Boeing Aircraft. Each team should use the library, Internet, and other data sources to make its projections. Each team member should examine at least one data source. The team should then pool the data and prepare its response. A spokesperson for each team should present the findings to the class.

WORKING THE NET

1. Go to **www.ipo.org**/. Tell the class what is new at this site. Explain to the class how a business might use the information from the **ipo** site. Be sure to provide an example.

2. Go to an Internet search engine, such as Excite, Infoseek, Lycros, or Altavista, and look up the "North Korean economy." North Korea is probably the best example of a command economy in the world. Write a report on the current economic conditions in North Korea.

3. Go to **www.mbda.gov/youth.html** and describe to the class "The Youth Entrepreneurship Initiative." Explain the training opportunities, the electronic center, and the internship program. How could this site be valuable to you or your classmates?

4. Go to **www.quality.nist.gov**/ and learn about the Malcolm Baldrige National Quality Award. How does a company apply to compete? Who won recently? What is the "library of quality"? Tell the class what is new about the quality award program. Report on the CEO survey on quality.

5. Go to an Internet search engine and look up "resume writing." Describe the Internet resources available on résumé preparation to the class.

CREATIVE THINKING CASE

The New England Aquarium—Just What Is It That People Are Eating?

Visitors to the New England Aquarium hoping to see specimens like yellowfin tuna and Atlantic lobster need look no farther than their plates. The aquarium's eateries offer up these and other marine delicacies, including Dover sole and grilled shrimp. Inside the aquarium, salmon swim in glass tanks; in its kitchens, their baked brethren swim in a lime cilantro *beurre blanc.*

"People like seafood," says Sue Knapp, a spokeswoman for the aquarium. "This is New England. It's part of our heritage."

But some visitors aren't taking the bait. After receiving a number of questions from perplexed patrons, the aquarium is preparing an information sheet explaining how it reconciles preservation with dinner. Dawn Carr, an official with People for the Ethical Treatment of Animals, equates the menu offerings to "eating poodle burgers at a dog show."

Knapp acknowledges the irony of "trying to help people appreciate wildlife while we're serving it." Yet she sees nothing wrong with menu offerings. "Obviously," she says, "they don't come from our tanks or exhibits." Knapp says the staff makes every effort to ensure that the creatures on the menu come from healthy stocks and are caught using acceptable practices.

The New England Aquarium, situated on Boston's waterfront, isn't the only one struggling with this slippery issue. On the West Coast, the Monterey Bay Aquarium says it did an extensive study about 18 months ago to reduce its seafood menu to eliminate catches it considers overfished, including swordfish, Atlantic bluefin tuna, and Atlantic lobster. Although Atlantic shrimp made the cut, Monterey serves only crustaceans caught by trawlers certified by the Earth Island Institute, a nonprofit conservation group, as using turtle-safe nets.

The New England Aquarium's conservation policies allow for a few more menu choices. It says it will serve even swordfish, which is widely believed to be overfished. Knapp says the institution looks carefully to ensure that the swordfish that grace its plates were caught from regions with healthy stocks.

The New England Aquarium has a long history of promoting aquatic delights. A decade ago, it published a seafood cookbook called "A Feast of Fishes." Given the current depleted state of the world's fisheries, Knapp says, "We'd probably take a hard look before we would reprint it."

Critical Thinking Questions

1. Is the New England Aquarium a business or a not-for-profit organization? Defend your position.
2. Explain the conflicts that may rise between a not-for-profit organization's goals and its need for revenue.
3. Give some examples of trends that may affect the New England Aquarium.
4. Go to **www.neaq.org**/ and report on the latest tactics that the New England Aquarium is using to raise money.

VIDEO CASE

Burton Snowboards and the External Business Environment

The modern sport of snowboarding began in 1964 when Sherman Poppen screwed a pair of children's skis together to enable his kids to surf on the snow near their Michigan home. Poppen's device—called the Snurfer—was soon marketed as a $12 toy. The Snurfer caught on with youngsters, but it took an entrepreneur named Jake Burton to promote snowboarding as a sport and to develop high-quality snowboarding equipment.

Burton Snowboards, founded by Jake Burton in the winter of 1978–1979, is a highly successful, privately held producer and distributor of snowboards and snowboarding accessories and apparel. The Burton name has become synonymous with quality in snowboarding products. Marketing quality products is part of Burton's formula for success. Another part—indeed, a major part—is being appropriately responsive to the external business environment. Known as the Burton Way, the company's formula for success emphasizes "knowing and respecting the consumer, keeping one eye on the market and another on the product."

One important response to the external environment has been Burton's commitment to developing snowboarding as a sport. Snowboarding was not permitted at ski resorts until the 1980s. In the early years of that decade, Burton Snowboards "spearheaded the effort to legalize snowboarding at ski resorts." According to Jake Burton, "while other companies were saying 'our boards are great,' we were saying 'snowboarding is great.'" By focusing on developing the sport, Burton Snowboards helped create a growth market for snowboarding equipment. Snowboarding has developed to such an extent that it was included in the 1998 Winter Olympics. However, Jake Burton maintains that "the Olympics provided some energy to the growth of the sport, but nothing huge."

Traditionally, snowboarding appealed to males in their teens and early 20s but in recent years, the snowboarding market has changed significantly. "Snowboarding suppliers realize that their demographic stretches far beyond the 14- to 22-year-old male and well into the middle-aged disposable income demographic. Women, meanwhile, are almost half the market." Burton Snowboards has responded accordingly. While remaining committed to its traditional core customers, the company has embraced a broader, more diverse clientele.

Another element of Burton's responsiveness to the external business environment is the company's history of sensitivity to foreign markets. In the early 1980s, Jake Burton and his spouse spent nearly two years in Austria—Jake worked with and learned from ski manufacturers, and his spouse worked on setting up distribution for the company. Today, Jake Burton encourages employees at the Burlington, Vermont, operation "to spend as much time as possible overseas because it's such a great place to learn."

The sport of snowboarding has been growing in the three major markets for snowboarding equipment: North America, Europe, and Japan. Burton Snowboards is sensitive to consumers' expectations in each market, but it does not develop a different product line for each area. Rather, the company has one global line with products that appeal to the different markets.

Will the Burton Way enable Burton Snowboards to continue to be successful as a privately held company? Jake Burton thinks so. He has no plans to take the company public. He does, however, expect the company to expand and diversify by knowing and respecting its customers—and to continue to be successful.

Critical Thinking Questions

1. Describe some of the key external environmental conditions that are influencing Burton Snowboards.
2. How does the Burton Way address the external environmental conditions identified in question (1)?
3. Explain how a business can help shape the external environment in which it operates.

APPENDIX 1: GETTING YOUR CAREER OFF ON THE RIGHT TRACK

>lg 7

There is no sure-fire recipe for finding the perfect job right out of school. Yet, there are ways to improve your chances of success.

Who Am I?

The first step is to ask "Who am I?" This question is the start of *self-assessment*, examining your likes and dislikes and basic values. You may want to ask yourself the following questions:

- Do I want to help society?
- Do I want to help make the world a better place?
- Do I want to help other people directly?
- Is it important for me to be seen as part of a big corporation?
- Do I prefer working indoors or outdoors?
- Do I like to meet new people, or do I want to work alone?

What Can I Do?

After determining what your values are, take the second step in career planning by asking "What can I do?" This question is the start of *skill assessment*, evaluating your key abilities and characteristics for dealing successfully with problems, tasks, and interactions with other people. Many skills—for instance, the ability to speak clearly and strongly—are valuable in many occupations.

Be sure to consider the work experience you already have including part-time jobs while going to school, summer jobs, volunteer jobs, and internships (short-term jobs for students, related to their major field of study). These jobs teach you skills and make you more attractive to potential employers. It's never too early or too late to take a part-time job in your chosen field. For instance, someone with an interest in accounting would do well to try a part-time job with a CPA firm.

In addition to examining your job-related skills, you should also look at your leisure activities. Some possible questions: Am I good at golf? Do I enjoy sailing? Tennis? Racquetball? In some businesses, transactions are made during leisure hours. In that case, being able to play a skillful, or at least adequate, game of golf or tennis may be an asset.

Finding My First Professional Job

The next step is landing the job that fits your skills and desires. You need to consider not only a general type of work but also your lifestyle and leisure goals. If you like to be outdoors most of the time, you might be very unhappy spending eight hours a day in an office. Someone who likes living in small towns may dislike working at the headquarters of a big corporation in Los Angeles or New York City or Chicago. But make sure that your geographic preferences are realistic. Some parts of the country will experience much greater growth in jobs than others (see Exhibit 1A-1).

Want to check out the Occupational Outlook Handbook on line? Go to http://stats.bls.gov/oco-home.htm

You might start answering the question "What will I do?" by studying the *Career Employment Opportunities Directory—Business Administration*. The directory lists several hundred up-to-date sources of employment with businesses, government agencies, and professional organizations.

Another important source of job information is the *Occupational Outlook Handbook*, published every two years by the U.S. Department of Labor. The introduction in the current *Handbook* projects job opportunities by industry though the year 2000. The *Handbook* is divided into 19 occupational clusters describing 200 jobs (with a section on military careers). Among the clusters are

Where the Jobs Are: Projected U.S. Employment, 1988–2010

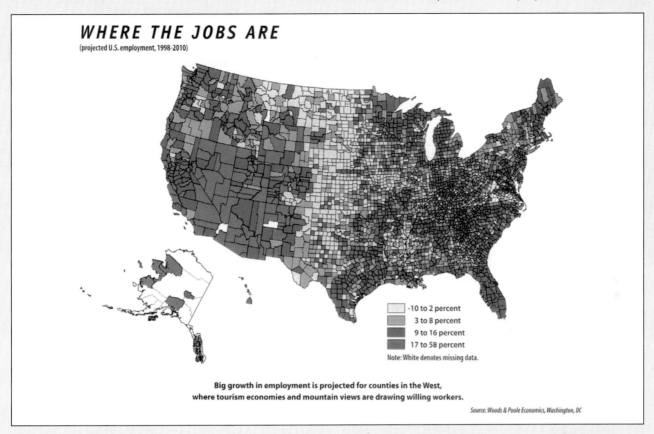

WHERE THE JOBS ARE
(projected U.S. employment, 1998-2010)

-10 to 2 percent
3 to 8 percent
9 to 16 percent
17 to 58 percent
Note: White denotes missing data.

Big growth in employment is projected for counties in the West,
where tourism economies and mountain views are drawing willing workers.

Source: Woods & Poole Economics, Washington, DC

education, sales and marketing, transportation, health, and social services. Each job description tells about the nature of the work, working conditions, required training, other qualifications, chances for advancement, employment outlook, earnings, related occupations, and sources of more information. Two other good sources of job information are *Changing Times Annual Survey: Jobs for New College Graduates* and *Peterson's Business and Management Jobs*.

The career appendixes at the end of each part of this book are another good source of career information. They contain short job descriptions and explain what parts of the country are most likely to have openings in certain fields, the skills required, the employment outlook through 2010, and salary information. Each career appendix features a "dream career," a career worth striving for.

Using the Internet to Jump-Start Your Job Search

Build a Résumé

>lg 8

There are about 100,000 job-related sites and 2.5 million résumés on the Internet.[1] To break through the clutter, you must start with a great résumé—a written description of your education, work experience, personal data, and interests. Professional WebResume software (available through **www.mysoftware.com**) can make your résumé preparation task a lot easier. WebResume software not only helps you format your résumé but also lets you control who sees it. A "confidential" option enables you to create a two-tiered résumé. The first tier offers professional information but doesn't include your name or address. The second tier contains contact information but is password-protected—and you decide who can get the password. WebResume understands what's different about looking for a job online. Its "Search Engine Keywords" function inserts the "tags" that major search engines use to index résumés. And WebResume will submit your résumé to 11 job sites, including CareerMosaic, JobTrak, and IntelliMatch. Exhibit 1A-2 offers seven tips for preparing your cyber résumé.

Once you have created a great résumé, the next step is to get it noticed. There are tens of thousands of places to send your résumé; Exhibit 1A-3 suggests several great places to begin.

Oh My Gosh—I've Got a Job Interview

If some of the companies you contacted want to speak with you, your résumé achieved its goal of getting you a job interview. Look at the interview as a chance to describe your knowledge and skills and interpret them in terms of the employer's specific needs. To make this kind of presentation, you need to do some research on the company. A great place to start looking is **www.hovers.com.** This site offers profiles and financial data on more than 12,000 companies worldwide. It also provides links to other sites where you can dig further.

Experience Online (**www.experienceonline.com**) lets you look inside 200 large companies. The site's Snapshot describes life in the company. Go to NestléUSA, and you learn that life is buttoned-down from Monday through Thursday, but casual on Friday, complete with "chocolate martinis on Hollywood Boulevard."

> e x h i b i t   1 A - 2 <

Tips for Preparing Your Cyber Résumé

- **Think nouns, not verbs.** Career counselors used to advise job seekers to pepper their résumés with action verbs that would impress human resource staffers. Web résumés also get scanned—by digital eyeballs. Companies then use software that combs through résumés for words that signal job titles, technical skills, and levels of education or experience. And most of those words are nouns. Now employees search for nouns such as what software programs you can use.

- **The more buzzwords, the better.** Career counselors also used to advise students to avoid buzzwords in their résumés. Today buzzwords are all the buzz. "Applicant-tracking systems" rank résumés by the number of keywords in them. If a company is looking for an accountant trainee with knowledge of Lotus 1-2-3, Microsoft Excel, and Peachtree Office Accounting, it can rank résumés according to whether they include all three programs, two of them, and so on.

- **Don't forget to describe your personality and attitude.** Just because most résumé searches are computerized doesn't mean that companies don't look for human qualities. A tracking system can identify behavioral traits—dependability, responsibility, a high energy level—as easily as it can technical skills. Be enthusiastic and let your passion show.

- **Personal home pages should be all business.** Like many job seekers, you may want to include a link in your Web résumé to a personal Web page, where you can post detailed information about your career. But don't use up your page with photos of you, your family, or your pets. An HR manager at a big chemical company puts it this way: "I'm not looking for a pretty face. I'm looking for a skill. What you look like is not a skill."

- **It's not a résumé—it's a movie trailer.** Electronic résumés do eventually get read by real human beings—on a computer screen. You have about 20 lines to grab their attention. So don't waste precious real estate on details such as your address. Lead with your technical skills and personal qualities. Identify yourself as a solution to someone's problem.

- **Break the one-page rule.** Limiting your résumé to what will fit on a single piece of paper doesn't mean much in the online world. If you can hold your readers' attention, they'll keep scrolling. But don't overdo it: At some point, most executives do print out résumés that they find interesting.

- **Ask the wizard.** These days, most word processing programs come with good résumé templates and with "wizards"—step-by-step guides that walk you through the templates. If you're looking for a real wizard, visit the Professional Association of Resume Writers (**www.parw.com**).

SOURCE: Gina Imperato, "35 Ways to Land a Job Online," *Fast Company* (August 1998), pp. 194–195.

> e x h i b i t   1 A - 3 <

Some Places to Send Your Cyber Résumé

Site	Description	Key Features
The Monster Board www.monster.com	Resume City, the site's job bank, posts more than 25,000 openings and more than 300,000 résumés. It *is* a monster.	Creative resources and events, such as weekly career fairs, feature companies from specific geographic areas or industries. Even the ads feature information about companies and their employment opportunities.
America's Job Bank www.ajb.dni.us	This government site posts an average of 5,000 new openings per day. Companies contribute another 3,000.	This powerful site has easy-to-use search capabilities. Use any of three options: a keyword search, a menu search (which lets you choose from 22 job categories), or a military-code search.
Careerpath.com www.careerpath.com	This site features classified ads from more than 65 newspapers, including the *New York Times*, the *Los Angeles Times*, and the *Boston Globe*.	In some case, you get a jump on the Sunday papers. Ads from the *New York Times* appear on Saturday afternoon.
HotJobs.com www.hotjobs.com	This member-based site charges companies a hefty fee to post openings or to search through résumés.	Job seekers can create a personal home page to manage their search. The page tracks all the jobs they've applied for and collects statistics on how many companies have retrieved their résumé.
Online Career Center www.occ.com	A pioneer in online recruiting, OCC started in 1992 and moved to the Web in 1993.	The site's "search within a search" feature lets you narrow your search criteria so that you can find jobs that are right for you.
NationJob NetWork www.nationjob.com	This site includes more than 15,000 jobs nationwide with emphasis on those in the Midwest.	"P.J. Scout," the site's personal search agent, is the best out there. If it finds five matching jobs or fewer, it e-mails you the complete listings. If it finds more than five, it sends links to the postings.
4Work www.4work.com	Specify the state where you want to work and your skill set, and 4Work e-mails you the appropriate postings.	This is one of the few sites that includes listings of internships and volunteer opportunities.
America's Employers www.americasemployers.com	Maintained by career consultants, this site offers several thousand updated listings, along with real-time seminars.	The site's networking forums help you develop new contacts and job leads. There's even a chat room for online interviews.
ESPAN www.espan.com	Another pioneer in online employment services, ESPAN is easy to navigate.	The site notifies you every week of job postings that match criteria that you specify. These notifications arrive via e-mail, complete with links to job specs and company information.
The CareerBuilder Network www.careerbuilder.com	This site focuses on the needs of companies rather than job seekers. But it does include a database of 20,000 openings.	Don't want to use an e-mail address from your current company? Career-Builder, in cooperation with Who Where? (**www.whowhere.com**), will give you a special e-mail account that you can access from the CareerBuilder site.

SOURCE: Gina Imperato, "35 Ways to Land a Job Online," *Fast Company* (August 1998), pp. 196–197.

The **Company Blueprint** describes history, strategy, and culture. The site warns about Nestlé's uptight style, but approves of its "diverse and genuine people." Next, visit the **How to Break In** section and get the inside scoop on interviews: what the company may ask you and what you should ask in return.

An interview tends to have three parts: ice-breaking (about five minutes), in which the interviewer tries to put the applicant at ease; questioning (directly or indirectly) by the interviewer; and questioning by the applicant. Almost every recruiter you meet will be trying to rate you in 5 to 10 areas. The questions will be designed to assess your skills and personality.

For the interview you should dress conservatively. Plan to arrive about 10 to 15 minutes ahead of time. Try to relax. Smile and make eye contact with (but do not stare at) the interviewer. Body language is an important communicator. The placement of your hands and feet and your overall posture say a good deal about you.

Many firms start with a *screening interview,* a rather short interview (about 30 minutes) to decide whether to invite you back for a second interview. Only about 20 percent of job applicants are invited back. The second interview is a half day or a day of meetings set up by the human resource department with managers in different departments. After the meetings, someone from the human resource department will discuss other application materials with you and tell you when a letter of acceptance or rejection is likely to be sent. (The wait may be weeks or even months.) Many applicants send follow-up letters in the meantime to show they are still interested in the firm.

Selecting the Right Job for You

Hard work and a little luck may pay off with multiple job offers. Your happy dilemma is deciding which one is best for you. Start by considering the FACTS:

- *Fit.* Do the job and the employer fit your skills, interests, and lifestyle?
- *Advancement and growth.* Will you have the chance to develop your talents and move up within the organization?
- *Compensation.* Is the employer offering a competitive salary and benefits package?
- *Training.* Will the employer provide you with the tools needed to be successful on the job?
- *Site.* Is the job location a good match for your lifestyle and your pocketbook?

A great way to evaluate a new location is through HOMEFAIR (**www.homefair.com**). This site offers tools to help you calculate the cost of moving, the cost of living, and the quality of life in various places. The **Moving Calculator** helps you figure out how much it will cost to ship your worldly possessions to a particular city. The **Relocation Crime Lab** compares crime rates in various locations. The **City Snapshots** feature compares demographic, economic, and climate information for two cities of your choosing. The **Salary Calculator** computes cost-of-living differences between hundreds of U.S. and international cities and tells you how much you'd need to make in your new city to maintain your current standard of living.

Companies Where Multiculturalism Thrives. To determine which companies are truly inclusive in hiring, promoting, and retaining people of color, *Fortune* magazine conducts a yearly corporate diversity survey. A list of the recent "top ten" are shown in Exhibit 1A-4. You may want to obtain a complete list of the magazine's latest survey before deciding which job to accept.

When It's Time to Start Your New Job

No time is more crucial, and possibly nerve-racking, than the first few months at a new job. During this breaking-in period, the employer decides whether a new employee is valuable enough to keep and, if so, in what capacity. Sometimes the

>lg 9

| Rank COMPANY 1997 revenues (millions) | Number of Minorities | | Percentage of Minorities | WORKFORCE* ASIAN | | |
	BOARD OF DIRECTORS	TOP 25 PAID	OFFICIALS AND MANAGERS	BLACK HISPANIC	DIVERSITY PROGRAMS	
1 Pacific Enterprises Los Angeles $2,777	2 of 8	2	34.1%	50.7%	5	Allows people to nominate themselves for the company's fast-track management training programs. That's one reason PE has the highest percentage of minority officials and managers of any company on the list.
2 Advantica Spartanburg, S.C. $2,609	4 of 12	2	29.9%	46.0%	4	Talk about a turnaround. The parent company of Denny's now has a diverse group of suppliers and franchisees. Every penny of charitable giving goes to groups that primarily benefit minorities.
3 BankAmerica San Francisco $23,585	2 of 13	3 (of 45)	25.9%	43.8%	8	BankAmerica's approach to diversity: Make the company a comfortable place for everyone to work, and the cream—black white, Hispanic, Asian, whatever— will rise to the top.
4 Fannie Mae Washington, D.C. $27,777	3 of 18	3	22.8%	38.8%	7	In breaking down barriers to home ownership for blacks and Hispanics, Fannie Mae has found a new growth business. Last year 18% of the single-family homes it financed were bought by minorities, versus 13% in 1993.
5 Marriott International Bethesda, Md. $12,034	2 of 9	•	18.5%	50.3%	6	In 1999, only one franchise was owned by a person of color. Now 29 are: 20 by Asians, 5 by blacks, 4 by Hispanics. As many as 30 languages are spoken at some Marriotts.
6 Applied Materials $4,074	1 of 9	8	16.4%	32.2%	0	The semiconductor company recruits at historically black Howard University and at the National Hispanic University in San Jose. Among its 25 highest-paid executives, 8 are minorities, the best showing on the list.
7 Edison International Rosemead, Calif. $9,235	4 of 18	2	24.3%	41.0%	2	Another turnaround tale. The utility paid $11.25 million to settle a 1996 discrimination case; since then the number of minority corporate officers has gone from one to five.
8 Computer Associates Islandia, N.Y. $4,040	2 of 7	6	11.7%	18.5%	6	Founder and CEO Charles Wang is from China. President and COO Sanjay Kumar is Sri Lankan. Wang donated $25 million to the State University of New York for an Asian-American center.

(Continued)

Exhibit 1A-4 *(Continued)*

	Number of Minorities			Percentage of Minorities		
Rank COMPANY 1997 revenues (millions)	BOARD OF DIRECTORS	TOP 25 PAID	OFFICIALS AND MANAGERS	WORKFORCE* ASIAN BLACK HISPANIC	DIVERSITY PROGRAMS	
9 Ryder System Miami $5,351	0 of 11	8	12.6%	25.3%	6	Ryder ties Applied Materials, with the most minorities among the 25 highest-paid employees. Many senior executives also take part in the company's extensive minority mentoring program.
10 Pitney Bowes Stamford, Conn $4,101	2 of 11	2	19.4%	39.3%	7	Three years ago the postage-meter makers set a goal of spending $52 million with minority and women suppliers by 2000 (it spent $52.8 million in 1997). Minorities accounted for nearly half of new hires in the past year.

•Not available *The overall percentage of minorities includes Native Americans.

SOURCE: "The Diversity Elite," *Fortune* (August 3, 1998), pp. 144–145. ©1998 Time Inc. Reprinted by permission.

employee's whole future with the company rides on the efforts of the first few weeks or months.

Most firms offer some sort of formal orientation. But generally speaking, they expect employees to learn quickly—and often on their own. You will be expected to become familiar with the firm's goals; its organization, including your place in the company; and basic personnel policies, such as coffee breaks, overtime, and parking.

Here are a few tips on making your first job rewarding and productive:

- *Listen and learn:* When you first walk into your new job, let your eyes and ears take everything in. Do people refer to one another by first names, or is the company more formal? How do people dress? Do the people you work with drop into one another's open offices for informal chats about business matters? Or have you entered a "memo mill," where anything of substance is put on e-mail and talks with other employees are scheduled through secretaries? Size up where the power lies. Who seems to most often assume a leadership role? Who is the person others turn to for advice? Why has that person achieved that position? What traits have made this person a "political leader"? Don't be misled by what others say, but also don't dismiss their evaluations. Make your own judgments based on what you see and hear.
- *Do unto others:* Be nice. Nice people are usually the last to be fired and among the first to be promoted. Don't be pleasant only with those who can help you in the company. Be nice to everyone. You never know who can help you or give you information that will turn out to be useful. Genuinely nice people make routine job assignments, and especially pressure-filled ones, more pleasant. And people who are dealt with pleasantly usually respond in kind.

> e x h i b i t   1 A - 5 <

How to Move Up

> - Love what you do, which entails first figuring out who you are.
> - Never stop learning about new technologies and new management skills.
> - Try to get international experience even if it is only a short stint overseas.
> - Create new business opportunities—they could lead to a promotion.
> - Be really outstandingly terrific at what you're doing now, this week, this month.

- *Don't start out as a maverick:* If every new employee tried to change tried-and-true methods to suit his or her whims, the firm would quickly be in chaos. Individual needs must take a back seat to established procedures. Devote yourself to getting things done within the system. Every manager realizes that it takes time for a new person to adjust. But the faster you start accomplishing things, the faster the boss will decide that you were the right person to hire.

- *Find a great mentor:* The leading cause of career unhappiness is working for a bad boss.[2] Good jobs can easily be ruined by supervisors who hold you back. In contrast, your career will soar (and you will smile every day) when you have a great mentor helping you along the way. If you find a job with a super mentor, jump at the change to take it.

Movin' On Up

Once you have been on the job for a while, you will want to get ahead and be promoted. Exhibit 1A-5 offers several suggestions for improving your chances of promotion. The first item might seem a bit strange, yet it's there for a practical reason. If you don't really like what you do, you won't be committed enough to compete with those who do. The passionate people are the ones who go the extra mile, do the extra work, and come up with fresh out-of-the-box ideas.

Seek out business opportunities in your company. Act like an entrepreneur (but not as a new employee). That's exactly what P. J. Smoot, head of training and development at International Paper in Chicago, did. When she joined International Paper, she was in the finance department. "I noted that there wasn't a lot of career development or training going on, except at the college recruitment level, and I saw a real need for it," she recalls.[3]

So she wrote a proposal to the human resources department; they liked it so much that they hired her to put her ideas into practice. What started as an 18-month assignment has evolved into a full-fledged companywide training program. Smoot, who oversees the program, has since won six promotions—all because she saw a way to help her company and then acted on it.

So there you have it! In the next chapter we will begin our journey through the world of business so that you can determine what areas of business are most interesting to you. Remember, it's never too early to begin planning your career—the future is now.

APPENDIX NOTES

1. Gina Imperato, "35 Ways to Land a Job Online," *Fast Company* (August 1998), pp. 193–198.
2. John Sullivan, "What Makes a Great Job," *Fast Company* (October 1998), p. 166.
3. Anne Fisher, "Six Ways to Supercharge Your Career," *Fortune* (January 13, 1998), pp. 46–49.

chapter two

Understanding Evolving Economic Systems and Competition

learning goals

>lg 1   What is economics, and how are the three sectors of the economy linked?

>lg 2   How do economic growth, full employment, and price stability indicate a nation's economic health?

>lg 3   What is inflation, how is it measured, and what causes it?

>lg 4   How does the government use monetary policy and fiscal policy to achieve its macroeconomic goals?

>lg 5   What are the basic microeconomic concepts of demand and supply, and how do they establish prices?

>lg 6   What are the four types of market structure?

>lg 7   Which trends are reshaping micro- and macroeconomic environments?

The Smart car—today Europe, tomorrow the world

It's as big as an oversized go-cart with a plastic exterior that never rusts or dents. It can be swapped for another color for about the price of an evening dress. Designed for city commuting, it can turn on a dime, goes easy on fuel, and barely pollutes.

Alexis Mannes, a Brussels car dealer, says, "This may be the car that will change the car business." That's just what Daimler-Benz AG has in mind for its joint project with Société Cease de Microelectronic et d'Horlogerie SA, (SMH), maker of Swatch watches. Nicknamed the "Smart" car, the ultra-light, ultrafuel-efficient two-seater is being marketed as the ideal European city car, selling for the equivalent of $8,500.

Daimler-Benz has no current plans to market the Smart car in the United States, but both Daimler and its new partner, Chrysler Corp., view the project as a laboratory. Both see the Smart car as an idea factory for the automotive technology and industrial cooperation of the future. "Daimler sees the Smart as a playground to test things," says Peter Soliman, a consultant with Booz-Allen Hamilton in Düsseldorf. "Even if it never makes any money, it has already taught the operation a lot about manufacturing, research and development and distribution that they can carry over to their main business."

Some rival auto makers scoff at the idea of plastic doors, hoods, and trunks. But the lightweight materials are critical in increasing fuel efficiency, which is important in Europe where auto makers have agreed to reduce their fleets' carbon dioxide emissions by some 25 percent by the year 2008. The Smart car is one of Europe's most fuel-efficient autos, using just 4.8 liters of gasoline per 100 kilometers—or roughly 1 gallon per 59 miles—compared with 6.8 liters for Ford Motor Co.'s Ka and 6.6 liters for a Volkswagen Polo.

To make the car dramatically smaller than existing subcompacts, Micro Compact Car, the Daimler-SMH joint venture that makes the Smart, was forced to redesign the basic "three-box" concept of the traditional car, which has a hood, a cockpit, and a trunk. Designers put the engine in the back, as in the original VW Beetle. Then they shoved the rest of the car's mechanics below the passenger cabin, something that had previously been done only with minivans. As a result, the Smart factory in Hambach, France, is capable of building 900 cars a day with virtually no parts inventory of its own. Because only 25 percent of the Smart's value is added in final assembly, it takes just 4.5 hours to assemble one, compared with 20 hours for a VW Polo.

Critical Thinking Questions

As you read this chapter, consider the following questions as they relate to the Smart car:

- What factors determine the price of the Smart?
- In what type of environment does Daimler-Benz compete?
- How can the changing economic environment affect the demand for the Smart?

Business in the 21st Century

Auto history is littered with cars of tomorrow that landed on the scrap heap, including the Edsel, the Tucker, and the DeLorean sports car. And for every Smart enthusiast there seems to be a Smart skeptic. "Too expensive," says Shuhei Toyoda, chief engineer for Toyota Motor Corp.'s new Yaris, another small city car. Ferdinand Piech, chairman of rival Volkswagen AG, suggests that the Smart car isn't even new: "We already have a city car," he scoffs, referring to the VW Polo. "And it has four seats."[1]

BUSINESS IN THE 21ST CENTURY

economic system
The combination of policies, laws, and choices made by a nation's government to establish the systems that determine what goods and services are produced and how they are allocated.

Whether the Smart car will be a success will depend in part on the economic system of the countries where it is marketed. A nation's **economic system** is the combination of policies, laws, and choices made by its government to establish the systems that determine what goods and services are produced and how they are allocated. Capitalism and a planned economy, which we discussed in Chapter 1, are examples of economic systems. In a planned economy, government bureaucrats would determine whether to build a car like the Smart car. Historically, planned economies have done a much worse job of stimulating economic growth and creating a higher standard of living for their citizens than capitalist economies have. Even though the Smart car is not very expensive, most people in planned economies like Cuba and North Korea could not afford one.

Daimler Chrysler considered the economic system of European nations in developing its compact, affordable, and highly fuel-efficient Smart car.

This chapter will help you understand how economies provide jobs for workers and also create and deliver products to consumers and businesses. You will also learn how governments attempt to influence economic activity through policies such as lowering or raising taxes. Next, we discuss how supply and demand determine prices for goods and services. We conclude by examining trends in evolving economic systems and competition.

HOW BUSINESSES AND ECONOMIES WORK

>lg 1

economics
The study of how a society uses scarce resources to produce and distribute goods and services.

Economics is the study of how a society uses scarce resources to produce and distribute goods and services. The resources of a person, a firm, or a nation are limited. Hence, economics is the study of choices—what people, firms, or nations choose from among the available resources. Every economy is concerned with what types and amounts of goods and services should be produced, how they should be produced, and for whom. These decisions are made by the marketplace, the government, or both. In the

United States the government and the free market system together guide the economy.

You probably know more about economics than you realize. Every day many news stories deal with economic matters: a union wins wage increases at General Motors; the Federal Reserve Board lowers interest rates; Wall Street has a record day; the president proposes a cut in income taxes; consumer spending rises as the economy grows; or retail prices are on the rise, to mention just a few examples.

Macroeconomics and Microeconomics

The state of the economy affects both people and businesses. How you spend your money (or save it) is a personal economic decision. Whether you continue in school and whether you work part-time are also economic decisions. Every business also operates within the economy. Based on their economic expectations, businesses decide what products to produce, how to price them, how many people to employ, how much to pay these employees, how much to expand the business, and so on.

Economics has two main subareas. **Macroeconomics** is the study of the economy as a whole. It looks at *aggregate* data, data for large groups of people, companies, or products considered as a whole. In contrast, **microeconomics** focuses on individual parts of the economy, such as households or firms.

Both *macroeconomics* and *microeconomics* offer a valuable outlook on the economy. For example, Ford might use both to decide whether to introduce a new line of cars, like the Smart car, from Europe. The company would consider such macroeconomic factors as the national level of personal income, the unemployment rate, interest rates, fuel costs, and the national level of sales of imported cars. From a microeconomic viewpoint, Ford would judge consumer demand for new cars versus the existing supply, competing models, labor and material costs and availability, and current prices and sales incentives.

Economics as a Circular Flow

Another way to see how the sectors of the economy interact is to examine the **circular flow** of inputs and outputs among households, businesses, and governments as shown in Exhibit 2-1. Let's review the exchanges by following the purple circle around the inside of the diagram. Households provide inputs (natural resources, labor, capital, entrepreneurship) to businesses, which convert these inputs into outputs (goods and services) for consumers. In return, consumers receive income from rent, wages, interest, and ownership profits (green circle). Businesses receive income from consumer purchases of goods and services.

The other important exchange in Exhibit 2-1 takes place between governments (federal, state, and local) and both individuals and businesses. Governments supply many types of publicly provided goods and services (highways, schools, police, courts, health services, unemployment insurance, Social Security) that benefit individuals and businesses. Government purchases from businesses also contribute to business profits. The contractor who repairs a local stretch of state highway, for example, is paid by government for the work. As the diagram shows, government receives taxes from individuals and businesses to complete the flow.

Changes in one flow affect the others. If government raises taxes, households have less to spend on goods and services. Lower consumer spending

macroeconomics

The subarea of economics that focuses on the economy as a whole by looking at aggregate data for large groups of people, companies, or products.

microeconomics

The subarea of economics that focuses on individual parts of the economy such as households or firms.

circular flow

The movement of inputs and outputs among households, businesses, and governments; a way of showing how the sectors of the economy interact.

> e x h i b i t　　2 - 1　<

Economics as a Circular Flow

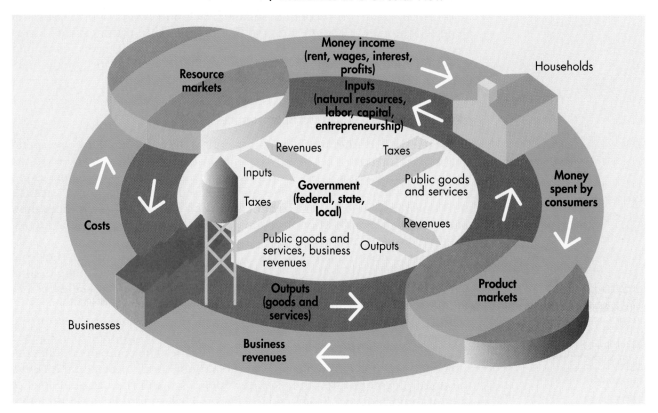

concept check

- What is economics?
- What is the difference between macro-economics and microeconomics?
- How do resources flow among the household, business, and government sectors?

causes businesses to reduce production, and economic activity declines; unemployment may rise. In contrast, cutting taxes can stimulate economic activity. Keep the circular flow in mind as we continue our study of economics. The way economic sectors interact will become more evident as we explore macroeconomics and microeconomics.

MACROECONOMICS: THE BIG PICTURE

>lg 2

Have you ever looked at Headline News on the Internet or turned on the radio or television and heard something like, "Today the Labor Department reported that for the second straight month unemployment declined"? Statements like this are macroeconomic news. Understanding the national economy and how changes in government policies affect households and businesses is a good place to begin our study of economics.

Let's look first at macroeconomic goals and how they can be met. The United States and most other countries have three main macroeconomic goals: economic growth, full employment, and price stability. A nation's economic well-being depends on carefully defining these goals and choosing the best economic policies to reach them.

Striving for Economic Growth

Perhaps the most important way to judge a nation's economic health is to look at its production of goods and services. The more the nation produces, the higher its standard of living. An increase in a nation's output of goods and services is **economic growth.**

Economic growth is usually a good thing, but it also has a bad side. Increased production yields more pollution. Growth may strain public facilities, such as roads, electricity, schools, and hospitals. Thus, the government tries to apply economic policies that will keep growth to a level that does not reduce the quality of life.

economic growth
An increase in a nation's output of goods and services.

As we saw in Chapter 1, the most basic measure of economic growth is the *gross domestic product (GDP).* GDP is the total market value of all final goods and services produced within a nation's borders each year. It is reported quarterly and is used to compare trends in national output. When GDP rises, the economy is growing.

The U.S. Bureau of Economic Analysis tracks national and regional economic statistics, including the GDP. To find the latest GDP statistics, visit the BEA at
www.bea.doc.gov

The *rate* of growth in real GDP (GDP adjusted for inflation) is also important. Recently, the U.S. economy has been growing at about 3 to 4 percent annually. This growth rate has meant a slow, steady increase in output of goods and services and low unemployment. When the growth rate slides toward zero, the economy will begin to stagnate and perhaps decline.

business cycles
Upward and downward changes in the level of economic activity.

recession
A decline in GDP that lasts for at least two consecutive quarters.

The level of economic activity is constantly changing. These upward and downward changes are called **business cycles.** Business cycles vary in length, in how high or low the economy moves, and in how much the economy is affected. Changes in GDP trace the patterns as economic activity expands and contracts. An increase in business activity results in rising output, income, employment, and prices. Eventually, these all peak, and output, income, and employment decline. A decline in GDP that lasts for two consecutive quarters (each a three-month period) is called a **recession.** It is followed by a recovery period when economic activity once again increases. The most recent recession began in 1990 and ended in March 1991. Since that time the United States has enjoyed a long period of steady growth and prosperity.

The housing industry is a leading economic indicator. A rise in new home construction typically translates into a robust economy.

Businesses must monitor and react to the changing phases of business cycles. When the economy is growing, companies often have a difficult time hiring good employees and finding scarce supplies and raw materials. When a recession hits, many firms find they have more capacity than the demand for their goods and services requires. During the recession of the early 1990s, many firms operated at 75 percent or less of their capacity. When plants use only part of their capacity, they operate inefficiently and have higher costs per unit produced. Let's say that Mars Corp. has a plant that can produce one million Milky Way candy bars a day, but because of a recession Mars can sell only half a million candy bars a day. Mars has a huge plant with large, expensive machines designed to produce a million candy bars a day. Producing Milky Ways at 50 percent capacity does not efficiently utilize Mars's investment in the plant and equipment.

Keeping People on the Job

full employment

The condition when all people who want to work and can work have jobs.

Another macroeconomic goal is **full employment,** or having jobs for all who want to and can work. Full employment doesn't actually mean 100 percent employment. Some people choose not to work for personal reasons (attending school, raising children) or are temporarily unemployed while they wait to start a new job. Thus, the government defines full employment as the situation when about 94 to 96 percent of those available to work actually have jobs. During the late 1990s, the economy operated at close to full employment.

Measuring Unemployment To determine how close we are to full employment, the government measures the **unemployment rate.** This rate indicates the percentage of the total labor force that is not working but is *actively looking for work.* It excludes "discouraged workers," those not seeking jobs because they think no one will hire them. Each month the Department of Labor releases statistics on employment. These figures help us understand how well the economy is doing. In the past two decades, unemployment rose as high as 9.7 percent in 1982, which was a recession year. It then declined steadily through the remainder of the 1980s and most of the 1990s. In 1999, the rate fell to about 4 percent, which was the lowest rate in almost 30 years.[2]

unemployment rate

The percentage of the total labor force that is actively looking for work but is not actually working.

HOT links

How are the job prospects in your area? Your region's unemployment statistics can give you an idea of how hard it will be to find a job. Find the most recent unemployment statistics from the Bureau of Labor Statistics at **www.bls.gov**

Types of Unemployment Economists classify unemployment into four types: frictional, structural, cyclical, and seasonal. The categories are of small consolation to someone who is unemployed, but they help economists understand the problem of unemployment in our economy.

frictional unemployment

Short-term unemployment that is not related to the business cycle.

Frictional unemployment is short-term unemployment that is not related to the business cycle. It includes people who are unemployed while waiting to start a better job, those who are reentering the job market, and those entering for the first time such as new college graduates. This type of unemployment is always present and has little impact on the economy.

structural unemployment

Unemployment that is caused by a mismatch between available jobs and the skills of available workers in an industry or region; not related to the business cycle.

Structural unemployment is also unrelated to the business cycle but is involuntary. It is caused by a mismatch between available jobs and the skills of available workers in an industry or a region. For example, if the birthrate declines, fewer teachers will be needed. Or the available workers in an area may lack the skills that employers want. Retraining and skill-building programs are often required to reduce structural unemployment.

cyclical unemployment

Unemployment that occurs when a downturn in the business cycle reduces the demand for labor throughout the economy.

Cyclical unemployment, as the name implies, occurs when a downturn in the business cycle reduces the demand for labor throughout the economy. In a long recession, cyclical unemployment is widespread, and even people with good job skills can't find jobs. The government can partly counteract cyclical unemployment with programs that boost the economy.

In the past, cyclical unemployment affected mainly less skilled workers and those in heavy manufacturing. Typically, they would be rehired when economic growth increased. During the 1990s, however, competition forced many American companies to downsize so they could survive in the global marketplace. Motorola cut 15,000 jobs, or 10 percent of its workforce, to lower costs so that it could compete with Asian, European, and other U.S. semiconductor and telecommunications firms.[3]

seasonal unemployment

Unemployment that occurs during specific seasons in certain industries.

>lg 3

inflation

The situation in which the average of all prices of goods and services is rising.

purchasing power

The value of what money can buy.

demand-pull inflation

Inflation that occurs when the demand for goods and services is greater than the supply.

cost-push inflation

Inflation that occurs when increases in production costs push up the prices of final goods and services.

During busy summer months, theme parks like Disney World hire many young people and adults—a group of employees subject to seasonal unemployment.

The last type is **seasonal unemployment,** which occurs during specific seasons in certain industries. Employees subject to seasonal unemployment include retail workers hired for the Christmas buying season, lettuce pickers in California, and restaurant employees in Aspen during the summer.

Keeping Prices Steady

The third macroeconomic goal is to keep overall prices for goods and services fairly steady. The situation in which the average of all prices of goods and services is rising is called **inflation.** Inflation's higher prices reduce **purchasing power,** the value of what money can buy. If prices go up but income doesn't rise or rises at a slower rate, a given amount of income buys less. For example, if the price of a basket of groceries rises from \$30 to \$40 but your salary remains the same, you can buy only 75 percent as many groceries (\$30 ÷ \$40). Your purchasing power declines by 25 percent (\$10 ÷ \$40).

Inflation affects both personal and business decisions. When prices are rising, people tend to spend more—before their purchasing power declines further. Businesses that expect inflation often increase their supplies, and people often speed up planned purchases of cars and major appliances.

During the 1990s, inflation in the United States was in the 2 to 4 percent range. This level is generally viewed as quite low. In the 1980s we had periods of inflation in the 12 to 13 percent range. Some nations have had triple-digit inflation or even higher in recent years. In the late 1990s, Bulgaria had an annual rate of inflation of 123 percent; Turkmenistan, 992 percent; and Angola, 4,145 percent!

Want to know where the consumer price index stands today? Go to **http://stats.bls.gov/cpi-home.htm**

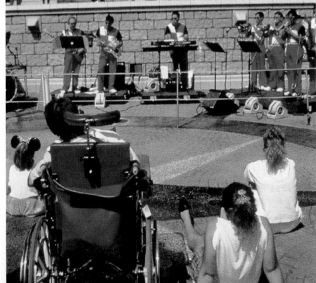

Types of Inflation There are two types of inflation. **Demand-pull inflation** occurs when the demand for goods and services is greater than the supply. Would-be buyers have more money to spend than the amount needed to buy available goods and services. Their demand, which exceeds the supply, tends to pull prices up. This situation is sometimes described as "too much money chasing too few goods." The higher prices lead to greater supply, eventually creating a balance between demand and supply.

Cost-push inflation is triggered by increases in production costs, such as expenses for materials and wages. These increases push up the prices of final goods and services. Wage increases are a major cause of cost-push inflation, creating a "wage-price spiral." For example, assume the United Auto Workers union negotiates a three-year labor agreement that raises wages 3 percent per year and increases overtime pay. Car makers will then raise car prices to cover their higher labor costs. Also, the higher wages will give auto workers more money to buy goods and services, and this increased demand may pull up other prices. Workers in other industries will demand higher wages to keep up with the increased prices, and the cycle will push prices even higher.

consumer price index (CPI)

An index of the prices of a market basket of goods and services purchased by typical urban consumers.

producer price index (PPI)

An index of the prices paid by producers and wholesalers for various commodities such as raw materials, partially finished goods, and finished products.

How Inflation Is Measured   The rate of inflation is most commonly measured by looking at changes in the **consumer price index (CPI),** an index of the prices of a "market basket" of goods and services purchased by typical urban consumers. It is published monthly by the Department of Labor. Major components of the CPI, which are weighted by importance, are food, clothing, transportation, housing, health, and recreation. Data are collected from about 23,000 retail and service businesses in 87 areas around the country.

The CPI sets prices in a base period at 100. The base period, which now is 1982–1984, is chosen for its price stability. Current prices are then expressed as a percentage of prices in the base period. A rise in the CPI means prices are increasing. For example, the CPI was 163.4 in August 1998, meaning that prices had increased 63.4 percent from the 1982–1984 base period.

Changes in wholesale prices are another important indicator of inflation. The **producer price index (PPI)** measures the prices paid by producers and wholesalers for such commodities as raw materials, partially finished goods, and finished products. The PPI is actually a family of indexes for many different product categories. For example, the PPI for finished goods was 130.2 in August 1998. Examples of other PPI indexes include containers, fuels and lubricants, and construction. Because the PPI measures prices paid by producers for raw materials, energy, and other commodities, it may foreshadow subsequent price changes for businesses and consumers.

The Impact of Inflation   Inflation has several negative effects on people and businesses. For one thing, inflation penalizes people who live on fixed incomes. Let's say that a couple receives $1,000 a month retirement income beginning in 1999. If inflation is 10 percent in 2000, then the couple can buy only 90 percent of what they could purchase in 1999. Similarly, inflation hurts savers. As prices rise, the real value, or purchasing power, of a nest egg of savings deteriorates.

HOT links

How do the PPI and the CPI differ? Get the answers to this and other questions about the PPI by visiting the Bureau of Labor Statistics PPI site at

www.bls.gov/ppihome.htm

concept check

- What is a business cycle? How do businesses adapt to periods of contraction and expansion?
- Why is full employment usually defined as a target percentage below 100 percent? How is unemployment measured?
- What is the difference between demand-pull and cost-push inflation?

ACHIEVING MACROECONOMIC GOALS

>lg 4

To reach macroeconomic goals, countries must often choose among conflicting alternatives. Sometimes political needs override economic ones. For example, bringing inflation under control may call for a politically difficult period of high unemployment and low growth. Or, in an election year, politicians may resist raising taxes to curb inflation. Still, the government must try to guide the economy to a sound balance of growth, employment, and price stability. The two main tools it uses are monetary policy and fiscal policy.

Monetary Policy

monetary policy

A government's programs for controlling the amount of money circulating in the economy and interest rates.

Monetary policy refers to a government's programs for controlling the amount of money circulating in the economy and interest rates. Changes in the money

Federal Reserve System (the Fed)

The central banking system of the United States.

contractionary policy

The use of monetary policy by the Fed to tighten the money supply by selling government securities or raising interest rates.

expansionary policy

The use of monetary policy by the Fed to increase the growth of the money supply.

fiscal policy

The government's use of taxation and spending to affect the economy.

supply affect both the level of economic activity and the rate of inflation. The **Federal Reserve System (the Fed),** the central banking system, prints money and controls how much of it will be in circulation. The money supply is also controlled by the Fed's regulation of certain bank activities.

When the Fed increases or decreases the amount of money in circulation, it affects interest rates (the cost of borrowing money and the reward for lending it). The Fed can change the interest rate on money it lends to banks to signal the banking system and financial markets that it has changed its monetary policy. Banks, in turn, may pass along this change to consumers and businesses that receive loans from the banks. If the cost of borrowing increases, the economy slows because interest rates affect consumer and business decisions to spend or invest. The housing industry, business, and investments react most to changes in interest rates.

As you can see, the Fed can use monetary policy to contract or expand the economy. With **contractionary policy,** the Fed restricts, or tightens, the money supply by selling government securities or raising interest rates. The result is slower economic growth and higher unemployment. Thus, contractionary policy reduces spending and, ultimately, lowers inflation. With **expansionary policy,** the Fed increases, or loosens, growth in the money supply. An expansionary policy stimulates the economy. Interest rates decline, so business and consumer spending go up. Unemployment rates drop as businesses expand. But increasing the money supply also has a negative side: more spending pushes prices up, increasing the inflation rate.

HOT links

Eight times a year, the Federal Reserve Board issues the Beige Report with up-to-the-minute information abut the state of the U.S. economy. Find it at the Federal Reserve's home page, **www.bog.frb.fed.us.**

Fiscal Policy

The other economic tool used by the government is **fiscal policy,** its program of taxation and spending. By increasing its spending or by cutting taxes, the government can stimulate the economy. Look again at Exhibit 2-1. The more government buys from businesses, the greater business revenues and output are. Likewise, if consumers or businesses have to pay less in taxes, they will have more income to spend for goods and services. Tax policies in the United States therefore affect business decisions. High corporate taxes can make it harder for U.S. firms to compete with companies in countries with lower taxes. As a result, companies may choose to locate facilities overseas to reduce their tax burden.

Nobody likes to pay taxes, although we grudgingly accept that we have to. Although most U.S. citizens complain that they are overtaxed, we pay lower taxes per capita (per person) than citizens in many countries similar to ours, as Exhibit 2-2 shows.

Taxes are, of course, the major source of revenue for our government. Every year the president prepares a budget for the coming year based upon estimated revenues and expenditures. Congress receives the president's report and recommendations and then, typically, debates and analyzes the proposed budget for several months. The president's original proposal is always modified in numerous ways. Exhibit 2-3 shows sources of revenue and expenses for the U.S. budget.

While fiscal policy has a major impact on businesses and consumers, continual increases in government spending raise another important issue. When government takes more money from businesses and consumers (the private sector) and uses these funds for increased government spending (the public

Tax Revenues, by Country (Per Capita and Percentage of GDP)

	Per Capita	Percentage of GDP
United States	$ 7,234	27.6%
Japan	10,434	27.8
Australia	5,589	29.9
United Kingdom	5,968	34.1
Canada	6,858	36.1
Germany	12,197	39.3
Norway	11,706	41.2
Italy	7,416	41.7
France	10,129	44.1
The Netherlands	9,983	45.9
Belgium	10,500	46.6
Sweden	11,481	51.0
Denmark	14,460	51.6

crowding out

The situation that occurs when government spending replaces spending by the private sector.

sector), a phenomenon known as **crowding out** occurs. Here are three examples of crowding out:

1. The government spends more on public libraries, and individuals buy fewer books at bookstores.
2. The government spends more on public education, and individuals spend less on private education.
3. The government spends more on public transportation, and individuals spend less on private transportation.

In other words, government spending is crowding out private spending.

Revenues and Expenses for the Federal Budget

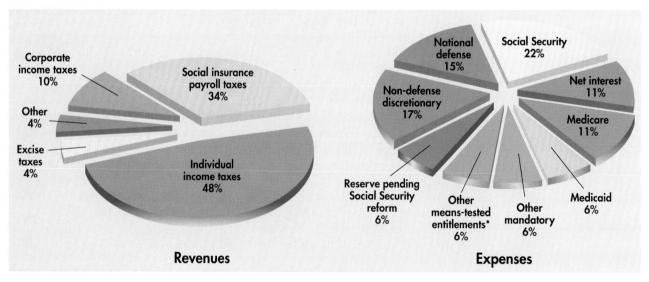

Revenues

Expenses

federal budget deficit
The condition that occurs when the federal government spends more for programs than it collects in taxes.

If the government spends more for programs (social services, education, defense) than it collects in taxes, the result is a **federal budget deficit.** To balance the budget, the government can cut its spending, increase taxes, or do some combination of the two. When it cannot balance the budget, the government must make up any shortfalls by borrowing (just like any business or household).

In 1998, for the first time in a generation, there was a federal budget surplus (revenue exceeded spending) of about $70 billion.[4] This surplus is expected to grow to over $150 billion annually by 2002. Whenever the government finds itself with a surplus, Congress begins an often heated debate about what to do with the money. Some members of Congress, for example, want to spend more on social programs or for defense. Others say that this money belongs to the people and should be returned in the form of tax cuts. Another alternative is to reduce the national debt.

See how the national deficit has changed since the nation began by visiting
budget.org/NationalDebt/Deficit

national debt
The accumulated total of all of the federal government's annual budget deficits.

Despite the recent federal budget surplus, the U.S. government has run budget deficits for many years. The accumulative total of these past deficits is the **national debt,** which now amounts to about $5 trillion or about $20,000 for every man, woman, and child in the United States. Interest on the debt is more than $360 billion a year. To cover the deficit, the U.S. government borrows money from people and businesses in the form of Treasury bills, Treasury notes, and Treasury bonds. These are federal IOUs that pay interest to the owners.

The national debt is an emotional issue debated not only in the halls of Congress, but by the public as well. Some believe that deficits contribute to economic growth, high employment, and price stability. Others have the following reservations about such a high national debt.

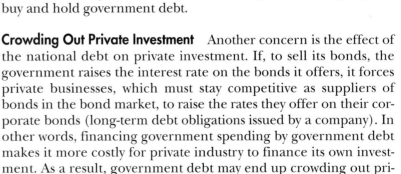

Want to know the current public debt per citizen? Go to
www.publicdebt.treas.gov/opd/opdpenny.htm

Not Everyone Holds the Debt   One issue is who actually bears the burden of the national debt. If only the rich were bondholders, then they alone would receive the interest payments. Depending on how many bonds they held, they could end up receiving more in interest than they paid in taxes. In the meantime, poorer people, who held no bonds, would end up paying taxes that would be transferred to the rich as interest. Under these conditions, the debt would indeed be a burden to some.

The government is very conscious of this burden effect and has kept a watchful eye on who holds what bonds. For example, it has at times instructed commercial banks to reduce their total debt by divesting some of their bond holdings. That's also why the Treasury created **savings bonds.** Because these bonds are issued in relatively small denominations, they allow more people to buy and hold government debt.

savings bond
Government bonds of relatively small denominations.

concept check

- What are the two kinds of monetary policy? How does the government use monetary policy to achieve its macroeconomic goals?
- What is fiscal policy? What fiscal policy tools can the government use to achieve its macroeconomic goals?
- What problems can a large national debt present?

Crowding Out Private Investment   Another concern is the effect of the national debt on private investment. If, to sell its bonds, the government raises the interest rate on the bonds it offers, it forces private businesses, which must stay competitive as suppliers of bonds in the bond market, to raise the rates they offer on their corporate bonds (long-term debt obligations issued by a company). In other words, financing government spending by government debt makes it more costly for private industry to finance its own investment. As a result, government debt may end up crowding out private investment and slowing economic growth in the private sector.

MICROECONOMICS: ZEROING IN ON BUSINESSES AND CONSUMERS

>lg 5

Now let's shift our focus from the whole economy to *microeconomics,* the study of households, businesses, and industries. This field of economics is concerned with how prices and quantities of goods and services behave in a free market. It stands to reason that people, firms, and governments try to get the most from their limited resources. Consumers want to buy the best quality at the lowest price. Businesses want to keep costs down and revenues high to earn larger profits. Governments also want to use their revenues to provide the most effective public goods and services possible. These groups choose among alternatives by focusing on the prices of goods and services.

As consumers in a free market, we influence what is produced. If Mexican food is popular, the high demand attracts entrepreneurs who open more Mexican restaurants. They want to compete for our dollars by supplying Mexican food at a lower price, of better quality, or with different features such as Santa Fe Mexican food rather than Tex-Mex. This section explains how business and consumer choices influence the price and availability of goods and services.

The Nature of Demand

demand

The quantity of a good or service that people are willing to buy at various prices.

demand curve

A graph showing the quantity of a good or service that people are willing to buy at various prices.

Demand is the quantity of a good or service that people are willing to buy at various prices. The higher the price, the lower the quantity demanded, and vice versa. A graph of this relationship is called a **demand curve.**

Let's assume you own a store that sells jackets for snowboarders. From past experience you know how many jackets you can sell at different prices. The demand curve in Exhibit 2-4 depicts this information. The *x*-axis (horizontal axis) shows the quantity of jackets, and the *y*-axis (vertical axis) shows the related price of those jackets. For example, at a price of $60, customers will buy (demand) 500 snowboard jackets.

In the graph the demand curve slopes downward and to the right. This means that as the price falls, people will want to buy more jackets. Some people

> e x h i b i t   2 - 4 <

Demand Curve for Jackets for Snowboarders

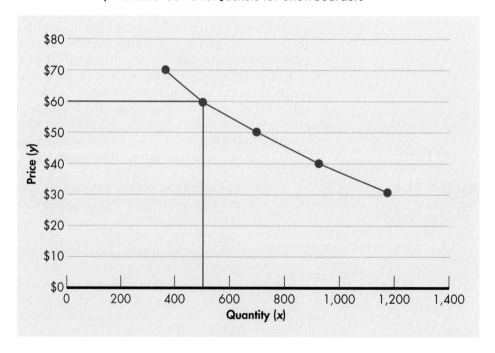

who were not going to buy a jacket will purchase one at the lower price. Also, some snowboarders who already have a jacket will buy a second one. The graph also shows that if you put a large number of jackets on the market, you will have to reduce the price to sell all of them.

The Nature of Supply

supply

The quantity of a good or service that businesses will make available at various prices.

supply curve

A graph showing the quantity of a good or service that a business will make available at various prices.

Demand alone is not enough to explain how the market sets prices. We must also look at **supply,** the quantity of a good or service that businesses will make available at various prices. The higher the price, the greater the amount a jacket manufacturer is willing to supply, and vice versa. A graph of the relationship between various prices and the quantities a manufacturer will supply is a **supply curve.**

We can again plot the quantity of jackets on the x-axis and the price on the y-axis. As Exhibit 2-5 shows, 900 jackets will be available at a price of $60. Note that the supply curve slopes upward and to the right, the opposite of the demand curve. If snowboarders are willing to pay higher prices, manufacturers of jackets will buy more inputs (Goretex, dye, machinery, labor) and produce more jackets. The quantity supplied will be higher at higher prices, because producers can earn higher profits.

How Demand and Supply Interact to Determine Prices

In a stable economy, the number of jackets that snowboarders demand depends on the jackets' price. Likewise, the number of jackets that suppliers provide depends on price. But at what price will consumer demand for jackets match the quantity suppliers will produce?

To answer this question, we need to look at what happens when demand and supply interact. By plotting both the demand curve and the supply curve on the same graph in Exhibit 2-6, we see that they cross at a certain quantity and price. At that point, labeled E, the quantity demanded equals the quantity supplied.

> e x h i b i t   2 - 5 <

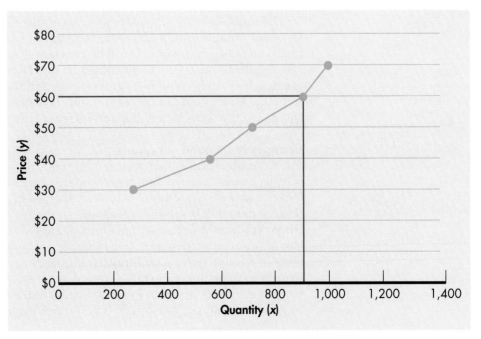

Supply Curve for Jackets for Snowboarders

Equilibrium Price and Quantity

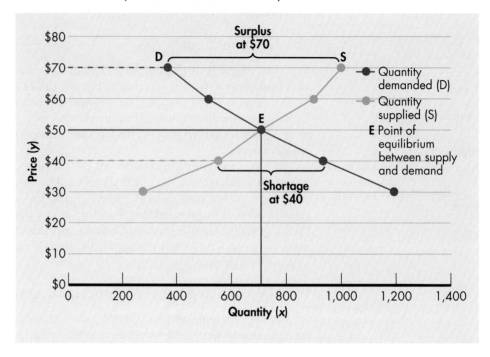

equilibrium

The point at which quantity demanded equals quantity supplied.

This is the point of **equilibrium.** The equilibrium price is $50; the equilibrium quantity is 700 jackets. At that point there is a balance between the amount consumers will buy and the amount the manufacturers will supply.

Market equilibrium is achieved through a series of quantity and price adjustments that occur automatically. If the price increases to $70, suppliers produce more jackets than consumers are willing to buy, and a surplus results. To sell more jackets, prices will have to fall. Thus, a surplus pushes prices downward until equilibrium is reached. When the price falls to $40, the quantity of jackets demanded rises above the available supply. The resulting shortage forces prices upward until equilibrium is reached at $50.

The number of snowboarder jackets produced and bought at $50 will tend to rest at equilibrium unless there is a shift in either demand or supply. If demand increases, more jackets will be purchased at every price, and the demand curve shifts to the right (as illustrated by line D_2 in Exhibit 2-7). If demand decreases, less will be bought at every price, and the demand curve shifts to the left (D_1). When demand decreased, snowboarders bought 500 jackets at $50 instead of 700 jackets. When demand increased, they purchased 800.

Changes in Demand A number of things can increase or decrease demand. For example, if snowboarders' incomes go up, they may decide to buy a second jacket. If incomes fall, a snowboarder who was planning to purchase a jacket may wear an old one instead. Changes in fashion or tastes can also influence demand. If snowboarding were suddenly to go out of fashion, demand for jackets would decrease quickly. A change in the price of related products can also influence demand. For example, if the average price of a snowboard rises to $1,000, people will quit snowboarding and jacket demand will fall. Another factor that can shift demand is expectations about future prices. If you expect jacket prices to increase significantly in the future, you may decide to go ahead and get one today. If you think prices will fall, you will postpone

Shifts in Demand

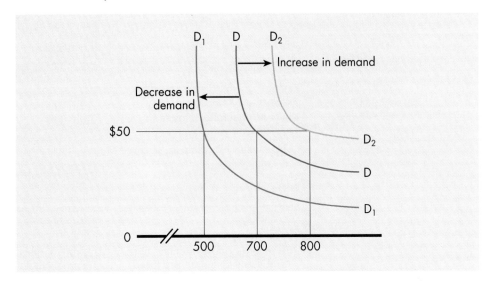

your purchase. Finally, changes in the number of buyers will affect demand. Snowboarding is a young person's sport. The number of teenagers will increase in the next few years. Therefore, the demand for snowboarding jackets should increase.

Changes in Supply   New technology typically lowers the cost of production. For example, North Face, a manufacturer of ski and snowboarder jackets, has just purchased laser-guided pattern-cutting equipment and computer-aided pattern-making equipment. Each jacket is now cheaper to produce, resulting in a higher profit per jacket. This becomes an incentive to supply more jackets at every price. If the price of resources such as labor or fabric goes up, North Face will earn a smaller profit on each jacket, and the amount supplied will decrease at every price. The reverse is also true. Changes in the prices of other goods can also affect supply. Let's say that snow skiing becomes a really hot sport. The number of skiers jumps dramatically and the price of ski jackets soars. North Face can use its machines and fabrics to produce either ski or snowboard jackets. If the company can make more profit from ski jackets, it will produce fewer snowboarding jackets at every price. Also, simply a change in the number of producers will shift the supply curve. If the number of manufacturers increases, more jackets will be placed on the market at every price and vice versa. Taxes can also affect supply. If the government decides, for some reason, to tax the manufacturer for every snowboard jacket produced, then profits will fall and fewer jackets will be offered at every price. Exhibit 2-8 summarizes the factors that can shift demand and supply curves.

concept check

- What is the relationship between prices and demand for a product?
- How is market equilibrium achieved?
- Draw a graph that shows an equilibrium point.

COMPETING IN A FREE MARKET

>lg 6

market structure

The number of suppliers in a market.

One of the characteristics of a free market system is that suppliers have the right to compete with one another. The number of suppliers in a market is called **market structure.** Economists identify four types of market structures: (1) perfect competition, (2) pure monopoly, (3) monopolistic competition, and (4) oligopoly.

Factors That Cause Demand and Supply Curves to Shift

	Shift Demand	
Factor	To the Right if:	To the Left if:
Buyers' incomes	increase	decrease
Buyers' preferences/tastes	increase	decrease
Prices of substitute products	increase	decrease
Expectations about future prices	will rise	will fall
Number of buyers	increases	decreases
	Shift Supply	
Technology	lowers costs	increases costs
Resource prices	fall	increase
Changes in prices of other products that can be produced with the same resources	profit of other product falls	profit of other product increases
Number of suppliers	increases	decreases
Taxes	lowered	increased

Perfect Competition

perfect (pure) competition
A market structure in which a large number of small firms sell similar products, buyers and sellers have good information, and businesses can be easily opened or closed.

Characteristics of **perfect (pure) competition** include:

- A large number of small firms are in the market.
- The firms sell similar products; that is, each firm's product is very much like the products sold by other firms in the market.
- Buyers and sellers in the market have good information about prices, sources of supply, and so on.
- It is easy to open a new business or close an existing one.

In a perfectly competitive market, firms sell their products at prices determined solely by forces beyond their control. Because the products are very similar and because each firm contributes only a small amount to the total quantity supplied by the industry, price is determined by supply and demand. A firm that raised its price even a little above the going rate would lose customers. In the wheat market, for example, the product is essentially the same from one wheat producer to the next. Thus, none of the producers has control over the price of wheat.

Perfect competition is an ideal. No industry shows all its characteristics, but the stock market and some agricultural markets, such as those for wheat and corn, come closest. Farmers, for example, can sell all of their crops through national commodity exchanges at the current market price.

Pure Monopoly

pure monopoly
A market structure in which a single firm accounts for all industry sales and in which there are barriers to entry.

barriers to entry
Factors, such as technological or legal conditions, that prevent new firms from competing equally with a monopoly.

At the other end of the spectrum is **pure monopoly,** the market structure in which a single firm accounts for all industry sales. The firm is the industry. This structure is characterized by **barriers to entry**—factors that prevent new firms from competing equally with the existing firm. Often the barriers are technological or legal conditions. Polaroid, for example, has held major patents on instant photography for years. When Kodak tried to market its own instant camera, Polaroid sued, claiming patent violations. Polaroid collected millions of dollars from Kodak. Another barrier may be one firm's control of a natural resource. DeBeers Consolidated Mines Ltd., for example, controls most of the world's supply of uncut diamonds.

Public utilities like gas and water are pure monopolies. Some monopolies are created by a government fiat that outlaws competition. The U.S. Postal Service is currently one such monopoly.

Monopolistic Competition

monopolistic competition

A market structure in which many firms offer products that are close substitutes and in which entry is relatively easy.

Three characteristics define the market structure known as **monopolistic competition:**

- Many firms are in the market.
- The firms offer products that are close substitutes but still differ from one another.
- It is relatively easy to enter the market.

Under monopolistic competition, firms take advantage of product differentiation. Industries where monopolistic competition occurs include clothing, food, and similar consumer products. Firms under monopolistic competition have more control over pricing than do firms under perfect competition because consumers do not view the products as exactly the same. Nevertheless, firms must demonstrate those product differences to justify their prices to customers.

> m a k i n g   e t h i c a l   c h o i c e s <

GASOLINE PRICE GYRATIONS AND OPEC

In March 1999, gasoline prices skyrocketed in anticipation that the Organization of Petroleum Exporting Countries (OPEC) would decide, at a meeting on March 23, to restrict the world's supply of crude oil. OPEC was expected to approve cuts in petroleum production totaling 2.1 million barrels a day. The purpose was to strengthen the price of crude oil. Over the preceding 18 months, crude oil prices had fallen from $22 per barrel to around $11 per barrel. At one point, crude oil prices had sunk as low as $9 per barrel.

The average price of all grades of gasoline at U.S. service stations increased by more than 9 percent in the two-week period preceding OPEC's March 23 meeting. About half of the price increase was blamed on refiners who were quick to pass crude oil cost increases through to consumers. The other half was attributed to dwindling supplies of refined gasoline that resulted from the depletion of the huge refined gasoline inventories of the preceding autumn and winter.

Historically, OPEC has been unable "to maintain supply discipline among its members for very long." Some industry observers expected petroleum prices to fall back rather quickly due to an oversupply of crude oil in the global market. Analysts pointed out that a major problem for OPEC was that other oil-producing countries were ready to increase their production if OPEC members restricted their output of crude oil.

Critical Thinking Questions

1. Should businesses raise prices in anticipation of cost increases? Or should they wait to raise prices until the cost increases actually occur?
2. In your opinion, is it ethical or unethical for a group of nations to restrict the supply of a commodity such as crude oil so as to force a price increase?

Capitalizing on Trends in Business

Types of Market Structures

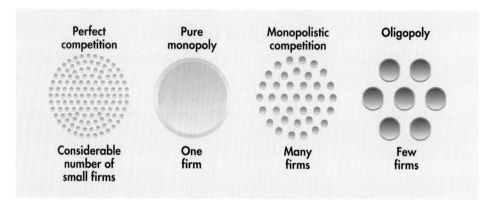

Consequently, companies use advertising to distinguish their products from others. Such distinctions may be significant or superficial. For example, Nike says "Just Do It," and Tylenol is advertised as being easier on the stomach than aspirin.

Oligopoly

oligopoly

A market structure in which a few firms produce most or all of the output and in which large capital requirements or other factors limit the number of firms.

An **oligopoly** has two characteristics:

- A few firms produce most or all of the output.
- Large capital requirements or other factors limit the number of firms.

Boeing and McDonnell Douglas (aircraft manufacturers) and USX (formerly U.S. Steel) are major firms in different oligopolistic industries.

With so few firms in an oligopoly, what one firm does has an impact on the other firms. Thus, the firms in an oligopoly watch one another closely for new technologies, product changes and innovations, promotional campaigns, pricing, production, and other developments. Sometimes they go so far as to coordinate their pricing and output decisions, which is illegal. Many antitrust cases—legal challenges arising out of laws designed to control anticompetitive behavior—occur in oligopolies. Exhibit 2-9 summarizes the primary types of market structures.

c o n c ə p t   c h ə c k

- What is meant by market structure?
- Describe the four types of market structure.

CAPITALIZING ON TRENDS IN BUSINESS

>lg 7

Trends in business occur at both the macroeconomic and the microeconomic level. We will begin by taking a look at some microeconomic trends.

Delivering Value and Quality

Companies today are facing accelerating change in many areas, including better educated and more demanding consumers, new technology, and the globalization of markets. As a result, competition is the toughest it has ever been. More and more, the key to building and sustaining a long-range advantage is a commitment to delivering superior customer value.

customer value

The customer's perception of the ratio of benefits (functionality, performance, durability, design, ease of use, and serviceability) to the sacrifice (of money, time, and effort) necessary to obtain those benefits.

Customer value is the customer's perception of the ratio of benefits to the sacrifice necessary to obtain those benefits. Customers receive benefits in the form of functionality, performance, durability, design, ease of use, and serviceability. To receive those benefits, they give up money, time, and effort.

Customer value is not simply a matter of high quality. A high-quality product that is available only at a high price will not be perceived as a value. Nor will bare-bones service or low-quality goods selling for a low price. Instead, customers value goods and services of the quality they expect that are sold at prices they are willing to pay. Value marketing can be used to sell a $150,000 Rolls Royce as well as a $3 Tyson frozen chicken dinner.

Businesses provide customer value by:

- *Offering products that perform.* This is the bare minimum. Consumers have lost patience with shoddy merchandise.
- *Giving consumers more than they expect.* Soon after Toyota launched Lexus, the company had to order a recall. The weekend before the recall, dealers personally phoned all the Lexus owners in the United States and arranged to pick up their cars and provide replacement vehicles.
- *Avoiding unrealistic pricing.* Consumers couldn't understand why Kellogg's cereals commanded a premium over other brands, so Kellogg's market share fell 5 percent.
- *Giving the buyer facts.* Today's sophisticated consumer wants informative advertising and knowledgeable salespeople.

In today's business world, if a firm doesn't deliver customer value it doesn't survive. Firms that provide customer value end up with satisfied customers. Exhibit 2-10 lists some companies that are especially good at satisfying customers.

> e x h i b i t   2 - 1 0 <

Some Companies and Products That Deliver Satisfaction

Company or Division

Mercedes-Benz
H. J. Heinz (food processing)
Colgate-Palmolive (pet foods)
H. J. Heinz (pet foods)
Mars (food processing)
Maytag
Quaker Oats
Cadillac
Hershey Foods
Coca-Cola
Toyota
Volvo
Zenith Electronics
Buick
Cadbury Schweppes

Creating Long-Term Relationships

relationship management
The practice of building, maintaining, and enhancing interactions with customers and other parties in order to develop long-term satisfaction through mutually beneficial partnerships.

Customer satisfaction helps build long-term relationships between a company and its clients. Today, companies are focusing on **relationship management,** which involves building, maintaining, and enhancing interactions with customers and other parties so as to develop long-term satisfaction through mutually beneficial partnerships. In general, the longer a customer stays with a company, the more that customer is worth. Long-term customers buy more, take less of a company's time, are less sensitive to price, and bring in new customers. Best of all, they require no acquisition or start-up costs. Good long-standing customers are worth so much that in some industries, reducing customer defections by as little as five points—from, say, 15 percent to 10 percent per year—can double profits.

Travelodge practices relationship management by launching Travelodge Miles, a guest rewards program featuring swipe-card technology. The program thanks frequent Travelodge and Thriftlodge guests for their patronage with value-added rewards such as frequent-flyer miles, free hotel nights, free rental cars, and other travel perks. Guests earn one Travelodge Mile for each qualified lodging dollar spent at participating economy Travelodge and Thriftlodge properties. With 250 Miles, members can redeem them for Sleepy Bear dolls, T-shirts, or a road atlas or keep saving the Miles for other rewards at higher levels. The enhanced level is already paying off with an increase in the average stay of preferred guests—almost a full night longer per stay.[5] The system makes it easy to track and gather data on the company's best customers and enabled the creation of a "Gold Level" for preferred customers. These Gold Level customers receive preferred rates and free local phone calls.

strategic alliance
A cooperative agreement between business firms; sometimes called a *strategic partnership.*

Relationship management also means creating long-term relationships with suppliers. Suppliers are making major adjustments in their thinking, management styles, and methods of responding to purchaser's standards and operational requirements. A satisfied customer is one of the best sources of new business because the customer already knows that the supplier can meet expectations and deliver on its promises. Thus, the supplier has created trust, and trust is the foundation of most successful relationships.

A **strategic alliance,** sometimes called a strategic partnership, is a cooperative agreement between business firms. The trend toward forming strategic alliances is accelerating rapidly, particularly among high-tech firms. These companies have realized that strategic partnerships are more than just important—they are critical. Xerox management, for example, has decided that to maintain its leadership position in the reprographics industry, the company must "include suppliers as part of the Xerox family." This strategy often means reducing the number of suppliers, treating those that remain as allies, sharing strategic information freely, and drawing on supplier expertise in developing new products that can meet the quality, cost, and delivery standards of the marketplace.

By building strong customer relationships, retailers can turn a one-time buyer into a loyal, long-term customer.

Another way to build long-term relationships is to provide products designed specifically for the individual customer and then make it very easy to reorder. Could a mass producer like Levi Strauss implement such a strategy? Absolutely, with the help of technology, as the Applying Technology box describes.

LEVI'S ORIGINAL SPIN PROGRAM CREATES JEANS JUST FOR YOU

Finding a pair of jeans that fit as if they were made for you and you alone is one of life's perfect moments. It certainly beats the wasted hours spent in dressing rooms, yanking on and peeling off pair after pair of denim duds. Thanks to technology, the perfect jeans, just for you, can be a reality.

Levi's Original Spin Program allows you to create the perfect jeans for your lifestyle and your figure. Here is how it works: Go to a Levi's store that features the Original Spin Program. There you can choose from three basic jean models: relaxed, classic, or low cut. Plus, you can make your jeans as baggy or as fitted as you want and pick a color. Next, choose from five leg openings: flare, wide, boot cut, straight, or tapered. Finally, pick a fly: button or zipper.

When you've made your choices, the clerk will measure your waist, rear, and inseam and then hunt up a test pair for you to try on. If you like what you see, all that info goes into the computer and is zapped to the Levi's factory in Tennessee, where your personal pair will be stitched. The jeans cost about $55, plus $6 if you want them shipped to your home. (There's no charge if you go back to the store to pick them up.) All this takes about two weeks. Want more jeans but perhaps a different model or color? Call the Original Spin Store or go to the Web site at **www.levi.com/originalspin/**

Critical Thinking Questions

1. Do you think the Original Spin Program will help build long-term relationships?
2. How might other types of manufacturers or retailers create similar programs?
3. Would you use the Original Spin Program? Why or why not?

Creating a Competitive Workforce

Creating customer value and building long-term relationships require a world-class workforce. The goal of leading companies such as Coca-Cola and Intel is for all workers to add value to every job they do every day. Such firms place a strong emphasis on training and the use of technology to improve worker productivity.

For example, the state of California employs around 200,000 workers who, for the most part, stay and build their careers in state government. Taxpayer investment in training state workers can result in significant savings for the state. California is one of the first states to offer Internet courses for its employees. Now workers are getting high-quality training from their computers either at work or home.[6]

Entrepreneurial Spirit in Former Command Economies

A key trend in macroeconomics is the surprising entrepreneurial spirit among many citizens of former command economies.

Russia and China have inched away from planned economies. Today, China has a population of 1.3 billion and they all want more and better goods and services.[7] Already there are 21 million *ge-ti-hu* (entrepreneurs) in China.

One entrepreneur, Robert Kuok, helped bring Coca-Cola to China. Kuok grew up in Hong Kong, where he started a chain of hotels. When Coca-Cola decided to enter mainland China, the company realized that careful handling would be needed to sell the most American product in the world (Coca-Cola) to the Chinese. Every entrepreneur in Asia coveted the opportunity to license Coke in China, a deal that could in time be worth $8 billion.[8] Coke chose Robert Kuok. "I thought, 'My God, this is a gift from Heaven,' " Kuok recalls. Kuok is being modest. It was not a gift. Coke knew what it was doing. Soft drinks were not Kuok's business, but Coke didn't need expertise in soft drinks. It needed a smart guy with contacts. And that's Kuok, a 73-year-old hotel owner, commodities trader, investor, and cosmopolite. Keeping 12.5 percent of the bottling venture, Coke granted 87.5 percent to Kerry Group, Kuok's Hong Kong-based conglomerate.[9]

Another example of an entrepreneur is Russia's Konstantin Borovoi. Borovoi was a math professor until he made a small fortune selling his knowledge of computer software. When the floodgates opened for capitalism, he started the Russian

MONEY OFFERS NEW HOPE TO STRUGGLING ENTREPRENEURS

Sekororo, South Africa, is a place of abundant sunshine and scarce opportunity. Nurse Leshabane had lived for years in a cycle of subsistence, surviving on odd jobs and the charity of family and friends. Then, in the spring of 1998, hope arrived at her door in the form of Ben Nkuna. He couldn't offer her a job because virtually none were to be had in this dusty village of tin shacks and grass huts in South Africa's Northern Province, one of the country's most impoverished regions. But if she could find three or four friends willing to go in with her, Nkuna would provide money to start a small business.

This wasn't an offer of charity: Leshabane and her friends would be expected to repay the money in regular quarterly installments at an interest rate of about 20 percent, slightly below South Africa's prime rate at the time. Many Africans avoid credit, but Leshabane accepted the offer—after some hesitation.

Today, Leshabane operates a tiny vending stand at a busy Sekororo crossroads, selling fruit and a kind of porridge called *pap* to passersby. For the first time in her life, she has a steady income, however small, to help support her extended family of 11. "I thought it was some kind of robbery," says Leshabane of

Nkuna and his associates. "But this has changed my life."

Neither robber nor loan shark, Nkuna represents the Small Enterprise Foundation, a nonprofit organization in the vanguard of those bringing "microcredit" to Africa. Known also as microfinance, the program provides small amounts of start-up capital to the poor as a way of helping them out of poverty. The notion has made some headway in Asia, where almost 13 million people living below the World Bank's official poverty line—defined as those subsisting on $1 a day or less—participate in microcredit programs.

Critical Thinking Questions

1. Do you think that programs like the Small Enterprise Foundation can help lift rural Africa out of poverty?

2. Do you think that a 20 percent interest rate is fair?

3. Won't Leshabane basically end up working for Nkuna because she will be unable to get out of debt?

Commodities and Raw Materials Exchange and ended up indirectly controlling about 12 percent of Russia's economy.[10] The Russian economy is divided into two parts—the very profitable part and the rest. The very profitable part is under the patronage of the state, which has created a host of privileges that favor tycoons such as Borovoi. "Without these privileges," says Olga Kryshtanovska, a specialist on Russian elites, "all the other enterprises experience all the difficulties that exist in this country. No one helps them. They are completely defenseless."[11]

The entrepreneurial spirit is not limited to the evolving old command economies. Struggling developing countries are also creating their own share of entrepreneurs. The Focusing on Small Business box tells one such story.

c o n c ə p t c h ə c k

- How do businesses provide customer value?
- How does relationship management make a business more competitive?
- Explain the entrepeneurial movement in former command economies.

APPLYING THIS CHAPTER'S TOPICS

This chapter has been about micro- and macroeconomics. Economics is not something you should learn for an exam and then forget. Economics is an analytical science that will help you understand the world around you. It can help you be more imaginative and insightful in everyday life. You should now better understand why prices are going up or down, when interest rates will fall, and when and why the unemployment rate will fall. Understanding these basic economic concepts can help you decide whether to change jobs

> t r y i t n o w ! <

1. Understand Your Tax Commitment Soon you will enter the permanent job market, if you are not there already. Typically, your earnings will rise over the next 35 years, but as your earnings increase, so will your taxes. The average American works five months out of every year just to cover taxes. Are taxes too high in our country? Since taxes will be a major part of your financial life for the next 35 to 45 years, you need to be informed. Visit a few organizations that advocate tax reform, such as Americans for Tax Reform (**www.atr.ort/**) and Citizens for Tax Justice (**www.ctj.org/**).

2. Learn a Foreign Language Consider taking a job outside the United States for a while. If you decide to work overseas, having basic skills in a second language will go a long way toward ensuring that you have a rewarding and pleasant experience. Learning a second language can also bring a lot of self-satisfac-tion. Go to **www. acceleratedlearning.net/benefitslang.htm** and learn more about the benefits of learning a foreign language. Another excellent source for accelerated language training is **www. learnalanguage. com**.

(and how much money to ask for) and whether to buy a car now or wait until next year. When you hear that Ford Motor Co. has 115 days of inventory, understanding supply and demand will tell you that now may be the time to buy that new car.

at Daimler-Benz AG

Consider the opening story about the Smart car. The two basic determinants of price for the Smart car are demand and supply: the number of people who want to purchase the car at various prices, and the number of cars Daimler-Benz is willing to produce at various price points. Daimler-Benz competes in a market with a few large competitors. What one auto manufacturer does will have an impact on the others. Therefore, Daimler-Benz competes in an oligopolistic market. How will changes in the economy such as a recession or inflation affect the Smart car? During a recession, demand for the Smart car might decline, but it could also increase if people look for a low-price alternative to a traditional car. With inflation prices of resources used to produce the Smart car will increase, so Daimler-Benz would probably raise the price of the car.

Similarly, economics will help you become a better informed citizen. Almost every political issue is, in some way, grounded in economic concepts. You should now know what it means to balance the budget and what problems occur with monopoly power. In short, economics can help you make more thoughtful and informed decisions.

Economics can also help you understand what is happening in other countries and can help you become aware of opportunities there. As more and more countries have moved away from command economies, American and foreign multinational firms are moving in to take advantage of ground floor opportunities. Consider accepting a foreign assignment. It's a wonderful way to experience other cultures and, at the same time, get ahead in your career. More and more large organizations are requiring that their middle and upper-level managers have foreign field experience. When you have an opportunity for a foreign assignment, don't let it slip by.

KEY TERMS

barriers to entry 50
business cycles 39
circular flow 37
consumer price
   index (CPI) 42
contractionary
   policy 43
cost-push inflation
   41
crowding out 44
customer value 53
cyclical
   unemployment 40
demand curve 46
demand 46
demand-pull
   inflation 41

SUMMARY OF LEARNING GOALS

>lg 1 **What is economics, and how are the three sectors of the economy linked?**
Economics is the study of how individuals, businesses, and governments use scarce resources to produce and distribute goods and services. The two major areas in economics are macroeconomics, the study of the economy as a whole, and microeconomics, the study of particular markets. The individual, business, and government sectors of the economy are linked by a series of two-way flows. The government provides public goods and services for the other two sectors and receives income in the form of taxes. Changes in one flow affect the other sectors.

>lg 2 **How do economic growth, full employment, and price stability indicate a nation's economic health?**
A nation's economy is growing when the level of business activity, as measured by gross domestic product, is rising. GDP is the total value of all goods and services produced in a year. The goal of full employment is to have a job for all who can and want to work. How well a nation is meeting its employment goals is measured by the unemployment rate. There are four types of unemployment: frictional, structural, cyclical, and seasonal. With price stability, the

economic growth
39
economic system
36
economics 36
equilibrium 48
expansionary
policy 43
federal budget
deficit 45
Federal Reserve
System (the Fed)
43
fiscal policy 43
frictional
unemployment 40
full employment 40
inflation 41
macroeconomics
37
market structure 49
microeconomics
37
monetary policy
42
monopolistic
competition 51
national debt 45
oligopoly 52
perfect (pure)
competition 50
producer price
index (PPI) 42
purchasing power
41
pure monopoly 50
recession 39
relationship
management 54
savings bonds 45
seasonal
unemployment 41
strategic alliance
54
structural
unemployment 40
supply 47
supply curve 47
unemployment rate
40

overall prices of goods and services are not moving very much either up or down.

>lg 3 **What is inflation, how is it measured, and what causes it?**
Inflation is the general upward movement of prices. When prices rise, purchasing power falls. The rate of inflation is measured by changes in the consumer price index (CPI) and the producer price index (PPI). There are two main causes of inflation. If the demand for goods and services exceeds the supply, prices will rise. This is called demand-pull inflation. With cost-push inflation, higher production costs, such as expenses for materials and wages, increase the final prices of goods and services.

>lg 4 **How does the government use monetary policy and fiscal policy to achieve its macroeconomic goals?**
Monetary policy refers to actions by the Federal Reserve System to control the money supply. When the Fed restricts the money supply, interest rates rise, the inflation rate drops, and economic growth slows. By expanding the money supply, the Fed stimulates economic growth.

The government also uses fiscal policy—changes in levels of taxation and spending—to control the economy. Reducing taxes or increasing spending stimulates the economy; raising taxes or decreasing spending does the opposite. When the government spends more than it receives in tax revenues, it must borrow to finance the deficit. Some economists favor deficit spending as a way to stimulate the economy; others worry about our high level of national debt.

>lg 5 **What are the basic microeconomic concepts of demand and supply, and how do they establish prices?**
Demand is the quantity of a good or service that people will buy at a given price. Supply is the quantity of a good or service that firms will make available at a given price. When the price increases, the quantity demanded falls but the quantity supplied rises. A price decrease leads to increased demand but a lower supply. At the point where the quantity demanded equals the quantity supplied, demand and supply are in balance. This equilibrium point is achieved by market adjustments of quantity and price.

>lg 6 **What are the four types of market structure?**
Market structure is the number of suppliers in a market. Perfect competition is characterized by a large number of buyers and sellers, very similar products, good market information for both buyers and sellers, and ease of entry and exit into the market. In pure monopoly, there is a single seller in a market. In monopolistic competition, many firms sell close substitutes in a market that is fairly easy to enter. In an oligopoly, a few firms produce most or all of the industry's output. An oligopoly is also difficult to enter and what one firm does will influence others.

>lg 7 **Which trends are reshaping the micro- and macroeconomic environments?**
One micro trend is that firms are placing more emphasis on delivering value and quality to the customer. Companies are also establishing long-term relationships with both customers and suppliers. To compete in today's environment, companies and industries must build a competitive workforce. At the macro level, budding entrepreneurial spirit in former command economies is sparking wealth among individual business owners and fueling the growth of capitalism.

PREPARING FOR TOMORROW'S WORKPLACE

1. Assume that the U.S. economy is sluggish and the government wants to stimulate it just before a national election. Write a paper explaining which type of policy—monetary or fiscal—the government is more likely to use and why.

2. Use the Internet or go to the library and determine the current trends in GDP growth, unemployment, and inflation. What do these trends tell you about the level of business activity and the business cycle? If you owned a personnel agency, how would this information affect your decision making?

3. Divide the class into four teams. One pair of teams will debate the pros and cons of airline deregulation. The other pair will debate electric utility deregulation. One team should take the pro and the other the con for each issue. If you have Internet access, use the Dow Jones news service or Lexis-Nexis to obtain current articles on the subjects.

4. As a manufacturer of in-line roller skates, you are questioning your pricing policies. You note that over the past five years, the CPI increased an average of 2 percent per year, but the price of a pair of skates increased an average of 8 percent per year for the first three years and 2 percent for the next two years. What does this information tell you about demand, supply, and other factors influencing the market for these skates?

5. Divide the class into teams of four persons. Each team should make an appointment with an entrepreneur who has started a business within the last two years. Ask about the person's biggest successes and failures. Also ask what the entrepreneur would change if she or he could start over again. Each team should make an oral report to the class.

6. Write a paper describing an occasion when you received outstanding customer value and an occasion when you received very poor customer value.

WORKING THE NET

1. Point your browser toward the Bureau of Economic Analysis Regional Accounts Data at **www.bea.doc.gov/bea/dr1.htm.** Find the historical information for your state's gross domestic product (GDP). What trends do you see? Can you think of reasons for these trends? How does your state's GDP compare with the U.S. GDP overall? Federal GDP figures are available at **www.bea.doc.gov/bea/dn1.htm.**

2. Read more about how the consumer price index (CPI) is computed at **stats.bls.gov/cpifacts.htm.** Look at the relative importance of each category included in the CPI. How well do these weightings match your own expenditures on each of these categories? What are some of the drawbacks of computing the CPI this way? Do you think these categories give a realistic picture of how most Americans spend their money? Why or why not?

3. For the next week, track the daily updates for the Federal Reserve interest rate at **bog.frb.fed.us/release/h115/about.htm.** At the end of the week, note any changes in the rate. Can you think of any events that may have influenced the rate change? If there was no change, what factors were involved?

4. Ever think about what you'd do differently if you were president? Here's your chance to find out how your ideas would affect the federal budget. The

National Budget Simulator at **garnet.berkeley.edu:3333/budget/budget.html** lets you see how government officials make tradeoffs in planning the federal budget. Experiment with your own budget ideas at the site. What are the effects of your decisions?

CREATIVE THINKING CASE

Should Network Solutions Have a "Dot-Com" Monopoly on the Internet

It's often said that no one owns the Internet. But a little company in Herndon, Virginia, comes pretty close. Since 1994, Network Solutions, Inc. has held an exclusive federal contract to handle distribution of addresses for the World Wide Web, including its most widely recognized feature: the ".com" suffix. Currently appended to more than two million Web addresses, .com covers the preeminent domain for doing cyberbusiness. If Web addresses were California real estate, Network Solutions would own the coastline.

Like most monopolies, this one is lucrative. Registering Web addresses for $70 a pop, Network Solutions has metamorphosed from a minority contractor scrambling for government computer jobs into a publicly traded Internet player with revenues at $77 million.

But now that monopoly is under siege. Network Solutions's original contract with the government has expired, and competitors are demanding a piece of the action. To fight back, the company has hired top-dollar lobbyists.

When Network Solutions received its monopoly, there were only 7,500 Web addresses; now there are millions. Network Solutions argues that taking away its monopoly will create chaos in cyberspace. The federal government agrees that stability of the Internet is very important. Government officials also claim that maintaining a monopoly will stifle competition and strangle the growth of the global network.

The company does more than merely collect registrations. Each evening, Network Solutions adds the day's newly registered names to the Internet's master list of addresses. And at midnight Eastern Standard Time, the company releases this updated master list to engineers around the world who maintain the Internet's 13 "root servers." Without the updated list, these digital hubs wouldn't know where to direct traffic. Right now, Network Solutions is the sole guardian of the master list.

The critical nature of that task in today's economy was demonstrated on July 17, 1997, when a software bug rendered portions of Network Solutions's nightly master list invisible. The following day, roughly a third of all Internet sites were inaccessible. Since then, Network Solutions has upgraded its software and installed a number of safety features. The company's competitors argue that the breakdown shows precisely why Network Solutions needs competition. But the company and its defenders counter that such problems are more manageable with one experienced company.

Critical Thinking Questions

1. Should Network Solutions maintain its ".com" monopoly? Why or why not?

2. What might be a possible compromise solution?

3. What can Network Solutions do to try and maintain its monopoly?

4. Go to **www.networksolutions.com** and learn how to register a Web address. How do you determine if someone has already registered the name that you want? What is the current cost to register? Go to the site's "The Internet in Action" discussion. Describe what you found to the class.

VIDEO CASE

Black Forest Motors: The Mercedes-Benz Strategy in Action

Mercedes-Benz (**www.mercedescenter.com**), a manufacturer headquartered in Germany, produces luxury and near-luxury automobiles for distribution in Germany, the United States, and elsewhere. To increase its sales and perceived customer value in the U.S. market, Mercedes-Benz decided to pursue a corporate strategy called the "Customer Value Triad." This strategy had three components: goods quality, service quality, and value-based pricing. While goods quality and value-based pricing are established by the manufacturer, dealerships are the key element in service quality.

Black Forest Motors is a Mercedes-Benz dealership located in North Acme, Michigan, near Lake Michigan's Grand Traverse Bay. Black Forest Motors is a prime example of the Mercedes-Benz corporate strategy in action, particularly the service quality component of the Customer Value Triad. Black Forest prides itself on exceeding customers' expectations of product quality, price, and service. As a result, Black Forest's customer base, fondly referred to as its "family of owners," has continued to grow. Black Forest Motors describes itself as "a great place to purchase a car."

Some employees have been with Black Forest Motors since its founding. Black Forest views this as evidence that the dealership is also a great place to work. This translates directly into quality customer service and helps the dealership to be a great place to purchase a vehicle.

The sales, service, and parts departments powerfully demonstrate Black Forest's commitment to service quality, as well as to goods quality and value-based pricing. The sales department's sole purpose is to exceed customer expectations from test drive to delivery of the vehicle. This commitment begins with the test drive, which customers can schedule online through Black Forest's Web page. The sales staff is dedicated to providing the information that customers need to make an educated buying decision. Black Forest wants all of its customers to drive away in a Mercedes-Benz that they feel is the perfect choice. Among the Mercedes-Benz automobiles sold by Black Forest are all five models that were voted "1998 Best Overall Value of the Year in Their Class" by IntelliChoice:

- Mercedes-Benz C230, the Best Overall Value, Near-Luxury Cars.
- Mercedes-Benz C280, the Best Overall Car Value over $20,000.
- Mercedes-Benz C280 sedan, the Best Overall Value, Luxury Cars.
- Mercedes-Benz E320, a Best Overall Value, Luxury Cars.
- Mercedes-Benz S320 Series sedan, a Best Overall Value, Luxury Cars.

The service department has a state-of-the-art facility, featuring the latest diagnostic and repair equipment used by highly trained, factory technicians. The department's operations are based on the premise that "you and your vehicle deserve only the best of care." Goods quality and service quality are also emphasized in the parts department. It is stocked with a large inventory of the same high-quality parts used in manufacturing Mercedes-Benz vehicles.

With its commitment to the Customer Value Triad of goods quality, service quality, and value-based pricing, Black Forest Motors asks only one thing of its clients: "If you were treated well, your expectations met, and the service was good, please tell others."

Critical Thinking Questions

1. Do you think the Mercedes-Benz Customer Value Triad is an effective way to formulate a corporate strategy?

2. How might a strategy based on the Customer Value Triad help Mercedes-Benz and its dealerships to compete effectively in the American marketplace?

3. Why are product and service quality important elements of operating a successful business? What is the impact on the price of the cars?

4. Does Mercedes-Benz operate in an oligopolistic marketplace?

chapter three

Competing in the Global Marketplace

learning goals

>lg 1   Why is global trade important to the United States?

>lg 2   How is global trade measured?

>lg 3   Why do nations trade?

>lg 4   What are the barriers to international trade?

>lg 5   How do governments and institutions foster world trade?

>lg 6   What are international economic communities?

>lg 7   How do companies enter the global marketplace?

>lg 8   What threats and opportunities exist in the global marketplace?

>lg 9   What are the advantages of multinational corporations?

>lg 10   What are the trends in the global marketplace?

Selling Saturn in Japan

General Motors Corp.'s Saturn division came to Japan on a mission—to break into the Japanese automobile market. So far, the gung ho effort has been a flop.

Unlike other foreign auto manufacturers, which positioned their cars as upscale novelty items, Saturn's strategy was to compete with Japanese rivals on their home turf by introducing the Saturn as an everyday car. Saturn adapted its U.S. model to the needs of Japanese consumers by installing right-hand drive steering and adding folding side mirrors—practically a necessity on Japan's narrow streets. Saturn also established its own dealership network to set itself apart from other imports. To counter some widely held perceptions about U.S. companies, Saturn even blitzed the airwaves with ads depicting it as a cozy company with friendly Japanese employees.

The effort, which coincided with the nosedive in Japan's economy, hasn't paid off. Saturn sold just 1,400 vehicles in its first 16 months. "We knew we'd have to have patience, but we didn't know we'd need this much patience," says Keith Wicks, general director of Saturn Japan.

Can a U.S. automaker ever be more than a niche player in Japan? Since 1996, all three large U.S. automakers have failed to sell American cars to the Japanese mass market. Chrysler Corp.'s Neon—once dubbed the "Japanese-car killer"—has gone nowhere in Japan, and Ford Motor Co.'s right-hand drive Taurus bombed here. Sales of GM's Cavalier, produced in the United States and sold under the Toyota Motor Corp. badge, also have been disappointing.

Some analysts say Saturn is using the wrong strategy for Japan where the typical foreign car buyer wants to stand out from the crowd. Distinctive European models accounted for almost two-thirds of all imported vehicles sold in Japan in 1998. Successful imports from the United States have included such quintessentially "American" cars as GM's Cadillac Seville and Chrysler's Jeep Cherokee.

Saturn wanted to buck the pattern. It priced Saturns at about $14,000—competitive with Japanese models and below the price of most foreign imports. Ads have included scenes of Saturn's U.S. headquarters in the Tennessee countryside and Japanese salespeople sporting Saturn's casual look—polo shirts and white knit sweaters instead of the typical suit. Print ads feature young parents describing how much they like their Saturns: to court parents, Saturn has even put a play area and toys in every showroom.[1]

As the Saturn story illustrates, selling in the global marketplace isn't always easy. Competition, for example, can be very difficult on Japanese automakers' home turf.

Critical Thinking Questions

As you read this chapter, consider the following questions as they relate to Saturn:

- What are several other factors that can make success difficult in the global marketplace?
- What can governments do to protect domestic competitors?
- What cultural differences did Saturn consider when entering Japan's auto market?

BUSINESS IN THE 21ST CENTURY

global vision

The ability to recognize and react to international business opportunities, be aware of threats from foreign competition, and effectively use international distribution networks to obtain raw materials and move finished products to customers.

Today, global revolutions are under way in many areas of our lives: management, politics, communications, technology. The word *global* has assumed a new meaning, referring to a boundless mobility and competition in social, business, and intellectual arenas. No longer just an option, having a global vision has become a business imperative. Having a **global vision** means recognizing and reacting to international business opportunities, being aware of threats from foreign competitors in all markets, and effectively using international distribution networks to obtain raw materials and move finished products to the customer.

U.S. managers must develop a global vision if they are to recognize and react to international business opportunities, as well as remain competitive at home. Often a U.S. firm's toughest domestic competition comes from foreign companies. Moreover, a global vision enables a manager to understand that customer and distribution networks operate worldwide, blurring geographic and political barriers and making them increasingly irrelevant to business decisions. Sometimes, too, as Saturn discovered, that global vision must be fine-tuned. The purpose of this chapter is to explain how global trade is conducted. We also discuss the barriers to international trade and the organizations that foster global trade. The chapter concludes with trends in the global marketplace.

AMERICA GOES GLOBAL

>lg 1

Over the past two decades, world trade has climbed from $200 billion a year to more than $4 trillion. Countries and companies that were never considered major players in global markets are now contributing to this growth in world trade. Gillette, for example, derives two-thirds of its revenue from its international division. Although this has contributed tremendously to the company's growth, it has also opened the company to new problems. In 1998 Gillette was unable to meet its 20 percent annual profit growth goal because of recessions in Asia. At the same time, global financial turmoil also presents opportunities to buy small consumer products companies outside the United States at a very good price. Gillette has agreed to an extensive licensing and supply arrangement with Rocket Electric Co., one of South Korea's largest battery makers. For a payment of about $60 million, Gillette effectively doubled its share of the world's 10th-largest battery market, to about 22 percent. Although best known as a maker of razors, Gillette bought battery maker Duracell International, Inc. in late 1996 and is now a world leader in that industry as well.[2]

Although Cheetos and Ruffles haven't done very well in Japan, the potato chip has been quite successful. PepsiCo's (owner of Frito-Lay) overseas snack business brings in more than $3.25 billion annually. Recently, Frito-Lay spent $20 million on advertising in Europe in one month to convince European consumers to eat more tortilla chips.[3]

Global business is not a one-way street, where only U.S. companies sell their wares and services throughout the world. Foreign competition in

In pursuing its global vision of selling cars to Japan's mass market, General Motors' Saturn Division faces stiff competition from Japanese automakers as well as foreign imports.

the domestic market used to be relatively rare but now occurs in almost every industry. In fact, U.S. makers of electronic goods, cameras, automobiles, fine china, tractors, leather goods, and a host of other consumer and industrial products have struggled to maintain their domestic market shares against foreign competitors. Nevertheless, the global market has created vast, new business opportunities for many U.S. firms.

The Importance of Global Business to the United States

Many countries depend more on international commerce than the United States does. For example, France, Great Britain, and Germany all derive more than 19 percent of their gross domestic product (GDP) from world trade, compared to about 12 percent for the United States. Nevertheless, the impact of international business on the U.S. economy is still impressive:

- The United States exports about a fifth of its industrial production and a third of its farm products.
- One of every 16 jobs in the United States is directly or indirectly supported by exports.
- U.S. businesses export nearly $850 billion in goods to foreign countries every year, and almost a third of U.S. corporate profits is derived from international trade and foreign investment.
- Exports account for almost one-third of America's economic growth.
- Chemicals, office machinery, computers, automobiles, aircraft, and electrical and industrial machinery make up almost half of all nonagricultural exports.[4]

The U.S. International Trade Administration (ITA) helps U.S. firms do business in foreign markets. To get the inside scoop on what it takes to do business in hundreds of countries, visit the ITA's Trade Compliance Center at

www.mac.doc.gov/tcc

These statistics might seem to imply that practically every business in the United States is selling its wares throughout the world, but nothing could be further from the truth. About 85 percent of all U.S. exports of manufactured goods are shipped by 250 companies. Only the very large multinational companies have seriously attempted to compete worldwide. Fortunately, more small companies are now aggressively pursuing international markets.

concept check

- What is global vision, and why is it important?
- What impact does international trade have on the U.S. economy?

MEASURING TRADE BETWEEN NATIONS

>lg 2

International trade improves relationships with friends and allies, helps ease tensions among nations, and—economically speaking—bolsters economies, raises people's standard of living, provides jobs, and improves the quality of life. The value of international trade is over $4 trillion a year and growing. This section takes a look at some key measures of international trade: exports and imports, the balance of trade, the balance of payments, and exchange rates.

Exports and Imports

exports

Goods and services produced in one country and sold in other countries.

imports

Goods and services that are bought from other countries.

The developed nations (those with mature communication, financial, educational, and distribution systems) are the major players in international trade. They account for about 70 percent of the world's exports and imports. **Exports** are goods and services made in one country and sold to others. **Imports** are goods and services that are bought from other countries. The United States is both the largest exporter and the largest importer in the world. During a four-year period

The United States is the world leader in exports and imports, which are a key measure of international trade.

ending in 1998, U.S. exports accounted for almost one-third of U.S. economic growth and 2.2 million additional American jobs. Today, U.S. exports amount to approximately $850 billion annually. Exports support more than 12 million U.S. jobs.[5]

Each year the United States exports more food, animal feed, and beverages than the year before. A third of U.S. farm acreage is devoted to crops for export. The United States is also a major exporter of engineering products and other high-tech goods, such as computers and telecommunications equipment. For more than 40,000 U.S. companies (the majority of them small), international trade offers exciting and profitable opportunities. Among the largest U.S. exporters are Boeing Co., General Motors Corp., General Electric Co., Ford Motor Co., and IBM.

Despite our impressive list of resources and great variety of products, imports to the United States are also growing. Some of these imports are raw materials that we lack, such as manganese, cobalt, and bauxite, which are used to make airplane parts, exotic metals, and military hardware. More modern factories and lower labor costs in other countries make it cheaper to import industrial supplies (like steel) and production equipment than to produce them at home. Most of Americans' favorite hot beverages—coffee, tea, and cocoa—are imported. We also import Scotch whiskey, English bicycles, German and Japanese automobiles, Italian and Spanish shoes, Central American bananas, Philippine plywood, Hong Kong textiles, and French wines.

Balance of Trade

balance of trade

The difference between the value of a country's exports and the value of its imports during a certain time.

trade surplus

A favorable balance of trade that occurs when a country exports more than it imports.

trade deficit

An unfavorable balance of trade that occurs when a country imports more than it exports.

balance of payments

A summary of a country's international financial transactions showing the difference between the country's total payments to and its total receipts from other countries.

The difference between the value of a country's exports and the value of its imports during a certain time is the country's **balance of trade.** A country that exports more than it imports is said to have a *favorable* balance of trade, called a **trade surplus.** A country that imports more than it exports is said to have an *unfavorable* balance of trade, or a **trade deficit.** When imports exceed exports, more money flows out of the country than flows into it.

Check out the current U.S. balance of trade with various countries at

www.bea.doc.gov/bea/di1.htm

Although U.S. exports have been booming, we still import more than we export. We have had an unfavorable balance of trade throughout the 1990s. In 1998 the United States had a trade deficit of approximately $110 billion.[6] Part of the problem is that most U.S. companies still avoid the export market. Many medium-size and small producers think "going global" is more trouble than it's worth. And as we've seen, Americans are buying more foreign goods than ever before. As long as we continue to import more than we export, the United States will continue to have a trade deficit.

Balance of Payments

Another measure of international trade is called the **balance of payments,** which is a summary of a country's international financial transactions showing the difference between the country's total payments to and its total receipts from other countries. The balance of payments includes imports and exports (balance of trade), long-term investments in overseas plants and equipment, government loans to and from other countries, gifts and foreign aid, military expenditures made in other countries, and money transfers in and out of foreign banks.

From 1900 until 1970, the United States had a trade surplus, but in the other areas that make up the balance of payments, U.S. payments exceeded receipts, largely due to the large U.S. military presence abroad. Hence, almost every year since 1950, the United States has had an unfavorable balance of payments. And since 1970, both the balance of payments *and* the balance of trade have been unfavorable. What can a nation do to reduce an unfavorable balance of payments? It can foster exports, reduce its dependence on imports, decrease its military presence abroad, or reduce foreign investment.

In the late 1990s, the countries of Asia including Japan, Russia, and much of the rest of the developing world were in a recession. America's relatively strong economy drew in the exports of crisis-stricken countries at the same time that foreign demand for American products weakened. As a result, the U.S. balance of payments deficit soared, rising from $236 billion in 1998 to an estimated $290 billion in 1999.[7]

The Changing Value of Currencies

The exchange rate is the price of one country's currency in terms of another country's currency. If a country's currency *appreciates,* less of that country's currency is needed to buy another country's currency. If a country's currency *depreciates,* more of that currency will be needed to buy another country's currency.

How do appreciation and depreciation affect the prices of a country's goods? If, say, the U.S. dollar depreciates relative to the Japanese yen, U.S. residents have to pay more dollars to buy Japanese goods. To illustrate, suppose the dollar price of a yen is $0.012 and that a Toyota is priced at 2 million yen. At this exchange rate, a U.S. resident pays $24,000 for a Toyota ($0.012 × 2 million yen = $24,000). If the dollar depreciates to $0.018 to one yen, then the U.S. resident will have to pay $36,000 for a Toyota.

As the dollar depreciates, the prices of Japanese goods rise for U.S. residents, so they buy fewer Japanese goods—thus, U.S. imports decline. At the same time, as the dollar depreciates relative to the yen, the yen appreciates relative to the dollar. This means prices of U.S. goods fall for the Japanese, so they buy more U.S. goods—and U.S. exports rise.

Get up-to-the-minute exchange rates at **xe.net/currency**

floating exchange rates
A system in which prices of currencies move up and down based upon the demand for and supply of the various currencies.

devaluation
A lowering of the value of a nation's currency relative to other currencies.

Currency markets operate under a system called **floating exchange rates.** Prices of currencies "float" up and down based upon the demand for and supply of each currency. Global currency traders create the supply of and demand for a particular currency based on that currency's investment, trade potential, and economic strength.

If a country decides that its currency is not properly valued in international currency markets, the government may step in and adjust the currency's value. In a **devaluation,** a nation lowers the value of its currency relative to other currencies. In August 1998, Russia devalued the ruble by 34 percent.[8] A month later, Colombia and Ecuador also devalued their currencies but by much less than Russia. Russia not only devalued its currency but also restructured government short-term debt to long term and imposed strict financial controls on Russian banks and companies. As a result, companies and banks could not meet their foreign debt obligations.

concept check

- Describe the position of the United States in world trade.
- Explain the difference between balance of trade and balance of payments.
- Explain the impact of a currency devaluation.

WHY NATIONS TRADE

>lg 3

One might argue that the best way to protect workers and the domestic economy is to stop trade with other nations. Then the whole circular flow of inputs and outputs would stay within our borders. But if we decided to do that, how would we get resources like cobalt and coffee beans? The United States simply can't produce some things, and it can't manufacture some products, such as steel and most clothing, at the low costs we're used to. The fact is that nations—like people—are good at producing different things: you may be better at balancing a ledger than repairing a car. In that case you benefit by "exporting" your bookkeeping services and "importing" the car repairs you need from a good mechanic. Economists refer to specialization like this as *advantage*.

Absolute Advantage

absolute advantage

The situation when a country can produce and sell a product at a lower cost than any other country or when it is the only country that can provide the product.

A country has an **absolute advantage** when it can produce and sell a product at a lower cost than any other country or when it is the only country that can provide a product. The United States, for example, has an absolute advantage in reusable spacecraft and other high-tech items.

Suppose that the United States has an absolute advantage in air traffic control systems for busy airports and that Brazil has an absolute advantage in coffee. The United States does not have the proper climate for growing coffee, and Brazil lacks the technology to develop air traffic control systems. Both countries would gain by exchanging air traffic control systems for coffee.

Comparative Advantage

principle of comparative advantage

The concept that each country should specialize in the products that it can produce most readily and cheaply and trade those products for those that other countries can produce most readily and cheaply.

free trade

The policy of permitting the people of a country to buy and sell where they please without restrictions.

protectionism

The policy of protecting home industries from outside competition by establishing artificial barriers such as tariffs and quotas.

Even if the United States had an absolute advantage in both coffee and air traffic control systems, it should still specialize and engage in trade. Why? The reason is the **principle of comparative advantage,** which says that each country should specialize in the products that it can produce most readily and cheaply and trade those products for goods that foreign countries can produce most readily and cheaply. This specialization ensures greater product availability and lower prices. Even small businesses have learned how to capitalize on comparative advantage as demonstrated in the Focusing on Small Business box.

For example, Mexico and China have a comparative advantage in producing clothing because of low labor costs. Japan has long held a comparative advantage in consumer electronics because of technological expertise. America has an advantage in computer software, airplanes, some agricultural products, heavy machinery, and jet engines.

Thus, comparative advantage acts as a stimulus to trade. When nations allow their citizens to trade whatever goods and services they choose without government regulation, free trade exists. **Free trade** is the policy of permitting the people of a country to buy and sell where they please without restrictions. The opposite of free trade is **protectionism,** in which a nation protects its home industries from outside competition by establishing artificial barriers such as tariffs and quotas. In the next section, we'll look at the various barriers, some natural and some created by governments, that restrict free trade.

concept check

- Explain the difference between absolute advantage and comparative advantage.
- Describe the principle of comparative advantage.
- Describe the policy of free trade and its relationship to comparative advantage.

BARRIERS TO TRADE

>lg 4

International trade is carried out by both businesses and governments—as long as no one puts up trade barriers. In general, trade barriers keep firms from sell-

SMALL AMERICAN BUSINESSES SCRAMBLE
FOR SUCCESS IN CHINA

From an office overlooking Beijing's crowded streets, former Beverly Hills businessman Jian Lin plots what he hopes will become China's next cultural revolution: family entertainment American style. "We found a lot of young Chinese are doing well in business. They are starving for entertainment," Jian said.

Along with big corporations such as Microsoft and Motorola, small business entrepreneurs from the United States are starting to launch their own businesses and joint ventures across China. The obstacles to success can be daunting. Language is a barrier for most Americans. They also must deal with bureaucratic corruption and an unfamiliar business culture based on *guanxi*, the contacts needed to cut through governmental red tape. "A lot of Americans come here with a lot of hope, a lot of money, but they are killed by doing business with the wrong people," said Jian.

To business people like Jian and his Chinese partner, Liu Tie, China represents a vast, largely untapped market. The joint venture launched by Liu's Beijing Dazhong Trading Group and Jian's Innovation Capital Corp. includes a traveling carnival, complete with cotton candy, corn dogs and midway games, that played through the summer in Chinese coastal cities. They are renovating space in Beijing's main railroad station to house a motion simulation theater and two bars, one with a theme of outer space and the other of New Orleans' Bourbon Street. The pair also won rights to turn a quiet park into a family-fun center with rides, arcades, and a cowboy-themed restaurant. Eventually, Jian and Liu want to create an entertainment empire of similar ventures in cities across China.

A Chinese native who immigrated to the United States as a child, Jian speaks fluent Mandarin Chinese and knows China's culture. In Liu, chairman of a $5 million-a-year real estate and food services company, Jian gained a partner with money to invest and connections needed to secure permits and leases. Jian brings American connections to the deal. He bought equipment for the traveling carnival and hired an American carnival company to run it. He also negotiated the purchase of a $700,000, 45-seat motion simulation theater from Los Angeles-based Showscan Entertainment.

Younger Chinese business people, such as Liu, 30, understand capitalism and are eager to reap its rewards, said Jian, who is 44. "The easiest way to do business in China is to find a young entrepreneur," he said. "They will take command of the problem. All that you have to do is assist them in the way a normal American does business. They love that."

Critical Thinking Questions

1. How is the principle of comparative advantage working here?
2. What type of American small businesses might do best in China?
3. In what areas does America have an absolute advantage over China?

ing to one another in foreign markets. The major obstacles to international trade are natural barriers, tariff barriers, and nontariff barriers.

Natural Barriers

Natural barriers to trade can be either physical or cultural. For instance, even though raising beef in the relative warmth of Argentina may cost less than raising beef in the bitter cold of Siberia, the cost of shipping the beef from South America to Siberia might drive the price too high. *Distance* is thus one of the natural barriers to international trade. Jet airplanes cut the time needed to ship goods long distances, but weight is a factor. Thus, air cargo is limited to products with a high value per pound. For example, it would not make sense to ship coal or gravel by air, although orchids, seafood, computers, and replacement parts for machinery are often moved this way. With advances in technology, liquefied natural gas, asphalt, and other hard-to-transport products can now be moved by ship or barge—something not feasible 15 or 20 years ago. Further improvements in technology should help lower other distance barriers as well.

Language is another natural trade barrier. People who can't communicate effectively may not be able to negotiate trade agreements or may ship the wrong goods.

Tariff Barriers

tariff

A tax imposed on imported goods.

A **tariff** is a tax imposed by a nation on imported goods. It may be a charge per unit, such as per barrel of oil or per new car; it may be a percentage of the value of the goods, such as 5 percent of a $500,000 shipment of shoes; or it may be a combination. No matter how it is assessed, any tariff makes imported goods more costly, so they are less able to compete with domestic products.

protective tariffs

Tariffs that are imposed in order to make imports less attractive to buyers than domestic products are.

Protective tariffs make imports less attractive to buyers than domestic products are. The United States, for instance, has protective tariffs on imported poultry, textiles, sugar, and some types of steel and clothing. On the other side of the world, Japan imposes a tariff on U.S. cigarettes that makes them cost 60 percent more than Japanese brands. U.S. tobacco firms believe they could get as much as a third of the Japanese market if there were no tariffs on cigarettes. With tariffs, they have under 2 percent of the market.

Arguments for and against Tariffs Congress has debated the issue of tariffs since 1789. The main argument against tariffs is that they discourage free trade, and free trade lets the principle of comparative advantage work most efficiently. The main argument for tariffs is that they protect domestic businesses and workers.

One of the oldest arguments in favor of protectionism is the *infant-industry argument.* By protecting new domestic industries from established foreign competitors, so this argument goes, a tariff can give a struggling industry time to become an effective competitor. A tariff protected the infant U.S. motorcycle industry against British firms. But eventually the Japanese drove most European and American producers from the market. Harley-Davidson is the only remaining large U.S. motorcycle maker.

A second argument for tariffs is the *job-protection argument.* Supporters—especially unions—say we should use tariffs to keep foreign labor from taking away U.S. jobs. U.S. jobs are lost, they say, when low-wage countries sell products at lower prices than those charged in the United States. The higher prices charged by the U.S. firms help pay the higher wages of U.S. workers. More than 200,000 U.S. manufacturing jobs have been lost since 1997 because of high U.S. wages.

Defense suppliers and the military often use the *preparedness argument* for tariffs. They say that industries and technology that are vital to our military should be protected during peace-

Tariffs on the imported goods arriving on this foreign ship at a port in Seattle, Washington, make the products more expensive than those of U.S. competitors.

time because these industries will be needed in the event of war. U.S. ship-builders, gunpowder manufacturers, and uniform manufacturers are helped by this sort of tariff.

An argument against tariffs is that they raise prices, thereby decreasing consumers' purchasing power. Over the long run tariffs may also be too protective, if they cause domestic companies to stop innovating and fall behind technologically. An example is the Italian car builder Fiat. Protective tariffs helped keep Fiat's Italian market share very high. As Europe's trade barriers fell, foreign competitors moved in with cars that Italian drivers preferred. Fiat is now desperately spending billions of dollars to revamp its factories and design new models.

Details about Japan's tariffs and regulations for foreign companies are available at www.ita.doc.gov/region/japan/japan.html

Nontariff Barriers

Governments also use other tools besides tariffs to restrict trade. Among them are import quotas, embargoes, buy-national regulations, custom regulations, and exchange controls.

import quota

A limit on the quantity of a certain good that can be imported.

Import quotas   One type of nontariff barrier is the **import quota** or limits on the quantity of a certain good that can be imported. The goal of setting quotas is to limit imports to the optimum amount of a given product. America protects its shrinking textile industry with quotas. In 1998, for example, China sold over $6.5 billion in textiles in the United States whereas U.S. textile manufacturers shipped only $64 million in garments and fabric to China. Because Chinese textile exports to the United States far exceeded the quota, the U.S. government threatened to impose millions of dollars in fines on China. Bejiing countered by threatening to place quotas on U.S. fruit, beverages, and other goods. U.S. negotiators finally decided to eliminate the fines.[9]

embargo

A total ban on imports or exports of a product.

Embargoes   A complete ban against importing or exporting a product is an **embargo.** Often embargoes are set up for defense purposes. For instance, the United States does not allow various high-tech products, such as supercomputersand lasers, to be exported to countries that are not allies. Although this embargo costs U.S. firms billions of dollars each year in lost sales, it keeps enemies from using the latest technology in their military hardware.

Buy-national regulations   Government rules that give special privileges to domestic manufacturers are called buy-national regulations. One such regulation in the United States bans the use of foreign steel in constructing U.S. highways. Many state governments have buy-national rules for supplies and services.

Custom regulations   In a more subtle move, a country may make it hard for foreign products to enter its markets by establishing custom regulations that are different from generally accepted international standards, such as requiring bottles to be quart size rather than liter size. The French seem most adept at using this tactic. For example, to reduce imports of foreign VCRs, at one time France ruled that all VCRs had to enter through the customs station at Poitiers. This customs house is located in the middle of the country, was woefully understaffed, and was open only a few days each week. What's more, the few customs agents at Poitiers opened each package separately to inspect the merchandise. Within a few weeks, imports of VCRs in France came to a halt.

c o n c e p t c h e c k

- Discuss the concept of natural trade barriers.
- Describe several tariff and nontariff barriers to trade.

Exchange controls **Exchange controls** are laws that require a company earning foreign exchange (foreign currency) from its exports to sell the foreign exchange to a control agency, usually a central bank. For example, assume that Rolex, a Swiss company, sells 300 watches to Zales Jewelers, a U.S. chain, for $120,000 (U.S.). If Switzerland had exchange controls, Rolex would have to sell its U.S. dollars to the Swiss central bank and would receive Swiss francs.

FOSTERING GLOBAL TRADE

exchange controls

Laws that require a company earning foreign exchange (foreign currency) from its exports to sell the foreign exchange to a control agency, such as a central bank.

dumping

The practice of charging a lower price for a product in foreign markets than in the firm's home market.

From our discussion so far, it might seem that governments act only to restrain global trade. On the contrary, governments and international financial organizations work hard to increase it as this section explains.

Antidumping Laws

U.S. firms don't always get to compete on an equal basis with foreign firms in international trade. To level the playing field, Congress has passed antidumping laws. **Dumping** is the practice of charging a lower price for a product (perhaps below cost) in foreign markets than in the firm's home market. The company might be trying to win foreign customers, or it might be seeking to get rid of surplus goods. Sometimes, too, to help create an export market, a government will subsidize certain industries so that they can sell their goods for less. In the past, Japanese steel was sold below cost in world markets, and the losses were covered by government subsidies.

When the variation in price can't be explained by differences in the cost of serving the two markets, dumping is suspected. Most industrialized countries have antidumping regulations. They are especially concerned about *predatory dumping,* the attempt to gain control of a foreign market by destroying competitors with impossibly low prices. Many businesspeople feel that Japan has engaged in predatory dumping of semiconductors in the U.S. market. Without import quotas, companies such as Intel wouldn't exist.

One of the most famous dumping cases in U.S. history involved Japanese color television sets during the 1960s and 1970s. In 1971 U.S. television makers filed a complaint, alleging that Japanese television makers were selling below cost and offering distributors rebates, while also restricting imports into Japan. The Treasury Department, which then enforced the antidumping laws, took no action for three years and then failed to collect duties even though it had determined that dumping was occurring. The U.S. television industry was effectively destroyed. Today, there are no U.S.-owned television makers. As a result of that experience, Congress transferred the authority to enforce antidumping laws from the Treasury Department to the Commerce Department.[10]

The Uruguay Round and the World Trade Organization

Uruguay Round

A 1994 agreement by 117 nations to lower trade barriers worldwide.

The **Uruguay Round** of trade negotiations is an agreement to dramatically lower trade barriers worldwide. Adopted in 1994, the agreement was signed by 117 nations in Marrakesh, Morocco. The most ambitious global trade agreement ever negotiated, the Uruguay Round reduced tariffs by one-third worldwide, a move that is expected to increase global income by $235 billion annually by 2005. Perhaps the most notable aspect of the agreement is its recognition of new global realities. For the first time, an agreement covers services, intellectual property rights, and trade-related investment measures such as exchange controls.

FOREIGN STEEL: FRIEND OR FOE OF AMERICAN STEEL?

As a result of the global competitive pressures that emerged during the 1980s, the American steel industry eliminated hundreds of thousands of jobs in an effort to cut costs and become more competitive and more profitable. As part of this downsizing, many U.S. steel producers closed some or all of their basic steelmaking operations but retained their more profitable rolling mills. Consequently, American steelmakers began importing more steel slabs—the output from the basic steelmaking operation. In fact, imports of steel slabs increased from 155,343 tons in 1980 to 6.8 million tons in 1998. Steel slabs are finished into various hot-rolled, cold-rolled, or galvanized products.

The American steel industry is still fighting for survival. Interestingly, the beleaguered industry has begun to attack the very imports that it has embraced in the past several years. Complaining that foreign steel producers are engaging in unfair trade practices, American steel producers have lobbied the U.S. Congress to provide legislative relief from foreign companies that are dumping steel into the American market.

The legal test for product dumping is based on two criteria. First, the product must be priced unfairly low—either below its production costs or below the selling price in the home country. Second, the imported product must harm the domestic industry.

Steel producers in Brazil, Japan, and Russia, among others, have been accused of dumping steel into the American market. Meanwhile, U.S. steel producers say they will not import steel that is priced below fair market value. However, "one steel trader scoffs at the notion that U.S. steelmakers would pay the fair-value price of steel they import if others are paying a price below fair value."

Critical Thinking Questions

1. Is it ethical for the steel industry to benefit from pricing policies and practices that it complains are unfair?
2. How might the ethical climate of a steel producer be affected by simultaneously complaining about and benefiting from dumping?
3. What role, if any, can government play in establishing an ethical position with regard to dumping?

The Uruguay Round made several major changes in world trading practices:

- *Entertainment, pharmaceuticals, integrated circuits, and software.* Under new rules, patents, copyrights, and trademarks are protected for 20 years. Computer programs are protected for 50 years and semiconductor chips for 10 years. Many developing nations will have a decade to phase in patent protection for drugs. However, France, which limits the number of U.S. movies and television shows that can be shown, refused to liberalize market access for the U.S. entertainment industry.

- *Financial, legal, and accounting services.* Services were brought under international trading rules for the first time, potentially creating a vast opportunity for these competitive U.S. industries. Now it is easier to admit managers and key personnel into a country.

- *Agriculture.* Europe will gradually reduce farm subsidies, opening new opportunities for such U.S. farm exports as wheat and corn. Japan and Korea will begin to import rice. But subsidies for U.S. growers of sugar, citrus fruit, and peanuts will be reduced.

- *Textiles and apparel.* Strict quotas limiting imports from developing countries are being phased out over 10 years, causing further job losses in the U.S. clothing industry. But retailers and consumers will be the big winners because quotas now add $15 billion a year to clothing prices.

- *A new trade organization.* The new **World Trade Organization (WTO)** replaces the old General Agreement on Tariffs and Trade (GATT), which was created in 1948. The GATT contained extensive loopholes that enabled countries to evade agreements to reduce trade barriers. Today, all WTO members must fully comply with all agreements under the Uruguay Round. The WTO also has an effective dispute settlement procedure with strict time limits to resolve disputes.

The WTO has emerged as the world's most powerful institution for reducing trade barriers and opening markets. Approximately 135 nations now belong to the organization. The advantage of WTO membership is that member countries lower trade barriers among themselves. Countries that don't belong must negotiate trade agreements individually with all their trading partners. To date, China and Russia are the largest countries that have not qualified for WTO membership.

The United States has had some success in winning trade disputes at the WTO. Of the 41 cases the United States has brought before the WTO, 18 have been settled; only 2 cases were lost, and 16 were settled in favor of the United States or won outright. Of 19 cases brought by other countries, against the United States, 11 have been settled; the United States lost 4, and 7 were settled in its favor. America's biggest loss came in 1998 when a WTO panel ruled that the Japanese government's attempt to protect Fuji Photo Film from competition by Kodak was not illegal. This decision still has U.S. trade officials fuming.

The World Bank and International Monetary Fund

Two international financial organizations are instrumental in fostering global trade. The **World Bank** offers low-interest loans to developing nations. Originally, the purpose of the loans was to help these nations build infrastructure such as roads, power plants, schools, drainage projects, and hospitals. Now the World Bank offers loans to help developing nations relieve their debt burdens. To receive the loans, countries must pledge to lower trade barriers and aid private enterprise. In addition to making loans, the World Bank is a major source of advice and information for developing nations. The United States has granted the organization $60 million to create knowledge databases on nutrition, birth control, software engineering, creating quality products, and basic accounting systems.[11]

The **International Monetary Fund (IMF)** was founded in 1945, one year after the creation of the World Bank, to promote trade through financial cooperation and eliminate trade barriers in the process. The IMF makes short-term loans to member nations that are unable to meet their budgetary expenses. It operates as a lender of last resort for troubled nations. In exchange for these emergency loans, IMF lenders frequently extract significant commitments from the borrowing nations to address the problems that led to the crises. These steps may include curtailing imports or even devaluing the currency.

World Trade Organization (WTO)

An organization established by the Uruguay Round in 1994 to oversee international trade, reduce trade barriers, and resolve disputes among member nations.

The World Trade Organization tracks the latest trade developments between countries and regions around the world. For the most recent global trading news, visit the WTO's site at

www.wto.org

World Bank

An international bank that offers low-interest loans, as well as advice and information, to developing nations.

International Monetary Fund (IMF)

An international organization, founded in 1945, that promotes trade, makes short-term loans to member nations, and acts as a lender of last resort for troubled nations.

In the late 1990s, South Korea, Thailand, Malaysia, and Indonesia were hit by a severe recession. IMF intervention to rescue these economies did not seem to work as unemployment and interest rates soared. The crisis also hit Russia and several countries of Latin America including Brazil. Private money for economic development simply quit flowing into these economies. The basic problem was that capital (money) had flowed into these emerging economies with little attention paid to the creditworthiness of the borrowers. With easy money, borrowers took on more debt than they could repay. To make matters worse, banks and other financial institutions were so closely intertwined with governments that decisions were made for political reasons and not based on sound economics.

Gain additional insight into the workings of the International Monetary Fund at

www.imf.org

Such global financial problems do not have a simple solution. One option would be to pump a lot more funds into the IMF, giving it enough resources to bail out troubled countries and put them back on their feet. In effect, the IMF would be turned into a real lender of last resort for the world economy.

The danger of counting on the IMF, though, is the "moral hazard" problem. Investors would assume that the IMF would bail them out and would therefore be encouraged to take bigger and bigger risks in emerging markets, leading to the possibility of even deeper financial crises in the future.

concept check

- Describe the purpose and role of the WTO.
- What are the roles of the World Bank and the IMF in world trade?

INTERNATIONAL ECONOMIC COMMUNITIES

>lg 6

Nations that frequently trade with each other may decide to formalize their relationship. The governments meet and work out agreements for a common economic policy. The result is an economic community or, in other cases, a bilateral trade agreement (an agreement between two countries to lower trade barriers). For example, two nations may agree upon a **preferential tariff,** which gives advantages to one nation (or several nations) over others. For instance, when members of the British Commonwealth trade with Great Britain, they pay lower tariffs than do other nations. In other cases, nations may form free-trade associations. In a **free-trade zone,** few, if any, duties or rules restrict trade among the partners, but nations outside the zone must pay the tariffs set by the individual members. A *customs union* sets up a free-trade area and specifies a uniform tariff structure for members' trade with nonmember nations. In a *common market,* or economic union, members go beyond a customs union and try to bring all of their government trade rules into agreement.

preferential tariff

A tariff that is lower for some nations than for others.

free-trade zone

An area where the nations allow free, or almost free, trade among each other while imposing tariffs on goods of nations outside the zone.

North American Free Trade Agreement (NAFTA)

North American Free Trade Agreement (NAFTA)

A 1993 agreement creating a free-trade zone including Canada, Mexico, and the United States.

The **North American Free Trade Agreement (NAFTA)** created the world's largest free-trade zone. The agreement was ratified by the U.S. Congress in 1993. It includes Canada, the United States, and Mexico, with a combined population of 360 million and an economy of $6 trillion.

Canada, the largest U.S. trading partner, entered a free-trade agreement with the United States in 1988. Thus, most of the new long-run opportunities opened for U.S. business under NAFTA are in Mexico, America's third largest trading partner. Before NAFTA, tariffs on Mexican exports to the United States averaged just 4 percent, and most goods entered the United States duty-free, so

Want to learn the latest info about NAFTA? Go to http://www.NAFTA-customs.org

NAFTA's primary impact was to open the Mexican market to U.S. companies. When the treaty went into effect, tariffs on about half the items traded across the Rio Grande disappeared. Since NAFTA came into effect, U.S.-Mexican trade has increased by 250 percent, from $80 billion to $200 billion annually.[12] The pact removed a web of Mexican licensing requirements, quotas, and tariffs that limited transactions in U.S. goods and services. For instance, the pact allows U.S. and Canadian financial services companies to own subsidiaries in Mexico for the first time in 50 years.

The real test of NAFTA will be whether it can deliver rising prosperity on both sides of the Rio Grande. For Mexicans, NAFTA must provide rising wages, better benefits, and an expanding middle class with enough purchasing power to keep buying goods from the United States and Canada. That scenario is plausible in the long run, but not guaranteed. As for the United States, the full implementation of NAFTA will add about $30 billion to GDP annually. But for Americans, the trade agreement will need to prove that it can produce more well-paying jobs than it destroys. Although estimates of the employment effects of NAFTA vary widely, almost every study agrees that there will be gains. The Labor Department has certified—under a program that gives displaced workers retraining and unemployment relief—that 128,303 U.S. workers have lost their jobs so far because of increased competition from Mexico and Canada. That compares with 2.2 million jobs created each year since NAFTA took effect.[13]

Ultimately, some U.S. politicians would like to expand NAFTA to include other Latin American countries and perhaps even Great Britain. Chile was to be the first new entrant, but wrangling within the U.S. Congress has blocked NAFTA expansion so far. Concerns that NAFTA will eventually cost more American jobs than it creates have stalled congressional expansion of the agreement. As a result, countries south of the U.S. border have been forming their own trade agreements.

The largest new trade agreement is **Mercosur,** which includes Brazil, Argentina, Uruguay, and Paraguay. The elimination of most tariffs among the trading partners has resulted in trade revenues that currently exceed $16 billion annually.[14] The economic boom created by Mercosur will undoubtedly cause other nations to either seek trade agreements on their own or enter Mercosur. The European Union, discussed next, hopes to have a free-trade pact with Mercosur by 2005.

The European Union

In 1993, the member countries of the European Community (EC) ratified the **Maastricht Treaty,** which proposed to take the EC further toward economic, monetary, and political union. Officially called the Treaty on European Union, the document outlined plans for tightening bonds among the member states and creating a single market. The European Commission, which drafted the treaty, predicts that Maastricht will create 1.8 million new jobs by 2001. Also, retail prices in the **European Union (EU),** as the EC is now called, are expected to fall by a minimum of 6 percent. Exhibit 3-1 shows the members of the EU.

Although much of the treaty deals with developing a unified European market, Maastricht is also intended to increase integration among the EU members in areas much closer to the heart of national sovereignty. The treaty called for economic and monetary coordination, including a common currency and an

Mercosur

A trade agreement among Argentina, Brazil, Paraguay, and Uruguay that eliminates most tariffs among the member nations.

Maastricht Treaty

A 1993 treaty concluded by the members of the European Community (now the European Union) that outlines plans for tightening bonds among the members and creating a single market; officially called the Treaty on European Union.

European Union (EU)

An organization of 15 European nations (as of 1999) that works to foster political and economic integration in Europe; formerly called the European Community.

Member Countries of the European Union (highlighted in color)

independent central bank. In addition, EU members will eventually share foreign security and defense policies as well as European citizenship—any EU citizen will be able to live, work, vote, and run for office in any member country. The treaty also coordinated health and safety regulations and standardized trade rules, duties, customs procedures, and taxes. A driver hauling cargo from Amsterdam to Lisbon can now clear four border crossings by showing a single piece of paper. Before the Maastricht Treaty, a driver had to carry two pounds of paper to cross the same borders. By setting uniform standards, the treaty's goal is to eliminate the need for manufacturers to produce a separate product for each country—one Braun electric razor for Italy, a slightly different one for Germany, and a third one for France, for example. Goods marked GEC (goods for EC) can be traded freely without being retested at each border.

Some economists have called the EU the "United States of Europe." It is an attractive market, with 320 million consumers and purchasing power almost equal to that of the United States. But the EU will probably never be a United States of Europe. For one thing, even in a united Europe, businesses will not be able to produce a single Europroduct for a generic Euroconsumer. With nine languages and different national customs, Europe will always be far more diverse than the United States. Thus, product differences will continue. It will be a long time, for instance, before the French begin drinking the same instant coffee that Britons enjoy. Even preferences for washing machines differ: British homemakers want front-loaders, and the French want top-loaders; Germans like lots of settings and high spin speeds, while Italians like lower speeds.

The eurodollar replaces the individual currencies of eleven European Union nations. The new common currency enables the countries to do business as a single trading bloc.

An entirely different type of problem facing global businesses is the possibility of a protectionist movement by the EU against outsiders. For example, European automakers have proposed holding Japanese imports at roughly their current 10 percent market share. The Irish, Danes, and Dutch don't make cars and have unrestricted home markets; they are unhappy at the prospect of limited imports of Toyotas and Datsuns. Meanwhile France has a strict quota on Japanese cars to protect its own Renault and Peugeot. These local automarkers could be hurt if the quota is raised at all.

Interestingly, a number of big U.S. companies are already considered more "European" than many European companies. Coke and Kellogg's are considered classic European brand names. Ford and General Motors compete for the largest share of auto sales on the continent. IBM and Dell dominate their markets. General Electric, AT&T, and Westinghouse are already strong all over Europe and have invested heavily in new manufacturing facilities there.

Although many U.S. firms are well prepared to contend with European competition, the rivalry is perhaps more intense there than anywhere else in the world. In the long run, it is questionable whether Europe has room for eight mass-market automakers, including Ford and GM, when the United States sustains just three. Similarly, an integrated Europe probably doesn't need 12 national airlines.

The Euro

Eleven of the 15 members of the European Union are converting their currencies to the eurodollar, or "euro" for short, a new currency that will circulate in all 11 nations. Due to internal policies, Great Britain, Portugal, Spain, and Sweden will not convert to the euro; the currencies that will become obsolete are listed in Exhibit 3-2. The conversion began in January 1999 and will be completed in 2002 when the euro notes begin circulating. With the conversion, the participating European nations will be doing business as a single trading bloc, which will become the largest economy in the world in terms of percentage of world GDP.

concept check ✔

• Explain the pros and cons of NAFTA.
• What is the European Union? Will it ever be a United States of Europe?
• Discuss the concept of the euro.

PARTICIPATING IN THE GLOBAL MARKETPLACE

>lg 7

Companies decide to "go global" for a number of reasons. Perhaps the most urgent reason is to earn additional profits. If a firm has a unique product or technological advantage not available to other international competitors, this advantage should result in major business successes abroad. In other situations, management may have exclusive market information about foreign customers, marketplaces, or market situations not known to others. In this case, although exclusivity can provide an initial motivation for going global, managers must realize that competitors will eventually catch up. Finally, saturated domestic markets, excess capacity, and potential for cost savings can also be motivators to expand into international markets. A company can enter global trade in several ways, as this section describes.

Converting to the Eurodollar Means That Eleven Currencies Will Disappear

Countries Converting to the Eurodollar/Currency to be Replaced

Austria/Schilling	Greece/Drachma
Belgium/Franc	Ireland/Pound
Denmark/Krone	Italy/Lira
Finland/Markka	Luxembourg/Franc
France/Franc	Netherlands/Guilder
Germany/Deutsche mark	

IBM's entry in global markets includes exporting, which helps the company to expand the global distribution of products like the OS/2 Warp operating system to businesses and consumers in Japan.

Exporting

When a company decides to enter the global market, usually the least complicated and least risky alternative is **exporting,** or selling domestically produced products to buyers in another country. A company, for example, can sell directly to foreign importers or buyers. Exporting is not limited to huge corporations such as General Motors or Westinghouse. Indeed, small companies account for 96 percent of all U.S. exporters, but only 30 percent of the export volume.[15] The United States is the world's largest exporter. Many small businesses claim that they lack the money, time, or knowledge of foreign markets that exporting requires. The U.S. Small Business Administration (SBA) now offers the Export Working Capital Program, which helps small and medium-size firms obtain working capital (money) to complete export sales. The SBA also provides counseling and legal assistance for small businesses that wish to enter the global marketplace. Companies such as American Building Restoration Products of Franklin, Wisconsin, have benefited tremendously from becoming exporters. American Building is now selling its chemical products to building restoration companies in Mexico, Israel, Japan, and Korea. Exports account for more than 5 percent of the firm's total sales.[16]

The Internet is an excellent source of information for any firm that is considering entering the global marketplace by exporting. The Applying Technology box describes some of the new information sources found on the Web.

exporting

The practice of selling domestically produced goods to buyers in another country.

Licensing

Another effective way for a firm to move into the global arena with relatively little risk is to sell a license to manufacture its product to a firm in a foreign country. **Licensing** is the legal process whereby a firm (the *licensor*) agrees to let another firm (the *licensee*) use a manufacturing process, trademark, patent, trade secret, or other proprietary knowledge. The licensee, in turn, agrees to pay the licensor a royalty or fee agreed on by both parties.

> a p p l y i n g   t e c h n o l o g y <

INTERNET RESOURCES FOR SMALL BUSINESS EXPORTING

The Internet offers excellent resources for any company that wants to start exporting. Help is available from both private and government sources. Several outstanding private sites include:

- **www.exportzone.com/** This site provides numerous trade leads for exporters.
- **www.tradelcorp.com/** Export assistance for firms wanting to do business in China is available here.
- **www.uscib.org** This is the site of the United States Council for International Business, which advances the global interests of American businesses abroad. It officially represents U.S. companies' positions to foreign businesses and governments.

The federal government also provides numerous sites for export assistance. For example:

- **www.lowe.org/data/7/7541.txt** This site lists names, addresses, and phone numbers of key contacts at all 16 Export Assistance Centers

(EACs) in the United States. EACs provide hands-on assistance with exporting and exporting finance.

- **www.sba.gov/oit/info/pubs_ei.html** This site provides the text version of the book *Breaking into the Trade Game,* as well as links to "opportunities in exporting," "international trade assistance," "international trade loan program," and a "trade events calendar."
- **www.otexa.ita.doc.gov/exports/NEW-EXP.STM** This site is a comprehensive resource for information on all federal government export assistance programs.

Critical Thinking Questions

1. Assume that you want to export in-line skates and have no idea how to do it or where to start. Check the sites listed here to see what information you can find.
2. What other data would you need before making the export decision?

licensing

The legal process whereby a firm agrees to allow another firm to use a manufacturing process, trademark, patent, trade secret, or other proprietary knowledge in exchange for the payment of a royalty.

U.S. companies have eagerly embraced the licensing concept. For instance, Philip Morris licensed Labatt Brewing Company to produce Miller High Life in Canada. The Spaulding Company receives more than $2 million annually from license agreements on its sporting goods. Fruit-of-the-Loom lends its name through licensing to 45 consumer items in Japan alone, for at least 1 percent of the licensee's gross sales.

The licensor must make sure it can exercise sufficient control over the licensee's activities to ensure proper quality, pricing, distribution, and so on. Licensing may also create a new competitor in the long run, if the licensee decides to void the license agreement. International law is often ineffective in stopping such actions. Two common ways that a licensor can maintain effective control over its licensees are by shipping one or more critical components from the United States and by locally registering patents and trademarks in its own name.

Franchising, covered in Chapter 5, is a form of licensing that has grown rapidly in recent years. Over 350 U.S. franchisors operate more than 32,000 outlets in foreign countries, bringing in sales of $6 billion. More than half of the international franchises are for fast-food restaurants and business services. McDonald's's international division is responsible for over 50 percent of the chain's sales and 60 percent of its profits.[17]

Contract Manufacturing

contract manufacturing
The practice in which a foreign firm manufactures private-label goods under a domestic firm's brand name.

In **contract manufacturing,** a foreign firm manufactures private-label goods under a domestic firm's brand. Marketing may be handled by either the domestic company or the foreign manufacturer. Levi Strauss, for instance, entered into an agreement with the French fashion house of Cacharel to produce a new Levi's line called "Something New" for distribution in Germany.

The advantage of contract manufacturing is that it lets a company "test the water" in a foreign country. By allowing the foreign firm to produce a certain volume of products to specification, and put the domestic firm's brand name on the goods, the domestic firm can broaden its global marketing base without investing in overseas plants and equipment. After establishing a solid base, the domestic firm may switch to a joint venture or direct investment, explained below.

Joint Ventures

joint venture
An agreement in which a domestic firm buys part of a foreign firm or joins with a foreign firm to create a new entity.

Joint ventures are somewhat similar to licensing agreements. In a **joint venture,** the domestic firm buys part of a foreign company or joins with a foreign company to create a new entity. A joint venture is a quick and relatively inexpensive way to enter the global market. It can also be very risky. Many joint ventures fail. Others fall victim to a takeover, in which one partner buys out the other.

E*Trade, one of the hottest U.S. Internet-based stockbrokers, recently entered into a joint venture with Softbank Corp. of Japan to offer online investing services in Asia. E*Trade also entered a second joint venture with the British company Electronic Share Information (ESI). The agreement provides E*Trade the opportunity to serve ESI's 170,000 customers and gives ESI access to E*Trade's software and brand name.[18]

In a successful joint venture, both parties gain valuable skills from the alliance. In the General Motors–Suzuki joint venture in Canada, for example, both parties have contributed and gained. The alliance, CAMI Automotive, was formed to manufacture low-end cars for the U.S. market. The plant, which is run by Suzuki management, produces the Geo Metro/Suzuki Swift—the smallest, most fuel-efficient GM car sold in North America—as well as the Geo Tracker/Suzuki Sidekick sport utility vehicle. Through CAMI, Suzuki has gained access to GM's dealer network and an expanded market for

Find out more about Suzuki's international joint ventures at
202.238.79.16/cpd/ koho_e/kaigai

parts and components. GM avoided the cost of developing low-end cars and obtained models it needed to revitalize the lower end of its product line and its average fuel economy rating. The CAMI factory may be one of the most productive plants in North America. There GM has learned how Japanese automakers use work teams, run flexible assembly lines, and manage quality control.

Direct Foreign Investment

direct foreign investment
Active ownership of a foreign company or of manufacturing or marketing facilities in a foreign country.

Active ownership of a foreign company or of overseas manufacturing or marketing facilities is **direct foreign investment.** Direct investors have either a controlling interest or a large minority interest in the firm. Thus, they stand to receive the greatest potential reward but also face the greatest potential risk. A firm may make a direct foreign investment by acquiring an interest in an existing company or by building new facilities. It might do so because it has trouble transferring some resources to a foreign operation or obtaining that resource locally. One important resource is personnel, especially managers. If the local labor market is tight, the firm may buy an entire foreign firm and retain all its employees instead of paying higher salaries than competitors. Sometimes firms make direct investments because they can find no suitable local partners. Also, direct investments avoid the communication problems and conflicts of interest that can arise with joint ventures. IBM, for instance, insists on total ownership of its foreign investments because it does not want to share control with local partners.

Kodak paid more than $1 billion to acquire and upgrade three government-owned film manufacturers in China. In return, the Chinese government granted Kodak a virtual monopoly to manufacture film in the country. In the past, the Chinese government would simply erect more trade barriers to keep companies like Kodak and Fuji out. In a more pragmatic move, the government decided to sell the debt-ridden, inefficient plants to outside investors and exit the film manufacturing business.[19]

HOT
links

How does Atwood Richards help companies like Nestlé and Sherwin Williams conduct business internationally? Find out by reading some of the case studies at the Atwood Richards Co. home page,
www.atwoodrichards.com

countertrade

A form of international trade in which part or all of the payment for goods or services is in the form of other goods and services.

Countertrade

International trade does not always involve cash. Today, countertrade is a fast-growing way to conduct international business. In **countertrade,** part or all of the payment for goods or services is in the form of other goods or services. Countertrade is a form of barter (swapping goods for goods), an age-old practice whose origins have been traced back to cave dwellers. The U.S. Commerce Department says that roughly 30 percent of all international trade involves countertrade. Each year about 300,000 U.S. firms engage in some form of countertrade. American companies, including General Electric, Pepsi, General Motors, and Boeing, barter about $7.5 billion of goods and services every year.[20]

The Atwood Richards Co. is the world's largest countertrade organization. Atwood reviews a client's unsold products and issues trade credits in exchange. The credits can be used to obtain other products and services Atwood has acquired—everything from hotel rooms and airline tickets to television advertising time, forklift trucks, carpeting, pulp, envelopes, steel castings, or satellite tracking systems.

concept check

- Discuss several ways that a company can enter international trade.
- Explain the concept of countertrade.

THREATS AND OPPORTUNITIES IN THE GLOBAL MARKETPLACE

>lg 8

To be successful in a foreign market, companies must fully understand the foreign environment in which they plan to operate. Politics, cultural differences, and the economic environment can represent both opportunities and pitfalls in the global marketplace.

Political Considerations

We have already discussed how tariffs, exchange controls, and other governmental actions threaten foreign producers. The political structure of a country may also jeopardize a foreign producer's success in international trade.

nationalism

A sense of national consciousness that boosts the culture and interests of one country over those of all other countries.

Intense nationalism, for example, can lead to difficulties. **Nationalism** is the sense of national consciousness that boosts the culture and interests of one country over those of all other countries. Strongly nationalistic countries, such as Iran and New Guinea, often discourage investment by foreign companies. In other, less radical forms of nationalism, the government may take actions to hinder foreign operations. France, for example, requires that pop music stations play at least 40 percent of their songs in French. This law was enacted because the French love American rock and roll. Without airtime, American CDs sales suffer. Coca-Cola recently attempted to purchase Orangina, France's only domestically owned and distributed soft drink. The French government blocked the sale saying that it would be "anticompetitive."[21] The real reason was nationalism.

In a hostile climate, a government may *expropriate* a foreign company's assets, taking ownership and compensating the former owners. Even worse is *confiscation*, when the owner receives no compensation. This happened during rebellions in several African nations during the 1990s.

Cultural Differences

Central to any society is the common set of values shared by its citizens that determine what is socially acceptable. Culture underlies the family, educational system, religion, and social class system. The network of social organizations generates overlapping roles and status positions. These values and roles have a tremendous effect on people's preferences and thus on marketers' options. Inca Kola, a fruity, greenish yellow carbonated drink, is the largest selling soft drink in Peru. Despite being described as "liquid bubble gum," the drink has become a symbol of national pride and heritage. The drink was invented in Peru and contains only fruit indigenous to the country. A local consumer of about a six-pack a day says, "I drink Inca Kola because it makes me feel like a Peruvian." He tells his young daughter, "This is our drink, not something invented overseas. It is named for your ancestors, the great Inca warriors."

Language is another important aspect of culture. Marketers must take care in selecting product names and translating slogans and promotional messages so as not to convey the wrong meaning. For example, Mitsubishi Motors had to rename its Pajero model in Spanish-speaking countries because the term refers to a sexual activity. Toyota Motors' MR2 model dropped the number 2 in France because the combination sounds like a French swearword. The literal translation of Coca-Cola in Chinese characters means "bite the wax tadpole."

Each country has its own customs and traditions that determine business practices and influence negotiations with foreign customers. In many countries, personal relationships are more important than financial considerations. For instance, skipping social engagements in Mexico may lead to lost sales. Negotiations in Japan often include long evenings of dining, drinking, and entertaining; only after a close personal relationship has been formed do business negotiations begin. Exhibit 3-3 presents some cultural "dos and don'ts."

Economic Environment

The level of economic development varies considerably, ranging from countries where everyday survival is a struggle, such as the Sudan and Eritrea, to countries that are highly developed, such as Switzerland and Japan. In general, complex, sophisticated industries are found in developed countries, and more basic industries are found in less developed nations. Average family incomes are higher in the more developed countries than in the least developed markets. Larger incomes mean greater purchasing power and demand not only for consumer goods and services but also for the machinery and workers required to produce consumer goods. Exhibit 3-4 provides a glimpse of what families earn throughout the world.

Business opportunities are usually better in countries that have an economic infrastructure in place. **Infrastructure** is the basic institutions and public facilities

infrastructure
The basic institutions and public facilities upon which an economy's development depends.

> e x h i b i t   3 - 3 <

Cultural Dos and Don'ts

DO:
- **Read up** on the culture of the country where you will be doing business. Pointing or beckoning with the forefinger is considered rude in some Asian countries, for example; pointing your foot at another person is considered rude in Thailand.
- **Remember** that pleasure and personal relationships are often a determining factor when Latin Americans and Asians do business.
- **Treat business cards** seriously almost everywhere. In many cultures, a business card is as important as a résumé. Don't glance at the card and shove it in your pocket. Take the card in your right hand, carefully examine it, and memorize the person's name, title, and company and the company's address. You may be tested later.
- **Be aware** of dietary taboos. Pork is considered unclean, for example, by Muslims. Nor should you offer a Hindu a meal containing beef; the cow is considered a sacred animal in the Hindu religion.

DON'T:
- **Dress too casually.** Americans view casual as comfortable or even as part of the breakdown of phony corporate hierarchical rules. In many Asian and Latin American countries, though, casual equals sloppy.
- **Use your left hand** to eat, or to give or receive objects, unless you are certain it is acceptable. In many Asian, Middle Eastern, and African cultures, the left hand is used for personal hygiene and is considered unclean.

Some Examples of Cultural Differences That Can Affect Business Dealings

- The Japanese do not like to say no. If your Japanese business partner tells you that your proposition would "be very difficult," she means "no, we don't want to do it that way."
- In Asia, companies usually do not provide employee evaluations, or performance reviews, unless the employee is about to be fired.
- A powerful Chinese buyer will buy the highest-quality product. He doesn't care about marketing or advertising pitches.
- In many parts of Latin America, the business day begins about 11 A.M., and proceeds until about 3 P.M., when there is a two-to-three-hour break; the last part of the work day runs from about 6 to 9 P.M.
- Hype doesn't sell in many countries, such as Germany and China. A good product stands on its own merits. If you have to hype a product, people believe that something must be wrong with it.
- European and Asian résumés include only the facts: a complete professional history and a copy of every degree, certificate or award earned. Expressions of professional accomplishment on the job are frowned on.
- Cultural norms vary from culture to culture. You might have to turn your head to avoid being kissed on the lips by another man in Russia, for example, as a sign of affection or expression of celebration. But a Chinese businessperson, even one who is a close friend, would generally be uncomfortable with physical contact beyond a handshake.

SOURCE: Bill Bowen, "Culture Clash," *Fort Worth Star Telegram* (September 28, 1998), pp. 14–15.

concept check

- Explain how political factors can affect international trade.
- Describe several cultural factors that a company involved in international trade should consider.
- How can economic conditions affect trade opportunities?

upon which an economy's development depends. When we think about how our own economy works, we tend to take our infrastructure for granted. It includes the money and banking system that provides the major investment loans to our nation's businesses; the educational system that turns out the incredible varieties of skills and basic research that actually run our nation's production lines; the extensive transportation and communications systems—interstate highways, railroads, airports, canals, telephones, Internet sites, postal systems, television stations—that link almost every piece of our geography into one market; the energy system that powers our factories; and, of course, the market system itself, which brings our nation's goods and services into our homes and businesses.

> e x h i b i t   3 - 4 <

What the World Earns
High consumption levels are concentrated in a small share of
households worldwide.

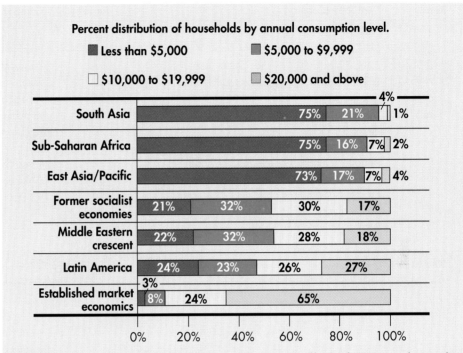

Percent distribution of households by annual consumption level.

■ **Less than $5,000**   ■ **$5,000 to $9,999**

□ **$10,000 to $19,999**   ■ **$20,000 and above**

South Asia	75%	21%	4% / 1%
Sub-Saharan Africa	75%	16%	7% / 2%
East Asia/Pacific	73%	17%	7% / 4%
Former socialist economies	21%	32%	30% / 17%
Middle Eastern crescent	22%	32%	28% / 18%
Latin America	24%	23%	26% / 27%
Established market economics	3% / 8%	24%	65%

0%   20%   40%   60%   80%   100%

Note: Consumption is in U.S. dollars on a purchase-power-parity basis. Percentages may add to more than 100 percent due to rounding.

SOURCE: World Bank and Global Business Opportunities.

THE IMPACT OF MULTINATIONAL CORPORATIONS

>lg 9

multinational corporations

Corporations that move resources, goods, services, and skills across national boundaries without regard to the country in which their headquarters are located.

Corporations that move resources, goods, services, and skills across national boundaries without regard to the country in which their headquarters are located are **multinational corporations.** Some are so rich and have so many employees that they resemble small countries. For example, the sales of both Exxon and General Motors are larger than the GDP of all but 22 nations in the world. Multinational companies are heavily engaged in international trade. The successful ones take political and cultural differences into account.

Today, dozens of America's top names—including General Electric, Gillette, Xerox, Dow Chemical, and Hewlett-Packard—sell more of their products outside the United States than they do at home. U.S. service companies—such as McDonald's, Service Master (cleaning services), and Federal Express—are close behind.

A multinational company may have several worldwide headquarters, depending on the location of its markets or technologies. Britain's APV, a maker of food-processing equipment, has a different headquarters for each of its worldwide businesses. Hewlett-Packard recently moved the headquarters of its personal computer business to Grenoble, France. Siemens A.G., Germany's electronics giant, is relocating its medical electronics division headquarters from Germany to Chicago. Honda is planning to move the worldwide headquarters for its power-products division to Atlanta, Georgia. The largest multinational corporations in the world are shown in Exhibit 3-5.

> e x h i b i t   3 - 5 <

The World's Largest Multinational Corporations

Rank	Company (Country)	Rank	Company (Country)
1	General Electric (U.S.)	14	Berkshire Hathaway (U.S.)
2	Microsoft (U.S.)	15	IBM (U.S.)
3	Coca-Cola (U.S.)	16	Glaxo Wellcome (U.K.)
4	Royal Dutch/Shell (Netherlands/U.K.)	17	Novartis (Switzerland)
5	Exxon (U.S.)	18	American International Group (U.S.)
6	Merck (U.S.)	19	Johnson & Johnson (U.S.)
7	Pfizer (U.S.)	20	Toyota Motor (Japan)
8	Wal-Mart Stores (U.S.)	21	Philip Morris (U.S.)
9	Nippon Telegraph & Telephone (Japan)	22	Cisco Systems (U.S.)
10	Intel (U.S.)	23	AT&T (U.S.)
11	Procter & Gamble (U.S.)	24	Unilever Group (Netherlands/U.K.)
12	Bristol-Myers Squibb (U.S.)	25	British Petroleum (U.K.)
13	Lucent Technologies (U.S.)		

SOURCE: "The World's 100 Largest Public Companies," *Wall Street Journal* (September 28, 1998), p. R27.

The Multinational Advantage

Procter & Gamble employees test different detergents formulated at P&G facilities worldwide, giving the company a technology advantage as a multinational corporation.

Large multinationals have several advantages over other companies. For instance, multinationals can often overcome trade problems. Taiwan and South Korea have long had an embargo against Japanese cars for political reasons and to help domestic automakers. Yet Honda USA, a Japanese-owned company based in the United States, sends Accords to Taiwan and Korea. In another example, when the environmentally conscious Green movement challenged the biotechnology research conducted by BASF, a major German chemical and drug manufacturer, BASF moved its cancer and immune-system research to Cambridge, Massachusetts.

Another advantage for multinationals is their ability to sidestep regulatory problems. U.S. drugmaker SmithKline and Britain's Beecham decided to merge in part so that they could avoid licensing and regulatory hassles in their largest markets. The merged company can say it's an insider in both Europe and the United States. "When we go to Brussels, we're a member state [of the European Union]," one executive explains. "And when we go to Washington, we're an American company."[22]

Multinationals can also shift production from one plant to another as market conditions change. When European demand for a certain solvent declined, Dow Chemical instructed its German plant to switch to manufacturing a chemical that had been imported from Louisiana and Texas. Computer models help Dow make decisions like these so it can run its plants more efficiently and keep costs down.

Multinationals can also tap new technology from around the world. Xerox has introduced some 80 different office copiers in the United States that were designed and built by Fuji Xerox, its joint venture with a Japanese company. Versions of the superconcentrated detergent that Procter & Gamble first formulated in Japan in response to a rival's product are now being sold under the Ariel brand name in Europe and being tested under the Cheer and Tide labels in the United States. Also, consider Otis Elevator's development of the Elevonic 411, an elevator that is programmed to send more cars to floors where demand is high. It was developed by six research centers in five countries. Otis's group in Farmington, Connecticut, handled the systems integration, a Japanese group designed the special motor drives that make the elevators ride smoothly, a French group perfected the door systems, a German group handled the electronics, and a Spanish group took care of the small-geared components. Otis says the international effort saved more than $10 million in design costs and cut the process from four years to two.

Finally, multinationals can often save a lot in labor costs, even in highly unionized countries. For example, when Xerox started moving copier-rebuilding work to Mexico to take advantage of the lower wages, its union in Rochester, New York, objected because it saw that members' jobs were at risk. Eventually, the union agreed to change work styles and to improve productivity to keep the jobs at home.

concept check

- What is a multinational corporation?
- What are the advantages of multinationals?

CAPITALIZING ON TRENDS IN BUSINESS

>lg 10

In this section we will examine several underlying trends that will continue to propel the dramatic growth in world trade. These trends are market expansion, resource acquisition, competition, technological change, and governmental actions.

Market Expansion

The need for businesses to expand their markets is perhaps the most fundamental reason for the growth in world trade. The limited size of domestic markets often motivates managers to seek markets beyond their national frontiers. The economies of large-scale manufacturing demand big markets. Domestic markets, particularly in smaller countries like Denmark and the Netherlands, simply can't generate enough demand. Nestlé was one of the first businesses to "go global" because its home country, Switzerland, is so small. Nestlé was shipping milk to 16 different countries as early as 1875. Today, hundreds of thousands of businesses are recognizing the potential rich rewards to be found in international markets.

Resource Acquisition

More and more companies are going to the global marketplace to acquire the resources they need to operate efficiently. These resources may be cheap or skilled labor, scarce raw materials, technology, or capital. Nike, for example, has opened manufacturing facilities in many Asian countries in order to use cheap labor. Honda opened a design studio in southern California to put that "California flair" into the design of some of its vehicles. Large multinational banks such as Bank of New York and Citigroup have offices in Geneva, Switzerland. Geneva is the private banking center of Europe and attracts capital from around the globe.

Competition

As multinational firms continue to enter new markets, their competitors will often do the same to maintain their competitive position. Starbucks, for example, recently entered Great Britain. Nestlé quickly developed Starbucks-type stores and moved into London shortly after Starbucks. Mazda has struggled for years in Japan because it lacked the resources of its larger domestic competitors—Toyota and Nissan. It entered the U.S. market in an effort to keep pace with its Japanese rivals by gaining market share and profitability. With the opening of Eastern Europe and China, thousands of businesses are racing to capture new customers. Each realizes that if it falls behind its competitors, it may have a difficult time catching up.

Technological Change

New technology, particularly the Internet, transportation systems, and information processing, fosters continued growth in international trade. Transportation improvements from computerized container ships to cargo jetliners have dramatically improved the efficiency of distribution throughout the world. Moreover, Federal Express and other shippers use advanced computerized tracking software to tell shippers where their packages are at any point in time. Shippers can use special software that enables them to enter FedEx's database and track the packages themselves, if they so desire. It's a far cry from the sailing ships of yesteryear when voyages took weeks or months, and there was no way to communicate with the ship once it left port.

The Internet opens up the world to any seller with a Web site. Markets no longer have geographic boundaries. E-mail enables a manager in London to receive reports from Dallas, Moscow, Capetown, and Tokyo in a matter of minutes rather than days. Thus, coordinating global business strategies is now a workable reality.

Government Actions

Governments around the globe, working with the WTO, have significantly lowered barriers to world trade. Sellers in the global marketplace have a more level playing field than ever before. Regional trade organizations, such as the European Union, NAFTA, and Mercosur, also have reduced trade barriers in large geographic areas. As these governmental actions continue to make it easier to "go global," world trade will continue to grow.

c o n c e p t c h e c k

- What trends will foster continued growth in world trade?
- Describe some of the ways businesses can take advantage of these trends to "go global."

APPLYING THIS CHAPTER'S TOPICS

Continue Your Education

The handwriting is on the wall. Low-skilled jobs are rapidly disappearing in America. U.S. businesses know that to compete globally, they must find cheap labor for labor-intensive businesses. This means establishing plants in Mexico, Asia, or other places in the world where labor in inexpensive. It also means that unskilled or low-skilled American workers will find it increasingly difficult to secure a permanent job. By continuing your education, you won't fall into this very undesirable trap.

Study the Role of a Global Manager

As business becomes more global, chances are that you may become a global manager. Start learning right now what this means and if it's right for you. The life of a global manager can be hectic, as these examples illustrate:

> As president of DoubleClick International, a unit of the New York Internet advertising company, Barry Salzman spends about 75% of his time traveling. He takes a laptop and four battery packs so he can wade through the 200 e-mail messages he averages daily. Welcome to the world of global management. It's a punishing pace, but it's the only way Mr. Salzman knows how to manage his network of 13 offices world-wide.
>
> Global managers spend proportionately more of their energy combating the sense of isolation that tends to gnaw at employees in remote offices. Mr. Salzman conducts a conference call every Monday morning for international managers in Canada, Europe and Asia. Only those who are flying somewhere are excused. "We try to maintain voice contact," he says. "We lose that with computers and e-mail."
>
> Top overseas performers at Secure Computing, a San Jose, Calif., software developer, are treated to a dinner for two by Christine Hughes, senior vice president of marketing and business development. Ms. Hughes supervises a 24-person staff in North and South America and Asia. One of her missions on trips is to combat the tendency of foreign-based employees to think the organization is "U.S.-centric," she says. Because they take much longer flights than the typical corporate road warrior, global managers wind up turning airplanes into offices. When she is overseas, Ms. Hughes has her office ship her a package of paperwork overnight, so she can work on the flight home. Mr. Salzman considers flight time some of his most productive; he uses it to answer e-mail and review contracts.
>
> Indeed, a global manager's workday never really ends. Wherever they are, it's still business hours somewhere else. When she's working in Australia, Ms. Hughes usually ends her day in a hotel room, talking with someone at the home office. "I'm on the phone until two in the morning dealing with issues," she says. "You just have to accept that."[23]

Your position may not be as hectic as that of Salzman or Hughes, but you can easily see the differences between a person who is a global manager and one who is not. Is this the life for you? Would you enjoy living abroad? Can you adapt easily to other cultures?

Changing Money Abroad   If you travel, work, or study abroad, you are going to need to change U.S. dollars to foreign currency. Making mistakes when changing money can cost you 10 to 20 percent of your bankroll. Here are a few tips about changing money abroad.

1. Know the exchange rate between U.S. dollars and the currencies of the countries you plan to visit before you go. Go to **www.cnntn.com/ markets/currencies/** for the latest quotations. Keep up with the changing rates by reading *USA Today International* or the *International Herald Tribune* everyday.

2. Avoid changing money at airports, train stations, and hotels. These places usually have the worst rates. Ask local people where they change money. Locals know where the best rates are.

3. Try to bargain with the clerk. Sometimes you can do better than the posted rate simply by asking.

4. Rather than making several small transactions, make one large exchange. This will often get you a better rate.

5. Don't change more than you will need. You'll pay another fee to change the foreign currency back to U.S. dollars.

6. Use a credit card. Typically, any major credit card will give you a better rate than a change booth or bank. Sometimes the spread is substantial, so minimize cash and use credit.

7. Traveler's checks usually have a worse exchange rate than cash. In other words, a $100 American Express travelers check will give you less in exchange than a $100 bill. If your traveler's checks are lost or stolen, however, they will be replaced, so the peace of mind is usually worth the added expense.

One way to see if you might be cut out to be a global manager is to spend some time abroad. The ideal situation is to find a job overseas during the summer months. This experience will help you decide if you want to be a global manager. Also, it will look good on your résumé. One source of international jobs information is **www.internationaljobs.org**/.

If you can't find a job overseas, save your money and travel abroad. Seeing how others live and work will broaden your horizons and give you a more enlightened view of the world. Even international travel can help you decide what you want to do in the global marketplace.

SUMMARY OF LEARNING GOALS

>lg 1   **Why is global trade important to the United States?**
International trade improves relations with friends and allies, eases tensions among nations, helps bolster economies, raises people's standard of living, and improves the quality of life. The United States is still the largest importer and exporter in the world. We export a fifth of our industrial production and about a third of our farm crops. One out of every 16 jobs in the United States is supported by exports.

>lg 2   **How is global trade measured?**
Two concepts important to global trade are the balance of trade (the difference in value between a country's exports and its imports over some period) and the

>looking ahead
at Saturn

Look back at the opening story about Saturn selling cars in Japan. Cultural factors, domestic competition, economic conditions, government actions, and regional trade agreements can all make selling in the global marketplace more difficult. Governments can take a number of actions to protect domestic competitors. Some common tactics are tariffs, quotas, embargoes, exchange controls, and buy-national regulations.

Saturn seems to face two major problems. First, the Japanese economy has been in a lengthy recession, which is dampening the demand for new cars. Second, when the Japanese decide to buy a foreign car, they want something "highly distinctive," like a Jeep. They generally do not regard the Saturn as a distinctive vehicle. Saturn will need to continue studying consumer preferences, cultural differences, and local competition to help build a market presence in Japan.

balance of payments (the difference between a country's total payments to other countries and its total receipts from other countries). The United States now has both a negative balance of trade and a negative balance of payments. Another import concept is the exchange rate, which is the price of one country's currency in terms of another country's currency. Currencies float up and down based upon the supply of and demand for each currency. Sometimes a government steps in and devalues its currency relative to the currencies of other countries.

>lg 3 Why do nations trade?
Nations trade because they gain by doing so. The principle of comparative advantage states that each country should specialize in the goods it can produce most readily and cheaply and trade them for those that other countries can produce most readily and cheaply. The result is more goods at lower prices than if each country produced by itself everything it needed. Free trade allows trade among nations without government restrictions.

>lg 4 What are the barriers to international trade?
The three major barriers to international trade are natural barriers, such as distance and language; tariff barriers, or taxes on imported goods; and nontariff barriers. The nontariff barriers to trade include import quotas, embargoes, buy-national regulations, customs regulations, and exchange controls. The main argument against tariffs is that they discourage free trade and keep the principle of comparative advantage from working efficiently. The main argument for using tariffs is that they help protect domestic companies, industries, and workers.

>lg 5 How do governments and institutions foster world trade?
The World Trade Organization created by the Uruguay Round has dramatically lowered trade barriers worldwide. For the first time a trade agreement covers services, intellectual property rights, and exchange controls. The World Bank makes loans to developing nations to help build infrastructures. The International Monetary Fund makes loans to member nations that cannot meet their budgetary expenses.

>lg 6 What are international economic communities?
International economic communities reduce trade barriers among themselves while often establishing common tariffs and other trade barriers toward nonmember countries. The best-known economic communities are the European Union, NAFTA, and Mercosur.

>lg 7 How do companies enter the global marketplace?
There are a number of ways to enter the global market. The major ones are exporting, licensing, contract manufacturing, joint ventures, and direct investment.

KEY TERMS

absolute advantage 70
balance of payments 68
balance of trade 68
contract manufacturing 83
countertrade 84
devaluation 69
direct foreign investment 83
dumping 74
embargo 73
European Union (EU) 78
exchange controls 74
exporting 81
exports 67
floating exchange rates 69
free trade 70
free-trade zone 77
global vision 66
import quota 73
imports 67
infrastructure 85
International Monetary Fund (IMF) 76
joint venture 83
licensing 81
Maastricht Treaty 78
Mercosur 78
multinational corporations 87
nationalism 84
North American Free Trade Agreement (NAFTA) 77
preferential tariff 77
principle of comparative advantage 70
protectionism 70
protective tariffs 72
tariff 72
trade deficit 68
trade surplus 68
Uruguay Round 74
World Bank 76
World Trade Organization (WTO) 76

>lg 8 **What threats and opportunities exist in the global marketplace?**
Domestic firms entering the international arena need to consider the politics, economies, and culture of the countries where they plan to do business. For example, government trade policies can be loose or restrictive, countries can be nationalistic, and governments can change. In the area of culture, many products fail because companies don't understand the culture of the country where they are trying to sell their products. Some developing countries also lack an economic infrastructure, which often makes it very difficult to conduct business.

>lg 9 **What are the advantages of multinational corporations?**
Multinational corporations have several advantages. First, they can sidestep restrictive trade and licensing restrictions because they frequently have headquarters in more than one country. Multinationals can also move their operations from one country to the next depending on which location offer more favorable economic conditions. In addition, multinationals can tap into a vast source of technological expertise by drawing upon the knowledge of a global workforce.

>lg 10 **What are the trends in the global marketplace?**
Global business activity will continue to escalate due to several factors. Firms that desire a larger customer base or need additional resources will continue to seek opportunities outside their country's borders. When an organization moves into a new global market, competitors typically follow its lead and enter the same new market. In addition, technological improvements in communication and transportation will continue to fuel growth in global markets by making it easier to sell and distribute products internationally.

PREPARING FOR TOMORROW'S WORKPLACE

1. Divide the class into teams of four persons. Each team should go to the Internet and look up information about America's trade imbalance with Japan. Every team should present its solution for solving the problem.
2. How can a country's customs create barriers to trade? Ask foreign students to describe such barriers in their country. American students should give examples of problems that foreign businesspeople might experience with American customs.
3. Divide the class into four teams. One team will represent Russia and another China. The Chinese team and Russian team should take the position that their country should be admitted to the WTO; the other two teams will oppose the position.
4. Should Great Britain be admitted to NAFTA? Why might Britain not wish to join?
5. Write a paper on how the euro may affect American business.
6. Divide the class into teams. Each team should choose a country and research its infrastructure to determine how it will help or hinder trade. Include a variety of countries, ranging from the most highly developed to the least developed.
7. What do you think is the best way for a small company to enter international trade? Why?
8. What impact have foreign multinationals had on the U.S. economy? Give some examples.
9. Write a paper on why countertrade will probably continue to grow.
10. Identify some U.S. multinational companies that have been successful in world markets. How do you think they have achieved their success?

WORKING THE NET

1. Go to the market access database maintained by the U.S. International Trade Department at **www.mac.doc.gov/tcc/country.** Pick a country that interests you from the index and read either the Commercial Guide or the Report on Trade Practices for that country. Would this country be a good market for a small U.S. clothing manufacturer interested in expanding internationally? Why or why not? What are the main barriers to trade the company might face?

2. Review the historical data about exchange rates between the U.S. dollar and the Japanese yen available at **www.ita.doc.gov/region/japan/exchange.html.** List any trends you spot. What years would have been best for a U.S. company to enter the Japanese marketplace? Given current exchange rate conditions, do you think Japanese companies are increasing or decreasing their exporting efforts in the United States?

3. Pretend that you are the president of a mid-sized U.S. software company who is trying to decide whether to export. Read several of the articles in the Software Report Export Guide at **www.swexport.com.** What opportunities might exporting hold for your firm? What barriers might you face?

4. Copenhagen is trying to attract foreign businesses. Visit the city's page at **www.copcap.dk.** Do you think Copenhagen would be an attractive location for a U.S. firm hoping to expand? What U.S. products and services might do well in Copenhagen? Why?

5. Visit *Export Today* magazine's online site at **www.exporttoday.com.** Read one of the articles from the current issue. Make a list of additional information you would need if you were the owner of a business effected by the events described in the article. Do a search on the search engine Alta Vista, **www. altavista.digital.com,** to uncover additional Internet sites related to the topic. Pick one site and write a review of the information and resources available on it. Rate the usefulness of the site and the information it offers. What additional information would you need?

CREATIVE THINKING CASE

Adaptive Eyecare Limited

Glasses propped on his nose, Joshua Silver drives carefully through this old college town. The thick, round frames make him look owlish. But he knows there is no better way to prove that these unusual glasses work than by wearing them himself. "I'm on a bit of a mission, you see," he says, "I can help all those people who need vision correction."

Professor Silver is a physicist at Oxford University who spends much of his time exploring the mysteries of subatomic particles. But for the last 13 years he has quietly pursued a more earthly passion: to devise low-cost adjustable spectacles for the one billion people in the world who need glasses, but don't have them. He also hopes to turn some of these people into paying customers.

The lenses of Silver's glasses are made from pairs of transparent plastic membranes, filled with a colorless silicone fluid. Attached to the spectacle frame are two circular "focus adjusters," which contain the fluid. A user can adjust the power of the lenses by twirling the adjusters. This injects fluid through a tiny hole in the frame.

A fatter lens increases magnification, helping those who are nearsighted; a thinner lens reduces magnification, helping the farsighted. Once each eye has been properly focused, the adjusters are snapped off, sealing the holes, and the spectacles are ready for use.

Tube carrying
fluid to the lens

Focus adjuster.
By turning the wheel,
a user sends more
fluid into the lens.
Once the lenses are
adjusted, the wheels
are removed.

Silicone fluid acts as a lens. More
fluid thickens the lens, correcting
nearsightedness; a thinner lens
corrects farsightedness.

Flexible Mylar
membranes

SOURCE: WSJ, Joshua Silver   Dan Ion/The Wall Street Journal

A pair could cost as little as $10. There is no need for a vision test, a visit to an optician, or an expensive prescription. "There's a strong argument to get these specs out to the millions of people who need them," says Bjorn Thylefors, who heads the World Health Organization's campaign to prevent blindness and has seen Silver's glasses. He calls the lack of spectacles "a sizable health problem in the developing world, with economic and educational repercussions."

Silver's start-up, Adaptive Eyecare Ltd., hopes to sell the glasses, for a profit, in developing countries. It has assembled a management group, including two manufacturing optometrists and a business consultant.

Critical Thinking Questions

1. Should Professor Silver "go global"?
2. If so, how should he enter the global marketplace?
3. What are several threats and opportunities Adaptive Eyecare may face?
4. Will the product be successful in the United States? In Ghana?

VIDEO CASE

Enforcement Technology, Inc.

Enforcement Technology, Inc., or ETEC (**www.autocite.com/**), located in Irvine, California, specializes in utilizing computer technology to address selected law enforcement challenges. ETEC's products are used primarily in parking and traffic enforcement and related purposes. AutoCITE and AutoPARK form the core of ETEC's business.

AutoCITE (Automated Citation Issuance System) is a portable citation system used by police and campus parking enforcement departments worldwide for issuing parking and traffic tickets. The AutoCITE device has a built-in printer, display, and user-friendly keyboard. It weighs less than three pounds and is designed to be held in one hand. In addition to the primary function of issuing parking and traffic tickets, AutoCITE is programmed to schedule court appearances and "also uses the violator's birth date to reassign juveniles to a juvenile court appearance." With AutoCITE, a police officer can quickly check driver's license information against law enforcement databases. "Using a prestored 'hotsheet,' the AutoCITE will alert the officer with 'wants or warrants' keyed to the driver's license number and/or name." AutoCITE can also be used for parking time limit marking, overnight parking, broken meter reporting, license plate inventory reporting, field interviews, false alarm responses, abandoned vehicle reports, witness forms, and automatic "hotsheet" searches.

AutoPARK is an automated parking citation management system and ticket processing service. Used to handle millions of citations for clients, AutoPARK covers all aspects of processing parking citations and collecting parking fines. The system's features include handheld computer issuance of parking tickets, ticket book inventory management, Department of Motor Vehicle (DMV) registered owner address inquiries, generation and mailing of notices, court scheduling, collections, a residential/parking permit system, and interfaces with DMV reporting systems.

ETEC markets its AutoCITE and AutoPARK systems throughout the United States and the world. One method that ETEC uses to reach potential customers is by being an exhibitor at trade shows such as the International Parking Conference and Exposition. This conference is attended by representatives from small, medium, and large cities throughout North America, Latin America, Asia, and Europe, as well as from American colleges and universities, domestic and international airports, major hospital systems in North America, commercial parking operations in North and Central America, and large theme parks in the United States.

ETEC's pursuit of a global distribution strategy is not without its challenges, however. In particular, ETEC must adapt the AutoCITE and AutoPARK systems to the language and legal requirements of the various nations where it markets its products and services.

Critical Thinking Questions

1. Why would a company like ETEC wish to pursue global marketing of its products?
2. How can trade shows help a company implement its business strategy?
3. What trends have influenced and will continue to influence ETEC's global business strategy?

chapter four

Making Ethical Decisions and Managing a Socially Responsible Business

learning goals

>lg 1   What philosophies and concepts shape personal ethical standards, and what are the stages of ethical development?

>lg 2   How can managers influence organizational ethics?

>lg 3   What are the techniques for creating employee ethical awareness?

>lg 4   What is social responsibility?

>lg 5   How do businesses meet their social responsibilities to various stakeholders?

>lg 6   What are the global and domestic trends in ethics and social responsibility?

Appendix:

>lg 7   How does the legal system govern business transactions and settle business disputes?

>lg 8   What are the required elements of a valid contract; and what are the key types of business law?

>lg 9   What are the most common taxes paid by businesses?

Searching for Solutions at the Miami International Airport

Smarte Carte luggage carts can be found in most major airports. But are they available at the Miami International Airport, the world's twelfth largest airport? No way. Each year, tens of millions of passengers pass through Miami International toting everything from tractor tires to swing sets. Yet there are no luggage carts.

Letters from disgruntled travelers pour in to the airport offices, pleading for carts. "I can't carry six bags and do not intend on paying a porter each time I need to use the bathroom," writes Nomi Lyonns of Vancouver, British Columbia. Even airport officials profess shame. "Last year, I was in an airport in Foz do Iguacu" (on Brazil's border with Paraguay), says Hernando Vergara, a spokesman for the Miami airport. "It had carts. It's kind of embarrassing we don't have them."

From Smarte Carte, Inc. headquarters in White Bear Lake, Minnesota, Miami airport looks like the mother lode of luggage concessions. Smarte Carte's chief executive officer, Brad Stanius, has lusted after its business for at least 12 years. "It's a no-brainer," says Stanius, whose company has a virtual lock on the U.S. market, with carts in 159 U.S. airports and 21 abroad.

But managers at the Miami airport do business in ways that leave outsiders and investors dumbfounded, especially at the airport. "No one seems to get a deal in the airport unless they have a local contractor in partnership who has the right political connections," complains Allen Harper, a real estate executive and chairman of the transportation commission at the Greater Miami Chamber of Commerce. "It really ties things up."

Smarte Carte, however, has been nothing if not persistent. For years, airport directors balked at luggage carts, fretting that they would jam the narrow concourses. By 1990, however, airport officials began warming to the idea. The lack of carts had become the No. 1 complaint among passengers. Smarte Carte, at the airport's invitation, brought down a couple of demonstration carts.

Airport executives spent weeks rolling them down ramps and handing them off to passengers. "Wherever we went, people asked us, 'Where did you get the cart?'" says Rick Elder, the airport director at the time. In 1994, airport officials took off on a 10-day around-the-world trip to airports in Singapore, Hong Kong, San Francisco, Frankfurt, and New York to study cart concessions and other amenities—bathrooms, for instance. (Frankfurt, which has carts that can scale escalators, was their favorite.) They returned home energized. "The vision was to make Miami International Airport the best airport in the world," says John Van Wezel, who headed the cart effort.

Critical Thinking Questions

As you read this chapter, consider the following questions as they relate to the Miami International Airport:

- Has the Miami Airport Authority acted in an ethical and responsible manner?

- Was it ethical for airport officials to go on an around-the-world trip to evaluate carts?

- Would it be ethical for Smarte Carte to enter into a partnership with Albo?

About that same time, Lazaro Albo, a prominent political fund-raiser here and a close friend of several county commissioners, had a vision of his own. He formed his own airport-cart company, called Miami Baggage Cart, Inc. He didn't have any carts, employees, or experience. But he did have one thing Smarte Carte lacked: connections. "Politics is my hobby," says Albo, a Cuban exile. "I have lived in Miami for 40 years. I have friends—lawyers, judges, county commissioners. I help my friends."

Albo says he got Smarte Carte's phone number off a cart at some other airport and arranged a meeting with the company in Minnesota. But the negotiations went nowhere. Smarte Carte, which charges passengers about $1.50 to use its carts, was willing to give Albo 20 percent of the proceeds to satisfy a county requirement that any airport service contract must include a "minority" partner with a 20 percent interest. (A long list of approved minorities includes women, African Americans, Hispanics, Asians, and Native Americans.) Albo wanted 50 percent of the profits and a consulting contract to help oversee operations.[1]

BUSINESS IN THE 21ST CENTURY

ethics

A set of moral standards for judging whether something is right or wrong.

Every day, managers and business owners like Lazaro Albo make business decisions based on what they believe to be right and wrong. Through their actions, they demonstrate to their employees what is and is not acceptable behavior and shape the moral standard of the organization. **Ethics** is a set of moral standards for judging whether something is right or wrong. As you will see in this chapter, personal and professional ethics are important cornerstones of an organization and shape its ultimate contributions to society. First, let's consider how individual business ethics are formed.

INDIVIDUAL BUSINESS ETHICS

Individual business ethics are shaped by personal choices and the environments in which we live and work. In addition, the laws of our society are guideposts for choosing between right and wrong. This section describes personal philosophies and legal factors that influence the choices people make when confronting ethical dilemmas.

utilitarianism

A philosophy that focuses on the consequences of an action to determine whether it is right or wrong; holds that an action that affects the majority adversely is morally wrong.

Utilitarianism

One of the philosophies that may influence choices between right and wrong is **utilitarianism,** which focuses on the consequences of an action taken by a person or organization. The notion that "people should act so as to generate the greatest good for the greatest number" is derived from utilitarianism. When an action affects the majority adversely, it is morally wrong. One problem with this philosophy is that it is nearly impossible to accurately determine how a decision will affect a large number of people. Another problem is that utilitarianism always involves both winners and losers. If sales are slowing and a manager decides to fire 5 people rather than putting everyone on a 30-hour workweek, the 20 people who keep their full-time jobs are winners, but the other 5 are losers.

A final criticism of utilitarianism is that some "costs," although small relative to the potential good, are so negative that some segments of society find them unacceptable. Reportedly, the backs of up to 3,000 animals a year are deliberately broken so that scientists can conduct spinal cord research that could someday lead to a cure for spinal cord injuries. To a number of people, however, the "costs" are simply too horrible for this type of research to continue.

Individual Rights

In our society, individuals and groups have certain rights that exist under certain conditions regardless of any external circumstances.[2] These rights serve as guides when making individual ethical decisions. The term *human rights* implies that certain rights—to life, to freedom, to the pursuit of happiness—are conveyed on birth and cannot be arbitrarily taken away. Denying the rights of an individual or group is considered to be unethical and illegal in most, though not all, parts of the world. Certain rights are guaranteed by the government and its laws, and these are considered *legal rights*. The U.S. Constitution and its amendments, as well as state and federal statutes, define the rights of American citizens. Those rights can be disregarded only in extreme circumstances, such as during wartime. Legal rights include the freedom of religion, speech, and assembly; protection from improper arrest and searches and seizures; and proper access to counsel, confrontation of witnesses, and cross-examination in criminal prosecutions. Also held to be fundamental is the right to privacy in many matters. Legal rights are to be applied without regard to race, color, creed, gender, or ability.

Justice—The Question of Fairness

justice
What is considered fair according to the prevailing standards of society; in the twentieth century, an equitable distribution of the burdens and rewards that society has to offer.

Another factor influencing individual business ethics is **justice,** or what is fair according to prevailing standards of society.[3] We all expect life to be reasonably fair. You expect your exams to be fair, the grading to be fair, and your wages to be fair, based on the type of work being done.

In the twenty-first century, we take *justice* to mean an equitable distribution of the burdens and rewards that society has to offer. The distributive process varies from society to society. Those in a democratic society believe in the "equal pay for equal work" doctrine, in which individuals are rewarded based on the value the free market places on their services. Because the market places different values on different occupations, the rewards, such as wages, are not necessarily equal. Nevertheless, many regard the rewards as just. A politician who argued that a supermarket clerk should receive the same pay as a physician, for example, would not receive many votes from the American people. At the other extreme, communist theorists have argued that justice would be served by a society in which burdens and rewards were distributed to individuals according to their abilities and their needs, respectively.

Stages of Ethical Development

preconventional ethics
A stage in the ethical development of individuals in which people behave in a childlike manner and make ethical decisions in a calculating, self-centered, selfish way, based on the possibility of immediate punishment or reward.

We can view an individual's ethical development as having reached one of three levels: preconventional, conventional, or postconventional. The behavior of a person at the level of **preconventional ethics** is childlike in nature; it is calculating, self-centered, and even selfish, based on the possibility of immediate

conventional ethics
The second stage in the ethical development of individuals in which people move from an egocentric viewpoint to consider the expectations of an organization of society.

Find out which companies test their products on animals and which don't at **www.petaonline.org/ shoppingguid/donttest.html**

postconventional ethics
The third stage in the ethical development of individuals in which people adhere to the ethical standards of a mature adult and are less concerned about how others view their behavior than about how they will judge themselves in the long run.

c o n c ə p t c h ə c k

- Define ethics.
- What is utilitarianism?
- Discuss the stages of ethical development.

punishment or reward. Thus, a student may not cheat on a test because she is afraid of receiving a failing grade for the course. The student's behavior is based not on a sense of what's right or wrong, but instead on the threat of punishment.

Conventional ethics moves from an egocentric viewpoint toward the expectations of society. Loyalty and obedience to the organization (or society) become paramount. At the conventional ethics level, a businessperson might say, "I know that our advertising is somewhat misleading, but as long as it will increase sales we should continue the campaign." Right or wrong is not the issue; the only question is whether the campaign will benefit the organization.

Postconventional ethics represents the ethical standards of the mature adult. At the postconventional level, businesspeople are concerned less about how others might see them and more about how they see and judge themselves over the long run. A person who has attained this ethical level might ask, "Even though this action is legal and will increase company profits, is it right in the long run? Might it do more harm than good in the end?" A manager at a soda bottler might refuse to offer disposable cans because he knows a certain percentage would end up as litter. An advertising agency manager might refuse a tobacco account because of the health hazards of smoking. A lab technician might refuse to recommend a new whitener for a detergent because it could harm the environment. All of these individuals are exhibiting postconventional morality.

Many people believe that the Internet is a vast anonymous place where they can say and do just about anything. When they think that they can't be caught, they sometimes revert to preconventional ethics. Yet e-mail servers owned by businesses and governmental agencies can quickly tell what is being sent and to whom. In the state of Washington, state auditors and ethics officials are trying to stem Internet ethics violations, as the Applying Technology box describes.

HOW ORGANIZATIONS INFLUENCE ETHICAL CONDUCT

>lg 2

People choose between right and wrong based on their personal code of ethics. They are also influenced by the ethical environment created by their employers. Consider the following newspaper headlines that announce legal claims against organizations that failed to manage their employees ethically:

- "Texaco's $176M Race Bias Settlement Gets Tentative OK." Then, adding to this financial hit: "Rights Groups Urge Boycott of Texaco" and "Stock Drops in Latest Fallout from Bias Case." Still more: "Texaco Agrees to Report to EEOC on Promotion of Racial Minorities."
- "Publix Super Markets Will Pay $81.5 Million to Settle Bias Suit." This figure includes plaintiffs' legal fees and "$2.5 million for monitoring the company's compliance."
- "Home Depot Pays $87.5 Million for Not Promoting More Women" and "Home Depot's Agreement to Settle Suit Could Cut 3rd-Quarter Earnings by 21%."[4]

As these headlines illustrate, poor business ethics can be very expensive for a company. Organizations can reduce the potential for these types of liability claims by educating their employees about ethical standards through various

WANTA' BUY SOME FLIES?

Washington state law prohibits use of public computers for private work or play. Yet, according to the state auditor's office, in two years, 14 investigations of whistle-blower complaints about computer misuse have been substantiated and three more are pending. The activities investigated have included using the Internet to run sports betting pools, conducting private business or hobbies, and installing and playing recreational games during work time.

Taxpayers don't have to wait for the auditor's office or curious reporters to catch Web weasels in the act. Watchdogs can use technology to fight back. Using a free, online search tool called DejaNews, Dave Wickham of Cle Elum discovered the variety of ways state workers waste their time online. His Web site (**www.adsnet.net/wickhamd/indexs.htm**) blows the whistle on cyber-slacking public employees throughout the country. By identifying the government domain

name on e-mail messages posted to Internet bulletin boards, Wickham found:

- A worker at the state Department of Health and Human Services running a fly-fishing business online.
- A Department of Ecology official giving advice on making homemade explosives.
- Another Health and Human Services employee posting more than a dozen messages about her favorite episodes of *The Simpsons*.

Critical Thinking Questions

1. Although what Washington state employees were doing was against the law, was their behavior unethical in each case?
2. At what level of ethical development are these workers?

informal and formal programs. The first step, however, in making a good ethical decision is to recognize unethical business activities when they occur.

Recognizing Unethical Business Actions

Researchers from Brigham Young University tell us that all unethical business activities will fall into one of the following categories:

1. *Taking things that don't belong to you.* The unauthorized use of someone else's property or taking property under false pretenses is taking something that does not belong to you. Even the smallest offense, such as using the postage meter at your office for mailing personal letters or exaggerating your travel expenses, belongs in this category of ethical violations.

2. *Saying things you know are not true.* Often, when trying for a promotion and advancement, fellow employees discredit their coworkers. Falsely assigning blame or inaccurately reporting conversations is lying. Although "This is the way the game is played around here" is a common justification, saying things that are untrue is an ethical violation.

3. *Giving or allowing false impressions.* The salesperson who permits a potential customer to believe that cardboard boxes will hold the customer's tomatoes

The *Online Journal of Ethics* reports on cutting-edge research into business and professional ethical questions. To read the *Journal's* articles, visit

www.depaul.edu/ethics/ethg1.html

for long-distance shipping when the salesperson knows the boxes are not strong enough has given a false impression. A car dealer who fails to disclose that a car has been in an accident is misleading potential customers.

4. *Buying influence or engaging in a conflict of interest.* A conflict of interest occurs when the official responsibilities of an employee or government official are influenced by the potential for personal gain. Suppose a company awards a construction contract to a firm owned by the father of the state attorney general while the state attorney general's office is investigating that company. If this construction award has the potential to shape the outcome of the investigation, a conflict of interest has occurred.

5. *Hiding or divulging information.* Failing to disclose the results of medical studies that indicate your firm's new drug has significant side effects is the ethical violation of hiding information that the product could be harmful to purchasers. Taking your firm's product development or trade secrets to a new place of employment constitutes the ethical violation of divulging proprietary information.

6. *Taking unfair advantage.* Many current consumer protection laws were passed because so many businesses took unfair advantage of people who were not educated or were unable to discern the nuances of complex contracts. Credit disclosure requirements, truth-in-lending provisions, and new regulations on auto leasing all resulted because businesses misled consumers who could not easily follow the jargon of long, complex agreements.

7. *Committing improper personal behavior.* Although the ethical aspects of an employee's right to privacy are still debated, it has become increasingly clear that personal conduct outside the job can influence performance and company reputation. Thus, a company driver must abstain from substance abuse because of safety issues. Even the traditional company Christmas party and picnic have come under scrutiny due to the possibility that employees at and following these events might harm others through alcohol-related accidents.

8. *Abusing another person.* Suppose a manager sexually harasses an employee or subjects employees to humiliating corrections in the presence of customers. In some cases, laws protect employees. Many situations, however, are simply interpersonal abuse that constitutes an ethical violation.

9. *Permitting organizational abuse.* Many U.S. firms with operations overseas, such as Levi Strauss, The Gap, and Esprit, have faced issues of organizational abuse. The unfair treatment of workers in international operations appears in the form of child labor, demeaning wages, and excessive work hours. Although a business cannot change the culture of another country, it can perpetuate—or stop—abuse through its operations there.

10. *Violating rules.* Many organizations use rules and processes to maintain internal controls or respect the authority of managers. Although these rules may seem burdensome to employees trying to serve customers, a violation may be considered an unethical act.

11. *Condoning unethical actions.* What if you witnessed a fellow employee embezzling company funds by forging her signature on a check that was to be voided? Would you report the violation? A winking tolerance of others' unethical behavior is itself unethical.[5]

Resolving Ethical Problems in Business

In many situations, there are no right or wrong answers. Instead, organizations must provide a process to resolve the dilemma quickly and fairly. Two approaches for resolving ethical problems are the "three-questions test" and the newspaper test.

The Three-Questions Test

In evaluating an ethical problem, managers can use the three-questions test to determine the most ethical response: "Is it legal?" "Is it balanced?" and "How does it make me feel?" Companies such as Southwest Airlines, Texas Instruments, Marriott, and McDonald's rely on this test to guide employee decision making. If the answer to the first question is "no," then don't do it. Many ethical dilemmas, however, involve situations that aren't illegal. For example, the sale of tobacco is legal in the United States. But, given all the research that shows that tobacco use is dangerous to one's health, is it an ethical activity?

The second question, "Is it balanced?" requires you to put yourself in the position of other parties affected by your decision. For example, as an executive, you might not favor a buyout of your company because you will probably lose your job. Shareholders, however, may benefit substantially from the price to be paid for their shares in the buyout. At the same time, the employees of the business and their community may suffer economically if the purchaser decides to close the business or focus its efforts in a different product area. The best situation, of course, is when everybody wins or shares the burden equally.

The final question, "How does it make me feel?" asks you to examine your comfort with a particular decision. Many people find that after reaching a decision on an issue they still experience discomfort that may manifest itself in a loss of sleep or appetite. Those feelings of conscience can serve as a guide in resolving ethical dilemmas.

Front Page of the Newspaper Test

Many managers use the "front page of the newspaper test" for evaluating ethical dilemmas. The question to be asked is how a critical and objective reporter would report your decision in a front-page story. Some managers rephrase the test for their employees: How will the headline read if I make this decision? This test is helpful in spotting and resolving potential conflicts of interest. When Salomon Brothers experienced difficulties with federal regulators over securities transactions, its new CEO explained to employees that before making any choice or decision they should reflect on whether they would be willing to see it reported in a newspaper that their family, friends, and communities would read.[6]

Leading by Example

Employees often follow the examples set by their managers. That is, leaders and managers establish patterns of behavior that determine what's acceptable and what's not within the organization. While Ben Cohen was president of Ben & Jerry's ice cream, he followed a policy that no one could earn a salary more than seven times the lowest-paid worker. He wanted all employees to feel that they were equal (remember the "balance

HOT links

Read more about the ethical issues facing businesses at **www.depaul.edu/ethics/ethg1.html**

Employees of Ben & Jerry's are influenced by the ethical values of company founders Ben Cohen and Jerry Greenfield, who created an environment of equity in compensating employees.

question"). At the time he resigned, company sales were $140 million and the lowest-paid worker earned $19,000 per year. Ben Cohen's salary was $133,000 based on the "seven times" rule. A typical top executive of a $140 million company might have earned ten times Cohen's salary. Ben Cohen's actions helped shape the ethical values of Ben & Jerry's.

Ethics Training

In addition to providing a system to resolve ethical dilemmas, organizations also provide formal training to develop an awareness of questionable business activities and practice appropriate responses. About 35 percent of all American companies have some type of ethics training programs.[7] The ones that are most effective, like those created by Levi Strauss, American Express, and Campbell Soup Company, begin with techniques for solving ethical dilemmas such as those discussed earlier. Next, employees are presented with a series of situations and asked to come up with the "best" ethical solution. One of these ethical dilemmas is shown in Exhibit 4-1.[8] Some companies have tried to add a bit of excitement and fun to their ethics training programs by presenting them in the form of games. Citigroup, for example, has created The Work Ethic, a board game in which participants strive to correctly answer legal, regulatory, policy-related, and judgment ethics questions.

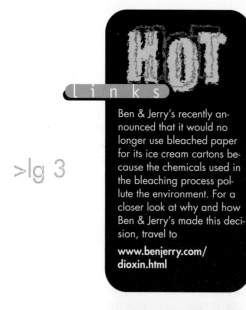

>lg 3

Ben & Jerry's recently announced that it would no longer use bleached paper for its ice cream cartons because the chemicals used in the bleaching process pollute the environment. For a closer look at why and how Ben & Jerry's made this decision, travel to

www.benjerry.com/ dioxin.html

Discover what Texas Instruments's "Ethics Quick Test" includes at

www.ti.com/corp/docs/ ethics/quicktest.html

> e x h i b i t   4 - 1 <

An Ethical Dilemma Used for Employee Training

Donations and Vendors

As CEO of a large Chicago hotel, you and your purchasing manager are in the midst of the annual review of several vendors' contracts. One of the suppliers is Sherman Distributors, a restaurant supply company that furnishes straws, salt, pepper, condiments, and related items for the restaurants and room service in your hotel. Your spouse, an associate dean at a local university's business school, has informed you that Sherman's CEO, who serves on the school's council of advisers, has mentioned Sherman's supply contract and a willingness to endow a scholarship fund. Your spouse's primary area of responsibility at the school is fund-raising.

Discussion Questions
1. What ethical issues does the situation raise?
2. Would it make a difference if Sherman's bid were the lowest?
3. Would renewing Sherman's contract create an appearance of impropriety?
4. What would you do to avoid negative perceptions?
5. Should the university be concerned about perceptions?

Establishing a Formal Code of Ethics

code of ethics
A set of guidelines prepared by a firm to provide its employees with the knowledge of what the firm expects in terms of their responsibilities and behavior toward fellow employees, customers, and suppliers.

Most large companies and thousands of smaller ones have created, printed, and distributed codes of ethics. In general, a **code of ethics** provides employees with the knowledge of what their firm expects in terms of their responsibilities and behavior toward fellow employees, customers, and suppliers. Some ethical codes offer a lengthy and detailed set of guidelines for employees. Others are not really codes at all but rather summary statements of goals, policies, and priorities. Some companies have their codes framed and hung on office walls or printed on cards to be carried at all times by executives. The code of ethics for Costco Wholesale, the chain of membership warehouse clubs, is shown in Exhibit 4-2.

Do codes of ethics make employees behave in a more ethical manner? Some people believe that they do. Others think that they are little more than public relations gimmicks. One research study found that corporate codes of ethics were not influential in determining a person's ethical decision-making behavior.[9]

Fortunately, most workers only rarely face an ethical dilemma. A survey of 1,002 American adults found that 75 percent had never been asked or told to do something that they thought was unethical on the job.[10] Of those who were asked to do something unethical, 4 out of 10 people did the unethical act. When asked what they would do if they found their boss doing something unethical, most (78 percent) said that they would try to talk to the boss or otherwise try to resolve the situation without losing their jobs. Nine percent said that they would "look the other way" and 5 percent claimed that they would quit. The rest weren't sure what they would do.

When faced with an ethical dilemma, entrepreneurs and large-business managers responded differently, however, as shown in the Focusing on Small Business box.

concept check

- Discuss two approaches to resolving ethical problems.
- What is the role of top management in organizational ethics?
- What is a code of ethics?

MANAGING TO BE SOCIALLY RESPONSIBLE

>lg 4

social responsibility
The concern of businesses for the welfare of society as a whole; consists of obligations beyond those required by law or contracts.

Acting in an ethical manner is one of the four components of the pyramid of corporate social responsibility. **Social responsibility** is the concern of businesses for the welfare of society as a whole. It consists of obligations beyond those required by law or union contract. This definition makes two important points. First, social responsibility is voluntary. Beneficial action required by law, such as cleaning up factories that are polluting air and water, is not voluntary. Second, the obligations of social responsibility are broad. They extend beyond investors in the company to include workers, suppliers, consumers, and communities.

Exhibit 4-3 portrays economic performance as the foundation for the other three responsibilities. At the same time that a business pursues profits (economic responsibility), however, it is expected to obey the law (legal responsibility); to do what is right, just, and fair (ethical responsibility); and to be a good corporate citizen (philanthropic responsibility). These four components are distinct but together constitute the whole. Still, if the company doesn't make a profit, then the other three responsibilities are moot.

Many companies are already working to make the world a better place to live. Consider these examples:

- Colby Care Nurses, Inc., a home health care service located in Los Angeles County, is offering much-needed health care to predominantly African American and Hispanic communities that are often not covered by other providers. The company prides itself on giving back to the community by employing its residents and providing role models for its young people.

Costco Wholesale's Code of Ethics

CODE OF ETHICS

By   Jim   Sinegal

OBEY THE LAW

The law is irrefutable! Absent a moral imperative to challenge a law, we must conduct our business in total compliance with the laws of every community where we do business.

- Comply with all statutes.

- Cooperate with authorities.

- Respect all public officials and their positions.

- Avoid all conflict of interest issues with public officials.

- Comply with all disclosure and reporting requirements.

- Comply with safety and security standards for all products sold.

- Exceed ecological standards required in every community where we do business.

- Comply with all applicable wage and hour laws.

- Comply with all applicable anti-trust laws.

- Protect "inside information" that has not been released to the general public.

TAKE CARE OF OUR MEMBERS

The member is our key to success. If we don't keep our members happy, little else that we do will make a difference.

- Provide top-quality products at the best prices in the market.

- Provide a safe shopping environment in our warehouses.

- Provide only products that meet applicable safety and health standards.

- Sell only products from manufacturers who comply with "truth in advertising/packaging" standards.

- Provide our members with a 100% satisfaction guaranteed warranty on every product and service we sell, including their membership fee.

- Assure our members that every product we sell is authentic in make and in representation of performance.

- Make our shopping environment a pleasant experience by making our members feel welcome as our guests.

- Provide products to our members that will be ecologically sensitive.

> Our member is our reason for being. If they fail to show up, we cannot survive. Our members have extended a "trust" to Costco by virtue of paying a fee to shop with us. We can't let them down or they will simply go away. We must always operate in the following manner when dealing with our members:
> Rule #1 – The member is always right.
> Rule #2 – In the event the member is ever wrong, refer to rule #1.
>
> There are plenty of shopping alternatives for our members. We will succeed only if we do not violate the trust they have extended to us. We must be committed at every level of our company, with every ounce of energy and grain of creativity we have, to constantly strive to "bring goods to market at a lower price."

> **If we do these four things throughout our organization, we will realize our ultimate goal, which is to REWARD OUR SHAREHOLDERS.**

TAKE CARE OF OUR EMPLOYEES

To claim "people are our most important asset" is true and an understatement. Each employee has been hired for a very important job. Jobs such as stocking the shelves, ringing members' orders, buying products and paying our bills are jobs we would all choose to perform because of their importance. The employees hired to perform these jobs are performing as management's "alter egos." Every employee, whether they are in a Costco warehouse or whether they work in the regional or corporate offices, is a Costco ambassador trained to give our members professional, courteous treatment.

Today we have warehouse managers who were once stockers and callers and vice presidents who were once in clerical positions for our company. We believe that Costco's future executive officers are currently working in our warehouses, depots, buying offices and accounting departments, as well as in our home offices.

To that end, we are committed to these principles:

- Provide a safe work environment.

- Pay a fair wage.

- Make every job challenging, but make it fun!

- Consider the loss of any employee as a failure on the part of the company and a loss to the organization.

- Teach our people how to do their jobs and how to improve personally and professionally.

- Promote from within the company to achieve the goal of a minimum of 80% of management positions being filled by current employees.

- Create an "open door" attitude at all levels of the company that is dedicated to "fairness and listening."

RESPECT OUR VENDORS

Our vendors are our partners in business, and for us to prosper as a company, they must prosper with us. It is important that our vendors understand that we will be tough negotiators but fair in our treatment of them.

- Treat all vendors and their representatives as you would expect to be treated if visiting their places of business.

- Pay all bills within the allocated time frame.

- Honor all commitments.

- Protect all vendor property assigned to Costco as though it were our own.

- Always be thoughtful and candid in negotiations.

- Provide a careful review process with at least two levels of authorization before terminating business with an existing vendor of more than two years.

- Do not accept gratuities of any kind from a vendor.

> These guidelines are exactly that - guidelines, some common sense rules for the conduct of our business. Intended to simplify our jobs, not complicate our lives, these guidelines will not answer every question or solve every problem. At the core of our philosophy as a company must be the implicit understanding that not one of us is required to lie or cheat on behalf of Costco. In fact, dishonest conduct will not be tolerated. To do any less would be unfair to the overwhelming majority of our employees who support and respect Costco's commitment to ethical business conduct.
>
> If you are ever in doubt as to what course of action to take on a business matter that is open to varying ethical interpretations, take the high road and do what is right.
>
> If you want our help, we are always available for advice and counsel. That's our job, and we welcome your questions or comments.
>
> Our continued success depends on you. We thank each of you for your contribution to our past success and for the high standards you have insisted upon in our company.

97HR1005

ARE ENTREPRENEURS MORE ETHICAL?

In a recent survey of 165 entrepreneurs and 128 large-company business managers, the entrepreneurs proved more apt to regard certain business activities as unethical. Seventy-four percent of the entrepreneurs and 71 percent of the managers said a prescribed code of ethics would help them in making decisions.

The following table presents the actions described to the survey participants and shows the percentage of entrepreneurs and business managers who said each action was unethical.

Critical Thinking Questions

1. Does the survey prove that entrepreneurs are more ethical than business managers?
2. Why would it make a difference if one group were more ethical than the other?
3. Are you surprised at the results? Why or why not?

	Percentage Considered Unethical	
Business Activity	Entrepreneurs	Business Managers
Using company services for personal purposes	82%	72%
Using company supplies for personal purposes	93	86
Overstating an expense account by more than 10%	99	95
Overstating an expense account by less than 10%	93	87
Using company time for personal benefit	81	70
Taking longer than necessary to do a job	91	78

- Wrigley, the Chicago chewing gum maker, is producing a $10 million commercial campaign aimed at getting African, Asian, and Hispanic Americans to use doctors for regular health maintenance instead of as a last resort.
- Ben & Jerry's, the premium ice cream maker, sent seven workers to live with Cree Indians in Canada to see how they've been displaced by a new hydroelectric power complex.
- Jantzen, the world's leading swimsuit manufacturer, makes direct grants through its clean water campaign to organizations that preserve and clean up beaches and waterways.
- Apple Computer donates almost $10 million in computer equipment and advice to U.S. schools annually.
- Ricoh, a Japanese office equipment maker, has developed a reverse copier that strips away the toner and allows the copy paper to be used again.[11]

The Pyramid of Corporate Social Responsibility

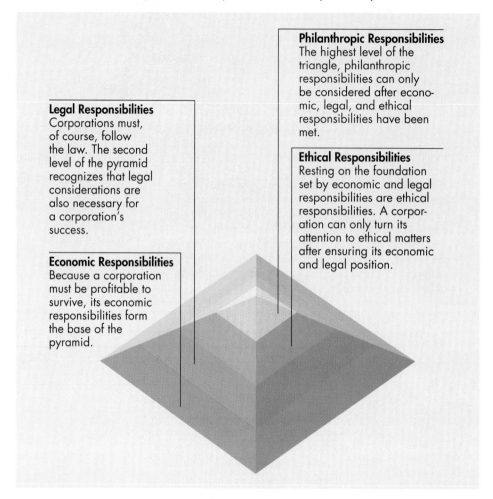

Philanthropic Responsibilities
The highest level of the triangle, philanthropic responsibilities can only be considered after economic, legal, and ethical responsibilities have been met.

Ethical Responsibilities
Resting on the foundation set by economic and legal responsibilities are ethical responsibilities. A corporation can only turn its attention to ethical matters after ensuring its economic and legal position.

Legal Responsibilities
Corporations must, of course, follow the law. The second level of the pyramid recognizes that legal considerations are also necessary for a corporation's success.

Economic Responsibilities
Because a corporation must be profitable to survive, its economic responsibilities form the base of the pyramid.

Understanding Social Responsibility

Peter Drucker, a management expert, said that we should look first at what an organization does *to* society and second at what it can do *for* society. This idea suggests that social responsibility has two basic dimensions: legality and responsibility.

Illegal and Irresponsible Behavior   The idea of social responsibility is so widespread today that it is hard to conceive of a company continually acting in illegal and irresponsible ways. Nevertheless, such actions do sometimes occur. For example, Royal Caribbean Cruise Lines, the world's second-largest cruise line, had to pay a $9 million fine for dumping oily bilge waste into the ocean and then lying about it.[12] In another case, Louisiana-Pacific Corp. pleaded guilty to pollution violations and agreed to pay $37 million in penalties, including the biggest criminal fine in the 28-year history of the Clean Air Act. The Portland, Oregon–based timber company was fined $5.5 million under the act for higher-than-allowed emissions from a plant in Colorado that makes floorboards and siding. It was fined an additional $31 million for offenses such as doctoring reports, tampering with pollution-monitoring equipment, and lying to inspectors. U.S. District Judge Lewis Babcock in Denver also placed the company on probation for five years. Louisiana- Pacific will also donate $500,000 to environmental groups under the agreement.[13]

Federal, state, and local laws determine whether an activity is legal or not. The laws that regulate business are discussed in the appendix to this chapter.

Irresponsible but Legal Behavior   Sometimes companies act irresponsibly, yet their actions are legal. For example, in 1998 Congress was considering comprehensive tobacco legislation that would curb industry promotion and open the industry to liability lawsuits from the health hazards of smoking. A key aspect of the legislation focused on the 3,000 teenagers who become addicted to smoking each day. The bill included all manner of protections aimed at teenagers: no billboard advertising near schools, serious restrictions on advertising in publications with significant teen readership, and in-store restrictions on cigarette merchandising. The five major U.S. tobacco companies began a six-month, $60 million advertising campaign to kill the legislation. The campaign successfully shifted the focus from the ills of tobacco to the tax and spend policies of Washington. Once the legislation died, the campaign was dropped.[14] Other controversial advertising campaigns include Budweiser's ad featuring talking frogs and lizards and the cuddly Spuds McKenzie. Joe Camel, however, was perhaps the advertising symbol most disliked by activists.

Legal and Responsible Behavior The vast majority of business activities fall into the category of behavior that is both legal and responsible. Most firms act legally, and most try to be socially responsible. Lucent Technologies (formerly Bell Labs) each year has 10,000 employees participate in "Global Days of Caring," assisting community projects worldwide. Richard McGinn, chairman of Lucent, says, "Global Days are a celebration of the generosity and spirit of Lucent people who live the value of social responsibility year around."[15] A recent Global Days of Caring found employees working on specific projects in 25 states and 20 countries. The projects included engaging in environmental cleanup, fixing up child care and senior citizens centers, and assisting organizations like Camp DaKaNi in Oklahoma City, home to the local Camp Fire Boys and Girls, which was significantly damaged during a tornado. Ongoing projects include painting maps on elementary school playgrounds to help teach geography and making "smart" teddy bears for children to ease the trauma of a hospital stay. Lucent gives employees paid time off for the projects and provides coordination and money. The company also engages in a number of other socially responsible activities including hiring and training the unemployed, giving equipment and grants to schools, and making grants to community agencies where Lucent employees volunteer.

JCPenney's national sponsorship of the Race for the Cure represents a legal and socially responsible activity. The nationwide series of 98 running and fitness walks that draw more than 700,000 participants benefit the Susan G. Komen Breast Cancer Foundation.

COSTAS FOODS

Should business be socially responsible? Can business be socially responsible? Some executives, like Jack Welch, General Electric's CEO, believe that business can and should be socially responsible, but say that the marketplace alone is insufficient for achieving social responsibility. These executives are "calling faith in value-free, self-regulating markets a dangerous illusion and urging governments to protect people and the planet before it's too late." Other people, however, believe that business should be ethically neutral and focus on "profit as the primary measure of corporate success." They argue that the most socially responsible thing a business can do is to make as much profit as possible.

One business that operates on the basis of values and commitment to social responsibility is Costas Foods, an independently owned and operated grocer based in Valparaiso, Indiana. Not only does Costas Foods operate a values-driven business, but it emphasizes a particular set of values—Christian values.

When new employees watch a training video made by owner Bill Costas, they hear about the company's Christian values, not the ins and outs of the grocery business. Costas talks "to employees about values, how to treat customers, God and the Bible (handed out along with the W-2 forms to every new hire)." But Costas is not holier-than-thou. He also talks of his early days in the grocery business; his struggles with alcohol, marital infidelity, and tax cheating; and how he conquered those challenges through religious faith. That faith became the foundation for Bill Costas, the grocer and businessman. He operates Costas Foods according to Christian values, and all new employees are told that.

Critical Thinking Questions

1. Is it ethical for a business not to be socially responsible? Explain you answer.
2. Should a particular doctrine or set of principles, such as the Christian tradition, be used as the basis of running an ethical business? Why or why not?
3. How might the ethical actions of a business that operates on the basis of religious principles differ, if at all, from those of one that does not?

concept check

- What are the four components of social responsibility?
- Give an example of legal but irresponsible behavior.

Many other companies are also trying to do more. For example, Bristol-Myers, Coca-Cola, General Motors, Exxon, Ford Motor, Citigroup, J. P. Morgan, and many others have agreed to help the National Black MBA Association persuade young African Americans to look for executive jobs. The group, which has about 2,000 members, has built a scholarship fund that hands out $450,000 a year.

RESPONSIBILITIES TO STAKEHOLDERS

>lg 5

stakeholders

Individuals or groups to whom a business has a responsibility; include employees, customers, the general public, and investors.

What makes a company admired or perceived as socially responsible? Such a company meets its obligations to its stakeholders. **Stakeholders** are the individuals or groups to whom a business has a responsibility. The stakeholders of a business are its employees, customers, the general public, and investors.

Responsibility to Employees

An organization's first responsibility is to provide a job to employees. Keeping people employed and letting them have time to enjoy the fruits of their labor is the finest thing business can do for society. Beyond this fundamental responsibility, employers must provide a clean, safe working environment that is free from all forms of discrimination. Companies should also strive to provide job security whenever possible.

Enlightened firms are also empowering employees to make decisions on their own and suggest solutions to company problems. Empowerment contributes to an employee's self-worth, which, in turn, increases productivity and reduces absenteeism. The Ritz Carlton hotel chain, for example, empowers *all* employees to solve *any* guest problem on the spot. Dana Corp., an automotive-components manufacturer based in Toledo, Ohio, has created a culture where empowerment has become a reality. The company has implemented a number of programs and practices that encourage and recognize individual contributions. These include a commitment to 40 hours of education for each employee every year; an internal promotion policy in which the people who help create the company's success share in the rewards; a suggestion system in which each employee is encouraged to submit two ideas per month and the company strives for 80 percent implementation of those ideas; an organizational structure that supports individual responsibility; a retirement program that encourages longevity; and a stock-purchase program that encourages eligible employees to own a share of the company.

Levi Strauss's unique corporate culture rewards and recognizes employee achievements. To learn about working for a company that values employee efforts, go to the Levi Strauss home page at

www.levistrauss.com

Many companies are doing an excellent job in meeting their responsibilities toward their employees. Each year *Fortune* conducts an extensive survey of the best places to work in America. The top 10 are shown in Exhibit 4-4. Some companies offer unusual benefits to their employees. CMP Media gives employees $30,000 for infertility treatments and adoption aid. FedEx allows free rides in the jump seats of company planes. Steelcase has a 1,200-acre camping and recreational area for employee use.

Responsibility to Customers

A central theme of this text is that to be successful in the new millennium a company must satisfy its customers. Satisfied customers lead to long-term relationships and a long-term stream of revenue and profits for the firm. Poor customer service or shoddy products will drive customers away. However, nothing drives customers away faster or breaks the bonds of a long-term relationship quicker than failure to treat a customer fairly or honestly.

consumer fraud

The practice of deceiving customers by such means as failing to honor warranties or other promises or selling goods or services that do not meet advertised claims.

IOMEGA Corp. learned this lesson the hard way. Recently, the company agreed to provide free customer support via the Internet or by telephone as part of a settlement of a **consumer-fraud** lawsuit. The lawsuit accused the disk drive maker of not honoring product warranties and failing to provide adequate technical support. Customers said they had trouble installing IOMEGA products despite packaging claims that installation was easy. When they tried to call IOMEGA, they learned the company charged up to $19.99 for the help. Even then, they had trouble getting help because technical-support lines were severely understaffed. Customers were often left waiting on hold for an hour or more.[16]

See how IOMEGA now supports customers online at

www.IOMEGA.com/ support/suportpage

Allegations of consumer fraud have also been made in a case involving Computer Learning Centers. Based in Fairfax, Virginia,

> e x h i b i t   4 - 4 <

America's Best Places to Work

Company (Headquarters Location; Number of U.S. Sites)	Comments
1 Southwest Airlines (Dallas; 61)	Why is Southwest No. 1? Listen to a typical comment from the more than 100 received from enthusiastic employees: "Working here is truly an unbelievable experience. They treat you with respect, pay you well, and empower you. They use your ideas to solve problems. They encourage you to be yourself. I love going to work!!"
2 Kingston Technology (Fountain Valley, CA; 2)	Nearly everyone in the US wanted to work at this manufacturer of computer memory devices after last year's stories about its year-end bonus averaging $75,000 per employee. This bonus was in line with company policies: free soft drinks and cups of noodles at all times and a golf driving range in the back of the plant.
3 SAS Institute (Cary, NC; 36)	The world's largest privately held computer software company, SAS Institute offers superb on-site child care for $200 a month, an on-site clinic that offers primary medical care at zero cost to employees, and an award-winning cafeteria, where a pianist plays during lunch. It's no surprise that turnover, at 4% a year, is among the lowest in the software industry.
4 Fel-Pro (Skokie, IL; 8)	Fel-Pro makes auto, truck, and motorcycle gaskets in a sprawling plant just north of Chicago. It is ultra-family-friendly: $1,000 savings bond at child's birth, affordable on-site child care, summer camp on company's 200-acre recreation area, summer jobs for employees' kids, and $3,500 annual college scholarships.
5 TDIndustries (Dallas; 6)	TDI installs and services air-conditioning and plumbing systems in six Texas cities. All stock is in the hands of employees, with no one owning more than 9%. A monthly meeting fills in all employees on financial results. Employees are wildly upbeat. One said, "This company makes you feel like a human being again."
6 MBNA (Wilmington, DE; 20)	This house of plastic, the second-largest issuer of credit cards, pampers employees so they will be nice to customers. The coddling includes four on-site child care centers, one-week paid leave for new fathers and adoptive parents, adoption aid of up to $10,000. No. 1 hiring criterion: "People who like other people."
7 W. L. Gore (Newark, DE; 31)	W. L. Gore is the maker of Gore-Tex waterproof fabrics, glide dental floss, and dozens of other high-tech materials. It employs avant-garde management theories that seem to work. Instead of a traditional hierarchy topped by bosses and managers, the company uses an organization in which dozens of so-called sponsors set the pace.
8 Microsoft (Redmond, WA; 18)	Microsoft offers a remarkably challenging atmosphere for the brainy. Everybody gets stock options, and most professionals hired before 1992 have thus become millionaires; six became billionaires. All company picnics include a rodeo and five bands. And Bill (never Mr. Gates) personally answers all e-mail from employees.
9 Merck (Whitehouse Station, NJ; 68)	The corporate credo is to put patients before profits, and that sense of mission permeates this drug company's culture. Employees take obvious pride in the fact that Merck provides a low-cost anti-AIDS drug and gives away a medicine in developing countries that prevents river blindness. Some 31% of managers are women.
10 Hewlett-Packard (Palo Alto, CA; 30)	The godfather of Silicon Valley, Hewlett-Packard is still a trailblazer in people practices. It recently added domestic-partner benefits and nursing-home-care insurance for spouses, parents, and grandparents to an already lush benefits package. "They 'walk the talk' when they say their people are their most important asset," one worker told us.

SOURCE: Robert Levering and Milton Moskowitz, "The 100 Best Companies to Work For in America," *Fortune* (January 12, 1998), pp. 84–85. ©1999 Time Inc. Reprinted by permission.

the company provides training in computer programming, network administration, and other computer skills at 25 centers across the country. The Illinois Attorney General's Office accused the company of making misrepresentations to students who enrolled at its Illinois campus. The company allegedly made unrealistic promises of high earning potential and job placement to entice students to sign up for courses. Some students paid the school thousands of dollars. "When students enrolled, they often found overcrowded classrooms, unprepared instructors, few computers, books or other necessary materials," the attorney general said.[17]

Responsibility to the General Public

A business must also be responsible to the general public. A business provides a community with jobs, goods, and services. It also pays taxes that go to support schools, hospitals, and better roads. Most companies try to be good citizens in their communities. Corning, Inc., for example, located in Corning, New York, has made a point of acting responsibly toward its namesake. When the company constructed new headquarters in the early 1990s, it deliberately kept the building's height low enough to avoid overshadowing the town. The corporation also distributes leaflets warning of the dangers of smoking, bulimia, anorexia nervosa, and herpes to its employees, who include half of the town's 12,000 inhabitants.

corporate philanthropy

The practice of charitable giving by corporations; includes contributing cash, donating equipment and products, and supporting the volunteer efforts of company employees.

To preserve the environment, businesses must become more environmentally responsible. These digital images of Earth illustrate how a strip mining firm altered the same area over a 24-year period.

Environmental Protection Business is also responsible for protecting and improving the world's fragile environment. The world's forests are being destroyed fast. Every second, an area the size of a football field is laid bare. Plant and animal species are becoming extinct at the rate of 17 per hour. A continent-size hole is opening up in the earth's protective ozone shield. Each year we throw out 80 percent more refuse than we did in 1960; as a result, more than half of the nation's landfills are filled to capacity.

Want to see how the global environment is changing? Go to:
www.usgs.gov/earthshots

To slow the erosion of the world's resources, many companies are becoming more environmentally responsible. Toyota is now using "renewable" energy sources to power its facilities, making it the largest single user of clean power in the world. Toyota's first step in the United States was to turn to renewable sources such as solar, wind, geothermal, and water power for the electricity at its headquarters in Torrance and Irving, California.

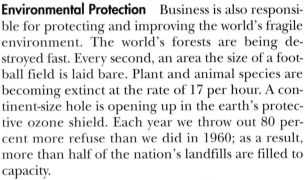

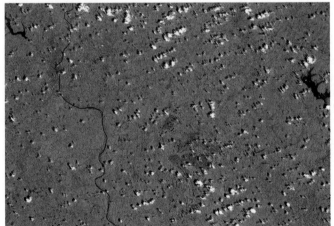

Corporate Philanthropy Companies also display their social responsibility through corporate philanthropy. **Corporate philanthropy** includes cash contributions, donations of equipment and products, and support for the volunteer efforts of company employees as at Lucent Technologies. Corporate philanthropy totals about $9 billion a year.[18] Coca-Cola has a multiyear $60 million strategic partnership with the Boys and Girls Clubs of America. It funds concerts, sports tournaments, and other activities for club members. Restaurant chain Denny's has become Save the Children's largest corporate supporter—contributing $2.5 million over three years from selling special meals, scarves, and neckties. Tanqueray has spent more than $2 million a year in major markets around the country to sponsor its Tanqueray AIDS Rides—bicycle races that get the attention of consumers between the ages of 25 and 40. The AIDS Rides have picked up a few hitchhikers, including Gatorade and Starbucks.

More and more companies are donating products and research findings rather than cash. IBM,

for example, donates about $100 million a year to various organizations. About $70 million of IBM's donations are in noncash items. In a recent year, Merck, the giant pharmaceutical firm, donated $5 million in cash and $116 million in noncash items.[19] Such giving makes business sense because companies can value their donations at fair-market prices, rather than the cost to produce them. Better yet, a generous tax law allows corporations to write off the cost of producing the donation as well as the difference between the cost and retail value. In contrast, a business that donates $1 million in cash can write off only that amount.

Responsibilities to Investors

Companies' relationships with investors also entail social responsibility. Although a company's economic responsibility to make a profit might seem to be its main obligation to its shareholders, many investors increasingly are putting more emphasis on other aspects of social responsibility.

> **social investing**
> The practice of limiting investments to securities of companies that behave in accordance with the investor's beliefs about ethical and social responsibility.

Some investors are limiting their investments to securities that fit within their beliefs about ethical and social responsibility. This is called **social investing.** For example, a social investment fund might eliminate from consideration the securities of all companies that make tobacco products or liquor, manufacture weapons, or have a history of polluting. Not all social investment strategies are alike. Some ethical mutual funds will not invest in government securities because they help to fund the military; others freely buy government securities, with managers noting that federal funds also support the arts and pay for AIDS research. Today, about $100 billion is invested in social investment funds.

When investors are dissatisfied with corporate managers, they are less passive than in the past. They are pressuring corporations with tactics such as exposés on television and other media and calling government attention to perceived wrongdoings. Groups of owners are pressuring companies to increase profits, link executive pay to performance, and oust inefficient management. Consequently, executives and managers are giving more weight to the concerns of owner stakeholders in the decision-making process. For example, shareholders of pharmaceutical giant Pfizer forced the company to stop selling flavoring agents to tobacco companies. In the 1990s, a number of chief executives from major corporations—General Motors, IBM, Apple, and Eastman Kodak, to name a few—were expelled by dissatisfied investors.[20]

c o n c e p t   c h e c k

- How do businesses carry out their social responsibilities to consumers?
- What is corporate philanthropy?
- Is a company's only responsibility to its investors to make a profit? Why or why not?

CAPITALIZING ON TRENDS IN BUSINESS

>lg 6

Three important trends related to ethics and social responsibility for the new millennium are changes in corporate philanthropy, a new social contract between employers and employees, and the growth of global ethics and social responsibility. This section will examine each trend in turn.

Trends in Corporate Philanthropy

> **strategic giving**
> The practice of tying philanthropy closely to the corporate mission or goals and targeting donations to regions where a company operates.

Corporate philanthropy has typically involved seeking out needy groups and then giving them money or company products. Today, the focus is shifting to **strategic giving,** which ties philanthropy more closely to the corporate mission or goals and targets donations to regions where a company operates.

Thomas Kimble is the chairman of the General Motors Foundation, which is GM's philanthropic organization. Kimble notes, "Prior to 1997 our giving was simply for unselfish purposes. Now our thinking is that we need to balance unselfish giving with strategic donations to target groups." Most of the foundation's gifts now go to areas such as education, health and human services, and public policy that are related to GM's corporate goals such as lowering costs. Funding for research on a major health threat such as cancer makes both social and economical sense, GM believes. "Health care was the company's highest cost, so funding health, especially cancer-related research, became a priority," explains Kimble.[21]

Similarly, IBM "focuses like a laser beam" on areas related to its mission as "an information technology solutions provider," says Stanley Litow, IBM's director of community relations.[22] As we noted earlier, product and research donations account for most of the more than $100 million IBM contributes to philanthropic causes each year. IBM launched its nationwide Reinventing Education effort by singling out a number of school systems, including Philadelphia's public schools, to serve as test centers. The computer giant committed $2 million in research, products, and some 50 employees, including researchers and marketing and technology professionals, who worked over a 22-month period to find ways to boost literacy and improve teaching methods. As a result, IBM adapted the voice recognition technology used in its products to young children's high-pitched voices and pronunciations to come up with software that would enable a child working on a computer to recognize word and sentence patterns.

Corporate philanthropy has also become a target for special-interest groups. AT&T, General Electric, and Eastman Kodak have come under attack by abortion foes for their donations to Planned Parenthood. The conservative Capital Research Center has criticized Anheuser-Busch, Hewlett-Packard, and other manufacturers for supporting what the center claims are radical groups seeking to undermine the capitalist system. When Philip Morris gave money to conservative political causes, the gay activist group ACT-UP encouraged consumers to stop buying its products.

General Motors is often recognized as a top participant in philanthropic activities. Which charities and organizations does GM support, and how? Read GM's Annual Philanthropic Report online at

www.gm.com

Computer firms that link their product donations to schools with their corporate goals represent the corporate philanthropy trend of strategic giving.

A New Social Contract Trend between Employer and Employee

Another trend in social responsibility is the effort by organizations to redefine their relationship with their employees. Many people have viewed social responsibility as a one-way street that focuses on the obligations of business to society, employees, and others. Now, companies are telling employees that they also have a responsibility when it comes to job security. The new contract goes like this: "There will never be job security. You will be employed by us as long as you add value to the organization, and *you* are continuously responsible for finding ways to add value. In return, you have the right to demand interesting and important work, the freedom and resources to perform it well, pay that reflects your contribution, and the experience

Applying This Chapter's Topics

Human rights problems plague athletic shoemaker Nike. When Phil Knight, Nike's chief executive, visited Stanford University, students and faculty protested the company's practice of paying employees working at its contract plants in Asia wages too low to support an adequate living standard.

and training needed to be employable here or elsewhere." Coca-Cola, for example, requires extensive employee retraining each year. The idea, according to a Coke executive, is to become a more valuable employee by adding 25 percent to your existing knowledge every year.

Trends in Global Ethics and Social Responsibility

As U.S. businesses expand into global markets, their corporate codes of ethics and policies on social responsibility must travel with them. As a citizen of several countries, a multinational corporation has several responsibilities. These include respecting local practices and customs, ensuring that there is harmony between the organization's staff and the host population, providing management leadership, and developing a cadre of local managers who will be a credit to their community. When a multinational makes an investment in a foreign country, it should commit to a long-term relationship. That means involving all stakeholders in the host country in decision making. Finally, a responsible multinational will implement ethical guidelines within the organization in the host country. By fulfilling these responsibilities, the company will foster respect for both local and international laws.

Multinational corporations often must balance conflicting interests of stakeholders when making decisions regarding social responsibilities, especially in the area of human rights. Questions involving child labor, forced labor, minimum wages, and workplace safety can be particularly difficult. Levi Strauss was strongly praised when it announced it was leaving China in 1993 because of the country's poor human rights record. China is also an inexpensive place to manufacture clothing, and the temptation to stay there was simply too great. In fact, Levi Strauss never stopped making clothes in China; its Hong Kong subsidiary continues to manufacture clothes on a contract basis. Levi recently announced that it would begin selling clothes in China. One might argue that Levi Strauss must remain competitive and profitable, or it will not be able to be a leader in the cause of social responsibility. When the announcement came, however, human rights activists quickly set up a picket at Levi's San Francisco headquarters.[23]

c o n c ə p t c h ə c k

- Describe strategic giving.
- What role do employees have in improving their job security?
- How do multinational corporations demonstrate social responsibility in a foreign country?

APPLYING THIS CHAPTER'S TOPICS

Are you at the preconventional, conventional, or postconventional stage of ethical development? If you determine that you are at the preconventional level, you should begin striving for a more mature ethical outlook. This may mean taking an ethics course, reading a book on ethics, or engaging in a lot of introspection about yourself and your values. A person with preconventional ethics will probably have a difficult time succeeding in today's business world.

Ethics Are Part of Everyday Life

Realize that ethics plays a part in our lives every day. We all must answer questions such as these:

How do I balance the time and energy obligations of my work and my family? How much should I pay my employees? What should I do with the child of my husband's first marriage who is disrupting our new family? How am I spending my money? Should I "borrow" a copy of my friend's software? If I know my employee is having troubles at home, should I treat her differently? What should I do if I know a neighbor's child is getting into serious trouble? How do I react to a sexist or racist joke?

Too many people make decisions about everyday questions without considering the underlying moral and ethical framework of the problems. They are simply swept along by the need to get through the day. Our challenge to you is to always think about the ethical consequences of your actions. Make doing so a habit.

Waiting for dramatic events before consciously tackling ethical considerations is like playing a sport only on the weekend. Just as a weekend warrior often ends

> t r y   i t   n o w ! <

1. **Support a Good Cause** You don't have to wait until graduation to start demonstrating your social responsibility. Go to HubHeaven right now at **www.HubHeaven.org**. Heaven seeks to bring about positive social change through a unique mix of innovative initiatives and celebrity involvement. An innovative ANGELS program couples computer training with community service. Heavenly programs include the following:
   - Heavenly Bodies. Features celebrities who serve as role models. They describe causes they care about and explain how to get involved in supporting the cause. Participating celebrities include models Tyra Banks, Frederique, and Lauren Wacht; actors Martin Sheen, Billy Baldwin, Malik Yoba, and Andrew Shue; musicians MC Hammer and Adam Yauch; dancer Reg E. Gaines; and political commentator Chris Cuomo.
   - Good Company. Profiles and publicizes companies and organizations that effect change.
   - Do Something. Provides leadership training, guidance, and grants to those who take action to improve their communities.

   - Volunteer Now! Connects young adults with local volunteer opportunities in their areas of interest.
   - Cloud Nine. Features issue-oriented articles and essays by leading writers, activists, and artists and encourages participation in dialogue and debate.
   - ANGELS (America's Network of Givers, Educators, Linkers, and Servers). Administers a real-world computer training and community service program for inner-city high school students. ANGELS is a nationwide effort to lessen the divide between the information haves and have-nots.

2. **Know Your Ethical Values** To get a better idea of your own level of ethical development, take an ethics test. Go to **www.polley-edu.com/ethics.htm**. Check your responses against others' responses and read their comments. This test will give you better insight into yourself.

up with pulled muscles and poor performance, people who seldom consider the ethical implications of daily activities won't have the coordination to work through the more difficult times in their lives. Don't let this happen to you.

>looking ahead
at Miami International Airport

Given the hardship that the lack of luggage carts at the Miami International Airport imposed on passengers, many people would argue that the Miami Airport Authority had not acted in an ethical and responsible manner. Mr. Albo seems to be selling his political connections. Although this is done routinely in the United States and most other countries, many people view this practice as unethical. Also, it is highly unlikely that airport officials needed to go on an around-the-world trip to evaluate luggage carts. Many would also consider this action unethical.

Work for a Firm That Cares about Its Social Responsibilities

When you enter the job market, make certain that you are going to work for a socially responsible organization. Ask a prospective employer "how the company gives back to society." If you plan to work for a large company, check out *Fortune*'s current list of America's most admired corporations. It appears around March 1.

If you plan to work for a multinational, examine *Fortune*'s most globally admired corporations, which appears in October. The list is broken down by industry and includes 10 to 15 companies in each industry. Working for an ethical, socially responsible organization will make you proud of the place where you work.

SUMMARY OF LEARNING GOALS

>lg 1 **What philosophies and concepts shape personal ethical standards, and what are the stages of ethical development?**
Ethics is a set of moral standards for judging whether something is right or wrong. A utilitarianism approach to setting personal ethical standards focuses on the consequences of an action taken by a person or organization. According to this approach, people should act so as to generate the greatest good for the greatest number. Every human is entitled to certain rights such as freedom and the pursuit of happiness. Another approach to ethical decision making is justice, or what is fair according to accepted standards.

There are three stages of ethical development. At the level of preconventional ethics, behavior is childlike in nature and self-centered. Conventional ethics moves from an egocentric point of view toward the expectations of society or an organization. Postconventional ethics represents the ethical standards of the mature adult.

>lg 2 **How can managers influence organizational ethics?**
The first step management should take is to recognize the categories of unethical business actions. Managers should educate employees to use the three-questions test or the front page of the newspaper test when faced with ethical dilemmas. Top management must shape the ethical culture of the organization. They should lead by example.

>lg 3 **What are the techniques for creating employee ethical awareness?**
The most common way companies raise employee ethical awareness is through ethics training. Typically, this involves analyzing and discussing ethical dilemmas. Companies also create and distribute codes of ethics to heighten ethical awareness.

>lg 4 **What is social responsibility?**
Social responsibility is the concern of businesses for the welfare of society as a whole. It consists of obligations beyond just making a profit. Social responsibility also goes beyond what is required by law or union contract. Companies may engage in illegal and irresponsible behavior, irresponsible but legal behavior,

KEY TERMS

code of ethics 107
consumer fraud
   113
conventional ethics
   102
corporate
   philanthropy 115
ethics 100
justice 101
postconventional
   ethics 102
preconventional
   ethics 101
social investing
   116
social responsibility
   107
stakeholders 112
strategic giving
   116
utilitarianism 100

or legal and responsible behavior. The vast majority of organizations act legally and try to be socially responsible.

>lg 5   **How do businesses meet their social responsibilities to various stakeholders?**
Stakeholders are individuals or groups to whom business has a responsibility. Businesses are responsible to employees. They should provide a clean, safe working environment. Organizations can build employees' self-worth through empowerment programs. Businesses also have a responsibility to customers to provide good, safe products and services. Organizations are responsible to the general public to be good corporate citizens. Firms must help protect the environment and provide a good place to work. Companies also engage in corporate philanthropy, which includes contributing cash, donating goods and services, and supporting volunteer efforts of employees. Finally, companies are responsible to investors. They should earn a reasonable profit for the owners.

>lg 6   **What are the global and domestic trends in ethics and social responsibility?**
Today, corporate philanthropy is shifting away from simply giving to any needy group and is focusing instead on strategic giving, in which the philanthropy relates more closely to the corporate mission or goals and targets donations to areas where the firm operates. Corporate philanthropy is coming under increasing attacks from special-interest groups, however.

   A second trend is toward a new social contract between employer and employee. Instead of the employer having the sole responsibility for maintaining jobs, now the employee must assume part of the burden and find ways to add value to the organization.

   As the world increasingly becomes a global community, multinational corporations are now expected to assume a global set of ethics and responsibility. Global companies must understand local customs. They should also involve local stakeholders in decision making. Multinationals must also make certain that their suppliers are not engaged in human rights violations.

>lg 7   **How does the legal system govern business transactions and settle business disputes?**
Laws are the rules governing a society's conduct that are created and enforced by a controlling authority. The U.S. court system governs the legal system and includes both federal and state courts, each organized into three levels. The courts settle disputes by applying and interpreting laws. Most cases start in trial courts. Decisions can be appealed to appellate courts. The U.S. Supreme Court is the nation's highest court and the court of final appeal. To avoid the high costs of going to court, many firms now use private arbitration or mediation as alternatives to litigation.

>lg 8   **What are the required elements of a valid contract; and what are the key types of business law?**
A contract is an agreement between two or more parties that meets five requirements: mutual assent, capacity, consideration, legal purpose, and legal form. If one party breaches the contract terms, the remedies are damages, specific performance, or restitution.

   Tort law settles disputes involving civil acts that harm people or their property. Torts include physical injury, mental anguish, and defamation. Product-liability law governs the responsibility of manufactures and sellers for product defects. Bankruptcy law gives business or individuals who cannot meet their financial obligations a way to be relieved of their debts. Some laws are designed to keep the marketplace free from influences that would restrict competition such as price fixing and deceptive advertising. Laws protecting consumer rights are another important area of government control.

>lg 9   **What are the most common taxes paid by businesses?**
Income taxes are based on the income received by businesses and individuals. Congress determines the income taxes that are to be paid to the federal

government. In addition to income taxes, individuals and businesses also pay property taxes (assessed on real and personal property), payroll taxes (the employer's share of Social Security taxes and federal and state unemployment taxes), sales taxes (levied on goods), and excise taxes (levied against specific products such as gasoline, alcoholic beverages, and tobacco).

PREPARING FOR TOMORROW'S WORKPLACE

1. Divide the class into two teams. Representatives from each team should debate whether ethics can be taught.
2. Write a paper that explains how utilitarianism may conflict with human rights.
3. Divide the class into teams. Each team should select 1 of the 11 categories of unethical behavior discussed in the chapter and find an example of that behavior through the personal experience of a team member or through research in the library or on the Internet. Use one of the techniques recommended in the chapter for resolving the ethical problem. Present your findings to the class.
4. You have been asked to give a speech on creating employee ethical awareness. Prepare an outline for your speech.
5. Go to the library and find examples of firms meeting their responsibilities to the four categories of stakeholders.
6. Divide the class into teams. Debate whether the only social responsibility of the employer to the employee is to provide a job. Include a discussion of the employee's responsibility to bring value to the firm.
7. Identify the potential ethical and social responsibility issues confronting the following organizations: Microsoft, Columbia Hospitals, Nike, American Cancer Society, and R.J. Reynolds. Use the library and the Internet to gather data, and then make some potential recommendations on how these issues should be handled.

WORKING THE NET

1. Visit the Web site of the People for the Ethical Treatment of Animals (PETA) at **furisdead.com.** Read about PETA's view of the fur industry. Do you agree or disagree with this view? Why? How do you think manufacturers who make fur clothing would justify their actions to someone from PETA? Would you work for a store that offered fur-trimmed clothing in addition to other items? Explain your answer.
2. Use a major search engine such as Yahoo (**www.yahoo.com**) or Lycos (**www.lycos.com**) to look for several examples of corporate codes of ethics. What common elements appear in the examples you found? Suggest how one of the codes could be improved.
3. Read the article "The National Litigious Environment" at **www.diversitydtg.com/articles/litigious.html**. Can a firm whose primary motivation for ethical action is to avoid lawsuits still be an ethical firm?
4. At **www.goodmoney.com/wpubco.htm**, you will find a list of public companies that have been identified as being socially responsible. Pick one of the companies and find its Internet home page (Yahoo at **www.yahoo.com** is one way to find this). Read about the firm's operations and marketing efforts. Do you agree or disagree that this firm is socially responsible? Give specific examples from the company's Web site to support your answer.
5. Read about Bank of America's community development and environmental protection programs at **www.boa.com**. Why do you think Bank of

America runs these programs? How do these programs benefit Bank of America's stockholders/investors? Customers? Employees? Use a search engine like Dogpile (**www.dogpile.com**) to find other examples of corporate philanthropy.

CREATIVE THINKING CASE

Limited Too Helps Girl Scouts Earn a Merit Badge in Shopping

Draped shoulder to waist, the Kelly-green Girl Scout sash is the showcase of its wearer's badges and patches. The insignia denote achievement in fields such as first aid, plants and animals, folk art, or shopping. Yes, shopping. It's part of the Fashion Adventure program, offered nationwide inside Limited Too stores, which merchandise clothing specifically for girls age seven to 14. To earn the patch, the Girl Scouts must troop off to a Limited Too, where they learn about fabrics, markdowns, store security, and what merchandisers do. The girls get to browse among clothes racks, choose their favorite outfits and model in front of others. They also get 15 percent off coupons from the store.

One Fashion Adventurer, Junior Girl Scout Kari Chambers of Hilliard, Ohio, went camping one recent week with the girls in Troop 2213, heating 'smores by a glowing bonfire. Another week, it was off to the sprawling Mall at Tuttle Crossing in a Columbus suburb. At a Limited Too packed with the latest girls' fashions, the 10-year-old tried on a white dress and sashayed in front of her troop. "You model in a circle," she says, "and everyone would be there to see you." She twirls to demonstrate.

Limited is just one of a handful of corporate sponsors tapping into the Girl Scouts. General Motors Corp.'s Saturn division offers the Saturn Girl Scout Auto Workshop course to older Girl Scouts. "It's nauseating," says Peggy Charren, consumer activist and founder of Action for Children's Television. The Fashion Adventure program, she says, is a "pure and simple sales pitch under the auspices of the Girl Scouts."

"We're trying to make sure that our program activities remain contemporary," says Marianne Ilaw, spokeswoman for the Girl Scouts of the U.S.A. Defending business-sponsored programs such as Fashion Adventure, she says, "It's a real life experience for girls who will be working. It's just a learning environment." Ilaw says participating companies must present a full educational program. The Fashion Adventure patch comes with a 13-page booklet suggesting exercises before the store visit, such as hemming a pant leg and identifying parts of a shirt (distinguishing, for instance, darts from yokes).

Officials at Limited Too stress that the three-year-old Fashion Adventure program is strictly a community service, to educate the girls about fashion and grooming. Michael Rayden, president and chief executive of Limited Too, says the program is part of any good corporation's "three legs of the stool: community, family and business."

Critical Thinking Questions

1. Do you think it is ethical for the Girl Scouts to offer a Fashion Adventure merit badge tied in with Limited Too? Why or why not?

2. Is the Limited Too simply meeting its public social responsibility, as it claims?

3. Would you view the situation differently if the Fashion Adventure badge could be earned at any retailer of the girls' choosing? Why or why not?

4. Limited Too has planned a catalog strictly for preteen girls. It will be mailed directly to preteen girls, not their parents. Is this an ethical act? Why?

5. Go to the Limited Too's Web site at **www.pages.prodigy.com/Limited_Too/**. Comment on the site and how it relates to this chapter.

VIDEO CASE

The Bank of Alma

The Bank of Alma (**www.firstbank-alma.com**) began more than a 100 years ago as a community-oriented banking institution known as W. S. Turck & Co. With acquisitions and mergers over the years, W. S. Turck's successor became known as the Bank of Alma in 1957. As of early 1999, the Bank of Alma consisted of 10 offices and seven automatic teller machines (ATMs) located throughout Gratiot County in central Michigan and the surrounding communities. The Bank of Alma also became the lead bank in Firstbank Corporation, a multibank holding company.

The Bank of Alma has a four-point mission that guides its operations. First and foremost, it is committed to customer satisfaction. Second, it is cognizant of employee needs. Third, it supports the communities that it serves. Fourth, it aims to enhance shareholder value.

John McCormack, the president and chief executive officer, says that the Bank of Alma has been around a long time because it has never lost its customer focus. The overarching goal is to make each customer's "experience with the Bank of Alma delightful in every way." Continuously focusing on exceptional customer service is the key to the bank business strategy.

Delighting the customers is accomplished in several ways. One way is through the range of products and services offered to the local community. The Bank of Alma offers a variety of checking services that are designed to fit customers' lifestyles; a wide selection of savings account options to meet customers' future needs; a wide range of loan options, including consumer loans, personal lines of credit, mortgage loans, home equity loans, construction loans, commercial loans, check overdraft protection, and credit cards; and other products and services, such as trust and investment management services, employee benefit plans, business accounts, ATM and check cards, safety deposit boxes, electronic payroll direct deposits, and electronic tax payments.

Another way the Bank of Alma delights customers is by relying on local decision making so that it can provide quick and effective service. For instance, the bank has a well-established reputation for providing loans that customers qualify for and can afford. The Bank of Alma also makes banking convenient by providing both a telephone banking center and an extensive branch and ATM network.

The Bank of Alma also seeks to delight its customers through vigorous enforcement of its policies regarding confidentiality, honesty, inappropriate disclosure of information, and privacy. Managerial and nonmanagerial employees at the Bank of Alma view these policies, and the actions governed by them, as essential to developing trusting relationships with the bank's customers. Adhering to these ethical standards is important because customers entrust their financial assets and a variety of financial information to the bank.

An additional, though less obvious, means of delighting customers is through outreach to local communities. The Bank of Alma is committed to the communities that it serves. It not only provides significant financial support to those communities, but it also encourages bank employees to be involved meaningfully in the communities where they work.

Critical Thinking Questions

1. Is the Bank of Alma operated as an ethical business? Explain your answer.
2. Why is trust so crucial for the Bank of Alma? To what extent can (or should) trust be applied to other businesses?
3. To what extent do you apply standards such as confidentiality, honesty, privacy, and nondisclosure of information to your own interactions with other people?

APPENDIX 4: UNDERSTANDING THE LEGAL AND TAX ENVIRONMENT

>lg 7

Our legal system affects everyone who lives and does business in the United States. The smooth functioning of society depends on the law, which protects the rights of people and businesses. The purpose of law is to keep the system stable while allowing orderly change. The law defines which actions are allowed or banned and regulates some practices. It also helps settle disputes. The legal system both shapes and is shaped by political, economic, and social systems. As Judge Learned Hand wrote in *The Spirit of Liberty,* "Without [the law] we cannot live; only with it can we insure the future which by right is ours."

In any society **laws** are the rules of conduct created and enforced by a controlling authority, usually the government. They develop over time in response to the changing needs of people, property, and business. The legal system of the United States is thus the result of a long and continuing process. In each generation new social problems occur, and new laws are created to solve them. For instance, in the late 1800s corporations in certain industries, such as steel and oil, merged and became dominant. The Sherman Antitrust Act was passed in 1890 to control these powerful firms. Eighty years later, in 1970, Congress passed the National Environmental Policy Act. This law dealt with pollution problems, which no one had thought about in 1890. Today new areas of law are developing to deal with the Internet.

The Main Sources of Law

Common law is the body of unwritten law that has evolved out of judicial (court) decisions rather than being enacted by legislatures. It is also called case law. It developed in England and came to America with the colonists. All states except Louisiana, which follows the Napoleonic Code inherited from French settlers, follow the English system. Common law is based on community customs that were recognized and enforced by the courts.

Statutory law is written law enacted by legislatures at all levels, from city and state governments to the federal government. Examples of statutory law are the federal and state constitutions, bills passed by Congress, and *ordinances,* which are laws enacted by local governments. Statutory law is the chief source of new laws in the United States. Among the business activities governed by statutory law are securities regulation, incorporation, sales, bankruptcy, and antitrust.

Related to statutory law is **administrative law,** or the rules, regulations, and orders passed by boards, commissions, and agencies of federal, state, and local governments. The scope and influence of administrative law have expanded as the number of these government bodies has grown. Federal agencies issue more rulings and settle more disputes than all the courts and legislatures combined. Some federal agencies that issue rules are the Civil Aeronautics Board, the Internal Revenue Service, the Securities and Exchange Commission, the Federal Trade Commission, and the National Labor Relations Board.

Business Law

Business law is the body of law that governs commercial dealings. These laws provide a protective environment within which businesses can operate. They serve as guidelines for business decisions. Every businessperson should be familiar with the laws governing his or her field. Some laws, such as the Internal Revenue Code,

laws
The rules of conduct in a society, created and enforced by a controlling authority, usually the government.

common law
The body of unwritten law that has evolved out of judicial (court) decisions rather than being enacted by a legislature; also called *case law.*

statutory law
Written law enacted by a legislature (local, state, or federal).

administrative law
The rules, regulations, and orders passed by boards, commissions, and agencies of government (local, state, and federal).

business law
The body of law that governs commercial dealings.

apply to all businesses. Other types of business laws may apply to a specific industry, such as Federal Communications Commission laws that regulate radio and TV stations.

In 1952 the United States grouped many business laws into a model that could be used by all the states. The **Uniform Commercial Code (UCC)** sets forth the rules that apply to commercial transactions between businesses and between individuals and businesses. It has been adopted by 49 states; Louisiana uses only part of it. By standardizing laws, the UCC simplifies the process of doing business across state lines. It covers the sale of goods, bank deposits and collections, letters of credit, documents of title, and investment securities. Many articles of the UCC are covered later in this appendix.

The Court System

The United States has a highly developed court system. This branch of government, the **judiciary,** is responsible for settling disputes by applying and interpreting points of law. Although court decisions are the basis for common law, the courts also answer questions left unanswered by statutes and administrative rulings. They have the power to assure that these laws do not violate the federal or state constitutions.

Trial Courts   Most court cases start in the **trial courts,** also called courts of general jurisdiction. The main federal trial courts are the U.S. district courts. There is at least one federal district court in each state. These courts hear cases involving serious federal crimes, immigration, postal regulations, disputes between citizens of different states, patents, copyrights, and bankruptcy. Specialized federal courts handle tax matters, international trade, and claims against the United States.

Appellate Courts   The losing party in a civil (noncriminal) case and a losing defendant in a criminal case may appeal the trial court's decision to the next level in the judicial system, the **appellate courts (courts of appeals).** There are 12 U.S. circuit courts of appeals. Cases that begin in a federal district court are appealed to the court of appeals for that district. These courts may also review orders from administrative agencies. Likewise, the states have appellate courts and supreme courts for cases tried in state district or superior courts.

No cases start in appellate courts. Their purpose is to review decisions of the lower courts and affirm, reverse, or modify the rulings.

The Supreme Court   The U.S. Supreme Court is the highest court in the nation. It is the only court specifically established by the U.S. Constitution. Any cases involving a state or in which an ambassador, public minister, or consul is a party are heard directly by the Supreme Court. Its main function is to review decisions by the U.S. circuit courts of appeals. Parties not satisfied with a decision of a state supreme court can appeal to the U.S. Supreme Court. But the Supreme Court accepts only those cases that it believes will have the greatest effect on the country, only about 200 of the thousands of appeals it gets each year.

Administrative Agencies   Administrative agencies have limited judicial powers to regulate their special areas. These agencies exist at the federal, state, and local levels. For example, in 1998 the Federal Trade Commission enacted the "Federal Universal Service Fund," which subjects each pager phone to a $0.18 fee. This fund was created by the Federal Trade Commission to ensure that all citizens, schools, libraries, and hospitals in rural areas have access to telecommunications service (like the Internet) at prices comparable to those charged in urban and suburban areas. A list of selected federal agencies is shown in Exhibit 4A-1.

Nonjudicial Methods of Settling Disputes

Settling disputes by going to court is both expensive and time-consuming. Even if the case is settled prior to the actual trial, sizable legal expenses can be

Uniform Commercial Code (UCC)

A model set of rules that apply to commercial transactions between businesses and between businesses and individuals; has been adopted by all states except Louisiana, which uses only part of it.

judiciary

The branch of government that is responsible for settling disputes by applying and interpreting points of law; consists of the court system.

trial courts

The lowest level of courts, where most cases begin; also called *courts of general jurisdiction.*

appellate courts (courts of appeals)

The level of courts above the trial courts; the losing party in a civil case and the defendant in a criminal case may appeal the trial court's decision to an appellate court.

> e x h i b i t   4 A - 1 <

Federal Regulatory Agencies

Agency	Function
Federal Trade Commission (FTC)	Enforces laws and guidelines regarding unfair business practices and acts to stop false and deceptive advertising and labeling.
Food and Drug Administration (FDA)	Enforces laws and regulations to prevent distribution of adulterated or misbranded foods, drugs, medical devices, cosmetics, veterinary products, and hazardous consumer products.
Consumer Products Safety Commission	Ensures compliance with the Consumer Product Safety Act and seeks to protect the public from unreasonable risk of injury from any consumer product not covered by other regulatory agencies.
Federal Communications Commission (FCC)	Regulates wire, radio, and TV communication in interstate and foreign commerce.
Environmental Protection Agency (EPA)	Develops and enforces environmental protection standards and researches the effects of pollution.

arbitration

A method of settling disputes in which the parties agree to present their case to an impartial third party and are required to accept the arbitrator's decision.

mediation

A method of settling disputes in which the parties submit their case to an impartial third party but are not required to accept the mediator's decision.

contract

An agreement that sets forth the relationship between parties regarding the performance of a specified action; creates a legal obligation and is enforceable in a court of law.

express contract

A contract in which the terms are specified in either written or spoken words.

implied contract

A contract that depends on the acts and conduct of the parties to show agreement; the terms are not specified in writing or orally.

incurred in preparing for trial. Therefore, many companies now use private arbitration and mediation firms as alternatives to litigation. Private firms offer these services, which are a high growth area within the legal profession.

With **arbitration,** the parties agree to present their case to an impartial third party and are required to accept the arbitrator's decision. **Mediation** is similar, but the parties are not bound by the mediator's decision. The mediator suggests alternative solutions and helps the parties negotiate a settlement. Mediation is more flexible than arbitration and allows for compromise. If the parties cannot reach a settlement, they can then go to court, an option not available in most arbitration cases.

In addition to saving time and money, corporations like the confidentiality of testimony and settlement terms in these proceedings. Arbitration and mediation also allow businesses and medical professionals to avoid jury trials, which can result in large settlements in certain types of lawsuits, such as personal injury, discrimination, medical malpractice, and product liability.

Contract Law

Linda Price, a 22-year-old college student, is looking at a car with a sticker price of $12,000. After some negotiating, she and the salesperson agree on a price of $11,000, and the salesperson writes up a contract, which they both sign. Has Linda legally bought the car for $11,000? The answer is yes, because the transaction meets all the requirements for a valid contract.

A **contract** is an agreement that sets forth the relationship between parties regarding the performance of a specified action. The contract creates a legal obligation and is enforceable in a court of law. Contracts are an important part of business law. Contract law is also incorporated into other fields of business law, such as property and agency law (discussed later in this appendix). Some of the business transactions that involve contracts are buying materials and property, selling goods, leasing equipment, and hiring consultants.

A contract can be an **express contract,** which specifies the terms of the agreement in either written or spoken words, or an **implied contract,** which depends on the acts and conduct of the parties to show agreement. An example of an express contract is the written sales contract for Linda Price's new car. An implied contract exists when you order and receive a sandwich at Jason's Grill. You and the restaurant have an implied contract that you will pay the price shown on the restaurant's menu in exchange for an edible sandwich.

Contract Requirements   Businesses deal with contracts all the time, so it's important to know the requirements of a valid contract. For a contract to be legally enforceable, all of the following elements must be present:

- *Mutual assent.* Voluntary agreement by both parties to the terms of the contract. Each party to the contract must have entered into it freely, without duress. Using physical or economic harm to force the signing of the contract—threatening injury or refusing to place another large order, for instance—invalidates a contract. Likewise, fraud—misrepresenting the facts of a transaction—makes a contract unenforceable. Telling a prospective used-car buyer that the brakes are new when in fact they have not been replaced makes the contract of sale invalid.

- *Capacity.* Legal ability of a party to enter into contracts. Under the law, minors (those under 18), mental incompetents, drug and alcohol addicts, and convicts cannot enter into contracts.

- *Consideration.* Exchange of some legal value or benefit between the parties. Consideration can be in the form of money, goods, or a legal right given up. Suppose that an electronics manufacturer agrees to rent an industrial building for a year at a monthly rent of $1,500. Its consideration is the rent payment of $1,500, and the building owner's consideration is permission to occupy the space. But if you offer to type a term paper for a friend for free and your offer is accepted, there is no contract. Your friend has not given up anything, so you are not legally bound to honor the deal.

- *Legal purpose.* Absence of illegality. The purpose of the contract must be legal for it to be valid. A contract cannot require performance of an illegal act. A contract to smuggle drugs into a state for a specified amount of money would not be legally enforceable.

- *Legal form.* Oral or written form, as required. Many contracts can be oral. For instance, an oral contract exists when Bridge Corp. orders office supplies by phone from Ace Stationery Store and Ace delivers the requested goods. Written contracts include leases, sales contracts, and property deeds. Some types of contracts must be in writing to be legally binding. In most states, written contracts are required for the sale of goods costing more than $500, for the sale of land, for contract performance that cannot be carried out within a year, and for guarantees to pay the debts of someone else.

As you can see, Linda Price's car purchase meets all the requirements for a valid contract. Both parties have freely agreed to the terms of the contract. Linda is not a minor and presumably does not fit any of the other categories of incapacity. Both parties are giving consideration, Linda by paying the money and the salesperson by turning over the car to her. The purchase of the car is a legal activity. And the written contract is the correct form because the cost of the car is over $500.

breach of contract
The failure by one party to a contract to fulfill the terms of the agreement without a legal excuse.

Breach of Contract   A **breach of contract** occurs when one party to a contract fails (without legal excuse) to fulfill the terms of the agreement. The other party then has the right to seek a remedy in the courts. There are three legal remedies for breach of contract:

- *Payment of damages.* Money awarded to the party who was harmed by the breach of contract, to cover losses incurred because the contract wasn't fulfilled. Suppose that Ajax Roofing contracts with Fred Wellman to fix the large hole in the roof of his factory within three days. But the roofing crew doesn't show up as promised. When a thunderstorm four days later causes $45,000 in damage to Wellman's machinery, Wellman can sue for damages to cover the costs of the water damage because Ajax breached the contract.

- *Specific performance of the contract.* A court order requiring the breaching party to perform the duties under the terms of the contract. Specific performance is the most common method of settling a breach of contract. Wellman might ask the court to direct Ajax to fix the roof at the price and conditions in the contract.

- *Restitution.* Canceling the contract and returning to the situation that existed before the contract. If one party fails to perform under the contract, neither party has any further obligation to the other. Because Ajax failed to fix Wellman's roof under the terms of the contract, Wellman does not owe Ajax any money. Ajax must return the 50 percent deposit it received when Wellman signed the contract.

Warranties

Express warranties are specific statements of fact or promises about a product by the seller. This form of warranty is considered part of the sales transaction that influences the buyer. Express warranties appear in the form of statements that can be interpreted as fact. The statement "This machine will process 1,000 gallons of paint per hour" is an express warranty, as is the printed warranty that comes with a computer or a telephone answering machine.

Implied warranties are neither written nor oral. These guarantees are imposed on sales transactions by statute or court decision. They promise that the product will perform up to expected standards. For instance, a man bought a used car from a dealer, and the next day the transmission fell out as he was driving on the highway. The dealer fixed the car, but a week later the brakes failed. The man sued the car dealer. The court ruled in favor of the car owner because any car without a working transmission or brakes is not fit for the ordinary purpose of driving. Similarly, if a customer asks to buy a copier to handle 5,000 copies per month, she relies on the salesperson to sell her a copier that meets those needs. The salesperson implicitly warrants that the copier purchased is appropriate for that volume.

Patents, Copyrights, and Trademarks

The U.S. Constitution protects authors, inventors, and creators of other intellectual property by giving them the rights to their creative works. Patents, copyrights, and registration of trademarks and servicemarks are legal protection for key business assets.

A **patent** gives an inventor the exclusive right to manufacture, use, and sell an invention for 17 years. The U.S. Patent Office, a government agency, grants patents for ideas that meet its requirements of being new, unique, and useful. The physical process, machine, or formula is what is patented. Patent rights— pharmaceutical companies' rights to produce drugs they discover, for example—are considered intangible personal property.

The government also grants copyrights. A **copyright** is an exclusive right, shown by the symbol ©, given to a writer, artist, composer, or playwright to use, produce, and sell her or his creation. Works protected by copyright include printed materials (books, magazine articles, lectures), works of art, photographs, and movies. Under current copyright law, the copyright is issued for the life of the creator plus 50 years after the creator's death. Patents and copyrights, which are considered intellectual property, are the subject of many lawsuits today.

patent
A form of protection established by the government for inventors; gives an inventor the exclusive right to manufacture, use, and sell an invention for 17 years.

copyright
A form of protection established by the government for creators of works of art, music, literature, or other intellectual property; gives the creator the exclusive right to use, produce, and sell the creation during the lifetime of the creator and for 50 years thereafter.

trademark

A design, name, or other distinctive mark that a manufacturer uses to identify its goods in the marketplace.

servicemark

A symbol, name, or design that identifies a service rather than a tangible object.

>lg 8

tort

A civil, or private, act that harms other people or their property.

product liability

The responsibility of manufacturers and sellers for defects in the products they make and sell.

A **trademark** is a design, name, or other distinctive mark that a manufacturer uses to identify its goods in the marketplace. Apple Computer's multicolored apple logo (symbol) is an example of a trademark. A **servicemark** is a symbol, name, or design that identifies a *service* rather than a tangible object. The Travelers Insurance umbrella logo is an example of a servicemark.

Most companies identify their trademark with the ® symbol in company ads. This symbol shows that the trademark is registered with the Register of Copyrights, Copyright Office, Library of Congress. The trademark is followed by a generic description: Fritos corn chips, Xerox copiers, Scotch brand cellophane tape, Kleenex tissues.

Trademarks are valuable because they create uniqueness in the minds of customers. At the same time, companies don't want a trademark to become so well known that it is used to describe all similar types of products. For instance, *Coke* is often used to refer to any cola soft drink, not just those produced by the Coca-Cola Company. Companies spend millions of dollars each year to keep their trademarks from becoming *generic words,* terms used to identify a product class rather than the specific product. Coca-Cola employs many investigators and files 70 to 80 lawsuits each year to prevent its trademarks from becoming generic words.

Once a trademark becomes generic (which a court decides), it is public property and can be used by any person or company. Names that were once trademarked but are now generic include *aspirin, thermos, linoleum,* and *toll house cookies.*

Tort Law

A **tort** is a civil, or private, act that harms other people or their property. The harm may involve physical injury, emotional distress, invasion of privacy, or *defamation* (injuring a person's character by publication of false statements). The injured party may sue the wrongdoer to recover damages for the harm or loss. A tort is not the result of a breach of contract, which would be settled under contract law. Torts are part of common law. Examples of tort cases are medical malpractice, *slander* (an untrue oral statement that damages a person's reputation), *libel* (an untrue written statement that damages a person's reputation), product liability (discussed in the next section), and fraud.

A tort is generally not a crime, although some acts can be both torts and crimes. (Assault and battery, for instance, is a criminal act that would be prosecuted by the state and also a tort because of the injury to the person.) Torts are private wrongs and are settled in civil courts. *Crimes* are violations of public law punishable by the state or county in the criminal courts. The purpose of criminal law is to punish the person who committed the crime. The purpose of tort law is to provide remedies to the injured party.

For a tort to exist and damages to be recovered, the harm must be done through either negligence or deliberate intent. *Negligence* occurs when reasonable care is not taken for the safety of others. For instance, a woman attending a New York Mets baseball game was struck on the head by a foul ball that came through a hole in the screen behind home plate. The court ruled that a sports team charging admission has an obligation to provide structures free from defects and seating that protects spectators from danger. The Mets were found negligent. Negligence does not apply when an injury is caused by an unavoidable accident, an event that was not intended and could not have been prevented even if the person used reasonable care. This area of tort law is quite controversial, because the definition of negligence leaves much room for interpretation.

Product-Liability Law

Product liability refers to manufacturers' and sellers' responsibility for defects in the products they make and sell. It has become a specialized area of law combining aspects of contracts, warranties, torts, and statutory law (at both the state and federal levels). A product-liability suit may be based on negligence or strict liability (both of which are torts) or misrepresentation or breach of warranty (part of contract law).

An important concept in product-liability law is **strict liability.** A manufacturer or seller is liable for any personal injury or property damage caused by defective products or packaging—even if all possible care was used to prevent such defects. The definition of *defective* is quite broad. It includes manufacturing and design defects and inadequate instructions on product use or warnings of danger.

Product-liability suits are very costly. More than 100,000 product-liability suits were filed against hundreds of companies that made or used asbestos, a substance that causes lung disease and cancer but was once used widely in insulation, brake linings, textiles, and other products. Eighteen companies were forced into bankruptcy as a result of asbestos-related lawsuits, and the total cost of asbestos cases to defendants and their insurers exceeds $10 billion (most of which was paid not to the victims but to lawyers and experts).

Bankruptcy Law

Congress has given financially distressed firms and individuals a way to make a fresh start. **Bankruptcy** is the legal procedure by which individuals or businesses that cannot meet their financial obligations are relieved of their debts. A bankruptcy court distributes any assets to the creditors.

Bankruptcy can be either voluntary or involuntary. In a *voluntary bankruptcy,* the debtor files a petition with the court, stating that debts exceed assets and asking the court to declare the debtor bankrupt. In an *involuntary bankruptcy,* the creditors file the bankruptcy petition.

The Bankruptcy Reform Act of 1978, amended in 1984 and 1986, provides for the quick and efficient resolution of bankruptcy cases. Under this act, two types of bankruptcy proceedings are available to businesses: *Chapter 7* (liquidation) and *Chapter 11* (reorganization). Most bankruptcies, an estimated 70 percent, use Chapter 7. After the sale of any assets, the cash proceeds are given first to secured creditors and then to unsecured creditors. A firm that opts to reorganize under Chapter 11 works with its creditors to develop a plan for paying part of its debts and writing off the rest.

Laws to Promote Fair Competition

Many measures have been taken to try to keep the marketplace free from influences that would restrict competition. These efforts include **antitrust regulation,** laws that prevent companies from entering into agreements to control trade through a monopoly. The first act regulating competition was the Sherman Antitrust Act, passed in 1890 to prevent large companies from dominating an industry and making it hard for smaller firms to compete. This broad act banned monopolies and contracts, mergers, or conspiracies in restraint of trade. In 1914 the Clayton Act added to the more general provisions of the Sherman Antitrust Act. It outlawed the following:

- *Price discrimination.* Offering a customer discounts that are not offered to all other purchasers buying on similar terms.
- *Exclusive dealing.* Refusing to let the buyer purchase a competitor's products for resale.
- *Tying contracts.* Requiring buyers to purchase merchandise they may not want in order to get the products they do want.
- *Purchase of stock in competing corporations so as to lessen competition.* Buying competitors' stock in such quantity that competition is reduced.

The 1950 *Celler-Kefauver Act* amended the Clayton Act. It bans the purchase of one firm by another if the resulting merger decreases competition within

---

strict liability

A concept in product-liability law under which a manufacturer or seller is liable for any personal injury or property damage caused by defective products or packaging even though all possible care was used to prevent such defects.

bankruptcy

The legal procedure by which individuals or businesses that cannot meet their financial obligations are relieved of their debt.

antitrust regulation

Laws that prevent companies from entering into agreements to control trade through a monopoly.

the industry. As a result, all corporate acquisitions are subject to regulatory approval before they can be finalized.

Most antitrust actions are taken by the U.S. Department of Justice, based on federal law. Violations of the antitrust acts are punishable by fines, imprisonment, or civil damage payments that can be as high as three times the actual damage amount. These outcomes give defendants an incentive to resolve cases.

The *Federal Trade Commission Act,* also passed in 1914, bans unfair trade practices. This act created the Federal Trade Commission (FTC), an independent five-member board with the power to define and monitor unfair trade practices, such as those prohibited by the Sherman and Clayton Acts. The FTC investigates complaints and can issue rulings called *cease-and-desist orders* to force companies to stop unfair business practices. Its powers have grown over the years. Today the FTC is one of the most important agencies regulating the competitive practices of business.

Regulation of Advertising and Pricing A number of federal laws directly affect the promotion and pricing of products. The *Wheeler-Lea Act* of 1938 amended the Federal Trade Commission Act and gave the FTC authority to regulate advertising. The FTC monitors companies' advertisements for false or misleading claims.

The most important law in the area of pricing is the *Robinson-Patman Act,* a federal law passed in 1936 that tightened the Clayton Act's prohibitions against price discrimination. An exception is made for circumstances like discounts for quantity purchases, as long as the discounts do not lessen competition. But a manufacturer cannot sell at a lower price to one company just because that company buys all its merchandise from the manufacturer. Also, if one firm is offered quantity discounts, all firms buying that quantity of goods must get the discounts. The FTC and the antitrust division of the Justice Department monitor pricing.

consumerism

A social movement that seeks to increase the rights and powers of buyers vis-à-vis sellers.

Consumer Protection Laws **Consumerism** reflects the struggle for power between buyers and sellers. Specifically, it is a social movement seeking to increase the rights and powers of buyers vis-à-vis sellers. Sellers' rights and powers include the following:

- To introduce into the marketplace any product, in any size and style, that is not hazardous to personal health or safety, or if it is hazardous, to introduce it with the proper warnings and controls.
- To price the product at any level they wish, provided they do not discriminate among similar classes of buyers.
- To spend any amount of money they wish to promote the product, so long as the promotion does not constitute unfair competition.
- To formulate any message they wish about the product, provided that it is not misleading or dishonest in content or execution.
- To introduce any buying incentives they wish.

Meanwhile, buyers have the following rights and powers:

- To refuse to buy any product that is offered to them.
- To expect products to be safe.
- To expect a product to be essentially as the seller represents it.
- To receive adequate information about the product.

Many laws have been passed to protect consumer rights. Exhibit 4A-2 lists the major consumer protection laws.

deregulation

The removal of rules and regulations governing business competition.

Deregulation of Industries During the 1980s and 1990s, the U.S. government has actively promoted **deregulation,** the removal of rules and regulations governing business competition. Deregulation has drastically changed some once-regulated industries (especially the transportation, telecommunications, and

> e x h i b i t   4 A - 2 <
| Key Consumer Protection Laws

Mail Fraud Act (1872)	Makes it a federal crime to defraud consumers through use of the mail.
Pure Food and Drug Act (1906)	Created the Food and Drug Administration (FDA); protects consumers against the interstate sale of unsafe and adulterated foods and drugs.
Food, Drug, and Cosmetic Act (1938)	Expanded the power of the FDA to cover cosmetics and therapeutic devices and to establish standards for food products.
Flammable Fabrics Act (1953)	Prohibits sale or manufacture of clothing made of dangerously flammable fabric.
Child Protection Act (1966)	Prohibits sale of harmful toys and gives the FDA the right to remove dangerous products from the marketplace.
Cigarette Labeling Act (1965)	Requires cigarette manufacturers to put labels warning consumers about health hazards on cigarette packages.
Fair Packaging and Labeling Act (1966)	Regulates labeling and packaging of consumer products.
Consumer Credit Protection Act (Truth-in-Lending Act) (1968)	Requires lenders to fully disclose to borrowers the loan terms and the costs of borrowing (interest rate, application fees, etc.).
Fair Credit Reporting Act (1971)	Requires consumers denied credit on the basis of reports from credit agencies to be given access to their reports and to be allowed to correct inaccurate information.
Consumer Product Safety Act (1972)	Created the Consumer Product Safety Commission, an independent federal agency, to establish and enforce consumer product safety standards.
Equal Credit Opportunity Act (1975)	Prohibits denial of credit on the basis of gender, marital status, race, religion, age, or national origin.
Magnuson-Moss Warranty Act (1975)	Requires that warranties be written in clear language and that terms be fully disclosed.
Fair Debt Collection Practice Act (1978)	Makes it illegal to harass or abuse any person, to make false statements, or to use unfair methods when collecting a debt.
Alcohol Labeling Legislation (1988)	Provides for warning labels on liquor saying that women shouldn't drink when pregnant and that alcohol impairs our abilities.
Nutrition Labeling and Education Act (1990)	Requires truthful and uniform nutritional labeling on every food the FDA regulates.
Children's Television Act (1990)	Limits the amount of advertising to be shown during children's television programs to not more than 10.5 minutes per hour on weekends and not more than 12.0 minutes per hour on weekdays.
Americans with Disabilities Act (ADA) (1990)	Protects the rights of people with disabilities; makes discrimination against the disabled illegal in public accommodations, transportation, and telecommunications.
Brady Law (1998)	Imposes a 5-day waiting period and a background check before a gun purchaser can take possession of the gun.

financial services industries) and created many new competitors. The result has been entries into and exits from some industries. One of the latest industries to deregulate is the electric power industry. With almost 200 investor-owned electric utilities, it is the largest industry to be deregulated so far. California became the first state to deregulate electricity. Consumers can now buy electricity from several different suppliers, either local utilities or those in other states. In some parts of California, electric rates have risen rather than fallen, however. As a result, there is a movement to re-regulate electricity in California.

Despite the California experience, consumers typically benefit from deregulation. Increased competition often means lower prices. Businesses also benefit because they have more freedom to operate and can avoid the costs associated with government regulations. But more competition can also make it hard for small or weak firms to survive.

Regulation of the Internet Although 70 million Americans are signing onto the Web regularly, only a minority do so to purchase products. The majority of electronic commerce remains business-to-business transactions. Americans are still far more likely to get the latest news, rather than the latest fashions, in cyberspace. Yet there are clear successes: Amazon.com is America's biggest bookstore. Egghead Software holds hyperauctions in cyberspace to sell off surplus items. Loyal Wal-Mart shoppers can browse for discounts at the retail giant's Web site.

Many states would like to tax commerce on the Internet. Washington, however, has promised to stop any such activity. In June 1997, the White House released "A Framework for Global Electronic Commerce," which advocated a minimalist approach to government intervention in electronic commerce. After providing a Universal Commercial Code for Electronic Commerce and protecting intellectual property, there's not much more for the government to do, according to the framework. And in November 1997, the TransAtlantic Business Dialogue, an international group composed of executives from such giants as Coca-Cola, Erickson, Ford, France Telecom, Goodyear, Pfizer, and Time Warner, released a report that called for governments to sit back and let markets evolve standards for privacy protection and encryption. Governments, the report asserted, should refrain from levying special taxes on electronic transactions, while working with the private sector to harmonize international legal standards and protecting intellectual property.

Taxation of Business

Taxes are sometimes seen as the price we pay to live in this country. Taxes are assessed by all levels of government on both business and individuals, and they are used to pay for the services provided by government. The federal government is the largest collector of taxes, accounting for 54 percent of all tax dollars. States are next, followed closely by local government taxes. The average American family pays about 37 percent of its income for taxes, 28 percent to the federal government and 9 percent to state and local governments.

Income Taxes **Income taxes** are based on the income received by businesses and individuals. The income taxes paid to the federal government are set by Congress, regulated by the Internal Revenue Code, and collected by the Internal Revenue Service. These taxes are *progressive,* meaning that rates increase as income increases. Most of the states and some large cities also collect income taxes from individuals and businesses. The state and local governments establish their own rules and tax rates.

Other Types of Taxes Besides income taxes, individuals and businesses pay a number of other taxes. The four main types are property taxes, payroll taxes, sales taxes, and excise taxes.

Property taxes are assessed on real and personal property, based on the assessed value of the property. They raise quite a bit of revenue for state and local governments. Most states tax land and buildings. Property taxes may be based on fair market value (what a buyer would pay), a percentage of fair market value, or replacement value (what it would cost today to rebuild or buy something like the original). The value on which the taxes are based is the assessed value.

Any business that has employees and meets a payroll must pay **payroll taxes,** the employer's share of Social Security taxes and federal and state unemployment taxes. These taxes must be paid on wages, salaries, and commissions. State unemployment taxes are based on the number of employees in a firm who have become eligible for unemployment benefits. A firm that has never had an employee become eligible for unemployment will pay a low rate of state

>lg 9

income taxes
Taxes that are based on the income received by businesses and individuals.

property taxes
Taxes that are imposed on real and personal property based on the assessed value of the property.

payroll taxes
The employer's share of Social Security taxes and federal and state unemployment taxes.

sales taxes

Taxes that are levied on goods when they are sold; calculated as a percentage of the price.

excise taxes

Taxes that are imposed on specific items such as gasoline, alcoholic beverages, airline tickets, and guns.

unemployment taxes. The firm's experience with employment benefits does not affect federal unemployment tax rates.

Sales taxes are levied on goods when they are sold and are a percentage of the sales price. These taxes are imposed by states, counties, and cities. They vary in amount and in what is considered taxable. Some states have no sales tax. Others tax some categories (such as appliances) but not others (such as clothes). Still others tax all retail products except food, magazines, and prescription drugs. Sales taxes increase the cost of goods to the consumer. Businesses bear the burden of collecting sales taxes and sending them to the government.

Excise taxes are placed on specific items, such as gasoline, alcoholic beverages, cigarettes, airline tickets, cars, and guns. They can be assessed by federal, state, and local governments. In many cases, these taxes help pay for services related to the item taxed. For instance, gasoline excise taxes are often used to build and repair highways. Other excise taxes—like those on alcoholic beverages, cigarettes, and guns—are used to control practices that may cause harm.

chapter five

Forms of Business Ownership

learning goals

>lg 1   What are the three main forms of business organization, and what factors should a company's owners consider when selecting a form?

>lg 2   What are the advantages and disadvantages of sole proprietorships?

>lg 3   Why would a new business venture choose to operate as a partnership, and what downside would the partners face?

>lg 4   How does the corporate structure provide advantages and disadvantages to a company, and what are the major types of corporations?

>lg 5   Does a company have any business organization options besides sole proprietorship, partnership, and corporation?

>lg 6   Why is franchising growing in importance?

>lg 7   Why would a company use mergers and acquisitions to grow?

>lg 8   What trends will affect business organization in the future?

It's a Match with JobDirect, Inc.

Sometimes the best ideas are born out of desperation. Sharing a taxi in Boston in June 1995 and commiserating about their difficulties finding jobs, college juniors Sara Sutton and Rachel Bell wondered why there wasn't an Internet service geared toward entry-level jobs and internships. Taking Bell's father's advice—"When you go out into the real world, you don't have to work for a company. You can start one yourself."—the two women spent several months testing the feasibility of using Internet technology to match students with jobs. Although they had no business or technical experience, they believed that their idea had merit and took leaves of absence—Sutton from the University of California at Berkeley and Bell from Hobart & William Smith College—to start JobDirect (**www.jobdirect.com**).

After developing a business plan and raising about $60,000 from family and friends, they were ready to start the company. But what form should their business take? Should they be partners or form a corporation? Although partnerships are easy to set up, Sutton and Bell would be personally liable for all the company's financial obligations. And could a partnership attract enough money to grow the company? In June 1996, they formed an S corporation because of tax advantages and limited liability.

Bell and Sutton also realized they needed professional managers and technology experts. In the spring of 1996, they hired former Tufts University professor and small business consultant Robert Ford as president and chief operating officer and Microsoft alumnus Jesse Keller as vice president, development in charge of Web systems, along with sales and marketing staff.

As the scope of their venture grew, so did the need for additional funding. "We wanted to have our corporate house in order from the earliest stages, giving us credibility and flexibility to attract investors in a fast moving Internet business environment," explains president Rob Ford. "We also wanted a structure that allowed us to develop JobDirect as a national brand." In August 1996, JobDirect incorporated in Connecticut as a regular, or C, corporation, which was better suited to the company's long-term growth plan. Soon after, the company's new law firm—a specialist in small high-growth companies—advised JobDirect to reincorporate in Delaware to avoid Connecticut's restrictive securities laws.

To differentiate JobDirect from other Web database services, the management group decided to take their service directly to college campuses to create awareness of their free Internet service and build

Critical Thinking Questions

As you read this chapter, consider the following questions as they relate to JobDirect, Inc.:

- What factors should Bell and Sutton consider when selecting a form of business organization?
- What are some of the pros and cons they would encounter if they organized as a partnership?
- How does incorporating benefit their business?

relationships. They also developed the technology to cross-reference the qualifications on posted résumés with current positions and notify the students directly about appropriate positions via e-mail. Students could also search the job database, and employers could perform targeted searches of student résumés.

In September 1996, Bell and Sutton took their show on the road—literally. They visited 43 colleges in a "JobDrive" recreational vehicle with 15 laptop computers so students could submit résumés directly into JobDirect's database. Word of JobDirect's novel approach spread as people learned about this efficient way for entry-level job seekers and potential employers to exchange information. By June 1997, JobDirect, Inc. had three JobDrive RVs traveling throughout the United States, 50,000 student résumés in its database, and 80 employer clients listing 15,000 positions. Through 1998 the corporation raised $3.5 million from about 60 private stockholders and venture capital firms (institutional investors that finance young companies).[1]

BUSINESS IN THE 21ST CENTURY

Selecting the corporate form of business ownership allows Job-Direct to attract the investors it needs to finance the company's growth in the fast-paced Internet environment.

As business novices, Rachel Bell and Sara Sutton knew very little about choosing a form of business organization for their new venture. They were fortunate to have good advisers who helped them understand the pros and cons of partnerships, limited liability companies, and corporations. They also learned that a company may need to change its legal form as it grows.

If you, like Rachel and Sara, dream of owning your own business, you are not alone. In 1997, for example, almost 900,000 new companies opened their doors for business—and that includes only firms with employees. If one-person businesses were counted, the number would be even higher.

Regardless of size, every new business must choose a form of business organization that reflects its goals. In this chapter we will look at the different ways to organize a business. The three main types of business organization—sole proprietorships, partnerships, and corporations—all have advantages and disadvantages. Other business structures, such as cooperatives, joint ventures, and franchising, are appropriate for special situations. Next we will explore how corporations use mergers and acquisitions to grow. Finally, we'll look ahead at trends shaping business organization in the future.

TYPES OF BUSINESS ORGANIZATION

>lg 1

Congratulations! You've decided to start a company. You've got a great idea and some start-up funding. Before you go any further, however, you must set up your business entity. Which form of business organization best suits the needs of your particular business?

To choose wisely, you must ask several key questions: Do you want to own the business alone or with other participants? How much operating control do the owners want? Who will be liable for the firm's debts and taxes? Can the firm attract employees? What costs are associated with the chosen ownership structure? How easy will it be to find financing? How will the business be taxed? The answers determine the legal ownership structure you will select.

Most businesses fall into one of three major ownership categories: sole proprietorships, partnerships, or corporations. As Exhibit 5-1 illustrates, sole proprietorships are the most popular form of business ownership. They account for 73 percent of all businesses, compared to 20 percent for corporations and 7 percent for partnerships. Most sole proprietorships and partnerships remain small, however, so corporations generate about 90 percent of total business sales and 72 percent of the profits.

Each form of business ownership has advantages and disadvantages. As we'll discover in the following sections, the form that offers the most advantages in the early stages of a company's life may no longer meet its needs as it grows.

SOLE PROPRIETORSHIPS

>lg 2

Starting Hot Pots, a San Diego company that specializes in container gardens for small spaces, gave owner Gail Cecil the chance to combine her love of gardening

> e x h i b i t 5 - 1 <

Comparison of Forms of Business Organization

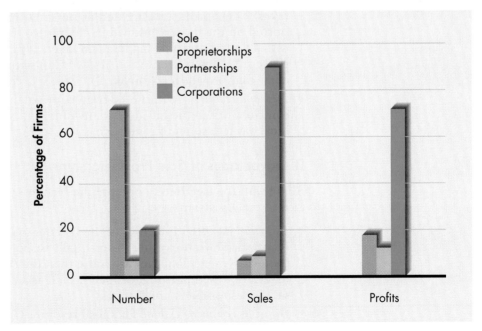

SOURCE: Internal Revenue Service, as reported in U.S. Bureau of the Census, *Statistical Abstract of the United States, 1998,* 118th ed. (Washington, DC.: Government Printing Office, 1998), p. 540.

with her desire to bring beauty into people's homes. All she needed to get started was her expertise in horticulture, a business license, and the money for business cards, plants, pots, and related materials. "I love being my own boss and the challenge of creating new designs for each location," she says. At the same time, Gail has no guaranteed paycheck, and the work can be lonely: "It's hard to stay motivated. Some days I really have to push myself to look for new clients."[2]

sole proprietorship
A business that is established, owned, operated, and often financed by one person.

Gail Cecil formed Hot Pots as a **sole proprietorship,** a business that is established, owned, operated, and often financed by one person. Your neighborhood florist, shoe repair shop, construction company, and hair salon are usually sole proprietorships. Small service businesses, such as lawyers, accountants, consultants, landscapers, and real estate agents, often operate as sole proprietorships. In fact, almost half of all sole proprietorships offer services.

Advantages of Sole Proprietorships

Sole proprietorships have several advantages that make them popular:

- *Easy and inexpensive to form.* As Gail Cecil discovered, sole proprietorships have few legal requirements, and forming one doesn't cost much. Once the owner obtains the start-up funds and necessary local licenses and permits, he or she can start the business.
- *Profits that all go to the owner.* The owner of a sole proprietorship gets all the profits the business earns. The more efficiently the firm operates, the higher the profits.
- *Direct control of the business.* Successful sole proprietors like Gail Cecil thrive on their independence. They like being their own boss and controlling all business decisions without having to consult anyone else. It's easy to respond quickly to changing business conditions.
- *Freedom from government regulations.* Although all businesses are subject to some government controls, sole proprietorships have more freedom than other business forms.
- *No special taxation.* Proprietorships do not pay special franchise or corporate taxes. Their profits are treated as personal income of the owner and reported on the owner's individual tax return. Business income is combined with all other personal income and taxed at personal rates ranging from 15 percent to 39.6 percent (as of 1998). Combining business and personal income may provide a tax break.
- *Ease of dissolution.* With no co-owners or partners involved, the proprietor can close or sell the business at any time. Thus, sole proprietorships are an ideal way to test new business ideas.

Disadvantages of Sole Proprietorships

Along with the freedom to operate the business as they wish, sole proprietors face several disadvantages:

- *Unlimited liability.* In the eyes of the law, the sole proprietor and the firm are identical. Thus, the owner is personally responsible for all the debts of the business—even when they are more than the company is worth. The owner may have to sell personal property, such as a car, house, or investments, to satisfy claims against the business.
- *Difficulty in raising capital.* Financial resources are more limited for sole proprietorships. Business lenders view the owner's unlimited liability as a high risk. Business assets are not protected from claims of personal creditors. Owners must often use personal funds—borrowing on credit cards, taking

second mortgages on their homes, and selling investments—to finance the business. Inability to raise additional funding may curtail expansion plans.

- *Limited managerial expertise.* The success of a sole proprietorship depends entirely on the owner's skills and talents. The owner is fully responsible for all business decisions and must be a "jack-of-all-trades." Not all owners are equally skilled in all areas. An inventor who creates a new product may not be a good salesperson, production manager, or accountant.

- *Trouble finding qualified employees.* Sole proprietors have difficulty finding and keeping good employees. Small firms cannot offer the same fringe benefits and opportunities for advancement as larger companies.

- *Personal time commitment.* Running a sole proprietorship requires a huge time commitment and often dominates the owner's life. The owner must be willing to make sacrifices, often working 12 or more hours a day, six or seven days a week.

- *Unstable business life.* The life span of a sole proprietorship is uncertain. If the owner loses interest, retires, or dies, the business will cease to exist unless the owner finds a buyer.

- *Losses that all go to the owner.* The sole proprietor is responsible for all losses. However, tax law allows the proprietor to deduct these losses from other types of personal income.

The sole proprietorship may be a suitable choice for a one-person start-up operation that has no employees and little risk of liability exposure, like Hot Pots. For many sole proprietors, however, this is a temporary choice. As the business grows, the owner may not have the managerial and financial resources to operate alone. At this point she or he may decide to go into partnership with one or more co-owners.

concept check

- What is a sole proprietorship?
- Why do so many businesspeople choose this form of business organization?
- What are the drawbacks to being a sole proprietor?

PARTNERSHIPS

>lg 3

Brett Cosor had an idea for a company that provides big-screen multimedia installations for special events. However, he realized that his strengths were in the creative vision rather than the nuts-and-bolts details of the business. In 1988 he recruited his cousin Jeff Studley to handle the operational side of CPR MultiMedia Solutions, based in Gaithersburg, Maryland. The cousins' abilities were complementary. "Brett is a goal-oriented guy; I'm a task-oriented guy," explains Studley. By 1998, their partnership had grown into a business with two divisions, 47 employees, and revenues of $10 million.[3]

For those like Brett Cosor who don't want to "go it alone," the partnership offers another form of business ownership. A **partnership** is an association of two or more persons who agree to operate a business together for profit. Some professional services firms—for example, law firms, accounting firms, investment banks, stock brokerages, and real estate companies—are set up as partnerships.

Forming a partnership is simple. The parties agree, either orally or in writing, to share in the profits and losses of a joint enterprise. Written partnership agreements that spell out the terms and conditions of the partnership can prevent later conflicts between the partners. These agreements typically include the name and purpose of the partnership, contributions of each partner (financial, talent, equipment, etc.), management responsibilities and duties of each partner, compensation arrangements (salaries and shares of profits), provisions covering the addition of new partners and sale of partnership interests, and procedures for resolving conflicts, dissolving the business, and distributing assets.

partnership

An association of two or more persons who agree to operate a business together for profit.

general partnership

A partnership in which all partners share in the management and profits. Each partner can act on behalf of the firm and has unlimited liability for all its business obligations.

limited partnership

A partnership with one or more general partners, who have unlimited liability, and one or more limited partners, whose liability is limited to the amount of their investment.

general partners

Partners who have unlimited liability for all of the firm's business obligations and who control its operations.

limited partners

Partners whose liability for the firm's business obligations is limited to the amount of their investment. They help to finance the business, but do not participate in the firm's operations.

There are two basic types of partnerships: general and limited. In a **general partnership,** all partners share in the management and profits. They co-own assets, and each can act on behalf of the firm. Each partner has unlimited liability for all the business obligations of the firm. A **limited partnership** has two types of partners: one or more **general partners,** who have unlimited liability, and one or more **limited partners,** whose liability is limited to the amount of their investment. In return for limited liability, limited partners agree not to take part in the day-to-day management of the firm. They help to finance the business, but the general partners maintain operational control.

Advantages of Partnerships

Some advantages of partnerships come quickly to mind:

- *Ease of formation.* Like sole proprietorships, partnerships are easy to form. The partners agree to do business together and develop a partnership agreement. For most partnerships, applicable state laws are not complex.
- *Availability of capital.* Because two or more people contribute financial resources, partnerships can raise funds more easily for operating expenses and business expansion. The partners' combined financial strength also increases the firm's ability to raise funds from outside sources.
- *Diversity of skills and expertise.* Partners share the responsibility for managing and operating the business. Ideal partnerships bring together people with complementary backgrounds, rather than those with similar experience. Combining partner skills to set goals, manage the overall direction of the firm, and solve problems increases the likelihood of the partnership's success. Finding the right partner entails looking at your own strengths and weaknesses and examining what you're looking for in a partner. In Exhibit 5-2 you'll find some advice on choosing a partner.
- *Flexibility.* General partners take an active role in managing their firm and can respond quickly to changes in the business environment.
- *No special taxes.* Partnerships pay no income taxes. A partnership must file a partnership return with the Internal Revenue Service that reports the amount of profit and how it was divided among the partners. Each partner's profit or loss is then reported on the partner's personal income tax return, with profits taxed at personal tax rates.
- *Relative freedom from government control.* Except for state rules for licensing and permits, the government has little control over partnership activities.

Disadvantages of Partnerships

Despite their advantages, partnerships also have their downside:

- *Unlimited liability.* All general partners have unlimited liability for the debts of the business. In fact, any one partner can be held personally liable for all partnership debts and legal judgments (like malpractice)—regardless of who caused them. As with sole proprietorships, business failure can lead to a loss of the general partners' personal assets. To overcome this disadvantage, many states now allow the formation of limited liability partnerships (LLPs). The LLP limits each individual partner's liability to harm resulting from his or her own acts, but not for the acts of the other partners.
- *Potential for conflicts between partners.* Partners may have different ideas—personal or business—about such matters as how and when to expand the business, which employees to hire, and how to allocate responsibilities. As CPR MultiMedia's business grew, so did the strain of managing a larger company. Differences in their personalities and work styles caused major clashes and a communications breakdown between Cosor and Studley. "We stopped

> e x h i b i t   5 - 2 <

Picking the Right Partner

Picking a partner is an art, not a science. Be prepared to talk, talk, talk—about everything. On paper someone may have all the right business credentials. But does that person share the ideas you have for your company? And honesty, integrity, and ethics are equally, if not more, important. After all, you may be liable for what your partner does. Be willing to trust your intuition. "Trust those gut feelings—they're probably right," advises Irwin Gray, author of *The Perils of Partners*. First, ask yourself the following questions. Then ask a potential partner and see how well your answers match.

1. Why do you want a partner?
2. What characteristics and talents does each person bring to the partnership?
3. How will you divide partnership responsibilities? Consider every aspect of the business, from long-range planning to daily operations. Who will handle marketing, sales, accounting, customer service?
4. What is your long-term vision for the business (size, life span, financial commitment, etc.)?
5. What are your personal reasons for forming this company—for example, steady paycheck, independence, creating a company that stays small, building a large company?
6. Are all parties willing to put in the same amount of time, and if not, is there an alternative arrangement that is acceptable to everyone?
7. Do you have similar work ethics and values on how to run the company? Is the person honest?
8. What requirements should be included in the partnership agreement?

SOURCES: Julie Bawden Davis, "Buddy System," *Business Start Ups* (June 1998), downloaded from **www.entrepreneurmag.com;** Azriela Jaffe, "'Till Death Do Us Part' Is No Way to Start a Business," *Business Week Online* (October 23, 1998), downloaded from **www.businessweek.com/ smallbiz;** Jerry Useem, "Partners on the Edge," *Inc.* (August 1998), pp. 54, 59.

pulling in the same direction in the same harness," says Studley. "All of a sudden there were two moons pushing tides in different directions, and that creates a lot of turbulence." To save the business, the cousins began working through their differences with the help of a psychologist who specialized in counseling troubled business partners.[4]

- *Sharing of profits.* Dividing the profits is relatively easy if all partners contribute about the same amount of time, expertise, and capital. But if one partner provides more money and the other puts in more time, it is more difficult to arrive at a fair profit-sharing formula.

- *Difficulty in leaving or ending a partnership.* Partnerships are easier to form than to leave. Suppose one partner wants to leave. How much is that partner's share worth? Is there a buyer who is acceptable to the other partners? If a partner owning more than 50 percent of the entity withdraws, dies, or becomes disabled, the partnership must reorganize or end. To avoid these problems, most partnership agreements include specific guidelines for transfer of partnership interests and buy-sell agreements so that surviving partners can buy a deceased partner's interest. Partners often buy special life insurance policies on each partner that fund this purchase.

You can see why business partnerships are often compared to marriages. As with marriage, choosing the right partner is critical. If you're considering forming a partnership, allow plenty of time to evaluate both your own and your potential partner's goals, personalities, business values, and work habits. You might even decide to go into partnership with your spouse. Learn more about this growing trend in the Focusing on Small Business box.

c o n c ə p t c h ə c k

- How does a partnership differ from a sole proprietorship?
- Describe briefly the three types of partnerships and explain the difference between a general partner and a limited partner.
- What are the main advantages and disadvantages of partnerships, and how do they compare to sole proprietorships?

PERFECT PARTNERS

Looking for the perfect partner for your business? Sometimes the best person is close at hand—your spouse. It worked for Paula Mae Schwartz, who needed a partner to handle the growing demands of her public relations (PR) firm for high-tech companies. She convinced her husband Steve, a vice president at a software developer, to join her in 1990. It was a natural fit. He understood the services her target clients required and could also "talk the talk," while Paula Mae knew how to pull together PR campaigns. The business partnership worked as well as their personal one. Today, Schwartz Communications is one of the country's fastest growing high-tech PR agencies, with 150 employees, East and West Coast offices, and over 80 clients.

The Schwartzes represent two growing trends: married couples teaming up for business ventures and people leaving corporate life to start their own companies. Whether they organize as a partnership or become co-owners of a corporation, spouses have a head start. They know each other's strengths and weaknesses and can also structure the firm to allow for more family time, perhaps by working at home.

Going into business with a spouse has pitfalls as well, however. "You have to have a strong marriage going in to it," advises Fran Rogers of Work/Family Directions, a national consulting firm (who also partners with her husband). One risk is too much togetherness. The Schwartzes avoided problems from the start by carefully structuring their business relationship and setting rules. They acknowledged their separate identities, allocating responsibilities based on individual strengths and weaknesses. Steve ran sales and marketing; Paula Mae, internal operations. Physical separation—offices at opposite ends of the company—helped, too. Mutual respect is also important. They learned to trust each other's judgment, to compromise, and to keep personal issues and egos out of the business—no easy task.

Critical Thinking Questions

1. What are the pros and cons of going into business with your spouse, as opposed to a non-family partner?
2. How did the Schwartzes' approach to their business venture contribute to its success?
3. Suggest some ground rules to help the Schwartzes separate their work and personal lives.

CORPORATIONS

corporation

A legal entity with an existence and life separate from its owners, who therefore are not personally liable for the entity's debts. A corporation is chartered by the state in which it is formed and can own property, enter into contracts, sue and be sued, and engage in business operations under the terms of its charter.

When people think of corporations, they typically think of major, well-known corporations like IBM, Microsoft, General Electric, and Procter & Gamble. Corporations range in size from large multinational corporations like these, with sales in the billions of dollars and thousands of employees, to small firms with a few employees and revenues under $25,000.

A **corporation** is a legal entity with an existence and life separate from its owners. Because of this separation, the owners are not personally liable for the corporation's debts. A corporation is subject to the laws of the state in which it is formed. The state issues a charter that gives the corporation the right to operate as a business and specifies its business goals. A corporation can own property, enter into contracts, sue and be sued, and engage in business operations under the terms of its charter. Unlike sole proprietorships and partnerships, corporations are taxable entities.

Corporations play an important role in the U.S. economy. As we saw in Exhibit 5-1, corporations account for only 20 percent of all businesses but generate about 90 percent of all revenues and 72 percent of the profits. Just scan

Exhibit 5-3, the 10 largest U.S. corporations, and you will see many familiar names that affect our lives every day. In 1998, the top 500 industrial and service corporations, as ranked by *Fortune,* accounted for over $5.5 trillion in sales and almost $325 billion in profits. Yet many individuals and small businesses also incorporate to benefit from the advantages of this form of business organization. Over 70 percent of all corporations have sales under $500,000.

The Incorporation Process

Setting up a corporation is more complex than starting a sole proprietorship or partnership. Most states base their laws for chartering corporations on the Model Business Corporation Act of the American Bar Association. Nevertheless, registration procedures, fees, taxes, and laws regulating corporations do vary from state to state.

Which Fortune 500 company had the biggest revenue increase? The highest profits? Highest return to investors? What is the largest entertainment company? Get all the details on the largest U.S. companies at

www.pathfinder.com/ fortune/fortune500/

A firm doesn't have to incorporate in the state where it is based. It may benefit by comparing the rules in several states before choosing a state of incorporation. Although it is a small state with few corporations actually based there, Delaware's pro-corporate policies have made it the state of incorporation for many companies, including about half of the Fortune 500.

Incorporating a company involves five main steps:

1. Selecting the company's name
2. Writing the *articles of incorporation* (see Exhibit 5-4) and filing them with the appropriate state office, usually the secretary of state
3. Paying required fees and taxes
4. Holding an organizational meeting
5. Adopting bylaws, electing directors, and passing the first operating resolutions

> e x h i b i t   5 - 3 <

The 10 Largest U.S. Corporations (Ranked by 1998 Sales)

1998 Rank	Company	Sales ($ Millions)	Profits ($ Millions)
1	General Motors	$161,315	$ 2,956
2	Ford Motor	144,416	22,070
3	Wal-Mart Stores	139,208	4,430
4	Exxon	100,697	6,370
5	General Electric	100,469	9,296
6	IBM	81,667	6,328
7	Citigroup	76,431	5,807
8	Philip Morris	57,813	5,372
9	Boeing	56,154	1,120
10	AT&T	53,588	6,398

SOURCE: "The Fortune 500," *Fortune* (April 26, 1999), p. F-1.

The state issues the corporate charter based on the information in the articles of incorporation. Once the corporation has its charter, it holds an organizational meeting to adopt bylaws, elect directors, and pass initial operating resolutions. *Bylaws* provide the legal and managerial guidelines for operating the firm.

The Corporate Structure

As Exhibit 5-5 shows, corporations have their own organizational structure with three important components: stockholders, directors, and officers.

The owners of a corporation are its **stockholders,** or *shareholders,* who hold shares of stock that provide certain rights. They may receive a share of the corporation's profits in the form of dividends, and they can sell or transfer their ownership in the corporation (the shares of stock) at any time. Stockholders can attend annual meetings, elect the board of directors, and vote on matters that affect the corporation, as the charter and bylaws specify. They generally have one vote for each share of stock they own.

Stockholders elect a **board of directors** to govern the corporation. The directors handle overall management of the corporation. They set major corporate goals and policies, hire corporate officers, and oversee the firm's operations and finances. Small firms may have as few as 3 directors, whereas large corporations usually have 15 to 25. Large corporations typically include both corporate executives and *outside directors* (not employed by the organization) chosen for their professional and personal expertise. Because they are inde-

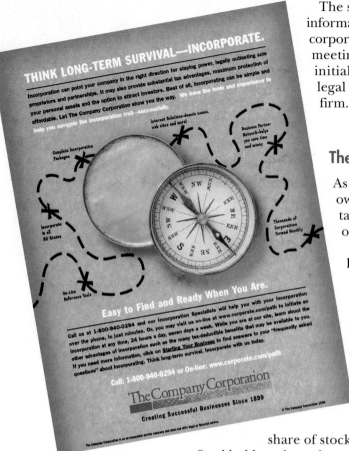

The Company Corporation guides firms through the steps of incorporating and informs them of the corporate structure's many tax-deductible benefits.

stockholders

The owners of a corporation, who hold shares of stock that provide certain rights; also known as *shareholders.*

board of directors

A group of people elected by the stockholders to handle the overall management of a corporation, such as setting corporate goals and policies, hiring corporate officers, and overseeing the firm's operations and finances.

> e x h i b i t   5 - 4 <

Articles of Incorporation

Articles of incorporation are prepared on a form authorized or supplied by the state of incorporation. Although they may vary slightly from state to state, all articles of incorporation include the following key items:

- Name of the corporation
- The company's goals
- Types of stock and number of shares of each type to issue
- Life of the corporation (usually "perpetual," meaning with no time limit)
- Minimum investment by the owners

- Methods for transferring shares of stock
- Address of the corporate office
- Names and addresses of the first board of directors
- Names and addresses of the incorporators
- Other public information the incorporators wish to include

Organizational Structure of Corporations

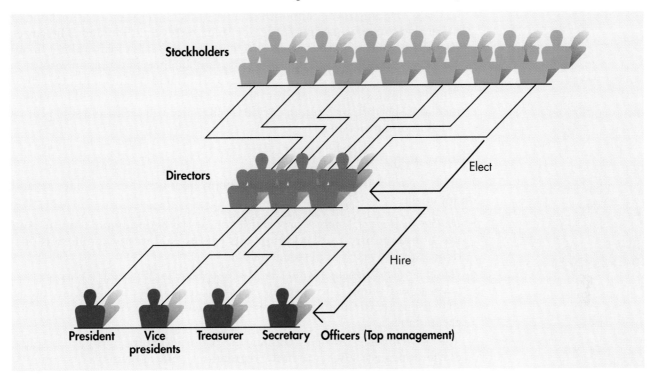

pendent of the firm, outside directors can bring a fresh view to the corporation's activities.

The *officers* of a corporation are its top management. Hired by the board, they include the president and chief executive officer (CEO), vice-presidents, treasurer, and secretary and are responsible for achieving corporate goals and policies. Officers may also be board members and stockholders.

Advantages of Corporations

Certain features enable corporations to merge financial and human resources into enterprises with great potential for growth and profits:

- *Limited liability.* This is one of the key advantages of corporations. Because a corporation is a legal entity that exists apart from its owners, a stockholder's liability for the debts of the firm is limited to the amount of the stock owned. If the corporation goes bankrupt, creditors can look only to the assets of the corporation for payment.

- *Ease of transferring ownership.* Stockholders of public corporations can sell their shares to someone else at any time without affecting the status of the corporation.

- *Unlimited life.* The life of a corporation is unlimited. Although corporate charters specify a number of years of life, they also include rules for renewal. The corporation is separate from its owners, so unlike a sole proprietorship or partnership, death or withdrawal of an owner does not affect its existence.

- *Tax deductions.* Corporations also are allowed certain tax deductions, such as for operating expenses, that reduce their taxable income. Under the current

(1998) tax code, corporate tax rates range from 15 to 35 percent, compared to 15 to 39.6 percent for individuals.

- *Ability to attract financing.* Corporations can raise money by selling new shares of stock. Dividing ownership into smaller units makes it more affordable to more investors, who can purchase one share or several thousand. The larger size and stability of corporations also help them get bank loans. These financial resources allow corporations to invest in facilities and human resources and grow much larger than sole proprietorships and partnerships. Clearly, it would be impossible to make automobiles, provide nationwide telecommunications services, or build major oil or chemical refineries as a sole proprietorship or partnership.

Disadvantages of Corporations

Although corporations offer businesses many benefits, they also have several disadvantages:

- *Double taxation of profits.* Corporations must pay federal and state income taxes on their profits. In addition, any profits paid to stockholders as dividends are also taxed as personal income.
- *Cost and complexity of formation.* As discussed earlier, forming a corporation takes several steps. The cost can run into thousands of dollars, including state filing, registration, and license fees, as well as the cost of attorneys and accountants.
- *More government restrictions.* Unlike sole proprietorships and partnerships, corporations are subject to many regulations and reporting requirements. For example, corporations must register in each state where they want to do business. Before selling stock to the public, they must register with the Securities and Exchange Commission (SEC). Unless it is closely held, the firm must publish financial reports on a regular basis. It must also file other special reports with the SEC and state and federal agencies. These reporting requirements impose substantial costs. Publishing information on corporate operations may also give an advantage to competitors.

Types of Corporations

Three types of corporate business organization provide limited liability. The "basic" corporate form of organization is the *conventional,* or *C, corporation.* Small businesses can also achieve limited liability through two other options: the S corporation and the limited liability company.

S Corporations   Double taxation of corporate profits is a major disadvantage for some small corporations. To avoid this problem, firms that meet certain size and ownership constraints can organize as S corporations. An **S corporation** is a hybrid entity that is organized like a corporation, with stockholders, directors, and officers, but taxed like a partnership. Income and losses flow through to the stockholders and are taxed as the personal income of the stockholders. S corporations can have only 75 qualifying shareholders and one class of stock. The owners of an S corporation are not personally liable for the debts of the corporation. About 2.2 million U.S. businesses enjoy the benefits of limited liability and special tax treatment that S corporations offer.

S corporation

A hybrid entity that is organized like a corporation, with stockholders, directors, and officers, but taxed like a partnership, with income and losses flowing through to the stockholders and taxed as their personal income.

limited liability company (LLC)

A hybrid organization that offers the same liability protection as a corporation but may be taxed as either a partnership or a corporation.

Confused about the differences between regular corporations, S corporations, and LLCs? Compare the three business structures at **www.4inc.com/compare.htm**

Limited Liability Companies A newer type of business entity, the **limited liability company (LLC)** is also a hybrid organization. Although LLCs are not corporations, like S corporations they appeal to small businesses. LLCs are easy to set up and are not subject to many restrictions. LLCs provide the same liability protection as corporations but offer the option of being taxed as either a partnership or a corporation. First authorized by Wyoming in 1977, LLCs became popular after a 1988 tax ruling that treats them like partnerships for tax purposes. Today, all states allow the formation of LLCs.

Exhibit 5-6 summarizes the advantages and disadvantages of each form of business ownership.

> e x h i b i t 5 - 6 < Advantages and Disadvantages of Major Types of Business Organization

	Sole Proprietorship	Partnership	Corporation
Advantages			
	Owner receives all profits.	More expertise and managerial skill available	Limited liability protects owners from losing more than they invest.
	Low organizational costs	Relatively low organizational costs	Can achieve large size due to marketability of stock (ownership)
	Income taxed as personal income of proprietor.	Income taxed as personal income of partners.	Ownership is readily transferable.
	Independence	Fund-raising ability is enhanced by more owners.	Long life of firm (not affected by death of owners)
	Secrecy		Can attract employees with specialized skills
	Ease of dissolution		Greater access to financial resources allows growth.
			Receives certain tax advantages
Disadvantages			
	Owner receives all losses.	Owners have unlimited liability; may have to cover debts of other, less financially sound partners.	Double taxation because both corporate profits and dividends paid to owners are taxed
	Owner has unlimited liability; total wealth can be taken to satisfy business debts.	Dissolves or must reorganize when partner dies	More expensive and complex to form
	Limited fund-raising ability can inhibit growth.	Difficult to liquidate or terminate	Subject to more government regulation
	Proprietor may have limited skills and management expertise.	Potential for conflicts between partners	Financial reporting requirements make operations public.
	Few long-range opportunities and benefits for employees	Difficult to achieve large-scale operations	
	Lacks continuity when owner dies		

SPECIALIZED FORMS OF BUSINESS ORGANIZATION

>lg 5

In addition to the three main forms, several specialized types of business organization play a role in our economy. We'll look at cooperatives and joint ventures in this section and take a more detailed look at franchising in the following section.

Cooperatives

cooperatives

Legal entities typically formed by people with similar interests, such as customers or suppliers, to reduce costs and gain economic power. A cooperative has limited liability, an unlimited life span, and an elected board of directors; all profits are distributed to the member-owners in proportion to their contributions.

Have you eaten a Sunkist orange or spread Land O' Lakes butter on your toast? If so, you've used items produced by cooperatives. **Cooperatives** are typically formed by people with similar interests, such as customers or suppliers, to reduce costs and gain economic power. The member-owners pay annual fees and share in any profits. Cooperatives may be organized to provide just about any good or service, such as business services, child care, financial services, food, health care, marketing of agricultural and other products, and utilities and cable television. Today, over 100 million people are members of 48,000 U.S. cooperatives with revenues of over $120 billion. In 1997, the top 100 cooperatives, led by the agriculture, grocery, and hardware/lumber industries, generated over $4 billion in revenues.[5]

Did you know that cooperatives market about 30 percent of farmers' products in the United States? For more co-op statistics, head to the National Cooperative Business Association Web site,

www.ncba.org/stats.cfm

A cooperative is a legal entity with several corporate features, such as limited liability, an unlimited life span, an elected board of directors, and an administrative staff. Cooperatives distribute all profits to the members in proportion to their contributions. Because they do not keep any profits, cooperatives do not pay taxes.

There are two types of cooperatives. *Seller cooperatives* are popular in agriculture. Individual producers join to compete more effectively with large producers. Member dues support market development, national advertising, and other business activities. In addition to Sunkist and Land O' Lakes, other familiar cooperatives are Calavo (avocados), Ocean Spray (cranberries and juices), and Blue Diamond (nuts). Farmland Industries, the largest cooperative in the United States, earned more than $9 billion from sales of feed, fertilizer, petroleum, and grain. *Buyer cooperatives* combine members' purchasing power. Buying in volume results in lower prices. Food cooperatives are one example. College bookstores may operate as buyer cooperatives. At the end of the year, members get shares of the profits based on how much they bought.

Cooperatives help small-business owners like the proprietor of this TrueValue hardware store compete with larger corporations.

By forming cooperatives to obtain discounts, small companies can lower costs, increase their efficiency, and compete with larger corporations. Many independent hardware store owners belong to True Value, Doing It Best, or Ace cooperatives. Robin Bryant, owner of a Doing It Best hardware store in Burlington, North Carolina, paid $2,700 to join that cooperative. In return, she received training in store management, as well as support from the cooperative. "They always get the answers I need quickly," she says. "They work with owners like myself because they really want us to succeed."

For Bryant, the cooperative route was the only way to survive against chain discounters like Home Depot and Lowe's. Among the benefits are the lower prices and greater merchandise variety she gets by ordering from the cooperative's centralized purchasing system.[6]

Joint Ventures

In a *joint venture* (defined in Chapter 3), two or more companies form an alliance to pursue a specific project, usually for a specific time period. There are many reasons for joint ventures. The project may be too large for one party to handle on its own. By forming joint ventures, companies can gain access to new markets, products, or technology. Both large and small companies benefit from joint ventures. Software giant Microsoft Corp. teamed up with Citibank and other partners for its TransPoint joint venture to offer nationwide online billing and bill-paying services. Young technology companies often form joint ventures with more established players to get wider distribution for their products. The joint venture brings the larger company access to the latest technology.

FRANCHISING

franchising

A form of business organization based on a business arrangement between a franchisor, which supplies the product concept, and the franchisee, who sells the goods or services of the franchisor in a certain geographic area.

franchisor

In a franchising arrangement, the company that supplies the product concept to the franchisee.

franchisee

In a franchising arrangement, the individual or company that sells the goods or services of the franchisor in a certain geographic area.

franchise agreement

A contract setting out the terms of a franchising arrangement, including the rules for running the franchise, the services provided by the franchisor, and the financial terms. Under the contract, the franchisee is allowed to use the franchisor's business name, trademark, and logo.

Andrea Brinkman, a critical care nurse, was burned out after seven years working for large health care organizations. After researching various franchise concepts, she joined the more than 500,000 Americans who own franchises. In 1996 she decided to capitalize on the growing demand for used retail goods and opened Children's Orchard, a resale franchise specializing in children's clothing, toys, and equipment. In addition to being her own boss, running her own retail outlet gave Brinkman the opportunity to develop personal relationships with her customers.[7]

Franchises come in all sizes, from McDonald's, with 23,000 franchises in over 100 countries, to Children's Orchard with about 80 units in several states, to new concepts still on the drawing boards. Chances are you deal with one of the more than 2,100 franchise systems in the United States and Canada almost every day. When you have lunch at Taco Bell or Jamba Juice, make copies at Kinko's, change your oil at Jiffy Lube, buy candles at Wicks 'n' Sticks, or drop your film off at Moto Photo, in each case you are dealing with a franchised business. These and other familiar name brands have come to mean quality, consistency, and value to customers.

Franchising, one of the fastest growing segments of the economy, provides a way to own a business without starting it from scratch. **Franchising** is a form of business organization that involves a business arrangement between a **franchisor,** the company that supplies the product concept, and the **franchisee,** the individual or company that sells the goods or services in a certain geographic area. With a franchise, the business owner buys a package: a proven product, proven operating methods, and training in managing the business.

The **franchise agreement** is a contract allowing the franchisee to use the franchisor's business name and its trademark and logo. The agreement outlines the rules for running the franchise, the services provided by the franchisor, and the financial terms. The franchisee agrees to keep inventory at certain levels, buy a standard equipment package, keep up sales and service levels, follow the franchisor's operating rules, take part in the franchisor's promotions, and maintain a relationship with the franchisor. In return, the franchisor generally provides the use of a proven company name and symbols, building plans and help finding a site, guidance and training, management assistance, managerial and accounting procedures, employee training, wholesale prices on supplies, and financial assistance.

Advantages of Franchises

Like other forms of business organization, franchising offers some distinct advantages:

- *Increased ability for franchisor to expand.* Because franchisees finance their own units, franchisors can grow without making a major investment. Although franchisors give up a share of profits to their franchisees, they receive ongoing revenues in the form of royalty payments. In 1998 Diedrich Coffee, Inc., a 36-unit specialty coffee chain based in southern California, turned to franchising to expand nationally. It signed a franchise agreement with Tacala, Inc., the largest U.S. Taco Bell franchisee, to develop 44 coffee houses and 35 carts and kiosks in North Carolina. Through 2003 Diedrich plans to add 1,500 coffee houses through regional franchising agreements in new geographic areas. "It would take us 10 years to build out what we can do in less than half that time using franchisees," said Tim Ryan, Diedrich's president. He added that franchisees are in a better position to adapt the company's concepts to local markets.[8]

- *Recognized name, product, and operating concept.* The franchisee gets a widely known and accepted business with a proven track record, as well as operating procedures, standard goods and services, and national advertising. Consumers know they can depend on products from such franchises as Pizza Hut, Hertz, and Holiday Inn. As a result, the franchisee's risk is reduced and the opportunity for success rises.

> m a k i n g   e t h i c a l   c h o i c e s <

JOHN PARK'S UNUSUAL BUSINESS PRACTICES

John Park, one of the hottest Athlete's Foot franchisees in the nation, owns nine stores in some of Chicago's toughest neighborhoods. Park estimates that about 90 percent of his sales staff have criminal records. Occasionally, he hires people right out of prison.

Park has a rather unusual working arrangement with his sales staff. Park says, "From 9:30 to 6 is my time . . . whatever you do after that is your time." He does not ask many questions about his employees' outside activities, yet he is ready with bail money or short-term loans. Of course, such financial favors are eventually deducted from the employee's wages. None of the sales staff are allowed to work the cash register. A Korean American himself, Park hires only Korean American managers to handle the money.

By hiring people who have criminal records, "Park gets something that has proved indispensable (in the rough neighborhoods where his stores are located):

salesmen who have genuine currency on these streets— and clout." Park has never been robbed, but two of his stores have been burglarized. After one of the burglaries, a sales clerk—who was also a gang member— was called to guard the store through the night. The clerk subsequently talked to another local gang member, and Park's stores have not been burglarized since. Having sales people who are in touch with the street can also prove beneficial in moving the store's merchandise. "Stock changes from neighborhood to neighborhood, sometimes depending on gang allegiances."

Critical Thinking Questions

1. In your judgment, are Park's business practices ethical or unethical?
2. Suppose that you represent the franchisor, Athlete's Foot. Would you be concerned about Park's business practices?

- *Management training and assistance.* The franchisor provides a structured training program that gives the new franchisee a crash course in how to start and operate the business. Ongoing training programs for managers and employees are another plus. In addition, franchisees have a peer group to provide support and share ideas.
- *Financial assistance.* Being linked to a nationally known company can help a franchisee obtain funds from a lender. Also, the franchisor typically gives the franchisee advice on financial management, referrals to lenders, and help in preparing loan applications. Many franchisors also offer payment plans, short-term credit for buying supplies from the franchise company, and loans to buy real estate and equipment.

Disadvantages of Franchises

Franchising also has disadvantages, of course:

- *Loss of control.* The franchisor has to give up some control over operations and has less control over its franchisees than over company employees.
- *Costs of franchising.* Franchising can be a costly form of business. A recent Gallup survey reports that the average franchise start-up cost is about $143,000. These costs vary, depending on the type of business, and may include expensive facilities and equipment. The franchisee also pays ongoing fees or royalties (usually a percentage of sales). Fees for national and local advertising and management advice may add to the franchisee's cost. Franchise fees are higher for better known franchises, but even newer companies may charge $10,000 to $25,000 or more. Industry averages range from a low of $12,000 for real estate franchises to $36,000 in the lodging industry. Lodging franchises require the highest average total initial investment—$1.8 million, excluding real estate.[9] Exhibit 5-7 compares the total start-up costs and ongoing royalty fees for several types of franchise units.

> e x h i b i t   5 - 7 <

Cost Comparison of Selected Franchises

Name	Description	Total Start-up Costs, including Franchise Fee	Royalty
Precision Auto Wash	Car wash	$360,200–$461,600	10%
McDonald's	Fast-food restaurant	$413,100–$1.3 million	12.5%+
Tutor Time Child Care	Child care learning center	$196,900–$1.7 million	6%
Chem-Dry	Carpet, drapery, upholstery cleaning	$19,900–$55,600	$190 per month
Jani-King	Commercial cleaning services	$8,400–$34,800	10%
Mrs. Field's Original Cookies	Cookies and bakery products	$44,900–$412,100	6–8%
Super 8 Motels	Economy motels	$240,600–$2.2 million	5%
Hilton Inns, Inc.	Hotels and resorts	$30–$45 million	5%
Re/Max International	Real estate services	$20,000–$192,000	Varies
Liberty Tax Service	Income tax preparation	$5,500–$18,600	14%

SOURCE: "Franchise 500," *Entrepreneur* (January 1999), pp. 212–297.

- *Restricted operating freedom.* The franchisee agrees to conform to the franchisor's operating rules and facilities design, as well as inventory and supplies standards. Some franchises require franchisees to purchase only from the franchisor or approved suppliers. The franchisor may restricted the franchisee's territory or site, which can limit growth. Failure to conform to franchisor policies can mean loss of the franchise.

Franchise Growth

Many of today's major names in franchising, such as McDonald's and Kentucky Fried Chicken, started in the 1950s. Franchising grew rapidly in the 1960s and 1970s as more types of businesses—clothing, business services, convenience stores, and many others—used franchising to distribute their goods and services. The popularity of franchising continued as more business owners turned to franchising as a way to expand operations quickly and in new geographic areas, with limited capital investment. For example, between 1980 and 1999 the number of franchise units counted by *Entrepreneur* magazine's Franchise 500 nearly doubled.

Today, there are more than 2,100 franchise systems in the United States and Canada. The more than 500,000 business units in the United States employ over 8 million people and generate revenues of $800 billion. Franchises account for an estimated 50 percent of U.S. retail sales.[10] Fast food is the industry with the largest number of franchises, as Exhibit 5-8 shows.

HOT links

Have a sweet tooth? Indulge yourself by finding out the requirements for owning a Rocky Mountain Chocolate Factory franchise at
www.rmcfusa.com

> e x h i b i t   5 - 8 <

Franchise Population by Industry

Industry	Percentage of Total Units
Fast food	17%
Retail	11
Service businesses	9
Restaurants	9
Automotive	8
Maintenance	7
Building and construction	6
Business services	5
Retail food	5
Other*	23

*3 percent or less: Baked goods, personnel services, sports and recreation, real estate, lodging, education, printing, child-related, travel.
SOURCE: *Profile of Franchising*, vol. 1 (Washington, DC: IFA Educational Foundation, 1998), p. 21, Chart 1.1.

International Franchising

Like other areas of business, franchising is part of the global marketplace. Most franchise systems either operate units internationally already or plan to expand overseas as the demand for all types of goods and services grows. "Our research has shown us that this is an ideal time to move into the Korean market," says Doug Dwyer, president of Worldwide Refinishing Systems, a bath and kitchen remodeling franchise. "Because the average living standard now is fairly high in Korea, people not only desire but also can afford a better living environment that refinishing and restoring can provide."[11] Currently, among the most popular types of international franchises are restaurants, hotels, business services, educational products, car rentals, and nonfood retail stores.

Franchisors in foreign countries face many of the same problems as other firms doing business abroad. In addition to tracking the market and currency changes, franchisors must be aware of the local culture, language differences, and political risks.

Franchisors in foreign countries also face the challenge of aligning their business operations with the goals of their franchisees, who may be located half a globe away. Technology improves communication with the franchisee and unites worldwide suppliers and customers, as described in the Applying Technology box.

concept check

- Describe franchising and the main parties to the transaction.
- Summarize the major advantages and disadvantages of franchising.
- Why has franchising proved so popular?

CORPORATE GROWTH THROUGH MERGERS AND ACQUISITIONS

>lg 7

As the 20th century came to a close, corporations continued to merge at record levels. In 1998 alone, the total value of mergers worldwide was $2.5 trillion, and in the United States acquisition plans involving more than 12,500 U.S. companies and $1.7 trillion were announced! Exhibit 5-9 lists the top 10 mergers of 1998, which include the seven largest mergers of all time.

> e x h i b i t   5 - 9 <

Top 10 Mergers of 1998

Rank	Acquirer	Target	Industry	Value ($Billions)*
1	Exxon	Mobil	Oil and gas	$86.4
2	Travelers Group	Citicorp	Financial services	72.6
3	SBC Communications	Ameritech	Telecommunications	72.4
4	Bell Atlantic	GTE	Telecommunications	71.3
5	AT&T	Tele-Communications	Telecommunications/Cable	69.9
6	NationsBank	Bank of America	Banking	61.6
7	British Petroleum	Amoco	Oil and gas	55.0
8	Daimler-Benz	Chrysler	Motor vehicles	40.5
9	Norwest	Wells Fargo	Banking	34.4
10	Banc One	First Chicago NBD	Banking	29.6

*Based on stock value on announcement date; includes debt of target assumed by acquirer.
SOURCE: "Top Ten Deals of 1998," *Fortune* (January 11, 1999), p. 71.

FOR MENUS, CLICK HERE

Imagine trying to coordinate operations for Tricon Restaurants International's 10,000 Kentucky Fried Chicken (KFC), Pizza Hut, and Taco Bell franchises around the world. "When you're in 83 countries, it's nearly impossible to get consistency and discipline in building a global brand," comments Elana Gold, Tricon's KFC brand manager. "We needed to get everyone on the same page." Frustrated by the inadequacies and expense of paper-filled marketing binders, Tricon turned to an electronic business solution for global marketing management. In collaboration with Chicago software developer DNA Visual Solutions, Tricon created Brand Toolkit, a multimedia CD-ROM application with marketing resources. The CD-ROM provides Tricon franchisees with clearly organized information in an easy-to-use, cost-effective format.

With the click of a mouse, franchisees access detailed information about brand history, advertising, promotions, menu management, pricing, and operations. Guidelines on the best marketing practices and samples of effective ads teach franchisees how to develop ads to meet corporate standards. After working through a tutorial on menu guidelines, the franchisee can download actual menu models.

The CD-ROM format allows Tricon to design graphically rich interactive content such as video, three-dimensional (3-D) images, photographs, and animation that would take too long to send via the Internet. Adding an Internet connection to the next version of Brand Toolkit will allow franchisees to receive current news and updates to the CD-ROM and eventually do online transactions. In addition, the CD will take franchisees on a virtual reality tour through a 3-D restaurant model and show them the effect of layout and decorating modifications.

Since implementing the Brand Toolkit, relationships between Tricon and its franchisees have improved. As Howard Weinzimmer, DNA vice president, explains, "What does a franchise really have to sell? Product, methodology, and brand. Our technology helps them deliver that to all of their constituents."

Critical Thinking Questions

1. Summarize Brand Toolkit's benefits to both Tricon and its franchisees.
2. Describe several other ways Tricon could use different forms of technology to improve communications and franchise operations.

---

merger

The combination of two or more firms to form a new company, which often takes on a new corporate identity.

acquisition

The purchase of a corporation by another corporation or by an investor group; the identity of the acquired company may be lost.

A **merger** occurs when two or more firms combine to form one new company, which often takes on a new corporate identity. In an **acquisition,** a corporation or an investor group buys a corporation, and the identity of the acquired company may be lost. (A company can also acquire divisions or subsidiaries of another firm.) In Travelers Group's 1998 $73 billion acquisition of Citicorp, Travelers was the *acquirer* and Citicorp the *target*. Normally, an acquiring company finds a target company and, after analyzing the target carefully, negotiates with its management or stockholders.

Merger Motives

Although the headlines tend to focus on mega-mergers, the current "merger mania" affects small companies as well. The motives for undertaking mergers and acquisitions are similar regardless of size. Often the goal is strategic: improving the overall performance of the merged firms through cost savings, elimination of overlapping operations, improved purchasing power, increased market share, or reduced competition. Growth, widening of product lines, and the ability to quickly acquire technology or management skill are other mo-

In announcing their merger, Exxon CEO Lee Raymond and Mobil CEO Lucio Noto stated that the merged firms will improve their profitability with annual cost savings of almost $3 billion.

tives. Acquiring a company is often faster, less risky, and less costly than developing products internally or expanding internationally.

Two of 1998's largest mergers, for example, involved giant oil companies: Exxon acquired Mobil and British Petroleum acquired Amoco. In the oil industry, size counts; larger companies have historically earned higher returns. With crude oil prices at record lows, these major oil companies had already cut costs as much as possible and saw the merger route as the only way to improve profitability. Exxon and Mobil merged the two companies' technological expertise with Exxon's lower exploration and production costs and Mobil's larger reserves outside the United States. Although the new corporation has more operating units, it eliminated duplication in nonoperational areas such as headquarters facilities, executive team, and marketing organization. The result was annual cost savings of $2.8 billion.[12]

Another motive for acquisitions is financial restructuring—cutting costs, selling off units, laying off employees, refinancing the company—to increase the value of the company to its stockholders. Financially motivated mergers are based not on the potential to achieve economies of scale, but rather on the acquirer's belief that the target has hidden value that can be unlocked through restructuring. Most financially motivated mergers involve larger companies.

Types of Mergers

The three main types of mergers are horizontal, vertical, and conglomerate. In a **horizontal merger,** companies at the same stage in the same industry merge to reduce costs, expand product offerings, or reduce competition. Many of the large mergers in the late 1990s were horizontal mergers to achieve economies of scale. For example, in 1998 SBC Communications acquired both Ameritech and Pacific Telesis, reuniting three regional Bell operating companies that were split up in 1984. SBC's goal was to create a larger company to dominate the newly deregulated telecommunications industry.

In a **vertical merger,** a company buys a firm in its same industry that is involved in an earlier or later stage of the production or sales process. Buying a supplier of raw materials, a distribution company, or a customer gives the acquiring firm more control. America Online (AOL), Inc. acquires companies that address different Internet-related markets and capabilities. In 1998 AOL announced its $4.2 billion acquisition of Netscape Communications Corp. AOL had focused on the consumer market, while Netscape had a strong presence in the corporate market. AOL gained Netscape's software technology, including powerful Web browser software and the behind-the-scenes software to run Web sites and conduct electronic commerce.[13]

horizontal merger
A merger of companies at the same stage in the same industry; done to reduce costs, expand product offerings, or reduce competition.

vertical merger
A merger of companies at different stages in the same industry; done to gain control over supplies of resources or to gain access to different markets.

conglomerate merger
A merger of companies in unrelated businesses; done to reduce risk.

To learn more about the latest information technology industry mergers, explore the Broadview Associates site at **www.broadview.com**

A **conglomerate merger** brings together companies in unrelated businesses to reduce risk. Combining with a company whose products have a different seasonal pattern or that respond differently to the business cycle can result in a more stable sales pattern. GE Capital Corp., the financial unit of General Electric Co., targets acquisitions that balance each other: risky companies

leveraged buyout (LBO)
A corporate takeover financed by large amounts of borrowed money; can be done by outside investors or by a company's own management.

concept check

- Differentiate between a merger and an acquisition.
- What are the most common motives for corporate mergers and acquisitions?
- Describe the different types of corporate mergers.

whose performance fluctuates with changing financial markets and companies that perform consistently regardless of market conditions. GE Capital has 28 separate business lines in five major product groups: specialty insurance; consumer services such as credit card operations and auto and home financing; equipment leasing, ranging from aircraft to satellites to portable toilets; commercial financing; and financing for smaller businesses. Recently, it entered the rapidly growing information technology services market as well.[14]

A specialized financially motivated type of merger, the **leveraged buyout (LBO),** became popular in the 1980s but is less common today. LBOs are corporate takeovers financed by large amounts of borrowed money—as much as 90 percent of the purchase price. LBOs can be started by outside investors or the corporation's management. Believing that the company is worth more than the value of all the stock, they buy the stock and take the company private. The purchasers expect to generate cash flow by improving operating efficiency or by selling off some units for cash that can be used to pay the debt. Although some LBOs did improve efficiency, many did not live up to investor expectations or generate enough cash to pay the debt.

CAPITALIZING ON TRENDS IN BUSINESS

>lg 8

As we learned in Chapter 1, an awareness of trends in the business environment is a critical component of business success. Many of the social, demographic, and technology trends described in that chapter affect how businesses organize. When studying options for organizing a business or choosing a career path, consider the following trends in franchising and mergers and acquisitions.

Niche Markets

More franchises are catering to niche markets. For example, former Denver dentist Scott Menough now operates two Colorado Wild Birds Unlimited, Inc. franchises. Started by Jim Carpenter in 1981, this franchise system now has more than 250 units around the United States. Used goods are another growing segment of the retail market. GrowBiz offers franchisees resale outlets in six concepts: Once Upon a Child, Computer Renaissance, It's About Games, Play It Again Sports, Music Go Round (instruments), and ReTool. Within 10 years the company opened 1,200 outlets. At its 700 Play It Again Sports stores, used items sell so quickly that the units now carry new items as well, amounting to about 60 percent of inventory.[15]

To boost its share of the $18 million coffee market, Starbucks is expanding beyond coffee cafes by operating kiosks in airports, providing coffee service to businesses, and selling its coffee in supermarkets.

New Twists for Existing Franchises

As more franchise systems crowd into growing industry categories, established franchises must find ways to differentiate themselves:

- *Multiple franchise concepts.* Like GrowBiz, other franchisors offer more than one type of outlet. Precision Tune Auto Care's 650 franchisees like the option of choosing from Precision Auto Care, Precision Lube Express, or Precision Auto Wash stores. Many operate all three. Precision is also taking its successful multiple-option concept overseas to countries where people drive older cars.[16]

- *New types of outlets and expanded product offerings.* Pioneering postal service franchisor Mail Boxes Etc. added MBE Business Express, 24-hour self-service business centers in hotel lobbies. Coffee franchises like Diedrich's operate coffee carts in office complexes. Food franchises now offer broader menus. Smoothie franchise Jamba Juice added soup and snacks, and bagel franchises serve soups, salads, and gourmet sandwich creations.

- *Cross-branding.* Operating two or more franchises in one location generates more customer traffic and maximizes space, personnel, and management utilization. Jim Hobold of Cincinnati runs a Burger King and Frullati Cafe and Bakery (healthy fast food) franchises. "Every day mothers come into Burger King for chicken tender meals or burgers and fries for their kids, then come to Frullati for fruit smoothies and salads or sandwiches for themselves," he says. "With both operations in one place, we only need one general manager."[17]

The Big Get Bigger

As noted earlier, consolidation to achieve economies of scale is driving strategic mergers in industries such as automobiles, defense, oil, telecommunications, utilities, and financial services. These and other industries overexpanded due to an abundance of investment capital, globalization, better information technology, deregulation, and privatization. The result was fierce price competition and a search for other ways to improve financial performance.[18] Consolidation is affecting companies of all sizes, from small businesses to industry leaders like Mobil and Citicorp, which surprised many when they became targets.

In addition to the oil and telecommunications mergers described earlier, consolidation is changing the competitive environment in other industries as well. In the supermarket industry, announced mergers as of year-end 1998 will increase the market share of the top 10 supermarket chains to almost 50 percent, compared to 30 percent in 1993. And between 1986 and 1998, the number of grocery wholesalers plummeted from 366 to 97 firms. Bank consolidations represented over 25 percent of 1998's total deal value.[19]

Hands across the Sea

Because size is also an advantage when competing in the global marketplace, cross-border mergers are also on the rise. In particular, U.S. and European companies want new markets around the world. German automaker Daimler-Benz's 1998 acquisition of Chrysler, the number three U.S. automaker, created the world's third largest auto manufacturer based on revenues. Other trans-Atlantic acquisitions in recent years include Deutsche Bank AG, a major German bank, acquiring Banker's Trust for about $10 billion in 1998 and the $56 billion 1999 merger between Britain's Vodaphone Group and its joint venture partner AirTouch Communications to create the world's largest cellular phone company.

European companies are also seeking partners closer to home. In 1998 Hoechst AG (Germany) and France's Rhone-Poulenc SA merged to form the world's largest life sciences company. Both U.S. and European companies are buying Latin American companies, especially in the telecommunications, utility, and financial services industries.

Cross-border mergers present special challenges for the combined entity. It must contend with differences in language and social and workplace cultures in addition to the usual complexities of merging two companies.

concept check

- What are the important trends in franchising?
- How will the performance of the stock market affect future merger activity?
- What are the important trends in mergers and acquisitions?

APPLYING THIS CHAPTER'S TOPICS

Clearly, you need to understand the benefits of different forms of business organization if you start your own company. If you decide to work for someone else, this information will help you match a business entity with your goals. Suppose you are considering two job offers for computer programming positions: a two-year-old consulting firm with 10 employees owned by a sole proprietor or a publicly traded software developer with sales of $500 million. In addition to comparing the specific job responsibilities, consider the following:

- Which company offers the better training? Do you prefer the on-the-job training you'll get at the small company, or do you want formal training programs as well?
- Which position offers the chance to work on a variety of assignments?
- What are the opportunities for advancement? Employee benefits?
- What happens if the owner of the young firm gets sick or decides to sell the company?
- Which company offers a better work environment for you?

Answering these and similar questions will help you decide which job meets your particular needs.

Is Franchising in Your Future?

If the franchise route to business ownership interests you, begin educating yourself about the franchise process and investigate various types of franchise opportunities. You should research a franchise company thoroughly before making a financial commitment, because there are considerable differences among the more than 2,100 franchise systems. Once you've narrowed your choices to several specific franchises, ask for the *Uniform Franchise Offering Circular (UFOC)* for that franchisor and read it thoroughly. The Federal Trade Commission (FTC) requires franchisors to prepare this document. The UFOC provides a wealth of information about the franchisor, including its history, operating style and management, past or pending litigation against the franchisor, the franchisee's financial obligations, and any restrictions on the sale of units. Interviewing current and past franchisees is another essential step.

Would-be franchisees should check recent issues of small business magazines such as *Entrepreneur, Inc., Business Start Ups,* and *Success* for industry trends, ideas on promising franchise opportunities, and advice on how to choose and run a franchise. The International Franchise Association Web site at **www.franchise.org** has links to *Franchise World* magazine and other useful sites. (For other franchise-related sites, see the Try It Now box and the Working the Net questions.)

Is franchising for you? Assertiveness, desire to be your own boss, willingness to make a substantial time commitment, passion about the franchise concept, optimism, patience, and integrity rank high on franchisors' lists. Prior business experience is also a definite plus, and some franchisors prefer or require experience in their field. The information in Exhibit 5-10 can help you make a realistic self-assessment and increase your chances of success.

1. **Learn the Laws**   Before starting your own company, you should know the legal requirements in your area. Call the appropriate city or county departments, such as licensing, health, and zoning, to find out what licenses and permits you need and any other requirements you must meet. Do the requirements vary depending on the type of company? Are there restrictions on starting a home-based business? Then contact your secretary of state or other agency that handles corporations to get information on how to incorporate.

2. **Study Franchise Opportunities**   Franchising offers an alternative to starting a business on your own. Do you have what it takes to be successful? Start by making a list of your interests and skills, and do a self-assessment using some of the suggestions in the last section of this chapter. Next you need to narrow the field of thousands of different franchise systems. At Franchise Handbook Online **www.franchise1. com**, you'll find articles with checklists to help you thoroughly research a franchise and its industry, as well as a directory of franchise opportunities. Armed with this information, you can develop a questionnaire to evaluate a prospective franchise.

> e x h i b i t   5 - 1 0 <

Are You a Perfect Franchisee?

What traits do franchisors look for in a prospective franchisee? Specific preferences vary depending on the type of franchise company. For example, most lodging franchisors want prior experience in hotel management. The following questions are based on characteristics franchisors cited in a *Nation's Business* magazine survey:

• How long have you wanted to own a business?
• Are you willing to work hard and put in long hours?
• Do you have the required financial resources for your chosen franchise?
• Does the idea of running *all* aspects of a small business, from dealing with customers to bookkeeping and maintenance, appeal to you?
• Are you excited about the specific franchise concept?
• Do you have prior business experience? In what fields?
• Can you balance your entrepreneurial tendencies with the need to follow the franchisor's operating procedures?
• Are you competitive and a high achiever?
• Do your expectations and personal goals match the franchisor's?

SOURCE: Adapted from Thomas Love, "The Perfect Franchisee," *Nation's Business* (April 1, 1998), downloaded from **business.elibrary.com**.

Mergers and You

The high level of merger and acquisition activity changes the business environment for employees, business owners, and customers. You may work for an acquiring or a target company. What does this mean careerwise?

It's important in any job to take opportunities to develop a portfolio of transferable skills. This increases your chances of finding another job, either at the new company or at a new firm. Announcement of a merger increases the stress level for all employees. You will have to live with uncertainty for many months while the companies work out the details of integrating two operations. You may lose your job when overlapping departments are combined. According to outplacement firm Challenger, Gray & Christmas, in 1998 mergers were responsible for almost 74,000 lost jobs, or about 11 percent of all job cuts.[20] Even if you keep your job, the corporate culture may change, whether the acquirer is a U.S. company or one based overseas. The best approach is keep the quality and quantity of your work at the highest levels and be flexible.

If you own a small company, you may become a target. Or your customers may disappear as they are acquired by other companies. Should the large number of mergers discourage you from starting your own company? Not at all! Even though size is an advantage in many industries, the worldwide economy still needs small, entrepreneurial firms. Despite consolidation trends, large corporations still prefer to outsource many projects to companies with specialized expertise in such areas as design and technology. Also, many niche markets exist where being small provides benefits such as personal service and quick, creative solutions to customer problems.

Mergers also affect vendors, competing firms, and customers. If you own or work for a supplier in an industry with lots of merger activity, increase your efforts to acquire new customers, perhaps in different sectors. Maintain and nurture customer contacts. Those employees often move to other companies where they can recommend your firm. As a customer, you may find that your local bank branch or supermarket disappears after a merger. If competition decreases as a result of a merger, you may face fewer choices and higher prices.

>looking ahead
at JobDirect, Inc.

Choosing the corporate structure early in its life paid off for JobDirect, Inc. Despite competition from other job search Web sites, in just a few years JobDirect has carved out a special niche in entry-level job placements. Its student database has résumés from about 225,000 current job seekers. The employer database, with more than 20,000 job listings from over 150 clients, includes major firms like PaineWebber, Sears, Oracle, Xerox, and Macy's, as well as smaller companies and not-for-profits like the Peace Corps and Teach for America. In a nationwide survey, college students ranked JobDirect first among Web job search services. Revenues from corporate client fees were about $1.5 million for 1998. Corporate and online partnerships with companies like Barnes and Noble College Bookstores and Yahoo! help JobDirect reach more students.

What challenges does JobDirect face? "We must continue to differentiate ourselves from the clutter in the marketplace by maintaining our technology and marketing lead over other job posting companies," says president Rob Ford. "Our interactive matching service is unique and sets us apart from what are essentially electronic classified advertisements." The company will also have to evaluate future financing strategies such as whether to become a public company.[21]

SUMMARY OF LEARNING GOALS

>lg 1   **What are the three main forms of business organization, and what factors should a company's owners consider when selecting a form?**
A sole proprietorship is a business owned and operated by an individual. A partnership is an association of two or more people who operate a business as

co-owners. A corporation is a legal entity with an existence separate from its owners. When choosing a form of organization for a business, evaluate the owner's liability for the firm's debts, the ease and cost of forming the business, the ability to raise funds, the taxes, the degree of operating control the operator can retain, and the ability to attract employees.

>lg 2   What are the advantages and disadvantages of sole proprietorships?

The advantages of sole proprietorships include ease and low cost of formation, the owner's rights to all profits, the owner's control of the business, relative freedom from government regulation, absence of special taxes, and the ease of dissolution. Disadvantages include unlimited liability of the owner for debts, difficulty in raising capital, limited managerial expertise, large personal time commitment, unstable business life, difficulty in attracting qualified employees, and the owner's personal absorption of all losses.

>lg 3   Why would a new business venture choose to operate as a partnership, and what downside would the partners face?

Partnerships can be formed as either general partnerships or limited partnerships. In a general partnership, the partners co-own the assets and share in the profits. Each partner is individually liable for all debts and contracts of the partnership. The operations of a limited partnership are controlled by one or more general partners, who have unlimited liability. Limited partners are financial partners whose liability is limited to their investment; they do not participate in the firm's operations. The advantages of partnerships include ease of formation, availability of capital, diversity of managerial expertise, flexibility to respond to changing business conditions, and relative freedom from government control. Disadvantages include unlimited liability for general partners, potential for conflict between partners, limited life, sharing of profits, and difficulty in leaving a partnership.

>lg 4   How does the corporate structure provide advantages and disadvantages to a company, and what are the major types of corporations?

A corporation is a legal entity chartered by a state. Its organizational structure includes stockholders, who own the corporation; the board of directors, who are elected by the stockholders and govern the firm; and officers who carry out the goals and policies set by the board. Stockholders can sell or transfer their shares at any time and are entitled to receive profits in the form of dividends.

Advantages of corporations include limited liability, ease of transferring ownership, stable business life, and ability to attract financing. Disadvantages are double taxation of profits, the cost and complexity of formation, and government restrictions.

>lg 5   Does a company have any business organization options besides sole proprietorship, partnership, and corporation?

Businesses can also organize as limited liability companies, cooperatives, joint ventures, and franchises. A limited liability company (LLC) provides limited liability for its owners but is taxed like a partnership. These two features make LLCs an attractive form of business organization for many small firms.

Cooperatives are collectively owned by individuals or businesses with similar interests that combine to achieve more economic power. Cooperatives distribute all profits to their members. Two types of cooperatives are buyer and seller cooperatives.

A joint venture is an alliance of two or more companies formed to undertake a special project. Joint ventures can be set up in various ways, such as through partnerships or special-purpose corporations. By sharing management expertise, technology, products, and financial and operational resources, companies can reduce the risk of new enterprises.

>lg 6   Why is franchising growing in importance?

Franchising is one of the fastest growing forms of business ownership. It involves an agreement between a franchisor, the supplier of goods or services, and a

KEY TERMS

acquisition 156
board of directors
146
conglomerate
merger 157
cooperatives 150
corporation 144
franchise
agreement 151
franchisee 151
franchising 151
franchisor 151
general partners
142
general partnership
142
horizontal merger
157
leveraged buyout
(LBO) 158
limited liability
company (LLC)
149
limited partners
142
limited partnership
142
merger 156
partnership 141
S corporation 148
sole proprietorship
140
stockholders 146
vertical merger
157

franchisee, the individual or company that buys the right to sell the franchisor's products in a specific area. With a franchise, the business owner does not have to start from scratch but buys a business concept with a proven product and operating methods. The franchisor provides management training and assistance; use of a recognized brand name, product, and operating concept; and financial assistance. Franchises can be costly to start, however, and restrict operating freedom because the franchisee must conform to the franchisor's standard procedures.

>lg 7   **Why would a company use mergers and acquisitions to grow?**

In a merger, two companies combine to form one company; in an acquisition, one company or investor group buys another. Companies merge for strategic reasons, such as growth, diversification of product lines, increased market share, and economies of scale. The other main motive for merging is financial restructuring—cutting costs, selling off units, laying off employees, refinancing the company—to increase the value of the company to its stockholders.

There are three types of mergers. In a horizontal merger, companies at the same stage in the same industry combine to have more economic power, to diversify, or to win greater market share. A vertical merger involves the acquisition of a firm that serves an earlier or later stage of the production or sales cycle, such as a supplier or sales outlet. In a conglomerate merger, unrelated businesses come together to reduce risk through diversification.

>lg 8   **What trends will affect business organization in the future?**

Americans continue to open new businesses, from sole proprietorships to multi-unit franchise operations, at record rates. The service sector is growing fastest to meet the increased demand for convenience from working women and two-income families. Good franchise opportunities include those providing services for children and senior citizens, as well as resale shops and other specialty markets. To remain competitive, established franchisors are offering multiple concepts, new types of outlets, and expanded products. Key merger trends include increasing numbers of mergers between companies that wish to consolidate to achieve economies of scale and cross-border mergers.

PREPARING FOR TOMORROW'S WORKPLACE

1. Interview the sole proprietor of a local business. Prepare a brief report outlining his or her experiences, including reasons for starting this particular business as a sole proprietorship, start-up costs, time commitment, biggest surprises, mistakes to avoid, what he or she likes best/least, and plans for the future.

2. Susan Atkinson is thinking about opening a business to sell her homemade barbeque sauces over the Internet. Although she has enough money saved to start the business on her own, she is worried about her lack of knowledge of accounting and finance. A friend mentions that he knows someone with 10 years of business management experience who wants to get involved with a start-up company. As Susan's business consultant, prepare a memo for Susan that recommends a form of business organization, including the issues she should consider, advantages, disadvantages, and risks involved, and reasons for your choice.

3. At the end of a late night study session, you wonder why someone doesn't provide an on-campus coffee delivery service and decide this is a great business for you. There's just one catch: you're broke, so you'll need a partner. Summarize the management and technical skills and financial resources you need for your company; then make a list of the qualities and resources you bring to the team and what you want in a partner. Select a potential partner

from your class to interview using the advice in Exhibit 5-2 as a starting point. Evaluate the proposed partnership.

4. You and a partner co-own Glow Auto, a successful car-detailing business. Because sales at the first location have tapered off, you want to open additional outlets in a large city about 20 miles away. Because of the cost of expanding, you decide to sell Glow Auto franchises. The idea takes off, and soon you have 25 units throughout the region. Your success results in an invitation to speak at the local Rotary Club. Prepare a brief presentation that describes how you evaluated the benefits and risks of becoming a franchisor, the problems you encountered, and how you've established good working relationships with your franchisees.

5. In the pharmaceutical industry, new products are a key to continued growth. Many major drug firms like SmithKline Beecham and Glaxo see mergers and acquisitions as a way to beef up their research and development efforts. In contrast, Merck & Co.'s CEO believes a merger would distract the company from its strategic goals. Although new competitors created through mergers are spending more on research and development than Merck can, he points out that Merck remains the world's biggest drug maker. Create two teams to debate the pros and cons of the merger issue as it applies to Merck.

6. Select one of the top 10 mergers of 1998 from Exhibit 5-9. Research the background of the merger using a variety of sources, including the acquirer's corporate Web site and news articles from business periodicals like *Business Week, Fortune,* and the *Wall Street Journal.* Report on the motives behind the merger, the problems facing the new entity, and the company's progress toward achieving its objectives.

WORKING THE NET

1. Visit the JobDirect Web site at **www.jobdirect.com.** Click on "JobDirect Guide" to read a brief company profile, and then follow links to get more details about the company's founders and team and the story of how they developed their idea. What qualifications did Rachel Bell and Sara Sutton bring to the venture? How did they compensate for resources they lacked? What were some of the lessons they learned about organizing a company?

2. Consult *Entrepreneur* magazine's guide to business start-ups, "One Step at a Time," at **www.entrepreneurmag.com/startup/52steps/** and link to the articles at Step 12 on choosing a form of business organization. Summarize for the class the reasons that the entrepreneurs profiled chose a particular structure. Do you agree with their choices?

3. Research how to form a corporation and an LLC in your state using a search engine to find relevant sites. Here are two to get you started: **www.corporate.com** and **www.incorporate-usa.com.** What steps are necessary to set up a corporation in your state? How do the fees compare to other states? If you were incorporating a business, what state would you choose and why?

4. Select three franchises that interest you. Research them at sites such as the Franchise Handbook Online (**www.franchise1.com/directory.html**), *Entrepreneur* magazine's Franchise 500 (**www.entrepreneurmag.com/franchise500/**), and Be the Boss (**www.betheboss.com**). Prepare a chart comparing them, including history, number and location of units, financial requirements (initial franchise fee, other start-up costs, royalty and advertising fees), and any other information that would help you evaluate the franchise.

5. Check out the latest merger trends at Industry Week (**www.industryweek.com**). Find examples of a horizontal merger and a merger that failed.

CREATIVE THINKING CASE

Should Jason take the Subway?

Jason Braden's dream of starting and running a business in his hometown became reality when he inherited $35,000 from his grandfather. Jason, who wanted a low-risk venture that provided a decent income, decided that his town needed a sandwich store near two large office parks. Jason had worked during college at a Subway Sandwich store and knew that designing the store, rent, and equipment and supply costs would quickly eat up his $35,000, leaving little for advertising or promotion. Jason also didn't know much about finding suppliers, setting up an accounting system, and hiring employees.

Jason contacted his former boss José Gonzalez, who owned five Subway franchises. Mr. Gonzalez was very positive about his experiences, telling Jason that Subway was one of the lowest cost food franchises to start and pointing to his late-model sports car and house in an affluent neighborhood as proof of the income potential.

Jason requested information about becoming a franchisee from Subway's corporate offices. He learned that his total initial investment could range from $60,000 to $103,000, depending on store size and location. The company could help with financing for most of the costs and provide training to help him set up an efficient operation. The only cash down payment was the $10,000 franchise fee. After the store opened, out of weekly gross sales Jason would pay 8 percent royalties and 3.5 percent to Subway's fund for national advertising.

Before he submitted his application, however, Jason searched the Internet for more information. He discovered that many Subway franchisees had filed lawsuits against the company for reasons such as not completely explaining their rights and obligations as franchisees or opening too many franchises in their neighborhoods. "Subway is the biggest problem in franchising," said one congressional economist. "If anyone in my family ever asked whether they should buy a Subway franchise, I would say absolutely not, no way."

Jason spoke again to Mr. Gonzalez, who assured him that many of the lawsuits had been filed by unsuccessful franchisees who had not followed Subway's operating procedures. Also, the company had resolved some issues raised by the disgruntled franchisees.

Jason had two other options. His parents would lend him $20,000 to open his own independent sandwich store or to buy a different type of franchise. His girlfriend said she'd contribute about $30,000, so they could pool their funds and go into business as partners. After all, they got along really well and this would give them a chance to spend more time together.

Critical Thinking Questions

1. Should Jason purchase a Subway Sandwich franchise? Defend your answer.
2. How could Jason minimize the potential risks of opening an independent sandwich shop? Would you recommend this course of action? Why?
3. What potential problems might Jason encounter if he goes into partnership with his girlfriend? How could they reduce these problems?
4. If you were Jason, which course of action would you take? Why?

VIDEO CASE

Second Chance Body Armor

Imagine yourself working on a job where being shot at or knifed is a real possibility. What measures could you take to protect yourself as a law enforcement officer, a prison guard, a firefighter, a pizza delivery person, a convenience store clerk, or a worker in some other hazardous occupation? Second Chance

Body Armor (**www.sruniforms.com/second.html**) provides one possible solution in the form of protective clothing—body armor that is worn underneath a person's street clothes.

Second Chance Body Armor produces comfortable, concealable, everyday body armor. It is made with lightweight materials that stop the penetration of a bullet or a knife, thereby protecting the wearer against serious or fatal injury. The armor is designed to be comfortable so that people will wear it on a daily basis.

Richard Davis, president of Second Chance Body Armor, invented the concept of concealable body armor in 1971. Though he had a good product, he found that the market was not aware of it. To promote market awareness, Davis developed advertisements in which he shot himself at point-blank range while wearing the body armor. He survived, sustaining only superficial abrasions.

Since those early days, Second Chance Body Armor has expanded its line of personal protection products. Second Chance's business strategy is quite simple: focus on customer needs for comfortable, custom-fit body armor. Carrying out this strategy requires strong customer service, the use of new technology, and the creation and maintenance of brand identity.

Second Chance now produces several different types of concealable body armor. The SUPERfeatherlite Body Armor, advertised as its "good" armor, is made with DuPont Kevlar 129. The SUPERfeatherlite SC229 is billed as the "better" model. It is made with Akzo-Nobel TWARON T-2000 Microfilament fibers and Butterfly Lite fabrication technology. Second Chance's "best" body armor, the Monarch, combines three fourth-generation ballistics technologies "to produce revolutionary improvement in wearability and performance." The Monarch model incorporates ARAFLEX IV ballistics fibers; Butterfly Lite stitch patterns to protect against multihits, multiangle hits, and blunt trauma; and Gore-Tex ComfortCOOL ballistic pad covers for moisture protection and breathability. Second Chance also produces the Monarch +P+, which combines antiballistic properties and antipuncture properties into a single body armor model. Promoted as Second Chance's "bonus" model, this product provides protection from both gunshots and penetration by knives and other sharp instruments. No matter which type of body armor a Second Chance customer purchases, it is designed for comfort and custom fit to the customer using five different body measurements.

The Second Chance brand has become so widely accepted in law enforcement circles that it has become a generic name just as Kleenex has for facial tissue. There is only one Second Chance brand, but people commonly refer to any body armor as "providing them with their second chance." By following the business strategy of focusing on customer needs for comfortable, custom-fit body armor, Second Chance has developed into the worldwide leader in body armor.

Critical Thinking Questions

1. As the proprietor of Second Chance Body Armor, Richard Davis focused on serving customer needs for comfortable, custom-fit body armor. He also went to great lengths to create market awareness of his invention. Do you think Davis used a wise business strategy? What do you think of his approach to creating market awareness? Explain your answer.

2. What advantages and disadvantages of the sole proprietorship might Davis have experienced?

3. Suppose that you wish to go into business for yourself in the future. What insights does the Second Chance Body Armor experience provide for you?

chapter six

Entrepreneurship: Starting and Managing Your Own Business

learning goals

>lg 1   Why do people become entrepreneurs, and what are the different types of entrepreneurs?

>lg 2   Which characteristics do successful entrepreneurs share?

>lg 3   How do small businesses contribute to the U.S. economy?

>lg 4   What are the advantages and disadvan-

>lg 5   How does the Small Business Administration help small businesses?

>lg 6   What are the first steps to take if you are starting your own firm?

>lg 7   Why does managing a small business present special challenges for the owner?

>lg 8   What trends are shaping the small business

The Juice Guys Squeeze Their Way to Success

From a small boat in Nantucket Harbor to a $60 million company named one of *Inc.* magazine's fastest growing firms—that kind of success is every potential entrepreneur's dreams. "If I were on the outside looking in, I would say, 'These guys were an overnight success,'" says Tom Scott, co-president of Nantucket Nectars **(www.juiceguys.com).** "Being on the inside, it's been a long, long time. We almost went out of business a thousand times." As Scott and his partner and co-president Tom First acknowledge, "Nantucket Nectars is one big collection of mistakes." But they learned through experience, relying on their creativity and instincts.

Scott didn't set out to develop a multimillion dollar juice company. During the summer of 1988, he started Allserve from a small boat in Nantucket Harbor. "It was like a floating 7-Eleven," Scott recalls. He made the rounds of the yachts in the harbor, selling newspapers and snacks, taking trash, and doing laundry. Despite the 18-hour days, seven days a week, Scott loved being his own boss and vowed to find a way to make enough money to live on Nantucket.

Classmate Tom First became Scott's partner in Allserve the summer following graduation. During the winter, however, business was nonexistent. With lots of time on their hands, the Toms and their friends would gather for dinner. One night First re-created a fresh peach juice he'd tasted in Spain. It was an instant hit, so the two Toms named it Nantucket Nectar, bottled it in recycled wine bottles, and sold it the next summer from the boat and a small store.

Though the peach juice was a success, Allserve was too seasonal and too small to support both partners. Pooling their $17,000 savings, they hired a bottler to produce 1,400 cases of Nantucket Nectars. The initial production run sold out so quickly that they began investigating mass production. By 1993, Nantucket Nectars reached $400,000 in sales.

To expand, Scott and First needed to raise more money. One of the investors they contacted was Michael Egan, then chairman of Alamo Rent a Car and a former Allserve customer. Egan liked Scott, First, and their company so much that he provided $500,000 in first-round financing. "It was very hard to dissuade them from their mistakes," he says. "But I've never been involved with two such fast learners in my life."

As demand increased, the "juice guys" encountered their first major problem: distributing their juice to enough markets. In 1994 they lost $2 million by handling their own distribution. In 1995, after Egan contributed an additional $1.5 million, they hired outside distributors and made a profit of $850,000 on $15 million in sales.

Critical Thinking Questions

As you read this chapter, consider the following questions as they relate to Nantucket Nectars, Inc.:

- What type of entrepreneur is Scott? What were his motives in starting Nantucket Nectars?

- What personal characteristics contributed to Scott and First's success?

- What advantages and disadvantages did Scott and First face as small business owners, and how did they overcome them?

Business in the 21st Century

By 1997, Nantucket Nectars was a $50 million company and one of *Inc.* magazine's 20 fastest growing private companies. In November of that year, Scott and First sold a large ownership stake to Ocean Spray Cranberries, Inc., retaining about half the company. They are still active in management, and although their corporate offices are now in Cambridge, Massachusetts, the company maintains its original entrepreneurial feeling. "Employees don't walk into the job with a procedures manual," says First. "We figure it out ourselves. Trial and error. That's entrepreneurial. That's fun."[1]

BUSINESS IN THE 21ST CENTURY

The entrepreneurial spirit is capturing the interest of people from all backgrounds and age groups. Teenagers are starting fashion clothing and high-tech companies. Recent college graduates like Tom Scott and Tom First shun the "jacket and tie" corporate world to make it on their own. Downsized employees and midcareer executives form another large group of small business owners. Retirees who worked for others all their lives may form the company they always wanted to own.

New businesses continue to be formed in the United States at high rates. A study by the Entrepreneurial Research Consortium found that more than one-third of all households include someone involved with starting or funding a small business. These small companies are the lifeblood of the U.S. economy. In fact, 98 percent of all U.S. companies have fewer than 100 employees, yet they account for about 38 percent of all workers. Other firms will start small but grow into multimillion dollar corporations.

Companies started by entrepreneurs and small business owners make significant contributions to the global economy. They are hotbeds of innovation, taking leadership roles in technological change and the development of new goods and services. They account for 51 percent of the gross domestic product and 47 percent of all retail sales. Small businesses create most of the new jobs in the United States. Firms with fewer than 500 employees provide jobs for over half the labor force. In addition, they provide women, minorities, and immigrants with opportunities for economic and social advancement.

You may be one of the millions of Americans who's considering joining the ranks of business owners. As you read this chapter, you'll get the information and tools you need to help you decide whether owning your own company is the right career path for you. You'll discover why entrepreneurship continues to be one of the hottest areas of business activity, as well as the characteristics you need to become a successful entrepreneur. Then we'll look at the importance of small businesses in the economy, their advantages and disadvantages, and the role of the Small

In launching Nantucket Nectars, entrepreneurs Tom Scott and Tom First join the growing number of college graduates who choose to start their own businesses rather than working for someone else.

Business Administration. Next, the chapter offers guidelines for starting and managing a small business. Finally, it explores the trends that will shape entrepreneurship and small business ownership in the 21st century.

ENTREPRENEURSHIP TODAY

>lg 1

Although he's only 25, Jared Schutz already has five companies to his credit. At 16, he started a company to trade government scrap metal. While in college he used those earnings to open a technical consulting firm, American Information Systems, Inc. (AIS), with two partners. Soon after he founded Stardot Consulting to create Web sites for politicians, he helped a friend start Internet athletic equipment dealer Sportscape.com. His latest venture is Proflowers.com, an Internet flower retailer that's growing 25 percent a month. A high-energy person described by his partners as "a classic idea man," Schutz also has top marketing and strategy skills and knows how to use Internet technology to his advantage.[2]

The United States is blessed with a wealth of entrepreneurs like Schutz. According to research by the Small Business Administration, 16 million Americans—about 13 percent of all nonagricultural workers—are involved in either full- or part-time entrepreneurial activities. And their ranks continue to swell as up-and-coming entrepreneurs aspire to become the next Bill Gates or Marc Andreessen (co-founder of Netscape).

Why has entrepreneurship remained a strong part of the foundation of the U.S. business system for so many years? Today's global economy rewards innovative, flexible companies that respond quickly to changes in the business environment. These companies are started by **entrepreneurs,** people with vision, drive, and creativity who are willing to take the risk of starting and managing a business to make a profit.

entrepreneurs
People with vision, drive, and creativity who are willing to take the risk of starting and managing a new business to make a profit or of greatly changing the scope and direction of an existing firm.

Entrepreneur or Small Business Owner?

The term *entrepreneur* is often used in a broad sense to include most small business owners. But there is a difference between entrepreneurship and small business management. Entrepreneurship involves taking a risk, either to create a new business or to greatly change the scope and direction of an existing firm. Entrepreneurs typically are innovators who start companies to pursue their ideas for a new product or service. They are visionaries who spot trends.

While entrepreneurs may be small business owners, not all small business owners are entrepreneurs. They are managers or people with technical expertise who started a business or bought an existing business and made a conscious decision to stay small. For example, the proprietor of your local independent bookstore is a small business owner. Jeff Bezos, founder of Amazon.com, also sells books. But Bezos is an entrepreneur: he developed a new model—a Web-based book retailer—that revolutionized the world of book selling. The two groups share some of the same characteristics, and we'll see that some of the reasons for becoming an entrepreneur or a small business owner are very similar. However, entrepreneurs are less likely to accept the status quo and generally take a longer-term view than the small business owner.

Types of Entrepreneurs

Entrepreneurs fall into several categories: classic entrepreneurs, multipreneurs, and intrapreneurs.

Classic Entrepreneurs

Classic entrepreneurs are risk takers who start their own companies based on innovative ideas. Some classic entrepreneurs are *micropreneurs* who start small and plan to stay small. They often start businesses just for personal satisfaction and the lifestyle. Michael McVey got the entrepreneurial urge after the 1994 baseball players' strike when he lost his job selling hot dogs at Colorado Rockies baseball games. McVey developed Treebats, roughly cut decorative baseball bats carved from recycled Colorado Christmas trees, to combine his love of baseball with an opportunity to recycle the wood. His company, Colorado Rules, sells Treebats to baseball teams, to tourists as souvenirs, and to corporations that want to give the Colorado-inspired bats as gifts instead of coffee mugs or T-shirts.[3]

In contrast, *growth-oriented entrepreneurs* want their businesses to grow into major corporations. Most high-tech companies are formed by growth-oriented entrepreneurs. Jeff Bezos's recognized that with Internet technology he could compete with large chains of traditional book retailers. Bezos' goal was to build his company into a high-growth enterprise—and he even chose a name that reflected this strategy: Amazon.com. Now he's moving beyond books in an effort to make his company a one-stop shopping site.[4]

Multipreneurs

Then there are *multipreneurs,* entrepreneurs who start a series of companies. Jim Clark is the quintessential multipreneur, starting three high-tech companies with market values of more than $1 billion each. A

How can Jim Clark help you? Get answers to your medical questions at the consumer solutions area or learn more about the company at the Healtheon Web site

www.healtheon.com

former Stanford professor, Clark founded Silicon Graphics, Inc., which makes powerful high-end graphics computers, in 1982. His next venture, Internet pioneer Netscape, was formed in 1994 and went public in 1995. While Clark was still Netscape's chairman, he shifted his attention to his newest company, Healtheon, which he founded in 1996 and took public in early 1999. Healtheon provides online medical data for physicians, insurers, and hospitals. A visionary who's better at creating companies, putting together a management team, and advising the company than at day-to-day management, Clark began looking for his next start-up before Netscape went public.[5]

Intrapreneurs

intrapreneurs

Entrepreneurs who apply their creativity, vision, and risk taking within a large corporation, rather than starting a company of their own.

Some entrepreneurs don't own their own companies but apply their creativity, vision, and risk taking within a large corporation. Called **intrapreneurs,** these employees enjoy the freedom to nurture their ideas and develop new products, while their employers provide regular salaries and financial backing. Intrapreneurs have a high degree of autonomy to run their own mini-companies within the larger enterprise. They share many of the same personality traits as classic entrepreneurs but take less personal risk. According to Gifford Pinchot, who coined the term *intrapreneur* in 1985, corporations have lost billions of dollars by rejecting ideas from employees who then leave to start their own companies. Corporations that create supportive environments for intrapreneurship retain their most innovative employees—as well as ownership of the products they develop.[6] Xerox Technology Ventures (XTV) funds promising research projects that don't quite fit the overall corporate objectives until the projects are ready for outside financing. This gives them the chance to develop into profitable businesses, rather than be shunted aside.[7]

Why Become an Entrepreneur?

As the examples in this chapter show, entrepreneurs are found in all industries and have different motives for starting companies. The most common reason cited by CEOs of the *Inc.* 500, the magazine's annual list of fastest growing private companies, is the desire to control their own destiny. Related to this is a desire for job security now that large corporations regularly downsize staff and streamline operations. Other reasons, as Exhibit 6-1 shows, include making money and building a new company. Two other important basic motives mentioned in other surveys are feeling personal satisfaction with your work and creating the lifestyle that you prefer.

Do entrepreneurs feel that going into business for themselves is worth it? The answer is a resounding yes. In one survey, over 80 percent said they would do it over again. And as we've seen, many thrive on creating multiple companies around their ideas. "The first time, you go and take a risk and push it, and you succeed, then the next time, you take more risk; you push further," says Kamran Elahan, who's started seven successful technology companies. "It becomes an addiction. Each time you want to push it further, further, further."[8]

c o n c ə p t   c h ə c k

- What is an entrepreneur? Describe several types of entrepreneurs.
- What differentiates an entrepreneur from a small business owner?
- What are some major factors that motivate entrepreneurs to start businesses?
- Describe the personality traits and other skills characteristic of successful entrepreneurs.
- What does it mean to say that an entrepreneur should work on the business, not in it?

CHARACTERISTICS OF SUCCESSFUL ENTREPRENEURS

>lg 2

Do you have what it takes to become an entrepreneur? Being an entrepreneur requires special drive, perseverance, passion, and a spirit of adventure in addition to managerial and technical ability. Having a great concept is not enough. An entrepreneur must also be able to develop and manage the company that implements the idea. In addition, entrepreneurs *are* the company; they cannot leave problems at the office at the end of the day. Most entrepreneurs tend to work longer hours and take fewer vacations once they have their own company. They also share other common characteristics, as described in the next section.

> e x h i b i t   6 - 1 <

Reasons Entrepreneurs Start Companies

Reason	Percentage Citing
To be my own boss or control my own life	41%
To make money	16
To create something new	12
To prove I could do it	9
Because I was not rewarded at my old job	6
Because I was laid off from my old job	5
Other	11

SOURCE: "Inc. 500 Almanac," *Inc. 500* (October 22, 1996), p. 24.

The Entrepreneurial Personality

Many of the studies of the entrepreneurial personality have found similar traits.[9] In general, entrepreneurs are:

- *Ambitious.* Entrepreneurs have a high need for achievement and are competitive.

- *Independent.* They are self-starters who prefer to lead rather than follow. They are also individualists. "I've done between 400 and 500 acquisitions in my career, so I know a lot about entrepreneurs. Entrepreneurs don't march left, right, left, right. They march left, left, right, right, left, hop, skip," comments Paul M. Verrochi, chairman and CEO of Provant, a Boston company that provides business training services.[10]

- *Self-confident.* They understand the challenges of starting a business but are decisive and have faith in their abilities to resolve problems. Entrepreneurs trust their hunches and act on them.

- *Risk taking.* Though they are not averse to risk, most successful entrepreneurs prefer situations with a moderate degree of risk, where they have a chance to control the outcome, to highly risky ventures that depend on luck.

- *Visionary.* "Entrepreneurs believe they can create the future," says Marc Andreessen, Netscape co-founder.[11] Their ability to spot trends and act on them sets entrepreneurs apart from small business owners and managers.

- *Creative.* To compete with larger firms, entrepreneurs need to have creative product designs, marketing strategies, and solutions to managerial problems.

- *Energetic.* Starting a business takes long hours. Some entrepreneurs start companies while still employed full-time. Each week, Elle Hamm, founder of the Beverly Hills–based Rudwear Collection, worked 40 hours at a hotel job and another 40 hours developing her line of funky clothing and accessories.[12]

- *Passionate.* Entrepreneurs love their work. "If you're not passionate about what you're doing, you can't be an entrepreneur," says Judy Estrin, founder of three successful high-tech companies. "It just takes too many compromises and too much effort."[13]

- *Committed.* They make personal sacrifices to achieve their goals. Because they are so committed to their companies, entrepreneurs are persistent in seeking solutions to problems. Tom Scott and Tom First, for example, believed in their product and refused to lower their quality standards, even if it meant financial hardship.

The Edward Lowe Foundation's mission is to "champion the entrepreneurial spirit." Find out how it accomplishes that goal by exploring its site at **www.lowe.org**

The Hagberg Consulting Group, a leadership development consulting firm, studied over 2,000 executives for 12 years. In addition to the characteristics already mentioned, the study found that in comparison to the average executive, entrepreneurs are much more opinionated, emotionally aloof, impatient, focused, and aggressive. They also tend to get upset when things don't go their way.[14]

Managerial Ability and Technical Knowledge

A person with all the characteristics of an entrepreneur might still lack the business skills to run a successful business. As we'll discuss later in this chapter, entrepreneurs believe they can learn many of these technical skills.

Entrepreneurs need managerial ability to organize a company, develop operating strategies, obtain financing, and manage day-to-day activities. Good interpersonal and communication skills are also essential in dealing with employees, customers, and other businesspeople, such as bankers, accountants, and attorneys. They also need the technical knowledge to carry out their ideas. For instance, an entrepreneur may have a great idea for a new computer game and be a self-confident, hardworking, motivated person with good interpersonal skills. But without a detailed knowledge of computers, that entrepreneur would find it nearly impossible to produce a computer game that would sell.

Michael Gerber, author of *The E-Myth Revisited,* agrees that entrepreneurs need both managerial ability and technical skills to succeed. "Everybody who goes into business is actually three people in one: the Entrepreneur, the Manager, and the Technician," Gerber says. He explains that the technician can do the work but cannot run and grow the business; those are the jobs of the other two. Owners need to get their roles straight: work *on* the business, not *in* it.[15]

Working on the business often requires entrepreneurs to take Jim Clark's approach: focus on what they do best and hire others to do the rest. As Lillian Vernon, founder of the successful mail-order business that bears her name, explains, "My biggest mistake was trying to do it all. As the business grew, I had a hard time relinquishing responsibility. I finally realized the only healthy way to grow a business is with a qualified, dedicated management team."[16]

SMALL BUSINESS

>lg 3

Although large corporations dominated the business scene for many decades, in recent years small businesses have once again come to the forefront of the U.S. economy. In fact, about 98 percent of the businesses in the United States have fewer than 100 employees. Small businesses are important to the U.S. economy. By some estimates, U.S. small businesses in the aggregate would rank fourth among the world's economic powers based on the total value of goods and services they produce.[17]

Let's look at some of the main reasons behind the increase in small business formation:

- *Independence and a better lifestyle.* Large corporations no longer represent job security or offer as many fast-track career opportunities. Midcareer employees leave the corporate world in search of new opportunities. Many new college and business school graduates shun the corporate world altogether and start their own companies or look for work in small firms.
- *Personal satisfaction from work.* Many small business owners cite this as one of the primary reasons for starting their companies. They love what they do.
- *Best route to success.* Small businesses offer their owners the potential for profit. Also, business ownership provides greater advancement opportunities for women and minorities, as we discuss later in this chapter.
- *Rapidly changing technology.* Advances in computer and telecommunications technology, as well as the sharp decrease in the cost of this technology, have given individuals and small companies the power to compete in industries that were formerly closed to them. The arrival of the Internet and World Wide Web is responsible for the formation of many small businesses, as we'll discuss in the trends section later in this chapter.
- *Outsourcing.* As a result of downsizing, corporations often contract with outside firms for services they used to provide in-house. This "outsourcing"

creates opportunities for smaller companies, many of which offer specialized goods and services.

- *Major corporate restructurings and downsizings.* These force many employees to look for other jobs or careers.

What Is a Small Business?

How many small businesses are there in the United States? Estimates range from over 5 million to almost 20 million, depending on how government agencies and other groups define a business and the size limits they use. The database of the federal Small Business Administration, which uses the number of business enterprises, lists about 5.4 million firms with fewer than 500 employees as of 1995. The Bureau of Labor Statistics estimates that another 10.5 million individuals are self-employed.[18]

So what makes a business "small"? As we've seen, there are different interpretations, and the range is extremely broad. Generally, though, a **small business** has the following characteristics:

- Independently managed
- Owned by an individual or a small group of investors
- Based locally (although the market it serves may be widespread)
- Not a dominant company (thus it has little influence in its industry)

Exhibit 6-2 shows some of the characteristics of the typical American small business.

Small businesses in the United States can be found in almost every industry group, as shown in Exhibit 6-3. Small businesses include the following:

- *Services.* Service firms are the most popular category of small businesses because they are easy and low cost to start. They are often small; very few service-oriented companies are national in scope. They include repair services, restaurants, specialized software companies, accountants, travel agencies, management consultants, and temporary help agencies.
- *Wholesale and retail trade.* Retailers sell goods or services directly to the end user. Wholesalers link manufacturers and retailers or industrial buyers; they assemble, store, and distribute products ranging from heavy machinery to produce. About 85 percent of all wholesale firms have fewer than 20 employees. Most retailers also qualify as small businesses, whether they operate one store or a small chain.

small business

A business that is independently owned, is owned by an individual or a small group of investors, is based locally, and is not a dominant company in its industry.

> e x h i b i t 6 - 2 <

The Typical American Small Business

Median number of employees	3
Median annual revenues	$150,000–$200,000
Average annual earnings of owner	$40,000
Average hours per week owner works	50.4
Percentage with Internet access	47%
Percentage that maintain a Web site	35%

SOURCES: "17th Annual D&B Small Business Study Says Minority Business Owners Expect Highest Profit Growth; Profile of Typical U.S. Small Business Revealed," *Business Wire* (February 18, 1998); and "Small Business: An Economic Powerhouse," National Federation of Independent Businesses (1998), downloaded from **www.nfibonline.com.**

Types of Small Business, by Industry

Industry	Percentage of All Small Businesses
Services	39.2%
Retail trade	20.4
Construction	11.8
Finance, insurance, real estate	8.0
Wholesale trade	7.4
Manufacturing	6.0
Transportation, public utilities	3.9
Agriculture, mining, other	3.3

SOURCE: Office of Advocacy, U.S. Small Business Administration, as reported in *Statistical Abstract of the United States*, 118th ed. (Washington, D.C.: Government Printing Office, 1998), p. 548.

- *Manufacturing.* This category is dominated by large companies, but many small businesses produce goods. Machine shops, printing firms, clothing manufacturers, beverage bottlers, electronic equipment manufacturers, and furniture makers are often small manufacturers. In some industries, small manufacturing businesses have an advantage because they can focus on customized products that would not be profitable for larger manufacturers.

- *Construction.* Firms employing under 20 people account for about 90 percent of the nation's construction companies. They include independent builders of industrial and residential properties and thousands of contractors in such trades as plumbing, electrical, roofing, and painting.

- *Agriculture.* Small businesses dominate agriculture-related industry, including forestry and fisheries. The Small Business Administration estimates that 99 percent of all agricultural firms have fewer than 100 employees.

Advantages of Small Business

Small businesses have advantages directly related to their size:

- *Greater flexibility.* Because most small businesses are owner-operated, they can react more quickly to changing market forces. They can develop product ideas and market opportunities without going through a lengthy approval process.

- *More efficient operation.* Small businesses are less complex than large organizations. They have fewer employees doing things that are not directly related to producing or selling the company's product (such as accounting and legal work). Thus, they can keep their total costs down.

- *Greater ability to serve specialized markets.* Small businesses excel in serving specialized markets. Large firms tend to focus on goods and services with an established demand and the potential for high sales.

>lg 4

Thousands of small manufacturers like this metal platemaker flourish because of their flexibility, efficiency, and ability to serve specialized markets.

BEING AN INFORMATION BROKER

Are you interested in going into business for yourself? Do you have access to the Internet? If you answered yes to both questions, you might be interested in becoming the proprietor of an information brokerage service.

Information brokers "specialize in hunting down confidential financial data" for lawyers working on behalf of their clients and individuals or firms seeking to collect payments on bills, among others. Some firms in this fast-growing industry use only legitimate public records to conduct their searches. Other information brokers use unscrupulous methods. Indeed, Julie Williams, acting Comptroller of the Currency for the United States, says that dishonest information brokering is both "growing and alarming."

According to federal and state authorities, "the most widely used [information brokering] practice involves impersonating an account holder to obtain balances." The Internet has enabled information brokers to easily gather information on individuals. In turn, this information makes it easier for the broker to impersonate an account holder when calling a financial institution. Other tactics used by unscrupulous information brokers

include mailing phony rebate checks to targets in order to obtain their bank account numbers from returned checks and using bogus offers of preapproved credit to trick people into revealing bank information and Social Security numbers.

An investigation of Summer Associates Information Services in Stamford, Connecticut, shows how easy it is for someone to start an information brokerage business. Summer was a small operation located in a three-room suite in a converted factory in Stamford. The entire business operated with just a few people, a telephone, and a computer modem.

Critical Thinking Questions

1. How does the information brokerage industry reflect trends in business?
2. What should an information broker do to ensure that the business is operated ethically?
3. Suppose that you wish to become an entrepreneur. What insights, if any, does the information brokerage industry provide?

Many products would not exist were it not for small firms' ability to provide them cost-effectively. Narrative Television Network (NTN), for example, is a Tulsa firm that provides narrated movies and television shows for the visually impaired and blind. Founders Jim Stovall, totally blind since age 29, and Kathy Harper, a legally blind legal researcher, wanted careers that they could manage despite their disability. Stovall came up with the idea of providing narration to supplement the soundtracks on movies and television shows (similar to the closed captioning service for the hearing impaired).[19]

- *More personal service.* Another advantage of small businesses is their ability to give the personal touch. In businesses like gourmet restaurants, health clubs, fashion boutiques, and travel agencies, customers place a high value on personal attention. Through this direct relationship with customers, the owner-manager also gets feedback on how well the firm is meeting customer needs.

Disadvantages of Small Business

Small businesses also face several disadvantages:

- *Limited managerial skill.* Small business owners may not have the wide variety of skills they need to respond quickly to change. As noted earlier, they often lack knowledge in areas like finance, marketing, taxation, and business law. They may have experience in one area of business but not in the specific type of business they choose to start. Others have the technical skills but not the management ability. Nantucket Nectars' founders, Scott and First, were business novices with no experience in managing a company or producing, distributing, or marketing juice. They learned on the job—and quickly. Other entrepreneurs hire consultants to help them solve problems. Later this chapter discusses how these problems can be overcome when starting and managing a small business.

- *Fund-raising difficulty.* Another big problem for small businesses is obtaining adequate financing. Small firms must compete with larger, more established firms for the same pool of investment funds. Getting loans can be difficult because new businesses are obviously more risky than established ones. And the interest rates charged by banks and private investors are usually higher for small firms than for large ones. Sources of financing are examined in greater detail later in the chapter.

- *Burdensome government regulations.* The addition of new federal, state, and local regulations creates more compliance and reporting requirements for small businesses. Expanded federal, state, and local environmental regulations on water pollution and toxic wastes are especially burdensome. Local laws regulate noise pollution and traffic related to home-based businesses. With limited staff and financial resources, small firms may have to hire outside consultants to help prepare the many types of reports the government requires.

- *Extreme personal commitment of the owner.* Starting and managing a small business requires a major commitment by the owner. According to Dun & Bradstreet's 17th Annual Small Business Survey, more than half of all entrepreneurs work more than 51 hours a week, and 26 percent work over 60 hours a week. Long hours, the need for owners to do much of the work themselves, and the stress of being personally responsible for the success of the business are big disadvantages.

The Small Business Administration

>lg 5

Small Business Administration (SBA)

A government agency that helps people start and manage small businesses, helps small business owners win federal contracts, and speaks on behalf of small business.

Many small business owners turn to the **Small Business Administration (SBA)** for assistance. The SBA's mission is to help people start and manage small businesses, help them win federal contracts, and speak on behalf of small business. Through its national network of local offices, the SBA advises and helps small businesses in the areas of finance and management. Its toll-free number—1-800-U-ASK-SBA (1-800-827-5722)—provides general information, and its Web site at **www.sba.gov** offers details on all its programs.[20]

Financial Assistance Programs The SBA offers financial assistance to qualified small businesses that cannot obtain financing on reasonable terms through normal lending channels. This assistance takes the form of guarantees on loans made by private lenders. (The SBA no longer provides direct loans.) These loans can be used for most business purposes, including purchasing real estate, equipment, and materials. The SBA manages almost 500,000 loans totaling about $40 billion. For fiscal year 1998, the SBA made over 47,000 guaranteed loans totaling almost $10.8 billion.

Small Business Investment Company (SBIC)

Privately owned and managed investment companies that are licensed by the Small Business Administration and provide long-term financing for small businesses.

More than 300 SBA-licensed **Small Business Investment Companies (SBICs)** provide long-term funding for small businesses. These privately owned and managed investment companies hope to earn a substantial return on their investments as the small

What does it take to qualify for one of the many SBA loan programs? Find out at **www.sba.gov/financing**

businesses grow. In 1998, SBICs invested a record $3.2 billion in about 3,460 small businesses. The SBA's Angel Capital Electronic Network (ACE-Net) offers a matching service for small businesses seeking funding from individual investors.

Management Assistance Programs   The SBA also provides a wide variety of management advice. Its Business Development Library has publications on most business topics. Its "Starting Out" series offers more than 30 brochures on how to start a business in different fields (from ice cream stores to fish farms).

The Office of Business Development and local Small Business Development Centers offer advice, training, and educational programs. Business development officers counsel small-business owners. The SBA also offers free management consulting through two volunteer groups, the Service Corps of Retired Executives (SCORE) and the Active Corps of Executives (ACE). Executives in these programs use their business background to help small business owners.

The more than 12,000 SCORE volunteers and approximately 1,000 Small Business Development Centers provide management and technical assistance to about 900,000 small businesses each year. The Internet is helping SCORE expand its outreach into new markets by offering e-mail counseling through its Web site (**www.score.org**).

The SBA is committed to helping minority-owned businesses through its Office of Minority Enterprise Development. It has special programs and support services for socially and economically disadvantaged persons, including women, Native Americans, and Hispanics. The SBA also makes a special effort to help veterans go into business for themselves.

concept check

- What is a small business? Why are small businesses becoming so popular?
- Discuss the major advantages and disadvantages of small business ownership.
- What is the Small Business Administration? Describe the financial and management assistance programs offered by the SBA.

STARTING YOUR OWN BUSINESS

>lg 6

You may have decided that you'd like to go into business for yourself. If so, what's the best way to go about it? You can (1) start from scratch, (2) buy an existing business, or (3) buy a franchise. The first two options are covered in this section. Franchising was covered in Chapter 5.

Getting Started

The first step in starting your own business is a self-assessment to determine whether you have the personal traits you need to succeed and, if so, what type of business would be best for you. The Your Career feature that follows this chapter includes a questionnaire and other information to help you make these decisions. Finding the idea and choosing a form of business organization come next.

Finding the Idea   Entrepreneurs get ideas for their businesses from many sources. It is not surprising that 60 percent of Inc. 500 executives got the idea for their company while working in the same industry. Starting a firm in a field where you have experience improves your chances of success. Other sources of inspiration are hobbies and personal interests; suggestions from customers, family, and friends; and college courses or other education.

Ideas are all around you. Do you have a problem that you need to solve or a product that doesn't work as well as you'd like? Maybe one of your coworkers has a complaint. Raising questions about the way things are done is a great way to generate ideas. Many successful businesses get started because someone notices problems and needs and then finds a way to fill them. In 1996 Bill Gross founded Idealab, a company that develops Internet-related companies based on his ideas, on that premise. "Just about every idea I've ever pursued has been something that I . . . passionately feel I would want in my life," Gross says.[21]

What Pennsylvania interior designer Julie Margaret wanted was convenience. Tired of struggling with heavy mattresses and box springs when she arranged model homes, she wondered if there was a way to make beds look real without incurring the expense and hassle of real mattresses. The answer was Mimics, cardboard box "mattresses" reinforced with ribs so they won't collapse if someone sits on them. Margaret began selling the lightweight, reusable substitute cardboard beds in 1996. Mimics, which are easy to ship and cost only $30 to $50 depending on size, quickly became popular with contractors, department stores, bedding manufacturers, and photography studios.[22] Later in this chapter we'll offer more suggestions for ways to generate business ideas.

For tips on how to start, grow, or manage your business, check out *Entrepreneur* magazine's "Smart Tip of the Day" at **www.entrepreneurmag.com/smarttip.hts**

Choosing a Form of Business Organization Another key decision for a person starting a new business is whether it will be a sole proprietorship, partnership, corporation, or limited liability company. As discussed in Chapter 5, each type of business organization has advantagest and disadvantages. The choice depends on the type of business, number of employees, capital requirements, tax considerations, and level of risk involved.

Developing the Business Plan

Once you have the basic concept for a product, you must develop a plan to create the business. The planning process is one of the most important steps in starting a business and helps minimize the risks involved. A good business plan can be a critical determinant of whether a firm succeeds or fails. Debbie Gallagher, head of the Center for Entrepreneurship at New York's Nassau Community College, points out that two-thirds of all businesses fail in the first five years. "Why are these businesses failing? They haven't educated themselves as to what it takes to run a business," she says.[23]

One of the best ways to get that education is by preparing a formal, written **business plan** that describes in detail the idea for the new business and how it will be carried out. A well-prepared, comprehensive business plan helps business owners take an objective and critical look at their business venture and set goals that will help them manage the business and monitor its growth and performance.

Key features of a business plan are a general description of the company, the qualifications of the owner(s), a description of the product or service, an analysis of the market (demand, customers, competition), and a financial plan. It should focus on the uniqueness of the business and explain why customers will be attracted to it. Exhibit 6.4 is a brief outline of what a business plan should include.

Writing a good business plan may take many months. Many businesspeople, in their eagerness to begin doing business, neglect planning. They immediately get caught up in day-to-day operations and have little time for planning. But taking the time to develop a good business plan pays off. Writing the plan forces you to analyze your concept carefully and make decisions about marketing, production, staffing, and financing. A venture that seems sound at the idea stage may not look so good after closer analysis. The business plan also serves as the first operating plan for the business.

business plan

A formal written statement that describes in detail the idea for a new business and how it will be carried out; includes a general description of the company, the qualifications of the owner(s), a description of the product or service, an analysis of the market, and a financial plan.

Outline for a Business Plan

Title page: Provides names, addresses, and phone numbers of the venture and its owners and management personnel; date prepared; copy number; and contact person.

Table of contents: Provides page numbers of the key sections of the business plan.

Executive summary: Provides a one- to three-page overview of the total business plan. Written after the other sections are completed, it highlights their significant points and, ideally, creates enough excitement to motivate the reader to continue reading.

Vision and mission statement: Concisely describes the intended strategy and business philosophy for making the vision happen.

Company overview: Explains the type of company, such as manufacturing, retail, or service; provides background information on the company if it already exists; describes the proposed form of organization—sole proprietorship, partnership, or corporation. This section should be organized as follows: company name and location, company objectives, nature and primary product or service of the business, current status (startup, buyout, or expansion) and history (if applicable), and legal form of organization.

Product and/or service plan: Describes the product and/or service and points out any unique features; explains why people will buy the product or service. This section should offer the following descriptions: product and/or service; features of the product or service providing a competitive advantage; available legal protection—patents, copyrights, trademarks—and dangers of technical or style obsolescence.

Marketing plan: Shows who the firm's customers will be and what type of competition it will face; outlines the marketing strategy and specifies the firm's competitive edge. This section should offer the following descriptions: analysis of target market and profile of target customer; methods of identifying and attracting customers; selling approach, type of sales force, and distribution channels; types of sales promotions and advertising; and credit and pricing policies.

Management plan: Identifies the key players—active investors, management team, and directors—citing the experience and competence they possess. This section should offer the following descriptions: management team, outside investors, and/or directors and their qualifications, outside resource people and their qualifications, and plans for recruiting and training employees.

Operating plan: Explains the type of manufacturing or operating system to be used; describes the facilities, labor, raw materials, and product processing requirements. This section should offer the following descriptions: operating or manufacturing methods, operating facilities (location, space, and equipment), quality-control methods, procedures to control inventory and operations, sources of supply, and purchasing procedures.

Financial plan: Specifies financial needs and contemplated sources of financing; presents projections of revenues, costs, and profits. This section should offer the following descriptions: historical financial statements for the last three to five years or as available; pro forma financial statements for three to five years, including income statements, balance sheets, cash flow statements, and cash budgets (monthly for first year and quarterly for second year); break-even analysis of profits and cash flows; and planned sources of financing.

Appendix of supporting documents: Provides materials supplementary to the plan. This section should offer the following descriptions: management team biographies, any other important data that support the information in the business plan, and the firm's ethics code.

SOURCE: From *Small Business Management, 11th edition,* by Justin G. Longenecker and Carlos W. Moore. © 2000. Reprinted with permission of South-Western College Publishing, a division of Thomson Learning. Fax 800 730-2215.

The most common use of business plans is to persuade lenders and investors to finance the venture. The detailed information in the business plan helps them decide whether to invest. Even though the business plan may have taken months to write, it must capture the potential investor's interest in only a few minutes. For that reason, the basic business plan should be written with a particular reader in mind; it should be tailored to the type of investor you plan to approach and his or her investment goals.

The business plan should not be set aside once financing is obtained and the company is operational. Entrepreneurs who think the business plan is only for raising money make a huge mistake. Owners should review the plan on a regular basis—monthly, quarterly, or annually, depending on how fast their particular industry changes. "A business plan is a dynamic plan," says Jerry Kleinman, co-founder of Optimal Resolutions, Inc., a Manhasset (New York) family business consulting group. "It needs to be constantly updated as both internal and external conditions change. . . . As you meet your projections, you then want to set higher goals." Reviewing your plan will help you identify strengths and weaknesses in marketing strategies and management and also help you analyze possible opportunities for expansion in light of current trends and your original mission.[24]

Many business students get firsthand experience writing business plans by participating in their school's business plan competitions. As the Focus on Small Business box explains, many contest winners launch successful companies.

Financing the Business

Once the business plan is complete, the next step is to get the financing to set up the business. The amount required depends on the type of business and the

> f o c u s i n g   o n   s m a l l   b u s i n e s s <

FROM CLASSROOM TO COMPANY

What do 1-800 Contacts, Direct Hit Technologies, and Ampersand Art Supply have in common? These companies were all winners of major business plan competitions. 1-800 Contacts, for example, won the 1995 Brigham Young University tournament. The mail-order contact lens replacement company sold almost $4 million in lenses the following year.

About 35 business schools sponsor the contests, where students (usually in MBA programs) present plans for a new business. Students compete first at intramural contests at their own schools. Winners of those contests go on to intercollegiate contests at the University of Texas, Austin; San Diego State University (SDSU); the University of Oregon; or the University of Nebraska.

By creating a business from the ground up, students use every aspect of their business education. "Going through a competition teaches students how to present a plan and exposes them to the type of questions investors will be asking," says Alex de Noble, SDSU professor of management and entrepreneurship and director of its tournament. The contest also provides valuable networking opportunities and exposes would-be entrepreneurs to businesspeople who can advise them as they refine their plans.

Elaine Salazar, CEO and president of Ampersand Art Supply, which manufactures and sells art supplies at over 400 U.S. and overseas outlets, won the Texas and

California competitions. "I didn't just get an education on putting together a good business plan at the University of Texas," she says. "I had access to people and resources that helped me launch my business." One of the judges liked the company so much that he invested $300,000.

Winning does not guarantee success, however. University of Texas student Eric Hills, whose computer software start-up won second place at the San Diego contest, was unable to raise financing for Partnerware Technologies. "Some folks automatically assumed the company . . . was more of an academic exercise than a real business," he says. Hayes Batson, another software developer who placed second at the University of Chicago, fared better: "Coming in second helped provide us with the credibility we needed to raise $1 million."

Critical Thinking Questions

1. You and a friend decide to enter your school's business plan competition with an idea for a new interactive computer game based on the stock market. How would you prepare a business plan to convince judges that your idea is a winner?
2. As a judge at a business plan competition, what characteristics would you look for in a winning business plan, and why?

debt

A form of business financing consisting of borrowed funds that must be repaid with interest over a stated time period.

equity

A form of business financing consisting of funds raised through the sale of stock in a business.

angel investors

Individual investors or groups of experienced investors who provide funding for start-up businesses.

venture capital

Financing obtained from investment firms that specialize in financing small, high-growth companies and receive an ownership interest and a voice in management in return for their money.

Looking for your own angel? Visit the SBA's Angel Capital Electronic Network (ACE-Net) at **ace-net.sr.unh.edu/pub** (Note: ACE-Net operates from a secure server. If you cannot access it, read more about ACE-Net at **www.sba.gov/advo/acenet/**)

entrepreneur's planned investment. Businesses started by lifestyle entrepreneurs require less financing than growth-oriented businesses. The National Federation of Independent Businesses estimates that about half of all small business owners started their companies with less than $20,000, and 37 percent of the 1998 Inc. 500 were started with $10,000 or less.[25] Of course, manufacturing and high-tech companies generally require a larger initial investment.

The two forms of business financing are **debt,** borrowed funds that must be repaid with interest over a stated time period, and **equity,** funds raised through the sale of stock in the business. Those who provide equity funds get a share of the profits. Lenders usually limit debt financing to no more than a quarter to a third of the firm's total needs. Thus, equity financing usually amounts to about 65 to 75 percent of total start-up financing.

Two sources of equity financing for young companies are angel investors and venture capital firms. **Angel investors** are individual investors or groups of experienced investors who provide funding for start-up businesses. Angels often get involved with companies at a very early stage. **Venture capital** is financing obtained from investment firms that specialize in financing small, high-growth companies and receive an ownership interest and a voice in management in return for their money. They typically invest at a later stage than angel investors. We'll discuss venture capital in greater detail in Chapter 21.

Who provides the start-up funding, whether debt or equity, for small companies? Almost 80 percent of all business owners contribute personal savings to their new companies. Exhibit 6-5 shows how the founders of the Inc. 500 companies financed their start-ups.

Buying a Small Business

Another route to small business ownership is buying an existing business. Although this approach is less risky, it still requires careful and thorough analysis. Several important questions must be answered: Why is the owner selling? Does he or she want to retire or move on to another challenge, or are there some problems with the business? Is the business operating at a profit? If not, can the problems be corrected? What are the owner's plans after selling the company? Depending on the type of business, customers may be more loyal to the owner than to the product or service. They could leave the firm if the current owner decides to open a similar business. To protect against this situation, a "noncompete clause" can be included in the contract of sale.

Many of the same steps for starting a business from scratch apply to buying an existing company. A business plan that thoroughly analyzes all aspects of the business should be prepared. Get answers to all your questions, and determine, via the business plan, that the business is a good one. Then you must negotiate the purchase price and other terms and get financing. This can be a difficult process, and it may require the use of a consultant.

Risks of Small Business Ownership

Running your own business may not be as easy as it sounds. Despite the many advantages of being your own boss, the risks are great as well. Many businesses fail each year. The SBA estimates that about a quarter of all new businesses fail after two years, half after three years, and almost two out of every three by the end of the sixth year.[26]

Sources of Start-up Funding

Source	Percentage Using
Owner's personal savings	79%
Family members	16
Partners	14
Personal charge cards	10
Friends	7
Bank loans	7
Angel investors	5
Mortgaged property	4
Venture capital	3
Other	8

SOURCE: "The Inc. 500 Almanac," *Inc. 500* (October 21, 1997), p. 28.

Businesses close down for many reasons. Here are the most common causes:

- Economic factors—business downturns and high interest rates
- Financial causes—inadequate capital, low cash balances, and high expenses
- Lack of experience—inadequate business knowledge, management experience, and technical expertise

Many of the causes of business failure are interrelated. For example, low sales and high expenses are often directly related to poor management.

Inadequate planning is often at the core of business problems. As described earlier, a thorough feasibility analysis, from market assessment to financial plan, is critical to business success. And even with the best plans, business conditions change and unexpected situations arise. An entrepreneur may start a company based on a terrific new product only to find that a large firm with more marketing and distribution clout introduces a similar item.

The stress of managing a business can take its toll. The business can consume your whole life. Owners may find themselves in over their heads and unable to cope with the pressures of business operations, from the long hours to being the main decision maker.

Even successful businesses may have to deal with many of these difficulties. For example, growing too quickly can cause as many problems as sluggish sales. Growth can strain a company's finances. Additional capital is required to fund the expanded operations, from hiring additional staff to purchasing more equipment. Successful business owners must respond quickly as the business changes and develop plans to manage growth.

concept check

- How can potential business owners find new business ideas?
- Why is it important to develop a business plan? What should such a plan include?
- What financing options do small business owners have?
- Summarize the risks of business ownership.

MANAGING A SMALL BUSINESS

>lg 7   Whether you start a business from scratch or buy an existing one, you must be able to keep it going. The main job of the small business owner is to carry out the business plan through all areas of the business—from personnel to

production and maintenance. The small business owner must be ready to solve problems as they arise and move quickly when market conditions change. Hiring, training, and managing employees is another crucial responsibility. Clearly, managing a small business is quite a challenge.

Over time, the owner's role will change. As the company grows, others will make many of the day-to-day decisions while the owner focuses on managing employees and making plans for the firm's long-term success. The owner must always watch performance, evaluate company policies in light of changing conditions, and develop new policies as required. She or he must nurture a continual flow of ideas to keep the business growing. The type of employees needed may also change as the firm grows. A larger firm may need more managerial talent and technical expertise.

Using Outside Consultants

One way to ease the burden of managing a business is to hire outside consultants. Nearly all small businesses need a good certified public accountant (CPA) who can help with financial record keeping, tax planning, and decision making. An accountant who works closely with the owner to help the business grow is a valuable asset. An attorney who knows about small business law can provide legal advice and draw up essential documents. Consultants in other areas, such as marketing, employee benefits, and insurance, can be hired as needed. Outside directors with business experience are another way for small companies to get advice. Resources like these free the small business owner to concentrate on planning and day-to-day operations.

Want to know more about Employease? Read about its services at its Web site,
www.employease.com

Some aspects of the business can be *outsourced,* or contracted out to specialists in that area. For example, Employease is an Internet-based human resources system that manages benefits information for small and mid-size companies. At a secure Web site, a company's employees can review, change, or update benefits information. The company's personnel managers can analyze its benefits data to see how employees are using the benefits. The service costs less than buying the sophisticated software, which would be too expensive for most small firms.[27]

Hiring and Retaining Employees

Attracting good employees can be hard for a small firm, which may not be able to match the salaries, benefits, and advancement potential offered by larger firms. Compounding the problem is the general labor shortage. With unemployment rates below 5 percent, as they were at the end of the 1990s, small companies are finding it even harder to compete for qualified workers.

Small companies may have to be creative to find new employees and to convince applicants to join their firm. Jonathan Hirshon knew that Horizon Communications, a public relations (PR) firm in Silicon Valley, couldn't afford to compete with established high-tech PR firms for experienced staffers. Instead, he hires career changers with no PR background and trains them. "I can train people about technology, but I can't train them to be smart," he says. Hirshon's strategy is working: revenues jumped from $300,000 in 1996 to an anticipated $1 million in 1998. Horizon also benefits from the fresh perspective these employees bring.[28]

Once they hire employees, small business owners must promote employee satisfaction to retain them. Comfortable working conditions, flexible hours,

Small firms can use the Internet as a recruiting source by listing positions at job banks such as The Monster Board, which reach millions of job seekers.

concept check

- How does the small business owner's role change over time?
- Discuss strategies small business owners can use to acquire the expertise they need to help them run the business, either from outside sources or employees.
- Why should a small business consider exporting?

employee benefit programs, opportunities to help make decisions, and a share in profits and ownership are some of the ways to do this.

Later chapters of the book present detailed discussions of management, production, human resources, marketing, accounting, computers, and finance, all of which are useful to small business owners.

Operating Internationally

More and more small businesses are discovering the benefits of looking beyond the United States for markets. As we learned in Chapter 4, the global marketplace represents a huge opportunity for U.S. businesses, both large and small. About 40 percent of the Inc. 500 companies do business overseas, and more companies are joining their ranks each year. According to the Department of Commerce (DOC), 60 percent of American firms that export have fewer than 100 employees. Small businesses decide to export because of foreign competition in the United States, new markets in growing economies, economic conditions (such as recession) in the United States, and the need for increased sales and higher profits.

Many small businesses hire international trade specialists to get started selling overseas. They have the time, knowledge, and resources that most small businesses lack. Export trading companies buy goods at a discount from small businesses and resell them abroad. *Export management companies (EMCs)* act on a company's behalf. For fees of 5 to 15 percent of gross sales and multiyear contracts, they handle all aspects of exporting, including finding customers, billing, shipping, and helping the company comply with foreign regulations.

Want a quick course on how to expand into global markets? Check out Deloitte & Touche's Expanding Your Business Globally at

www.dtonline.com/expand/excover.htm

CAPITALIZING ON TRENDS IN BUSINESS

>lg 8   Social and demographic trends, combined with the challenges of operating in the fast-paced technology-dominated business climate of the 1990s, have changed the face of entrepreneurship and small business ownership. About

two-thirds of all new business owners launch their ventures from home. New ownership trends are emerging as well as more young people choose entrepreneurship over traditional career paths. The number of women and minority business owners continues to grow. Finally, the Internet is creating numerous opportunities for new types of small businesses.

Home Is Where the Office Is

For an increasing number of business owners, their daily commute is a walk down the hall to their home office. Since 1990, the number of Americans running home-based businesses has doubled to an estimated 12.6 million, and about two-thirds of all new businesses start at home. About half of all businesses with sales between $50,000 and $500,000 are home based.[29] Home-based businesses cover a wide variety of fields, as Exhibit 6-6 illustrates.

Considering starting a business at home? You'll find tips and advice at the American Association of Home Based Businesses Web site,

www.aahbb.org

No longer does running a business from home carry a stigma. In fact, many home-based entrepreneurs who could afford outside offices choose to stay home. "The home office used to be a stage in growth for many businesses," comments Sandy Weinberg, professor of entrepreneurship at Muhlenberg College in Allentown, Pennsylvania. "Now there's less of a need for many to ever move out of the home." Two trends that contribute to the rising popularity of working at home are the availability of low-cost technology—from voice mail to powerful computers and the Internet—and the large number of former corporate executives who consult or start businesses from home.[30]

Ownership Trends

At one time, most entrepreneurs were career changers starting second or third careers and corporate executives deciding to go out on their own. Today, many

> e x h i b i t 6 - 6 <

Top 10 Home-Based Business Start-Ups, 1997

Business	Number Started
1. General contracting	28,887
2. Construction	21,697
3. Computer services	17,669
4. Business consulting	15,261
5. Cleaning services	12,505
6. Real estate	7,007
7. Painting	6,518
8. Crafts	5,437
9. Trucking	5,279
10. Marketing services	5,028

SOURCE: "Almanac: Where the Start-ups Are," *Inc. State of Small Business 1998* (May 19, 1998), p. 136.

young people are choosing entrepreneurship as their first career. For women and minorities, entrepreneurship and small business ownership are a route to economic independence and personal and professional fulfillment. These groups are starting small businesses at rates far above the general population.

Entrepreneurs are getting younger all the time. About 30 percent of new entrepreneurs are age 30 or younger. An even higher number—over 60 percent of Americans ages 14 to 29—want to start their own business. A Wells Fargo Bank–National Federation of Independent Business (NFIB) study showed that Generation X-ers are among the most entrepreneurial of all age groups. "Instead of marching to the beat of corporate drums, many Gen. X-ers are opting to build or buy their own drum, allowing them to pound out their own beat," explains study author William J. Dennis of the NFIB Education Foundation. As Exhibit 6-7 shows, almost half of the people starting their own businesses, either from scratch or buying a business, were under 35. Another key factor is the Internet, which makes it easier for technology-literate people in their teens and 20s to get into business.

Women start businesses at a rate twice the national average, making them one of the most dynamic small business segments. The SBA Office of Advocacy estimates that about 8.5 million American women own businesses that generate $3.1 trillion in revenue and employ almost 24 million workers. Growth of this segment has been phenomenal, with sales soaring more than 350 percent from 1987 to 1997.[31]

What motivates women to start their own firms? A study sponsored by three major women's business organizations found that the two leading reasons are the inspiration of an entrepreneurial idea and frustration with the previous work environment. More women business owners than men report dissatisfaction with their corporate jobs, mentioning inflexibility, the "glass ceiling" (lack of promotional opportunities), contributions not valued, unpleasant environment, and lack of challenge as specific reasons for going the entrepreneurial route.

Women-owned businesses make a significant contribution to today's business environment. They favor such workplace innovations as flexible scheduling, employee autonomy, and a family-like work environment and are more likely to commit to socially responsible business practices. Phyllis Adams found success in a nontraditional field for women—highway and heavy construction.

> e x h i b i t   6 - 7 <

People Starting a Business, by Age

Age	Percentage of Total
Under 26	12.5%
26–35	34.1
36–45	30.1
46–55	16.9
56–65	4.9
Over 65	1.5

SOURCE: Wells Fargo/NFIB series on Business Starts and Stops, cited in "Generation X Leads the Way in Small Business Starts," NFIB Press Release, March 26, 1998, downloaded from **www.nfib.org.**

Women entrepreneurs like Heather Howitt, founder of Oregon Chai Tea Company, are launching their own firms at twice the rate of the national average.

After 16 years in her father's general contracting business, she started Phylway Construction in Thibodaux, Louisiana, in 1992 with just $10,000 and an old truck. Her dedication to getting the work done during the cleanup after the devastation of Hurricane Andrew gave her company a good reputation right from the start. By 1998, sales were over $10 million and growing. Adams attributes her success to her positive attitude and team-building management style. "As a company, we've worked on building open communication and trust," she says.[32]

Firms owned by minorities—nonwhite people—are another high-growth sector. From 1987 through 1992 (the most recent Census Bureau data available), the number of minority-owned firms rose 63 percent to a total of 2 million, compared to 26 percent for all firms. Even more striking is the increase in sales they generated: 128 percent, compared to 67 percent for all start-ups during the period. Hispanic-owned businesses experienced the highest growth rate, 83 percent.

Like women business owners, today's minority entrepreneurs have more education and prior business experience than their predecessors and are branching out into new industries. "Traditionally, minorities owned businesses in retail, but in the late 1980s and the 1990s, we've seen a diversification into high tech, construction, and the service industries," says George Herrera, president of the U.S. Hispanic Chamber of Commerce. Contributing to this trend is the increase in government high-tech contracting and the globalization of U.S. business.[33]

The passage of NAFTA has opened doors for Hispanic entrepreneurs in particular. Their bilingual and bicultural skills help them form stronger trade relationships with Mexico. Javier Pacheco's firm, Mercantile Transport, Inc., has grown over 20 percent a year. Based near Los Angeles with offices in El Paso, San Diego, and Tijuana, the firm carries textiles, computer components, and other products between *maquiladora* plants in Mexico and the United States. Pacheco attributes part of his success to his understanding of Mexican business culture, which makes it easier to work effectively with Mexican customs officials.[34]

African Americans are less likely than other minorities to own their own enterprises. Although self-employment has been a route to advancement for other minority groups in the United States, the rate of self-employment for blacks is one-third that of whites. The 621,000 African American–owned businesses represent less than 4 percent of all operating businesses, and about 75 percent have sales under $25,000 a year. A major obstacle for African American business owners is poor access to financing. Though other minority businesses also have problems obtaining financing, loan rejection rates for African American business owners were twice that of white-owned businesses, even after taking into account that African American–owned businesses tended to be younger, smaller, and owned by less experienced managers. This lack of financing discour-

For an overview of SBA services for women and links to its Online Women's Business Center and other program sites, visit the SBA Office of Women's Business Ownership site at
www.sba.gov/womeninbusiness/

ages African Americans from becoming business owners. To remedy this situation, the SBA has pledged to double the number of loan guarantees for African Americans.[35]

The Internet Explosion

As noted earlier, advances in technology make it easier than ever to start companies and develop a loyal customer following. Instead of pouring money into rent and fancy stores, entrepreneurs can launch businesses over the World Wide Web—and compete with long-established companies.

What services does the Minority Business Development Agency provide for small business owners? Click over to

www.mbda.gov/

to find out.

> a p p l y i n g   t e c h n o l o g y <

COLD FUSION GETS SOME BIG AIR

Cold Fusion Sports runs its discount snowboard business from a tiny, crowded San Francisco storefront. Its conference table rests on two sawhorses, and corrugated metal and used doors create separate spaces within its rooms. But co-founders and long-time snowboarders Tom Williams, Neil McKinnel, and Mark Horton couldn't be happier. Sales are soaring—from $78,000 in 1997 to $550,000 in 1998 and headed toward $6 million in 1999—as the company added skateboards, surfboards, wakeboards, and related equipment to its product lines.

How can Cold Fusion do so well in such a tiny space? Most of its customers never set foot in the physical store but order from the company's virtual store on the World Wide Web, www.boardshop.com.

"Today it's easy to set up an e-commerce site using packaged programs," says president Williams. "But it's much harder to build a successful e-commerce site that offers more than essentially an online classified ad or catalog. We wanted to 'humanize' our site, to create a lifestyle-oriented destination site for snowboarders." Adds CEO McKinnel, "The biggest challenge. . . is making the site look professional. That's what makes people comfortable giving us money."

The founders designed their first Web site, basically an order-taking site, in-house. They quickly registered keywords like "snowboard" with Yahoo! and America Online so that Cold Fusion's ad showed up when consumers searched for those terms.

Sales took off, but the high volume of traffic soon overwhelmed the site. Even though McKinnel ran a mail-order snowboard business and Williams was president of a computer leasing company, the partners soon discovered that they lacked the resources and technological expertise to manage inventory and a growing Web business. Although McKinnel handles most of the design, they now outsource Web site management to an Internet specialist, Pandesic LLC, which set up a fully automated e-commerce site. The result is a sophisticated Web site that integrates the entire online marketing and sales process, including secure Internet technology for online ordering, and tracks inventory.

The partners are pleased with their decision to outsource the Web site. "Partnering with Pandesic allows us to focus on our mission—providing consumers with a huge selection of premium equipment at discount prices and the finest customer service and product knowledge—while Pandesic focuses on providing the technology," says Williams.

Critical Thinking Questions

1. What are the advantages to Cold Fusion of operating as a virtual store? Disadvantages?
2. Would you buy board sports equipment from Cold Fusion? Why or why not? What features should Cold Fusion offer at its site to improve the buying process?

What's topping the pop music charts? Find out at CDNow's site, **cdnow.com**

CDNow took on the major music chains with its virtual music store. Instead of spending money on warehouses and distribution systems to place CDs on racks in stores around the country, the company focused on creating an informative and entertaining site. Visitors can search a huge inventory of all types of music, read interviews with their favorite artists, download sound clips, and, of course, order CDs and music in all categories.

Companies like Go2Net, Inc. simplify the process of setting up Web stores. Its Hypermart (**www.hypermart.com**) gives free space to small businesses that allow Hypermart to run ads on their Web pages. Its clients range from high-tech companies to home-based entrepreneurs selling handcrafts, and over 90,000 companies have taken advantage of the service in two years.[36]

Only about 20 percent of small businesses with Web sites can take orders and have the security to accept credit card numbers online. Nevertheless, the Web can boost sales in other ways by providing a convenient, always available source of product information. Cold Fusion Sports, profiled in the Applying Technology box, tapped into the full power of the Web to create a discount sports equipment retailer serving board sports enthusiasts.

c o n c ə p t   c h ə c k

- What significant trends are occurring in small business management?
- How is the Internet affecting small business?

APPLYING THIS CHAPTER'S TOPICS

After reading Chapters 5 and 6, you may be ready to go into business. Perhaps you believe you have just the "better mousetrap" the world needs. Maybe you want to be your own boss or seek financial rewards. Job security or quality of life issues may be your primary motives.

Whatever your reasons, you'll have to do a lot of groundwork before taking the plunge. Do you know what you want from life and how the business fits into your overall goals? Do you have what it takes to start a business, from personal characteristics like energy and persistence to money to fund the venture? You'll also have to research the feasibility of your product idea and develop a business plan. No question about it, becoming an entrepreneur or small business owner is hard work.

Taking the First Steps

Maybe you know that you want to run your own business but don't know what type of business to start. In addition to the advice provided earlier in the chapter, here are some ways to gather possible ideas:

- Brainstorm with family and friends without setting any limits, and then investigate the best ideas, no matter how impossible they may seem at first.
- Look at products that don't meet your needs and find ways to change them.
- Focus on your interests and hobbies. Attorneys Tim and Nina Zagat turned a love of dining out into a publishing company that sells restaurant guides.

- Use your skills in new ways. Are you computer-savvy? You could start a business providing in-home consulting to novices who don't know how to set up or use their computers.
- Be observant—look for anything that catches your interest wherever you are, in your hometown or when you travel. What's special about it? Is there a niche market you can fill?
- Pay attention to the latest fads and trends.
- Surf the Web, especially the "What's New" or "What's Hot" sections of search engines.[37]

Working at a Small Business

Working for a small company can be a wonderful experience. Many people enjoy the less structured atmosphere and greater flexibility that often characterize the small business workplace. Several years' experience at a small company can be a good stepping-stone to owning your own company. You'll get a better understanding of the realities of running a small business before striking out on your own. Other potential benefits include:

- *More diverse job responsibilities.* Small companies may not have formal job descriptions, giving you a chance to learn a wider variety of skills to use later. At a large company your job may be strictly defined.

> t r y   i t   n o w !   <

1. **Explore the Possibilities** Starting a business at home is one of the easiest ways to become self-employed. Using the businesses listed in Exhibit 6.6 and the Home Office Association of America (HOAA) Web site (**www.hoaa.com**) for ideas, choose a possible business opportunity that interests you. Then explore both the HOAA site and the American Association of Home-Based Businesses Web site (**www.aahbb.org**) to learn more about how to set up your business.

2. **Learn from an Entrepreneur** What does it really take to become an entrepreneur? Find out by interviewing a local entrepreneur or researching an entrepreneur you've read about in this chapter or in the business press. Get answers to the following questions, as well as any others you'd like to ask:

- How did you develop your vision for the company?
- What are the most important entrepreneurial characteristics that helped you succeed?
- Where did you learn the business skills you needed to run and grow the company?
- How did you research the feasibility of your idea? Prepare your business plan?
- What were the biggest challenges you had to overcome?
- Where did you obtain financing for the company?
- What are the most important lessons you learned by starting this company?
- What advice do you have for would-be entrepreneurs?

- *Less bureaucracy*. Small companies typically have fewer formal rules and procedures. This creates a more relaxed working atmosphere.
- *Your ideas more likely to count*. You'll have greater access to top management and be able to discuss your ideas.
- *Greater sense of your contribution to business*. You can see how your work contributes to the firm's success.

However, you should also be aware of the disadvantages of being a small business employee:

- *Lower compensation packages*. Although the gap between large and small businesses is narrowing, salaries are likely to be lower at small businesses. In addition, there may be few, if any, employee benefits such as health insurance and retirement plans.
- *Less job security*. Small businesses may be more affected by changing economic and competitive conditions. A change in ownership can put jobs at risk as well.
- *Greater potential for personality clashes*. When two employees don't get along, their hostility really stands out. Such conflicts can affect the rest of the staff. Also, if you have a problem with your boss, you don't have anyone to go to if the boss owns the company.
- *Fewer opportunities for career advancement*. After a few years, you may outgrow a small firm. There may be no chances for promotion. And with fewer people within the firm with whom to network, you'll have to join outside organizations for these connections.

Evaluating these factors will help you decide whether working at a small business is the right opportunity for you.

>looking ahead
at Nantucket Nectars, Inc.

Nantucket Nectars now has about 120 employees and five different lines of all-natural fruit juices, juice cocktails, iced teas, and lemonades. Despite its growth, Tom Scott and Tom First have kept the unique touches that made the company special, from homey labels and company trivia under the bottlecaps to the casual dress code. And the sentimental duo still owns their first business, Nantucket Allserve.

Although they are enjoying their financial success, they are far from complacent. "We're both paranoid people," Scott says. "Neither of us goes home and says, 'All right, now we're where we want to be.'" With competitors nipping at their heels, they are experimenting with new packaging, increased nutritional content for their Super Nectar line, and other products such as the Protein Smooth nutritional drink and an all-natural lemonade. The company also opened smoothie bars on Nantucket and in Boston. Their long-range plan is to grow Nantucket Nectars to $200 million in sales by 2002 and eventually become the country's largest juice producer. What could stand in their way? "Only ourselves—if we're not willing to improve ourselves and to strengthen our product over the next few years," says First.[38]

SUMMARY OF LEARNING GOALS

>lg 1   Why do people become entrepreneurs, and what are the different types of entrepreneurs?
Entrepreneurship involves taking the risk of starting and managing a business to make a profit. Entrepreneurs are innovators who start firms either to have a certain lifestyle or to develop a company that will grow into a major corporation. People become entrepreneurs for four main reasons: the opportunity for profit, independence, personal satisfaction, and lifestyle. Classic entrepreneurs may be micropreneurs, who plan to keep their businesses small, or growth-oriented entrepreneurs. Multipreneurs start multiple companies, while intrapreneurs work within large corporations.

>lg 2   **Which characteristics do successful entrepreneurs share?**

Successful entrepreneurs are ambitious, independent, self-confident, creative, energetic, passionate, and committed. They have a high need for achievement and a willingness to take moderate risks. They have good interpersonal and communication skills. Managerial skills and technical knowledge are also important for entrepreneurial success.

>lg 3   **How do small businesses contribute to the U.S. economy?**

A small business is independently owned and operated, has a local base of operations, and is not dominant in its field. The Small Business Administration further defines small business by size, according to the industry. Small businesses play an important role in the economy. About 98 percent of U.S. businesses have fewer than 100 employees. Small businesses are found in every field, but they dominate the construction, wholesale, and retail categories. Most new private-sector jobs created in the United States over the past decade were in small firms. Small businesses also create about twice as many new goods and services as larger firms.

>lg 4   **What are the advantages and disadvantages facing owners of small businesses?**

Small businesses have flexibility to respond to changing market conditions. Because of their streamlined staffing and structure, they can be efficiently operated. Small firms can serve specialized markets more profitably than large firms and provide a higher level of personal service. Disadvantages include limited managerial skill, difficulty in raising the capital needed for start-up and expansion, the burden of complying with increasing levels of government regulation, and the major personal commitment required on the part of the owner.

>lg 5   **How does the Small Business Administration help small businesses?**

The Small Business Administration is the main federal agency serving small businesses. It provides guarantees of private lender loans for small businesses. The SBA also offers a wide range of management assistance services, including courses, publications, and consulting. It has special programs for veterans, minorities, and women.

>lg 6   **What are the first steps to take if you are starting your own firm?**

After finding an idea that satisfies a market need, the small business owner should choose a form of business organization. The process of developing a formal business plan helps the business owner to analyze the feasibility of his or her idea. This written plan describes in detail the idea for the business and how it will be implemented. The plan also helps the owner obtain both debt and equity financing for the new business.

>lg 7   **Why does managing a small business present special challenges for the owner?**

At first, small business owners are involved in all aspects of the firm's operations. Wise use of outside consultants can free up the owner's time to focus on planning and strategy in addition to day-to-day operations. Other key management responsibilities are finding and retaining good employees and monitoring market conditions.

>lg 8   **What trends are shaping the small business environment?**

Women are starting businesses at a faster rate than any other group. Currently, they own about 30 percent of all businesses. Women often choose self-employment for lifestyle reasons and to overcome limited opportunities in large firms. Minority-owned businesses are another high-growth category. Minorities view business ownership as a way to overcome racial discrimination and economic hardship. Both women and minorities have made strides in overcoming

KEY TERMS

angel investors
  184
business plan 181
debt 184
entrepreneur 171
equity 184
intrapreneur 172
small business 176
Small Business
  Administration
  (SBA) 179
Small Business
  Investment
  Company (SBIC)
  179
venture capital
  184

barriers to entrepreneurship, such as discrimination, lack of formal business education, and limited business experience. Special training programs and financial assistance have helped increase business ownership among women and minorities. The Internet is also fueling small business growth by making it easier to open Web-based businesses.

PREPARING FOR TOMORROW'S WORKPLACE

1. After working in marketing with a major food company for 12 years, you are becoming impatient with corporate "red tape" (regulations and routines). You have an idea for a new snack product for nutrition-conscious consumers and are thinking of starting your own company. What are the entrepreneurial characteristics you will need? What other factors should you consider before quitting your job? Divide the class into two groups: one takes the role of the entrepreneurial employee, and the other takes the role of his or her current boss. Each should develop notes for a script. The employee will focus on why this is a good idea, reasons he/she will succeed, and so on, while the employer will play devil's advocate to convince him/her that staying on at the large company is a better idea.

2. Interview a small business owner in your community. Ask the owner why she/he chose this business, what she/he likes and dislikes most about running it, and the biggest challenges, advantages, and disadvantages. What would she/he do differently if starting over again today? Summarize your interview and prepare a brief report to present to your class.

3. Your class decides to participate in a local business plan competition. Divide the class into small groups and choose one of the following ideas:

   - A new computer game based on the stock market
   - A company with an innovative design for a skateboard
   - Travel services for college and high school students

   Prepare a detailed outline for the business plan, including the objectives for the business and the types of information you would need to develop product, marketing, and financing strategies. Each group will then present their outline for the class to critique.

4. A small catering business in your city is for sale for $150,000. The company specializes in business luncheons and smaller social events. The owner has been running the business for four years from her home but is expecting her first child and wants to sell. You will need outside investors to help you purchase the business. Develop questions to ask the owner about the business and its prospects and a list of documents you'd want to see. What other types of information would you need before making a decision to buy this company? Summarize your findings in a memo to a potential investor that explains the appeal of the business for you and how you plan to investigate the feasibility of the purchase.

5. Research the various types of assistance available to women and minority business owners. Call or visit the nearest SBA office to find out what services and resources it offers. Contact trade associations such as the National Alliance of Black Entrepreneurs, the U.S. Hispanic Chamber of Commerce, the National Foundation for Women Business Owners (NFWBO), and the Department of Commerce Minority Business Development Agency (MBDA). Call these groups or use the Web to develop a list of their resources and how a small business owner could use them.

WORKING THE NET

1. If you want to start a business, you need to have a plan to show investors and bankers. Visit Sample Business Plans at **www.bplans.com**/ to review sample plans for all types of businesses. You'll also get information about making a presentation of your plan, tips on international business plans, advice on business start-ups, an Ask the Experts page, and more. Select an idea for a company in a field that interests you, and using information from this site, prepare an outline for its business plan.

2. Visit the American Venture Capital Exchange site (**www.avce.com**), look through some of the listings, and find a business idea you like or dislike. Explain why you think this is a good business idea or not. List additional information the entrepreneur should have about starting this business and research the industry on the Web using a search engine.

3. Check out the international trade Web links at the State University of New York's Sites for Entrepreneurs, **www.smallbiz.sunycentral.edu/trade.htm.** Pick two or three of the suggested global business Web sites. Compare them in terms of the information offered to small businesses that want to venture into overseas markets. Which is the most useful, and why?

4. What can the Small Business Administration do to help you start and operate a business? Explore the SBA Web site at **www.sba.gov.** Read the latest news headlines about small businesses. What resources are available to you locally? What classes does the Small Business Classroom offer? What about financing assistance? Do you think the site lives up to the SBA's goal of being a one-stop shopping resource for the small business owner? Why or why not?

5. The Small Business Knowledge Base offers a wealth of information on all phases of small business start-ups and management. Select a type of business that interests you and go through the checklist presented at **www.bizmove. com/starting/m1b.htm,** Starting a Business: Determining the Feasibility of Your Business Idea. It will help you evaluate your suitability to be a business owner and analyze your idea for a business. Based on your feasibility study, should you continue to investigate this opportunity? Take time to explore the rest of the site as well.

CREATIVE THINKING CASE

They Keep Going and Going . . .

For many entrepreneurs, once is not enough. Even if their first attempts are less than successful, they learn from their mistakes and become "multipreneurs," starting other companies. In the technology sector, failure is almost a status symbol rather than a blot on an entrepreneurial résumé. Investors like entrepreneurs who are willing to learn from their mistakes and plunge back in. "We prefer to back smart people who have stubbed their toes to backing smart people who have experienced nothing but smooth sailing," says Michael Moritz, a partner at venture firm Sequoia Capital. The entrepreneurs themselves agree that failure can provide better experience than easy successes. Dealing with the failure helps them to identfy their strengths and weaknesses more clearly—and to do whatever is necessary to avoid making the same mistakes the next time.

Take Jerry Kaplan. In 1987 he founded Go Corporation, a pen-based computer company whose "Penpoint" computer won praise. Even though he had a great management team, Go's visionary, next-generation technology was ahead of its time and never gained market acceptance. Although Go failed, Kaplan turned the experience into a success by writing *Startup. A Silicon Valley Adventure,* a best-selling chronicle of his experiences.

Today, Kaplan is riding high on the Internet sea as chief executive officer of Onsale, a leading interactive online auction house (**www.onsale.com**) he founded in 1995 with partner Alan Fisher. No auction buff himself, Kaplan had the vision to combine two popular trends—the Internet and people's love of auctions—to create a major retail distribution channel through the Internet. This venture was in many ways the opposite of Go's pen-based computing: low technical risk, low capital risk, and quick time to market.

Starting with computer-related products, Onsale soon branched out into other categories such as consumer electronics, sports equipment, and travel services. It resells new, refurbished, or remanufactured goods that it buys at a discount from manufacturers as well as goods offered on consignment.

At first, investors did not share the co-founders' enthusiasm for online auctions. The pair provided $500,000 in start-up funding themselves. After their early success, they raised $4 million from venture capital investors in 1996 and went public in April 1997 at $6 a share. By early 1999, Onsale had over 1 million registered users and annual sales of over $200 million, and it was trading at $45. "Onsale has pioneered a new form of retailing that . . . combines the bargains of a warehouse club, the entertainment of television shopping, the skill of the stock market, and the fun of Las Vegas," explains Kaplan. "Customers don't just buy, they win."

Critical Thinking Questions

1. Do you agree with Michael Moritz's preference for funding companies run by people who have experienced failure? Why?
2. How did Kaplan's experiences at Go help him to build Onsale into a successful company?
3. Many other companies such as eBay also offer online auctions. Visit the Onsale and eBay sites (**www.onsale.com** and **www.ebay.com**) to see how they compare.

VIDEO CASE

Yahoo!

Yahoo!,(**www.yahoo.com** and **www.yahoo.com/doc/pr/**), the Internet media company, started out as an idea, grew into a hobby, and became a rapidly expanding business. In April 1994, as a diversion from their doctoral studies in electrical engineering at Stanford University, David Filo and Jerry Yang began to categorize the sites they visited on the Internet. They started their guide as a way to keep track of their personal interests. During 1994, Filo and Yang transformed their guide "into a customized database designed to serve the needs of the thousands of users that began to use the service through the closely bound Internet community."

Filo and Yang's service soon grew into an entrepreneurial venture as a Web search engine. This search engine has been supplemented with a variety of services that, when taken together, constitute what is now Yahoo! Yahoo! Inc. has become "a global Internet media company that offers a branded network of comprehensive information, communication, and shopping services to millions of users daily."

Yahoo! has vigorously pursued a strategy of innovation, responding rapidly to user feedback, creating new services, and monitoring the Web for new content. Its services now include direct marketing; online shopping; Internet auctions; travel reservations and ticketing; communications tools such as *Yahoo! Mail, Yahoo! Pager, Yahoo! Chat,* and *Yahoo! Calendar*; audio content on *Yahoo! News*; a guide to locating career information on *Yahoo! Employment*; sports coverage on *Yahoo! Sports;* snow conditions, resort, and travel information on *Yahoo! Ski and Snow;* 18 *World Yahoo!* sites, and local sites for major American cities.

All of this made the company's most recent fiscal year (1998) a landmark success. Net revenue for fiscal 1998 was approximately $203 million, nearly triple that of the preceding fiscal year. Tim Koogle, the company's chairman and CEO, commented: "Our performance exceeded expectations and is the result of relentless expansion of the value-added choices and services we offer users, advertisers, and merchants. While giving users the best experience available on the Web, we delivered a uniquely powerful platform on which advertisers and merchants can build their online businesses. We look forward to continuing to maintain and strengthen our leadership position in the coming year."

In February 1999, Yahoo! announced the launch of "a new set of services designed to help small businesses and merchants create a Web presence and promote their business online." These services, in conjunction with those launched during the preceding summer, address the needs of the increasing numbers of merchants and small businesses that wish to use the Internet to reach new customers. *Yahoo! Site,* one of the new services, provides businesses with a fast, easy way to create a professional-quality Web site and immediately market their products or services online. *Yahoo! Site* can be upgraded to *Yahoo! Store,* which was launched in June 1998, to conduct commercial transactions online. *Yahoo! Connected Office* enables small companies to create their own intranet, a shared company calendar, and customizable business news and information. *Yahoo! Small Business,* launched in August 1998, provides useful tools and general small business information, products, and services.

Critical Thinking Questions

1. Do you think David Filo and Jerry Yang have entrepreneurial personalities? Explain your answer.
2. What type of entrepreneurial business do you think Yahoo! is? Do you think it will continue to grow at the same rate over the next five years?
3. Are you interested in going into business for yourself? Can you derive any insights from Yahoo!'s example to help you to act on your own entrepreneurial tendencies?

Your Career as an Entrepreneur

Do you have what it takes to own your own company? Or are you better suited to working for a corporation? To find out, you need to determine whether you have the personal traits for entrepreneurial success. If the answer is yes, you need to identify the type of business that is best for you.

Know Yourself

Owning a business is challenging and requires a great deal of personal sacrifice. You must take a hard and honest look at yourself before you decide to strike out on your own. The quiz in Exhibit YC-1 can help you evaluate whether you have the personality traits to become a successful entrepreneur. Think about yourself and rate yourself—honestly!—on each of these characteristics.

Which Business Is for You?

If you are well suited to owning your own company, the next question is what type of business to start. You need to consider your expertise, interests, and financial resources. Start with a broad field, then choose a specific good or service. The business can involve a new idea or a refinement of an existing idea. It may bring an existing idea to a new area.

To narrow the field, ask yourself the following questions:

- What do I like to do?
- What am I good at?
- How much can I personally invest in my business?
- Do I have access to other financial resources?
- What is my past business experience?
- What are my personal interests and hobbies?
- How can I use my experience and interests in my own business?
- Do I want or need partners?

Spending time on these and similar questions will help you identify some possible business opportunities and the resources you will need to develop them.

> e x h i b i t   Y C - 1 <

How Do You Rate?

	High	Above Average	Average	Below Average	Low
Ability to handle uncertainty	○	○	○	○	○
Confidence	○	○	○	○	○
Discipline	○	○	○	○	○
Drive/ambition	○	○	○	○	○
Energy	○	○	○	○	○
Flexibility	○	○	○	○	○
Independence	○	○	○	○	○
Ability to seize opportunity	○	○	○	○	○
Persistence	○	○	○	○	○
Problem solving	○	○	○	○	○
Total	____	____	____	____	____

Scoring: Give yourself 5 points for every "high," 4 points for every "above average," 3 points for every "average," 2 points for every "below average," and 1 point for every "low."

Score results

- 50–46: You are already in business for yourself or should be!
- 45–40: Your entrepreneurial aptitude and desires are high.
- 39–30: A paid staff job and owning your own business rate equally.
- 29–20: Entrepreneurial aptitude is apparently not one of your strong suits.
- 19–10: You might find the going tough and the rewards slim if you owned your own business.

Prior job experience is the number-one source of new business ideas. Starting a firm in a field where you have specialized product or service experience improves your chances for success.

Personal interests and hobbies are another major source of ideas. Gourmet food enthusiasts have started many restaurants and mail-order food businesses. For example, The Hot Shop is an online retailer selling only hot sauces and related products (**www.hotstuff4u.com**). Jean McGraw, a British nanny who lives near San Francisco, got rave reviews about the buttery shortbread cookies she made as gifts. In 1996 she started McGraw's Shortbread with $10,000 in savings. The company was so successful that she outgrew her rented kitchen space and leased a larger bakery and warehouse.[1]

chapter seven

Management and Leadership in Today's Organization

learning goals

>lg 1 What is the role of management?

>lg 2 What are the four types of planning?

>lg 3 What are the primary responsibilities of managers in organizing activities?

>lg 4 How do leadership styles influence a corporate culture?

>lg 5 How do organizations control activities?

>lg 6 What roles do managers take on in different organizational settings?

>lg 7 What set of managerial skills is necessary for managerial success?

>lg 8 What trends will affect management in the future?

Using Toyota Techniques to Build Toys

It took a savvy group of investors to see the potential of Alexander Doll Co. (www.alexanderdollco.com), a small low-tech company located in the middle of Harlem. After 70 plus years, the company that handcrafts Madame Alexander collectible dolls found itself hoping to salvage its profitability by adopting the manufacturing and management methods used by one of the world's largest automakers. Headed for bankruptcy in 1995, Alexander Doll Co. was purchased by an investment group organized by TBM Consulting of North Carolina. The TBM partners specialize in teaching Toyota's lean management and manufacturing methods to American companies. TBM's investment group seeks out underperforming firms and changes the way their manufacturing process is managed, while retaining the company's original location and workforce.

The makeover at Alexander Doll Co. started with a change in leadership. New CEO Herbert Brown had lots of expertise in manufacturing, developed at companies such as Black & Decker, and he convinced employees to work with him in developing a new approach to making dolls. Empowering employees to share in decision making is one of the many lessons gleaned from the Toyota approach.

Managers and employees alike had to refocus on planning accurately for future production. Doll fabric is purchased in very small quantities that can't be reordered, and 75 percent of the styles change every year. Therefore, accurate forecasting of materials and production scheduling is crucial. In addition to reemphasizing accurate planning, the company needed to reorganize the entire production process. In contrast to the batch manufacturing method previously used at the company, Brown introduced employees to Toyota-style work teams. By working as teams, rather than producing parts individually, employees are able to fill orders much more quickly and have reduced work in progress by an astounding 96 percent. The company uses standard quality-control methods to provide feedback for the continuous improvement of the production process.

And how did the Alexander Doll Co. respond to the Toyota techniques? Projected sales for 1998 were $32 million, up from $23.8 million in 1995. The company is showing signs of financial good health and is predicting a profit for 2000, testimony to the ability of sound management techniques to cross the boundaries of culture, industry, and firm.[1]

Critical Thinking Questions

As you read this chapter, consider the following questions as they relate to Alexander Doll Co.

- What is the role of management?
- Why did good planning at Alexander Doll make a difference?
- Was reorganization into work teams a key to success for Alexander Doll?

BUSINESS IN THE 21ST CENTURY

Using current management techniques appropriate to the production process is essential to the success of the Alexander Doll Co. Today's companies rely on managers to guide the daily process using human, technological, financial, and other resources to create competitive advantage. For many beginning business students, being in "management" is an attractive, but somewhat vague, future goal. This vagueness is due in part to an incomplete understanding of what managers do and how they contribute to organizational success or failure. This chapter introduces the basic functions of management and the skills required by managers to drive an organization toward its goals. We will also discuss how leadership styles influence a corporate culture and highlight the trends that are shaping the future role of managers.

THE ROLE OF MANAGEMENT

>lg 1

management
The process of guiding the development, maintenance, and allocation of resources to attain organizational goals.

planning
The process of deciding what needs to be done to achieve organizational objectives; identifying when and how it will be done; and determining by whom it should be done.

concept check

- Define the term *management*.
- What are the four key functions of managers?

Management is the process of guiding the development, maintenance, and allocation of resources to attain organizational goals. Managers are the people in the organization responsible for developing and carrying out this management process. Management is dynamic by nature and evolves to meet needs and constraints in the organization's internal and external environments. In a global marketplace where the rate of change is rapidly increasing, flexibility and adaptability are crucial to the managerial process. This process is based in four key functional areas of the organization: planning, organization, leadership, and control. Although these activities are discussed separately in the chapter, they actually form a tightly integrated cycle of thoughts and actions. From this perspective, the managerial process can be described as (1) anticipating potential problems or opportunities and designing plans to deal with them, (2) coordinating and allocating the resources needed to implement plans, (3) guiding personnel through the implementation process, and (4) reviewing results and making any necessary changes. This last stage provides information to be used in ongoing planning efforts, and thus the cycle starts over again.

As shown in Exhibit 7-1, managerial work can be divided into four activities: planning, organizing, leading, and controlling. The four functions are highly interdependent, with managers often performing more than one of them at a time and each of them many times over the course of a normal workday. As you will learn in the following sections, all of the functions require sound decision making and communication skills.

PLANNING

>lg 2

Planning begins by anticipating potential problems or opportunities the organization may encounter. Managers then design strategies to solve current problems, prevent future problems, or take advantage of opportunities. These strategies serve as the foundation for goals, objectives, policies, and procedures. Put simply, planning is deciding what needs to be done to achieve organizational objectives, identifying when and how it will be done, and determining by whom it should be done. Effective planning requires extensive information

> e x h i b i t   7 - 1 <

> e x h i b i t   7 - 1 <

What Managers Do and Why

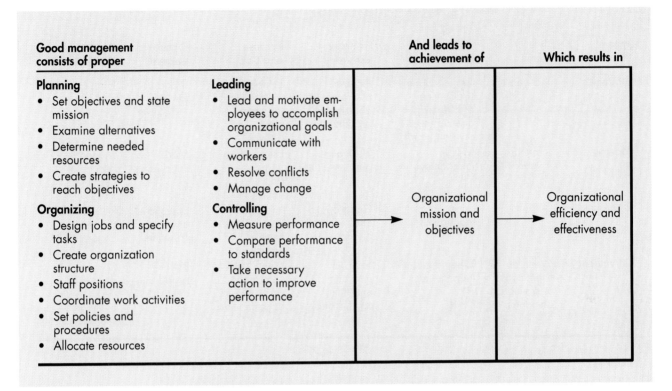

Good management consists of proper		And leads to achievement of	Which results in
Planning • Set objectives and state mission • Examine alternatives • Determine needed resources • Create strategies to reach objectives **Organizing** • Design jobs and specify tasks • Create organization structure • Staff positions • Coordinate work activities • Set policies and procedures • Allocate resources	**Leading** • Lead and motivate employees to accomplish organizational goals • Communicate with workers • Resolve conflicts • Manage change **Controlling** • Measure performance • Compare performance to standards • Take necessary action to improve performance	Organizational mission and objectives →	Organizational efficiency and effectiveness

about the external business environment in which the firm competes, as well as its internal environment.

There are four basic types of planning: strategic, tactical, operational, and contingency. Most of us use these different types of planning in our own lives. Some plans are very broad and long term (more strategic in nature), such as planning to attend graduate school after earning a bachelor's degree. Some plans are much more specific and short term (more operational in nature), such as planning to spend a few hours in the library this weekend. Your short-term plans support your long-term plans. If you study now, you have a better chance of achieving some future goal, such as getting a job interview or attending graduate school. Like you, organizations tailor their plans to meet the requirements of future situations or events. A summary of the four types of planning appears in Exhibit 7-2.

Strategic planning involves creating long-range (one to five years), broad goals for the organization and determining what resources will be needed to accomplish those goals. An evaluation of external environmental factors such as economic, technological, and social issues is critical to successful strategic planning. Strategic plans, such as the organization's long-term **mission,** are formulated by top-level managers and put into action at lower levels in the organization. For example, in a recent memo called "The Era Ahead," sent to hundreds of Microsoft managers, CEO Bill Gates outlines his company's long-term course.[2] Currently, Microsoft is the king of the desktop software industry, but Gates wants the company to become a major player in the field of information appliances. This grand vision for the company sets the stage for planning at all levels of the organization.

strategic planning

The process of creating long-range (one to five years), broad goals for the organization and determining what resources will be needed to accomplish those goals.

mission

An organization's purpose and reason for existing; its long-term goals.

Types of Planning

Type of Planning	Time Frame	Level of Management	Extent of Coverage	Purpose and Goal	Breadth of Content	Accuracy/ Predictability
Strategic	1–5 years	Top management (CEO, vice-presidents, directors, division heads)	External environment and entire organization	Establish mission and long-term goals	Broad and general	High degree of uncertainty
Tactical	Less than 1 year	Middle management	Strategic business units	Establish midrange goals for implementation	More specific	Moderate degree of certainty
Operational	Current	Supervisory management	Geographic and functional divisions	Implement and activate specific objectives	Specific and concrete	Reasonable degree of certainty
Contingency	When an event occurs or a situation demands	Top and middle management	External environment and entire organization	Meet unforeseen challenges and opportunities	Both broad and detailed	Reasonable degree of certainty once event or situation occurs

mission statement

A formal document that states an organization's purpose and reason for existing and describes its basic philosophy.

tactical planning

The process of beginning to implement a strategic plan by addressing issues of coordination and allocating resources to different parts of the organization; has a shorter time frame (less than one year) and more specific objectives than strategic planning.

operational planning

The process of creating specific standards, methods, policies, and procedures that are used in specific functional areas of the organization; helps guide and control the implementation of tactical plans.

How does Ben & Jerry's mission statement translate into company action? Visit Ben & Jerry's home page at **www.benjerry.com** to learn more.

How have Mickey Drexler's plans for Gap, Inc. panned out? Read about the company's latest performance history under "company information" at **www.gap.com**

An organization's mission is formalized in its **mission statement,** a document that states the purpose of the organization and its reason for existing. For example, Ben & Jerry's mission statement addresses three fundamental issues and states the basic philosophy of the company (see Exhibit 7-3).

In all organizations, plans and goals at the tactical and operational levels should clearly support the organization's mission statement.

Tactical planning begins the implementation of strategic plans. Tactical plans have a shorter (less than 1 year) time frame than strategic plans and more specific objectives designed to support the broader strategic goals. Tactical plans begin to address issues of coordinating and allocating resources to different parts of the organization.

Operational planning creates specific standards, methods, policies, and procedures that are used in specific functional areas of the organization. Operational objectives are current, narrow, and resource focused. They are designed to help guide and control the implementation of tactical plans.

All of these types of planning are apparent in the history of Gap, Inc. Mickey Drexler is the driving force behind the company's strategic vision, namely, to become a global brand on the level of Coca-Cola, Gillette, and Disney.[3] On a strategic planning level, Drexler hopes to make Gap clothing a universal wardrobe staple by saturating the market with retail

> e x h i b i t   7 - 3 <

| Ben & Jerry's Mission Statement

"Ben & Jerry's is dedicated to the creation and demonstration of a new corporate concept of linked prosperity. Our mission consists of three interrelated parts:

Product

To make, distribute and sell the finest quality all natural ice cream and related products in a wide variety of innovative flavors made from Vermont dairy products.

Economic

To operate the Company on a sound financial basis of profitable growth, increasing value for our shareholders, and creating opportunities and financial rewards for our employees.

Social

To operate the Company in a way that actively recognizes the central role that business plays in the structure of society by initiating ways to improve the quality of life of a broad community—local, national, and international. Underlying the mission of Ben & Jerry's is the determination to seek new and creative ways of addressing all three parts, while holding a deep respect for individuals inside and outside the Company and for the communities of which they are a part."

SOURCE: Ben & Jerry's, Inc.

stores and supplying the world with fundamental clothing such as pocket-Ts, khakis, and denim. At the tactical level, Drexler's planning focuses on different ways the company can grow the Gap brand. Creation of GapKids and Old Navy were both tactical plans designed to extend the Gap brand and increase market coverage. Even at the operational level, Drexler has a say in the planning process. After noticing that some stores were looking increasingly shabby, Drexler introduced a plan for completely remodeling every store every seven years. Such attention to detail at every level of planning has paid off for Drexler and his company. As of 1998, Gap's 10-year annualized total return to investors was 38.8 percent.

The key to effective planning is anticipating future situations and events. Yet even the best-prepared organization must sometimes cope with unforeseen circumstances such as a natural disaster, an act of terrorism, or a radical new technology. Therefore, many companies have developed **contingency plans** that identify alternative courses of action for very unusual or crisis situations. The contingency plan typically stipulates the chain of command, standard operating procedures, and communication channels the organization will use during an emergency. Failure to have adequate contingency plans for emergencies can have serious consequences for an organization, as Potomac Electric Power Co. (Pepco) discovered on a cold night in January 1999.[4]

The ice storm that struck the Washington, D.C. area that night was, according to Pepco officials, the most devastating ever to hit the region. An estimated 400,000 residents and businesses were left powerless, some for as long as five days. A review of Pepco's response to the situation identified the following weaknesses in the company's planning: (1) despite forecasts of freezing rain, Pepco had only its standard number of line crews on duty; (2) customer service agents

contingency plans

Plans that identify alternative courses of action for very unusual or crisis situations; typically stipulate the chain of command, standard operating procedures, and communication channels the organization will use during an emergency.

HOT links

To learn more about how firms develop contingency plans for all sorts of crises, visit *Contingency Planning* magazine's Web site at **www.contingencyplanning. com**

had little or no information about what was happening in the field during the crisis; (3) due to inadequate tracking mechanisms, Pepco could not always tell whether power had been restored to individual houses; and (4) repair staff had been reduced by one-third over the previous three years to trim costs. In the weeks following the power outage, Pepco executives spent long hours analyzing what went wrong and devising a new contingency plan to enable them to cope more effectively during the next emergency.

concept check

- What is the purpose of planning, and what is needed to do it effectively?
- Identify the unique characteristics of each type of planning.

ORGANIZING

>lg 3

organizing
The process of coordinating and allocating a firm's resources in order to carry out its plans.

A second key function of managers is **organizing,** which is the process of coordinating and allocating a firm's resources in order to carry out its plans. Organizing includes developing a structure for the people, positions, departments, and activities within the firm. Managers can arrange the structural elements of the firm to maximize the flow of information and the efficiency of work processes. They accomplish this by doing the following:

- Dividing up tasks *(division of labor)*
- Grouping jobs and employees *(departmentalization)*
- Assigning authority and responsibilities *(delegation)*

These and other elements of organizational structure are discussed in detail in Chapter 8. In this chapter, however, you should understand the three levels of a managerial hierarchy. This hierarchy is often depicted as a pyramid as in Exhibit 7-4. The fewest managers are found at the highest level of the pyramid.

> e x h i b i t 7 - 4 <

The Managerial Pyramid

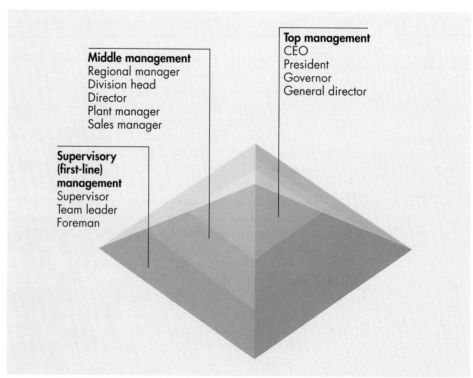

top management

The highest level of managers; includes CEOs, presidents, and vice-presidents, who develop strategic plans and address long-range issues.

middle management

Managers who design and carry out tactical plans in specific areas of the company.

supervisory management

Managers who design and carry out operation plans for the ongoing daily activities of the firm.

Called **top management,** they are the small group of people at the head of the organization (such as the CEO, presidents, and vice-presidents). Top-level managers develop *strategic plans* and address long-range issues such as which industries to compete in, how to capture market share, and what to do with profits. These managers design and approve the firm's basic policies and represent the firm to other organizations. They also define the company's values and ethics and thus set the tone for employee standards of behavior. For example, at Booz Allen & Hamilton, Inc., a New York consulting company, employees are expected to model their behavior on that of the senior partners. Martha Gross Clark, vice-president and chief financial officer (CFO) of the company, explains that employees are much more likely to take their cues from how top managers behave than to follow written rules.[5]

The second and third tiers of the hierarchy are called **middle management** and **supervisory management,** respectively. Middle managers (such as division heads, departmental managers, and regional sales managers) are responsible for beginning the implementation of strategic plans. They design and carry out *tactical plans* in specific areas of the company. They begin the process of allocating resources to meet organizational goals, and they oversee supervisory managers throughout the firm. Supervisors, the most numerous of the managers, are at the bottom of the managerial pyramid. These managers design and carry out *operational plans* for the ongoing daily activities of the firm. They spend a great deal of their time guiding and motivating the employees who actually produce the goods and services.

c o n c ə p t   c h ə c k

- Explain the managerial function of organizing.
- What is the managerial pyramid?

LEADING

>lg 4

leadership

The process of guiding and motivating others toward the achievement of organizational goals.

power

The ability to influence others to behave in a particular way.

legitimate power

Power that is derived from an individual's position in an organization.

reward power

Power that is derived from an individual's control over rewards.

coercive power

Power that is derived from an individual's ability to threaten negative outcomes.

expert power

Power that is derived from an individual's extensive knowledge in one or more areas.

referent power

Power that is derived from an individual's personal charisma and the respect and/or admiration the individual inspires.

Leadership, the third key management function, is the process of guiding and motivating others toward the achievement of organizational goals. Managers are responsible for directing employees on a daily basis as the employees carry out the plans and work within the structure created by management. Organizations need strong effective leadership at all levels in order to meet goals and remain competitive.

To be effective leaders, managers must be able to influence others' behavior. This ability to influence others to behave in a particular way is called **power.** Researchers have identified five primary sources, or bases, of power:

- **Legitimate power,** which is derived from an individual's position in an organization
- **Reward power,** which is derived from an individual's control over rewards
- **Coercive power,** which is derived from an individual's ability to threaten negative outcomes
- **Expert power,** which is derived from an individual's extensive knowledge in one or more areas
- **Referent power,** which is derived from an individual's personal charisma and the respect and/or admiration the individual inspires

Many leaders use a combination of all of these sources of power to influence individuals toward goal achievement. Bill Gates, for example, gets his legitimate power from his position as CEO of Microsoft. He is able to offer incentives such as stock options to reward high-performing employees and to threaten low performers with undesirable

Want to learn more about Bill Gates's management style? Go to **www.microsoft.com/BillGates** to read his official biography, speeches, and other information. For a different view, visit **www.zpub.com/un/bill**

Microsoft CEO Bill Gates uses all five bases of power—legitimate, reward, coercive, expert, and referent—in leading his employees to achieve organizational goals.

leadership style

The relatively consistent way that individuals in leadership positions attempt to influence the behavior of others.

consequences. His technical expertise in computer software, technological innovation, and financial management allows him to greatly influence the decisions made at Microsoft, and many people find his strong focus and ability to convey his vision compelling enough to warrant great respect and admiration.

Leadership Styles

Individuals in leadership positions tend to be relatively consistent in the way they attempt to influence the behavior of others, meaning that each individual has a tendency to react to people and situations in a particular way. This pattern of behavior is referred to as **leadership style.** As Exhibit 7-5 shows, leadership styles can be placed on a continuum that encompasses three distinct styles: autocratic, participative, and free rein.

Autocratic leaders are directive leaders, allowing for very little input from subordinates. These leaders prefer to make decisions and solve problems on their own and expect subordinates to implement solutions according to very specific and detailed instructions. In this leadership style, information typically flows in one direction, from manager to subordinate. The military, by necessity, is generally autocratic. When autocratic leaders treat employees with fairness and respect, they may be considered knowledgeable and decisive. But often autocrats are perceived as narrow-minded and heavy-handed in their unwillingness to share power, information, and decision making in the organization. The trend in organizations today is away from the directive, controlling style of the autocratic leader.

In 1997 a merger took place that initially had Wall Street investors jumping for joy. HFS, one of the world's biggest franchisers of real estate brokerages, and

> e x h i b i t   7 - 5 <

Leadership Styles of Managers

Amount of authority held by the leader

Autocratic Style	Participative Style (democratic, consensual, consultative)	Free-Rein (Laissez-Faire) Style
• Manager makes most decisions and acts in authoritative manner. • Manager is usually unconcerned about subordinates' attitudes toward decisions. • Emphasis is on getting task accomplished. • Approach is used mostly by military officers and some production line supervisors.	• Manager shares decision making with group members and encourages teamwork. • Manager encourages discussion of issues and alternatives. • Manager is concerned about subordinates' ideas and attitudes. • Manager coaches subordinates and helps coordinate efforts. • Approach is found in many successful organizations.	• Manager turns over virtually all authority and control to group. • Members of group are presented with task and given freedom to accomplish it. • Approach works well with highly motivated, experienced, educated personnel. • Approach is found in high-tech firms, labs, and colleges.

Amount of authority held by group members

Many successful organizations use participative leadership styles that involve group members in discussing issues and making decisions.

autocratic leaders

Directive leaders who prefer to make decisions and solve problems on their own with little input from subordinates.

participative leadership

A leadership style in which the leader shares decision making with group members and encourages discussion of issues and alternatives; includes democratic, consensual, and consultative styles.

democratic leaders

Leaders who solicit input from all members of the group and then allow the members to make the final decision through a vote.

consensual leaders

Leaders who encourage discussion about issues and then require that all parties involved agree to the final decision.

CUC International, a billion dollar seller of club memberships, appeared at first to be a match made in heaven. But the partnership was a disaster, due at least in part to two very different leadership styles.[6] Henry Silverman, CEO of HFS, was an autocratic leader. He wanted to be in total control, to make every decision, and to know what was going on in every corner of his company. In contrast, Walter Forbes, CEO of CUC International, viewed himself as a visionary leader who left the operational details of running the company to others. Forbes's leadership style was so hands-off that he appeared to be unaware of massive accounting irregularities discovered in his organization after the merger. The distinctly different leadership styles of these two men resulted in a culture clash and a battle for power that ended up costing shareholders billions of dollars in lost earnings. In hindsight, perhaps both parties could have benefited from a more participative approach to management. There are three types of participative leadership: democratic, consensual, and consultative.

Democratic leaders solicit input from all members of the group and then allow the group members to make the final decision through a voting process. This approach works well with highly trained professionals. The president of a physicians' clinic might use the democratic approach. **Consensual leaders** encourage discussion about issues and then require that all parties involved agree to the final decision. This is the general style used by labor mediators. **Consultative leaders** confer with subordinates before making a decision, but retain the final decision-making authority. This technique has been used to dramatically increase the productivity of assembly-line workers.

The third leadership style, at the opposite end of the continuum from the autocratic style, is **free-rein** or **laissez-faire** (French for "leave it alone") **leadership.** Managers who use this style turn over all authority and control to subordinates. Employees are assigned a task and then given free rein to figure out the best way to accomplish it. The manager doesn't get involved unless asked. Under this approach, subordinates have unlimited freedom as long as they do not violate existing company policies. This approach is also sometimes used with highly trained professionals as in a research laboratory. Although one might at first assume that subordinates would prefer the free-rein style, this approach can have several drawbacks. If free-rein leadership is accompanied by unclear expectations and lack of feedback from the manager, the experience can be frustrating for an employee. Employees may perceive the manager as being uninvolved and indifferent to what is happening or as unwilling or unable to provide the necessary structure, information, and expertise.

Employee Empowerment

Participative and free-rein leaders use a technique called empowerment to share decision-making authority with subordinates. **Empowerment** means giving employees increased autonomy and discretion to make their own decisions, as well as control over the resources needed to implement those decisions. When decision-making power is shared at all levels of the organization, employees feel a greater sense of ownership in, and responsibility for, organizational outcomes.

consultative leaders

Leaders who confer with subordinates before making a decision, but who retain the final decision-making authority.

free-rein (laissez-faire) leadership

A leadership style in which the leader turns over all authority and control to subordinates.

empowerment

The process of giving employees increased autonomy and discretion to make decisions, as well as control over the resources needed to implement those decisions.

corporate culture

The set of attitudes, values, and standards that distinguishes one organization from another.

What management leadership traits do business executives believe are necessary to succeed in today's competitive business world? Read the results of a survey in *Entrepreneur* magazine at **www.entrepreneurmag. com** by doing a search for "leadership."

Jack Welch, CEO of General Electric Corp. and a consummate manager, says that "Giving people self-confidence is by far the most important thing that I can do. Because then they will act."[7]

There is no one best leadership style. Each of the three styles described here works best in a particular type of business environment or situation. The most effective style for a given situation depends on elements such as the characteristics of the subordinates, the complexity of the task, the source of the leader's power, and the stability of the environment.

Corporate Culture

The leadership style of managers in an organization is usually indicative of the underlying philosophy, or values, of the organization. The set of *attitudes, values,* and *standards of behavior* that distinguishes one organization from another is called **corporate culture.** A corporate culture evolves over time and is based on the accumulated history of the organization, including the vision of the founders. It is also influenced by the dominant leadership style within the organization. Evidence of a company's culture is seen in its heroes (e.g., Andy Grove of Intel), myths (stories about the company that are passed from employee to employee), symbols (e.g., the Nike swoosh), and ceremonies. Procter & Gamble's corporate culture is so strong that it is sometimes referred to as a cult, and employees are said to be "Procterized," rather than socialized.[8]

Although culture is intangible and its rules are often unspoken, it can have a strong impact on a company's success. Therefore, managers must try to influence the corporate culture so that it will contribute to the success of the company. The 1998 merger of America's Chrysler Corp. with Germany's Daimler-Benz AG presented just such a challenge. Andreas Renschler, head of executive management development at DaimlerChrysler AG, was put in charge of "one of the world's biggest efforts to bridge corporate cultural differences."[9] Among the issues to be addressed in this corporate marriage are differences in language, customs, labor-management relations, worker autonomy, and compensation. What does Renschler see as the key to successfully combining the two corporate cultures? He plans to wed them by developing trust through team building and promoting managers who show a willingness to embrace change. Consider how a corporate culture may influence the success of a new technology business such as the one described in the Focusing on Small Business box.

In merging their companies, Chrysler's CEO Robert Eaton (front left) and Daimler-Benz's CEO Jurgen Schrempp (front right) are combining the firms' two different cultures by building trust through team building and rewarding managers who can adapt to change.

concept check

- How do leaders influence other people's behavior?
- How can managers empower employees?
- What is corporate culture?

HOW THE INTERNET CHANGED A LIFELONG GOAL

Gary Cullis spent years preparing to be a patent attorney. He earned his law degree from Harvard in 1997. But Cullis never practiced law for even one day. Instead, he took a leap of faith and started an Internet company. Now he is one of hundreds of young entrepreneurs with innovative ideas who have cashed in on the phenomenal growth of the World Wide Web. The hardest thing he's had to do so far? Tell his mom he's not going to be a lawyer.

Cullis's idea began to take shape as he worked on patent research during his law school years. He wanted a more efficient way to search the Web, so he wouldn't have to wade through thousands of irrelevant information sites before finding what he needed. Frustrated with the lack of existing alternatives, Cullis developed his own software program and named it Direct Hit. Called a "popularity engine," Cullis's software ranks Internet search results by using information such as length of viewing time to calculate how popular each Web site has been with people who ran similar searches. In early 1998 Cullis entered his idea in the prestigious Entrepreneurship Competition at the Massachusetts Institute of Technology and won $50,000.

"Within three months of his graduation, Cullis had founded a company dedicated to making Internet searching easier, raised $1.4 million in venture capital and landed contracts with America Online Inc., Apple Computer Inc. and Wired Digital Inc. Without stopping for fancy planning and the usual business school stuff, Direct Hit raised another $2 million in the fall, hired 30 people, signed up more high-profile customers, released a string of new search features and . . . moved into 9,000 square foot digs near Boston." To make all of this happen in such a short time, Cullis needed help, and he found it in a man named Mike Cassidy, a man with some striking similarities to Cullis himself. Cassidy had also attended Harvard, and while there had won the same MIT contest. At age 22 Cassidy formed a technology company called Stylus Innovation, Inc., which he sold in 1996 for $13 million. In 1998 Cassidy went looking for a new challenge and found Cullis's Direct Hit. Cullis and Cassidy met, and after spending four hours together, Cullis offered Cassidy the CEO position in his new company. Cassidy accepted. Knowing how quickly business happens in the cyberworld, Cassidy immediately arranged an appointment with a large venture capital firm. By late afternoon of the day they presented their idea, Cullis and Cassidy had a check in hand, and Direct Hit became a reality.

Critical Thinking Questions

1. How did Cullis combine an entrepreneurial spirit with planning skills to make Direct Hit a success?
2. What type of management style should Mike Cassidy use to be most popular with Direct Hit employees?
3. Do you think that there will be a lot of employee empowerment at Direct Hit?

CONTROLLING

>lg 5

controlling

The process of assessing the organization's progress toward accomplishing its goals; includes monitoring the implementation of a plan and correcting deviations from the plan.

The fourth key function that managers perform is controlling. **Controlling** is the process of assessing the organization's progress toward accomplishing its goals. It includes monitoring the implementation of a plan and correcting deviations from that plan. As Exhibit 7-6 on p. 214 shows, controlling can be visualized as a cyclical process made up of five stages:

1. Setting performance standards (goals)
2. Measuring performance
3. Comparing actual performance to established performance standards
4. Taking corrective action (if necessary)
5. Using information gained from the process to set future performance standards

How Organizations Control Activities

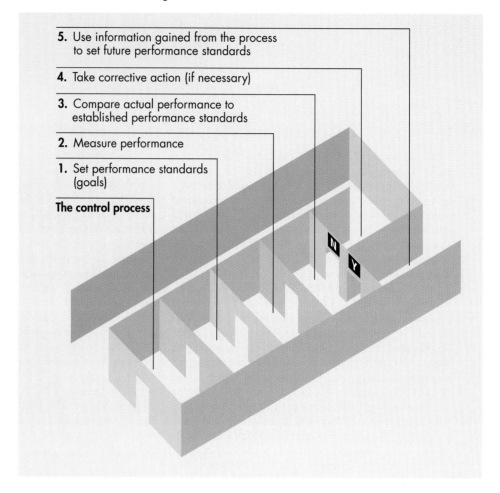

5. Use information gained from the process to set future performance standards

4. Take corrective action (if necessary)

3. Compare actual performance to established performance standards

2. Measure performance

1. Set performance standards (goals)

The control process

Performance standards are the levels of performance the company wants to attain. These goals are based on its strategic, tactical, and operational plans. The most effective performance standards state a measurable behavioral objective that can be achieved in a specified time frame. For example, the performance objective for the sales division of a company could be stated as "$100,000 in gross sales for the month of January." Each individual employee in that division would also have a specified performance goal. Actual firm, division, or individual performance can be measured against performance standards to see if a gap exists between the desired level of performance and the actual level of performance. If a performance gap does exist, the reason for it must be determined and corrective action taken.

Feedback is essential to the process of control. Most companies have a reporting system that identifies areas where performance standards are not being met. A feedback system helps managers detect problems before they get out of hand. If a problem exists, the managers take corrective action. Toyota uses a simple but effective control system on its automobile assembly lines. Each worker serves as the customer for the process just before his or hers. Each worker is empowered to act as a quality control inspector. If a part is defective or not installed properly, the next worker won't accept it. Any worker can alert the supervisor to a problem by tugging on a rope that turns on a warning light (i.e., feedback). If the problem isn't corrected, the worker can stop the entire assembly line.

MANAGERIAL CHALLENGES IN A GARMENT FACTORY

For a number of years, the Mehserjian family ran a garment factory in Los Angeles, where they did contract sewing of T-shirts and other budget-priced clothing for a variety of clients. In 1997, their best year, they generated $2.9 million in sales from 120 sewing machines and made a profit of $400,000. The following year their business began a nose-dive. Their profits dwindled as some of their biggest customers shifted their contract sewing to factories in Mexico where labor costs were substantially lower.

Departing customers repeatedly said that they would continue to place orders with the Mehserjians if the family had a factory in Mexico. The Mehserjians reacted with a two-point strategy. First, they began sewing higher-priced garments in the Los Angeles factory. Second, they opened a factory on the outskirts of Guadalajara, Mexico, to sew lower-priced garments.

About half of the 100 sewing machines in the Mehserjians' Mexican factory are sitting idle. Finding enough workers to keep the Mexican facility running—even at half capacity—is a daily struggle. Improving productivity is a constant challenge as well. An even greater challenge, though, is trying to change the workers' attitudes. The Mehserjians pay above the prevailing market rate for the locale. Yet they still have difficulty getting employees to show up to work on a regular basis. To solve the attendance problem, the Mehserjians offered employees a 10 percent bonus for coming to work as scheduled for the entire week. In spite of this, absenteeism is still rampant.

Critical Thinking Questions

1. Can a business remain ethical while responding to the competitive pressures of the marketplace?
2. Do incentives for coming to work constitute bribery?
3. How far should companies go to ensure that employees conform to minimal work standards?

c o n c ə p t   c h ə c k

- Describe the control process.
- Why is the control process important to the success of the organization?

Why is controlling such an important part of a manager's job? First, it helps managers to determine the success of the other three functions: planning, organizing, and leading. Second, control systems direct employee behavior toward achieving organizational goals. Third, control systems provide a means of coordinating employee activities and integrating resources throughout the organization.

MANAGERIAL ROLES

>lg 6

informational roles

A manager's activities as an information gatherer, an information disseminator, or a spokesperson for the company.

interpersonal roles

A manager's activities as a figurehead, company leader, or liaison.

decisional roles

A manager's activities as an entrepreneur, resource allocator, conflict resolver, or negotiator.

In carrying out the responsibilities of planning, organizing, leading, and controlling, managers take on many different roles. A role is a set of behavioral expectations, or a set of activities that a person is expected to perform. Managers' roles fall into three basic categories: **informational roles, interpersonal roles,** and **decisional roles.** These roles are summarized in Exhibit 7-7. In an *informational role*, the manager may act as an information gatherer, an information distributor, or a spokesperson for the company. A manager's *interpersonal roles* are based on various interactions with other people. Depending on the situation, a manager may need to act as a figurehead, a company leader, or a liaison. When acting in a *decisional role*, a manager may have to think like an entrepreneur, make decisions about resource allocation, help resolve conflicts, or negotiate compromises.

Managerial Decision Making

In every function performed, role taken on, and set of skills applied, a manager is a decision maker. Decision making means choosing among alternatives.

> e x h i b i t   7 - 7 <

The Many Roles That Managers Play in an Organization

Role	Description	Example
Informational Roles		
Monitor	Seeks out and gathers information relevant to the organization.	Finding out about legal restrictions on new product technology.
Disseminator	Provides information where it is needed in the organization.	Providing current production figures to workers on the assembly line.
Spokesperson	Transmits information to people outside the organization.	Representing the company at a shareholders' meeting.
Interpersonal Roles		
Figurehead	Represents the company in a symbolic way.	Cutting the ribbon at ceremony for the opening of a new building.
Leader	Guides and motivates employees to achieve organizational goals.	Helping subordinates to set monthly performance goals.
Liaison	Acts as a go-between among individuals inside and outside the organization.	Representing the retail sales division of the company at a regional sales meeting.
Decisional Roles		
Entrepreneur	Searches out new opportunities and initiates change.	Implementing a new production process using new technology.
Disturbance handler	Handles unexpected events and crises.	Handling a crisis situation such as a fire.
Resource allocator	Designates the use of financial, human, and other organizational resources.	Approving the funds necessary to purchase computer equipment and hire personnel.
Negotiator	Represents the company at negotiating processes.	Participating in salary negotiations with union representatives.

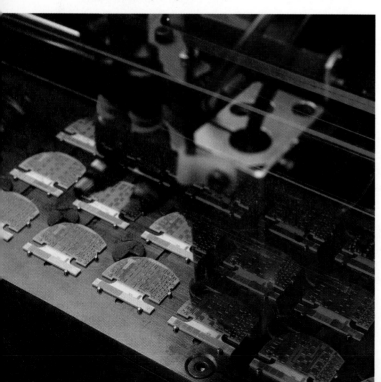

Managers made nonprogrammed decisions in preparing their automated production facilities like the microchip manufacturing system shown here for the unique situation presented by the year 2000.

Decision making occurs in response to the identification of a problem or an opportunity. The decisions managers make fall into two basic categories: programmed and nonprogrammed. Programmed decisions are made in response to routine situations that occur frequently in a variety of settings throughout an organization. For example, the need to hire new personnel is a common situation for most organizations. Therefore, standard procedures for recruitment and selection are developed and followed in most companies.

Infrequent, unforeseen, or very unusual problems and opportunities require **nonprogrammed decisions** by managers. Because these situations are unique and complex, the manager rarely has a precedent to follow. Preparing manufacturing companies for the year 2000 is an example of nonprogrammed decision making. The problem was that manufacturing equipment failed to operate properly when the computers that control their operations, which were designed to handle only two-digit years, failed to recognize the new millennium.[10] Although most of the attention was focused on mainframe computers, factories were actually the biggest "Y2K" challenge for managers. Because factory automation systems tend to be made by numerous manufacturers and assembled piecemeal using specialized software, there is no one blueprint for finding all

nonprogrammed decisions
Responses to infrequent, unforeseen, or very unusual problems and opportunities where the manager does not have a precedent to follow in decision making.

the electrical components and fixing all of the software. The final decision on how to adjust each manufacturing system must be made after carefully gathering information and weighing alternative courses of action.

Addressing the Y2K problem required a systematic approach to decision making as illustrated in Exihibit 7-8. Managers typically follow five steps in the decision-making process:

1. Recognize or identify a problem or opportunity. Although it is more common to focus on problems because of their obvious negative effects, managers who do not take advantage of new opportunities may lose competitive advantage to other firms.
2. Gather information so as to identify alternative solutions or actions.
3. Choose one or more alternative after evaluating the strengths and weaknesses of each possibility.
4. Put the chosen alternative into action.
5. Gather information to obtain feedback on the effectiveness of the chosen plan. Some very practical questions to ask during the decision-making process are shown in Exhibit 7-9.

c o n c ə p t   c h ə c k

- What are the three types of managerial roles?
- Give examples of things managers might do when acting in each of the different types of roles.
- List the five steps in the decision-making process.

MANAGERIAL SKILLS

>lg 7

In order to be successful in planning, organizing, leading, and controlling, managers must use a wide variety of skills. A *skill* is the ability to do something proficiently. Managerial skills fall into three basic categories: conceptual, human relations, and technical skills. The degree to which each type of skill is used depends upon the level of the manager's position as seen in Exhibit 7-10. Additionally, in an increasingly global marketplace, it pays for managers to develop a special set of skills to deal with global management issues.

technical skills
A manager's specialized areas of knowledge and expertise, as well as the ability to apply that knowledge.

Technical Skills

Specialized areas of knowledge and expertise and the ability to apply that knowledge make up a manager's **technical skills.** Preparing a financial statement,

> e x h i b i t   7 - 8 <

The Decision-Making Process

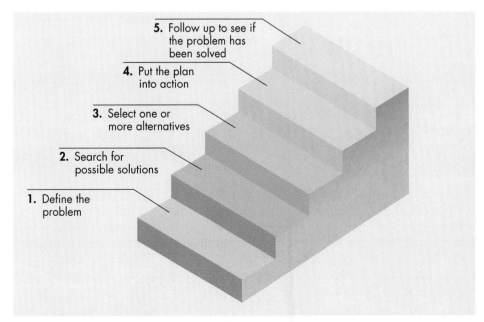

5. Follow up to see if the problem has been solved
4. Put the plan into action
3. Select one or more alternatives
2. Search for possible solutions
1. Define the problem

> e x h i b i t   7 - 9 <

Questions to Ask Yourself to Help Make Better Decisions

1. *What's my decision problem?* What, broadly, do I have to decide? What specific decisions do I have to make as a part of the broad decision?
2. *What are my fundamental objectives?* Have I asked "Why?" enough times to get to my bedrock wants and needs?
3. *What are my alternatives?* Can I think of more good ones?
4. *What are the consequences of each alternative in terms of the achievement of each of my objectives?* Can any alternatives be safely eliminated?
5. *What are the trade-offs among my more important objectives?* Where do conflicting objectives concern me the most?
6. *Do any uncertainties pose serious problems?* If so, which ones? How do they impact consequences?
7. *How much risk am I willing to take?* How good and how bad are the possible consequences? What are ways of reducing my risk?
8. *Have I thought ahead, planning out into the future?* Can I reduce my uncertainties by gathering information? What are the potential gains and costs in time, money, and effort?
9. *Is the decision obvious or pretty clear at this point?* What reservations do I have about deciding now? In what ways could the decision be improved by a modest amount of added time and effort?
10. *What should I be working on?* If the decision isn't obvious, what do the critical issues appear to be? What facts and opinions would make my job easier?

SOURCE: Reprinted by permission of Harvard Business School Press. From *Smart Choices: A Practical Guide to Making Better Decisions,* by John S. Mannond, Ralph L. Keeney, and Howard Raiffa. Boston, MA 1998. Copyright © 1998 by the President and Fellows of Harvard College; all rights reserved.

programming a computer, designing an office building, and analyzing market research are all examples of technical skills. These types of skills are especially important for supervisory managers because they work closely with employees who are producing the goods and/or services of the firm. Supervisory managers need to be knowledgeable about the specific production and operation tools, techniques, and methods relevant to their specific area of the organization, as demonstrated in the Applying Technology box.

> e x h i b i t   7 - 1 0 <

The Importance of Managerial Skills at Different Management Levels

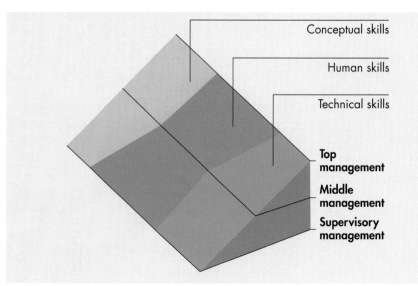

> a p p l y i n g   t e c h n o l o g y <

ADVANCED INFORMATION TECHNOLOGY IS A KEY TO DELL'S SUCCESS

Successful managers use new information technology to enhance corporate fitness. One of the best measures of corporate fitness is return on investment capital (ROIC). The two components that combine to create a high ROIC are the ability to charge a price much higher than actual cost (operating margin) and the ability to generate sales from a small base of invested capital (asset utilization). Dell Computers provides an excellent example of how both these elements can be significantly increased by effectively managing information technology. Dell's entrepreneurial approach to computer sales combines cutting-edge knowledge of Internet technology with sophisticated enterprise software that streamlines order processing and delivery, resulting in something known as mass customization.

Dell's reliance on advanced information technology systems allows it to build millions of personal computers a year to exact customer specifications and provide investors with a very comfortable ROIC. How does the company do it? Dell uses information technology in a number of ways to increase both operating margin and asset utilization. It uses sophisticated logistics software to reduce the cost of customization; yet it is able to charge a premium for the unique configurations customers want, thus increasing the operating margin. Asset utilization is improved by shortening the supply chain and tying up far less capital in inventory. Dell's managers use information technology aggressively to create value for their customers at a lower cost than the competition.

Critical Thinking Questions

1. Are technology skills important at all levels of management at Dell?
2. What other managerial skills are important at Dell?
3. Are technology skills important at other computer manufacturers like IBM and Gateway?

Human Relations Skills

human relations skills

A manager's interpersonal skills that are used to accomplish goals through the use of human resources.

Human relations skills are the interpersonal skills managers use to accomplish goals through the use of human resources. This set of skills includes the ability to understand human behavior, to communicate effectively with others, and to motivate individuals to accomplish their objectives. Giving positive feedback to employees, being sensitive to their individual needs, and showing a willingness to empower subordinates are all examples of good human relations skills.

Karl Eberle, general manager at Harley-Davidson's newest assembly plant, uses strong human relations skills to build cohesive self-directed work teams that run the production process.[11] Working closely with line workers and union representatives, Eberle empowers employees to make decisions about how to build a better bike and improve the work environment. This commitment to building relationships with Harley employees is in part responsible for the recent revitalization of the company and is a key to its continued success.

Conceptual Skills

conceptual skills

A manager's ability to view the organization as a whole, understand how the various parts are interdependent, and assess how the organization relates to its external environment.

Conceptual skills include the ability to view the organization as a whole, understand how the various parts

Most successful managers work hard at continually updating their managerial skills. One organization that offers many ongoing training and education programs is the American Management Association. Visit its site at

www.amanet.com

Capitalizing on Trends in Business

are interdependent, and assess how the organization relates to its external environment. These skills allow managers to evaluate situations and develop alternative courses of action. Good conceptual skills are especially necessary for managers at the top of the management pyramid where strategic planning takes place.

Global Management Skills

global management skills
A manager's ability to operate in diverse cultural environments.

The increasing *globalization* of the world market, as discussed in Chapter 3, has created a need for managers who have **global management skills,** that is, the ability to operate in diverse cultural environments. With more and more companies choosing to do business in multiple locations around the world, employees are often required to learn the geography, language, and social customs of other cultures. It is expensive to train employees for foreign assignments and pay their relocation costs; therefore, choosing the right person for the job is especially important. Individuals who are open-minded, flexible, willing to try new things, and comfortable in a multicultural setting are good candidates for international management positions.

c o n c ə p t c h ə c k

- Define the basic managerial skills.
- How important is each of these skill sets at the different levels of the management pyramid?
- What new challenges do managers face due to increasing globalization?

CAPITALIZING ON TRENDS IN BUSINESS

>lg 8

Three important trends in management today are: increasing employee empowerment, the growing use of information technology, and the increasing need for global management skills. Each will be examined in turn.

Managers Empowering Employees

The employee empowerment trend allows employers to tap the knowledge and talent of all employees and gives workers a greater sense of ownership in their work and commitment to their employers.

Most of the firms discussed in this chapter, including Ben & Jerry's, General Electric, and Harley-Davidson, are including more employees in the decision-making process than ever before. This increased level of employee involvement comes from the realization that people at all levels in the organization possess unique knowledge, skills, and abilities that can be of great value to the company. With empowerment, managers share information and responsibility with employees at all levels in the organization. Along with the authority to make decisions, empowerment also gives employees the control over resources needed to implement those decisions. Empowering employees enhances their commitment to the organization by giving them a feeling of ownership in the firm and an increased sense of competency.

In order for empowerment to work, managers have to facilitate employee decision making by providing access to necessary information, clear expectations for results, behavioral boundaries, and the resources employees need to carry out their decisions. This concept is illustrated by Steve Miller, group managing director of the Royal Dutch/Shell Group of Companies. Royal Dutch/Shell is one of the largest companies in the world with a strong sense of tradition and a very structured way of doing things. When Miller set out to change the way things were done at his company, he knew he would have to involve the people on the front lines, the "grassroots" positions of the company. He calls his form of empowerment *grassroots leadership*. Grassroots leadership means finding a way to empower the frontline people, "to challenge them, to provide them with the resources they need, and then to hold them accountable."[12]

Managers and Information Technology

The second trend having a major impact on managers is the proliferation of information technology. An increasing number of organizations are selling technology, and an increasing number are looking for cutting-edge technology to make and market the products and services they sell. A brief look at PeopleSoft, a rapidly growing provider of automated human resource functions, provides some insight into the crucial role information technology can play in today's organizations.[13] Plenty of new technology is being used at PeopleSoft, but it is "people-oriented" technology, and it starts with a backpack. Every new employee is issued a backpack filled with a laptop, pager, cell phone, and digital assistant. Steve Zarate, chief information officer at PeopleSoft, calls it "information-to-go." Every employee has access to PeopleSoft's "massive information infrastructure that spans continents and time zones." PeopleSoft uses information systems to create an "infomacracy," an organization where members have access to the information they need to make and implement decisions. By using the latest technology to empower people and keep members of the organization connected, PeopleSoft has grown to be a $10 billion company.

Managing in a Global Marketplace

Find out more about how DoubleClick manages its worldwide operations by visiting the company's home page at

www.doubleclick.com

Geographic boundaries no longer constrain businesses the way they once did. To fully realize their potential, many companies must look to international markets to expand the sales of their products and services. This presents significant new challenges to managers. Global management can mean flying thousands of miles a week to keep up with business units spread across the world. Although new information technology makes communication easier than ever before, sometimes it cannot substitute for face-to-face contact. Ensuring that employees in far-flung locations still feel part of a cohesive organizational team can be difficult. Global managers often have to adapt to a new culture, learn a new language, manage a diverse workforce, and operate in a foreign economic system. For many managers, accepting an international position also means helping their spouses and children adapt to the new environment. And in some companies, managers must try to translate an entire company philosophy into another language and culture.

c o n c e p t c h e c k

- What steps must managers take if employee empowerment is to work?
- How can information technology aid in decision-making?
- What special problems do global managers face?

APPLYING THIS CHAPTER'S TOPICS

Many of the skills managers use to accomplish organizational goals can be applied outside the organizational setting. You could be using these skills in your life right now to accomplish your personal goals. This section provides some examples.

Effective Time Management

Successful managers use their time wisely. Adopting the following time management techniques will help you become a more successful student now and will help prepare you for the demands of your future workplace:

- *Plan ahead.* This is first and most obvious. Set both long-term and short-term goals. Review your list often and revise it when your situation changes.
- *Establish priorities.* Decide what is most important and what is most urgent. Sometimes they are not the same thing. Keep in mind the 80–20 rule: 20 percent of one's effort delivers 80 percent of the results.
- *Delegate.* Ask yourself if the task can be accomplished as effectively by someone else. Empower other people, and you may be surprised by the quality of the outcome.
- *Learn to say no.* Be stingy with your time. Be realistic about how long tasks will take. Don't feel guilty when you don't have the time, ability, or inclination to take on an additional task.
- *Batch.* Group activities together so they take up less of your day. For example, set aside a certain time to return phone calls, answer e-mail, and do any necessary written correspondence.
- *Stay on task.* Learn how to handle diversions. For example, let your answering machine take messages until you finish a particular task. Create a routine that helps you stay focused.
- *Set deadlines.* Don't let projects drag on. Reward yourself each time you cross a certain number of items off your "to do" list.

Decision-Making Skills

One of the best ways to prepare for any career, including a career in business, is to improve your ability to make good decisions. But what is a "good" decision? Is it one that is made quickly, but with incomplete information? Or is it one that is made more slowly, but with more facts and figures to support it? Is a good decision always objective? Or should it be based on a gut feeling? And, if you practice making decisions, do you actually get better at making them? Some recognized decision makers offer these guidelines:[14]

- *Have confidence in your judgment, and always go by the evidence,* says Ed Koch, former mayor of New York City.
- *Think about the long-term consequences of your decision,* says Pamela Lopker, CEO of QAD, Inc. and America's richest self-made woman.
- *Listen to your inner wisdom,* says W. Brian Arthur, Citigroup Professor at the Santa Fe Institute.
- *Be flexible,* says Chung-Jen Tan, senior manager at IBM's Watson Research Center.
- *Listen to your intuition,* says Deborah Triant, CEO of Check Point Software Technologies, Inc.
- *Ask yourself how you want things to turn out and how things could go wrong,* says Roger Rainbow, vice-president at Shell International Ltd.
- *Think in terms of opportunities instead of problems,* says Howard Raiffa, Professor Emeritus at Harvard Business School.
- *Sometimes the "wrong" decision is the right thing to do,* says Chris Newell, executive director at the Lotus Institute.

Save Time and Money Successful managers use both their time and their money well. As a student, you may feel that you never have enough of either of these resources. You can save yourself some time and money by taking advantage of some of the bargains on the following Web sites:[15]

- Student Advantage (**www.studentadvantage. com**). One way to cut costs on everything from transportation to food to clothing is to use a student discount card. The Student Advantage Card is one such discount card, accepted at over 20,000 businesses nationwide.
- FastWeb.com (**www.fastweb.com**) and Sallie Mae (**www.scholarships.salliemae.com**). Save valuable time and find out about "free" money available through academic scholarships and grants. These sites offer free online searches for scholarships and grants.

- VarsityBooks.com (**www.varsitybooks.com**), **Follett College Stores (www.efollett.com)**, and BigWords. com (**www.BIGWORDS.com**). Students can spend hundreds of dollars per semester on textbooks and other course materials. Save up to 40 percent on textbooks by buying online.
- Travelocity (**www.travelocity.com**), Expedia Travel (**www.expedia.com**), United College Plus (**www.collegeplus.com**). Save time and money by using sites that make your travel arrangements for you, and do it at a discount price.
- Apple Computer (**www.apple.com/education/ hed/students**) and Campus Essentials (**www. dell.com/client/edu/essentials.htm**). Take advantage of special deals (discounts and rebates) on personal computers, and then use your new computer to find even more good deals on the Internet!

>looking ahead
at Alexander Doll Co.

Can the Alexander Doll Co. stay in Harlem and continue to increase its competitive position? Making collectible dolls is a labor-intensive process, so most of the company's competitors manufacture overseas to take advantage of cheaper labor. Alexander Doll has chosen to reduce costs by focusing on new production methods. In the coming years, the company will need to emphasize its commitment to mass customization in order to increase its customer base and remain profitable.

SUMMARY OF LEARNING GOALS

>lg 1 What is the role of management?
Management is the process of guiding the development, maintenance, and allocation of resources to attain organizational goals. Managers are the people in the organization responsible for developing and carrying out this management process. The four primary functions of managers are planning, organizing, leading, and controlling.

>lg 2 What are the four types of planning?
Planning is deciding what needs to be done, identifying when and how it will be done, and determining by whom it should be done. Managers use four different types of planning: strategic, tactical, operational, and contingency planning. Strategic planning involves creating long-range (one to five years), broad goals and determining the necessary resources to accomplish those goals. Tactical planning has a shorter time frame (less than one year) and more specific objectives that support the broader strategic goals. Operational planning creates specific standards, methods, policies, and procedures that are used in specific functional areas

KEY TERMS

autocratic leaders
210
coercive power
209
conceptual skills
219
consensual leaders
211
consultative leaders
211
contingency plans
207
controlling 212
corporate culture
212
decisional roles
215
democratic leaders
211
empowerment 211
expert power 209
free-rein (laissez-
faire) leadership
211
global management
skills 220
human relations
skills 219
informational roles
215
interpersonal roles
215
leadership style
210
leadership 209
legitimate power
209
management 204
middle
management 209
mission 205
mission statement
206
nonprogrammed
decisions 216
operational
planning 206
organizing 208
participative
leadership 211
planning 204
power 209
referent power
209
reward power 209
strategic planning
205
supervisory
management 209
tactical planning
206
technical skills 217
top management
209

of the organization. Contingency plans identify alternative courses of action for very unusual or crisis situations.

>lg 3   **What are the primary responsibilities of managers in organizing activities?**
Organizing involves coordinating and allocating a firm's resources in order to carry out its plans. It includes developing a structure for the people, positions, departments, and activities within the firm. This is accomplished by dividing up tasks (division of labor), grouping jobs and employees (departmentalization), and assigning authority and responsibilities (delegation).

>lg 4   **How do leadership styles influence a corporate culture?**
Leading is the process of guiding and motivating others toward the achievement of organizational goals. Managers have unique leadership styles that range from autocratic to free rein. The set of *attitudes, values,* and *standards of behavior* that distinguishes one organization from another is called corporate culture. A corporate culture evolves over time and is based on the accumulated history of the organization, including the vision of the founders. The dominant leadership style within the organization is a powerful determinant of corporate culture.

>lg 5   **How do organizations control activities?**
Controlling is the process of assessing the organization's progress toward accomplishing its goals. The control process is as follows: (1) set performance standards (goals), (2) measure performance, (3) compare actual performance to established performance standards, (4) take corrective action (if necessary), and (5) use information gained from the process to set future performance standards.

>lg 6   **What roles do managers take on in different organizational settings?**
Managers' roles fall into three categories. In an *informational role,* the manager may act as an information gatherer, an information distributor, or a spokesperson for the company. A manager's *interpersonal roles* are based on various interactions with other people. Depending on the situation, a manager may need to act as a figurehead, a company leader, or a liaison. When acting in a *decisional role,* a manager may have to think like an entrepreneur, make decisions about resource allocation, help resolve conflicts, or negotiate compromises.

>lg 7   **What set of managerial skills is necessary for managerial success?**
Managerial skills fall into three basic categories: technical, human relations, and conceptual skills. Specialized areas of knowledge and expertise and the ability to apply that knowledge make up a manager's technical skills. Human relations skills are the interpersonal skills managers use to accomplish goals through the use of human resources. This set of skills includes the ability to understand human behavior, to communicate effectively with others, and to motivate individuals to accomplish their objectives. Conceptual skills include the ability to view the organization as a whole, understand how the various parts are interdependent, and assess how the organization relates to its external environment.

>lg 8   **What trends will affect management in the future?**
Three important trends in management today are increasing employee empowerment, the increasing use of information technology, and the growing need for global management skills. Empowerment means giving employees increased autonomy and discretion to make their own decisions, as well as control of the resources needed to implement those decisions. When decision-making power is shared at all levels in the organization, employees feel a greater sense of ownership in, and responsibility for, organizational outcomes. Using the latest information technology, managers can make quicker, better-informed decisions. It also keeps organization members connected. As more companies "go global," the need for global management skills is growing.

Global managers often have to adapt to a new culture, learn a new language, manage a diverse workforce, and operate in a foreign economic system.

PREPARING FOR TOMORROW'S WORKPLACE

1. The board of directors of Biogen Labs, a high-tech medical research organization, has asked you to prepare a memo describing the most desirable managerial style for the company's next president. The members of the presidential search committee will use this information as they consider job candidates.

2. Do not-for-profit organizations like the Red Cross and Boy Scouts of America need managers? Why or why not?

3. Form small groups with three or four members each. Each group should then go to a business headquartered in the area. Try to speak to the president of the organization and several top subordinates. Report on the management styles of these individuals.

4. You have been asked to speak to the Rotary Club on sources of managerial power. Prepare an outline of your speech.

5. Talk to the dean or department head at your school. Ask for examples of strategic planning, tactical planning, and contingency planning at your university or college that can be shared with the class. Make your presentation.

6. Write a short paper on how you are using the four management functions to accomplish your goal of graduating.

7. Using a McDonald's restaurant manager as an example, give an example of a decision for each of the managerial functions: planning, organizing, leading, and controlling.

WORKING THE NET

1. Develop a management profile for McDonald's restaurant corporation. Begin by doing a search on the Hoover's Industry Research site (**www.hoovers.com**) for information about the company. Follow the links to McDonald's home page and to articles that have been written about McDonald's management. Describe the management style of McDonald's top executives from this information. If possible, explain how this has affected McDonald's performance.

2. Find information about how to develop a business plan by doing a search on the Dogpile mega-search engine (**www.dogpile.com**). Make a list of the resources available and suggest which ones would be most useful for (a) top executives of a large corporation, (b) a small business owner, and (c) a middle manager in a large corporation preparing an operational plan for her or his department. See if you can also find a site that has examples of completed business plans.

3. Go to the Management General Web site at **www.mgeneral.com.** Click on "leaders" and pick one of the short essays about management and leadership. Do you agree or disagree? Try to find real-world examples that support your argument by searching the archives of business magazines such as *Forbes* (**www.forbes.com**), *Fortune* (**www.fortune.com**), or *Business Week* (**www.businessweek.com**).

4. How do entrepreneurs develop corporate culture in their organizations? Do a search on the term "corporate culture" at the site of either *Inc.* magazine (**www.inc.com**) or *Entrepreneur* magazine (**www.entrepreneurmag.com**) to find answers to this question.

Prepare a short presentation for your class explaining your findings.

CREATIVE THINKING CASE

Anatomy of Dragonflies and Empowerment

Once a week, Duncan Highsmith closets himself for two hours in a small room adjacent to his office and tries to wrap his brain around the world. Seated at a large wooden table, the president and CEO of Highsmith, Inc. sifts through stacks of articles on subjects ranging from juvenile crime to semiotics to the anatomy of dragonflies. In this eclectic mix he is searching for nascent trends, provocative contradictions, and, most important, *connections* that could eventually reshape his business. Joining Highsmith in these sessions—which he considers paramount to his company's future success—is a single trusted business associate named Guedea Carreño. She is a librarian.

Highsmith's pursuit—called Life, the Universe, and Everything—springs from his conviction that you can't take a narrow approach to the future. "We tend to behave as though the future will be like the present, only bigger and faster," says Highsmith, whose $55 million business is the country's leading mail order supplier of equipment such as book displays, audio-video tools, and educational software for schools and libraries.

Life, the Universe, and Everything is significant for the information it gathers, but Highsmith also intends it as a teaching tool that will ultimately prod everyone in the company to see and understand the kinds of big-picture connections CEOs generally make in isolation. Toward that end, he's beginning to broaden participation in the project, asking other staff members to pass along scraps of intriguing information and using his discussions with Carreño as the basis for presentations at executive meetings.

"I think it's starting to create a demand on the part of executives to spend time in the long-term development of the business rather than on routing operations," says Highsmith. "A big part of my job is to make myself unnecessary, and I hope this will help me do that."

Highsmith was trying to build an organization rich in human potential in an area poor in actual humans. "We have a very limited labor market, so I wanted to make the most of the people we had by helping them become decision makers, by providing them with information and the context to make good decisions," he says. The idea was to create an environment in which warehouse workers, for example, could resolve issues as small as what kind of packing material to use by reading news articles about environmentally sound alternatives and as large as how their duties should be structured in a flat organization by reading case studies in business books.

Highsmith's overarching goal is for all employees in the company to shed their tactical blinders and begin thinking strategically—about customers, about the industry, and about forces for which the words *big picture* seem inadequate. "Life, the Universe, and Everything is in many ways in its infancy," says Highsmith. "The concrete benefits still have more to do with my role than with the rest of the organization. But thinking about what's next is becoming part of the routine work of the organization."

Critical Thinking Questions

1. How would you describe Duncan Highsmith's leadership style?
2. Is Life, the Universe, and Everything a tool for employee empowerment? Why or why not?
3. Is Life, the Universe, and Everything more beneficial for strategic planning or tactical planning, or is it equally beneficial for both?

VIDEO CASE

The Department Store Division of Dayton Hudson

Hudson's, Dayton's, and Marshall Field's are the components of the Department Store Division of Dayton Hudson Corp. (**www.dhc.com**). Each has a long history in general merchandise retailing. Marshall Field's was established in 1852, Hudson's in 1881, and Dayton's in 1902. In 1985 Dayton's and Hudson's merged into one department store company, which was joined by Marshall Field's in 1990. Currently, Dayton Hudson's Department Store Division operates 19 Dayton's, 20 Hudson's, and 24 Marshall Field's stores—a total of 63 stores—in eight states.

The stores refer to their customers as guests. The typical guest is female, married, and in her mid-40s. Approximately 40 percent of the guests have children living at home. Nearly 60 percent of the guests have earned at least an undergraduate degree, and about two-thirds hold white-collar jobs. The median household income of guests is about $58,000 annually.

Each store is "dedicated to providing guests with great service, exciting, distinctive merchandise, fashion leadership and a convenient shopping environment." In short, every Hudson's, Dayton's, and Marshall Field's store seeks to be "the best store in town"—a mission they embarked on in 1996. The Department Store Division says, "We have a single-minded focus on being the best store in town—with a passion for great merchandise and superior service."

Fashion leadership is the core of the division's business. The stores try to provide their guests with the widest possible assortment of the latest fashions and home products. The division's merchandising strategy has three objectives: (1) to be dominant in national brands, with the best assortments and the newest items; (2) to differentiate product offerings through high-quality private brands that fill the gaps between the national brands and that are available only at Hudson's, Dayton's, or Marshall Field's; and (3) to constantly monitor brand assortments, eliminating those brands that are inconsistent with the company's desired market position.

To improve guest experiences and to enhance market share in its core upper Midwest markets, the Department Store Division launched a remodeling program in 1998 to make its stores more guest-friendly. As part of a disciplined, multiyear campaign, eight stores were remodeled in 1998, and nine more stores were scheduled for remodeling in 1999.

The division recognizes that a wide assortment of trendy merchandise and guest friendly physical facilities are only part of the formula for making Hudson's, Dayton's, and Marshall Field's "the best store in town." The stores' employees are also a crucial element in this formula. Accordingly, the stores are investing significant sums in training their "team members to deliver consistently superior service."

The division's efforts have been well received by the company's customers. As a result, the Department Store division has enjoyed two consecutive years of strong earnings growth.

Critical Thinking Questions

1. How, if at all, are planning, organizing, leading, and controlling being used in Dayton Hudson Corp.'s Department Store Division?

2. What managerial roles appear to be necessary for carrying out Dayton Hudson's "best store in town" mission?

3. Explain why conceptual, human relations, and technical skills are important to the development and successful execution of strategies to fulfill "the best store in town" mission.

chapter eight

Designing Organizational Structures

learning goals

>lg 1   What are the five structural building blocks that managers use to design organizations?

>lg 2   What are the five types of departmentalization?

>lg 3   How can the degree of centralization/decentralization be altered to make an organization more successful?

>lg 4   How do mechanistic and organic organizations differ?

>lg 5   What is the difference between line positions and staff positions?

>lg 6   What is the goal of reengineering?

>lg 7   How does the informal organization affect the performance of the company?

>lg 8   What trends are influencing the way businesses organize?

Procter & Gamble Reorganizes to Sell $70 Billion in 2005

The people who bring you Crest toothpaste, Pringles potato chips, and Hugo Boss cologne are really shaking things up. In an attempt to increase sales worldwide and bring new products to market more quickly, Procter & Gamble (www.pg.com) is reorganizing its corporate structure.[1] The company, which for decades has encouraged organizational secrecy, is even soliciting advice on redesign from sources outside the company.[2] CEO John Pepper visited Jack Welch at General Electric and Lewis Platt at Hewlett Packard, among other executives, asking them to share their wisdom on global marketing, new-product development, and organizational effectiveness. The consensus of consumers, chain-store customers, and industry insiders is that P&G needs to be simpler and to move faster.

To achieve these goals, the company has undertaken "Organization 2005!" To achieve its 2005 sales goal of $70 billion and reinvigorate its corporate culture, P&G is revamping its entire corporate management structure. The old P&G bureaucracy was based on geography, with four executive vice-presidents overseeing the North American, Asian, Latin American, European, Middle Eastern, and African operations. Under this system, senior regional managers had wide latitude in setting prices and handling products. The old structure is being replaced by seven product-based global business units organized by category, such as baby care, food and beverage, and laundry and cleaning. These global business units will develop and sell products on a worldwide basis. P&G hopes that this shift from geographic departmentalization to a product-based structure will lead to faster product innovation and increase flexibility and response time.

As part of the restructuring process, P&G is streamlining its corporate staff and creating a global business services organization. Services that are currently spread throughout the organization, such as finance, accounting, and information technology, are being consolidated. According to top management, this will provide P&G with greater economies of scale and will improve both the quality and speed of those service areas. Additionally, P&G plans to introduce a new compensation system that will encourage employee innovation, flexibility, and customer service.

To implement the new structure, current CEO John Pepper is stepping down and handing over the reins to chief operations officer (COO) Durk Jager. Jager faces many challenges in winning acceptance for the new structure from the tradition-bound managers at P&G. The structural change will result in a drastic reduction in senior executives, from the previous 144 to a lean 8 positions. Jager's style, described as determined and often abrasive, is to push hard for rapid change. In the 1980s his aggressive turnaround of P&G's failing Japanese operations earned him the nickname "Crazy Man Durk." Time will tell if Durk can build cohesiveness and unity of purpose throughout the new structure and achieve the growth P&G needs to sustain it in the new century.

Critical Thinking Questions

As you read this chapter, consider the following questions as they relate to Procter & Gamble:

- What are the structural building blocks that Procter & Gamble can use in its reorganization?
- How does decentralization enter into the reorganization?
- How can the informal organization affect the reorganization?

BUSINESS IN THE 21ST CENTURY

In today's dynamic business environment, organizational structures need to be designed so that the organization can quickly respond to new competitive threats and changing customer needs. In the future, companies such as Procter & Gamble will achieve long-term success only if they have the ability to manage change and organize their resources effectively. In this chapter, we'll present the five structural building blocks of organizations and look at how each can be used to build unique organizational structures. We'll explore how communication, authority, and job specialization are combined to create both formal and informal organizational structures. Finally, we'll consider how reengineering and new business trends are changing the way businesses organize.

STRUCTURAL BUILDING BLOCKS

>lg 1

As you learned in Chapter 7, the key functions that managers perform include planning, organizing, leading, and controlling. This chapter focuses specifically on the organizing function. Organizing involves coordinating and allocating a firm's resources so that the firm can carry out its plans and achieve its goals. This organizing, or structuring, process is accomplished by

- determining work activities and dividing up tasks (*division of labor*),
- grouping jobs and employees (*departmentalization*), and
- assigning authority and responsibilities (*delegation*).

formal organization

The order and design of relationships within a firm; consists of two or more people working together with a common objective and clarity of purpose.

The result of the organizing process is a formal organizational structure. A **formal organization** is the order and design of relationships within the firm. It consists of two or more people working together with a common objective and clarity of purpose. Formal organizations also have well-defined lines of authority, channels for information flow, and means of control. Human, material, financial, and information resources are deliberately connected to form the business organization. Some connections are long lasting, such as the links among people in the finance or marketing department. Others can be changed at almost any time, as when a committee is formed to study a problem.

Five structural building blocks are used in designing an efficient and effective organizational structure. They are division of labor, departmentalization, managerial hierarchy, span of control, and centralization of decision making.

Division of Labor

division of labor

The process of dividing work into separate jobs and assigning tasks to workers.

specialization

The degree to which tasks are subdivided into smaller jobs.

The process of dividing work into separate jobs and assigning tasks to workers is called **division of labor.** In a fast-food restaurant, for example, some employees take or fill orders, others prepare food, a few clean and maintain equipment, and at least one supervises all the others. In an auto assembly plant, some workers install rearview mirrors, while others mount bumpers on bumper brackets. The degree to which the tasks are subdivided into smaller jobs is called **specialization.** Employees who work at highly specialized jobs, such as assembly-line workers, perform a limited number and variety of tasks. Employees who become specialists at one task, or a small number of tasks, develop greater skill in doing that particular job. This can lead to greater efficiency and consistency in production and other work activities. However, a high degree of specialization can also result in employees who are disinterested or bored due to the lack of variety and challenge.

Currently, most managers recognize that there is a trade-off between the economic benefits and the human costs associated with specialization. At Harley-Davidson's Kansas City assembly plant, managers and workers together have created an environment that maximizes the benefits and minimizes the drawbacks of highly specialized motorcycle assembly jobs.[3] To streamline the production process and at the same time keep employees involved and motivated, line workers are *required* to share their opinions and to make decisions about how to build better bikes. There is no denying the benefits of specialization in designing an efficient production system. But Harley has discovered that those benefits are best realized in an atmosphere that allows employees to experience challenge, empowerment, and ownership.

Departmentalization

>lg 2

departmentalization

The process of grouping jobs together so that similar or associated tasks and activities can be coordinated.

organization chart

A visual representation of the structured relationships among tasks and the people given the authority to do those tasks.

The second building block used to create a strong organizational structure is called **departmentalization.** After the work is divided into jobs, jobs are then grouped together so that similar or associated tasks and activities can be coordinated. This grouping of people, tasks, and resources into organizational units facilitates the planning, leading, and control processes.

An **organization chart** is a visual representation of the structured relationships among tasks and the people given the authority to do those tasks. In the organization chart in Exhibit 8-1, each figure represents a job, and each job includes several tasks. The sales manager, for instance, must hire salespeople, establish sales territories, motivate and train the salespeople, and control sales operations. The chart also indicates the general type of work done in each position.

> e x h i b i t   8 - 1 <

Organizational Chart for a Typical Appliance Manufacturer

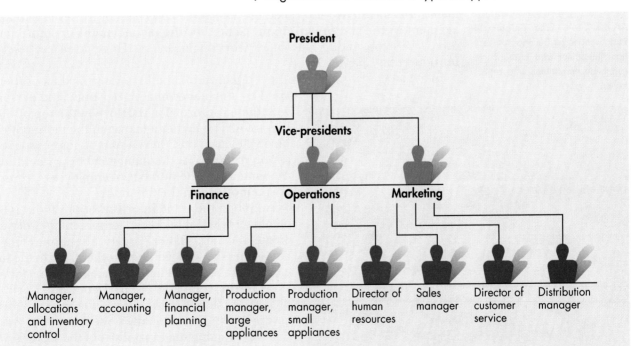

As Exhibit 8-2 shows, five basic types of departmentalization are commonly used in organizations:

- **Functional departmentalization,** which is based on the primary functions performed within an organizational unit (marketing, finance, production, sales, and so on).
- **Product departmentalization,** which is based on the goods or services produced or sold by the organizational unit (such as outpatient/emergency services, pediatrics, cardiology, and orthopedics).
- **Process departmentalization,** which is based on the production process used by the organizational unit (such as lumber cutting and treatment, furniture finishing, shipping).
- **Customer departmentalization,** which is based on the primary type of customer served by the organizational unit (such as wholesale or retail purchasers).
- **Geographic departmentalization,** which is based on the geographic segmentation of organizational units (such as U.S. and Canadian marketing, European marketing, South American marketing).

People are assigned to a particular organizational unit because they perform similar or related tasks, or because they are jointly responsible for a product, client, or market. Decisions about how to departmentalize affect the way management assigns authority, distributes resources, rewards performance, and sets up lines of communication. Many large organizations use several types of departmentalization. For example, a global company may be departmentalized first geographically (North American, European, and Asian units), then by product line (foods/beverages and health care), and finally by functional area (marketing, operations, finance, and so on). As Procter & Gamble illustrates, the type(s) of departmentalization an organization uses can directly affect organizational performance.

Managerial Hierarchy

The third building block used to create effective organizational structure is the **managerial hierarchy** (also called the *management pyramid*), or the levels of management within the organization. Generally, the management structure has three levels: top, middle, and supervisory management. These three levels were introduced in Chapter 7.

In a managerial hierarchy, each organizational unit is controlled and supervised by a manager in a higher unit. The person with the most formal authority is at the top of the hierarchy. The higher a manager, the more power he or she has. Thus, the amount of power *decreases* as you move down the management pyramid. At the same time, the number of employees *increases* as you move down the hierarchy.

Although the trend in organizations today is to eliminate layers of middle management in order to create a leaner, "flatter" organization, sometimes companies find that adding another layer to the hierarchy can actually simplify the reporting relationships in the company. Home Depot, the world's biggest home improvement retailer, recently discovered this.[4] The company's phenomenal growth rate was straining the capabilities of the six division heads who reported directly to the CEO. So the company hired four new group presidents, adding

Sidebar definitions

functional departmentalization

Departmentalization that is based on the primary functions performed within an organizational unit.

product departmentalization

Departmentalization that is based on the goods or services produced or sold by the organizational unit.

process departmentalization

Departmentalization that is based on the production process used by the organizational unit.

customer departmentalization

Departmentalization that is based on the primary type of customer served by the organizational unit.

geographic departmentalization

Departmentalization that is based on the geographic segmentation of the organizational units.

At the Santa Cruz Amusement Park, a manager (second from left) has the power and authority to supervise employees who report to her.

Five Ways to Organize

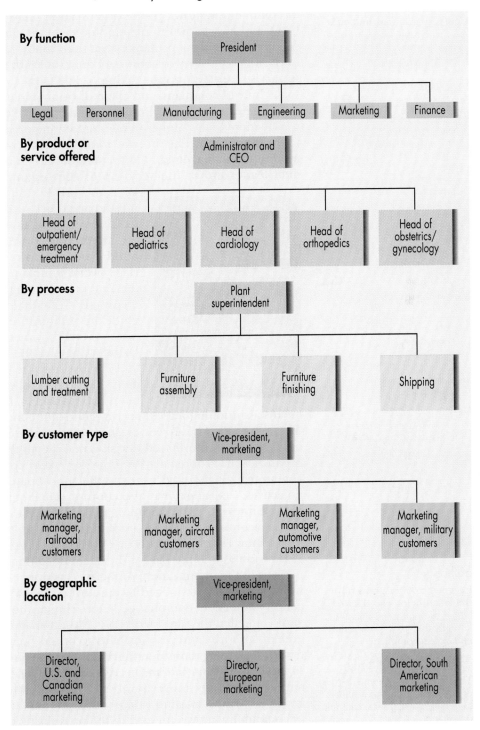

By function

President

Legal | Personnel | Manufacturing | Engineering | Marketing | Finance

By product or service offered

Administrator and CEO

Head of outpatient/ emergency treatment | Head of pediatrics | Head of cardiology | Head of orthopedics | Head of obstetrics/ gynecology

By process

Plant superintendent

Lumber cutting and treatment | Furniture assembly | Furniture finishing | Shipping

By customer type

Vice-president, marketing

Marketing manager, railroad customers | Marketing manager, aircraft customers | Marketing manager, automotive customers | Marketing manager, military customers

By geographic location

Vice-president, marketing

Director, U.S. and Canadian marketing | Director, European marketing | Director, South American marketing

managerial hierarchy

The levels of management within an organization; typically, includes top, middle, and supervisory management.

a layer of management between the CEO and the division heads. As often happens when a structure is changed, there was some initial negative reaction to the decision. Eventually, most of the resistance was overcome as managers realized the new positions were needed to deal with business areas outside the company's traditional core competencies (for example, a direct marketing expert and a retail sales expert). Adding the new positions actually freed the division heads to concentrate on the duties central to their particular area of the business.

chain of command

The line of authority that extends from one level of an organization's hierarchy to the next, from top to bottom, and makes clear who reports to whom.

An organization with a well-defined hierarchy has a clear **chain of command,** which is the line of authority that extends from one level of the organization to the next, from top to bottom, and makes clear who reports to whom. The chain of command is shown in the organization chart and can be traced from the CEO all the way down to the employees producing goods and services. Under the *unity of command* principle, everyone reports to and gets instructions from only one boss. Unity of command guarantees that everyone will have a direct supervisor and will not be taking orders from a number of different supervisors. Unity of command and chain of command give everyone in the organization clear directions and help coordinate people doing different jobs.

The increasing number of mergers among organizations has given rise to an interesting trend. The unity of command principle used to be clearly evident in most top management hierarchies, but now a number of firms are choosing dual leadership at the very top of the organization.[5] At Ford Motor Co.,

How is Ford Motor Co.'s CEO partnership working? Get the latest performance statistics by clicking on "investors" at
www.ford.com

William Ford Jr. and Jacques Nasser have settled into adjacent offices and parallel responsibilities. At Citigroup, co-CEOs Sandy Weill and John Reed are attempting to work out their differences and build synergies to make their managerial "marriage" work. Rampant globalization and the blistering rate of technological change have made it increasingly difficult for just one top manager to guide an organization toward success. Huge businesses created by megamergers such as Citigroup, DaimlerChrysler, Bell Atlantic/GTE, and Exxon Mobil must find creative ways to merge management hierarchies as well as corporate cultures. For many top managers, this new model of leadership means abandoning a competitive, stand-alone mentality for a more collaborative approach. The power-sharing concept can be very beneficial when top managers push the shared decision making all the way down the ranks of the organization. Problems arise, however, when co-executives cannot agree on common goals and objectives and the appropriate strategies for attaining those objectives. Co-leaders may also confuse and alienate their managerial subordinates if lines of communication and authority are not clear. And just like parents, co-commanders have to stand together on their decisions, being careful not to show favoritism to any one individual or group within the organization.

authority

Legitimate power, granted by the organization and acknowledged by employees, that allows an individual to request action and expect compliance.

delegation of authority

The assignment of some degree of authority and responsibility to persons lower in the chain of command.

Individuals who are part of the chain of command have authority over other persons in the organization. **Authority** is legitimate power, granted by the organization and acknowledged by employees, that allows an individual to request action and expect compliance. Exercising authority means making decisions and seeing that they are carried out. Most managers *delegate*, or assign, some degree of authority and responsibility to others below them in the chain of command. The **delegation of authority** makes the employees accountable to their supervisor. *Accountability* means responsibility for outcomes. Typically, authority and responsibility move downward through the organization as managers assign activities to, and share decision making with, their subordinates. Accountability moves upward in the organization as managers in each successively higher level is held accountable for the actions of their subordinates.

Span of Control

The fourth structural building block is the managerial span of control. Each firm must decide how many managers are needed at each level of the management hierarchy to effectively supervise the work performed within organiza-

span of control
The number of employees a manager directly supervises; also called *span of management*.

tional units. A manager's **span of control** (sometimes called *span of management*) is the number of employees the manager directly supervises. It can be as narrow as 2 or 3 employees or as wide as 50 or more. In general, the larger the span of control, the more efficient the organization. As Exhibit 8-3 shows, however, both narrow and wide spans of control have benefits and drawbacks.

If hundreds of employees perform the same job, one supervisor may be able to manage a very large number of employees. Such might be the case at a clothing plant, where hundreds of sewing machine operators work from identical patterns. But if employees perform complex and dissimilar tasks, a manager can effectively supervise only a much smaller number. For instance, a supervisor in the research and development area of a pharmaceutical company might oversee just a few research chemists due to the highly complex nature of their jobs.

The optimal span of control is determined by the following five factors:

* *Nature of the task.* The more complex the task, the narrower the span of control.
* *Location of the workers.* The more locations, the narrower the span of control.
* *Ability of the manager to delegate responsibility.* The greater the ability to delegate, the wider the span of control.
* *Amount of interaction and feedback between the workers and the manager.* The more feedback and interaction required, the narrower the span of control.
* *Level of skill and motivation of the workers.* The higher the skill level and motivation, the wider the span of control.

centralization
The degree to which formal authority is concentrated in one area or level of an organization.

Centralization of Decision Making

>lg 3

The final component in building an effective organizational structure is deciding at what level in the organization decisions should be made. **Centralization** is the degree to which formal authority is concentrated in one

> e x h i b i t 8 - 3 <
Narrow and Wide Spans of Control

	Advantages	Disadvantages
Narrow span of control	• High degree of control. • Fewer subordinates may mean manager is more familiar with each individual. • Close supervision can provide immediate feedback.	• More levels of management, therefore more expensive. • Slower decision making due to vertical layers. • Isolation of top management. • Discourages employee autonomy.
Wide span of control	• Fewer levels of management means increased efficiency and reduced costs. • Increased subordinate autonomy leads to quicker decision making. • Greater organizational flexibility. • Higher levels of job satisfaction due to employee empowerment.	• Less control. • Possible lack of familiarity due to large number of subordinates. • Managers spread so thin that they can't provide necessary leadership or support. • Lack of coordination or synchronization.

Entrepreneur David Pomije of FuncoLand changed from centralized decision making to decentralization after realizing that employees with specialized knowledge made better decisions in their area of expertise than he did. He willingly gave up authority to employees who were eager to accept more responsibility.

decentralization
The process of pushing decision-making authority down the organizational hierarchy.

concept check

- What are the five building blocks of organizational structure?
- List the five types of departmentalization.
- What factors determine the optimal span of control?
- What are the primary characteristics of a decentralized organization?

area or level of the organization. In a highly centralized structure, top management makes most of the key decisions in the organization, with very little input from lower-level employees. Centralization lets top managers develop a broad view of operations and exercise tight financial controls. It can also help to reduce costs by eliminating redundancy in the organization. But centralization may also mean that lower-level personnel don't get a chance to develop their decision-making and leadership skills and that the organization is less able to respond quickly to customer demands.

Decentralization is the process of pushing decision-making authority down the organizational hierarchy, giving lower-level personnel more responsibility and power to make and implement decisions. Benefits of decentralization can include quicker decision making, increased levels of innovation and creativity, greater organizational flexibility, faster development of lower-level managers, and increased levels of job satisfaction and employee commitment. But decentralization can also be risky. If lower-level personnel don't have the necessary skills and training to perform effectively, they may make costly mistakes. Additionally, decentralization may increase the likelihood of inefficient lines of communication, incongruent or competing objectives, and duplication of effort.

Several factors must be considered when deciding how much decision-making authority to delegate throughout the organization. These factors include the size of the organization, the speed of change in its environment, managers' willingness to give up authority, employees' willingness to accept more authority, and the organization's geographic dispersion. Decentralization is usually desirable when the following conditions are met:

- The organization is very large, like Exxon, Ford, or General Electric.
- The firm is in a dynamic environment where quick, local decisions must be made, as in many high-tech industries.
- Managers are willing to share power with their subordinates.
- Employees are willing and able to take more responsibility.
- The company is spread out geographically, such as JC Penney, Mobil Oil, or Procter & Gamble.

As organizations grow and change, they continually reevaluate the organizational structure to determine whether it is helping the company to achieve its goals. Firms can alter the degree of centralization/decentralization in the organizational structure as the needs of the company change. For example, Motorola has recently *centralized* functions and activities in an effort to increase operational efficiency and recapture market share. Motorola is restructuring both its cell phone division and its semiconductor business in a major effort to regain competitiveness in these markets.[6] The reorganization involves consolidating previously autonomous communications divisions. Motorola hopes this increased centralization will enable the divisions to share resources more efficiently and respond more quickly to customers.

Have Motorola's plans to centralize the functions and operations of its divisions been successful? Find out by clicking on "About Motorola" at

www.mot.com

MECHANISTIC VERSUS ORGANIC STRUCTURES

>lg 4

mechanistic organization

An organizational structure that is characterized by a relatively high degree of job specialization, rigid departmentalization, many layers of management, narrow spans of control, centralized decision making, and a long chain of command.

organic organization

An organizational structure that is characterized by a relatively low degree of job specialization, loose departmentalization, few levels of management, wide spans of control, decentralized decision making, and a short chain of command.

Using different combinations of the building blocks described above, organizations can build a wide variety of organizational structures. Nevertheless, structural design generally follows one of the two basic models described in Exhibit 8-4: mechanistic or organic. A **mechanistic organization** is characterized by a relatively high degree of job specialization, rigid departmentalization, many layers of management (particularly middle management), narrow spans of control, centralized decision making, and a long chain of command. This combination of elements results in what is called a *tall organizational structure*. Military organizations typically have tall structures. In contrast, an **organic organization** is characterized by a relatively low degree of job specialization, loose departmentalization, few levels of management, wide spans of control, decentralized decision making, and a short chain of command. This combination of elements results in what is called a *flat organizational structure*. Colleges and universities tend to have flat organizational structures, with only two or three levels of administration between the faculty and the president. Exhibit 8-5 shows examples of flat and tall organizational structures.

Although few organizations are purely mechanistic or purely organic, most organizations tend more toward one type or the other. The decision to create a more mechanistic or a more organic structural design is based on factors such as the firm's overall strategy, the size of the organization, the types of technologies used in the organization, and the stability of its external environment.

concept check

- Compare and contrast mechanistic and organic organizations.
- What factors determine whether an organization should be mechanistic or organic?

> e x h i b i t   8 - 4 <

Mechanistic versus Organic Structure

Structural Characteristic	Mechanistic	Organic
Job specialization	High	Low
Departmentalization	Rigid	Loose
Management hierarchy (levels of management)	Tall (many levels)	Flat (few levels)
Span of control	Narrow	Wide
Decision-making authority	Centralized	Decentralized
Chain of command	Long	Short

Tall versus Flat Organizational Structures

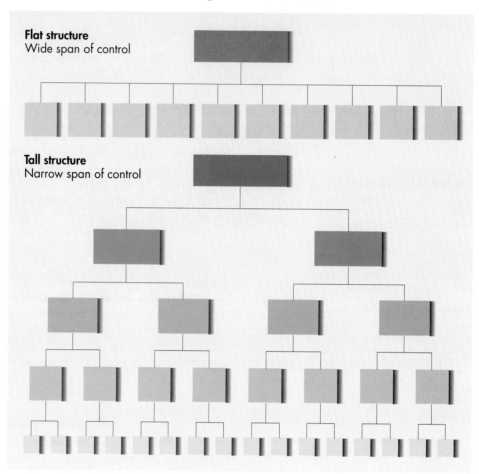

Flat structure
Wide span of control

Tall structure
Narrow span of control

Apple Computer's interim chief executive Steve Jobs uses an organic structure to develop new products like the iMac computer. Organic structures allow firms like Apple to succeed in rapidly changing environments.

>lg 5

COMMON ORGANIZATIONAL STRUCTURES

There is no single best way to design an organization. Within the basic mechanistic and organic models and the hybrids that contain elements of both, an almost infinite variety of organizational structures can be developed. Many organizations use a combination of elements from different structural types to meet their unique organizational needs. Some of the most common structural designs are discussed in this section.

line organization

An organizational structure with direct, clear lines of authority and communication flowing from the top managers downward.

line-and-staff organization

An organizational structure that includes both line and staff positions.

line positions

All positions in the organization directly concerned with producing goods and services and which are directly connected from top to bottom.

staff positions

Positions in an organization held by individuals who provide the administrative and support services that line employees need to achieve the firm's goals.

committee structure

An organizational structure in which authority and responsibility are held by a group rather than an individual.

Line Organization

The **line organization** is designed with direct, clear lines of authority and communication flowing from the top managers downward. Managers have direct control over all activities, including administrative duties. An organization chart for this type of structure would show that all positions in the firm are directly connected via an imaginary line extending from the highest position in the organization to the lowest (where production of goods and services takes place). This structure with its simple design, clear chain of command, and broad managerial control is often well suited to small, entrepreneurial firms.

Line-and-Staff Organization

As an organization grows and becomes more complex, the line organization can be enhanced by adding staff positions to the design. Staff positions provide specialized advisory and support services to line managers in the **line-and-staff organization,** shown in Exhibit 8-6. In daily operations, those individuals in **line positions** are directly involved in the processes used to create goods and services. Those individuals in **staff positions** provide the administrative and support services that line employees need to achieve the firm's goals. Line positions in organizations are typically in areas such as production, marketing, and finance. Staff positions are found in areas such as legal counseling, managerial consulting, public relations, and human resource management.

Committee Structure

In **committee structure,** authority and responsibility are held by a group rather than an individual. Committees are typically part of a larger line-and-staff organization. Often the committee's role is only advisory, but in some situations the committee has the power to make and implement decisions. Committees can make the coordination of tasks in the organization much easier. At Toyota, for

> e x h i b i t   8 - 6 <

Line-and-Staff Organization

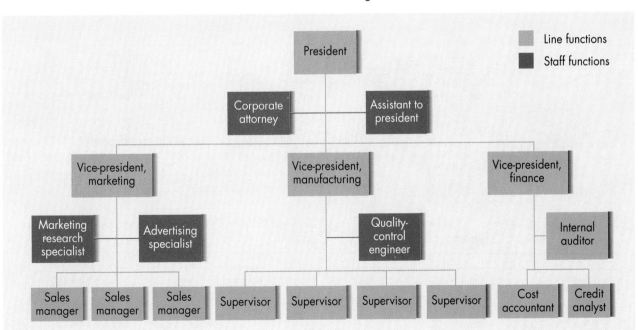

example, product and manufacturing engineers work together in committees. Using this process, factory machinery is developed concurrently with new car prototypes so it is able to accommodate them. Committees bring diverse viewpoints to a problem and expand the range of possible solutions, but there are some drawbacks. Committees can be slow to reach a decision and are sometimes dominated by a single individual. It is also more difficult to hold any one individual accountable for a decision made by group.

Committee meetings can sometimes go on for long periods of time with little seemingly being accomplished. This is why many workers quickly develop an aversion to serving on committees. Stan Richards, president of the Richards Group, a Dallas-based advertising agency, developed a few simple tricks to creating short, effective committee meetings.[7] These are explained in the Focusing on Small Business box.

Matrix Structure

matrix structure (project management)

An organizational structure that combines functional and product departmentalization by bringing together people from different functional areas of the organization to work on a special project.

The **matrix structure** (also called the **project management** approach) is sometimes used in conjunction with the traditional line-and-staff structure in an organization. Essentially, this structure combines two different forms of departmentalization, functional and product, that have complementary strengths and weaknesses. The matrix structure brings together people from different functional areas of the organization (such as manufacturing, finance, and marketing) to work on a special project. Each employee has two direct supervisors: the line manager from her or his specific functional area and the project manager. Exhibit 8-7 shows a matrix organization with four special project groups (A, B, C, D), each with its own project manager. Because of the dual chain of command, the matrix structure presents some unique challenges for both managers and subordinates.

> e x h i b i t   8 - 7 <

Matrix Organization

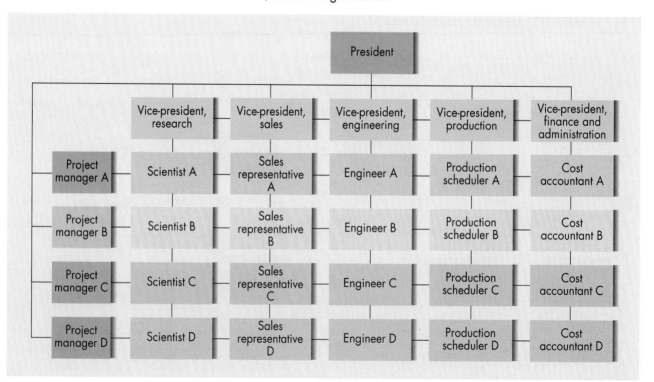

CREATING A STAIRWAY TO COMMITTEE HEAVEN

In 1987, when the Richards Group got big enough to take over a second floor in the building where it was then based, founder Stan Richards got worried that something special would get lost. "Everything changes when you move to multiple floors," he says. "People become tribal. Communication becomes more formal—and less effective." So Richards began convening regular committee meetings in the stairwell that connected the two floors. The idea: to gather everyone to hear news straight from the founder. Today those meetings seem downright quaint. The small agency has grown rapidly but the stairwell meetings continue.

Stairwell meetings are part of a strategy to maintain the spirit of small-company communication inside a fast-growing outfit. "Agencies can be hotbeds of paranoia," says Richards. "The best way to combat that tendency is simply not to keep secrets from each other."

Richards notes, "Being together is the key—all of us hearing something at exactly the same time. The event that brings us together varies. Another key point: Meeting in the staircase lets us be a little theatrical. Once, when we were courting an airline client, we even dropped oxygen masks from the fourth floor."

"If I call a committee meeting, we announce it over the loudspeaker, and people gather in the stairwell," says Richards. "I usually stand on the second level, so that everyone can hear me. We try to keep it short: I announce the news and offer a brief explanation. Then I might answer a question or two."

Critical Thinking Questions

1. How effective would stairwell meetings be in a large organization?
2. What are the advantages of a stairwell meeting?
3. What are other ways a large organization can retain the spirit of a small company?

Advantages of the matrix structure include:

- *Teamwork.* By pooling the skills and abilities of various specialists, the company can increase creativity and innovation and tackle more complex tasks.
- *Efficient use of resources.* Project managers use only the specialized staff they need to get the job done, instead of building large groups of underused personnel.
- *Flexibility.* The project structure is flexible and can adapt quickly to changes in the environment; the group can be disbanded quickly when it is no longer needed.
- *Ability to balance conflicting objectives.* The customer wants a quality product and predictable costs. The organization wants high profits and the development of technical capability for the future. These competing goals serve as a focal point for directing activities and overcoming conflict. The marketing representative can represent the customer, the finance representative can advocate high profits, and the engineers can push for technical capabilities.
- *Higher performance.* Employees working on special project teams may experience increased feelings of ownership, commitment, and motivation.
- *Opportunities for personal and professional development.* The project structure gives individuals the opportunity to develop and strengthen technical and interpersonal skills.

Disadvantages of the matrix structure include:

- *Power struggles.* Functional and product managers may have differing goals and management styles.
- *Confusion among team members.* Reporting relationships and job responsibilities may be unclear.
- *Lack of cohesiveness.* Team members from different functional areas may have difficulty communicating effectively and working together as a team.

How do you keep project teams on track in a matrix structure? Chris Higgins, BankAmerica's "Mr. Project," has some basic rules for getting things done.[8] Higgins joined the bank five years ago as a vice-president in charge of project management in the payment services division. His span of control has increased from a team of 8 to 140 project managers, with a current combined budget of $100 million. Higgins gives this advice for keeping projects on track in a matrix organization:

1. Spend less time doing and more time planning. Higgins believes teams are often quick at acting, but slow to think things through. Planning is particularly important when the team is made up of members from different functional areas.
2. Don't rely on electronic communication. Face-to-face communication can prevent confusion, clarify expectations, and build relationships—all of which can be lost when only e-mail is used to transmit information. Take time to communicate with team members.
3. Look for the commonality among projects. Although project teams often have unique challenges, not every challenge requires a unique plan of operation.
4. Project work isn't just about problem solving and timetables—it also requires encouraging employees to maintain momentum and keep up morale. Celebrate the achievement of interim goals, and make the project challenging as well as fun!

concept check

- How do line and staff positions differ?
- Why does the matrix structure have a dual chain of command?
- What are advantages of a matrix structure? Disadvantages?

REENGINEERING ORGANIZATIONAL STRUCTURE

>lg 6

reengineering

The complete redesign of business structures and processes in order to improve operations.

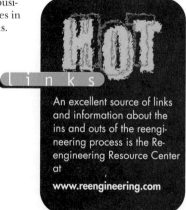

An excellent source of links and information about the ins and outs of the reengineering process is the Reengineering Resource Center at

www.reengineering.com

Periodically, all businesses must reevaluate the way they do business. This includes assessing the effectiveness of the organizational structure. To meet the formidable challenges of the future, companies are increasingly turning to **reengineering**—the complete redesign of business structures and processes in order to improve operations. An even simpler definition of reengineering is "starting over." In effect, top management asks, "If we were a new company, how would we run this place?" The purpose of reengineering is to identify and abandon the outdated rules and fundamental assumptions that guide current business operations. Every company has many formal and informal rules based on assumptions about technology, people, and organizational goals that no longer hold. Thus, the goal of reengineering is to redesign business processes to achieve improvements in cost control, product quality, customer service, and speed. The reengineering process

REENGINEERING THE IOC

In early 1999, the International Olympic Committee (IOC) received a wake-up call for reform when the Salt Lake City organizing committee "disclosed that it gave more than $1 million in cash and gifts to two dozen IOC members before it won the 2002 Winter Games." A report prepared by a panel appointed by the United States Olympic Committee (USOC) "offered a stinging rebuke of the IOC's structure and procedures and condemned it for failing to respond to warning signs about abuse as long ago as 1991." In the scandal's aftermath, 30 members—more than one-fourth of the IOC—were removed from the committee.

In addition to expelling the offending members, the IOC adopted some structural reforms in response to the scandal. The committee changed its process for selecting Olympics host cities and reduced the role of members. The IOC also agreed to create an ethics commission and a panel to recommend structural changes in the organization.

While praising the committee for taking quick action, corporate sponsors said the reforms had only begun and that they would monitor future IOC actions. A Visa International spokesperson said, "We expect the IOC to review other opportunities to rebuild public trust and support." An executive from another Olympics sponsor was more critical. He observed that "[Juan Antonio] Samaranch [the IOC's president] could have taken his mandate and put it behind some very specific reforms. . . Instead they set up study groups."

The corporate world—and at least some of the IOC membership—recognizes that the scandal could reduce the number of corporate sponsors or lower the fees that sponsors are willing to pay. Some observers fear, however, that not all IOC members are serious about reform.

Critical Thinking Questions

1. Why might someone take a bribe or accept a substantial gift voting in favor of a specific bidding city?
2. How might the IOC use reengineering to make structural changes to its organization?

should result in a more efficient and effective organizational structure that is better suited to the current (and future) competitive climate of the industry.

The many challenges of reengineering are well exemplified by the massive makeover currently in progress at VF Corp., a $5.5 billion-a-year apparel manufacturer headquartered in Greensboro, North Carolina. The project has been underway for four years and has already cost more than $70 million just for new software. Will the results be worth the cost? VF's reengineering goals include increasing annual revenue to $7 billion by the year 2000 by focusing on meeting the customer's needs, centralizing corporate functions, reducing costs, and pumping up marketing efforts. This requires structural change and new information technology. And if all goes well, VF's reengineering effort will have prepared the company to meet the competition head on in the 21st century.

Is VF's reengineering effort paying off? Find out by clicking on "investor relations" at **www.vfc.com**

concept check

- What is meant by reengineering?
- What is the purpose of reengineering?

THE INFORMAL ORGANIZATION

>lg 7

informal organization
The network of connections and channels of communication based on the informal relationships of individuals inside an organization.

Thus far in the chapter we have focused on the elements of formal organizational structures, many of which can be seen in the boxes and lines of the organization chart. Yet many important relationships within an organization do not show up on an organization chart. Nevertheless, these relationships can affect the decisions and performance of employees at all levels of the organization. The network of connections and channels of communication based on the informal relationships of individuals inside the organization is known as the **informal organization.** Informal relationships can be between people at the same hierarchical level or between people at different levels and in different departments. Some connections are work related, such as those formed among people who carpool or ride the same train to work. Others are based on nonwork commonalties such as belonging to the same church or health club or having children who attend the same school. The informal channels of communication of the informal organization are often referred to as the grapevine, the rumor mill, or the intelligence network.

Informal relationships between co-workers promote friendships among employees and keep employees informed about what's happening in their firm.

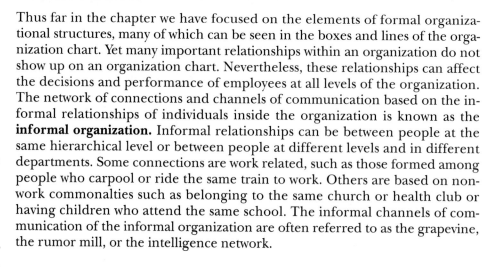

Functions of the Informal Organization

The informal organization has several functions: First, it provides a source of friendships and social contact for organization members. Second, the interpersonal relationships and informal groups help employees feel better informed and connected with what is going on in their firm, thus giving them some sense of control over their work environment. Third, the informal organization can provide status and recognition that the formal organization cannot or will not provide employees. Fourth, the network of relationships can aid the socialization of new employees by informally passing along rules, responsibilities, basic objectives, and job expectations. Finally, the organizational grapevine helps employees to be more aware of what is happening in their workplace by transmitting information quickly and conveying it to places that the formal system does not reach.

Although the informal organization can help the formal organization to achieve its goals, it can also create problems if not managed well. Group *norms* (commonly accepted standards of behavior) may conflict with the company's standards and cause problems. For instance, during a merger or acquisition, informal groups may strongly resist change (especially structural change), spread incorrect information through the grapevine, and foster fear and low morale among employees. With this in mind, managers need to learn to use the existing informal organization as a tool that can potentially benefit the formal organization. An excellent way of putting the informal organization to work for the good of the company is to bring informal leaders into the decision-making process. For another approach to the informal organization, see the Applying Technology box.

concept check

- What is the informal organization?
- How can informal channels of communication be used to improve operational efficiency?

IT IS A SMALL WORLD AFTER ALL!

Ever been to Disneyland's "small, small world"? The reality may be closer than you think. Two Cornell University researchers have come up with a recipe for turning any large network of components into a "small world." This is an intriguing concept for managers looking for more effective ways to structure their organizations. The small-world model could be used to improve the operational efficiency of very large corporations like General Motors and Procter & Gamble. The key to the small-world model is shortcuts: well-connected individuals or components that can cut across traditional organizational boundaries. These shortcuts could significantly speed up the flow of information through a company. Using mathematical modeling, the researchers discovered that it takes only a very few random connections, or shortcuts, to reduce a large world to a small one. Of primary importance is linking well-connected people from each level, as in the accompanying illustration.

The small-world model is based on Stanley Millgram's "six degrees of separation" concept. In the 1960s Millgram, a social psychologist at Harvard, theorized that we were all much more closely connected by our web of social interactions than any of us realized. Millgram conducted an experiment that showed it took on average only five intermediaries to connect a person in the Midwest with a complete stranger in Massachusetts—hence the phrase "six degrees of separation." The Cornell researchers used experimental mathematics, a discipline that combines mathematical analysis with computer simulations, to explore different models of social interaction. To test the random network model, the two researchers applied it to three different fully mapped networks (including the nation's western electric power grid) and found that it is indeed a small, small world.

Critical Thinking Questions

1. What are shortcuts in the small-world model? What purpose do they serve?
2. How could an organization use the small-world model internally to improve efficiency?
3. How could an organization use the small-world model in its external environment?

MISSING LINK

The key to an efficient organization is the creation of shortcuts between different levels.

1. In what researchers call a "locally ordered system," communication occurs only between people on the same level.

2. Random shortcuts can be introduced into such a network—that is, people meet members of other levels at the water cooler and pass along information.

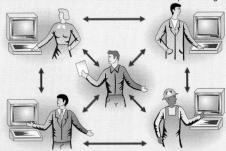

3. Only a few such shortcuts are needed to create a "a small world" in which information flows freely throughout the group. Productivity rises as a result.

SOURCE: Reprinted from August 17, 1998 issue of Business Week by special permission © by the McGraw Hill Companies Inc.

CAPITALIZING ON TRENDS IN BUSINESS

>lg 8

To achieve long-term objectives, organizations constantly evaluate and alter their organizational structures. The increased use of information technology and globalization are creating new options for organizing a business.

The Virtual Corporation

One of the biggest challenges for companies today is adapting to the technological changes that are affecting all industries. Organizations are struggling to find new organizational structures that will help them transform information technology into a competitive advantage. One alternative that is becoming increasingly prevalent is the **virtual corporation,** which is a network of independent companies (suppliers, customers, even competitors) linked by information technology to share skills, costs, and access to one another's markets. This network structure allows companies to come together quickly to exploit rapidly changing opportunities. The key attributes of a virtual corporation are:

virtual corporation

A network of independent companies linked by information technology to share skills, costs, and access to one another's markets; allows the companies to come together quickly to exploit rapidly changing opportunities.

- *Technology.* Information technology helps geographically distant companies form alliances and work together.

For an inside look at a virtual corporation, point your browser to GeneraLife's corporate home page at
www.generalife.com

- *Opportunism.* Alliances are less permanent, less formal, and more opportunistic than in traditional partnerships.
- *Excellence.* Each partner brings its core competencies to the alliance, so it is possible to create an organization with higher quality in every functional area and increase competitive advantage.
- *Trust.* The network structure makes companies more reliant on each other and forces them to strengthen relationships with partners.
- *No borders.* This structure expands the traditional boundaries of an organization.

In the concept's purest form, each company that links up with others to create a virtual corporation is stripped to its essence. Ideally, the virtual corporation has neither central office nor organization chart, no hierarchy, and no vertical integration. It contributes to an alliance only its core competencies, or key capabilities. It mixes and matches what it does best with the core competencies of other companies and entrepreneurs. For example, a manufacturer would only manufacture, while relying on a product design firm to decide what to make and a marketing company to sell the end result.

How does Cisco handle continual change without chaos? Read about the company's strategies at
www.cisco.com

Although firms that are purely virtual organizations are still relatively scarce, many companies are embracing several of the characteristics of the virtual structure. One of the best examples is Cisco Systems, Inc., the global leader of networking for the Internet.[9] Cisco produces the tools needed to build the powerful networks that link businesses to their customers and suppliers—access products, Web scaling products, security products, and many more. Perhaps because of the nature of its products, Cisco has been at the forefront of developing a new approach to organizational structure and management, incorporating information technology in every conceivable way. Along with an innovative organizational design, Cisco has built a unique corporate culture, relentlessly pursued alliances to acquire and retain intellectual capital, focused obsessively on customer needs, and developed some of the most progressive human resource policies in the industry. Cisco CEO John Chambers believes strongly that organizations should be built on change, not stability; organized as networks, not hierarchies; based on interdependencies, not self-sufficiency; and, above all, based on technological advantage. According to Chambers, Cisco has found "the sweet spot" where technology and the future meet to transform not just business, but all of life.

Structuring for Global Mergers

Recent mergers creating megafirms (such as DaimlerChrysler and Exxon Mobil) raise some important questions regarding corporate structure. How can managers hope to organize the global pieces of these huge, complex new firms into a cohesive, successful whole? Should decision making be centralized or decentralized? Should the firm be organized around geographic markets or product lines? And how can managers consolidate distinctly different corporate cultures? These issues and many more must be resolved if mergers of global companies are to succeed. The merger of Pharmacia AB of Sweden and Michigan-based Upjohn Co. provides some insight into these structural dilemmas. Forging one company from two, while also boosting profits, presented some unique challenges to Fred Hassan, CEO of newly merged Pharmacia & Upjohn.[10]

The merger of Upjohn Co. and Pharmacia AB required restructuring the operations of both firms. Has the strategy worked? Uncover the details at **www.upjohn.com**

When Hassan took over, sales and earnings were declining, turf wars were raging between regional offices, and the company's best talent was being hired away by its competitors. Hassan began his restructuring by reducing the number of senior executives from 19 to 8 so that they could make decisions as a team and collaborate more closely across different functional areas. Hassan lobbied to move the company's headquarters to a more strategic location that would be closer to other pharmaceutical firms and enable outside talent to be recruited more easily. Additionally, as is the case with many mergers, Hassan consolidated overlapping marketing, research, and administrative functions at the company's three regional offices. By restructuring the company, Hassan hopes his firm is now better positioned to compete with the other giants in the global pharmaceutical industry.

APPLYING THIS CHAPTER'S TOPICS

How is organizational structure relevant to you? A common thread linking all of the companies profiled in this chapter is you, the consumer. Companies structure their organizations to facilitate achieving their overall organizational

Build a Web Site   How computer literate are you? Have you ever built your own Web page? Could you build one for someone else? Find out what it takes to be a freelance Web builder! Visit **www.builder.cnet.com** to get information about building Web sites for fun and profit. You can set your own hours, name your own price, and choose your own projects. This site gives you a wide variety of information about Web-based businesses. Not sure whether you have the right skills, or uncertain what skills you should develop to work in this field? Don't know the difference between a content creator and a technical developer? Answers to those questions and many more can be found at this site. Companies are adapting their organizations to compete in cyberspace. Learn the skills you need to be a part of these new organizations.

goals. In order to be profitable, companies must have a competitive advantage, and competition is based on meeting customer expectations. The company that best satisfies customer wants and demands is the company that will lead the competition.

When companies make changes to their organizational structures, they are attempting to increase in some way their ability to satisfy the customer. For example, several of the companies profiled in this chapter were consolidating or centralizing parts of their operation. Why? Those companies hope to become more efficient and reduce costs, which should translate into better customer service and more reasonable prices. Some companies are decentralizing operations, giving departments or divisions more autonomy to respond quickly to changes in the market or to be more flexible in their response to customer demands. Many companies are embracing new information technology because it brings them closer to their customers faster than was previously possible. Internet commerce is benefiting consumers in a number of ways. When you buy books at **www.amazon.com** or use **www.ebay.com** to sell a used bicycle, you are sending the message that the virtual company is a structure you will patronize and support. Increasing globalization and use of information technology will continue to alter the competitive landscape, and the big winner should be the consumer, in terms of increased choice, increased access, and reduced price!

>looking ahead

at Procter & Gamble

In 1997 Procter & Gamble promised to double its sales to $70 billion by the year 2005. Midway through its pursuit of this goal P&G is switching CEOs. Whether the company achieves its 2005 objective may depend largely on how well the company adapts to the distinctly different style of its new chief executive, Durk Jager.[11] In a company known for its traditional, insular corporate culture, Jager is preaching "stretch, innovation, and speed." He wants P&G to take more risks and foster innovation by looking for ideas outside its core business areas. Excited at the prospect of Jager shaking things up at P&G, Wall Street analysts anticipate higher stock prices as the company works to become a more nimble competitor. If he survives the cultural backlash, Jager may indeed prove to be just what P&G needs to attain that $70 billion goal.

KEY TERMS

authority 234
centralization 235
chain of command 234
committee structure 239
customer departmental-ization 232
decentralization 236
delegation of authority 234
departmentalization 231
division of labor 230
formal organization 230
functional departmental-ization 232
geographic departmental-ization 232
informal organization 244
line-and-staff organization 239
line organization 239
line positions 239
managerial hierarchy 232
matrix structure (project management) 240
mechanistic organization 237
organic organization 237
organization chart 231
process departmental-ization 232
product departmental-ization 232
reengineering 242
span of control 235
specialization 230
staff positions 239
virtual corporation 246

SUMMARY OF LEARNING GOALS

>lg 1 What are the five structural building blocks that managers use to design organizations?

The five structural building blocks that are used in designing an efficient and effective organizational structure are (1) division of labor, which is the process of dividing work into separate jobs and assigning tasks to workers; (2) departmentalization; (3) the managerial hierarchy (or the *management pyramid*), which is the levels of management within the organization (generally consists of top, middle, and supervisory management); (4) the managerial span of control (sometimes called *span of management*), which is the number of employees the manager directly supervises; and (5) the amount of centralization or decentralization in the organization, which entails deciding at what level in the organization decisions should be made. Centralization is the degree to which formal authority is concentrated in one area or level of the organization.

>lg 2 What are the five types of departmentalization?

Five basic types of departmentalization (see Exhibit 8-2) are commonly used in organizations:

- *Functional.* Based on the primary functions performed within an organizational unit.
- *Product.* Based on the goods or services produced or sold by the organizational unit.
- *Process.* Based on the production process used by the organizational unit.
- *Customer.* Based on the primary type of customer served by the organizational unit.
- *Geographic.* Based on the geographic segmentation of organizational units.

>lg 3 How can the degree of centralization/decentralization be altered to make an organization more successful?

In a highly centralized structure, top management makes most of the key decisions in the organization with very little input from lower-level employees. Centralization lets top managers develop a broad view of operations and exercise tight financial controls. In a highly decentralized organization, decision-making authority is pushed down the organizational hierarchy, giving lower-level personnel more responsibility and power to make and implement decisions. Decentralization can result in faster decision-making and increased innovation and responsiveness to customer preferences.

>lg 4 How do mechanistic and organic organizations differ?

A mechanistic organization is characterized by a relatively high degree of work specialization, rigid departmentalization, many layers of management (particularly middle management), narrow spans of control, centralized decision making, and a long chain of command. This combination of elements results in a *tall organizational structure.* In contrast, an organic organization is characterized by a relatively low degree of work specialization, loose departmentalization, few levels of management, wide spans of control, decentralized decision making, and a short chain of command. This combination of elements results in a *flat organizational structure.*

>lg 5 What is the difference between line positions and staff positions?

In daily operations, those individuals in *line positions* are directly involved in the processes used to create goods and services. Those individuals in *staff positions* provide the administrative and support services that line employees need to achieve the firm's goals. Line positions in organizations are typically in areas such as production, marketing, and finance. Staff positions are found in areas such as legal counseling, managerial consulting, public relations, and human resource management.

>lg 6   **What is the goal of reengineering?**
Reengineering is a complete redesign of business structures and processes in order to improve operations. The goal of reengineering is to redesign business processes to achieve improvements in cost control, product quality, customer service, and speed.

>lg 7   **How does the informal organization affect the performance of a company?**
The informal organization is the network of connections and channels of communication based on the informal relationships of individuals inside the organization. Informal relationships can be between people at the same hierarchical level or between people at different levels and in different departments; the relationships can be based on connections made inside or outside the workplace. Informal organizations give employees more control over their work environment by delivering a continuous stream of company information throughout the organization, thereby helping employees stay informed.

>lg 8   **What trends are influencing the way businesses organize?**
The virtual corporation is a network of independent companies (suppliers, customers, even competitors) linked by information technology to share skills, costs, and access to one another's markets. This network structure allows companies to come together quickly to exploit rapidly changing opportunities. The key attributes of a virtual corporation are technology, opportunism, excellence, trust, and no borders.

Large global mergers, like DaimlerChrysler created from the merger of America's Chrysler Corp. and Germany's Daimler Benz, raise important issues in organizational structure. The ultimate question is how does management take two huge global organizations and create a single, successful, cohesive organization?" Should it be centralized or decentralized? Should it be organized along product or geographic lines? These are some of the questions management must answer.

PREPARING FOR TOMORROW'S WORKPLACE

1. The dean of your school has asked you to organize a new honor society in business. The group will hold an annual banquet with a businessperson as speaker, publish a quarterly newsletter, raise money to fund its activities, and recruit new student members. Write a memo to the dean explaining some of the factors to consider in organizing the new honor society. Also, suggest an organization chart for the group.

2. Divide the class into groups of five. Each group should be assigned a different type of organization: manufacturer, product retailer, service retailer, nonprofit organization, and governmental agency. Each group should interview managers at their assigned organization and report to the class on the structure of the organization. Be sure to ask the managers if they are satisfied with the current organizational structure and how it might be improved.

3. Would you like to work in a virtual organization? Why or why not?

4. Write a paper on why organizing is an important process. Give an example of how being disorganized can cause severe problems.

5. As the person in charge of homecoming, would you centralize or decentralize your operation? Explain why.

6. Why do you think that reengineering has become popular? Give an example of a company that has gone through reengineering.

7. Draw an organization chart of the firm you work for, your college, or a campus student organization. Show the lines of authority and formal communication. Describe the informal relationships that you think are important for the success of the organization.

8. Describe how the group norms in an informal organization with which you are familiar have influenced the company or organization. How can managers make informal organizations work for the good of the company?

WORKING THE NET

1. Find at least three examples of organization charts on the Internet by searching on Alta Vista (**www.altavista.digital.com**) for the term "company organizational charts." Analyze each company's organizational structure. Are the companies organized by function, product/service, process, customer type, or geographic location?

2. At either the *Fortune* magazine (**www.fortune.com**) or the *Forbes* (**www.forbes.com**) Web site, search the archives for stories about companies that have reengineered. Find an example of a reengineering effort that succeeded and one that failed and discuss why.

3. Visit the *Inc.* magazine Web site (**www.inc.com**) and use the search engine to find articles about virtual corporations. Using a search engine, find the Web site of at least one virtual corporation and look for information about how the company uses span of control, informal organization, and other concepts from this chapter.

4. At every level of the business, time management plays an important role in smoothing the chain of command and span of control. Research time management skills at **www.mindtools.com.** Make a list of how you can use this information to improve your school performance.

CREATIVE THINKING CASE

Organizing the Monster

Tyrannosaurus rex, pterodactyl, and brontosaurus—dinosaurs all. But what's a trumpasaurus? In fact, he's no dinosaur at all, but a friendly monster—a 10-foot-high, bright green-and-purple mascot, affectionately dubbed "Trump"—who greets you as you step off the fifth-floor elevator at the new 75,000-square-foot headquarters of the Monster Board, a job search Web site. Founded in April 1994 by Jeffrey Taylor, the Monster Board became part of the interactive division of TMP Worldwide in 1995. Today the company, based in Maynard, Massachusetts, boasts that it is the most successful career center on the Internet. Serving both job seekers and recruiters, the site receives more than 2.5 million visits per month, contains more than 50,000 job postings from 40,000 companies, and posts nearly 500,000 résumés.

The Monster Board Web site makes it easy for job hunters and recruiters to find each other. That business model is reflected in the design principle behind the company's new headquarters—and especially in the 22 team areas built into the space. The goal: to make sure that people can connect with one another whenever and wherever they need to—without having to wait for an empty room.

Teams are encouraged to name their rooms—the Creative Group meets in "Brian Forest"; the Alliance Team convenes in "Raise the Roof"—and each group has a small budget for decorating its rooms. "There's something that happens when you get together in your own comfortable space," says Danielle McCabe, the creative director of the Monster Board. "Ideas start to happen."

The largest, most-often-used meeting spot is the Monster Den—a cavernous area that features a kitchen, pool and ping-pong tables, oversize armchairs, and a mural decorated with monsters. Every Monday morning, all 180 Monster Board employees gather in the Den for a meeting whose purpose is to ensure that everyone in the company is on the same (Web) page.

Critical Thinking Questions

1. How would you describe the organizational structure at the Monster Board?
2. Do you think that the informal organization might be very important at the Monster Board?
3. Would you be happy working in this type of organizational structure? Why or why not?

VIDEO CASE

JIAN: A Virtual Organization

On its Web page (**www.jian.com**), JIAN, located in Mountain View, California, comments on the company's unusual name. "While a black belt is a master of the martial arts, a 'jian' is a *master of every art*—the ultimate human with extraordinary acumen, power and resourcefulness." JIAN describes itself as a contemporary software company that applies modern techniques to the art of building businesses. JIAN provides "expert knowledge and effective, time-saving tools that work with familiar Windows and Macintosh word processing and spreadsheet software."

Included among JIAN's software products are: BizPlan*Builder,* the company's original product for developing a business plan; Marketing*Builder* Interactive, a package that simplifies the creation of a marketing plan; EmployeeFile*Builder,* which provides a quick, easy, safe way to manage employee information; and EmployeeManual*Maker,* a program that facilitates the preparation and publication of customized employee handbooks. Other JIAN software products help with the safety, financial, and legal aspects of running a business. Most of JIAN's software products can be electronically downloaded from its Web site for immediate implementation anywhere in the world. User manuals are shipped separately from Web downloads.

JIAN, founded in July 1986 by Burke Franklin, was originally named Tools For Sales and focused on the development of sales promotion materials. Franklin also applied his experience to helping clients with their business plans. In 1988, Franklin took the best materials from each of these projects and developed BizPlan*Builder,* which became the flagship product for JIAN.

JIAN experienced rapid early growth. Franklin's challenge was to design an organization that would enable the company to continue to grow. Because it would be expensive and take him away from his software development and marketing expertise, Franklin rejected the common business approach of purchasing the equipment and hiring the people necessary to produce and distribute JIAN's products. Instead, Franklin decided to design JIAN as a virtual organization. He outsourced the production and distribution of JIAN's software to BINDCO and the human resources functions to EXECUSTAFF. BINDCO produces the software, packaging, manuals, and labels for JIAN's products, then assembles the products, and distributes them through JIAN's distribution channels. BINDCO also manages JIAN's inventory, takes its orders, and collects customer payments. EXECUSTAFF provides complete human resources services from hiring to firing and everything in between, including payroll, benefits administration, and worker's compensation claims. This virtual organization allows JIAN to concentrate on its core activities of designing business software and to increase its productivity and flexibility.

The success of a virtual organization is very dependent on how relationships among the partners are managed. The partners in a virtual relationship need to understand how the others operate. They also need to establish appropriate expectations. Communication and trust are crucial to a successful virtual relationship Progressive thinking and the willingness to try new programs are additional keys to success. The JIAN team says, "By the year 2000, we will have contributed to the success of more than 1,000,000 entrepreneurs and business owners."

Critical Thinking Questions

1. What differentiates a virtual organization from other organizational structures?
2. What are the advantages and disadvantages of a virtual organization?
3. Would you like to work for a virtual organization? Why or why not?

chapter nine

Managing Human Resources

learning goals

>lg 1   What is the human resource management process?

>lg 2   How are human resource needs determined?

>lg 3   How do human resource managers find good people to fill the jobs?

>lg 4   What is the employee selection process?

>lg 5   What types of training and development do organizations offer their employees?

>lg 6   What is a performance appraisal?

>lg 7   How are employees compensated?

>lg 8   What is organizational career management?

>lg 9   What are the key laws and federal agencies affecting human resource management?

>lg 10   What trends are affecting human resource management?

An Employee Problem at Don Pablos

James Taylor is an assistant restaurant manager at Don Pablos (**www.avado.com**), a Mexican restaurant chain of 25 units, most of which are located in larger cities of the Southwest. In addition to being a shift manager several days a week, he is responsible for hiring and training employees and scheduling their weekly shift assignments. Most of the wait staff work part-time and attend the local university. After the restaurant closes at 11:00 P.M., James stays to check liquor and food inventories, count cash and credit card receipts, and clean. One recent morning, he came early to the restaurant to prepare work schedules for the next two weeks, check employee time sheets, prepare payroll information for electronic transfer to corporate headquarters, and decide how to address a performance problem with Sharon Young, a waitress who has worked at the restaurant for nearly a year.

Sharon had been 30 minutes late for work the previous night, the fifth time in the last four weeks she had been late. Her attendance record for the last three months revealed six absences; each time she called only a few minutes before the start of her work shift to say she could not come to work. Punctuality and attendance had obviously become a problem. As a part-time employee, Sharon was not eligible for any paid sick leave or health insurance coverage. At the same time, James was aware that Sharon was an excellent waitress; her service and customer relations skills are the best among the current wait staff, and several repeat customers ask for her table.

As James contemplated his approach and options in dealing with Sharon, he quickly reviewed job and performance requirements for waitstaff employees. They had to have good communication skills, a strong service (or helpfulness) orientation, reasonably detailed knowledge of menu items, be neat and clean in physical appearance, and possess sufficient strength to carry large trays of food. Most importantly, however, they had to be dependable, or work when scheduled and report to work a few minutes before the start of the work shift. Sharon was obviously becoming less dependable. Training, counseling, a disciplinary warning, or termination were feasible options for dealing with her situation. Discharging her, however, won't improve her performance or correct her behavior.

Critical Thinking Questions

As you read this chapter, consider the following questions as they relate to Don Pablos Mexican restaurant:

- Is James faced with a typical human resource problem?
- What areas does human resource management cover?
- How should James proceed in solving this employee problem?

BUSINESS IN THE 21ST CENTURY

Human resource management in contemporary organizations is instrumental in driving an organization toward its objectives. Today, human resource professionals face numerous challenges in recruiting, selecting, and retaining employees:

- Organizations are competing with each other for a shrinking pool of applicants.
- Workers seek to balance work and home/life activities.
- Technology is reshaping the way business is done.
- Laws govern many aspects of the employee-employer relationship.

Each day, human resource experts and front line supervisors deal with these challenges while sharing responsibility for attracting and retaining skilled, motivated employees. Whether faced with a large or small human resource problem, managers like James at Don Pablos need to understand the process for finding and retaining excellent employees.

In this chapter, you will learn about the role of human resource management in building and maintaining an exceptional workforce. We will explore human resource planning, recruiting and selection, training, and motivating employees toward reaching organizational objectives. The chapter will also cover employee job changes within an organization and the laws guiding human resource decisions. Finally, we will look at important trends influencing human resource management.

DEVELOPING PEOPLE TO HELP REACH ORGANIZATIONAL GOALS

>lg 1

human resource management
The process of hiring, developing, motivating, and evaluating employees to achieve organizational goals.

Human resource management is the process of hiring, developing, motivating, and evaluating employees to achieve organizational goals. Organizational strategies and objectives form the basis for making all human resource management decisions. All companies strive to hire and develop well-trained, motivated employees. The human resources management process includes these steps, illustrated in Exhibit 9-1:

- Job analysis and design
- Human resource planning and forecasting
- Employee recruitment
- Employee selection
- Training and development
- Performance planning and evaluation

> e x h i b i t   9 - 1 <

> e x h i b i t   9 - 1 <

Human Resource Management Process

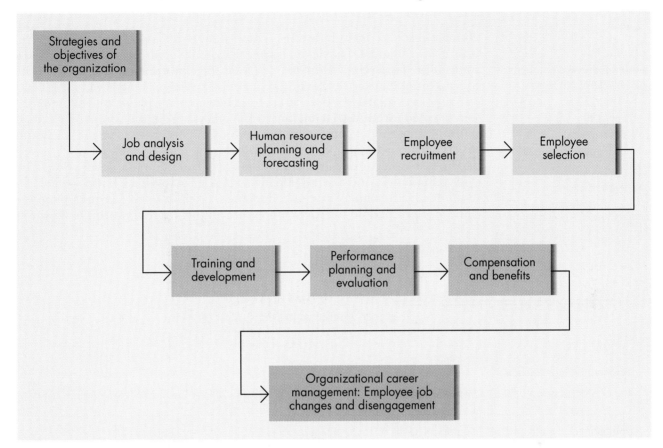

The flowchart shows the process with boxes: Strategies and objectives of the organization → Job analysis and design → Human resource planning and forecasting → Employee recruitment → Employee selection → Training and development → Performance planning and evaluation → Compensation and benefits → Organizational career management: Employee job changes and disengagement

c o n c ə p t   c h ə c k

- Define human resource management.
- Describe the human resource management process.

- Compensation and benefits
- Organizational career management: employee job changes and disengagement.

In the following sections, you will learn more about each of these important functions.

HUMAN RESOURCE PLANNING

>lg 2

Firms need to have the right number of people, with the right training, in the right jobs, to do the organization's work when it needs to be done. Human resource specialists are the ones who must determine future human resource needs. Then they assess the skills of the firm's existing employees to see if new people must be hired or existing ones retrained.

Creating a strategy for meeting future human resource needs is called **human resource (HR) planning.** Two important aspects of HR planning are job analysis and forecasting the firm's people needs. The HR planning process begins with a review of corporate strategy and policy. By understanding the mission of the organization, planners can understand its human resource needs. When Compaq Computer bought Digital Equipment Corp. (DEC), the acquisition resulted in several thousand DEC employees losing their jobs, while hundreds of

human resource (HR) planning

Creating a strategy for meeting future human resource needs.

Compaq employees were transferred to DEC's former headquarters in Boston. Many transferred employees assumed managerial positions.

Job Analysis and Design

Human resource planners must know what skills different jobs require. Information about a specific job is typically assembled through a **job analysis,** a study of the tasks required to do a job well. This information is used to specify the essential skills, knowledge, and abilities. For instance, when General Dynamics was awarded the contract for a new military plane, several new jobs were created for industrial engineers. Job analysts from the company's human resource department gathered information from other department heads and supervisors to help recruiters hire the right people for the new jobs.

The tasks and responsibilities of a job are listed in a **job description.** The skills, knowledge, and abilities a person must have to fill a job are spelled out in a **job specification.** These two documents help human resource planners find the right people for specific jobs. A sample job description is shown in Exhibit 9-2.

job analysis

A study of the tasks required to do a particular job well.

job description

The tasks and responsibilities of a job.

job specification

A list of the skills, knowledge, and abilities a person must have to fill a job.

> e x h i b i t   9 - 2 <

Job Description

Position: College Recruiter

Reports to: Vice-President of Human Resources

Location: Corporate Offices

Classification: Salaried/Exempt

Job Summary: Member of HR corporate team. Interacts with managers and department heads to determine hiring needs for college graduates. Visits 20 to 30 college and university campuses each year to conduct preliminary interviews of graduating students in all academic disciplines. Following initial interviews, works with corporate staffing specialists to determine persons who will be interviewed a second time. Makes recommendations to hiring managers concerning best qualified applicants.

Job Duties and Responsibilities:

Estimated time spent and importance

15% Working with managers and department heads, determines college recruiting needs.

10% Determines colleges and universities with degree programs appropriate to hiring needs to be visited.

15% Performs college relations activities with numerous colleges and universities.

25% Visits campuses to conduct interviews of graduating seniors.

15% Develops applicant files and performs initial applicant evaluations.

10% Assists staffing specialists and line managers in determining who to schedule for second interviews.

5% Prepares annual college recruiting report containing information and data about campuses, number interviewed, number hired, and related information.

5% Participates in tracking college graduates who are hired to aid in determining campuses that provide the most outstanding employees.

Job Specification (Qualifications):

Bachelor's degree in human resource management or a related field. Minimum of two years of work experience with the firm in HR or department that annually hires college graduates. Ability to perform in a team environment, especially with line managers and department heads. Very effective oral and written communication skills. Reasonably proficient in Excel, Word, and Windows computer environment and familiar with People Soft.

Human Resource Planning and Forecasting

Forecasting an organization's human resource needs, known as an HR *demand forecast,* is an essential aspect of HR planning. This process involves two forecasts: (1) determining the number of people needed by some future time (in one year, for example), and (2) estimating the number of people currently employed by the organization who will be available to fill various jobs at some future time. This is an *internal* supply forecast.

Does TeamStaff, a PEO, live up to its motto "Simply a better way to employ people"? Find out at

www.teamstaff.com

By comparing human resource demand and supply forecasts, a future personnel surplus or shortage can be determined and appropriate action taken. For example, United Airlines hired approximately 2,000 additional flight attendants when it developed the Star Alliance, an air transport network consisting of United, Lufthansa, SAS, Thai, Varig, and Air Canada. On the other hand, One Plus Financial terminated hundreds of employees when it withdrew from the mortgage banking industry. Exhibit 9-3 summarizes the process of forecasting an organization's needs.

> e x h i b i t 9 - 3 <

Human Resource Planning Process

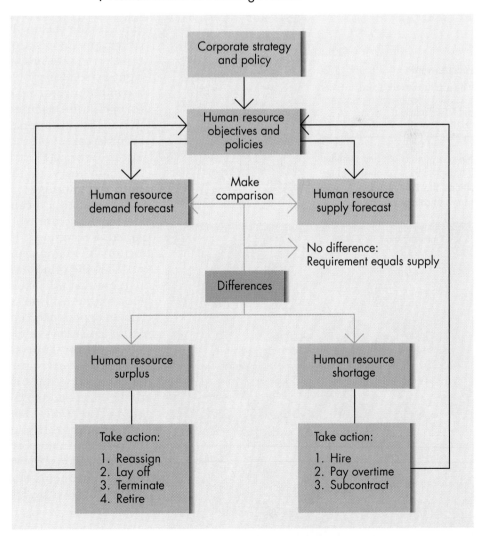

contingent workers

Persons who prefer temporary employment, either part-time or full-time.

concept check

- Describe the job analysis and design process.
- What is the process for human resource forecasting?

In recent years many firms with employee shortages are hiring **contingent workers,** or persons who prefer temporary employment, either part-time or full-time. College students and retired persons comprise a big portion of America's contingent workforce. Other people who want to work but don't want to be permanent employees join a professional employer organization (PEO). A PEO performs staffing, training, and compensation functions by contracting with a business to provide employees for a specified period of time. A firm with a shortage of accountants can rent or lease an accountant from the PEO for the expected duration of the shortage.

EMPLOYEE RECRUITMENT

>lg 3

When a firm creates a new position or an existing one becomes vacant, it starts looking for people with qualifications that meet the requirements of the job. Two sources of job applicants are the internal and external labor markets. The internal labor market consists of employees currently employed by the firm; the external labor market is the pool of potential applicants outside the firm.

recruitment

The attempt to find and attract qualified applicants in the external labor market.

Many organizations find qualified job applicants for professional positions through recruitment programs at college campuses.

Search the database of CareerPath.com (**www.careerpath.com**) for a job in a new city. It combines the listings of the *New York Times, Washington Post, Boston Globe, Chicago Tribune, Los Angeles Times,* and *San Jose Mercury News.*

Most companies including UPS, Southwest Airlines, and Wal-Mart follow a policy of promotion from within and try to fill positions with their existing employees. The internal search for job applicants usually means that a person must change his or her job. People are typically either promoted or transferred. A firm's *skills inventory* can help find the right person for a job opening. A skills inventory is a computerized employee database containing information on each employee's previous work experience, educational background, performance records, career objectives, and job location preferences. General Electric has used a skills inventory for many years as a means of determining promotions and transfers.

If qualified job candidates cannot be found inside the firm, the external labor market must be tapped. **Recruitment** is the attempt to find and attract qualified applicants in the external labor market. The type of position determines which recruitment method will be used and which segment of the labor market will be searched. Boeing will not recruit an experienced engineer the same way it would recruit a secretary or clerk typist.

Nontechnical, unskilled, and other nonsupervisory workers are recruited through newspaper, radio, and sometimes even television help wanted ads in local media. Starbucks placed ads in the *Beijing Youth Daily* to attract workers for its Beijing coffee shops.[1] Entry-level accountants, engineers, and systems analysts are commonly hired through college campus recruitment efforts. Each year Texas Instruments sends recruiters to dozens of colleges across the United States that have engineering degree programs. To recruit inexperienced technicians, National SemiConductor visits junior and community college campuses with electronic and related technical programs that are within 50 to 100 miles of its facilities.

A firm that needs executives and other experienced professional, technical, and managerial employees may employ the services of an executive search firm such as Korn Ferry. The hiring firm pays the search firm a fee equivalent to one to four months of the employee's first-year salary. Many search firms specialize in a particular occupation, industry, or geographic location.

Many firms participate in local job fairs. A **job fair** is typically a one-day event held at a convention center to bring together thousands of job seekers and hundreds of firms searching for employees.

Some firms now use the Internet exclusively to attract new employees. A firm can post job announcements at its Web site, and applicants send their résumés via the Internet. Beacon Application Services Corp., a systems integration company, recruits only over the Internet. According to Dan Maude, president of the firm, "A year's worth of Web recruiting for us costs less than one agency fee. . . . it's also faster."[2] The Applying Technology box describes how Career Central uses the Internet to match job applicants with job openings.

job fair
An event, typically one day, held at a convention center to bring together thousands of job seekers and hundreds of firms searching for employees.

> a p p l y i n g   t e c h n o l o g y <

CAREER CENTRAL USES TECHNOLOGY TO HELP PROFESSIONALS FIND THE RIGHT JOB

Although large companies increasingly are using executive search firms to recruit professional and managerial employees, small firms, which collectively have the majority of available professional and managerial positions, often cannot afford the fees charged by the search firms. Likewise, many recent business school graduates who want to work for small to medium-sized firms have difficulty finding out about job opportunities. Jeff Hyman launched Career Central (**www.careercentral.com**) to remedy this situation.

Career Central's goal is to bring together MBAs and the firms seeking them. It has three sets of customers: MBA job seekers, business schools with MBA programs, and employers. An individual searching for a position provides education and work information to Career Central's Web site, which then posts the information online. Business schools also distribute Career Central's registration diskettes to graduate business students and alumni. Employers, the only paying customers, can access Career Central's applicant data-

base for about $3,000 per search. Career Central guarantees employers data for at least 10 qualified job applicants per search. The employer then contacts these candidates to conduct further screening. Career Central's fee is 10 percent or less of the fee normally charged by a headhunter.

When you graduate, you very likely will use an electronic job search service like that provided by Career Central as part of your job search. Your campus may have its own computerized service, or it may subscribe to such a service and make it available to students.

Critical Thinking Questions

1. What are the benefits of an electronic job search for the applicant?
2. What are the benefits to the employer?
3. How can an electronic job search improve the match between the applicant's skills and the job's requirements?

concept check

- What is a skills inventory, and what are the two labor markets?
- Describe different ways that employees are recruited.
- How is technology helping firms find the right recruits?

Other firms including Coca-Cola, Paine Webber, and NationsBank utilize artificial intelligence software to scan and track résumés.[3] Restrac and Resumix scan résumés for key words to identify qualified job candidates. Each system can scan and search thousands of résumés in minutes. With such systems, the words you use to describe your education, background, and work experience become very important.

EMPLOYEE SELECTION

>lg 4

selection

The process of determining which persons in the applicant pool possess the qualifications necessary to be successful on the job.

After a firm has attracted enough job applicants, employment specialists begin the selection process. **Selection** is the process of determining which persons in the applicant pool possesses the qualifications necessary to be successful on the job. The steps in the employee selection process are shown in Exhibit 9-4 and described below:

1. *Initial screening.* During the initial screening, an applicant usually completes an application form and has a brief interview of 30 minutes or less. The application form includes questions about education, work experience, and previous job duties. A personal résumé may be substituted for the application form. The interview is normally structured and consists of a short list of specific questions. For example: Are you familiar with any accounting software packages? Did you supervise anyone in your last job? Did you use a company car when making sales calls?

2. *Employment testing.* Following the initial screening, an applicant may be asked to take one or more employment tests, such as the Minnesota Clerical Test or the Wonderlic Personnel Test, a mental ability test. Some tests are designed to measure special job skills, others measure aptitudes, and some are intended to capture characteristics of one's personality. The Myers-Briggs

> e x h i b i t　9 - 4 <

Steps of the Employee Selection Process

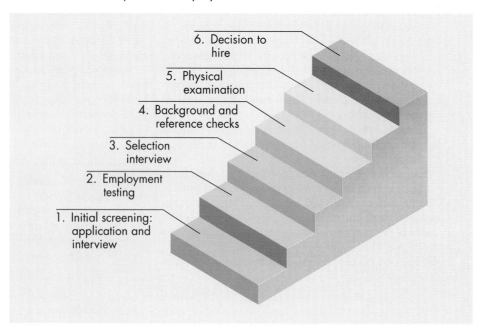

Type Indicator is a personality and motivational test widely used on college campuses as an aid in providing job and career counseling. Companies are increasingly using general attitude tests in job screening. John Pate, vice president of BT: Employee Screening Services, says, "You like to know what people are thinking. You don't want to hire their problems."[4]

selection interview

An in-depth discussion of an applicant's work experience, skills and abilities, education, and career interests.

3. *Selection interview.* The tool most widely used in making hiring decisions by Intel, Merck, and other firms is the **selection interview,** an in-depth discussion of an applicant's work experience, skills and abilities, education, and career interests. For managerial and professional positions, an applicant may be interviewed by several persons, including the line manager for the position to be filled. This interview is designed to determine an applicant's communication ability and motivation. It is also a means for gathering additional factual information from the applicant such as college major, years of part-time work experience, computer equipment used, and reason for leaving the last job. The applicant may be asked to explain how to solve a particular management problem or how she or he provided leadership to a group in a previous work situation when an important problem had to be solved quickly. United Airlines asks prospective flight attendants how they handled a conflict with a customer or coworker in a previous job.

Get advice for brushing up your interview skills at the Job Hunting Advice page of the *Wall Street Journal's* Career site,

careers.wsj.com/

Carolyn Murray, a recruiter for W. C. Gore and Associates, makers of Gore-Tex, says she pays little attention to a candidate's carefully scripted responses to her admittedly easy questions. Instead, she listens for a casual remark that reveals the reality behind an otherwise thought-out reply. Using a baseball analogy, Carolyn gives examples of how three job candidates struck out in Exhibit 9-5.[5]

4. *Background and reference check.* If applicants pass the selection interview, most firms examine their background and check their references. In recent years an increasing number of employers such as American Airlines, Disney, and Microsoft are carefully researching applicants' backgrounds, particularly

> e x h i b i t   9 - 5 <

Striking Out with Gore-Tex

The Pitch (Question to Applicant)	The Swing (Applicant's Response)	The Miss (Interviewer's Reaction to Response)
"Give me an example of a time when you had a conflict with a team member."	"Our leader asked me to handle all of the Fed Exing for our team. I did it, but I thought that Fed Exing was a waste of my time."	"At Gore, we work from a team concept. Her answer shows that she won't exactly jump when one of her teammates needs help."
"Tell me how you solved a problem that was impeding your project."	"One of the engineers on my team wasn't pulling his weight, and we were closing in on a deadline. So I took on some of his work."	"The candidate may have resolved the issue for this particular deadline, but he did nothing to prevent the problem from happening again."
"What's the one thing that you would change about your current position?"	"My job as a salesman has become mundane. Now I want the responsibility of managing people."	"He's not maximizing his current position. Selling is never mundane if you go about it in the right way."

their legal history, reasons for leaving previous jobs, and even creditworthiness. Retail firms such as Men's Warehouse, JC Penney, Tandy, and TD Industries, where employees have extensive contact with customers, tend to be very careful about checking applicant backgrounds. Some checking can be easily done using the Internet. In fact, many retired law enforcement officers have started their own firms that specialize in these investigations.

5. *Physical exams.* Companies frequently require job candidates to have a medical checkup to ensure they are physically able to perform a job. Drug testing is becoming a routine part of physical exams. Companies such as American Airlines, Burlington Northern Railroad, and the U.S. Postal Service use drug testing for reasons of workplace safety, productivity, and employee health. A comprehensive study by the Postal Service found that employees who tested positive for drugs were 50 percent more likely to be fired, injured, disciplined, or absent than those who tested negative. Drug users also had lower performance ratings.[6]

6. *Decision to hire.* If an applicant progresses satisfactorily through all the selection steps, a decision to hire the individual is made. The decision to hire is nearly always made by the manager of the new employee.

concept check

- What are the steps in the employee selection process?
- Describe some ways that applicants are tested.

EMPLOYEE TRAINING AND DEVELOPMENT

>lg 5

training and development

Activities that provide learning situations in which an employee acquires additional knowledge or skills to increase job performance.

To ensure that both new and experienced employees have the knowledge and skills to perform their jobs successfully, organizations invest in training and development activities. **Training and development** involves learning situations in which the employee acquires additional knowledge or skills to increase job performance. Training objectives specify performance improvements, reductions in errors, job knowledge to be gained, and/or other positive organizational results. The design of training programs at General Electric, for example, includes determining instructional methods, number of trainees per class, printed materials (cases, notebooks, manuals, and the like) to be used, location of training, use of audiovisual equipment and software, and many other matters. The process of creating and implementing training and development activities is shown in Exhibit 9-6.

> e x h i b i t   9 - 6 <

Employee Training and Development Process

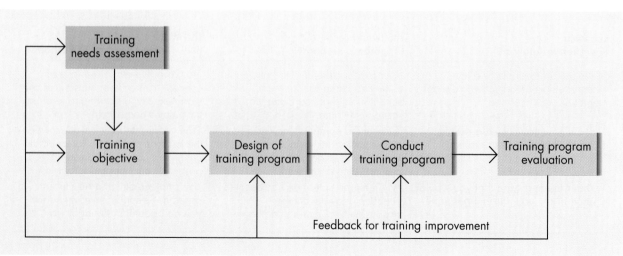

Training for new employees is instrumental in getting them up to speed and familiar with their job responsibilities. A study at MCI Worldcom found that in the first three months a new hire can accomplish only 60 percent as much as an experienced worker. And even a 5 percent drop in overall employee efficiency can cut MCI Worldcom's annual revenue by "several hundred million dollars."[7] The first type of training that new employees experience is **employee orientation,** which entails getting the new employee ready to perform on the job. Formal orientation (a half-day classroom program) provides information about company policies, salary and benefits, and parking. Although this information is very helpful, the more important orientation is about job assignments, work rules, equipment, and performance expectations provided by the new employee's supervisor and coworkers. This second briefing tends to be more informal and may last for several days or even weeks.

employee orientation

Training that prepares a new employee to perform on the job; includes information about job assignments, work rules, equipment, and performance expectations, as well as about company policies, salary and benefits, and parking.

On-the-Job Training

Continuous training for both new and experienced employees is important to keep job skills fresh. Job-specific training, designed to enhance a new employee's ability to perform a job, includes **on-the-job training,** during which the employee learns the job by doing it with guidance from a supervisor or experienced coworker.

On-the-job training takes place at the job site or workstation and tends to be directly related to the job. This training involves specific job instructions, coaching (guidance given to new employees by experienced ones), special project assignments, or job rotation. **Job rotation** is the reassignment of workers to several different jobs over time. At Sears, management trainees work sequentially in two or three merchandise departments, customer service, credit, and human resources during their first year on the job.

An **apprenticeship** usually combines specific on-the-job instruction with classroom training. It may last as long as four years and can be found in the skilled trades of carpentry, plumbing, and electrical work.

With **mentoring,** another form of on-the-job training, a senior manager or other experienced employee provides job- and career-related information to a protégé. Mentoring is becoming increasingly popular with many firms, including Federal Express, Texaco, Merrill Lynch, and Bank of America, which uses "quad squads" composed of a mentor and three new hires (a male, female, and a minority group member). At Coca-Cola Roberto Goizueta mentored Douglas Ivester to become CEO of the company. When Goizueta died suddenly in 1997, Ivester's transition to CEO went very smoothly. The company clearly benefited from this mentoring relationship.

The primary benefits of on-the-job training are that it provides instant feedback about performance and is inexpensive. Trainees produce while learning, and no expensive classroom or learning tools are needed.

on-the-job training

Training in which the employee learns the job by doing it with guidance from a supervisor or experienced coworker.

job rotation

Reassignment of workers to several different jobs over time so that they can learn the basics of each job.

apprenticeship

A form of on-the-job training that combines specific job instruction with classroom instruction.

mentoring

A form of on-the-job training in which a senior manager or other experienced employee provides job- and career-related information to a protégé.

Off-the-Job Training

Even with the advantages of on-the-job training, many firms recognize that it is often necessary to train employees away from the workplace. With off-the-job training, employees learn the job away from the job. There are numerous popular methods of off-the-job training. Frequently, it takes place in a classroom where cases, role-play exercises, films, videos, lectures, and computer demonstrations are utilized to develop workplace skills.

Another form of off-the-job training takes place in a facility called a vestibule or a training simulator. In **vestibule training,** used by Honda and Kroger, trainees learn about products, manufacturing processes, and selling in a scaled-down version of an assembly line or retail outlet. When mistakes

vestibule training

A form of off-the-job training in which trainees learn in a scaled-down version or simulated work environment.

By using vestibule training, airlines can teach pilots flight maneuvers and the controls of new aircraft in a safe and controlled off-the-job training environment.

concəpt chəck

- Describe several types of on-the-job training.
- Explain vestibule training and programmed instruction.

are made, no customers are lost or products damaged. A training simulator, such as American Airlines' flight simulator for pilot training, is much like a vestibule facility. Pilots can practice hazardous flight maneuvers or learn the controls of a new aircraft in a safe, controlled environment with no passengers.

In a very rapidly developing trend that will undoubtedly accelerate in the 21st century, many companies including Compaq and Microsoft are using computer-assisted, electronically delivered training and development courses and programs. Many of these courses have their origins in **programmed instruction,** a self-paced, highly structured training method that presents trainees with concepts and problems using a modular format. Each module consists of a set of concepts, math rules, or task procedures with test questions at the end of the module. When the trainee or student masters all material presented in a module, he or she advances to the next module, which is somewhat more difficult. Some courses taught on your campus probably use programmed instructional materials.

Finally, trade associations, colleges and universities, and professional organizations offer professional and executive education courses at training centers or professional organization meetings.

Usually, off-the-job training is more expensive then on-the-job training, and its impact is less direct or the transfer of learning to the job is less immediate. Nevertheless, despite these shortcomings, some training can only be done away from the job.

PERFORMANCE PLANNING AND EVALUATION

>lg 6

programmed instruction
A form of computer-assisted off-the-job training.

performance appraisal
A comparison of actual performance with expected performance to assess an employee's contributions to the organization.

Along with employee orientation and training, new employees learn about performance expectations through performance planning and evaluation. Managers provide employees with expectations about the job. These are communicated as job objectives, schedules, deadlines, and product and/or service quality requirements. As an employee performs job tasks, the supervisor periodically evaluates the employee's efforts. A **performance appraisal** is a comparison of actual performance with expected performance to assess an employee's contributions to the organization and to make decisions about training, compensation, promotion, and other job changes. The performance planning and appraisal process is shown in Exhibit 9-7 and described below.

1. The manager establishes performance standards.

2. The employee works to meet the standards and expectations.

3. The employee's supervisor evaluates the employee's work in terms of quality and quantity of output and various characteristics such as job knowledge, initiative, relationships with others, and attendance and punctuality.

4. Following the performance evaluation, reward (pay raise) and job change (promotion) decisions can be made.

5. Rewards are positive feedback and provide reinforcement, or encouragement, for the employee to work harder in the future.

> e x h i b i t   9 - 7 <

Performance Planning and Evaluation

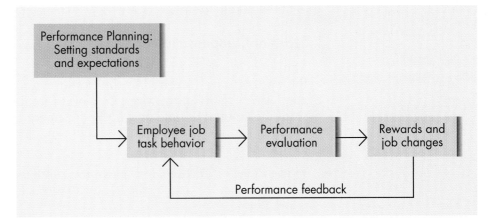

Performance Planning:
Setting standards
and expectations

→ Employee job
task behavior → Performance
evaluation → Rewards and
job changes

Performance feedback

concept check

- What are the steps in the performance planning and appraisal process?
- What purposes do performance appraisals serve?

Performance appraisals serve a number of purposes, but they are most often used to make decisions about pay raises, training needs, and advancement opportunities.

EMPLOYEE COMPENSATION AND BENEFITS

>lg 7

Compensation, which includes both pay and benefits, is closely connected to performance appraisal. Employees who perform better tend to get bigger pay raises.[8] Several factors affect an employee's pay.

1. *Pay structure and internal influences.* Wages, salaries, and benefits usually reflect the importance of the job. The jobs that management considers more important are compensated at a higher rate; president, chief engineer, and chief financial officer are high-paying jobs. Likewise, different jobs of equal importance to the firm are compensated at the same rate. For instance, if a drill-press operator and a lathe operator are considered of equal importance, they may both be paid $21 per hour.

2. Pay level and external influences. In deciding how much to pay workers, the firm must also be concerned with the salaries paid by competitors. If competitors are paying much higher wages, a firm may lose its best employees. Larger firms conduct salary surveys to see what other firms are paying. Wage and salary surveys conducted by the Chamber of Commerce or the U.S. Department of Labor can also be useful.

   An employer can decide to pay at, above, or below the going rate. Most firms try to offer competitive wages and salaries within a geographic area or an industry. If a company pays below-market wages, it may not be able to hire skilled people. The level, or competitiveness, of a firm's compensation is determined by the firm's financial condition (or profitability), efficiency, and

External influences affect employee pay and benefits. With a high demand for skilled workers and high turnover rates, firms in the information technology industry offer high wages and many benefits to attract and retain workers like this Netscape employee.

employee productivity, as well as the going rates paid by competitors. Miller Brewing Co. is considered a high-paying firm ($22–$25 per hour for production employees); McDonald's is a lower paying company ($6–$8 per hour for counter employees).

Types of Compensation or Pay

There are two basic types of compensation: direct and indirect. Direct pay is the wage or salary received by the employee; indirect pay consists of various employee benefits and services. Employees are usually paid directly on the basis of the amount of time they work, the amount they produce, or some combination of time and output. The following are the most common types of compensation:

- *Hourly wages.* Technicians, machinists, and assembly-line workers at Miller Brewing Co. are paid by the hour with wages ranging from $22.50 to $26.50 per hour.

- *Salaries.* Managerial and professional employees are paid an annual salary either on a biweekly or a monthly basis. The annual salary of our U.S. president is $200,000.

- *Piecework and commission.* Some employees are paid according to how much they produce or sell. A car salesperson might be paid $500 for each car sold or a 3 percent commission on the car's sale price. Thus, a salesperson who sold four cars in one week at $500 per car would earn $2,000 in pay for that week. Alternatively, a 3 percent commission on four cars sold with total sales revenue of $70,000 would yield $2,100 in pay.

  Increasingly, business firms are paying employees using a base wage or salary and an incentive. The incentive feature is designed to increase individual employee, work group, and/or organizational performance. Incentive pay plans are commonly referred to as variable or contingent pay arrangements.

- *Accelerated commission schedule.* A salesperson could be paid a commission rate of 3 percent on the first $50,000 of sales per month, 4 percent on the next $30,000, and 5 percent on any sales beyond $80,000. For a salesperson who made $90,000 of sales in one month, the monthly pay would be as follows:

$$
\begin{array}{rcl}
3\% \times \$50,000 &=& \$1,500 \\
4\% \times \$30,000 &=& \$1,200 \\
5\% \times \underline{\$10,000} &=& \underline{\$\ \ 500} \\
\$90,000 && \$3,200
\end{array}
$$

- *Bonus.* A bonus is a payment for reaching a specific goal; it may be paid on a monthly, quarterly, or annual basis. A bank with several offices or branches might set monthly goals for opening new accounts, making loans, and customer service. Each employee of a branch that meets all goals would be paid a monthly bonus of $100. Although the bonuses are paid to the employees individually, the employees must function as an effective, high-performing group to reach the monthly goals.

- *Profit sharing.* A firm that offers profit sharing pays employees a portion of the profits over a preset level. For example, profits beyond 10 percent of gross sales might be shared at a 50 percent rate with employees. The company retains the remaining profits. All employees may receive the same profit shares, or the shares may vary according to base pay.

- *Fringe benefits.* **Fringe benefits** are indirect compensation and include pensions, health insurance, vacations, and many others. Some fringe benefits are

fringe benefits

Indirect compensation such as pensions, health insurance, and vacations.

required by law: unemployment compensation, worker's compensation, and Social Security, which are all paid in part by employers. *Unemployment compensation* provides former employees with money for a certain period while they are unemployed. To be eligible, the employee must have worked a minimum number of weeks, be without a job, and be willing to accept a suitable position offered by the state Unemployment Compensation Commission. Some state laws permit payments to strikers. *Worker's compensation* pays employees for lost work time caused by work-related injuries and may also cover rehabilitation after a serious injury. *Social Security* is mainly a government pension plan, but it also provides disability and survivor benefits and benefits for people undergoing kidney dialysis and transplants. Medicare (health care for the elderly) and Medicaid (health care for the poor) are also part of Social Security.

Many employers also offer fringe benefits not required by law. Among these are paid time off (vacations, holidays, sick days, even pay for jury duty), insurance (health and hospitalization, disability, life, dental, vision, and accidental death and dismemberment), pensions and retirement savings accounts, and stock purchase options.

Some firms with numerous fringe benefits allow employees to mix and match benefit items or select items based on individual needs. This is a flexible or cafeteria-style benefit plan. A younger employee with a family may desire to purchase medical, disability, and life insurance, whereas an older employee may want to put more benefit dollars into a retirement savings plan. All employees are allocated the same number of benefit dollars but can spend these dollars on different items and in different amounts.

concept check

- How does a firm establish a pay scale for its employees?
- What is the difference between direct and indirect pay?

ORGANIZATIONAL CAREER MANAGEMENT

>lg 8

An important aspect of the human resource management process is organizational career management, or facilitating employee job changes, including promotions, transfers, demotions, layoffs, terminations, and retirements.

Job Changes within the Organization

promotion

An upward move in an organization to a position with more authority, responsibility, and pay.

A **promotion** is an upward move in an organization to a position with more authority, responsibility, and pay. Promotion decisions are usually based on merit (ability and performance) and seniority (length of service). Union employees usually prefer a strict seniority system for employee advancement. Managers and technical employees strongly prefer promotions based on merit.

transfer

A horizontal move in an organization to a position with about the same salary and at about the same organizational level.

A **transfer** is a horizontal move in an organization to a position with about the same salary and at about the same organizational level. An employee may seek a transfer for personal growth, for a more interesting job, for convenience (better work hours, work location, or training opportunity), or for a job that offers more potential for advancement. Employers may transfer workers from positions where they are no longer needed to ones where they are needed. Or the goal may be to find a better fit for the employee within the firm. Sometimes transfers are made to give employees a different perspective or to reenergize them. Consider Randy Lagman, a staff support technician for Internet operations at Lands' End, a billion-dollar clothing catalog company based in Dodgeville, Wisconsin. Randy was transferred from a self-described "Web-geek" position to a job with the title "technical adventurer outfitter."

Randy's transfer had a big impact on his work style. For most people, bringing work home means reading reports in front of the TV or analyzing spreadsheets in an office carved out of a spare bedroom. For Lagman, it means wearing a raincoat, sitting under a lawn sprinkler, and testing a weatherproof laptop. "I'm getting a reputation as the neighborhood crackpot," he jokes. His work has also had an impact on his understanding of risk and stress. Lots of information technology people believe that they work in high-stakes, high-pressure environments. But Lagman's role as technical adventurer outfitter brings him into contact with people who know the *real* meaning of risk.[9]

When a person is downgraded or reassigned to a position with less responsibility, it is called a **demotion.** This usually occurs when an employee isn't performing satisfactorily. In most companies, a person is given several warnings before a demotion takes place.

Separations

A **separation** occurs when an employee leaves the company. Layoffs, terminations, resignations, and retirements are all types of separations. Sometimes separations occur because companies are trying to remain competitive in the global marketplace. When oil prices dropped significantly early in 1997, many energy firms laid off or terminated workers. UPR, Inc., an oil exploration and drilling company, initially terminated 400 employees and later offered early retirement packages to other employees to encourage them to retire.

A **layoff** is a temporary separation arranged by the employer, usually because business is slow. Layoffs can be planned, such as seasonal reductions of employees, or unplanned, as when sales unexpectedly decline. Generally, employees with the least seniority are laid off first.

There are several alternatives to a layoff. With a *voluntary reduction in pay,* all employees agree to take less pay so that everyone can keep working. Other firms arrange to have all or most of their employees take vacation time during slow periods. Major league baseball teams, the Houston Astros, for example, encourage their full-time year-round employees to take vacations during the off-season from November through April. Other employees agree to take *voluntary time off,* or work fewer hours, which again has the effect of reducing the employer's payroll and avoiding the need for a layoff. Control Data Corp. avoids layoffs with what it calls a *rings of defense* approach. Temporary employees are hired with the specific understanding that they may be laid off at any time. When layoffs are needed, the temporary workers are the first "ring of defense." Permanent Control Data employees know they probably will never be laid off.

A **termination** is a permanent separation arranged by the employer. Reasons for terminations include failure to perform as expected, violation of work rules, dishonesty, theft, sexual harassment, excessive absenteeism, or insubordination (disobedience).

Most companies follow a series of steps before terminating an employee. First, the employee is given an oral warning. The second step is a written statement that the employee's actions are not acceptable. If the employee fails to improve, he or she is suspended from work for a time. If the employee persists in wrongdoing after suspension, his or her employment is terminated.

Resignation is a permanent form of separation that is undertaken voluntarily by the employee, whereas layoff and termination are involuntary. An employee may resign for almost any reason: to seek a new career, move to a different part of the country, accept an employment offer with a significant pay raise, or join a fast-growing firm with numerous advancement opportunities.

For companies in high-growth industries, keeping employees from resigning and moving to "greener pastures" is a number-one priority. This is particularly true in smaller entrepreneurial firms where losing a key employee can be disastrous. A good example of a company that emphasizes employee retention is Trilogy Software, discussed in the Focusing on Small Business box.

demotion

The downgrading or reassignment of an employee to a position with less responsibility.

separation

The departure of an employee from the organization; can be a layoff, termination, resignation, or retirement.

layoff

A temporary separation of an employee from the organization; arranged by the employer, usually because business is slow.

termination

A permanent separation of an employee from the organization, arranged by the employer.

resignation

A permanent separation of an employee from the organization, done voluntarily by the employee.

AT TRILOGY SOFTWARE, RESIGNATION IS A DIRTY WORD

At age 28, Danielle Rios has it all—a BS degree in computer science from Stanford, a great track record as a software developer for IBM, and the energy and savvy to market herself. With all that going for her, Rios could be a free-agent winner in the new economy, adding value by juggling different projects with different firms. Or she could have her pick of well-established corporate launch pads for her career.

But for the last three years, Rios has worked with Trilogy Software, Inc., a small, rapidly growing software firm based in Austin, Texas. Trilogy is on the cutting edge of sales-and-marketing software, and Rios is part of a team that shows potential customers how the software can work for them.

Joe Liemandt founded Trilogy in 1989, after dropping out of Stanford only a few months before graduation. To finance the start-up, Liemandt charged up 22 credit cards. Four years ago, Trilogy had 100 employees. Today it has almost 1,000 and plans to add another 1,000 soon. But to call Trilogy workers "employees" misses the point. They're all shareholders. They're all managers. They're all partners. That's how Liemandt, Trilogy's CEO, has chosen to run his company—and that's what makes it successful.

Liemandt knows that Trilogy depends on talented people. He also knows that people can go anywhere. Which means that his biggest competitive headache isn't companies like SAP AG, Baan Co., and PeopleSoft, Inc.—businesses he has to face down in the marketplace. His biggest worry is holding onto people like Rios. "There's nothing more important than recruiting and growing people," he says. "That's my number-one job."

It's a seller's market for talent. People with the right combination of savvy and ambition can afford to shop for the right boss, the right colleagues, the right environment. In the old economy, it was a buyer's market: Companies had their pick of the crop, and the question they asked was "Why hire?" Now the question is "Why join up?"

Critical Thinking Questions

1. Do you think that Trilogy overemphasizes the importance of employees?
2. What are some things that Trilogy can do to keep those workers in high demand?
3. Would you want to work for Trilogy?

---

retirement
The separation of an employee from the organization at the end of his or her career.

concept check

- What is organizational career management?
- Define promotion, transfer, termination, and retirement.

Retirement usually ends one's career. Common retirement ages are 55, 62, 65, and 70, but no one can be required to retire, according to the Age Discrimination Act. The law does, however, allow mandatory retirement in a few occupations, such as firefighter, police officer, and commercial airline pilot.

Workers in companies with too many employees may be offered early-retirement incentives. This option offers retirement benefits to younger employees or adds extra retirement benefits or both. Employees can thus retire more comfortably without working longer. Xerox, General Motors, IBM, Hewlett-Packard, and Phillips Petroleum, among others, have used early-retirement plans to reduce their workforces.

LAWS AFFECTING HUMAN RESOURCE MANAGEMENT

>lg 9

Federal laws help ensure that job applicants and employees are treated fairly and not discriminated against. Hiring, training, and job placement must be unbiased. Promotion and compensation decisions must be based on

> m a k i n g   e t h i c a l   c h o i c e s <

AN UNFAIR DISMISSAL?

Alex Lambros, Jr., a stockbroker, has had just one customer complaint in 25 years in the business. Recruited in 1989 to work for Merrill Lynch & Co., Lambros soon became a top producer. He developed a "$88 million book of brokerage business" and was recognized by the company as one of the elite performers in the brokerage industry.

Several years later, when he was the acting branch manager of a Merrill Lynch office in Cape Coral, Florida, Lambros was fired for destroying company property. His apparent offense was that he tore open a payroll envelope addressed to the office's branch manager.

Lambros filed a complaint of wrongful termination and defamation with the New York Stock Exchange—one of several oversight authorities for the brokerage industry. Lambros contended that he was terminated because he "had repeatedly questioned the propriety of actions by superiors." He further contended that Merrill Lynch's managers were tempted by his "lush client base." High-performing brokers get a larger share of the commissions paid by clients. By redistributing Lambros's client base to brokers with lower commissions or by having managers take over the accounts, the company could retain a greater percentage of the commissions, and the managers would benefit. In addition, a brokerage firm benefits if client accounts are actively traded—"something that top producers with trusted relationships with their clients don't always do." Were Lambros's claims true? Merrill Lynch contends that his claims "were baloney from the start."

Critical Thinking Questions

1. In your opinion, was Lambros's dismissal fair and just?
2. How would you evaluate the action of a brokerage firm's managers who obtain new clients by firing a broker and taking his accounts?

performance. These laws help all Americans who have talent, training, and the desire to get ahead.

New legislation and the continual interpretation and reinterpretation of existing laws will continue to make the jobs of human resource managers challenging and complicated. In 1999, for example, the National Academy of Sciences reported a link between muscle and skeletal injuries and certain workplace activities, such as lifting. In response, OSHA, a federal agency discussed below, issued new standards for the handling and lifting of objects by employees. Of course, human resource managers must now integrate these standards into their organizations. The key laws that currently affect human resource management are shown in Exhibit 9-8.

Several laws govern wages, pensions, and unemployment compensation. For instance, the Fair Labor Standards Act sets the minimum wage, which is periodically raised by Congress. Many minimum-wage jobs are found in service businesses, such as restaurants and car washes. The Pension Reform Act protects the retirement income of employees and retirees. Federal tax laws also affect compensation, including employee profit-sharing and stock purchase plans.

Employers must also be aware of changes to laws concerning employee safety, health, and privacy. The Occupational Safety and Health Act requires employers to provide a workplace free of health and safety hazards. For instance, manufacturers must require employees working on loading docks to wear steel-toed shoes so their feet won't be injured if materials are dropped. Drug and AIDS testing are also governed by federal laws.

> e x h i b i t   9 - 8 <

> e x h i b i t   9 - 8 <

Laws Impacting Human Resource Management

Law	Purpose	Agency of enforcement
Social Security Act (1935)	Provides for retirement income and old age health care	Social Security Administration
Fair Labor Standards Act (1938)	Sets minimum wage, restricts child labor, sets overtime pay	Wage and Hour Division, Department of Labor
Equal Pay Act (1963)	Eliminates pay differentials based on gender	Equal Employment Opportunity Commission
Civil Rights Act (1964), Title VII	Prohibits employment discrimination based on race, color, religion, gender, or national origin	Equal Employment Opportunity Commission
Age Discrimination Act (1967)	Prohibits age discrimination against those over 40 years of age	Equal Employment Opportunity Commission
Occupational Safety and Health Act (1970)	Protects worker health and safety, provides for hazard-free workplace	Occupational Safety and Health Administration
Vietnam Veterans Readjustment Act (1974)	Requires affirmative employment of Vietnam War veterans	Veterans Employment Service, Department of Labor
Employee Retirement Income Security Act (1974)—also called Pension Reform Act	Establishes minimum requirements for private pension plans	Internal Revenue Service, Department of Labor, and Pension Benefit Guaranty Corporation
Pregnancy Discrimination Act (1978)	Treats pregnancy as a disability, prevents employment discrimination based on pregnancy	Equal Employment Opportunity Commission
Immigration Reform and Control Act (1986)	Verifies employment eligibility, prevents employment of illegal aliens	Employment Verification Systems, Immigration and Naturalization Service
Americans with Disabilities Act (1990)	Prohibits employment discrimination based on mental or physical disabilities	Department of Labor
Family and Medical Leave Act (1993)	Requires employers to provide unpaid leave for childbirth, adoption, or illness	Equal Employment Opportunity Commission

Human resource managers must ensure that their firms accommodate the needs of disabled employees like wheelchair-bound workers who need ramps to facilitate their mobility.

Another employee law that continues to strongly affect the work of human resource managers is the Americans with Disabilities Act. To be considered disabled, a person must have a physical or mental impairment that greatly limits one or more major life activities. More than 54 million Americans fall into this category.[10] Employers may not discriminate against disabled persons. They must make "reasonable accommodations" so that qualified disabled employees can perform the job, unless doing so would cause "undue hardship" for the business. Altering work schedules, modifying equipment so a wheelchair-bound person can use it, and making buildings accessible by ramps and elevators are considered reasonable. Two companies often praised for their efforts to hire the disabled are McDonald's and DuPont.

The Family and Medical Leave Act went into effect in 1993. The law applies to employers with 50 or more employees. It requires these employers to provide unpaid leave of up to 12 weeks during any 12-month period to workers who have been employed for at least a year and work a minimum of 25 hours a week. The reasons for the leave include the birth or adoption of a child; the serious illness of a child, spouse, or parent; or a serious illness that prevents the worker from doing the job. Upon return, the employee must be given her or his old job back. The worker cannot collect unemployment compensation while on leave. A company can deny leave to a salaried employee in the highest-paid 10 percent of its workforce, if letting the worker take leave would create a "serious injury" for the firm.

The Role of Government Agencies in Human Resource Management

Several federal agencies oversee employment, safety, compensation, and related areas. The Occupational Safety and Health Administration (OSHA) sets workplace safety and health standards, provides safety training, and inspects places of work (assembly plants, construction sites, and warehouse facilities, for example) to determine employer compliance with safety regulations.

The Wage and Hour Division of the Department of Labor enforces the federal minimum-wage law and overtime provisions of the Fair Labor Standards Act. Employers covered by this law must pay certain employees a premium rate of pay (or time and one-half) for all hours worked beyond 40 in one week.

How does the Equal Employment Opportunity Commission promote equal opportunity in employment? Visit **www.eeoc.gov** to learn what the agency does.

The Equal Employment Opportunity Commission, created by the 1964 Civil Rights Act, investigates and resolves charges of discrimination. It also files lawsuits on its own against employers. Violators can be forced to promote, pay back wages to, or provide additional training for employees against whom they discriminated. Sears, Motorola, and AT&T have had to make large back-pay awards and to offer special training to minority employees after the courts found they had been discriminated against.

The Office of Federal Contract Compliance Programs (OFCCP) oversees firms with U.S. government contracts to make sure that applicants and employees get fair treatment. A big part of its job is to review federal contractors' affirmative action programs. Employers set up **affirmative action programs** to expand job opportunities for women and minorities. In the case of a major violation, the OFCCP can recommend cancellation of the firm's government contract.

Making Affirmative Action Work in the New Millennium

Many firms have appointed an affirmative action officer to help ensure that they comply with antidiscrimination laws. At firms such as Coca-Cola, Snap-on Tools, Hilton Hotels, and Santa Fe Southern Pacific Railroads, the affirmative action officer makes sure that job applicants and employees get fair treatment. He or she often reports directly to the company president rather than to the vice-president of human resources.

Affirmative action officers watch for signs of *adverse impact,* or unfair treatment of certain classes of employees. **Protected classes** are the specific groups (women, African Americans, Native Americans, and others) who have legal protection against employment discrimination.

One example of adverse impact is a job qualification that tends to weed out more female applicants than male applicants. Suppose that an airline automatically rules out anyone under five feet seven inches tall who wants to

affirmative action programs

Programs established by organizations to expand job opportunities for women and minorities.

protected classes

The specific groups who have legal protection against employment discrimination; include women, African Americans, Native Americans, and others.

concept check

- What are the key federal laws affecting employment?
- List and describe the functions of the two federal agencies that enforce employment discrimination laws.
- What is affirmative action?

be a pilot. Many more female applicants than male applicants would be rejected because women tend to be shorter than men. But height has nothing to do with a pilot's ability, so this height requirement would be discriminatory.

The overall affirmative action record of the past decade has been mixed. The employment of women in professional occupations continues to grow, but minority representation among professionals has not significantly increased, even though professional jobs have been among the fastest growing areas. Technical jobs have the most equitable utilization rates of minorities.

CAPITALIZING ON TRENDS IN BUSINESS

>lg 10

Social change, evolving demographics, advancing technology, and global competition are driving the trends in human resource management in the 21st century.

Social Change

The most dramatic social change that is occurring is the increasing number of women joining the labor force—a trend that began in the 20th century and continues today. Today, women comprise about 45 percent of the American labor force. The entry of women into the workforce has created some new human resource management issues including dual-career couples, child and elder care, and workplace sexual harassment. American Airlines, for example, recently offered a new employee benefit called Life Balance Work/Life Services to assist employees in coping with some nonwork lifestyle issues. According to Allison Payne, the airline's Vice President of Human Resources, Life Balance functions like a personal assistant who can help with child care arrangements, car repair services, mortgage rate information, parenting, and many other personal and family issues.[11]

Another social change is the new attitude toward changing jobs. Only a few years ago, recent college graduates could expect to change jobs and employers three to five times during their 25 to 40 years of professional experience. Now, a 22- to 25-year-old college graduate can expect 6 to 10 of these changes and one or two significant occupational changes, such as from engineer to accountant. This increased frequency of job changes may mean that employees and employers are less loyal to one another.

Demographics

Changes in demographics have resulted in a more diverse workforce, as shown in Exhibit 9-9. **Diversity** refers to employee differences in age, race and ethnicity, gender, educational background, and work experiences. Managing a diverse work group is more difficult than managing a homogeneous group, such as all white males, for example, because each group brings its own ideas, habits, culture, and communication skills to the work environment. Progressive human

diversity
Employee differences in age, race and ethnicity, gender, educational background, and work experience.

HOT links

For the latest news in the human resources field, visit the Web site of the Society for Human Resource Management at

www.shrm.org

The Diversity of the American Labor Force

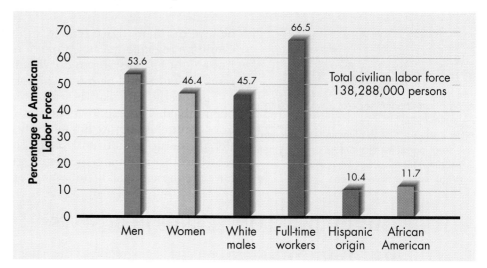

resource practices of diversity management focus on mentoring women and minority persons and removing the *glass ceiling,* or the invisible barrier in many firms that prevents women, minorities, and others from advancing to high-level management and executive positions. Nothing has prevented Darla Moore from advancing in her professional fields of banking and investments. She is CEO of Rainwater, Inc., and in 1998 she became the first woman ever to have a college of business named for her—the Darla Moore College of Business Administration at the University of South Carolina.[12]

Advancing Technology

Advances in information technology have greatly improved the efficiency of handling many transaction-based aspects (payroll and expense reimbursement) of employee services. Technology enables instant communication of human resource data from far-flung branches to the home office. Ease of communication has also led many companies to outsource some or all of their human resource functions. **Outsourcing** is the assignment of various functions, like human resources, accounting, or legal work, to outside organizations. The National Geographic Society outsourced all of its employee benefits programs to Workforce Solutions. Administaff is a large company that handles compensation and benefits processing, training, and even performance appraisal for many large corporate clients. Without computer databases and networks, such outsourcing would be impossible.

Technology has also made telecommuting a reality for almost 29 million workers. **Telecommuting** is now commonplace. In this arrangement, employees work at home and are linked to the office by phone, fax, and computer.[13] At Cisco Systems, a computer-networking giant based in San Jose, California, telecommuters have improved their productivity by up to 25 percent, while the company has saved about $1 million on overhead and retained key employees who might otherwise have left. What's more, those who have traded suits for sweats say they love setting their own schedules, skipping rush hour, spending more time with their kids, and working at least part-time in comfortable surroundings. "It's surprising the number of engineers who will respond to a question at 11:00 on a Saturday night," says John Hotchkiss, Cisco's human resource manager. "We can solve a problem that would not have been solved until Monday morning."[14]

outsourcing
The assignment of various functions, such as human resources, accounting, or legal work, to outside organizations.

telecommuting
An arrangement in which employees work at home and are linked to the office by phone, fax, and computer.

Telecommuting has also grown because of a strong economy in which employers must do what they can to attract the best and brightest workers. Telecommuting also offers environmental and political benefits as companies respond to Clean Air Act provisions aimed at reducing traffic. It also enables businesses to cut real estate costs by creating "hoteling" arrangements in which, say, 10 people share a single cubicle on an as-needed basis. Exhibit 9-10 lists some of the companies most friendly to telecommuting.

Global Competition

As more firms "go global," they are sending an increasing number of employees overseas. Proctor and Gamble, IBM, Caterpillar, Microsoft, Federal Express, and many others have tens of thousands of employees abroad. Such companies face somewhat different human resource management issues than do firms that operate only within the United States. For example, criteria for selecting employees include not only technical skills and knowledge of the business, but also the ability to adapt to a local culture and to learn a foreign language.

Once an individual is selected for an overseas assignment, language training and cultural orientation become important. Salary and benefits, relocation expenses, and special allowances (housing, transportation, and education) can increase human resource costs by as much as three times normal annual costs. After an overseas assignment of one year or more, the firm must repatriate the employee, or bring the individual back home. Job placement and career progression frequently become issues during repatriation because the firm has changed and the employee's old job may no longer exist. After spending a year in Brussels, Belgium, Mike Rocca, a financial executive with Honeywell, experienced "reentry shock" when he returned to his corporate office in Minneapolis and saw how new software had changed accounting.

concept check

- How is the entry of more women into the workforce affecting human resource management?
- What is diversity, and how does it affect human resource management?
- What benefits does telecommuting offer?
- What issues does "going global" present for human resource management?

> e x h i b i t   9 - 1 0 <

Telecommuting-Friendly Employers

Company	Percentage of Workforce that Telecommutes	Special Features
Aetna	2%	Telecommuter is assigned an office "buddy."
Arthur Andersen	20	Conducts safety inspections of home offices.
AT&T	55	Manager and employee work out details.
Boeing	1	Rules differ for each business unit.
Cisco Systems	66	24-hour technical support, ergonomic furniture required.
Georgia Power	5	May soon allow some to work at company sites near home.
Hewlett-Packard	8	Recommends ergonomically correct office.
IBM	20	Teleworkers use shared space in the office.
Merrill Lynch	5	Employees can test telecommuting in two-week simulation.
The Leisure Co./America West	16	Arranges monthly potluck team dinners to keep everyone in touch.

APPLYING THIS CHAPTER'S TOPICS

It's never too early to start thinking about your career in business. No, you don't have to decide today, but it's important to decide fairly soon how you will spend your life's work. A very practical reason for doing so is that it will save you a lot of time and money. We have seen too many juniors, seniors, or even graduate students who aren't really sure what they want to do upon graduation.

Interested in a career in human resources? At **www.ipma-hr.org/ research/stud2.html** you'll find valuable tips to point you in the right direction.

The longer you wait to choose a profession, the more credit hours you may have to take in your new field and the longer it will be before you starting earning real money.

A second reason to choose a career field early is that you can get a part-time or summer job and "test-drive" the profession. If it's not for you, you can find out very quickly.

Your school placement office can give you plenty of information about various careers in business. We also describe many career opportunities at the end of each part of this text. Another source of career information is the Internet. Go to any search engine,

> t r y   i t   n o w ! <

Make Telecommuting Work for You Maybe a part-time job might require too much driving time. Perhaps there are simply no jobs in the immediate area that suit you. Try telecommuting right now. Is telecommuting for you? Nearly 75 percent of teleworkers responding to an AT&T survey said they were more satisfied with their personal and family lives than before they started working at home.[16] But telecommuting is not for every person or every job, and you'll need plenty of self-discipline to make it work for you. Ask yourself if you can perform your duties without close supervision. Also, think about whether you would miss your coworkers.

If you decide to give telecommuting a try, consider these suggestions to maintain your productivity:

- *Set ground rules with your family.* Spouses and small children have to understand that even though you're in the house, you are busy earning

a living. It's fine to throw in a few loads of laundry and answer the door when the plumber comes. It's another thing to take the kids to the mall or let them play games on your office PC.

- *Clearly demarcate your work space by using a separate room with a door you can shut.* Let your family know that, emergencies excepted, the space is off-limits during working hours.
- *If you have small children, you may want to arrange for child care during your working hours.*
- *Stay in touch with your coworkers and professional colleagues.* Go into the office from time to time for meetings to stay connected.

Above all, you can make telecommuting work for you by being productive. Doing your job well whether on-site or telecommuting will help assure you of a bright future.

such as Excite or Lycos, and enter "careers in business," or narrow your search to a specific area such as management or marketing.

Career planning will not end when you find your first professional job. It is a life-long process that ends only with retirement. Your career planning will include conducting a periodic self-assessment of your strengths and weaknesses, gathering information about other jobs both within the firm and externally, learning about other industries, and setting career goals for yourself.[15] You must always think about your future in business.

You Will Be Involved in Human Resources Decision Making

During your professional career in business, you will likely have the opportunity to become a manager. As a manager, you will have to make many human resource decisions, including hiring, firing, promoting, giving a pay raise, sending an employee to a training program, disciplining a worker, approving a college tuition reimbursement request, and reassigning an employee to a different job. In short, you will be involved in virtually every human resource decision or activity affecting the employees you manage.

Always treat people as you wish to be treated when making human resource decisions. Be fair, be honest, offer your experience and advice, and communicate frequently with your employees. If you follow this simple advice, you will be richly rewarded in your own career.

>looking ahead

at Don Pablos

James was faced with a typical human resource problem with Sharon, the tardy waitperson. As presented in this chapter, James should utilize his human resource management skills and redirect Sharon toward improved performance. One approach is to offer additional training on company policies and the importance of good customer service. He might remind her that if she is late or doesn't come to work on a particular day, then her work must be shared by other waitpersons, which may lead to poor customer service. Finally, James may have to make the difficult decision to demote or fire Sharon if her performance does not meet desired levels.

Don Pablos is expanding the number of its units and is part of a larger organization called Avado Brands. In addition to Don Pablos, the company owns Canyon Cafe restaurants (southwestern theme), Hops (a microbrewery with an American-style menu), and McCormick and Schmicks (seafood). The firm plans to open 200 new restaurants by 2001, which will create many new human resource challenges and opportunities.

SUMMARY OF LEARNING GOALS

>lg 1 What is the human resource management process?
The human resource management process consists of a sequence of activities that begins with job analysis and HR planning; progresses to employee recruitment and selection; then focuses on employee training, performance appraisal, and compensation; and ends when the employee leaves the organization. Human resource decisions and activities along this series of events increase the value and contributions the employee makes to the firm. Over several years for a given employee, training, performance appraisal, and changes in compensation form a repeated set of activities that facilitate career development and increase a person's contributions to the firm.

>lg 2 How are human resource needs determined?
Creating a strategy for meeting human resource needs is called human resource planning, which begins with job analysis. Job analysis is a process for studying a job to determine its tasks and duties for setting pay, determining

KEY TERMS

affirmative action
  programs 274
apprenticeship
  265
contingent workers
  260
demotion 270
diversity 275
employee
  orientation 265
fringe benefits 268
human resource
  (HR) planning
  257
human resource
  management 256
job analysis 258
job description
  258
job fair 261
job rotation 265
job specification
  258
layoff 270
mentoring 265
on-the-job training
  265
outsourcing 276
performance
  appraisal 266
programmed
  instruction 266
promotion 269
protected classes
  274
recruitment 260
resignation 270
retirement 271
selection 262
selection interview
  263
separation 270
telecommuting 276
termination 270
training and
  development 264
transfer 269
vestibule training
  265

employee job performance, specifying hiring requirements, and designing training programs. Information from the job analysis is used to prepare a job description, which lists the tasks and responsibilities of the job. A job specification describes the skills, knowledge, and abilities a person needs to fill the job described in the job description. By examining the human resource demand forecast and the *internal* supply forecast, human resource professionals can determine if the company faces a personnel surplus or shortage.

>lg 3   **How do human resource managers find good people to fill the jobs?**
When a job vacancy occurs, most firms begin by trying to fill the job from within. If a suitable *internal* candidate is not available, the firm begins an external search. Firms use local media to recruit nontechnical, unskilled, and nonsupervisory workers. To locate highly trained recruits, employers use college recruiters, executive search firms, job fairs, and company Web sites to promote job openings.

>lg 4   **What is the employee selection process?**
Typically, an applicant submits an application, or résumé, and then receives a short, structured interview. If an applicant makes it past the initial screening, he or she may be asked to take an aptitude, personality, or skills test. The next step is the selection interview which is an in-depth discussion of the applicant's work experience, skills and abilities, education, and career interests. An applicant seeking a professional or managerial position will typically be interviewed by several people. After the selection interview, successful applicants may be asked to undergo a physical exam before being offered a job.

>lg 5   **What types of training and development do organizations offer their employees?**
Training and development programs are designed to increase employees' knowledge, skills, and abilities in order to foster job performance improvements. Formal training (usually classroom in nature and off-the-job) takes place shortly after being hired. Development programs prepare employees to assume positions of increasing authority and responsibility. Job rotation, executive education programs, mentoring, and special project assignments are examples of employee development programs.

>lg 6   **What is a performance appraisal?**
A performance appraisal compares an employee's actual performance with the expected performance. Performance appraisals serve several purposes but are typically used to determine an employee's compensation, training needs, and advancement opportunities.

>lg 7   **How are employees compensated?**
Direct pay is the hourly wage or monthly salary paid to an employee. In addition to the base wage or salary, direct pay may include bonuses and profit shares. Indirect pay consists of various benefits and services. Some benefits are required by law: unemployment compensation, worker's compensation, and Social Security. Others are voluntarily made available by employers to employees. These include paid vacations and holidays, pensions, health and other insurance products, employee wellness programs, and college tuition reimbursement.

>lg 8   **What is organizational career management?**
Organizational career management is the facilitation of employee job changes, including promotions, transfers, layoffs, and retirements. A promotion is an upward move with more authority, responsibility, and pay. A transfer is a horizontal move in the organization. When a person is downgraded to a position with less responsibility, it is a demotion. A layoff is a temporary separation arranged by the employer, usually when business is slow. A termination is a permanent separation arranged by the employer. A resignation is a voluntary separation by the employee. Retirement is a permanent separation that ends one's career.

>lg 9   **What are the key laws and federal agencies affecting human resource management?**

A number of federal laws (listed in Exhibit 9-8) affect human resource management. Federal law prohibits discrimination based on age, race, gender, color, national origin, religion, or disability. The Americans with Disabilities Act bans discrimination against disabled workers and requires employers to change the work environment to accommodate the disabled. The Family and Medical Leave Act requires employers, with certain exceptions, to provide employees up to 12 weeks of unpaid leave a year. The leave can be for the birth or adoption of a child or due to serious illness of a family member.

Federal agencies that deal with human resource administration are the Equal Employment Opportunity Commission (EEOC), the Occupational Safety and Health Administration (OSHA), the Office of Federal Contract Compliance Programs (OFCCP), and the Wage and Hour Division of the Department of Labor. The EEOC and OFCCP are primary agencies for enforcement of employment discrimination laws; OSHA enforces safety regulation; and the Wage and Hour Division enforces the minimum wage and related laws. Many companies employ affirmative action and safety officers to ensure compliance with antidiscrimination and workplace safety laws.

>lg 10   **What trends are affecting human resource management?**

Women now comprise 45 percent of the workforce in America. As a result, we are seeing growing numbers of dual-career couples. In turn, companies are now facing issues like sexual harassment and nonwork lifestyle issues such as child care and elder care. Workers also now change jobs three to five times during their career. This lessens the loyalty between employer and employee. As the American workforce becomes increasingly more diverse, companies are offering diversity training and mentoring of minorities.

Technology continues to improve the efficiency of human resource management. It also enables firms to outsource many functions done internally in the past. Telecommuting is becoming increasingly popular among employers and employees.

As more firms enter the international market, they are sending an increasing number of employees overseas. In addition to normal job requirements, selected workers must have the ability to adapt to a local culture and perhaps to learn a foreign language.

PREPARING FOR TOMORROW'S WORKPLACE

1. Divide the class into teams of five. Each group should select a form of applicant testing: drug, honesty, skill, intelligence, personality, AIDS, and physical exams. Each group should defend why their form of testing should be used to screen applicants. The other groups should offer reasons not to use the specific test.
2. Write a memo explaining why the employee selection process in your company should be different for hiring a custodial employee and a chemist.
3. What kind of training and development program would be best for assembly-line workers? For first-line supervisors? For industrial sales representatives? For maintenance workers? For computer programmers?
4. Many human resource tasks can be computerized. These include payroll processing, insurance, pension and other benefit plan enrollments, application forms and résumé evaluation, and communications with retirees. The president of your company is thinking about computerizing many human resource operations but is worried that doing so will "dehumanize" employee/employer relations. Write a memo to the president addressing

the "dehumanizing" concern and explaining why the firm should computerize these operations.

5. Would an overseas job assignment be good for your career development? If you think so, what country would you prefer to live and work in for two or three years, and what type of job would you like to have in that country?

6. The fringe benefit package of many employers includes numerous voluntarily provided items such as health insurance, life insurance, pension plan, paid vacations, tuition reimbursement, employee price discounts on products of the firm, and paid sick leave. At your age, what are the three or four most important benefits? Why? Twenty years from now, what do you think will be your three or four most important benefits? Why?

7. Select two teams of five. One team will take the position that employees are simply a business expense to be managed. The second team will argue that employees are an asset to be developed to enable the firm to gain a competitive advantage. The remainder of the class will judge which team provided the stronger argument.

8. How important is training likely to be in the future? What changes that are facing organizations will increase the importance of training?

9. Is reducing the number of employee resignations always a good thing? Why or why not?

10. You are applying for a job as a manager. Write down five critical questions that you would ask your prospective employer. Share these with the class.

WORKING THE NET

1. Many companies now use special scanning software to read résumés and accept résumés in electronic form. Because scannable résumés differ from traditional résumés, you should prepare a separate résumé for these companies. Go to the Monster Board at **content.monster.com/resume/** to learn how to prepare an electronic résumé that will get results. Develop a list of rules for creating effective electronic résumés, and revise your own résumé into electronic format.

2. Working as a contingent employee can help you explore your career options. Visit the Manpower Web site at **www.manpower.com,** and search for several types of jobs that interest you. What are the advantages of being a temporary worker? What other services does Manpower offer job seekers?

3. As a corporate recruiter, you must know how to screen prospective employees. A good starting point is the Integrity Center Web site at **www.integctr.com.** If offers a brief tutorial on pre-employment screening, a glossary of key words and phrases, and related information. Prepare a short report that tells your assistant how to go about this process.

4. You've been asked to give a speech about the current status of affirmative action and equal employment to your company's managers. Starting with the Web site of the American Association for Affirmative Action (**www.affirmativeaction.org**) and its links to related sites, research the topic and prepare an outline for your talk. Include current legislation and recent court cases.

5. Web-based training is becoming popular at many companies as a way to bring a wider variety of courses to more people at lower costs. The Web-Based Training Information Center site at **www.filename.com/wbt** provides a good introduction. Learn about the basics of online training at its Primer page. Then link to the Resources section, try a demo, and explore other areas that interest you. At the Lucent Technologies Center for Excellence in Distance Learning (CEDL) at **www.lucent.com/cedl,** you can get ideas on

how a company can use distance learning to train its workforce without disrupting the daily routine. Prepare a brief report on your findings, including the pros and cons of distance learning, to present to your class.

CREATIVE THINKING CASE

"Do-It-Yourself" Human Resource Management at Spectrum Signal Processing

Some companies are now managing all or part of their human resource functions with employee teams. Martin McConnell decided that this was the way to go at Spectrum Signal Processing, Inc. McConnell is vice-president of finance for Spectrum, a hardware and software designer with 180 employees in Burnaby, British Columbia. He says his company has no human resource department at all. Instead, it uses rotating human resource committees.

In a 1996 employee-satisfaction survey, Spectrum's managers discovered that its employees were not all that satisfied with the way the company was dealing with human resource issues. So Spectrum created a cross-functional employee team to focus on those issues. McConnell initially thought the committee would be only short term; it would deal with the immediate problems and then disband. "But it gained so much interest and momentum, it became part of our culture," he says.

Now the committee regularly discusses and addresses most of the company's typical human resource functions: performance appraisals and the employee handbook, as well as company training, recognition, mentoring, and orientation programs. (Payroll and benefits administration are handled by the accounting department.)

The committee consists of 12 elected members from various job functions. Member-involvement dates are staggered, so the committee is constantly getting new members and perspectives. McConnell and CEO Barry Jinks also serve on the team, albeit in an advisory role. According to group chair Carol Schulz, the bosses' presence doesn't present a hindrance. "They have the same say as anybody else," says Schulz. "Plus it gives employees the feeling that they really do care."

McConnell admits that at first he worried that the committee might establish some overly expensive policies. "But it's not us versus them," he says. "Whatever decision they made would be modified for what works for the environment. Or maybe we'd implement it in stages."

Critical Thinking Questions

1. What are the advantages and possible disadvantages of a do-it-yourself human resource department?
2. Would this concept work at a large company like Ford Motor Co., or is it best suited for smaller organizations?
3. One problem that has surfaced at Spectrum is that serving on the committee takes a lot of time and distracts committee members from their jobs. McConnell is thinking about using a co-op student from a local university to do detail and leg work. Do you think that this is a good idea? Why or why not?

VIDEO CASE

Valassis Communications: Matching People to the Company's Culture

Valassis Communications, Inc.(**www.valassis.com:**) headquartered in Livonia, Michigan, has been a leader in marketing services for over a quarter of a century. Valassis maintains that it has set the standard in its industry "for quality, reliability, service and expertise." A publicly held company with annual sales exceeding $740 million, Valassis has more than 1,300 employees across the United States and Canada.

The company's flagship product is the Free-Standing Insert (FSI), which is "distributed through newspapers to over 57 million households nearly every Sunday." The FSI is a booklet containing coupons, refunds, and other values from America's largest packaged goods companies. Other Valassis products include solo inserts that promote a single company's products or services; delivery of manufacturers' product samples and promotional messages through Sunday newspapers; direct placement of newspaper ads for clients; and oversight of clients' games and sweepstakes promotions.

Valassis Communications has a unique corporate culture that it calls "Change to Grow." Valassis recognizes "that in order to remain successful, companies must continue to change; to generate new ideas and pursue new business opportunities; to stay ahead of the trends and the competition!" Consequently the company has adopted a corporate philosophy that both embraces change and uses it as a catalyst for growth.

The Change to Grow philosophy and culture are based on eight fundamental principles:

- Change is good.
- Don't point fingers—solve problems.
- Go—with speed.
- Create positive energy.
- Set the high bar high—don't fear failure.
- Be empowered, and be accountable.
- Communicate clearly and openly.
- Stick to fundamentals.

Executives at Valassis Communications believe the company's competitive advantage in the marketplace is based on its very capable and highly motivated employees. Accordingly, Valassis strives to match the abilities and motivation of the people it hires with the company's Change to Grow culture. With over 14,000 applicants for approximately 100 job openings annually, Valassis puts prospective employees through a rigorous screening and interview process to determine which individuals are most likely to embody and adhere to the eight fundamental principles of the "Change to Grow" culture.

Those who are fortunate enough to be hired by Valassis embark on unique career paths. The company does not "believe in rigid, standardized training methods or career paths, because . . . each employee has their own strengths, talents, and ultimate career goals."

Valassis also prefers to promote from within the company. Consequently, it invests heavily in employee training. Valassis University, a company-run educational program, "offers professional and personal development courses, as well as courses that cover specific areas and functions of the company. . . . Employees can work toward a variety of Valassis 'degrees' including a Bachelor and Master of Leadership." Valassis also supports continuing education for employees through an educational assistance reimbursement program.

When it comes to people, the bottom line for Valassis is to hire the right people through its recruitment and selection process and then to develop those people with appropriate training.

Critical Thinking Questions

1. What are the advantages of Valassis Communications' approach of hiring people with abilities and motivation that match the company's Change to Grow culture?

2. How does the Valassis approach to training and development help reinforce the company's culture?

3. Would you like to work for a company like Valassis Communications, given its Change to Grow culture? Why or why not?

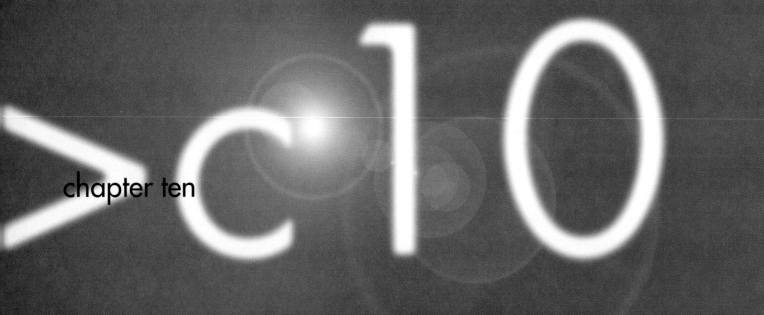

> c 10

chapter ten

Motivating Employees and Creating Self-Managed Teams

learning goals

>lg 1   What are the basic principles of Frederick Taylor's concept of scientific management?

>lg 2   What did Elton Mayo's Hawthorne studies reveal about worker motivation?

>lg 3   What is Maslow's hierarchy of needs, and how do these needs relate to employee motivation?

>lg 4   How are McGregor's Theories X and Y used to explain worker motivation?

>lg 5   What are the basic components of

>lg 6   What three contemporary theories on employee motivation offer insights into improving employee performance?

>lg 7   How can managers redesign existing jobs to increase employee motivation and performance?

>lg 8   What different types of teams are being used in organizations today?

>lg 9   What initiatives are organizations using to-day to motivate and retain employees?

Motivating Employees at SAS Institute, Inc.

What would a company need to do to motivate you to work hard and stay committed? How would you feel about a 35-hour full-time work-week? What about two on-site day-care facilities so you'll know your children are safe and well cared for? And perhaps some fitness and recreational facilities to help you stay in shape and deal with job stress? Maybe a 36,000-square-foot gym, some pool and Ping-Pong tables, two basketball courts, a dance studio, and a yoga room? And to make workouts more convenient, your dirty gym clothes would be laundered for you each day. To help you stay healthy and happy, you might want full health insurance coverage (at no cost to you) and, of course, an on-site health clinic to make visiting the doctor more convenient. Are you motivated yet? Well, let's add on-site massages, elder-care referrals, casual dress every day of the week, and unlimited sick days. Not possible you say? Well, let me introduce you to SAS Institute, Inc. (**www.sas.com**), a software giant you've probably never heard of.[1]

On a secluded 200-acre campus in North Carolina is a company that believes in spoiling its employees. SAS Institute, the world's largest privately held software company,[2] has created a work environment that fosters intense loyalty. "I like happy people," explains cofounder, CEO, and majority owner James H. Goodnight, when discussing company perks such as bonuses, profit sharing, extra paid vacation time, private offices, fully stocked break rooms, discounted memberships to the local country club, and a pianist in the subsidized lunchroom. But the numbers tell the real story.

In a hypercompetitive industry where employee turnover is often around 20 percent, the annual turnover rate at SAS has hovered around 4 percent for years. High-performance employees at SAS seldom defect to the competition, and the company has hundreds of applications for any job openings. Revenue has increased by double-digit percentages each year for the past 22 years and is expected to hit $850 million this year. The company is valued at about $5 billion, and Goodnight's personal net worth is an estimated $3.5 billion. Stanford University business professor Jeffrey Pfeffer has studied SAS and figures the company saves approximately $50 million a year from its low turnover rate. What may look like excessive employee coddling to outsiders makes good business sense to Goodnight. For instance, the free company clinic costs $1 million a year to operate, but that is about $500,000 less than the company would have to pay if employees were treated elsewhere.

The salaries at SAS are only average for the industry, and the company doesn't offer stock options like many of its high-tech competitors. Goodnight also refuses to pay sales commissions to SAS salespeople, claiming commissions encourage high-pressure sales tactics. Yet the company, recently named one of the "100 best companies to work for in America" by *Fortune* magazine,[3] is thriving. By providing a wide array of incentives that motivate SAS employees to achieve high levels of productivity and foster intense company loyalty, SAS seems to have found the magic formula.

Critical Thinking Questions

As you read this chapter, consider these questions as they relate to SAS Institute:

- Why don't most companies offer perks like those at SAS Institute?

- How do SAS Institute's generous benefits contribute to its low employee turnover rate?

- What else can SAS do to motivate its workers?

BUSINESS IN THE 21ST CENTURY

People can be a firm's most important resource. They can also be the most challenging resource to manage well. Employees who are motivated and work hard to achieve personal and organizational goals can become a crucial competitive advantage for a firm. The key then is understanding the process of motivation, *what* motivates individuals, and *how* an organization like SAS can create a workplace that allows people to perform to the best of their abilities. Motivation is basically a need-satisfying process. A need is the lack of something, the gap between what is and what one desires. An unsatisfied need pushes (motivates) the individual to pursue behavior that will result in the need being met.

Successful managers help employees to achieve organizational goals and guide workers through the motivation process using the leadership skills discussed in Chapter 7. To succeed, managers must understand human relations, how employees interact with one another, and how managers interact with employees to improve effectiveness. Human relations skills include the ability to motivate, lead, communicate, build morale, and teach others. This chapter presents the traditional theories on human motivation and the modern application of these theories. We also explore the use of teams in creating and maintaining a motivated workforce.

THE EVOLUTION OF MOTIVATION THEORY

How can managers and organizations promote enthusiastic job performance, high productivity, and job satisfaction? Many studies of human behavior in organizations have contributed to our current understanding of these issues. A look at the evolution of management theory and research shows how managers have arrived at the practices used today to manage human behavior in the workplace. A sampling of the most influential of these theorists and research studies are discussed in this section.

Frederick Taylor's Scientific Management

scientific management

A system of management developed by Frederick W. Taylor and based on four principles: developing a scientific approach for each element of a job, scientifically selecting and training workers, encouraging cooperation between workers and managers, and dividing work and responsibility between management and workers according to who can better perform a particular task.

One of the most influential figures of the *classical era* of management, which lasted from about 1900 to the mid-1930s, was Frederick W. Taylor, a mechanical engineer sometimes called the "father of **scientific management.**" Taylor's approach to improved performance was based on economic incentives and the premise that there is "one best way" to perform any job. As a manager at the Midvale and Bethlehem Steel companies in Philadelphia in the early 1900s, Taylor was frustrated at the inefficiency of the laborers working in the mills.

Convinced that productivity could be improved, Taylor studied the individual jobs in the mill and redesigned the equipment and the methods used by workers. Taylor timed each job with a stopwatch and broke down every task into separate movements. He then prepared an instruction sheet telling exactly how each job should be done, how much time it should take, and what motions and tools should be used. Taylor's ideas led to dramatic increases in productivity in the steel mills and resulted in the development of four basic principles of scientific management:

1. Develop a scienctific approach for each element of a person's job.
2. Scientifically select, train, teach, and develop workers.
3. Encourage cooperation between workers and managers so that each job can be accomplished in a standard, scientifically determined way.
4. Divide work and responsibility between management and workers according to who is better suited to each task.

Taylor published his ideas in *The Principles of Scientific Management*. His pioneering work vastly increased production efficiency and contributed to the specialization of labor and the assembly-line method of production. Taylor's approach is still being used nearly a century later in companies such as United Parcel Service (UPS), where industrial engineers maximize efficiency by carefully study-

Employers of factory workers in the early 1900s applied scientific methods to improve productivity. During this classical era of management, employers believed employee performance was motivated only by economic incentives.

ing every step of the delivery process looking for the quickest possible way to deliver packages to customers. Though Taylor's work was a giant step forward in the evolution of management, it had a fundamental flaw in that it assumed that all people are primarily motivated by economic means. Taylor's successors in the study of management found that motivation is much more complex than he envisioned.

Want to find out more about organizational efficiency at United Parcel Service? Visit www.ups.com

The Hawthorne Studies

>lg 2

The classical era of management was followed by the *human relations era,* which began in the 1930s and focused primarily on how human behavior and relations affect organizational performance. The new era was ushered in by the Hawthorne studies, which changed the way many managers thought about motivation, job productivity, and employee satisfaction. The studies began when engineers at the Hawthorne Western Electric plant decided to examine the effects of varying levels of light on worker productivity—an experiment that might have interested Frederick Taylor. The engineers expected brighter light to lead to increased productivity, but the results showed that varying the level of light in either direction (brighter or dimmer) led to increased output from the experimental group. In 1927, the Hawthorne engineers asked Harvard professor Elton Mayo and a team of researchers to join them in their investigation.

From 1927 to 1932, Mayo and his colleagues conducted experiments on job redesign, length of workday and workweek, length of break times, and incentive plans. The results of the studies indicated that increases in performance were tied to a complex set of employee attitudes. Mayo claimed that both experimental and control groups from the plant had developed a sense of group pride because they had been selected to participate in the studies. The pride that came from this special attention motivated the workers to increase their productivity. Supervisors who allowed the employees to have some

Hawthorne effect

The phenomenon that employees perform better when they feel singled out for attention or feel that management is concerned about their welfare.

control over their situation appeared to further increase the workers' motivation. These findings gave rise to what is now known as the **Hawthorne effect,** which suggests that employees will perform better when they feel singled out for special attention or feel that management is concerned about employee welfare. The studies also provided evidence that informal work groups (the social relationships of employees) and the resulting group pressure have positive effects on group productivity. The results of the Hawthorne studies enhanced our understanding of what motivates individuals in the workplace. They indicate that in addition to the personal economic needs emphasized in the classical era, social needs play an important role in influencing work-related attitudes and behaviors.

Maslow's Hierarchy of Needs

>lg 3

Another well-known theorist from the behavioral era of management history, psychologist Abraham Maslow, proposed a theory of motivation based on universal human needs. Maslow believed that each individual has a hierarchy of needs, consisting of physiological, safety, social, esteem, and self-actualization needs, as shown in Exhibit 10-1.

> e x h i b i t   1 0 - 1 <

Maslow's Hierarchy of Needs

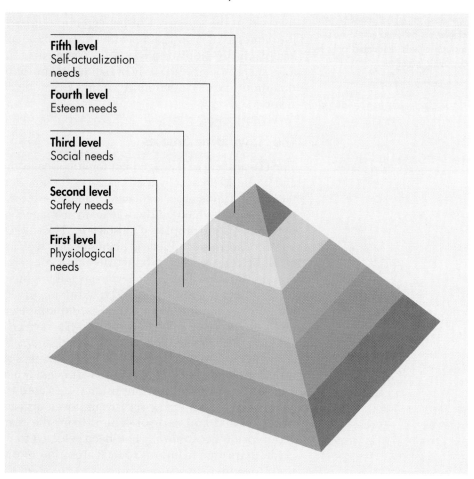

Fifth level
Self-actualization needs

Fourth level
Esteem needs

Third level
Social needs

Second level
Safety needs

First level
Physiological needs

Maslow's theory of motivation contends that people act to satisfy their unmet needs. When you're hungry, for instance, you look for and eat food, thus satisfying a basic physiological need. Once a need is satisfied, its importance to the individual diminishes, and a higher-level need is more likely to motivate the person.

Maslow's hierarchy of needs

A theory of motivation developed by Abraham Maslow; holds that humans have five levels of needs and act to satisfy their unmet needs. At the base of the hierarchy are fundamental physiological needs, followed in order by safety, social, esteem, and self-actualization needs.

According to **Maslow's hierarchy of needs,** the most basic human needs are physiological needs, that is, the needs for food, shelter, and clothing, In large part, it is the physiological needs that motivate a person to find a job. People need to earn money to provide food, shelter, and clothing for themselves and their families. Once people have met these basic needs, they reach the second level in Maslow's hierarchy, which is safety needs. People need to feel secure, to be protected from physical harm, and to avoid the unexpected. In work terms, they need job security and protection from work hazards. Companies such as Southwest Airlines, Harley-Davidson, and FedEx help meet employees' safety needs with their official "no layoffs" policies.[4]

Find out more about three companies that made *Fortune* magazine's "100 best companies to work for" by visiting www.southwest.com, www.harleydavidson.com, and www.fedex.com

Physiological needs and safety are physical needs. Once these are satisfied, individuals focus on needs that involve relationships with other people. At Maslow's third level are social needs, or needs for belonging (acceptance by others) and for giving and receiving friendship and love. Informal social groups on and off the job help people satisfy these needs. At the fourth level in Maslow's hierarchy are esteem needs, which are needs for the respect of others and for a sense of accomplishment and achievement. Satisfaction of these needs is reflected in feelings of self-worth. Praise and recognition from managers and others in the firm contribute to the sense of self-worth. Dana Corp., an automotive-components manufacturer based in Ohio, has created a corporate culture designed to encourage and recognize the contributions of its employees.[5] The company helps employees meet esteem needs by implementing employee suggestions, promoting from within, delegating decision-making authority, and formally recognizing individuals who reach or exceed their goals.

Self-actualization needs motivate Jim Clark, co-founder of Netscape Communications and Silicon Graphics. Having satisfied the lower-order needs in Maslow's hierarchy, Clark continues to embrace challenges that help him achieve high personal goals.

Finally, at the highest level in Maslow's hierarchy are self-actualization needs, or needs for fulfillment, for living up to one's potential, and for using one's abilities to the utmost. The Army recruiting slogan "Be all that you can be" describes the human need for self-actualization. Many mid- and upper-level managers, who have satisfied all of the lower-order needs, are driven by very personal self-actualization goals. Jim Clark

How is Jim Clark's latest venture going? Find out by visiting Healtheon Corp. at www.healtheon.com

is an excellent example.[6] Clark cofounded Silicon Graphics and Netscape Communications Corp. With a personal worth of $500 million, three university degrees (including a Ph.D. in computer science), lavish homes in Florida and California, a Boeing helicopter, and a $30 million sailboat, what motivated Clark to start yet another technology company, Healtheon Corp.? Obviously, Clark is easily able to meet all needs at the first four levels of Maslow's hierarchy. Yet his personal goal to be the very best in his field, his need for self-actualization, pushes Clark to find new challenges. Clark's latest goal is to be known as the guy who started three technology companies with market values of over $1 billion—something no one else has yet done. Clark, who says, "I'm never content," is always looking for new ways to achieve the very best that he can be.

Managers who accept Maslow's ideas attempt to improve employee motivation by modifying organizational and managerial practices to increase the likelihood that employees will meet all levels of needs. Maslow's theory has also helped managers understand that it is hard to motivate people by appealing to already satisfied needs. For instance, overtime pay may not motivate employees who earn a high wage and value their leisure time.

McGregor's Theories X and Y

Douglas McGregor, one of Maslow's students, influenced the study of motivation with his formulation of two contrasting sets of assumptions about human nature—Theory X and Theory Y.

The **Theory X** management style is based on a pessimistic view of human nature and assumes the following:

- The average person dislikes work and will avoid it if possible.
- Because people don't like to work, they must be controlled, directed, or threatened with punishment to get them to make an effort.
- The average person prefers to be directed, avoids responsibility, is relatively unambitious, and wants security above all else.

This view of people suggests that managers must constantly prod workers to perform and must closely control their on-the-job behavior. Theory X managers tell people what to do, are very directive, like to be in control, and show little confidence in employees. They often foster dependent, passive, and resentful subordinates.

In contrast, a **Theory Y** management style is based on a more optimistic view of human nature and assumes the following:

- Work is as natural as play or rest. People want to and can be self-directed and self-controlled and will try to achieve organizational goals they believe in.
- Workers can be motivated using positive incentives and will try hard to accomplish organizational goals if they believe they will be rewarded for doing so.
- Under proper conditions, the average person not only accepts responsibility but seeks it out. Most workers have a relatively high degree of imagination and creativity and are willing to help solve problems.

Managers who operate on Theory Y assumptions recognize individual differences and encourage workers to learn and develop their skills. A secretary might be given the responsibility for generating a monthly report. The reward for doing so might be recognition at a meeting, a special training class to enhance computer skills, or a pay increase. In short, the Theory Y approach builds on the idea that worker and organizational interests are congruent.

Theory X

A management style, formulated by Douglas McGregor, that is based on a pessimistic view of human nature and assumes that the average person dislikes work, will avoid it if possible, prefers to be directed, avoids responsibility, and wants security above all.

Theory Y

A management style, formulated by Douglas McGregor, that is based on a relatively optimistic view of human nature; assumes that the average person wants to work, accepts responsibility, is willing to help solve problems, and can be self-directed and self-controlled.

motivating factors

Intrinsic job elements that lead to worker satisfaction.

hygiene factors

Extrinsic elements of the work environment that do not serve as a source of employee satisfaction or motivation.

According to Herzberg's motivation theory, the job factors that motivate these Pacific Bell employees who install fiber optic cable are the work itself, achievement, recognition, responsibility, advancement, and growth.

Marilyn Nelson, CEO of Carlson Co., is determined to create a corporate culture based on Theory Y assumptions.[7] Carlson Co. is one of the largest privately held companies in the world, with holdings that include Radisson Hotels, TGIFriday franchises, and Carlson Travel Network. CEO Nelson is determined to replace the patriarchal micro-management style of her father (and predecessor) with leadership that empowers all levels of employees. Nelson's motto is "I want to lead with love, not fear," and she is changing the company culture by introducing expanded benefits, profit sharing, flextime schedules, and on-site day care.

Herzberg's Motivator-Hygiene Theory

Another important contribution to our understanding of individual motivation came from Frederick Herzberg's studies, which addressed the question, "What do people really want from their work experience?" In the late 1950s Herzberg surveyed numerous employees to find out what particular work elements made them feel exceptionally good or bad about their jobs. The results indicated that certain job factors are consistently related to employee job satisfaction while others can create job dissatisfaction. According to Herzberg, **motivating factors** (also called *job satisfiers*) are primarily intrinsic job elements that lead to satisfaction. **Hygiene factors** (also called *job dissatisfiers*) are extrinsic elements of the work environment. A summary of motivating and hygiene factors appears in Exhibit 10-2.

One of the most interesting results of Herzberg's studies was the implication that the opposite of satisfaction is not dissatisfaction. Herzberg believed that proper management of hygiene factors could prevent employee dissatisfaction, but that these factors could not serve as a source of satisfaction or motivation. Good working conditions, for instance, will keep employees at a job but won't make them work harder. But poor working conditions, which are job dissatisfiers, may make employees quit. According to Herzberg, a manager who wants to increase employee satisfaction needs to focus on

> e x h i b i t   1 0 - 2 <

Herzberg's Motivating and Hygiene Factors

Motivating Factors	Hygiene Factors
Achievement	Company policy
Recognition	Supervision
Work itself	Working conditions
Responsibility	Interpersonal relationships at work
Advancement	Salary and benefits
Growth	Job security

the motivating factors, or satisfiers. A job with many satisfiers will usually motivate workers, provide job satisfaction, and prompt effective performance. But a lack of job satisfiers doesn't always lead to dissatisfaction and poor performance; instead, a lack of job satisfiers may merely lead to workers doing an adequate job, rather than their best.

Although Herzberg's ideas have been widely read and his recommendations implemented at numerous companies over the years, there are some very legitimate concerns about Herzberg's work. Although his findings have been used to explain employee motivation, in fact his studies focused on job satisfaction, a different (though related) concept from motivation. Other criticisms focus on the unreliability of Herzberg's methodology, the fact that the theory ignores the impact of situational variables and the assumed relationship between satisfaction and productivity. Nevertheless, the questions raised by Herzberg about the nature of job satisfaction and the effects of intrinsic and extrinsic factors on employee behavior have proved a valuable contribution to the evolution of theories of motivation and job satisfaction.

concept check

- What are the four principles of scientific management?
- What did Elton Mayo's studies reveal about employee productivity?
- How can a manager use an understanding of Maslow's hierarchy to motivate employees?
- How do the Theory X and Theory Y management styles differ?
- What is the difference between job satisfiers and job dissatisfiers?

CONTEMPORARY VIEWS ON MOTIVATION

>lg 6

The early management scholars laid a foundation that enabled managers to better understand their workers and how best to motivate them. Since then, new theories have given us an even better understanding of worker motivation. Three of these theories are explained in this section: the expectancy theory, the equity theory, and the goal-setting theory.

Expectancy Theory

expectancy theory

A theory of motivation that holds that the probability of an individual acting in a particular way depends on the strength of that individual's belief that the act will have a particular outcome and on whether the individual values that outcome.

One of the best-supported and most widely accepted theories of motivation is expectancy theory, which focuses on the link between motivation and behavior. According to **expectancy theory,** the probability of an individual acting in a particular way depends on the strength of that individual's belief that the act will have a particular outcome and on whether the individual values that outcome. The degree to which an employee is motivated depends on three important relationships, shown in Exhibit 10-3:

1. The link between *effort and performance,* or the strength of the individual's expectation that a certain amount of effort will lead to a certain level of performance.
2. The link between *performance and outcome,* or the strength of the expectation that a certain level of performance will lead to a particular outcome.

> e x h i b i t   1 0 - 3 <

How Expectations Can Lead to Motivation

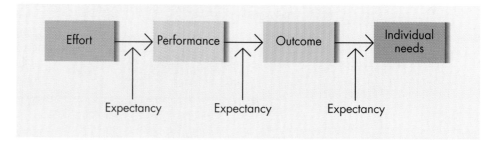

3. The link between *outcomes and individual needs,* or the degree to which the individual expects the anticipated outcome to satisfy personal needs. Some outcomes have more valence, or value, to individuals than others do.

Based on the expectancy theory, managers should do the following to motivate employees:[8]

- Determine the rewards valued by each employee.
- Determine the desired performance level and then communicate it clearly to employees.
- Make the performance level attainable.
- Link rewards to performance.
- Determine what factors might counteract the effectiveness of a award.
- Make sure the reward is adequate for the level of performance.

For an example of expectancy theory at work, see the discussion of Trilogy Software in the Focusing on Small Business box on the next page.

Equity Theory

equity theory
A theory of motivation that holds that worker satisfaction is influenced by employees' perceptions about how fairly they are treated compared with their coworkers.

Another contemporary explanation of motivation, **equity theory** is based on individuals' perceptions about how fairly they are treated compared with their coworkers. Equity means justice or fairness, and in the workplace it refers to employees' perceived fairness of the way they are treated and the rewards they earn. Employees evaluate their own *outcomes* (e.g., salary, benefits) in relation to their *inputs* (e.g., number of hours worked, education, and training) and then compare the outcomes-to-inputs ratio to one of the following: (1) the employee's own past experience in a different position in the current organization, (2) the employee's own past experience in a different organization, (3) another employee's experience inside the current organization, or (4) another employee's experience outside the organization.

According to equity theory, if employees perceive that an inequity exists, they will make one of the following choices:

- *Change their work habits* (exert less effort on the job).
- *Change their job benefits and income* (ask for a raise, steal from the employer).
- *Distort their perception of themselves* ("I always thought I was smart, but now I realize I'm a lot smarter than my coworkers").
- *Distort their perceptions of others* ("Joe's position is really much less flexible than mine").
- *Look at the situation from a different perspective* ("I don't make as much as the other department heads, but I make a lot more than most graphic artists").
- *Leave the situation* (quit the job).

Managers can use equity theory to improve worker satisfaction. Knowing that every employee seeks equitable and fair treatment, managers can make an effort to understand an employee's perceptions of fairness and take steps to reduce concerns about inequity.

Goal-Setting Theory

goal-setting theory
A theory of motivation based on the premise that an individual's intention to work toward a goal is a primary source of motivation.

Goal-setting theory is based on the premise that an individual's intention to work toward a goal is a primary source of motivation. Once set, the goal clarifies for the employee what needs to be accomplished and how much effort will be required for completion. The theory has three main components: (1) specific goals lead to a higher level of performance than do more generalized goals ("do your best"); (2) more difficult goals lead to better performance than do easy goals (provided the individual accepts the goal); and (3) feedback on

TRILOGY REWARDS RISK TAKERS

Does expectancy theory really explain employee motivation? A visit to Trilogy Software Inc. in Austin, Texas, might convince you that it does. Joe Liemandt, the 30-year-old founder and CEO of Trilogy, is an entrepreneur with a vision, as well as a knack for motivating high-performing employees. In Liemandt's words, "at a software company, people are everything," so Trilogy focuses on recruiting the best people it can find, getting those recruits "up to speed" as quickly as possible, and then turning them loose so they can make immediate contributions. But once it has wooed them, how does Trilogy get its people to stay? That's where the expectancy model comes in.

According to expectancy theory, employees will be motivated when three important factors are addressed. First, Liemandt makes sure Trilogy recruits feel confident that exerting a given level of effort will result in a certain level of performance. Liemandt hires the most talented graduates he can find and thrusts responsibility on them immediately, giving them the power to make decisions and the resources to implement their decisions. Liemandt calls this the "just-do-it-now" spirit.

Expectancy theory is based not only on the link between effort and performance, but also on the link between *performance and outcomes.* Here again Liemandt has succeeded in creating a workplace conducive to high levels of motivation. On arriving at the company, all Trilogy recruits take part in a three-month "boot camp" called Trilogy University. Liemandt's goal

is to develop creative people who work well in teams, adapt swiftly to changes in customer demands, and are willing to take risks. New employees are immediately shown the clear link between performance and rewards. At the end of "boot camp," Liemandt takes 300 new employees on an all-expenses-paid trip to Las Vegas as a reward for their hard work.

The last component of expectancy theory is the *valence* of employee outcomes or rewards. Employees must meet very high performance goals, but if they do, the rewards include high salaries, bonuses, stock options, and participation in a unique corporate culture. Trilogy employees wear what they want, set their own hours, and socialize at the weekly company-sponsored happy hour. For some employees, the best reward of all is the chance to work with people like themselves—people who are creative, talented, and ambitious. In the words of one new recruit, "Trilogy hires people who are smart, talented, interesting, and cool. Those are exactly the sort of people I want to be around."

Critical Thinking Questions

1. Do you think expectancy theory works best in high-tech companies like Trilogy?
2. How does Liemandt's taking new employees to Las Vegas fit into expectancy theory?
3. Do you think that you would be highly motivated if you worked for Trilogy?

Are you bright, talented, and ambitious? Are you willing to take a risk? Find out how to become a Trilogian by visiting
www.trilogy.com

progress toward the goal enhances performance. Feedback is particularly important because it helps the individual identify the gap between the *real* (the actual performance) and the *ideal* (the desired outcome defined by the goal).

Bruce Tulgan, founder of Rainmaker Thinking, a consulting firm, emphasizes the relationship between goal achievement and feedback in his book *FAST Feedback.*[9] According to Tulgan, feedback that allows employees to meet their goals is FAST—frequent, accurate, specific, and timely. Because businesses operate in a dynamic environment, FAST feedback is necessary to ensure that employees stay in tune with what is working and what needs to be changed.[10] Managers can help employees meet goals by creating a feedback system based on day-to-day interactions and a variety of communication channels, such as routine meetings, memos, social events, e-mail, and voice mail.

Want to order Tulgan's *FAST Feedback* or look for other books about giving feedback? Visit

www.amazon.com or **www.barnesnoble.com**

Given the trend toward employee empowerment in the workplace, more and more employees are participating in the goal-setting process. Are employees who set their own work goals more motivated to achieve them? Research on the benefits of shared goal setting versus assigned goals has produced mixed results. Still, it is clear that when employees are encouraged to participate in the goal-setting process, they are more likely to accept a goal as desirable, especially if the goal is difficult.

concept check

- Discuss the three relationships central to expectancy theory.
- Explain the comparison process that is a part of equity theory.
- How does goal-setting theory contribute to our understanding of motivation?

FROM MOTIVATION THEORY TO APPLICATION

>lg 7

The material presented thus far in this chapter demonstrates the wide variety of theorists and research studies that have contributed to our current understanding of employee motivation. Now we turn our attention to more practical matters, to ways that these concepts can be applied in the workplace to meet organizational goals and improve individual performance.

Motivational Job Design

How might managers redesign or modify existing jobs to increase employee motivation and performance? The following three options have been used extensively in the workplace.

job enlargement

The horizontal expansion of a job by increasing the number and variety of tasks that a person performs.

The horizontal expansion of a job, increasing the number and variety of tasks that a person performs is called **job enlargement.** Increasing task diversity can enhance job satisfaction, particularly when the job is mundane and repetitive in nature. A potential drawback to job enlargement is that employees may perceive that they are being asked to work harder and do more with no change in their level of responsibility or compensation. This can cause resentment and lead to dissatisfaction.

job enrichment

The vertical expansion of a job by increasing the employee's autonomy, responsibility, and decision-making authority.

Job enrichment is the vertical expansion of an employee's job. Whereas job enlargement addresses the breadth or scope of a job, enrichment attempts to increase job depth by providing the employee with more autonomy, responsibility, and decision-making authority. In an enriched job, the employee can use a variety of talents and skills and has more control over the planning, execution, and evaluation of the required tasks. In general, job enrichment has been found to increase job satisfaction and reduce absenteeism and turnover.

job rotation

The shifting of workers from one job to another; also called *cross-training*.

Also called *cross-training*, **job rotation** is the shifting of workers from one job to another. This may be done to broaden an employee's skill base or because an employee has ceased to be interested in or challenged by a particular job. The organization may benefit from job rotation because it increases flexibility in scheduling and production, since employees can be shifted to cover for absent workers or changes in production or operations. It is also a valuable tool for training lower-level managers in a variety of functional areas. Drawbacks of job rotation include an increase in training costs and decreased productivity while employees are getting "up to speed" in new task areas.

Work-Scheduling Options

As companies try to meet the needs of a diverse workforce and retain quality employees, while remaining competitive and financially prosperous, managers are challenged to find new ways to keep workers motivated and satisfied. Increasingly popular are alternatives to the traditional work schedule, such as the compressed workweek, flextime, job sharing, and telecommuting.

One option for employees who want to maximize their leisure hours, indulge in three-day weekends, and avoid commuting during morning and evening rush hours is the compressed workweek. Employees work the traditional 40 hours, but fit those hours into a shorter workweek. Most common is the 4-40 schedule, where employees work four 10-hour days a week. By the mid-1990s, 25 percent of large U.S. companies offered a compressed workweek to some of their employees, double the percentage in the late 1980s.[11] Organizations that offer this option claim benefits ranging from increased motivation and productivity to reduced absenteeism and turnover.

Another scheduling option, called flextime, allows employees to decide what their work hours will be. Employees are generally expected to work a certain number of hours per week, but have some discretion as to when they arrive at work and when they leave for the day. The flexible work hours schedule offers many of the benefits of the compressed workweek, including increased morale and productivity and reduced absenteeism. Additionally, flextime may reduce employee tardiness and increase satisfaction due to the increased feelings of autonomy. A significant drawback is that flextime cannot be adapted to every job, particularly service jobs where customers expect personnel to be present at specific times.

Job sharing is a scheduling option that allows two individuals to split the tasks, responsibilities, and work hours of one 40-hour-per-week job. Though used less frequently than flextime and the compressed workweek, this option can also provide employees with job flexibility. The primary benefit to the company is that it gets "two for the price of one"—the company can draw on two sets of skills and abilities to accomplish one set of job objectives.

Telecommuting, described in Chapter 8, is a work-scheduling option that allows employees to work from home via a computer that is linked with their office, headquarters, or colleagues. It is the fastest growing of the four scheduling options. Working at home allows employees a high degree of flexibility and autonomy—they can wear what they want, set their own hours, work at their own pace, and control their own work environment. Telecommuting also gives employees the option of living geographically distant from their employer without the headaches of traditional long-distance commuting. Potential drawbacks to telecommuting include lost productivity due to distractions at home, feelings of isolation, and lack of inclusion in the corporate culture and informal communication network.

Recognition, Empowerment, and Economic Incentives

All employees have unique needs that they seek to fulfill through their jobs. Organizations must devise a wide array of incentives to ensure that a broad spectrum of employee needs can be addressed in the work environment, thus increasing the likelihood of motivated employees. A sampling of these motivational tools is discussed here.

Formal recognition of superior effort by individuals or groups in the workplace is one way to enhance employee motivation. Recognition serves as positive feedback and reinforcement, letting employees know what they have done well and that their contribution is valued by the organization. Recognition can take many forms, both formal and informal. Some companies use formal

job sharing

A scheduling option that allows two individuals to split the tasks, responsibilities, and work hours of one 40-hour-per-week job.

awards ceremonies to acknowledge and celebrate their employees' accomplishments. Others take advantage of informal interaction to congratulate employees on a job well done and offer encouragement for the future. Recognition can take the form of an employee of the month plaque, a monetary reward, a day off, a congratulatory e-mail, or a verbal "pat on the back."

Employee empowerment, sometimes called employee involvement or participative management, involves delegating decision-making authority to employees at all levels of the organization. Employees are given greater responsibility for planning, implementing, and evaluating the results of decisions. Empowerment is based on the premise that human resources, especially at lower levels in the firm, are an underutilized asset. Employees are capable of contributing much more of their skills and abilities to organizational success if they are allowed to participate in the decision-making process and are given access to the resources needed to implement their decisions.

Any discussion of motivation has to include the use of monetary incentives to enhance performance. Currently, companies are using a variety of variable-pay programs such as piece-rate plans, profit sharing, gain sharing, and bonuses to encourage employees to be more productive. Unlike the standard salary or hourly wage, **variable pay** means that a portion of an employee's pay is directly linked to an individual or organizational performance measure. In *piece-rate pay plans,* for

variable pay

A systems of paying employees in which a portion of an employee's pay is directly linked to an individual or organizational performance measure.

example, employees are paid a given amount for each unit they produce, directly linking the amount they earn to their productivity. *Profit-sharing plans* are based on overall company profitability. Using an established formula, management distributes some portion of company profits to all employees. *Gain-sharing plans* are incentive programs based on group productivity. Employees share in the financial gains attributed to the increased productivity of their group. This encourages employees to increase productivity within their specific work area regardless of the overall profit picture for the organization as a whole. A *bonus* is simply a one-time lump-sum monetary reward.

Want to earn stock options working for Microsoft? Check out employment possibilities by visiting www.microsoft.com

Although all of these monetary incentives can be used very successfully to enhance employee motivation and performance, the incentive that is fast becoming most popular with new members of the workforce is the stock option.[12] One of the most successful companies to use employee stock options (ESOPs) as a recruiting and performance tool is Microsoft. Early on, Bill Gates recognized the advantages of offering employees the opportunity to accumulate wealth through stock ownership. Employees are often willing to forgo larger salaries and other benefits in favor of stock that may be worth a great deal in the future. And, if managers want talented employees who will work for the company with the enthusiasm that comes with ownership, then they must be willing to trade equity for talent.

concept check

- Explain the difference between job enlargement and job enrichment.
- What are the four work-scheduling options that can enhance employee performance?
- Are all employees motivated by the same economic incentives? Explain.

USING TEAMS TO ENHANCE MOTIVATION AND PERFORMANCE

>lg 8

One of the most apparent trends in business today is the use of teams to accomplish organizational goals. Using a team-based structure can increase individual and group motivation and performance. This section gives a brief overview of group behavior, defines work teams as specific types of groups, and provides suggestions for creating high-performing teams.

Understanding Group Behavior

Teams are a specific type of organizational group. Every organization contains *groups,* social units of two or more people who share the same goals and cooperate to achieve those goals. Understanding some fundamental concepts related to group behavior and group processes provides a good foundation for understanding concepts about work teams. Groups can be formal or informal in nature. Formal groups are designated and sanctioned by the organization; their behavior is directed toward accomplishing organizational goals. Informal groups are based on social relationships and are not determined or sanctioned by the organization.

Formal organizational groups must operate within the larger organizational system. To some degree, elements of the larger system, such as organizational strategy, policies and procedures, available resources, and corporate culture, determine the behavior of smaller groups within the organization. Other factors that affect the behavior of organizational groups are individual member characteristics (e.g., ability, training, personality), the roles and norms of group members, and the size and cohesiveness of the group. Norms are the implicit behavioral guidelines of the group, or the standards for acceptable and nonacceptable behavior. These standards are conveyed through socialization, a process by which new group members learn:

- The basic goals of the group.
- The preferred means for reaching those goals.
- The behavior patterns expected for effective performance within the group.
- The basic rules and attitudes that help maintain the group's identity and integrity.

Work socialization occurs both formally in training programs and informally by watching and talking with other group members. Group performance is related to how rapidly new members are socialized.

group cohesiveness
The degree to which group members want to stay in the group and tend to resist outside influences.

Group cohesiveness refers to the degree to which group members want to stay in the group and tend to resist outside influences (such as a change in company policies). When group performance norms are high, group cohesiveness will have a positive impact on productivity. Cohesiveness tends to increase when the size of the group is small, individual and group goals are congruent, the group has high status in the organization, rewards are group-based rather than individual based, and the group competes with other groups within the organization. Work group cohesiveness can benefit the organization in several ways including increased productivity, enhanced worker self-image because of group success, increased company loyalty, reduced employee turnover, and reduced absenteeism. On the other hand, cohesiveness can also lead to restricted output, resistance to change, and conflict with other work groups in the organization.

Members of formal work groups share the same organizational goals and work together to achieve those goals. Group members are guided by norms that dictate acceptable behavior needed to accomplish effective group performance.

The opportunity to turn the decision-making process over to a group with diverse skills and abilities is one of the arguments for using work groups (and teams) in organizational settings. For group decision making to be most effective, however, both managers and group members must acknowledge its strengths and weaknesses (see Exhibit 10-4).

Strengths and Weaknesses of Group Decision Making

Strengths	Weaknesses
• Groups bring more information and knowledge to the decision process.	• Groups typically take a longer time to reach a solution than an individual takes.
• Groups offer a diversity of perspectives and, therefore, generate a greater number of alternatives.	• Group members may pressure others to conform, reducing the likelihood of disagreement.
• Group decision making results in a higher-quality decision than individual decision making.	• The process may be dominated by one or a small number of participants.
• Participation of group members increases the likelihood that a decision will be accepted.	• Groups lack accountability, because it is difficult to assign responsibility for outcomes to any one individual.

Work Groups versus Work Teams

work groups

Groups of employees who share resources and coordinate efforts so as to help members better perform their individual duties and responsibilities. The performance of the group can be evaluated by adding up the contributions of the individual group members.

work teams

Groups of employees who not only coordinate their efforts, but also collaborate by pooling their knowledge, skills, abilities, and resources in a collective effort to attain a common goal; causing the performance of the team to be greater than the sum of the members' individual efforts.

problem-solving teams

Teams of employees from the same department or area of expertise and from the same level of the organizational hierarchy who meet regularly to share information and discuss ways to improve processes and procedures in specific functional areas.

We have already noted that teams are a special type of organizational group, but we also need to differentiate between work groups and work teams. **Work groups** share resources and coordinate efforts to help members better perform their individual duties and responsibilities. The performance of the group can be evaluated by adding up the contributions of the individual group members. **Work teams** require not only coordination but also *collaboration,* the pooling of knowledge, skills, abilities, and resources in a collective effort to attain a common goal. A work team creates *synergy,* causing the performance of the team as a whole to be greater than the sum of team members' individual contributions. Simply assigning employees to groups and labeling them a team does not guarantee a positive outcome. Managers and team members must be committed to creating, developing, and maintaining high-performance work teams. Factors that contribute to their success are discussed later in this section.

Types of Teams

The evolution of the team concept in organizations can be seen in three basic types of work teams: problem solving, self-managed, and cross-functional. Japanese companies used problem-solving teams, known as quality circles, as early as the 1950s to improve quality and efficiency in manufacturing processes. **Problem-solving teams** are typically made up of employees from the same department or area of expertise and from the same level of the organizational hierarchy. They meet on a regular basis to share information and discuss ways to improve processes and procedures in specific functional areas. Problem-solving teams generate ideas and alternatives and may recommend a specific course of action, but they typically do not make final decisions, allocate resources, or implement change.

Many organizations that experienced success using problem-solving teams were willing to expand the team concept to allow team members greater responsibility in making decisions, implementing

Visit Harley-Davidson's recent annual report at **www.harleydavidson.com** to learn how the circle organizational design promotes interdependent work teams.

ARE TEAMWORK AND EMPOWERMENT FOR EVERYONE?

Eaton Corp.'s plant in South Bend, Indiana, makes heavy-duty transmission gears. The manufacturing process requires employees to perform some very hot, heavy, noisy, dirty jobs. Large forge presses stamp hot steel into various shapes for transmission gear blanks. Long-handled tongs are used to lift white-hot parts and work them across the dies in the forge presses. The presses are so noisy that workers must communicate with hand signals.

Job success at Eaton's South Bend plant depends on teamwork. Each of the 106 employees is on at least three teams as well as a functional team. Work teams are self-directing; the employees are their own bosses. Employees are empowered to solve problems on their own, and they are expected to enforce the work rules themselves. Although there are no bosses, everyone watches everyone else, and "it can feel like having a hundred bosses."

Effective empowerment and teamwork at the South Bend plant rest on four pillars: trust, respect, communication, and involvement. Eaton's culture of empowerment, though resilient, is also delicate: a single breach of trust, respect, communication, or involvement can cause distrust to enter and the culture to atrophy.

Eaton's employees are expected to assume a great deal of responsibility in performing their jobs. As Alexander Cutler, Eaton's president and CEO, observes, however, "[T]he admission ticket for this kind of responsibility is accountability—and not everyone necessarily wants accountability." Indeed, some people try to work around the system, finding subtle ways to resist policies that they dislike. For instance, one worker refuses to note any problems when he does the daily locker check as part of the plant's general cleanliness campaign. His reasoning is that he is empowered and he is making the decision to ignore any problems.

The bottom line for Eaton is twofold: many workers thrive in a culture of teamwork and empowerment, but some discover that this culture is not for them.

Critical Thinking Questions

1. Does Eaton—or any business that relies on a culture of empowerment and teamwork—have an ethical responsibility to ensure that employees fit in with the culture and are motivated by it? Explain your answer.
2. Do employees of businesses like Eaton's South Bend plant have an ethical responsibility to do everything possible to function effectively as empowered team members? Explain your answer.

---

self-managed work teams

Highly autonomous teams of employees who manage themselves without any formal supervision and take responsibility for setting goals, planning and scheduling work activities, selecting team members, and evaluating team performance.

cross-functional teams

Teams of employees who are from about the same level in the organizational hierarchy but from different functional areas; for example, task forces, organizational committees, and project teams.

solutions, and monitoring outcomes. These highly autonomous groups are called **self-managed work teams.** They manage themselves without any formal supervision, taking responsibility for setting goals, planning and scheduling work activities, selecting team members, and evaluating team performance. PepsiCo, Hewlett-Packard, Digital Equipment Corp., and Xerox are just a few of the well-known, highly successful companies using self-managed work teams.

The most recent adaptation of the team concept is called a **cross-functional team.** These teams are made up of employees from about the same hierarchical level, but different functional areas of the organization. Many task forces, organizational committees, and project teams are cross-functional. Often the team members work together only until they solve a given problem or complete a specific project. Cross-functional teams allow people with various levels and areas of expertise to pool their resources, develop new ideas, solve problems, and coordinate complex projects. Both problem-solving teams and self-managed teams may also be cross-functional teams. The Applying Technology box describes yet another type of team that is becoming more common—the virtual team.

VIRTUAL TEAMS

Increasing globalization and advances in information technology are changing the competitive landscape and forcing organizations to reevaluate organizational structures and work processes. Downsizing is common, and many organizations have become increasingly decentralized and geographically dispersed. The problem? Given these trends, it has become more and more challenging for organizations to retain the advantages of team-based organizational structures. The answer? Virtual teams.

Virtual teams are made up of employees in different geographic or organizational locations who come together as a team via a combination of telecommunications and information technologies. Virtual teams work together to accomplish a common goal, but rarely (if ever) meet in a face-to-face setting. Membership is often dynamic, changing to accommodate project or task requirements. The emergence of virtual teams can be attributed to five factors:

1. The increase in flat (horizontal) organizational structures.
2. Increased interorganizational cooperation (e.g., strategic alliances).
3. Changing employee expectations regarding the use of technology (i.e., increased technological sophistication).
4. The ongoing shift from production to service/knowledge work environments.
5. The increasing globalization of business activities.

Virtual teams can exist because of relatively recent advances in computer and telecommunications technology. The infrastructure of virtual teamwork is made up of three basic types of technology: desktop videoconferencing systems (DVCS), collaborative software systems, and Internet/Intranet systems. These technologies allow virtual team members to interact and facilitate the accomplishment of complex work assignments.

Virtual teams provide an exciting opportunity to change the way in which work gets done, but they also present unique management challenges:

- The lack of traditional social interaction that facilitates trust and commitment.
- Increased team diversity (e.g., geographic location, language, culture, functional area, company outsiders).
- The need for team members to be technologically savvy.
- Increased difficulty coordinating resources and tasks (the teams are virtual, but the work is real).
- Increased difficulty monitoring individual and team performance.

In the workplace today, the use of virtual teams is an innovative way for companies to create competitive advantage. In the future such teams may become a necessity, perhaps even a dominant organizational form.

Critical Thinking Questions

1. What is meant by "virtual teams"?
2. Describe the technology that has enabled virtual teams to become a reality.
3. Would you like to be a member of a virtual team?

Building High-Performance Teams

What are the factors that contribute to highly motivated and productive teams? Based on a study of teams in organizations, researchers have identified some basic building blocks of high-performance teams: (1) the skills of team members, (2) the accountability of the team, and (3) the commitment of the team members.[13] Exhibit 10-5 identifies some specific aspects of those building blocks that contribute to high performance.

The following are some guidelines for enhancing team performance:[14]

- Team work assignments should focus on specific, concrete issues.
- Work should be broken down and delegated to individuals or subgroups (teams are not the same as group meetings).

> e x h i b i t 1 0 - 5 <

Building Blocks of High-Performance Teams

Skills	Accountability	Commitment
• Problem solving	• Small number of members	• Specific goals
• Technical/functional	• Mutual accountability	• Common approach
• Interpersonal	• Individual accountability	• Meaningful purpose

con c ə p t c h ɔ c k

- What is the difference between a work team and a work group?
- Identify and describe three types of work teams.
- What are some ways to build a high-performance team?

- Team membership should be based on skills and abilities rather than formal authority or organizational position.
- Team members should do roughly the same amount of work to maintain equity within the group.
- Traditional hierarchical patterns of communication and interaction must be broken down.
- Teams must work to create an atmosphere of openness, commitment, and trust.

>lg 9

CAPITALIZING ON TRENDS IN BUSINESS

Firms that train workers in new technologies such as videoconferencing increase employee motivation and satisfaction. Employers benefit from their investment in training and education with a more loyal, productive, and skilled workforce.

According to a recent *Industry Week* article on the "100 best managed companies," people are the only real source of competitive advantage, and the only way companies can stay competitive is by "unleashing the full creative power of people at all levels of the organization."[15] This chapter has focused on understanding what motivates people and how employee motivation and satisfaction affect productivity and organizational performance. Organizations can improve performance by investing in people. In reviewing the ways companies are currently choosing to invest in their human resources, we can spot three obvious trends: (1) education and training, (2) employee ownership, and (3) work-life benefits. Every company in *Fortune* magazine's 1999 list of the "100 best companies to work for" has employee programs in at least one of those areas, and many offer programs in all three categories.[16]

Education and Training

Companies that provide educational and training opportunities for their employees reap the benefits of a more motivated, as well as a more skilled, workforce. Employees who are properly trained in new technologies are more productive and less resistant to job change. Education and training provide additional benefits by increasing employees' feelings of competence and self-worth. When companies spend money to upgrade employee knowledge and skills, they convey the message "we value you and are committed to your growth and development as an employee." One of Allied Signal's goals is to better prepare its employees to take on new job assignments within the organization.[17] In 1991 only 20 percent of job openings at Allied were filled internally. The company's training and educational program, called a learning initiative, began in 1992, and today approximately 70 percent of job openings at Allied are filled with internal candidates.

Employee Ownership

Companies are always looking for new ways to increase employee commitment and thus decrease absenteeism and turnover. Jim Porter, vice-president at Honeywell, Inc., claims that competitive advantage boils down to employees who are committed to making the company successful, and that commitment is driven by a sense of ownership in the organization.[18] In Porter's words, "owners behave very differently from hired hands." Like an increasing number of companies today, Honeywell creates a sense of economic ownership by giving employees stock options in the company. Employee stock ownership increases employees' feelings of responsibility for the performance of the organization.

Work-Life Benefits

c o n c e p t   c h e c k

- What benefits can an organization derive from offering training and educational opportunities for its employees?
- How can employee stock ownership programs benefit both the employees and the organization?
- How can work-life benefits help both an organization and its employees?

In another growing trend in the workplace, companies are helping their employees to manage the numerous and sometimes competing demands in their lives. Organizations are taking a more active role in helping employees achieve a balance between their work responsibilities and their personal obligations. The desired result is employees who are less stressed, better able to focus on their jobs, and, therefore, more productive. Ford Motor Co. is a leader in providing work-life benefits for employees. The company offers telecommuting, part-time positions, job sharing, subsidized child care, elder-care referral, and on-site fitness centers.

APPLYING THIS CHAPTER'S TOPICS

We've come a long way from the days of *scientific management*. Organizations now offer a wide variety of incentives to attract and retain high-quality employees. A knowledgeable, creative, committed, and highly skilled workforce provides a company with a source of sustainable competitive advantage in an increasingly competitive business environment. What does that mean to you? It means that companies are working harder than ever to meet employee needs. It means that when you graduate from college or university you may choose a prospective employer on the basis of its day-care facilities and fitness programs as well as its salaries. It means that you need to think about what motivates you. Would you forgo a big salary to work for a smaller company that gives you lots of freedom to be creative and make your own decisions? Would you trade extensive health coverage for a share of ownership in the company? Most organizations try to offer a broad spectrum of incentives to meet a variety of needs, but each company makes trade-offs, and so will you in choosing an employer. Do a little research on a company you are interested in working for (paying particular attention to its corporate culture); then use the exercise in the Try It Now section to help you determine how well your values fit with the company's values.

> t r y   i t   n o w ! <

The accompanying table lists 17 personal characteristics and 13 institutional values you might encounter at a company.[19] Select and rank order the 10 personal characteristics that best describe you; do the same for the 10 institutional values that would be most evident in your ideal workplace. Test your fit at a firm by seeing whether the characteristics of the company's environment match your top 10 personal characteristics.

The Choice Menu

Rank Order (1–17)	You Are	Rank Order (1–13)	Your Ideal Company Offers
_____	1. Flexible	_____	1. Stability
_____	2. Innovative	_____	2. High expectations of performance
_____	3. Willing to experiment	_____	3. Opportunities for professional growth
_____	4. Risk taking	_____	4. High pay for good performance
_____	5. Careful	_____	5. Job security
_____	6. Autonomy seeking	_____	6. A clear guiding philosophy
_____	7. Comfortable with rules	_____	7. A low level of conflict
_____	8. Analytical	_____	8. Respect for the individual's rights
_____	9. Team oriented	_____	9. Informality
_____	10. Easygoing	_____	10. Fairness
_____	11. Supportive	_____	11. Long hours
_____	12. Aggressive	_____	12. Relative freedom from rules
_____	13. Decisive	_____	13. The opportunity to be distinctive, or different from others
_____	14. Achievement oriented		
_____	15. Comfortable with individual responsibility		
_____	16. Competitive		
_____	17. Interested in making friends at work		

SUMMARY OF LEARNING GOALS

>lg 1   **What are the basic principles of Frederick Taylor's concept of scientific management?**

Scientific management is based on the belief that employees are motivated by economic incentives and that there is "one best way" to perform any job. The four basic principles of scientific management developed by Taylor are as follows:

1. Develop a scientific approach for each element of a person's job.
2. Scientifically select, train, teach, and develop workers.
3. Encourage cooperation between workers and managers so that each job can be accomplished in a standard, scientifically determined way.

>looking ahead

There is no doubt that most employees would say SAS Institute, Inc. is a great place to work. SAS's revenue growth and its very low employee turnover reflect its happy, motivated workers. The future, indeed, looks very bright. Nevertheless, SAS will have to continuously adapt its employee benefits to match employees' changing needs. One area SAS must monitor is employee salaries, which are only average for the industry. Perhaps some workers would rather have a fatter paycheck than a pianist in the lunchroom. A second challenge is the incredible wealth that managers and top executives of software and other high-tech companies are accumulating when their companies go public (issue common stock). SAS is still privately owned and simply can't match the wealth-generating opportunities of a public company. If SAS goes public, will it retain its intense employee loyalty and high job satisfaction ratings?

4. Divide work and responsibility between management and workers according to who is better suited to each task.

>lg 2 **What did Elton Mayo's Hawthorne studies reveal about worker motivation?**
From 1927 to 1932, Mayo and his colleagues conducted experiments at the Hawthorne Western Electric plant on job redesign, length of workday and workweek, length of break times, and incentive plans. The results of the studies indicated that increases in performance were tied to a complex set of employee attitudes. Mayo claimed that both the experimental and the control groups at the plant had developed a sense of group pride because they had been selected to participate in the studies. The pride that came from this special attention motivated the workers to increase their productivity. Supervisors who allowed the employees to have some control over their situation appeared to further increase the workers' motivation. These findings gave rise to what is now known as the Hawthorne effect, which suggests that employees will perform better when they feel singled out for special attention or feel that management is concerned about employee welfare.

>lg 3 **What is Maslow's hierarchy of needs, and how do these needs relate to motivation?**
Maslow believed that each individual has a hierarchy of needs, consisting of physiological, safety, social, esteem, and self-actualization needs. The most basic needs are physiological such as air, food, clothing, and shelter. After these are satisfied, we have safety needs. People need to feel secure and to be protected from harm. At the third level are social needs, or needs for belonging (acceptance by others) and for giving and receiving friendship and love. At the fourth level in Maslow's hierarchy are esteem needs, which are needs for the respect of others and for a sense of accomplishment and achievement. Finally, at the highest level are self-actualization needs—the needs for fulfillment, for living up to one's potential, and for using one's abilities to the utmost.

Managers who accept Maslow's ideas attempt to increase employee motivation by modifying organizational and managerial practices to increase the likelihood that employees will meet all levels of needs. Maslow's theory has also helped managers understand that it is hard to motivate people by appealing to already satisfied needs.

>lg 4 **How are McGregor's Theories X and Y used to explain worker motivation?**
Douglas McGregor influenced the study of motivation with his formulation of two contrasting sets of assumptions about human nature—designated Theory X and Theory Y. Theory X says people don't like to work and will avoid it if they can. Because people don't like to work, they must be controlled, directed, or threatened to get them to make an effort. The average worker wants to avoid responsibility but wants job security. Theory Y says work is as natural as play or rest. People want to be self-directed and will try to accomplish goals that they

KEY TERMS

cross-functional
    teams 302
equity theory 295
expectancy theory
    294
goal-setting theory
    295
group cohesiveness
    300
Hawthorne effect
    290
hygiene factors
    293
job enlargement
    297
job enrichment
    297
job rotation 297
job sharing 298
Maslow's hierarchy
    of needs 291
motivating factors
    293
problem-solving
    teams 302
scientific
    management 288
self-managed work
    teams 302
Theory X 292
Theory Y 292
variable pay 299
work groups 301
work teams 301

believe in. Workers can be motivated with positive incentives. The average person wants and seeks responsibility and is willing to help solve problems. McGregor personally believed that Theory Y assumptions describe most employees and that managers seeking to motivate subordinates should develop management practices based on those assumptions.

>lg 5   **What are the basic components of Herzberg's motivator-hygiene theory?**
Frederick Herzberg's studies indicated that certain job factors are consistently related to employee job satisfaction while others can create job dissatisfaction. According to Herzberg, motivating factors (also called satisfiers) are primarily intrinsic job elements that lead to satisfaction, such as achievement, recognition, the (nature of) work itself, responsibility, advancement, and growth. What Herzberg termed hygiene factors (also called dissatisfiers) are extrinsic elements of the work environment such as company policy, relationships with supervisors, working conditions, relationships with peers and subordinates, salary and benefits, and job security. These are factors that can result in job dissatisfaction if not well-managed. One of the most interesting results of Herzberg's studies was the implication that the opposite of satisfaction is not dissatisfaction. Herzberg believed that proper management of hygiene factors could prevent employee dissatisfaction, but that these factors could not serve as a source of satisfaction or motivation.

>lg 6   **What three contemporary theories on employee motivation offer insights into improving employee performance?**
According to expectancy theory, the probability of an individual acting in a particular way depends on the strength of that individual's belief that the act will have a particular outcome and on whether the individual values that outcome. The degree to which an employee is motivated depends on three important relationships: the link between *effort and performance,* the link between *performance and outcome,* and the link between *outcomes and personal needs.*

Equity theory is based on individuals' perceptions about how fairly they are treated compared with their coworkers. Equity means justice or fairness, and in the workplace it refers to employees' perceived fairness of the way they are treated and the rewards they earn. Employees evaluate their own *outcomes* (e.g., salary, benefits) in relation to *inputs* (e.g., number of hours worked, education and training) and then compare the outcomes-to-inputs ratio to their own past experiences or the experiences of another person whose situation is similar.

Goal-setting theory states that employees are highly motivated to perform when specific goals are established and feedback on progress is offered.

>lg 7   **How can managers redesign existing jobs to increase employee motivation and performance?**
The horizontal expansion of a job by increasing the number and variety of tasks that a person performs is called job enlargement. Increasing task diversity can enhance job satisfaction, particularly when the job is mundane and repetitive in nature. Job enrichment is the vertical expansion of an employee's job to provide the employee with more autonomy, responsibility, and decision-making authority. In general, job enrichment has been found to increase employee job satisfaction and reduce absenteeism and turnover. Job rotation, also called cross-training, is the shifting of workers from one job to another. This may be done to broaden an employee's skill base or when an employee ceases to be interested in or challenged by the job.

As companies try to meet the needs of a diverse workforce and retain quality employees, while remaining competitive and financially prosperous, managers are challenged to find new ways to keep workers motivated and satisfied, thereby increasing individual and organizational performance and decreasing absenteeism and turnover. Popular motivational tools include work-scheduling options, employee recognition programs, empowerment, and variable-pay programs.

>lg 8 **What different types of teams are being used in organizations today?**
Work groups share resources and coordinate efforts to help members better perform their individual duties and responsibilities. The performance of the group can be evaluated by adding up the contributions of the individual group members. Work teams require not only coordination but also *collaboration,* the pooling of knowledge, skills, abilities, and resources in a collective effort to attain a common goal. The work team creates *synergy,* causing the performance of the team as a whole to be greater than the sum of team members' individual contributions.

Four types of work teams are used: problem solving, self-managed, cross-functional, and virtual teams. *Problem-solving teams* are typically made up of employees from the same department or area of expertise and from the same level of the organizational hierarchy; they meet on a regular basis to share information and discuss ways to improve processes and procedures in specific functional areas. *Self-managed work teams* are highly autonomous groups that manage themselves without any formal supervision. They take responsibility for setting goals, planning and scheduling work activities, selecting team members, and evaluating team performance. *Cross-functional teams* are made up of employees from about the same hierarchical level, but different functional areas of the organization. These teams allow people with various areas of expertise to pool their resources, develop new ideas, solve problems, and coordinate complex projects. In a *virtual team,* employees in different geographic or organizational locations come together as a team via a combination of telecommunications and information technologies. Virtual teams work together to accomplish a common goal, but rarely (if ever) meet face-to-face. Membership is often dynamic, changing to accommodate project or task requirements.

>lg 9 **What initiatives are organizations using today to motivate and retain employees?**
Today, firms are using three key tactics to motivate and retain workers. First, companies are investing more in employee education and training, which make workers more productive and less resistant to job change. Second, managers are offering employees a chance for ownership in the company. This can strongly increase employee commitment. Finally, enlightened employers are providing work-life benefits to help employees achieve a better balance between work and personal responsibilities. Examples include telecommuting, job sharing, subsidized child care, and on-site fitness centers.

PREPARING FOR TOMORROW'S WORKPLACE

1. Do you think the concept of scientific management is applicable today? Why or why not?
2. How are job satisfaction and employee morale linked to job performance? Do you work harder when you are satisfied with your job? Explain your answer.
3. Review the assumptions of Theories X and Y. Under which set of assumptions would you prefer to work? Is your current or former supervisor a Theory X manager or a Theory Y manager? Explain by describing the person's behavior.
4. Think about several of your friends who seem to be highly self-motivated. Talk with each of them and ask them what factors contribute the most to their motivation. Make a list of their responses and compare them to the factors that motivate you.

5. Is money a job satisfier or a job maintenance factor for you? Explain.

6. Both individual motivation and group participation are needed to accomplish certain goals. Describe a situation you're familiar with in which cooperation achieved a goal that individual action could not. Describe one in which group action slowed progress and individual action would have been better.

7. Explain the differences between equity theory and expectancy theory.

8. Using expectancy theory, analyze how you have made and will make personal choices, such as a major area of study, a career to pursue, or job interviews to seek.

9. If a famous executive or sports figure were to give a passionate motivational speech, trying to persuade people to work harder, what do you think the impact would be? Why?

10. Give some examples of situations in which you wanted to do a great job but were prevented from doing so. What was the impact on you? What does your response suggest about your efforts to motivate other people to perform?

WORKING THE NET

1. Looking for 1,001 ways to motivate or reward your employees? Bob Nelson can help. Visit his Nelson Motivation site at **www.nelson-motivation.com/** to get some ideas you can put to use to help you do a better job, either as a manager or as an employee.

2. More companies are offering their employees stock ownership plans. To learn the differences between an employee stock ownership plan (ESOP) and stock options, visit the National Center for Employee Ownership (NCEO) at **www.nceo.org** and the Foundation for Enterprise Development (FED) at **www.fed.org.** Which stock plan would you rather have? Why?

3. Open-book management is one of the better known ways to create a participatory work environment. Over 2,000 companies have adopted this practice, which involves sharing financial information with nonmanagement employees and training them to understand financial information. Does it really motivate employees and improve productivity? The NCEO's Open Book Management site, **www.openbookmanagement.org/,** offers survey results, case studies, related activities, and links that will help you answer this question.

4. You've been asked to develop a staff recognition program for your company but don't have a clue where to start! The U.S. Navy Bureau of Medicine and Surgery has a Web site that can help: **www.nmimc.med.navy.mil/toolkit/ staffrec/index.htm.** Its Staff Recognition Toolkit has resources for both informal and formal employee recognition programs. You can even download and print a variety of full-color thank-you notes or view model recognition nomination forms. Using the information at the site, outline the plan you would recommend for your company.

5. How do you keep your employees satisfied? The Business Research Lab has a series of articles on this topic at **busreslab.com/tips/tipses.htm.** Compile a list of the best ideas—the ones that would motivate *you.*

6. Knowing how to build and manage effective teams is a necessary skill in today's workplace. Team Building News, **www.teambuildingnews.com,** is a newsletter featuring ways America's top corporations use innovative team building to improve team performance. For a good summary of major issues facing teams, review the Team Building handout at the site for the Poynter Institute School for Journalists, **www.poynter.org/research/lm/lm_team. htm.**

CREATIVE THINKING CASE

A Clash of Cultures as Ford Meets Volvo

In Gothenburg, Sweden, Volvo car workers are nervous about what life will be like under their new owner, Ford Motor Co. After all, they might lose their badminton courts. At Volvo's flagship factory here, employees have the use of a company gym, Olympic-size swimming pool, badminton and tennis courts, an outdoor track, and tanning beds. There's also a hot-water pool, where workers go for physical therapy sessions after a hard day on the assembly line.

Some 1,800 Volvo workers, or roughly 9 percent of the total workforce at the company's headquarters, use the facilities. Unions and workers worry that Ford, which bought Volvo, may consider it all a bit too lavish. Although workers have to pay $1.50 a day to get in, Volvo pays as much as five million kronor ($605,500) a year to support the center. "Everybody at Volvo is wondering what Ford's takeover really means to our future," says Claes Andersson, vice-president of the plant workers union. "Will our Volvo traditions continue?"

For Ford, the Volvo purchase raises a big question of benefit equality. Ford workers in the United States are considerably less pampered than Swedish workers. Ford plants usually have free-of-charge fitness centers for employees, as well as weight-reduction programs, but U.S. workers have to do without the tanning beds and other goodies normally found only at the most exclusive health clubs.

Ford has been vague about its plans. "I respect the Swedish heritage," said Jacques Nasser, Ford's CEO. But he added that "nothing is safe in this world; there are no guarantees."

It's not just the health club that workers worry about, but a host of issues ranging from job security to quality of life. For example, Nasser said he wanted to make Volvo a "volume car" in the United States, which could mean a three-shift, round-the-clock production schedule, just like in the United States. Volvo employees currently work two shifts.

Nasser's comments disturbed 40-year-old Jari Saarelainen, a Volvo night-shift worker. He now works fewer than 30 hours a week, but gets paid about the same as day-shift workers, who work as many as 40 hours a week, because of a government-mandated allocation for late-shift employees. The setup allows him to spend lots of time with his wife and four children. "It's a human way of work," he says.

Saarelainen realizes he has it good, but argues that his relatively undemanding workload also helps the company because productivity and morale are higher than they would be under a more conventional employer. "We hope that Ford can grasp that this system is better for the company and the workers," he says. Indeed, the absentee rate at Volvo is roughly 4 percent a day, down from well over 10 percent in the late 1980s. "We like to think that the gym contributed to that," says Mats Edenborg, spokesman for Volvo Group.

Critical Thinking Questions

1. Do you think that Volvo has carried employee benefits and perks too far?

2. Swedish income taxes are far higher than in the United States. High salaries are taxed away, so many companies try to do a few things extra for their employees. Is this a sufficient reason for Ford to maintain Volvo's benefits for its workers?

3. A Ford worker in the United States can earn over $100,000 a year with overtime. A typical Volvo worker earns about $30,275 (U.S.) per year. Should Ford cut the perks and raise wages at Volvo? The government would take slightly over 50 percent.

4. Should Nasser simply leave benefits and perks at both places as they are? What if Ford workers start to complain or Volvo workers start demanding higher salaries?

VIDEO CASE

Motivational Initiatives at Valassis Communications

Valassis Communications, Inc. (**www.valassis.com**) has set the standard in the marketing services industry "for quality, reliability, service and expertise." The company's products include the free-standing insert (FSI) in Sunday newspapers, which contains coupons, refunds, and other values from America's largest packaged goods companies; solo inserts that promote a single company's products or services; delivery of manufacturers' product samples and promotional messages through Sunday newspapers; direct placement of newspaper ads for customers; and oversight of customers' games and sweepstakes promotions.

Executives at Valassis Communications believe the company's success results from having highly motivated employees. The company has many programs that are intended to foster employee motivation. Three of the more notable programs involve employee recognition, perks, and employee communications.

Valassis has a variety of employee recognition programs that are designed to ensure that employees at all levels of the company understand the importance of their contributions. One program recognizes outstanding employees in four categories: Idea of the Year, Change to Grow (which reflects the company's corporate philosophy and culture), Team Player, and Employee of the Year. Employees nominate candidates for each category, and an election is held to select the winner. The winners receive an award as well as shares of the company's stock; their names are permanently listed in the company's "Hall of History," and their accomplishments are featured in the annual report. Other employee recognition programs include sales awards for the top performing account managers, various divisional recognition programs for outstanding performance, length of service awards, and perfect attendance awards.

In addition to a comprehensive benefits plan, Valassis provides employees with a variety of perks that address work/family issues. These benefits include flextime scheduling, job sharing, child care and dependent care reimbursement programs, and an adoption expense program. Health-related perks include an employee assistance plan and on-site fitness centers. At its corporate headquarters, Valassis also provides such amenities as an on-site hair salon/manicurist, an on-site automatic teller machine (ATM), dry cleaning pickup and delivery service, and an on-site cafeteria with indoor and outdoor dining. Many company locations offer summer half-days before holiday weekends, summer barbecues, free legal consultation services, rollover vacation days, and personal computer purchase assistance.

Valassis also provides timely information to employees and seeks suggestions and feedback from employees. Among the primary communication vehicles are a monthly newsletter, a quarterly video magazine, public posting of all company press releases and outside articles written about the company, and a program in which employees have a brown bag lunch with the company's leaders. Other communication initiatives include a suggestion program to encourage employees to provide ideas; a semiannual survey that allows employees to provide feedback on any aspect of the company and its operations; and an annual daylong review where "employees receive a detailed update on company performance, learn about the corporate goals and initiatives for the upcoming year, and meet with their areas to set departmental and individual initiatives." The "Welcome Binder" tells new employees "everything they need to know about VCI and the surrounding community."

One result of these motivational initiatives is that Valassis Communications has acquired a reputation of being a great place to work. In 1997, *Fortune* magazine placed Valassis 67th in its list of the "100 best companies to work for." In 1998, Valassis placed 37th in the *Fortune* rankings.

Critical Thinking Questions

1. How could the motivational programs at Valassis be explained in the context of Maslow's needs hierarchy? Herzberg's motivator-hygiene theory?
2. How have Valassis's motivational programs contributed to the company being selected as one of the "100 best companies to work for"?
3. To what extent are the motivational methods used by Valassis Communications transferable to other companies?

chapter eleven

>c11

Understanding Labor-Management Relations

learning goals

>lg 1   What is the historical development of American labor unions?

>lg 2   What role did federal law play in the development of the union-management relationship?

>lg 3   What is the union organizing process?

>lg 4   What is the collective bargaining process, and what key issues are included in the union contract?

>lg 5   How do employees file a grievance?

>lg 6   What economic tactics do unions and employers use in labor-management conflicts?

>lg 7   What trends will affect American workers and labor-management relations?

A Slowdown at American Airlines

For decades, American unions have exercised the right to strike and picket as a means of exerting economic pressure (lost sales and profits) on an employer to force the company to settle a dispute with a union. Strikes are not the only tactic unions have at their disposal, however, as one airline discovered to its dismay.

Early in 1999 American Airlines (AA) pilots represented by the Allied Pilots Association engaged in several days of work slowdown. Many pilots refused to fly overtime hours and others called in sick. The airline's daily flight schedules assume that about 10 to 15 percent of its pilots will be willing to work overtime. On February 7, 1999, the lack of pilots forced the airline to cancel 10 percent, or 240, of its scheduled flights. Through their work slowdown, the pilots and their union were bringing attention to their dispute with the company and applying economic pressure. The individual pilots' refusal to fly overtime was legal because their labor agreement with the airline specified that overtime would be voluntary, not mandatory. The pilots who called in sick when they were not were violating the agreement, however.

This work slowdown and the pilots' dispute with AA revolved around the firm's purchase of Reno Air late in 1998. Reno Air was a small regional air carrier that operated primarily in the western states. Its 300 pilots were paid about 50 percent less than AA pilots. The Allied Pilots Association wanted to integrate the Reno pilots into AA's pilot seniority lists and pay them at higher rates as quickly as possible. The company wanted to take as long as 18 months to merge the Reno pilots and raise their pay. Consequently, a dispute developed.[1]

Critical Thinking Questions

As you read this chapter, consider these questions as they relate to American Airlines:

- Donald Carty, CEO of AA, was faced with a difficult choice of actions: (1) give in to the union, (2) continue to resist and suffer more losses, or (3) seek some relief from the economic pressure by asking a federal judge to order the sick pilots back to work. What should he have done?

- What are some of the tactics that the union could use against American?

- What are some of the tactics American could employ against the union?

BUSINESS IN THE 21ST CENTURY

Tens of thousands of American firms are unionized and millions of American workers belong to unions. Worker organizations have existed in the United States since before the signing of the Declaration of Independence. If you work in the mining, manufacturing, construction, or transportation industries, you will probably deal with or be affected by labor unions.

A **labor union,** such as the International Brotherhood of Teamsters, is an organization that represents workers in dealing with management over disputes involving wages, hours, and working conditions. The labor relations process that produces a union-management relationship consists of three phases: union organizing, negotiating a labor agreement, and the day-to-day administering of the agreement. The second phase constitutes **collective bargaining,** which is the process of negotiating labor agreements that provide for compensation and working arrangements mutually acceptable to the union and to management.

Labor unions have a rich history in American business. We begin this chapter by exploring their historical development. Next, we discuss the critical role federal law has played and continues to play in labor-management relations. We will see how unions are organized and how they bargain with management. We then discuss important issues and items in labor agreements and the economic tactics available to unions and to management. We conclude with trends in labor-management relations.

labor union

An organization that represents workers in dealing with management over disputes involving wages, hours, and working conditions.

collective bargaining

The process of negotiating labor agreements that provide for compensation and working arrangements mutually acceptable to the union and to management.

THE EMERGENCE OF UNIONS AND COLLECTIVE BARGAINING

Early labor organizations began to develop toward the end of the 1700s, as the United States started to shift from an agricultural to an industrial economy. Craft guilds or societies, as they were called, were made up of skilled artisans (shoemakers and tailors) who pushed for better working conditions. They resisted shop owners who wanted to lower wages. Many of the early guilds threatened to stop working unless business owners paid higher wages, provided some of the tools needed for work, and shortened the workday. Employers opposed these efforts, often successfully, and the guilds would disband.

In 1869 a small group of clothing workers secretly founded the Noble Order of the Knights of Labor. The **Knights of Labor** was the first major national labor organization. By about 1880 its local assemblies had more than 500,000 members. But it was never very successful at improving the employment situation of working people. Instead, the organization was more concerned with broad social and economic issues such as child labor, public education, and business monopolies.

Knights of Labor

The first important national labor organization in the United States; founded in 1869.

American Federation of Labor

Many of the craft groups within the Knights of Labor were unhappy with its social reform policy and political activities. In 1881 they broke away and formed the Federation of Organized Trades and Labor Unions, which five years later was renamed the **American Federation of Labor (AFL).** Under Samuel Gompers, who was its president for more than 35 years, the AFL dropped the philosophy of the Knights of Labor. In its place, the AFL pressed for better

American Federation of Labor (AFL)

A national labor organization made up of numerous craft unions; founded in 1881 by splinter groups from the Knights of Labor. In 1955, the AFL merged with the Congress of Industrial Organizations (CIO) to form the AFL-CIO.

recognition and more power for member unions, collective bargaining, and the right to conduct temporary work stoppages (*strikes*) to improve wages, hours, and working conditions.

    The AFL consisted of numerous craft unions joined together under the banner of one large labor organization. A **craft union** represents skilled workers in a single craft or occupation, such as bricklaying, carpentry, or plumbing. Each craft union had exclusive jurisdiction over its trade or craft and respected the jurisdictions of other craft unions; that is, each had the right to organize all workers within a single skilled trade or craft. The carpenters' union, for example, represented only carpenters; it did not represent plumbers. Each union also developed its own constitution, chose its own leaders, and formulated its own strategy for collective bargaining.

    Gompers emphasized *business unionism,* a philosophy and approach that encouraged unions to be businesslike in their dealings with employers. The union and company would negotiate and sign a contract, or a written labor agreement, much as two business firms might reach a written purchase or sales contract.

Congress of Industrial Organizations

The AFL was the major force on the labor scene for nearly 50 years. But with the Great Depression of the 1930s came severe unemployment in the building and skilled trades and a loss of power for the AFL. Then, just as the economy began to improve, the AFL faced a crisis. Mass-production workers wanted to be represented by unions, but the craft unions thought the factory workers would jeopardize the high labor standards that had been gained through collective bargaining and did not want to represent them.

    Under the leadership of John L. Lewis, the United Mine Workers (UMW) of America challenged the AFL's position. For several decades the UMW had been a member of the AFL. But it had developed as a mining industry union, containing both skilled and unskilled workers. Thus, it went against the AFL's doctrine of exclusive jurisdiction based on craft. Lewis argued that a union organized along industry lines would be better than a craft union for representing workers in large-scale, mass-production industries. Each industry could have its own union. Under the leadership of Lewis, Sidney Hillman, and Walter Ruether, industry-wide union membership drives began in the automobile, steel, tire, and oil industries. In each case a different **industrial union** was formed under the slogan "one industry, one union."

    In 1935 Lewis took his union and a handful of others and left the AFL. They formed the **Congress of Industrial Organizations (CIO).** As a collection of industrial unions, the CIO succeeded in organizing unions in the mass-production industries of food processing, electrical equipment manufacturing, auto assembly, and oil refining. After a brief period, the AFL counterattacked and also recruited thousands of industrial workers to its ranks.

The AFL and CIO: Rivalry and Merger

Until the early 1950s, the AFL and the CIO competed for new members and frequently attempted to steal each other's members. Unfortunately, some workers got caught in the crossfire. These efforts cost both organizations a lot of money and produced few membership gains overall. Finally, the two decided to end their rivalry. On December 5, 1955, the AFL and CIO merged into one organization with

craft union

A union that represents skilled workers in a single craft or occupation such as bricklaying, carpentry, or plumbing.

industrial union

A union that represents all of the workers in a particular industry, such as auto workers or steel workers.

Congress of Industrial Organizations (CIO)

A national labor organization made up of numerous industrial unions; founded in 1935. In 1955, the CIO merged with the American Federation of Labor (AFL) to form the AFL-CIO.

Industrial unions were formed in the mid-1930s to represent workers in mass-production industries. They organized factory workers like the automotive employees shown here in 1937 protesting work conditions at General Motor's assembly plant in Flint, Michigan.

What diverse types of unions are affiliated with the AFL-CIO today? Find out at this AFL-CIO site:

www.aflcio.org/unionand/unions.htm

George Meany as its president. The combined AFL-CIO spoke for more than 16 million workers.

Today, the AFL-CIO is an umbrella organization for most American labor unions. It represents about 80 unions and approximately 85 percent of all rank-and-file union members—those who are not elected officials of the union. The AFL-CIO provides research, education, legal, and public relations services to member unions. It does not take part in collective bargaining. It does sponsor and coordinate union membership and organizes drives. Lobbying and political involvement are also prominent activities. John Sweeny, president of the AFL-CIO, pledged to spend $40 million on the 2000 elections for voter registration drives, television ads, newsletters, and telephone banks primarily in support of Democratic candidates.[2]

The Labor Movement Today

In 1945, the high-water mark for the U.S. labor movement, union members accounted for 35.5 percent of all employed Americans. Today, that share stands at about 15 percent, or 19,217,000 workers. This total includes about 2.5 million professional employees who belong to employee associations, such as the National Education Association, an organization of public school teachers. The general trend of union membership during the last quarter of the 20th century was one of decline. As indicated in Exhibit 11-1, membership in traditional unions since the merger of the AFL and the CIO in 1955 peaked at about 20,250,000 in the late 1970s and dropped to about 16,400,000 by the turn of the century. The decline would have been sharper had unions in service industries (hospitals and food service) and in the public sector (postal, state, county, and municipal) not experienced significant growth in the 1980s and 1990s.

Today, a labor union may represent an industry or a skilled trade or a geographic area. There are still craft unions (often found in the building trades) and industrial unions (such as the United Auto Workers and the United Steelworkers of America). A more recent type is the **conglomerate union,** which represents a wide variety of workers and industries. For instance, the Teamsters Union represents not only truck drivers but also nurses, teachers, police officers, sanitation engineers, firefighters, secretaries, and flight attendants.

The basic structure of the modern labor movement consists of three parts: local unions, national and international unions, and the AFL-CIO, as described earlier. There are approximately 60,000 local unions and 80 national and international unions.

Local Unions   A **local union** is a branch or unit of a national union that represents workers at a specific plant or over a specific geographic area. Local 276 of the United Auto Workers represents assembly employees at the General Motors plant in Arlington, Texas. In conformance to national union rules, local unions determine the number of local union officers, procedures for electing officers, the schedule of local meetings, financial arrangements with the national organization, and the local's role in negotiating labor agreements.

The three main functions of the local union are collective bargaining, worker relations and membership services, and community and political activities. Collective bargaining takes place every two or three years. Local union officers and shop stewards in the plant oversee worker-management relations on a day-to-day basis. A **shop steward** is an elected union official who represents union

conglomerate union

A union that represents a wide variety of workers in various industries.

local union

A branch or unit of a national union that represents workers at a specific plant or in a specific geographic area.

shop steward

An elected union official who represents union members to management when workers have complaints.

Union Membership Trends, 1955–2000

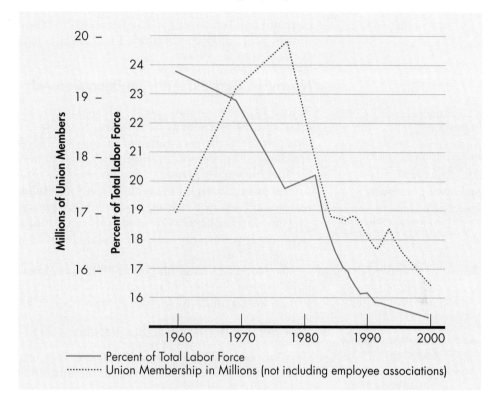

— Percent of Total Labor Force
············ Union Membership in Millions (not including employee associations)

SOURCE: Bureau of Labor Statistics, Washington, D.C.: U.S. Department of Labor.

members to management when workers have complaints. Union issues are discussed at monthly meetings. Financial and other reports are given, officers are elected, committee appointments are announced, and special events are planned. Members may also get a union newsletter and other information from the national union at these meetings.

national union

A union that consists of many local unions in a particular industry, skilled trade, or geographic area and thus represents workers throughout an entire country.

National and International Unions   **National unions** range in size from a few thousand members (Screen Writers Guild) to more than a million members (Teamsters with 1.4 million). National unions that have locals and members in Canada, like the United Auto Workers and the United Steelworkers, are frequently described as international unions; American unions represent workers only on the North American continent, however, and do not extend overseas.

The number of national unions has steadily declined since the early 20th century. Much of this decline has resulted from union mergers. Early in 1999, for example, the United Papermakers International Union (UPIU) and the Oil, Chemical and Atomic Workers Union (OCAW) agreed to merge under the new name of PACE, or Paper, Allied-Industrial, Chemical and Energy International Union. PACE has 320,000 members and has set an aggressive growth goal of adding 10,000 new members a year, according to Robert Wages, executive vice-president of the new organization.[3] The Service Employees International Union (SEIU) added 124,000 members in May 1998 when it merged with the local National Health and Human Service Employees Union.[4]

c o n c ə p t c h ə c k

• Trace the development of the labor movement in the United States.
• What is the AFL-CIO, and how does it operate?
• What are the functions of a local union?
• What is the trend in union membership?

THE LEGAL ENVIRONMENT OF UNIONS

>lg 2
Although today unions and employers nearly always resolve their differences without disruptions, union-management relations have not always been so peaceful and businesslike. The respectful relationship that now exists between unions and employers has resulted, in part, from laws passed from the early 1930s to the late 1950s.

Norris–La Guardia Act (Anti-Injunction Act)

Before 1932, a company faced with striking or picketing workers could get the courts to order them back to work. It did so by requesting an **injunction,** a court order barring certain union activities. Only rarely did a judge deny the employer's request for an injunction. Union members who didn't obey could be fined or sent to prison.

Employers also used the courts to enforce **yellow-dog contracts,** in which employees agreed not to join a labor union as a condition of being hired. Employees who broke a yellow-dog contract could be fired. Blacklists of workers who were involved with unions circulated among employers to keep the workers from being hired.

The **Norris–La Guardia Act** of 1932 (also known as the Anti-Injunction Act) largely ended the use of injunctions by employers. It banned their use to prevent strikes, among other things. The act also made yellow-dog contracts unenforceable.

Wagner Act (National Labor Relations Act)

The Norris–La Guardia Act opened the door to more union organizing, especially in mass-production industries. But employers were still not obliged to bargain with unions. The unions urged Congress to pass a law that would require employers to deal with them.

Congress responded with the National Labor Relations Act of 1935, commonly known as the **Wagner Act.** This law encouraged the formation of unions and the use of collective bargaining. It also provided a means for peacefully resolving disputes over union representation. The cornerstone of this important act is in Section 7:

> Employees shall have the right to self-organization, to form, join, or assist labor organizations, to bargain collectively through representatives of their own choosing, and to engage in other concerted activities for the purpose of collective bargaining or other mutual aid or protection.

In addition to making it illegal for an employer to refuse to bargain with a union about wages, hours, and other job conditions, the Wagner Act also protected workers from unfair labor practices. For instance, an employer cannot discriminate against (or treat unfairly) an employee who is involved in union activities. Nor can an employer fire an employee for joining a union.

The **National Labor Relations Board (NLRB)** was established to enforce the Wagner Act. Its five members are appointed by the president; the agency's main office is in Washington, D.C., and regional and field offices are scattered throughout the United States. NLRB field agents investigate charges of employer and union wrongdoing (or unfair labor practices) and supervise elections held to decide union representation. Administrative law judges conduct hearings to determine whether employers and unions have violated the law. In 1998 the NLRB allowed unfair labor practice charges and election petitions to be made on its Web site.[5]

injunction

A court order barring certain union activities.

yellow-dog contracts

Contracts in which employees agreed not to join a labor union as a condition of being hired.

Norris–La Guardia Act

A statute enacted in 1932 that barred the use of injunctions to prevent strikes and other union activities and made yellow-dog contracts unenforceable; also called the *Anti-Injunction Act.*

Wagner Act

A statute enacted in 1935 that established that employees have a right to organize and join labor unions and to engage in collective bargaining; also known as the *National Labor Relations Act.*

National Labor Relations Board (NLRB)

An agency established by the Wagner Act of 1935 to enforce the act and investigate charges of employer and union wrongdoing and supervise elections for union representatives.

At the NLRB Web site, **www.nlrb.gov,** you'll learn about the agency's many activities and how it protects workers' rights.

Taft-Hartley Act (Labor-Management Relations Act)

Taft-Hartley Act

A statute enacted in 1947 that defined unfair union practices, outlined the rules for dealing with strikes of major economic impact, broadened employer options for dealing with unions, and further defined the rights of employees as individuals.

Employers resisted the Wagner Act and in some cases disobeyed it, until the Supreme Court upheld the law in 1937. Many employers saw the Wagner Act as too pro-labor. In 1947 Congress amended it with the Labor-Management Relations Act, commonly known as the **Taft- Hartley Act.** This act:

- Defined unfair union practices.
- Outlined the rules for dealing with strikes of major economic impact.
- Broadened employer options for dealing with unions.
- Further defined the rights of employees as individuals.

Among the unfair union practices banned by the Taft-Hartley Act were excessive or discriminatory fees and dues. (For example, monthly dues of $200 would be too much for a union member who earns only $2,000 per month.) Also, the act made it unlawful for picketing union members to block nonstriking employees from entering the business to go to work.

Emergency Strike Procedures   Immediately after World War II, union strike activity increased dramatically. Lengthy strikes disrupted business, and many firms and citizens suffered. In response, Congress included national emergency strike procedures in the Taft-Hartley Act. Under these provisions, the president can declare a national emergency if a strike threatens the health and safety of Americans. The President can temporarily stop the strike by having a federal judge issue an injunction. The injunction forces the strikers back to work for up to 80 days (known as the *cooling-off period*) while the employer and labor negotiators try to resolve their differences. If they don't reach an agreement within 80 days, the strike can resume. The president cannot issue a second injunction.

conciliation

A method of attempting to settle labor disputes in which a specialist from the Federal Mediation and Conciliation Service helps management and the union focus on the issues and acts as a go-between.

mediation

A method of attempting to settle labor disputes in which a specialist from the Federal Mediation and Conciliation Service serves as a mediator.

Federal Mediation and Conciliation Service   Congress also created the Federal Mediation and Conciliation Service as part of the Taft-Hartley Act. This service helps unions and employers negotiate labor agreements. Agency specialists, who serve as impartial third parties between the union and the employer, use two processes: conciliation and mediation. In **conciliation,** the specialist helps management and the union focus on the issues and acts as a go-between.

The specialist takes a stronger role in **mediation,** a process of settling disputes in which the parties present their case to a neutral mediator. The mediator (the specialist) holds talks with union and management negotiators at separate meetings and at joint sessions. The mediator also suggests compromises. Mediators cannot issue binding decisions. Their only tools are communication and persuasion. Mediation almost always produces a settlement between the union and a firm, but sometimes the process takes months or even a year. As an example, a mediator tried for more than eight months to settle a strike between Local 850 of the United Steelworkers Union and Continental General Tire that started in September 1998. As of late February 1999, the strike was still in progress, but the firm continued operations by hiring 700 permanent strike replacements.[6]

Landrum-Griffin Act (Labor-Management Reporting and Disclosure Act)

Landrum-Griffin Act

A statute enacted in 1959 to regulate the internal affairs of unions; contains a bill of rights for union members, rules for electing union officers, and safeguards to keep unions financially sound.

Shortly after the merger of the AFL and the CIO in 1955, some national unions including the Teamsters and Bakery Workers were accused of poor financial management, rigged elections for officers, and bribery of union officials. After an investigation, Congress passed the Labor-Management Reporting and Disclosure Act of 1959, often called the **Landrum-Griffin Act.** Unlike the Wagner and Taft-Hartley Acts, this law deals mostly with the internal affairs of labor unions. It contains a bill of rights for union members, a set of rules for electing union officers, and safeguards to help make unions financially sound. It also requires that unions file detailed annual financial reports with the U.S. secretary of labor. The Department of Labor enforces the Landrum-Griffin Act.

In the late 1990s, the Departments of Labor and Justice, under the Landrum-Griffin Act, were pursuing internal union reforms aimed at ridding the Laborers' International Union of corrupt influences and association with organized crime. Supervision of the election of union officers in 2001 was turned over to the Justice Department.[7] The Laborers' International is one of the nation's largest unions with 600 locals and over 700,000 members.

UNION ORGANIZING

>lg 3

Unions can be formed or gain new members in two ways:
1. A unionized employer hires more workers, who choose, or are required, to join the union.
2. The employees of a nonunion employer form or join a union.

> m a k i n g   e t h i c a l   c h o i c e s <

TRYING TO ORGANIZE IMMIGRANT WORKERS

Organized labor is working vigorously to reverse a 30-year decline in power and membership. Like other unions, the Teamsters are focusing on organizing immigrants as one way of reversing this decline.

Doug Martin, a union organizer for Teamsters Local 174 in Seattle and Tacoma, Washington, faces some interesting challenges in his work on the Teamsters' campaign to unionize owner-operators in the trucking business in the area. These truckers mostly "haul containers between ship lines and rail lines or warehouses for the freight companies." On average, the truckers earn about $40 per short-haul round trip, with two or three trips daily and more during peak periods. Although their trucks are leased to the freight companies, all of the truckers' operating expenses are out-of-pocket costs.

Many of the short-haul truckers that Martin is trying to persuade to join the Teamsters union are immigrants. They include Mexicans, Hungarians, Eritreans from East Africa, East Indians, and Poles, but a substantial proportion are Russian immigrants.

Martin's union organizing efforts meet with failure and frustration more often than with success. Many of the Russian truckers in Seattle are reluctant to join be-

cause they associate unions with the Communist government of the former Soviet Union. Additionally, many of the Russians are devout Pentecostal Christians who worry that membership in other organizations will conflict with their church.

Immigrant truckers are difficult to organize for other reasons as well. Some are fearful of alienating the owners of the freight companies. Others do not want to be viewed as troublemakers. Some believe that unions will not really help them—that unions are biased in favor of Americans. Some of the Russian truckers also think that "unions are for lazy people."

Critical Thinking Questions

1. What fundamental ethical issue does Doug Martin face in trying to organize the immigrant truckers?
2. What basic ethical issue do the immigrant truckers face?
3. Should cultural differences be considered in evaluating whether actions are fair and just?

A nonunion employer becomes unionized through an *organizing campaign*. The campaign is started either from within, by unhappy employees, or from outside, by a union that has picked the employer for an organizing drive. Once workers and the union have made contact, a union organizer tries to convince all the workers to sign *authorization cards*. These cards prove the workers' interest in having the union represent them. In most cases, employers resist this card-signing campaign by speaking out against unions in letters, posters, and employee assemblies. However, it is illegal for employers to interfere directly with the card-signing campaign or to coerce employees into not joining the union.

Once the union gets signed authorization cards from at least 30 percent of the employees, it can ask the National Labor Relations Board for a **union certification election.** This election, by secret ballot, determines whether the workers want to be represented by the union. The NLRB posts an election notice and defines the **bargaining unit**—employees who are eligible to vote and who will be represented by the particular union if it is certified. Supervisors and managers cannot vote. The union and the employer than engage in a preelection campaign conducted through speeches, memos, and meetings. Both try to convince

union certification election

An election in which workers vote, by secret ballot, on whether they want to be represented by a union; conducted by the National Labor Relations Board.

bargaining unit

The employees who are eligible to vote in a union certification election and who will be represented by the union if it is certified.

> f o c u s i n g   o n   s m a l l   b u s i n e s s <

UNION OR NO UNION?

Late Friday afternoon, Hudson Gray, a 32-year-old entrepreneur who owned a building maintenance and cleaning business with 78 employees, was contemplating next Thursday's NLRB representation election. For nearly six weeks he had carefully followed the advice of Tom Parker, a labor relations consultant, concerning the union organizing and representation election campaign. For the last week Gray's job-site supervisors and general manager had been telling him that only about one-third of the employees seemed to favor the union. Though he was confident of winning the election, Gray knew he couldn't take the situation for granted. He had aggressively campaigned against the union, but had done so within the law; no unfair labor practice charges had been filed against him.

Now Gray had to decide how to end the campaign next week. He had three basic options. He could continue his hard-charging campaign with the posters, brochures, and employee letters Tom Parker had helped to draft. The centerpiece of these materials was a booklet in which Gray posed various questions about the union, including such things as union dues, its strike

record, and its willingness to represent part-time employees. As a second option, he could back off and instruct his supervisors to respond only to employee questions. As a third option, he could prepare to give a pre-election speech to the employees on Tuesday afternoon. If he did, he would talk for 20 to 30 minutes about how the close working relationships that he and his management team had achieved with the employees had contributed to the firm's success. A union could jeopardize these relationships.

Critical Thinking Questions

1. If Gray decides to give a speech, what points should he make?
2. Assume the company wins the election (a majority of the workers vote "no union"). What can Gray do over the next several months to prevent the same union or another one from trying to organize his workforce?
3. If the union wins, how might Gray's business change?

Benefits Stressed by Unions in Organizing Campaigns

Almost Always Stressed	Often Stressed	Seldom Stressed
Grievance procedures	More influence in decision making	Higher-quality products
Job security		Technical training
Improved benefits	Better working conditions	More job satisfaction
Higher pay	Lobbying opportunities	Increased production

workers to vote in their favor. Exhibit 11-2 lists the benefits usually stressed by the union during a campaign. See the Focusing on Small Business box for an example of how a small business owner might deal with a union organizing campaign.

Sometimes two unions compete for the same group of workers. In 1999 the Teamsters Union and the United Auto Workers Union were both organizing workers at the Coors brewery in Golden, Colorado, the largest single brewery plant in the world. More than 1,400 workers in the brewery and approximately 800 employees at an adjacent bottle and can plant were combined into one bargaining unit by the NLRB.[8]

The election itself is conducted by the NLRB. If a majority vote for the union, the NLRB certifies the union as the exclusive bargaining agent for all employees who had been designated as eligible voters. The employer then has to bargain with the union over wages, hours, and other terms of employment. The complete organizing process is summarized in Exhibit 11-3. In August 1995 the United Steelworkers Union won an election at Magnetic Specialty, Inc. by a vote of 65 to 33. In March 1997 the union called a strike to force the company to recognize the union and bargain. The NLRB ordered the firm to bargain. The AFL-CIO had assisted the union with rallies, marches, and demonstrations urging the company to negotiate.[9]

In some situations, after one year, if the union and employer don't reach an agreement, the workers petition for a **decertification election,** which is similar to the certification election, but allows workers to vote out the union. Decertification elections are also held when workers become dissatisfied with a union that has represented them for a longer time. In the 1990s, the number of decertification elections increased to several hundred per year.

decertification election

An election in which workers vote, by secret ballot, on whether they want to continue to be represented by their union.

c o n c ə p t   c h ə c k

- Describe the union organizing process.
- What is a union certification election?
- How is the NLRB involved in union organizing campaigns and representation elections?

NEGOTIATING UNION CONTRACTS

>lg 4

A union contract is created through collective bargaining. Typically, both management and union negotiating teams are made up of a few persons. One person on each side is the chief spokesperson.

Bargaining begins with union and management negotiators setting a *bargaining agenda,* a list of contract issues that will be discussed. Much of the bargaining over the specific details takes place through face-to-face meetings and the exchange of written proposals. Demands, proposals, and counterproposals are exchanged during several rounds of bargaining. The resulting contract

Union Organizing Process and Election

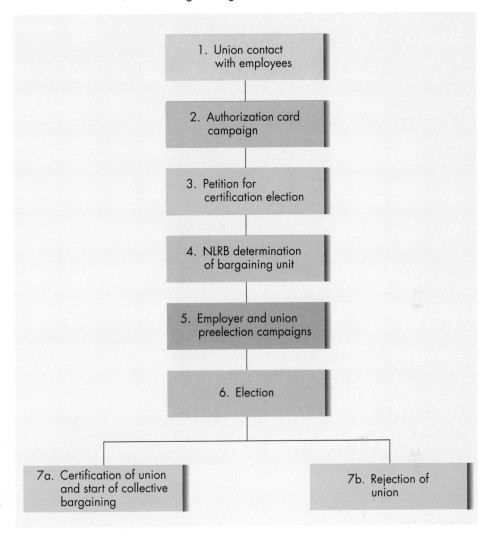

1. Union contact with employees

2. Authorization card campaign

3. Petition for certification election

4. NLRB determination of bargaining unit

5. Employer and union preelection campaigns

6. Election

7a. Certification of union and start of collective bargaining

7b. Rejection of union

The lead negotiators representing the employer and the union during collective bargaining shake hands after agreeing on a contract that must be approved by top management and union members.

must then be approved by top management and by union members. The collective bargaining process is shown in Exhibit 11-4.

Early in 1999 a local union of the United Food and Commercial Workers (UFCW) finalized a 54-month master contract with five New Jersey food chains (Grand Union, Pathmark, Food Town, Shop Rite, and Edwards). Five separate but essentially identical contracts covering 8,000 workers at 325 stores were signed. Almost 97 percent of the workers approved, or ratified, the contracts according to John Niccollai, national union president.[10]

The contract negotiated by the union and the employer may range from a few pages to as many as 500. It is a legally binding agreement that typically covers such issues as union security, management rights, wages, job benefits, and job security. Each of these is discussed in this section.

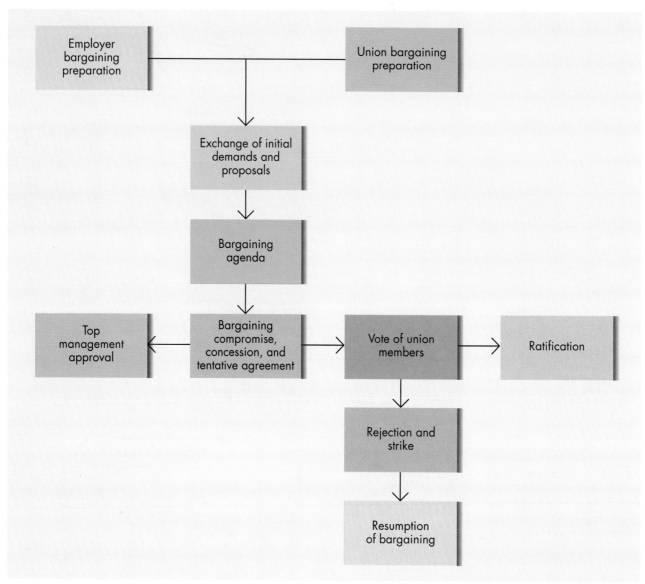

closed shop

A company where only union members can be hired; made illegal by the Taft-Hartley Act.

union shop

A company where nonunion workers can be hired but must then join the union.

agency shop

A company where employees are not required to join the union but must pay it a fee to cover its expenses in representing them.

Union Security

One of the key issues in a contract is union security. From the union's perspective, the most secure arrangement is the **closed shop,** a company where only union members can be hired. The union serves, in effect, as an employment agency for the firm. The Taft-Hartley Act made closed shops illegal, however. Today, the most common form of union security is the **union shop.** Nonunion workers can be hired, but then they must join the union, normally within 30 or 60 days.

An **agency shop** does not require employees to join the union. But to keep working at the company, employees must pay the union a fee to cover its expenses in representing them. The union must fairly represent all workers, including those who do not become members.

States with Right-to-Work Laws

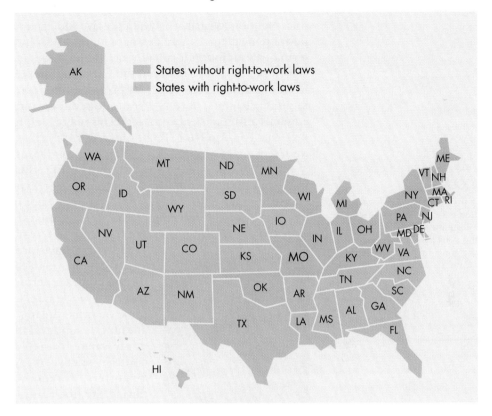

Under the Taft-Hartley Act, any state can make all forms of union security illegal by enacting **right-to-work laws.** In the 21 states that have these laws (see Exhibit 11-5), employees can work at a unionized company without having to join the union. This is commonly known as an **open shop** arrangement. Workers don't have to join the union or pay dues or fees to the union.

Closely related to union security is the *dues checkoff*. When a labor contract includes a dues checkoff clause, the employer deducts union dues from members' paychecks. The funds are sent to the union at the end of each pay period. The automatic checkoff ensures that union dues will be paid on time.

Management Rights

When a company becomes unionized, management loses some of its decision-making abilities. But management still has certain rights that can be negotiated in collective bargaining.

One way to resist union meddling in management matters is to put a *management-rights clause* in the labor agreement. Most union contracts have one. A typical clause gives the employer all rights to manage the business except as specified in the contract. For instance, if the contract does not specify the criteria for promotions, with a management rights clause managers will have the right to use any criteria they wish. Another way to preserve management rights is to list areas that are not subject to collective bargaining. This list might secure management's right to schedule work hours, hire and fire workers, set production standards, determine the number of supervisors in each department, and promote, demote, and transfer workers. These rights, also known as *management prerogatives*, are not governed by any hard and fast rules. They vary from one contract to another.

right-to-work laws

State laws that allow employees to work at a unionized company without having to join the union.

open shop

A company where employees do not have to join the union or pay dues or fees to the union; established under right-to-work laws.

Wages

Much bargaining effort goes into wage increases and improvements in fringe benefits. Once agreed to, they remain in effect for the life of the contract. In the contract mentioned earlier between the five supermarket chains and the UFCW, journeymen meatcutters' weekly wages increased from $800 to $894 over the contract term of about four and a half years.[11] The three-year contract (January 6, 1999 to December 31, 2001) between the SEIU and the Realty Advisory Board on Labor Relations, Inc. in New York City provided for 3 percent annual wage increases for building cleaners, porters, elevator operators, and handypersons.[12] Exhibit 11-6 contains a summary of contract terms negotiated by many employers and unions in 1999. The Applying Technology box describes a situation in which workers were seeking more control over working conditions as well as higher wages.

cost-of-living adjustment (COLA)

A provision in a labor contract that calls for wages to increase automatically as the cost of living rises (usually measured by the consumer price index).

Some contracts provide for a **cost-of-living adjustment (COLA),** under which wages increase automatically as the cost of living goes up. A typical COLA clause might call for a wage increase of one cent per hour for each two-fifths of a point rise in the consumer price index. Often the adjustments are made only after the cost of living rises a certain amount, typically 4 percent in a year.

Visit the Social Security Administration site to track the latest cost-of-living adjustment at
www.ssa.gov/OACT/COLA/latestCOLA.html

Other contracts provide for *lump-sum wage adjustments.* The workers' base pay remains unchanged for the contract period (usually two or three years), but each worker receives a bonus (or lump sum) once or twice during the contract. The lump-sum amount depends on the profitability of the firm and might range from $200 to $2,000. Under the 1998 contract between Airborne Express and the Teamsters, workers received a lump sum of $750 during the first contract year along with a $1.40 per hour increase over five years.[13]

The union and the employer are usually both concerned about the firm's ability to pay higher wages. The firm's ability to pay depends greatly on

> e x h i b i t   1 1 - 6 <

Summary of Labor Agreement Provisions for 1999

- Modest pay hikes of 2.0 to 3.9 percent annually.
- Three-year contracts.
- Incentive and variable-pay systems, including profit sharing, in one-third of contracts.
- Pay for performance and training or skill-based pay in many contracts.
- Increase in 401k and defined contribution retirement plans but traditional defined benefit plans still included in 80 percent of agreements.
- Continued emphasis on job security with layoff protection and recall rights and increased severance pay arrangements.
- Additional focus on rising health care costs through cost containment and employee cost sharing of insurance premiums.
- In many contracts, special training programs aimed at employee diversity, drug and alcohol rehabilitation, sexual harassment, and absenteeism control.

SOURCE: *Daily Labor Report* (December 21, 1998).

PILOTS AND FEDEX NEGOTIATE THEIR FIRST CONTRACT

Federal Express, one of the nation's largest employers and one of the world's largest transportation companies, specializes in moving letters and packages for overnight delivery. Fred Smith founded the company in 1973 and continues to be its CEO. Except for its 3,500 pilots, FedEx is a nonunion firm. The pilots have attempted unionization several times, but they didn't become sufficiently organized for collective bargaining purposes until the late 1990s. In 1998, in the midst of negotiating its first labor agreement with the pilots, FedEx introduced The Optimizer, a high-tech plane scheduling and routing system aimed at increasing pilot and system productivity.

Unfortunately, The Optimizer changed pilot schedules and routes, particularly for less senior pilots, much more significantly than the firm anticipated. Hundreds of pilots complained, and antagonism to The Optimizer galvanized the 3,500 pilots into a cohesive group for the first time. FedEx had never experienced a strike but in mid-October 1998, it faced the prospect of one. As

it turned out, however, the pilots accepted a tentative agreement, and the strike was averted.

In early February 1999, the pilots approved their first contract by a vote of 2,516 to 395. Under the contract, pilot pay will increase 17 percent over five years, and pension benefits will increase from 41 percent of the pilot's final year's pay to 72.5 percent. Pilots were also given a greater say in schedules and routes, and a special union-management committee was created to handle complaints.

Critical Thinking Questions

1. Do you think it was wise for FedEx to introduce a major change (The Optimizer) in pilot aircraft assignments and flight schedules when trying to negotiate its first labor agreement?
2. Should airline pilots be permitted to strike?
3. If FedEx pilots went out on strike, could the firm easily replace them with nonunion pilots?

---

its profitability. But even if profits have declined, average to above-average wage increases are still possible if labor productivity increases. For 1998 and 1999, the productivity of the American economy as a whole increased about 3.5 percent each year. Negotiated wage increases for those years averaged slightly less than 3 percent each year.

Benefits

In addition to requests for wage increases, unions usually want better fringe benefits. In some industries, such as steel and auto manufacturing, fringe benefits are 40 percent of the total cost of compensation. Benefits may include higher wages for overtime work, holiday work, and less desirable shifts; insurance programs (life, health and hospitalization, dental care); payment for certain nonwork time (rest periods, vacations, holidays, sick time); pensions; and income-maintenance plans. A fairly common income-maintenance plan is a *supplementary unemployment benefits fund* set up by the employer to help laid-off workers.

Before the mid-1980s, unions gradually extended the list of benefits. But because of poor economic conditions, major technological changes, government deregulation, and increased competition, many unions then found themselves in a weaker bargaining position and lost some of the benefits they had won earlier. Lost benefits are known as **give-backs,** or *concession bargaining.* Give-backs

give-backs

Benefits given up by a union; also called *concession bargaining.*

were most common in the auto, airline, steel, mining, and construction industries. As economic conditions improved in the late 1990s, many unions pushed to reinstate some of the lost benefits. In the 54-month contract between the UFCW and the New Jersey food chains, pension benefits were increased from $1,350 to $1,925 per month for those with 35 years of service to make up for earlier years when pension benefits had been cut.

Job Security and Seniority

Cost-of-living adjustments, supplementary unemployment benefits, and certain other benefits give employees some financial security. But most financial security is directly related to job security—the assurance, to some degree, that workers will keep their jobs. Of course, job security depends primarily on the continued success and financial well-being of the company.

Seniority, the length of an employee's continuous service with a firm, is discussed in about 90 percent of all labor contracts. Seniority is a factor in job security; usually, unions want the workers with the most seniority to have the most job security. Seniority also serves other purposes in collective bargaining. One is to determine an employee's eligibility for vacations. It is also important in calculating severance pay (additional pay given to employees who leave the company) and pension benefits. Seniority in these areas is called *benefit rights*. Seniority is also used to determine job assignments. Under *competitive status seniority*, people with job rights seniority have first choice of higher-paying jobs, the preferred shift, overtime work, and job transfers.

concept check

- Explain the collective bargaining process.
- What do unions want from collective bargaining?
- What are management rights?
- What are the different forms of seniority, and why is it important to employees?

GRIEVANCE AND ARBITRATION

>lg 5

grievance

A formal complaint, filed by an employee or by the union, charging that management has violated the contract.

The union's main way of policing the contract is the grievance procedure. A **grievance** is a formal complaint, by an employee or by the union, that management has violated some part of the contract. Under a typical contract, the employee starts by presenting the grievance to the supervisor, either in person or in writing. The typical grievance procedure is illustrated in Exhibit 11-7. A shop steward may be at the meeting or may just get a copy of the grievance.

If the problem isn't solved, the grievance is put in writing (if it hasn't been already). The employee, one or more union officials, the supervisor, and perhaps the plant manager then discuss the grievance. If the matter still can't be resolved, another meeting takes place with higher-level representatives of both parties present. If top management and the local union president can't resolve the grievance, it goes to arbitration.

arbitration

The process of settling a labor-management dispute by having a third party—a single arbitrator or a panel—make a decision, which is binding on both the union and the employer.

Arbitration is the process of settling a labor-management dispute by having a third party—a single arbitrator or a panel—make a decision. The decision is final and binding on the union and the employer. The arbitrator reviews the grievance at a hearing and then makes the decision, which is presented in a document called the *award*. The decision is not reviewable by the courts, but once in a great while, an appeal is made. For example, when the Norfolk and Western Railway Co. fired David Lyons for failing to produce a urine sample for a random drug test, Lyons protested by filing a grievance. An arbitrator upheld the company's action. Lyons appealed, but the court affirmed the arbitrator's award even though aspects of the drug test were improper.[14]

Sometimes a case rests on whether the grievance steps shown in Exhibit 11-7 are carried out in a timely manner. In a widely publicized case involving 28 Chicago firefighters, arbitrator Edwin Benn ruled that the fire department's at-

> e x h i b i t   1 1 - 7 <

Typical Grievance Procedure

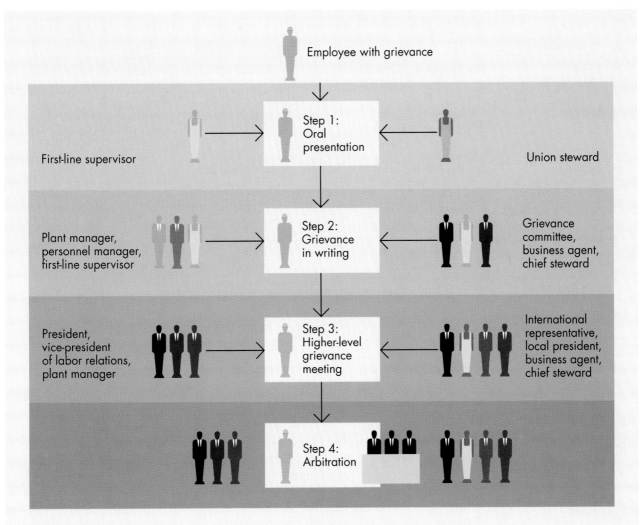

Employee with grievance

First-line supervisor → Step 1: Oral presentation ← Union steward

Plant manager, personnel manager, first-line supervisor → Step 2: Grievance in writing ← Grievance committee, business agent, chief steward

President, vice-president of labor relations, plant manager → Step 3: Higher-level grievance meeting ← International representative, local president, business agent, chief steward

Step 4: Arbitration

concept check

- Describe the grievance procedure.
- Explain the arbitration process.
- In what ways do arbitrators act like judges?

tempt to discipline the firefighters was untimely. The firefighters had participated in a station house party where alcoholic beverages were consumed before going on fire calls. Unfortunately for the firefighters, the party had been videotaped, but the tape wasn't revealed until seven years after the incident. Additionally, after getting the tape the internal affairs division of the fire department waited more than six months to launch its investigation. The arbitrator ruled that the six-month delay was not timely under contract provisions.[15]

MANAGING LABOR-MANAGEMENT CONFLICT

>lg 6   Both sides to labor-management conflicts have powerful tools for exerting economic (or financial) pressure. Unions can fight with strikes, product boycotts, picketing, and corporate campaigns. Employers can fight with lockouts, strike replacements, and mutual-aid pacts and can also shift production to nonunion plants or out of the country. Exhibit 11-8 lists the methods used by both sides.

Strategies of Unions and Employers

Union Strategies		Employer Strategies	
• **Strike:**	Employees refuse to work.	• **Lockout:**	Employer refuses to let employees enter plant to work.
• **Boycott:**	Employees try to keep customers and others from doing business with employer.	• **Strike replacements:**	Employer uses nonunion employees to do jobs of striking union employees.
• **Picketing:**	Employees march near entrance of firm to publicize their view of dispute and discourage customers.	• **Mutual-aid pact:**	Employer receives money from other companies in industry to cover some of income lost because of strikes.
• **Corporate campaign:**	Union disrupts stockholder meetings or buys company stock to have more influence over management.	• **Shift production:**	Employer moves production to nonunion plant or out of country.

wildcat strike

A strike by a group of union members or an entire local union without the approval of the national union while the contract is still in effect.

selective strike strategy

A union strategy of conducting a strike at (shutting down) a critical plant that supplies parts to other plants.

The union strategy of the sick-out used by American Airlines pilots represented by the Allied Pilot Association resulted in angry customers, overworked employees who had to find alternate flights for passengers, and a $100 million loss in revenues for the airline.

Union Strategies

The strike is the most powerful union tool, but it is usually the means of last resort. Although a strike may hurt the employer, it also means loss of pay to employees. On the average, fewer than 2 percent of U.S. workers are involved in strikes each year. And with few exceptions, strikes tend to last under a month. However, strikes by the United Auto Workers at Caterpillar in 1982 and 1992 lasted many months each time.

Strikes occur most often over economic issues such as wages, pensions, vacation time, and other benefits. A strike normally starts immediately after the old union contract has expired, if management and labor can't agree on new contract terms. Sometimes a group of union members or an entire local union will strike without the approval of the national union, while the contract is still in effect. This action, which is often illegal because it violates the contract, is called a **wildcat strike.**

Another union strike strategy is to shut down (strike) a critical plant that supplies parts to other plants. Because the other plants don't receive parts from the struck plant, the firm has to curtail production and loses sales. The United Auto Workers used this **selective strike strategy** in the summer of 1998 against the General Motors stamping and parts facility in Flint, Michigan. The 54-day strike at one plant caused the company to stop production at virtually all of its assembly plants because critical parts were not available. GM lost approximately $2.2 billion during this dispute. From 1992 to early 1999, GM endured 22 strikes, losing 286 days of production, worth about $4 billion.[16]

A different form of refusal to work is the **sick-out,** which occurs when a group of employ-

sick-out

A union strategy in which a group of employees claim they cannot work because of illness, thereby disrupting the company.

picketing

Union members parade in front of the employer's plant carrying signs and trying to persuade nonstriking workers to stop working and customers and suppliers from doing business with the company.

corporate campaign

A union strategy in which a union disrupts a corporation's relations with its shareholders or investors as a means of attacking the company.

lockout

An employer tactic in a labor dispute in which the employer refuses to allow workers to enter a plant or building to work, which means that the workers do not get paid.

The owners of NBA teams used the employer strategy of a lockout during a pay dispute with its unionized basketball players. The NBA players and their union representatives are shown here voicing their demands for better pay during a press conference held before the dispute was settled.

ees claim they can't work because of illness. As the chapter's opening feature described, nearly 30 percent of American Airlines pilots called in sick on different days one week in February 1999. Flight operations were severely disrupted, tens of thousands of customers were inconvenienced and angered, and the company lost more than $100 million.

The tactic most often used by unions is **picketing.** When a union calls a strike, it usually sets up picket lines to advertise the strike and discourage the employer from staying open. Union members parade back and forth in front of the employer's site, carrying signs saying the employer is unfair. The picketers try to persuade nonstriking workers to stop working and other people (customers and suppliers) to stop doing business with the company.

Another union weapon is the consumer and product boycott. If a union has a dispute with a firm that produces a consumer product, it asks its own and other union members to stop purchasing the product. Product sales drop and the company suffers financially. In the 1970s, under the leadership of Cesar Chavez, the United Farm Workers Union in California organized nationwide boycotts of table grapes and lettuce. Lettuce and grape growers lost millions because many customers supported the farm workers. The Textile Workers Union conducted a boycott of J. P. Stevens in the 1980s, but it was not particularly successful because the company's products couldn't be easily identified by consumers who might have been supportive.

Use the LaborNet site at **www.igc.org/igc/labornet/** to find out if any product boycotts are currently in progress.

The **corporate campaign** is a fairly new union strategy. With this strategy, a union may try to disrupt the stockholder meetings of a company it wants to pressure. Sometimes the union buys stock in the company, so it can have more influence. The union may also threaten to withdraw great sums of money from banks that do business with the firm. Unions have recently conducted corporate campaigns against the Diamond Walnut Cooperative, Fisher Scientific, Hood Furniture Co., and the Frontier Hotel (Las Vegas).

Employer Strategies

Employers have their own strategies in labor disputes. One of the most effective is the **lockout,** in which the company refuses to let workers enter a plant or building to work. If the workers can't perform their jobs, they don't get paid. Also, management can hire temporary workers during a lockout. Sometimes, however, a lockout can benefit the union. Overhead costs (costs for lease payments, insurance premiums, and management salaries) continue whether a plant is open or closed, putting pressure on management to end the lockout. One of the most widely publicized lockouts took place from August 1998 to early January 1999. NBA team owners locked out their players over player compensation issues. After six months and the cancellation of nearly 1,000 professional basketball games, NBA Commissioner David Stern and Billy Hunter, executive director of the

strike replacements

Nonunion employees hired to replace striking union members; also known as *scabs*.

mutual-aid pact

An agreement by companies in an industry to create a fund that can be used to help cover fixed costs of any member company whose workers go on strike.

union busting

The process by which a company avoids unionization by moving to another region of the country or shifting operations offshore.

c o n c e p t   c h e c k

- What strategies can unions use against employers in labor conflicts?
- What strategies does management have?
- Whose strategies seem to be the strongest and most effective?

players' union, reached a contract settlement. An abbreviated 50-game schedule started in February 1999. Although both parties lost (the players lost several months of salary, and the teams lost ticket and TV revenues), the owners were considered to have won the dispute.[17]

Strike replacements (or "scabs") are nonunion employees hired to replace striking union members. If suitable replacements can be found, the company can stay open and keep making sales and earning profits. The problem with strike replacements is finding qualified people. Major league baseball teams were ready to field minor league players in the spring of 1995. Many fans, however, were ready to stay home and not attend the games. A settlement was reached, but some early season games were canceled. In 1995 President Clinton signed an executive order prohibiting the hiring of replacement workers in firms with government contracts. Employers, in general, have strongly disagreed with this action.

Another strategy used by employers in some industries is the **mutual-aid pact.** Companies in the industry pool some of their financial resources in a fund that can be used to help cover fixed costs of any member company whose workers go on strike. These pacts have been used with some success in the airline, tire, and newspaper industries.

Avoiding unionization by moving to another region of the country or shifting operations offshore is another employer option. Union officials refer to this anti-union strategy as **union busting.** Over nearly 20 years Ingersoll-Rand Co. reduced its unionized facilities from 100 percent to 25 percent. It did this by building and buying new plants in open shop states, relocating production from union to nonunion plants, and vigorously opposing union organizing drives.[18]

CAPITALIZING ON TRENDS IN BUSINESS

>lg 7

Several labor-management trends that began during the last years of the 20th century will continue into the next century. Among the most notable is the unions' effort to reverse the decline in their memberships. Shortages of skilled labor in the unionized crafts, particularly construction, will continue to be a problem. Both of these issues are examined here.

Union Organizing and Membership

Most unions saw their memberships decline in the 1980s and 1990s. The greatest losses were experienced by unions that represent significant numbers of manufacturing employees (United Auto Workers, United Steelworkers, Machinists, Communication Workers, and Electrical Workers). Corporate restructuring (mergers, acquisitions, and downsizing), technological changes (automation and industrial robots), and the shifting of manufacturing offshore to countries such as Mexico, China, and Korea reduced manufacturing employment, and therefore union membership dropped. These changes will continue.

In contrast, however, many unions that represent service sector workers increased their memberships in the late 1990s (Service Employees International, United Food and Commercial Workers, Hotel and Restaurant, and State, County and Municipal Workers). In particular, significant union membership gains took place in the health care industry. In 1998, for example, the SEIU unionized 1,400 nurses and 500 professional and scientific personnel at the state hospital and medical school on the campus of the University of Iowa.[19] The SEIU also won the right to represent 2,500 hospital employees at the Columbia/HCA–owned Sunrise Hospital and Medical Center in Las Vegas.[20] The California Nurses Association won a representation election at Good Samaritan Hospital in Los Angeles that netted over 500 new members.[21] The United Steelworkers Union gained representational rights for 3,500 University of Toronto administrative and technical employees.[22]

The unions' efforts to maintain or increase membership are also apparent in labor contracts. With low unemployment and very good economic conditions during most of the 1990s, unions are becoming more aggressive in pushing for larger annual wage increases and for more job security. During the late 1990s, the wage terms of labor agreements showed modest annual gains (2 to 3 percent), but larger demands are likely if the economy remains strong.

Despite the booming economy, nearly 700,000 workers, many of them union members, were laid off in the 1990s, largely as a result of mergers and acquisitions.[23] Consequently, unions are putting more emphasis on job security when negotiating contracts. Unions have also increased their efforts to slow the trend of outsourcing work to nonunion firms; outsourcing is another cause of worker layoffs. Many unions (particularly the United Auto Workers) have negotiated job retraining programs as a way of preserving union jobs.

To reverse the trend of shortages in skilled labor, union and employers need to cooperate to attract more people to skilled trades. Their joint sponsorship of apprenticeship programs in skilled trades such as carpentry shown will help to alleviate the shortage of skilled labor.

Shortages of Skilled Labor

A trend that may become more pronounced as we move further into the 21st century is the developing shortage of skilled workers in nearly all of the construction crafts. Early in 1999, approximately 75 percent of construction firms of all sizes reported shortages of skilled labor.[24] Most of these shortages can be traced to falling enrollments in apprenticeship programs. Many apprenticeship programs in the trades of plumbing, carpentry, painting, sheet metal work, electrical work, and tile laying are sponsored jointly by unions and management. Machinist and millwright craft workers are also in short supply in many manufacturing industries. Enrollments in apprenticeship programs in manufacturing are also declining. Unions and employers of skilled workers will need to cooperate more closely to entice sufficient numbers of young people into apprenticeship programs so that they can become journeymen and eventually master craftsmen.[25]

concept check

• What trends are occurring in union membership?
• Why are shortages of skilled labor developing in some areas, and what can be done to alleviate them?

Applying This Chapter's Topics

APPLYING THIS CHAPTER'S TOPICS

Even though the labor movement has declined in recent years, you are very likely to encounter unions and union members if you work in the airline, railroad, trucking, construction, health care, and various manufacturing indus-

> t r y   i t   n o w !   <

An important activity of the union-management relationship and collective bargaining is negotiating. Whether you pursue a career in labor relations or some other field, you will negotiate in your job. Purchasing agents, sales representatives, and stockbrokers negotiate on a daily basis. To negotiate successfully, you must be prepared. Two aspects of this preparation are (1) identifying items or aspects of a situation that are negotiable and (2) for these items, determining a range of acceptable alternatives or outcomes.

After you graduate from college and have two or three years of work experience, you will probably have several job advancement opportunities either with your current employer or other business organizations. This situation will involve a test of your negotiating skills. Start preparing now. The accompanying table lists some items or considerations you may need to take into account when changing jobs. First, circle the items that you think you will be able to negotiate. Second, for these negotiable items, identify possible outcomes ranging from pessimistic to realistic to optimistic. For example, a pessimistic outcome on a company car might be no car at all, a realistic outcome might be a Ford Taurus, and an optimistic outcome might be a BMW.

	Range of Alternatives/Outcomes		
Item/Consideration	Pessimistic	Realistic	Optimistic
Company car			
Expense account			
Travel allowance			
Salary			
Health insurance			
Training			
Bonus/other incentives			
Relocation expenses			
Work location			
Home office and equipment			
College tuition reimbursement			
Country club membership			

tries, as well as the federal government. In fact, if you work in a nonsupervisory position, you may become a union member.

If you advance into a management position in a unionized firm, you will deal with union stewards and other union officials. You might even become a member of the firm's bargaining team and assist in negotiating a labor agreement. As a manager in such a situation, you need to possess and exercise effective interpersonal skills, especially communication and perceptual skills. Perceptual skill in a unionized environment is the ability to quickly understand a situation with conflict potential. Many union-management conflicts are caused by misunderstandings and lack of communication. Those who are successful in the union-management arena, whether they be managers, union officials, or mediators, are especially effective communicators with outstanding perceptual skills.

How can you develop these important interpersonal skills? These skills obviously improve with experience, but you can accelerate skill development by (1) taking courses that will challenge your oral and written communication skills, (2) joining student organizations and becoming an officer or committee chair, and (3) being an effective group member in business courses where student teams solve business problems, make investment decisions, or devise ways to implement changes in the work environment.

>looking ahead
at American Airlines and Its Pilots

After nearly a week of pilot sick-outs in February 1999, Donald Carty, CEO of American Airlines, sought an injunction from a federal judge to stop the pilots' job action and require them to return to work. The judge, Joe Kendall, ordered the pilots back to work and instructed the union to urge the pilots to return. When the union was slow to respond, Judge Kendall fined the union $10 million. The union appealed the judge's ruling and fine. It was several months after the pilot sick-out before the company and union resolved their dispute over pilot pay and seniority.

SUMMARY OF LEARNING GOALS

>lg 1 What is the historical development of American labor unions?

Early labor organizations were craft guilds formed to further their members' interests. Unfavorable economic conditions and the courts contributed to the demise of many of these guilds. The Knights of Labor was one of the first national labor organizations, but it was not very good at improving the lot of workers. In 1881 many of the craft groups left the Knights of Labor to form the American Federation of Labor (AFL). Under Samuel Gompers, the AFL pursued such practical matters as union rights and better wages, hours, and working conditions for members.

In 1935 John L. Lewis and the United Mine Workers of America left the AFL to form the Congress of Industrial Organizations (CIO). Until the early 1950s, the AFL and the CIO competed for membership. The two groups merged to form the AFL-CIO in 1955. Today, the U.S. labor movement consists of the AFL-CIO labor federation, national and international unions, and local unions. As an umbrella organization, the AFL-CIO represents about 12 to 13 percent of the total U.S. workforce. A national union consists of many local unions in a particular industry, skilled trade, or geographic area. The main functions of the local unions are collective bargaining, worker relations and membership services, and community and political activities.

KEY TERMS

agency shop 326
American
  Federation of
  Labor (AFL) 316
arbitration 330
bargaining unit
  323
closed shop 326
collective
  bargaining 316
conciliation 321
conglomerate union
  318
Congress of
  Industrial
  Organizations
  317
corporate
  campaign 333
cost-of-living
  adjustment
  (COLA) 328
craft union 317
decertification
  election 324
give-backs 329
grievance 330
industrial union
  317
injunction 320
Knights of Labor
  316
labor union 316
Landrum-Griffin Act
  321
local union 318
lockout 333
mediation 321
mutual-aid pact 334
National Labor
  Relations Board
  (NLRB) 320
national union 319
Norris–La Guardia
  Act 320
open shop 327
picketing 333
right-to-work laws
  327
selective strike
  strategy 332
shop steward 318
sick-out 332
strike replacements
  334
Taft-Hartley Act 321
union busting 334
union certification
  election 323
union shop 326
Wagner Act 320
wildcat strike 332
yellow-dog
  contracts 320

>lg 2   **What role did federal law play in the development of the union-management relationship?**
The Norris–La Guardia Act of 1932 banned employers' use of injunctions and greatly limited yellow-dog contracts. This law essentially ended the use of the courts as a means of settling a labor dispute. In 1935 Congress passed the Wagner Act, which encouraged the formation of unions, defined unfair labor practices, and created the NLRB. The Wagner Act was amended in 1947 by the Taft-Hartley Act, which placed some constraints on labor union organizing activities. In 1959 Congress passed the Landrum-Griffin Act, which dealt mainly with the internal affairs of unions, or such things as officer elections, financial record keeping, and constitution and bylaw provisions.

>lg 3   **What is the union organizing process?**
A company is unionized through an organizing drive that begins either inside, with a small group of existing employees, or outside, with an established union that targets the employer. When the union gets signed authorization cards from 30 percent of the firm's employees, the NLRB conducts a union certification election. A majority vote is needed to certify the union as the exclusive bargaining agent. The union and the employer then begin collective bargaining and have one year in which to reach an agreement.

>lg 4   **What is the collective bargaining process, and what key issues are included in the union contract?**
Collective bargaining is the process of negotiating, administering, and interpreting labor agreements. Both union and management negotiators prepare a bargaining proposal. The two sides meet and exchange demands and ideas. Bargaining consists of compromises and concessions that lead to a tentative agreement. Top management then approves or disapproves the agreement for the management team. Union members vote to either approve or reject the contract.

One of the most important issues for the union in negotiating an agreement is union security. Closely related is the dues checkoff. To protect its rights, the employer often includes a management-rights clause in the labor agreement. Much of the effort that goes into negotiations is devoted to deciding on wage increases and improvements in fringe benefits. Job security, another union concern, is assured mainly through seniority provisions that determine employee layoffs, promotions, and job transfers.

>lg 5   **How do employees file a grievance?**
In most labor agreements the grievance procedure consists of three or four steps. In the initial step, the employee files a grievance; this is an oral and/or written presentation to the supervisor and may involve a union steward as representative of the grievant. Steps two and three involve meetings of the employee and one or more union officials and the appropriate supervisor and one or more management officials. If the grievance is not resolved at step three, either party (union or management) can request that an arbitrator, or neutral third party, hear and decide the grievance.

>lg 6   **What economic tactics do unions and employers use in labor-management conflicts?**
The union's primary weapon is the strike—union members stop working. During a strike, union members may picket, or parade back and forth in front of the struck employer carrying signs that alert the public to the union's dispute with the employer. An additional union action is the product boycott

where the union attempts to convince consumers to discontinue purchase of products of the firm with which the union has a dispute. Employers' weapons include the lockout, strike replacements, mutual-aid pacts, and shifting of production to nonunion locations. Of these, the lockout and strike replacements are the most common. The employer may simply close (lock) the plant and prevent workers from reporting for work and then hire temporary, nonunion workers as strike replacements.

>lg 7   **What trends will affect American workers and labor-management relations?**
Decline in union members will cease, and the growth in members that began in the last half of 1998 will continue. Union demands for wage increases and improvements in fringe benefits will stimulate new membership. These demands will be commonplace as long as the economy remains strong. Shortages of skilled workers will likely persist into the 21st century. To drive more interest in skilled craft positions, unions and employers will need to build strong apprenticeship programs that provide sound foundations for careers in the skilled crafts.

PREPARING FOR TOMORROW'S WORKPLACE

1. Divide the class into two groups. One group will take the position that workers should be required to join unions and pay dues. The other group will take the position that workers should not be required to join unions. Hold a debate in which a spokesperson from each group is given 10 minutes to present the group's arguments.

2. Assume you have been asked to speak at a local meeting of human resource and labor relations professionals. The topic is whether union membership will increase or decline in the 21st century. Take either the increase or the decline position and outline your presentation.

3. Under what circumstances, if any, should police officers, firefighters, teachers, and nurses be allowed to strike? If you believe any or all of these groups should not be allowed to strike under any circumstances, how can they deal with poor supervision, low salaries, stressful job situations, and inadequate equipment?

4. Go to the government documents section in your college or university library and inspect publications of the Department of Labor (DOL), including *Employment and Earnings, Compensation and Working Conditions, Monthly Labor Review, Occupational Outlook Handbook,* and *Career Guide to Industries.* Alternatively, go to the DOL, Bureau of Labor Statistics Web site at **http://stats.bls.gov.** Access the most recent DOL publications and locate the following information:

   - Number of persons in the American workforce
   - Unemployment rate for last year
   - Demographic characteristics of the American workforce: race, ethnic status, age, marital status, and gender
   - Occupations where there are projected shortages for the next 5 or 10 years
   - Union membership by major industry category: manufacturing, banking and finance, health care, business and personal services, sports and entertainment, and any other area of interest to you

5. Assume you are a director of labor relations for a firm faced with a union certification election in 30 days. Draft a letter to be sent to your employees in which you urge them to vote "no union"; be persuasive in presenting your arguments against the union.

6. Divide the class into four groups; each group will focus on one of the major professional sports (baseball, football, basketball, and hockey). Within each group students should engage in a discussion/debate concerning whether the athletes of that sport should unionize and engage in collective bargaining.

7. Divide the class into union and management teams and negotiate the following union demands:
   a. Wage increases of 10 percent
   b. Union shop
   c. Cost-of-living allowance or adjustment
   d. Fully paid (by employer) health insurance
   e. No outsourcing or subcontracting

8. Go to the library and skim recent issues of the *Wall Street Journal, Business Week,* and/or the *Daily Labor Report* until you find articles about either a recent strike or a labor contract settlement. Report to your class the specifics of the strike or settlement.

9. Assume you are a union member. Would you participate in an employee sick-out? Why or why not?

10. Have you or a member of your family ever been a union member? If so, name the union and describe it in terms of membership size, membership characteristics, strike history, recent bargaining issues, and employers under union contracts.

WORKING THE NET

1. How are labor unions using the Internet to expand their influence and recruit new members? Use a search engine like Google (**www.google.com**) or the AFL-CIO Web site (**www.aflcio.org**) to find individual union Web sites. Describe in a brief report how the Internet helps three unions in different industries.

2. The 50th anniversary of the Taft-Hartley Act in 1997 resulted in many articles opposing this law. Through Internet research, find out why the act has been called a worker's nightmare. Start at sites such as **www.labornet.org,** which has an article on "Taft-Hartley: 50 Years," and "Taft-Hartley Act: How long can a bad law stay on the books?" found at **www.ns.net/~rrhan/taft.html.** Do you agree with these articles?

3. Workers of America (**www.woa.org**) is a pro-union organization whose mission is to provide information about existing conditions and trends in the American workplace and to improve conditions for American workers. How does it achieve its goals?

4. Not everyone believes that unions are good for workers. The National Right to Work Legal Defense Foundation offers free legal aid to employees whose "human and civil rights have been violated by compulsory unionism abuses." Visit its Web site (**www.nrtw.org**) and summarize its position on the disadvantages of labor unions. Contrast this with the views of the Workers of America (see the preceding activity).

5. Although we tend to think of labor unions as representing manufacturing employees, many office and service industry employees and professionals

belong to unions. Visit the Web sites of several nonmanufacturing unions and discuss how they help their members. Here are some suggestions: the Office and Professional Employees International Union (**www.opeiu.org**), the National Education Association (**www.nea.org**), Actors' Equity Association (**www.actorsequity.org**), and the American Federation of Musicians (**www.afm.org**). What are the differences, if any, between these unions and those in other industries?

CREATIVE THINKING CASE

Union Organizing at Iowa Plastics

You are the plant manager of Iowa Plastics Corp., a company that manufactures keyboard pads, plastic shells for computer monitors, tower boxes for computer hard-drives, and other items for computer equipment. The plant employs several hundred production workers who use state-of-the-art plastics manufacturing technology. The production process is highly automated. Most of the workers are semiskilled assemblers, but numerous skilled craftsmen and technicians are also employed.

The plant is located in Iowa, a right-to-work state. The company's other plants are located in Tennessee, North Carolina, and Missouri. The firm has always been nonunion, although two years ago the Teamsters Union attempted to unionize the Missouri plant. A certification election was held, and the company won by a 3-to-1 margin.

Each Monday morning you meet for about an hour with the production supervisors, plant engineer, and human resource manager to review the week's production schedule, product shipments, raw material inventories, employee staffing levels, and related matters. Four weeks ago at one of these meetings, one of the production supervisors reported that he had overheard some workers talking about forming a union. Since that time, two other supervisors have indicated they think employees want a union.

In this morning's mail (Tuesday), you received a registered letter from the Teamsters Union informing you that it represents your employees and that a union organizing drive has been in progress for 60 days. You are surprised, even somewhat shocked. You have never worked in a unionized environment and don't plan to now. Your mind quickly fills with questions:

- What went wrong?
- Should I talk to the workers who have started this?
- Do I call corporate headquarters?
- Should I call a meeting of supervisors for later this morning?
- What do I do if the workers strike?
- Why did the Teamsters do this?
- Should I announce a pay increase to show employees that I run the plant, not the Teamsters?
- Do I need a labor lawyer?

Critical Thinking Questions

1. You are obviously faced with a significant problem. How should you proceed?
2. Outline a general course of action and indicate specifically what you can do over the next several days and weeks, assuming you want the plant to remain union-free.

VIDEO CASE

Promoting Cooperation at the Mt. Pleasant Police Department

Like many other police departments, the Mt. Pleasant, Michigan Police Department is transforming the way it does business. Located in Isabella County in central Michigan, Mt. Pleasant has adopted a community policing approach. "Community policing . . . employs customer-based organizational strategies, partnerships, and problem-solving processes to reduce or prevent crime and disorder and to improve the community's quality of life."

The Mt. Pleasant community policing approach fosters cooperation with other law enforcement units in Isabella County. Public safety agencies in the area have developed three specialized units—the Traffic Enforcement Team, the Containment Unit, and the Youth Services Unit—that work cooperatively to handle specific programs or projects. Funding for the personnel, equipment, vehicles, and operating costs of these teams is provided by the Saginaw-Chippewa Indian Tribe. This is done in accordance with Tribe's 1993 gaming compact with the state of Michigan regarding the operation of its Soaring Eagle Casino.

Effective community policing relies on cooperation—between the police department and members of the community, as well as among members of the police department itself. In the former case, police departments must draw on available resources to develop and maintain effective working relationships with not only different constituencies in the community but also with other law enforcement agencies in the area. In the latter case, cooperative and effective working relationships must be established between labor and management—or equivalently between the patrolmen and the command officers.

One way in which the Mt. Pleasant Police Department has established cooperative working relationships with community constituencies and other law enforcement agencies is by drawing on the resources of the Regional Community Policing Institute (RCPI). RCPI is a joint project of the School of Criminal Justice, the School of Labor and Industrial Relations, the Urban Affairs Program, and the Department of Psychology at Michigan State University. The Mt. Pleasant Police Department is one of approximately two dozen police agencies and partner communities in Michigan that work with the Regional Community Policing Institute. The Saginaw-Chippewa Indian Tribal Police is also a partner member.

Drawing on RCPI resources is a necessary but insufficient condition for making Mt. Pleasant's community policing program a success. Arguably more important is effective cooperation among members of the Mt. Pleasant Police Department in implementing community policing. Indeed, the Regional Community Policing Institute indicates that many of the impediments to community policing are rooted in labor-management relations. Some of these impediments are: (1) The failure to integrate community policing with traditional policing responsibilities. (2) The lack of involvement of union leaders in the design, implementation, and monitoring of community policing. (3) Perceptions that community-based policing is a tool for the department's leadership to circumvent a labor contract. (4) Poor communication between the department leadership and the union. (5) Lack of a team focus. (6) Preferential treatment for community-based police officers.

The RCPI message is quite clear! An effective cooperative working relationship between a police department's leadership and its line officers—or equivalently between management and labor—must exist if community policing is to be effective. Such needed cooperation presents an interesting challenge for the Mt. Pleasant Police Department. It's employees are affiliated with two unions—a fairly unique challenge in union-management relations within police departments, in general. Mt. Pleasant's command officers are represented by the Command Officers Association of Michigan (COAM). Patrolmen are represented by the Police Officers Association of Michigan (POAM).

The Police Officers Association of Michigan, for instance, is a labor organization that serves the needs of law enforcement officers in Michigan. POAM provides various labor related services, including negotiations, grievance processing, arbitration, and legal representation. Working with the business agents representing local union bargaining committees, the POAM staff provides information about a variety of issues that are of interest to the police unions. As input into contract negotiations, POAM supplies wage and benefits information regarding other police departments in the region. POAM also provides members with actuarial data regarding the costs—and this information can be decisive in gaining improvements. POAM provides analytical support in other areas as well. These include Social Security questions, health care issues, work-practice surveys, and cost-of-living analyses.

The Police Officers Association of Michigan exists to serve and support its union locals—including the patrolmen of the Mt. Pleasant Police Department. The challenge for the local bargaining unit is to represent the interests of the Mt. Pleasant patrolmen while building cooperative relationships within the department—relationships that are crucial for the success of Mt. Pleasant's community policing program.

Critical Thinking Questions

1. How might community-based policing affect the way police officers do their jobs?
2. Why would a good working relationship between "management" and "labor" be essential for community policing to be effective?
3. How might a police agency overcome impediments in the working relationship between "management"/*- and "labor"?

chapter twelve

>c 12

Achieving World-Class Operations Management

learning goals

>lg 1   Why is production and operations management important in both manufacturing and service firms?

>lg 2   What types of production processes are used by manufacturers and service firms?

>lg 3   How do organizations decide where to put their production facilities? What choices must be made in designing the facility?

>lg 4   Why are resource planning tasks like inventory management and supplier relations critical to production?

>lg 5   How do operations managers schedule and control production?

>lg 6   How can quality management and lean manufacturing techniques help firms improve production and operations management?

>lg 7   What roles do technology and automation play in manufacturing and service industry operations management?

>lg 8   What key trends are affecting the way companies manage production and operations?

Harley-Davidson Revs up Production

Harley-Davidsons **(www.harley-davidson.com)** aren't just motorcycles. They're an American legend, known for their unique style, sound, and power ever since the first one was assembled in a backyard workshop in 1903. "People want more than two wheels and a motor," explains Harley-Davidson CEO Jeffrey Bleustein. "Harleys represent something very basic—a desire for freedom, adventure and individualism."

Back in the 1980s, Harleys also represented everything that was wrong with American manufacturing. The company's main factory in York, Pennsylvania, was outdated and inefficient, keeping prices high. Quality was so poor that owners sometimes joked they needed two Harleys—one to ride and one for parts. Fed-up consumers started buying motorcycles made by Japanese and German manufacturers. Harley-Davidson's future looked grim.

To turn things around, the company designed new models and borrowed state-of-the-art quality and production techniques from Japanese manufacturers. It cut the number of parts stored in inventory at the company's factories, keeping costs—and prices—under control. As quality improved and prices stabilized, Harley-Davidson's sales began to climb.

By the mid-1990s, however, Harley's existing factories were having trouble keeping up with demand. Customers often had to wait a year or longer to get a new Harley. The choice was clear: either the firm must rev up its production capability, or it would risk losing customers to foreign competitors once again.

First order of business? A new $86 million factory in Kansas City. The 330,000-square-foot plant, opened in 1998, puts Harley-Davidson at the forefront of modern manufacturing and management practice.

In a special lightproof room, lasers automatically pierce holes in fenders for tail lights and other attachments. Robots then polish the finished fenders, along with gas and oil tanks, while other robots paint the various components needed to build a Harley. The components are loaded onto three dozen specially designed carts that swivel 360 degrees and can be lowered or raised to suit different workers or tasks. The carts move among workstations where employees assemble motorcycle frames. By the end of the line, 70 employees have assembled 650 parts at 20 different workstations.

No motorcycle leaves the plant without a final stop at Station 20. A team of test drivers revs up and rides each motorcycle, checking operating quality and listening for the classic

Critical Thinking Questions

As you read this chapter, consider the following questions as they relate to Harley-Davidson:

- How has a focus on manufacturing supported Harley-Davidson's growth?
- What factors outside the company have led to this focus?
- What future production changes will Harley need to make in order to continue to grow?

Harley sound. Any bikes that don't meet rigid standards are sent back to the factory for adjustments and fine-tuning.

Employees are integral to the success of Harley's new factory. They are grouped in work teams, and every employee is cross-trained to perform a variety of production tasks. Each work team must constantly look for ways to build a better Harley. The result has been many employee-generated ideas for better equipment, factory layout, and production processes.

Looking back, CEO Bleustein believes production and operations have been vital to Harley-Davidson's continued growth. "In the last 10 years, we were very much internally focused," he says. "We had to fix our manufacturing and bring it to a new level. With that in place, our focus can be more external, bringing new and exciting products to the marketplace."[1]

BUSINESS IN THE 21ST CENTURY

>lg 1

Assembly-line employees at Harley-Davidson's new Kansas City plant suggested production process improvements that contributed to their firm's continued growth.

Finding the most efficient and effective methods of making the goods it sells to customers is an ongoing focus of nearly every type of business organization. Today more than ever, changing consumer expectations, technological advances, and increased competition are all forcing business organizations to rethink where, when, and how they will produce products or services.

Like Harley-Davidson in the chapter's opening story, manufacturers are discovering that it is no longer enough to simply push products through the factory and onto the market. Consumers are demanding higher quality at reasonable prices. They also expect products to be delivered in a timely manner. Firms that can't meet these expectations often face strong competition from businesses that can. To compete, many manufacturers are reinventing how they make their products by automating their factories, developing new production processes, and tightening their relationships with suppliers.

Service organizations are also facing challenges. Their customers are demanding better service, shorter waits, and more individualized attention. Just like manufacturers, service organizations are using new methods to deliver what customers need and want. Banks, for example, are using technology such as ATMs and the Internet to make their services more accessible to customers. Many colleges now offer weekend courses for working students. Tax services are filing tax returns via computer.

In this chapter, we will examine how manufacturers and service firms manage and control the creation of products and services. Following a brief overview, we'll discuss production planning, including the choices firms must make concerning the type of production process they will use, the location where production will occur, and the management of resources needed in production. Next, we'll explain routing and scheduling, two critical tasks for controlling production and operations efficiency. Many businesses are improving productivity by employing new methods like quality control and automation. We'll discuss these methods before summarizing some of the trends affecting production and operations management.

PRODUCTION AND OPERATIONS MANAGEMENT—AN OVERVIEW

production

The creation of products and services by turning inputs, such as natural resources, raw materials, human resources, and capital, into outputs.

operations management

Management of the production process.

Production, the creation of products and services, is an essential function in every firm. Production turns inputs, such as natural resources, raw materials, human resources, and capital, into outputs, products and services. This process is shown in Exhibit 12-1. Managing this conversion process is the role of **operations management.**

In the 1980s, many U.S. industries, such as automotive, steel, and electronics, lost customers to foreign competitors because their production systems could not provide the quality customers demanded. As a result, most American companies, both large and small, now consider a focus on quality to be a central component of effective operations management.

The goal of customer satisfaction, closely linked to quality, is also an important part of effective production and operations. In the past, the manufacturing

> e x h i b i t   1 2 - 1 <

Production Process for Goods and Services

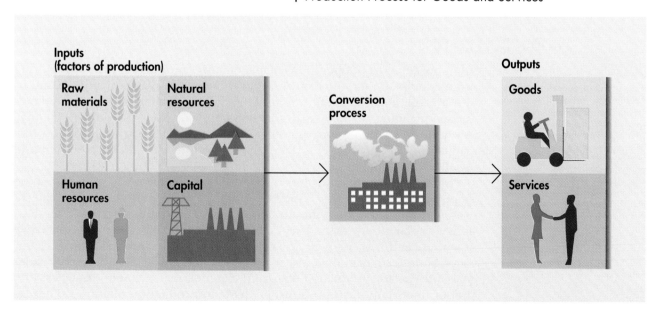

function in most companies was inwardly focused. Manufacturing had little contact with customers and didn't always understand their needs and desires. Today, however, stronger links between marketing and manufacturing have encouraged production managers to be more outwardly focused and to consider decisions in light of their effect on customer satisfaction. Service companies have also found that making operating decisions with customer satisfaction in mind can be a competitive advantage.

Operations managers, the personnel charged with managing and supervising the conversion process, play a vital role in today's firm. They control about three-fourths of a firm's assets, including inventories, wages, and benefits. They work closely with other major functions of the firm, such as marketing, finance, accounting, and human resources, to help ensure that the firm continually provides customer satisfaction. They face the challenge of combining people and other resources to produce high-quality goods, on time and at a reasonable cost. Working with marketing, they help to decide which products to make or which services to offer. They become involved with the development and design of goods and determine what production processes will be most effective.

Production and operations management involves three main types of decisions that are made at three different stages:

1. *Production planning.* The first decisions facing operations managers come at the *planning stage.* At this stage, decisions are made regarding where, when, and how production will occur. Resources are obtained and site locations determined.

2. *Production control.* At this stage, the decision-making process focuses on scheduling, controlling quality and costs, and the actual day-to-day operations of running a factory or service facility.

3. *Improving production and operations.* In the final stage, operations management focuses on developing more efficient methods of producing the firm's goods.

It is important to remember that these three types of decisions are ongoing and often occur simultaneously. In the following sections, we will take a closer look at the decisions and considerations firms face in each of these stages of production and operations management.

concept check

- Define production and explain how operations management is related to it.
- What are the three main types of decisions operations managers must make?

PRODUCTION PLANNING

production planning

The aspect of operations management in which the firm considers the competitive environment and its own strategic goals in an effort to find the best production methods.

An important part of operations management is **production planning.** During production planning, the firm considers the competitive environment and its own strategic goals in an effort to find the best production methods. Good production planning balances goals that may conflict such as providing high-quality service while keeping operating costs down, or keeping profits high while maintaining adequate inventories of finished products. Sometimes accomplishing all of these goals is quite difficult.

Production planning involves three phases. Long-term planning has a time frame of three to five years. It focuses on which goods to produce, how many to produce, and where they should be produced. Medium-term planning decisions cover about two years. They concern the layout of factory or service facilities, where and how to obtain the resources needed for production, and labor issues. Short-term planning, with a one-year time frame, converts these broader goals into specific production plans and materials management strategies.

Four important decisions must be made in production planning. They involve the type of production process that will be used, site selection, facilities layout, and purchasing issues.

Production Process

In production planning, the first decision to be made is which type of **production process**—the way a good is made—best fits with the company's goals and customer demands. Another important consideration is the type of good or service being produced, as different goods may require different production processes. In general, there are three types of production: mass production, mass customization, and customization.

production process
The way a good is made.

mass production
The ability to manufacture many identical goods at once.

Mass Production   **Mass production,** the ability to manufacture many identical goods at once, was a product of the Industrial Revolution. Henry Ford's Model-T

automobile is a good example of mass production. Each car turned out by Ford's factory was identical, right down to its color. If you wanted a car in any color except black, you were out of luck. Canned goods, over-the-counter drugs, and household appliances are examples of goods that are still mass-produced. The emphasis in mass production is on keeping manufacturing costs low by producing highly uniform products.

Increasingly, however, manufacturers are finding that mass production is becoming more complex. Many products are more complicated to produce. Automobile manufacturers, for example, are incorporating more sophisticated electronics into their car designs. As a result, the number of assembly stations in an auto assembly plant has increased. In many industries, customers are also demanding a wider array of choices and even customization. These trends have led to changes in the processes used to produce many goods.

A quality control employee inspects the uniformity of Trix yogurt, a product that is mass-produced to keep manufacturing costs low.

mass customization
A manufacturing process in which goods are mass-produced up to a point and then custom tailored to the needs or desires of individual customers.

customization
The production of goods or services one at a time according to the specific needs or wants of individual customers.

job shop
A manufacturing firm that produces goods in response to customer orders.

Mass Customization and Customization   In **mass customization,** a relatively new concept in manufacturing, goods are produced using mass production techniques, but only up to a point. At that point, the product or service is custom tailored to the needs or desires of individual customers. Golf club maker Taylor Made Golf devotes part of its production plant to mass customization. Customers needing longer club shafts, customized grips, or other options order through pro shops and golf instructors. Workers at Taylor Made's plant add the parts to the clubs based on the customer's requirements.[2]

Customization is the opposite of mass production. In customization, the firm produces goods one at a time according to the specific needs or wants of individual customers. Unlike mass customization, each product or service produced is unique. For example, a print shop may handle a variety of projects, including newsletters, brochures, stationery, and reports. Each print job varies in quantity, type of printing process, binding, color of ink, and type of paper. A manufacturing firm that produces goods in response to customer orders is called a **job shop.**

Some types of service businesses also deliver customized services. Doctors, for instance, usually must consider the individual illnesses and circumstances of each patient before developing a customized treatment plan. Real estate agents also develop a customized service plan for each customer based on the type of house the person is selling or wants to buy. The differences between mass production, mass customization, and customization are summarized in Exhibit 12-2.

In addition to production type, operations managers also classify production processes in two ways: (1) by how inputs are converted into outputs and (2) by the timing of the process.

Converting Inputs to Outputs   Production involves converting inputs (raw materials, parts, human resources) into outputs (products or services). In a manufacturing company, the inputs, the production process, and the final outputs are usually obvious. Harley-Davidson, for instance, converts steel, rubber, paint, and other inputs into motorcycles. The production process in a service company involves a less obvious conversion. For example, Columbia Health Care converts the knowledge and skills of its medical personnel, along with equipment and supplies from a variety of sources, into health care services for patients. Examples of the inputs and outputs used by other types of businesses are shown in Exhibit 12-3.

There are two basic processes for converting inputs into outputs. In **process manufacturing,** the basic input (raw materials, parts) is *broken down* into one or more outputs (products). For instance, bauxite (the input) is processed to extract aluminum (the output). The **assembly process** is just the opposite. The basic inputs, like parts, raw materials, or human resources, are either *combined* to create the output or *transformed* into the output. An airplane, for example, is created by assembling thousands of parts. Iron and other materials are combined and transformed by heat into steel. In services, customers may play a role in the transformation process. For example, a tax preparation service combines the knowledge of the tax preparer with the customer's information about personal finances in order to complete tax returns.

Production Timing   A second consideration in choosing a production process is timing. A **continuous process** uses long production runs that may last days, weeks, or months without equipment shutdowns. It is best for high-volume, low-variety products with standardized parts, such as nails, glass, and paper.

---

process manufacturing

A production process in which the basic input is broken down into one or more outputs (products).

assembly process

A production process in which the basic inputs are either combined to create the output or transformed into the output.

continuous process

A production process that uses long production runs lasting days, weeks, or months without equipment shutdowns; generally used for high-volume, low-variety products with standardized parts.

> e x h i b i t   1 2 - 2 <

Classification of Production Types

Mass Production	Mass Customization	Customization
Highly uniform products or services. Many products made sequentially.	Uniform and standardized production to a point, then unique features added to each product.	Each product or service produced according to individual customer requirements
Examples: Breakfast cereals, soft drinks, and computer keyboards.	Examples: Dell computers, tract homes, and Taylor Made Golf clubs.	Examples: Custom homes, legal services, and haircuts.

Converting Inputs to Outputs

Type of Organization	Input	Output
Airline	Pilots, crew, flight attendants, reservations system, ticketing agents, customers, airplanes, fuel, maintenance crews, ground facilities	Movement of customers and freight
Grocery store	Merchandise, building, clerks, supervisors, store fixtures, shopping carts, customers	Groceries for customer sales
High school	Faculty, curriculum, buildings, classrooms, library, auditorium, gymnasium, students, staff, supplies	Graduates, public service
Manufacturer	Machinery, raw materials, plant, workers, managers	Finished products for consumers and other firms
Restaurant	Food, cooking equipment, serving personnel, chefs, dishwashers, host, patrons, furniture, fixtures	Meals for customers

Some services also use a continuous process. Your local electric company is one example. Per-unit costs are low and production is easy to schedule.

In an **intermittent process,** short production runs are used to make batches of different products. Machines are shut down to change them to make different products at different times. This process is best for low-volume, high-variety products such as those produced by mass customization or customization. Job shops are examples of firms using an intermittent process.

Although some service companies use continuous processes, most service firms rely on intermittent processes. For instance, a restaurant preparing gourmet meals, a physician performing physical examinations or surgical operations, and an advertising agency developing ad campaigns for business clients all customize their services to suit each customer. They use the intermittent process. Note that their "production runs" may be very short—one grilled salmon or one eye exam at a time.

intermittent process

A production process that uses short production runs to make batches of different products; generally used for low-volume, high-variety products.

Site Selection

>lg 3

One big decision that must be made early in production and operations planning is where to put the facility, be it a factory or a service office. Site selection affects operating costs, the price of the product or service, and the company's ability to compete. For instance, the costs of shipping raw materials and finished goods can be as much as 25 percent of a manufacturer's total cost. Locating a factory where these and other costs are as low as possible can make a major contribution to a firm's success. Mistakes made at this stage can be expensive. It is hard and costly to move a factory or service facility once production begins. Firms must weigh a number of factors to ensure that the right decision is made.

Availability of Production Inputs

As we discussed earlier, organizations need certain resources in order to produce goods for sale. Access to these resources, or inputs, is a huge consideration in site selection. For example, the availability and cost of labor are very important to both manufacturing and service businesses. Payroll costs can vary widely from one location to another

because of differences in the cost of living, the number of jobs available, and the skills and productivity of the local workforce. The unionization of the local labor force is another point to consider in many industries. Low labor costs were one reason AlliedSignal, a U.S. manufacturer, chose Ireland as the site for a new factory. Ireland has a skilled workforce, but high unemployment rates in the country have kept the cost of labor down. AlliedSignal and other companies pay employees significantly less in salary and fringe benefits in Ireland than they do in the United States.[3]

Executives must also assess the availability of raw materials, parts, and equipment for each production site under consideration. It can be costly to ship these resources long distances so companies that use heavy or bulky raw materials may choose to be located near suppliers. Mining companies want to be near ore deposits, oil refiners near oil fields, paper mills near forests, and food processors near farms.

Marketing Factors

Businesses must also evaluate how the location of their facility will affect their ability to serve their customers. For some firms, it may not be necessary to be located near customers. Instead, the firm will need to assess the difficulty and costs involved with distributing its goods to customers from the location chosen.

Other firms may find that locating near customers can provide marketing advantages. When a factory or service center is close to customers, the firm can often offer better service at a lower cost. Other firms may gain a competitive advantage by locating their facilities so that customers can easily buy their products or services. The location of competitors may also be a factor. Businesses with more than one facility may also need to consider how far to spread their locations in order to maximize market coverage.

Local Incentives

Incentives offered by countries, states, or cities may also influence site selection. Tax breaks are a common incentive. The locality may reduce the amount of taxes the firm will pay on income, real estate, utilities, or payroll. Tax incentives offered by state and city governments were a deciding factor in Mitsubishi's selection of Illinois as the site for its factory. For 13 years, Mitsubishi has enjoyed a 50 percent exemption from real estate taxes and receives a 50 percent rebate on its utility taxes.[4]

Other government incentives can also convince businesses to choose one location over another. Local governments sometimes offer exemption from certain regulations or financial assistance in order to attract or keep production

Detroit, Michigan, is a world-class manufacturing city where a high percentage of the local workforce is employed by General Motors and other firms in the automotive industry.

facilities in their area. When financial services firm Fidelity Mutual was looking for a site for its administrative and customer service operations, the company chose Cincinnati, Ohio. Cincinnati officials gave the firm a tax break equal to about 5 percent of the firm's construction costs. The city also constructed a free highway to the new site and built a center at Northern Kentucky University. There, 200 students answer customer telephone inquiries for less pay than Fidelity's former telephone center employees.[5]

Manufacturing Environment   Another factor to consider is the manufacturing environment in a potential location. Some localities have a strong existing manufacturing base. When a large number of manufacturers, perhaps in a certain industry, are already located in an area, that area is likely to offer greater availability of resources, such as manufacturing workers, better accessibility to suppliers and transportation, and other factors that can increase a plant's operating efficiency.

Every year, *Industry Week* evaluates the manufacturing climate of 315 U.S. cities. Each city is rated based on the productivity of its manufacturing sector, the percentage of the local workforce employed by manufacturing firms, the contribution of manufacturing to the area's overall economy, and several other factors. Though not necessarily the largest manufacturing cities in the United States, the top-ranked cities are considered "world-class" manufacturing cities by *Industry Week*. As Exhibit 12-4 shows, Kokomo, Indiana, and Detroit, Michigan, topped the most recent *Industry Week* survey.

What characteristics make a city a world-class manufacturing site? Read the full *Industry Week* article at **www.industryweek.com**

International Location Considerations   In recent years, manufacturers in many industries have opened new production facilities outside the United States. There are often sound financial reasons for considering a foreign location. Labor costs are considerably lower in countries like

> e x h i b i t   1 2 - 4 <

Top 10 World-Class U.S. Manufacturing Cities

1. Kokomo, Indiana
2. Detroit, Michigan
3. Wilmington-Newark, Delaware
4. Houston, Texas
5. San Jose, California
6. Flint, Michigan
7. Elkhart-Goshen, Indiana
8. Chicago, Illinois
9. Austin-San Marcos, Texas
10. Janesville-Beloit, Wisconsin

SOURCE: "World Class Manufacturing Cities," *Industry Week Special Report* (April 1998), downloaded from *Industry Week* Web site, **www.industryweek.com**.

Singapore, Ireland, and Mexico. Foreign countries may also have fewer regulations governing how factories operate. Or with a foreign location, production may be closer to new markets. That's exactly why Cabot Corp.'s Microelectronics Materials Division decided to open a plant in Japan. The company, which makes industrial slurries that are used to form computer chips, recognized a growing demand for its product in Asia. Opening a plant in Japan gave the company the ability to take advantage of this market growth.[6]

Facility Layout

After the site location decision has been made, the next focus in production planning is the facility's layout. Here, the goal is to determine the most efficient and effective design for the particular production process. A manufacturer might opt for a U-shaped production line, for example, rather than a long, straight one, to allow products and workers to move more quickly from one area to another.

Service organizations must also consider layout, but they are more concerned with how it affects customer behavior. It may be more convenient for a hospital to place its freight elevators in the center of the building, but doing so may block the flow of patients, visitors, and medical personnel between floors and departments.

There are three main types of facility layouts: process, product, and fixed-position layouts. All three layouts are illustrated in Exhibit 12-5.

process layout

A facility arrangement in which work flows according to the production process. All workers performing similar tasks are grouped together, and products pass from one workstation to another.

Process Layout The **process layout** arranges work flow around the production process. All workers performing similar tasks are grouped together. Products pass from one workstation to another (but not necessarily to every workstation). For example, all grinding would be done in one area, all assembling in another, and all inspection in yet another. The process layout is best for firms that produce small numbers of a wide variety of products, typically using general-purpose machines that can be changed rapidly to new operations for different product designs. For example, a manufacturer of custom machinery would use a process layout.

product (assembly-line) layout

A facility arrangement in which workstations or departments are arranged in a line with products moving along the line.

Product Layout The **product** (or **assembly-line**) **layout** is used for a continuous or repetitive production process. When large quantities of a product must be processed on an ongoing basis, the workstations or departments are arranged in a line with products moving along the line. Automobile and appliance manufacturers, as well as food-processing plants, usually use a product layout. Service companies may also use a product layout for routine processing operations. For example, overnight film processors use assembly-line techniques.

fixed-position layout

A facility arrangement in which the product stays in one place and workers and machinery move to it as needed.

Fixed-Position Layout Some products cannot be put on an assembly line or moved about in a plant. A **fixed-position layout** lets the product stay in one place while workers and machinery move to it as needed. Products that are impossible to move—ships, airplanes, and construction projects—are typically produced using a fixed-position layout. Limited space at the project site often means that parts of the product must be assembled at other sites, transported to the fixed site, and then assembled. The fixed-position layout is also common for on-site services like housecleaning services, pest control, and landscaping.

Resource Planning

>lg 4

As part of the production planning process, firms must ensure that the resources needed for production, such as raw materials, parts, and equipment, will be available at strategic moments in the production process. This can be a

Facility Layouts

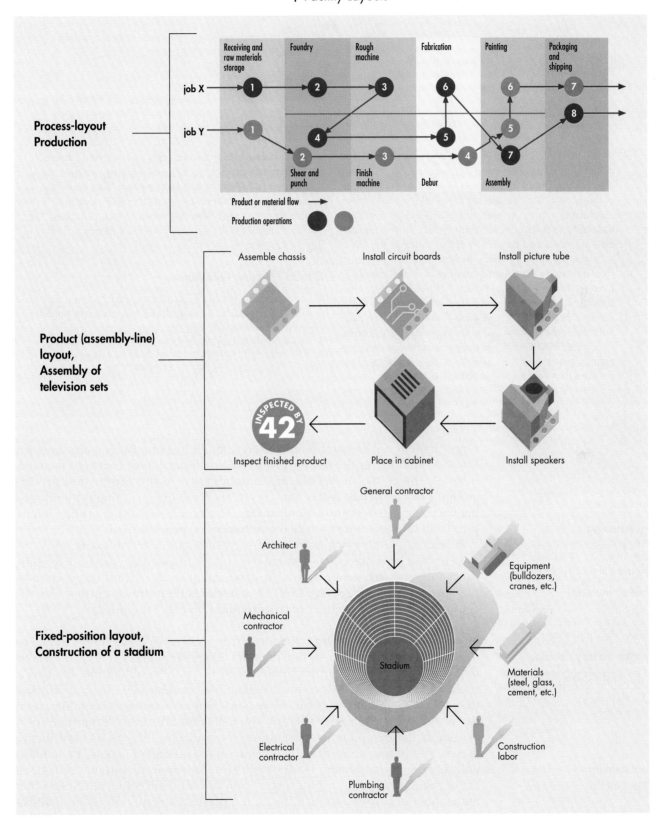

Process-layout Production

Product (assembly-line) layout, Assembly of television sets

Fixed-position layout, Construction of a stadium

SOURCE: From *Production and Operations Management, 8th edition,* by Gaither/Frazier. © 1999. Reprinted with permission of South-Western College Publishing, a division of Thomas Learning. Fax 800-730-2215

huge challenge. The components used to build just one Boeing airplane, for instance, number in the millions. Cost is also an important factor. In many industries, the cost of materials and supplies used in the production process amounts to as much as half of sales revenues. Resource planning is therefore a big part of any firm's production strategy. The process of buying production inputs from various sources is called **purchasing,** or procurement.

Resource planning begins by specifying which raw materials, parts, and components will be required, and when, to produce finished goods. To determine the amount of each item needed, the expected quantity of finished goods to be produced must be forecast. A **bill of material** is then drawn up that lists the components and the number of each required to make the product.

Insourcing and Outsourcing   Next, the firm must decide whether to make its own production materials or buy them from outside sources. This is the **make-or-buy decision.** The quantity of items needed is one consideration. If a part is used in only one of many products, buying the part may be more cost-effective than making it. Buying standard items, such as screws, bolts, rivets, and nails, is usually cheaper and easier than producing them internally. Sometimes purchasing larger components from another manufacturing firm is cost-effective as well. Purchasing items from an outside source instead of making them internally is called **outsourcing.** Harley-Davidson, for example, purchases its tires, brake systems, and other motorcycle components from other businesses that make them to Harley's specifications. If a product has special design features that need to be kept secret to protect a competitive advantage, however, a firm may decide to produce all parts internally.

---

purchasing

The process of buying production inputs from various sources; also called *procurement.*

bill of material

A list of the components and the number of each required to make a given product.

make-or-buy decision

The determination by a firm of whether to make its own production materials or buy them from outside sources.

outsourcing

The purchase of items from an outside source rather than making them internally.

In deciding whether to make or buy, a firm must also consider whether outside sources can provide high-quality supplies in a reliable manner. Having to shut down production because vital parts weren't delivered on time can be a costly disaster. For example, General Motors relies on hundreds of suppliers for parts. When workers in two of the plants that supplied parts went on strike, GM was forced to shut down virtually all of its North American production.[7] Just as bad are inferior parts or materials, which can damage a firm's reputation for producing high-quality goods. Therefore, firms that buy some or all of their production materials from outside sources need to pay close attention to building strong relationships with quality suppliers.

inventory

The supply of goods that a firm holds for use in production or for sale to customers.

Inventory Management   A firm's **inventory** is the supply of goods it holds for use in production or for sale to customers. Deciding how much inventory to keep on hand is one of the biggest challenges facing operations managers. On the one hand, with large inventories, the firm can meet most production and customer demands. Buying in large quantities can also allow a company to take advantage of quantity discounts. On the other hand, large inventories can tie up the firm's money, are expensive to store, and can become obsolete.

inventory management

The determination of how much of each type of inventory a firm will keep on hand and the ordering, receiving, storing, and keeping track of inventory.

Inventory management involves deciding how much of each type of inventory to keep on hand and the ordering, receiving, storing, and keeping track of it. The goal of inventory management is to keep down the costs of ordering and holding inventories while maintaining enough on hand for production and sales. Good inventory management enhances product quality, makes operations more efficient, and increases profits. Poor inventory management can result in dissatisfied customers, financial difficulties, and even bankruptcy.

One way to determine the best inventory levels is to look at three costs: the cost of holding inventory, the cost of reordering frequently, and the cost of not keeping enough inventory on hand. Managers must measure all three costs and try to minimize them.

perpetual inventory

A continuously updated list of inventory levels, orders, sales, and receipts.

To control inventory levels, managers often track the use of certain inventory items. Most companies keep a **perpetual inventory,** a continuously updated list of inventory levels, orders, sales, and receipts, for all major items. Today, companies often use computers to track inventory levels, calculate order quantities, and print purchase orders at the right times.

materials requirement planning (MRP)

A computerized system of controlling the flow of resources and inventory. A master schedule is used to ensure that the materials, labor, and equipment needed for production are at the right places in the right amounts at the right times.

Computerized Resource Planning   Many manufacturing companies have adopted computerized systems to control the flow of resources and inventory. **Materials requirement planning (MRP)** is one such system. MRP uses a master schedule to ensure that the materials, labor, and equipment needed for production are at the right places in the right amounts at the right times. The schedule is based on forecasts of demand for the company's products. It says exactly what will be manufactured during the next few weeks or months and when the work will take place. Sophisticated computer programs coordinate all the elements of MRP. The computer comes up with materials requirements by comparing production needs to the materials the company already has on hand. Orders are placed so items will be on hand when they are needed for production. MRP helps ensure a smooth flow of finished products.

manufacturing resource planning II (MRPII)

A complex computerized system that integrates data from many departments to control the flow of resources and inventory.

Manufacturing resource planning II (MRPII) was developed in the late 1980s to expand on MRP. It uses a complex computerized system to integrate data from many departments, including finance, marketing, accounting, engineering, and manufacturing. MRPII can generate a production plan for the firm, as well as management reports, forecasts, and financial statements. The system lets managers make more accurate forecasts and assess the impact of production plans on profitability. If one department's plans change, the effects of these changes on other departments are transmitted throughout the company.

enterprise resource planning (ERP)

A computerized resource planning system that includes information about the firm's suppliers and customers as well as data generated internally.

Whereas MRP and MRPII systems are focused internally, **enterprise resource planning (ERP)** systems go a step further and incorporate information about the firm's suppliers and customers into the flow of data. ERP unites all of a firm's major departments into a single software program. For instance, production can call up sales information and know immediately how many units must be produced to meet customer orders. By providing information about the availability of resources, including both human resources and materials needed for production, the system allows for better cost control and eliminates production delays. The system automatically notes any changes, such as the closure of a plant for maintenance and repairs on a certain date or a supplier's inability to meet a delivery date, so that all functions can adjust accordingly. ERP is being used to improve operations not only in large corporations, such as Boeing, Lockheed Martin, and General Motors, but in small businesses as well, as the Focusing on Small Business box describes.

> f o c u s i n g   o n   s m a l l   b u s i n e s s <

PUTTING ANTHRO'S PRODUCTION TOGETHER WITH ERP

Anthro Corp. executives are clear about their strategic goal. They want to be the McDonald's of the furniture industry. To get there, they know they must find a way to make producing custom office furniture as simple as turning out burgers.

In its plant in Tualatin, Oregon, Anthro's 65 employees make furniture to hold electronic gear like personal computers, medical instruments, and video equipment. Once customers place their orders over the phone, the manufacturing workers assemble prefabricated parts to each customer's specifications. Anthro promises to ship the finished furniture within 24 hours.

Anthro's problems began when sales took off. Suddenly, the company was struggling to keep up with the 30,000 different production orders that streamed in each year. Managing inventory also became more difficult. The plant sometimes ran out of critical items like castors just when workers needed them.

The solution? Anthro purchased an enterprise resource planning (ERP) system from software maker SAP. The $500,000 system runs on 30 PCs and links together everyone from senior executives to production workers. When a customer places an order, it is immediately entered into the ERP system, which automatically calculates the costs of producing the order.

At the same time, the system releases a production order to the factory floor that alerts workers to the details of the customer's order. The system also checks on-hand inventory. If a part needed for assembly isn't available, the system either sends a purchase order to Anthro's suppliers or tells assembly workers what needs to be done.

It took Anthro six months to implement the system, but company president Shoaib Tareer says he expects benefits like faster production times to continue for many years. "You have to have a long-term focus, because the advantage is, once you get it going, you can grow with it."

Critical Thinking Questions

1. How might the benefits from ERP affect Anthro's other functions such as marketing, human resources, or financial management?
2. Why do you think Anthro decided to install an ERP system instead of an MRP or MRPII system?
3. Do you agree with Anthro's president that the $500,000 investment in ERP was worthwhile? What other changes in production planning could the company have made to improve operating efficiency?

Supply Chain Management

In the past, the relationship between purchasers and suppliers was often competitive and antagonistic. Businesses used many suppliers and switched among them frequently. During contract negotiations, each side would try to get better terms at the expense of the other. Communication between purchasers and suppliers was often limited to purchase orders and billing statements.

supply chain

The entire sequence of securing inputs, producing goods, and delivering goods to customers.

Today, however, many firms are moving toward a new concept in supplier relationships. The emphasis is increasingly on developing a strong **supply chain.** The supply chain can be thought of as the entire sequence of securing inputs, producing goods, and delivering goods to customers. If any of the links in this process are weak, chances are customers—the end point of the supply chain—will end up dissatisfied.

supply chain management

The process of smoothing transitions along the supply chain so that the firm can satisfy its customers with quality products and services; focuses on developing tighter bonds with suppliers.

Strategies for Supply Chain Management Ensuring a strong supply chain requires that firms implement supply chain management strategies. **Supply chain management** focuses on smoothing transitions along the supply chain, with the ultimate goal of satisfying customers with quality products and services. A critical element of effective supply chain management is to develop tighter bonds with suppliers. In many cases, this means reducing the number of suppliers used and asking those suppliers to offer more services or better prices in return for an ongoing relationship. Instead of being viewed as "outsiders" in the production process, many suppliers are now playing an important role in supporting the operations of their customers. They are expected to meet higher quality standards, offer suggestions that can help reduce production costs, and even contribute to the design of new products.

One company that is seeking to forge stronger bonds with its suppliers is AMD. AMD manufactures integrated circuits that are used to build computers and communications equipment. The company has manufacturing facilities in the United States, Asia, and Europe and regards its suppliers as partners in the production process. Before a company can sell to AMD, it must pass a rigorous evaluation by AMD managers and executives. Each supplier must show that it is willing to match AMD's dedication to quality, reliability, service, and flexibility in meeting demand. Suppliers who meet AMD's requirements are rewarded with a long-term relationship with the company.[8]

Get a bird's eye view of AMD's manufacturing by viewing the quick-time video at

www.amd.com/video/manufac-qt.html

Improving Supplier Communications Underlying supply chain management is the development of strong communications with suppliers. Technology is providing new ways to do this. Some manufacturing firms are using the Internet to keep key suppliers informed about their requirements. Intel, for example, has set up a special Web site for its suppliers and potential suppliers. Would-be suppliers can visit the site to get information about doing business with Intel; once they are approved, they can access a secure area to make bids on Intel's current and future resource needs. The Internet also streamlines purchasing

Want to do business with Intel? Check out the company's supplier site at

www.supplier.intel.com

by providing firms with quick access to a huge database of information about the products and services of hundreds of potential suppliers. The number of businesses using the Internet to buy materials, supplies, and services is skyrocketing. According to market research firm International Data Corp., $32 billion of business-to-business purchases were made on the Internet in 1998 alone. By the year 2002, expect to see $331 billion of purchasing activity on the Web.[9]

Another communications tool is **electronic data interchange (EDI),** in which two trading partners exchange information electronically. EDI can be conducted via a linked computer system or over the Internet. The advantages of exchanging information with suppliers electronically include speed, accuracy, and lowered communication costs.

PRODUCTION AND OPERATIONS CONTROL

>lg 5

electronic data interchange (EDI)
The electronic exchange of information between two trading partners.

Every company needs to have systems in place to see that production and operations are carried out as planned and to correct errors when they are not. The coordination of materials, equipment, and human resources to achieve production and operating efficiencies is called production control. Two of its key aspects are routing and scheduling.

Routing Production

Routing is the first step in controlling production. It sets out a work flow, that is, the sequence of machines and operations through which a product or service progresses from start to finish. Routing depends on the type of goods being produced and the facility layout. Good routing procedures increase productivity and cut unnecessary costs.

McDonald's is experimenting with new food preparation routes in many of its restaurants. The changes are part of McDonald's "Made For You" program, a strategic decision to offer customers more choices in how their orders are prepared. First, the restaurant chain redesigned its kitchens to improve the way orders are prepared and routed through the kitchen. New high-tech food preparation equipment that automates much of the order preparation process was added. Finally, a centralized computer system improved the flow of communications between the customer counter and the kitchen. When a customer orders a Big Mac, the order taker enters it into a specially designed cash register that simultaneously sends the information to a video screen in the kitchen. Before the customer has even finished paying, kitchen workers have almost a third of the order completed. Within a few moments, the order, including customizations such as extra ketchup or tomatoes, is on its way out to the customer.[10]

Scheduling

Closely related to routing is **scheduling.** Scheduling involves specifying and controlling the time required for each step in the production process. The operations manager prepares timetables showing the most efficient sequence of production and then tries to ensure that the necessary materials and labor are in the right place at the right time.

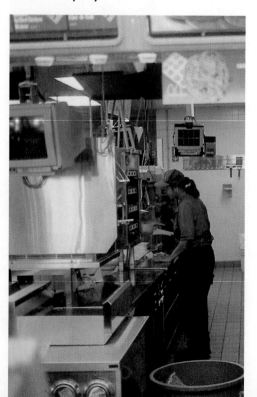

Redesigned food preparation routes and a computer system that links kitchen workers with order takers is helping McDonald's to serve customized food quickly.

routing

The aspect of production control that involves setting out the work flow—the sequence of machines and operations through which the product or service progresses from start to finish.

scheduling

The aspect of production control that involves specifying and controlling the time required for each step in the production process.

Scheduling is important to both manufacturing and service firms. The production manager in a factory schedules material deliveries, work shifts, and production processes. Trucking companies schedule drivers, clerks, and truck maintenance and repair with customer transportation needs. Scheduling at a college entails deciding when to offer which courses in which classrooms with which instructors. A museum must schedule its special exhibits, ship the works to be displayed, market its services, and conduct educational programs and tours.

Scheduling can range from simple to complex. Giving numbers to customers waiting in a bakery and making interview appointments with job applicants are examples of simple scheduling. Organizations that must produce large quantities of products or services, or service a diverse customer base, face more complex scheduling problems.

Three common scheduling tools used for complex situations are Gantt charts, the critical path method, and PERT.

Gantt charts

Bar graphs plotted on a time line that show the relationship between scheduled and actual production.

Gantt Charts   Named after their originator, Henry Gantt, **Gantt charts** are bar graphs plotted on a time line that show the relationship between scheduled and actual production. Exhibit 12-6 is an example. On the left, the chart lists the activities required to complete the job or project. Both the scheduled time and the actual time required for each activity are shown, so the manager can easily judge progress.

Gantt charts are most helpful when only a few tasks are involved, when task times are relatively long (days or weeks rather than hours), and when job routes are short and simple. One of the biggest shortcomings of Gantt charts is that they are static. They also fail to show how tasks are related. These problems can be solved, however, by using two other scheduling techniques, the critical path method, and PERT.

> e x h i b i t   1 2 - 6 <

A Typical Gantt Chart

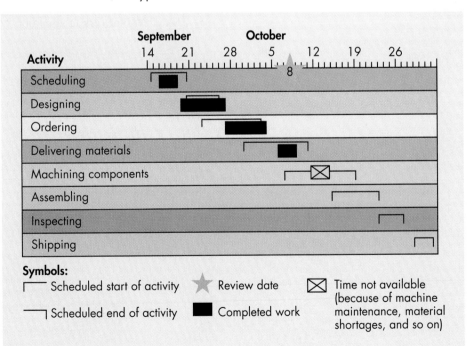

The Critical Path Method and PERT To control large projects, operations managers need to closely monitor resources, costs, quality, and budgets. They also must be able to see the "big picture"—the interrelationships of the many different tasks necessary to complete the project. Finally, they must be able to revise scheduling and divert resources quickly if any tasks fall behind schedule. The critical path method (CPM) and the program evaluation and review technique (PERT) are related project management tools that were developed in the 1950s to help managers accomplish this.

In the **critical path method (CPM)**, the manager identifies all of the activities required to complete the project, the relationships between these activities, and the order in which they need to be completed. Then, the manager develops a diagram that uses arrows to show how the tasks are dependent on each other. The longest path through these linked activities is called the **critical path.** If the tasks on the critical path are not completed on time, the entire project will fall behind schedule.

To better understand how CPM works, look at Exhibit 12-7, which shows a CPM diagram for constructing a house. All of the tasks required to finish the house and an estimated time for each have been identified. The arrows indicate the links between the various steps and their required sequence. As you can see, most of the jobs to be done can't be started until the house's foundation and frame are completed. It will take five days to finish the foundation and another seven days to erect the house frame. The activities linked by red arrows form the critical path for this project. It tells us that the fastest possible time the house can be built is 38 days, the total time needed for all of the critical path tasks. The noncritical path jobs, those connected with black arrows, can be delayed a bit or done early. Short delays in installing appliances or roofing won't delay construction of the house because these activities don't lie on the critical path.

Like CPM, **program evaluation and review technique (PERT)** helps managers identify critical tasks and assess how delays in certain activities will affect operations or production. In both methods, managers use diagrams to see how

critical path method (CPM)

A project management tool that enables a manager to determine the critical path of activities for a project—the activities that will cause the entire project to fall behind schedule if they are not completed on time.

critical path

In a critical path method network, the longest path through the linked activities.

program evaluation and review technique (PERT)

A project management tool that is similar to the CPM method but assigns three time estimates for each activity (optimistic, most probable, and pessimistic); allows managers to anticipate delays and potential problems and schedule accordingly.

> e x h i b i t   1 2 - 7 <

A CPM Network for Building a House

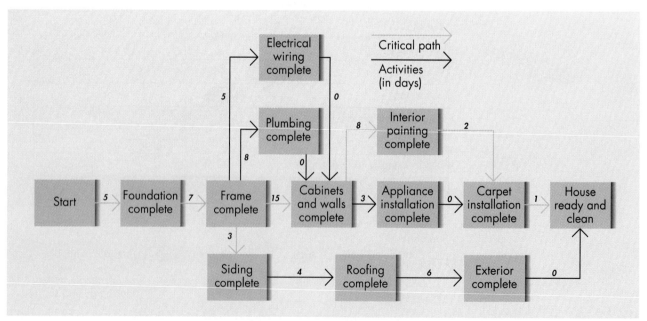

operations and production will flow. PERT differs from CPM in one important respect, however. CPM assumes that the amount of time needed to finish a task is known with certainty; therefore, the CPM diagram shows only one number for the time needed to complete each activity. In contrast, PERT assigns three time estimates for each activity: an optimistic time for completion, the most probable time, and a pessimistic time. These estimates allow managers to anticipate delays and potential problems and schedule accordingly.

c o n c ə p t   c h ə c k

- What is production control, and what are its key aspects?
- Identify and describe three commonly used scheduling tools.

IMPROVING PRODUCTION AND OPERATIONS

>lg 6

Competing in today's business world is difficult. The process of producing and delivering goods and services is becoming increasingly complex. Customers are demanding higher levels of quality and satisfaction. The lower production costs enjoyed by many foreign competitors can be difficult to compete against. In light of these challenges, businesses are continually looking for new ways to keep quality high, costs low, and production processes flowing smoothly. Among the methods that many companies have successfully implemented are total quality management, lean manufacturing, and automation.

Total Quality Management

Successful businesses recognize that quality and productivity must go hand in hand. Defective products waste materials and time, increasing costs. Worse, poor quality causes customer dissatisfaction, which usually means lost sales.

quality control

The process of creating standards for quality and then measuring finished products and services against them.

To a consumer, quality is how well a good serves its purpose. From the company's point of view, quality is the degree to which a good conforms to a set of predetermined standards. **Quality control** involves creating those quality standards and measuring finished products and services against them. Once quality control was simply a matter of inspecting products before they went out the door. Today, it's a company-wide commitment that involves every facet of operations.

One of the first to say that quality control should be a company-wide goal was an American, Dr. W. Edwards Deming. His ideas were adopted by the Japanese in the 1950s but largely ignored in the United States until the 1970s. Deming suggested that merely inspecting products after they are produced is not enough to ensure quality. He believed that quality control must start with top management, who must foster a culture dedicated to producing quality. Teamwork between managers and workers helps to identify ways to improve the production process, leading to better quality.

total quality management (TQM)

The use of quality principles in all aspects of a company's production and operations.

Total quality management (TQM) refers to the use of quality principles in all aspects of a company's production and operations. It emphasizes that all employees involved with bringing a product or service to customers—marketing, purchasing, accounting, shipping, manufacturing—contribute to its quality. TQM focuses on improving operations to achieve greater efficiency and, in turn, higher quality. Nearly every decision involved in production and operations management can affect a firm's ability to produce high-quality products and services. In Chapter 14, we'll look at some specific methods businesses are using to control and improve quality.

lean manufacturing

Streamlining production by eliminating steps in the production process that do not add benefits that customers are willing to pay for.

The Move toward Lean Manufacturing

Manufacturers are discovering that they can better respond to rapidly changing customer demands, while keeping inventory and production costs down, by adopting lean manufacturing techniques. **Lean manufacturing** can be defined as streamlining production by eliminating steps in the production process that do not add benefits that customers are willing to pay for. In other words, non-value-added production processes are cut so that the company can concentrate its production and operations resources on items essential to satisfying customers. Toyota was a pioneer in developing these techniques, but today manufacturers in many industries have also adopted the lean manufacturing philosophy.

just-in-time (JIT)

A system in which materials arrive just when they are needed for production rather than being stored on site.

Another Japanese concept, **just-in-time (JIT),** goes hand in hand with lean manufacturing. JIT is based on the belief that materials should arrive exactly when they are needed for production, rather than being stored on site. Relying closely on computerized systems such as MRP, MRPII, and ERP, manufacturers determine what parts will be needed and when, and then order them from suppliers so they arrive "just in time." Under the JIT system, inventory and products are "pulled" through the production process in response to customer demand. JIT requires close teamwork between vendors and production and purchasing personnel because any delay in deliveries of supplies could bring JIT production to a halt. If employed properly, however, a JIT system can greatly reduce inventory holding costs and can also smooth production highs and lows.

Automation in Productions and Operations Management

>lg 7

Technology is helping many firms improve their operating efficiency and ability to compete. Computer systems, in particular, are enabling manufacturers to automate factories in ways never before possible.

Travel through Winnebago's production processes at
www.winnebagoind.com/companyinfo

Consider how technology and automation have helped Winnebago. Plagued with production problems, the recreational-vehicle maker decided to use technology to streamline production and improve product quality. Since 1995, the company has spent approximately $5 million annually to automate its factory. Now a single worker is able to oversee the routing of panels needed to produce customized models with the touch of a button. A $400,000 computer tells the plant's production machines how to cut materials to fit the desired floor plan and accessories. Using computerized equipment, one worker can now do tasks that previously required several workers.[11]

computer-aided design (CAD)

The use of computers to design and test new products and modify existing ones.

computer-aided manufacturing (CAM)

The use of computers to develop and control the production process.

CAD/CAM systems

Linked computer systems that combine the advantages of computer-aided design and computer-aided manufacturing. The system helps design the product, control the flow of resources, and operate the production process.

Among the technologies helping to automate manufacturing are computer aided-design and manufacturing, robotics, flexible manufacturing systems, and computer-integrated manufacturing.

Computer-Aided Design and Manufacturing Systems Computers have transformed the design and manufacturing processes in many industries. In **computer-aided design (CAD),** computers are used to design and test new products and modify existing ones. Engineers use these systems to draw products and look at them from different angles. They can analyze the products, make changes, and test prototypes before making even one item. **Computer-aided manufacturing (CAM)** uses computers to develop and control the production process. The systems analyze the steps required to make the product. They then automatically send instructions to the machines that do the work. **CAD/CAM systems** combine the advantages of CAD and CAM by integrating design, testing, and manufacturing control into one linked computer system. The system helps design the product, control the flow of resources needed to produce the product, and operate the production process.

Automakers like General Motors have relied on CAD/CAM technology for some time. Using CAD/CAM systems, automotive designers are able to see a three-dimensional version of the car they are designing and make subtle adjustments to the design that can make a car model stand out in consumers' minds. The systems also detail and track all of the materials, parts, and processes necessary to move each car from the design stage to the showroom.[12]

Robotics   Robots are computer-controlled machines that can perform tasks independently. **Robotics** is the technology involved in designing, constructing, and operating robots. The first robot, or "steel-collar worker," was used by General Motors in 1961.

Robots can be mobile or fixed in one place. Fixed robots have an arm that moves and does what the computer instructs. Some robots are quite simple, with limited movement for a few tasks such as cutting sheet metal and spot welding. Others are complex, with hands or grippers that can be programmed to perform a series of movements. Some robots are even equipped with sensing devices for sight and touch.

Robots usually operate with little or no human intervention. Replacing human effort with robots is most effective for tasks requiring accuracy, speed, or strength. Although manufacturers, such as Harley-Davidson as described at the beginning of this chapter, are most likely to use robots, some service firms are also finding them useful. Loyola University Medical Center in Chicago uses a $500,000 robot to sort and process hundreds of blood samples daily, freeing medical personnel from a tedious, and sometimes hazardous, repetitive task. The hospital estimates it saves about $200,000 a year in lab operating costs.[13]

Flexible Manufacturing Systems   A relatively new way to automate a factory is to blend computers, robots, machine tools, and materials- and parts-handling machinery into a **flexible manufacturing system (FMS).** These systems combine automated workstations with computer-controlled transportation devices. Automatic guided vehicles (AGVs) move materials between workstations and into and out of the system.

Flexible manufacturing systems are expensive. Once in place, however, a system requires little labor to operate and provides consistent product quality. The system can be changed easily and inexpensively. FMS equipment can be programmed to perform one job and then quickly be reprogrammed to perform another. These systems work well when small batches of a variety of products are required or when each product is made to individual customer specifications.

Computer-Integrated Manufacturing   Computer-integrated manufacturing **(CIM)** combines computerized manufacturing processes (like robots and FMS) with other computerized systems that control design, inventory, production, and purchasing. With CIM, when a part is redesigned in the CAD system, the changes are quickly transmitted both to the machines producing the part and to all other departments that need to know about and plan for the change.

robotics
The technology involved in designing, constructing, and operating robots (computer-controlled machines that can perform tasks independently).

flexible manufacturing system (FMS)
A system that combines automated workstations with computer-controlled transportation devices—automatic guided vehicles (AGVs)—that move materials between workstations and into and out of the system.

computer-integrated manufacturing (CIM)
The combination of computerized manufacturing processes such as robots and flexible manufacturing systems with other computerized systems that control design, inventory, production, and purchasing.

With computer-aided design, engineers can design, analyze, modify, and test prototypes before products are manufactured.

Technology and Automation in Nonmanufacturing Operations

Manufacturers are not the only businesses benefiting from technology. Nonmanufacturing firms are also using automation to improve customer service and productivity. Banks now offer services to customers through automated teller machines (ATMs), via automated telephone systems, and even over the Internet. Retail stores of all kinds use point-of-sale (POS) terminals that track inventories, identify items that need to be reordered, and tell which products are selling well. Wal-Mart, the leader in retailing automation, has its own satellite system connecting POS terminals directly to its distribution centers and headquarters. As the Applying Technology box discusses, the restaurant industry is also streamlining operations with automation technology.

concept check

- Define total quality management, lean manufacturing, and just-in-time, and explain how each can help a firm improve its production and operations.
- How are both manufacturing and nonmanufacturing firms using technology and automation to improve operations?

> a p p l y i n g t e c h n o l o g y <

AUTOMATION SPEEDS UP FAST FOOD

Tired of long lines at fast-food restaurants? Chains like McDonald's, Arby's, and Burger King are hoping technology can put the "fast" back into fast food by automating many of the processes used in taking and preparing food orders.

You may have already noticed changes on drive-thru menu boards. McDonald's and Hardee's restaurants have rotating menu boards that automatically change according to the time of day. Pull up at breakfast and the board will show only breakfast items. Visit at lunch time and you'll see lunch items. By limiting the choices displayed on the menu board, the restaurant makes it easier and quicker for customers to order. McDonald's and Burger King have also put special LCD screens at the drive-thru that show what you've ordered so you can instantly see if your order isn't right. Next innovation for the drive-thru? Face-to-face video technology that will let you see the face of the cashier (and let the cashier see you) as you're ordering.

Inside, fast-food restaurants are also changing. Most chains have high-tech point-of-sale (POS) computer systems. When you order at the counter, the clerk enters the information at the register, and it is automatically transmitted to the kitchen. These systems also let managers keep track of customer sales and operating efficiency. Soon, some fast-food chains will be adding self-service terminals so that you can punch in and pay for your order without waiting in line.

In the kitchen, technology is speeding up food preparation. FAST, Inc. (**www.fastinc.com**), a computer automa-

tion company, has developed the SMART Commercial Kitchen system, which links computer technology with the cooking controls of all the kitchen's appliances. The system automatically tells appliances such as ovens, fryers, and holding cabinets when to turn on, how long and at what temperature to cook, and when to turn off. Arby's has connected its SMART system to its POS system. When customer orders reach a certain level, the SMART system tells workers in the kitchen to put more beef in the ovens and then instantly sets the right cooking times.

Perhaps the most intriguing technologies on the horizon are automated handwashing systems. Spurred by recent incidents of food contamination, many chains are looking into equipping workers with electronic handwashing badges. The badges will beep at selected intervals to remind employees to wash their hands or change their gloves. They'll also keep track of whether the employee does as told—and report any handwashing deadbeats to the restaurant manager!

Critical Thinking Questions

1. How is automation likely to change customers' opinions of fast-food restaurants? Why?
2. Discuss the effect of automation and technology on the employees of fast-food restaurants.
3. Do you think some of the technology being used in fast-food restaurants would work for the cafeteria in your school? How about for an expensive steakhouse? Defend your answers.

CAPITALIZING ON TRENDS IN BUSINESS

>lg 8

The past decade has seen the U.S. economy grow at an unprecedented rate. Stock prices and corporate profits in many industries have soared, and unemployment and inflation have plummeted. Changes in production and operations management have made a huge contribution to this success and are likely to continue to propel productivity and economic growth in the new millennium.

Although traditional manufacturing firms generate over $3 trillion in sales each year, their role in the economy is changing.[14] The number of jobs provided by manufacturing companies is shrinking; manufacturing now accounts for just 15 percent of U.S. jobs, down from 35 percent in the 1950s.[15] Faced with growing global competition, more complex products, and more demanding consumers, manufacturers are having to rethink how, when, and where they produce the goods they sell. Because product prices in most industries have not risen over the past decade, it is also vital that manufacturers uncover new production techniques that keep production costs as low as possible.

Nonmanufacturing firms also face operating challenges. Like manufacturers, they must keep up with the constant pace of change and carefully manage how they use and deploy resources. As the service sector grows, so do customer expectations about the speed and quality of service. This puts increased pressure on nonmanufacturing firms to be ever vigilant in their search for new ways of streamlining service production and operations. In this section, we will look at some of the trends likely to alter how companies manage and control the production of goods and services in the future.

Modular Production

The executives at Palm Computing knew they had a good idea: a small electronic personal organizer called the Pilot. They also knew that their competitive advantage would depend on getting the Pilot on the market as quickly as possible, a schedule that would be impossible to meet without help. The Pilot's designers wrote detailed specifications for how the product should be produced; then the company invited 3,500 other firms to create different parts of the product. Working together, Palm and its suppliers soon had the Pilot on the market. It became one of history's hottest products, selling more than 1 million units in its first 18 months.

Palm Computing's success highlights a growing trend in the business world, *modular production.* Modular production involves breaking a complex product, service, or process into smaller pieces that can be created independently and then combined quickly to make a whole. Modular production not only cuts the cost of developing and designing innovative products, but it also gives businesses a tool for meeting rapidly changing conditions. Modular production also makes it easier to implement mass customization or pure customization strategies. With access to a variety of components that can be assembled in different ways, endless combinations of product features are possible.

Palm Computing's modular production process have helped the company compete effectively. Learn more about Palm Computing at http://palm.3com.com

Agile Manufacturing

Another concept businesses are using to stay flexible and move fast is *agile manufacturing*. Investing millions of dollars in production processes, resources, and equipment that can be used only to produce one particular product doesn't always make economic sense. When customer demands shift or new technological innovations occur, the firm must be able to adapt. In agile manufacturing, firms strive to develop a production system comprised of flexible tools and processes that can be quickly changed to produce new or different products. Toyota uses agile manufacturing methods at its Kentucky plant. The factory builds both Camry and Avalon cars and the Siena minivans on the same assembly line. All three vehicles basically rely on the same underlying body platform. As the vehicles move through the plant, different components and parts are added depending on whether workers are producing a minivan or a car.[16]

Trends in Facility Layout

Work cell design, also sometimes called module design or cellular manufacturing, is an innovation that some manufacturers are finding can help improve quality and production efficiency. Work cells are small, self-contained production units that include several machines and workers arranged in a compact, sequential order. Each work cell performs all or most of the tasks necessary to complete either a product or a major production sequence. There are usually between 5 and 10 workers in a cell, and they are trained to be able to do any of the steps in the production process. The goal is to create a team environment where team members are involved in production from beginning to end.

Work cell design can have dramatic results. Berne Apparel, a maker of cotton coveralls and jackets, has been using the concept for a year. Workers in each group now work together to complete entire garments, rather than just parts of a garment. Because they can communicate with each other better and fill different production roles to get the job done, production time has been cut and quality improved. The company also has less employee turnover.[17]

concept check

- Explain modular production.
- How can agile manufacturing help a company obtain a competitive advantage?
- Explain how work cell design can help a company improve quality and efficiency.

APPLYING THIS CHAPTER'S TOPICS

As we've seen throughout this chapter, every organization produces something. Cereal manufacturers turn grains into breakfast foods. Law firms turn the skills and knowledge of attorneys into legal services. Retailers provide a convenient way for consumers to purchase a variety of goods. Colleges and universities convert students into educated individuals. Therefore, no matter what type of organization you end up working for in the future, you will be involved, to one degree or another, with your employer's production and operations processes.

In some jobs, such as plant manager and quality-control manager, you will have a direct role in the production process. But employees of manufacturing firms are not the only ones involved with production. Software developers, bank tellers, medical personnel, magazine writers, and a host of other jobs are also actively involved in turning inputs into outputs. If you manage people in these types of jobs, you'll need insight into the tools used to plan, schedule, and control production processes. Understanding production processes, resource management, and techniques for increasing productivity is vital to be-

Track a Project with a Gantt Chart   Your teacher has just announced a huge assignment, due in three weeks. Where do you start? How can you best organize your time? A Gantt chart can help you plan and schedule more effectively. First, break the assignment down into smaller tasks. Say, for instance, that you have a 10-page research paper due in three weeks. Your list of tasks would include picking a topic, researching information at the library and on the Internet, organizing your notes, developing an outline, and writing and proofreading the paper. Next, estimate how much time each task will take.

Try to be realistic. There's no sense saying it will only take you a day to write the paper when you know you have spent a week or more writing similar papers in the past. At the top of a piece of paper, list all of the days until the assignment is due. Along the side of the paper, list all of the tasks you've identified in the order they need to be done. Starting with the first task, block out the number of days you estimate each task will take. If you run out of days, you'll know you need to adjust how you've scheduled your time. If you know that you will not be able to work on some days, note them on the chart as well. Hang the chart where you can see it. Your Gantt chart will give you a visual tool for tracking your progress. Instead of worrying about the entire project all at once, you'll be able to see exactly what you should be doing on a particular day. The end result should be a terrific paper turned in on time!

coming a more valuable employee, who sees how his or her job fits into "the big picture" of the firm's operating goals.

Other professionals also need to understand production and operations management in order to help the firm reach its goals. Want to be a sales representative? An awareness of how, when, and where goods or services are made will help you better serve customer needs. Or, perhaps you plan to work in new product development. The best idea for a new product will fail if production cannot produce it in a timely, cost-effective manner. Human resource managers need to know the type of work operations personnel do in order to do a good job of recruiting and retaining employees. Financial personnel, such as accountants, also need to understand what goes on in production and operations. That knowledge helps them in budgeting, pricing products, and managing financial resources.

If you plan to start your own business, you'll also face many production and operations decisions. You can use the information from this chapter to help you find suppliers, design an operating facility (no matter how small), and put customer-satisfying processes in place. This information can also help you make decisions about whether to manufacture goods yourself or rely on outside contractors to handle production.

SUMMARY OF LEARNING GOALS

>lg 1   **Why is production and operations management important in both manufacturing and service firms?**
In the 1980s, many U.S. manufacturers lost customers to foreign competitors because their production and operations management systems did not support the high-quality, reasonably priced products consumers demanded. Service organizations also rely on effective operations management in order to satisfy consumers.

Operations managers, the personnel charged with managing and supervising the conversion of inputs into outputs, work closely with other functions in organizations to help ensure quality, customer satisfaction, and financial success.

>looking ahead

at Harley-Davidson

Harley-Davidson's new Kansas City manufacturing plant is up and running. After less than a year of operation, the new factory has helped the company increase the number of motorcycles it produces and do a better job at meeting consumer demand. But the company's executives want more. They plan to increase production from about 150,000 motorcycles in 1999 to 200,000 a year by 2003. At the same time, they hope to save $40 million in production and inventory costs.

How will Harley-Davidson increase production while slashing costs? By making an enormous technology investment. The company is spending $50 million in 1999 alone—about 2 percent of projected sales—to install new computer systems that will eventually automate how production and operations information is managed and used throughout the company.

Topping the list of purchases is a new computer system that will help Harley-Davidson manage its relationships with suppliers. Since 1995, the company has cut the number of its suppliers from 1,000 to just over 425. Now the company hopes to streamline its $1 billion annual spending for parts, components, and materials. The new system will boost the company's ability to order electronically and will involve suppliers more closely in the design and development of new products.

Although some analysts criticize Harley-Davidson's slow and deliberate pace of incorporating technology and other changes into production, others are convinced that's the secret to the motorcycle manufacturer's success. "This is a company that gets better every quarter," says one analyst. "There's nothing wrong with being an intelligent tortoise as opposed to a hare."[18]

>lg 2 What types of production processes are used by manufacturers and service firms?

Products are made using one of three types of production processes. In mass production, many identical goods are produced at once, keeping production costs low. Mass production, therefore, relies heavily on standardization, mechanization, and specialization. When mass customization is used, goods are produced using mass production techniques up to a point, after which the product or service is custom tailored to individual customers by adding special features. In general, mass customization is more expensive than mass production, but consumers are often willing to pay more for mass-customized products. When a firm's production process is built around customization, the firm makes many products one at a time according to the very specific needs or wants of individual customers.

>lg 3 How do organizations decide where to put their production facilities? What choices must be made in designing the facility?

Site selection affects operating costs, the price of the product or service, and the company's ability to compete. In choosing a production site, firms must weigh the availability of resources—raw materials, human resources, and even capital—needed for production, as well as the ability to serve customers and take advantage of marketing opportunities. Other factors include the availability of local incentives and the manufacturing environment. Once a site is selected, the firm must choose an appropriate design for the facility. The three main production facility designs are process, product, and fixed-position layouts.

>lg 4 Why are resource planning tasks like inventory management and supplier relations critical to production?

Production converts input resources, such as raw materials and labor, into outputs, finished goods and services. Firms must ensure that the resources needed

KEY TERMS

assembly process 350
bill of material 356
CAD/CAM systems 364
computer-aided design (CAD) 364
computer-aided manufacturing (CAM) 364
computer-integrated manufacturing (CIM) 365
continuous process 350
critical path 362
critical path method (CPM) 362
customization 349
electronic data interchange (EDI) 360
enterprise resource planning (ERP) 358
fixed-position layout 354
flexible manufacturing system (FMS) 365
Gantt charts 361
intermittent process 351
inventory 357
inventory management 357
job shop 349
just-in-time (JIT) 364
lean manufacturing 363
make-or-buy decision 356
manufacturing resource planning II (MRPII) 357
mass customization 349
mass production 349
materials requirement planning (MRP) 357
operations management 347
outsourcing 356
perpetual inventory 357
process layout 354
process manufacturing 350

for production will be available at strategic moments in the production process. If they are not, productivity, customer satisfaction, and quality may suffer. Carefully managing inventory can help cut production costs while maintaining enough supply for production and sales. Through good relationships with suppliers, firms can get better prices, reliable resources, and support services that can improve production efficiency.

>lg 5   **How do operations managers schedule and control production?**
Routing is the first step in scheduling and controlling production. Routing analyzes the steps needed in production and sets out a work flow, the sequence of machines and operations through which a product or service progresses from start to finish. Good routing increases productivity and can eliminate unnecessary cost. Scheduling involves specifying and controlling the time and resources required for each step in the production process. It can range from simple to complex. Operations managers use three methods to schedule production: Gantt charts, the critical path method, and PERT.

>lg 6   **How can quality management and lean manufacturing techniques help firms improve production and operations management?**
Quality and productivity go hand in hand. Defective products waste materials and time, increasing costs. Poor quality also leads to dissatisfied customers. By implementing quality-control methods, firms often reduce these problems and streamline production. Lean manufacturing also helps streamline production by eliminating unnecessary steps in the production process. When activities that don't add value for customers are eliminated, manufacturers can respond to changing market conditions with greater flexibility and ease.

>lg 7   **What roles do technology and automation play in manufacturing and service industry operations management?**
Many firms are improving their operational efficiency by using technology to automate parts of production. Computer-aided design and manufacturing systems, for example, help design new products, control the flow of resources needed for production, and even operate much of the production process. By using robotics, human time and effort can be minimized. Robots are especially useful for tasks that require accuracy, speed, and strength. Factories are being automated by blending computers, robots, and machinery into flexible manufacturing systems that require less labor to operate. Service firms are automating operations too. Banks, law firms, and utility companies have used technology to cut labor costs and control quality.

>lg 8   **What key trends are affecting the way companies manage production and operations?**
Faced with growing global competition, increased product complexity, and more demanding consumers, manufacturers are rethinking how, when, and where they produce the goods they sell. Agile manufacturing is a concept that helps manufacturers stay fast and flexible. Firms strive to develop production systems composed of tools and processes that can be quickly changed to produce new or different products. Cellular manufacturing creates small, self-contained production units that include several machines and workers. Each work cell performs all or most of the tasks necessary to complete a product or production sequence. Because of these trends and the increased use of technology in production, firms are recognizing that smarter, better motivated workers are an asset. Both manufacturing and nonmanufacturing firms are therefore putting new emphasis on empowering employees—giving them greater say in deciding how their jobs should be done and a larger role in company decision making.

product (or
  assembly-line)
  layout 354
production 347
production
  planning 348
production process
  349
program evaluation
  and review
  technique (PERT)
  362
purchasing 356
quality control 363
robotics 365
routing 360
scheduling 360
supply chain 359
supply chain
  management 359
total quality
  management
  (TQM) 363

PREPARING FOR TOMORROW'S WORKPLACE

1. Reliance Systems, headquartered in Oklahoma City, is a manufacturer of computer keyboards. The company plans to build a second factory and hopes to find a location with access to low-cost but skilled workers, national and international transportation, and favorable government incentives. The company has zeroed in on three possible states for the site: Connecticut, Kentucky, and Louisiana. Divide the class into four groups. Assign one state to each of three groups, while the fourth group will represent the company's board of directors. The state groups should read information about their state, available at **www.corporatelocation.com,** and develop a case for that state. The board group should read about all three states. Each group will make a brief presentation to the board on behalf of their state. The board will choose the new site. After the presentations, have a general discussion about the board's decision: whether you agree with it, the factors the board used to support the decision, and other factors Reliance should consider in the site selection process.

2. Tom Lawrence and Sally Zickle are co-owners of L-Z Marketing, an advertising agency. Last week, they landed a major aerospace manufacturer as a client. The company wants the agency to create its annual report. Tom, who develops the art for the agency, needs about a week to develop the preliminary report design, another two weeks to set the type, and three weeks to get the report printed. Sally writes the material for the report and doesn't need as much time: two days to meet with the client to review the company's financial information and about three weeks to write the report copy. Of course, Tom can't set type until Sally has finished writing the report. The client will also need two days between each step to review and approve Tom and Sally's work. Sally will also need three days to proofread the report before it goes to the printer. Divide the class into three or four groups. Each team should develop either a Gantt chart or a critical path diagram for Tom and Sally to use in scheduling the project. Explain why you chose the method you did. How long will it take Tom and Sally to finish the project if there are no unforeseen delays? Compare the groups' answers and discuss any variations.

3. Look for ways that technology and automation are used at your school, in the local supermarket, and at your doctor's office. As a class, discuss how automation affects the service you receive from each of these organizations. Does one organization use any types of automation that might be effectively used by one of the others? Explain.

4. Pick a small business in your community. Make a list of the resources critical to the firm's production and operations. What would happen if the business suddenly couldn't acquire any of these resources? Divide the class into small groups and discuss strategies that small businesses can use to manage their supply chain.

5. Pretend the class has been assigned the task of making sandwiches for the annual school homecoming party. The homecoming committee wants 120 peanut butter and jelly sandwiches, 179 ham and cheese sandwiches, 87 cheese sandwiches, and 99 turkey sandwiches. All of the peanut butter and jelly sandwiches must be on white bread. Half of the remaining sandwiches should be on white, a quarter on whole wheat, and the rest on rye bread. All of the ham and cheese sandwiches should have pickles and mustard. Half of the cheese and turkey sandwiches should have mayonnaise only and the other half both mayo and mustard. As a class, decide which production layout and processes will be most effective for producing the sandwich order.

Move different class members into place. Explain the advantages and disadvantages of your choices. How would you adapt if the order was doubled? Cut in half? If the committee decided it needed the sandwiches a day early?

WORKING THE NET

1. Go to **purchasing.miningco.com/msub-corp.htm.** Pick two or three of the companies listed and visit their supplier information Web sites. Compare the requirements the companies set for their suppliers. How do the requirements differ? How are they similar? Which company demands the most from its suppliers? Why do you think this is?

2. Visit *Corporate Location* magazine's Web site **www.corporatelocation.com.** Under corporate location tips, you will find a database that compares locations for these industries: general services, telecommunications, automotive manufacturing, and electronics manufacturing. Do a search to see which U.S. states are best for each industry. Are there differences? Which industry seems to have the broadest choice of locations? Why do you think this is? Which industry seems to have the narrowest choice? Why do you think this is?

3. *Industry Week* magazine's Web site at **www.industryweek.com** has a wide variety of articles covering manufacturing methods and techniques. Choose three of these production methods: lean manufacturing, work cell design, CAD/CAM systems, ERP, supply chain management. Then do a search in the site's database to find an example of a firm that has adopted one of the methods you chose. Find an example for each of the three methods. Write a paragraph about each firm, describing how it has applied the method you chose and the results it has achieved. What problems did the firm encounter? How did it solve those problems?

4. Manufacturers face many federal, state, and local regulations. Visit the National Association of Manufacturers at **www.nam.org.** Pick two or three of the legislative or regulatory issues discussed there and use a search engine like Yahoo (**www.yahoo.com**) to find more information.

5. Using a search engine like Excite (**www.excite.com**) or Info Seek (**www.infoseek.com**), search for information about technologies like robotics, CAD/CAM systems, or ERP. Find at least three suppliers for one of these technologies. Visit their Web sites and discuss how their clients are using their products to automate production.

CREATIVE THINKING CASE

New Patterns for Jody B Fashions

Jody Branson is the owner of Jody B Fashions, a small manufacturer of women's dresses. Jody designs the dresses herself and personally orders fabrics, trims, and other materials needed for production from a number of different suppliers. Jody has a work crew of 40. Production begins when the fabric is cut using Jody's patterns. After cutting, the pieces for each dress style are placed into bundles, which are then moved through the factory from worker to worker. Each worker opens each bundle and does one assembly task, such as sewing on collars, hemming the dresses, or adding decorative items like appliqués and lace. Then the worker puts the bundle back together and passes it on to the next person in the production process. Finished dresses are pressed and packaged for shipment.

Things were running smoothly until recently when Jody sold her first big order to Kmart. Unlike the small boutique stores Jody usually sells to, Kmart wants to buy hundreds of dresses in different style and fabric combinations all at one time. If Kmart is pleased with this first order, chances are good it will give Jody a steady stream of future business. In the past, some of Jody's suppliers haven't sent their fabrics on time, so she has always ordered extra material to avoid shortages. She tried to do the same to prepare for the Kmart order, but her inventory room has become a disorganized nightmare. Jody had to shut down production twice this week because the workers who do the cutting couldn't find the fabric she had specified.

Jody knows she is beginning to fall behind on the Kmart order. She needs to cut the amount of time her workers take to finish each dress, but she doesn't want to sacrifice quality. Luckily, Jody has set aside some emergency capital that she can use to help solve this problem. She sees only three options:

- Hire additional workers for her production crew and hope to speed up production.
- Automate some of her production systems.
- Call Kmart's buyer and ask for an extension on the order delivery deadline.

Critical Thinking Questions

1. Evaluate Jody's production processes. Could she change them in any way to increase production?
2. Discuss the effectiveness of Jody's supply chain. Make recommendations for improvement.
3. Draw a diagram of how work flows through Jody's factory. Could Jody improve production by using a different layout? Draw a diagram of how this might look.
4. What do you think Jody should do? Are there any other options she could consider? Discuss whether each option is a short-term or long-term solution.

VIDEO CASE

The Vermont Teddy Bear Company

The Vermont Teddy Bear Co. (**www.vtbear.com**), operating out of a factory in Shelburne, Vermont, uses mass customization to produce handcrafted teddy bears of such quality that each bear is guaranteed for life. Vermont Teddy Bears are targeted toward customers who are seeking quality, personalized gifts.

A Vermont Teddy Bear can easily be personalized for a specific occasion because the company produces a wide variety of teddy bears. There are numerous birthday teddy bears, get-well bears, new baby bears, "I love you" bears, summer bears, sports and hobby bears, holiday bears, graduation bears, bears for kids, occupational bears, and all-occasion bears. The occupational bears include a businessman and businesswoman, a doctor, a nurse, a teacher, and a police officer. The sports and hobby bears include a soccer bear, a golfer bear, a martial arts bear, a cheerleader bear, a fitness bear, a referee/soccer mom bear, and the Bahama Mama teddy bear, among others. Outfits for the teddy bears are sold separately.

A Vermont Teddy Bear can also be personalized with a creative card message of 35 words or less that accompanies the gift. To help customers who are at a loss for a personalized message, the company offers a variety of suggestions that can be used as is or adapted.

Another personalized service is the Bear-Gram delivery service, which is the company's core business. "By calling 1-800-829-BEAR, a customer is assisted by a Bear Counselor sales agent to design a perfect gift for a special holiday, to commemorate a life event such as a birthday, an anniversary, or the birth of a new baby, or to wish someone well during a stay in the hospital. The added value to the Bear-Gram delivery service includes a Vermont Teddy Bear customized to fit the occasion, optional embroidery, a personalized greeting card, a colorful gift box equipped with an AirHole and B'Air Bag to ensure a safe journey, all delivered with a candy treat."

The Vermont Teddy Bear Co. strives to make the best teddy bears in the world. By "combining unparalleled design innovation, unmatched product quality, and a passion for service, the Vermont Teddy Bear Company creates those moments and memories to love, cherish, and share from generation to generation."

The Vermont Teddy Bear Co. is committed to its various stakeholders. Customers are viewed as the foundation of the business, and exceeding their expectations is the backbone of the company's corporate culture. Employees, who are viewed as internal customers, function in "a results-oriented environment that encourages fairness, collaboration, mutual respect, and pride" in the company. Finally, the company engages vendors in a partnership focusing on innovative product development and unsurpassed customer service.

Critical Thinking Questions

1. What characteristics of the Vermont Teddy Bear Co.'s manufacturing operations point to the use of mass customization?
2. How does mass customization benefit the Vermont Teddy Bear Co.?
3. Why is quality control important for the Vermont Teddy Bear Co.?

Your Career in Management

Many students in business schools choose management as their major. Management principles and practices apply in any kind of organization, regardless of the product, service, or process. A person who wants to become a manager needs a strong background in psychology, sociology, group dynamics, social psychology, and human relations.

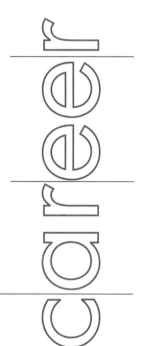

Managers must respect the individuality, dignity, and needs of the people who report to them. They must also be able to motivate others to perform needed tasks. In turn, good managers are always motivated to do the best possible job. They also are confident—and their confidence is based on continual self-evaluation of their abilities and past successes.

The new millennium will be a good time for college graduates to seek careers in management. However, a college degree does not lead immediately to a management position. The career path for a manager typically begins with a position as a management trainee. Trainees learn about company policy, the nature of the industry, operating procedures, and organization structures. They may also spend some time on the production line, work in a warehouse, or perform some other blue-collar job. The training program may last from several weeks to several years. After completing the program, new managers may specialize in sales, production, accounting, personnel, industrial relations, credit, finance, or research and development. Middle-level and upper-level managers are chosen from the ranks of sales managers, production managers, controllers, and so on.

If you enjoy working with people, consider human resource management. This field requires the ability to get along with different types of people and to communicate effectively. You do not have to be outgoing to have strong interpersonal skills. In fact, a quiet, friendly manner can be an asset. Take speech, writing, and other communication courses in college to strengthen your interpersonal skills.

A career in human resource management offers many challenges and opportunities. For instance, if you choose this field, you will have a chance to help ensure that all employees are treated fairly. All decisions must be made fairly, whether they involve who to hire, promote, and train; how much to pay; or how to help dissatisfied employees. When employees sense that the employer is unfair, their work attitudes and behaviors suffer. Absenteeism, low motivation, lack of concern for the quality of products, lack of commitment, and even sabotage may result. These attitudes and behaviors affect costs, productivity, and profits. As a communicator and an advocate, the human resource professional helps the organization succeed.

DREAM CAREER: HOTEL AND MOTEL MANAGEMENT

Hotel and motel management is a sophisticated field. Managers must understand computers, finance, and labor relations. They also need to know the seven other areas that make up the backbone of the operation: rooms, food and beverage, personnel, sales and marketing, hotel accounting, conventions, and catering. The emphasis in hotel and motel management has evolved from technical skills to management skills. Recently, the industry has become much more competitive because more companies are pursuing a limited number of travelers.

The preferred way to advance is through the management training program of a major hotel chain. Prospective managers receive 6 to 15 months of intensive training, rotating through all the major departments. The fastest way to become a general manager is to specialize in room sales or food and beverage, which are the most operations-oriented areas.

- *Places of employment.* Throughout the country and abroad, with most jobs in medium-size to large cities.
- *Skills required.* A two-year degree for some jobs, but the quickest route to management is a four-year degree. A second language is mandatory for employment overseas, and it helps in some U.S. metropolitan areas.
- *Employment outlook through 2010.* Good.
- *Salaries.* $22,000–$26,000 for trainees; $40,000–$55,000 for assistant managers; $70,000–$100,000+ for general managers in major cities.

WHERE THE OPPORTUNITIES ARE
City Manager

With the increase in urban problems—decaying inner cities, for example—cities have a great need for people with managerial skills. City managers are usually ap-

pointed by a governing body, such as a city council, and are responsible to that body. The major duties of city managers are managing tax collection and disbursement, law enforcement, and public works projects; hiring department heads and supporting staffs; and preparing annual budgets (to be approved by city officials). Other duties may include collecting rents, designing traffic controls, and planning for expansion.

- *Places of employment.* Generally, cities with populations over 50,000, although some smaller communities now hire city managers.
- *Skills required.* Master's degree in public administration, although some cities accept people with a four-year degree and several years' experience as an assistant city manager.
- *Employment outlook through 2010.* Very good. More and more cities are seeking professional managers rather than politicians to handle complex city affairs.
- *Salaries.* $30,000–$60,000 for assistant city managers; $55,000–$100,000+ for city managers, with the higher figure for medium-size to large cities.

Quality-Control Manager

If significant numbers of a product break down during the warranty period, the cost of repairs eats into corporate profits. Thus many firms hire quality-control employees for all phases of the design and manufacturing process. Others spend their money on inspection procedures. A quality-control manager supervises quality-control inspectors. The inspectors decide whether products and materials meet quality standards. To do so, they either examine every item produced or check a sample of the items.

- *Places of employment.* Everywhere, but the best opportunities are in areas where high-tech industries are concentrated, such as Austin, Boston, and Marin County, California.
- *Skills required.* Two-year degree for inspectors; two-year or four-year degree plus experience for managers; four-year degree or master's degree for quality-control engineers.
- *Employment outlook through 2010.* Above average in high-tech industries.
- *Salaries.* $28,000–$44,000 for inspectors; $40,000–$60,000 for managers; $70,000+ for managers with an engineering degree and an MBA.

Purchasing Manager

If materials, supplies, and equipment are not on hand when they're needed, the entire work flow of an organization could stop. Keeping a big enough supply on hand is the purchasing manager's responsibility. It includes more than just buying goods and services, however. Market forecasting, production planning, and inventory control are all part of the job. Purchasing managers supervise purchasing agents or industrial buyers, who do the actual buying. More than half of all purchasing managers work for moderate-size to large manufacturers. The rest work in government agencies, construction companies, hospitals, and schools.

- *Places of employment.* Throughout the country, especially in large industrial and government centers, such as Washington, D.C., Atlanta, Chicago, Pittsburgh, and Los Angeles.
- *Skills required.* Generally, a two-year or four-year degree, but many employers now require an MBA.
- *Employment outlook through 2010.* Good in general; very good with MBA.
- *Salaries.* $29,000–$32,000 for junior purchasing agents (but less for entry-level purchasing agents in the federal government); $60,000–$100,000 for purchasing managers.

Industrial Production Manager

Production managers are usually responsible for all production in a factory. In large plants with several operations—aircraft assembly, for instance—a manager is in charge of each operation, such as machining, assembly, or finishing. Production managers are typically responsible for production scheduling, staffing, equipment, quality control, inventory control, and coordination with other departments. Production managers, in essence, plan the production schedule. They determine which machines will be used, whether overtime or extra shifts are necessary, the sequence of production, and related matters.

- *Places of employment.* Throughout the United States.
- *Skills required.* Two-year or four-year degree, depending on employer. More are requiring a four-year degree, and some are requiring an MBA.
- *Employment outlook through 2010.* Very good with undergraduate engineering degree and MBA.
- *Salaries.* $27,000–$33,000 for assistant production managers; $40,000–$65,000 for production managers. Some employers give performance bonuses.

Manager of Corporate Training

The training and development of employees will be of great importance in the new millennium. U.S. companies spend over $240 billion a year on formal and informal training. That's only slightly less than is spent nationally each year on elementary, secondary, and higher education. Technical training in robotics and automation and basic education for those who have not finished high school are two areas of growth in the field of training.

A manager of corporate training supervises specialists who design training programs, conduct those programs, and assess them. The training manager may also oversee a reimbursement program for employees who take outside courses, arrange for special noncredit courses for employees on college campuses, and represent the firm in designing apprenticeship programs with labor unions.

- *Places of employment.* Any relatively large firm (1,000 or more employees).
- *Skills required.* Four-year or master's degree with a major in human resource management, adult education, psychology, or occupational education.
- *Employment outlook through 2010.* Very good.
- *Salaries.* $28,000–$35,000 to start for corporate training specialists; $65,000–$95,000 for managers; higher salaries for those with more experience or an advanced college degree.

Plant Health and Safety Officer

The Occupational Safety and Health Act of 1970 requires that manufacturing facilities and offices be safe and healthy places to work. Virtually all firms that employ 500 or more workers have a safety officer, who conducts safety inspections, keeps accident and injury records, provides safety training, and may help design safety features into equipment.

- *Places of employment.* Any business or other type of establishment that employs several hundred or more people. Even large office buildings often have a health and safety officer.
- *Skills required.* Four-year degree with a major in industrial engineering, safety engineering, industrial hygiene, occupational nursing, industrial administration, or some area of business administration.
- *Employment outlook through 2010.* Very good, especially in manufacturing firms and health care organizations.
- *Salaries.* $40,000–$75,000. The higher salaries are associated with positions requiring an engineering background.

Human Resource Development Specialist

The past decade has seen much corporate restructuring through mergers, acquisitions, and retrenchments. Some firms have created internal consulting jobs for people who can smooth corporate change and development. The duties of a development specialist include counseling employees about their performance, conducting stress-management programs, mediating disputes between departments, helping employees find new jobs, and counseling employees with personal or career problems.

- *Places of employment.* Large organizations, which are most likely to be located in metropolitan areas.
- *Skills required.* Master's (even doctoral) degree in psychology, business administration, human resource management, industrial or organizational psychology, or related behavioral or social sciences.
- *Employment outlook through 2010.* Good. Only very large firms are likely to hire human resource development specialists.
- *Salaries.* $45,000–$110,000. The lower salaries are for people with a master's degree; the higher salaries are for those with experience or a doctoral degree.

College Recruiter

Many firms, especially large ones, recruit graduates from colleges and universities. A corporate college recruiter is involved in employment planning and assessing human resource needs for professional, technical, and managerial employees; selecting colleges to visit; interviewing graduating students at those colleges; performing preliminary screening of these applicants; and recommending applicants to line managers for in-depth interviews. The job can involve a lot of travel, especially in the late fall and early spring. The recruiter may also be responsible for developing recruiting brochures for distribution to applicants through college placement offices across the country.

- *Places of employment.* Any firm, government agency, or other type of organization that hires large numbers of college graduates.

- *Skills required.* Four-year college degree with almost any major. Very good oral and written communication skills are essential.
- *Employment outlook through 2010.* Good, although fewer positions are available in manufacturing firms. This job is usually reserved for those who know about the organization.
- *Salaries.* $32,000–$70,000. Larger firms in metropolitan areas pay higher salaries.

MANAGEMENT CAREERS: A FINAL NOTE

This discussion has not begun to exhaust the list of managerial positions. There are managers for every possible business function: traffic managers, public relations managers, office managers, department managers, and administrators at all levels.

Many opportunities for advancement from line operations, sales positions, or general administrative work are available for those who wish to move up and take more responsibility. Higher-level managers need many more administrative skills than lower-level managers do, but most companies train people for those positions. Many companies also encourage potential managers to continue their education. Some even pay tuition. The future looks promising for those willing to make the effort to move into management.

chapter thirteen

Understanding the Customer and Creating Goods and Services that Satisfy

learning goals

>lg 1   What are the marketing concept and relationship building?

>lg 2   How do managers create a marketing strategy?

>lg 3   What is the marketing mix?

>lg 4   How do consumers and organizations make buying decisions?

>lg 5   What are the five basic forms of market segmentation?

>lg 6   How is marketing research used in marketing decision making?

>lg 7   What are the trends in understanding the consumer?

Targeting Baby Boomers at DaimlerChrysler

In 1955, Chrysler needed an icon. It had no Corvette, no Thunderbird for crew cut young men in blue jeans to drool over. That year the company found its muscle car: the C-300. Touted as "America's most powerful car," the C-300 tore up the tracks at NASCAR and Daytona, positioning Chrysler as a leader in high-performance, upscale American automobiles. The company launched a new model in its "letter-car" series every year until 1965's 300L and then discontinued the line.

Now, 45 years later, Chrysler had merged with Germany's Daimler Benz, and the new company, DaimlerChrysler (**www.daimlerchrysler.de/**) needed an icon to catch the attention of 40-something baby boomers. "Bringing a car to market is a $1 billion to $4 billion investment," says Steven Bruyn, large-car marketing executive at the Chrysler division of DaimlerChrysler. "As a result, you like to be right." The company didn't have to go far for its concept: it resurrected the 300 letter series from the 1950s and 1960s, and simply picked up where it left off in the alphabet. After three years of development, engineering tinkering, and intense market research, the car maker launched the 300M in 1998. Sales have been booming since, and it was named the Motor Trend 1999 Car of the Year.

Steering the 300M from drafting table to dealer has been no easy task. At the start of the project, Bruyn and his team studied the potential of the near-luxury car market by looking at population trends and forecasts for its target customers. America's baby boomers were aging and well educated, and their personal income was growing, courtesy of a strong national economy. They wanted room for their expanding waistlines—and were willing to pay for it.

Factors like these indicated a robust future for near-luxury car sales, but how did the 300M fit into the picture? Through marketing research, DaimlerChrysler honed its profile of the car's typical driver. "To 300M drivers, the car is more than just something to get them from point A to point B," says Bruyn.

Target customers are real car enthusiasts. They read Motor Trend and other car magazines. And, says Paul Leinberger, senior vice-president at Roper Starch Worldwide, they're looking for a product that represents who they are. "It's not about status, but their sense of identity," he says.

America's mood swing toward nostalgia also influenced the design of the 300M, both inside and out. The egg-crate grille harks back to earlier styles in the letter series, and simple analog dials dot the dashboard. Chrysler restored the series's vintage silver-winged badge, which now appears on the hood of all of the brand's cars and trucks. Of course, not everything about the 300M recalls the 1950s—standard features include leather seats, climate control, and a stereo system with nine speakers. "We marketed the 300M with an 'American heritage' wrapper," Bruyn says. "It differentiated us from the others in the market."[1]

Critical Thinking Questions

As you read this chapter, consider the following questions as they relate to DaimlerChrysler:

- Why do companies identify target customers for their products?

- Why is it important to differentiate a product?

- How does a company like DaimlerChrysler find out what customers and potential customers want in a car?

BUSINESS IN THE 21ST CENTURY

marketing
The process of discovering the needs and wants of potential buyers and customers and then providing goods and services that meet or exceed their expectations.

exchange
The process in which two parties give something of value to each other to satisfy their respective needs.

In marketing its 300M model, DaimlerChrysler conducted research to find out what potential buyers wanted and needed and then designed the car to satisfy those wants and needs.

Marketing played an important role in DaimlerChrysler's successful launch of its 300M. Marketing is the process of getting the right goods or services to the right people at the right place, time, and price, using the right promotion techniques. This concept is referred to as the *"right" principle*. We can say that **marketing** is finding out the needs and wants of potential buyers and customers and then providing goods and services that meet or exceed their expectations. Marketing is about creating exchanges. An **exchange** takes place when two parties give something of value to each other to satisfy their respective needs. In a typical exchange, a consumer trades money for a good or service.

To encourage exchanges, marketers follow the "right" principle. If your local DaimlerChrysler dealer doesn't have the right car for you when you want it, at the right price, you will not exchange money or credit for a new car. Think about the last exchange (purchase) you made: What if the price had been 30 percent higher? What if the store or other source had been less accessible? Would you have bought anything? The "right" principle tells us that marketers control many factors that determine marketing success. In this chapter, you will learn about the marketing concept and how organizations create a marketing strategy. You will learn how the marketing mix is used to create sales opportunities. Next, we examine how and why consumers and organizations make purchase decisions. Then, we discuss the important concept of market segmentation, which helps marketing managers focus on the most likely purchasers of their wares. We conclude the chapter by examining how marketing research and decision support systems help guide marketing decision making.

CHRYSLER 300 m

THE MARKETING CONCEPT

>lg 1

marketing concept
Identifying consumer needs and then producing the goods or services that will satisfy them while making a profit for the organization.

If you study today's best organizations, you'll see that they have adopted the **marketing concept,** which involves identifying consumer needs and then producing the goods or services that will satisfy them while making a profit. The marketing concept is oriented toward pleasing consumers by offering value. Specifically, the marketing concept involves:

- Focusing on customer wants so the organization can distinguish its product(s) from competitors' offerings.
- Integrating all of the organization's activities, including production, to satisfy these wants.

- Achieving long-term goals for the organization by satisfying customer wants and needs legally and responsibly.

Today, companies of every size in all industries are applying the marketing concept. McDonald's, for example, found that burger eaters like to determine what's on their burger rather than buying a hamburger that is already dressed in a heated bin. Now, its restaurants deliver fresh sandwiches made to order. After McDonald's changed its procedures to satisfy this customer need, its sales rose 9 percent and profits increased 25 percent.[2]

Firms have not always followed the marketing concept. Around the time of the Industrial Revolution in America (1860–1910), firms had a **production orientation,** which meant that they worked to lower production costs without a strong desire to satisfy the needs of their customers. To do this, organizations concentrated on mass production, focusing internally on maximizing the efficiency of operations, increasing output, and ensuring uniform quality. They also asked such questions as What can we do best? What can our engineers design? What is economical and easy to produce with our equipment?

There is nothing wrong with assessing a firm's capabilities. In fact, such assessments are necessary in planning. But the production orientation does not consider whether what the firm produces most efficiently also meets the needs of the marketplace. By implementing the marketing concept, an organization looks externally to the consumers in the marketplace and commits to customer value, customer satisfaction, and relationship marketing as explained in this section.

production orientation

An approach in which a firm works to lower production costs without a strong desire to satisfy the needs of customers.

Customer Value

Customer value is the ratio of benefits to the sacrifice necessary to obtain those benefits. The customer determines the value of both the benefits and the sacrifices. Creating customer value is a core business strategy of many successful firms. Customer value is rooted in the belief that price is not the only thing that matters. A business that focuses on the cost of production and price to the customer will be managed as though it were providing a commodity differentiated only by price. In contrast, businesses that provide customer value believe that many customers will pay a premium for superior customer service. Sir Colin Marshall, chairman of the board of British Airways (BA), is explicit about his commitment to superior customer service, insisting that BA can succeed only by meeting all of its customers' value-driven needs, not just price. In a highly competitive industry, BA has used this customer-value-based strategy to become the world's most profitable airline.[3]

The automobile industry also illustrates the importance of creating customer value. To penetrate the fiercely competitive luxury automobile market, Lexus adopted a customer-driven approach, with particular emphasis on service. Lexus stresses product quality with a standard of zero defects in manufacturing. The service quality goal is to treat each customer as one would treat a guest in one's home, to pursue the perfect person-to-person relationship, and to strive to improve continually. This strategy has enabled Lexus to establish a clear quality image and capture a significant share of the luxury car market.

customer value

The ratio of benefits to the sacrifice necessary to obtain those benefits, as determined by the customer; reflects the willingness of customers to actually buy a product.

Customer Satisfaction

Customer satisfaction is the customer's feeling that a product has met or exceeded expectations. New York State Electric and Gas Corp. says that its top priority is customer satisfaction. "We're committed to providing superior customer service and earning our customers' business every day," said Ralph Tedesco, senior vice-president of the Customer Service Business Unit. "We're

customer satisfaction

The customer's feeling that a product has met or exceeded expectations.

very proud that our customers acknowledge our restoration efforts following devastating storms and give us high marks for customer service."[4]

Read Embassy Suites's
Guest Guarantee at
www.embassy-suites.com

At Double Tree Hotels, guests are asked to fill out a CARE card several times during their stay to let staff know how they are doing. Managers check the cards daily to solve guests' problems before they check out. Guests can also use a CARE phone line to call in their complaints at the hotel. A CARE committee continually seeks ways to improve guest services. The goal is to offer a solution to a CARE call in 15 minutes. Embassy Suites goes one step further by offering a full refund to guests who are not satisfied with their stay.

Who delivers the most customer satisfaction in America? Exhibit 13-1 suggests that it's the German auto manufacturer Mercedes-Benz, a division of DaimlerChrysler.

Customer satisfaction may indicate how consumers feel about a product, but it may not indicate their willingness to actually purchase that product. General Motors' Cadillac Division, for example, was quite pleased that more than 90 percent of its customers reported that they were either "satisfied" or "highly satisfied" with their recent purchase of a new Cadillac, figures comparable with those reported by purchasers of Japanese automobiles. But Cadillac was quite dismayed to learn that only 30 to 40 percent of these new Cadillac owners would buy another Cadillac, compared with more than 80 percent of Japanese auto purchasers.[5] GM had been asking only about customer satisfaction, not customer value, the willingness of customers to actually buy a new Cadillac.

> e x h i b i t   1 3 - 1 <

Companies That Deliver the Highest Levels of Customer Satisfaction

Rank	Company or Division
1	Mercedes-Benz
2	H. J. Heinz food processing
3	Colgate-Palmolive pet foods
4	H. J. Heinz pet foods
5	Mars food processing
6	Maytag
7	Quaker Oats
8	Cadillac
9	Hershey Foods
10	Coca-Cola
11	Toyota
12	Volvo
13	Zenith Electronics
14	Buick
15	Cadbury Schweppes

SOURCE: "The 1998 Satisfaction Index," *Fortune* (February 16, 1998), p. 162.

Building Relationships

relationship marketing

A strategy that focuses on forging long-term partnerships with customers by offering value and providing customer satisfaction.

Relationship marketing is a strategy that focuses on forging long-term partnerships with customers. Companies build relationships with customers by offering value and providing customer satisfaction. Companies benefit from repeat sales and referrals that lead to increases in sales, market share, and profits. Costs fall because it is less expensive to serve existing customers than to attract new ones. Keeping a customer costs about one-fourth of what it costs to attract a new customer, and the probability of retaining a customer is over 60 percent, whereas the probability of landing a new customer is less than 30 percent.[6]

Customers also benefit from stable relationships with suppliers. Business buyers have found that partnerships with their suppliers are essential to producing high-quality products while cutting costs. Customers remain loyal to firms that provide them greater value and satisfaction than they expect from competing firms.

> f o c u s i n g   o n   s m a l l   b u s i n e s s <

IF YOU WANT TO BUY A CROCK-POT, TRY SOMEPLACE ELSE

With Wal-Marts and Home Depots overrunning the landscape, it looked as though Josh and Michael Bracken's small nursery in Dallas, Texas, would quickly wilt. So how is it that profit at the Brackens' Nicholson-Hardie Nursery & Garden Center rose 11 percent last year and the brothers are talking of expansion? Well, they make house calls, for one thing. One afternoon, 29-year-old Josh responds to a plea from retiree Jon Bauman, who is fretting over a bed of withering azaleas. "These are way dry," the nurseryman says, prodding the brittle plants and snapping off a twig. He advises Bauman to either water his shrubs more often or find a plant that is better suited to the dense clay soil. "At the Gap, anyone with a smile can sell a shirt," Josh boasts. "But it takes a couple of years to learn about plants."

In industry after industry, chain competitors have driven independents into the ground. The same thing almost happened in the nursery business, where big retailers now control two-thirds of the $71 billion lawn-and-garden market. But today, many of the nation's 10,000 independent nurseries are stubbornly holding their own by stocking plants suited for local conditions, pampering customers, and luring them with inventive promotions. Homestead Gardens in Davidsonville, Maryland, holds an herb festival, with local chefs demonstrating how to make herbal marinades and garnishes.

Because the Brackens can't buy in bulk as the chains do, they don't even attempt to match the chains' prices. Instead, they offer superior customer service by stocking more than 1,000 plant varieties, far more than the chains carry. Rare perennial flowers as tapien verbena and Mount Fuji phlox, which sell for between $3 and $6, can be found only at Brackens.

To distinguish themselves, the brothers aim for the sort of customer who "would buy a Land Rover versus a Chevrolet," says Josh. Thus, the stores stock top-of-the-line tools one might find in Martha Stewart's garden, including $35 British sheep shears for trimming grass and $45 Swiss pruners. There are dozens of brass and animal-shaped fountains, some selling for thousands of dollars. Nicholson-Hardie even carries a $20.95 imported British rosemary-scented herbal hand cream. It can't be found anywhere else in Dallas except at Neiman Marcus. Michael Bracken, who handles the company's finances, says he loves the association with the fancy retailer. "It adds to the aura."

Critical Thinking Questions

1. What else could the Brackens do to build long-term relationships with customers?
2. Would a frequent purchaser program work?
3. What about giving away airline miles with purchases?

Frequent buyer clubs are an excellent way to build long-term relationships. All major airlines including American and United have frequent flyer programs. After you fly a certain number of miles, you become eligible for a free ticket. Now, cruise lines, hotels, car rental agencies, credit card companies, and even mortgage companies give away "airline miles" with purchases. Consumers patronize the airline and its partners because they want the free tickets. Thus, the program helps to create a long-term relationship with the customer.[7]

If an organization is to build relationships with customers, its employees' attitudes and actions must be customer oriented. Any person, department, or division that is not customer oriented weakens the positive image of the entire organization. An employee may be the only contact a potential customer has with the firm. In that person's eyes, the employee is the firm. If greeted discourteously, the potential customer may well assume that the employee's attitude represents the whole firm.

Building long-term relationships with customers is an excellent way for small businesses to compete against the big chains. Sometimes small firms, with few employees, are in a better position to "go the extra mile," as explained in the Focusing on Small Business box on p. 385.

concept check

- What is marketing?
- Explain the marketing concept.
- Explain the difference between customer value and customer satisfaction.
- What is meant by relationship marketing?

CREATING A MARKETING STRATEGY

>lg 2

There is no secret formula for creating goods and services that provide customer value and customer satisfaction. An organization that is committed to providing superior customer satisfaction puts customers at the very center of its marketing strategy. Creating a customer-focused marketing strategy involves four main steps: understanding the external environment, defining the target market, creating a competitive advantage, and developing a marketing mix. This section will examine the first three steps, and the next section will discuss how a company develops a marketing mix.

Understanding the External Environment

Unless marketing managers understand the external environment, a firm cannot intelligently plan for the future. Thus, many organizations assemble a team of specialists to continually collect and evaluate environmental information, a process called **environmental scanning.** The goal in gathering the environmental data is to identify future market opportunities and threats.

environmental scanning
The process in which a firm continually collects and evaluates information about its external environment.

For example, as technology continues to blur the lines between personal computers, television, and compact disc players, a company like Sony may find itself competing against a company like Compaq. Research shows that children would like more games bundled with computer software, while adults desire various types of word-processing and business-related software. Is this information an opportunity or a threat to Compaq marketing managers?

In general, six categories of environmental data shape marketing decisions:

- *Social forces* such as the values of potential customers and the changing roles of families and women working outside the home.
- *Demographic forces* such as the ages, birth and death rates, and locations of various groups of people.
- *Economic forces* such as changing incomes, inflation, and recession.
- *Technological forces* such as advances in communications and data retrieval capabilities.

- *Political and legal forces* such as changes in laws and regulatory agency activities.
- *Competitive forces* from domestic and foreign-based firms.

Defining the Target Market

target market

The specific group of consumers toward which a firm directs its marketing efforts.

Managers and employees focus on providing value for a well-defined target market. The **target market** is the specific group of consumers toward which a firm directs its marketing efforts. It is selected from the larger overall market.

For instance, Carnival Cruise Lines says its main target market is "blue-collar entrepreneurs," people with an income of $25,000 to $50,000 a year who own auto supply shops, dry cleaners, and the like. Unlike other cruise lines, it does not seek affluent retirees. Quaker Oats targets its grits to blue-collar consumers in the South. Kodak targets Ektar color print film, designed for use only in rather sophisticated cameras, to advanced amateur photographers. The Limited, Inc. has several different types of stores, each for a distinct target market: Express for trendy younger women, Lerner for budget-conscious women, Lane Bryant and Roaman's for full-size women, and Henri Bendel's for upscale, high-fashion women. These target markets are all part of the overall market for women's clothes.

Identifying a target market helps a company focus its marketing efforts on those who are most likely to buy its products or services. Concentrating on potential customers lets the firm use its resources efficiently. The target markets for Marriott International's lodging alternatives are shown in Exhibit 13-2. The latest in the Marriott family is SpringHill Suites. The SpringHill idea came from another Marriott chain, Fairfield Suites, an offshoot of Marriott's Fairfield Inns. The suites, opened in 1997, were roomy but devoid of most frills: the closets didn't have doors, and the lobby floors were covered with linoleum. Some franchisees complained to Marriott that the suites were *under*priced: Fairfield Suites guests were saying they would pay a little more for a few more frills.

The National Fluid Milk Processor Promotion Board creates ads targeted at different market segments to promote the consumption of milk. It targets the youth market with ads featuring celebrities such as NASCAR driver Jeff Gordon.

So Marriott began planning an upgrade. To create each of the first 20 or so SpringHill locations, Marriott spent $200,000 renovating an existing Fairfield Suites unit, adding ergonomic chairs, ironing boards, and other amenities. Lobbies at SpringHill hotels are fancier than the rooms themselves: the lobbies have fireplaces, breakfast rooms, crown moldings at the ceiling, and granite or ceramic tile floors.

Creating a Competitive Advantage

competitive advantage

A set of unique features of a company and its products that are perceived by the target market as significant and superior to those of the competition; also called *differential advantage.*

A **competitive advantage**, also called a differential advantage, is a set of unique features of a company and its products that are perceived by the target market as significant and superior to those of the competition. As Andrew Grove, CEO of Intel, says, "You have to understand what it is you are better at than anybody else and mercilessly focus your efforts on it." Competitive advantage is the factor or factors that cause customers to patronize a firm and not the competition. There are three types of competitive advantage: cost, product/service differential, and niche.

HOT *links*

Look for other ways Marriott builds customer relationships at

www.marriott.com

> e x h i b i t 1 3 - 2 <
| The Target Markets for Marriott International

	Price Range	Target Market
Fairfield Inn	$45–65	Economizing business and leisure travelers
TownePlace Suites	$55–70	Moderate-tier travelers who stay three to four weeks
SpringHill Suites	$75–95	Business and leisure travelers looking for more space and amenities
Courtyard	$75–105	Travelers seeking quality and affordable accommodations designed for the road warrior
Residence Inn	$85–110	Travelers seeking a residential-style hotel
Marriott Hotels, Resorts, and Suites	$90–235	Grounded achievers who desire consistent quality
Renaissance Hotels and Resorts	$90–235	Discerning business and leisure travelers who seek creative attention to detail
Ritz-Carlton	$175–300	Senior executives and entrepreneurs looking for a unique, luxury, personalized experience

SOURCE: Christina Binkley, "Marriott Outfits an Old Chain for New Market," *Wall Street Journal* (October 13, 1998), pp. B1, B3.

cost competitive advantage

A firm's ability to produce a product or service at a lower cost than all other competitors in an industry while maintaining satisfactory profit margins.

Cost Competitive Advantage A firm that has a **cost-competitive advantage** can produce a product or service at a lower cost than all its competitors while maintaining satisfactory profit margins. Firms become cost leaders by obtaining inexpensive raw materials, making plant operations more efficient, designing products for ease of manufacture, controlling overhead costs, and avoiding marginal customers. DuPont, for example, has an exceptional cost competitive advantage in the production of titanium dioxide. Technicians created a production process using low-cost feedstock that gives DuPont a 20 percent cost advantage over its competitors. The cheaper feedstock technology is complex and can be accomplished only by investing about $100 million and several years of testing time.

A cost competitive advantage enables a firm to deliver superior customer value. Chapparal Steel, for example, is the leading low-cost U.S. steel producer because it uses only scrap iron and steel and a very efficient continuous-casting process to make new steel. In fact, Chapparal is so efficient that it is the only U.S. steel producer that ships to Japan. Similarly, Fort Howard Paper's competitive advantage lies in its cost-saving manufacturing process. Fort Howard Paper uses only recycled pulp, rather than the more expensive virgin pulp, to make toilet paper and other products. The quality, however, is only acceptable to the commercial market, such as office buildings, hotels, and restaurants. Therefore, the company does not try to sell to the home market through grocery stores.

differential competitive advantage

A firm's ability to provide a unique product or service that offers something of value to buyers besides simply a lower price.

Differential Competitive Advantage A product/service **differential competitive advantage** exists when a firm provides something unique that is valuable to buyers beyond simply offering a low price. Differential competitive advantages tend to be longer lasting than cost competitive advantages because cost advantages are subject to continual erosion as competitors catch up. Cost advantages fail to last for two reasons. For one thing, technology is transferable. For example, Bell Labs invented fiber optic cable that reduced the cost of voice and data transmission by dramatically increasing the number of calls that could be transmitted simultaneously through a two-inch cable. Within five years, however, fiber optic technology had spread throughout the industry. Second, for most production processes or product categories (e.g., running shoes and laptop computers), there are alternative suppliers. Over time, high-cost producers tend to seek out lower-cost suppliers and they can compete more effectively with the industry's low-cost producers.

The durability of a differential competitive advantage tends to make this strategy more attractive to many top managers. Common differential advantages are brand names (Lexus), a strong dealer network (Caterpillar Tractor for construction work), product reliability (Maytag washers), image (Neiman Marcus in retailing), and service (Federal Express). Brand names such as Coca-Cola, BMW, and Cartier stand for quality the world over. Through continual product and marketing innovations and attention to quality and value managers at these organizations have created enduring competitive advantages. Arthur Doppelmayer, an Austrian manufacturer of aerial transport systems, believes his main differential advantage, besides innovative equipment design, is his service system, which allows the company to come to the assistance of users anywhere in the world within 24 hours. Doppelmayer uses a worldwide system of warehouses and skilled personnel prepared to move immediately in emergency cases.

niche competitive advantage

A firm's ability to target and effectively serve a single segment of the market within a limited geographic area.

Niche Competitive Advantage A company with a **niche competitive advantage** targets and effectively serves a single segment of the market within a limited geographic area. For small companies with limited resources that potentially face giant competitors, "niche-ing" may be the only viable option. A market segment that has good growth potential but is not crucial to the success of major competitors is a good candidate for a niche strategy. Once a potential segment has been identified, the firm needs to make certain it can defend against challengers through its superior ability to serve buyers in the segment. For example, Pea-in-the-Pod is a small chain of retail stores that sells maternity clothes. Its quality materials, innovative designs, and reasonable prices serve as a barrier against competition.

concept check

- What is environmental scanning?
- What is a target market, and why should a company have one?
- What is a competitive advantage?
- Explain the three types of competitive advantages.

DEVELOPING A MARKETING MIX

>lg 3

marketing mix

The blend of product offering, pricing, promotional methods, and distribution system that brings a specific group of consumers superior value.

four Ps

Product, price, promotion, and place (distribution), which together make up the marketing mix.

Once a firm has defined its target market and identified its competitive advantage, it can create the **marketing mix,** that is, the blend of product offering, pricing, promotional methods, and distribution system that brings a specific group of consumers superior value. Distribution is sometimes referred to as place, so the marketing mix is based on the **four Ps:** product, price, promotion, and place. Every target market requires a unique marketing mix to satisfy the needs of the target consumers and meet the firm's goals. A strategy must be constructed for each of the four Ps and blended with the strategies for the other elements. Thus, the marketing mix is only as good as its weakest part. An excellent product with a poor distribution system could be doomed to failure.

A successful marketing mix requires careful tailoring. For instance, at first glance you might think that McDonald's and Wendy's have roughly the same marketing mix. After all, they are both in the fast-food business. But McDonald's targets parents with young children through Ronald McDonald, heavily promoted children's Happy Meals, and

Compare McDonald's and Wendy's marketing efforts by visiting their home pages at **www.mcdonalds.com** and **www.wendys.com**

playgrounds. Wendy's is targeted to a more adult crowd. Wendy's has no playgrounds but it does have carpeting (a more adult atmosphere), and it pioneered fast-food salad bars.

Product Strategy

Marketing strategy typically starts with the product. You can't plan a distribution system or set a price if you don't know what you're going to market. Marketers use the term *product* to refer to both *goods,* such as tires, stereos, and clothing, and *services,* such as hotels, hair salons, and restaurants. Thus, the heart of the marketing mix is the good or service. Creating a **product strategy** involves choosing a brand name, packaging, colors, a warranty, accessories, and a service program.

Marketers view products in a much larger context than you might imagine. They include not only the item itself but also the brand name and the company image. The names Yves St. Laurent and Gucci, for instance, create extra value for everything from cosmetics to bath towels. That is, products with those names sell at higher prices than identical products without the names. We buy things not only for what they do, but also for what they mean. (Product strategies are discussed further in Chapter 14.)

Pricing Strategy

Pricing strategy is based on demand for the product and the cost of producing it. Some special considerations can also influence the price. Sometimes, for instance, a special introductory price is used to get people to try a new product. Some firms enter the market with low prices and keep them low, such as Carnival Cruise Lines and Suzuki cars. Others enter a market with very high prices and then lower them over time, such as producers of high-definition televisions and personal computers. (You can learn more about pricing strategies in Chapter 14.)

Distribution Strategy

Distribution is the means (the channel) by which a product flows from the producer to the consumer. One aspect of **distribution strategy** is deciding how many stores and which specific wholesalers and retailers will handle the product in a geographic area. Cosmetics, for instance, are distributed in many different ways. Avon has a sales force of several hundred thousand representatives who call directly on consumers. Clinique and Estee Lauder are distributed through selected department stores. Cover Girl and Del Laboratories use mostly chain drugstores and other mass merchandisers. Redken sells through beauticians. Revlon uses several of these distribution channels. (Distribution is examined in detail in Chapter 15.)

Promotion Strategy

Many people feel that promotion is the most exciting part of the marketing mix. **Promotion strategy** covers personal selling, advertising, public relations, and sales promotion. Each element is coordinated with the others to create a promotional blend. An advertisement, for instance, helps a buyer get to know the company and paves the way for a sales call. A good promotion strategy can dramatically increase a firm's sales. (Promotion is the topic of Chapter 16.)

Public relations plays a special role in promotion. It is used to create a good image of the company and its products. Bad publicity costs nothing to send out, but it can cost a firm a great deal in lost business. Good publicity, such as a television or magazine story about a firm's new product, may be the result of much time, money, and effort spent by a public relations department.

product strategy

The part of the marketing mix that involves choosing a brand name, packaging, colors, a warranty, accessories, and a service program for the product.

pricing strategy

The part of the marketing mix that involves establishing a price for the product based on the demand for the product and the cost of producing it.

distribution strategy

The part of the marketing mix that involves deciding how many stores and which specific wholesalers and retailers will handle the product in a geographic area.

promotion strategy

The part of the marketing mix that involves personal selling, advertising, public relations, and sales promotion of the product.

OMNILIFE: THE STORY OF A CONTEMPORARY MEDICINE MAN?

Jorge Vergara got his start in the weight-loss and nutritional supplement business by working for Herbalife when it expanded into Mexico following investigations into its sales methods by the U.S. Food and Drug Administration and the California attorney general's office. To satisfy the investigating authorities, Herbalife agreed to stop making excessive product claims and engaging in questionable sales practices.

Thinking he could do better on his own, Vergara left Herbalife in 1991 and started his own business, Omnilife, geared to the Mexican market. Rather than selling diet pills and diet formulas, Vergara put vitamins and minerals in sweetened canned drinks, teas, coffees, and chewing gum. He focused on smaller communities where nutritional products are rare. Additionally, he used cash-and-carry distribution centers to supply the company's distributors, who operated in a multilevel marketing system similar to that used by Herbalife and Amway, among others.

Arturo Rodriguez, an Omnilife distributor, says the company is concerned about customers' health and consequently sells delicious products that make customers feel better. Another distributor, Pepe Vergara, who is also Jorge Vergara's cousin, provides a different perspective on Omnilife products. He says the company sells junk food—but that it is nutritional junk food!

Omnilife's sales pitches rely heavily on testimonials. They include claims that Omnilife products have helped customers "to avoid cancer operations or to walk again." Jorge Vergara admits "that he and his distributors sometimes make claims that wouldn't pass regulatory muster in the U.S." The spouse of an Omnilife distributor compares Vergara to the "medicine men who can still be found touting herbal potions in town squares throughout Latin America."

Critical Thinking Questions

1. How would you describe Omnilife's marketing mix?
2. Is Omnilife's marketing mix managed in an ethical fashion? Explain your answer.

Sales promotion directly stimulates sales. It includes trade shows, catalogs, contests, games, premiums, coupons, and special offers. McDonald's contests offering money and food prizes are an example. The company also issues discount coupons from time to time.

Not-for-Profit Marketing

HOT links

Considering a career in marketing? Visit
www.ama.org

Profit-oriented companies are not the only ones that analyze the marketing environment, find a competitive advantage, and create a marketing mix. The application of marketing principles and techniques is also vital to not-for-profit organizations. Marketing helps not-for-profit groups identify target markets and develop effective marketing mixes. In some cases, marketing has kept symphonies, museums, and other cultural groups from having to close their doors. In other organizations, such as the American Heart Association and the U.S. Army, marketing ideas and techniques have helped managers do their jobs better. The army, for instance, has identified the most effective ways to get men and women between the ages of 18 and 24 to visit a recruiter.

social marketing
The application of marketing techniques to social issues and causes.

In the private sector, the profit motive is both an objective for guiding decisions and a criterion for evaluating results. Not-for-profit organizations do not seek to make a profit for redistribution to owners or shareholders. Rather, their focus is often on generating enough funds to cover expenses. For example, the Methodist Church does not gauge its success by the amount of money left in offering plates. The Museum of Science and Industry does not base its performance evaluations on the dollar value of tokens put into the turnstile.

Not-for-profit marketing is also concerned with **social marketing,** that is, the application of marketing to social issues and causes. The goals of social marketing are to effect social change (for instance, by creating racial harmony), further social causes (for instance, by helping the homeless), and evaluate the relationship between marketing and society (for instance, by asking whether society should allow advertising on television shows for young children). Individual organizations also engage in social marketing. The Southern Baptist Radio and Television Convention promotes brotherhood and goodwill by promoting religion and good deeds. M.A.D.D. counsels against drunk driving, and the National Wildlife Federation asks your help in protecting endangered animals and birds.

concept check

- What is meant by the marketing mix?
- What are the components of the marketing mix?
- How can marketing techniques help not-for-profit organizations?
- Define social marketing.

BUYER BEHAVIOR

>lg 4

buyer behavior
The actions people take in buying and using goods and services.

An organization cannot reach its goals without understanding buyer behavior. **Buyer behavior** is the actions people take in buying and using goods and services. Marketers who understand buyer behavior, such as how a price increase will affect a product's sales, can create a more effective marketing mix.

To understand buyer behavior, marketers must understand how consumers make buying decisions. The decision-making process has several steps, which are shown in Exhibit 13-3. The entire process is affected by a number of personal and social factors. A buying decision starts (step 1) with a stimulus. A *stimulus* is anything that affects one or more of our senses (sight, smell, taste, touch, or hearing). A stimulus might be the feel of a sweater, the sleek shape of a new-model car, the design on a package, or a brand name mentioned by a friend. The stimulus leads to problem recognition (step 2): "This sweater feels so soft and looks good on me. Should I buy it?" In other words, the consumer decides that there's a purchase need.

The consumer next gets information about the purchase (step 3). What other styles of sweaters are available? At what price? Can this sweater be bought at a lower price elsewhere? Next, the consumer weighs the options and decides whether to make the purchase (step 4). If the consumer buys the product (step 5), certain outcomes are expected. These outcomes may or may not become reality: the sweater may last for years, or the shoulder seams may pull out the first time it's worn. Finally, the consumer assesses the experience with the product (step 6) and uses this information to update expectations about future purchases (step 7).

Influences on Consumer Decision Making

As Exhibit 13-3 shows, individual and social factors can influence the consumer decision-making process. *Individual factors* are within the consumer and are unique to each person. They include perception, beliefs and attitudes, values, learning, self-concept, and personality. Companies often conduct research to better understand individual factors that cause consumers to buy or not to buy. For instance, Hyatt Hotels found that people who stayed at Hyatt while on busi-

Consumer Decision-Making Process

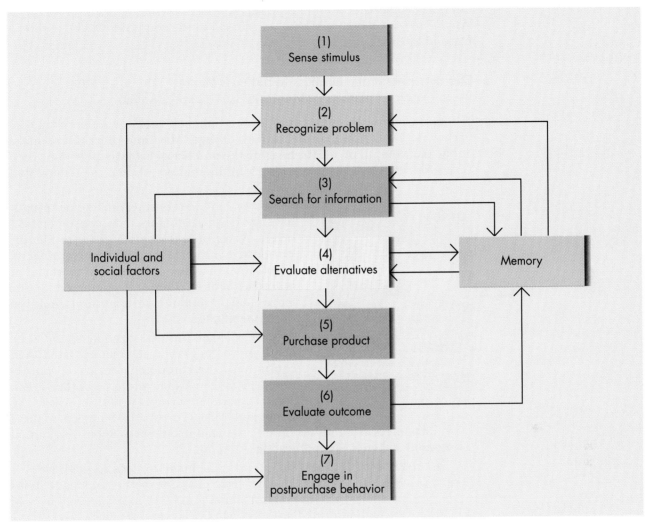

ness chose other hotels when they traveled on vacation with their children. Hyatt was perceived as a businessperson's hotel. So Hyatt came up with a program called Camp Hyatt, which caters to children with a year-round program that varies by season. It combines attractive rates that appeal to parents with lots of activities for kids.

Social factors that affect the decision-making process include all interactions between a consumer and the external environment: family, opinion leaders, social class, and culture. Families may be the most important of these social factors. Yet families have limited resources, so many buying decisions are compromises. Since a number of decisions include input from several family members, marketing managers sometimes promote products using a family theme, such as Camp Hyatt.

Business-to-Business Purchase Decision Making

Business buyer behavior and business markets are different from consumer markets. Business markets include institutions such as hospitals and schools, manufacturers, wholesalers and retailers, and various branches of government.

The key difference between a consumer product and a business product is the intended use. If you purchase a certain model Dell computer for your home so you can surf the Internet, it is a consumer good. If a purchasing agent for MTV buys exactly the same computer for an MTV script writer, it is a business good. Why? The reason is that MTV is a business, so the computer will be used in a business environment.

Characteristics of the Business-to-Business Market   The main differences between consumer markets and business markets are as follows:

1. *Purchase volume.* Business customers buy in much larger quantities than consumers. Think how many truckloads of sugar Mars must purchase to make one day's output of M&Ms. Imagine the number of batteries Sears buys each day for resale to consumers. Think of the number of pens the federal government must use each day.

Who are the business-to-business marketing superstars? Find out at www.adage.com/news_and _features/specialreports/ bm100-1995

2. *Number of customers.* Business marketers usually have far fewer customers than consumer marketers. As a result, it is much easier to identify prospective buyers and monitor current needs. Think about how few customers for airplanes or industrial cranes there are compared to the more than 70 million consumer households in the United States.

3. *Location of buyers.* Business customers tend to be much more geographically concentrated than consumers. The computer industry is concentrated in Silicon Valley and a few other areas. Aircraft manufacturing is found in Seattle, St. Louis, and Dallas/Fort Worth. Suppliers to these manufacturers often locate close to the manufacturers to lower distribution costs and facilitate communication.

4. *Direct distribution.* Business sales tend to be made directly to the buyer because such sales frequently involve large quantities or custom-made items like heavy machinery. Consumer goods are more likely to be sold through intermediaries like wholesalers and retailers.

5. *Rational purchase decisions.* Unlike consumers, business buyers usually approach purchasing rather formally. Businesses use professionally trained purchasing agents or buyers who spend their entire career purchasing a limited number of items. They get to know the items and the sellers quite well.

concept check

- Explain the consumer decision-making process.
- How do business markets differ from consumer markets?

MARKET SEGMENTATION

>lg 5

market segmentation

The process of separating, identifying, and evaluating the layers of a market in order to design a marketing mix.

The study of buyer behavior helps marketing managers better understand why people make purchases. To identify the target markets that may be most profitable for the firm, managers use **market segmentation,** which is the process of separating, identifying, and evaluating the layers of a market to design a marketing mix. For instance, a target market might be segmented into two groups: families with children and families without children. Families with young children are likely to buy hot cereals and presweetened cereals. Families with no children are more likely to buy health-oriented cereals. You can be sure that cereal companies plan their marketing mixes with this difference in mind. A business market may be segmented by large customers and small customers or by geographic area.

The five basic forms of consumer market segmentation are demographic, geographic, psychographic, benefit, and volume. Their characteristics are summarized in Exhibit 13-4 and discussed in the following sections.

Demographic Segmentation

demographic segmentation
The differentiation of markets through the use of categories such as age, education, gender, income, and household size.

Demographic segmentation uses categories such as age, education, gender, income, and household size to differentiate among markets. This form of market segmentation is the most common. The U.S. Census Bureau provides a great deal of demographic data. For example, marketing researchers can use census data to find areas within cities that contain high concentrations of high-income consumers, singles, blue-collar workers, and so forth.

Find a vast array of census data at
www.census.gov

You don't have to be an adult to have market clout. One study found that aggregate spending by or on behalf of children ages 4 to 12 roughly doubled every decade in the 1960s, 1970s, and 1980s. It tripled in the 1990s to more than $24 billion.[8] And whereas children in the 1960s spent almost all their money on candy, today only one-third of the money goes to food and drink, with the balance spent on toys, clothes, movies, and games.

Mature Americans (those born before 1945), baby boomers (consumers born between 1946 and 1967), and Generation Xers (younger consumers born between 1968 and 1979) all have different needs, tastes, and consumption patterns. Exhibit 13-5 shows some of these generational differences; note that baby boomers tend to be nostalgic and prefer the old to the new, whereas Generation Xers tend to be video oriented and would rather see the movie than read the book.

Certain markets are segmented by gender. These include clothing, cosmetics, personal care items, magazines, jewelry, and footwear. Gillette, for

> e x h i b i t   1 3 - 4 <

Forms of Consumer Market Segmentation

Form	General Characteristics
Demographic segmentation	Age, education, gender, income, race, social class, household size
Geographic segmentation	Regional location (e.g., New England, Mid-Atlantic, Southeast, Great Lakes, Plains States, Northwest, Southwest, Rocky Mountains, Far West); population density (urban, suburban, rural); city or county size; climate
Psychographic segmentation	Lifestyle, personality, interests, values, attitudes
Benefit segmentation	Benefits provided by the good or service
Volume segmentation	Amount of use (light versus heavy)

> e x h i b i t   1 3 - 5 <

Preferences of Mature Adults, Baby Boomers, and Generation Xers

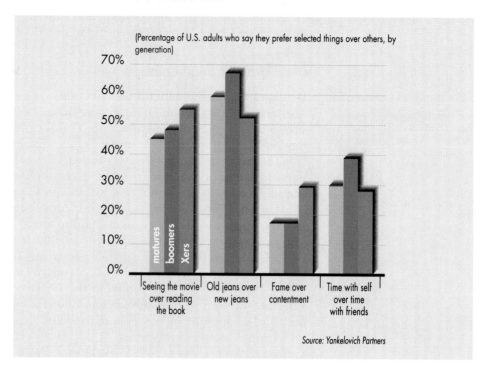

(Percentage of U.S. adults who say they prefer selected things over others, by generation)

Source: Yankelovich Partners

example, is one of the world's best-known marketers of personal care products and has historically targeted men for the most part. Yet women's products have generated most of Gillette's growth since 1992. Gillette's shaving line for women has expanded into a $400 million global business, growing nearly 20 percent annually. Gillette has increased its advertising budget to help it reach a goal of $1 billion in revenues from women's shaving products worldwide by 2001.[9] In the United States, women's blades and disposables now make up about one-fifth of Gillette's sales.

Income is another popular way to segment markets. Income level influences consumers' wants and determines their buying power. Housing, clothing, automobiles, and alcoholic beverages are among the many markets segmented by income. Budget Gourmet frozen dinners are targeted to lower-income groups, whereas the Le Menu line is aimed at higher-income consumers.

Geographic Segmentation

geographic segmentation

The differentiation of markets by region of the country, city or county size, market density, or climate.

Geographic segmentation means segmenting markets by region of the country, city or county size, market density, or climate. *Market density* is the number of people or businesses within a certain area. Many companies segment their markets geographically to meet regional preferences and buying habits. Pizza Hut, for instance, gives easterners extra cheese, westerners more ingredients, and midwesterners both. Both Ford and Chevrolet sell more pickup trucks and truck parts in the middle of the country than on either coast. The well-defined "pickup truck belt" runs from the upper Midwest south through Texas and the Gulf states. Ford "owns" the northern half of this truck belt, and Chevrolet the southern half.

Psychographic Segmentation

psychographic segmentation
The differentiation of markets by personality or lifestyle.

Race, income, occupation, and other demographic variables help in developing strategies but often do not paint the entire picture of consumer needs. Demographics provide the skeleton, but psychographics add meat to the bones. **Psychographic segmentation** is market segmentation by personality or lifestyle. People with common activities, interests, and opinions are grouped together and given a "lifestyle name."

Benefit Segmentation

benefit segmentation
The differentiation of markets based on what a product will do rather than on customer characteristics.

Benefit segmentation is based on what a product will do rather than on consumer characteristics. For years Crest toothpaste was targeted toward consumers concerned with preventing cavities. Recently, Crest subdivided its market. It now offers regular Crest, Crest Tartar Control for people who want to prevent cavities and tartar buildup, Crest for kids with sparkles that taste like bubble gum, and another Crest that prevents gum disease. Another toothpaste, Topol, targets people who want whiter teeth—teeth without coffee, tea, or tobacco stains. Sensodyne toothpaste is aimed at people with highly sensitive teeth.

Volume Segmentation

volume segmentation
The differentiation of markets based on the amount of the product purchased.

The fifth main type of segmentation is **volume segmentation**, which is based on the amount of the product purchased. Just about every product has heavy, moderate, and light users, as well as nonusers. Heavy users often account for a very large portion of a product's sales. Thus, a firm might want to target its marketing mix to the heavy-user segment. Kraft recently ran a $30 million advertising campaign directed at heavy users of Miracle Whip. A heavy user consumes 550 servings or 17 pounds of Miracle Whip a year.[10]

Retailers are aware that heavy shoppers not only spend more, but also visit each outlet more frequently than other shoppers. Heavy shoppers visit the grocery store 122 times per year, compared with 93 annual visits for the medium shopper. They visit discount stores more than twice as often as medium shoppers, and they visit convenience/gas stores more than five times as often. On each trip, they consistently spend more than their medium-shopping counterparts.[11]

HOT links

Links to major marketing research firms are available at **www.quirks.com/source/sb.html**

concept check

- Define market segmentation.
- List and discuss the five basic forms of market segmentation.

USING MARKETING RESEARCH TO SERVE EXISTING CUSTOMERS AND FIND NEW CUSTOMERS

>lg 6

marketing research
The process of planning, collecting, and analyzing data relevant to a marketing decision.

How do successful companies learn what their customers value? Through marketing research, companies can be sure they are listening to the voice of the customer. **Marketing research** is the process of planning, collecting, and analyzing data relevant to a marketing decision. The results of this analysis are then communicated to management. The information collected through marketing research includes the preferences of customers, the perceived benefits of products, and consumer lifestyles. Research helps companies make better use of their marketing budgets. Marketing research has a range of uses from fine-tuning products to discovering whole new marketing concepts.

For example, everything at the Olive Garden restaurant chain from the decor to the wine list is based on marketing research. Each new menu item is put through a series of consumer taste tests before being added to the menu. Hallmark Cards uses marketing research to test messages, cover designs, and even the size of the cards. Hallmark's experts know which kinds of cards will sell best in which places. Engagement cards, for instance, sell best in the Northeast, where engagement parties are popular. Birthday cards for "Daddy" sell best in the South because even adult southerners tend to call their fathers Daddy.

This section examines the marketing research process, which consists of the following steps:

1. Define the marketing problem.
2. Choose a method of research.
3. Collect the data.

USING THE WEB TO GATHER DECISION-MAKING INFORMATION

Web-based marketing research studies are changing the way marketing research will be conducted in the future. Web-based surveys have many advantages over traditional methods. For starters, no interviewers are involved, so interviewer errors are eliminated, as is interviewer bias. If the interviewer is in a bad mood or doesn't like certain types of people or subjects, then the data can be affected. In Web-based surveys, every respondent has exactly the same interviewer—one that is never tired, moody, prejudiced, impatient, or opinionated. Telephone interviews are limited to audio, but Web surveys can be truly multimedia. For example, a recent study of a new computer game showed respondents a variety of screen shots as well as a video clip of sample game play.

In contrast to traditional market research surveys, which can take six weeks to process, Web-based surveys are fast. Questionnaires are posted on a secure Web site, and respondents are directed to the site from banner ads or personal invitations issued by e-mail. Respondents drop by the survey site whenever they want to (even at 3 A.M.) and complete their surveys. Often, a sufficiently large sample, say, 300 or 400 respondents, can be completed over a weekend.

Any research project has two major cost components: data collection and analysis. Data collection costs for a Web-based survey are almost zero. With over 170 million Internet users worldwide by 2001, you can find just about any type of respondent on the Web. Analysis costs are also reduced because with advanced software programs data can be analyzed as quickly as consumers fill out a questionnaire online.

Overall, Web-based surveys offer tremendous potential to the marketing research industry because they are faster, generate more accurate information, and cost less than traditional surveys. Used properly, Web-based marketing research soon will vastly increase the amount of customer feedback on which managers base critical business decisions.

Critical Thinking Questions

1. Do you see any disadvantages of Internet surveys?
2. Would you participate in a Web survey? Why or why not?

4. Analyze the research data.
5. Make recommendations to management.

Define the Marketing Problem

The most critical step in the marketing research process is defining the marketing problem. This involves either writing a problem statement or a list of research objectives. If the problem is not defined properly, the remainder of the research will be a waste of time and money. Two key questions can help in defining the marketing problem correctly:

1. Why is the information being sought? By discussing with managers what the information is going to be used for and what decisions might be made as a result, the researcher can get a clearer grasp of the problem.
2. Does the information already exist? If so, money and time can be saved and a quick decision can be made.

Choose a Method of Research

After the problem is correctly defined, a research method is chosen. There are three basic research methods: survey, observation, and experiment.

With **survey research,** an interviewer interacts with respondents, either in person or by mail, to obtain facts, opinions, and attitudes. A questionnaire is used to provide an orderly and structured approach to data gathering. Face-to-face interviews may take place at the respondent's home, in a shopping mall, the Internet or at a place of business.

Observation research is research that monitors respondents' actions without direct interaction. In the fastest growing form of observation research, researchers use cash registers with scanners that read tags with bar codes to identify the item being purchased. Technological advances are rapidly expanding the future of observation research. For example, A. C. Nielsen has been using black boxes for years on television sets to silently obtain information on a family's viewing habits. But what if the set is on and no one is in the room? To overcome that problem, researchers will soon rely on infrared passive "people meters" that will identify the faces of family members watching the television program. Thus, the meter will duly record when the set is on and no one is watching.

In the third research method, **experiment,** the investigator changes one or more variables—price, package, design, shelf space, advertising theme, or advertising expenditures—while observing the effects of those changes on another variable (usually sales). The objective of experiments is to measure causality. For example, an experiment may reveal the impact that a change in package design has on sales.

survey research

A marketing research method in which an interviewer interacts with respondents, either in person, by mail, a mall, or the Internet to obtain facts, opinions, and attitudes.

observation research

A marketing research method in which the investigator monitors respondents' actions without interacting directly with the respondents; for example, by using cash registers with scanners.

experiment

A marketing research method in which the investigator changes one or more variables—price, packaging, design, shelf space, advertising theme, or advertising expenditures—while observing the effects of these changes on another variable (usually sales).

Interviewing people in a shopping mall is a popular survey research method that allows firms to gather information about consumer opinions and attitudes.

Collect the Data

primary data

Information collected directly from the original source to solve a problem.

secondary data

Information that has already been collected for a project other than the current one, but which may be used to solve the current problem.

Two types of data are used in marketing research: **primary data,** which are collected directly from the original source to solve a problem; and **secondary data,** which is information that has already been collected for a project other than the current one but may be used to help solve it. Secondary data can come from a number of sources, among them government agencies, trade associations, research bureaus, universities, the Internet, commercial publications, and internal company records. Company records include sales invoices, accounting records, data from previous research studies, and historical sales data.

Primary data are usually gathered through some form of survey research. As described earlier, survey research often relies on interviews (see Exhibit 13-6 for the different types of interviews). Today, conducting surveys over the Internet is the fastest growing form of survey research, as the Applying Technology box on p. 398 describes.

See examples of the secondary research available from CACI at **demographics.caci.com**

> e x h i b i t   1 3 - 6 <

Types of Interviews Used in Survey Research

Type	Description
Door-to-door	Interviewer interviews consumer in consumer's home.
Executive interview	Interviewer interviews industrial product user (e.g., engineer, architect, doctor, executive) or decision maker at place of business regarding an industrial product.
Mall intercept	Interviewer interviews consumer in shopping mall or other high-traffic location. Interviews may be done in public areas of the mall, or the respondent may be taken to a private test area.
Central location telephone interview	Interviewing is conducted from a telephone facility set up for that purpose. These facilities typically have equipment that permits the supervisor to unobtrusively monitor the interview while it is taking place. Some facilities have Wide Area Telephone Service (WATS) to permit national sampling from a single location. The questionnaire is programmed into a computer. The interviewer enters responses directly.
Self-administered questionnaires	These are most frequently employed at high-traffic locations such as shopping malls or in captive audience situations such as classrooms and airplanes. Respondents are given general information on how to fill out the questionnaire and are left to complete it on their own.
Ad hoc (one-shot) mail surveys	Questionnaires are mailed to a sample of consumers or industrial users. Instructions are included. Respondents are asked to fill out the questionnaire and return it via mail. Sometimes a gift or monetary incentive is provided.
Mail panels	Several companies, including Market Facts, NPD Research, and National Family Opinion Research, operate large (more than 100,000 households) consumer panels and ad hoc mail surveys. The company has contacted the people on the panel earlier and explained the panel concept to them. They have agreed to participate for a certain period of time. In addition, participants are offered gratuities to participate in mail panels.
Point-of-service touch-screen monitors	Kiosks, equipped with touch-screen monitors, provide a new way to capture information from individuals in stores, health clinics, and other shopping or service environments.
Internet surveys	This is the fastest growing form of survey research. As the number of individuals connected to the Internet increases, this approach will become increasingly attractive. Internet surveys are discussed in the Applying Technology box.

Analyze the Data

After the data have been collected, the next step in the research process is data analysis. The purpose of this analysis is to interpret and draw conclusions from the mass of collected data. Many software statistical programs such as SAS and SPSS are available to make this task easier for the researcher.

Make Recommendations to Management

After completing the data analysis, the researcher must prepare the report and communicate the conclusions and recommendations to management. This is a key step in the process because marketing researchers who want their conclusions acted upon must convince the manager that the results are credible and justified by the data collected. Today, presentation software like PowerPoint and Astound provides easy-to-use tools for creating reports and presentations that are more interesting, compelling, and effective than was possible just a few years ago.

concept check

- Define marketing research.
- Explain the marketing research process.
- What are the three basic marketing research methods?

CAPITALIZING ON TRENDS IN BUSINESS

>lg 7

To discover exactly what customers value most, organizations are using innovative techniques for collecting customer information. Some of the more sophisticated marketing research techniques that are growing in popularity are advanced observation research methods, decision support systems (DDSs), and database marketing.

Advanced Observation Research Methods

All forms of observation research are increasingly using more sophisticated technology. The major television networks, for example, are supporting an advanced technology that provides highly accurate market data about television viewers' behavior. The networks have been discouraged by the data flowing from A. C. Nielsen media research, which indicate that the networks are losing market share. The networks say that Nielsen's research is faulty and are backing a new measurement system created by Statistical Research Inc. (SRI). The stakes are about $13 billion in advertising revenue generated annually by the major networks.[12] SRI has developed Systems for Measuring And Reporting Television, or SMART, at a cost of $160 million. The SMART setup consists of meters with sensors that can pick up signals from the air. The meter looks like a VCR and sits on top of the television. Users log in and out before and after watching television by pressing a device similar to a TV remote control, which was designed for ease of use. The device accurately tracks which program is being watched and by whom.

Technology is also being applied to measure Internet traffic. By 2002, online advertising revenue is expected to reach $9 billion, and advertisers want to make certain that people are seeing their Web ads.[13] Web sites measure their own popularity, largely by the number of "hits," or the times a page or parts of a page are called up. Sites then try to convert that measurement into "unique visitors" so that one person calling up several pages is not counted more than once. Web researchers like Relevant-Knowledge have a group of people, or "panel," who agree to install software on their PCs to monitor their movements online. Relevant-Knowledge now has a panel of 20,000 people. The data show the number of first-time users who visit a site each month.

Perhaps most astounding of all is the new technology that is allowing us to learn how the brain receives and processes information. Brain science has come so far that researchers are now able to routinely eavesdrop on brains while they think. The new technology offers insights about how we perceive, think, and make decisions. This information will enable researchers to uncover consumers' root motivations—or hot buttons. These come from the subliminal regions of our brains, where values, needs, and motivations originate.[14]

Decision Support Systems

decision support system (DSS)

An interactive, flexible, computerized information system that allows managers to make decisions quickly and accurately; used to conduct sales analyses, forecast sales, evaluate advertising, analyze product lines, and keep tabs on market trends and competitors' actions.

More and more managers are turning to another form of technology called a **decision support system (DSS),** an interactive, flexible computerized information system that allows managers to make decisions quickly and accurately. Managers use DSS to conduct sales analyses, forecast sales, evaluate advertising, analyze product lines, and keep tabs on market trends and competitors' actions. A DSS not only allows managers to ask "what if" questions, but enables them to slice the data any way they want. A DSS has the following characteristics:

1. *Interactive.* The manager gives simple instructions and sees results generated on the spot. The process is under the manager's direct control; no computer programmer is needed.
2. *Flexible.* It can sort, regroup, total, average, and manipulate the data in a variety of ways. It will shift gears as the user changes topics, matching information to the problem at hand. For example, the chief executive can see highly aggregated figures, while the marketing analyst views detailed breakouts.
3. *Discovery oriented.* It helps managers probe for trends, isolate problems, and ask new questions.
4. *Easy to learn and use.* Managers need not be particularly computer knowledgeable. Novice users can elect a standard, or "default," method of using the system that enables them to bypass optional features and work with the basic system while they gradually learn its possibilities. This minimizes the frustration that frequently accompanies new computer software.

Using Databases for Micromarketing

database marketing

The creation of a large computerized file of the profiles and purchase patterns of customers and potential customers; usually required for successful micromarketing.

Perhaps the fastest growing use of DSS is for **database marketing,** which is the creation of a large computerized file of the profiles and purchase patterns of customers and potential customers. Using the very specific information in the database, a company can, if it wishes, direct a different individualized message to every customer or potential customer.

Beginning in the 1950s, network television enabled advertisers to "get the same message to everyone simultaneously." Database marketing can get a customized, individual message to everyone simultaneously through direct mail. This is why database marketing is sometimes called *micromarketing*. Specifically, database marketing can:

- Identify the most profitable and least profitable customers.
- Identify the most profitable market segments or individuals and target efforts with greater efficiency and effectiveness.

- Aim marketing efforts to those goods, services, and market segments that require the most support.
- Increase revenue through repackaging and repricing products for various market segments.
- Evaluate opportunities for offering new products and services.
- Identify products and services that are best-sellers and most profitable.

Database marketing can create a computerized form of the old-fashioned relationship that people used to have with the corner grocer, butcher, or baker. "A database is sort of a collective memory," says Richard G. Barlow, president of Frequency Marketing, Inc., a Cincinnati-based consulting firm. "It deals with you in the same personalized way as a mon-and-pop grocery store, where they knew customers by name and stocked what they wanted."[15] American Express, for example, can pull from its database all cardholders who made purchases at golf pro-shops in the past six months, attended symphony concerts, or traveled to Europe more than once in the last year.

c o n c ə p t   c h ə c k

- How is technology being used in marketing research?
- What is a decision support system (DSS) and what is its purpose?
- Explain what database marketing is and describe some of its uses.

APPLYING THIS CHAPTER'S TOPICS

As a consumer, you participate in shaping consumer products by the choices you make and the products and services you buy. You can become a better consumer by actively participating in marketing surveys and learning more about the products you buy.

Participate in Marketing Research Surveys

All of us get tired of telephone solicitations where people try to sell us everything from new carpet to chimney cleaning. Recognize that marketing research surveys are different. A true marketing research survey will *never* involve a sales pitch nor will the research firm sell your name to a database marketer. The purpose of marketing research is to build better goods and services for you and me. Help out the researchers and ultimately help yourself. The Council for Marketing and Opinion Research (CMOR) is an organization of hundreds of marketing research professionals that is dedicated to preserving the integrity of the research industry. If you receive a call from someone who tries to sell you something under the guise of marketing research, get the name and address of the organization. Call CMOR at 1-800-887-CMOR and report the abuse.

Understand Cognitive Dissonance

cognitive dissonance
The condition of having beliefs or knowledge that are internally inconsistent or that disagree with one's behavior.

When making a major purchase, particularly when the item is expensive and choices are similar, consumers typically experience **cognitive dissonance;** that is, they have beliefs or knowledge that are internally inconsistent or that disagree with their behavior. In other words, instead of feeling happy with their new purchase, they experience doubts, feel uneasy, and wonder if they have done the right thing. Understand that this feeling of uneasiness is perfectly normal and goes away over time. Perhaps the best way to avoid cognitive

1. **Stop junk mail**   If you are upset about junk mail, contact the Direct Marketing Association and have your name removed from mailing lists. The e-mail address is **www.the-dma.org/.** You can also join an umbrella organization dedicated to stopping the flood of junk e-mail, intrusive tele-marketing calls, and junk mail. One such organi-zation is Zero Junk Mail. It can be found at **www.zerojunkmail.com.**

2. **Know Your Profile**   Do you wonder where mar-keters place you in their psychographic profiles? To find out, go to **www.future.sri.com/vals/ques-nt.html** and take the Values and Life-Styles self-test. Where do you fit in?

dissonance is to insist on a strong warranty or money-back guarantee. A second approach is to read everything you can find about your purchase. Go to the Internet and use the search engines to find articles relevant to your purchase. Find Internet chat rooms about your product and join in the discussion. And, before you buy, check out the *Consumer Reports* ratings on your product at **www.consumerreports.org.**

SUMMARY OF LEARNING GOALS

>lg 1   **What are the marketing concept and relationship building?**
Marketing includes those business activities that are designed to satisfy con-sumer needs and wants through the exchange process. Marketing managers use the "right" principle—getting the right goods or services to the right peo-ple at the right place, time, and price, using the right promotional techniques. Today, many firms have adopted the marketing concept. The marketing con-cept involves identifying consumer needs and wants and then producing goods or services that will satisfy them while making a profit. Relationship marketing entails forging long-term relationships with customers, which can lead to repeat sales, reduced costs, and stable relationships.

>lg 2   **How do managers create a marketing strategy?**
A firm creates a marketing strategy by understanding the external environ-ment, defining the target market, determining a competitive advantage, and developing a marketing mix. Environmental scanning enables companies to understand the external environment. The target market is the specific group of consumers toward which a firm directs its marketing efforts. A com-petitive advantage is a set of unique features of a company and its products that are perceived by the target market as significant and superior to those of the competition.

>lg 3   **What is the marketing mix?**
To carry out the marketing strategy, firms create a marketing mix—a blend of products, distribution systems, prices, and promotion. Marketing managers use

this mix to satisfy target consumers. The mix can be applied to nonbusiness as well as business situations.

at DaimlerChrysler

Before a company can create a marketing mix, it must identify the target market for the product. Thus, DaimlerChrysler first had to identify the target market for the 300M. To be successful, the company had to identify one or more competitive advantages unique to the 300M. DaimlerChrysler used marketing research to identify the target market for the 300M and then determined the needs and desires of these potential buyers. With this information, the company could build customer value into the 300M. The automaker must continue to use marketing research to identify the ever-changing desires of the target market. DaimlerChrysler can retain its leadership position with the 300M by continuing to deliver value to target buyers.

>lg 4   How do consumers and organizations make buying decisions?
Buyer behavior is what people and businesses do in buying and using goods and services. The consumer decision-making process consists of the following steps: responding to a stimulus, recognizing a problem or opportunity, seeking information, evaluating alternatives, purchasing the product, judging the purchase outcome, and engaging in postpurchase behavior. A number of factors influence the process. Individual factors are within the individual consumer and are unique to each person. Social factors include all interactions between a consumer and the external environment, such as family, social classes, and culture. The main differences between consumer and business markets are purchase volume, number of customers, location of buyers, direct distribution, and rational purchase decisions.

>lg 5   What are the five basic forms of market segmentation?
Success in marketing depends on understanding the target market. One technique used to identify a target market is market segmentation. The five basic forms of segmentation are demographic (population statistics), geographic (location), psychographic (personality or lifestyle), benefit (product features), and volume (amount purchased).

>lg 6   How is marketing research used in marketing decision making?
Much can be learned about consumers through marketing research, which involves collecting, recording, and analyzing data important in marketing goods and services and communicating the results to management. Marketing researchers may use primary data, which are gathered through door-to-door, mall-intercept, telephone, the Internet and mail interviews. The Internet is becoming a quick, cheap, and efficient way to gather primary data. Secondary data are available from a variety of sources including government, trade, and commercial associations. Secondary data save time and money, but they may not meet researchers' needs. Both primary and secondary data give researchers a better idea of how the market will respond to the product. Thus, they reduce the risk of producing something the market doesn't want.

>lg 7   What are the trends in understanding the consumer?
New technology has increased the sophistication of observation research techniques and improved the accuracy of data, such as measurements of the size of television audiences and Web traffic to specific sites. Researchers are also analyzing the brain to better understand how people think. A second trend is the growing use of decision support systems. These enable managers to make decisions quickly and accurately. A third trend is the growing use of databases for micromarketing.

KEY TERMS

benefit
  segmentation
  397
buyer behavior
  392
cognitive
  dissonance 403
competitive
  advantage 387
cost competitive
  advantage 388
customer
  satisfaction 383
customer value
  383
database marketing
  402
decision support
  system (DSS) 402
demographic
  segmentation
  395
differential
  competitive
  advantage 388
distribution strategy
  390
environmental
  scanning 386
exchange 382
experiment 399
Four Ps 389
geographic
  segmentation
  396
market
  segmentation
  394
marketing 382
marketing concept
  382
marketing mix 389
marketing research
  397
niche competitive
  advantage 389
observation
  research 399
pricing strategy
  390
primary data 400
product strategy
  390
production
  orientation 383
promotion strategy
  390
psychographic
  segmentation
  397
relationship
  marketing 385

PREPARING FOR TOMORROW'S WORKPLACE

1. Can the marketing concept be applied effectively by a sole proprietorship, or is it more appropriate for larger businesses with more managers? Explain.

2. Break the class into seven teams and have each team choose one of the following organizations: United Airlines; Henrietta's Hair Styling Salon; Caterpillar Tractor Co.; Revlon (cosmetics); the American Cancer Society chapter in Evanston, Illinois (population 80,000); Burger King; George and Harry's machine tool–rebuilding shop. Each team should present a description of its organization's marketing mix. After the presentations, have the class discuss why the marketing mix differs among the organizations.

3. Write a memo to your manager explaining why it is important for his small business (a restaurant) to have a competitive advantage.

4. Divide the class into two groups. Debate the following propositions: (1) business buyer behavior can be just as emotional as consumer buyer behavior; (2) consumer buyer behavior can be just as rational as business buyer behavior.

5. "Market segmentation is the most important concept in marketing." Why do you think some marketing professionals make this statement? Give an example of each form of segmentation.

6. Write a paper explaining when a marketer would want to use primary data and when it would be better to use secondary data.

7. Divide the class into two teams. Debate the concept that marketing research is an invasion of privacy.

8. Can marketing research be carried out in the same manner all over the world? Why or why not?

9. Divide the class into teams of four or five. Each team should choose a company and determine its competitive advantage, the type of competitive advantage, and whether the advantage can be sustained over the next five years.

WORKING THE NET

1. You've been hired by a snack food manufacturer that is interested in adding popcorn snacks to its product line. First, however, the company asks you to find some secondary data on the current market for popcorn. Go to the Dogpile Search Engine (**www.dogpile.com**) and do a search for "popcorn consumption." Can you find how much popcorn is sold annually? The geographic locations with the highest popcorn sales? The time of the year when the most popcorn is sold? What are the limitations of doing research like this on the Internet?

2. Read the *Business Week* article about marketing to children at **www.businessweek. com/1997/26/635331.html**. Do you think it is ethical for companies to use children as a marketing segment? Why or why not?

3. You and a friend want to start a new magazine for people who work at home. Do a search of the U.S. Census database at **www.census.gov** to get information about the work-at-home market.

4. Take the VALS-2 lifestyle survey at **future.sri.com/vals/valsindex.html** and find out which psychographic segment you're in. Do you agree or disagree with the results? Why or why not?

secondary data
400
social marketing
392
survey research
399
target market 387
volume
segmentation
397

5. Knight Marketing Corp. (**www.knightmkt.com**) markets cleaning products to businesses in the automotive, marine, and industrial industries. Do a search on Yahoo (**www.yahoo.com**) for businesses that sell consumer cleaning products. Pick one or two companies; compare and contrast their marketing strategies and visit their home pages. Compare and contrast their marketing with Knight Marketing Corp.'s marketing.

CREATIVE THINKING CASE

The American Automobile Association—Building Long-Term Relationships?

This case is built upon the experience of Don Schultz, a marketing professor at Northwestern University. He tells his story in the first person.

Almost every car owner knows about the American Automobile Association. They're the people who slog through rain and snow to rescue stranded motorists. Whether it's a flat tire on the expressway or a broken axle or keys locked in a car parked in a lot, the AAA professionals come running. And they do a good job. I've been a member of the Chicago Motor Club, a "Triple A" affiliate, for 20 years. They have given good service to me, my wife, my children, and my mother.

In recent months, my car has had a problem. For reasons known only to the car, the battery discharges at random. Sometimes it happens overnight, sometimes weeks go by without a problem. When the battery discharges itself, I call AAA. No matter where I am, they come out and give me a jump. Seemingly my problem is no problem for them. They provide cheerful, friendly service, day and night.

Until recently, that is, when apparently I triggered their brand relationship destroying mechanism. While other service suppliers were sending end-of-the-year calendars and thank-you letters, I got threats from AAA. In a letter, Gerald F. Svarz, manager of member relations, wrote:

> Our records indicate that you have requested Emergency Road Service four times during the past 12 months. As outlined in the Member's Handbook, the Club reserves the right to notify a member when they have used four or more service calls in the previous 12 months. Excessive use of Emergency Road Service can result in the nonrenewal or the cancellation of a membership. The nonrenewal or cancellation of membership is based solely on the number of calls in a membership year.

Wow, talk about *building* brand *relationships!* Here's an organization that's going to kick me out of its club, whose primary claim to fame and only reason for being—at least for most of its members—is emergency road service. Only don't use our service too much, they say, or we'll cancel your membership. We reserve that right.

Just to make sure I wasn't overlooking something, I checked out AAA in the Yellow Pages. "Emergency Road Service," the ad says. Same for the newspaper ads I found. And "Emergency Road Service" is splashed all over the relation-*building* magazine they send me every few months. Their promotional literature says "Emergency Road Service" in big bold letters.

The problem is, they reserve the right to limit the Emergency Road Service you need. Am I a better AAA *customer* if I don't ever use their services? It sure sounds like it. What about all those years I paid the membership fee and never used the service? They didn't write to thank me for that, nor did they adjust my membership fee the way auto insurance companies do for safe drivers.

Critical Thinking Questions

1. Is AAA following the marketing concept?
2. Doesn't it make economic sense to "weed out" people who use the service too much?
3. Insurance companies cancel people's auto insurance if they get too many speeding tickets. Isn't AAA's policy the same thing?
4. Would you make any changes in AAA's operations? If so, what?

VIDEO CASE

Burke Marketing Research

Burke Marketing Research (**www.burke.com**), with offices and affiliates in 40 countries throughout the world, provides marketing research services to a wide range of clients. They include companies in the following industries: agricultural/chemical; computer hardware and software; communications/technology; consumer goods and services; entertainment, television, and cable; insurance and financial; pharmaceutical and health care; publishing; and travel services. Across this broad spectrum of industries, Burke deals with both quantitative and qualitative marketing issues. Each project is customized to fit the specific client's marketing needs and decision-making requirements.

As a 100 percent employee-owned firm, Burke has a special commitment to its clientele. "Every employee is personally committed to providing the best possible service" to clients. Clients work directly with an account team which is charged with ensuring that the client's "objectives are met efficiently, economically, and on time."

To generate information for its studies, Burke uses a variety of data collection methods including focus groups, mail surveys, Internet online surveys, phone surveys, and mall intercept interviews. From its experience in "dealing with recurrent marketing problems across many industry and product categories," the company has developed a variety of marketing research protocols for examining and diagnosing common marketing problems. These protocols include onsite vendor/customer focus groups, image and positioning analysis, advertising campaign evaluation, new product demand and pricing analysis, product testing analysis, brand equity analysis, marketing performance analysis, and an integrated concept evaluation system. Each account team shapes the protocols to deal with the client's unique issues. In using each protocol, Burke follows a generally accepted approach to marketing research: defining the marketing problem; selecting and adapting the appropriate protocol for collecting the data; collecting and analyzing the data; and, finally, generating a report for the client that contains useful results and recommendations.

Based on its marketing research, Burke provides "an interpretative and decision-oriented analysis" of the client's situation. Burke's research reports include "accurate, reliable information that can significantly improve [the client's] . . . decision-making process." The overarching goal is to provide clients with marketing information that will enable them to develop better products and services, to become better informed marketers, and to have more satisfied customers.

Burke's executives believe that effective "marketing research consists of much more than telephone surveys." They say that good marketing research requires knowledgeable, experienced people who are familiar with the client's industry and the challenges the client faces every day. Good marketing research also requires "attention to detail and a commitment to finding . . . results."

Critical Thinking Questions

1. How would you describe Burke's competitive advantage in the marketing research marketplace?
2. How does Burke Marketing Research use market segmentation in its own business?
3. Do you think Burke's approach to marketing research is effective? Why or why not?

>c14

chapter fourteen

Developing Quality Products at the Right Price

learning goals

>lg 1   What is a product, and how is it classified?

>lg 2   How does branding distinguish a product from its competitors?

>lg 3   What are the functions of packaging?

>lg 4   How do organizations create new products?

>lg 6   What is the role of pricing in marketing?

>lg 7   How are product prices determined?

>lg 8   What strategies are used for pricing products?

>lg 9   What trends are occurring in products and pricing?

Sales of Soaps Prove Bubbly for Artemis

One of the fastest-selling new products for urban teens comes with a warning sticker: users run "the risk of serious bodily harm, including head injury, spinal injury or death." Pretty scary stuff for a pair of sneakers. These sneakers are called Soaps, and they're no ordinary shoes. Embedded in each sole is a smooth plastic plate that lets wearers slide along handrails, curbs, ledges, and other structures—like skating without the skates. Practitioners call this "grinding."

Introduced in 1998, the fad is picking up speed. Soaps are becoming a hit among thrill-seeking teens and preteens who are no longer content—or allowed—to perform their stunts on skateboards and in-line skates, which are banned in many public places. Artemis Innovations, Inc., Soaps' closely held maker, says that Soaps are now sold in about 2,000 stores. With a retail price of $70 to $80, Soaps are a financially attractive alternative to skateboards and in-line skates, which usually cost $120 or more. They also open a whole new recreational frontier. Skateboards are generally forbidden indoors, but Soaps can work anywhere, transforming a flight of school stairs or a study-hall windowsill into a playground. Artemis says 90 percent of wearers are male.

Billed by Artemis as the "stepchild" of skateboards and in-line skates, Soaps were born in 1994 during a casual lunch chat between Chris Morris, founder of Artemis, and Dave Inman, an industry consultant. Morris had worked at Rollerblades, and Inman wondered whether a shoe could be built in the spirit of Rollerblades' product. Both men recalled how sliding—on a patch of ice or in stockings on a hardwood floor—was a favorite childhood pastime. Morris went home, fetched a pair of Nikes out of the closet, hollowed out the center portion of the sole, stuck in a homemade plate, and tried a little grinding himself. He has since applied for patents for 23 components of his contraption. He launched the shoe with little seed money and almost none for advertising. To help spread the word, he formed a small band of a dozen teenage daredevils who agreed to wear the shoe and grind from time to time in public.

Aficionados say grinding in sneakers is easier than on skates or skateboards, but injuries aren't uncommon. Morris says the company has received reports of several broken ankles, sprains, and other injuries, but no fatalities and no lawsuits.[1]

Critical Thinking Questions
As you read this chapter, consider the following questions as they relate to Artemis Innovations:

- Is this typical of the way new products are developed?
- How should Soaps be classified?
- What is Artemis's price strategy for Soaps?

Business in the 21ˢᵗ Century

BUSINESS IN THE 21ˢᵀ CENTURY

The creation of a marketing mix normally begins with the first of the four Ps, product. Only when there is something to sell can marketers create a promotional theme, set a price, and establish a distribution channel. Organizations prepare for long-term success by creating and packaging products that add value and pricing them to meet the organization's financial objectives. In addition, organizations respond to changing customer needs by creating new products. This chapter will examine products, brands, and the importance of packaging. We discuss how new products are created and how they go through periods of sales growth and then decline. Next, you will discover how managers set prices to reach pricing goals. Alternative pricing strategies used to reach specific target markets are then discussed. We conclude with a look at trends in products and pricing.

WHAT IS A PRODUCT?

product

In marketing, any good or service, along with its perceived attributes and benefits, that creates value for the customer.

In marketing, a **product** is any good or service, along with its perceived attributes and benefits, that creates value for the customer. Attributes can be tangible or intangible. Among the tangible attributes are packaging and warranties as illustrated in Exhibit 14-1. Intangible attributes are symbolic, such as brand image. People make decisions about which products to buy after considering both tangible and intangible attributes of a product. For example, when you buy a pair of jeans, you consider price, brand, store image, and style before you buy. These factors are all part of the marketing mix.

> e x h i b i t   1 4 - 1 <   Tangible and Intangible Attributes of a Product Create Value for the Buyer

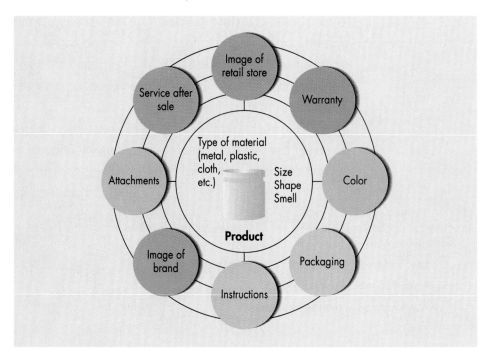

Products are often a blend of goods and services as shown in Exhibit 14-2. For example, Honda Accord (a good) would have less value without Honda's maintenance agreement (a service). Although Burger King sells such goods as sandwiches and french fries, customers expect quality service as well, including quick food preparation and cleanliness. When developing a product, an organization must consider how the combination of goods and services will provide value to the customer.

Classifying Consumer Products

Because most things sold are a blend of goods and services, the term *product* can be used to refer to both. After all, consumers are really buying packages of benefits that deliver value. The person who buys a plane ride on United Airlines is looking for a quick way to get from one city to another (the benefit). Providing this benefit requires goods (a plane, food) and services (ticketing, maintenance, piloting).

Marketers must know how consumers view the types of products their companies sell so that they can design the marketing mix to appeal to the selected target market. To help them define target markets, marketers have devised product categories. Products that are bought by the end user are called *consumer products.* They include electric razors, sandwiches, cars, stereos, magazines, and houses. Consumer products that get used up, such as Breck hair mousse and Lays potato chips, are called *consumer nondurables.* Those that last for a long time, such as Whirlpool washing machines and computers, are *consumer durables.*

Another way to classify consumer products is by the amount of effort consumers are willing to make to acquire them. The four major categories of consumer products are unsought products, convenience products, shopping products, and specialty products, as summarized in Exhibit 14-3.

unsought products
Products that either are unknown to the potential buyer or are known but the buyer does not actively seek them.

Unsought products are products unknown to the potential buyer or known products that the buyer does not actively seek. New products fall into this category until advertising and distribution increase consumer awareness of them. Some goods are always marketed as unsought items, especially products we do not like to think about or care to spend money on. Insurance, burial plots, encyclopedias, and similar items require aggressive personal selling and highly persuasive advertising. Salespeople actively seek leads to potential buyers. Because consumers usually do not seek out this type of product, the company

> e x h i b i t   1 4 - 2 <

Products Are Typically a Blend of Goods and Services

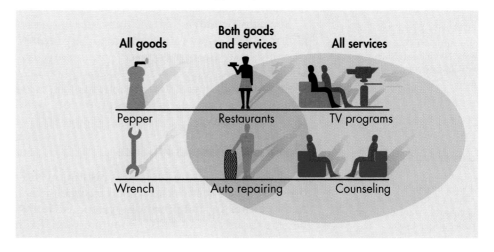

All goods	Both goods and services	All services
Pepper	Restaurants	TV programs
Wrench	Auto repairing	Counseling

> e x h i b i t   1 4 - 3 <

Classification of Consumer Products by the Effort Expended to Buy Them

Consumer Product	Examples	Degree of Effort Expended by Consumer
Unsought products	Life insurance Burial plots New products	No effort
Convenience products	Soft drinks Bread Milk Coffee	Very little or minimum effort
Shopping products	Automobiles Homes Vacations	Considerable effort
Specialty products	Expensive jewelry Gourmet dinners Limited-production automobiles	Maximum effort

must go directly to them through a salesperson, direct mail, telemarketing, or direct-response advertising.

convenience products

Relatively inexpensive items that require little shopping effort and are purchased routinely without planning.

Convenience products are relatively inexpensive items that require little shopping effort. Soft drinks, candy bars, milk, bread, and small hardware items are examples. We buy them routinely without much planning. This does not mean that such products are unimportant or obscure. Many, in fact, are well known by their brand names—such as Pepsi-Cola, Pepperidge Farm breads, Domino's pizza, Sure deodorant, and UPS shipping.

Find out about Domino's recipe for success with pizza at **www.dominos.com**

In contrast to convenience products, **shopping products** are bought only after a brand-to-brand and store-to-store comparison of price, suitability, and style. Examples are furniture, automobiles, a vacation in Europe, and some items of clothing. Convenience products are bought with little planning, but shopping products may be chosen months or even years before their actual purchase.

shopping products

Items that are bought after considerable planning, including brand-to-brand and store-to-store comparisons of price, suitability, and style.

specialty products

Items for which consumers search long and hard and for which they refuse to accept substitutes.

Specialty products are products for which consumers search long and hard and for which they refuse to accept substitutes. Expensive jewelry, designer clothing, state-of-the-art stereo equipment, limited-production automobiles, and gourmet dinners fall into this category. Because consumers are willing to spend much time and effort to find specialty products, distribution is often limited to one or two sellers in a given region, such as Neiman-Marcus, Gucci, or the Porsche dealer.

Classifying Business Products

capital products

Large, expensive items with a long life span that are purchased by businesses for use in making other products or providing a service.

Products bought by businesses or institutions for use in making other products or in providing services are called *business* or *industrial products*. They are classified as either capital products or expense items. **Capital products** are usually large, expensive items with a long life span. Examples are buildings, large ma-

expense items

Items, purchased by businesses, that are smaller and less expensive than capital products and usually have a life span of less than one year.

chines, and airplanes. **Expense items** are typically smaller, less expensive items that usually have a life span of less than a year. Examples are printer ribbons and paper. Industrial products are sometimes further classified in the following categories:

1. *Installations.* These are large, expensive capital items that determine the nature, scope, and efficiency of a company. Capital products like General Motors' Saturn assembly plant in Tennessee represent a big commitment against future earnings and profitability. Buying an installation requires longer negotiations, more planning, and the judgments of more people than buying any other type of product.

2. *Accessories.* Accessories do not have the same long-run impact on the firm as installations, and they are less expensive and more standardized. But they are still capital products. Minolta copy machines, IBM personal computers (PCs), and smaller machines such as Black and Decker table drills and saws are typical accessories. Marketers of accessories often rely on well-known brand names and extensive advertising as well as personal selling.

3. *Component parts and materials.* These are expense items that are built into the end product. Some component parts are custom-made, such as a drive shaft for an automobile, a case for a computer, or a special pigment for painting U.S. Navy harbor buoys; others are standardized for sale to many industrial users. Intel's pentium chip for PCs and cement for the construction trade are examples of standardized component parts and materials.

4. *Raw materials.* Raw materials are expense items that have undergone little or no processing and are used to create a final product. Examples include lumber, copper, and zinc.

5. *Supplies.* Supplies do not become part of the final product. They are bought routinely and in fairly large quantities. Supply items run the gamut from pencils and paper to paint and machine oil. They have little impact on the firm's long-run profits. Bic pens, Champion copier paper, and Pennzoil machine oil are typical supply items.

6. *Services.* These are expense items used to plan or support company operations; for example, janitorial cleaning and management consulting.

concept check
- What is a product?
- What are the classes of consumer goods?
- Explain how business products are classified.

BUILDING BRAND EQUITY AND MASTER BRANDS

>lg 2

Most industrial and consumer products have a brand name. If everything came in a plain brown wrapper, life would be less colorful and competition would decrease. Companies would have less incentive to put out better products because consumers would be unable to tell one company's products from those of another.

The product identifier for a company is its **brand.** Brands appear in the form of words, names, symbols, or designs. They are used to distinguish a company's products from those of its competitors. Examples of well-known brands are Kleenex tissues, Jeep automobiles, and IBM computers. A **trademark** is the legally exclusive design, name, or other identifying mark associated with a company's brand. No other company can use that same trademark.

brand

A company's product identifier that distinguishes the company's products from those of its competitors.

trademark

The legally exclusive design, name, or other identifying mark associated with a company's brand.

Find out how to trademark a design, name or other identifying mark by visiting the U.S. Patents and Trademark Office at
www.uspto.gov

These brand names for laundry detergents are effective because they are short, distinctive, and easy to pronounce, recognize, and remember.

brand equity
The value of company and brand names.

Benefits of Branding

Branding has three main purposes: product identification, repeat sales, and new product sales. The most important purpose is *product identification*. Branding allows marketers to distinguish their products from all others. Exhibit 14-4 identifies the characteristics of an effective brand name. Many brand names are familiar to consumers and indicate quality. The term **brand equity** refers to the value of company and brand names. A brand that has high awareness, perceived quality, and brand loyalty among customers has high brand equity. Brand equity is more than awareness of a brand—it is the personality, soul, and emotion associated with the brand. Think of the feelings you have when you see the brand name Harley-Davidson, Nike, or even Microsoft. A brand with strong brand equity is a valuable asset. Some brands such as Coke, Kodak, Marlboro, and Chevrolet are worth millions of dollars.

A brand so dominant in consumers' minds that they think of it immediately when a product category, use, attribute, or customer benefit is mentioned is a **master brand.** Exhibit 14-5 lists some of America's master brands in several product categories.

U.S. brands command substantial premiums in many places around the world. Procter & Gamble's Whisper sanitary napkins sell for 10 times the price of local brands in China. Johnson & Johnson brands like Johnson's baby shampoo and Band-Aids command a 500 percent premium in China.

> e x h i b i t   1 4 - 4 <

Characteristics of Effective Brand Names

- Easy to pronounce (by both domestic and foreign buyers)
- Easy to recognize
- Easy to remember
- Short
- Distinctive, unique
- Describes the product
- Describes the product's use
- Describes the product's benefits
- Has a positive connotation
- Reinforces the desired product image
- Is legally protectable in home and foreign markets of interest

> e x h i b i t   1 4 - 5 <

> e x h i b i t   1 4 - 5 <

America's Master Brands

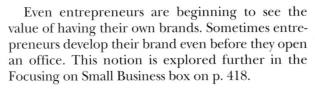

Product Category	Master Brand
Adhesive bandages	Band-Aid
Antacids	Alka-Seltzer
Baking soda	Arm & Hammer
Cellophane tape	Scotch Tape
Fast food	McDonald's
Gelatin	Jell-O
Rum	Barcardi
Salt	Morton
Soft drinks	Coca-Cola
Soup	Campbell's

master brand

A brand so dominant that consumers think of it immediately when a product category, use, attribute, or customer benefit is mentioned.

brand loyalty

A consumer's preference for a particular brand.

In launching his line of cologne and personal care products, entrepreneur Michael Jordan enjoys high brand equity because people associate the brand with Jordan's status as one of the world's best athletes.

Even entrepreneurs are beginning to see the value of having their own brands. Sometimes entrepreneurs develop their brand even before they open an office. This notion is explored further in the Focusing on Small Business box on p. 418.

Building Repeat Sales with Brand Loyalty

A consumer who tries one or more brands may decide to buy a certain brand regularly. The preference for a particular brand is **brand loyalty.** It lets consumers buy with less time, thought, and risk. Brand loyalty ensures future sales for the firm. It can also help protect a firm's share of the market, discourage new competitors, and thus prolong the brand's life. Brand loyalty even allows companies to raise prices. Quaker Oats Co., maker of Cap'n Crunch, Life, and Quaker oatmeal, recently raised its prices 3.8 percent. Analysts said that Quaker could do this, even though other cereal makers didn't raise prices, because of the strong consumer loyalty to Quaker products.[2]

What makes people loyal to a brand? Though pricing, promotion, and product quality are important, customer interaction with the company may be most critical. A recent study found that 90 percent of consumers who were delighted with their experience say they will continue to buy the product/service whereas only 37 percent of the customers who were dissatisfied with their experience say they will remain loyal.[3] Brand loyalty to a particular company's products is a marketer's dream come true.

HOT links

See how one consulting firm helps clients pick the right name by pointing your Web browser to

www.namebase.com

LITTLE GUYS CAN WIN THE BRANDING WAR

Small companies are embracing branding in part because they've seen the Fortune 500 corporations concentrating on building and leveraging their brands more than ever before. Coca-Cola Co. made the new Braves baseball stadium in Atlanta a shrine to Coke; giant Nikeworld stores extend the icon of the Nike swoosh into the realm of "experiential" retailing.

Entrepreneurs thinking about creating their own brands should consider these suggestions:

1. *Establish your uniqueness.* That's what Cape Cod Chips has done as it has battled with snack-industry giants for supermarket shelf space and a share of the dollars spend by potato chip lovers across the country. The company, which is based in Hyannis, Massachusetts, focuses on its self-developed "batch" processing of potatoes, which yields a distinctive taste and texture; extends its product line with chips made from different varieties of potatoes rather than just dusting on flavorings as some of its bigger competitors do; relies on product sampling instead of traditional advertising as its marketing workhorse; and supports its regional identity with everything from tours of its factory to its product packaging, which features a lighthouse.
2. *Stay within your core.* China Mist Tea Co. in Phoenix has grown to a $4 million company in just a few years by providing only iced tea and selling

only to restaurants and institutions. Along with that growth, however, has come the temptation to expand beyond its core business or to partner with a beverage giant such as Coca-Cola or PepsiCo. "We have such fanatically loyal customers that even Coke has noticed it and commented to us about it, and that's the key to our growth," says Dan Schweiker, co-owner of the company. "The reason is we know what our niche is and pay attention to it. We're not trying to become Lipton tea."

3. *Dominate a geographic or niche market.* Coke may have taught the world to sing, but a savvy small brander can dominate southwestern Mississippi or Schenectady, New York. Utz Potato Chip Co. of Hanover, Pennsylvania, for instance, has built a whole advertising campaign around the fact that people outside the mid-Atlantic region can't buy Utz products in stores. Small regional brewer Point Brewing Co. stopped a five-year sales decline last year by paring back to the 12-county region around its headquarters in Stevens Point, Wisconsin.

Critical Thinking Questions

1. Should all small businesses try to build a brand? Why or why not?
2. What other suggestions do you have for an entrepreneur attempting to build a brand?

Facilitating New Product Sales

The third main purpose of branding is to facilitate *new product sales.* Let's assume that your class forms a company to market frozen tarts and pies under the name "University Frozen Desserts." Now, assume that Pepperidge Farms develops a new line of identical frozen tarts and pies. Which ones will consumers try? The Pepperidge Farm products, without doubt. Pepperidge Farm is known for its quality frozen bakery products. Consumers assume that its new tarts and pies will be of high quality and are therefore willing to give them a try. The well-known Pepperidge Farm brand is facilitating new product introduction.

manufacturer brands

Brands that are owned by national or regional manufacturers and widely distributed; also call *national brands.*

Types of Brands

Brands owned by national or regional manufacturers and widely distributed are **manufacturer brands.** (These brands are sometimes called national brands, but since some of the brands are not owned by nationwide or international manufacturers, *manufacturer brands* is a more accurate term.) A few well-known manufacturer brands are Polaroid, Liz Claiborne, Nike, and Sony.

Manufacturer brands can bring new customers and new prestige to small retailers. For instance, a small bicycle repair shop in a midwestern college town got the franchise to sell and repair Schwinn bicycles. The shop's profits grew quickly, and it became one of the most successful retail businesses in the university area. Because manufacturer brands are widely promoted, sales are often high. Also, most manufacturers of these brands offer frequent deliveries to their retailers. Thus, retailers can carry less stock and have less money tied up in inventory.

dealer brands

Brands that are owned by the wholesaler or retailer rather than the name of the manufacturer.

Brands that are owned by the wholesaler or retailer, rather than that of the manufacturer, are **dealer brands.** Sears has several well-known dealer (or private) brands, including Craftsman, Diehard, and Kenmore. The Independent Grocers Association (IGA), a large wholesale grocery organization, uses the brand name Shurfine on its goods. Dealer brands tie consumers to particular wholesalers or retailers. If you want a Kenmore washing machine, you must go to Sears.

Although profit margins are usually higher on dealer brands than on manufacturer brands, dealers must still stimulate demand for their products. Sears's promotion of its products has made the company one of the largest advertisers in the United States. But promotion costs can cut heavily into profit margins. And if a dealer-brand item is of poor quality, the dealer must assume responsibility for it. Sellers of manufacturer brands can refer a disgruntled customer to the manufacturer.

generic products

Products that carry no brand name, come in plain containers, and sell for much less than brand-name products.

Many consumers don't want to pay the costs of manufacturer or dealer brands. One popular way to save money is to buy **generic products.** These products carry no brand name, come in plain containers, and sell for much less than brand-name products. They are typically sold in black and white packages with such simple labels as "liquid bleach" or "spaghetti." Generic products are sold by 85 percent of U.S. supermarkets. Sometimes manufacturers simply stop the production line and substitute a generic package for a brand package, though the product is exactly the same. The most popular generic products are garbage bags, jelly, paper towels, coffee cream substitutes, cigarettes, and paper napkins.

HOT links

Curious about how generic and private label products are manufactured? Visit the Private Label Manufacturers Association at

www.plma.com

concept check

- Define the terms *brand* and *trademark*.
- Describe the three benefits of branding.
- Explain the differences between manufacturer brands and dealer brands.
- What is a generic product?

THE IMPORTANCE OF PACKAGING IN A SELF-SERVICE ECONOMY

>lg 3

Just as a brand gives a product identity, its packaging also distinguishes it from competitors' products and increases its customer value. When you go to the store and reach for a bottle of dishwashing detergent, the package is the last chance a manufacturer has to convince you to buy its brand over a competitor's. A good package may cause you to reach for Joy rather than Palmolive.

The Functions of a Package

A basic function of packaging is to protect the product from breaking or spoiling and thus extend its life. A package should be easy to ship, store, and stack on a shelf and convenient for the consumer to buy. Many new packaging methods have been developed recently. Aseptic packages keep foods fresh for months without refrigeration. Examples are Borden's "sipp' packs" for juices, the Brik Pak for milk, and Hunt's/Del Monte's aseptic boxes for tomato sauce. Some package developers are creating "micro-atmospheres" that allow meat to stay fresh in the refrigerator for weeks.

Why do people usually skip drinks when they buy take-out from a restaurant? According to research conducted by Pepsi, consumers dislike paper cups because they get soggy and can easily spill if jostled, so customers stop someplace else to pick up a bottle or can.[4] But restaurants don't like selling drinks in bottles and cans, which have lower margins than soda from the fountain. Pepsi's solution is a plastic "twist'n go" cup with a dome-shaped lid that is screwed on (see Exhibit 14-6). The cup, designed to carry 32 ounces, also has a narrow bottom that fits car cupholders. It costs more than a paper cup, but Pepsi is betting it will pay for itself with extra volume.

A second basic function of packaging is to help promote the product by providing clear brand identification and information about the product's features. For example, Ralston Purina Co.'s Dog Chow brand, the leading dog food, was losing market share. The company decided that the pictures of dog breeds on the package were too old-fashioned and rural. With a new package featuring a photo of a dog and a child, sales have increased.

Adding Value through Warranties

warranty
A guarantee of the quality of a good or service.

implied warranty
An unwritten guarantee that a product is fit for the purpose for which it is sold.

express warranty
A written guarantee about a product, such as that it contains certain materials, will perform a certain way, or is otherwise fit for the purpose for which it was sold.

A **warranty** guarantees the quality of a good or service. An **implied warranty** is an unwritten guarantee that the product is fit for the purpose for which it was sold. All sales have an implied warranty under the Uniform Commercial Code (a law that applies to commercial dealings in most states). An **express warranty** is made in writing. Express warranties range from simple statements, such as "100 percent cotton" (a guarantee of raw materials) and "complete satisfaction guaranteed" (a statement of performance), to extensive documentation that accompanies a product.

> e x h i b i t   1 4 - 6 <

Pepsi Builds a Better Cup for Restaurant Take-Out Customers

full warranty

The manufacturer's guarantee to meet certain minimum standards, including repair or replacement of the product or refunding the customer if the product does not work.

c o n c ə p t   c h ə c k

- What are the functions of a package?
- Explain the differences between an implied warranty, an express warranty, and a full warranty.

In 1975, Congress passed the Magnuson-Moss Warranty–Federal Trade Commission Improvement Act to help consumers understand warranties and to help them get action from manufacturers and dealers. A **full warranty** means the manufacturer must meet certain minimum standards, including repair of any defects "within a reasonable time and without charge" and replacement of the merchandise or a full refund if the product does not work "after a reasonable number of attempts" at repair. Under the law, any warranty that does not live up to this tough standard must be "conspicuously" promoted as a limited warranty.

CREATING PRODUCTS THAT DELIVER VALUE

>lg 4

New products pump life into company sales, enabling the firm not only to survive but also to grow. Companies like Allegheny Ludlum (steel), Corning (fiber optics), Dow (chemicals), Hewlett-Packard (computers), Campbell Soup (foods), and Stryker (medical products) get most of their profits from new products. Companies that lead their industries in profitability and sales growth get 49 percent of their revenues from products developed within the last five years.

Marketers have several different terms for new products, depending on how the product fits into a company's existing product line. When a firm introduces a product that has a new brand name and is in a product category new to the organization, it is classified as a new product.

line extension

A new flavor, size, or model using an existing brand name in an existing category.

A new flavor, size, or model using an existing brand name in an existing category is called a **line extension.** Diet Cherry Coke and caffeine-free Coke are line extensions. The strategy of expanding the line by adding new models has enabled companies like Seiko (watches), Kraft (cheeses), Oscar Mayer (lunch meats), and Sony (consumer electronics) to tie up a large amount of shelf space and brand recognition in a product category.

Organizing the New Product Effort

In large organizations, such as Procter & Gamble and Kraft General Foods, new product departments are responsible for generating new products. The department typically includes people from production, finance, marketing, and engineering. In smaller firms, committees perform the same functions as a new product department.

For major new product development tasks, companies sometimes form venture teams. IBM, for example, formed a venture group to create the first PC. Like a new product department, a venture team includes members from most departments of the company. The idea, however, is to isolate the team members from the organization's day-to-day activities so that they can think and be creative. IBM is headquartered in New York, but the PC venture team was located in Florida.

Line extensions of Pace salsa products include new flavors such as roasted pepper and garlic, which help Pace increase its shelf space and brand recognition.

Steps to Develop New Products That Satisfy Customers

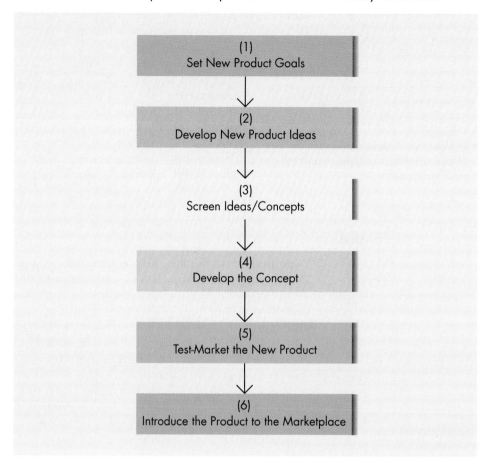

(1)
Set New Product Goals

(2)
Develop New Product Ideas

(3)
Screen Ideas/Concepts

(4)
Develop the Concept

(5)
Test-Market the New Product

(6)
Introduce the Product to the Marketplace

How New Products Are Developed

Developing new products is both costly and risky. About 67 percent of all new products fail.[5] To increase their chances for success, most firms use the following product development process, which is also summarized in Exhibit 14-7.

1. *Set new product goals.* New product goals are usually stated as financial objectives. For example, a company may want to recover its investment in three years or less. Or it may want to earn at least a 15 percent return on the investment. Nonfinancial goals may include using existing equipment or facilities.

2. *Develop new product ideas.* Smaller firms usually depend on employees, customers, investors, and distributors for new ideas. Larger companies use these sources and more structured marketing research techniques, such as focus groups and brainstorming. A **focus group** consists of 8 to 12 participants led by a moderator in an in-depth discussion on one particular topic or concept. The goal of focus group research is to learn and understand what people have to say and why. The emphasis is on getting people talking at length and in detail about the subject at hand. The intent is to find out how they feel about a product, concept, idea, or organization, how it fits into their lives,

focus group

A group of 8 to 12 participants led by a moderator in an in-depth discussion on one particular topic or concept.

and their emotional involvement with it. Focus groups often generate excellent product ideas. A few examples are the interior design of the Ford Taurus, Stick-Up room deodorizers, Dustbusters, and Wendy's salad bar. In the industrial market, machine tools, keyboard designs, aircraft interiors, and backhoe accessories evolved from focus groups.

brainstorming

A method of generating ideas in which group members suggest as many possibilities as they can without criticizing or evaluating any of the suggestions.

Brainstorming is also used to generate new product ideas. With **brainstorming** the members of a group think of as many ways to vary a product or solve a problem as possible. Criticism is avoided, no matter how ridiculous an idea seems at the time. The emphasis is on sheer numbers of ideas. Evaluation of these ideas is postponed to later steps of development.

3. *Screen ideas and concepts.* As ideas emerge, they are checked against the firm's new product goals and its long-range strategies. Many product concepts are rejected because they don't fit well with existing products, needed technology is not available, the company doesn't have enough resources, or the sales potential is low.

4. *Develop the concept.* Developing the new product concept involves creating a prototype of the product, testing the prototype, and building the marketing strategy. The type and amount of product testing vary, depending on such factors as the company's experience with similar products, how easy it is to make the item, and how easy it will be for consumers to use it. Suppose that Seven Seas is developing a new salad dressing flavor. The company already has a lot of experience in this area, so the new dressing will go directly into advanced taste tests and perhaps home-use tests. To develop a new line of soft drinks, however, Seven Seas would most likely do a great deal of testing. It would study many aspects of the new product before actually making it.

While the product is tested, the marketing strategy is refined. Channels of distribution are selected, pricing policies are developed and tested, the target market is further defined, and demand for the product is estimated. Management also continually updates the profit plan.

As the marketing strategy and prototype tests mature, a communication strategy is developed. A logo and package wording are created. As part of the communication strategy, promotion themes are developed, and the product is introduced to the sales force.

test-marketing

The process of testing a new product among potential users.

5. *Test-market the new product.* **Test-marketing** is testing the product among potential users. It allows management to evaluate various strategies and to see how well the parts of the marketing mix fit together. Few new product concepts reach this stage. For those that pass this stage, the firm must decide whether to introduce the product on a regional or national basis.

6. *Introduce the product.* A product that passes test-marketing is ready for market introduction, called *rollout*, which requires a lot of logistical coordination. Various divisions of the company must be encouraged to give the new item the attention it deserves. Packaging and labeling in a different language may be required. Sales training sessions must be scheduled, spare parts inventoried, service personnel trained, advertising and promotion campaigns readied, and wholesalers and retailers informed about the new item. If the new product is to be sold internationally, it may have to be altered to meet the requirements of the target countries. For instance, electrical products may have to run on different electrical currents.

Delve deeper into Procter & Gamble's marketing and brand management strategies at the firm's home page, **www.pg.com**

The Role of the Product Manager

When a new product enters the marketplace in large organizations, it is often placed under the control of a product or brand manager. A **product manager** develops and implements a complete strategy and marketing program for a specific product or brand. Product management first appeared at Procter & Gamble in 1929. A new company soap, Camay, was not doing well, so a young Procter & Gamble executive was assigned to devote his exclusive attention to developing and promoting this product. He was successful, and the company soon added other product managers. Since then, many firms, especially consumer products companies, have set up product management organizations.

concept check

- How do companies organize for new product development?
- What are the steps in the new product development process?
- Explain the role of the product manager.

THE PRODUCT LIFE CYCLE

>lg 5

product manager
The person who develops and implements a complete strategy and marketing program for a specific product or brand.

product life cycle
The pattern of sales and profits over time for a product or product category; consists of an introductory stage, growth stage, maturity, and decline (and death).

Product managers create marketing mixes for their products as they move through the life cycle. The **product life cycle** is a pattern of sales and profits over time for a product (Ivory dishwashing liquid) or a product category (liquid detergents). As the product moves through the stages of the life cycle, the firm must keep revising the marketing mix to stay competitive and meet the needs of target customers.

Stages of the Life Cycle

As illustrated in Exhibit 14-8, the product life cycle consists of the following stages:

1. *Introduction.* When a product enters the life cycle, it faces many obstacles. Although competition may be light, the *introductory stage* usually features frequent product modifications, limited distribution, and heavy promotion. The failure rate is high. Production and marketing costs are also high, and sales volume is low. Hence profits are usually small or negative.

2. *Growth stage.* If a product survives the introductory stage, it advances to the *growth stage* of the life cycle. In this stage, sales grow at an increasing rate, profits are healthy, and many competitors enter the market. Large companies may start to acquire small pioneering firms that have reached this stage. Emphasis switches from primary demand promotion to aggressive brand advertising and communicating the differences between brands. For example, the goal changes from convincing people to buy compact disc players to convincing them to buy Sony versus Panasonic or RCA.

    Distribution becomes a major key to success during the growth stage, as well as in later stages. Manufacturers scramble to acquire dealers and distributors and to build long-term relationships. Without adequate distribution, it is impossible to establish a strong market position.

    Toward the end of the growth phase, prices normally begin falling and profits peak. Price reductions result from increased competition and from cost reductions from producing larger quantities of items (economies of scale). Also, most firms have recovered their development costs by now, and their priority is in increasing or retaining market share and enhancing profits.

3. *Maturity.* After the growth stage, sales continue to mount—but at a decreasing rate. This is the *maturity stage*. Most products that have been on the market for a long time are in this stage. Thus, most marketing strategies are designed for mature products. One such strategy is to bring out several variations of a basic product (line extension). Kool-Aid, for instance, was originally offered in three flavors. Today there are more than 10, as well as sweetened and unsweetened varieties.

Sales and Profits during the Product Life Cycle

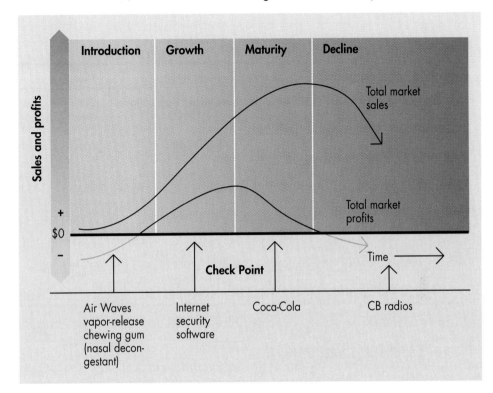

4. *Decline (and death).* When sales and profits fall, the product has reached the *decline stage.* The rate of decline is governed by two factors: the rate of change in consumer tastes and the rate at which new products enter the market. Sony turntables are an example of a product in the decline stage. The demand for turntables has now been surpassed by the demand for compact disc players and cassette players.

The Product Life Cycle as a Management Tool

The product life cycle may be used in planning. Marketers who understand the cycle concept are better able to forecast future sales and plan new marketing strategies. Exhibit 14-9 is a brief summary of strategic needs at various stages of the product life cycle.

Marketers must be sure that a product has moved from one stage to the next before changing its marketing strategy. A temporary sales decline should not be interpreted as a sign that the product is dying. Pulling back marketing support can become a self-fulfilling prophecy that brings about the early death of a healthy product.

c o n c ə p t c h ə c k

- What is the product life cycle?
- Describe each stage of the product life cycle.
- What are the marketing strategies for each stage of the product life cycle?

PRICING PRODUCTS RIGHT

>lg 6

An important part of the product development process is setting the right price. Price is the perceived value that is exchanged for something else. Value in our society is most commonly expressed in dollars and cents. Thus, price is typically the amount of money exchanged for a good or service. Note that *perceived value* refers to the time of the transaction. After you've used a product you've bought, you may decide that its actual value was less than its perceived

Strategies for Success at Each Stage of the Product Life Cycle

	Life Cycle Stage			
Category	**Introduction**	**Growth**	**Maturity**	**Decline**
Marketing objectives	Encourage trial, establish distribution	Get triers to repurchase, attract new users	Seek new users or uses	Reduce marketing expenses, keep loyal users
Product	Establish competitive advantage	Maintain product quality	Modify product	Maintain product
Distribution	Establish distribution network	Solidify distribution relationships	Provide additional incentives to ensure support	Eliminate trade allowances
Promotional	Build brand awareness	Provide information	Reposition product	Eliminate most advertising and sales promotions
Pricing	Set introductory price (skimming or penetration pricing)	Maintain prices	Reduce prices to meet competition	Maintain prices

value at the time you bought it. The price you pay for a product is based on the *expected satisfaction* you will receive and not necessarily the *actual satisfaction* you will receive.

Although price is usually a dollar amount, it can be anything with perceived value. When goods and services are exchanged for each other, the trade is called *barter*. If you exchange this book for a math book at the end of the term, you have engaged in barter.

Pricing Objectives

Price is important in determining how much a firm earns. The prices charged customers times the number of units sold equals the *gross revenue* for the firm. Revenue is what pays for every activity of the company (production, finance, sales, distribution, and so forth). What's left over (if anything) is profit. Managers strive to charge a price that will allow the firm to earn a fair return on its investment.

The chosen price must be neither too high nor too low. And the price must equal the perceived value to target consumers. If consumers think the price is too high, sales opportunities will be lost. Lost sales mean lost revenue. If the price is too low, consumers may view the product as a great value, but the company may not meet its profit goals. Three common pricing objectives are maximizing profits, achieving a target return on the investment, and offering good value at a fair price.

Maximizing Profits

profit maximization

A pricing objective that entails getting the largest possible profit from a product by producing the product as long as the revenue from selling it exceeds the cost of producing it.

Profit maximization means producing a product as long as the revenue from selling it exceeds the cost of producing it. In other words, the goal is to get the largest possible profit from the product. For example, suppose Carl Morgan, a builder of houses, sells each house for $100,000. His revenue and cost projections are shown in Exhibit 14-10. Notice in column 3 that the cost of building

> e x h i b i t   1 4 - 1 0 < Revenue, Cost, and Profit Projections for Morgan's Houses

(1) Unit of Output (House)	(2) Selling Price (Revenue)	(3) Cost of Building House	(4) Profit on House	(5) Total Profit
1st	$100,000	$ 76,000	$ 24,000	$ 24,000
2nd	100,000	75,000	25,000	49,000
3rd	100,000	73,000	27,000	76,000
4th	100,000	70,000	30,000	106,000
5th	100,000	70,000	30,000	136,000
6th	100,000	77,000	23,000	159,000
7th	**100,000**	**90,000**	**10,000**	**169,000**
8th	100,000	115,000	(15,000)	154,000

each house drops for the second through the fifth house. The lower cost per house results from two things: First, by having several houses under construction at the same time, Morgan can afford to hire a full-time crew. The crew is more economical than the independent contractors to whom he would otherwise subcontract each task. Second, Morgan can order materials in greater quantities than usual and thus get quantity discounts on his orders.

Morgan decides that he could sell 15 houses a year at the $100,000 price. But he knows he cannot maximize profits at more than seven houses a year. Inefficiencies begin to creep in at the sixth house. (Notice in column 3 that the sixth house costs more to build than any of the first five houses.) Morgan can't supervise more than seven construction jobs at once, and his full-time crew can't handle even those seven. Thus, Morgan has to subcontract some of the work on the sixth and seventh houses. To build more than seven houses, he would need a second full-time crew.

The table also shows why Morgan should construct seven houses a year. Even though the profit per house is falling for the sixth and seventh houses (column 4), the total profit is still rising (column 5). But at the eighth house, Morgan would go beyond profit maximization. That is, the eighth unit would cost more than its selling price. He would lose $15,000 on the house, and total profit would fall to $154,000 from $169,000 after the seventh house.

Achieving a Target Return on Investment

target return on investment
A pricing objective where the price of a product is set so as to give the company the desired profitability in terms of return on its money.

Another pricing objective used by many companies is **target return on investment** where a price is set to give the company the desired profitability in terms of return on its money. Among the companies that use target return on investment as their main pricing objective are 3M, Procter & Gamble, General Electric, and DuPont.

To get an idea of how target return works, imagine that you are a marketing manager for a cereal company. You estimate that developing, launching, and marketing a new hot cereal will cost $2 million. If the net profit for the first year is $200,000, the return on investment will be $200,000 ÷ $2,000,000, or 10 percent. Let's say that top management sets a 15 percent target return on investment. (The average target return on investment for large corporations is now about 14 percent.) Since a net profit of $200,000 will yield only a 10 percent return, one of two things will happen: either the cereal won't be produced, or the price and marketing mix will be changed to yield the 15 percent target return.

Value Pricing

value pricing

A pricing strategy in which the target market is offered a high-quality product at a fair price and with good service.

Value pricing has become a popular pricing strategy. **Value pricing** means offering the target market a high-quality product at a fair price and with good service. It is the notion of offering the customer a good value. Value pricing doesn't mean high quality that's available only at high prices. Nor does it mean bare-bones service or low-quality products. Value pricing can be used to sell a variety of products, from a $35,000 Jeep Grand Cherokee to a $2.99 package of L'eggs hosiery.

A value marketer does the following:

• *Offers products that perform.* This is the price of entry because consumers have lost patience with shoddy merchandise.

> a p p l y i n g   t e c h n o l o g y <

THE INTERNET IS HELPING CONSUMERS MAKE BETTER PRICING DECISIONS

The Internet has taken some control over prices away from managers by making pricing information and comparison shopping more readily available than ever before. For example, price cutting has been relentless in the business of trading stocks online. At least 70 brokers have been lured to the Internet, expecting paper-free transactions to be more profitable. For most, however, these efficiencies haven't increased profits because commission rates have been slashed to stay competitive.

In 1997, a commission of $19.95 for trading 1,000 shares was considered fair. Now commissions are as low as $7. Because of their trusted brand names, Fidelity Investments and Charles Schwab & Co. have been successful at charging higher rates. A newer competitor, E*Trade Group, Inc., is profitable but is having to spend heavily to increase its visibility and must charge well below Schwab's prices to get business.

Consumers have increasing power to drive down prices in other markets, too. Search engines run by Excite, Inc. include a comparison-shopping service called Jango (**www.jango.com**), which scans a myriad of online vendors and finds the best prices for books, compact discs, and other goods. The Hotbot search engine run by Wired Ventures, Inc. (**www.hotbot.com**) offers a similar service, operated by Junglee, Inc., of Sunnyvale, California.

Anyone wanting to buy videos online, for example, can quickly see what a dozen vendors are charging for today's hit movies. A $21.99 quote from CD Now, Inc. doesn't look so good compared to the $20.99 at Reel.com, Inc. or the $20.45 at Video On-line Express. And all those prices lose out to the $16.99 asking price at Videoflicks Canada Ltd.—matching the price at Viacom, Inc.'s Blockbuster stores. As online competition intensifies, whatever savings retailers can achieve from paperless record keeping are likely to slip into customers' fingers instead of pumping up profit margins.

Critical Thinking Questions

1. Do you think that the Internet will drive traditional retailers out of business?
2. Do you think that low prices are the main reason people shop online?

- *Gives consumers more than they expect.* Soon after Toyota launched Lexus, the company had to order a recall. The weekend before the recall, dealers phoned every Lexus owner in the United States and arranged to pick up their cars and provide replacement vehicles.
- *Gives meaningful guarantees.* DaimlerChrysler offers a 70,000-mile power train warranty. Michelin recently introduced a tire warranted to last 80,000 miles.
- *Gives the buyer facts.* Today's sophisticated consumer wants informative advertising and knowledgeable salespeople.
- *Builds long-term relationships.* American Air Lines' Advantage program, Hyatt's Passport Club, and Whirlpool's 800-number hot line all help build good customer relations.

The Internet has influenced managerial pricing decisions like no other phenomenon in recent history. It has also given consumers more pricing power than ever before, as the Applying Technology box on p. 428 explains.

concept check

- Explain the concept of price.
- What is meant by target return on investment, and how does it differ from profit maximization?
- What is value pricing?

HOW MANAGERS SET PRICES

>lg 7

After establishing a pricing objective, managers must set a specific price for the product. Two techniques that are often used to set a price are markup pricing and breakeven analysis.

Markup Pricing

markup pricing
A method of pricing in which a certain percentage (the markup) is added to the product's cost to arrive at the price.

One of the most common forms of pricing is **markup pricing.** In this method, a certain percentage is added to a product's cost to arrive at the retail price. (The retail price is thus *cost plus markup.*) The cost is the expense of manufacturing the product or acquiring it for resale. The markup is the amount added to the cost to cover expenses and leave a profit. For example, if Banana Boat suntan cream costs Walgreen's drugstore $5 and sells for $7, it carries a markup of 29 percent:

Cost	$5	Cost to Walgreen's
Markup	+2	Walgreen's markup to cover expenses (utilities, wages, etc.)
Retail price	$7	Banana Boat suntan cream price paid by the consumer

$$\text{Walgreen's markup percentage} = \frac{\text{Markup}}{\text{Retail price}}$$

$$= \frac{\$2}{\$7}$$

$$= 29\%$$

Several elements influence markups. Among them are tradition, the competition, store image, and stock turnover. Traditionally, department stores used a 40 percent markup. But today competition has forced retailers to respond to consumer demand and meet competitors' prices. A department store that tried to sell household appliances at a 40 percent markup would lose customers to such discounters as Wal-Mart and Target. However, a retailer trying to develop a prestige image will use markups that are much higher than those used by a retailer trying to develop an image as a discounter.

Breakeven Analysis

Manufacturers, wholesalers (companies that buy from manufacturers and sell to retailers and institutions), and retailers (firms that sell to end users) need to know how much of a product must be sold at a certain price to cover all costs. The point at which the costs are covered and additional sales result in profit is the **breakeven point.**

To find the breakeven point, the firm measures the various costs associated with the product:

- **Fixed costs** do not vary with different levels of output. The rent on a manufacturing facility is a fixed cost. It must be paid whether production is one unit or a million units.
- **Variable costs** change with different levels of output. Wages and expenses of raw materials are considered variable costs.
- The **fixed-cost contribution** is the selling price per unit (revenue) minus the variable costs per unit.
- **Total revenue** is the selling price per unit times the number of units sold.
- **Total cost** is the total of the fixed costs and the variable costs.
- **Total profit** is total revenue minus total cost.

Knowing these amounts, the firm can calculate the breakeven point:

$$\text{Breakeven point in units} = \frac{\text{Total fixed cost}}{\text{Fixed-cost contribution}}$$

Let's see how this works: Grey Corp., a manufacturer of aftershave lotion, has variable costs of $3 per bottle and fixed costs of $50,000. Grey's management believes the company can sell up to 100,000 bottles of aftershave at $5 a bottle without having to lower its price. Grey's fixed-cost contribution is $2 ($5 selling price per bottle minus $3 variable costs per bottle). Therefore, $2 per bottle is the amount that can be used to cover the company's fixed costs of $50,000.

To determine its breakeven point, Grey applies the previous equation:

$$\text{Breakeven point in bottles} = \frac{\$50,000 \text{ fixed cost}}{\$2 \text{ fixed-cost contribution}}$$

$$= 25,000 \text{ bottles}$$

Grey Corp. will therefore break even when it sells 25,000 bottles of after-shave lotion. After that point, at which the fixed costs are met, the $2 per bottle becomes profit. If Grey's forecasts are correct and it can sell 100,000 bottles at $5 a bottle, its total profit will be $150,000 ($2 per bottle × 75,000 bottles).

By using the equation, Grey Corp. can quickly find out how much it needs to sell to break even. It can then calculate how much profit it will earn if it sells more units. A firm that is operating close to the breakeven point may change the profit picture in two ways. Reducing costs will lower the breakeven point and expand profits. Increasing sales will not change the breakeven point, but it will provide more profits.

breakeven point
The price at which a product's costs are covered, so additional sales result in profit.

fixed costs
Costs that do not vary with different levels of output; for example, rent.

variable costs
Costs that change with different levels of output; for example, wages and cost of raw materials.

fixed-cost contribution
The selling price per unit (revenue) minus the variable costs per unit.

total revenue
The selling price per unit times the number of units sold.

total cost
The sum of the fixed costs and the variable costs.

total profit
Total revenue minus total cost.

c o n c ə p t c h ə c k

- Explain how markups are calculated.
- Describe breakeven analysis.
- What does it mean to "break even"?

PRODUCT PRICING

>lg 8

Managers use various pricing strategies when determining the price of a product, as this section explains. Price-skimming and penetration pricing are strategies used in pricing new products; other strategies such as leader pricing and bundling may be used for established products as well.

Price Skimming

price skimming
The strategy of introducing a product with a high initial price and lowering the price over time as the product moves through its life cycle.

The practice of introducing a new product on the market with a high price and then lowering the price over time is called **price skimming.** As the product moves through its life cycle, the price usually is lowered because competitors are entering the market. As the price falls, more and more consumers can buy the product.

Price skimming has four important advantages. First, a high initial price can be a way to find out what buyers are willing to pay. Second, if consumers find the introductory price too high, it can be lowered. Third, a high introductory price can create an image of quality and prestige. Fourth, when the price is lowered later, consumers may think they are getting a bargain. The disadvantage is that high prices attract competition.

Price skimming can be used to price virtually any new products such as high-definition televisions, PCs, and color computer printers. Recently, Gillette introduced the Oral-B Cross Action toothbrush. The bristles on the new brush don't stand up straight. Instead, three rows of multicolored bristles of varying sizes are angled in opposing directions, an innovation that the company says enables the brush to remove 25 percent more plaque than the leading toothbrush. The Cross Action was introduced at a price of $5.00 compared with $2.50 for a typical toothbrush. Products don't have to be expensive to use a skimming strategy.

Penetration Pricing

penetration pricing
The strategy of selling new products at low prices in the hope of achieving a large sales volume.

A company that doesn't use price skimming will probably use **penetration pricing.** With this strategy, the company offers new products at low prices in the hope of achieving a large sales volume. Penetration pricing requires more extensive planning than skimming does because the company must gear up for mass production and marketing. When Texas Instruments entered the digital-watch market, its facilities in Lubbock, Texas, could produce 6 million watches a year, enough to meet the entire world demand for low-priced watches. If the company had been wrong about demand, its losses would have been huge.

Penetration pricing has two advantages. First, the low initial price may induce consumers to switch brands or companies. Using penetration pricing on its jug wines, Gallo has lured customers away from Taylor California Cellars and Inglenook. Second, penetration pricing may discourage competitors from entering the market. Their costs would tend to be higher, so they would need to sell more at the same price to break even.

Leader Pricing

leader pricing
The strategy of pricing products below the normal markup or even below cost to attract customers to a store where they would not otherwise shop.

loss leader
A product priced below cost as part of a leader pricing strategy.

Pricing products below the normal markup or even below cost to attract customers to a store where they wouldn't otherwise shop is **leader pricing.** A product priced below cost is referred to as a **loss leader.** Retailers hope that this type of pricing will increase their overall sales volume and thus their profit.

Items that are leader priced are usually well known and priced low enough to appeal to many customers. They also are items that consumers will buy at a lower price, even if they have to switch brands. Supermarkets often feature coffee and bacon in their leader pricing. Department stores and specialty stores also rely heavily on leader pricing.

Bundling

bundling
The strategy of grouping two or more related products together and pricing them as a single product.

Bundling means grouping two or more related products together and pricing them as a single product. Marriott's special weekend rates often include the room, breakfast, and one night's dinner. Department stores may offer a washer and dryer together for a price lower than if the units were bought separately.

Capitalizing on Trends in Business

The idea behind bundling is to reach a segment of the market that the products sold separately would not reach as effectively. Some buyers are more than willing to buy one product but have much less use for the second. Bundling the second product to the first at a slightly reduced price thus creates some sales that otherwise would not be made. Aussie 3-Minute Miracle Shampoo is typically bundled with its conditioner because many people use shampoo more than conditioner so they don't need a new bottle of conditioner.

Odd-Even Pricing

odd-even (psychological) pricing

The strategy of setting a price at an odd number to connote a bargain and at an even number to suggest quality.

Psychology often plays a big role in how consumers view prices and what prices they will pay. **Odd-even pricing** (or **psychological pricing**) is the strategy of setting a price at an odd number to connote a bargain and at an even number to imply quality. For years, many retailers have priced their products in odd numbers—for example, $99.95 or $49.95—to make consumers feel that they are paying a lower price for the product.

Some retailers favor odd-numbered prices because they believe that $9.99 sounds much less imposing to customers than $10.00. Other retailers believe that an odd-numbered price signals to consumers that the price is at the lowest level possible, thereby encouraging them to buy more units. Neither theory has ever been conclusively proved, although one study found that consumers perceive odd-priced products as being on sale.

Even-numbered pricing is sometimes used to denote quality. Examples include a fine perfume at $100 a bottle, a good watch at $500, or a mink coat at $3,000.

prestige pricing

The strategy of increasing the price of a product so that consumers will perceive it as being of higher quality, status, or value.

Prestige Pricing

The strategy of raising the price of a product so consumers will perceive it as being of higher quality, status, or value is called **prestige pricing.** This type of pricing is common where high prices indicate high status. In the specialty shops on Rodeo Drive in Beverly Hills, which cater to the super-rich of Hollywood, shirts that would sell for $15 elsewhere sell for at least $50. If the price were lower, customers would perceive them as being of low quality.

c o n c ə p t c h ə c k

- What is the difference between penetration pricing and price skimming?
- What is the objective of leader pricing?
- Explain the concept of price bundling.
- Describe odd-even pricing and prestige pricing.

CAPITALIZING ON TRENDS IN BUSINESS

>lg 9

As customer expectations increase and competition becomes fiercer, perceptive managers will find innovative strategies to satisfy demanding consumers and establish unique products in the market. For example, strategies that build instant brand recognition and use technology to meet individual consumer needs will help ensure the ultimate success of new products.

Building Immediate Brand Recognition

Building brand recognition has traditionally been a long-term process. Popular brand names like Coca-Cola, Chevrolet, Sony, and Whirlpool took decades to become household words. Start-up technology companies, however, don't have decades to build brand recognition. To survive and thrive, they must use powerful, precise strategies for building rapid brand awareness. Consider that half of U.S. households are familiar with America Online (AOL) and 42 percent know Yahoo.[6] And PalmPilot, the electronic personal

WHO HAS THE COMMERCIAL RIGHTS TO INFORMATION ABOUT THE HUMAN DNA STRUCTURE?

In the highly competitive world of pharmaceutical research, development, and manufacturing, major companies usually do not share basic science with each other. That is changing, however—at least with respect to developing the biological blueprint for all human life. The major drug companies are developing a plan for working together to create a map of genetic landmarks (called SNPs or "snips") in the human DNA structure. The companies believe open access to SNPs is "crucial" to the testing and development of new drugs.

The ultimate goal of this research is to create personalized medicine that will enable treatment to be customized to a person's unique genetic profile. For example, scientists could use the SNPs on the human genome map to determine which of the approximately 100,000 genes in human DNA "predispose people to such common but hard-to-treat ills as diabetes, depression, cancer, arthritis, memory loss and cardiovascular problems." If the biological causes of these illnesses could be identified, the commercial implications for the development of new medicines would be enormous.

The major drug companies fear that small biotechnology companies might be ahead in the race to unravel the human genome. If these small companies succeed, they "will patent their discoveries and monopolize crucial gene information—then be able to either keep it private or charge drug companies huge fees for access to it."

Critical Thinking Questions

1. What do you think of the actions of the major pharmaceutical companies from an ethical perspective?
2. Should any individual or organization have the right to a monopoly on information about the human genetic structure?
3. Should society protect the legitimate interests of those who have unraveled the mysteries of the human genome?

organizer, sold one million units in only 18 months, surpassing even the Sony Walkman.

How did these high-tech start-ups accomplish levels of brand recognition that took Procter & Gamble a generation? For one thing, they gave away lots of product. AOL is the leader in giveaways. For several years it has been blanketing the country with diskettes and CD-ROMs offering consumers a one-month free trial. For another, these companies rely heavily on public relations. Sun has built the visibility of Java—its flagship software platform—within the corporate community almost entirely through public relations techniques such as sending managers out on speaking tours and making high-profile announcements every time a licensing agreement is signed.

A third way to quickly build a brand is to use the Internet effectively. Amazon.com strives to make every customer interaction highly personal, the antithesis of the anonymous strip-mall experience. When customers log on to the site, they are welcomed by name and offered a list of recommended books based on previous purchases. Through a service called BookMatcher, Amazon.com asks customers to rate 10 books. The ratings give it more

See how Amazon.com uses the Internet to deliver personal customer service at

www.amazon.com

insight into readers' preferences and enable it to suggest additional titles they might like. All of this adds up to relationship marketing that land-based retailers can only dream about.

Mass Customization

A silent revolution is changing the way many goods are made and services are delivered. Companies as diverse as BMW, Dell Computer, Levi Strauss, Mattel, McGraw-Hill, Wells Fargo, and many leading Web businesses are adopting mass customization to maintain or obtain a competitive edge. As we described in an earlier chapter, **mass customization** involves tailoring mass-market goods and services to the unique needs of the individuals who buy them.

Mass producers dictate a one-to-many relationship, whereas mass customizers engage in a continual dialogue with customers. Although production is cost-efficient, the flexibility of mass customization can cut inventory. And mass customization offers two other advantages over mass production: it provides superior customer service, and it makes full use of cutting-edge technology.

A number of technological advances are making customization possible. Computer-controlled factory equipment and industrial robots make it easier to quickly readjust assembly lines. Bar-code scanners make it possible to track virtually every part and product. Databases now store trillions of bytes of information, including individual customers' preferences for everything from cottage cheese to cowboy boots. Digital printers make it easy to change product packaging.

And then there's the Internet, which ties these disparate pieces together. Says Joseph Pine, author of the pioneering book *Mass Customization*: "Anything you can digitize, you can customize." The Internet makes it easy for companies to move data from an online order form to the factory floor. The Internet makes it easy for manufacturing to communicate with marketers. Most of all, the Internet makes it easy for a company to conduct an ongoing, one-on-one dialogue with each of its customers to learn about and respond to their exact preferences.[7]

The Growth of Internet Auctions

The Internet is also becoming the source of information on competitive prices. Name the product—computers, airline tickets, rare coins—and chances are, there's a Web site where you can name your price. The Internet Auction List counted more than 1,500 auction-related Web sites in more than 40 product categories in 1998.[8] You can think of Internet auctions as a new distribution outlet where companies with excess inventory can reach eager customers. Web auctions aren't necessarily a great place to save money. The advantage of the auctions is that they give consumers access to products that are hard to find (like a concert poster from an old Rolling Stones tour) or that aren't available in stores (like overstocked computer inventory, refurbished laser printers, or last year's fancy consumer electronics equipment).

mass customization

A flexible manufacturing technique in which mass-market goods and services are tailored to the unique needs of the individuals who buy them.

concept check

• How can a new company build immediate brand recognition?
• What advantages does mass customization offer over mass production?
• What advantages do Internet auctions offer to companies and to consumers?

APPLYING THIS CHAPTER'S TOPICS

This chapter makes several important points that can affect your life right now. First, businesses are using mass customization to deliver low-cost, specialized products and services that meet the unique needs of individual customers. The Internet has helped usher in mass customization and has opened up vast sources of information on business and consumer products as explained in this section.

Custom Products and Services

Mass customization means that now, more than ever, you can get exactly the product that will fit your needs. A number of companies have adapted this strategy for competition, including AT&T, Coke and Pepsi, and fast-food companies such as McDonalds. The Internet is frequently the primary avenue for delivering customized products, giving you easy access to product and pricing information. For example, customerdisc.com allows music lovers to pick their favorite songs from various music categories and organize them on their own personalized CD. Consumers may even choose title and cover art for their customized CD. Mass customization is not limited to consumer products. As a business manager, you will find many companies are creating new product and pricing strategies designed to meet your specific company needs.

Looking for cheap airfares? Priceline.com lets consumers bid on air and hotel rates. Check out

www.priceline.com

> t r y   i t   n o w ! <

1. **Name Your Price** Priceline.com lets you "name your own price" for airline tickets, hotel rooms, and home mortgages. No, you won't get an airline ticket from New York to Los Angeles for $100. Priceline's airline tickets are best for last-minute travelers who can be flexible. You can name a destination and travel dates, but you cannot request flight times or a specific airline (though all flights are booked on major carriers). Priceline sells many of its tickets for about the same price as the 21-day advance fare even when the flight is booked only 2 days prior to departure.

If you like checking out airlines' last-minute online travel deals but hate sifting through all those weekly e-mails, here's a solution: Smarter Living (**www.smarterliving.com**), is a service that sorts through the special deals of 20 major airlines and sends them out weekly in a single electronic newsletter. Sign up free at the Web site.

2. **Know When to Bid** If you decide to bid at an Internet auction, visit Auction Insider (**www. auctioninsider.com**) on the Web and learn how to be a smart bidder. This site offers strategies and tactics for the first-time bidder—including tips on how to avoid winning an auction that you're better off losing. For example, Auction Insider advises against bidding on used items (not to be confused with refurbished items, which can be a good deal). It also provides updated rankings of the top 10 auction sites for computers, electronics, and collectibles and lists hundreds of other auctions as well.

Using the Internet to Find Product Information

It has been said that people can raise their standard of living by one-third by becoming intelligent consumers. Now the Internet makes intelligent shopping easier than ever. You can go to *Consumer Reports* on the Net and find out how products are ranked. Go to CompareNet and compare products feature-by-feature and dollar-for-dollar. You can shop price for an infinite variety of products and then ask your local retailer to meet or beat the price. You can also bid on almost anything in an Internet auction.

>looking ahead
at Soaps by Artemis

In large organizations, new products are typically developed using the process described in the chapter. Smaller companies may simply improvise. For most consumers, soaps would be a specialty product. An argument can be made that Artemis will use a skimming strategy and then lower prices as competition enters. Others might say that Artemis is using a modified penetration strategy because Soaps are priced under alternative products like in-line skates and skateboards.

SUMMARY OF LEARNING GOALS

>lg 1 **What is a product, and how is it classified?**
A product is any good or service, along with its perceived attributes and benefits, that creates customer value. Tangible attributes include the good itself, packaging, and warranties. Intangible attributes are symbolic like a brand's image.

Most items are a combination of goods and services. Services and goods are often marketed differently. Products are categorized as either consumer products or industrial products. Consumer products are goods and services that are bought and used by the end users. They can be classified as unsought products, convenience products, shopping products, or specialty products, depending on how much effort consumers are willing to exert to get them.

Industrial products are those bought by organizations for use in making other products or in rendering services. Capital products are usually large, expensive items with a long life span. Expense items are typically smaller, less expensive items that usually have a life span of less than a year.

>lg 2 **How does branding distinguish a product from its competitors?**
Products usually have brand names. Brands identify products by words, names, symbols, designs, or a combination of these things. The two major types of brands are manufacturer (national) brands and dealer (private) brands. Generic products carry no brand name. Branding has three main purposes: product identification, repeat sales, and new product sales.

>lg 3 **What are the functions of packaging?**
Often the promotional claims of well-known brands are reinforced in the printing on the package. Packaging is an important way to promote sales and protect the product. A package should be easy to ship, store, and stack on a store shelf. Companies can add value to products by giving warranties. A warranty guarantees the quality of a good or service.

>lg 4 **How do organizations create new products?**
To succeed, most firms must continue to design new products to satisfy changing customer demands. But new product development can be risky. Many new products fail. To be successful, new product development requires input from production, finance, marketing, and engineering personnel. In large organizations, these people work in a new product development department. The steps

in new product development are setting new product goals, exploring ideas, screening ideas, developing the concept (creating a prototype and building the marketing strategy), test-marketing, and introducing the product. When the product enters the marketplace, it is often managed by a product manager.

>lg 5   **What are the stages of the product life cycle?**
After a product reaches the marketplace, it enters the product life cycle. This cycle typically has four stages: introduction, growth, maturity, and decline (and possibly death). Profits usually are small in the introductory phase, reach a peak at the end of the growth phase, and then decline. Marketing strategies for each stage are listed in Exhibit 14-9.

>lg 6   **What is the role of pricing in marketing?**
Price indicates value, helps position a product in the marketplace, and is the means for earning a fair return on investment. If a price is too high, the product won't sell well, and the firm will lose money. If the price is too low, the firm may lose money even if the product sells well. Prices are set according to pricing objectives. Among the most common objectives are profit maximization, target return on investment, and value pricing.

>lg 7   **How are product prices determined?**
A cost-based method for determining price is markup pricing. A certain percentage is added to the product's cost to arrive at the retail price. The markup is the amount added to the cost to cover expenses and earn a profit. Breakeven analysis determines the level of sales that must be reached before total cost equals total revenue. Breakeven analysis provides a quick look at how many units the firm must sell before it starts earning a profit. The technique also reveals how much profit can be earned with higher sales volumes.

>lg 8   **What strategies are used for pricing products?**
The two main strategies for pricing a new product are price skimming and penetration pricing. Price skimming involves charging a high introductory price and then, usually, lowering the price as the product moves through its life cycle. Penetration pricing involves selling a new product at a low price in the hope of achieving a large sales volume.

Pricing tactics are used to fine-tune the base prices of products. Among these tactics are leader pricing, bundling, odd-even pricing, and prestige pricing. Sellers that use leader pricing set the prices of some of their products below the normal markup or even below cost to attract customers who might otherwise not shop at those stores. Bundling is grouping two or more products together and pricing them as one. The notion is that the seller will sell more items than if the products were priced separately. Psychology often plays a role in how consumers view products and in determining what they will pay. Setting a price at an odd number tends to create a perception that the item is cheaper than the actual price. Prices in even numbers denote quality or status. Raising the price so an item will be perceived as having high quality and status is called prestige pricing. Consumers pay more because of the perceived quality or status.

>lg 9   **What trends are occurring in products and pricing?**
Two important trends in product design and branding are building immediate brand recognition and using technology to meet individual customer needs.

PREPARING FOR TOMORROW'S WORKPLACE

1. Prepare a memo explaining how most products are a combination of goods and services; provide examples.

KEY TERMS

brainstorming 423
brand 415
brand equity 416
brand loyalty 417
breakeven point 430
bundling 431
capital products 414
convenience products 414
dealer brands 419
expense items 415
express warranty 420
fixed costs 430
fixed-cost contribution 430
focus group 422
full warranty 421
generic products 419
implied warranty 420
leader pricing 431
line extension 421
loss leader 431
manufacturer brands 418
markup pricing 429
mass customization 434
master brand 416
odd-even (psychological) pricing 432
penetration pricing 431
prestige pricing 432
price skimming 431
product 412
product life cycle 424
product manager 424
profit maximization 426
shopping products 414
specialty products 414
target return on investment 427
test-marketing 423
total cost 430
total profit 430
total revenue 430
trademark 415
unsought products 413
value pricing 428
variable costs 430
warranty 420

2. Divide the class into teams of four persons each. Each team should go to a different type of store (e.g., hardware, supermarket, discount, department, or specialty store) and identify two new products. Each team should report to the class on the attributes of the new products, indicate whether the team believes the products will be successful, and explain why or why not.

3. Your company plans to start selling gourmet frozen foods through the Internet. You are chairing a committee to name this new service. Write a memo to committee members suggesting things that they should consider in creating a brand name.

4. Divide the class into two groups. Have the two groups debate whether consumers will readily accept the following products as generic products: automobile tires, ice cream, staples, scientific calculators, running shoes, panty hose, gasoline, and men's briefs. One group should argue that the products will be accepted; the other should argue that they will not.

5. Under what circumstances would a jeans maker market the product as a convenience product? A shopping product? A specialty product?

6. Dick Storinger, the owner of Oakton Pharmacy, needed a personal computer to keep track of prescriptions, print labels, and maintain his financial records. At Computercraft, Dick tried out a few models and decided on the small one that his daughter bought for her work in graduate business school. Did Storinger buy a consumer product or an industrial product? Explain.

7. Go to the library and look through magazines and newspapers to find examples of price skimming, penetration pricing, and value pricing. Make copies and show them to the class.

8. Write down the names of two brands to which you are loyal. Indicate the reasons for your loyalty.

9. Explain how something as obvious as a retail price can have a psychological dimension.

WORKING THE NET

1. Thousands of new products are introduced each year, but many don't stay on store shelves for long. The New Products Showcase and Learning Center tracks new product flops and successes. Go to the Center's Trade Show list at **www.showlearn.com/showlist.html**. Pick one of the trade shows on the list and read about the new products that are scheduled to be introduced there. Choose one or two new products to review. What type of good is it (i.e., convenience, shopping, or specialty)? Evaluate its chances of succeeding. What pricing issues do you think the manufacturer will face?

2. You're working for a company that plans to introduce gourmet treats for pets. Your job is to determine the market for this new product and the marketing issues that may need to be addressed. Start your information search at the American Demographics site, **www.marketingtools.com**. Do a search for articles on pet ownership, pet food, and pet products. Write a short report summarizing the information.

3. DVD is a new video and music technology that some claim will make compact discs obsolete. Read about the DVD in DVD Review (**www.dvdreview.com**). Look under "editorial" for information about the current status of DVD sales and marketing. Where on the product life cycle is DVD today? Where do you think it will be five years from now? Where are CDs on the product life cycle today? Where are cassette tapes?

4. Visit an online retailer such as Amazon.com (**www.amazon.com**) or eToys (**www.eToys.com**). At the site, try to identify examples of leader pricing, bundling, odd pricing, and other pricing strategies. Do online retailers have different pricing considerations than real-world retailers? Explain.

5. Do a search on Yahoo (**www.yahoo.com**) for online auctions for a product you are interested in buying. Visit several auctions and get an idea of how the product is priced. How do these prices compare with the price you might find in a local store? What pricing advantages or disadvantages do companies face in selling their products through online auctions? How do online auctions affect the pricing strategies of other companies? Why?

CREATIVE THINKING CASE

Personality Puffs and Cardio Chips

There was a time when potato chips were just potato chips, their greasy crunch leaving the snacker with an aftertaste of delicious guilt. No more. A new kind of chips aims at tackling the psyche rather than tickling the taste bud, promising to turn Americans into kinder, happier, and gentler souls.

The secret? Herbs and plant extracts, such as St. John's wort, gingko biloba, and kava kava, are added to the chips along with essences of edible flowers—violet, chamomile, peppermint, and passion flower—to help combat depression, promote long life, and improve memory. "It's just one of those next steps in the evolution of snacks and food," said the chips' manufacturer, Robert Ehrlich. "There are definitely benefits from the product."

But not everyone is swallowing that claim. Some nutritionists have expressed concern that all the feel-good messages about the snacks are just advertising gimmicks to sell chips. "They're just ridiculous," said Norman Rosenthal, clinical professor of psychiatry and author of *St. John's Wort: The Herbal Way to Feeling Good.* "It would be like having a penicillin pie or an antibiotic apple strudel."

The Food and Drug Administration's chief of special nutrition, Elizabeth Yetley, said Ehrlich does not have an obligation to discuss his products with the FDA. But he is responsible for making sure that food products are safe before he markets them. "Even though there are critics, people love them," Ehrlich said.

Ehrlich began making his mood-enhancing snacks four years ago. A group of herbalists, zen masters, a psychiatrist, and young consumers help put the products together. At 99 cents for a 2-ounce bag, the chips are sold in supermarkets—in the health food section—in the United States and in some parts of Europe, Asia, and South America.

His latest product, Personality Puffs, came out recently. Low-fat Cardio Chips containing a blend of natural herbs to improve cardiovascular health, metabolic conditions, the immune system, and aging also recently arrived on the market. His other herbal products include St. John's Wort Tortilla Chips to improve moods, Gingko Biloba Rings to enhance memory, and Kava Corn Chips to promote relaxation. Personality Puffs, which come in the shape of little people, are made up of a blend of flowers, St. John's wort, and gingko biloba.

Unlike other herbal products, Personality Puffs come with a set of printed rules that will "open you to the magic that is ready to happen in your life." Snackers are asked to buy at least two bags and give one away to a stranger within one hour of purchase. That, Ehrlich said, will create goodwill and kindness.

Critical Thinking Questions

1. How would you classify these consumer goods?
2. Using the criteria discussed in the chapter, evaluate Ehrlich's brand names.
3. Would you recommend that Ehrlich issue an express warranty with his products? Why or why not?
4. Describe the pricing strategy for the herbal chips.

VIDEO CASE

The Toronto Blue Jays Approach to Value Pricing

Prior to the 1999 baseball season, the Toronto Blue Jays (**wqww.bluejays.ca**) had a ticket-pricing structure with only five different prices. After a thorough study of their ticket prices, the Blue Jays established a new pricing structure that provides many more options. Each option gives fans different product value in terms of price and seating location in the Toronto SkyDome.

Under the new pricing structure, seats in the premium dugout level, SkyClub infield, and field-level infield are sold only as season tickets and are priced, respectively, at $40, $38, and $37 per seat per game. All other tickets can be purchased on a single-game basis. SkyClub baseline seats are priced at $36, and field-level seats by the bases are priced at $32 each. Field-level, baseline seats and SkyClub outfield seats sell for $29.50 apiece. SkyDeck infield and 100 Level outfield seats go for $22. SkyDeck base seats are priced at $15 and SkyDeck baseline seats at $6. Group ticket sales, an important component of the Blue Jays product mix, are targeted toward the seats priced at $32 and under.

As part of Toronto's effort to provide a high-quality product at a fair price, four regularly occurring special promotions are offered for the team's home games. These are TIM-BR Mart Tuesdays, the Blue Light $1,000,000 Blast, Honda Jr. Jays Saturdays, and Spectacular Sundays.

At every home game played on Tuesdays, TIM-BR Mart collaborates with the Blue Jays in a three-part promotion called TIM-BR Mart Tuesdays. When a Toronto player hits the official TIM-BR Mart target, a fan chosen at random wins a cottage supplied and built by TIM-BR Mart. Another fan chosen at random gets to watch the game from a custom-built wood deck in the Toronto SkyDome. This fan is also provided food and beverage service. A third lucky fan wins a custom-built deck for his or her home by TIM-BR Mart.

Before every Friday home game, selected fans participate in an onfield batting challenge where they can win a variety of prizes, including $1 million. In addition, when a Blue Jays player hits a home run, fans chosen randomly win one of the many prize packs that are available in the Blue Light $1,000,000 Blast.

Saturday home games have special promotions for children. On Honda Jr. Jays Saturdays, children "experience a day filled with activities, contests, prizes, autographs, and more!" Children 14 and under are admitted at discounted prices. The gates open early so fans can watch batting practice; children can enter a drawing to throw out the ceremonial first pitch at the next Honda Jr. Jays Saturday game; nine youngsters get to take the field along with the Blue Jays starting lineup (they also receive an autographed Blue Jays collectible item); a child is selected to announce the Blue Jays batters for one inning; and children can run the bases following the game. Each child 14 and under also receives Blue Jays souvenir giveaways.

Spectacular Sundays are designed to ensure that fans do not leave the ballpark empty-handed. Using prizes and giveaways provided by corporate sponsors, fans are "treated to a day packed full of fun, value and great baseball for the entire family."

Through a well-planned package of special promotions, along with different ticket prices for seats providing different amenities, the Toronto Blue Jays are regaining their fan base and market success.

Critical Thinking Questions

1. How would you describe the Toronto Blue Jays baseball franchise as a product?
2. What decision criteria do you think the Blue Jays used in establishing their new ticket price structure?
3. The Toronto Blue Jays could be described as a value marketer. What aspect of the team's marketing strategy indicate that it is a value marketer?

>c15

chapter fifteen

Distributing Products in a Timely and Efficient Manner

learning goals

>lg 1   What are physical distribution (logistics) and logistics management?

>lg 2   What are distribution channels and their functions?

>lg 3   How can channels be organized?

>lg 4   When would a marketer use exclusive

>lg 6   What are the different kinds of retail operations?

>lg 7   What are the components of a successful retailing strategy?

>lg 8   What are functions of physical distribution?

>lg 9   What are the trends in distribution?

Serving the Customer at Home Depot

Home Depot (**www.HomeDepot.com/**) is growing like angry crabgrass these days. Its stores, resembling monstrous bright orange boxes, are already as much Americana as the Golden Arches. Two new stores open every week. By 2001, the landscape will be covered with 1,350 Home Depot centers—three times as many as in 1996. Sales were a record $30 billion in 1998, 25 percent higher than in 1997 and two and a half times the revenue of Home Depot's main competitor, Lowe's. Today, the typical Home Depot generates $43 million in annual sales, up from $29 million in 1990.

Home Depot succeeded where others faltered by being the first on the block (now almost every block) to recognize just what the core customer wanted: everything. It built radical "big box" stores (the typical new store is 108,000 square feet) and loaded them with every imaginable home product, under one humongous roof. The stores contain nothing fancy, just rows and rows of building materials and good old-fashioned toolbox stuff. Then Home Depot hired carpenters, plumbers, contractors, and other industry professionals to stroll the aisles in bright orange aprons with their names handwritten on the front and drilled them in the founder's mantra: This is a service business, not a discount hardware store. Help customers solve their problems, don't just sell them a wrench. "It's not what we do, it's what happens in the stores," says founder Bernie Marcus. "He who gives the best service wins."[1]

Critical Thinking Questions

As you read this chapter, consider the following questions as they relate to Home Depot:

- Is distribution a large part of Home Depot's success?
- Home Depot is already a market leader. If it continues to blanket the market with "orange boxes," is any further innovation necessary?
- How will the Internet affect Home Depot?

An efficient distribution system allows Home Depot to offer customers a vast assortment of building materials, appliances, and tools.

At the core of Home Depot's success is knowing the needs of its customers and responding to those needs by designing a distribution system that gives customers access to a vast array of home improvement products under one roof. Because value and convenience matter most to its customers, Home Depot put its money where its customers' most critical desires are. Home Depot shoppers define value as well-stocked shelves, dependably low prices, and variety. Home Depot responded by investing in a world-class operating system that delivers that value expertly.

BUSINESS IN THE 21ˢᵀ CENTURY

This chapter explores how organizations use a distribution system to enhance the value of a product and examines the methods they use to move products to locations where consumers wish to buy them. First, we'll discuss the functions and members of a distribution system. Next, we'll explore the role of wholesalers and retailers in delivering products to customers. We'll also discuss how physical distribution increases efficiency and customer satisfaction. Finally, we'll look at trends in distribution.

THE ROLE OF DISTRIBUTION

physical distribution (logistics)

The movement of products from the producer to industrial users and consumers.

manufacturer

A producer; an organization that converts raw materials to finished products.

logistics management

The management of the physical distribution process.

supply chain management

Management of activities in a supply chain to minimize inventory and move goods efficiently from producers to end users.

Physical distribution (logistics) is the movement of products from the producer or **manufacturer,** to industrial users and consumers. Physical distribution activities are usually the responsibility of the marketing department and are part of the large series of activities included in the supply chain. As discussed in Chapter 12, a supply chain is the system through which an organization acquires raw material, produces products, and delivers the products and services to its customers. Exhibit 15-1 illustrates a supply chain. The physical distribution process is managed through **logistics management,** which involves managing (1) the movement of raw materials, (2) the movement of materials and products within plants and warehouses, and (3) the movement of finished goods to intermediaries and buyers. **Supply chain management** helps increase the efficiency of logistics service by minimizing inventory and moving goods efficiently from producers to the ultimate users.[2]

A recent innovation in logistics management is **vendor-managed inventory,** which was pioneered by Wal-Mart when it challenged the traditional roles of suppliers and distributors in building its superb supply chain. Using its vast wealth of sales information and working directly with manufacturers, the company surrendered responsibility for managing its warehouse inventories to its suppliers in exchange for having the right products delivered to the right store exactly when needed. Key manufacturers like Procter & Gamble placed managers at Wal-Mart's headquarters; there they managed the restocking of stores, replacing Wal-Mart

> e x h i b i t   1 5 - 1 <

Supply Chain

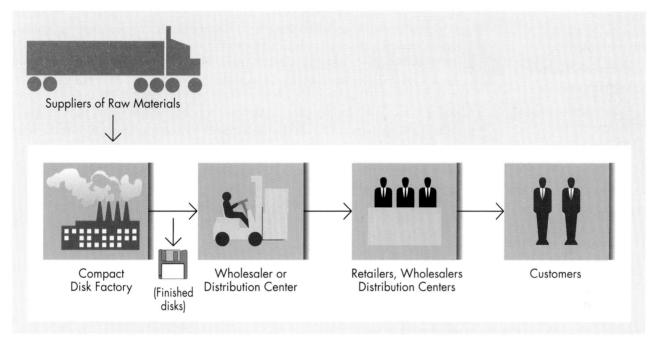

Suppliers of Raw Materials

Compact
Disk Factory

(Finished
disks)

Wholesaler or
Distribution Center

Retailers, Wholesalers
Distribution Centers

Customers

concept check

- Define physical distribution and logistics management.
- What are the advantages of vendor-managed inventory?

buyers. The outside managers also pooled sales information and market research with Wal-Mart executives, helping the retailer improve store sales and the manufacturers to focus their marketing efforts. Vendor-managed inventory is now sweeping across a variety of industries from processed foods to health care.

THE NATURE AND FUNCTIONS OF DISTRIBUTION CHANNELS

>lg 2

On their way from producers to end users and consumers, goods and services pass through a series of marketing entities known as a **distribution channel.** This section will look first at the entities that make up a distribution channel and then will examine the functions that channels serve.

vendor-managed inventory

A system of managing inventory in which the supplier manages the distributor's inventory, thereby reversing the traditional arrangement.

distribution channel

The series of marketing entities through which goods and services pass on their way from producers to end users.

marketing intermediaries

Organizations that assist in moving goods and services from producers to end users.

Marketing Intermediaries in the Distribution Channel

A distribution channel is made up of **marketing intermediaries,** or organizations that assist in moving goods and services from producers to end users and consumers. Marketing intermediaries are so called because they are in the middle of the distribution process between the producer and the end user. The following marketing intermediaries most often appear in the distribution channel:

- *Agents and brokers.* **Agents** are sales representatives of manufacturers and wholesalers, and **brokers** are entities that bring buyers and sellers together. Both agents and brokers are usually hired on commission basis by either a

agents

Sales representatives of manu-facturers and wholesalers.

brokers

Go-betweens that bring buyers and sellers together.

industrial distributors

Independent wholesalers that buy related product lines from many manufacturers and sell them to industrial users.

wholesalers

Firms that sell finished goods to retailers, manufacturers, and institutions.

retailers

Firms that sell goods to con-sumers and to industrial users for their own consumption.

buyer or a seller. Agents and brokers are go-betweens whose job is to make deals. They do not own or take possession of goods.

- *Industrial distributors.* **Industrial distributors** are independent wholesalers that buy related product lines from many manufacturers and sell them to industrial users. They often have a sales force to call on purchasing agents, make deliveries, extend credit, and provide information. Industrial distributors are used in such industries as aircraft manufacturing, mining, and petroleum.
- *Wholesalers.* **Wholesalers** are firms that sell finished goods to retailers, manu-facturers, and institutions (such as schools and hospitals). Historically, their function has been to buy from manufacturers and sell to retailers.
- *Retailers.* **Retailers** are firms that sell goods to consumers and to industrial users for their own consumption.

At the end of the distribution channel are final consumers, like you and me, and industrial users. Industrial users are firms that buy products for internal use or for producing other products or services. They include manufacturers, utilities, airlines, railroads, and service institutions, such as hotels, hospitals, and schools.

Exhibit 15-2 shows various ways marketing intermediaries can be linked. For instance, a manufacturer may sell to a wholesaler that sells to a retailer that in

> e x h i b i t   1 5 - 2 <

Channels of Distribution for Industrial and Consumer Products

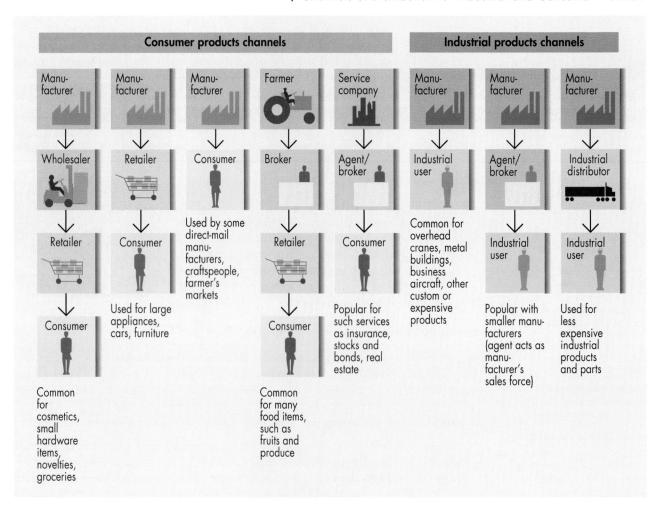

turn sells to a customer. In any of these distribution systems, goods and services are physically transferred from one organization to the next. As each takes possession of the products, it may take legal ownership of them. As the exhibit indicates, distribution channels can handle either consumer products or industrial products.

The Functions of Distribution Channels

Why do distribution channels exist? Why can't every firm sell its products directly to the end user or consumer? Why are go-betweens needed? Channels serve a number of functions.

Channels Reduce the Number of Transactions   Channels make distribution simpler by reducing the number of transactions required to get a product from the manufacturer to the consumer. Assume for the moment that only four students are in your class. Also assume that your professor requires five textbooks, each from a different publisher. If there were no bookstore, 20 transactions would be necessary for all students in the class to buy the books, as shown in Exhibit 15-3. If the bookstore serves as a go-between, the number of transactions is reduced to nine. Each publisher sells to one bookstore rather than to four students. Each student buys from one bookstore instead of from five publishers.

Dealing with channel intermediaries frees producers from many of the details of distribution activity. Producers are traditionally not as efficient or as enthusiastic about selling products directly to end users as channel members are.

> e x h i b i t   1 5 - 3 <   How Distribution Channels Reduce the Number of Transactions

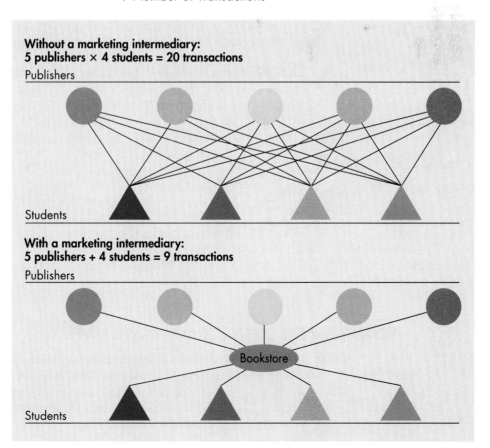

First, producers may wish to focus on production. They may feel that they cannot both produce and distribute in a competitive way. Some firms also may not have the resources to invest in distributing their products.

Channels Ease the Flow of Goods   Channels make distribution easier in several ways. The first is by *sorting*, which consists of the following:

- *Sorting out.* Breaking many different items into separate stocks that are similar. Eggs, for instance, are sorted by grade and size.
- *Accumulating.* Bringing similar stocks together into a larger quantity. Twelve large grade A eggs could be placed in some cartons and 12 medium grade B eggs in other cartons.
- *Allocating.* Breaking similar products into smaller and smaller lots. (Allocating at the wholesale level is called **breaking bulk**.) For instance, a tank-car load of milk could be broken down into gallon jugs. The process of allocating generally is done when the goods are dispersed by region and as ownership of the goods changes.

breaking bulk

The process of breaking large shipments of similar products into smaller, more usable lots.

Without the sorting, accumulating, and allocating processes, modern society would not exist. We would have home-based industries providing custom or semi-custom products to local markets. In short, we would return to a much lower level of consumption.

A second way channels ease the flow of goods is by locating buyers for merchandise. A wholesaler must find the right retailers to sell a profitable volume of merchandise. A sporting goods wholesaler, for instance, must find the retailers who are most likely to reach sporting goods consumers. Retailers have to understand the buying habits of consumers and put stores where consumers want and expect to find the merchandise. Every member of a distribution channel must locate buyers for the products it is trying to sell.

Channel members also store merchandise so that goods are available when consumers want to buy them. The high cost of retail space often means that goods are stored by the wholesaler or the manufacturer.

Channels Perform Needed Functions   The functions performed by channel members help increase the efficiency of the channel. Yet consumers sometimes feel that the go-betweens create higher prices. They doubt that these intermediaries perform useful functions. Actually, however, if channel members did not perform important and necessary functions at a reasonable cost, they would cease to exist. If firms could earn a higher profit without using certain channel members, they would not use them.

A useful rule to remember is that, although channel members can be eliminated, their functions cannot. The manufacturer must either perform the functions of the intermediaries itself or find new ways of getting them carried out. Publishers can bypass bookstores, for instance, but the function performed by the bookstores then has to be performed by the publishers or by someone else.

c o n c ə p t   c h ə c k

- List and define the marketing intermediaries that make up a distribution channel.
- How do channels reduce the number of transactions?
- What is meant by sorting out and accumulating?
- Define breaking bulk.

HOW CHANNELS ORGANIZE AND COVER MARKETS

>lg 3

In an efficient distribution channel, all the channel members work smoothly together and do what they're expected to do. A manufacturer expects wholesalers to promote its products to retailers and to perform several other functions as well. Not all channels have a leader or a single firm that sets channel policies. But all channels have members who rely on one another.

Vertical Marketing Systems

To increase the efficiency of distribution channels, many firms have turned to vertical marketing systems. In a **vertical marketing system,** firms are aligned in a hierarchy (manufacturer to wholesaler to retailer). Such systems are planned, organized, formalized versions of distribution channels. The three basic types of vertical marketing systems are corporate, administrative, and contractual.

vertical marketing system

An organized, formal distribution channel in which firms are aligned in a hierarchy from manufacturer to wholesaler to retailer.

corporate distribution system

A vertical marketing system in which one firm owns the entire distribution channel.

Corporate Distribution Systems In a **corporate distribution system,** one firm owns the entire channel of distribution. Corporate systems are tops in channel control. A single firm that owns the whole channel has no need to worry about channel members. The channel owner will always have supplies of raw materials and long-term contact with customers. It will have good distribution and product exposure in the marketplace.

Examples of corporate distribution systems abound. Evans Products Co. (a manufacturer of plywood), for instance, bought wholesale lumber distributors to better market its products to retail dealers. This move was an example of forward integration. **Forward integration** occurs when a manufacturer ac-

forward integration

The acquisition by a manufacturer of a marketing intermediary closer to the customer, such as a wholesaler or retailer.

quires a marketing intermediary closer to the customer, such as a wholesaler or retailer. A wholesaler could integrate forward by buying a retailer. Other examples of forward integration include Sherwin-Williams, a paint maker that operates over 2,000 paint stores, and Hart Schaffner and Marx, a long-established menswear manufacturer that owns more than 100 clothing outlets. Or a manufacturer might integrate forward by buying a wholesaler. For decades, Pepsi-Cola focused on supplying syrup and concentrate to independent bottlers. But in the 1980s, it decided it could best satisfy retailers' demands by serving them itself.

Details of how forward integration contributes to Sherwin-Williams's success can be found in the firm's investor information at

www.s-w.com

After spending several billion dollars to buy out independent bottlers, Pepsi-Cola today owns bottling and distributing operations that account for half the soda in its system. This strategy created many opportunities for supply chain improvement through a reorganization of its bottling and distribution network. To guide those decisions, Pepsi analyzed demographic trends to identify locations that would yield long-term growth and warrant future expansion. It coupled this information with soft drink consumption trends and marketing forecasts, thus determining when and where new plants should be located. But none of this would have been possible without the purchase of its bottling and distribution outlets.[3]

backward integration

The acquisition of the production process by a wholesaler or retailer.

Backward integration is just the reverse of forward integration. It occurs when a wholesaler or retailer gains control over the production process. Many large retail organizations have integrated backward. Sears has part ownership of production facilities that supply over 30 percent of its inventory. Wal-Mart bought McLane Co., a Texas wholesaler with a reputation as one of the best specialty distributors of cigarettes, candy, and perishables in the United States. With McLane, Wal-Mart can avoid outside distributors and can lower overall costs.

administrative distribution system

A vertical marketing system in which a strong organization takes over as leader and sets policies for the distribution channel.

Administrative Distribution Systems In an **administrative distribution system,** a strong organization takes over as leader and sets channel policies. The leadership role is informal; it is not written into a contract. Companies such as Gillette, Hanes, Campbell's, and Westinghouse are administrative system leaders. They can often influence or control the policies of other channel members without the costs and expertise required to set up a corporate distribution system. They

RITE AID'S SUPPLIER RELATIONSHIPS

Rite Aid, the third largest drugstore chain in America, has more than 3,800 stores with annual revenue of almost $13 billion. Recently, however, earnings have suffered. In late March 1999, Rite Aid announced that net income for the fiscal quarter just completed was 39 percent below the year earlier quarter. Rite Aid attributed the earnings decline to problems related to its acquisition of the Thrifty Payless, Harco, and K&B chains.

At the end of the February 1999 fiscal quarter, Rite Aid took deductions on its payments to numerous suppliers, including the U.S. consumer products unit of Bayer AG, Dial Corp., Bic Corp., and the M&M/Mars unit of Mars, Inc. The notice to Bayer "cited damaged and outdated merchandise removed from acquired and remodeled stores" as the reason for the deductions. According to Rite Aid officials, "the company's rapid pace of acquisitions and store openings, closings and

remodelings . . . [resulted] in many items being classed as outdated, damaged or otherwise unwanted, and suppliers are expected to take them back or give credit if the merchandise is destroyed or marked down."

Many of the suppliers are not buying Rite Aid's explanation, however. They point out that the Thrifty Payless acquisition was completed in late 1996, while the Harco and K&B deals were closed in 1997.

Critical Thinking Questions

1. Do you think Rite Aid handled its supplier relationships in a fair and just manner?
2. Why are honesty and trust essential to effective working relationships in a distribution channel?
3. Can business practices be ethical in the absence of honesty and trust? Explain your answer.

---

may be able to dictate how many wholesalers will be in the channel or require that the wholesalers offer 60-day credit to retail customers, among other things.

contractual distribution system

A vertical marketing system in which a network of independent firms at different levels (manufacturer, wholesaler, retailer) coordinate their distribution activities through a written contract.

Contractual Distribution Systems   The third form of vertical marketing is a **contractual distribution system.** It is a network of independent firms at different levels (manufacturer, wholesaler, retailer) that coordinate their distribution activities through a written contract. Franchises are a common form of the contractual system. The parent companies of McDonald's and Chemlawn, for instance, control distribution of their products through the franchise agreement each franchisee signs.

The Intensity of Market Coverage

>lg 4

All types of distribution systems must be concerned with market coverage. How many dealers will be used to distribute the product in a particular area? As Exhibit 15-4 shows, the three degrees of coverage are exclusive, selective, and intensive. The type of product determines the intensity of the market coverage.

exclusive distribution

A distribution system in which a manufacturer selects only one or two dealers in an area to market its products.

When a manufacturer selects one or two dealers in an area to market its products, it is using **exclusive distribution.** Only items that are in strong demand can be distributed exclusively because consumers must be willing to travel some distance to buy them. If Wrigley's chewing gum were sold in only one drugstore per city, Wrigley's would soon be out of business. However, Bang and Olufsen stereo components, Jaguar automobiles, and Adrienne Vittadini designer clothing are distributed exclusively with great success.

Different Products Require Different Degrees of Market Coverage

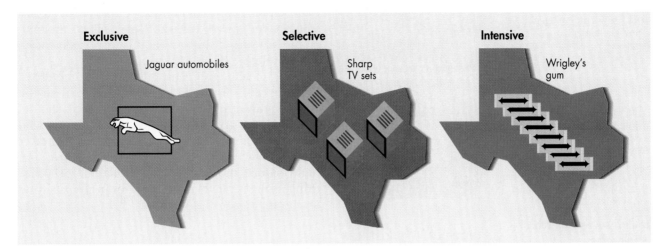

selective distribution

A distribution system in which a manufacturer selects a limited number of dealers in an area (but more than one or two) to market its products.

concept check

- What is meant by an efficient channel of distribution?
- What are the three types of vertical marketing systems?
- Name the three degrees of market coverage.

A manufacturer that chooses a limited number of dealers in an area (but more than one or two) is using **selective distribution.** Since the number of retailers handling the product is limited, consumers must be willing to seek it out. Timberline boots, a high-quality line of footwear, are distributed selectively. So are Sony televisions, Maytag washers, Waterford crystal, and Tommy Hilfiger clothing. When choosing dealers, manufacturers look for certain qualities. Sony may seek retailers that can offer high-quality customer service. Tommy Hilfiger may look for retailers with high-traffic locations in regional shopping malls. All manufacturers try to exclude retailers that are a poor credit risk or that have a weak or negative image.

A manufacturer that wants to sell its products everywhere there are potential customers is using **intensive distribution.** Such consumer goods as bread, tape, and lightbulbs are often distributed intensively. Usually, these products cost little and are bought frequently, which means that complex distribution channels are necessary. Coca-Cola is sold in just about every type of retail business, from gas stations to supermarkets.

WHOLESALING

>lg 5

intensive distribution

A distribution system in which a manufacturer tries to sell its products wherever there are potential customers.

Wholesalers are channel members that buy finished products from manufacturers and sell them to retailers. Retailers in turn sell the products to consumers. Manufacturers that use selective or exclusive distribution normally sell directly to retailers. Manufacturers that use intensive distribution often rely on wholesalers.

Wholesalers also sell products to institutions, such as manufacturers, schools, and hospitals, for use in performing their own missions. A manufacturer, for instance, might buy typing paper from Nationwide Papers, a wholesaler. A hospital might buy its cleaning supplies from Lagasse Brothers, one of the nation's largest wholesalers of janitorial supplies.

Sometimes wholesalers sell products to manufacturers for use in the manufacturing process. A builder of custom boats, for instance, might buy batteries from a battery wholesaler and switches from an electrical wholesaler. Some wholesalers even sell to other wholesalers, creating yet another stage in the distribution channel.

merchant wholesaler

An institution that buys goods from manufacturers (takes ownership) and resells them to businesses, government agencies, other wholesalers, or retailers.

full-service merchant wholesalers

Wholesalers that provide many services for their clients, such as providing credit, offering promotional and technical advice, storing and delivering merchandise, or providing installation and repairs.

limited-service merchant wholesalers

Wholesalers that typically carry a limited line of fast-moving merchandise and do not offer many services to their clients.

Many publishers use wholesaler Ingram Book Group to distribute their books, audiotapes, and periodicals to bookstores and libraries. For a closer look at the services this wholesaler provides, visit Ingram's Web site at

www.ingrambook.com

About half of all wholesalers offer financing for their clients. They sell products on credit and expect to be paid within a certain time, usually 60 days. Other wholesalers operate like retail stores. The retailer goes to the wholesaler, selects the merchandise, pays cash for it, and transports it to the retail outlet.

Because wholesalers usually serve limited areas, they are often located closer to retailers than the manufacturers are. Retailers can thus get faster delivery at lower cost from wholesalers. A retailer who knows that a wholesaler can restock store shelves within a day can keep a low level of inventory on hand. More money is then available for other things because less cash is tied up in items sitting on the shelves or in storerooms.

Types of Wholesalers

The two main types of wholesalers are merchant wholesalers and agents and brokers, as shown in Exhibit 15-5. Merchant wholesalers take title to the product (ownership rights); agents and brokers simply facilitate the sale of a product from producer to end user.

> e x h i b i t   1 5 - 5 <

The Two Categories of Wholesalers

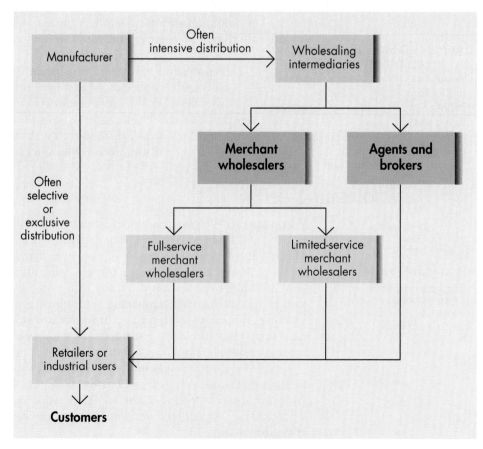

cash and carry wholesaler
A limited-service merchant wholesaler that does not offer credit or delivery services.

manufacturers' representatives
Salespeople who represent non-competing manufacturers; function as independent agents rather than as salaried employees of the manufacturers.

Business and retail customers pay cash for and carry their purchases from Costco, a limited-service wholesaler that doesn't offer credit or delivery service.

Merchant Wholesalers Merchant wholesalers make up 80 percent of all wholesaling establishments and conduct slightly under 60 percent of all wholesale sales. A **merchant wholesaler** is an institution that buys goods from manufacturers and resells them to businesses, government agencies, other wholesalers, or retailers. All merchant wholesalers take title to the goods they sell. Most merchant wholesalers operate one or more warehouses where they receive goods, store them, and later reship them. Customers are mostly small or moderate-size retailers, but merchant wholesalers also market to manufacturers and institutional clients. Merchant wholesalers can be categorized as either full-service or limited-service wholesalers, depending on the number of channel functions they perform.

Full-service merchant wholesalers perform many functions. They assemble an assortment of products for their clients, provide credit, and offer promotional help and technical advice. In addition, they maintain a sales force to contact customers, store and deliver merchandise, and perhaps offer research and planning support. Depending on the product line, full-service merchant wholesalers sometimes provide installation and repair as well. Full service also means "going the extra mile" to meet special customer needs, such as offering fast delivery in emergencies.

As the name implies, **limited-service merchant wholesalers** perform only a few of the full-service merchant wholesaler's activities. Generally, limited-service merchant wholesalers carry a limited line of fast-moving merchandise. They do not extend credit or supply market information. One type of limited-service merchant wholesaler is the **cash and carry wholesaler.** This wholesaler doesn't offer credit or delivery, hence the term "cash and carry" wholesaler. Sam's Clubs and Costco are nationally known cash and carry wholesalers. About 60 percent of Sam's volume is done with small businesses. These companies are unique because they are not only wholesalers but also do business with consumers. Government employees, credit union members, and employees of large corporations, among others, can pay an annual fee (usually $35) and shop at Costco or Sam's. Retail customers typically pay a 5 percent markup as well. Exhibit 15-6 lists additional types of limited-service merchant wholesalers.

Agents and Brokers As mentioned earlier, agents represent manufacturers and wholesalers. **Manufacturers' representatives** (also called **manufacturers' agents**) represent noncompeting manufacturers. These salespeople function as independent agents rather than as salaried employees of manufacturers. They do not take title to or possession of merchandise. They get commissions if they make sales—and nothing if they don't. They are found in a variety of industries, including electronics, clothing, hardware, furniture, and toys.

Brokers bring buyers and sellers together. Like agents, brokers do not take title to merchandise, they receive commissions on sales, and they have little say over company sales policies. They are found in markets where the information that would join buyers and sellers is scarce. These markets include real estate, agriculture, insurance, and commodities.

concept check

- Define wholesaling and describe what wholesalers do.
- Describe merchant wholesalers and the categories of merchant wholesalers.
- Explain the difference between agents and brokers.

Limited-Service Merchant Wholesalers

- **Cash-and-carry wholesalers:** Have a limited line of fast-moving goods and sell to small retailers for cash. Normally do not deliver.

- **Truck wholesalers:** Perform primarily a selling and delivery function. Carry a limited line of semiperishable merchandise (such as milk, bread, snack foods), which they sell for cash as they make their rounds of supermarkets, small groceries, hospitals, restaurants, factory cafeterias, and hotels.

- **Drop shippers:** Operate in bulk industries, such as coal, lumber, and heavy equipment. Do not carry inventory or handle the product. Upon receiving an order, they select a manufacturer, who ships the merchandise directly to the customer on the agreed-upon terms and time of delivery. The drop shipper assumes title and risk from the time the order is accepted to its delivery to the customer.

- **Rack jobbers:** Serve grocery and drug retailers, mostly in the area of non-food items. They send delivery trucks to stores, and the delivery people set up toys, paperbacks, hardware items, health and beauty aids, and so on. They price the goods, keep them fresh, set up point-of-purchase displays, and keep inventory records. Rack jobbers retain title to the goods and bill the retailers only for the goods sold to consumers. They do little promotion because they carry many branded items that are highly advertised.

- **Producers' cooperatives:** Owned by farmer members and assemble farm produce to sell in local markets. The co-op's profits are distributed to members at the end of the year. Co-ops often attempt to improve product quality and promote a co-op brand name, such as Sun Maid raisins, Sunkist oranges, or Diamond walnuts.

THE COMPETITIVE WORLD OF RETAILING

>lg 6

Some 30 million Americans are engaged in retailing. Of this number, almost 16 million work in service businesses like barber shops, lawyers' offices, and amusement parks. Although most retailers are involved in small businesses, most sales are made by the giant retail organizations, such as Sears, Wal-Mart, Kmart, and JC Penney. Half of all retail sales come from fewer than 10 percent of all retail businesses. This small group employs about 40 percent of all retail workers. Retailers feel the impact of changes in the economy more than many other types of businesses. Survival depends on keeping up with changing lifestyles and customer shopping patterns.

At the National Retail Federation's Web site, you'll find current retail statistics, links to retailing resources, and information about retailing careers. Check it out at **www.nrf.com**

Types of Retail Operations

There is a great deal of variety in retail operations. The major types of retailers are described in Exhibit 15-7, which divides them into two main categories: in-store and nonstore retailing. Examples of *in-store retailing* include Sears, Wal-Mart, Kmart, Saks, and Dayton Hudson. These retailers get most

Retailing Takes Many Forms

Types of In-Store Retailing	Description	Examples
Department store	Houses many departments under one roof with each treated as a separate buying center to achieve economies of buying, promotion, and control	JC Penney, Saks, May Co., Rich's, Bloomingdale's
Specialty store	Specializes in a category of merchandise and carries a complete assortment	Toys 'R Us, Radio Shack, Zales Jewelers
Variety store	Offers a variety of inexpensive goods	Ben Franklin, Woolworths
Convenience store	Offers convenience goods with long store hours and quick checkout	7-Eleven, Circle K
Supermarket	Specializes in a wide assortment of food, with self-service	Safeway, Kroger, Winn Dixie
Discount store	Competes on the basis of low prices and high turnover; offers few services	Wal-Mart, Target, Kmart
Off-price retailer	Sells at prices 25% or more below traditional department store prices in spartan environment	Robs, T. J. Maxx, Clothestime
Factory outlet	Owned by manufacturer; sells close-outs, factory seconds, and canceled orders	Levi Strauss, Ship 'n Shore, Dansk
Catalog store	Sends catalogs to customers and displays merchandise in showrooms where customers can order from attached warehouse	Best, Service Merchandise, Lurias
Hypermart	Offers huge selection of food and general merchandise with very low prices; sometimes called "mall without a wall"	Hypermart USA, American Fare
Types of Nonstore Retailing	**Description**	**Examples**
Vending machine	Sells merchandise by machine	Canteen
Direct selling	Sells face-to-face, usually in the person's home	Fuller Brush, Avon, Amway
Direct-response marketing	Attempts to get immediate consumer sale through media advertising, catalogs, or direct mail	K-Tel, L. L. Bean, Ronco
Home shopping networks	Selling via cable television	Home Shopping Network QVC
Internet retailing (e-commerce)	Selling over the Internet	Bluefly.com, CDnow, eToys, Amazon.com

of their revenue from people who come to the store to buy what they want. Many in-store retailers also do some catalog and telephone sales.

Nonstore retailing includes vending, direct selling, direct-response marketing, home shopping networks, and Internet retailing. Vending uses machines to sell food and other items, usually as a convenience in institutions like schools and hospitals.

Direct selling involves face-to-face contact between the buyer and seller, but not in a retail store. Usually, the seller goes to the consumer's home. Sometimes contacts are made at the place of work. Mary Kay Cosmetics, Avon, Herbalife, and Amway each employ

Want to be a Mary Kay Cosmetics representative? Find out more about the company and how to get started at

www.marykay.com

Avon is a direct selling retailer that employs representatives to sell its cosmetics and personal care merchandise at the buyer's home or place of business.

over 100,000 direct salespeople. Some companies, such as Tupperware and Longaberger baskets, specialize in parties in a person's home. Most parties are a combination social affair and sales demonstration. The hostess usually gets a discount and a special gift for rounding up a group of friends. Such parties seem to be replacing door-to-door canvassing. The sales of many direct-sales companies have suffered, however, as women continue to enter the workforce on a full-time basis.

Direct-response marketing is conducted through media that encourage a consumer to reply. Popular direct-response media are catalogs, direct mail, television, newspapers, and radio. The ads invite a person to "call the toll-free number now" or to fill out an order blank. Direct-response marketing includes K-Tel selling "golden oldies" and Ed McMahon shouting from an envelope that "you may have just won $10 million." It also includes the catalogs sent out by Lands' End, L. L. Bean, J. Crew, Lillian Vernon, and countless others.

Internet retailing, also called e-commerce, is the selling of merchandise over the Internet. E-commerce sales are exploding and will have a profound impact on retailers around the world. It is also going to change how you shop. Internet retailing is discussed later in this chapter. Meanwhile, some of the hottest entrepreneurs around are those starting e-commerce businesses on the Net. Winning in cyberspace is discussed in the Focusing on Small Business box.

Components of a Successful Retailing Strategy

>lg 7

Retailing is a very competitive business. Managers have to develop an effective strategy to survive. The key tasks in building a retail strategy are defining a target market, developing a product offering, creating an image and a promotional strategy, choosing a location, and setting prices.

Stores magazine has hundreds of ideas for putting together a successful retailing strategy. Visit the magazine's Web site at
www.stores.org

Defining a Target Market The first and foremost task in developing a retail strategy is to define the target market. This process begins with market segmentation, the topic of an earlier chapter, and the determination of a target market. For example, Target's merchandising approach for sporting goods is to match its product assortment to the demographics of the local store and region. Target stores in the Northeast stock a variety of ski equipment to satisfy the local interest in downhill and cross-country skiing. The amount of space devoted to sporting goods, as well as in-store promotions, also varies according to each store's target market.

Target markets in retailing are often defined by demographics. Dollar General and Family Dollar stores target households earning less than $25,000 per year.[4] Eddie Bauer targets suburban 25- to 45-year-olds.[5] Claire's, a retailer selling inexpensive costume jewelry, such as Y-shaped necklaces, wire tricep bracelets and headbands, targets 12- to 14-year-old girls.[6]

WINNING RETAIL BUSINESS IN CYBERSPACE

A few years ago, Pierre M. Omidyar decided to launch a Web site. Inspired by his fiancée's passion for collecting Pez dispensers, the Silicon Valley entrepreneur hit on the idea of building a flea market in cyberspace—where people could buy and sell anything to anybody. There was one snag, though. How could he persuade complete strangers to trust one another enough to hand over merchandise or cash without ever having met?

Omidyar's solution was to devise a system where buyers and sellers can rate their experiences with different traders. eBay, Inc. assigns a point for positive comments, zero for neutral responses, and minus 1 for negative feedback. Anyone who accumulates a score of minus 4 is not allowed to use the service anymore. That provided the assurance people needed to feel comfortable trading with one another—and it helped Omidyar's eBay become the largest person-to-person auction site on the Web, selling $400 million in merchandise a year.

In cyberspace, successful shopkeepers start by doing what all good merchants do: they offer customers a special reason to stop by—to get the widest selection, the greatest convenience, top-notch service, the best products, or their deep knowledge of whatever they're selling. Then they add an extra digital twist. That can mean playing into the psychology of the Net—the way eBay and online auction site Onsale tap into cybershoppers' penchants for bargains, competition, and interaction with other buyers and sellers. Or it can mean using the Internet's unique ability to provide personalized service, the way 1-800-Flowers, Inc. will send you an e-mail reminder of your wife's birthday, or Amazon.com, Inc. will recommend a book you might like. "The pattern of all the successful Internet companies is that they're doing things that can only be done online," says Jeffrey P. Bezos, chief executive of Amazon.com.

Critical Thinking Questions

1. Can everything be sold on the Internet?
2. Will manufacturers that sell through traditional department and specialty stores have to start selling on the Web to be competitive?
3. Is e-commerce going to drive some retailers out of business?

Developing the Product Offering The second element in determining a retail strategy is the product offering, also called the product assortment or merchandise mix. Retailers decide what to sell on the basis of what their target market wants to buy. They can base their decision on market research, past sales, fashion trends, customer requests, and other sources. For example, after more companies began promoting office casual days, Brooks Brothers, the upscale retailer of men's and women's conservative business wear, updated its product line with khaki pants, casual shirts, and a selection of brightly colored shirts and ties.

After determining what products will satisfy target customers' desires, retailers must find sources of supply and evaluate the products. When the right products are located, the retail buyer negotiates a purchase contract. The buying function can be performed in-house or delegated to an outside firm. The goods must then be moved from the seller to the retailer, which means shipping, storing, and stocking the inventory. The trick is to manage the inventory by cutting prices to move slow goods and by keeping adequate supplies of hot-selling items in stock.

One of the more efficient new methods of managing inventory and streamlining the way products are moved from supplier to distributor to retailer is

efficient consumer response (ECR)

A method of managing inventory and streamlining the movement of products from supplier to distributor to retailer; relies on electronic data interchange to communicate information such as automatic shipping notifications, invoices, inventory data, and forecasts.

electronic data interchange (EDI)

Computer-to-computer exchange of information, including automatic shipping notifications, invoices, inventory data, and forecasts; used in efficient consumer response systems.

called **efficient consumer response (ECR).** At the heart of ECR is **electronic data interchange (EDI),** the computer-to-computer exchange of information, including automatic shipping notifications, invoices, inventory data, and forecasts. In a full implementation of ECR, products are scanned at the retail store when purchased, which updates the store's inventory lists. Headquarters then polls the stores to retrieve the data needed to produce an order. The vendor confirms the order, shipping date, and delivery time, then ships the order, and transmits the invoice electronically. The item is received at the warehouse, scanned into inventory, and then sent to the store. The invoice and receiving data are reconciled, and payment via an electronic transfer of funds completes the process. Many retailers are experimenting with or have successfully implemented ECR and EDI. Dillard's, one of the fastest-growing regional department store chains, has one of the most technologically advanced ECR systems in the industry.

The pioneer and market leader in ECR systems is Wal-Mart, discussed in the Applying Technology box.

> applying technology <

WAL-MART KNOWS WHAT YOU LIKE

Many retailers talk a good game when it comes to mining data collected at cash registers as a way to build sales. Wal-Mart, the nation's largest retailer, has been doing it since about 1990. Now, it is sitting on a treasure trove of information so vast and detailed that it far exceeds what many manufacturers know about their own products.

Wal-Mart's database is second in size only to that of the U.S. government. Along with raw sales, profit margin, and inventory numbers, Wal-Mart also collects "market-basket data" from customer receipts at all its stores, so it knows what products are likely to be purchased together. The company receives about 100,000 queries a week from suppliers and its own buyers looking for purchase patterns or checking on a product.

At 192,000 square feet, Wal-Mart supercenters are about the size of four football fields. Wal-Mart quickly found customers were having trouble navigating them. To address customers' frustrations, Wal-Mart dug through heaps of purchase data from its supercenters and unearthed lots of ways to help people find things they didn't even know they needed. Kleenex tissues are in the paper-goods aisle and also mixed in with the cold medicine. Measuring spoons are in housewares and also hanging next to Crisco shortening. In October, flashlights are in the hardware aisle and also with the Halloween costumes.

To get real-time reports on sales, profitability, and inventory position, Wal-Mart managers can use a hand-held computer that scans bar codes on store shelves. The information is crucial for pricing and shipping decisions, but it doesn't leave much room for creativity: "Everybody thinks they have a feel for what people like, but we keep data," says Randy Mott, Wal-Mart's chief information officer.

The data also help Wal-Mart time merchandise deliveries so that its shelves stay stocked—but not overstocked. The supercenters have cut back on how high they stack merchandise, making stores feel less crowded. The data have also helped keep inventory levels leaner and turning faster—a must for a retailer of perishable produce as well as of perishable fashion.

Critical Thinking Questions

1. Do you think that Wal-Mart's database could help in creating displays?
2. How can Wal-Mart's database be used in stocking a new Wal-Mart?
3. Is it a good idea to continually change a store's merchandise layout?

Creating an Image and Promotional Strategy   The third task in developing a retail strategy is to create an image and a promotional strategy. Promotion combines with the store's merchandise mix, service level, and atmosphere to make up a retail image. We will discuss promotion in more detail in the next chapter. *Atmosphere* refers to the physical layout and decor of the store. They can create a relaxed or busy feeling, a sense of luxury, a friendly or cold attitude, and a sense of organization or clutter.

These are the most influential factors in creating a store's atmosphere:

- *Employee type and density.* Employee type refers to an employee's general characteristics—for instance, neat, friendly, knowledgeable, or service oriented. Density is the number of employees per 1,000 square feet of selling space. A discounter such as Kmart has a low employee density that creates a "do-it-yourself" casual atmosphere.
- *Merchandise type and density.* The type of merchandise carried and how it is displayed add to the atmosphere the retailer is trying to create. A prestigious retailer such as Saks or Marshall Field's carries the best brand names and displays them in a neat, uncluttered arrangement.
- *Fixture type and density.* Fixtures can be elegant (rich woods), trendy (chrome and smoked glass), or old, beat-up tables, as in an antique store. The fixtures should be consistent with the general atmosphere the store is trying to create. By displaying its merchandise on tables and shelves rather than on traditional pipe racks, the Gap creates a relaxed and uncluttered atmosphere that enables customers to see and touch the merchandise more easily.
- *Sound.* Sound can be pleasant or unpleasant for a customer. Classical music at a nice Italian restaurant helps create ambiance, just as country and western music does at a truck stop. Music can also entice customers to stay in the store longer and buy more or encourage them to eat quickly and leave a table for others.
- *Odors.* Smell can either stimulate or detract from sales. The wonderful smell of pastries and breads entices bakery customers. Conversely, customers can be repulsed by bad odors, such as cigarette smoke, musty smells, antiseptic odors, and overly powerful room deodorizers.

Choosing a Location   The next task in creating a retail strategy is figuring out where to put the store. First, a community must be chosen. This decision depends on the strength of the local economy, the nature of the competition, the political climate, and so forth. Then a specific site must be selected. One important decision is whether to locate in a shopping center. Large retailers like Kmart and Target and sellers of shopping goods like furniture and cars can use a free-standing store because customers will seek them out. Such a location also has the advantages of low-cost land or rent and no direct competitors close by. It may be harder to attract customers to a free-standing location, however. Another disadvantage is that the retailer can't share costs for promotion, maintenance, and holiday decorating, as do stores in a mall.

Setting Prices   Another strategic task of the retail manager is to set prices. The strategy of pricing was presented in Chapter 14. Retailing's goal is to sell products, and the price is critical in ensuring that sales take place.

Price is also one of the three key elements in the store's image and positioning strategy. Higher prices often imply quality and help support the prestige image of such retailers as Lord and Taylor, Saks Fifth Avenue, Gatch, Carrier, and Neiman-Marcus. On the other hand, discounters and off-price retailers offer good value for the money.

concept check
- Describe at least five types of in-store retailing and four forms of nonstore retailing.
- Discuss the components of a successful retail strategy.

USING PHYSICAL DISTRIBUTION TO INCREASE EFFICIENCY AND CUSTOMER SATISFACTION

>lg 8

Physical distribution is an important part of the marketing mix. Retailers don't sell products they can't deliver, and salespeople don't (or shouldn't) promise deliveries they can't make. Late deliveries and broken promises may mean loss of a customer. Accurate order filling and billing, timely delivery, and arrival in good condition are important to the success of the product.

Distribution managers are responsible for making decisions that affect the successful delivery of a product to the end consumer. These decisions, presented in this section, include choosing a warehouse location and type, setting up a materials-handling system, and choosing among the available modes of transportation.

Choosing a Warehouse Location and Type

Deciding where to put a warehouse is mostly a matter of deciding which markets will be served and where production facilities will be located. A *storage warehouse* is used to hold goods for a long time. For instance, Jantzen makes bathing suits at an even rate throughout the year to provide steady employment and hold down costs. It then stores them in a warehouse until the selling season.

distribution centers

Warehouses that specialize in changing shipment sizes, rather than in storing goods.

Distribution centers are a special form of warehouse. They specialize in changing shipment sizes rather than storing goods. Such centers make bulk (put shipments together) or break bulk. They strive for rapid inventory turnover. When shipments arrive, the merchandise is quickly sorted into orders for various retail stores. As soon as the order is complete, it is delivered. Distribution centers are the wave of the future, replacing traditional warehouses. Companies simply can't afford to have a lot of money tied up in idle inventory.

Setting Up a Materials-Handling System

Water is one of the five major modes of transportation that distribution managers can choose from in moving products from the producer to the buyer.

A materials-handling system moves and handles inventory. The goal of such a system is to move items as quickly as possible while handling them as little as possible. When Kodak built a new plant for making photographic coated paper, for example, it designed a way to minimize materials handling. It built a 10-level concrete rack to hold the one-ton rolls of raw paper. A computer handles inventory control and commands machines that can retrieve and carry the rolls without damage and then load the paper onto the assembly line.

Making Transportation Decisions

Transportation typically accounts for between 5 and 10 percent of the price of goods.[7] Physical distribution managers must decide which mode of transportation to use to move products from producer to buyer. This decision is, of course, related to all other physical distribution decisions. The five major modes of transportation are railroads, motor carriers, pipelines, water transportation, and airways. Distribution managers generally choose a mode of transportation on the basis of several criteria:

- *Cost.* The total amount a specific carrier charges to move the product from the point of origin to the destination.

- *Transit time.* The total time a carrier has possession of goods, including the time required for pickup and delivery, handling, and movement between the point of origin and the destination.
- *Reliability.* The consistency with which the carrier delivers goods on time and in acceptable condition.
- *Capability.* The carrier's ability to provide the appropriate equipment and conditions for moving specific kinds of goods, such as those that must be transported in a controlled environment (for example, under refrigeration).
  - *Accessibility.* The carrier's ability to move goods over a specific route or network.
  - *Traceability.* The relative ease with which a shipment can be located and transferred.[8]

The Freight World Web site offers detailed information on various transportation modes and links to transportation companies. Visit it at

www.freightworld.com

c o n c ə p t c h ə c k

- Discuss the functions of physical distribution.
- What factors are considered when selecting a mode of transportation?

Using these six criteria, a shipper selects the mode of transportation that will best meet its needs. Exhibit 15-8 shows how the basic modes of transportation rank in terms of these criteria.

CAPITALIZING ON TRENDS IN BUSINESS

>lg 9

Companies are using new distribution strategies to boost their profits and gain a competitive edge. The Internet is spurring many of these new strategies by opening up a whole new avenue for buying goods and services. In this section we'll discuss two emerging trends in distribution, stocklifting and the growth of the physical distribution of services. Chapter 18 will explore how the Internet is offering vast new methods for distributing products and services.

> e x h i b i t 1 5 - 8 <

Criteria for Ranking Modes of Transportation

	Highest				Lowest
Relative cost	Air	Truck	Rail	Pipe	Water
Transit time	Water	Rail	Pipe	Truck	Air
Reliability	Pipe	Truck	Rail	Air	Water
Capability	Water	Rail	Truck	Air	Pipe
Accessibility	Truck	Rail	Air	Water	Pipe
Traceability	Air	Truck	Rail	Water	Pipe

The Rough and Tumble Practice of Stocklifting

At the giant Lowe's Home Improvement Warehouse store in Athens, Georgia, in aisle 23 near the lawn mowers, hundreds of garden gloves recently vanished. The missing merchandise was manufactured by Wells Lamont, the nation's largest garden-glove company. Almost overnight, the empty shelves were restocked with gloves made by Wells Lamont's archrival, Midwest Quality Gloves, Inc. The same scene played out in 100 other Lowe's stores: Wells Lamont gloves were replaced by Midwest gloves—floral, pigskin, cowhide, and others. Behind the inventory switch was Midwest. It had struck a deal with Lowe's to buy 225,000 pairs of Wells Lamont gloves and clear them all out so that it could fill shelf after shelf with its own product.

stocklift (buyback)
The practice in which a company purchases all of a competitor's products from retailers and replaces the merchandise with its own products.

This shadowy tactic—called a **stocklift** or **buyback**—is spreading. Makers of everything from party napkins to bicycle chains are lifting truckloads of competitors' products everywhere from Kmarts to Revco drugstores. Then they dump the merchandise into an underground distribution network for resale by faraway, sometimes foreign, retailers. Wells Lamont, the stocklift victim, had no immediate recourse. "Of course we mind it, but that's not illegal," shrugs Richard Stoller, a Wells Lamont vice-president, referring to any stocklift. "We sold the product to the customer," the retailer. "It's their inventory, not ours."[9]

Manufacturers say store managers increasingly consider stocklifts the normal way to do business with vendors. "It costs a ton of money," says Nicolaus Bruns, group product manager for humidifiers and other housewares at Bemis Manufacturing Co. But "if you want to land a major [retail] account, you're going to have to do it."[10]

Services and Physical Distribution

The fastest-growing part of our economy is the service sector. Although distribution in the service sector is difficult to visualize, the same skills, techniques, and strategies used to manage goods inventory can also be used to manage service inventory, such as hospital beds, bank accounts, or airline seats. The quality of the planning and execution of distribution can have a major impact on costs and customer satisfaction. Because service industries are so customer oriented, customer service is a priority. Service distribution focuses on three main areas:

- *Minimizing wait times.* Minimizing the amount of time customers wait to deposit a check, obtain their food at a restaurant, or see a doctor for an appointment is a key factor in maintaining the quality of service. FedEx, for example, revolutionized the delivery market when it introduced guaranteed overnight delivery of packages and documents to commercial and residential customers.

- *Managing service capacity.* For a product manufacturer, inventory acts as a buffer, enabling it to provide the product during periods of peak demand without extraordinary efforts. Service firms don't have this luxury. If they don't have the capacity to meet demand, they must either turn down some prospective customers, let service levels slip, or expand capacity. For instance, at tax time so many customers may desire tax preparation services that a tax preparation firm will have to either turn business away or add temporary offices or preparers.

- *Improving delivery through new distribution channels.* Like manufacturers, service firms are now experimenting with different distribution channels for

concept check

- What is stocklifting, and why do companies engage in it?
- How are service firms changing their distribution systems to improve customer service?
- How does physical distribution influence service delivery?

their services. These new channels can increase the time that services are available (like round-the-clock automated teller machines) or add to customer convenience (like pizza delivery or walk-in medical clinics). For example, alternatives to hospitals called medical malls now offer one-stop shopping for all types of medical services. Like traditional malls, these shopping areas are equipped with fountains, food courts, and other amenities. The only difference lies in their product assortment, which ranges from radiology and cardiac treatment to outpatient surgery.[11]

APPLYING THIS CHAPTER'S TOPICS

This chapter has two important implications for you, both of which involve the Internet. First, the Web is going to make it easier for you to shop. Second, just as the automobile transformed consumers' lives in the 20th century, the Web will change your life in this century.

> try it now! <

1. **Comparison Shop**   A beauty of the Internet is the ability to comparison shop like never before. To compare brands, features, and prices of products, go to one of these sites: **www.jango.excite.com, www.bottomdollar.com, www.mysimon.com,** or **www.compare.net.** If you already know exactly what you want but just need to find out where you can get it online cheaply or offline conveniently, use this shopping engine: **www.inktomi.com.**

2. **Kick the Tires Before You Buy**   At some point you are going to buy a car. The Web can simplify the process, help you make an intelligent decision, and save you money. Start at **www.edmunds. com.** The online version of the respected car-buying guide is crammed with information about new and used cars. The site offers thousands of car reviews

and current loan rates. Once you decide what you want, go to one or all of these sites to get the best price: **www.autobytel.com, www.autoconnect.com,** or **www.autoweb.com.** If you decide to buy a used car but are not sure about the strange sound or unexplained dent, go to **www.carfax.com** and plug in the car's vehicle identification number. In return you will get an immediate report of the car's public history that will tell you such things as whether the car has been auctioned and its emission test results. The report costs $20, but if there are no data, you don't pay. Once you have found the car of your dreams, go to **www.carfinance.com,** enter the make, model, and year, and NationsBank will give you a quote for a loan or a lease plan at no charge.

The Internet Makes Shopping a Breeze

If you want to sniff several new perfumes, mall walk, or simply be around other people and people watch, then the old familiar mall is the place to go. If you want convenience and the ability to comparison shop, go to the Net. To find the best fare for traveling, use one of the sites listed in Exhibit 15-9.

The Web Is Changing Your Life

The Net is about choice, freedom, and control. Online consumers can take out of cyberspace anything that interests them and leave behind what doesn't. In the offline world, products and services are built far in advance of customer needs, and customers can do little to configure those products and services to their own requirements. That situation is fading into history. The Net allows a vendor to build to demand. Already Gateway and Dell let customers configure personal computers and servers to their liking.

Consumers like you may save time and money by shopping online, which offers easy access to information and the opportunity to compare prices. Just about everything will soon be obtainable over the Web. Through the years retailers and manufacturers have made billions of dollars in profits from the inability of consumers to compare prices quickly. Now search engines and product comparison sites can save you time as never before. They can make you a smarter shopper. You may be able to raise your standard of living by one-third just by becoming an intelligent buyer. The Web can easily make this happen for you.

> e x h i b i t   1 5 - 9 <

Find a Good Deal on Travel Using One of These Sites

- **Microsoft Expedia (expedia.msn.com).** Microsoft's online travel site offers a vast array of information about vacation spots, cruises, and tours, as well as direct access to all major air, car, rail, and hotel reservation systems. You can compare airfares, check arrival times, get maps of cities and routes, and share tips and advice with other travelers.
- **Preview Travel (www.previewtravel.com).** This online travel agency devotes itself to helping Web surfers plan and book leisure-time travel. Its site provides live access to the reservation systems of virtually all air carriers, hotel chains, and car rental companies. You can search for low fares or browse the library of travel-related information.
- **priceline.com (www.priceline.com).** At priceline.com, you name the price for an airplane ticket, and airlines can sell off seats that would otherwise go empty. Just tell priceline your destination, travel dates up to six months in advance, and how much you're willing to pay.
- **Travelocity (www.travelocity.com).** A full-service travel site with millions of members, Travelocity's streamlined interface provides information for tourists and business travelers and books air, car, and hotel reservations worldwide. The search engine will find the three lowest fares available, and fare comparisons for popular air routes are published several times a day.
- **TravelWeb (www.travelweb.com).** Originally a travel agents' tool for booking hotel rooms, this site is now accessible to anyone who uses the Internet. The site provides information about some 22,000 hotels worldwide, both independent and chain owned. For most of the hotels, you can book and cancel online. The site has recently begun offering airline reservations and a large library of maps, photos, and weather forecasts.

SUMMARY OF LEARNING GOALS

>lg 1　**What are physical distribution (logistics) and logistics management?**
Physical distribution, or logistics, is the movement of products from the producer to industrial users and consumers. Logistics management involves managing (1) the movement of raw materials, (2) the movement of materials and products within plants and warehouses, and (3) the movement of finished goods to intermediaries and buyers. Supply chain management helps increase the efficiency of logistics service by minimizing inventory and moving goods efficiently.

at Home Depot

Look back at the story about Home Depot at the beginning of the chapter. Without an efficient distribution system, Home Depot would be out of business. Keeping thousands of items in stock and available when the customer wants them is one key to Home Depot's success. Home Depot, like all retailers, must continue to innovate to stay one step ahead of the competition. Home Depot recently began offering professional installation on many items that it sells. A second innovation, called Expo Design Centers, is a one-stop shopping venue for major home renovations. The Centers feature industry-certified interior designers and project managers to handle each renovation. Like virtually all retailers, Home Depot will be affected by the Internet. For repair items and other convenience products, the Web should have little impact, but it will increase price competition for major appliances and other big ticket items.

>lg 2　**What are distribution channels and their functions?**
Distribution channels are the series of marketing entities through which goods and services pass on their way from producers to end users. Distribution systems focus on the physical transfer of goods and services and on their legal ownership at each stage of the distribution process. Channels (1) reduce the number of transactions, (2) ease the flow of goods, and (3) increase channel efficiency.

>lg 3　**How can channels be organized?**
A vertical marketing system is a planned, hierarchical organized distribution channel. There are three types of vertical marketing systems: corporate, administrative, and contractual. In a corporate system, one firm owns the entire channel. In an administrative system, a strong organization takes over as leader and sets channel policies. In a contractual distribution system, the independent firms coordinate their distribution activities by written contract. Forward integration occurs in a distribution channel when a manufacturer acquires a marketing intermediary closer to the customer, such as a retailer. Backward integration occurs when a wholesaler or retailer gains control over the production process.

>lg 4　**When would a marketer use exclusive, selective, or intensive distribution?**
The degree of intensity depends in part on the type of product being distributed. Exclusive distribution (one or two dealers in an area) is used when products are in high demand in the target market. Selective distribution has a limited number of dealers per area, but more than one or two. This form of distribution is used for consumer shopping goods, some specialty goods, and some industrial accessories. Intensive distribution occurs when the manufacturer sells its products in virtually every store willing to carry them. It is used mainly for consumer convenience goods.

>lg 5　**What is wholesaling, and what are the types of wholesalers?**
Wholesalers typically sell finished products to retailers and to other institutions, such as manufacturers, schools, and hospitals. They also provide a wide variety

KEY TERMS

administrative
  distribution system
  449
agents 445
backward
  integration 449
breaking bulk 448
brokers 445
cash and carry
  wholesaler 453
contractual
  distribution system
  450
corporate
  distribution system
  449
distribution centers
  460
distribution channel
  445
efficient consumer
  response (ECR)
  458
electronic data
  interchange (EDI)
  458
exclusive
  distribution 450
forward integration
  449
full-service
  merchant
  wholesalers 453
industrial
  distributors 446
intensive
  distribution 451
limited-service
  merchant
  wholesalers 453
logistics
  management 444
manufacturer 444
manufacturers'
  representatives
  (manufacturers'
  agents) 453
marketing
  intermediaries
  445
merchant
  wholesaler 453
physical distribution
  (logistics) 444
retailers 446
selective
  distribution 451
stocklift (buyback)
  462
supply chain
  management 444
vendor-managed
  inventory 445
vertical marketing
  system 449
wholesalers 446

of services, among them storing merchandise, financing inventory, breaking bulk, providing rapid delivery to retailers, and supplying market information. The three main types of wholesalers are merchant wholesalers, and agents and brokers. Merchant wholesalers buy from manufacturers and sell to other businesses. Full-service merchant wholesalers offer a complete array of services to their customers, who are retailers. Limited-service merchant wholesalers typically carry a limited line of fast-moving merchandise and offer few services to their customers. Agents and brokers are essentially independents who provide buying and selling services. They receive commissions according to their sales.

>lg 6   **What are the different kinds of retail operations?**
Some 30 million Americans are engaged in retailing. Retailing can be either in-store or nonstore. In-store retail operations include department stores, mass-merchandising shopping chains, specialty stores, discount stores, off-price retailers, factory outlets, and catalog showrooms. Nonstore retailing includes vending machines, direct sales, direct-response marketing, and Internet retailing (e-commerce).

>lg 7   **What are the components of a successful retailing strategy?**
Creating a retail strategy is important in all kinds of retailing and involves defining a target market, developing a product offering, creating an image and a promotional strategy, choosing a location, and setting prices. The most important factors in creating a store's atmosphere are employee type and density, merchandise type and density, fixture type and density, sound, and odors.

>lg 8   **What are the functions of physical distribution?**
The functions of physical distribution include choosing a warehouse location and type, setting up a materials-handling system, and choosing modes of transportation (air, highway, rail, water, or pipeline). Criteria for selecting a mode of transportation include cost, transit time, reliability, capability, accessibility, and traceability.

>lg 9   **What are the trends in distribution?**
The tactic of stocklifting, or buyback, is becoming increasingly popular among large manufacturers. It occurs when a company buys all of its competitor's stock from a retailer and replaces the inventory with its own merchandise. Physical distribution for services is becoming increasingly important because service providers must build good relationships with customers. This involves minimizing wait times, managing service capacity, and improving service delivery through new distribution channels.

It is estimated that by 2005 everyone in the developed world will have Internet access. Millions of consumers are now engaged in e-commerce as a result. Web shopping is safe, quick, and convenient. It enables consumers to compare product features and prices like never before. Consumers can use the Internet to shop all over the world.

PREPARING FOR TOMORROW'S WORKPLACE

1. Divide the class into two groups with one taking the "pro" position and the other the "con" position on the following issue: "The only thing marketing intermediaries really do is increase prices for consumers. It is always best to buy direct from the producer."
2. Divide the class into teams of four. Trace the channel for some familiar product. Each group should tell why they think the channel has evolved as it has and how it is likely to change.

3. Write a memo explaining how e-commerce has changed business already and how it will affect business in the future.

4. Go to the various Web sites in Exhibit 15-9 and find the cheapest fare for a flight from Boston to San Francisco.

5. You work for a small chain of department stores (six stores total) located within a single state. Write a memo to the president explaining how e-commerce may affect the chain's business.

6. Go to a successful, independent specialty store in your area that has been in business for quite a while. Interview the manager and try to determine how the store successfully competes with the national chains.

7. Discuss why innovation is so important in retailing today. Be sure to give examples.

WORKING THE NET

1. Visit *Industry Week*'s Web site at **www.industryweek.com**. Under archives, do a search using the search term "supply chain management." Choose an article from the results that describes how a company has used supply chain management to improve customer satisfaction, performance, or profitability. Give a brief presentation to your class on your findings.

2. What are some of the logistics problems facing firms that operate internationally? Visit the *Logistics* magazine Web site at **www.manufacturing.net/magazine/logistic** and see if you can find information about how firms manage global logistics.

3. Search for information on retail careers at the Mining Company's retail industry information site, **www. Retail industry.miningco.com**. What type of careers are available in retailing? What skills are needed? Does a career in retailing appeal to you? Why or why not?

4. Your boss has asked you to find the quickest and least expensive way to ship a 28-pound box of parts to a customer in La Mesa, California (zip code 92120) from the factory in Hastings, New York (zip code 10706). Use the search engine at **www.smartship.com** to find the best transportation firm for this task.

CREATIVE THINKING CASE

Fame Proves Fleeting for Planet Hollywood

Is it possible to be star-struck by a plate of Cap'n Crunch–coated, deep-fried chicken strips? Of course not. It was the investor–movie stars—Demi Moore, Bruce Willis, Whoopi Goldberg, Arnold Schwarzenegger, and others—who generated the huge buzz around Planet Hollywood International. The lines that immediately formed at Planet Hollywood's growing number of theme eateries made it the envy of the restaurant business.

And then all those people waiting in line sat down to eat. They ordered the chicken-strips appetizer, $6.95, savoring its glazed-doughnut-over-a-McNugget taste. They squinted into halogen spotlights aimed annoyingly on tables and watched oversized video screens showing the movie stars now so conspicuously absent from the restaurant. On the way out, they bought $18 T-shirts to remember the experience.

"Not a whole lot to it," concludes David Blake, a 42-year-old computer consultant from Richmond, Virginia, emerging from the Chicago Planet Hollywood one recent evening. "I wouldn't make a point of coming back." Adds Martha Padilla of her family's only visit here: "The food was bad."

So much for buzz. Instead of an instant empire, Planet Hollywood is shaping up as a heap of hype, a company with restaurants that don't generate repeat business and a lot of high-concept entertainment ideas that haven't taken off. Same store sales fell in 1996, 1997, and 1998.

Few celebrities, of course, want to hang out where they can easily be found by the "common folk." Yet that is precisely the premise that Planet Hollywood and its backers sought to advance. Seen any stars lately? "We're pretty sure we had one of the Spice Girls in tonight, but she wouldn't identify herself," confides a hostess at the Indianapolis Planet Hollywood. Morris the cat made a recent appearance in Chicago and donated a feeding dish to the restaurant's memorabilia collection. Truth is, stars go to hip, expensive places that most consumers in the Planet Hollywood target market have never heard of: Moomba, Spy, and Max in New York, according to *New York Daily News* gossip reporter Marcus Baram.

Critical Thinking Questions

1. Is Planet Hollywood following the marketing concept?
2. Could the Internet play a role in rejuvenating the chain?
3. Is the basic concept of Planet Hollywood fundamentally flawed?
4. There are Planet Hollywoods in 87 locations such as New York, Paris, and Las Vegas. There are also Planet Hollywoods in Gurnee Mills, Illinois, home of an outlet mall, and in the Mall of America, near Minneapolis. Comment on the firm's distribution strategy.

VIDEO CASE

The Internet and Burton Snowboards' Distribution System: Reaching Out to Newbies

The Internet is rapidly becoming an important element in the distribution system of many companies. Burton Snowboards (**www.burton.com/main.asp**), a manufacturer of snowboards and outerwear for snowboard riders, is no exception. Located in Burlington, Vermont, Burton Snowboards uses its Web site to promote the sport of snowboarding as well as to market its products to professionals and amateurs alike.

Part of Burton Snowboards' Web site caters to "newbies"—people who are new to the sport of snowboarding. Burton's Newbie Guide takes the novice through seven steps to a "great day on the hill." First, the new snowboarder decides what type of snowboard to ride. The newbie can choose from freestyle, freeride, and carving snowboards. Second, the newbie is asked about performance requirements. At the third step, the newbie is linked to the "hardgoods" page of Burton's online catalog and asked to select from a specific board series in the product line and to choose a board length in light of the rider's weight. Next, the new rider chooses a boot/binding combination—known as an interface—from three options: FreeSole, Soft SI, and Direct Drive. At the fifth step, the Newbie Guide asks the novice what type of clothing she or he would like to wear when snowboarding. The newbie is then linked to the "softgoods" or outerwear page of Burton's online catalog. At the sixth step, the newbie is asked to head to a local retailer or to an on-snow demonstration. A link to a list of dealer locations is provided, and a demo calendar is installed on the Web site for the fall and winter months. Finally, the newbie is asked to take a snowboarding lesson.

Selected retailers sell Burton Snowboards' products to newbies as well as to those with more snowboarding experience. The products are intended to appeal to the discriminating buyer regardless of experience or ability level. Burton's snowboards are premium products—"equipment that starts where many companies reach their 'high-end.'" Burton's describes its snowboards in terms of "the scoop story"—a take-off on ice cream parlor confections. The "single scoop" represents Burton's basic snowboard; still, the technology used in its design was provided by Burton's pro rider development team. The "double scoop" reduces weight while adding performance and versatility. The "triple scoop" offers an advanced, lightweight design that translates into improved riding for any ability level. The "quadruple scoop" provides "lightness, speed, comfort, convenience, and durability" for an unmatched level of rider performance. The "banana split" incorporates the latest technological innovations in snowboards to provide riders with "access to the geeky wizardry of . . . [Burton's] R&D lab."

Burton's also produces clothing to wear while snowboarding or in the lodge afterward. Emphasizing a layered approach for maximum comfort and warmth, Burton's produces a first layer, a thermal layer, a heater layer, and an outer layer of snowboarding outerwear. Burton's sells gloves, hats, and lodge clothing as well.

Although Burton Snowboards maintains distribution relationships with selected retailers, it has discovered that the Internet can be an important vehicle for developing customer traffic to those retailers.

Critical Thinking Questions

1. What function does Burton Snowboards' Web site serve in its distribution channel?

2. What does the newbie guide accomplish in terms of servicing Burton's distribution channel?

3. Do you think using the Internet to reach prospective customers is a wise business decision?

chapter sixteen

Using Integrated Marketing Communications to Promote Products

learning goals

>lg 1   What are the goals of promotional strategy?

>lg 2   What is the promotional mix, and what are its elements?

>lg 3   What are the types of advertising?

>lg 4   What are the advertising media, and how

>lg 6   What are the goals of sales promotion, and what are several types of sales promotion?

>lg 7   How does public relations fit into the promotional mix?

>lg 8   What factors affect the promotional mix?

>lg 9   What are three important trends in

Putting Dockers on Urban Networkers

Mo Clancy does not dress rap singers for a living. She has never met Puff Daddy and refrains from using words like "jiggy" in conversation. These disclaimers are worth mentioning up front because the folks at Levi Strauss have dreamed up a rather unusual job title for this tiny strawberry blonde: urban networker.

The position is a way for Levi's to boost its cool quotient for Dockers **(www.store.us.dockers.com/store/),** the khaki pants that don't swing, groove, or rock. "The image of Dockers isn't all that great," sighs Mo, who refers to them as "fat-man pants" in less guarded moments. Dockers, the leader in the men's khaki market, has decided to plow 65 percent of its ad budget into "urban networking" programs—a nod to the fact that future growth depends on stitching up a younger, hipper market.

So Mo trolls San Francisco's clubs, galleries—anyplace she can connect with trendsetters. "My job," she deadpans, "is about forming relationships with consumers and having the community think that we're okay." For example, Mo recently named 100 "visionaries" in the city, then sent free khakis to the hipsters, aged 25 to 34, on the list. Some were so amused that they actually started wearing the pants. When the Dockers Classically Independent Film Festival was held in June 1998, Mo helped select three of the directors whose works were screened.

At 29, Mo is part Valley Girl, part home-girl—something that's apparent as she ducks into her white BMW 325i. She's off to drop in on a few people on her "hot list," a database of poets, magazine editors, Webheads, and the like. "The hard part of this job is to take these really nebulous things I observe, and to try to make them work for our company," says Mo, speeding past dueling billboards for the Gap and Dockers. "But if you see something, like the way young people are beginning to connect with larger groups, you can portray that in marketing."[1]

Critical Thinking Questions

As you read this chapter, consider the following questions as they relate to Mo Clancy's work at Levi Strauss:

- Would you say that Mo Clancy's work is a form of promotion?
- What means can Levi use to promote Dockers?
- Can Dockers be sold over the Internet?

BUSINESS IN THE 21ST CENTURY

promotion

The attempt by marketers to inform, persuade, or remind consumers and industrial users to engage in the exchange process.

differential advantage

A set of unique features of a product that the target market perceives as important and better than the competition's features.

Very few goods or services can survive in the marketplace without good promotion. Marketers, such as those touting Levi's Dockers, promote their products to build consumer demand. **Promotion** is an attempt by marketers to inform, persuade, or remind consumers and industrial users to engage in the exchange process. Once the product has been created, promotion is often used to convince target customers that it has a **differential advantage** over the competition. A differential advantage is a set of unique features that the target market perceives as important and better than the competition's features. Such features may include high quality, fast delivery, low price, good service, and the like. Lexus, for example, is seen as having a quality differential advantage over other luxury cars. Therefore, promotion for Lexus stresses the quality of the vehicle.

This chapter presents the goals of promotion, the last element of the marketing mix, and explores the elements of the promotional mix. You will also learn about advertising and how personal selling and public relations fit into the promotional mix.

PROMOTIONAL GOALS

>lg 1

Most firms use some form of promotion. The meaning of the Latin root word is "to move forward." Hence actions that move a company toward its goals are promotional in nature. Because company goals vary widely, so do promotional strategies. The goal is to stimulate action. In a profit-oriented firm, the desired action is for the consumer to buy the promoted item. Mrs. Smith's, for instance, wants people to buy more frozen pies. Not-for-profit organizations seek a variety of actions with their promotions. They tell us not to litter, to buckle up, join the army, and attend the ballet.

Promotional goals include creating awareness, getting people to try products, providing information, retaining loyal customers, increasing the use of products, and identifying potential customers. Any promotional campaign may seek to achieve one or more of these goals:

Marketers promote their goods and services by creating advertisements that stimulate consumers to purchase them.

1. *Creating awareness.* All too often, firms go out of business because people don't know they exist or what they do. Small restaurants often have this problem. Simply putting up a sign and opening the door is rarely enough. Promotion through ads on local radio or television, coupons in local papers, fliers, and so forth can create awareness of a new business or product.

2. *Getting consumers to try products.* Promotion is almost always used to get people to try a new product or to get nonusers to try an existing product. Sometimes free samples are given away. Lever, for instance, mailed over 2 million free samples of its Lever 2000 soap to target households. Coupons and trial-size containers of products are also common tactics used to

tempt people to try a product. Pepsi spent $100 million trying to get consumers to try Pepsi One when it was introduced.[2]

3. *Providing information.* Informative promotion is more common in the early stages of the product life cycle. An informative promotion may explain what ingredients (like fiber) will do for your health, tell you why the product is better (high-definition television versus regular television), inform you of a new low price, or explain where the item may be bought.

Star-Kist uses a variety of promotional methods to sell tuna. Get a peek at some of them at the company's consumer Web site

www.starkist.com

People typically will not buy a product or support a not-for-profit organization until they know what it will do and how it may benefit them. Thus, an informative ad may change a need into a want or stimulate interest in a product. Consumer watchdogs and social critics applaud the informative function of promotion because it helps consumers make more intelligent purchase decisions. Star-Kist, for instance, lets customers know that its tuna is caught in dolphin-safe nets.

4. *Keeping loyal customers.* Promotion is also used to keep people from switching brands. Slogans such as Campbell's "Soups are mmmmm good" and American Airlines' "Something special in the air" remind consumers about the brand. Marketers also remind users that the brand is better than the competition. Dodge Ram trucks claim that they have superior safety features. For years, Pepsi has claimed it has the taste that consumers prefer. Continental Airlines brags of its improvement in on-time ratings. Such advertising reminds customers about the quality of the product.

Firms can also help keep customers loyal by telling them when a product or service is improved. Blockbuster guarantees that the hit movie you want to rent is in stock or it's free.

5. *Increasing the amount and frequency of use.* Promotion is often used to get people to use more of a product and to use it more often. When smoking was banned on domestic flights, Wrigley's began promoting its chewing gum as a good alternative to smoking. The most popular promotion to increase the use of a product may be frequent flyer programs. American Airlines, the pioneer, has enrolled over five million frequent flyers. Hotel chains like Marriott and Hyatt now have frequent user programs.

6. *Identifying target customers.* Promotion helps find customers. One way to do this is to list a Web site. For instance, the *Wall Street Journal* and *Business Week* include Web addresses for more information on computer systems, corporate jets, color copiers, and other types of business equipment, to help target those who are truly interested. Charles Schwab ads trumpet "Learn more about investing online; go to **www.schwab.com**." A full-page ad in the *Wall Street Journal* for Compaq notebook computers invites potential customers to visit **www.compaq.com/whoa**, or call 1-800-AT-COMPAQ.

The Promotional Mix

>lg 2

promotional mix
The combination of advertising, personal selling, sales promotion, and public relations used to promote a product.

The combination of advertising, personal selling, sales promotion, and public relations used to promote a product is called the **promotional mix.** Each firm creates a unique mix for each product. But the goal is always to deliver the firm's message efficiently and effectively to the target audience. These are the elements of the promotional mix:

- *Advertising.* Any paid form of nonpersonal promotion by an identified sponsor.
- *Personal selling.* A face-to-face presentation to a prospective buyer.

- *Sales promotion.* Marketing activities (other than personal selling, advertising, and public relations) that stimulate consumer buying, including coupons and samples, displays, shows and exhibitions, demonstrations, and other types of selling efforts.
- *Public relations.* The linking of organizational goals with key aspects of the public interest and the development of programs designed to earn public understanding and acceptance.

The sections that follow examine the elements of the promotional mix in more detail.

concept check

- List and discuss the goals of promotion.
- What is the promotional mix?

ADVERTISING BUILDS BRAND RECOGNITION

advertising

Any paid form of nonpersonal presentation by an identified sponsor.

Most Americans are bombarded daily with advertisements to buy things. **Advertising** is any paid form of nonpersonal presentation by an identified sponsor. It may appear on television or radio; in newspapers, magazines, books, or direct mail; or on billboards or transit cards.

The money that big corporations spend on advertising is mind-boggling. Total advertising expenses in this country are estimated at more than $190 billion a year. The largest percentage of the money goes to network television, followed closely by newspapers.[3] Nearly 12¢ of every dollar spent on perfume and cosmetics goes to advertising, and 15¢ out of every dollar spent on dolls and stuffed toys goes for advertising.[4] Even the missile and space industry spends nearly 2¢ of every sales dollar on ads. Spending by companies such as Procter & Gamble, Kraft-General Foods, Philip Morris, and General Motors averages more than $100,000 an hour, 24 hours a day; much of it is used in the prime evening hours on network television.

Billboard advertisements help The Gap build recognition for its brand of jeans.

Super Bowl games cost about $1.5 million for a 30-second commercial. A "Monday Night Football" commercial costs about $430,000 for 30 seconds, but for that $430,000 the advertiser gets a chance to contact hard-to-reach men between the ages of 18 and 49. A typical Monday night spot might bring a maker of cars, beer, soft drinks, fast foods, or other products an 11.5 percent "male" rating, meaning that about 11.5 percent of the television-owning households with men in them watch the ads. That's about 11.3 million men.[5]

In this section, you will learn about the different types of advertising, the strengths and weaknesses of advertising media, the functions of an advertising agency, and how advertising is regulated.

>lg 3

product advertising

Advertising that features a specific good or service.

comparative advertising

Advertising that compares the company's product with competing, named products.

Types of Advertising

The form of advertising most people know is **product advertising,** which features a specific good or service. It can take many different forms. One special form is **comparative advertising,** in which the company's product is compared with competing, named products. Coca-Cola and Pepsi often use comparative advertising. MCI claims that the only major difference between it and AT&T is that AT&T is more expensive. Another special form is **reminder advertising,** which is used to keep the product name in the public's mind. It is most often used during the maturity stage of the product life cycle. Reminder advertising assumes that the target market has already been persuaded of the product's

THE FIREARMS ADVERTISING CHALLENGE

Prompted by stagnant sales and a wave of municipal lawsuits, the gun industry launched an advertising campaign "to publicize how safe firearms are" just a few weeks before the deadly shootings at Columbine High School in Littleton, Colorado. The National Shooting Sports Foundation, an industry trade group that represents 1,500 gun manufacturers, distributors, and retailers, initiated a three-year advertising campaign during the first week of April 1999. Expected to cost $1 million in its first year, the ad campaign is running in magazines such as the *Atlantic Monthly,* the *Economist,* and the *New York Times Book Review.*

Many urban Americans associate firearms with crime and violence rather than with hunting and skeet shooting. Doug Painter, executive director of the National Shooting Sports Foundation, attributes this negative image of firearms to the public's lack of familiarity with shooting sports.

The ad campaign focuses on increasing public familiarity with shooting sports. Some of the ads point out that shooting sports are found in 21 Olympic events. Another ad shows a bull's eye and links firing a gun with competition and achievement. The ad says, "Since the first cave man threw a stone, the challenge of hitting a target has been part of human nature. Target sports require skill." A photo of a gun appears nearby.

Critical Thinking Questions

1. What type of advertising is being used to promote the sale of firearms? Why does the National Shooting Sports Foundation find it necessary to use this form of advertising?
2. Is it ethical for a business to promote a product—in this instance, guns—that can be used for deadly purposes? Explain your answer.
3. What other types of businesses face the ethical challenge of promoting potentially lethal products?

reminder advertising
Advertising that is used to keep a product's name in the public's mind.

institutional advertising
Advertising that creates a positive picture of a company and its ideals, services, and roles in the community.

advocacy advertising
Advertising that takes a stand on a social or economic issue; also called *grassroots lobbying.*

advertising media
The channels through which advertising is carried to prospective customers; includes newspapers, magazines, radio, television, outdoor advertising, direct mail, and the Internet.

merits and just needs a memory boost. Miller beer, V-8 vegetable juice, and the FTD florist association use reminder promotion.

In addition to product advertising, many companies use **institutional advertising**. This type of advertising creates a positive picture of a company and its ideals, services, and roles in the community. Instead of trying to sell specific products, it builds a desired image and goodwill for the company. Some institutional advertising supports product advertising that targets consumers. Other institutional advertising is aimed at stockholders or the public. **Advocacy advertising** takes a stand on a social or economic issue. It is sometimes called *grassroots lobbying.* Energy companies often use this type of advertising to influence public opinion about regulation of their industry.

Choosing Advertising Media

The channels through which advertising is carried to prospective customers are the **advertising media.** Both product and institutional ads appear in all the major advertising media: newspapers, magazines, radio, television, outdoor advertising, direct mail, and the Internet. Exhibit 16-1 summarizes the advantages and disadvantages of these media. Each company

> e x h i b i t   1 6 - 1 <

Strengths and Weaknesses of Major Media

Medium	Strengths	Weaknesses
Newspapers	Geographic selectivity and flexibility Short-term advertiser commitments News value and immediacy Constant readership High individual market coverage Low cost	Little demographic selectivity Limited color facilities Short-lived
Magazines	Good reproduction, especially color Message permanence Demographic selectivity (can reach affluent audience) Regionality Local-market selectivity Special-interest possibilities Relatively long advertising life	Long-term advertiser commitments Slow audience buildup Limited demonstration capacities Lack of urgency Long lead time for ad placement May be expensive for national coverage
Radio	Low and negotiable costs High frequency Immediacy of message Relatively little seasonal change in audience Highly portable Short scheduling notice Short-term advertiser commitments Entertainment carryover	No visuals Advertising message short-lived Background sound Commercial clutter (a large number of ads in a short time)
Television	Widely diversified audience Creative visual and audio opportunities for demonstration Immediacy of message Entertainment carryover	High cost Limited demographic selectivity Advertising message short-lived Consumer skepticism about advertising claims
Network	Association with programming prestige	Long-term advertiser commitments
Local	Geographic selectivity Associated with programs of local origin and appeal Short lead time	Narrow audience on independent stations High cost for broad geographic coverage
Outdoor advertising	Repetition possibilities Moderate cost Flexibility	Short messages Lack of demographic selectivity Many distractions when observing the message
Direct mail	Very efficient with good mailing list Can be personalized by computer Can reach very specific demographic market Lengthy message with photos and testimony	Very costly with poor mailing list May never be opened
Internet	Inexpensive global coverage Available at any time Interactive personalized message via e-mail	Not everyone has access Difficult to measure ad effectiveness

must decide which media are best for its products. Two of the main factors in making that choice are the cost of the medium and the audience reached by it.

The Internet is the hot new medium for the new millennium. Some are concerned that the Web will soon be full of clutter, like network television, as explained in the Applying Technology box.

THE WEB IS NOT NETWORK TV

Will the rush to advertise on the Web turn it into bad TV? That's the key question facing the Internet as it catapults to center stage of the consumer marketplace—both as a new ad medium and as a vehicle to sell goods and services.

At its best, the Web is a service medium, not simply a mass-marketing medium. The adage "build it and they will come" does not apply here. Consumers want—and will eventually demand—more unique services, accessible information, easy-to-use features, and more intuitive navigation.

Consumers "sell" their attention and loyalty to the sites they visit. In exchange, they expect meaningful content and helpful service. Online ads disrupt this "agreement," and more consumers are starting to interpret ads as an intrusion. Though Internet ads have their place—in online magazines and similar media sites—they are not the right tool for companies looking to mass-market consumer goods.

Before attempting to extend brands and business strategies on the Web, marketers need to understand its advantages and appreciate its limitations. Most marketers have yet to accomplish this with any strong degree of success. They rush to establish a Web presence or simply invest in banner ads without well-thought-out strategic marketing objectives that capitalize on the

Web's one-to-one communication capabilities. As a result, many sites today lack a unique brand voice and offer no harmony of messages, imagery, and identity. They are awash in clutter and gratuitous nonsense and offer no real value or positive "experience" to users.

Kodak offers an example of a site that creates a positive user experience. "Kodak Professional" (**www.kodak.com/go/professional**) is an online community that targets photography and print-imaging professionals by empowering them to communicate with one another using Kodak as a facilitator. The strength of this site, which attracted more than 400,000 visitors in its second month, lies in such value-added features as behind-the-scenes stories, software upgrades for scanners and cameras, international copyright information, and a real-time sunrise/sunset calculator.

Critical Thinking Questions

1. Go to the Web and find examples of sites and ads that create a very positive experience. Also find some that don't. Print examples of both and bring them to class for discussion.
2. What do you see as the major advantages of Internet advertising?

---

cost per thousand (CPM)

Cost per thousand contacts is a term used in expressing advertising costs; refers to the cost of reaching 1,000 members of the target market.

reach

The number of different target consumers who are exposed to a commercial at least once during a specific period, usually four weeks.

frequency

The number of times an individual is exposed to an advertising message.

Advertising Costs and Market Penetration   Cost per contact is the cost of reaching one member of the target market. Naturally, as the size of the audience increases, so does the total cost. Cost per contact enables an advertiser to compare media vehicles, such as television versus radio, or magazine versus newspaper, or, more specifically, *Newsweek* versus *Time*. An advertiser debating whether to spend local advertising dollars for TV spots or radio spots could consider the cost per contact of each. The advertiser might then pick the vehicle with the lowest cost per contact to maximize advertising punch for the money spent. Often costs are expressed on a **cost per thousand** (**CPM**) contacts basis.

Reach is the number of different target consumers who are exposed to a commercial at least once during a specific period, usually four weeks. Media plans for product introductions and attempts at increasing brand awareness usually emphasize reach. For example, an advertiser might try to reach 70 percent of the target audience during the first three months of the campaign. Because the typical ad is short-lived and often only a small portion of an ad may be perceived at one time, advertisers repeat their ads so consumers will remember the message. **Frequency** is the number of times an individual is exposed to a message. Average frequency is used by advertisers to measure the intensity of a specific medium's coverage.

Media selection is also a matter of matching the advertising medium with the product's target market. If marketers are trying to reach teenage females, they might select *Seventeen* magazine. If they are trying to reach consumers over 50 years old, they may choose *Modern Maturity.* A medium's ability to reach a precisely defined market is its **audience selectivity.** Some media vehicles, like general newspapers and network television, appeal to a wide cross section of the population. Others—such as *Brides, Popular Mechanic, Architectural Digest,* MTV, ESPN, and Christian radio stations—appeal to very specific groups.

audience selectivity
An advertising medium's ability to reach a precisely defined market.

How can you find the right magazine in which to advertise? The MediaFinder Web site at **www.mediafinder.com** has a searchable database of thousands of magazines.

Advertising Agencies

advertising agencies
Companies that help create ads and place them in the proper media.

Advertising agencies are companies that help create ads and place them in the proper media. Many firms rely on agencies to both create and monitor their ad campaigns.

Full-service advertising agencies offer the five services shown in Exhibit 16-2. Members of the creative services group develop promotional themes and mes-

> e x h i b i t   1 6 - 2 <

Functions of an Advertising Agency

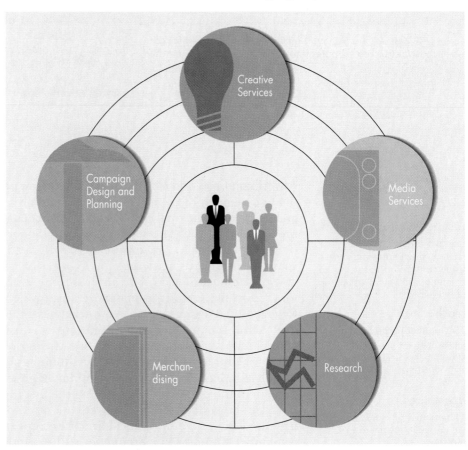

sages, write copy, design layouts, take photos, and draw illustrations. The media services group selects the media mix and schedules advertising. Researchers may conduct market research studies for clients or help develop new products or gauge the firm's or product's image. Merchandising advice may include developing contests and brochures for the sales force. Campaign design and planning are often wholly in the hands of the agency, although some firms prefer to do much of the work in-house, relying on the agency only for scheduling media and evaluating the campaign.

Advertising Regulation

Besides planning advertising campaigns and scheduling media, advertising agencies must also cope with the growing role and scope of advertising regulation.

National Advertising Division (NAD)

A subdivision of the Council of Better Business Bureaus that investigates complaints about advertising from consumers and other advertisers.

National Advertising Review Board (NARB)

A board that hears appeals from the decisions of the National Advertising Division (NAD) of the Council of Better Business Bureaus or resolves issues if the NAD is deadlocked.

Self-Regulation in the Advertising Industry   To avoid increasing government regulation, in 1971 advertising industry leaders set up procedures for self-regulation. The **National Advertising Division (NAD)** of the Council of Better Business Bureaus is a complaint bureau for consumers and advertisers. The **National Advertising Review Board (NARB)** is an appeals board that may be used if the NAD is deadlocked on an issue or if the losing party wishes to appeal.

After receiving a complaint about an advertisement, the NAD investigates. It collects and evaluates information and then decides whether the ad's claims are substantiated. If the ad is deemed unsatisfactory, the NAD negotiates with the advertiser to obtain a change in the ad or its discontinuation. Star-Kist, for example, recently complained that Bumblebee's ads claimed that its tuna was preferred 2 to 1. The NAD ruled that Bumblebee's research was not adequate to support the claim. Bumblebee agreed to drop the ads.

See which companies get the most complaints about their advertising at the Better Business Bureau's Web site: **www.bbb.org/advertising/ index.html**

Advertising managers want to avoid having to drop or modify advertisements or commercials. Not only does the controversy create ill will for the company, but the ad must be remade, which can be expensive. In addition, if a substitute commercial is unavailable, the timing of the campaign may be destroyed.

Federal Trade Commission (FTC)

An agency of the U.S. government that works to prevent deception and misrepresentation in advertising.

Federal Regulation of Advertising   When self-regulation doesn't work, in the United States the **Federal Trade Commission (FTC)** steps in. The FTC's main concern is with deception and misrepresentation in advertising. The FTC defines deception as "a representation, omission, or practice that is likely to mislead the consumer acting reasonably in the circumstances, to the consumer's detriment." The courts have ruled that deception can include what the consumer infers from the advertisement, as well as what is literally said.

Want to avoid legal problems with your ad campaign? Find detailed information about advertising law and FTC regulations at **www.advertisinglaw.com**

The FTC's traditional remedy for deceptive advertising is a cease-and-desist order barring use of the advertising claims found to be false or deceptive. In some cases, the FTC also requires a

concept check

- Define five different types of advertising, and give examples.
- Indicate some of the strengths and weaknesses of the seven main advertising media.
- Describe the services offered by advertising agencies.
- Name the groups that regulate advertising, and explain what remedies they may prescribe.

corrective advertising
An advertisement run to correct false impressions left by previous ads.

corrective message. **Corrective advertising** is an advertisement run to correct the false impressions left by previous ads. For example, after investigating several diet-program companies for false and deceptive advertising, the FTC required them to revise their weight-loss claims so that they accurately reflected the programs' success in helping customers keep off the weight they lose.

THE IMPORTANCE OF PERSONAL SELLING

personal selling
A face-to-face sales presentation to a prospective customer.

Advertising acquaints potential customers with a product and thereby makes personal selling easier. **Personal selling** is a face-to-face sales presentation to a prospective customer. Sales jobs range from salesclerks at clothing stores to engineers with MBAs who design large, complex systems for manufacturers. About 6.5 million people are engaged in personal selling in the United States. Slightly over 45 percent of them are women. The number of people who earn a living from sales is huge compared, for instance, with the half a million workers employed in the advertising industry.

Personal selling offers several advantages over other forms of promotion:

- Personal selling provides a detailed explanation or demonstration of the product. This capability is especially desirable for complex or new goods and services.
- The sales message can be varied according to the motivations and interests of each prospective customer. Moreover, when the prospect has questions or raises objections, the salesperson is there to provide explanations. In contrast, advertising and sales promotion can respond only to the objections the copywriter thinks are important to customers.
- Personal selling can be directed only to qualified prospects. Other forms of promotion include some unavoidable waste because many people in the audience are not prospective customers.
- Personal selling costs can be controlled by adjusting the size of the sales force (and resulting expenses) in one-person increments. In contrast, advertising and sales promotion must often be purchased in fairly large amounts.
- Perhaps the most important advantage is that personal selling is considerably more effective than other forms of promotion in obtaining a sale and gaining a satisfied customer.[6]

The Professional Salesperson

Companies that recruit college graduates to enter the field of selling want to develop professional salespeople. A professional salesperson has two main qualities: complete product knowledge and creativity. The professional knows the product line from A to Z and understands what each item can and cannot do. He or she also understands how to apply the product to meet customers' needs. For instance, a sales rep may find a way to install conveyor equipment that will lower the cost of moving products in the prospective customer's plant.

Professional salespeople develop long-term relationships with their clients. Most salespeople rely on repeat business, which depends, of course, on trust and honesty. Most professional selling is not high pressured. Instead, the sales process is more a matter of one professional interacting with another, such as a salesperson working with a purchasing agent. Professional salespeople are largely sources of information and creative problem solvers. They cannot bully a professional buyer into making an unwanted purchase.

Sales Positions

College graduates have many opportunities in sales. Among them are the following:

- *Selling to wholesalers and retailers.* When a firm buys products for resale, its main concerns are buying the right product and getting it promptly. Often retailers expect the manufacturer's salesperson to stock the merchandise on the shelves and to set up promotional materials approved by the store. Sometimes these sales jobs are entry-level training positions that can lead to better opportunities.

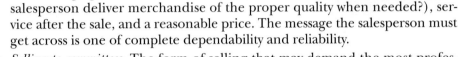

- *Selling to purchasing agents.* Purchasing agents are found in government agencies, manufacturing firms, and institutions (hospitals and schools). Purchasing agents look for credibility (Can the salesperson deliver merchandise of the proper quality when needed?), service after the sale, and a reasonable price. The message the salesperson must get across is one of complete dependability and reliability.
- *Selling to committees.* The form of selling that may demand the most professionalism and creativity is selling to a buying committee. When a purchase decision is so important that it will have a big impact on the buyer's long-run success, it is usually made by a committee. When United Airlines decides to order 100 new airplanes, for instance, a committee decides what type of plane to buy. A committee sales presentation requires careful analysis of the potential buyer's needs. It commonly includes an audiovisual display.

The Selling Process

>lg 5

Selling is a process that can be learned. Scholars have spelled out the steps of the selling process, shown in Exhibit 16-3, and professional salespeople use them all the time. These steps are as follows:

sales prospects
The companies and people who are most likely to buy a seller's offerings.

prospecting
The process of looking for sales prospects.

1. *Prospecting and qualifying.* To start the process, the salesperson looks for **sales prospects,** those companies and people who are most likely to buy the seller's offerings. This activity is called **prospecting.** Because there are no sure-fire ways to find prospects, most salespeople try many methods.

   For many companies, the inquiries generated by advertising and promotion are the most likely source of prospects. Inquiries are also known as sales leads. Leads usually come in the form of letters, cards, or telephone calls. Some companies supply salespeople with prospect lists compiled from external sources, such as Chamber of Commerce directories, newspapers, public records, club membership lists, Internet inquiries, and professional or trade publication subscription lists. Meetings, such as professional conventions and trade shows, are another good source of leads. Sales representatives attend such meetings to display and demonstrate their company's products and to answer the questions of those attending. The firm's files and records can be another source of prospects. Correspondence with buyers can be helpful. Records in the service department can identify people who already own equipment and might be prospects for new models. Finally, friends and acquaintances of salespeople can often supply leads.

   One rule of thumb is that not all prospects are "real." Just because someone has been referred or has made an inquiry does not mean that the person is a genuine prospect. Salespeople can avoid wasting time and increase their

> e x h i b i t   1 6 - 3 <

Steps in Making a Successful Sale

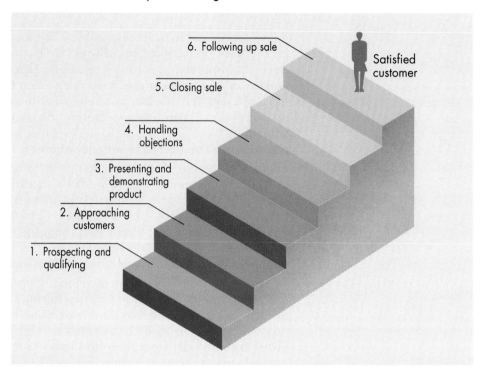

qualifying questions

Inquiries used by salespeople to separate prospects from those who do not have the potential to buy.

productivity by qualifying all prospects. **Qualifying questions** are used to separate prospects from those who do not have the potential to buy. The following three questions help determine who is a real prospect and who is not: (1) Does the prospect have a need for our product? (2) Can the prospect make the buying decision? (3) Can the prospect afford our product?

2. *Approaching customers.* After identifying a prospect, the salesperson explains the reason for wanting an appointment and sets a specific date and hour. At the same time, the salesperson tries to build interest in the coming meeting. One good way to do this is to impart an interesting or important piece of information—for instance, "I think my product can cut your shipping and delivery time by two days."

3. *Presenting and demonstrating the product.* The presentation and demonstration can be fully automated, completely unstructured, or somewhere in between. In a fully automated presentation, the salesperson shows a movie, slides, or a laptop and data projector and then answers questions and takes any orders. A completely unstructured presentation has no set format. It may be a casual conversation, with the salesperson presenting product benefits that might interest the potential buyer.

4. *Handling objections.* Almost every sales presentation, structured or unstructured, meets with some objection. Rarely does a customer say "I'll buy it" without asking questions or voicing concerns. The professional salesperson tries to anticipate objections so they can be countered quickly and with assurance. Read what Mack Jarvis, sales vice-president, Oracle Corporation, has to say about handling objections:

> Selling is a lot like seduction. That's especially true in the computer industry—where often you're selling a vision rather than a product. It requires

passion and emotion. When I'm in the selling zone, every cell in my body is working toward the same goal. I give myself instant feedback: If I'm emotionally drained after trying to make a sale, I know that I've done a good job.

When I prepare for a sales presentation, I try to think like my client *and* like my competitor. I try to pinpoint every objection that either of them could make to my presentation. I write these objections down, and then I figure out a way to respond to each one in three lines or less. I've given these "scripts" to sales reps, who then used them in their presentations. It's staggering how even the most boring sales rep can become a great salesperson simply by learning to convey a few simple points. If you can move a customer so that he or she can't argue against your point, then you've won.[7]

5. *Closing the sale.* After all the objections have been dealt with, it's time to close the sale. Even old pros sometimes find this part of the sales process awkward. Perhaps the easiest way to close a sale is to ask for it: "Ms. Jones, may I write up your order?" Another technique is to act as though the deal has been concluded: "Mr. Bateson, we'll have this equipment in and working for you in two weeks." If Mr. Bateson doesn't object, the salesperson can assume that the sale has been made.

6. *Following up on the sale.* The salesperson's job isn't over when the sale is made. In fact, the sale is just the start. The salesperson must write up the order properly and turn it in promptly. Often this part of the job is easy. But an order for a complex piece of industrial equipment may be a 100 pages of detail. Each detail must be carefully checked to ensure that the equipment is exactly what was ordered.

After the product is delivered to the customer, the salesperson must make a routine visit to see that the customer is satisfied. This follow-up call may also be a chance to make another sale. But even if it isn't, it will build goodwill for the salesperson's company and may bring future business. Repeat sales over many years are the goal of professional salespeople.

concept check

- What are the advantages of personal selling?
- Describe the professional salesperson.
- Explain the selling process.

SALES PROMOTION

sales promotions

Marketing events or sales efforts—not including advertising, personal selling, and public relations—that stimulate buying.

Sales promotion helps make personal selling and advertising more effective. **Sales promotions** are marketing events or sales efforts—not including advertising, personal selling, and public relations—that stimulate buying. Today, sales promotion is an $80 billion industry and growing. Couponing alone is a $6 billion industry with over 275 billion coupons being distributed annually.[8] Sales promotion is usually targeted toward either of two distinctly different markets. Consumer sales promotion is targeted to the ultimate consumer market. Trade sales promotion is directed to members of the marketing channel, such as wholesalers and retailers.

Immediate purchase is the goal of sales promotion, regardless of the form it takes. Therefore, it makes sense when planning a sales promotion campaign to target customers according to their general behavior. For instance, is the consumer loyal to your product or to your competitor's? Does the consumer switch brands readily in favor of the best deal? Does the consumer buy only the least expensive product, no matter what? Does the consumer buy any products in your category at all?

The objectives of a promotion depend on the general behavior of target consumers as described in Exhibit 16-4. For example, marketers who are targeting

> e x h i b i t   1 6 - 4 <

> e x h i b i t   1 6 - 4 <

Types of Consumers and Sales Promotion Goals

Type of Behavior	Desired Results	Sales Promotion Examples
Loyal customers: People who buy your product most or all of the time	Reinforce behavior, increase consumption, change purchase timing	• Loyalty marketing programs, such as frequent-buyer cards or frequent-shopper clubs
Competitor's customers: People who buy a competitor's product most or all of the time	Break loyalty, persuade to switch to your brand	• Bonus packs that give loyal consumers an incentive to stock up or premiums offered in return for proof-of-purchase
Brand switchers: People who buy a variety of products in the category	Persuade to buy your brand more often	• Sampling to introduce your product's superior qualities compared to their brand
Price buyers: People who consistently buy the least expensive brand	Appeal with low prices or supply added value that makes price less important	• Sweepstakes, contests, or premiums that create interest in the product
		• Any promotion that lowers the price of the product, such as coupons, cents-off packages, and bonus packs
		• Trade deals that help make the product more readily available than competing products
		• Coupons, cents-off packages, refunds, or trade deals that reduce the price of the brand to match that of the brand that would have been purchased

> e x h i b i t   1 6 - 5 <

Sign Language and Sample Displays in Sales Promotion

- *Aisle interrupter:* A cardboard sign that juts into the middle of the aisle
- *Dangler:* A sign hanging down from a shelf that sways when shoppers pass
- *Dump bin:* A box-shaped display holding products loosely dumped inside
- *Glorifier:* A small plastic "stage" that elevates one product above the rest
- *Wobbler:* A jiggling sign
- *Lipstick board:* A plastic surface on which messages are written with crayons
- *Necker:* A coupon hanging on a bottle neck
- *Y.E.S. unit:* "Your Extra Salesperson," a fact sheet that pulls down like a shade

SOURCE: Yumiko Ono, "Wobblers and Sidekicks Clutter Stores, Irk Retailers," *Wall Street Journal* (September 8, 1998), pp. B1, B4.

loyal users of their product don't want to change behavior. Instead, they want to reinforce existing behavior or increase product usage. Frequent-buyer programs that reward consumers for repeat purchases can be effective in strengthening brand loyalty. Other types of promotions are more effective with customers prone to brand switching or with those who are loyal to a competitor's product. Cents-off coupons, free samples, or an eye-catching display in a store will often entice shoppers to try a different brand. Store signs and displays have been given some catchy names by the sales promotion industry. Several are listed in Exhibit 16-5 on p. 484.

Sales promotion offers many opportunities for entrepreneurs. Entrepreneurs design contests and sweepstakes, fabricate displays, manufacture premiums, and deliver free samples, among other things. One successful entrepreneurial venture started when three people got together to plan their 22nd high school reunion. They created a company called Floorgraphics, Inc., which is featured in the Focusing on Small Business box.

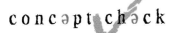

concept check

- How does sales promotion differ from advertising?
- Describe several types of sales promotion.

> focusing on small business <

A NEW FLOOR SHOW IN TOWN

In case you missed the billboard, television commercial, radio spot, or newspaper ad about Pepsi, just look down at the floor of your local Kmart. In front of the 12-packs of Pepsi, Diet Pepsi, and Mountain Dew lies a flat, 2-by-3-foot floor decal asking the question, "Thirsty?" next to the image of a Pepsi can.

This is only one of many floor ads that a company in Cherry Hill, New Jersey, has placed at the feet of consumers. Floorgraphics, Inc. designs ads and leases advertising floor space in stores—such as all 2,200 Kmarts nationally—to Pepsi and other companies. The concept of putting ads on the floor was developed by Floorgraphics president and chairman Fred Potok, who had previously worked on graphics and decals for buses, trucks, and vans. "It takes advantage of people's natural habits of looking down," Potok says. "This becomes a billboard on the floor."

Floorgraphics pays retailers a fee—the company would not disclose the amount—to use their floor space, usually for three to five years. Then the company talks with its customers about what type of ad they would like and sometimes designs it. The ad is always a digitally photographed decal that sticks to the floor. Floor ads remind consumers of brand names as they make their buying decisions.

Critical Thinking Questions

1. Do you think that floor ads will stimulate sales?
2. What other forms of sales promotion could a retailer use to increase sales?

PUBLIC RELATIONS HELPS BUILD GOODWILL

>lg 7

public relations

Any communication or activity designed to win goodwill or prestige for a company or person.

publicity

Information about a company or product that appears in the news media and is not directly paid for by the company.

Like sales promotion, public relations can be a vital part of the promotional mix. **Public relations** is any communication or activity designed to win goodwill or prestige for a company or person. Its main form is **publicity,** information about a company or product that appears in the news media and is not directly paid for by the company. Publicity can be good or bad. Children dying from eating tainted Jack-in-the-Box hamburgers is an example of negative publicity.

Naturally, firms' public relations departments try to create as much good publicity as possible. They furnish company speakers for business and civic clubs, write speeches for corporate officers, and encourage employees to take active roles in such civic groups as the United Way and the Chamber of Commerce. The main tool of the public relations department is the *press release*, a formal announcement of some newsworthy event connected with the company, such as the start of a new program, the introduction of a new product, or the opening of a new plant. Public relations departments may perform any or all of the functions described in Exhibit 16-6.

HOT links

Learn how to write a press release at

www.edgeonline.com/bbuilder/PRESREL/(PRESSREL.stml

New Product Publicity

Publicity is instrumental in introducing new products and services. Publicity can help advertisers explain what's different about their new product by prompting free news stories or positive word-of-mouth about it. During the introductory period, an especially innovative new product often needs more exposure than conventional, paid advertising affords. Public relations professionals write press releases or develop videos in an effort to generate news about their new product. They also jockey for exposure of their product or service at major events, on popular television and news shows, or in the hands of influential people.

concept check

- What are the functions of a public relations department?
- Explain the concept of event sponsorship.

> e x h i b i t   1 6 - 6 <

The Functions of a Public Relations Department

Public Relations Function	Description
Press relations	Placing positive, newsworthy information in the news media to attract attention to a product, a service, or a person associated with the firm or institution
Product publicity	Publicizing specific products or services
Corporate communication	Creating internal and external messages to promote a positive image of the firm or institution
Public affairs	Building and maintaining national or local community relations
Lobbying	Influencing legislators and government officials to promote or defeat legislation and regulation
Employee and investor relations	Maintaining positive relationships with employees, shareholders, and others in the financial community
Crisis management	Responding to unfavorable publicity or a negative event

By sponsoring sporting events like the Women's World Cup Soccer championship, McDonald's, Fuji Film, and other marketers increase their brand awareness and enhance their corporate image.

Event Sponsorship

Public relations managers may sponsor events or community activities that are sufficiently newsworthy to achieve press coverage; at the same time, these events also reinforce brand identification. Sporting, music, and arts activities remain the most popular choices of event sponsors. For example, almost all of the major college football bowls are sponsored by a product such as the Tostitos Fiesta Bowl, the FedEx Orange Bowl, and the Nokia Sugar Bowl. Many sponsors are also turning to more specialized events that have tie-ins with schools, charities, and other community service organizations.

FACTORS THAT AFFECT THE PROMOTIONAL MIX

Promotional mixes vary a great deal from product to product and from one industry to the next. Advertising and personal selling are usually a firm's main promotional tools. They are supported by sales promotion. Public relations helps develop a positive image for the organization and its products. The specific promotional mix depends on the nature of the product, market characteristics, available funds, and whether a push or a pull strategy is used.

The Nature of the Product

Selling toothpaste differs greatly from selling overhead industrial cranes. Personal selling is most important in marketing industrial products and least important in marketing consumer nondurables (consumer products that get used up). Broadcast advertising is used heavily in promoting consumer products, especially food and other nondurables. Print media are used for all types of consumer products. Industrial products may be advertised through special trade magazines. Sales promotion, branding, and packaging are roughly twice as important (in terms of percentage of the promotional budget) for consumer products as for industrial products.

Market Characteristics

When potential customers are widely scattered, buyers are highly informed, and many of the buyers are brand loyal, the promotional mix should include more advertising and sales promotion and less personal selling. But sometimes personal selling is required even when buyers are well informed and geographically dispersed, as is the case with mainframe computers. Industrial installations and component parts may be sold to knowledgeable people with much education and work experience. Yet a salesperson must still explain the product and work out the details of the purchase agreement.

detailing
The physical stocking of merchandise at a retailer by the salesperson who delivers the merchandise.

Salespeople are also required when the physical stocking of merchandise—called **detailing**—is the norm. Milk and bread, for instance, are generally stocked by the person who makes the delivery, rather than by store personnel. This practice is becoming more common for convenience products as sellers try to get the best display space for their wares.

Available Funds

Money, or the lack of it, is one of the biggest influences on the promotional mix. A small manufacturer with a tight budget and a unique product may rely heavily on free publicity. The media often run stories about new products.

If the product warrants a sales force, a firm with little money may turn to manufacturers' agents. They work on commission, with no salary, advances, or expense accounts. The Duncan Co., which makes parking meters, is just one of the many that rely on manufacturers' agents.

Push and Pull Strategies

push strategy

A promotional strategy in which a manufacturer uses aggressive personal selling and trade advertising to convince a wholesaler or retailer to carry and sell its merchandise.

pull strategy

A promotional strategy in which a manufacturer focuses on stimulating consumer demand for its product, rather than on trying to persuade wholesalers to carry the product.

Manufacturers may use aggressive personal selling and trade advertising to convince a wholesaler or a retailer to carry and sell their merchandise. This approach is known as a **push strategy.** The wholesaler, in turn, must often push the merchandise forward by persuading the retailer to handle the goods. A push strategy relies on extensive personal selling to channel members, or trade advertising, and price incentives to wholesalers and retailers. The retailer then uses advertising, displays, and other promotional forms to convince the consumer to buy the "pushed" products. This approach also applies to services. For example, the Jamaican Tourism Board targets promotions to travel agencies, which are members of its distribution channel.

At the other extreme is a **pull strategy,** which stimulates consumer demand in order to obtain product distribution. Rather than trying to sell to wholesalers, a manufacturer using a pull strategy focuses its promotional efforts on end consumers. As they begin demanding the product, the retailer orders the merchandise from the wholesaler. The wholesaler, confronted with rising demand, then places an order from the manufacturer. Thus, stimulating con-

> e x h i b i t   1 6 - 7 <

Push and Pull Promotional Strategies

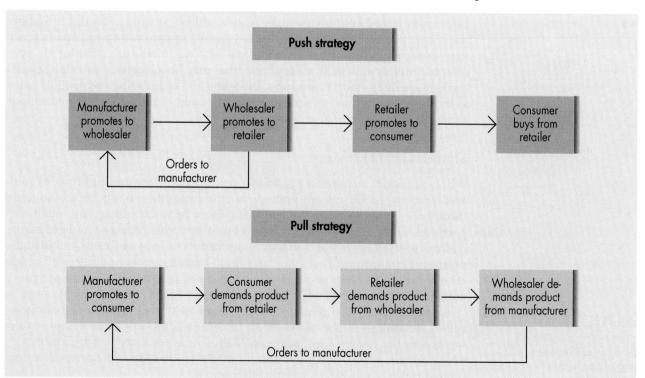

sumer demand pulls the product down through the channel of distribution. Heavy sampling, introductory consumer advertising, cents-off campaigns, and couponing may all be used as part of a pull strategy. For example, using a pull strategy, the Jamaican Tourism Board may entice travelers to come to its island by offering discounts on hotels or airfare. The push and pull promotional strategies are illustrated in Exhibit 16-7 on p. 488.

Rarely does a company use a pull or a push strategy exclusively. Instead, the mix will emphasize one of these strategies. For example, pharmaceutical company Marion Merrell Dow uses a push strategy, emphasizing personal selling and trade advertising, to promote its Nicoderm patch nicotine withdrawal therapy to physicians. Sales presentations and advertisements in medical journals give physicians the detailed information they need to prescribe the therapy to their patients who want to quit smoking. Marion Merrell Dow supplements its push promotional strategy with a pull strategy targeted directly to potential patients through advertisements in consumer magazines and on television. The advertisements illustrate the pull strategy in action: Marion Merrell Dow directs consumers to ask their doctors about the Nicoderm patch.

c o n c ə p t   c h ə c k

- Explain how the nature of the product, market characteristics, and available funds can affect the promotional mix.
- Distinguish between push and pull strategies.

CAPITALIZING ON TRENDS IN BUSINESS

>lg 9   Companies are adopting new promotional strategies to hone their marketing message and reach more customers. They are also reacting to new technologies, such as the digital VCR, that make it harder to measure audience size. Integrated marketing communications, the explosive growth of Internet advertising, and the impact of the digital VCR on television advertising are discussed in this section.

Integrated Marketing Communications

Ideally, marketing communications from each promotional mix element (personal selling, advertising, sales promotion, and public relations) should be integrated. That is, the message reaching the consumer should be the same regardless of whether it comes from an advertisement, a salesperson in the field, a magazine article, or a coupon in a newspaper insert.

From the consumer's standpoint, a company's communications are already integrated. Typical consumers do not think in terms of advertising, sales promotion, public relations, or personal selling. To them, everything is an "ad." Unfortunately, many marketers neglect this fact when planning promotional messages and fail to integrate the various elements of their communication efforts. The most common rift typically arises between personal selling and the other elements of the promotional mix.

This unintegrated, disjointed approach to promotion has propelled many companies to adopt the concept of **integrated marketing communications (IMC).** IMC involves carefully coordinating all promotional activities—media advertising, sales promotion, personal selling, and public relations, as well as direct marketing, packaging, and other forms of promotion—to produce a consistent, unified message that is customer focused. Following the concept of IMC, marketing managers carefully work out the roles the various promotional elements will play in the marketing mix. Timing of promotional activities is

integrated marketing communications (IMC)
The careful coordination of all promotional activities—media advertising, sales promotion, personal selling, and public relations, as well as direct marketing, packaging, and other forms of promotion—to produce a consistent, unified message that is customer focused.

coordinated, and the results of each campaign are carefully monitored to improve future use of the promotional mix tools. Typically, a marketing communications director is appointed who has overall responsibility for integrating the company's marketing communications.

Pepsi relied on IMC to launch Pepsi One. The $100 million program relied on personal selling in the distribution channels, a public relations campaign with press releases to announce the product, and heavy doses of advertising and sales promotion. The company toured the country's shopping malls setting up Pepsi One "lounges"—inflatable couches with plastic carpeting—for random taste tests. It also produced 11,000 end-cap displays for supermarket aisles and created stand-up displays for 12-packs to spark impulse purchases. It secured Oscar-winning actor Cuba Gooding Jr. as spokesperson for the ad campaign. The ads made their debut during the World Series. The tagline for the ad campaign was "Only One has it all."

The Growth of Web Advertising

The explosive growth of the Internet has led to similar growth in Web advertising. For companies whose businesses are based on the Internet, building a recognized brand name is important. With nothing to pick up or touch and hundreds of similar-sounding sites to choose from, online consumers have little to go on except a familiar name. In cyberspace, anyone with enough resources to rent space on a server and build some buzz for its brand is a potentially dangerous competitor.

There's a growing recognition among marketers, however, that the advertising tactics they have tried so far on the Web have been ineffective. The emotion-laden vignettes that work so well on TV simply don't excite viewers in cyberspace. Meanwhile, the established methods of Internet advertising don't do much better. Pop-up ads that just pop up on the screen are annoying interruptions to the online experience. Spending on banner ads is expected to drop as companies conclude that computer users are ignoring them. On the Internet, the consumer is in charge. That means marketers set on building their brands in the online world have to persuade consumers to participate in their marketing efforts. The latest theory on how to do that is called **rational branding.** The idea is to marry the emotional sell of traditional brand marketing—the message that links "Disney" with "family" or "Volvo" with "safety"—with a concrete service that is offered only online. Rational branding strives to both move and help the online consumer at the same time. In essence, the advertiser "pays" the consumer to endure the brand message by performing some kind of service. But the tactic poses a real challenge to makers of consumer products. There are very few ways to make soap or soda useful in the virtual world. Indeed, most of the top five buyers of TV advertising (General Motors, Procter & Gamble, Johnson & Johnson, Philip Morris, and Ford) are nearly invisible online.

MasterCard has found a way to use rational branding by offering Shop Smart, a type of MasterCard seal of approval given to e-commerce sites that use advanced credit card security systems. The program lets MasterCard slap its logo all over the hottest new online shopping sites. It also gives the company a chance to promote its Internet image.

The Impact of Digital VCRs on Television

Though the digital VCR is made of little more than a few integrated circuits, a power supply, and a massive multigigabyte hard drive, it will render traditional VCRs obsolete.[9] Here's why. Most people these days use VCRs to play prerecorded tapes. Although you can use a VCR to tape your favorite programs

rational branding

A tactic for advertising on the Internet that combines the emotional aspect of traditional brand marketing with a concrete service that is offered only online.

and watch them on your own time, that doesn't happen very often. The gadgets are too hard to use. This won't be the case with digital VCRs. With some simple programming through a remote control, a digital VCR will proactively record the shows you want to see. Tell it you are an Oprah Winfrey fan, and it automatically records all Oprah shows so that you can watch them when it's convenient. Type in a list of your favorite actors and directors, and over time the digital VCR will build a repository of their films. These devices take note of which programs you watch and recommend shows you didn't know about. They'll even record more than one show at a time.

Two technologies make this possible. First, digital VCRs continually scan databases of local program schedules, so they catch any show that matches your interests. Second, since the programs are delivered as digital bits, the device simply downloads those bits to the storage drive, just as you store documents on a floppy disk or a Zip drive. With this kind of open-ended access to programming, the concept of limitless channels will become a reality.

Why will this technology affect advertising? The reason is that TV advertisers—not to mention viewers—are used to a world of synchronous viewing. For the past 50 years, shows have belonged in time slots, and people have watched whatever is on at that particular time. As a result, ad sales are typically based on Nielsen audience ratings, which measure how many people are watching a show at a given moment.

But the digital VCR makes it very easy to watch shows on your own time—in other words, asynchronously. Watching TV will be more like surfing the Web than viewing a movie. That may reduce the Nielsen influence and make it even more difficult to measure the size of the audience watching any single program. This, in turn, will make it more difficult for the television networks to price their airtime for commercials. It will also make it difficult for advertisers to know if the price is fair.

concept check

- What is integrated marketing communications, and how can it help companies improve their promotional efforts?
- Define rational branding, and explain why it may not be useful for all products.
- How will digital VCRs affect television advertising?

APPLYING THIS CHAPTER'S TOPICS

Two important points from this chapter apply directly to you now. By understanding how advertising is changing to benefit you, you will be a better informed consumer. By realizing the importance of selling yourself, you will be better able to take advantage of life's opportunities.

Advertising Will Be More Beneficial to You

More and more advertising dollars will be directed to online promotion in the future. For the online advertiser, the challenge is to educate, entertain, or otherwise give you a benefit. Advertisers know that no one can be compelled to pay attention online—they must deliver benefits up front. If Colgate Palmolive wants to advertise toothpaste online, it needs more than photogenic lovers with toothy smiles. Unilever has created a Web site for Mentadent toothpaste that offers potential customers the chance to order a free sample, get oral-care advice, and send questions to a dental hygienist. Every week American Airlines sends e-mail to more than a million Net-SAAver subscribers listing rock-bottom

fares for undersubscribed flights on the coming weekend. You can and should expect to receive benefits from online advertisers.

E-mail advertising is also becoming more personal and more valuable to you. Although users of e-mail have long complained about unwanted direct marketing—commonly called spam—that hasn't stopped companies from looking for new and improved ways to exploit e-mail as a marketing tool. Now, by using sophisticated data-mining techniques to develop far more tailored messages, marketers may well be succeeding. Lured by the speed, cost savings, and personalized pitches that are possible online, companies such as 1-800-Flowers, Amazon.com, and Macy's are testing the tactic. "If the customer is willing, it's the ideal opportunity for a personalized dialogue," says Kent Anderson, president of Macys.com, the department store's online entity. "It gets us closer to a one-to-one relationship."[10] Macys.com, for example, will e-mail you to remind you of your spouse's birthday and anyone else you specify. Amazon.com e-mails you if a favorite author is conducting an online chat or has published a new work. It's a far cry from impersonal mass advertising. This is strictly for you.

>looking ahead

at MO Clancy's Job at Levi Strauss

Look back at the story about Mo Clancy working as an urban networker for Levi's. Mo's interaction with a younger, hipper set of customers is designed to increase demand for Levi's Dockers in a new market. Part of her work involves sales promotion and part is public relations. Levi can and does use each of the elements of the promotional mix to sell Dockers. Levi Strauss can and does use the Internet to sell Dockers. See for yourself. Go to **www.store.us.dockers.com/store/**.

Always Sell Yourself

If you stop and think about it, all of us must be salespeople. If you are going to be successful in business, and in life in general, you must be a salesperson. You must be able to effectively explain and sell your plans, ideas, and hopes. A straight "A" student who can't do this will not be successful. Conversely, a "C" student who can will be successful. *Always* be prepared to sell yourself and your ideas. It's the best way to get ahead in business and in life.

SUMMARY OF LEARNING GOALS

>lg 1   **What are the goals of promotional strategy?**
Promotion aims to stimulate demand for a company's goods or services. Promotional strategy is designed to inform, persuade, or remind target audiences about those products. The goals of promotion are to create awareness, get people to try products, provide information, keep loyal customers, increase use of a product, and identify potential customers.

>lg 2   **What is the promotional mix, and what are its elements?**
The unique combination of advertising, personal selling, sales promotion, and public relations used to promote a product is the promotional mix. Advertising is any paid form of nonpersonal promotion by an identified sponsor. Personal selling consists of a face-to-face presentation in a conversation with a prospective purchaser. Sales promotion consists of marketing activities—other than personal selling, advertising, and public relations—that stimulate consumers to buy. These activities include coupons and samples, displays, shows and exhibitions, demonstrations, and other selling efforts. Public relations is the marketing function that links the policies of the organization with the public interest and develops programs designed to earn public understanding and acceptance.

>lg 3   **What are the types of advertising?**
Institutional advertising creates a positive picture of a company. Advocacy advertising takes a stand on controversial social or economic issues. Product advertising features a specific good or service. Comparative advertising is product advertising in which the company's product is compared with competing, named products. Reminder advertising is used to keep a brand name in the public's mind.

>lg 4   **What are the advertising media, and how are they selected?**
The main types of advertising media are newspapers, magazines, radio, television, outdoor advertising, direct mail, and the Internet. Newspaper advertising delivers a local audience but has a short life span. Magazines deliver special-interest markets and offer good detail and color. Radio is an inexpensive and highly portable medium but has no visual capabilities. Television reaches huge audiences and offers visual and audio opportunities, but it can be very expensive. Outdoor advertising requires short messages but is only moderately expensive. Direct mail can reach targeted audiences, but it is only as good as the mailing list. The Internet is global in scope and can offer a personalized message response by e-mail, but as yet not everyone is on the Net. Media are evaluated on a CPM (cost per thousand contacts) basis and by reach and frequency.

>lg 5   **What is the selling process?**
About 6.5 million people in the United States are directly engaged in personal selling. Personal selling enables a salesperson to demonstrate a product and tailor the message to the prospect; it is effective in closing a sale. Professional salespeople are knowledgeable and creative. They also are familiar with the selling process, which consists of prospecting and qualifying, approaching customers, presenting and demonstrating the product, handling objections, closing the sale, and following up on the sale.

>lg 6   **What are the goals of sales promotion, and what are several types of sales promotion?**
Immediate purchase is the goal of sales promotion whether it is aimed at consumers or the trade (wholesalers and retailers). The most popular sales promotions are coupons, samples, premiums, contests, and sweepstakes. Trade shows, conventions, and point-of-purchase displays are other types of sales promotion.

>lg 7   **How does public relations fit into the promotional mix?**
Public relations is mostly concerned with getting good publicity for companies. Publicity is any information about a company or product that appears in the

KEY TERMS

advertising 474
advertising
 agencies 478
advertising media
 475
advocacy
 advertising 475
audience selectivity
 478
comparative
 advertising 474
corrective
 advertising 480
cost per thousand
 (CPM) 477
detailing 487
differential
 advantage 472
Federal Trade
 Commission (FTC)
 479
frequency 477
institutional
 advertising 475
integrated
 marketing
 communications
 (IMC) 489
National
 Advertising
 Division (NAD)
 479
National
 Advertising
 Review Board
 (NARB) 479
personal selling
 480
product advertising
 474
promotion 472
promotional mix
 473
prospecting 481
public relations
 486
publicity 486
pull strategy 488
push strategy 488
qualifying questions
 482
rational branding
 490
reach 477
reminder
 advertising 475
sales promotions
 483
sales prospects
 481

news media and is not directly paid for by the company. Public relations departments furnish company speakers for business and civic clubs, write speeches for corporate officers, and encourage employees to take active roles in civic groups. These activities help build a positive image for an organization, which is a good backdrop for selling its products.

>lg 8   **What factors affect the promotional mix?**

The factors that affect the promotional mix are the nature of the product, market characteristics, available funds, and whether a push or a pull strategy is emphasized. Personal selling is used more with industrial products, and advertising is used more heavily for consumer products. With widely scattered, well-informed buyers and with brand-loyal customers, a firm will blend more advertising and sales promotion and less personal selling into its promotional mix. A manufacturer with a limited budget may rely heavily on publicity and manufacturers' agents to promote the product.

>lg 9   **What are three important trends in promotion?**

Integrated marketing communications (IMC) is being used by more and more organizations. It is the careful coordination of all of the elements of the promotional mix to produce a consistent, unified message that is customer focused. A second trend is the growth of Web advertising. Traditional advertising techniques don't work very well on the Internet. Advertisers have found that they must use rational branding. A final trend is that digital VCRs may make the measurement of television audiences more difficult.

PREPARING FOR TOMORROW'S WORKPLACE

1. Divide the class into groups of five. Each group should select a firm in a different industry. Go to the Internet and library and analyze your firm's promotional strategy for several key products. Report your findings to the class.
2. Describe how the promotional mix will change at each stage of the product life cycle when digital VCRs become common.
3. The local Rotary club has asked you to give a speech on what it means to be a professional salesperson. Write an outline for your speech.
4. Divide the class into teams of five. Each team should choose a current advertising campaign, determine whether it is effective, and then explain why or why not. Each team should present its results to the class.
5. Go to the Internet or library and find out about a company that uses integrated marketing communications. Present your results to the class.
6. Do small business owners need to know much about personal selling? Why or why not?
7. How can advertising, sales promotion, and publicity work together? Give an example.

WORKING THE NET

1. Each week, *USA Today* polls its readers to determine the effectiveness of a major ad campaign. Visit *USA Today*'s AdTrack Index (**www.usatoday.com/money/index/ad001.htm**), pick one of the ad and campaigns listed, and read the article about it. Do you agree or disagree with consumer reaction to the campaign?
2. The Zenith Media site at **www.zenithmedia.com** is a good place to find links to Internet resources on advertising. At the site, click on "Leading Corporate and Brand Sites." Pick three of the company sites listed and review them, using the concepts in this chapter.

3. Read one of the topics listed under "FTC regulations" at the Arent and Fox Advertising Law Web site (**www.advertisinglaw.com**). Do you think most advertisers would self-regulate their advertising to comply with this regulation if the FTC did not enforce it? Why or why not?

4. Go to the *Sales and Marketing* magazine site at **www.salesandmarketing.com**. Find and read the magazine's monthly "What would you do?" article and the answers given by sales professionals. Would you handle the situation differently? Why or why not?

CREATIVE THINKING CASE

We Will Be Landing in Kansas So the Crew Can Grab a Steak

Flower Aviation in Salina, Kansas, uses lots of enticements to lure corporate jet pilots to land there for refueling. It promises low fuel prices and fast service. It even has two women dressed in short white skirts and sleeveless T-shirts waving bright orange flags to direct pilots to its facility.

But the real attraction is in the brown paper bag the women slip to the pilots once they have pulled in to fill 'er up: frozen Kansas City strip steaks. "The boss likes the fuel price, but I stop here for the steaks," says Bob Ricks, a pilot for a Melbourne (Florida) aircraft-sales corporation who has decided to pass over a competing refueler and taxi over to Flower. Flower hands out one eight-ounce steak for every 100 gallons of fuel purchased.

Gas-station giveaways and energetic attendants have all but disappeared from the roads, but gifts and rebates are soaring in the corporate jet refueling business. Since jets can refuel in many places along their routes, these "fixed-base operations," or FOBs as the refuelers and repair stations are known, battle not only competitors at the same airport, but also rivals hundreds of miles away.

With airplane fuel running about $1.79 a gallon, it can cost $1,800 or more to fill up a private jet, leaving the FBO with a profit of several hundred dollars. With so much money at stake, FBOs try to lure pilots with pricey enticements that include wine, frozen seafood, and top-of-the-line golf gear.

The competition to refill a jet's tanks is most intense at a few key midcontinent airports, including Lincoln, Grand Island, and North Platte, Nebraska. Located smack in the middle of most coast-to-coast air routes, many are also blessed with extralong runways built for now- abandoned military bases.

As planes line up to land in Lincoln, pickup trucks from the airport's three FBOs speed to the edge of the runway displaying "Follow Me" signs. Drivers say they try to cut off the competition to get the coveted first-in-line spot at the edge of the taxiway. "I've raced a couple down the ramp trying to get in the best position," admits Jackson Roth, a refueler at Silverhawk Aviation. "This is the playground out here." Such aggressiveness has, on occasion, angered pilots concerned for their safety.

Critical Thinking Questions

1. Are Flower's giveaways ethical?
2. What kind of promotion is Flower using?
3. What other promotional techniques could Flower use to attract customers?

VIDEO

Red Roof Inns

Red Roof Inns (**www.redroof.com/about_the_roof**/), founded in Columbus, Ohio, in 1973, is one of the leading economy lodging chains in the United

States. It was founded on "the philosophy of providing guests a clean, comfortable room at an affordable price." The company remained privately held until 1996, when it went public and began trading on the New York Stock Exchange. To facilitate expansion, Red Roof Inns is pursuing a threefold growth strategy. The first element of the strategy is to remain focused on the customer. The second is to expand the Red Roof Inns brand through franchising. The third is to develop new corporate-owned properties.

Red Roof Inns continues to provide business and leisure travelers with exceptional value in quality, convenience, and price. The chain employs nearly 6,500 people at its corporate offices, reservation centers, and inn locations. Currently, it has more than 270 properties, located in 36 states and the District of Columbia. Red Roof Inns has one of the highest systemwide occupancy rates in the lodging industry.

Red Roof Inns' goal is to be recognized as the best moderately priced lodging company by its guests, employees, investors, and franchisees. The chain's motto "Simply the best" captures this vision.

To support its vision, the company relies on three core values in managing its relationships with various stakeholder groups: dedication to customer service, respect for the individual, and a passion for excellence. Red Roof Inns applies these values to its relationships with guests, employees, investors, franchisees, suppliers, and the communities it serves.

One of the ways Red Roof Inns communicates its values is through its advertising campaigns. Using comedian and actor Martin Mull as a spokesperson, the company promotes its core values through various print media and television campaigns. Red Roof Inns even has video clips of its latest television advertising spots on its Web site. The advertising emphasizes that the inns provide excellent service to customers at a reasonable price.

Red Roof Inns is a strong brand, and the company reinvests in this brand through marketing and advertising. In 1997, Red Roof Inns made a number of improvements in its marketing and advertising. The company shifted resources from billboard advertising to more proactive sales efforts. The size of the sales staff was more than doubled. New sales practices, including intense telemarketing efforts and couponing, were implemented.

In early 1999, Red Roof Inns announced that it had been honored with six international advertising and public relations awards from the Hospitality Sales and Marketing Association International (HSMAI). Attracting more than 1,700 entries from 51 different countries, the HSMAI competition has become the largest and most prestigious in the industry. HSMAI presented Red Roof Inns and its creative agency, Diliberto, Inc., of Baltimore, Maryland, with five Adrian Advertising Awards (two gold, two silver, and one bronze) for their television and print media advertising campaigns. Red Roof Inns also received a bronze Golden Bell Public Relations Award from HSMAI for its involvement with children's hospitals.

Steve Parker, Red Roof Inns' senior vice-president of sales and marketing, says that the Adrian and Golden Bell Awards reflect the company's strength and creativity in both advertising and public relations. He goes on to point out that both are important parts of the overall marketing mix at Red Roof Inns.

Critical Thinking Questions

1. How would you describe the promotional mix used by Red Roof Inns?
2. How can Red Roof Inns' promotional mix help in executing the company's growth strategy?
3. What purpose is served by giving advertising or public relations awards to a company?

Your Career in Marketing

Marketing is critically important to American businesses. Top management realizes that a company must understand the marketplace and consumer needs and wants if it is to grow and compete effectively.

Marketing offers a rich variety of career opportunities, from marketing research to creative advertising. Some positions are desk jobs—for instance, market research analyst and product manager. Others—especially those in sales, public relations, and advertising—require wide contact with the public and with other firms. The outlook for careers in marketing will continue to be very bright through the year 2010.

DREAM CAREER:
ADVERTISING ACCOUNT MANAGER

Advertising account managers make sales to client firms. They are also responsible for keeping clients satisfied so they will stay with the advertising agency. These managers work on a day-to-day basis with clients and serve as the link between clients and the agency's creative, media, and research departments.

Account managers must understand each client's target consumers very well. To be successful, they have to help design the best possible advertising for their clients—advertising that will make a client's business grow. They also have to be able to identify the strengths and weaknesses of the brands to which they are assigned. Identifying brand differences is important, too, because these differences help set apart a client's products.

Human nature being what it is, clients can sometimes be difficult. With tact, insight, and a little humor, account managers should always tell clients what the agency believes is right for their business, even if this is not what the clients want to hear.

- *Places of employment.* Mainly New York City and Chicago, although there are more than 8,000 moderate-size and smaller agencies found in every metropolitan area.

- *Skills required.* Four-year degree.
- *Employment outlook through 2010.* Good.
- *Salaries.* $28,000–$35,000 for assistant account executives; $38,000–$75,000, for account executives; $50,000–$125,000 for account supervisors (who manage several account executives).

WHERE THE OPPORTUNITIES ARE
Retail Buyer

All merchandise sold in retail stores, from automobile tires to high-fashion clothing, appears through the decisions of buyers. Buyers for small stores may buy all the merchandise. Buyers for large stores often handle only one or two related lines, such as home furnishings and accessories. Buyers work with a limited budget and thus try to choose merchandise that will sell fast. They must understand customer likes and dislikes and be able to predict fashion and manufacturing trends.

- *Places of employment.* Throughout the country, with most jobs in major metropolitan areas.
- *Skills required.* Two-year degree for some jobs; four-year degree for most.
- *Employment outlook through 2010.* Good.
- *Salaries.* $26,000–$70,000, plus bonuses for some buyers.

Market Researcher

Market researchers provide information that marketing managers use to make decisions. Statisticians determine sample sizes, decide who is to be interviewed, and analyze data. Account executives in research firms sell research projects to advertising agencies, manufacturers, and retailers. They also act as go-betweens for research firms and clients in planning studies, giving progress reports, and presenting results. Field supervisors hire research field workers to do the interviewing. They are in charge of gathering data quickly, economically, and accurately.

- *Places of employment.* Mostly large research firms in New York City, Chicago, Dallas, and California. Other opportunities are available with manufacturers and large retailers throughout the country.
- *Skills required.* For research statisticians, an MBA; for account executives, a four-year degree; for field supervisors, usually a four-year degree but sometimes a two-year degree.
- *Employment outlook through 2010.* Good in the places mentioned here; fair elsewhere.
- *Salaries.* $38,000–$60,000 for research statisticians; $30,000–$50,000+ for account managers; $20,000–$40,000 for field supervisors.

Manufacturer's Representative

Manufacturer's sales reps sell mainly to other businesses: factories, railroads, banks, wholesalers, retailers, hospitals, schools, libraries, and other institutions. Most of these salespeople sell nontechnical products. Those who deal in highly technical goods, such as electronic equipment, are often called sales engineers or industrial sales workers. Some manufacturer's sales positions require much travel.

- *Places of employment.* Throughout the country.
- *Skills required.* For selling nontechnical products, usually a four-year degree; for selling technical products, a technical undergraduate degree and an MBA.
- *Employment outlook through 2010.* Very good.
- *Salaries.* $30,000–$65,000 for nontechnical sales reps; $30,000–$75,000+ for technical sales reps. Many companies also pay commissions or bonuses to salespeople.

Wholesaler Sales Representative

Wholesaler sales reps visit buyers for retail, industrial, and commercial firms and for schools, hospitals, and other institutions. They offer samples, pictures, or catalogs that list the items their company stocks. Some help retail store personnel improve and update systems for ordering and taking inventory. Sales reps who handle technical products, such as air-conditioning equipment, may help with installation and maintenance.

- *Places of employment.* Usually large cities (where the wholesalers are), but sales territories may be almost anywhere.
- *Skills required.* Either a two-year or a four-year degree, depending mainly on the product line and market.
- *Employment outlook through 2010:* Fair.
- *Salaries.* $30,000–$100,000, with the higher figure for experienced people in growth industries.

Public Relations Agent

Public relations agents help firms, government agencies, universities, and other organizations build and maintain a positive public image. They may handle press, community, or consumer relations; interest-group representation; fund-raising; speech writing; or plant tours. They often represent employers in community projects.

- *Places of employment.* Manufacturing firms, public utilities, transportation companies, insurance companies, trade and professional associations, and government agencies, mainly in large cities. More than half of the roughly 2,000 public relations firms are in New York City, Chicago, Los Angeles, and Washington, D.C.

- *Skills required.* Four-year degree.
- *Employment outlook through 2010.* Good.
- *Salaries.* $28,000–$75,000+, with the higher figure for public relations directors.

Product Manager

In large manufacturing firms, one key product may account for millions of dollars in sales. Such a product is too important to leave its success to chance. Product managers oversee its marketing program and are responsible for meeting profit objectives. They must coordinate the activities of the distribution department, market researchers, advertising agencies, and so on, to ensure that the product has the right marketing mix. Working with many departments without direct authority over any of them requires good human relations and planning skills.

- *Places of employment.* Major population centers and industrial centers.
- *Skills required.* Four-year degree usually, but some employers require an MBA.
- *Employment outlook through 2010.* Good.
- *Salaries.* $28,000–$90,000, with the higher figure for group product managers.

Advertising Media Planner

Advertising media planners supervise all media purchases and determine when commercials will be shown and which media will be used. They also select, recommend, and evaluate publications and programs that expose the advertising to best advantage. Media planners are responsible for achieving the right exposure in a campaign. They must be good negotiators because media rates can be flexible. Skilled planners can stretch their clients' media budgets.

- *Places of employment.* Mainly New York City and Chicago for large advertising agencies, but every metropolitan area for moderate-size and smaller agencies.
- *Skills required.* Four-year degree or MBA.
- *Employment outlook through 2010.* Fair.
- *Salaries.* $35,000–$75,000, with the higher amounts at major New York agencies.

Distribution Traffic Manager

Distribution traffic managers are responsible for inbound raw materials and products and outbound finished goods. They look for ways to avoid waste and damage and reduce time in transit, packaging costs, warehouse costs, and costs of intraplant movement. Most importantly, perhaps, traffic managers must understand the costs and services of the carriers so that they can reduce expense and improve service.

- *Places of employment.* Throughout the country, especially big industrial centers.
- *Skills required.* MBA.
- *Employment outlook through 2010.* Very good.
- *Salaries.* $35,000–$70,000, with the higher figure for senior traffic managers.

chapter seventeen

Using Technology to Manage Information

learning goals

>lg 1   How does information play a role in decision making?

>lg 2   What are the components of a computer, and how are computers categorized by size?

>lg 3   How does software make a computer useful?

>lg 4   Why are computer networks an important part of today's business information systems?

>lg 5   What is the structure of a typical information system?

>lg 6   How can companies manage information technology to their advantage?

>lg 7   What are the leading trends in information technology?

Unlocking KeyCorp's Customer Database for Greater Profits

Cleveland-based KeyCorp (**www.keybank. com**) wondered why its per-customer profitability was below average, even though it spent a considerable amount on marketing campaigns. The bank's executives knew that 18 percent of its customers generated 82 percent of bank revenue—but not which customers were the most profitable, the products they used, or which products to promote to different customer groups. Instead of targeting promotions effectively, salespeople based sales tactics on intuition, rather than hard data.

KeyCorp turned to a state-of-the-art data warehouse, a collection of data that supports management decision making, to solve these problems. Housed in its own IBM mainframe computer, the data warehouse consolidates all customer and prospect information from 40 separate databases. The data warehouse's customer profiles include 150 factors—from name and age to loan balances, services used, and frequency of automatic teller machine (ATM) usage. It is now the central information source for sales and marketing decisions throughout the bank.

With specialized software designed for financial services companies, KeyCorp marketing personnel look for hidden patterns and relationships in a group of data. They query the data warehouse to get answers to questions like:

- What kinds of customers purchase each KeyCorp product, when, and why?
- Who are the most profitable and least profitable customers?
- What distribution channels do different customers prefer?
- What would cause a customer to leave KeyCorp?

KeyCorp marketers work with technology personnel to get information to analyze consumer behavior and produce lists of customers most likely to respond to a product offer. The information is available in just a day or two, rather than the month it took with multiple databases.

Automated marketing campaign software identifies customers best suited to receive a particular offer, determines the best medium to reach them, and gathers data on campaign responses. By taking over much of the campaign execution, the software gives marketing managers more time for planning and evaluating campaigns and creating more effective strategies. They know what offers did well and the return on investment for the campaign and can allocate

Critical Thinking Questions

As you read this chapter, consider the following questions as they relate to KeyCorp:

- How does managing information give KeyCorp a competitive advantage?
- What problems might KeyCorp have while implementing the data warehouse?
- What steps could KeyCorp take to encourage acceptance of the new data warehouse and ensure that employees use it?

marketing dollars to the most profitable customer and prospect segments. "You set the rules and you take your hands off and measure results," says Todd Thompson, vice-president of corporate marketing. "Once you set it up, the technology just makes it happen."

Since implementing the data warehouse and installing the market automation software, higher direct mail response rates—5 to 10 percent, versus 1 to 2 percent in the past—are the rule rather than the exception, says Jo Ann Boylan, executive vice-president of Key Services Corp. Lower marketing costs are another benefit of targeted marketing campaigns. The bank reduced the number of total direct marketing messages by 20 percent yet increased the number of annual campaigns from seven major cross-selling programs to 45 smaller, targeted campaigns. The new marketing strategies have paid off: the number of people who buy the offered products is up 200 percent.[1]

BUSINESS IN THE 21ST CENTURY

As KeyCorp's executives discovered, harnessing the power of information technology gives a company a significant competitive advantage. The data warehouse helped KeyCorp cut costs, increase profits, spot market trends faster, and communicate more effectively with customers. It also showed the bank where to invest more marketing dollars to build stronger customer relationships.

Information systems like KeyCorp's data warehouse and the computers that comprise them are so much a part of our lives that we almost take them for granted. In less than 60 years, we have shifted from an industrial society to a knowledge-based economy driven by information. Businesses depend on information technology for everything from running daily operations to making strategic decisions. Computers are the tools of this information age, performing extremely complex operations as well as everyday jobs like word processing and creating spreadsheets. Through networks of linked computers, one manager can share information with hundreds of thousands of people around the world almost as easily as with a colleague on another floor of the same office building. Many companies now have a **chief information officer (CIO),** an executive with responsibility for managing all information resources.

Because most jobs today depend on managing information—obtaining, using, creating, and sharing it—this chapter begins with the role of information in decision making and the relationship between computers and information systems. Next it describes computer hardware, computer software, and computer networks. The following sections discuss business information systems and the management of information technology. Finally, we'll look at the latest

chief information officer (CIO)

An executive with responsibility for managing all information resources in an organization.

trends in information technology. Throughout the chapter, examples show how managers and their companies are using computers to make better decisions in a highly competitive world.

USING INFORMATION FOR DECISION MAKING

>lg 1

information technology (IT)
The equipment and techniques used to manage and process information.

Information technology (IT), the equipment and techniques used to manage and process information, has changed the way people make business decisions today. Only 30 years ago, well within the careers of many of today's top executives, few companies used computers. Today, IT is one of the fastest growing industries and includes not only computers but also telecommunications and Internet-related products and services. Computers now reside on almost every employee desktop and provide vast stores of information for decision making. Some of it is useful and some is not. To be useful, information must be:

- *Relevant.* Some kinds of information are more useful than others in making a given decision. For instance, when deciding whether to order raw materials, a manager is more likely to need information about inventories and future production plans than about overtime pay.
- *Accurate.* Obviously, inaccurate information can reduce a manager's ability to make good decisions.
- *Complete.* Partial information may cause a manager to focus on only one aspect of a decision. Other important aspects may be overlooked.
- *Timely.* Information that arrives too late is rarely more helpful than no information at all.

information system (IS)
The methods and equipment that provide information about all aspects of a firm's operations.

data
The many facts that together describe a company's status.

information
A meaningful and useful summary of data.

Managers use **information systems (ISs),** methods and equipment that provide information about all aspects of a firm's operations, to get the information they need to make decisions.

One function of an information system is to gather **data,** the many facts that together describe the company's status. For instance, the fact that a worker finished a unit of production on job 23-M-8735 at 2:17 P.M. on March 7 is a data item. When a manager must make a decision, a long list of data is generally not useful. For the production supervisor, a list of the times during the past hour when each unit was completed is far too detailed. Data must be turned into **information,** a meaningful and useful summary of data. The total number of units produced in the hour would be useful information.

Businesses collect a great deal of data. Only through well-designed IT systems and the power of computers can managers use such data to make better decisions. Companies are discovering that they can't operate well with a series of separate information systems geared to solving specific departmental problems. They need to integrate the systems throughout the firm. Company-wide systems that bring together human resources, operations, and technology are becoming an integral part of business strategy.

Technology experts are learning more about the way the business operates, and business managers are learning to use technology effectively to create new opportunities. Once companies know where they want to go, information systems can help them reach those goals. The Applying Technology box describes how PepsiCo's new purchasing system not only accomplished the company's original goals of automating the purchasing process but also improved inventory management and customer service.

concept check

- What are information systems? Why are they important?
- What makes information useful?
- Distinguish between data and information. How are they related?

> a p p l y i n g   t e c h n o l o g y <

PEPSI-COLA BOTTLES A NEW PURCHASING SYSTEM

An IT manager's job is never done. As soon as Pepsi-Cola North America completed the redesign of its vendor processing system in 1995, it began a related project to use the purchasing information in its new data warehouse to identify cost savings. Both projects were so successful that Pepsi-Cola improved its materials management, purchasing processes, and customer service—and saved more than $100 million over a three-year period.

Before revamping its purchasing systems, Pepsi bought supplies from 300,000 vendors who submitted 1.5 million invoices each year. It took 200 employees to manage this flood of paper and pay suppliers, leaving little time to analyze purchasing trends. By replacing local agreements with national contracts, Pepsi was able to purchase 90 percent of its supplies from just 1,000 vendors, who submit about half as many invoices.

Next, Pepsi centralized and automated its labor-intensive system. Now purchasers search an online catalog of approved items. Clicking on the item automatically enters it on a purchase order that fills in price and other data. The system automatically submits the completed form to the appropriate vendor. Once an employee confirms receipt, the system automatically generates payment in 30 days and records the purchase in the appropriate accounting files. Processing time dropped to 15 minutes per order, errors from 10 percent to less than 1 percent, and the cost of processing each invoice by over 60 percent.

The new system does more than cut costs. Pepsi's national supplier development staff now analyzes the centralized database for purchasing patterns. "We've found the biggest savings in the peripheral items—office supplies, lubricants, tires, uniforms, you name it—that used to be purchased regionally or locally," says controller and vice-president Peter Bridgman. "Using the data warehouse, we've been able to identify important items, find national suppliers for them, and leverage those relationships to reduce costs."

Not content to rest on his laurels, Bridgman put his team to work expanding the vendor processing system to inventory management and other stages of the supply chain. Company-wide, the beverage division is creating information system synergies with PepsiCo's Frito Lay snack foods division. By consolidating IT across product lines, PepsiCo will be able to offer more merchandising incentives and improve customer service.

Critical Thinking Questions

1. Why should companies view information systems' design as a dynamic and evolving process?
2. What different departments were involved in planning Pepsi's new purchasing systems? Why is this joint effort an important part of designing IT systems?
3. Make a list of the types of questions the technology specialists should raise. What questions are important to other departments?

COMPUTER HARDWARE

>lg 2

In 1943 IBM chairman Thomas Watson stated, "I think there is a world market for maybe 5 computers." And as recently as 1977, Ken Olsen, chairman and founder of Digital Equipment Corp. (now part of Compaq), said, "There is no reason why anyone would want a computer in their home."

How wrong they were! Computers have become a common feature of our lives today. Only rarely do we buy something or transact business without using computers in some way: scanning prices at a checkout, verifying a credit card through a network, getting cash from an ATM, using a spreadsheet to determine how much bank financing a company needs, or using a word processor to prepare a contract. Computers are essential to business operations, where they have greatly improved the quality, quantity, and accessibility of management information. They are part of the home scene as well. About 50 percent of all homes in the United States now have computers. In addition, many devices we use daily, from VCRs and microwave ovens to automobiles, contain miniature computers.

As useful as computers are, however, it's important to remember that a **computer** is just a machine that stores and manipulates symbols based on a set of instructions. It can't decide what information is needed to make a decision. Nor can it make the kinds of judgments that managers are expected to make. Nevertheless, computers have major advantages, including processing speed and accuracy and the ability to store vast amounts of data and programs. Because computers can process data millions of times faster than the human brain, they make it possible to manipulate and organize enormous amounts of data. Then managers assess the information and make decisions. Of course, computers are only as good as the data put into them and the instructions they are given. They cannot distinguish between right and wrong data. Let's now take a closer look at computer systems and the main types of computers.

Components of a Computer

Modern information systems combine computers, printers, terminals and displays, and many other hardware parts. **Hardware** is the equipment associated with the computer system. The list of hardware components can seem endless, but as shown in Exhibit 17-1, there are really only a few main categories: the input system, the central processing unit with primary storage, secondary storage, and the output system.

To be useful, computers must be able to receive data to process from an input system. Most data are entered into the computer using the keyboard and a mouse. Scanners are another type of input device. Optical scanners read text and bar codes, while magnetic scanners read routing and account codes on

computer

A machine that stores and manipulates symbols based on a set of instructions.

hardware

The equipment associated with a computer system; includes the input system, the central processing unit with primary storage, secondary storage, and the output system.

> e x h i b i t 1 7 - 1 <

Computer Hardware Components

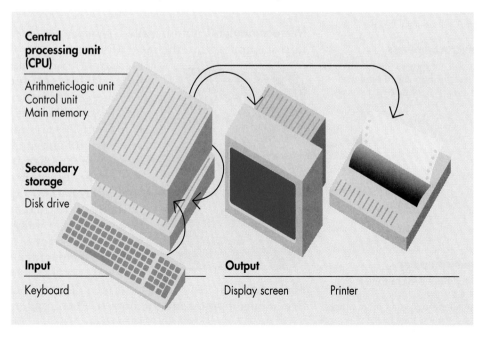

bank checks. Other types of automatic data entry devices include touch-screen display systems used in fast-food restaurants and point-of-sale terminals used in department stores. Voice recognition software is one of the newest forms of input.

central processing unit (CPU)

The central part of a computer system that performs all calculations, interprets program instructions, remembers information, and tells other parts of the computer what to do.

The brain of a computer system, the **central processing unit (CPU),** performs all calculations, interprets program instructions, remembers information, and tells other parts of the computer what to do. The microprocessor chips that comprise the CPU—for example, Intel's Pentium series and the Macintosh PowerPC—determine the computer's basic characteristics. The *primary storage* provides temporary storage for the instructions and data that the computer is processing. The primary type of memory in the CPU is **random access memory (RAM),** active, short-term memory that stores data and instructions for manipulating the data. These data are lost when the computer is turned off. The computer can quickly access any part of RAM.

random access memory (RAM)

The primary type of memory in a computer's central processing unit; an active, short-term memory that stores data and instructions for manipulating the data.

secondary storage

The part of a computer that provides long-term storage for programs and data.

Because primary storage is limited in amount and is only temporary, computers need a **secondary storage** system for long-term storage of programs and data. Secondary storage typically uses a combination of hard disk drives and other devices such as floppy disk drives, CD-ROM drives, tape drives, and Zip drives.

If you want to know more about a computer term or learn more about a topic, head to Webopaedia's on-line computer encyclopedia at

www.pcwebopaedia.com/

The main output devices are the video display screen (monitor) and the printer. The display screen shows both text and graphics on a television-like screen. The printer creates hard copy of the output, usually on paper. Printers vary in cost, speed, and quality of output. Today's laser printers provide high-speed output with quality like typesetting. Inkjet printers are a lower-cost alternative that have improved in quality. Some offer color as well as black and white printing.

Types of Computers

Most experts divide today's computers into four categories by size: microcomputers, minicomputers, mainframe computers, and supercomputers.

microcomputers

Small computers that can fit on a desktop; also called *personal computers (PCs)* or *desktop computers.*

Microcomputers Often called *personal computers (PCs)* or *desktop computers,* **microcomputers** are the most widely used type of computer. Their small size, increasing ease of use and power, and flexibility have enabled everyone, not just technology specialists, to enjoy the benefits of computers. Today most businesses and about 50 percent of all homes have PCs. Some PCs are single-user systems, while others are powerful enough to handle several users at the same time. Smaller, portable microcomputers are among the fastest growing segments of the microcomputer market. *Laptop* or *notebook computers* are portable units that rival desktops in computing power—yet can weigh just a few pounds. Smaller yet are *handheld* or *notepad computers,* some of which can read handwritten characters.

Handheld personal digital assistants are getting more powerful all the time. Find out what they can do at 3Com's Palm site,

www.palm.com/

minicomputers

Medium-sized computers that are too large for a desktop but small enough to fit in an office.

Minicomputers Too large to fit on a desktop but small enough to fit in an office, **minicomputers** are medium-sized computers often housed in one or two cabinets about the size of a file cabinet. They offer greater processing speed than microcomputers. The lines between minis and other types of computers are blurring, however. Many of today's minis would have been classified as mainframes five years ago. Minis are often at the heart of a company's *computer network,* which links together computers and related equipment such as printers so that employees can share data. They are also used in Internet networks. (Networks are discussed in greater detail in a later section of the chapter.)

To learn how companies in different industries use minicomputers like the IBM AS/400, read the case studies at

www.as400.ibm.com/ casest/CASEMENU.HTM

mainframe computers

Large computers that have much greater storage capacity than PCs or minicomputers.

Mainframe Computers   **Mainframe computers** have much greater storage capacity than PCs or minicomputers and can serve many users at the same time. Several units can be linked together to work as one unit to increase computing power. Other advantages include security and reliability. Today's mainframes are sleek, refrigerator-sized computers that cost far less to operate than their room-sized predecessors. They continue to be a major workhorse for companies with heavy data processing loads. About 70 percent of all corporate data resides on mainframe computers. Like minicomputers, they are used for networking.[2]

There is much more to a mainframe computer than its raw computing power. A mainframe computer is specially designed to efficiently handle very high volumes of data and manage vast amounts of stored information. Firms typically use mainframes to store and retrieve data that are directly used by employees across the company; the mainframe allows them to access data simultaneously.

In a large manufacturing company, for instance, people need to share information about inventories, customers, accounts, and production schedules. All that information can be stored in a central mainframe computer, which can run many large programs at once, handle heavy transaction volumes, and provide very rapid responses to requests. These capabilities make mainframes ideal for use in networks.

Fred Meyer, Inc., a large national retailer operating supermarkets and multi-department retail stores, runs its information systems on IBM System 390 mainframe computers linked together to achieve greater processing speed and capacity. "We want to know exactly what is selling, where and when," says Ron McEvoy, senior vice-president and CIO. With 225,000 different items in its inventory, the company needs powerful mainframes to handle the enormous volume of data its stores generate. Its merchandising, distribution, store, human resource, and finance systems have immediate access to the company's data warehouse at any time of day, across the enterprise. "We can make decisions within minutes of an event because of the quality of our information," says McEvoy. Mainframes also provide Fred Meyer with a cost-effective way to achieve 24-hour-a-day, 365-day-a-year reliability, improve productivity, and easily add capacity as the company grows.[3]

supercomputers

The most powerful computers. Only slightly larger than the typical microcomputer, they can perform many interrelated calculations quickly and are used to do complex computations to stimulate or predict difficult problems.

Supercomputers   The most powerful computers, **supercomputers** are used to do complex computations to simulate or predict difficult problems. They can perform many interrelated calculations quickly. Their size has ranged between minicomputers and mainframe computers, but the most recent models are only slightly larger than the typical microcomputer. Because the processors that make up a supercomputer can be linked together to share memory, these machines now have a processing speed of 3.1 teraflops—3.1 trillion calculations per second—and could reach 100 teraflops by 2004.

concept check

- Describe each of the main hardware components of a computer system and the main task of each.
- What are the four size categories of computers, and how do they differ?
- Why might a company purchase a mainframe computer instead of a less expensive microcomputer with almost the same computing power?

Once reserved for scientific analysis such as nuclear physics and mapping genes, supercomputers are now being used to solve government and business problems as well. For example, the Blue Mountain supercomputer at Los Alamos performs simulations to help cities manage traffic congestion and pollution, drug companies speed up new drug research, and automobile manufacturers design safer cars. Motorola uses the University of Illinois supercomputers to map cell phone systems in metropolitan areas. Computations that took months now take only hours.[4]

COMPUTER SOFTWARE

>lg 3

Computers have greatly increased worker productivity and efficiency at both large and small companies. For example, DaimlerChrysler uses powerful computers to conduct crash simulations, structural analyses, and other tests to improve auto safety and design. Compared to traditional crash testing, each virtual crash saves the company about $275,000.[5]

Companies now use computers for thousands of activities. The set of instructions that directs the computer's activities is called **software.** Some software is very complex and handles major information processing tasks for finance, accounting, production, sales, and marketing functions. Often companies customize their software to meet the needs of their particular industry. Software falls into two main categories: systems software and applications software.

Systems software controls the computer and provides program routines that enable applications programs to run on a particular computer. These program routines are part of an **operating system,** a collection of programs that manage the computer system's activities and run applications software. Commonly used operating systems include MS-DOS (Microsoft Disk Operating System), Windows (which makes MS-DOS easier to use by adding a *graphical user interface*), IBM's OS/2, Apple's Macintosh system, and UNIX.

Applications software is *applied* to a real-world task. It is used to perform a specific particular task or to solve a particular problem. If clerks need to record customer orders, they use an order-entry application program. If service representatives need to type letters in response to customer inquiries, they use a word processing application program. Applications software covers a wide range of programs, from the complex software that handles the large-scale processing needs of businesses to PC productivity software used by both businesses and individuals to games and other types of entertainment software.

Sabrina Tam, a sales representative for Homestyle Corp., a large furniture maker, provides a good example of how applications software is used. To help her better serve her customers, Homestyle has given Sabrina a powerful laptop computer with color display screen, communications modem, and CD-ROM drive that she can carry into a store owner's office and use during her presentations. Her laptop has word processing, spreadsheet, database management, graphics, and communications software. Sabrina can also use the modem to connect to Homestyle's central computers to find current product prices, check merchandise availability, and enter customers' orders while in their offices.

Word Processing

Sabrina uses **word processing software** to write, edit, and format letters to customers and reports to her manager. Special checkers verify both the spelling and grammar in her documents. Her word processing program makes it easy

software
The set of instructions that directs a computer's activities.

systems software
Software that controls the computer and provides program routines that enable applications programs to run on a particular computer.

operating system
A collection of programs that manages a computer system's activities and runs applications software.

applications software
Software that is *applied* to a real-world task; used to perform a specific particular task or to solve a particular problem.

word processing software
Software that is used to write, edit, and format letters and other documents.

to change documents without having to retype them. Sabrina can personalize letters to her customers by changing type styles and sizes, inserting graphics, and using various other features. Many word processing programs include features that enable Sabrina to design a simple newsletter for her customers and create documents for display on her company's Web site. Widely used word processing programs include Microsoft Word and WordPerfect.

Spreadsheets

spreadsheet software

Software that is used to prepare and analyze numerical data such as for financial statements, sales forecasts, and budgets.

Sabrina uses **spreadsheet software** to prepare sales and expense reports for her manager, price estimates and bids for customers, and other materials involving rows and columns of numbers. Spreadsheet software automatically calculates the rows and columns. Once the mathematical formulas are keyed into the spreadsheet, the data can be changed, and the solution will be recalculated instantaneously. Spreadsheets have many uses, including preparation and analysis of financial statements, sales forecasts, and budgets.

Sabrina's manager asked her to survey major customers and create a spreadsheet that could be used to estimate next year's sales. Sabrina entered the current year's sales into column B of her spreadsheet (see Exhibit 17-2). Her projections went into column C. At the bottom of each column, in the "total" row, she entered a formula that automatically computes the column total. For instance, the formula entered into cell B12 is "=SUM(B5:B11)," which tells the computer to enter into cell B12 the sum of the values in cells B5 through B11. Sabrina used another formula to get the percentage figures in column D. The minus signs indicate that Sabrina expects sales to decrease in the Honey Wood and Modern lines. The formulas let Sabrina change any of the numbers in the cells and automatically get new percentages and totals. This feature allows Sabrina to ask "what if" questions. For instance, she could do a second sales forecast that is 10 percent higher than the first.

Confused about how spreadsheets work? Learn some Spreadsheet Basics at

forum.swarthmore.edu/ sum95/math_and/ spreadsheets/basics.html

> e x h i b i t   1 7 - 2 <

Sample Spreadsheet

	A	B	C	D
1	Projected Sales by Product Line - District 19			
2				
3		Volume		
4	Product Line	Current	Projected	Increase
5	Honey Wood	43,441	35,000	–19.4%
6	Baroque	5,224,361	6,200,000	18.7%
7	Classic Oak	8,983,004	9,400,000	4.6%
8	Broadloom	92,495	240,000	159.5%
9	Modern	334,923	290,000	–13.4%
10	Provincial	4,903,027	5,500,000	12.2%
11	Broadway	284,043	410,000	44.3%
12	TOTAL	19,865,294	22,075,000	11.1%

Spreadsheets are very useful business tools. They are widely used to check the effects of different assumptions. Popular spreadsheet programs include Excel and Lotus 1-2-3.

Database Management

database software

Software that records, updates, and stores information.

Like electronic filing cabinets, **database software** records, updates, and stores information. Sabrina uses database management software to keep records on the 473 customers in her territory. She puts basic information on each customer into the database, including store name, address, name of owner or manager, telephone number, fax number, e-mail address, date of most recent call, furniture lines carried, and yearly volume of purchases. The records also include notes from previous sales calls, information on each customer's special needs, and a list of past purchases. The entries in each customer file form a record. Within each record are several columns, or *fields;* each contains a single piece of information about that customer—the store name, street address, city, and so on.

With this electronic research tool, Sabrina can search through data on her customers, sorting and organizing records in her customer database in many ways to more efficiently cover her territory. For instance, she can list customers in order of most recent visit and value of last year's furniture purchases. This information would help her focus on high-volume customers she has not visited recently. When new products are introduced, she can group customers by ZIP code, sort them by the volume of purchases, and schedule her visits to the best prospects on a region-by-region basis. Widely used database software includes Microsoft Access and FileMaker Pro.

Graphics

Sabrina uses graphics software to create tables and graphs for customer presentations and reports. She can summarize complex information in a visual rather than text form to make it more easily understood. For instance, she can depict a customer's profits from sales of her line of furniture. She can show profits for last year and then use similar graphs to show the potential profits from orders this year. Her graphics package, called *presentation graphics software,* is the simplest type. Yet the graphs it produces are more detailed than those produced by other types of programs. Sabrina can also use the graphics feature of her spreadsheet or word processing programs to illustrate her projections. Exhibit 17-3 is a bar graph of current versus projected sales for each product line. Widely used graphics systems include Adobe Illustrator and Freehand and Corel Draw.

Specialized programs such as Microsoft PowerPoint simplify the task of preparing presentation slides. They include tools to create charts, graphs, and pictures. The latest versions of presentation software include such features as multimedia and animation to enhance presentations.

Desktop Publishing

desktop publishing software

Software that combines word processing, graphics, and page layout software and is used to create documents such as sales brochures, catalogs, advertisements, and newsletters.

Homestyle uses **desktop publishing software** to design and produce sales brochures, catalogs, advertisements, and newsletters. This software combines word processing, graphics, and page layout software to create documents. Sabrina can design her newsletter with multiple columns of text on a page, along with titles, pictures, and graphs. For mailings to her customers, Sabrina sometimes uses her word processor to prepare text and a graphics program to prepare illustrations. Then she gives a floppy disk containing her text and graphs to a company designer, who uses a desktop publishing program to make a very handsome mailing piece. The company saves both time and money by not sending materials out to typesetters and other specialists. Widely used desk-

Graph Prepared with Spreadsheet Program

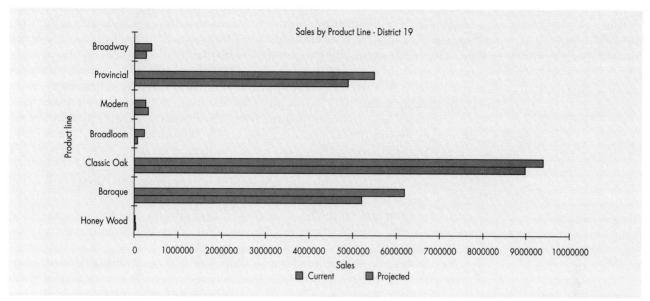

top publishing programs include PageMaker, QuarkXPress, and Microsoft Publisher.

Communications

modem

The part of a computer system that translates data into a form that can be transmitted.

Sabrina uses her computer's modem, communications software, and a telephone link to transfer customer orders, sales reports, expense reports, and other information to and from the home office. The **modem** translates data into a form that can be transmitted. Sabrina can call up her company's central computer system (which also has a modem and communications software) and transfer data. Systems like this are often used to connect microcomputers to larger company computers.

Integrated Software

Instead of using individual programs to perform each of the tasks described above, Sabrina could use an integrated software package or a software suite that combines several popular types of programs. The component programs are designed to work together, making it easy to switch between word processing and graphics, for example, and to import a picture or chart from one module to another. Integrated software packages like Microsoft Works and ClarisWorks include word processing, spreadsheet, database, graphics, and communications programs. Although the integrated applications are scaled-down versions of the individual programs, they have the features most users need and cost considerably less than buying separate software.

Software suites such as Microsoft Office and Lotus Smart Suite bundle together full versions of compatible applications at a reduced price. Like integrated software, suites typically include word processing, spreadsheet, database management, graphics presentation, and communications programs. The latest versions of suites now allow users to format documents for publication on Web pages.

concept check

- What is the difference between systems software and applications software?
- Discuss the main purpose of the five most common types of applications software.
- How do word processing software, desktop publishing software, and spreadsheet software differ? How can you use them together to create documents?

COMPUTER NETWORKS

>lg 4

computer network

A group of two or more computer systems linked together by communications channels to share data and information.

Today most businesses use networks to deliver information to employees, suppliers, and customers. A **computer network** is a group of two or more computer systems linked together by communications channels to share data and information. Networks have been widely used for about 20 years, but microcomputers have made networking much more affordable and popular. Whereas early networks could connect about 20 users and share only data, today's networks link thousands of users and can transmit audio and video as well as data.

By making it easy and fast to share information, networks have created new ways to work and increase productivity. They provide more efficient use of resources, permitting communication and collaboration across distance and time. With file sharing, all employees, regardless of location, have access to the same information. Shared databases also eliminate duplication of effort. Employees at different sites can "screen share" computer files, working on data as if they were in the same room. Their computers are connected by phone lines, they all see the same thing on their display, and anyone can make changes that are seen by the other participants. The employees can also use the networks for videoconferencing.

Networks make it possible for companies to run enterprise software, large programs with integrated modules that manage all of the corporation's internal operations. Enterprise resource planning (ERP) systems (first described in Chapter 12) run on networks. Typical subsystems include finance, human resources, engineering, sales and order distribution, and order management and procurement. These modules work independently and then automatically exchange information, creating a company-wide system that includes current delivery dates, inventory status, quality control, and other critical information. ERP applications can also be integrated with Web-based resources, as we'll see in Chapter 18. Let's now look at the two basic types of networks companies use to transmit data: local area networks and wide area networks.

Local Area Networks

local area network (LAN)

A network that connects computers at one site, enabling the computer users to exchange data and share the use of hardware and software from a variety of computer manufacturers.

A **local area network (LAN)** lets people at one site exchange data and share the use of hardware and software from a variety of computer manufacturers. LANs offer companies a more cost-effective way to link computers than linking terminals to a mainframe computer. The most common uses of LANs at small businesses, for example, are office automation, accounting, and information management.[6]

LANs can help companies reduce staff, streamline operations, and cut processing costs. United Science Industries, a fast-growing general contractor in Woodlawn, Illinois, invested $76,000 in a LAN with 15 networked computers. Instead of using field managers' handwritten sheets to produce invoices, the accounting department can access field manager files through the network. Invoices go out in 10 to 12 days instead of two months, the company collects accounts receivable 5 to 10 days faster, and its monthly labor costs dropped $20,000. "With the network, people spend less time hunting for information and more time working on tasks crucial to operations," says CEO Jay Koch.[7]

Wide Area Networks

wide area network (WAN)

A network that connects computers at different sites via telecommunications media such as phone lines, satellites, and microwaves.

A **wide area network (WAN)** connects computers at different sites via telecommunications media such as phone lines, satellites, and microwaves. A modem connects the computer or a terminal to the telephone line and transmits data almost instantly, in less than a second. The Internet is essentially a worldwide WAN. Long-distance telephone companies, such as AT&T, MCI WorldCom, and Sprint, operate very large WANs. Companies also connect LANs at various locations into WANs. WANs make it possible for companies to work on critical projects around the clock by using teams in different time zones.

Two forms of WANs—intranets and extranets—use Internet technology. We'll look at intranets, internal corporate networks, in this chapter and discuss extranets in the following chapter.

Intranets

intranet

An internal corporate-wide area network that uses Internet technology to link employees in many locations and with different types of computers.

Like LANs, **intranets** are private corporate networks. Many companies use both types of internal networks. However, because they use Internet technology to connect computers, intranets are WANs that link employees in many locations and with different types of computers. Essentially mini-Internets that serve only the company's employees, intranets operate behind a *firewall* that prevents unauthorized access. Employees navigate using a standard Web browser, which makes the intranet easier to use than a client/server system. They are also considerably less expensive to install and maintain and can take advantage of Internet interactive features such as chat rooms and team work spaces.

Until recently, intranets were too complicated and expensive for small businesses, but the cost has dropped as companies develop off-the-shelf programs. Children's Orchard, a franchiser whose stores sell new, secondhand, and manufacturer's overstock toys and children's clothing, uses an intranet to communicate with franchisees around the United States. It is the primary source of company news, corporate services, and peer support. Franchisees have a password to access the intranet through the company's regular Web site. There they can read newsletters, order supplies, and call up statistics on other stores to see how they compare. They can also chat with other franchisees to share ideas and solve problems. CEO Walter Hamilton estimates that the intranet saves the company at least $40,000 a year.[8]

concept check

- What is a computer network? How do a LAN and a WAN differ?
- What benefits do companies gain by using networks?
- You are an employee in the marketing department of a consumer products company. Make a list of the information you would expect to find on the company's intranet.

BUSINESS INFORMATION SYSTEMS

>lg 5

While individuals use business productivity software to accomplish a variety of tasks, the job of managing a company's information needs falls to information systems: users, hardware, and software that support decision making. Information systems collect and store the company's key data and produce the information needed by managers for analysis, control, and decision making.

As we learned in Chapter 12, factories use computer-based information systems to automate production processes and order and monitor inventory. Most companies use them to process customer orders and handle billing and vendor payments. Financial services companies like KeyCorp use a variety of information systems to process transactions such as deposits, ATM withdrawals, and loan payments. Most consumer transactions also involve information systems. When you check out at the supermarket, book a hotel room using a toll-free hotel reservations number, or buy CDs over the Internet, information systems record and track the transaction and transmit the data to the necessary places. Companies typically have several types of information systems:

- *Transaction processing systems* handle the daily business operations of the firm—for example, customer orders, pricing, employee payrolls, and inventory. These operational systems capture and organize raw data and convert these data into information.

- *Management support, or analytic, systems* are dynamic systems that help managers make decisions. These systems allow users to analyze data, including the transaction systems' operational data, to identify business trends, make forecasts, and model business strategies.

- *Office automation systems* use information technology tools such as e-mail, facsimile (fax) machines, and word processing to improve the flow of information throughout an organization. These systems support employees at all levels.

Each type of information system serves a particular level of decision making: operational, tactical, and strategic. Exhibit 17-4 shows the relationship between transaction processing and management support systems as well as the management levels they serve. Let's now take a more detailed look at how companies and managers use transaction processing and management support systems to manage information.

Transaction Processing Systems

The firm's integrated information system starts with its **transaction processing system (TPS).** The TPS receives raw data from internal and external sources and prepares these data for storage in a database similar to a microcomputer database but vastly larger. In fact, all the company's key data are stored in a single huge database that becomes the company's central information resource. A *database management system* tracks the data and allows users to query the database for the information they need.

The database can be updated in two ways. With **batch processing,** data are collected over some time period and processed together. Batch processing uses

transaction processing system (TPS)

An information system that handles the daily business operations of a firm. The system receives and organizes raw data from internal and external sources for storage in a database.

batch processing

A method of updating a database in which data are collected over some time period and processed together.

> e x h i b i t   1 7 - 4 <

A Company's Integrated Information System

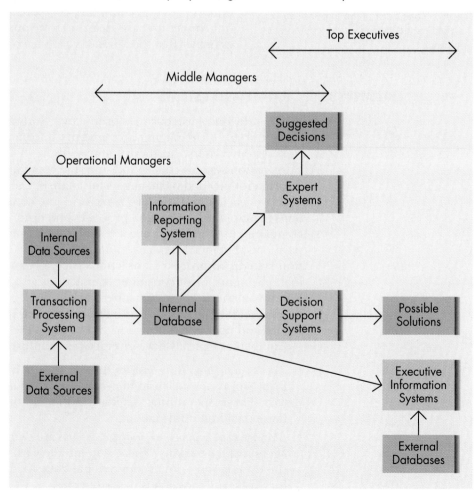

online (real-time) processing

A method of updating a database in which data are processed as they become available.

computer resources very efficiently and is well suited to applications such as payroll processing that require periodic rather than continuous processing. **Online,** or **real-time, processing** processes data as they become available. When you make an airline reservation, the agent enters your reservation directly into the airline's computer and quickly receives confirmation. Online processing keeps the company's data current. Because absolutely current data are needed for management decision making, many large companies use online processing systems.

The transaction processing systems of large companies are custom-designed to keep the records they need. But some applications in the areas of accounting and finance, human resource management, sales and marketing, and manufacturing are nearly universal. For example, the accounting information system diagrammed in Exhibit 17-5 is a typical TPS. It has subsystems for order entry, accounts receivable (for billing customers), accounts payable (for paying bills), payroll, inventory, and general ledger (for determining the financial status and profitability of the business). The accounting information system provides input to and receives input from the firm's other information systems, such as manufacturing (production planning data, for example) and human resources (data on hours worked and salary increases to generate paychecks).

Management Support Systems

Transaction processing systems were the first stage of information technology. By automating routine and tedious back-office processes such as accounting, order processing, and financial reporting, they reduced clerical expenses and provided basic operational information more quickly. As technology improved,

> e x h i b i t   1 7 - 5 <

Accounting Information System

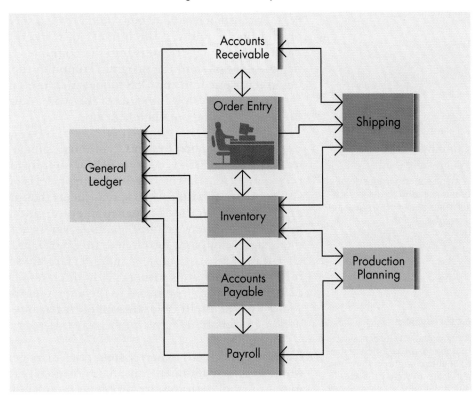

businesses realized that computers could do more than merely process data. Managers now have several types of **management support systems (MSSs)** that use the internal database to help them make better decisions.

As we saw in the KeyCorp opening vignette, information technologies such as data warehousing are part of more advanced MSSs. A **data warehouse** combines many databases across the whole company into one central database that supports management decision making. Data warehouses include software to extract data from operational databases, maintain the data in the warehouse, and provide data to users.

Information Reporting Systems   At the first level of a MSS is an *information reporting system,* which uses summary data collected by the TPS to produce reports with statistics that managers can use to make decisions. Some reports are scheduled and present information on a regular basis. For instance, Homestyle's payroll personnel get a weekly payroll report showing how each employee's paycheck was determined. The next level of report summarizes information. A payroll summary report might show higher-level managers total labor cost by department, overtime as a percentage of total payroll cost by department, and a comparison of current labor costs with those in the prior year. Exception reports help identify problems by telling about cases that fail to meet some standard. An accounts receivable exception report that lists all customers with overdue accounts would help collection personnel focus their work. Demand reports are special reports generated only when a manager requests them. The marketing manager for the Honey Wood furniture line might call for reports on sales by region and type of store to identify reasons for the sales decline.

Decision Support Systems   A **decision support system (DSS)** helps managers make decisions using computer models that describe real-world processes. The DSS also uses data from the internal database but looks for specific data that relate to the problems at hand. It is a tool for answering "what if" questions about what would happen if the manager made certain changes. In simple cases, a manager can create a spreadsheet and try changing some of the numbers. For instance, a manager could create a spreadsheet to show the amount of overtime required if the number of workers increases or decreases. With models, the manager enters into the computer the values that describe a particular situation, and the program computes the results. Homestyle's marketing executives could run DSS models that use sales data and demographic assumptions to develop forecasts of the types of furniture that would appeal to the fastest growing population groups.

Executive Information Systems   Although similar to a DSS, an **executive information system (EIS)** is customized for an individual executive. These systems provide specific information for strategic decisions. For example, Homestyle's CEO has an EIS with special spreadsheets that present financial data comparing Homestyle to its principal competitors and graphs showing current economic and industry trends. Belk, Inc., America's largest privately held department store company, developed an EIS for its buyers, assistant buyers, and executives. Its easy-to-understand interface allows users to quickly get answers to high-level questions such as, "How did last week's markdowns affect the sale of intimate apparel compared to the same time last year?" "Will our current inventory for Kenneth Cole shoes at our Charlotte store be sufficient, given the pending promotion?"[9]

Expert Systems   An **expert system** gives managers advice similar to what they would get from a human consultant. Artificial intelligence enables computers to reason and learn to solve problems in much the same way humans do. The

Medical professionals use expert systems to analyze patients' medications, ensuring that they do not cause allergic reactions and potentially dangerous interactions with patients' other prescriptions.

office automation system

An information system that uses information technology tools such as word processing systems, e-mail systems, cellular phones, pagers and fax machines, to improve communications throughout an organization.

use of expert systems is growing as more applications are found. To date, expert systems have been used to help explore for oil, schedule employee work shifts, and diagnose illnesses. Some expert systems take the place of human experts, while others assist them.

At Boston's Brigham and Women's Hospital, an expert system checks medication orders against patients' known allergies and potentially serious drug interactions. It pages doctors to alert them to problems within seconds. "Doctors just can't keep track of 1,000 facts on each patient," says Dr. Jonathan Teich. "The computer does it much better." It also suggests alternative medications. The system analyzes about 13,000 orders per day. Its fast response time—no longer does a lab technician have to call the pharmacist, who then finds the doctor—prevents about 400 serious medication errors daily.[10]

Office Automation Systems

Today's **office automation systems** make good use of the computer networks in many companies to improve communications. Office automation systems assist all levels of employees and enable managers to handle most of their own communication. The key elements include:

- *Word processing systems* for producing written messages.
- *E-mail systems* for communicating directly with other employees and customers and transferring computer files.
- *Departmental scheduling systems* for planning meetings and other activities.
- *Cellular phones* for providing telephone service away from the office, as in cars.
- *Pagers* that notify employees of phone calls. Some pagers have the ability to display more extensive written messages sent from a computer network.
- *Voice mail systems* for recording, storing, and forwarding phone messages.
- *Facsimile (fax) systems* for delivering messages on paper within minutes.
- *Electronic bulletin boards* and *computer conferencing systems* for discussing issues with others who are not present.

Office automation systems also make telecommuting and home-based businesses possible. An estimated 8 million people work at home, using microcomputers and other high-tech equipment to keep in touch with the office. Instead of spending time on the road twice a day, telecommuters work at home two or more days a week. As we discussed in Chapter 6, home offices are a popular trend among small business owners.

c o n c ə p t   c h ə c k

- What are the main components of an information system, and what does each do?
- Differentiate between the types of management support systems, and give examples of how each is used.
- How can office automation systems help employees work more efficiently?

MANAGING INFORMATION TECHNOLOGY

>lg 6

With the help of computers, people have produced more data in the last 30 years than in the previous 5,000 years combined. Companies today make sizable investments in information technology to help them manage this overwhelming amount of data, convert the data into knowledge, and deliver it to the people who need it. In many cases, however, the companies do not reap the desired benefits from these expenditures. Among the typical complaints from senior executives are that the payoff from IT investments is inadequate, IT investments do not relate to business strategy, the firm seems to be buying the latest technology for technology's sake, and communications between IT specialists and IT users are poor.[11]

Managing a company's information resources requires a coordinated effort among a firm's top executives, IT managers, and business unit managers. The goal is to develop an integrated, company-wide technology plan that achieves a balance between business judgment and technology expertise. Protecting company information and privacy concerns are other important aspects of knowledge management.

Technology Planning

Like any other business activity that involves the entire company, IT requires coordinated strategies and planning that take into account the company's strategic objectives. Then managers can select the right technology to help them reach those goals.

The goal of technology planning is to provide employees with the tools they need to perform their jobs at the highest levels of efficiency. The first step is a general needs assessment, followed by ranking of projects and the specific choices of hardware and software. Some basic questions departmental managers and IT specialists should ask when planning technology purchases include:

- What are the company's overall objectives?
- What problems does the company want to solve?
- How can technology help meet those goals and solve the problems?
- What are the company's priorities, both short- and long-term?
- Which technologies meet the company's requirements?
- Are additional hardware and software required? If so, will they integrate with the company's existing systems?

Once managers identify the projects that make business sense, they can choose the best products for the company's needs. The final step is to evaluate the potential benefits of the technology, in terms of efficiency and effectiveness. This requires developing specific criteria—not only quantitative measures like cost savings and profit improvement, but also qualitative factors such as employee satisfaction. For example, how will the new technology increase revenues? Will it get products to market faster by shortening the product development cycle or streamlining the production process? Will it save employees time and cut labor costs? What other benchmarks does the company want to achieve? How can prevention strategies guard against information loss?

Plans will change over time in response to company needs. "Basically, business and technology plans should become living documents that drive the company forward," says Cheryl Currid, a technology analyst.[12] The planning process can even be a catalyst for growth, as the Focusing on Small Business box demonstrates.

Protecting Computers and Information

Protecting the information stored in computers is no easy task. With the ever-increasing dependence on computers, companies must develop plans to cover power outages, equipment failure, human error, and disasters such as major

ACI BENEFITS FROM IT PLANNING

Sales at Actuarial Consultants, Inc. (ACI), a 38-person employee benefits consulting firm in Torrance, California, had been flat for four years. But before CEO Pat Byrnes could implement any growth strategies, ACI needed to revamp its business procedures and install centralized computer systems.

The company's benefits consultants each kept their own customer files and used whatever software they liked to prepare benefit plans. ACI's computer systems were a mess because it had no technology plan. Low-level tech support personnel bought hardware and software to fill immediate needs, without regard to compatibility with existing products. In addition, ACI had no marketing database or client tracking system. Its information sources were spread out all over the company, often on handwritten forms, and its accounting and record-keeping systems could barely keep track of its current accounts. "We are in a business that needs to move information quickly," said Byrnes. "We just couldn't go on like this any longer."

To avoid past mistakes, Byrnes hired an experienced IT executive to serve as the chief information officer and to build a solid IT infrastructure to support ACI's marketing, sales, and accounting operations and future growth. With experience at IBM and at another executive benefits consulting firm, Howard Moore understood technology as well as ACI's business and knew how to work with and train employees.

Moore developed a comprehensive technology plan to help ACI reach its goals. He first spent several months listening to employees' concerns and soliciting ideas about what they needed to work better. Next he standardized ACI's computer systems on one platform—the Windows operating system, Microsoft Office suite, and PCs from one manufacturer. Before installing additional applications such as e-mail and file sharing on the office's upgraded network, Moore had employees test them. If the employees weren't satisfied, he told the systems consultant to find something else.

Once the basics were in place, Moore began working on ACI's internal business processes. To improve customer acquisition methods, he created a prospect information form that could be shared over the network. For the first time, sales, marketing, and accounting personnel had access to information they needed. ACI could now forecast future staffing needs and do other long-range planning. And the ability to track business development per consultant allowed ACI to pay the consultants accordingly. Finally, Moore encouraged better communications through increased use of e-mail, instituted security and backup procedures, and developed a telecommuting program.

With the new IT systems in place, ACI was able to increase its client load without additional personnel. Byrnes was able to add two new business lines, compensation consulting and executive benefits—something he would not have considered before Moore took charge.

Critical Thinking Questions

1. How did the absence of technology planning cause problems at ACI?
2. Why did hiring a chief information officer, something usually found only at large companies, make sense for ACI?
3. If you were Moore, how you would evaluate ACI's technology needs to develop a technology plan?

fires, earthquakes, or floods. Many companies install fault-tolerant computer systems designed to withstand such disasters. Preventing costly problems can be as simple as regularly backing up applications and data. Companies should have systems in place that automatically back up the company's data every day. In addition, employees should back up their own work regularly.

Disasters are not the only threat to data. A great deal of data, much of it confidential, can easily be tapped or destroyed by anyone who knows about computers.

Data Security Issues Firms are taking steps to prevent computer crimes, which cost large companies hundreds of thousands of dollars every year. There are several major categories of computer crimes:

- *Unauthorized access and use.* This can create havoc with a company's systems. For example, employees at Bluebird Systems, a software company in Carlsbad, California, kept having unexplained system crashes and network slowdowns. A consultant traced the problem to Bluebird's network administrator, who was also a Sierra Club member and claimed that he'd asked permission to create and maintain the Sierra Club Web site on a Bluebird server. As the site expanded from a few pages to over 2,000, the heavy traffic affected Bluebird's network operations. Hal Tilbury, Bluebird's CEO, estimates that the network crashes cost the company several million dollars from lost employee productivity and missed deadlines—not to mention the risk of unauthorized access to the company's files and research.[13]

- *Security breaches and unauthorized access.* Employees can copy confidential new product information and provide it to competitors. Networking links make it easier for someone outside the organization to gain access to a company's computers. Computer crooks are getting more sophisticated all the time and find new ways to get into ultrasecure sites. For example, a British hacker was able to break into the network of the highly secret Rome Laboratory in New York by using computers in Latvia, Colombia, and Chile. Then he attacked defense and government systems.[14]

  To protect data, companies can encode confidential information so only the recipient can decipher it. Special authorization systems can help stop unwanted access from inside or outside. These can be as simple as a password or as sophisticated as fingerprint or voice identification. Companies can also install intrusion-detection systems to monitor networks for activities that signal the possibility of unauthorized access and document suspicious events. We'll revisit the issue of protecting confidential data in the next chapter's Internet discussion.

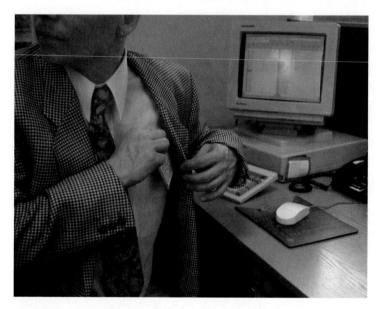

Employers can guard against employee theft of confidential information by installing special authorization systems that prevent unwanted access from inside their organization.

- *Software piracy.* The copying of copyrighted software programs by people who haven't paid for them is another form of unauthorized use. Piracy takes revenue away from the company that developed the program—usually at great cost. Thus, software firms take piracy seriously and go after the offenders. Many also make special arrangements so that large companies can get multiple copies of programs at a lower cost rather than use illegal copies.

- *Deliberate damage to information.* For example, an unhappy employee in the purchasing department could get into the computer system and delete information on past orders and future inventory needs. The sabotage could severely disrupt production and the accounts payable system. Willful acts to destroy or change the data in computers are hard to prevent. To lessen the damage, companies should back up critical information.

- *Computer viruses.* A computer program that copies itself into other software and can spread to other computer systems, a **computer virus** can destroy the contents of a computer's hard drive or damage files. Another form is called a

computer virus

A computer program that copies itself into other software and can spread to other computer systems.

> m a k i n g   e t h i c a l   c h o i c e s <

THE PAIRGAIN HOAX

At 9:27 A.M. on April 7, 1999, investors were jolted by a posting on the Yahoo! finance message board. The posting indicated that PairGain Technologies, Inc. had been acquired, and that the information had been found on the Internet site run by Bloomberg—a provider of news and financial data. The posting also provided "an electronic link to what appeared to be a news article on a Web site identified as Bloomberg.com."

As a result of this posting, heavy trading of PairGain's stock ensued, with the per share price rising by 32 percent at one point. Unfortunately for the buyers, the news story turned out to be fictitious. When investors began to discover the hoax, the stock fell, but was still up 10 percent at the end of the day. In all, 13.7 million shares were traded—more than six times PairGain's daily trading average of 2.1 million shares.

The fake news story, described as a very sophisticated example of "investors being duped by false or misleading postings on the Internet," illustrates "how cheaply and easily programmers can pull off Internet hoaxes using widely available technology and the anonymity afforded by the online world." The fake Bloomberg.com Web page was posted on the free Angelfire service provided by Lycos. To sign up for this free service, a person need only fill out a brief form, including "such unverifiable information as a name and address." A workable e-mail address is also required, but someone can easily use another person's e-mail address.

Critical Thinking Questions

1. Do Internet services have a moral or ethical responsibility to ensure that information provided on their free sites is not false or misleading?
2. What would you do if you discovered false or misleading information on an Internet site?

"worm" because it spreads itself automatically from computer to computer. Viruses can hide for weeks or months before starting to damage information. A virus that "infects" one computer or network can be spread to another computer by sharing disks or by downloading infected files over the Internet. To protect data from virus damage, software developers have created virus protection programs. This software automatically monitors computers to detect and remove viruses. Program developers make regular updates available to guard against newly created viruses. In addition, experts are becoming more proficient at tracking down virus authors, who are subject to criminal charges.

To find out if that e-mail alerting you to another virus threat is real or a hoax, check out the latest information at

www.sophos.com/virusinfo/analyses

Fixing the Millennium Bug As the year 2000 (Y2K) approached, computer users worried about the ability of their systems to recognize the new century's date. The problem stemmed from the long-standing practice of using two digits to refer to a year—12-31-99, for example. On January 1, 2000, some computers would either assume that the year was 1900, revert to some earlier date, or shut down entirely because they could not read "00." Any electronic device that depends on dates for any part of its processing could malfunction unless the software code for the date was fixed. The resulting loss of data could be catastrophic.

Once the so-called millennium bug was identified and gained widespread attention, companies began to tackle the problem. Though in concept the solution is simple—rewriting computer code instructions involving dates to accept the year 2000—in practice it was more difficult to find all the affected programs. For example, pharmaceutical company Eli Lilly had to test over 40,000 items to find devices that use a clock, while Texaco had 14,000 devices at just one refinery. Other companies chose to upgrade their software applications to newer Y2K-compliant versions such as ERP software. Regardless of approach, fixing the bug cost an estimated $300 billion in the United States alone. Many companies and governmental agencies underestimated their costs by 25 percent or more. Some economists predicted that Y2K damages to the flow of information could lead to a recession in 2000 or 2001.[15]

During 1999, companies tested their systems for Y2K readiness by running simulations that pretended it was the end of 1999 and watching what happened. In addition to fixing their own computer systems, companies made sure that their suppliers and customers also had Y2K-compliant systems.

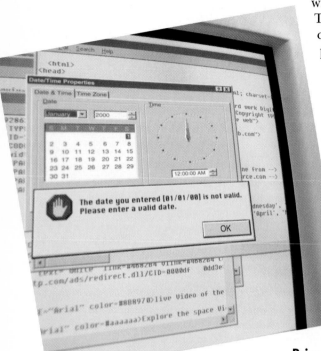

All organizations using computers were involved in the technology planning project of rewriting computer code instructions involving dates to accept the year 2000.

Privacy Concerns The very existence of huge electronic file cabinets full of personal information presents a threat to our personal privacy. Until recently, our financial, medical, tax, and other records were stored in separate computer systems. Computer networks make it easy to pool these data into data warehouses. Companies also sell the information they collect about you from sources like warranty registration cards, credit card records, registration at Web sites, and grocery store discount club cards. Telemarketers can combine data from different sources to create fairly detailed profiles of consumers.

Increasingly, consumers are fighting to regain control of personal data and how that information is used. Public outcry over a flaw in Microsoft's Windows 98 that allowed it to gather computer identification without the user's knowledge and electronic serial numbers in Intel's Pentium III chips resulted in changes to both products. Privacy advocates are working to block state governments from selling driver's license information. Legislation under discussion in California would restrict how businesses, nonprofit organizations, and government entities can collect and use personal information. For example, one proposal would prevent supermarkets from collecting and selling information gathered when shoppers use barcoded plastic discount cards. With information about their buying habits, advertisers can target consumers for specific marketing programs.[16]

The challenge to companies is to find a balance between collecting the information they need while at the same time protecting individual consumer rights. Most registration and warranty forms that ask questions about income and interests have a box for consumers to check to prevent the company from selling

c o n c ə p t   c h ə c k

- Why is technology planning an essential element of information management? What are its benefits?
- Describe the different threats to data security and the ways companies can protect information from destruction and from unauthorized use.
- Why are privacy rights advocates alarmed over the use of techniques such as data warehouses?

their names. Many companies now state their privacy policies to ensure consumers that they will not abuse the information they collect. Although supermarket chain Safeway records purchase data, it will not sell customer information to third parties like telemarketers and direct mail firms or manufacturers who want to send customers coupons. "What we're trying to assess is general shopping patterns," says Debra Lambert, Safeway's corporate director of public affairs.[17]

CAPITALIZING ON TRENDS IN BUSINESS

>lg 7

Information technology is a continually evolving field. The fast pace and amount of change, coupled with IT's broad reach, make it especially challenging to isolate industry trends. From the time we write this chapter to the time you read it—as little as six months—new trends will appear and those that seemed important may fade. However, three trends that are reshaping the IT landscape at the beginning of the 21st century are knowledge management, the emergence of information appliances, and the shortage of qualified IT personnel.

Managing Knowledge Resources

Although companies may have procedures to manage information, they are now tackling the more difficult task of knowledge management (KM). *Information management* involves collecting, processing, and condensing information. *Knowledge management,* however, focuses on gathering and sharing an organization's collective knowledge to improve productivity and foster innovation. Some companies are even creating a new position, chief knowledge officer, to head up this effort.

We've already seen how companies like KeyCorp and Belk use software tools to comb through company databases seeking information. But better software is not the only answer to KM. Effective KM calls for a cultural change within the company. It's a whole new way of working and communicating that encourages departments and employees to share knowledge. This attitude can be difficult to promote among employees who are used to protecting their own turf. KM's benefits can be significant in terms of both time and money. Chevron Corp.'s individual oil refineries had their own methods to improve efficiency. By mounting a formal effort to collect the best refinery management practices and make them available to all locations, Chevron saved $170 million.[18]

As KM has become an important company objective, the CIO has joined the top management team. No longer is IT an isolated department focused on keeping the company's computer systems running, managing IT costs, and dealing with IT suppliers. Today the CIO and his or her team are partners in the strategic planning process. IT managers provide input on how to leverage technology to improve business processes, change the business model, and better serve customers. As Joe Durocher, CIO at Hilton Hotel Corp., explains, IT has to be "an enabler, to help you do business in new and different ways."[19]

End of the Personal Computer Era?

"Information appliances," easy-to-use, inexpensive, consumer-oriented products that perform only one or two tasks, may soon replace the PC as our most popular information tool. In addition to simplicity and convenience, many of these appliances use wireless technology to make computing more portable.

These devices run counter to the recent trend to make PCs increasingly complex and powerful. Though businesses may need these PCs, most personal users don't. "The PC is so general purpose that very few of us use more than 5 percent of its capability," says former Hewlett-Packard CEO Lewis Platt. And for users who only want to do one thing—access the Internet, for example—a PC is more than they need. PCs won't disappear, however. They will co-exist with other alternatives, but will no longer dominate to the degree that they do now.

Fueled by such technological advances as tiny storage devices, efficient microprocessors, and wireless networks, information appliances could revolutionize the way we view computers. A wide variety of these devices are already available: palmtop personal digital assistants, hand-held scanners, cell phones that send and receive e-mail, portable music players for music downloaded from the Internet, set-top TV boxes that automatically save favorite programs, and Web phones with touch-screen access. Tiny microprocessors with Internet and digital capabilities make existing products "smarter." For example, fax machines that use the Internet rather than phone lines will save transmission costs.[20]

Like the palmtop personal digital assistant, information devices are becoming smalller, portable, and easier to use and are emerging as convenient alternatives to personal computers.

Searching for Information Technology Talent

The good news: the rapidly growing IT industry has created over 7.5 million new jobs since 1994. The bad news: there aren't enough qualified IT personnel to fill those jobs. The Meta Group's 1999 Staffing and Compensation Guide estimates that 400,000 programmer, systems analyst, and computer scientist positions are unfilled—more than twice the vacancy rate in 1997. At one point the 4,000-person Telecom Group Systems at Bell Atlantic Network Services had almost 800 openings. In fact, IT companies rank the lack of skilled workers as their most significant barrier to growth.[21]

If the shortage of IT talent continues, companies will be hard-pressed to keep up with the latest IT developments. According to Commerce Department predictions, demand for information systems analysts and computer engineers will almost double between 1998 and 2002. Yet the number of new college graduates with computer science degrees or programming skills has dropped in recent years. To attract and retain IT talent, companies are implementing new recruitment programs, partnering with educational institutions, increasing in-house training programs for individuals with no previous IT skills, and developing programs to improve employee satisfaction.

concept check

- Differentiate between information management and knowledge management. What steps can companies take to manage knowledge?
- What benefits do information appliances offer? Do you think they will diminish the importance of PCs?
- Why is the shortage of qualified IT personnel a serious problem?

APPLYING THIS CHAPTER'S TOPICS

Computer literacy is no longer a luxury. To succeed in business today, almost everyone must develop technological competence. Whether you have a part-time job in a fast-food restaurant that uses computerized ordering systems or perform financial analyses that guide the future of your own company, you will depend on computers. The more you increase your knowledge of technology, the more valuable you will be as an employee in today's information-driven businesses. In addition, the shortage of qualified IT personnel opens up new career avenues to those that enjoy working with technology. You can also take steps to protect your privacy.

Preparation Pays Off

Whether you are an employee or a business owner, you need to be aware of how technology affects the way your firm operates. New applications can change fundamental company operations and employees' roles. For example, companies that install ERP systems want individual employees to make more strategic, far-reaching decisions than before. This requires a dramatic shift in employee's roles and the way they should view their jobs. For example, an accountant's responsibilities might now include analyzing budgets,

> t r y   i t   n o w !   <

1. **Stay Current** Keeping up with the fast pace of technology change is a real challenge, but it is necessary if you wish to remain up-to-date on the latest IT developments. The Internet has simplified this task, however. Get into the habit of visiting news sites such as ZDNet (**www.zdnet.com**). Its Anchor Desk is updated daily with current news. You can also link to Ziff Davis publications such as *PC Week* and find online classes. Another excellent site is CNet's News.com (**www.news.com**), which updates the technology news headlines throughout the day. It has sections on enterprise computing, the Internet, IT services, telecommunications, and personal technology.

2. **Know Who's Hiring** you can benefit from the severe shortage of technology personnel—even if you don't think you want a job in IT. Read the classified employment ads in your local newspaper and the *Wall Street Journal*. Go online to browse the employment ads from almost any major newspaper and surf through the Web sites with job listings. Many technology company Web sites also post job openings. Make a list of jobs that interest you. In addition, read the general job listings to see how many require computer skills.

not just auditing expenses. A salesperson's role might expand to include more strategic decision making about customer issues. Your company will see the business benefits sooner if you prepare for these changing roles. A manager should begin teaching employees operational procedures before implementing the new system and help them acquire the necessary analytical skills. As an employee, you can take the initiative to learn as much as possible about the new technology and how it operates.

at KeyCorp

Unlike about one-third of all banking data warehouse projects, KeyCorp's data warehouse was a big success. A major factor was the support of top management, who emphasized to employees the important role the data warehouse played in the bank's ability to compete in the financial services marketplace. In developing the data warehouse, bank executives involved managers from all business units to ensure that the system would serve their needs and that they would contribute to its value. Compensation incentives encouraged staff members to use the data warehouse.

KeyCorp's data warehouse drives the bank's customer focus. The benefits go beyond improved results from marketing campaigns. Because the data warehouse generates monthly and annual customer profit reports, the bank can measure how well its sales force maximizes account profitability. The monthly profit reports highlight changing customer needs and behavior patterns so that the bank can identify potential problem accounts and prevent missing opportunities for more profit. Information from the data warehouse helps sales reps cross-sell by showing what services a customer is likely to buy next—or avoid. For example, trend analysis showed that customers who don't use ATMs aren't likely to try online banking. Removing those customers from prospect lists prevented KeyCorp from wasting money on mailings to customers who wouldn't be interested anyway.[23]

Acquiring IT skills will also open many career opportunities. If travel interests you, head for Europe, where an estimated 500,000 IT jobs are vacant. As a result, IT skills and experience are in demand—and salaries worldwide are climbing.

Keeping Secrets

By understanding how companies collect and use information, you can protect your personal data from being mined. The first step is simply saying no. You can usually get a store's discounts and products even if you withhold some personal information, explains Beth Givens of the Privacy Rights Clearinghouse in San Diego. "You don't have to give your name when you get a supermarket card. Safeway says you can register as an anonymous shopper." Also have your name removed from direct market lists to curb unwanted mail and data exchange.

Next, check your credit report for unfamiliar accounts and monthly charge card statements for fraudulent charges that signal that someone may have stolen your personal information. Then contact the creditors and let them know the information is not accurate. Major credit reporting agencies must correct the information. Finally, contact the major credit reporting agencies, Equifax, Experian, and TransUnion, and forbid prescreening credit rating checks. This puts a stop to unsolicited credit card offers, which can fall into the wrong hands.[22]

SUMMARY OF LEARNING GOALS

>lg 1 **How does information play a role in decision making?**
When making decisions, managers compare information about the company's current status to its goals and standards. Some of the information is provided by information systems, which collect and process data.

>lg 2 **What are the components of a computer, and how are computers categorized by size?**

Hardware components include the central processing unit (CPU), the secondary storage system, the input system, and the output system. The CPU consists of an arithmetic-logic unit, a control unit, and main memory.

Microcomputers are small enough to fit on a desktop. Minicomputers are too large for a desktop but small enough to fit into a normal office. Mainframe computers are about the size of a refrigerator and can quickly and reliably process high volumes of data. Supercomputers can perform complex computations to simulate or predict difficult problems.

>lg 3 **How does software make a computer useful?**

Software falls into two main categories: systems software and applications software. The most commonly used applications software are used for word processing, spreadsheets, graphics, databases, desktop publishing, and communications. Word processing systems aid in composing, editing, and formatting documents. Spreadsheets automatically manipulate rows and columns of numbers, making analysis easier. Graphics systems create graphs and drawings. Database systems store and retrieve records and create data presentations. Desktop publishing programs help create professional-looking documents with text and graphics. Communications systems can be used to share data among computer systems. Integrated software packages combine several types of applications software into one program or suite.

>lg 4 **Why are computer networks an important part of today's business information systems?**

Local area networks (LANs) and wide area networks (WANs) are used to link computers so they can share data and expensive hardware. Today companies use networks extensively to improve operating efficiency. Networking techniques like e-mail allow employees to communicate with each other quickly, regardless of their location.

>lg 5 **What is the structure of a typical information system?**

An information system consists of a transaction processing system, management support systems, and an office automation system. The transaction processing system collects and organizes operational data on the firm's activities. Management support systems help managers make better decisions. They include an information reporting system that provides information based on the data to the managers who need it; decision support systems that use models to assist in answering "what if" types of questions; and expert systems that give managers advice similar to what they would get from a human consultant. Executive information systems are customized to the needs of top management. All employees benefit from office automation systems that facilitate communication by using word processing, e-mail, fax machines, and similar technologies.

>lg 6 **How can companies manage information technology to their advantage?**

To get the most value from information technology (IT), companies must go beyond simply collecting and summarizing information. Technology planning involves evaluating the company's goals and objectives and using the right technology to reach them. Because companies are more dependent on computers than ever before, they need to protect data and equipment from natural disasters and computer crime such as unauthorized access and use and malicious damage. They must also take steps to protect customers' personal privacy rights.

KEY TERMS

applications
  software 508
batch processing
  514
central processing
  unit (CPU) 506
chief information
  officer (CIO) 502
computer 505
computer network
  512
computer virus 520
data 503
data warehouse
  516
database software
  510
decision support
  system (DSS) 516
desktop publishing
  software 510
executive
  information
  system (EIS) 516
expert system 516
hardware 505
information 503
information system
  (IS) 503
information tech-
  nology (IT) 503
intranet 513
local area network
  (LAN) 512
mainframe
  computers 507
management
  support system
  (MSS) 516
microcomputers
  506
minicomputers 506
modem 511
office automation
  system 517
online (real-time)
  processing 515
operating system
  508
random access
  memory (RAM)
  506
secondary storage
  506
software 508
spreadsheet
  software 509
supercomputers
  507
systems software
  508
transaction
  processing system
  (TPS) 514
wide area network
  (WAN) 512
word processing
  software 508

>lg 7   **What are the leading trends in information technology?**
Knowledge management focuses on sharing an organization's collective knowledge to improve productivity and foster innovation. The CIO plays a pivotal role in knowledge management. The emergence of simpler information appliances may make the PC a less important information tool. Consumers may prefer these easy-to-use devices to multifunction PCs. The shortage of qualified IT personnel is making it harder for companies to stay current with the latest IT developments.

PREPARING FOR TOMORROW'S WORKPLACE

1. Some people view the spread of computers with alarm, worrying that computers pose a threat to the job security of such workers as secretaries and factory workers and can lead to invasions of privacy, both in the workplace and at home. Others believe that computers bring benefits that far outweigh any of these concerns. Divide the class in half to debate these conflicting views.

2. Prepare a list of productivity applications software and campus-related information systems that would most benefit a full-time business student. What tasks would the software and systems support? How else could the student use technology to her or his advantage?

3. Visit or conduct a phone interview with a local small business owner about the different ways her or his firm uses information technology. Prepare a brief report on your findings that includes the hardware and software used, benefits of technology for the company, and any problems in implementing or using it.

4. Your school wants to automate the class registration process. Prepare a memo to the Dean of Information Systems describing an integrated information system that would help a student choose and register for courses. Include a graphic representation of the system similar to Exhibit 17-5 that shows how the data become useful information. Indicate the information a student needs to choose courses and its sources. Explain how several types of management support systems could help students make better course decisions. How could the school use the information it collects from this system?

5. Prior to January 1, 2000, alarming reports circulated about potential chaos from widespread system crashes due to the so-called Y2K bug. Predictions included power and telecommunications outages, disrupted transportation systems, inability to access accounts at banks, and stock market crashes—not to mention the general chaos at companies everywhere when their computers malfunctioned. Divide the class into small groups and discuss what really happened. In addition to general information, each group should select an industry—for example, banking, insurance, automobile manufacturers, computer hardware, telecommunications—and report on how it coped with the arrival of the year 2000.

WORKING THE NET

1. The size and cost of computer systems have fallen dramatically in the past year. Visit the Web site of eMachines, **www.e4me.com**/, a leading manufacturer of affordable PCs. What type of PC system can you buy for $500?

2. You are in the market for a new computer system for your five-employee consulting business. Using such resources as ZDNet Products (**www.zdnet.com/products**), ZDNet Computer Shopper (**www.zdnet.com/computershopper**), *Business Week's* Computer Buying Guide, Maven (**www.maven.businessweek.com**), and any other sites you find, conduct research on the latest hardware and software. Put together a list of your recommended purchases. Give reasons for your choices based on product reviews.

3. One of the fastest growing areas of business software is enterprise resource planning (ERP) applications. Visit the site of one of the following companies: SAP (**www.sap.com**); PeopleSoft (**www.peoplesoft.com**); Oracle (**www.oracle.com**); or Baan (**www.baan.com**). Prepare a short presentation for the class about the company's ERP product offerings and capabilities. Include examples of how companies use the ERP software.

4. The Internet has the answer to most computer equipment or software questions—from how to get your computer to stop crashing to which brand of scanner or printer is best for your system. Pick a hardware manufacturer, such as Apple, Compaq, Dell, Epson, Hewlett-Packard, or Iomega, and a software vendor—for example, Microsoft, Corel, Adobe, or any other whose products you use—and check out the technical support areas of their Web sites. Start at PC Help Online (**www.pchelponline.com**) and Support Help (**www.supporthelp.com/**), two sites that make it easy to link to a specific company or to find information. Then visit a third-party site that offers assistance from fellow computer users: America Online's Computing Channel's message boards, ZDHelp (**www.zdnet.com/zdhelp**), or CNET Message Boards (**www.cnet.com/cdoor/** and click on Community, then Message Boards). Which sites are the most helpful? Summarize your findings and prepare a brief report to share with the class.

CREATIVE THINKING CASE

Traci's Boutique

With a retailing degree and three years' experience in the highly competitive boutique business, Traci Steffinski decided to open her own small store in a city with a large university. The boutique sells an international collection of handcrafted jewelry, scarves, belts, and clothing. Because Traci's merchandise is reasonably priced, the boutique has been very successful, attracting a variety of customers, including students. After two profitable years, she is ready to open a second, larger boutique closer to campus.

Until now, Traci has managed the business without a computer. She realizes that with two stores she should computerize her operations. Traci has listed the activities that are involved in running her business: writing to potential suppliers for catalogs, ordering merchandise, approving credit card purchases, letting customers know about special sales and the new store, developing accounting and inventory systems, and hiring an artist to design an announcement and newspaper ads. Before opening the second store, Traci will need to hire additional staff and set up systems for paying them and tracking sales. She will also be traveling to more trade shows to find new items to sell.

Critical Thinking Questions

1. List the types of hardware and software that Traci will need. Be specific. Explain why each item will be needed and how it will be used.
2. Outline the steps Traci should take to develop her computer systems for inventory, financial information, and customer information.

3. How could Traci use spreadsheet software to run her business? Can you identify enough uses to justify an expense of, say, $300 for the software? Explain.

4. Should Traci also invest in networking and office automation equipment, and why? If so, what types of systems would you recommend?

VIDEO CASE

Information Management Challenges and Solutions at Archway Cookies

Archway Cookies (**www.archwaycookies.com** and **www.intermec.com/solutions/archway.htm**), family owned and headquartered in Battle Creek, Michigan, is the third largest cookie manufacturer in the United States and has a 5 percent share of the American cookie market. With two company-owned and four licensed bakeries in the United States and Canada, Archway produces more than one billion cookies annually.

Founding the company in 1936, Harold and Ruth Swanson "set the standard for what would become a one-of-a-kind cookie." The Swansons baked cookies that used only the finest quality ingredients and then delivered them fresh to the stores where they were sold. "This commitment to traditional quality and guaranteed freshness is the foundation of Archway Cookies."

Archway Cookies is a bake-to-order company. With over 60 different varieties of Home Style, Gourmet, Fat Free, Sugar Free, Bag, and Holiday cookies, Archway is a "bake today, ship tomorrow" manufacturing operation. Cookies are ordered by distributors, baked by the company, and shipped to distributors within 48 hours.

To "bake today" and "ship tomorrow," Archway must have accurate and timely information. Prior to 1991, the company managed its information using paper-based sales and tracking systems that were introduced in the 1930s. These systems did not provide for the fastest, most effective, and most efficient flow and use of data.

Archway's management recognized the need to automate data collection, improve data flow, and create a single database. Without these information management changes, achieving the company's sales growth goals would be difficult. So in 1991 Archway Cookies began using a system of hardware and software from Intermec Technologies Corp. Key components of the system were Intermec's Norand Base Bakery database software and Norand 4410 handheld computers.

Before 1991, distributors wrote everything down in route books, and Archway employed people to perform manual data entry. As a result, managers had difficulty understanding, comprehending, and analyzing data on a timely basis. This changed drastically when Archway supplied its distributors with the handheld computers and began using the route accounting software designed specifically for the baking industry. With the new management information system, Archway was able to track, analyze, and adjust sales to customers at the distributor level. In turn, this allowed "Archway to influence production at its two company-owned bakeries in Ashland, Ohio, and Boone, Iowa, as well as its four contract bakeries in Pennsylvania, New Jersey, Oregon and Canada." Orders are placed by downloading information to the bakeries on a daily basis.

According to Gene H. McKay III, Archway's chief of finance and operations, the use of information technology has produced considerable benefits. He says that "implementing this technology has saved the distributors an enormous amount of time on their routes, so the distributors have additional time for call-backs and for soliciting new sales." In turn, this has contributed to a 3 to 4 percent sales increase for Archway every year since the system was installed. The system has also provided better information access and information sharing throughout the company.

Critical Thinking Questions

1. Why is timely and accurate information essential for Archway's manufacturing operations?
2. How does Archway Cookies manage information technology to its advantage?
3. Do you think Archway Cookies would be able to achieve its sales growth goals without the use of computerized information technology?

>c18

chapter eighteen

Using the Internet for Business Success

learning goals

>lg 1   What is the Internet, and how does it work?

>lg 2   Who uses the Internet, and for what?

>lg 3   How has the Internet economy changed the business environment?

>lg 4   How can companies incorporate e-commerce into their overall business strategies?

>lg 5   What benefits do businesses achieve through e-commerce?

>lg 6   What steps are involved in launching an e-commerce venture?

>lg 7   What lies ahead for the Information Superhighway?

eToys Doesn't Play Around

The concept seems simple: set up an online store that just sells toys, take orders, and ship customers the merchandise. Edward "Toby" Lenk, founder and CEO of eToys, will tell you otherwise: "I can't tell you how amazingly complex this business is. To be really good at this is really hard."

Just two years after starting the company, Lenk succeeded in being "really good." eToys (**www.etoys.com**) is the leading Web toy retailer. In 1998 it sold $23 million in toys, video games, software, and music in the three months before Christmas, up from $500,000 a year earlier. Ranked number 5 on MediaMetrix's list of December's top shopping Web sites, eToys was also named most customer-focused online merchant of the 1998 holiday season by Patricia Seybold, technology consultant and author of a best-seller on Internet retailing.

Lenk got the idea for eToys while buying his niece a Christmas gift. Like most adults, he found the toy-buying experience unpleasant: long lines, noisy kids, poor service, and insufficient supplies of popular toys. The former Disney executive didn't know much about toys, but he saw an opportunity to use the Internet to give consumers what they wanted most: convenience, selection, and service.

Convenience was easy. Web stores are open 24 hours a day. The site's search engine quickly provides recommendations in categories like Picks of the Month, Toybox Essentials, and Favorites by Age. Shoppers click for detailed product information.

Selection proved harder. Book, music, and computer products e-tailers can buy from large distributors with a wide product range. The toy industry has no consolidated distributors, so eToys must deal with over 500 manufacturers. Today eToys features a much larger selection than any land-based store—10,000 products, both well-known brands and specialty brands that toy superstores don't carry—and keeps large inventories in its own warehouse.

Superior service won eToys rave reviews in the busy 1998 holiday season. Many Web merchants ran out of products, but Lenk was ready for the onslaught of cybershoppers. eToys shipped 95 percent of its orders within 24 hours, providing free shipping upgrades to deliver on time and $5 coupons if toys were out of stock. This focus on customer satisfaction paid off in customer retention and referrals. According to one study, each satisfied Web customer brings six new customers to the site.

Critical Thinking Questions

As you read this chapter, consider the following questions as they relate to eToys:

- What advantages does an online merchant like eToys have compared to traditional retailers? Disadvantages?
- Identify the reasons why eToys has jumped ahead of the well-known Toys "R" Us brand.
- Are toys well-suited for Web sales? Why or why not?

Like most "dot com" retailers, the Santa Monica, California company is still far from profitability. Web retailers incur huge marketing costs to acquire customers and build brand awareness. eToys spent $3 million for priority merchant status on America Online, formed partnerships with leading search engines, and pays its 250 Web site affiliates above-average commissions—25 percent of sales—for referrals. To reach the widest audience, eToys also runs print and television ads. Through promotional sweepstakes, such as giving away a Furby a day in holiday season and a Star Wars party in mid-1999, eToys collects e-mail addresses to build a customer database for future promotional e-mails.

eToys may have defined the rules of the game, but Toys "R" Us now wants to play, it opened its Web store in June 1998. Its delay hurt sales, however. eToys continued to build market share in the $23 billion toy industry at its rival's expense, with double the selection and three times as many site visits.[1]

BUSINESS IN THE 21ST CENTURY

As traditional retailers like Toys "R" Us learned all too well, taking a wait-and-see attitude with regard to the Internet can be disastrous. First-on-the-scene upstarts like eToys capture consumers' loyalty and wallets. As a 100 percent Web store, eToys can focus all its attention on providing the best online experience. Toys "R" Us arrived at the Internet party nine months late—a delay that in Internet time is equal to several years in traditional retailing.

Clearly, the Internet has transformed the business landscape in the same way that railroads and automobiles triggered earlier industrial revolutions. The computerization of businesses initiated the first stage of the Information Revolution. Now the Internet is a driving force in the second stage, moving us beyond the individual enterprise to an interconnected economy. In the virtual world of cyberspace, companies transact business without regard to traditional boundaries and constraints.

Fueled by Internet-related businesses, the information technology industry is growing at twice the rate of the economy in general. A whole new industry has sprung up around the Internet, and digital industries now represent about 40 percent of GDP. In addition, the Internet has changed the way most businesses operate and has forced companies and even whole industries to change their business models. The Internet creates new opportunities for growth through new products, greater speed to market, and enhanced cost competitiveness.

To succeed in business in the new millennium, you must understand how this relatively new communication and transaction medium is shaping business and society, as well as how to use the Internet to your advantage. We'll start our exploration of the Information Superhighway with some background on the Internet: how it works, its size, and how people use it. Next we'll look at the impact of the Internet on business operations and industry dynamics, examine the growth of electronic commerce in both the business-to-business and the business-to-consumer markets, and describe the steps required to launch an e-business. The chapter ends with a look at what lies ahead for the Internet.

THE INTERNET

Hard to believe, but just 10 years ago, hardly anyone knew what the Internet was. With unprecedented speed, the Internet has become a mainstay for businesses and individuals. Whereas radio took 38 years to gain 50 million users, television took 13 years, and PCs needed 16 years, the Internet took just 4 years.[2] Now the Internet is a fixture in our lives at home and work. Consider the following statistics about Internet users from the America Online/Roper Starch Cyberstudy 1998:

- 44 percent said Internet usage is becoming a necessity.
- 77 percent feel that the Internet has improved their lives.
- If stranded on a desert island, 67 percent would rather have a computer with Internet access, compared to 23 percent who chose a phone and 9 percent who preferred television.[3]

Just what is this phenomenon? The **Internet** represents the convergence of the computer's high-speed processing power with telecommunications networks' capability to transmit information around the world almost instantaneously. It is the world's largest computer network, essentially a worldwide "network of networks." All of the commercial and public networks that make up the Internet use **transmission control protocol/Internet protocol (TCP/IP)**, a communications technology that allows different computer platforms to communicate with each other to transfer data. The Internet is a truly unique entity—a decentralized, open network that almost anyone can access. It has no beginning or end. Networks can be added or removed at any time.

The Internet began life in 1969 as ARPAnet, a Defense Department network connecting various types of computers at universities doing military research. It subsequently developed into a larger system of networks for academic and research sites managed by the National Science Foundation (NSF). A major growth spurt began around 1993, when the introduction of browser technology made it easy to access graphics and sound as well as text over the World Wide Web. The **World Wide Web (WWW)**, a subsystem of the Internet, is an information retrieval system composed of **Web sites.** Each Web site contains a *home page*, the first document users see when they enter the site. The site might also contain other pages with documents and files. **Hypertext** within a Web page links users to documents at the same or other Web sites.

By April 1995, the Internet was so large that the NSF turned over its backbone—the major long-distance, high-speed, high-capacity transmission networks—to a group of commercial carriers. However, no one "owns" the Internet. Each private company operates its own networks. In addition to network administrators and users, the Internet also includes about several thousand **Internet service providers (ISPs),** commercial services that connect companies and individuals to the Net. All these players create a shared resource that becomes more useful as the number of networks expands.

Today, the terms *World Wide Web* and *Internet* are used interchangeably by most users. However, the Internet offers users other capabilities, including e-mail, file transfer, online chat sessions, and newsgroups (discussion groups on just about any topic). Thanks to **browsers,** software that allows users to

Internet
A worldwide computer network that includes both commercial and public networks and offers various capabilities including e-mail, file transfer, online chat sessions, and newsgroups.

transmission control protocol/Internet protocol (TCP/IP)
A communications technology that allows different computer platforms to communicate with each other to transfer data.

World Wide Web (WWW)
A subsystem of the Internet that consists of an information retrieval system composed of *Web sites.*

Web sites
Locations on the World Wide Web consisting of a home page and, possibly, other pages with documents and files.

hypertext
A file or series of files within a Web page that links users to documents at the same or other Web sites.

Internet service provider (ISP)
A commercial service that connects companies and individuals to the Internet.

browser
Software that allows users to access the World Wide Web with a graphical point and click interface.

access the Web with a graphical point and click interface, the Web has become the center of Internet activity, with the largest collection of online information in the world. As new technology makes it possible to send audio, video, voice (including telephone calls), 3-D animations, and videoconferencing over the Net, the Web is also becoming a multimedia delivery system.

How the Internet Works

To users around the world, the Internet operates as a single seamless network enabling them to send and receive text, graphics, movies, and sound files. With TCP/IP, the Internet's interconnected local and long-distance networks work together, regardless of the underlying hardware or software, to send and receive information. For example, suppose that you type in the address of a Web page for a company you are researching and hit the enter key. Exhibit 18-1 shows the route that these data might travel from your PC to the Web site's host computer and back again. A **host computer** stores services and data used by other computers on the network.

host computer

The central computer for a Web site that stores services and data used by other computers on the network.

The message travels across telephone lines from your computer to a bank of modems at your ISP. Then the request travels along a succession of interconnected national backbones to the network of the ISP that hosts the company's Web site. These national and international networks are run by network service providers (NSPs), major telecommunications companies that operate the high-speed long-distance networks. ISPs interconnect and share information at specific interchange points. Finally, your request reaches the company's Web server that stores the actual content of the Web site. *Servers* are computers that store data and "serve" information to other computers, called *clients*, upon request. Internet servers run specialized software for different applications, like the World Wide Web, e-mail, and Usenet (newsgroups). Each organization on the Web also has its own server with a unique site, or domain, name. The desired information then makes it way back to you over a similar route.

> e x h i b i t   1 8 - 1 <

Diagram of Internet Networks

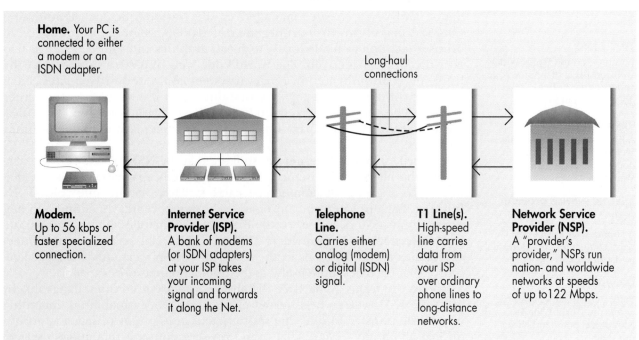

Home. Your PC is connected to either a modem or an ISDN adapter.

Long-haul connections

Modem. Up to 56 kbps or faster specialized connection.

Internet Service Provider (ISP). A bank of modems (or ISDN adapters) at your ISP takes your incoming signal and forwards it along the Net.

Telephone Line. Carries either analog (modem) or digital (ISDN) signal.

T1 Line(s). High-speed line carries data from your ISP over ordinary phone lines to long-distance networks.

Network Service Provider (NSP). A "provider's provider," NSPs run nation- and worldwide networks at speeds of up to 122 Mbps.

The Who, What, and Where of the Internet

>lg 2

The Internet's explosive growth is unparalleled. The number of host computers connected to the Internet grew from 1.3 million in 1993 to over 43 million in January 1999 and continues to increase by about 50 to 60 percent a year. The United States is home to about two-thirds of the world's host computers.[4] The amount of data being processed over the Internet doubles about every 100 days. The Web itself has grown at an astounding rate. Over 5 million Web sites with more than 350 million pages crowd the Web today, compared to a few hundred in 1993.

Who's Online?   According to surveys of Internet usage compiled by NUA Internet Surveys, about 170 million people were online worldwide as of May 1999. Of the about 85 million adult (over age 18) Internet users in the United States, about 64 million (75 percent) are regular Internet users. Although the Net was male dominated for many years, women now represent one of the fastest growing groups. One recent survey found that current Net users are 51.4 percent male and 48.6 percent female.[5]

Businesses are designing more Web sites that target women, one of the fastest-growing groups of Internet users. Women shown here using the Internet at a cybercafe can visit sites like iVillage that cater to their interests and tastes.

Web users tend to be better educated and wealthier than the U.S. population in general. About 43 percent have college degrees, compared to 31 percent for the country as a whole, and the average income is $55,000, versus $25,000 for the general population. The profile of Net users should become more mainstream over the next few years, however, as millions of new users log on. The average Web surfer will change from the technology-savvy 20-something to the "Mom and Pop" user as Net demographics move closer to national averages for age and ethnic groups. For example, the number of minority households surfing the Net has risen considerably in the past three years. The Internet is also gaining popularity among older users. About one-fifth of Net users are now over 50, pushing the average age of Internet users close to 40.[6]

As the characteristics of Internet users change, businesses must rethink the type of services they offer and change marketing campaigns to reach new groups. Merchants are simplifying their Web sites to make it easier for new users to find their way around. Because women are becoming an increasing force among online shoppers, businesses are responding with Web sites that cater to their tastes and interests. iVillage, the largest online community for women on the Internet, helps women find solutions to their problems. It has built itself into a major Internet brand and has numerous partnership agreements with companies that want to reach the iVillage audience, including America Online (AOL), NBC, and Intuit. Intuit, for example, helped iVillage develop a personal finance site.[7]

What Attracts Web Surfers   Using the Hot Links in each chapter of this book, you've discovered the wealth of resources available on the World Wide Web. From the five-day weather forecast for any city in the world to statistics on steel production in Russia to the best-selling CD albums of the week—it's all on the Web. The most visited Web sites are the ones offering news, travel,

> e x h i b i t   1 8 - 2 <

Most Popular Reasons to Use the Internet

Send e-mail	88%
Go to the WWW	85
Use search engines	77
Visit company or product sites	51
Research product purchases	47
Look up weather information	46
Visit reference sites	40
Read newspapers and magazines	33
Get stock quotes	27
Buy something	26
Visit sports sites	24
Online chats	23
Entertainment or product reviews	21
Play online games	21
Request customer service for products you own	19
Visit entertainment sites	18
Visit financial sites	13

SOURCE: Forrester Research survey of 100,000 Internet users, cited in "Information Please," *The Wall Street Journal* (December 7, 1998), p. R4.

entertainment, government, health/medicine, product information, sports, music, and games.

What do people do when they log on to the Internet? Sending e-mail is the most popular activity, followed closely by accessing the Web (85 percent). Once on the Web, they pursue a variety of interests, summarized in Exhibit 18-2.

How Businesses Tap the Net's Resources Corporations and business users are also active Web participants. In a recent study of major corporations, 89 percent of the respondents had a Web site. Of those, 56 percent offered customer service and 37 percent allowed visitors to make purchases online.[8] In addition to purchasing supplies and materials and selling products online, businesses use the Internet's vast resources to:

- Collect information on the latest economic conditions, competitors, industry trends, technology, and other developments.
  - Gather information on customers.
  - Allow employees in different locations to collaborate on projects.
  - Provide customer service.
  - Communicate with suppliers and customers.
  - Market their products.
  - Recruit and train employees.
  - Hold virtual meetings and conferences.

Exhibit 18-3 lists the top five responses of Inc. 500 executives when asked what their company's Web page helped them to achieve.

c o n c ə p t   c h ə c k

- How did the Internet develop into a global "network of networks"? Describe briefly how the Internet works.
- Who are today's Web users, and how will Web demographics change over the next five years?
- How can managers use the Internet to improve business operations?

Advantages of Corporate Web Site

More widespread marketing	84%
Increased sales	36
Improved customer service	32
Greater recruiting/hiring efficiency	30
Easier to find new business partners	10

SOURCE: Shane McLaughlin, "Web Sites We Love," *1998 Inc. 500* (October 20, 1998), p. 181.

THE NEW INTERNET ECONOMY

>lg 3

The Internet has significantly changed today's global economic framework. As companies rush to adapt Net technology to different tasks and industries, they promote another wave of technological innovation. In addition, the Internet has taken off in ways that its originators probably never imagined. It's more than just a communication tool, as first envisioned, or another way to get traditional information.

We're in the midst of a shift to a new Internet-centered economy. Existing companies must reinvent themselves to take advantage of Internet technology. Old business models no longer apply as the Net changes the rules of doing business. Many established companies waited for the Internet market to develop before moving online. Confident that their size would allow them to push the entrepreneurial upstarts out of the way, they were surprised to find themselves left in the dust. The Internet moved so quickly that they lost the advantage of being first to the Amazon.coms, Yahoo!s, and eToys. Let's now consider how the Internet affects competition, channel relationships, and marketing.

The New Face of Competition

The Internet is redefining the nature of competition by blurring the traditional barriers of geography and time. Store location and hours were once key factors in attracting customers. Your competition was in within easy driving distance. Now the competitive universe is unlimited. It doesn't matter whether a company is physically located in Portland, Oregon, or Portland, Maine. On the Web, competitors are just a click away.

In addition, new Internet businesses encounter fewer barriers than traditional businesses when entering a new market. To expand geographically or add new products, traditional retailers must incur substantial costs for a physical storefront and distribution. Once a company has a Web site, the cost to acquire a customer in New York is the same as adding one in New Zealand. And online companies find it easier to enter new markets. Amazon.com started with books but now offers CDs, videos, and gifts. In its quest to become a one-stop online transaction company, Amazon developed its own auction site to compete with eBay and is investing in other online retailers such as Pets.com and Homegrocer.com.[9]

Going Direct

The Internet is changing relationships among all channel members: manufacturers, distributors, retailers/service providers, and customers. No longer do

The Internet is changing channel relationships in the travel industry, as more consumers purchase tickets directly from airlines and reserve rooms at hotels over the Web rather than using the services of travel agents.

Experiment with online travel planning by researching a trip at Microsoft's Expedia travel site

www.expedia.msn.com

companies have to rely on intermediaries to connect with other participants in the supply chain. They can go directly to customers, bypassing traditional channels and displacing some intermediaries.

Take the travel industry, for example, which accounted for $3 billion of consumer spending in 1998. Travel agents are becoming less important as cybertravelers can now access much of the same information on the Web. Travelers can easily check airplane schedules, find the lowest fares and room prices, view panoramic photos of hotel rooms, obtain maps showing the best route between cities, get advice from experienced travelers in discussion groups, and then make their own reservations. The percentage of airline tickets sold by agents is dropping rapidly as more travelers buy tickets over the Web. Some airlines are encouraging this self-service by giving occasional discounts for Web ticket purchases. Microsoft's Expedia, with over 4 million registered users in North America, reports sales of over $10 million per week for just car rental, air travel, and hotel rooms. And additional services are on the horizon, such as virtual agents who take a customer's preferences and automatically develop a complete itinerary.[10]

Manufacturers with strong brands can also sell directly on the Web. Dell Computer's Internet sales now amount to more than $18 million a day. To the dismay of wholesalers and traditional retailers like Sears, Levi Strauss has begun selling direct. Iomega, which makes the popular Zip and Jaz hard drives, and Polaroid started selling directly to consumers in spring 1999. Manufacturers with brands carrying more weight than the retailer's—Estée Lauder and Tommy Hilfiger are two—may be able to bypass retailers entirely.

Most manufacturers, however, don't have the breadth of product to sell exclusively on the Web and will use it to provide information to support sales and refer customers to dealers. A retailer like Macy's can use the Web's interactivity to combine apparel and accessory products from several manufacturers into an outfit consumers will want to buy. Nor is it economically feasible for most manufacturers to fill small orders for individual customers. These limitations, along with the risk of alienating business partners, have discouraged many manufacturers from selling direct. They will continue to sell in large quantities to resellers.[11]

Distributors are using their customers' move to the Web to their advantage. They are providing warehousing, logistics, and e-commerce services to retailers and manufacturers. Distributors offer economies of scale to small retailers that want to set up Web shops. A new category of virtual merchant is emerging. Buy.com, for example, outsources order fulfillment and focuses only on selling products at extremely low prices to consumers. Merisel, a leading computer products distributor, expects the Internet to make distributors more important to retail customers because they will take on a larger share of retailers' expenses.[12]

In some industries, going direct takes on additional meaning. Customers no longer have to wait to get boxed software from many developers. They can download programs directly from a Web site, using a special password to unlock the software for their use. New technology to deliver music over the Web is changing the dynamics of the music industry.

Power to the Consumer

The radical shift in bargaining power from sellers to buyers is probably the most fundamental development being shaped by electronic commerce. As John Hagel III, author of *Net Gain* and *Net Worth*, says, "Information has been the key driver of negotiating power in economics for a long time, and electronic commerce is giving information to the customer, which in turn will dramatically enhance their bargaining power as they deal with vendors." All customers, from corporate purchasing agents to individuals, can search sites of various providers to compare products and prices. They can find the best products for their needs, rather than simply accepting what retailers offer. Vendors have a huge opportunity to build relationships by providing assistance in finding the right goods and services.[13]

The availability of neutral sources of product information gives consumers greater freedom of choice and control. For example, almost 20 percent of car buyers use the Web to shop for their cars, gathering information on dealer costs, options, and financing plans. They arrive at the dealership armed with the facts and ready to drive a hard bargain.

New types of "infomediaries" make it even easier for buyers by pulling together product information from many vendors. Thanks to *intelligent agents* that scour the Web's many databases, consumers no longer have to go from site to site to compare prices and obtain information. For example, CompareNet offers product reviews and online discussion forums as well as price and feature comparisons for a wide range of products. *Portals* are also becoming popular. These Web sites gather many resources into one convenient gateway to the Web. Some like Yahoo! are general portals with links to popular destination sites. Specialized portals like Intuit's financial services site also compete for viewer attention.

Service industries are also noticing a change in consumer buying patterns. In financial services, for example, customers can now comparison shop in a way never before possible for financial products such as personal loans, mortgages, auto insurance, and credit cards. Online stock brokerage and banking services attract more users daily. We'll discuss the Internet's impact on financial institutions in Chapters 20 and 22.

Keep these fundamental changes in mind as we now look at how companies in different industries are using e-commerce strategies.

concept check

- Describe the impact of the Internet on competition.
- How does the Internet change channel relationships among manufacturers, distributors, and retailers?
- Why does John Hagel consider the increasing power of the consumer the most important effect of the Internet on the business environment? Do you agree?

CAPITALIZING ON E-COMMERCE

>lg 4

electronic commerce (e-commerce)

The process of selling a product or service via the Internet; also called *electronic business (e-business)*.

The entire process of selling a product or service via the Internet is called **electronic commerce (e-commerce)** or *electronic business (e-business)*. E-commerce goes beyond selling products through an electronic catalog, however. Among the benefits of the Web's interactivity are convenience and increased efficiency, better customer service, lower transaction costs, and new relationship-building strategies.

E-commerce is moving into the business mainstream. More and more corporate and individual purchasers now go first to the Web to buy products ranging from diesel engine parts to consulting services to baby clothes. Although e-commerce barely existed in 1995, by early 1999, 44 percent of U.S. companies were selling online, and another 36 percent planned to start by 2000. Active commercial Web sites topped 400,000 in early 1998 and are expected to number 1.6 million by 2002. Companies with an online presence are rewarded with growing revenues. According to Forrester Research, e-commerce revenues went from zero to $51 billion in just four years—and are expected to reach $1.4 trillion by 2003. (Like the number of Internet users, the size of the e-commerce market is hard to estimate due to the different criteria used by various research firms.) In a recent survey, 85 percent of CEOs said e-commerce is vital to their company's future success.

E-commerce includes two distinct market segments. **Business-to-business e-commerce** involves transactions between companies—for example, purchasing raw materials to manufacture products or supplies. **Business-to-consumer e-commerce**, also called *"e-tailing,"* involves transactions between businesses and the end user of the goods or services. Although the consumer market has received more media attention, e-commerce between businesses accounted for 85 percent of 1998 e-commerce sales and is expected to exceed 90 percent by 2003.[14] In each of these sectors, companies have several business models from which to choose.

New E-Commerce Business Models Emerge

In the early days of e-commerce, companies could choose from three basic e-commerce revenue models:

- *Selling merchandise or services on the Internet.* Amazon.com and Travelocity are two examples of business-to-consumer sales sites. Cisco Systems sells about 75 percent of its computer networking products from its Web site. At the other end of the spectrum are niche businesses like Fridgedoor.com, which sells decorative refrigerator magnets.

- *Providing entertainment or information on a fee-for-service or subscription basis. The Wall Street Journal Interactive Edition* is one of the more successful paid news sites. Some online gaming sites charge players to play certain types of games. Travelers can now check e-mail or surf the Web using Internet kiosks located in airports on a pay-as-you-go basis.

- *Providing advertising or referral-supported entertainment or information sites.* CNet, ESPN SportsZone, and search engines like Yahoo! and Excite are examples of advertiser-supported sites that provide information to visitors. High-traffic sites, like Netscape's Netcenter, earn substantial revenue from ad sales. Other sites earn fees by referring consumers to merchant sites. CDNow has a corporate affiliate program that pays commissions when visitors order music from CDNow through special links on the affiliate site.

With the vast amount of free information on the Internet, the subscription model has not proved successful in most cases. Already new types of business models are emerging that use the Web to create more efficient marketplaces, especially in the business-to-business sector:[15]

- *Auctions to sell merchandise to businesses and consumers.* Examples of online auctions include eBay, the leading person-to-person auction site; OnSale, a merchant-to-buyer auction service; and Freemarkets, a business-to-business auction service for qualified buyers of industrial materials and components.

- *E-service providers that help other firms establish e-commerce operations.* The e-services market—from consultants to technology outsourcing companies—is poised for growth, from $22 billion in 1999 to a projected $220 billion by 2003. Services are driving revenue growth at IBM. On a smaller scale, Wazzu Corp. offers turnkey Internet solutions for small businesses.

---

business-to-business e-commerce

Electronic commerce that involves transactions between companies.

business-to-consumer e-commerce

Electronic commerce that involves transactions between businesses and the end user of the goods or services; also called *e-tailing*.

- *Industry exchanges and other information gatherers that serve as "infomediaries."* Industry exchanges bring together multiple buyers and sellers within one industry: Chemdex.com allows scientists to locate over 250,000 laboratory chemicals from 120 suppliers. Other infomediaries gather together vendors in many industries. SupplyBase brings together over 30,000 online supplier directories. Users can search a central database by geography, industry, technology, or other criteria.

- *Consumer infomediaries and portal sites.* These sites simplify the online experience by bringing together a combination of information, goods, and services from many individual companies. Catalog City and Shopping.com are two examples of shopping sites, while Intelihealth is a specialized portal offering medical data, health tips, and services such as online pharmacies and health insurance.

HOT links

What types of products can you find using SupplyBase's directories? Explore the DeveloPages at

www.supplybase.com

Companies often incorporate more than one business model into their e-commerce strategy. Yahoo!, for example, began as an advertising-supported Internet directory. It is now a leading portal where visitors can make travel reservations, shop, and bid at its own auction site.

The Business-to-Business Boom

Fortune 500 corporations and small businesses alike are embracing business-to-business e-commerce to save hundreds of millions of dollars through lower costs and reduced inventories. Business-to-business e-commerce includes all aspects of the supply chain, from product information to order, invoice, fulfillment, payment, and customer service. About 60 percent of purchasing managers rely on the Web to find supplies, and that number is quickly climbing. Companies without a Web site will lose business opportunities. In addition to Web-based e-commerce, many electronic data interchange (EDI) networks are moving to the Internet, replacing expensive proprietary networks.

It's no surprise that high-technology companies were early adopters of e-commerce. IBM purchases $4 billion of goods and services per year over the Internet, citing significant cost savings and improved connections with customers and business partners as clear benefits. The Applying Technology box describes how Cisco Systems uses the Web to its advantage.

E-commerce is no longer limited to high-tech companies, however; all types of manufacturing and transportation companies are becoming active participants. Customers of CSX Corp., one of the largest freight railroads in the United States, make 400,000 visits to the corporate Web site each month. They consult maps of CSX routes, book shipments, get price quotes, fill out their own bills of lading, calculate freight charges, and track shipments within the firm's 18,000-mile network. CSX's online system reduces transaction costs by replacing paper, phone, and fax communications and improving order accuracy. It also reduces staffing requirements. About 60 percent of CSX's shipments are booked electronically including those sent by General Motors,

Business customers of CSX use the railroad's Web site to book and track shipments of their merchandise, helping CSX to reduce transaction costs and improve order accuracy.

CISCO PRACTICES WHAT IT PREACHES

Cisco Systems, Inc., the world's leading provider of networking products for the Internet, is also a leader in applying this technology to its own management practices. Cisco does as much as possible on the Web, from product sales to financial reporting and employee travel plans. "We are the best example of how the Internet is going to change everything," claims CEO John Chambers.

Cisco's network links the company to its customers, prospects, business partners, suppliers, and employees. The network has been so successful in selling complex equipment online that Cisco now generates almost three-quarters of its customer orders over the Internet. Employees use the network extensively to make travel plans, file expense reports, check on benefits, and access more than 1.7 million pages of information. The Web has also improved purchasing and recruiting processes. The company receives about half of all job applications via the Internet.

In Cisco's high-technology, business-to-business market, quality of service can be more important than product features. Cisco was a pioneer in putting customer service online, launching Cisco Connection Online (CCO, **www. cisco.com**) in 1992. CCO provides customer service and technical support 24 hours a day. With CCO, the company has been able to build better customer relationships, reduce order cycle time, lower costs, and promote sales.

Existing customers can register to access the site's online sales, service, and technical support areas. At the site, they can place orders through an automatic system that calculates prices, including appropriate discounts, and links the order to the customer's sales representative. Customers can also check the status of their orders, track delivery with a link to the Federal Express site, get product data, register for seminars, and download software upgrades. Bug Alert notifies customers of software bugs within 24 hours of discovery.

CCO now handles 70–80 percent of Cisco's customer service and tech support inquiries. Cisco saves about $200 for every inquiry that goes to the Web rather than its call center, for total savings of over $250 million annually. Without CCO, Cisco would need three times as many call center personnel—including engineers who can now work on product development instead of tech support.

Critical Thinking Questions

1. What factors make Cisco's Internet strategy so successful?
2. Describe some of the differences companies should consider when developing a business-to-business Web site, versus a business-to-consumer site?
3. Why is customer service so important in the business-to-business market?

What's the best way to ship food and consumer commodities with CSX Corp.? Find out at the CSX Transportation site
www.csxt.com/com/food

extranet

A private computer network that uses Internet technology and a browser interface but is accessible only to authorized outsiders with a valid user name and password.

Home Depot, General Electric, and PepsiCo. In fact, customers like the system so much they check daily to follow the route of railcars carrying their merchandise.[16]

Extranets are becoming a popular business-to-business e-commerce tool for such activities as purchasing, inventory management, order fulfillment, information transmission, training, and sales presentations. Like an intranet, an **extranet** is a private network that uses Internet technology and a browser interface. Extranets, however, are accessible only to authorized outsiders with a valid user name and password. Companies can easily designate specific portions of their Web sites to share specific information and processes with suppliers, vendors, partners, customers, and other businesses at remote locations. For example, customers can find account balances and customized catalogs with account-specific pricing.

Extranets are a very efficient format for business-to-business e-commerce and could handle 40 percent of these transactions by 2002. Marine Power Europe, a manufacturer of boat parts, saves $1 million a year in order placement and processing costs. Thanks to a special multilingual extranet application, Marine Power's international distributors and dealers can get product information and transact business in their native languages. Multiple users from around the globe can even view the same live document in their native language.[17]

E-Tailing Hits Its Stride

Since Amazon.com turned the retailing world on its head in 1994, selling consumer goods over the Internet has become big business. By 1999, more than 90,000 established retailers and new businesses had opened the doors to their cybershops, with new merchants joining them daily.

The 1998 holiday shopping season marked a turning point in business-to-consumer online markets. Online sales of $3.5 billion—three time's higher than the fourth quarter of 1997—accounted for about 45 percent of the year's total online sales. More consumers, including new Web users and women—who had been more hesitant about Web purchases—accepted the Web as a shopping medium. And once they took the plunge, they came back, spending an average of $629 online.[18]

What do e-shoppers buy? Computer hardware and software account for by far the most revenues, as Exhibit 18-4 shows, followed by travel and books, music, and entertainment (including tickets). In general, electronics and low-risk, low-cost items sell best.

Although online sales represent less than 1 percent of total U.S. retail sales, e-tailing is becoming a driver of primary demand in the retail sector.

> exhibit 18 - 4 <

Most Popular Online Purchases

Category	1998 Revenues (Millions)
Computer hardware and software	$4,650
Travel	1,600
Books, music, and entertainment	1,300
Auction goods	500
Gifts	500
Household goods	500
Apparel	300
Food and wine	200
Automobiles	70
Toys	70

SOURCE: Boston Consulting Group, cited in Patricia Sellers, "Inside the First E-Christmas," *Fortune* (February 1, 1999), p. 71.

Successful early adopters like Costco, The Gap, and Office Depot recognized that the Web was another way to reach customers and complement their basic business. As Toys "R" Us learned, traditional retailers without an online presence lose sales to their more technologically up-to-date rivals. "We know we have to be there," states Jeffrey Cohen, Home Depot's head of direct marketing. In early 1999 the company tested the waters with a site for its Maintenance Warehouse unit, which sells supplies for commercial property maintenance.[19] Other companies like eToys went straight to the Web. Small businesses also found it easy to expand their reach and win new customers with a Web presence.

What makes a successful cybermerchant? The answer is convenience, selection, community service, and pricing. Consumers love the convenience of Web shopping. They can get more product choice and information in the same or less time. Chats and online discussion groups create a sense of community among shoppers with similar interests. Bargains are easy to find as intelligent agent software learns customer preferences and quickly scouts the Web for the best products and lowest prices.

Discover what's in style at The Gap and learn how a successful retailer uses the Web to its advantage at **www.gap.com**

Cyberspace also gives retailers a chance to break out of the size constraints of a physical store. A store might support 10,000 items, but on the Internet a retailer can offer millions of them without adding expensive shelf space. In addition to selling a broader merchandise mix, retailers can also use their Web sites for special promotions, merchandise that may be out of season in their regular stores, and excess inventory.

Where's the Profit?

Despite the increasing popularity of e-shopping, less than 5 percent of e-tailers are expected to show profits in the near term. Currently, the most profitable Internet-related companies are not the e-tailers, but rather the companies that provide infrastructure—computer, networking, and telecommunications equipment providers and telecommunications carriers. In these first stages of e-commerce, businesses are finding that they must focus on developing a solid infrastructure and building online relationships and brands, not on generating short-term profits.[20] It will take time for the financial benefits of e-commerce, such as reduced overhead, to reach the bottom line.

In the meantime, e-tailers are finding it hard to achieve a profit for several reasons:

- *Pricing.* It's so easy for shoppers to make price comparisons on the Internet that merchants get into price wars that cut margins considerably. After Amazon.com offered 30 percent off best-sellers, Barnes & Noble raised its discount to 40 percent, Wal-Mart followed with 45 percent, and Buy.com outdid them all with 50 percent.
- *Cannibalization.* Online sales may cannibalize higher margin sales from traditional retail stores.
- *Unexpected costs.* Although the Web can reduce brick-and-mortar costs, operating expenses are higher than anticipated. As the cost comparison in Exhibit 18-5 shows, online merchants must offer lower prices—but still incur higher expenses than a competing superstore. Online "real estate" (renting space at other sites through ads or other placements) and market-

> e x h i b i t 1 8 - 5 <

Cost Comparison: Superstore versus Online Store

	Superstore	Online
Average sale	$100	$100
Less: Discount	−10	−20
Shipping & handling (S&H)	—	11
Sales tax	7	—
Customer pays	$ 97	$ 91
Cost of sales, S&H	70	68
Gross profit	$ 27	$ 23
Operating expenses:		
Rent	1	5
Labor and store	11	—
Web site development	—	3
Marketing	3	17
Total	$ 15	$ 25
Operating profit per order	$ 12	−$2

SOURCE: Adapted from Mary Beth Grover, "Lost in Cyberspace," *Forbes* (March 8, 1999), pp. 124–128.

ing are expensive. Barnes & Noble paid AOL, the most popular online shopping mall, $40 million to be its exclusive bookseller for four years. In addition, online customer support hasn't eliminated the need for telephone support. Online shoppers jammed phone lines during the 1998 holiday season. Shopping.com had to double its call center support staff because of waits as long as an hour.[21]

Online shopping appeals to consumers because it's convenient and offers them an enormous selection of merchandise at competitive prices.

- *Aggressive growth.* Companies that want to grab a beachhead on the e-commerce shores have to grow quickly, and this growth is expensive. To build a brand name, market share, and a loyal customer base, companies make large investments in marketing and improved technology. Even as revenues soar, leaders like Amazon.com and @Home, a provider of high-speed cable Web service, continue to post losses. Industry analysts support this hypergrowth strategy and predict that profitability will follow.

Like many traditional retailers, the Borders bookstore chain reluctantly opened a Web store just to keep pace with Amazon and Barnes & Noble.

Borders spent $10 million to develop the site, plus another $15 million for a separate distribution center, and expects to incur high costs to upgrade and maintain the site. These expenses do not include marketing costs to attract visitors to the site, which can go as high as 65 percent of sales. Borders also worries that its Web site may take customers away from its stores and their higher margin sales. Nevertheless, Borders has found a good way to use the Web to its advantage: customers who can't find a book can place special orders right away using in-store terminals with Web access.[22]

Although e-tailers want to make money from their Web sites, most firms must also look beyond the bottom line. As the following section explains, e-commerce brings many other worthwhile benefits, such as substantial savings in costs and time, improved quality of service, and better customer relationships.

Benefiting from E-Commerce

>lg 5

As many examples in this book demonstrate, companies that use the Internet effectively gain clear advantages. Among the attractions of incorporating e-commerce into business strategies are the following:

1. *Lower prices.* Competition among online vendors leads to lower prices, for both businesses and individual consumers.

2. *Greater selection of products and vendors.* The Web makes it possible for corporate purchasing agents and individuals to find numerous vendors and retailers for almost any product.

3. *Access to customer and product sales data.* Companies can develop customer lists and learn their buying characteristics. They can also immediately learn which products are selling best.

4. *Around-the-clock ordering and customer service.* Company Web sites provide extensive product information for prospective customers around the world on a "24/7" basis, thereby expanding markets and facilitating more transactions—without hiring additional personnel. Customers themselves decide how much information they require by clicking on site links. Well-designed sites offer solutions to customer problems and make product suggestions.

5. *Lower costs.* As CSX and its customers learned, cost savings are a major benefit of e-commerce. These can take many forms, from the distribution savings shown in Exhibit 18-6 to staff reductions and lower costs of purchasing supplies. A report by the Organization for Economic Cooperation and Development (OECD) indicates that companies can reduce customer service costs by 10 to 50 percent and order processing time by 50 to 96 percent, depending on the type of business.[23]

6. *Customized products.* The Internet is revolutionizing product design and manufacturing. No longer do companies have to design and build products well in advance

Michael Dell (right), chief executive of Dell Computer, uses the Internet to allow customers to design their own computer systems, which has increased the company's efficiency and profitability.

> e x h i b i t   1 8 - 6 <

How E-Commerce Lowers Distribution Costs

Category	Traditional System	Internet	Percent Savings
Airline tickets	$8.00	$1.00	87%
Banking	1.08	0.13	89
Bill payment	2.22–3.32	0.65–1.10	67–71
Term life insurance policy	400–700	200–350	50
Software	15	0.20–0.50	97–99

SOURCE: Organization for Economic Cooperation and Development, "The Economic and Social Impact of Electronic Commerce," cited in Maryann Jones Thompson, "Spotlight: The Economic Impact of E-commerce," *The Industry Standard* (April 26, 1999), downloaded from **www.thestandard.com/metrics/**.

of the sale, basing product decisions on market research. They can use the Internet to take orders for products tailored to customer specifications. Dell Computers was one of the first to allow computer buyers to configure their ideal computer from menus at Dell's Web site. Even though Dell's build-to-order procedures were remarkably efficient when customers phone in their orders, the Web has increased its efficiency and profitability. Warehouses receive supply orders via Internet messages every two hours instead of daily faxes. Suppliers know about the company's inventory and production plans and get feedback on their performance in meeting shipping deadlines. Inventory on hand is a low 8 days, versus competitor Compaq's 26, and revenue is up 55 percent.[24]

Roadblocks on the E-Commerce Highway

Despite the increasing acceptance of e-commerce, companies are encountering some barriers along the Information Superhighway. Some of the problems include the following:

1. *Disruptions in channel relationships.* For example, manufacturers that start to sell directly to customers can jeopardize relationships with distributors.

2. *Poor customer service.* Although more consumers are venturing online to shop, they easily become frustrated when technology doesn't perform flawlessly. A survey of online shoppers conducted after the busy 1998 holiday season revealed that many were disappointed that online merchants were unprepared to fill orders. The percentage of satisfied customers dropped to 74 percent from 88 percent in June 1998. The top three reasons for dissatisfaction were product availability problems, high shipping and handling costs, and slow Web site performance.[25]

3. *Payment problems.* Because of a lack of standards for electronic payment methods, customers must enter personal information and credit card data at each online store. About 27 percent of Net shoppers find this enough of a nuisance to leave a site before completing their orders. Electronic commerce modeling language (ECML), a standard technology endorsed by a consortium of major technology companies and by Visa and

concept check

- Why are businesses incorporating e-commerce into their overall business strategies? Describe the different revenue models for e-commerce.
- Differentiate between the two major e-commerce market segments.
- Why do most businesses find it hard to show a profit on e-commerce? What barriers to success still exist?

MasterCard, may solve this problem. With ECML, shoppers enter information into their "digital wallet" just once, accessing it when they want to make a purchase.[26]

4. *Security and privacy issues.* Many consumers remain reluctant to order merchandise over the Web, even though they readily give out credit card numbers over the telephone or in retail stores. The increasing availability of special secure sites that encrypt personal data is solving this problem. We'll discuss privacy issues later in the chapter.

LAUNCHING A SUCCESSFUL E-BUSINESS

>lg 6

E-commerce involves more than building a flashy Web site to attract customers. It's also about adding value. Internet shoppers don't just want to duplicate the in-store experience when they visit a company's Web site—they want a *better* experience than they can get in their local store. In addition, e-commerce requires the right infrastructure to retain customers and encourage repeat purchases. In and of itself, e-commerce cannot make a company a winner. "If you don't have the right product, the right timing, and right distribution channels, the Internet won't change that," says Bruce Temkin of Forrester Research.[27]

Businesses can get involved with e-commerce in stages, as Exhibit 18-7 illustrates. A company might start with a simple promotional Web site (Level 1) or go a step further and add marketing and interactive capabilities that enhance the ability to get and keep customers (Level 2). Next, it can totally integrate

> e x h i b i t   1 8 - 7 <

Four Stages of E-Commerce

Level 1: Basic Presence	Level 2: Prospecting	Level 3: Business Integration	Level 4: Business Transformation
Basic site with corporate information, marketing materials. Updated at regular intervals.	Interactive, marketing-focused site with more corporate, product, and service information. Personalized content and e-mail customer support enhance the ability to get and keep customers.	More sophisticated sites with increased customer interaction. Greater process efficiencies, targeted marketing, self-service support, advanced search capabilities, online communities. Achieve profitability.	Total integration with back-office systems; more efficient supplier and customer communications; electronic transactions replace paper. Improved profitability from reduced operating costs, greater depth and breadth of sales channels.
Cost: $30,000–$100,000 for design and hosting	**Cost:** $400,000–$900,000	**Cost:** $1 million and up	**Cost:** $2 million and up
Example: Thompson Publishing Group, **www.thompson.com**	**Example:** Yahoo!, **www.yahoo.com**	**Example:** Charles Schwab & Co., **www.schwab.com**	**Example:** Dell Computer, **www.dell.com**

SOURCE: Adapted from Jane Asteroff and Maureen Fleming, "Four Ways to Increase a Web Site's Strategic Value," *Executive Edge* (September 1998), p. 7.

its Web activities into its existing business structure (Level 3). These three levels supplement rather than replace business procedures that can be performed offline. At Level 4, the highest level of strategic value, the company is transformed as it creates new business and shifts traditional business to the Internet.

As the potential benefits from the site increase, so do the costs. Developing a successful e-commerce strategy also takes time. Companies may not achieve positive returns on their Internet investment until they reach Level 3. Moving up the learning curve by working through the first levels before implementing more sophisticated technology is more likely to lead to success than attempting to transform the business in one step.[28]

Once a company decides to roll out or expand an e-commerce strategy, it faces a series of high-level decisions involving merchandising, Web site design, marketing, customer service and order fulfillment, Web site operations, and infrastructure. These decisions, summarized in Exhibit 18-8, form a road map leading to an Internet strategy that complements the firm's overall business strategy.

Merchandising

Many companies underestimate the effort required to effectively merchandise products on the Internet. First they must decide which products to sell and how to price them. Not all products can be sold successfully online. And slapping a picture of a product on a site with a basic description isn't sufficient. Successful

> e x h i b i t   1 8 - 8 <

Key Issues in Developing an E-Commerce Strategy

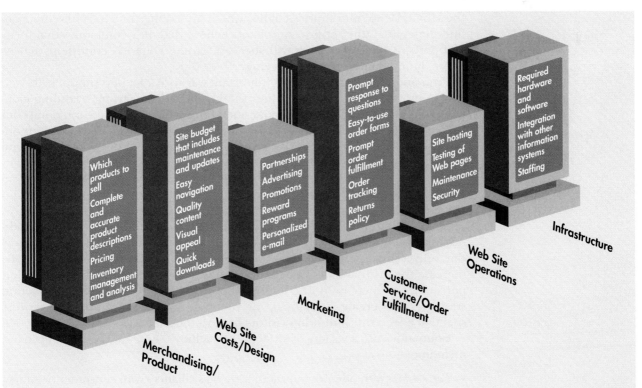

sites provide guidance and have accurate and lively product descriptions. Other merchandising issues include testing to make sure links to product pictures and descriptions are correct and designing easy-to-use order forms.

Site Costs and Design

Establishing an e-commerce Web site has become much easier in the past few years. Off-the-shelf software packages costing as little as $100 provide templates for sales-oriented Web sites. Packages with more sophisticated features like search engines and databases to manage inventory cost about $2,000 to $5,000. Companies can also hire a Web designer or outsource Web site development to a specialist. As Exhibit 18-7 shows, the cost of a corporate Web site ranges from $30,000 to over $2 million and includes not only the design and equipment but also updates to site content and technology and maintenance. On average, however, corporate Web sites cost about $250,000 to develop and $180,000 to maintain. For sites with online purchasing capabilities, the averages rise to $370,000 and $275,000, respectively.[29]

Regardless of who develops a site, managers responsible for the company's e-commerce strategy must plan carefully to ensure that the site meets the company's e-commerce objectives, in terms of both content and budget. Among the most important design considerations for e-commerce sites are simplicity, ease of navigation, visual appeal, download speed, and good product information. (For tips on creating an effective Web site, see Applying This Chapter's Topics.)

Marketing

Building brand equity is critical for e-commerce marketing. The first companies to build an online relationship with the consumer have a large advantage. Superbuild.com, a Seattle-based online home improvement merchant, hopes that "getting there first, getting the brand name out" will give it an edge over the Home Depot and Lowe's chains, which are taking time to refine their online strategies. Other online merchants believe that only companies that focus 100 percent on Web selling will succeed. Home Depot is confident that its strong brand name will give it leverage.[30]

Print and television ads are an important way to attract new shoppers to Web sites. Yahoo! soared ahead of other search sites with a strong branding campaign on television. Ben Boyd, spokesman for Barnesandnoble.com, points out that online advertising doesn't reach consumers who have yet to make an online purchase. Offline advertising makes them aware of a company's online presence. Executives at MotherNature.com, a new health products e-tailer, agree. Turning down a one-year, $5 million dollar deal with AOL in favor of radio and print ads, they saw both site traffic and the number of visitors who made purchases increase 500 percent.[31]

One of the underlying differences between Internet marketing and traditional marketing is the difficulty of turning shoppers into buyers. Studies show that only a small percentage of Web site visitors actually make a purchase. To increase the profitability of a Web site, e-businesses must raise that conversion percentage or increase traffic to obtain more volume. This requires marketing strategies that create "stickiness," an increase in the amount of time visitors spend at a Web site, and bring visitors back to the site.

Companies use a variety of strategies to achieve these marketing objectives, including:

- *Partnerships* with other organizations, such as alliances with consumer providers like AOL or with complementary retailers for placement of banner ads.

INTERNET MARKETING OF DIETARY SUPPLEMENTS

When Wayne Josephson took the dietary supplement androstenedione, he thought that he had discovered the fountain of youth. He says it "boosted his energy, built up his muscles, and even increased his sex drive." Invigorated and inspired by his personal experience, Josephson decided that androstenedione presented the opportunity for a new business—he would market the supplement over the Internet to older men.

So, in October 1998, Josephson set up a Web site to sell the dietary supplement that he called "The Stud Pill for Men." He issued a press release describing the supplement as a substance that was safe, proven, and approved by the Food and Drug Administration (FDA). The press release also indicated that the supplement would increase testosterone levels, reverse male aging, burn fat, build muscle, and boost strength, energy, and sex drive. In the first month that his Web site was operational, Josephson sold 1,000 bottles of "The Stud Pill for Men" for a sales volume of approximately $30,000.

Dietary supplements like androstenedione are not rigidly regulated by the FDA. Nonetheless, FDA rules and regulations prohibit vendors and manufacturers from making misleading claims about dietary products being used for the prevention or treatment of diseases. Additionally, the FDA must be provided with safety data on any product ingredients introduced after 1994. Interestingly, Josephson didn't bother to follow these regulations, let alone find out about them. When informed about these regulations, Josephson said that "he never hired a lawyer to learn about the regulations . . . because he didn't want to spend a lot of money starting the new business, and because he assumed his androstenedione supplier had taken care of all the legal requirements."

Critical Thinking Questions

1. Was Josephson acting ethically by promoting androstenedione as "The Stud Pill for Men"?
2. How would you characterize Josephson's failure to learn about and follow the FDA regulations? Was it an operational mistake or an ethical lapse?

- *Advertising* in both electronic and traditional media. In addition to banner ads, companies can buy sponsorships on Web pages that put their message into the content of the other Web sites.
- *Promotions, contests, and sweepstakes* at the Web site or through e-mail—for example, e-mail newsletters with notices of sale items, an e-mail dollars-off coupon for customers who haven't ordered for a while, and sweepstakes giving away trips and popular products.
- *"Frequent buyer" programs* for Internet retail sites, sponsored by individual merchants or companies like ClickRewards that offer awards for purchases at member sites.
- *Personalized e-mail* with links to Web sites, which increases sales by driving traffic to Web sites and improving customer retention. This type of e-mail marketing costs less than banner advertising and has a much higher "click-through" rate—an average of 18 percent, compared to 0.65 on banner ads.

Learn how you can earn "ClickMiles" from many different merchants at **www.clickrewards.com**

What brings site visitors back? For 75 percent of Web surfers, high-quality content is the key. Other criteria include ease of use, fast download time, and frequent updates.

Customer Service and Order Fulfillment

On the Internet, disgruntled shoppers usually don't wait around. Slow service? Poor information? Difficult ordering process? With just a click of the mouse, consumers find another site that makes shopping easier. Therefore, good customer service and order fulfillment are critical to gaining a competitive edge on the Internet.

With few exceptions, Internet customer service currently falls far below consumer expectations. A recent Jupiter Research study, for instance, found that 51 percent of Internet sites failed to respond to customer service questions within five days. Companies must set up an effective system and train customer service representatives to provide quick responses to customer questions about orders and products.

Web merchants must add more customer service staff and train them to sell and to advise online customers. Another option is to automate the process where possible. Customers see the Web as a way to speed up the entire buying process. Companies must be quick to learn from and adapt to this new selling medium.

Order fulfillment strategies are just as critical. Companies need new procedures to fill orders from the Web site without loss of data. Inventory management is critical for e-commerce sites. Many businesses are unprepared for the influx of new customers and do not have adequate inventory to fill customer orders. The many products that were out of stock was a major complaint of consumers during the 1998 holiday shopping season.

Companies are reevaluating operational strategies in response to the realities of e-commerce. As noted earlier, companies like Buy.com are outsourcing the distribution process to reduce warehouse and inventory holding costs. Amazon.com switched from outsourcing to in-house order fulfillment and distribution and now goes directly to publishers for most of its purchases.

Web Site Operations and Infrastructure

When planning an Internet strategy, managers must develop a plan for Web site operations and infrastructure. Some of the questions they need to ask include:

1. What hardware and software will we need?
2. Will design and operations, such as hosting the Web site on a server and distribution, be handled in-house or outsourced?
3. How will sales be integrated with the financial, accounting, and manufacturing systems?
4. What are our staffing needs?
5. Is the Web site secure so that customers feel comfortable ordering online? Have we created firewalls to protect internal company data from unauthorized access?

Once the Web site is online, managers must have a way to evaluate its effectiveness. They also need to know whose sites are best for their ads and promotions.

Measuring the return on an Internet investment is no easy task, however. As yet, the Web offers no standard measurement

concept check

- What are the four stages in developing an e-commerce strategy?
- How can a business increase the time visitors spend at its Web site?
- Describe several ways to ensure superior Internet customer service.

procedures. Auditing services use different methods to analyze Web-traffic data, often with conflicting results. Some common measurements include page impressions (number of times a page is seen), reach (number of unique visitors to a site), total number of site visits, time online, and click-throughs on linked ads. Companies must use caution in interpreting these results, however. A service that tells a company how many times its site is seen may not know if the visitor spends time on a page or quickly links to another site.

CAPITALIZING ON TRENDS IN BUSINESS

>lg 7   Predictions of a Jetsons-like future for the Internet abound. Within 10 years, we could live in a world where everything is interconnected through the Net. An in-home network would know to turn the coffeemaker on at a different time during the week and on weekends. Sprinkler systems would check the Web's weather reports and turn off if rain is expected. Manufacturers will use built-in Net links to diagnose and perhaps even fix problems with your kitchen appliances. Your refrigerator may be able to tell when supplies run low and generate orders from online grocers.[32] As discussed in Chapter 17, information appliances from Web-browsing phones to wireless handheld units will bring a wider range of services to consumers. Faster and more reliable Internet access will improve the quality of the Internet experience and make software and music downloads easier. Other trends include one-to-one marketing, better privacy policies, and industry consolidation.

Let's Get Personal

The Internet's ability to provide companies with a new, more effective link with customers could make it the most powerful direct marketing tool yet. Already it is creating new types of one-to-one marketing models. The Web's unique ability to provide immediate communication with and feedback from customers will allow merchants to meet customer demands on an individual basis. One year after implementing customized services, sites reported 47 percent growth in new customers and a 52 percent increase in sales.[33]

With the Internet, companies can:

- Target and deliver messages geared to a specific market segment based on demographics and interests.

- Create communities through chat sessions, newsgroups, and electronic personal shopping to build loyalty and enhance customer connections.

- Collect, track, and analyze customer data to identify consumer behavior and buying patterns.

- Convert online advertisements to sales transactions by allowing customers to link from the ad to the purchasing site.

Many different types of sites use personalization to create customer loyalty and increase purchases. Portal sites like Yahoo! and Excite let users create personalized pages with an e-mail box, news on specific topics, weather for their hometown, sports scores, and reminders of upcoming events like birthdays. American Airlines sends e-mail alerting customers to special fares on designated routes. CDNow's customers get personalized pages that recommend music according to past purchases, stated preferences, and ratings on performers and CDs. "It really is a music store for each of our 600,000-plus customers," says Jason Olim, CDNow's co-founder and CEO.[34] The Focusing on Small Business box describes how community building helped mail-order retailer Delia's break into e-tailing.

Privacy Policies Go Public

The Web's ability to provide personalized service comes at a price. Consumers have to supply personal information, raising concerns about privacy. The Web site's ability to follow an electronic trail is another issue. In early 1999, a study requested by the Federal Trade Commission showed that about two-thirds of all commercial Web sites warn the visitor that they collect personal information. Of those sites, only 10 percent also told customers that they could refuse to provide information and that they could review data collected at the site.

Make a contribution to protecting consumer privacy online. Submit your ratings of Web site privacy policies at the Privacy Watchdog site
watchdog.cdt.org/

In response to consumer concerns, companies are posting their privacy policies on their Web sites. These policies tell consumers what information the site collects and how it will be used. To reduce consumer fears and prevent possible future government regulation, companies such as IBM, Microsoft, and Disney are taking a strong privacy stance and leading a voluntary industry effort to protect customer privacy. They have announced that they will not advertise on Web sites that don't clearly state their privacy policies. Disney and its Web portal partner Infoseek Corp. went a step further. They will not accept advertising on any of their affiliated sites—including ESPN.com, ABC.com, ABCNews.com, and Family.com—from companies that do not have clear privacy policies. IBM also encouraged Web sites on which it advertises to allow visitors to prevent their personal information from being sold to outside marketers.[35]

Trying to Catch Amazon

In the early days of the Internet, small, nimble companies took the lead. In just a few years, many of those companies became major forces in e-commerce. Some forward-thinking established companies also recognized the Internet's power and joined the e-commerce community. Many others, however, decided to wait until the Net became more developed, sure that their size would enable them to trample the newcomers. But the fast pace of the Internet means that those who wait, lose. Those who arrived first have already moved to the next level of e-commerce.

No longer content to sell only books, e-tailing leader Amazon.com quickly branched out into related categories such as music, video, software, and gifts. By mid-1999 it had stepped up its expansion strategy with investments in Homegrocer.com, an Internet grocery-shopping service, online pharmacy Drugstore.com, and Pets.com, a pet care products company. It also established a partnership with Sotheby's, the fine arts auction house.[36]

Other online retailers are using strategic alliances to ward off Amazon's encroachment into their territory. CDNow's Jason Olim partnered with eToys,

DELIA'S TAPS INTO gURL POWER

Teenage girls today have lots of money to spend—$60 billion a year—and CEO Stephen Kahn wants them to spend it at Delia's, Inc. first. He and his college roommate Christopher Edgar founded the company in 1994, and by 1997 it was the leading direct marketer to the 28 million teenage girls in the United States.

"We felt that this group was not well served," Edgar said. "There wasn't a recognition of these kids as real consumers." With an upbeat catalog of cutting-edge clothes and trendy accessories, Delia's quickly grabbed the dominant market share. Its youthful image is real: most of its employees are under 30. Phone representatives dispense tips and fashion advice as well as take orders.

It didn't take long for copycat companies to invade Delia's territory. To maintain growth and market share, Delia's needed new distribution channels. And what could be more natural for its Generation Y consumers than the Internet?

Instead of simply opening an online Delia's store, in 1997 Kahn acquired gURL.com, an award-winning interactive entertainment and editorial site for teen girls. At **www.gurl.com**, teens found an online community, complete with chat rooms, games, an "e-zine" (online magazine), personal home pages, and e-mail. These services not only grabbed the attention and loyalty of Delia's target consumers but also helped Delia's track the likes and dislikes of the teen market and build brand awareness. Visitors to gURL.com could soon link to Delia's online store (**www.delias.com**), launched in May 1998.

Delia's shows that it takes its teen consumers seriously by using its Internet sites to build relationships. With a direct and humorous approach to topics that interest teens, its Web site is more than an online version of Delia's catalog. Like gURL.com, the site features chat rooms, teen-oriented news and entertainment stories, contests, and e-mail newsletters about the latest trends and sales. Visitors can order catalogs, purchase specially priced items available only online, join an on-line discount shopping club, and link to Delia's other sites.

The Internet has been a winning strategy for Delia's. "We consider our sites to be a powerful blend of content, community, and commerce for our target audience," says Kahn. In addition to generating sales revenue, Delia's Web site has proved to be an excellent way to build the company's database. More than 1,000 catalog requests come in over the Internet each day. Visitors download over 20 million monthly page views at the company's five Web sites, and several hundred thousand girls participate in the gURL.com community site. As a result of its success with teen girls, Delia's is expanding its strategy to other Generation Y consumers by adding catalogs and Web sites for its lines of boys' apparel, soccer products, and kids' home furnishings.

Critical Thinking Questions

1. What types of information should a company like Delia's include on its Web site to target teen consumers?
2. Visit the gURL.com and Delia's sites. Why do they attract teenage girls?
3. How can Internet communities enhance a company's relationship with a particular market segment?

concept check

- How can companies use the Internet to build customer relationships?
- What can online merchants do to lessen consumers' privacy concerns?
- How is industry consolidation changing the Internet business environment?

Cyberian Outpost, Reel.com, DatekOnline, Virtual Vineyards, Preview Travel, Garden Escape, and PC Flowers and Gifts to create ShopperConnection, a retail hub site.

Industry consolidation is also on the rise. Companies are acquiring rivals and buying companies in other e-commerce categories to stake out a larger claim on cyberspace. AOL has been a major acquirer of e-commerce companies such as When.com, which developed a personalized online calendar and event schedule, and ICQ, a developer of Internet instant messaging technology.

APPLYING THIS CHAPTER'S TOPICS

One of the biggest challenges you will face in your business career is keeping up with the Internet industry. By the time you read this chapter, new developments in access speed, voice and data transmission, and e-commerce will be making headlines. Just as in other areas of information technology, acquiring and maintaining Internet-related skills will serve you well in the future.

You may be called on to help your company go online or make its Web site more effective. A study by Boston information technology market researcher Yankee Group found that about 46 percent of small businesses still do not have a Web presence. And often small and medium-sized companies that are online do not know how to use the Internet to improve their business. Says Yankee Group's Michael Lauricella, "The Web site is more of a toy than a business tool."[37]

Creating a Successful Web Site

What makes a Web site a winner? According to four Web experts interviewed by *The Wall Street Journal Interactive Edition,* a site's overall look and "feel," layout, content, and ease of use are among the most important features. Simple, visually appealing layouts won praise. But the best Web sites have more than attractive design elements. The Web designers also included good prices and service in their list of "must-haves."[38]

Even the most attractive Web site will fail if the company doesn't fill orders promptly and provide good customer service. Here are some guidelines for creating effective Web sites:

- *Know what you want to accomplish.* Is the site mainly informational, or is it interactive, with searching and ordering capabilities?
- *Follow the 30-second rule.* Viewers have a short attention span and will move on to one of the millions of other sites unless they can see what the site is within 10 seconds, what it's about within the next 10, and how it's organized and what links it has in 10 more seconds.
- *Keep the design appropriate to the company.* The no-frills Cheap CDs site (**www.cheap-cds.com**) gives the customer the impression that this company offers the lowest prices—even if it doesn't always have the cheapest CDs.
- *Create strong content and update it regularly.* Quality content is the number one reason that users return to Web sites. Provide complete and accurate product information. Regular updates give visitors a reason to return to your site.
- *Flashy is not necessarily better.* Too many colors or graphic elements can be distracting. Strive for clarity, not clutter.
- *Make navigation easy.* Users want to move around a site as quickly as possible. Two common navigational tools are tabs along the top of the screen and a navigation bar on the left side. Search features also help visitors find what they need. Make sure links work.
- *Keep download times short.* Users like speedy sites. Multimedia effects can make pages slow to load. Customers quickly become frustrated and will leave a site without ordering if they have to wait for images to appear. Offering a text-only version of your site makes it easier for visitors with slower modems to access information.

1. **Create Your Own Web Site** Many ISPs now offer customers the chance to have their own Web site. Develop a proposal for a personal or business Web site, including the purpose, features, estimated cost, maintenance, update plan, and similar details. Refer to the guidelines in the "Applying This Chapter's Topics" section. For more help, visit Jakob Nielsen's Alertbox site **(www.useit.com)** for his biweekly columns on improving Web site usability. Check out his 1996 column "The Top Ten Mistakes of Web Design," which he recently updated. If possible, create and test the Web site.

2. **Build an E-commerce Site** If you're thinking of setting up a Web site to market products on the World Wide Web, check out the online e-commerce tutorial at **www.hotwired.com/ webmonkey/e-business/tutorials/ tutorial3.html.** You'll find five lessons that describe how to generate a realistic e-business plan, create an appropriate site design, market the site, handle payments, set up shipping procedures, and establish adequate security. With links to related articles on the HotWired site, this series guides you through the whole process, including whether to build your e-commerce site in-house or use outside experts.

- *Avoid long blocks of text.* Reading lots of text is difficult on the small screen. Users prefer to see headlines and article summaries, with links to the complete article for those who want more information.[39]

Gearing Up for E-Commerce

Suppose your company wants to start an online business venture. If you want your Web site to generate sales and repeat visits, you should start by analyzing the company's readiness for e-commerce. Here are some critical questions to ask:

1. Which customers are we trying to reach through the Internet: current customers, new customers, or a combination of both?
2. Will we offer a deep range of merchandise or only selected products?
3. Will we design our Web site in-house or outsource it?
4. How will we attract customers to our Web site?
5. How will we encourage purchases and repeat visits at our Web site?
6. How will we ensure that customers receive quality customer service?
7. What percentage of total sales do we hope to achieve through the Internet?
8. What internal operational changes do we need to make to support our Internet strategy?
9. Does our current technological infrastructure support our goals? If not, will we upgrade or outsource?
10. How will we mine customer information and purchases to improve service and profits?

You can also use similar questions to evaluate the success of an existing operation. In addition, you would determine the number of visitors, the percentage who buy, how well the order fulfillment and customer service procedures work, and what improvements and upgrades are necessary.

>looking ahead
at eToys

In the fast-paced world of Web retailing, a company cannot rest on its laurels. eToys is working hard to hold onto its lead as the Web's top toy retailer. The company raised additional capital to support expansion by going public in May 1999. A second warehouse on the East Coast will improve customer service. Lenk is adding more categories, including kids' sporting goods and maternity and baby products, to tap the larger children's products market—and its relatively high profit margins and attractive demographics. "Our anchor category is toys, but the vision for the company is to be the preeminent kids' retailing name for the 21st century," says eToys chief financial officer Steven Schoch.

Although eToys is well positioned in an industry tailor-made for the Net, it faces plenty of competition. Major retailers like Toys "R" Us are investing heavily in their sites. They also have the clout to put pressure on manufacturers. The manufacturers themselves could decide to sell directly to consumers from their own Web sites instead of selling to eToys. But perhaps the biggest threat comes from Amazon.com. In mid-1999 the online retailer everyone wants to copy announced that it, too, was opening an online toy store.[40]

SUMMARY OF LEARNING GOALS

>lg 1 What is the Internet, and how does it work?

The Internet is a global "network of networks" that is revolutionizing how businesses operate. It combines high-speed communications and computing power to transmit information immediately. All networks in the Internet use TCP/IP, a special language that allows different types of computers to communicate. In addition to the resources of the World Wide Web, the Internet provides file transfer capabilities, e-mail, chat sessions, and newsgroups. Data travel from the user's access point to the Internet service provider and then through a series of interlinked national backbones to the recipient's ISP.

>lg 2 Who uses the Internet, and for what?

About 170 million people worldwide use the Internet. About 64 million adults in the United States are regular users. Although adopters of the technology were younger, more affluent, and better educated than the general population, the profile of the Net user is moving closer to the national averages in these areas. Among the most popular Web sites are those with company and product information, news, reference materials, periodicals, financial quotes, and entertainment. Businesses use the Internet to research economic trends; gather industry information; learn about competitors; provide customer service; communicate with employees, vendors, and customers; market and sell products; and purchase supplies.

>lg 3 How has the Internet economy changed the business environment?
New types of companies provide enabling technology and services. The competitive arena is expanding as the Internet eliminates barriers of time and place and reduces barriers to entry. Channel relationships are changing as well. The Internet allows companies to sell directly to consumers without using distributors. Some distributors are finding new roles by providing services to online merchants who want to outsource order fulfillment. The Internet also em-

powers consumers by increasing access to information and making it easy to compare prices.

>lg 4 **How can companies incorporate e-commerce into their overall business strategies?**
E-commerce, the entire process of selling a product or service via the Internet, has two market segments: business-to-business and business-to-consumer. The business-to-business market accounts for about 85 percent of e-commerce revenue. Among the many models for e-commerce are selling goods and services over the Web, providing information for a fee, supporting an information or entertainment site with advertising or referral fees, facilitating sales through auctions, providing e-commerce-enabling services, and gathering industry or consumer information into "infomediary" sites.

>lg 5 **What benefits do businesses achieve through e-commerce?**
E-commerce reduces costs by streamlining company operating procedures. It offers the convenience of lower prices, greater selection of products and vendors, around-the-clock ordering and customer service availability (increasingly important in the global economy), ease of updating and distribution of product catalogs without incurring printing costs, and the ability to track customer and product sales data. Companies can eliminate intermediaries and sell directly to consumers and can offer customized products. The increased efficiency results in better customer service, lower transaction costs, and new relationship-building strategies.

>lg 6 **What steps are involved in launching an e-commerce venture?**
Companies can choose from several levels of e-commerce, starting with a basic promotional Web site and then adding order-taking and customer service features. More sophisticated strategies integrate Web activities into a company's existing business structure. To implement an e-commerce strategy, companies must consider merchandising, Web site design and costs, marketing, customer service and order fulfillment, operations, and infrastructure.

>lg 7 **What lies ahead for the Information Superhighway?**
One-to-one marketing is on the rise as e-commerce companies recognize the added value of personalization. Industry and consumer groups are developing solutions to protect customer privacy. Industry leaders are taking steps to protect their turf by acquiring other companies.

PREPARING FOR TOMORROW'S WORKPLACE

1. E-commerce may not provide a level playing field for small businesses. In fact, the Internet industry is consolidating as companies try to dominate their space. Divide the class into two teams and debate whether small businesses will continue to have an advantage in e-commerce or be pushed out by the "gorillas."

2. Divide the class into three groups representing retailers, distributors, and manufacturers. Each group should examine how the Web is changing channel relationships and prepare for a class discussion on the future of distributors.

3. Choose two of your favorite Web sites to explore and analyze. Using Exhibit 18-7 as a guide, decide which level of e-commerce strategy the site represents and explain why.

KEY TERMS

browser 535
business-to-business
  e-commerce 542
business-to-
  consumer
  e-commerce 542
electronic
  commerce
  (e-commerce)
  541
extranet 544
host computer 536
hypertext 535
Internet service
  provider (ISP)
  535
Internet 535
transmission control
  protocol/Internet
  protocol (TCP/IP)
  535
Web sites 535
World Wide Web
  (WWW) 535

4. How is eToys faring in the race to remain the number one online toy retailer? Using the Web and periodicals, prepare a brief update on the status of the company and its rivals Toys "R" Us, Amazon.com, and any others. What strategies is eToys using to maintain its edge?

5. How can a company determine whether a Web site is accomplishing its objectives? Research the techniques used by different ratings services such as Media Matrix, Nielsen, and Relevant Knowledge to measure site traffic. Develop a list of criteria that would be useful for evaluating a site that sells a product and a site that provides news information.

6. The Internet is changing the way travelers plan their trips. Comprehensive travel sites such as Preview Travel (**www.previewtravel.com**), Travelocity (**www.travelocity.com**), Internet Travel Network (**www.itn.com**), Expedia (**www.expedia.msn.com**), and The Trip.com (**www.thetrip.com**) provide information that once was available only to travel agents. Visit at least two of these sites to see what they offer. Do you think travel agents will become extinct in a few years? Why or why not? Suggest several ways travel agents can harness the Web to their advantage to counter this do-it-yourself trend.

WORKING THE NET

1. Compare the features of two Web-based grocery services such as Webvan (**www.webvan.com**), HomeGrocer (**www.homegrocer.com**), Peapod (**www.peapod.com**), NetGrocer (**www.netgrocer.com**), and ShopLink (**www.shoplink.com**). Which do you prefer, and why? How easy is it for consumers to shop at the site? Pick five items you regularly buy and compare the prices with those at your local market. Do you think consumers will eventually do more of their grocery shopping online?

2. Use the NUA Internet Surveys site at **www.nua.ie** to track the latest statistics and demographics on Internet users and to research the latest studies on e-commerce and business use. Summarize your findings in a brief report on key trends.

3. To avoid government intervention, Internet industry organizations are working toward self-regulation to protect consumer privacy. Visit the sites for the Online Privacy Alliance (**www.privacyalliance.org**) and TrustE (**www.truste.org**) and evaluate what they are doing. What criteria must firms meet to win the right to display the TrustE seal of approval?

4. What makes a good Web site? Check out the site for the Webbies Awards, **www.webbyawards.com**. Then compare the winning sites to the winners of the Muddies Awards for worst Web sites, **www.netstudio.com/mudbrick/**. Summarize the differences.

5. How good are "prebuilt" Web site templates for e-commerce? Compare the features and pricing offered by such companies as QuickSite (**www.quicksite.com**), VersaCheck Web Commerce (**www.mipsdla.com**), Maestro Commerce Suite (**bitsoftware.com**), Net.Commerce Start (**www.software.ibm.com/commerce/net.commerce**), and iCat (**www.icat.com**). If you were starting an online retail business, would you use one of these or hire an outside site designer?

CREATIVE THINKING CASE

Can Webvan Deliver in a Crowded Market?

Logging on to Webvan's Web site, **www.webvan.com**, customers can select from 20,000 products, including 300 kinds of vegetables, 350 types of cheese, and

700 different wines—at prices averaging 5 percent below supermarket prices. Customers then specify a 30-minute time period for delivery, which is free for orders over $50. They never have to deal with crowded supermarket aisles or lug heavy bags home.

The brainchild of Louis Borders, founder of Borders Books and Music, Webvan offers a new twist on an old idea: home delivery of groceries. It hopes to capture the minds and wallets of a very large group—the two-thirds of grocery shoppers who dislike the chore. Borders, CEO of the new venture, chose the San Francisco Bay area to introduce his service. "A concentration of busy, Web-savvy, and quality-conscious consumers makes the bay area an ideal choice," he says.

Webvan is plunging into a market that has been difficult for its competitors. Peapod, one of the first Internet grocers, has 100,000 customers but no profits after almost 10 years. According to market researcher Jupiter Communications, annual online grocery sales were $63 million in 1997 and are expected to reach $3.5 billion by 2002. Still, this is not even 1 percent of the total $415 billion U.S. grocery sales. Despite the convenience of shopping online, consumers worry that the bananas will not be ripe or the hamburger properly stored for delivery. Many shoppers still want to see what they buy.

Webvan is using technology to solve the problem of getting the product from the distribution center to the customer quickly—no simple task when dealing with perishable items like meat, milk, and ice cream. Its huge automated central distribution centers serve customers within a 40-mile radius. Instead of pushing carts up and down aisles to fill individual customers' shopping carts, employees at Webvan's facility in Oakland, California control robotic devices that pick items and place them on miles of conveyor belts. A single employee can pick 450 items an hour—about 10 times as fast as a human shopper.

Just one month after its debut, Webvan announced an arrangement with Bechtel Group to duplicate this automated distribution and delivery center in 26 large urban markets around the United States. Such ambitious expansion plans give Webvan an edge over its competitors. "There is no doubt that this will guarantee them customers," said Ken Cassar, a Jupiter analyst. "The real question is whether they will be profitable customers."

Webvan management says the lower inventory and distribution costs will make the company's prices comparable to those in local stores and lower than other online grocers' prices. In one test, Webvan charged $41.88 for 10 items including milk, diapers, and toothpaste—about 12 percent below Peapod's price for the same items. This is a big advantage in an industry where the average profit after taxes is a mere 1.3 percent of sales. To boost profits, Borders plans to use Webvan's home-delivery network for items such as office products and CDs and services like video and dry cleaning delivery.

Webvan's main competition could come from HomeGrocer.com, another online grocer based in the Seattle area. Founder and CEO Terry Drayton focuses more on customer service than technology to win customers. HomeGrocer hires its own drivers rather than use third party delivery services. These employees are trained to solicit feedback and build customer relationships. Wearing surgical slippers to protect customers' carpets, they deliver coupons for special offers along with orders.

Critical Thinking Questions

1. Contrast the strategies of Webvan and HomeGrocer. Which do you think will be more successful in the long run, and why? What do their approaches say about the requirements for building a successful Internet business?

2. Would you order groceries online? What steps could a Web-based grocery service take to encourage you to shop there?

3. Do you think online grocery shopping will catch on? What can traditional supermarkets do to compete with the convenience of online grocers?

VIDEO CASE

Elderly Instruments: Doing Business over the Internet

Elderly Instruments (**www.elderly.com**) located in Lansing, Michigan, "is a music store and mail-order service featuring a huge stock of new and used guitars, basses, amplifiers, banjos, mandolins, fiddles, dulcimers, harmonicas, accordions, bodhrans, and other instruments." Elderly Instruments also features "an extensive selection of instructional books and videos," as well as thousands of hard-to-find audio cassettes and CDs. The company focuses on low prices and fast, friendly, knowledgeable service.

Founded as a small retail outlet for musical instruments and accessories, Elderly Instruments soon expanded into mail-order sales. Then, recognizing the potential of the Internet, Elderly developed its own Web site to promote its musical instruments, accessories, recordings, books, and videos. To Elderly Instruments, doing business over the Internet is basically an electronic version of its mail-order sales—an area in which the company had already developed considerable expertise and become a significant player.

Elderly's Web site loads quickly and is organized for customer convenience. Its user-friendly format enables prospective customers to browse through the company's stock of vintage and used instruments, recordings, books, and videos. Special deals on closeout items are offered through the *Cheapo Depot* link. Product descriptions—and often pictures—are provided. Items can be selected for purchase, ordered, and paid for through the company's secure Web site. The site also explains shipping costs within the continental United States and internationally.

Customers can also order mail-order catalogs through the Web site. Elderly "publishes a full-color general mail-order catalog plus four specialized catalogs, each jam-packed with carefully selected musical merchandise." One specialty catalog features the finest in acoustic and electric instruments, strings, accessories, recordings, books, and videos. Another focuses only on acoustic and electric instruments and accessories. A third catalog is devoted to recordings, and the fourth covers books, instructional cassettes, and videos.

Prospective customers can become familiar with Elderly's showroom and employees through the Web site. The site contains a map of the showroom as well as a photographic tour of the showroom, back offices, repair shop, and warehouse and shipping areas. Photographs of Elderly's employees are included, and the *ElderlyCam* enables site visitors to see the latest snapshot of the showroom.

Another promotional and informational feature of the Web site is a calendar that provides information on the "extra-special events" taking place at Elderly's showroom in Lansing. Among these special events are in-store performances by various artists and instructional workshops where customers can learn to play various instruments or refine their skills. The artists' performances are typically provided free of charge, while a nominal fee is charged for the instructional workshops.

Taken as a whole, Elderly's Web site appears to be a remarkably effective instrument for conducting electronic commerce.

Critical Thinking Questions

1. How does doing business over the Internet enable Elderly Instruments to achieve low prices and fast, friendly, knowledgeable service?

2. What other benefits might Elderly Instruments achieve through electronic commerce?

3. Suppose that you are considering becoming a customer of Elderly Instruments. Would you be comfortable doing business with Elderly over the Internet? Why or why not?

>c19

chapter nineteen

Using Financial Information and Accounting

learning goals

>lg 1   Why are financial reports and accounting information important, and who uses them?

>lg 2   What are the differences between public and private accountants?

>lg 3   What are the six steps in the accounting cycle?

>lg 4   In what terms does the balance sheet describe the financial condition of an

>lg 5   How does the income statement report a firm's profitability?

>lg 6   Why is the statement of cash flows an important source of information?

>lg 7   How can ratio analysis be used to identify a firm's financial strengths and weaknesses?

>lg 8   What major trends are affecting the accounting industry today?

Testing 1, 2, 3

"My first accounting system—if you could call it that!—was a handheld electronic personal organizer to track tutoring appointments," says Jared Wells, owner of Wells Test Preparation Center in San Diego, California. When he opened a permanent location offering tutoring plus courses for SAT preparation, writing, and study skills, Wells wanted a better system to track revenues and expenses.

"When I started, I didn't even know what I wanted to get from my accounting system," he says. "That was probably one of my biggest problems. Unless you know the purpose of your system, you can't develop the right structure. It took me two years to find out that, as a sole proprietor, tax reporting was my primary need. I also wanted to have the information to make better business decisions."

With a friend's help he developed a client information system using Microsoft Access, a database program, to record client information, post transactions, and generate invoices and simple financial reports. Wells soon recognized that he needed specialized software for accurate tax reporting and professional assistance with bookkeeping and accounting. The firm he hired recommended QuickBooks Pro, popular small business accounting software that is easy to use—even for people who don't know much about accounting.

The transition to QuickBooks was anything but smooth, however. Wells still didn't understand the purpose of accounting other than tracking revenues and expenses. In addition, the basic format was geared to companies that made or sold goods, rather than service businesses. "That's what got me in to trouble in the first place," Wells recalls. "The general chart of accounts didn't fit my business." In addition, his first accounting firm worked mostly with larger companies with full-time controllers. Instead of advising him on the right way to proceed, the accountants let him make decisions and take shortcuts. "They set up more accounts and expense categories than we really needed, and because they didn't correspond to those on tax forms, we had a terrible time preparing our 1998 tax forms."

In early 1999 Wells started from scratch to create an entirely new QuickBooks accounting system. "I had learned enough accounting over two years to dive in and figure out the system myself," he says. "I now understood why I needed an accounting system—for tax reporting and to manage the business more efficiently—and what information I needed to accomplish these goals." Rather than using the program's standard account system, he set up the appropriate accounts for his firm. Expense records now have both a main category that relates to a line on the tax form and subcategories as needed for internal purposes. This makes tax filing easier and provides backup records in case of an audit.

Wells learned about accounting by trial and error. "I don't recommend this," he says. "If I'd had it to

Critical Thinking Questions

As you read this chapter, consider the following questions as they relate to Wells Test Preparation Center:

- If you were starting a new company, what planning steps would you take to avoid the difficulties Wells encountered?

- Jared Wells went through several different accounting firms before he found the right one. How could he have avoided these difficulties? Develop a questionnaire that he could have used to interview potential accountants.

- What factors should a company consider when selecting accounting software?

do over, I'd have taken business and accounting courses." Instead, he had to juggle financial reporting systems along with the other demands of a new company. "I went through three bookkeeping/accounting firms because of my naïveté," says Wells. "If I'd had some basic accounting background, I would have saved several thousand dollars in actual cash expenditures, plus who knows how much in lost time and wasted productivity."[1]

Understanding financial accounting information such as sales and inventory helps managers in all types of organizations make decisions that enhance operational effectiveness and efficiency.

BUSINESS IN THE 21ST CENTURY

As Jared Wells learned when he started his own company, accounting is the backbone of any business. He attributes many of his early problems to his lack of accounting knowledge. Because he was unable to evaluate the advice of his accounting firm, his first QuickBooks system did not meet his company's needs. Once he understood the basics of accounting, he could decide which financial information was important for his company, what those numbers meant, and how he could use them to make decisions.

Financial information is central to every organization. To operate effectively, businesses must have a way to track income, expenses, and assets in an organized manner. Financial information is also essential for decision making. Managers prepare financial reports using *accounting*, a set of procedures and guidelines for companies to follow when preparing financial reports. Unless you understand basic accounting concepts, you will not be able to "speak" the standard financial language of businesses.

This chapter starts by discussing why accounting is important for businesses and for users of financial information and then presents an overview of accounting procedures. Next the three main financial statements—the balance sheet, the income statement, and the statement of cash flows—are described. The chapter then discusses how to analyze financial statements using ratio analysis. Finally, it explores some of the trends affecting accounting.

THE PURPOSE OF ACCOUNTING

>lg 1

accounting

The process of collecting, recording, classifying, summarizing, reporting, and analyzing financial activities.

Accounting is the process of collecting, recording, classifying, summarizing, reporting, and analyzing financial activities. It results in reports that describe the financial condition of an organization. All types of organizations—businesses, hospitals, schools, government agencies, civic groups—use accounting procedures. Accounting provides a framework for looking at past performance, current financial health, and possible future performance. It also provides a frame-

In managerial accounting, internal reports detailing financial information such as the costs of labor and material in production are shared with other managers to assess the organization's performance.

managerial accounting
Accounting that provides financial information that managers inside the organization can use to evaluate and make decisions about current and future operations.

work for comparing the financial performances of different firms. Understanding how to prepare and interpret financial reports will enable you to evaluate two computer companies and choose the one that is more likely to be a good investment.

As Exhibit 19-1 shows, the accounting system converts the details of financial transactions (sales, payments, and so on) into a form that people can use to evaluate the firm and make decisions. Data become information, which in turn becomes reports. These reports describe a firm's financial position at one point in time and its financial performance during a specified period. Financial reports include *financial statements,* such as balance sheets and income statements, and special reports, such as sales and expense breakdowns by product line.

Who Uses Financial Reports?

The accounting system generates two types of financial reports, as shown in Exhibit 19-2: internal and external. Internal reports are used within the organization. As the term implies, **managerial accounting** provides financial information that managers inside the organization can use to evaluate and make decisions about current and future operations. For instance, the sales reports prepared by managerial accountants show how well marketing strategies are working. Production cost reports help departments track and control costs. Managers may prepare very detailed financial reports for their own use and provide summary reports for top management.

Financial accounting focuses on preparing external financial reports that are used by outsiders, that is, people who have an interest in the business but are not part of management. Although these reports also provide useful information for managers, they are primarily used by lenders, suppliers, investors, and government agencies to assess the financial strength of a business.

> e x h i b i t   1 9 - 1 <

The Accounting System

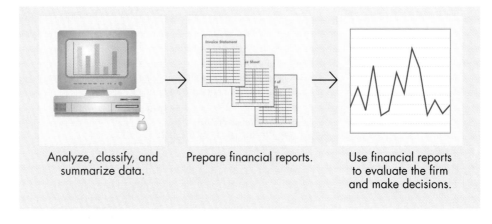

Analyze, classify, and summarize data.   Prepare financial reports.   Use financial reports to evaluate the firm and make decisions.

financial accounting

Accounting that focuses on preparing the financial reports used by outsiders such as lenders, suppliers, investors, and government agencies to assess the financial strength of a business.

generally accepted accounting principles (GAAP)

The financial accounting standards followed by accountants in the United States in preparing financial statements.

Financial Accounting Standards Board (FASB)

The private organization that is responsible for establishing financial accounting standards in the United States.

annual report

A yearly document that describes a firm's financial status and usually discusses the firm's activities during the past year and its prospects for the future.

>lg 2

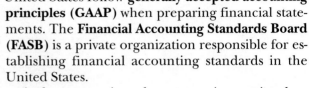

What issues is the FASB working on now? Check out the news section of
www.accountingnet.com

To ensure accuracy and consistency in the way financial information is reported, accountants in the United States follow **generally accepted accounting principles (GAAP)** when preparing financial statements. The **Financial Accounting Standards Board (FASB)** is a private organization responsible for establishing financial accounting standards in the United States.

At the present time, there are no international accounting standards, although the International Accounting Standards Committee is trying to develop them. Because accounting practices vary from country to country, a multinational company must make sure that its financial statements conform to both its own country's accounting standards and those of the parent company's country.

Financial statements are the chief element of the **annual report,** a yearly document that describes a firm's financial status. Annual reports usually discuss the firm's activities during the past year and its prospects for the future. Three primary financial statements included in the annual report are discussed and illustrated later in this chapter:

1. The balance sheet
2. The income statement
3. The statement of cash flows

The Accounting Profession

The accounting profession has grown rapidly due to the increased complexity, size, and number of businesses and the frequent changes in the tax laws. Accounting is now an over $40 billion industry. The more than one million

> e x h i b i t   1 9 - 2 <

Reports Provided by the Accounting System

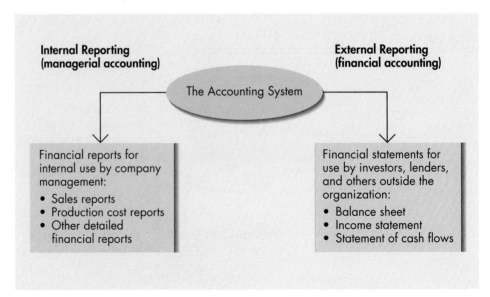

accountants in the United States are classified as either public accountants or private (corporate) accountants.

Public Accountants Independent accountants who serve organizations and individuals on a fee basis are called **public accountants.** Public accountants offer a wide range of services, including preparation of financial statements and tax returns, independent auditing of financial records and accounting methods, and management consulting. **Auditing,** the process of reviewing the records used to prepare financial statements, is an important responsibil-ity of public accountants. They provide a formal *auditor's opinion* indicating whether the statements have been prepared in accordance with accepted accounting rules. This written opinion is an important part of the annual report.

The largest public accounting firms, called the Big Five, operate worldwide and offer a variety of business consulting services in addition to accounting services. In order of size, they are Pricewaterhouse-Coopers, Andersen Worldwide, KPMG International, Ernst & Young, and Deloitte & Touche Tohmatsu International.

To become a **certified public accountant (CPA),** an accountant must complete an approved bachelor's degree program and pass a test prepared by the American Institute of Certified Public Accountants. Each state also has requirements for CPAs such as several years' on-the-job experience and continuing education. Only CPAs can provide the auditor's opinion on a firm's financial statements. Most CPAs first work for public accounting firms and later become private accountants or financial managers.

To find out more about the accounting profession and becoming a CPA, visit the American Institute of Certified Public Accountants' Web site at **www.aicpa.org/** and click on "Students."

Private Accountants Accountants employed to serve one particular organization are **private accountants.** Their activities include preparing financial statements, auditing company records to be sure employees follow accounting policies and procedures, developing accounting systems, preparing tax returns, and providing financial information for management decision making. Managerial accountants also have a professional certification program. Requirements to become a **certified management accountant (CMA)** are similar to those for the CPA.

BASIC ACCOUNTING PROCEDURES

Using generally accepted accounting principles, accountants record and report financial data in similar ways for all firms. They report their findings in financial statements that summarize a company's business transactions over a specified time period. As mentioned earlier, the three major financial statements are the balance sheet, income statement, and statement of cash flows.

People sometimes confuse accounting with bookkeeping. Accounting is a much broader concept. *Bookkeeping,* the system used to record a firm's financial transactions, is a routine, clerical process. Accountants take bookkeepers' transactions, classify and summarize the financial information, and then prepare and analyze financial reports. Accountants also develop and manage financial systems and help plan the firm's financial strategy.

---

public accountants

Independent accountants who serve organizations and individuals on a fee basis.

auditing

The process of reviewing the records used to prepare financial statements and issuing a formal *auditor's opinion* indicating whether the statements have been prepared in accordance with accepted accounting rules.

certified public accountant (CPA)

An accountant who has completed an approved bachelor's degree program, passed a test prepared by the American Institute of Certified Public Accountants, and met state requirements. Only a CPA can issue an auditor's opinion on financial statements.

private accountants

Accountants who are employed to serve one particular organization.

c o n c ə p t   c h ə c k

- Explain who uses financial information.
- Differentiate between financial accounting and managerial accounting.
- Compare the responsibilities of public and private accountants. How are they certified?

certified management accountant (CMA)

A managerial accountant who has completed a professional certification program, including passing an examination.

The Accounting Equation

assets
Things of value owned by a firm.

liabilities
What a firm owes to its creditors; also called *debts*.

owners' equity
The total amount of investment in the firm minus any liabilities; also called *net worth*.

The accounting procedures used today are based on those developed in the late fifteenth century by an Italian monk, Brother Luca Pacioli. He defined the three main accounting elements as assets, liabilities, and owners' equity. **Assets** are things of value owned by a firm. They may be *tangible*, such as cash, equipment, and buildings, or *intangible*, such as a patent or trademarked name. **Liabilities**—also called *debts*—are what a firm owes to its creditors. **Owners' equity** is the total amount of investment in the firm minus any liabilities. Another term for owners' equity is *net worth*.

The relationship among these three elements is expressed in the accounting equation:

$$Assets = Liabilities + Owners'\ equity$$

The accounting equation must always be in balance (that is, the total of the elements on one side of the equals sign must equal the total on the other side).

Suppose you start a bookstore and put $10,000 in cash into the business. At that point, the business has assets of $10,000 and no liabilities. This would be the accounting equation:

$$\begin{array}{ccccc}
Assets & = & Liabilities & + & Owners'\ equity \\
\$10,000 & = & \$0 & + & \$10,000
\end{array}$$

The liabilities are zero and owner's equity (the amount of your investment in the business) is $10,000. The equation balances.

double-entry bookkeeping
A method of accounting in which each transaction is recorded as two entries so that two accounts or records are changed.

To keep the accounting equation in balance, every transaction must be recorded as two entries. As each transaction is recorded, there is an equal and opposite event so that two accounts or records are changed. This method is called **double-entry bookkeeping.**

Suppose that after starting your bookstore with $10,000 cash, you borrow another $10,000 from the bank. The accounting equation will change as follows:

$$\begin{array}{ccccll}
Assets & = & Liabilities & + & Owners'\ equity & \\
\$10,000 & = & \$0 & + & \$10,000 & \text{Initial equation} \\
\$10,000 & = & \$10,000 & + & \$0 & \text{Borrowing transaction} \\
\$20,000 & = & \$10,000 & + & \$10,000 & \text{Equation after borrowing}
\end{array}$$

Now you have $20,000 in assets—your $10,000 in cash and the $10,000 loan proceeds from the bank. The bank loan is also recorded as a liability of $10,000 because it's a debt you must repay. Making two entries keeps the equation in balance.

The Accounting Cycle

>lg 3

The *accounting cycle* refers to the process of generating financial statements, beginning with a business transaction and ending with the preparation of the report. Exhibit 19-3 shows the six steps in the accounting cycle. The first step in the cycle is to analyze the data collected from many sources. All transactions that have a financial impact on the firm—sales, payments to employees and suppliers, interest and tax payments, purchases of inventory, and the like—must be documented. The accountant must review the documents to make sure they're complete.

Next each transaction is recorded in a *journal*, a listing of financial transactions in chronological order. Then the journal entries are recorded in *ledgers*, which show increases and decreases in specific asset, liability, and owners' equity accounts. The ledger totals for each account are summarized in a *trial balance*, which is used to confirm the accuracy of the figures. These values are used

The Accounting Cycle

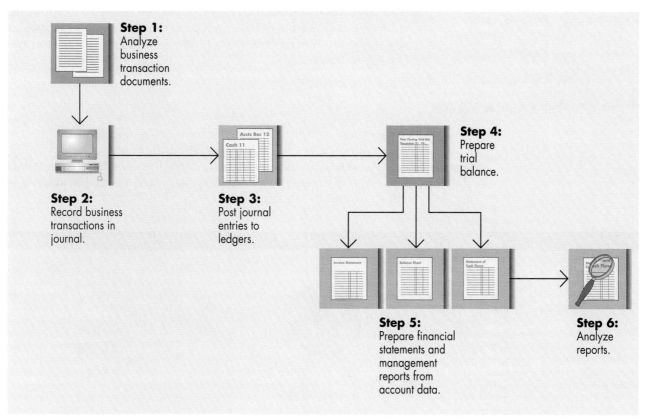

Step 1: Analyze business transaction documents.

Step 2: Record business transactions in journal.

Step 3: Post journal entries to ledgers.

Step 4: Prepare trial balance.

Step 5: Prepare financial statements and management reports from account data.

Step 6: Analyze reports.

to prepare financial statements and management reports. Finally, individuals analyze these reports and make decisions based on the information in them.

Computers in Accounting

As discussed in Chapter 17, computers have become part of the accounting activity in almost all firms, performing most of the mechanics of accounting. Because they can quickly and accurately handle large amounts of data, computers streamline the routine aspects of accounting so the accountant can focus on interpreting financial information. With computerized accounting systems, an entry generates the appropriate changes to other related parts.

Computerized accounting programs do many different things. Most accounting packages offer six basic modules that handle general ledger, sales order, accounts receivable, purchase order, accounts payable, and inventory control functions. Tax programs use accounting data to prepare tax returns and tax plans. Computerized point-of-sale terminals used by many retail firms automatically record sales and do some of the bookkeeping. The Big Five and many other large public accounting firms develop accounting software for themselves and for clients.

The Accounting Library site has a virtual consultant to help companies choose the best accounting applications for their needs. Check it out at

www.excelco.com/

concept check

- Explain the accounting equation.
- Describe the six-step accounting cycle.
- What role do computers play in accounting?

As the Applying Technology box explains, companies need to upgrade and reconfigure these critical computer systems regularly. Accounting and financial applications typically represent one of the largest portions of a company's software budget. Accounting soft-ware ranges from off-the-shelf programs for small businesses to full-scale customized enterprise resource planning systems for major corporations.

THE BALANCE SHEET

>lg 4

The **balance sheet,** one of three financial statements generated from the accounting system, summarizes a firm's financial position at a specific point in time. It reports the resources of a company (assets), the company's obligations (liabilities), and the difference between what is owned (assets) and what is owed (liabilities), or owners' equity.

> a p p l y i n g   t e c h n o l o g y <

CASE CLOSED

You'd think that Fortune 500 companies like $6.1 billion Case Corp. of Racine, Wisconsin, would be masters at designing corporate accounting systems. Yet when Case gained its independence from Tenneco in 1994, the manufacturer of farming and construction equipment had a hodgepodge of systems in its operating units around the world: 15 general ledger systems, 25 accounts payable systems, and 17 accounts receivable systems. In 1994, Case's financial managers began revamping its accounting systems to make them consistent throughout the company. Its overall financial reengineering was so successful that Case won *CFO* magazine's REACH awards for excellence in financial process reengineering in 1996, 1997, and 1998.

The first step was to benchmark other companies like Toyota and GM. "We took a serious look at what we were doing and how our competition was doing it," says Blaine Metzger, director of financial planning and analysis. "We unearthed some faults, to be frank, but these led us to improve our functional capabilities rather than outsource them."

Case began to consolidate, standardize, and automate its accounting systems. Representatives from payables, receivables, payroll, and ledger formed teams to develop standard processes for each accounting function. The result was three regional centers—in Racine, Paris, and Sydney—using the same system, standards, and processes. Each center handled all transaction processing in its region. "Our goal has been to eliminate the processing we don't need to do, automate those processes we do need, and standardize everything throughout the company," says Metzger.

Instead of multiple general ledger systems, for example, Case implemented Geac's SmartStream as its standard worldwide integrated client/server finance and accounting system. The need to make journal entries manually dropped 40 percent, reducing errors and providing faster and less costly financial closings. By 1998, Case had reduced the number of computer applications from 20 to 9, the error rate from 7.7 percent to 4.6 percent, and saved over $11 million a year. The cost of general accounting as a percentage of revenues dropped from 3.9 percent to 2.6 percent. Perhaps the most important benefit, however, was reducing the time employees spent on transaction processing from 70 percent to 30 percent so that they had significantly more time for business analysis.

Critical Thinking Questions

1. Why did the existence of many different computerized accounting systems create problems for Case Corp.?
2. What are the benefits of an integrated financial reporting system for a company? How does it help areas other than accounting and finance?

balance sheet

A financial statement that summarizes a firm's financial position at a specific point in time.

liquidity

The speed with which an asset can be converted to cash.

The assets are listed in order of their **liquidity,** the speed with which they can be converted to cash. The most liquid assets come first, and the least liquid are last. Because cash is the most liquid asset, it is listed first. Buildings, on the other hand, have to be sold to be converted to cash, so they are listed after cash. Liabilities are arranged similarly: liabilities due in the short term are listed before those due in the long term.

The balance sheet for Delicious Desserts, Inc., an imaginary bakery, is illustrated in Exhibit 19-4. The basic accounting equation is reflected in the three totals highlighted on the balance sheet: assets of $148,900 equal the sum of liabilities and owners' equity ($70,150 + $78,750). The three main categories of accounts on the balance sheet are explained below.

Assets

Assets can be divided into three broad categories: current assets, fixed assets, and intangible assets. **Current assets** are assets that can or will be converted to cash within the next 12 months. They are important because they provide the funds used to pay the firm's current bills. They also represent the amount of money the firm can quickly raise. Current assets include:

current assets

Assets that can or will be converted to cash within the next 12 months.

fixed assets

Long-term assets used by a firm for more than a year, such as land, buildings, and machinery.

depreciation

The allocation of an asset's original cost to the years in which it is expected to produce revenues.

- *Cash.* Funds on hand or in a bank
- *Marketable securities.* Temporary investments of excess cash that can readily be converted to cash
- *Accounts receivable.* Amounts owed to the firm by customers who bought goods or services on credit
- *Inventory.* Stock of goods being held for production or for sale to customers

On its balance sheet, this paper mill and wood processing plant would list long-term resources such as land, buildings, machinery, furniture, and fixtures as fixed assets.

Fixed assets are long-term assets used by the firm for more than a year. They tend to be used in production and include land, buildings, machinery, equipment, furniture, and fixtures. Except for land, fixed assets wear out and become outdated over time. Thus, they decrease in value every year. This declining value is accounted for through depreciation. **Depreciation** is the allocation of the asset's original cost to the years in which it is expected to produce revenues. A portion of the cost of a depreciable asset—a building or piece of equipment, for instance—is charged to each of the years it is expected to provide benefits. This practice helps match the asset's cost against the revenues it provides. Since it is impossible to know exactly how long an asset will last, estimates are used. They are based on past experience with similar items or IRS guidelines for assets of that type. Notice that, through 2000, Delicious Desserts has taken a total of $16,000 in depreciation on its bakery equipment.

intangible assets

Long-term assets with no physical existence such as patents, copyrights, trademarks, and goodwill.

Intangible assets are long-term assets with no physical existence. Common examples are patents, copyrights, trademarks, and goodwill. *Patents* and *copyrights* shield the firm from direct competition, so their benefits are more protective than productive. For instance, no one can use more than a small amount of copyrighted material without permission from the copyright holder. *Trademarks* are registered names that can be sold or licensed to others. Delicious Desserts' intangible asset is a trademark valued at $4,500. *Goodwill* occurs when a company pays more for an acquired firm than the value of its tangible assets.

Liabilities

Liabilities are the amounts a firm owes to creditors. Those liabilities coming due sooner—current liabilities—are listed first on the balance sheet, followed by long-term liabilities.

Balance Sheet for Delicious Desserts

Delicious Desserts, Inc.
Balance Sheet as of December 31, 2000

Assets

Current assets:		
Cash		$15,000
Marketable securities		4,500
Accounts receivable	$45,000	
Less: Allowance for doubtful accounts	1,300	43,700
Notes receivable		5,000
Inventory		15,000
Total current assets		$83,200
Fixed assets:		
Bakery equipment	$56,000	
Less: Accumulated depreciation	16,000	$40,000
Furniture and fixtures	$18,450	
Less: Accumulated depreciation	4,250	14,200
Total fixed assets		54,200
Intangible assets:		
Goodwill		$7,000
Trademark		4,500
Total intangible assets		11,500
Total assets		**$148,900**

Liabilities and Owners' Equity

Current liabilities:		
Accounts payable	$30,650	
Notes payable	15,000	
Accrued expenses	4,500	
Income taxes payable	5,000	
Current portion of long-term debt	5,000	
Total current liabilities		$60,150
Long-term liabilities:		
Bank loan for bakery equipment		
Total long-term liabilities		10,000
Total liabilities		**$70,150**
Owners' equity		
Common stock (10,000 shares)		$30,000
Retained earnings		48,750
Total owners' equity		**78,750**
Total liabilities and owners' equity		**$148,900**

current liabilities
Short-term claims that are due within a year of the date of the balance sheet.

Current liabilities are those due within a year of the date of the balance sheet. These short-term claims may strain the firm's current assets because they must be paid in the near future. Current liabilities include:

- *Accounts payable.* Amounts the firm owes for credit purchases due within a year. This account is the liability counterpart of accounts receivable.
- *Notes payable.* Short-term loans from banks, suppliers, or others that must be repaid within a year. For example, Delicious Desserts has a six-month, $15,000 loan from its bank that is a note payable.
- *Income taxes payable.* Taxes owed for the current operating period but not yet paid. Taxes are often shown separately because they are a large amount.
- *Current portion of long-term debt.* Any repayment on long-term debt due within the year. Delicious Desserts is scheduled to repay $5,000 on its equipment loan in the coming year.

long-term liabilities

Claims that come due more than one year after the date of the balance sheet.

Long-term liabilities come due more than one year after the date of the balance sheet. They include bank loans (such as Delicious Desserts' $10,000 loan for bakery equipment), mortgages on buildings, and the company's bonds sold to others.

retained earnings

The amounts left over from profitable operations since the firm's beginning; equal to total profits minus all dividends paid to stockholders.

Owners' Equity

Owners' equity is the owners' total investment in the business after all liabilities have been paid. For sole proprietorships and partnerships, amounts put in by the owners are recorded as capital. In a corporation, the owners provide capital by buying the firm's common stock. For Delicious Desserts, the total common stock investment is $30,000. **Retained earnings** are the amounts left over from profitable operations since the firm's beginning. They are total profits minus all dividends (distributions of profits) paid to stockholders. Delicious Desserts has $48,750 in retained earnings.

c o n c ǝ p t c h ǝ c k

- What is a balance sheet?
- What are the three main categories of accounts on the balance sheet, and how do they relate to the accounting equation?
- How do retained earnings relate to owners' equity?

THE INCOME STATEMENT

>lg 5

income statement

A financial statement that summarizes a firm's revenues and expenses and shows its total profit or loss over a period of time.

The balance sheet shows the firm's financial position at a certain point in time. The **income statement** summarizes the firm's revenues and expenses and shows its total profit or loss over a period of time. Most companies prepare monthly income statements for management and quarterly and annual statements for use by investors, creditors, and other outsiders. The primary elements of the income statement are revenues, expenses, and net income (or net loss). The income statement for Delicious Desserts for the year ended December 31, 2000, is shown in Exhibit 19-5.

Revenues

revenues

The dollar amount of a firm's sales plus any other income it received from sources such as interest, dividends, and rents.

gross sales

The total dollar amount of a company's sales.

net sales

The amount left after deducting sales discounts and returns and allowances from gross sales.

Revenues are the dollar amount of sales plus any other income received from sources such as interest, dividends, and rents. The revenues of Delicious Desserts arise from sales of its bakery products. Revenues are determined starting with **gross sales,** the total dollar amount of a company's sales. Delicious Desserts had two deductions from gross sales. *Sales discounts* are price reductions given to customers that pay their bills early. For example, Delicious Desserts gives sales discounts to restaurants that buy in bulk and pay at delivery. *Returns and allowances* is the dollar amount of merchandise returned by customers because they didn't like a product or because it was damaged or defective. **Net sales** is the amount left after deducting sales discounts and returns and allowances from gross sales. Delicious Desserts' gross sales were reduced by $4,500, leaving net sales of $270,500.

Income Statement for Delicious Desserts

Delicious Desserts, Inc.
Income Statement for the Year Ended December 31, 2000

Revenues

Gross sales	$275,000	
Less: Sales discounts	2,500	
Less: Returns and allowances	2,000	
Net Sales		$270,500

Cost of Goods Sold

Beginning inventory, January 1	$ 18,000	
Cost of goods manufactured	109,500	
Total cost of goods available for sale	$127,500	
Less: Ending inventory December 31	15,000	
Cost of goods sold		112,500

Gross profit　　　　　　　　　　　　　　　　　　　　**$158,000**

Operating Expenses

Selling expenses

Sales salaries	$31,000	
Advertising	16,000	
Other selling expense	18,000	
Total selling expenses		$65,000

General and administrative expenses

Professional and office salaries	$20,500	
Utilities	5,000	
Office supplies	1,500	
Interest	3,600	
Insurance	2,500	
Rent	17,000	
Total general and administrative expenses	50,100	
Total operating expenses		115,100

Net profit before taxes	**$42,900**
Less: Income taxes	10,725
Net profit	**$32,175**

Expenses

expenses

The costs of generating revenues.

cost of goods sold

The total expense of buying or producing a firm's goods or services.

Expenses are the costs of generating revenues. Two types are recorded on the income statement: cost of goods sold and operating expenses.

The **cost of goods sold** is the total expense of buying or producing the firm's goods or services. For manufacturers, cost of goods sold includes all costs directly related to production: purchases of raw materials and parts, labor, and factory overhead (utilities, factory maintenance, machinery repair). For wholesalers and retailers, it is the cost of goods bought for resale. For all sellers, cost of goods sold includes all the expenses of preparing the goods for sale, such as shipping and packaging.

Delicious Desserts' cost of goods sold is based on the value of inventory on hand at the beginning of the accounting period, $18,000. During the year, the company spent $109,500 to produce its baked goods. This figure includes the cost of raw materials, labor costs for bakery workers, and the cost of operating the bakery area. Adding the cost of goods manufactured to the value of beginning inventory, we get the total cost of goods available for sale, $127,500. To determine the cost of goods sold for the year, we subtract the cost of inventory at the end of the period:

$$\$127,500 - \$15,000 = \$112,500$$

The amount a company earns after paying to produce or buy its products but before deducting operating expenses is the **gross profit.** It is the difference between net sales and cost of goods sold. Since service firms do not produce goods, their gross profit equals net sales. Gross profit is a critical number for a company because it is the source of funds to cover all the firm's other expenses. Analyzing gross profits by product can translate into higher profits, as the Focusing on Small Business box demonstrates.

The other major expense category is **operating expenses.** These are the expenses of running the business that are not related directly to producing or buying its products. The two main types of operating expenses are selling expenses and general and administrative expenses. *Selling expenses* are those related to marketing and distributing the company's products. They include salaries and commissions paid to salespeople and the costs of advertising, sales supplies, delivery, and other items that can be linked to sales activity, such as insurance, telephone and other utilities, and postage. *General and administrative expenses* are the business expenses that cannot be linked to either cost of goods sold or sales. Examples of general and administrative expenses are salaries of top managers and office support staff; office supplies; fees for accounting, consulting, and legal services; insurance; rent; and utilities. Delicious Desserts' operating expenses totaled $115,100.

Net Profit or Loss

The final figure—or bottom line—on an income statement is the **net profit** (or **net income**) or **net loss.** It is calculated by subtracting all expenses from revenues. If revenues are more than expenses, the result is a net profit. If expenses exceed revenues, a net loss results.

Several steps are involved in finding net profit or loss. (These are shown in the right-hand column of Exhibit 19-5.) First, cost of goods sold is deducted from net sales to get the gross profit. Then total operating expenses are subtracted from gross profit to get the net profit before taxes. Finally, income taxes are deducted to get the net profit. As shown in Exhibit 19-5, Delicious Desserts earned a net profit of $32,175 in 2000.

It is very important to recognize that profit does not represent cash. The income statement is a summary of the firm's operating results during some time period. It does not present the firm's actual cash flows during the period. Those are summarized in the statement of cash flows, which is discussed briefly in the next section.

THE STATEMENT OF CASH FLOWS

>lg 6

Net profit or loss is one measure of a company's financial performance. However, creditors and investors are also keenly interested in how much cash a business generates and how it is used. The **statement of cash flows,** a summary of the money flowing into and out of a firm, is the financial statement used to

---

gross profit

The amount a company earns after paying to produce or buy its products but before deducting operating expenses.

operating expenses

The expenses of running a business that are not directly related to producing or buying its products.

net profit (net income)

The amount obtained by subtracting all of a firm's expenses from its revenues, when the revenues are more than the expenses.

net loss

The amount obtained by subtracting all of a firm's expenses from its revenues, when the expenses are more than the revenues.

statement of cash flows

A financial statement that provides a summary of the money flowing into and out of a firm.

concept check

- What is an income statement? How does it differ from the balance sheet?
- Describe the key parts of the income statement. Distinguish between gross sales and net sales.
- Define the two types of expenses. How is cost of goods sold calculated? How is net profit or loss calculated?

GROSS PROFITS SOLVE THE PROFITABILITY AND CASH FLOW MYSTERY

The owner of a small cosmetics accessories business should have been very pleased with herself. Just four years after starting her business, sales reached $1.5 million. But the fast sales growth did not translate into fatter profits, and the company had problems paying its bills each month. She suspected that she needed more sales volume and better marketing and sales promotions. However, small business consultant Norm Brodsky recognized that the problems were financial in origin.

Brodsky narrowed the trouble spots to two areas: either her gross profit was not high enough, or she didn't know where cash was going. Because the company sent orders to manufacturers who then shipped directly to retailers, it didn't carry inventory. Accounts receivable and accounts payable were at low levels. So Brodsky suspected they'd find the answer by analyzing the company's sales and cost of goods sold to see if gross profits were too low on some products. A quick review of the past three months' sales by customer proved him right.

Because the owner had no records of gross profit by product line and customer, Brodsky provided a form to record monthly sales, cost of goods sold, gross profit, and gross margin (gross profit as a percentage of sales) by product line. The owner also prepared a report by customer.

The analysis showed that in some areas gross profits were extremely low. The owner had set low profit goals when starting the business to help build sales, but she did not know how to increase profitability once she had a relationship with her customers. She was able to change her profit picture considerably by focusing on four areas: pricing, manufacturing costs, turning down low-profit customers, and adding products that sell at higher profits. For example, she now sells imported furniture, which has 38 percent gross margins versus 15 percent for her cosmetics lines.

Although compiling these reports took less than an hour a month using pencil and paper, they were an eye-opener for the owner. These numbers made it crystal clear that she had no idea where she generated profits and how her decisions affected profits. As she admitted, like many inexperienced small business owners she was "winging it," basing decisions on guesswork because she did not have the right information. The tracking system to analyze gross profit provided the clues to unravel her cash flow mystery.

Critical Thinking Questions

1. Why is it important to analyze the details of a company's financial statements once they are prepared?
2. Suggest other ways that a small business owner can delve into the numbers on the income statement to make better operating decisions.
3. Brodsky recommends tracking gross margins by hand rather than using a computer spreadsheet because calculating the percentages yourself makes the numbers more real. He says it's easy to overlook numbers on a printout because they all blend together. Do you agree? Why or why not?

assess the sources and uses of cash during a certain period, typically one year. All publicly traded firms must include a statement of cash flows in their financial reports to stockholders. The statement of cash flows tracks the firm's cash receipts and cash payments. It gives financial managers and analysts a way to identify cash flow problems and assess the firm's financial viability.

Using income statement and balance sheet data, the statement of cash flows divides the firm's cash flows into three groups:

- *Cash flow from operating activities.* Those related to the production of the firm's goods or services

Statement of Cash Flows for Delicious Desserts

Delicious Desserts, Inc.
Statement of Cash Flows for 2000

Cash Flow from Operating Activities

Net profit after taxes	$27,175	
Depreciation	1,500	
Decrease in accounts receivable	3,140	
Increase in inventory	(4,500)	
Decrease in accounts payable	(2,065)	
Decrease in accruals	(1,035)	
Cash provided by operating activities		$24,215

Cash Flow from Investment Activities

Increase in gross fixed assets	($5,000)	
Cash used in investment activities		($5,000)

Cash Flow from Financing Activities

Decrease in notes payable	($3,000)	
Decrease in long-term debt	(1,000)	
Cash used by financing activities		($4,000)
Net increase in cash and marketable securities		**$15,215**

- *Cash flow from investment activities.* Those related to the purchase and sale of fixed assets
- *Cash flow from financing activities.* Those related to debt and equity financing

c o n c ə p t c h ə c k

- What is the purpose of the statement of cash flows?

Delicious Desserts' statement of cash flows for 2000 is presented in Exhibit 19-6. It shows that the company's cash and marketable securities have increased over the last year. And the company had enough cash from operations to increase inventory and fixed assets and to reduce accounts payable, accruals, notes payable, and long-term debt.

ANALYZING FINANCIAL STATEMENTS

>lg 7

Individually, the balance sheet, income statement, and statement of cash flows provide insight into the firm's operations, profitability, and overall financial condition. By studying the relationships among the financial statements, however, one can gain even more insight into a firm's financial condition and performance.

ratio analysis

The calculation and interpretation of financial ratios taken from the firm's financial statements in order to assess a firm's condition and performance.

Ratio analysis involves calculating and interpreting financial ratios taken from the firm's financial statements to assess its condition and performance. A financial ratio states the relationship between amounts as a percentage. For instance, current assets might be viewed relative to current liabilities or sales relative to assets. The ratios can then be compared over time, typically three to five years. A firm's ratios can also be compared to industry averages or to those of another company in the same industry.

It's important to remember that ratio analysis is based on historical data and may not indicate future financial performance. Ratio analysis merely highlights

Technology and Information

potential problems; it does not prove that they exist. However, ratios can help managers understand operations better and identify trouble spots.

Ratios can be classified by what they measure: liquidity, profitability, activity, and debt. Using Delicious Desserts' 2000 balance sheet and income statement (Exhibits 19-4 and 19-5), we can calculate and interpret the key ratios in each group. Exhibit 19-7 summarizes the calculations of these ratios for Delicious Desserts.

Liquidity Ratios

liquidity ratios

Ratios that measure a firm's ability to pay its short-term debts as they come due.

current ratio

The ratio of total current assets to total current liabilities; used to measure a firm's liquidity.

Liquidity ratios measure the firm's ability to pay its short-term debts as they come due. These ratios are of special interest to the firm's creditors. The three main measures of liquidity are the current ratio, the acid-test (quick) ratio, and net working capital.

The **current ratio** is the ratio of total current assets to total current liabilities. Traditionally, a current ratio of 2 ($2 of current assets for every $1 of current liabilities) has been considered good. Whether it is sufficient depends on the industry in which the firm operates. Public utilities, which have a very steady cash

> e x h i b i t   1 9 - 7 <

Ratio Analysis for Delicious Desserts at Year-End 2000

Ratio	Formula	Calculation	Result
Liquidity Ratios			
Current ratio	$\dfrac{\text{Total current assets}}{\text{Total current liabilities}}$	$\dfrac{\$83,200}{\$60,150}$	1.4
Acid-test ratio	$\dfrac{\text{Total current assets} - \text{inventory}}{\text{Total current liabilities}}$	$\dfrac{\$83,200 - \$15,000}{\$60,150}$	1.1
Net working capital	Total current assets − Total current liabilities	$83,200 − $60,150	$23,050
Profitability Ratios			
Net profit margin	$\dfrac{\text{Net profit}}{\text{Net sales}}$	$\dfrac{\$32,175}{\$270,500}$	11.9%
Return on equity	$\dfrac{\text{Net profit}}{\text{Total owners' equity}}$	$\dfrac{\$32,175}{\$78,750}$	40.9%
Earnings per share	$\dfrac{\text{Net profit}}{\text{Number of shares of common stock outstanding}}$	$\dfrac{\$32,175}{10,000}$	$3.22
Activity Ratio			
Inventory turnover	$\dfrac{\text{Cost of goods sold}}{\text{Average inventory}}$		
	$\dfrac{\text{Cost of goods sold}}{(\text{Beginning inventory} + \text{Ending inventory})/2}$	$\dfrac{\$112,500}{(\$18,000 + \$15,000)/2}$	
		$\dfrac{\$112,500}{\$16,500}$	6.8 times
Debt Ratio			
Debt-to-equity ratio	$\dfrac{\text{Total liabilities}}{\text{Owners' equity}}$	$\dfrac{\$70,150}{\$78,750}$	89.1%

flow, operate quite well with a current ratio below 2. A current ratio of 2 might not be adequate for manufacturers and merchandisers that carry high inventories and have lots of receivables. The current ratio for Delicious Desserts for 2000, as shown in Exhibit 19-7, is 1.4. This means little without a basis for comparison. If the analyst found that the industry average for small bakeries was 2.4, Delicious Desserts would appear to have low liquidity.

acid-test (quick) ratio
The ratio of current assets excluding inventory to total current liabilities; used to measure a firm's liquidity.

The **acid-test (quick) ratio** is like the current ratio except that it excludes inventory, which is the least liquid current asset. The acid-test ratio is used to measure the firm's ability to pay its current liabilities without selling inventory. The name *acid-test* implies that this ratio is a crucial test of the firm's liquidity. An acid-test ratio of at least 1 is preferred. But again, what is an acceptable value varies by industry. The acid-test ratio is a good measure of liquidity when inventory cannot easily be converted to cash (for instance, if it consists of very specialized goods with a limited market). If inventory is liquid, the current ratio is better. Delicious Desserts' acid-test ratio for 2000 is 1.1. Because the bakery's products are perishable, it does not carry large inventories. Thus, the values of its acid-test and current ratios are fairly close. At a manufacturing company, however, inventory typically makes up a large portion of current assets, so the acid-test ratio will be lower than the current ratio.

> m a k i n g   e t h i c a l   c h o i c e s <

COOKING THE BOOKS

Cendant Corp. was created through the merger of HFS, Inc., a franchisor of lodging, real estate, and rental cars, and CUC, a conglomerate whose businesses included software, advertising publications, and an online venture. CUC's main revenue source, however, was from memberships in discount shopping, entertainment, and travel clubs.

In early April of 1998, Casper Sabatino and Steven Sparks, two CUC managers who stayed on after the merger, informed Michael Monaco, Cendant Corp.'s chief financial officer (CFO), that they had been ordered to "cook the books" at CUC by recording millions of dollars of fake orders and "arbitrarily adjust[ing] revenue up or expenses down." Sabatino and Sparks signed sworn affidavits a few days later, specifically naming Cosmo Corigliano, formerly CUC's CFO, and Anne Pember, CUC's former senior vice-president of finance and controller, as the executives who ordered them to falsify accounting records. Subsequently, Cendant officials announced that the company had uncovered evidence of wide-ranging

fraud. According to Cendant's announcement, "people just made things up." The following day Cendant's stock price fell by 46.5 percent.

Further investigation led Cendant officials to conclude that Corigliano and Pember falsified accounting records by using "consolidation entries" to increase revenues or cut expenses a few hundred thousand dollars at a time. Cendant officials also concluded that Corigliano and Pember ordered about half of CUC's divisional controllers to create fictitious consolidation entries.

As of mid-August 1998, investors had filed at least 71 lawsuits against Cendant Corp.

Critical Thinking Questions

1. What moral issues does this case raise?
2. Why is accurate information important in the operation of a business?
3. Suppose that you are working for someone who asks you to falsify information. What would you do? Why?

net working capital

The amount obtained by subtracting total current liabilities from total current assets; used to measure a firm's liquidity.

Net working capital, though not really a ratio, is often used to measure a firm's overall liquidity. It is calculated by subtracting total current liabilities from total current assets. Delicious Desserts' net working capital for 2000 is $23,050. Comparisons of net working capital over time often help in assessing a firm's liquidity.

Profitability Ratios

profitability ratios

Ratios that measure how well a firm is using its resources to generate profit and how efficiently it is being managed.

To measure profitability, a firm's profits can be related to its sales, equity, or stock value. **Profitability ratios** measure how well the firm is using its resources to generate profit and how efficiently it is being managed. The main profitability ratios are net profit margin, return on equity, and earnings per share.

net profit margin

The ratio of net profit to net sales; also called *return on sales.* It measures the percentage of each sales dollar remaining after all expenses have been deducted.

The ratio of net profit to net sales is the **net profit margin,** also called *return on sales.* It measures the percentage of each sales dollar remaining after all expenses, including taxes, have been deducted. Higher net profit margins are better than lower ones. The net profit margin is often used to measure the firm's earning power. "Good" net profit margins differ quite a bit from industry to industry. A grocery store usually has a very low net profit margin, perhaps below 1 percent, while a jewelry store's net profit margin would probably exceed 10 percent. Delicious Desserts' net profit margin for 2000 is 11.9 percent. In other words, Delicious Desserts is earning 11.9 cents on each dollar of sales.

return on equity (ROE)

The ratio of net profit to total owners' equity; measures the return that owners receive on their investment in the firm.

The ratio of net profit to total owners' equity is called **return on equity (ROE).** It measures the return that owners receive on their investment in the firm, a major reason for investing in a company's stock. Delicious Desserts has a 40.9 percent ROE for 2000. On the surface, a 40.9 percent ROE seems quite good. But the level of risk in the business and the ROE of other firms in the same industry must also be considered. The higher the risk, the greater the ROE investors look for. A firm's ROE can also be compared to past values to see how the company is performing over time.

earnings per share (EPS)

The ratio of net profit to the number of shares of common stock outstanding; measures the number of dollars earned by each share of stock.

Earnings per share (EPS) is the ratio of net profit to the number of shares of common stock outstanding. It measures the number of dollars earned by each share of stock. EPS values are closely watched by investors and are considered an important sign of success. EPS also indicates a firm's ability to pay dividends. Note that EPS is the dollar amount earned by each share, not the actual amount given to stockholders in the form of dividends. Some earnings may be put back into the firm. Delicious Desserts' EPS for 2000 is $3.22.

Activity Ratios

activity ratios

Ratios that measure how well a firm uses its assets.

Activity ratios measure how well a firm uses its assets. They reflect the speed with which resources are converted to cash or sales. A frequently used activity ratio is inventory turnover.

inventory turnover ratio

The ratio of cost of goods sold to average inventory; measures the speed with which inventory moves through a firm and is turned into sales.

The **inventory turnover ratio** measures the speed with which inventory moves through the firm and is turned into sales. It is calculated by dividing cost of goods sold by the average inventory. (Average inventory is estimated by adding the beginning and ending inventories for the year and dividing by 2.) On average, Delicious Desserts' inventory is turned into sales 6.8 times each year, or about once every 54 days (365 days ÷ 6.8). The acceptable turnover ratio depends on the line of business. A grocery store would have a high turnover ratio, maybe 20 times a year, whereas the turnover for a heavy equipment manufacturer might be only 3 times a year.

Debt Ratios

debt ratios

Ratios that measure the degree and effect of a firm's use of borrowed funds (debt) to finance its operations.

Debt ratios measure the degree and effect of the firm's use of borrowed funds (debt) to finance its operations. These ratios are especially important to lenders and investors. They want to make sure the firm has a healthy mix of debt and equity. If the firm relies too much on debt, it may have trouble meeting interest payments and repaying loans. The most important debt ratio is the debt-to-equity ratio.

The **debt-to-equity ratio** measures the relationship between the amount of debt financing (borrowing) and the amount of equity financing (owners' funds). It is calculated by dividing total liabilities by owners' equity. In general, the lower the ratio, the better. But it is important to assess the debt-to-equity ratio against both past values and industry averages. Delicious Desserts' ratio for 2000 is 89.1 percent. The ratio indicates that the company has 89 cents of debt for every dollar the owners have provided. A ratio above 100 percent means the firm has more debt than equity. In such a case, the lenders are providing more financing than the owners.

CAPITALIZING ON TRENDS IN BUSINESS

>lg 8

debt-to-equity ratio

The ratio of total liabilities to owners' equity; measures the relationship between the amount of debt financing and the amount of equity financing.

In the past accountants were portrayed primarily as "bean-counters" who over-analyzed financial data and were of little help to the managers and employees who produced the numbers the auditors examined. Although accountants still perform the important task of assuring that a company's financial reporting conforms to GAAP, they have become a valuable part of the financial team and consult with clients on information technology and other areas as well.

The increasing complexity of today's business environment creates additional challenges for the accounting profession. The information explosion means that the FASB must consider a greater number of new regulations and develop more position statements to keep up with the pace of change. The FASB also has an emerging issues task force that studies ways to make accounting standards more relevant for today's companies.

No longer can a company's assets be measured solely in terms of its bricks and mortar. Knowledge assets—brand names, patents, research and development (R&D) costs, and similar expenses—make up a large portion of the value of many information technology companies. As yet, however, there is no accepted way to value those assets; indeed, there is disagreement over whether companies should even try. In other areas GAAP is either unclear or subject to different interpretations.

Accountants Expand Their Role

Moving beyond their traditional task of validating a company's financial information, accountants now take an active role advising their clients on systems and procedures, accounting software, and changes in accounting regulations. They also delve into operating information to discover what's behind the numbers. By examining the risks and weaknesses in a company, they can help managers develop financial controls and procedures to prevent future trouble spots. For example, auditors in a manufacturing company may spend more time on inventory, a likely problem area.

Honeywell, Inc., the $8 billion building-controls company headquartered in Minneapolis, formed a collaborative relationship with Deloitte & Touche, its audit firm (Honeywell and Allied Signal merged in fall 1999). Instead of being a once-a-year event, Honeywell's audit included quarterly meetings to discuss changes in company operations and accounting regulations. In this way

Honeywell learned about upcoming changes in accounting regulations and avoided potential reporting problems before they happened. Thus, the company knew in advance how forthcoming changes would affect its financial statements, both at the operating division level and for the company as a whole. As a result, management avoided last-minute surprises in reported earnings.

Accounting firms have greatly expanded the consulting services they provide clients. As a result, accountants—especially the Big Five firms—have become more involved in the operations of their clients. This raises the question of potential conflicts of interest. Can auditors serve both the public and the client? Auditors' main purpose is to certify financial statements. Will they maintain sufficient objectivity to raise questions while auditing a client that provides significant consulting revenues? Can they review systems and methods that they recommended? Paul Danos, dean of Dartmouth's Amos Tuck School of Business Administration, believes that audit firms will act ethically to maintain their reputations. "If the financial markets don't believe in a firm's audit, the firm has nothing," he says.[2]

At their Web sites, you can learn about the types of consulting projects Big Five accounting firms handle. Go to the Mining Company's business majors page and click on Accounting for the links

businessmajors.miningco. com/mbody.htm

Valuing Knowledge Assets

As the world's economy becomes knowledge-based rather than industrial-based, more of a company's value may come from internally generated intangible intellectual assets such as R&D, brands, trademarks, and employee talent than from traditional tangible assets. Consider, for example, Dell Computer's direct marketing strategy, Gap's brand image, and AOL's subscriber base. How should these be valued? Today's accounting system is based on historical costs of physical assets. GAAP has no rules for estimating or reporting the value of investments in intangibles. The stock market, on the other hand, places a value on them. In fact, the value of knowledge assets now approaches or even exceeds the value of reported book assets. This is what creates the huge discrepancy between book value and market value.[3]

"The existing accounting system is failing us," says Amy Hutton, accounting professor at Harvard Business School. "The value is in the people, and that asset is not easily counted."[4] The majority of today's most successful companies—Microsoft, Intel, and Citigroup, to name a few—rose to the top because of their superior knowledge assets.

Whether and how to value intangibles is a controversial issue. Some people believe that because intangibles are uncertain and risky, they do not belong on the balance sheet. Costs related to intangibles may bear no relationship to their actual value. On the other hand, placing a value on intangibles allows companies to know whether they are earning adequate returns on R&D, whether patents are worth renewing, and whether they should invest more to build brands. Clearly, there are no quick and easy solutions to this issue, which will continue to be studied in the coming years.

Tightening the GAAP

Although GAAP is supposed to ensure uniformity of U.S. companies' financial reporting, in reality companies have some discretion in how they interpret certain accounting standards. Companies appear to be taking advantage of loopholes in GAAP to manipulate numbers. Cendant, for example, was accused of fraudulently inflating income by booking $500 million in fictitious revenues. Many companies are pushing accounting to the edge—and over it—to keep earnings rising to meet the expectations of investment analysts, who project earnings, and investors, who panic when a company misses the analysts' forecasts. This has raised serious concerns about the quality of earnings and questions about the validity of financial reports.

One of the most common issues involves write-offs of certain large one-time charges. What is a legitimate one-time charge, and what are normal operating costs that are written off as they are incurred? GAAP doesn't provide a clear answer. In this category are charges like restructuring charges (combining several years of expected future expenses and writing them off at once) and costs associated with acquisitions, such as "in-process R&D," the estimated value of R&D at an acquired company. The acquirer can write off the estimated value of products still in development. The benefits of this R&D are unknown and may be worthless in the future, so companies must take the charge against earnings now.

As of early 1999, the FASB was considering a proposal to eliminate the in-process R&D write-off. The Securities and Exchange Commission (SEC), which is also concerned with the decreasing quality of financial reporting, may ask for more disclosure about restructuring reserves, R&D write-offs, and similar items.[5]

HOT links

Has the FASB reached any decision on the in-process R&D write-off? Find out at its Web site

www.rutgers.edu/Accounting/raw/fasb

concept check

- What new roles are accountants playing? Do you see any potential problems from these new roles?
- What are knowledge assets, and why have they become so important?
- How can large one-time write-offs distort a company's financial results?
- What problems might the declining quality of financial reporting present for investors, lenders, and the economy in general?

APPLYING THIS CHAPTER'S TOPICS

By now it should be very clear that basic accounting knowledge is a valuable skill to have, whether you start your own company or work for someone else. Analyzing a company's financial statements before you take a job there can tell you quite a bit about its financial health. Once you are on the job, you need to understand how to read financial statements and how to develop financial information for business operations. It's almost impossible to operate effectively in a business environment otherwise. Especially in a small company, you will wear many hats, and having accounting skills may help you get the job. In addition, accounting will help you manage your personal finances.

If you own your own firm, you can't rely on someone else to take charge of your accounting system. You must decide what financial information you need to manage your company better and to track its progress. If you can't understand the reports your accountant prepares, you will have no idea whether they are accurate.

Managing your personal finances is also a lot easier if you understand accounting. Suppose your Great-Aunt Helen wants to buy you a few shares of stock to encourage your interest in business. Her stockbroker suggests two computer companies, and Aunt Helen asks you to choose one of them. The product lines of the companies are nearly identical. Where can you get more information to help you make your choice? Someone suggests that you should study

1. **Learn to Read Financial Statements** To become more familiar with annual reports and key financial statements, head for IBM's Guide to Understanding Financials at **www.ibm.com/investor/FinancialGuide/**. The material offers a good overview of financial reporting and shows you what to look for when you read these documents.

2. **Prepare Personal Financial Statements** One of the best ways to learn about financial statements is to prepare them. Put together your personal balance sheet and income statement, using Exhibits 19-4 and 19-5 as samples. You may want to use Entrepreneurial Edge Online's "Business Builders" section, with interactive modules that help prepare financial statements at **www.edgeonline.com/bbuilder/**.

You will have to adjust the account categories to fit your needs. Here are some suggestions:

- Current assets—cash on hand, balances in savings and checking accounts
- Investments—stocks and bonds, retirement funds
- Fixed assets—real estate, personal property (cars, furniture, jewelry, etc.)
- Current liabilities—charge card balances, loan payments due in one year
- Long-term liabilities—mortgage on real estate, loan balances that will not come due until after one year
- Income—employment income, investment income (interest, dividends)
- Expenses—housing, utilities, food, transportation, medical, clothing, insurance, loan payments, taxes, personal care, recreation and entertainment, and miscellaneous expenses

After you complete your personal financial statements, use them to see how well you are managing your finances. Consider the following questions:

- Should you be concerned about your debt ratio?
- Would a potential creditor conclude that it is safe or risky to lend you money?
- If you were a company, would people want to invest in you? Why or why not? What could you do to improve your financial condition?

their financial statements. The companies send you their financial statements upon request. Now that you have a basic understanding of accounting, you have an idea of what all those numbers mean and how you can use them to make your decision.

As you will see in Question 2 in the Try It Now box, accounting can also help you create personal financial statements. Budgeting, a key part of personal finance that we'll discuss in Chapter 23, also uses accounting concepts. And as noted above, financial statements are at the core of investment analysis.

SUMMARY OF LEARNING GOALS

>lg 1 **Why are financial reports and accounting information important, and who uses them?**

Accounting involves collecting, recording, classifying, summarizing, and reporting a firm's financial activities according to a standard set of procedures. The financial reports resulting from the accounting process give managers, employees, investors, customers, suppliers, creditors, and government agencies a way to analyze a company's past, current, and future performance. Financial accounting is

at Wells Test Preparation Center

Wells Test Preparation Center now has an accounting system that works smoothly. Jared Wells can generate financial statements and quickly get tax-related data. He also has the financial information he needs to make wise business decisions, such as whether he can afford to take on another instructor or rent more space. With his knowledge of accounting, he was able to analyze his products to see how much each service contributed to the center's overall profit picture. "It turned out to be very different than I thought it would be," Wells says. "I learned that the SAT preparation course has the highest profit margin." The center's primary growth was coming from referrals for tutoring for individual classes like math and science. Wells decided to market the SAT course more heavily in the future. He also began looking for ways to lower some of the costs of services with lower margins, thereby increasing profit margins.

In addition, Wells can now develop realistic forecasts, something that was impossible without basic accounting knowledge. "Now I not only have an accurate picture of where my firm is now but can also see where it could be down the road if I make certain decisions. This provides a reality check." For example, he discovered that profits would not be as high as expected in 1999, so he decided to defer some spending for both business and personal items. On a more positive note, projections showed steady growth and higher profits in the following year, so he was able to begin planning to expand his space. He also decided to work with a financial planner to develop a plan to invest his profits.[6]

concerned with the preparation of financial reports using generally accepted accounting principles. Managerial accounting provides financial information that management can use to make decisions about the firm's operations.

>lg 2 What are the differences between public and private accountants?
Public accountants work for independent firms that provide accounting services—such as financial report preparation and auditing, tax return preparation, and management consulting—to other organizations on a fee basis. Private accountants are employed to serve one particular organization and may prepare financial statements, tax returns, and management reports.

>lg 3 What are the six steps in the accounting cycle?
The accounting cycle refers to the process of generating financial statements. It begins with analyzing business transactions, recording them in journals, and posting them to ledgers. Ledger totals are then summarized in a trial balance that confirms the accuracy of the figures. Next the accountant prepares the financial statements and reports. The final step involves analyzing these reports and making decisions.

>lg 4 In what terms does the balance sheet describe the financial condition of an organization?
The balance sheet represents the financial condition of a firm at one moment in time, in terms of assets, liabilities, and owners' equity. The key categories of assets are current assets, fixed assets, and intangible assets. Liabilities are divided into current and long-term liabilities. Owners' equity, the amount of the owners' investment in the firm after all liabilities have been paid, is the third major category.

>lg 5 How does the income statement report a firm's profitability?
The income statement is a summary of the firm's operations over some period. The main parts of the statement are revenues (gross and net sales), cost of goods sold, operating expenses (selling and general and administrative expenses), taxes, and net profit or loss.

>lg 6 Why is the statement of cash flows an important source of information?
The statement of cash flows summarizes the firm's sources and uses of cash during a financial reporting period. It breaks the firm's cash flows into those from operating, investment, and financing activities. It shows the net change during the period in the firm's cash and marketable securities.

KEY TERMS

accounting 568
acid-test (quick)
   ratio 583
activity ratios 584
annual report 571
assets 572
auditing 571
balance sheet 575
certified
   management
   accountant (CMA)
   572
certified public
   accountant (CPA)
   572
cost of goods sold
   578
current assets 575
current liabilities
   575
current ratio 582
debt ratios 584
debt-to-equity ratio
   585
depreciation 575
double-entry
   bookkeeping 572
earnings per share
   (EPS) 584
expenses 578
financial
   accounting 570
Financial
   Accounting
   Standards Board
   (FASB) 571
fixed assets 575
generally accepted
   accounting
   principles (GAAP)
   571
gross profit 579
gross sales 577
income statement
   577
intangible assets
   575
inventory turnover
   ratio 584
liabilities 572
liquidity ratios 582
liquidity 575
long-term liabilities
   577
managerial
   accounting 569
net loss 579
net profit margin
   584
net profit (net
   income) 579
net sales 577
net working capital
   584

>lg 7   **How can ratio analysis be used to identify a firm's financial strengths and weaknesses?**

Ratio analysis is a way to use financial statements to gain insight into a firm's operations, profitability, and overall financial condition. The four main types of ratios are liquidity ratios, profitability ratios, activity ratios, and debt ratios. Comparing a firm's ratios over several years and comparing them to ratios of other firms in the same industry or to industry averages can indicate trends and highlight financial strengths and weaknesses.

>lg 8   **What major trends are affecting the accounting industry today?**

The accounting industry is responding to the rise in information technology in several ways. The role of accountants has expanded beyond the traditional audit and tax functions and now includes management consulting in areas such as computer systems, human resources, and electronic commerce. A major issue facing the industry is how to treat key intangible assets—knowledge assets such as patents, brands, research and development—and whether they should be valued and included on a company's balance sheet. In addition, both the FASB and the SEC have raised concerns about the quality of reported earnings. Loose interpretation of GAAP has given companies leeway in how they deal with items like restructuring charges and write-offs resulting from acquisitions.

PREPARING FOR TOMORROW'S WORKPLACE

1. Two years ago, Rebecca Mardon started a computer consulting business, Mardon Consulting Associates. Until now, she has been the only employee, but business has grown enough to support an administrative assistant and another consultant this year. Before she adds staff, however, she wants to hire an accountant and computerize her financial record keeping. Divide the class into small groups, assigning one person to be Rebecca and the others to represent members of a medium-size accounting firm. "Rebecca" should think about the type of financial information systems her firm requires and develop a list of questions for the firm. The accountants will prepare a presentation making recommendations to her as well as explaining why their firm should win the account.

2. Divide the class into small groups that represent accounting firms. Your firm has been hired to help several small businesses with their year-end financial statements.

   a. Based on the following account balances, prepare the Marbella Enterprise Co.'s balance sheet as of December 31, 2000:

Cash	$30,250
Accounts payable	28,500
Fixtures and furnishings	85,000
Notes payable	15,000
Retained earnings	64,450
Accounts receivable	24,050
Inventory	15,600
Equipment	42,750
Accumulated depreciation on fixtures and furnishings	12,500
Common shares (50,000 shares at $1)	50,000
Long-term debt	25,000
Accumulated depreciation on equipment	7,800

operating expenses
  579
owners' equity 572
private accountants
  572
profitability ratios
  584
public accountants
  571
ratio analysis 581
retained earnings
  577
return on equity
  (ROE) 584
revenues 577
statement of cash
  flows 579

| Marketable securities | 13,000 |
| Income taxes payable | 7,500 |

b. The following are the account balances for the revenues and expenses of the Windsor Gift Shop for the year ending December 31, 2000. Prepare the income statement for the shop.

Rent	$ 15,000
Salaries	23,500
Cost of goods sold	98,000
Utilities	8,000
Supplies	3,500
Sales	195,000
Advertising	3,600
Interest	3,000
Taxes	12,120

3. During the year ended December 31, 2000, Lawrence Industries sold $2 million worth of merchandise on credit. A total of $1.4 million was collected during the year. The cost of this merchandise was $1.3 million. Of this amount, $1 million has been paid, and $300,000 is not yet due. Operating expenses and income taxes totaling $500,000 were paid in cash during the year. Assume that all accounts had a zero balance at the beginning of the year (January 1, 2000). Write a brief report for the company controller that includes calculation of the firm's (a) net profit and (b) cash flow during the year. Explain why there is a difference between net profit and cash flow.

4. A friend has been offered a sales representative position at Draper Publications, Inc., a small publisher of computer-related books, but wants to know more about the company. Because of your expertise in financial analysis, you offer to help analyze Draper's financial health. Draper has provided the following selected financial information:

Account balances on December 31, 2000:

Inventory	$ 72,000
Net sales	450,000
Current assets	150,000
Cost of goods sold	290,000
Total liabilities	180,000
Net profit	35,400
Total assets	385,000
Current liabilities	75,000
Other information	
Number of common shares outstanding	25,000
Inventory at January 1, 2000	$ 48,000

Calculate the following ratios for 2000: acid-test (quick) ratio, inventory turnover ratio, net profit margin, return on equity (ROE), debt-to-equity ratio, and earnings per share (EPS). Summarize your assessment of the company's financial performance, based on these ratios, in a report for your friend. What other information would you like to have to complete your evaluation?

5. Divide the class into small groups and give each a copy of an annual report and a summary annual report. Have each group compare the two. What are the major differences between the two formats? If you were the investor relations manager for your company, which would you choose, and why?

6. Suppose that you are a member of the FASB's task force studying the issue of valuing knowledge assets. What would you recommend, and why?

WORKING THE NET

1. Do annual reports confuse you? ABC News' Business Section is one of many Web sites that can take the mystery out of this important document. "How to Read an Annual Report" has advice on analyzing the CEO's message and financial statements. Check it out at **abcnews.go.com/sections/business/dailynews/startstocks4/**.

2. Corporate reports filed with the SEC are now available on the Web at the EDGAR (Electronic Data Gathering, Analysis, and Retrieval system) Web site, **www.edgarhp.htm**. First, read about the EDGAR system; then go to the search page **www.sec.gov/edaux/searches.htm**. To see the type of information that companies must file with the SEC, use the search feature to locate a recent filing by a well-known company. What types of reports did you find, and what was the purpose of each report?

3. Can you judge an annual report by its cover? What are the most important elements of a top annual report? Go to Sid Cato's Official Annual Report Web site, **www.sidcato.com/**, to find his 15 standards for annual reports and read about the reports that receive his honors. Then get a copy of an annual report and evaluate it using Cato's 135-point scale. How well does it compare to his top picks?

4. Go to the Web site of the company whose annual report you evaluated in Question 3. Find the Web version of its annual report and compare it to the print version. What differences do you find, if any? Do you think companies should put their financial information online? Why or why not?

5. As mentioned in the Try It Now! box, Entrepreneurial Edge Online's Business Builders Toolkit includes modules on financial statements and ratio analysis. Using a corporate annual report, the module for ratio analysis, **www.edgeonline.com/bbuilder/FINRATIO/FINRATIO.stm**, and the ratio worksheet, **www.edgeonline.com/bbuilder/toolbox/passetws.stm**, analyze the financial condition of the company you chose.

CREATIVE THINKING CASE

Wrong Numbers Mean Wrong Decisions

R. S. Bacon Veneer Co. was selling $4 million in wood veneer products annually. Its accounting firm, one of the Big Five, produced reports that Bacon's president, Jim McCracken, couldn't understand: "We'd get this set of financial documents each month that would have made better sense for General Motors. We wanted to know if we were making money or losing money. But instead, we got all these numbers that were impossible for us to use." When McCracken forwarded these monthly reports to Bacon's bankers, he would include a letter explaining what he thought had actually happened during the month.

Using these financial reports, the accounting firm decided that Bacon was on the verge of financial disaster. It advised the company to sell everything and close up shop. McCracken shakes his head: "I'm still amazed that we had the courage to throw them and their reports out the door." Bacon switched to another, smaller accounting firm on the advice of its bankers.

The new firm found Bacon basically sound. One of the partners quizzed McCracken about the types of information he needed for management decisions. The result was a report of no more than 10 pages. McCracken could now see what each product cost. He used this information to plan ways to diversify. The clear, concise, informative reports convinced Bacon's bankers to increase the company's credit lines so it could expand. In the next five years, sales went up 300 percent. Profit margins remained more than adequate.

Critical Thinking Questions

1. If you were the president of R.S. Bacon Veneer, what financial data would you want from the new accounting system?
2. Why might the two accounting firms have come up with such different conclusions about Bacon's health? Why might a Big Five firm not be a good choice for a small business?
3. What role should a small company's banker play in choosing the right accounting firm?

VIDEO CASE

The Weathervane Terrace Inn and Suites

Charlevoix is a northern Michigan resort community located in a valley between Lake Charlevoix and Lake Michigan. With its majestic maple trees, picket fences, Victorian homes, three-masted schooners and gleaming yachts, blue water, and white sand beaches, Charlevoix is reminiscent of a summer resort town from the 1800s. In the winter, it offers scenic cross-country ski trails and snowmobiling trails. In short, Charlevoix is a year-round tourist destination.

One of Charlevoix's premier lodging facilities is the Weathervane Terrace Inn and Suites (**www.weathervane-chx.com/main.htm**). The Weathervane Inn, housed in an "architectural and historic masterpiece," provides "a special and unique lodging experience" for guests. The inn has special guest packages such as the Charlevoix Sampler and several different golf packages. The Weathervane's staff readily accommodates guests' special requests whether they involve organizing special outings, making reservations with other hotels on a guest's itinerary, arranging a charter fishing expedition, or renting a sailboat.

In addition to offering these services, the Weathervane Inn seeks to provide a luxurious and restful experience for its guests by providing numerous amenities including a pool, a hot tub spa, a massive stone fireplace in the game room, and spectacular views of Lake Michigan. All rental units are oversized. Each unit is furnished with a refrigerator, a microwave oven, and a videocassette recorder. Some rooms feature two-person Jacuzzi tubs and wet bars. The one-bedroom suites feature a kitchenette and fireplace. Conference and meeting facilities are available as well.

The Weathervane Inn has an interesting, if not unique, ownership structure. The rooms and suites are essentially condominium units that are owned by individual investors. A management team operates the inn for the owners. The managers' duties include promoting the inn, renting units to guests when they are not being used by the owners, cleaning and maintaining the rental units, and regularly reporting operating results to the owners. The managers strive to equitably allocate rentals across all the units. By doing this, they assure that all owners receive reasonable rental income from their condominium properties.

Essentially, the Weathervane's staff are sales and management agents for the condominium owners. As agents, they have a stewardship responsibility with regard to the investors' assets. This agency relationship also imposes important financial reporting requirements on the managers.

To enable them to do an effective and efficient job of financial reporting, the Weathervane Inn's managers use a computerized accounting information system. This system tracks all the accounting and financial data for each condominium unit, including rental activity and income, operating expenses, and maintenance expenses. This information is used to generate monthly accounting reports for each condominium owner. Thus, the owners are able to monitor and evaluate the management of their investment properties.

Critical Thinking Questions

1. Why is it important for the Weathervane Inn to have an effective and efficient accounting information system?

2. What types of accounting reports are likely to be most useful to the condominium owners? Explain your answer.

3. How can the condominium owners make use of financial accounting? How can they make use of managerial accounting?

Careers in Managing Information

Computers/information systems and accounting are among those fastest growing fields in the United States. Each offers many career opportunities at all levels.

With the increasing reliance on information technology, the number of traditional information-processing jobs—applications developer, programmers, systems analysts, and computer operators,

for instance—has increased. Many new jobs have opened up in networking, database administration, telecommunications, computer training and consulting, technical support, and microcomputer sales, service, and repair. In addition, the Internet has created new job opportunities, from Webmaster to Web site designer and software developer. Many other opportunities have been created by applying computer technology to existing jobs.

Some degree of computer knowledge is essential no matter what career you choose. Now every industry has computer jobs. Computers have also changed the way managers get data, make decisions, and do their work. If you enjoy working with computers, you may wish to try a career providing the computer-related services that senior managers need, especially development of information systems, decision support systems, and Internet-related systems.

A person who chooses a computer-oriented career needs more than just computer and math skills. People skills, organizational skills, analytical skills, and communication skills are all needed to enter one of today's hottest career paths.

New government regulations and the increased demand for good financial information have fueled the need for able accountants and auditors. To succeed in accounting, you need good basic math skills and an ability to analyze and interpret facts and figures. Good communication skills—both written and spoken—and computer skills are also important.

DREAM CAREER: WEB SITE DESIGNER

Professional Web page designers are responsible for most of what you see and hear on the Internet. Because

having a Web presence is becoming a must, businesses now spend almost $20 billion annually on Web site development. As a result, demand for skilled Web page designers is on the rise.

Using special coding languages, Web editing and graphics software, and tools like scanners and digital cameras, Web designers create Web sites to fit the client's image. The best designers make each site unique yet strive for simple, clean designs that are easy for users to navigate. In addition to developing new sites, they also maintain sites and redesign older sites to incorporate the latest Internet programming technology such as audio, videoconferencing, and other multimedia features. Keeping Web sites fresh and entertaining so that visitors return provides a steady stream of ongoing assignments.

The job calls for knowledge of Internet programming languages such as HTML, JavaScript, and Perl as well as creativity. The complexity of sites varies. As do-it-yourself resources become more available, designers who can build high-end sites with e-commerce and database applications will find jobs plentiful.

Designers may work in-house for one company or for specialized design firms that serve a variety of clients. Some firms do only page design, while others offer a full range of services, including Web site hosting, design, and marketing.

- *Places of employment.* Web site designers work both in-house and for specialized Internet services and consulting firms. Positions are available in most areas throughout the country.
- *Skills required.* Proficiency in Web programming languages, design experience.
- *Employment outlook through 2006.* Excellent.
- *Salaries.* $30,000–$74,000; average compensation is $47,000.

WHERE THE OPPORTUNITIES ARE

Systems Analyst

The people who diagnose computer-related business problems and offer solutions for them in the form of information systems are called systems analysts. They work with managers to define the problem and break it down into parts. For instance, if a firm needs a new inventory system, systems analysts will meet with purchasing and manufacturing managers to figure out what data to collect, what computer equipment will be required, and what steps to take to process the information.

Analysts use such techniques as accounting, sampling, and mathematical models to analyze a problem and design a new system. Then they translate the system into hardware needs and instructions for computer programmers and work with the programmers to set up the system.

Systems analysts need prior work experience. Nearly half of all systems analysts transfer from other careers, especially programming. In many industries, systems analysts begin as programmers and are promoted to systems analyst positions after gaining experience.

- *Places of employment.* Systems analysts work in all types of organizations. Positions are available in most large urban areas throughout the country.
- *Skills required.* A four-year degree in computer science or a related field such as business or engineering. Many positions require an MBA or an advanced degree in computer science.
- *Employment outlook through 2006.* Excellent.
- *Salaries.* $36,000–$65,000+ for experienced analysts.

Computer Programmer

Computer programmers work in a variety of companies. Software companies use programmers to develop packaged applications programs used by many companies and individuals. Hardware manufacturers may use programmers to write systems software for their equipment. Many companies hire programmers to develop customized computer applications. For example, a life insurance company programmer may write software to calculate policy premiums based on life expectancy tables, while a programmer at an educational software firm may develop math and reading games for elementary school children.

Computer programmers write programs based on design specifications from systems analysts. Then they determine the steps the program must take to accomplish the desired tasks and write the program in a series of coded instructions, using one of the languages developed especially for computers. Next, programmers test the program and correct any errors—a process called "debugging." Finally, the programmer prepares instructions for those who will run the program.

- *Places of employment.* Throughout the United States, especially in areas with many high-tech companies—including the San Francisco and Boston metropolitan areas, North Carolina, Texas, and southern California.
- *Skills required.* Bachelor's degree or higher, although some programmers qualify with two-year degrees or certificates. Technical or professional certification is becoming more common.
- *Employment outlook through 2006.* Above average.
- *Salaries.* $25,000 for beginning programmers; average starting salary for programmers with a bachelor's degree in computer science, $35,167;

$25,000–$75,000+ for experienced programmers; salaries are higher for those with proficiency in certain programming languages.

Database Manager

The huge growth of governmental and private databases has resulted in a high demand for people who can operate and monitor databases. The database manager (or administrator) normally is not involved in the design or development of the database software. Instead, these managers typically take over once the system has been installed at the organization.

A database manager is responsible for scheduling and coordinating user access as well as overall security. The manager arranges for the preparation of backup files and emergency recovery plans. He or she advises management as to which data should be included in the database, how the data should be organized, and how long the data should remain. Many database managers also compile and analyze statistics on the use and efficiency of the database and report these findings to management.

- *Places of employment.* Throughout the country, with most opportunities in large urban areas.
- *Skills required.* A bachelor's degree; many organizations also require relevant work experience and/or an MBA, as well as continuing education to upgrade technical expertise.
- *Employment outlook through 2006.* Excellent.
- *Salaries.* $54,000–$90,000+.

Network Administrator

As more companies turn to decentralized computer systems linked to networks, the demand is growing for network administrators to facilitate communications between computers. These specialists help managers define their computing needs and integrate their department's computer systems into the larger system. They purchase the network's equipment (PCs, workstations, printers, scanners, and databases) and maintain the network.

- *Places of employment.* Throughout the country, with most opportunities in large urban areas.
- *Skills required.* A bachelor of science degree in computer science and computer experience; certification from manufacturers of network systems hardware is desirable.
- *Employment outlook through 2006.* Excellent.
- *Salaries.* $43,000–60,000+.

Accountant

About 1 million accountants work in the United States today, and the field is still growing. Most accountants are involved in managerial accounting for businesses. Another 25 percent work in public accounting firms. The government and educational institutions also employ many accountants.

Managerial accountants work in all types of businesses, from small firms to large multinational corporations. Many are either certified management accountants (CMAs) or certified public accountants (CPAs). They prepare financial statements and other reports for management. They may also specialize in such areas as international, tax, or cost accounting, budgeting, or internal auditing. The top positions for managerial accountants are corporate controller and treasurer. The controller manages the accounting, audit, and budget departments. The treasurer is responsible for cash management, financial planning, and other financial activities.

Public accountants earn more than managerial accountants. More than 300,000 public accountants work in accounting firms throughout the United States and abroad. All levels of government have accounting positions as well. Most of these positions carry civil-service rank, and advancement depends on education and experience.

Accountants also establish businesses of their own, hanging out their shingles as CPAs, tax accountants, and accounting consultants.

Opportunities for minorities and women are excellent in the accounting field.

- *Places of employment.* Throughout the country, primarily in large urban areas.
- *Skills required.* A four-year degree in accounting or related field. Many large firms prefer a master's degree in accounting or an MBA. Computer skills are also important.
- *Employment outlook through 2006.* Average growth.
- *Salaries.* $26,000–$36,000 for beginning accountants and auditors with bachelor's degree; $27,000–$40,000 with master's degree; $36,000–$90,000+ for experienced accountants; $100,000–$300,000+ for partners in CPA firms.

chapter twenty

>c20

Understanding Money and Financial Institutions

learning goals

>lg 1   What is money, what are its characteristics and functions, and what are the three parts of the U.S. money supply?

>lg 2   What are the basic functions of the Federal Reserve, and what tools does it use to manage the money supply?

>lg 3   What are the key financial institutions, and what role do they play in the process of financial intermediation?

>lg 4   How does the Federal Deposit Insurance Corporation protect depositors' funds?

>lg 5   What role do U.S. banks play in the international marketplace?

>lg 6   What trends are reshaping the banking industry?

One-Stop Shopping at Citigroup

If you need a car loan, want to open a checking account, or decide to buy life insurance or invest some money, you might consider doing business with Citigroup (www.citi.com). Citigroup is the world's largest financial services firm, with $700 billion in assets and more than 100 million business and consumer customers worldwide. It was formed in April 1998 by the merger of Citicorp, a world banking powerhouse, and Travelers Group, an insurance and brokerage firm.

The Citicorp/Travelers merger represents a new era in banking. During the past decade, mergers between banks have increased steadily. But the marriage of Citicorp and Travelers combines two very different financial institutions. Current law—the Glass-Steagall Act—prevents banks from offering insurance and investment products. Citigroup hopes that Congress will approve pending legislation that would repeal the law, thus allowing it and other banks to integrate bank, insurance, and investment products.

Some industry experts say that the survival of banks depends on their ability to offer nonbanking financial services. Banks have lost a lot of commercial business as companies have turned to other institutions to finance their growth. Banks have also lost consumer business. In 1975, the typical American household had 36 percent of its financial assets at a bank. Today, that percentage has dropped to 17 percent. Rather than putting money in a bank for retirement or to save for college, Americans have shifted to money market funds, which pay higher interest rates than bank accounts, and the stock market. "What people want—and what they're going to continue to want—is investment vehicles," says bank consultant Edward Furash. He believes the Citicorp/Travelers merger "makes banking relevant again."

Citigroup expects to generate substantial earnings and cost savings from the cross-selling opportunities created by the merger. Citicorp and Travelers market products and services that can be sold in each other's distribution system. For example, Travelers can sell its investment and insurance products via Citicorp's vast global distribution system, which includes private bankers in 31 countries and some 1,100 Citibank branches. Citicorp gains access to Travelers' 20 million customers in the United States and can expand the sale of its bank products through the thousands of Travelers' financial consultants and salespeople.

Citigroup wants to expand its current customer base to 1 billion by 2012. It plans to use technology—primarily the Internet—to reach its goal. In addition to offering products online, it launched Finance.com, an online financial and investment

Critical Thinking Questions

As you read this chapter, consider the following questions as they relate to Citigroup:

- How is technology changing the way financial institutions interact with business and consumer customers?
- What are the benefits of banks merging with other banks and other financial services firms? What are the disadvantages?
- How does government regulation affect the financial services industry?

advisory service. It's also exploring the use of other technologies to broaden its distribution channels. In Singapore, for example, Citigroup formed a partnership with Mobile One that allows customers to open accounts and transfer money by using cell phones equipped with screens. A company goal is to let people use their cell phones as virtual credit cards to do banking, sell stocks, and buy insurance—the ultimate convenience in one-stop shopping.[1]

BUSINESS IN THE 21ST CENTURY

Imagine using your cell phone to open a bank account! The financial services industry is indeed moving in new directions, as demonstrated by Citigroup. Advanced technology, globalization of markets, and the relaxation of regulatory restrictions are accelerating the pace of change in financial services. The changes are giving businesses and consumers new options for conducting their financial transactions. The competitive landscape for financial institutions is also changing as they develop new ways to increase their market share and boost profits.

Because financial institutions connect people with money, this chapter begins with a discussion of money, its characteristics and functions, and the components of the U.S. money supply. Next it explains the role of the Federal Reserve System in managing the money supply. Then it describes different types of financial institutions and their services and the organizations that insure customer deposits. The chapter ends with a discussion of international banking and trends in the banking industry.

MONEY

money
Anything that is acceptable as payment for goods and services.

Money is anything that is acceptable as payment for goods and services. It affects our lives in many ways. We earn it, spend it, save it, invest it—and often wish we had more of it. Business and government use money in similar ways. Both require money to finance their operations. By controlling the amount of money in circulation, the federal government can promote economic growth and stability. For this reason, money has been called the lubricant for the machinery of our economic system. Our banking system was developed to ease the handling of money.

Characteristics of Money

For money to be a suitable means of exchange, it should have these key characteristics:

- *Scarcity.* Money should be scarce enough to have some value but not so scarce as to be unavailable. Pebbles, which meet some of the other criteria, would not work well as money because they are widely available. Too much money in circulation increases prices (inflation, as discussed in Chapter 2).

Governments control the scarcity of money by limiting the quantity of money produced.

- *Durability.* Any item used as money must be durable. A perishable item such as a banana becomes useless as money when it spoils. Even early societies used durable forms of money, such as metal coins and paper money, that lasted for a long time.
- *Portability.* Money must be easily moved around. Large or bulky items, such as boulders or heavy gold bars, cannot be transported easily from place to place.
- *Divisibility.* Money must be capable of being divided into smaller parts. Divisible forms of money help make possible transactions of all sizes and amounts.

How durable is U.S. money? To discover the life expectancy of U.S. bills, visit **www.ny.frb.org/pihome/fedpoint/fed01**

Functions of Money

Using several types of goods as money would be confusing. Thus, societies develop a uniform money system to measure the value of goods and services. For money to be acceptable, it must function as a medium of exchange, as a standard of value, and as a store of value.

As a *medium of exchange,* money makes transactions easier. Having a common form of payment in each country is much less complicated than having a barter system—where goods and services are exchanged for other goods and services. Money allows the exchange of products to be a simple process.

Money also serves as a *standard of value.* With a form of money whose value is accepted by all, goods and services can be priced in standard units. This makes it easy to measure the value of products and allows transactions to be recorded in consistent terms.

As a *store of value,* money is used to hold wealth. It retains its value over time. Someone who owns money can keep it for future use rather than exchange it today for other types of assets.

The U.S. Money Supply

The U.S. money supply has three parts: currency, demand deposits, and time deposits. *Currency* is cash held in the form of coins and paper money. Other forms of currency are traveler's checks, cashier's checks, and money orders. As of February 1999, the United States had about $470 billion of currency in circulation.

Demand deposits consist of money kept in checking accounts that can be withdrawn by depositors on demand. As of February 1999, U.S. demand deposits totaled $617 billion. Demand deposits include regular checking accounts as well as interest-bearing and other special types of checking accounts.

Time deposits are deposits at a bank or other financial institution that pay interest but cannot be withdrawn on demand. Examples are savings accounts, money market deposit accounts, and certificates of deposit. Time deposits totaled about $3.2 trillion as of February 1999.

Credit cards, sometimes referred to as "plastic money," are used as a substitute for cash and checks. Credit cards are simply a form of borrowing. When Citigroup issues a credit card to a small business owner, it gives a short-term loan to the business by directly paying the seller for the business's purchases. The business pays Citigroup when it receives its monthly statement.

Credit cards do not replace money; they simply defer payment.

demand deposits

Money kept in checking accounts that can be withdrawn by depositors on demand.

time deposits

Deposits at a bank or other financial institution that pay interest but cannot be withdrawn on demand.

concept check

- What is money, and what are its characteristics?
- What are the main functions of money?
- What are the components of the U.S. money supply?

THE FEDERAL RESERVE SYSTEM

>lg 2

Before the twentieth century, there was very little government regulation of the U.S. financial system. For most of its history, the country's banking system was decentralized because the public was afraid that a large central bank would negatively affect the financial system.

To learn more about how the Federal Reserve System works, visit the Web site of the Federal Reserve Bank of St. Louis at
www.stls.frb.org/ publications/pleng

In 1907 several large banks failed. These failures caused a public panic that resulted in a run on other banks by depositors who wanted to withdraw their money. This caused cash shortages and resulted in the failure of many other banks. The Panic of 1907 was so severe that Congress had to act. In 1913 it created the Federal Reserve System (commonly called the Fed) to correct weaknesses of the U.S. financial system.

The **Federal Reserve System** is the central bank of the United States. It consists of 12 district banks, each located in a major U.S. city. Originally, the Federal Reserve System was created to control the money supply, act as a borrowing source for banks, hold the deposits of member banks, and supervise banking practices. Its activities have since been broadened, making it the most powerful financial institution in the United States. Today, four of the Federal Reserve System's major activities are carrying out monetary policy, setting rules on credit, distributing currency, and making check clearing easier.

Federal Reserve System

The central bank of the United States consists of 12 district banks, each located in a major U.S. city.

Carrying Out Monetary Policy

The most important function of the Federal Reserve System is carrying out monetary policy. It uses its power to change the money supply in order to control inflation and interest rates, increase employment, and influence economic activity. Three tools used by the Federal Reserve System in managing the money supply are open market operations, reserve requirements, and the discount rate. Exhibit 20-1 summarizes the short-term effects of these tools on the economy.

Open market operations—the tool most frequently used by the Federal Reserve—involve the purchase or sale of U.S. government bonds. The U.S. Treasury issues bonds to obtain the extra money needed to run the government (if taxes and other revenues aren't enough). In effect, Treasury bonds are long-term loans (five years or longer) made by businesses and individuals

open market operations

The purchase or sale of U.S. government bonds by the Federal Reserve to stimulate or slow down the economy.

> e x h i b i t   2 0 - 1 < The Federal Reserve System's Monetary Tools and Their Effects

Tool	Action	Effect on Money Supply	Effect on Interest Rates	Effect on Economic Activity
Open market operations	Buy government bonds	Increases	Lowers	Stimulates
	Sell government bonds	Decreases	Raises	Slows Down
Reserve requirements	Raise reserve requirements	Decreases	Raises	Slows Down
	Lower reserve requirements	Increases	Lowers	Stimulates
Discount rate	Raise discount rate	Decreases	Raises	Slows Down
	Lower discount rate	Increases	Lowers	Stimulates

to the government. The Federal Reserve buys and sells these bonds for the Treasury. When the Federal Reserve buys bonds, it puts money into the economy. Banks have more money to lend so they reduce interest rates, and lower rates generally stimulate economic activity. The opposite occurs when the Federal Reserve sells government bonds.

reserve requirement

Requires banks that are members of the Federal Reserve System to hold some of their deposits in cash in their vaults or in an account at a district bank.

Banks that are members of the Federal Reserve System must hold some of their deposits in cash in their vault or in an account at a district bank. This **reserve requirement** ranges from 3 to 10 percent on different types of deposits. When the Federal Reserve raises the reserve requirement, banks must hold larger reserves and thus have less money to lend. As a result, interest rates rise and economic activity slows down. Lowering the reserve requirement increases loanable funds, causes banks to lower interest rates, and stimulates the economy. The Federal Reserve seldom changes reserve requirements, however.

discount rate

The interest rate that the Federal Reserve charges its member banks.

The Federal Reserve is called "the banker's bank" because it lends money to banks that need it. The interest rate that the Federal Reserve charges its member banks is called the **discount rate.** When the discount rate is less than the cost of other sources of funds (such as certificates of deposit), commercial banks borrow from the Federal Reserve and then lend the funds at a higher rate to customers. The banks profit from the *spread,* or difference, between the rate they charge their customers and the rate paid to the Federal Reserve. Changes in the discount rate usually produce changes in the interest rate that banks charge their customers. The Federal Reserve raises the discount rate to slow down economic growth and lowers it to stimulate growth.

Setting Rules on Credit

selective credit controls

The power of the Federal Reserve to use credit rules to influence the terms of consumer credit and margin requirements.

Another activity of the Federal Reserve System is setting rules on credit. It controls the credit terms on some loans made by banks and other lending institutions. This power, called **selective credit controls,** includes consumer credit rules and margin requirements. *Consumer credit rules* establish the minimum down payments and maximum repayment periods for consumer loans. The Federal Reserve uses credit rules to slow or stimulate consumer credit purchases. *Margin requirements* specify the minimum amount of cash an investor must put up to buy securities—investment certificates issued by corporations or governments. The balance of the purchase cost can be financed through borrowing from a bank or brokerage firm. By lowering the margin requirement, the Federal Reserve stimulates securities trading. Raising the margin requirement slows the trading. Margin requirements are discussed further in Chapter 22.

Distributing Currency

The Federal Reserve is distributing new paper currency that features larger and more detailed portraits, making the new notes harder to counterfeit than older currency.

The Federal Reserve distributes to banks the coins minted and the paper money printed by the U.S. Treasury. Most paper money is in the form of Federal Reserve notes. Look at a dollar bill and you'll see "Federal Reserve Note" at the top. The large letter seal on the left indicates which Federal Reserve Bank issued it. For example, bills bearing a D seal are issued by the Federal Reserve Bank of Cleveland, and those with an L seal are issued by the San Francisco district bank.

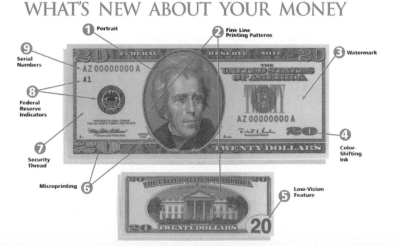

WHAT'S NEW ABOUT YOUR MONEY

Making Check Clearing Easier

Another important activity of the Federal Reserve is helping banks and other financial institutions clear checks. It handles about 18 billion checks a year. Its check-clearing system lets banks quickly convert

ARE BANKS TAKING ADVANTAGE OF BOUNCED CHECKS?

What happens when a checking account contains $1,000 and checks for $980, $30, $20, and $10 arrive at the bank for processing on the same day? The account is overdrawn by $40, but the customer may have to pay bounced-check fees amounting to as much as $120. With high-to-low check processing, which is used by six of the nine largest banks in the United States in at least some of their banks, when several checks arrive for processing on the same day, the bank processes the largest one first, thereby increasing the possibility that at least some checks will bounce.

High-to-low check processing can significantly increase a bank's profit because of the charges that are applied to bounced checks. Processing a bad check costs a bank between 50 cents and $1.50, yet most banks charge customers who write bad checks up to $30 per bad check processed. With high-to-low check processing, a bank is able to bounce as many checks as possible—and the fees paid by the customer are nearly all profit for the bank.

Increasingly, bank customers are beginning to protest high-to-low processing. One lawsuit accuses First Security Bank of New Mexico of "unfairly impos-ing unreasonable and excessive fees" and of adopting "high-to-low check processing without adequately notifying customers."

Banks defend high-to-low processing by pointing out that federal and state laws permit them to process checks in any order. A spokesperson for the American Bankers Association says, "If you want to avoid paying a fee, just don't write a bad check" or alternatively get overdraft protection.

Critical Thinking Questions

1. The practice of high-to-low check processing results in bouncing as many checks as possible. In your opinion, is this a fair banking practice?
2. Is it ethical for a bank to charge up to $30 for processing a customer's bad check when the bank's cost of processing is between 50 cents and $1.50?
3. Should a bank have an ethical responsibility to inform customers in advance that it uses high-to-low processing?

checks drawn on other banks—even distant ones—into cash. Checks drawn on banks within the same Federal Reserve district are handled locally and reported to the Federal Reserve, which uses a series of bookkeeping entries to transfer funds between the banks. The process is more complex for checks drawn on banks outside a bank's Federal Reserve district.

The time between when the check is written and when the funds are deducted from the check writer's account provides float. *Float* is the advantage gained from the time it takes a check to clear and the amount to be withdrawn from the check writer's account. Businesses open accounts at banks throughout the country that are known to have long check-clearing times. By "playing the float," firms can keep their funds invested for several extra days, thus earning more money. To reduce this practice, in 1988 the Fed established maximum check-clearing times.

concept check

- What are the four key functions of the Federal Reserve System?
- What three tools does the Federal Reserve System use in managing the money supply, and how does each affect economic activity?

THE U.S. FINANCIAL SYSTEM

>lg 3   The well-developed financial system in the United States supports our high standard of living. The system allows those who wish to borrow money to do so with

relative ease. It also gives savers a variety of ways to earn interest on their savings. For example, a computer company that wants to build a new headquarters in Atlanta might be financed partly with the savings of families in California. The Californians deposit their money in a local financial institution. That institution looks for a profitable and safe way to use the money and decides to make a real estate loan to the computer company. The transfer of funds from savers to investors enables businesses to expand and the economy to grow.

Households are important participants in the U.S. financial system. Although many households borrow money to finance purchases, they supply funds to the financial system through their purchases and savings. Overall, businesses and governments are users of funds. They borrow more money than they save.

Sometimes those who have funds deal directly with those who want them. A wealthy realtor, for example, may lend money to a client to buy a house. But most often, financial institutions act as intermediaries—or go-betweens—between the suppliers and demanders of funds. The institutions accept savers' deposits and invest them in financial products (such as loans) that are expected to produce a return. This process, called **financial intermediation,** is shown in Exhibit 20-2. Households are shown as suppliers of funds, and businesses and governments are shown as demanders. But a single household, business, or government can be either a supplier or a demander, depending on the circumstances.

Financial institutions are the heart of the financial system. They are a convenient vehicle for financial intermediation. They can be divided into two broad groups: depository institutions (those that accept deposits) and nondepository institutions (those that do not accept deposits).

financial intermediation

The process in which financial institutions act as intermediaries between the suppliers and demanders of funds.

> e x h i b i t   2 0 - 2 <

The Financial Intermediation Process

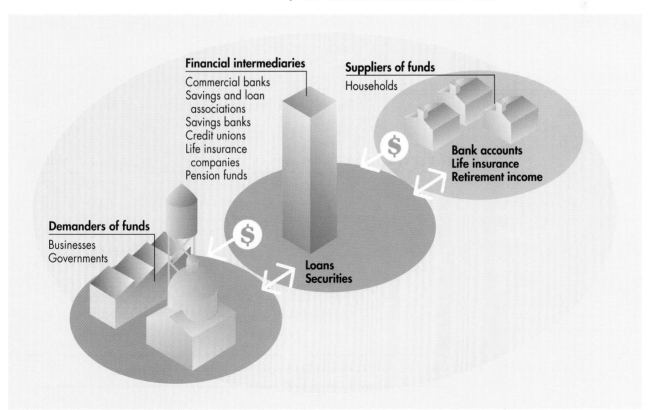

Depository Financial Institutions

Not all depository financial institutions are alike. Most people call the place where they save their money a "bank." Some of those places are indeed banks, but other depository institutions include thrift institutions and credit unions.

commercial banks

Profit-oriented financial institutions that accept deposits, make business and consumer loans, invest in government and corporate securities, and provide other financial services.

bank charter

An operating license issued to a bank by the federal government or a state government; required for a commercial bank to do business.

thrift institutions

Depository institutions formed specifically to encourage household saving and to make home mortgage loans.

credit unions

Not-for-profit, member-owned financial cooperatives.

Commercial Banks   A **commercial bank** is a profit-oriented financial institution that accepts deposits, makes business and consumer loans, invests in government and corporate securities, and provides other financial services. There are about 9,100 commercial banks in the United States accounting for $5 trillion in loans and investments (a bank's assets) and $3.4 trillion in deposits. Exhibit 20-3 lists the top 10 U.S. commercial banks.

Customers' deposits are a commercial bank's main source of funds; the main use of those funds is loans. The difference between the interest earned on loans and the interest paid on deposits, plus fees earned from other financial services, pays the bank's costs and provides a profit. Commercial banks are corporations owned and operated by individuals or other corporations. To do business, they must get a **bank charter**—an operating license—from either the federal government or a state government. Thus U.S. commercial banks can be either national or state banks.

National banks are chartered by the Comptroller of the Currency, who is part of the U.S. Treasury Department. These banks must belong to the Federal Reserve System and must carry insurance on their deposits from the Federal Deposit Insurance Corporation. *State banks* are chartered by the state in which they are based. Generally, state banks are smaller than national banks, are less closely regulated than national banks, and are not required to belong to the Federal Reserve System.

Thrift Institutions   A **thrift institution** is a depository institution formed specifically to encourage household saving and to make home mortgage loans. Thrift institutions include *savings and loan associations (S&Ls)* and *savings banks*. S&Ls keep large percentages of their assets in home mortgages. Compared with

> e x h i b i t   2 0 - 3 <

Top 10 U.S. Commercial Banks Based on Revenues, 1998

Rank by Revenue	Bank	Revenue (in Millions)
1	Bank of America Corp.	$50,777
2	Chase Manhattan Corp.	32,379
3	Bank One Corp.	25,595
4	First Union Corp.	21,543
5	Wells Fargo	20,482
6	J.P. Morgan & Co.	18,425
7	Bankers Trust Corp.	12,048
8	Fleet Financial Group	10,002
9	National City Corp.	8,071
10	PNC Bank	7,936

SOURCE: "Fortune 100 Ranked within Industries," *Fortune*, April 26, 1999, p. F-54.

S&Ls, savings banks focus less on mortgage loans and more on stock and bond investments. The 1,780 thrift institutions in the United States have about $1 trillion in assets and $704 billion in deposits.

Credit Unions A **credit union** is a not-for-profit, member-owned financial cooperative. Credit union members typically have something in common—their employer, union, professional group, or church, for example. The not-for-profit status of credit unions makes them tax-exempt, so they can pay good interest rates on deposits and offer loans at favorable interest rates. The approximately 12,000 credit unions in the United States have more than 75 million members. Credit union assets total almost $400 billion.

Commercial banks, thrift institutions, and credit unions offer a wide range of financial services for businesses and consumers. Typical services offered by depository institutions are listed in Exhibit 20-4. These services play an important role in helping to fuel the U.S. economy and foster individual financial security. One of the newest bank services is online banking. The Applying Technology box describes a bank that operates exclusively on the Internet.

One of the most popular services offered by depository institutions is the automated teller machine. ATMs on college campuses make it easy for students to deposit and withdraw money.

> e x h i b i t   2 0 - 4 <

Services Offered by Depository Institutions

Service	Description
Savings accounts	Pay interest on deposits
Checking accounts	Allow depositors to withdraw any amount of funds at any time up to the amount on deposit
Money market deposit accounts	Savings accounts on which the interest rate is set at market rates
Certificates of deposit (CDs)	Pay a higher interest rate than regular savings accounts, provided that the deposit remains for a specified period
Consumer loans	Loans to individuals to finance the purchase of a home, car, or other expensive items
Business loans	Loans to businesses and other organizations to finance their operations
Money transfer	Transfer of funds to other banks
Electronic funds transfer	Use of telephone lines and computers to conduct financial transactions
Automated teller machine (ATM)	Allows bank customers to make deposits and withdrawals from their accounts 24 hours a day
Debit cards	Allow customers to transfer money from their bank account directly to a merchant's account to pay for purchases
Smart card	Card that stores monetary value and can be used to buy goods and services instead of using cash, checks, and credit and debit cards
Online banking	Allows customers to conduct financial transaction via the Internet or through a dial-in line that operates with a bank's software

NETBANK OPENS ITS VIRTUAL DOORS

Many banks offer online banking services. But NetBank is different. It's a virtual bank with no physical location, no branches, and no tellers. It operates exclusively on the Internet yet offers all the services of brick-and-mortar banks. NetBank customers can open checking accounts, pay their bills, get a mortgage loan, and use their debit and credit cards online. And they can do all these things at any time because they have access to their accounts 24 hours a day, seven days a week. They also get *BankNotes,* an online newsletter, that keeps them informed about new products and services.

Many banks offer customers the convenience of banking at home via their computers. But NetBank gives its customers more than convenience. Because it has no tellers or physical locations, NetBank saves on overhead costs and passes the savings on to customers with lower service fees and higher interest rates on deposit accounts.

High rates and low fees are attracting people to NetBank. Since its opening in 1996, NetBank has amassed more than 17,000 customers. NetBank's CEO Danner Grimes plans to broaden the bank's line of products and services to attract more customers. But a major hurdle is convincing people that Internet-only

banking is safe. Grimes says that the two questions he is asked most frequently by potential customers are "Are my deposits safe?" and "How secure is banking on the Internet?"

NetBank assures customers that their deposits are safe because they are insured by the Federal Deposit Insurance Corporation for up to $100,000. And all online transactions are encrypted, which means that information customers give the bank is not available on the Internet in a form that can be read.

Still, customer doubts about security persist. One customer admits that as much as he loves to bank at NetBank, he still keeps half of his cash at a traditional bank and half at NetBank. "It's psychological," he explains.

Critical Thinking Questions

1. What can NetBank do to ease customers' concerns about the security of their deposits?
2. Do you think NetBank's strategy of targeting Internet users only is a sound business plan?
3. What business trends support NetBank's focus on technology as a competitive tool?

Nondepository Financial Institutions

Some financial institutions provide a few banking services but do not accept deposits. These nondepository financial institutions include insurance companies, pension funds, brokerage firms, and finance companies. They serve both individuals and businesses.

Insurance Companies   Insurance companies are major suppliers of funds. Policyholders make payments (called *premiums*) to buy financial protection from the insurance company. Insurance companies invest the premiums in stocks, bonds, real estate, business loans, and real estate loans for large projects. The insurance industry is discussed in detail in the appendix to Chapter 23, Managing Risk and Insurance.

pension funds

Large pools of money set aside by corporations, unions, and governments for later use in paying retirement benefits to their employees or members.

Pension Funds   Corporations, unions, and governments set aside large pools of money for later use in paying retirement benefits to their employees or members. These **pension funds** are managed by the employers or unions themselves or by outside managers, such as life insurance firms, commercial banks, and private investment firms. Pension plan members receive a specified monthly payment when they reach a given age. After setting aside enough money to pay near-term benefits, pension funds invest the rest in business loans, stock, bonds, or real estate. They often invest large sums in the stock of the employer. Pension fund assets total almost $4 trillion.

Brokerage Firms   A *brokerage firm* buys and sells securities (stocks and bonds) and provides related advice to clients. Many brokerage firms offer some banking services. They may offer customers a combined checking and savings account with a high interest rate and also make loans, backed by securities, to clients. Chapter 22 explains the activities of brokerage firms in more detail.

Finance Companies   A *finance company* makes short-term loans for which the borrower puts up tangible assets (such as an automobile, inventory, machinery, or property) as security. Finance companies often make loans to individuals or businesses that cannot get credit elsewhere. To compensate for the extra risk, finance companies usually charge higher interest rates than banks do. *Consumer finance companies* make loans to individuals. Beneficial Corp. and Household International, which recently merged, are two of the largest consumer finance companies. Together, they have more than 30 million customers. Promising new businesses with no track record and firms that can't get more credit from a bank often get loans from *commercial finance companies*. AT&T Capital Business Finance, GE Capital Small Business Finance, and The Money Store Commercial Lending are examples of commercial finance companies.

concept check

- What is the financial intermediation process?
- What are the three types of depository institutions and what services do they offer?
- What are the four main types of nondepository institution?

INSURING BANK DEPOSITS

>lg 4

The U.S. banking system worked fairly well from the establishment of the Federal Reserve System in 1913 until the 1929 stock market crash and the Great Depression that followed. Business failures caused by these events resulted in major cash shortages as people rushed to withdraw their money from banks. Many cash-starved banks failed because the Federal Reserve did not, as expected, lend money to them. The government's efforts to prevent bank failures were ineffective. In the next two years, 5,000 banks—about 20 percent of the total number—failed.

President Franklin D. Roosevelt made strengthening the banking system his first priority. After taking office in 1933, Roosevelt declared a bank holiday, closing all banks for a week so he could take corrective actions. Congress passed the Banking Act of 1933, which gave the Federal Reserve System power to regulate banks and reform the banking system. The act's most important provision was the creation of the **Federal Deposit Insurance Corporation (FDIC)** to insure deposits in commercial banks. The 1933 act also gave the Federal Reserve authority to set reserve requirements, ban interest on demand deposits, regulate the interest rates on time deposits, and prohibit banks from investing in specified types of securities. In 1934 the Federal Savings and Loan Insurance Corporation (FSLIC) was formed to insure deposits at S&Ls. When the FSLIC went bankrupt in the 1980s, the FDIC took responsibility for administering the fund that insures deposits at thrift institutions. Today, the major deposit insurance funds include the following:

Federal Deposit Insurance Corporation (FDIC)

An independent, quasi-public corporation backed by the full faith and credit of the U.S. government that insures deposits in commercial banks and thrift institutions for up to a ceiling of $100,000 per account.

- *The Bank Insurance Fund (BIF)*. Administered by the FDIC, this fund provides deposit insurance to commercial banks.
- *The Savings Association Insurance Fund (SAIF)*. Administered by the FDIC, this fund provides deposit insurance to thrift institutions.

• *The National Credit Union Share Insurance Fund.* Administered by the National Credit Union Administration, this fund provides deposit insurance to credit unions.

Role of the FDIC

The FDIC is an independent, quasi-public corporation backed by the full faith and credit of the U.S. government. It insures about 314 million deposit accounts in commercial banks and 79 million accounts in thrift institutions against loss if the financial institution fails. All member banks in the Federal Reserve System must be insured by the FDIC.

The ceiling on insured deposits is $100,000 per account. Each insured bank pays the insurance premiums, which are a fixed percentage of the bank's domestic deposits. The FDIC charged a flat rate for deposit insurance until 1993. Then, due to the large number of bank and thrift failures during the 1980s and early 1990s, it implemented a risk-based premium system that bases each bank's premium on the risk the bank poses to the insurance fund. Some experts argue that certain banks take too much risk because they view deposit insurance as a safety net for their depositors—a view many believe contributed to earlier bank failures.

HOT links

The FDIC gets so many requests about banks' insurance status that it added an option to determine "Is my bank insured?" on its Web site. Visit

www.fdic.gov

Enforcement by the FDIC

To ensure that banks operate fairly and profitably, the FDIC sets guidelines for banks and then reviews the financial records and management practices of member banks at least once a year. These reviews are performed by bank examiners, whose visits are unannounced. Bank examiners rate banks on their compliance with banking regulations. For example, banks must comply with the Equal Credit Opportunity Act, which states that a bank cannot refuse to lend money to people because of their color, religion, or national origin. Examiners also rate a bank's overall financial condition. They focus on loan quality, management practices, earnings, liquidity, and whether the bank has enough capital (equity) to safely support its activities.

When bank examiners conclude that a bank has serious financial problems, the FDIC can take several actions. It can lend money to the bank, recommend that the bank merge with a stronger bank, require the bank to use new management practices or replace its managers, buy loans from the bank, or provide extra equity capital to the bank. The FDIC may even cover all deposits at a troubled bank, including those over $100,000, to restore the public's confidence in the financial system.

concept check

• What is the FDIC, and what are its responsibilities?
• What are the major deposit insurance funds?
• What can the FDIC do to help financially troubled banks?

INTERNATIONAL BANKING

>lg 5

The financial marketplace spans the globe, with money routinely flowing across international borders. Multinational corporations need many special banking services, such as foreign currency exchange. Many U.S. banks started expanding into overseas markets by opening offices in Europe, Latin America, and the Far East. They provided better customer service than local banks in many countries and had access to more sources of funding. Citibank, for example, was the first bank in Japan to offer banking-by-phone and 24-hour-a-day ATM service. These services have helped Citibank earn a reputation as the most innovative bank in Japan.[2]

Competing against foreign banks can be difficult, however, Foreign banks are subject to fewer regulations, making it easier for them to undercut U.S. banks on the pricing of loans and services to multinational corporations and governments. Some governments protect their banks against foreign competition. In Singapore, for example, the government prohibits foreign banks from acquiring domestic banks, which are mostly family-owned businesses. Until recently, Singapore limited foreign ownership to 40 percent. By eliminating that restriction and permitting a limited number of foreign banks to open branches in Singapore and to install ATMs, the government is allowing more competition from foreign banks.[3]

International banking can be profitable, but it's also a high-risk business. For example, poorly regulated banking activities in East Asian countries caused an economic crisis in 1997 that Singapore Prime Minister Goh Chok Tong called "Asia's worst crisis since the Second World War." Some Asian banks made loans to finance highly speculative real estate ventures and corporate expansions that were fueling a booming economy in the Pacific Rim, which attracted many foreign investors. Japanese, U.S., German, French, and other European banks made billions of dollars worth of loans to Thailand, Indonesia, Malaysia, and Korea. The bank loans and foreign investments made the balance sheets of the Asian banks and their customers look better than they actually were. When investors started taking their money out of the Asian banks, the banks' assets plummeted, which forced currency devaluations. The situation severely injured the economies of several Asian countries, resulting in high inflation and deep debt. Lacking capital, Asian banks could not get loans to conduct business, and companies couldn't get loans to finance the production and export of their products. The crisis also hurt many foreign banks, including U.S. banks such as BankAmerica and Chase Manhattan, both of which have reduced the number of business loans in emerging markets.[4]

Which U.S. banks are the top global lenders? Click on Ranking the Banks at **www.americanbanker.com**

U.S. banks play an important role in global business by providing loans to foreign governments and businesses. They also offer trade-related services. For example, Bank Boston's global cash management services help firms manage their cash flows to improve their payment efficiency and reduce their exposure to operational risks. The bank's advanced information systems enable corporate customers to access their accounts electronically throughout the world. Other U.S. banks are hoping to take advantage of their technological expertise and information systems to sell more financial services throughout the world. Wells Fargo & Co., for example, is expanding internationally by using its automated telemarketing operations to make loans to Canadian small businesses.[5]

c o n c ə p t   c h ə c k

- What is the role of U.S. banks in international banking?
- What challenges do U.S. banks face in foreign markets?

CAPITALIZING ON TRENDS IN BUSINESS

>lg 6

Once a highly regulated industry offering limited services, the banking industry continues to change. Trends influencing the direction of banking are online banking, consolidation, and the integration of banking with brokerage and insurance services.

Online Banking

Banks are using Internet technology to expand their services. A research study from International Data Corp. predicts that 32 million U.S. households will bank online by 2003, up from 6.6 million households in 1998. The study estimates that the number of financial institutions offering online banking will grow from 1,150 in 1998 to more than 15,000 by 2003. "Online banking may be the critical service that enables banks to maintain their role as the dominant provider of financial services," says Paul Johnson, an analyst with International Data.[6]

To learn about the newest online banking products and services, visit www.electronicbanker.com/html/news

One service that offers banks tremendous profit potential is online bill presentment and payment. Although only 1 million bills were presented over the Internet in 1999, the number is expected to surge to 534 million bills by 2001.[7] Three large U.S banks—Chase Manhattan, First Union, and Wells Fargo—have formed a joint venture to create an online network for delivering consumers' monthly bills to the Web site that handles their checking account. The service will benefit many businesses, such as utility firms, because it will eliminate the time-consuming and costly process of printing bills, mailing them to customers, and waiting for the checks to arrive and clear.[8]

Consolidation

The number of depository institutions declined more than 40 percent over the past 25 years, falling from almost 19,000 in 1975 to less than 11,000 today. Although part of the decline can be attributed to the failure of banks and thrift institutions, most of it was due to consolidation through mergers and acquisitions.[9] Mergers increased substantially during the 1990s, with many banks acquiring local competitors to increase their market share within a region. In 1996 alone, more than 360 banks merged. Some banks, such as Bank of America and NationsBank, merged to create a nationwide customer base.

Proponents of bank consolidation believe that it will strengthen the U.S. banking system. They contend that a national banking system would reduce costs, improve operating efficiency, and increase customer convenience. Mergers can also help banks reduce the risks inherent in depending on one region's economy. For example, many local banks in Texas and New England failed when their regions experienced economic downturns.

Opponents of consolidation fear that it will concentrate power in large financial institutions. They worry that small banks' personal service and knowledge of the local economy will disappear. But, in a countertrend to consolidating, small banks are not only surviving, they are actually increasing in number. According to the Independent Bankers Association of America, there's been a resurgence in the creation of small banks because many peo-

Because many customers prefer the personalized service of small banks, community banks are growing in number at the same time that the banking industry as a whole is consolidating.

ple still prefer the personal service provided by the nation's 9,000 community banks. Other small banks are being formed to target niche markets. The Focusing on Small Business box shows how a community start-up plans to compete against larger banks by targeting a specific customer segment.

The Integration of Banking, Brokerage, and Insurance Services

As mentioned in the opening vignette, Citigroup awaits pending legislation—the Financial Services Modernization Act—that would repeal the Glass-Steagall Act of 1933, which prohibits banks from selling securities and insurance. Glass-Steagall was passed after federal investigations of bank failures following the 1929 stock market crash indicated that banks' practice of buying stock in their customers' firms had contributed to the failures. Banks argue that the law is outdated and puts them at a disadvantage in competing with security and investment firms, which are not bound by the same laws that regulate banks.

Passage of the Financial Services Modernization Act would allow banks to sell securities and insurance products. Industry experts say it will also result in a new wave of mergers and acquisitions between commercial banks and brokerage and insurance firms. The bank reform would benefit consumers by allowing them to structure their financial planning with one financial intermediary rather than using separate firms for their banking, investment, and insurance needs.

> f o c u s i n g   o n   s m a l l   b u s i n e s s <

A LITTLE BANK THAT CARES

Emma Chappell is the founder and chief executive of United Bank of Philadelphia. United Bank is an African American-owned community bank providing financial services to unserved and underserved communities, especially to African Americans, Hispanics, Asians, and women.

Chappell viewed the trend of bank mergers as an opportunity to start a community bank. "There are still a lot of people out there who want the specialized attention" that a small bank can offers, says Chappell.

United Bank focuses on the needs of entrepreneurs and small businesses—groups that have been hurt by the trend of mergers. For example, Lea Argiris, president of a small manufacturing firm, found that her line of credit was reduced and her loan payback period was shortened when her bank was acquired by a large bank. She learned that her six-employee firm was considered too small for the takeover bank.

United Bank offers special accounts for small businesses. Its Entrepreneurial-25 Business Checking targets firms that write 25 checks or less each month. It offers

a business money market deposit account, a business interest-bearing checking account, and customized loans and lines of credit. It also provides traveler's checks, wire transfers, safe deposit boxes, direct deposit, bank by mail, domestic and international collections, and international money transfers.

Chappell says mergers benefit small banks in other ways. For example, mergers eliminate the need for many employees and branches, leaving many bank professionals out of work. "The small community banks then have a pool by which they can acquire better-trained employees," says Chappell.

Critical Thinking Questions

1. What is United Bank of Philadelphia's advantage in competing against larger banks?
2. In what ways can Chappell help her bank's business customers beyond offering them banking products?

APPLYING THIS CHAPTER'S TOPICS

The bank you use today is vastly different from the bank your parents used 30 years ago. And the bank you will use in 2030 will be far different from your bank today. Because technology is driving many of the changes in banking, expect to use your computer and innovations like smart cards to conduct your financial transactions. Soon you may be getting your telephone bill via your computer rather than in the mailbox. Because technology-based banking options are cheaper for banks, you'll see more promotions like the Citigroup ad whose headline proclaims "Pay 2 bills online. Get $25." As banks introduce new ways to deliver their products and services, the prediction of a cashless, checkless society is becoming a reality.

New bank products and services mean consumers have many more choices. You can choose the convenience of online banking or opt for a more personal banking relationship at a community bank. Especially if you are an entrepreneur or a small business owner, you'll want to build a personal relationship with your banker.

1. **Stay Informed** To keep current with the changing trends and new products in the financial services industry, arm yourself with information. A banking Web site that will help you make informed decisions is **www.bankrate.com.** It has a How-To section that teaches the basics of banking and helps you calculate your payment on loans. The site's collection of interest rate information covers everything from car loans to money market accounts and enables you to compare rates from financial institutions in all 50 states. You can also check the fees different banks charge for their services and compare them to online banking service charges.

2. **Locate Lenders** More and more financial institutions are expanding their lending to entrepreneurs and small business owners. The following Web sites help start-ups and small businesses find financing:

- **www.cashfinder.com** Ten financial institutions participate in this program, which offers lines of credit, loans, credit cards, and leasing. You can download free software that lets you complete a loan application form and print it before faxing or mailing it to the lenders.
- **cgi.pathfinder.com** This site lists the top commercial lenders to small business. It provides links to national and regional bank holding companies, such as Wells Fargo, that make loans under $250,000.
- **www.ibaa.org** The Web site of the Independent Bankers Association of America provides leads to all U.S. community banks.

Getting Connected

Here's what you'll need to bank online. If you're going online through the World Wide Web, you'll need a computer with Internet capability—one with a 14.4 bps modem or faster, a Web browser, and service from an Internet or online service provider. Most providers charge about $20 per month for unlimited use. If you don't want to pay for Internet access or are concerned about the security of your transactions, you can get special software from your bank that connects you to the bank through a dial-in line. Most banks don't charge customers for the software. But online service fees vary among banks, so visit the Web sites of several banks to compare their fees and the services they offer.

Finding Financing

Entrepreneurs and small businesses have a more difficult time obtaining credit from a bank than do large firms that have proven track records and larger asset bases. The best way to improve your chances of getting a business loan is to give the bank information that can help it understand the strengths of your business. Prospective bankers are impressed by well-prepared presentations that include your business plan, financial history, and a management team that is committed to helping you achieve your goals.

When investigating banks, entrepreneurs and small business owners need to look at banks as more than just lending institutions. They need to ask what bank services and products can help them improve their efficiency and profitability. They should describe the type of relationship they want with their banker and the kinds of loans they'll need and the terms of payment they expect.

>looking ahead

at Citigroup

Citigroup wants to be the leading global provider of financial services. To achieve its goal, Citigroup is opening offices in emerging countries. It plans to open 25 new branches in Poland, a fast-growing market for consumer and corporate banking. In another global expansion move, Citigroup acquired Financiero Atlas, a consumer finance company based in Santiago, Chile, that operates 65 branches.

Citigroup's main hurdle in competing in global markets is the government's restrictions on the integration of banking, securities, and insurance services. "U.S. financial services companies must be able to offer customers the same array of products and services that their international competitors are now free to provide if we are to maintain our nation's leadership position around the world," said co-CEOs John Reed and Sanford Weill in announcing the merger. "This is particularly critical given the rapid pace of consolidation by global competitors."[10]

SUMMARY OF LEARNING GOALS

>lg 1 **What is money, what are its characteristics and functions, and what are the three parts of the U.S. money supply?**
Money is anything accepted as payment for goods and services. For money to be a suitable means of exchange, it should be scarce, durable, portable, and divisible. Money functions as a medium of exchange, a standard of value, and a store of value. The U.S. money supply consists of currency (coins and paper money), demand deposits (checking accounts), and time deposits (interest-bearing deposits that cannot be withdrawn on demand).

KEY TERMS

bank charter 606
commercial banks
 606
credit unions 606
demand deposits
 601
discount rate 603
Federal Deposit
 Insurance
 Corporation
 (FDIC) 609
Federal Reserve
 System 602
financial
 intermediation
 605
money 600
open market
 operations 602
pension funds 608
reserve requirement
 603
selective credit
 controls 603
thrift institutions
 606
time deposits 601

>lg 2 **What are the basic functions of the Federal Reserve, and what tools does it use to manage the money supply?**
The Federal Reserve System (the Fed) is an independent government agency that performs four main functions: carrying out monetary policy, setting rules on credit, distributing currency, and making check clearing easier. The three tools it uses in managing the money supply are open market operations, reserve requirements, and the discount rate.

>lg 3 **What are the key financial institutions, and what role do they play in the process of financial intermediation?**
Financial institutions can be divided into two main groups: depository institutions and nondepository institutions. Depository institutions include commercial banks, thrift institutions, and credit unions. Nondepository institutions include insurance companies, pension funds, brokerage firms, and finance companies. Financial institutions ease the transfer of funds between suppliers and demanders.

>lg 4 **How does the Federal Deposit Insurance Corporation protect depositors' funds?**
The Federal Deposit Insurance Corporation insures deposits in commercial banks through the Bank Insurance Fund and deposits in thrift institutions through the Savings Association Insurance Fund. The FDIC sets banking policies and practices and reviews banks annually to ensure that they operate fairly and profitably.

>lg 5 **What role do U.S. banks play in the international marketplace?**
U.S. banks provide loans and trade-related services to foreign governments and businesses. They also offer specialized services such as cash management and foreign currency exchange.

>lg 6 **What trends are reshaping the banking industry?**
By using Internet technology, banks are delivering more services online. Bank mergers and acquisitions continue to consolidate the banking industry, helping banks to improve their operating efficiency, reduce costs, and extend their geographic reach. Passage of bank reform legislation that will allow banks to market securities and insurance products will help banks compete with nondepository institutions and with banks in other countries.

PREPARING FOR TOMORROW'S WORKPLACE

1. According to bank regulators, about 80 percent of U.S. bank customers prefer the convenience of banking with a large bank while 20 percent prefer the personalized service of a small bank. Interview 10 people, asking them their preference and the reasons for it.
2. In 1983 the Federal Reserve Bank of Atlanta published a report predicting that check writing would almost disappear in the United States by 2000. The bank based its prediction on the spread of technology in the banking industry. Consumers, the report said, would prefer using debit cards and paying their bills via computer rather than writing checks. But Americans are writing more checks each year—twice the number they wrote 20 years ago and eight times more than the average European. Find articles in the business press to discover why Americans are reluctant to change their check-writing habits and why banks want customers to write fewer checks.
3. Interview a local small business owner about his or her relationship with a bank. What services does the bank provide for the owner? Why did the owner choose that particular bank over other banks?

4. Suppose that you are a loan officer for a bank. An entrepreneur calls to make an appointment with you regarding financing for her new venture—a juice bar. You tell the potential customer that she will need to be prepared for the meeting so that you can get a good understanding of her business and of her banking needs. Write a letter to the customer detailing the information she should bring to the meeting.

5. A growing number of banks use databases to identify profitable and unprofitable customers. Bankers say they lose money—about $500 a year—on unprofitable customers who typically keep less than $1,000 in their checking and savings accounts, frequently call the bank to check on their accounts, and often visit the bank. Profitable customers keep several thousand dollars in their accounts and seldom visit a teller or call the bank. To turn unprofitable customers into profitable ones, banks have assessed fees on almost 300 services, including using a bank teller. Many fees are waived for customers who maintain high account balances. Bankers justify the fees by saying they're in business to earn a profit. Divide your class into two groups and debate whether banks are justified in treating unprofitable and profitable customers differently.

WORKING THE NET

1. The convenience of online banking is appealing to you, but you're not sure if you should bank with an Internet-only bank like NetBank or an online service of a traditional bank. Use the Electronic Banking Association's Web site, **www.e-banking.org,** to find financial institutions online. Compare the services offered by Internet-only and traditional banks and their service fees. Which offers the best deal?

2. The growth in online banking is also creating opportunities for unscrupulous people to perpetrate fraud by taking advantage of the anonymity of the Internet. The FDIC encourages people to report suspicious Internet banking sites such as those offering extremely high interest rates on deposits or extremely low interest rates on loans. Learn about other suspicious practices and what you can do to report them to the FDIC by visiting **www.fdic.gov/consumer/suspicious.**

CREATIVE THINKING CASE

Starting a Niche Bank

Nat Padget worked in the banking industry for 21 years as a bank examiner, loan officer, and top manager. But he wanted a bank of his own. Padget knew that starting a traditional full-service bank was an enormous and expensive undertaking, so he decided to start a bank that targets a niche market. In 1998 Padget opened the Chattahoochee National Bank in Alpharetta, Georgia. The bank serves professional service firms such as insurance brokers and computer and engineering consulting firms that earn revenues ranging from $3 million to $30 million.

Chattahoochee is a no-frills bank. Padget leases space in an office building, but he doesn't have tellers or drive-up windows. Instead, he has six loan officers who visit customers and conduct transactions using laptop computers. He also provides a courier service that customers can use to deposit their checks. Padget charges his customers a slightly higher loan rate than that charged by competing banks. Since its opening, Chattahoochee has amassed assets of $23 million.

Critical Thinking Questions

1. Why do you think Chattahoochee's customers are willing to pay a higher rate on loans than they could get at competing banks?
2. What is Padget's strategy of operating a profitable bank?

VIDEO CASE

Roney & Co. and Firstbank Corp.

Founded in 1925 by William C. Roney Sr., Roney & Co. (**www.roney.com**), headquartered in Michigan, grew into the state's largest investment securities and investment banking firm. In November 1997, Roney & Co. announced that it had been purchased by First Chicago NBD Corp., the region's banking leader. On October 2, 1998, First Chicago NBD and Banc One Corp. merged to form Bank One Corp; eight months later, on May 28, 1999, Bank One divested Roney & Co. Roney then became a wholly owned subsidiary of Raymond James Financial Inc.

As a regional full-service investment firm, Roney & Co. strives "to build and preserve wealth for . . . clients." The firm does this by meeting virtually any investment need that its clients have "from stocks and bonds to mutual funds, options, unit investment trusts, money market funds, and insurance, along with investment management services, pension . . . [and] retirement plan services, plus complete investment banking capabilities." Roney's professional, knowledgeable, and ethical employees work as a team to provide outstanding service to all clients.

Firstbank Corp. (**www.firstbank-alma.com**) is a bank holding company consisting of a small network of affiliated community banks located in Michigan. The affiliated banks are the Bank of Alma, Firstbank of Mt. Pleasant, First Bank of West Branch, and the Bank of Lakeview. Offering a full range of deposit and loan products, Firstbank's affiliates seek to differentiate themselves from their banking competition by continuously focusing on exceptional customer service. The banks believe that integrity, customer satisfaction, and trust are the key elements of solid community banking. Each affiliate bank has its own president and board of directors. This helps each bank to make decisions that focus on the local community and local customers.

Firstbank of Mt. Pleasant, for instance, is headed by Thomas Sullivan. He emphasizes that Firstbank customers will have a more personal and flexible banking experience because the bank strives to tailor its services to individual customer needs. The bank offers "a wide variety of checking and savings accounts to fit . . . [customer's] individual or corporate needs, and all types of consumer, mortgage, and commercial loans." The bank also has an affiliation with SII Investments, Inc. to provide customers with access to stocks, bonds, mutual funds, annuities, and insurance products.

The Bank of Alma, another affiliate, is headed by John McCormack, who is also president and CEO of Firstbank Corp. As the head of the Bank of Alma, McCormack emphasizes making banking convenient for customers and knowing customers well so that the bank can recommend appropriate financial solutions whatever a customer's banking needs happen to be.

Another unit of Firstbank Corp. is 1st Armored, Inc., which provides several armored courier services for financial institutions in Michigan. These services include Federal Reserve shipping, individual bank deliveries, coin wrapping, and automated teller machine servicing.

Critical Thinking Questions

1. What roles do Roney & Co. and Firstbank Corp. play in the U.S. financial system?

2. What similarities do you see in how Roney & Co. and Firstbank Corp. conduct their respective businesses?

3. What differences do you see in how Roney & Co. and Firstbank Corp. conduct their respective businesses?

chapter twenty-one

Financial Management

learning goals

>lg 1   What roles do finance and the financial manager play in the firm's overall strategy?

>lg 2   How does a firm develop its financial plans, including forecasts and budgets?

>lg 3   What types of short-term and long-term expenditures does a firm make?

>lg 4   What are the main sources and costs of unsecured and secured short-term financing?

>lg 5   How do the two primary sources of long-term financing compare?

>lg 6   What are the major types, features, and costs of long-term debt?

>lg 7   When and how do firms issue equity, and what are the costs?

>lg 8   What trends are affecting the field of financial management?

Continental Airlines' New Routes to Profitability

What does it take to be a successful chief financial officer (CFO) today? CFOs are no longer behind-the-scenes players but key members of the executive team, setting the firm's overall strategy and participating in managerial activities that go well beyond traditional areas. Team building, strategic and operational planning, managing risks, selling and acquiring companies—it's all in a day's work for financial managers like Larry Kellner, executive vice president and CFO of Continental Airlines.

When Kellner took over the financial pilot's seat in 1995, the airline was about to crash into bankruptcy for the third time. At the end of 1994, Continental reported a net loss of $613 million, and its stock price was a mere $4.63 per share. The airline had very little credibility with investors and lenders: its debt amounted to more than $500 million, it owed $1 billion in overdue payments on leases from aircraft manufacturers, and it needed billions of dollars in additional financing to survive. "We had basically run out of cash," says Kellner.

Kellner and his financial staff set out to rebuild Continental's relationships with investors, analysts, banks, and trade creditors. They had to convince these key groups that the airline would not only take off but keep on flying this time.

The first step was to make sure Continental had the financial resources it needed to operate. Navigating through turbulent financial skies, Kellner negotiated with lenders and aircraft manufacturers to restructure high-interest debt on more favorable terms. From 1994 to 1997, annual interest expense dropped from $204 million to $75 million.

Kellner also raised over $6 billion in new financing at advantageous rates and increased cash reserves to over $1 billion. As a result, Continental operated more efficiently and had the resources to weather a future economic downturn. By the end of 1998, the company's net income was $383 million, earnings per share were $6.34, and its stock was selling for $33.50—quite a change from the situation when Kellner came on board.

Once the airline's financial house was in order, operational performance and customer service also improved. The airline had the resources to upgrade and expand its fleet, add services, and enter more international markets through partnerships with other airlines. Continental's reputation within the airline industry and the investment community soared. So did Kellner's; he was one of the 10 winners of *CFO* magazine's 1998 CFO Excellence Awards.[1]

Critical Thinking Questions

As you read this chapter, consider the following questions as they relate to Continental Airlines:

- In addition to raising funds for Continental Airlines, what other types of financial activities would Larry Kellner oversee?

- What types of economic, industry, and other information would be important to Continental's financial analysts in developing forecasts of revenues and operating expenses?

- Did Kellner's actions help to achieve the financial manager's primary goal of maximizing the value of the firm to its owners?

BUSINESS IN THE 21ˢᵀ CENTURY

In today's fast-paced global economy, managing a firm's finances is more complex than ever. For managers like Larry Kellner, a thorough command of traditional finance activities—financial planning, investing money, and raising funds—is only part of the job. Financial managers are more than number crunchers. As part of the top management team, chief financial officers (CFOs) need a broad understanding of their firm's business and industry, as well as leadership ability and creativity. They must never lose sight of the primary goal of the financial manager: to maximize the value of the firm to its owners.

Financial management—raising and spending a firm's money—is both a science and an art. The science part is analyzing numbers and flows of cash through the firm. The art is answering questions like these: Is the firm using its financial resources in the best way? Aside from costs, why choose a particular form of financing? How risky is each option?

This chapter focuses on the financial management of a firm. We'll start with an overview of the role of finance and of the financial manager in the firm's overall business strategy. Next we consider the basics of financial planning—forecasts and budgets. Discussions of investment decisions and sources of short- and long-term financing follow. Finally, we'll look at key trends affecting financial management in the 21st century.

THE ROLE OF FINANCE AND THE FINANCIAL MANAGER

financial management

The art and science of managing a firm's money so that it can meet its goals.

Finance is critical to the success of all companies. It may not be as visible as marketing or production, but management of a firm's finances is just as much a key to its success.

Financial management—the art and science of managing a firm's money so it can meet its goals—is not just the responsibility of the finance department. All business decisions have financial consequences. Managers in all departments must work closely with financial personnel. If you are a sales representative, for example, the company's credit and collection policies will affect your ability to make sales.

Any company, whether it's a two-attorney law partnership or General Motors, needs money to operate. To make money, it must first spend money—on inventory and supplies, equipment and facilities, and employee wages and salaries.

Revenues from sales of the firm's products should be the chief source of funding. But money from sales doesn't always come in when it's needed to pay the bills. Financial managers must track how money is flowing into and out of the firm (see Exhibit 21-1). They work with the firm's other department managers to determine how available funds will be used and how much money is needed. Then they choose the best sources to obtain the required funding.

For example, a financial manager will track day-to-day operational data such as cash collec-

When you come across a finance term you don't understand, visit the Hypertextual Finance Glossary at **www.duke.edu/~charvey/ Classes/wpg/glossary.htm.**

How Cash Flows through a Business

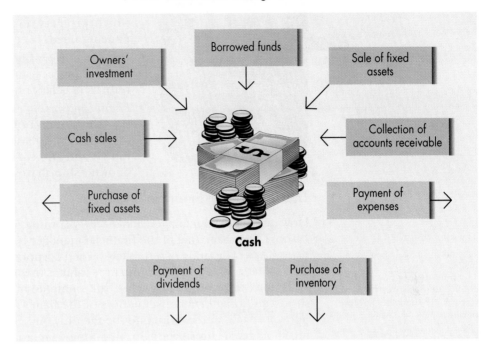

cash flows

The inflow and outflow of cash for a firm.

___

Financial managers at Ford Motor Company plan and monitor cash flow to ensure that funds are available to finance the labor and material costs of producing vehicles.

tions and disbursements to ensure that the company has enough cash to meet its obligations. Over a longer time horizon, the manager will thoroughly study whether and when the company should open a new manufacturing facility. The manager will also suggest the most appropriate way to finance the project, raise the funds, and then monitor the project's implementation and operation.

Financial management is closely related to accounting. In most firms both areas are the responsibility of the vice-president of finance or the CFO. But accountants' main function is to collect and present financial data. Financial managers use financial statements and other information prepared by accountants to make financial decisions. Financial managers focus on **cash flows,** the inflow and outflow of cash. They plan and monitor the firm's cash flows to ensure that cash is available when needed.

The Financial Manager's Responsibilities and Activities

Financial managers have a complex and challenging job. They analyze financial data prepared by accountants, monitor the firm's financial status, and prepare and implement financial plans. One day they may be developing a better way to automate cash collections,

the next they may be analyzing a proposed acquisition. The key activities of the financial manager are:

- *Financial planning.* Preparing the financial plan, which projects revenues, expenditures, and financing needs over a given period.
- *Investment (spending money).* Investing the firm's funds in projects and securities that provide high returns in relation to the risks.
- *Financing (raising money).* Obtaining funding for the firm's operations and investments and seeking the best balance between debt (borrowed funds) and equity (funds raised through the sale of ownership shares in the business).

The Goal of the Financial Manager

return

The opportunity for profit.

risk

The potential for loss or the chance that an investment will not achieve the expected level of return.

risk-return trade-off

A basic principle in finance that holds that the higher the risk associated with an investment, the greater the return that is required.

How can financial managers make wise planning, investment, and financing decisions? The main goal of the financial manager is *to maximize the value of the firm to its owners.* The value of a publicly owned corporation is measured by the share price of its stock. A private company's value is the price at which it could be sold.

To maximize the firm's value, the financial manager has to consider both short- and long-term consequences of the firm's actions. Maximizing profits is one approach, but it should not be the only one. Such an approach favors making short-term gains over achieving long-term goals. What if a firm in a highly technical and competitive industry did no research and development? In the short run, profits would be high because research and development is very expensive. But in the long run, the firm might lose its ability to compete because of its lack of new products.

Financial managers constantly strive for a balance between the opportunity for profit and the potential for loss. In finance, the opportunity for profit is termed **return;** the potential for loss, or the chance that an investment will not achieve the expected level of return, is **risk.** A basic principle in finance is that the higher the risk, the greater the return that is required. This widely accepted concept is called the **risk-return trade-off.** Financial managers consider many risk and return factors when making investment and financing decisions. Among them are changing patterns of market demand, interest rates, general economic conditions, market conditions, and social issues (such as environmental effects and equal employment opportunity policies).

concept check

- What is the role of financial management in a firm?
- How do the three key activities of the financial manager relate?
- What is the main goal of the financial manager? How does the risk-return trade-off relate to the financial manager's main goal?

FINANCIAL PLANNING

>lg 2

As we learned in Chapter 7, companies use several types of plans to determine how to achieve organizational objectives. A company's *financial plan* is part of the overall company plan and guides the firm toward its business goals and the maximization of its value. The financial plan enables the firm to estimate the amount and timing of its investment and financing needs.

To prepare a financial plan, the financial manager must first consider existing and proposed products, the resources available to produce them, and the financing needed to support production and sales. Forecasts and budgets are essential to the firm's financial planning. They should be part of an integrated planning process that links them to strategic plans and performance measurement. As the Applying Technology box describes, Avon Products, Inc. is using data marts to develop a comprehensive, real-time financial planning system to achieve its goals.

AVON'S FINANCIAL PLANNING GETS A MAKEOVER

Many managers would list forecasting and budgeting as their least favorite tasks. Even financial executives agree that these financial plans take too long to prepare. And even when a company has an excellent set of financial plans, they don't benefit managers unless the information is consistent and available. At about 75 percent of large companies, information is scattered throughout the company in multiple financial planning and reporting systems.

This is not the case at New York–based beauty-products company Avon Products, Inc., however. As part of its new financial discipline, which also includes $400 million in cost reductions and earnings growth of at least 16 percent a year, Avon recently completely revamped its worldwide planning and budgeting process.

Avon's goal is to integrate projections of all departments. With more than 40 international operating units and more than 6,000 products, this task, though essential, is far from easy. "Finance will come up with a forecast, and they don't see marketing and sales people. We need to make sure we have a coordinated forecast," says Stephen Ibbotson, Avon's director of global business process redesign. No longer can financial managers only be reporters of information. They must facilitate the process by serving as consultants to operations, marketing, and sales. In the end, "financial forecasts should be owned by operating management," says Edwina Woodbury, Avon's CFO.

As a first step, Avon implemented data marts for its United Kingdom operations. Data marts combine separate databases into one. Using special software, managers can go online to retrieve marketing, finance, and sales data for operational management, as well as executive decision making.

The next phase involves creating a coordinated forecast that is consistent around the world. This is especially important for a company that gets two-thirds of its revenues from outside the United States. "Our current business is geographical; each business unit reports to a regional head," says Ibbotson. "[Forecasting] needs to be a global process reflecting the global nature of manufacturing and procurement."

The ultimate goal is to link the integrated forecasts with strategic and tactical planning. "Our current process is inefficient," says CFO Woodbury. "We have to crunch a lot of numbers to come up with a forecast or a plan."

Critical Thinking Questions

1. Should the responsibility for developing a firm's forecasts and budgets lie with financial managers or operational managers? Why?
2. Why is it important to integrate financial plans with strategic plans?
3. How can Avon link forecasts and budgets to operational plans?

Forecasts

The financial planning process starts with financial forecasts, or projections of future developments within the firm. The estimated demand for the firm's products (the sales forecast) and other financial and operating data are key inputs. At Ford Motor Co., economic analysts estimate expected production and sales for each line of cars and trucks. Then financial analysts prepare detailed short- and long-term financial forecasts based on these assumptions.

short-term forecasts

Projections of revenues, costs of goods, and operating expenses over a one-year period.

Short-term forecasts, or *operating plans*, project revenues, costs of goods, and operating expenses over a one-year period. Using short-term forecasts, Ford's financial managers estimate the next year's expenses for inventory, labor, advertising, and other operating activities. These estimates form the basis for cash budgets, described below, which predict cash inflows and outflows over the same period.

long-term forecasts

Projections of a firm's activities and the funding for those activities over a period that is longer than one year, typically 2 to 10 years.

budgets

Formal written forecasts of revenues and expenses that set spending limits based on operational forecasts; include cash budgets, capital budgets, and operating budgets.

cash budgets

Budgets that forecast a firm's cash inflows and outflows and help the firm plan for cash surpluses and shortages.

capital budgets

Budgets that forecast a firm's outlays for fixed assets (plant and equipment), typically for a period of several years.

Long-term forecasts, or *strategic plans,* typically cover 2 to 10 years and take a broader view of the firm's financial activities. With these forecasts, management can assess the financial effects of various business strategies: What would be the financial results of investing in new facilities and equipment? Of developing new products? Of eliminating a line of business? Of acquiring other firms? Long-term forecasts also show where the funding for these activities is expected to come from.

Budgets

Firms prepare **budgets** to plan and control their future financial activities. These are formal written forecasts of revenues and expenses that set spending limits based on operational forecasts. All budgets begin with forecasts. Budgets are a way to control expenses and compare the actual performance to the forecast.

Firms use several types of budgets. Most cover a one-year period. **Cash budgets** forecast the firm's cash inflows and outflows and help the firm plan for cash surpluses and shortages. Because having enough cash is so critical to their financial health, many firms prepare annual cash budgets subdivided into months or weeks. Then they project the amount of cash needed in each shorter time period. **Capital budgets** forecast outlays for fixed assets (plant and equipment). They usually cover a period of several years and ensure that the firm will have enough funds to buy the equipment and buildings it needs. **Operating budgets** combine sales forecasts with estimates of production costs and operating expenses in order to forecast profits. They are based on individual budgets for sales, production, purchases of materials, factory overhead, and operating expenses. Operating budgets then are used to plan operations: dollars of sales, units of production, amounts of raw materials, dollars of wages, and so forth.

Budgets are routinely used to monitor and control the performance of a division, a department, or an individual manager. When actual outcomes differ from budget expectations, management must take action.

c o n c ə p t c h ə c k

- What is a financial plan? Name two types of financial planning documents.
- Distinguish between short- and long-term forecasts. How are both used by financial managers?
- Briefly describe three types of budgets.

HOW ORGANIZATIONS USE FUNDS

>lg 3

operating budgets

Budgets that combine sales forecasts with estimates of production costs and operating expenses in order to forecast profits.

To grow and prosper, a firm must keep investing money in its operations. The financial manager decides how best to use the firm's money. Short-term expenses support the firm's day-to-day activities. For instance, athletic apparel maker Nike regularly spends money to buy such raw materials as leather and fabric and to pay employee salaries. Long-term expenses are typically for fixed assets. For Nike, these would include outlays to build a new factory, buy automated manufacturing equipment, or acquire a small manufacturer of sports apparel.

Short-Term Expenses

Short-term expenses, often called *operating expenses,* are outlays used to support current production and selling activities. They typically result in current assets, which include cash and any other assets (accounts receivable and inventory) that can be converted to cash within a year. The financial manager's goal is to manage current assets so the firm has enough cash to pay its bills and to support its accounts receivable and inventory.

cash management

The process of making sure that a firm has enough cash on hand to pay bills as they come due and to meet unexpected expenses.

Cash Management: Assuring Liquidity Cash is the lifeblood of business. Without it, a firm could not operate. An important duty of the financial manager is **cash management,** or making sure that enough cash is on hand to pay bills as they come due and to meet unexpected expenses.

Businesses use budgets to estimate the cash requirements for a specific period. Many companies keep a minimum cash balance to cover unexpected expenses or changes in projected cash flows. The financial manager arranges loans to cover any shortfalls. If the size and timing of cash inflows closely match the size and timing of cash outflows, the company needs to keep only a small amount of cash on hand. A company whose sales and receipts are fairly predictable and regular throughout the year needs less cash than a company with a seasonal pattern of sales and receipts. A toy company, for instance, whose sales are concentrated in the fall, spends a great deal of cash during the spring and summer to build inventory. It has excess cash during the winter and early spring, when it collects on sales from its peak selling season.

Because cash held in checking accounts earns little, if any, interest, the financial manager tries to keep cash balances low and to invest the surplus cash. Surpluses are invested temporarily in **marketable securities,** short-term investments that are easily converted into cash. The financial manager looks for low-risk investments that offer high returns. Three of the most popular marketable securities are Treasury bills, certificates of deposit, and commercial paper. (**Commercial paper** is unsecured short-term debt (an IOU) issued by a financially strong corporation.)

In addition to seeking the right balance between cash and marketable securities, the financial manager tries to shorten the time between the purchase of inventory or services (cash outflows) and the collection of cash from sales (cash inflows). The three key strategies are to collect money owed to the firm (accounts receivable) as quickly as possible, to pay money owed to others (accounts payable) as late as possible without damaging the firm's credit reputation, and to minimize the funds tied up in inventory.

Find an introduction to the types of cash management services banks offer their customers at Centura Bank's site

www.centura.com/ business/cash/

marketable securities

Short-term investments that are easily converted into cash.

commercial paper

Unsecured short-term debt (an IOU) issued by a financially strong corporation.

accounts receivable

Sales for which a firm has not yet been paid.

Managing Accounts Receivable **Accounts receivable** represent sales for which the firm has not yet been paid. Because the product has been sold but cash has not yet been received, an account receivable amounts to a use of funds. For the average manufacturing firm, accounts receivable represent about 15 to 20 percent of total assets.

The financial manager's goal is to collect money owed to the firm as quickly as possible—while offering customers credit terms attractive enough to increase sales. Accounts receivable management involves setting *credit policies,* guidelines on offering credit, and *credit terms,* specific repayment conditions, including how long customers have to pay their bills and whether a cash discount is given for quicker payment. Another aspect of accounts receivable management is deciding on *collection policies,* the procedures for collecting overdue accounts.

Setting up credit and collection policies is a balancing act for financial managers. On the one hand, easier credit policies or generous credit terms (a longer repayment period or larger cash discount) result in increased sales. On the other hand, the firm has to finance more accounts receivable. The risk of uncollectible accounts receivable also rises. Businesses consider the impact on sales, timing of cash flow, experience with bad debt, customer profiles, and industry standards when developing their credit and collection policies.

Companies that want to speed up collections can use several strategies. They can actively manage their accounts receivable, rather than passively letting customers pay when they want to. Michael Churchman, owner of Rocky Mountain Radar, an electronics company in El Paso, Texas, waited three months for his first payment from the federal government. Not content to settle for the government's typically slow payment process, he took steps to be paid in 15 days:

good follow-up with both the buyer and the person who handles his accounts payable and offering a 5 percent cash discount for payment within 15 days. The benefits of faster collections offset the small discount.[2]

Technology can also help firms speed up collections. To cope with the meteoric rise in sales and, hence, accounts receivable, Dell Computer implemented an automated receivables collection system. Customized software improved order processing and collection methods. The new system also took over labor-intensive tasks such as sending letters to overdue accounts at specified times and creating activity reports with current account status. Dell's days receivables outstanding dropped from 50 to 37 days, freeing up a significant amount of cash.[3]

Inventory   Another use of funds is to buy inventory needed by the firm. In a typical manufacturing firm, inventory is nearly 20 percent of total assets. The cost of inventory includes not only its purchase price, but also ordering, handling, storage, interest, and insurance costs.

Production, marketing, and finance managers usually have differing views about inventory. Production managers want lots of raw materials on hand to avoid production delays. Marketing managers want lots of finished goods on hand so customer orders can be filled quickly. But financial managers want the least inventory possible without harming production efficiency or sales. Financial managers must work closely with production and marketing to balance these conflicting goals. Techniques for reducing the investment in inventory—efficient order quantities, the just-in-time system, and materials requirement planning—were described in Chapter 12.

Long-Term Expenditures

capital expenditures

Investments in long-lived assets, such as land, buildings, machinery, and equipment, that are expected to provide benefits over a period longer than one year.

capital budgeting

The process of analyzing long-term projects and selecting those that offer the best returns while maximizing the firm's value.

A firm also uses funds for its investments in long-lived assets, such items as land, buildings, machinery, and equipment. These are called **capital expenditures.** Unlike operating expenses, which produce benefits within a year, the benefits from capital expenditures extend beyond one year. For instance, a printer's purchase of a new printing press with a usable life of seven years is a capital expenditure. It appears as a fixed asset on the firm's balance sheet. Paper, ink, and other supplies, however, are expenses. Mergers and acquisitions, discussed in Chapter 5, are also considered capital expenditures.

Firms make capital expenditures for many reasons. The most common are to expand and to replace or renew fixed assets. Another reason is to develop new products. Most manufacturing firms have a big investment in long-term assets. Boeing Co., for instance, puts millions of dollars a year into airplane-manufacturing facilities.

Because capital expenditures tend to be costly and have a major effect on the firm's future, the financial manager must analyze long-term projects and select those that offer the best returns while maximizing the firm's value. This process is called **capital budgeting.** Decisions involving new products or the acquisition of another business are especially important. Another challenge managers face is assessing the value of proposed information technology expenditures, as the Focusing on Small Business box demonstrates.

c o n c ə p t   c h ə c k

- Distinguish between short- and long-term expenses.
- What is the financial manager's goal in cash management? List the three key cash management strategies.
- Describe the firm's main motives in making capital expenditures.

OBTAINING SHORT-TERM FINANCING

>lg 4

How do firms raise the funding they need? They borrow money (debt), sell ownership shares (equity), and retain earnings (profits). The financial manager must assess all these sources and choose the one most likely to help maximize the firm's value.

NET PAYOFFS

Do investments in the latest technology pay off? So far, the results are mixed. According to International Data Corp., a major information technology research firm, through 1998 companies received only $1.00 back for every $1.50 they invested.

One exception to this rule is Loanshop.com, the first online mortgage company. Profitability in this high-volume business depends on a company's ability to generate high-quality loan transactions at the lowest possible cost.

The company gets over half of its customer communications via e-mail, and quick response was the key to converting leads to sales. The conversion rate was greatest for replies within an hour of receipt and then dropped quickly, to less than 1 percent after 24 hours. Unless Loanshop could quickly separate incoming e-mail according to priority, it would miss promising sales opportunities.

Loanshop.com had two options to speed up the process of separating serious leads from routine questions: hire more staff or invest in special software to filter e-mail and route high-priority inquiries to mortgage counselors. But what were the relevant financial, operating, or process measurements that showed whether the new technology added value? While many of its rivals focused on the number of visitors to the Web site, Loanshop.com president Jack Rodgers disagreed: "It's a meaningless number if no one buys our product."

Loanshop.com's managers knew that one person could process 100 e-mail messages in an eight-hour day. The e-mail automation system could perform this task in just 15 minutes—a 96 percent reduction. Armed with these data, managers performed a capital budgeting analysis and determined that the technology solution was the better choice.

The new software acts as the company's inbound e-mail telemarketing agent. It filters e-mail, answers routine inquiries, and sends loan requests directly to loan counselors. It also can forward completed loan applications to the Federal National Mortgage Association's automated underwriting system. The results speak for themselves: Loanshop.com doubled its mortgage counselors' sales, reduced the number of employees handling e-mail by over one-third, and earned a 40 percent return on investment in 14 months. Customers are happy, too: they learn whether they qualify for a loan in five minutes and save an average of $1,500 in administrative costs.

Critical Thinking Questions

1. Describe the steps a company should take to evaluate a proposed investment in new information technology equipment.
2. What measures and performance outcomes were relevant for Loanshop.com's capital budgeting decision?
3. What mistakes could a company make by investing in new technology? How did Loanshop.com avoid them?

Like expenses, borrowed funds can be divided into short- and long-term loans. A short-term loan comes due within one year; a long-term loan has a maturity greater than a year. Short-term financing is shown as a current liability on the balance sheet. It is used to finance current assets and support operations. Short-term loans can be unsecured or secured.

Unsecured Short-Term Loans

unsecured loans
Short-term loans for which the borrower does not have to pledge specific assets as security.

Unsecured loans are made on the basis of the firm's creditworthiness and the lender's previous experience with the firm. An unsecured borrower does not have to pledge specific assets as security. The three main types of unsecured short-term loans are trade credit, bank loans, and commercial paper.

trade credit

The extension of credit by the seller to the buyer between the time the buyer receives the goods or services and when it pays for them.

accounts payable

Purchase for which a buyer has not yet paid the seller.

line of credit

An agreement between a bank and a business that specifies the maximum amount of unsecured short-term borrowing the bank will allow the firm over a given period, typically one year.

revolving credit agreement

A guaranteed line of credit whereby a bank agrees that a certain amount of funds will be available for a business to borrow over a given period.

Trade Credit: Accounts Payable   When Goodyear sells tires to General Motors, GM does not have to pay cash on delivery. Instead, Goodyear regularly bills GM for its tire purchases, and GM pays at a later date. This is an example of **trade credit**—the seller extends credit to the buyer between the time the buyer receives the goods or services and when it pays for them. Trade credit is a major source of short-term business financing. The buyer enters the credit on its books as an **account payable.** In effect, the credit is a short-term loan from the seller to the buyer of the goods and services. Until GM pays Goodyear, Goodyear has an account receivable from GM—and GM has an account payable to Goodyear.

Bank Loans   Unsecured bank loans are another source of short-term business financing. Companies often use these loans to finance seasonal (cyclical) businesses. For instance, a swimwear maker has strong sales in the spring and summer and lower sales during the fall and winter. It needs short-term bank financing to increase inventories before its strongest selling season and to finance accounts receivable during late winter and early spring, as shown in Exhibit 21-2. The company repays these bank loans when it sells the inventory and collects the receivables.

Unsecured bank loans include lines of credit and revolving credit agreements. A **line of credit** is an agreement between a bank and a business. It specifies the maximum amount of unsecured short-term borrowing the bank will allow the firm over a given period, typically one year. A line of credit is not a guaranteed loan; the bank agrees to lend funds only if it has money available. Usually, the firm must repay any borrowing within a year. It must also either pay a fee or keep a certain percentage of the loan amount (10 to 20 percent) in a checking account at the bank.

Another bank loan, the **revolving credit agreement,** is basically a guaranteed line of credit. Because the bank guarantees that funds will be available, it

> e x h i b i t   2 1 - 2 <

Swimwear Manufacturer's Seasonal Cash Flows

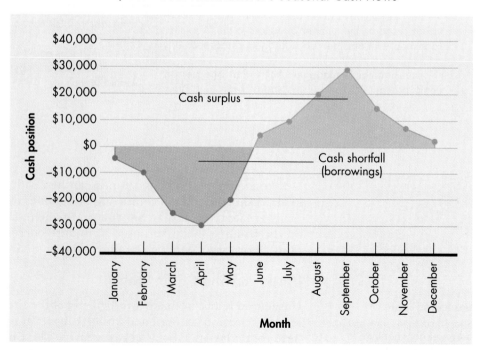

charges an extra fee in addition to interest. Revolving credit loans are often arranged for a two- to five-year period.

Firms often obtain annual lines of credit based on their expected seasonal needs. Then they can quickly borrow without having to reapply to the bank each time funds are needed. Suppose the swimwear maker projected a cash shortfall of $80,000 for the period from February to June. The financial manager might get a $100,000 line of credit from the bank. (The extra $20,000 would be there to cover any unexpected expenses.) The firm could borrow funds as needed—$10,000 in February, $25,000 in March, $30,000 in April. Then it could gradually repay the loan as it collects cash during the summer months.

Commercial Paper As noted earlier, *commercial paper* is an unsecured short-term debt (an IOU) issued by a financially strong corporation. Thus, it is a short-term investment for firms with temporary cash surpluses, and it is a financing option for major corporations. Corporations issue commercial paper in multiples of $100,000 for periods ranging from 30 to 270 days. Many big companies use commercial paper instead of short-term bank loans because the interest rate on commercial paper is usually 1 to 2 percent below bank rates.

BetzDearborn, a Pennsylvania manufacturer of water treatment chemicals, saved $800,000 a year by replacing a portion of its short-term financing with a $500 million commercial paper program. Not only was the interest rate lower, but commercial paper was more flexible, allowing BetzDearborn to issue it as needed. By fine-tuning the timing of its borrowing, the company reduced expenses even further.[4]

Secured Short-Term Loans

secured loans
Loans for which the borrower is required to pledge specific assets as collateral, or security.

Secured loans require the borrower to pledge specific assets as *collateral,* or security. The secured lender can legally take the collateral if the borrower doesn't repay the loan. Commercial banks and commercial finance companies are the main sources of secured short-term loans to business. Borrowers whose credit is not strong enough to qualify for unsecured loans use these loans.

Typically, the collateral for secured short-term loans is accounts receivable or inventory. Because accounts receivable are normally quite liquid (easily converted to cash), they are an attractive form of collateral. The appeal of inventory—raw materials or finished goods—as collateral depends on how easily it can be sold at a fair price.

factoring
A form of short-term financing in which a firm sells its accounts receivable outright at a discount to a factor.

Another form of short-term financing using accounts receivable is **factoring.** A firm sells its accounts receivable outright to a *factor,* a financial institution (usually a commercial bank or commercial finance company) that buys accounts receivable at a discount. Factoring is widely used in the clothing, furniture, and appliance industries. Factoring allows a firm to turn its accounts receivable into cash without worrying about collections. Because the factor assumes all the risks and expenses of collecting the accounts, firms that factor all of their accounts can reduce the costs of their credit and collection operations. Factoring is more expensive than a bank loan, however, because the factor buys the receivables at a discount from their actual value. But often a company has no choice because it has neither the track record to get unsecured financing nor other collateral to pledge as security for a loan.

Learn about the services and current rates offered by 21st Capital Corp., a factoring firm, at **www.21stcapital.com.**

concept check

- Distinguish between unsecured and secured short-term loans.
- Briefly describe the three main types of unsecured short-term loans.
- Discuss the two ways that accounts receivable can be used to obtain short-term financing.

SHAKY FINANCIAL MANAGEMENT

Paul Nussbaum assembled a $7 billion hotel empire in less than three years when he was CEO of Patriot American Hospitality, Inc. Patriot acquired a 450-hotel portfolio that included boutique hotels in England and the Wyndham Hotels chain in the United States, among others.

Patriot's buying spree was financed with large amounts of short-term debt and financial instruments called equity forward contracts, which were to be repaid in the future with Patriot stock. "The contracts were, in essence, a huge bet that Patriot's stock price would climb." If the stock price rose, Patriot would be able to pay off the equity forward contracts with fewer shares. If the stock price fell, more shares would be required to pay off the contracts.

Patriot's stock price declined during most of 1998, compromising the company's financial stability. Moreover, the company was forced to issue additional shares of common stock to cover its equity forward contracts, thereby "diluting its existing pool of stock and pushing its share price into a potentially fatal nose dive."

Patriot's financial position was further compromised by its load of short-term debt. Hundreds of millions of dollars of short-term debt were due in the first quarter of 1999. Nussbaum had planned to pay off that debt by selling long-term debt to investors, but because of the credit crunch set off by Russia's debt default, Patriot was unable to float its bond offering.

Patriot was hurt by other events as well. Nussbaum never established effective financial controls. Appropriate financial oversight was lacking for several months due to conflicts among the firm's key financial managers and the voluntary departure of the person who shared the chief financial officer's duties. Nussbaum also "lost credibility on Wall Street when the company repeatedly failed to meet earnings targets."

Critical Thinking Questions

1. Does Patriot's financial situation reflect questionable business ethics, or is it simply a case of poor management or unfortunate circumstances?
2. Is it unethical for a business firm to assume a high level of risk in its financial management?
3. Do publicly traded business firms have an ethical responsibility to their investors? Why or why not?

RAISING LONG-TERM FINANCING

A basic principle of finance is to match the term of the financing to the period over which benefits are expected to be received from the associated outlay. Short-term expenses should be financed with short-term funds, and long-term expenses should be financed with long-term funds. Long-term financing sources include both debt (borrowing) and equity (ownership). Equity financing comes either from selling new ownership interests or from retaining earnings.

Debt versus Equity Financing

>lg 5

financial risk

The chance that a firm will be unable to make scheduled interest and principal payments on its debt.

Say that the Boeing Co. plans to spend $2 billion over the next four years to build and equip new factories to make jet aircraft. Boeing's top management will assess the pros and cons of both debt and equity and then consider several possible sources of the desired form of long-term financing.

The major advantage of debt financing is the deductibility of interest expense for income tax purposes, which lowers its overall cost. In addition, there is no loss of ownership. The major drawback is **financial risk**—the chance that the firm will be unable to make scheduled interest and principal payments.

The lender can force a borrower that fails to make scheduled debt payments into bankruptcy. Most loan agreements have restrictions to ensure that the borrower operates efficiently.

Equity, on the other hand, is a form of permanent financing that places few restrictions on the firm. The firm is not required to pay dividends or repay the investment. However, equity financing gives common stockholders voting rights that provide them with a voice in management. Equity is more costly than debt. Unlike the interest on debt, dividends to owners are not tax-deductible expenses. Exhibit 21-3 summarizes the major differences between debt and equity financing.

Financial managers try to select the mix of long-term debt and equity that results in the best balance between cost and risk. Company policies about the mix of debt and equity vary. Some companies have high debt compared to equity. Debt as a percentage of equity is 72 percent at Navistar, a heavy equipment manufacturer. Others keep debt to a minimum. The debt-to-equity ratio for Bristol Myers-Squibb is about 15 percent; Exxon, 9 percent; Hewlett-Packard, 10 percent; and Microsoft, 0 percent.

Debt Financing

>lg 6

term loan
A business loan with a maturity of more than one year; can be unsecured or secured.

Long-term debt is used to finance long-term (capital) expenditures. The maturities of long-term debt typically range between 5 and 20 years. Three important forms of long-term debt are term loans, bonds, and mortgage loans.

A **term loan** is a business loan with a maturity of more than one year. Term loans generally have 5- to 12-year maturities and can be unsecured or secured. They are available from commercial banks, insurance companies, pension funds, commercial finance companies, and manufacturers' financing subsidiaries. A contract between the borrower and the lender spells out the amount and maturity of the loan, the interest rate, payment dates, the purpose of the loan, and other provisions such as operating and financial restrictions on the borrower to control the risk of default. Term loans may be repaid on a quarterly, semiannual, or annual schedule. The payments include both interest and principal, so

> e x h i b i t 2 1 - 3 <

Major Differences between Debt and Equity Financing

	Debt Financing	Equity Financing
Voice in management	Creditors typically have none, unless borrower defaults on payments. Creditors may be able to place restraints on management in event of default.	Common stockholders have voting rights.
Claim on income and assets	Debtholders rank ahead of equity holders. Payment of interest and principal is a contractual obligation of the firm.	Equity owners have a residual claim on income (dividends are paid only after interest and any scheduled principal payments are paid). The firm has no obligation to pay dividends.
Maturity	Debt has a stated maturity and requires repayment of principal by a specified maturity date.	The company is not required to repay equity, which has no maturity date.
Tax treatment	Interest is a tax-deductible expense.	Dividends are not tax-deductible and are paid from after-tax income.

bonds

Long-term debt obligations (liabilities) issued by corporations and governments.

mortgage loan

A long-term loan made against real estate as collateral.

common stock

A security that represents an ownership interest in a corporation.

the loan balance declines over time. Borrowers try to arrange a repayment schedule that matches the forecast cash flow from the project being financed.

Bonds are long-term debt obligations (liabilities) issued by corporations and governments. Like term loans, corporate bonds are issued with formal contracts that set forth the obligations of the issuing corporation and the rights of the bondholders. Most bonds are issued in multiples of $1,000 (par value) for maturities of 10 to 30 years. The stated interest rate, or *coupon rate,* is the percentage of the bond's par value that the issuer will pay each year as interest.

A **mortgage loan** is a long-term loan made against real estate as collateral. The lender takes a mortgage on the property, which lets the lender seize the property, sell it, and use the proceeds to pay off the loan if the borrower fails to make the scheduled payments. Long-term mortgage loans are often used to finance office buildings, factories, and warehouses. Life insurance companies are an important source of these loans. They make billions of dollars' worth of mortgage loans to businesses each year.

Equity Financing

Equity is the owners' investment in the business. In corporations, the preferred and common stockholders are the owners. A firm obtains equity financing by selling new ownership shares (external financing) or by retaining earnings (internal financing).

Selling New Issues of Common Stock   **Common stock** is a security that represents an ownership interest in a corporation. The prospectus for a new issue of common stock is shown in Exhibit 21-4. It shows that in May 1999, Juno Online Services offered 6.5 million shares priced at $13.00 per share. Underwriters' fees totaled $0.91 per share, leaving $12.09 per share for the company (a total of $78.6 million). The company also incurred several million dollars in issuance costs for printing, legal work, and accounting. Dividends, discussed below, are another potential cost of issuing common stock.

The Juno Online offering is an example of a company *going public*—its first sale of stock to the public. Usually, a high-growth company has an *initial public offering (IPO)* because it needs to raise more funds to finance continuing growth. (Companies that are already public can issue and sell additional shares of common stock to raise equity funds.) An IPO often enables existing stockholders, usually employees, family, and friends who bought the stock privately, to earn big profits on their investment.

But going public has some drawbacks. For one thing, there is no guarantee an IPO will sell. It is also expensive. Big fees must be paid to investment bankers, brokers, attorneys, accountants, and printers. Once the company is public, it is closely watched by regulators, stockholders, and securities analysts. The firm must reveal such information as operating and financial data, product details, financing plans, and operating strategies. Providing this information is often costly.

Going public can be successful when a company is well established and market conditions are right. Strong equity markets in the late 1990s prompted many companies to go public, especially very young Internet-related companies. Frequently companies that were only a year or two old rushed to go public to take advantage of market conditions. eToys, the online toy retailer profiled in

>lg 7

Yahoo co-founder Jerry Yang held a press conference to announce that his Internet search engine firm was going public to finance the expansion of Yahoo's online services.

Common Stock Prospectus

PROSPECTUS

6,500,000 Shares

Juno Online Services, Inc.

Common Stock

We are selling 6,500,000 shares of our common stock. The underwriters named in this prospectus may purchase up to 975,000 additional shares of our common stock to cover over-allotments.

This is an initial public offering of common stock. Our common stock has been approved for quotation on the Nasdaq National Market under the symbol "JWEB".

Investing in the common stock involves risks. See "Risk Factors" beginning on page 9.

Neither the Securities and Exchange Commission nor any state securities commission has approved or disapproved of these securities or determined if this prospectus is truthful or complete. Any representation to the contrary is a criminal offense.

	Per Share	Total
Initial Public Offering Price	$13.00	$84,500,000
Underwriting Discount[1]	$ 0.91	$ 5,915,000
Proceeds to Juno Online Services, Inc.	$12.09	$78,585,000

(1) For a further description of underwriting compensation, please see "Underwriting".

The underwriters are offering the shares subject to various conditions. The underwriters expect to deliver the shares to purchasers on or about June 1, 1999.

Salomon Smith Barney

Bear, Stearns & Co. Inc.

PaineWebber Incorporated

May 25, 1999

Chapter 18's opening story, went public in May 1999 at $20 a share. Its shares soared to $76.56 the first day of trading—even though the company was less than two years old and had not shown any profits. A month later, the stock was trading around $37—still a healthy increase over the initial offering price as investors showed confidence that the Internet-based retailer would grow faster than traditional toy stores.[5]

How is eToys' stock doing today? Check its price by typing the symbol ETYS in the Quotes Plus box at **dowjones.wsj.com/**

dividends

Payments to stockholders from a corporation's profits.

Dividends and Retained Earnings **Dividends** are payments to stockholders from a corporation's profits. A company does not have to pay dividends to stockholders. But if investors buy the stock expecting to get dividends and the firm does not pay

stock dividends

Payments to stockholders in the form of more stock; may replace or supplement cash dividends.

them, the investors may sell their stock. If too many sell, the value of the stock decreases. Dividends can be paid in cash or in stock. **Stock dividends** are payments in the form of more stock. Stock dividends may replace or supplement cash dividends. After a stock dividend has been paid, more shares have a claim on the same company, so the value of each share often declines.

At their quarterly meetings, the company's board of directors (with the advice of its financial managers) decides how much of the profits to distribute as dividends and how much to reinvest. A firm's basic approach to paying dividends can greatly affect its share price. A stable history of dividend payments indicates good financial health. If a firm that has been making regular dividend payments cuts or skips a dividend, investors start thinking it has serious financial problems. The increased uncertainty often results in lower stock prices. Thus, most firms set dividends at a level they can keep paying.

retained earnings

Profits that have been reinvested in a firm.

Retained earnings, profits that have been reinvested in the firm, have a big advantage over other sources of equity capital: they do not incur underwriting costs. Financial managers strive to balance dividends and retained earnings to maximize the value of the firm. Often the balance reflects the nature of the firm and its industry. Well-established firms and those that expect only modest growth, like public utilities, typically pay out much of their earnings in dividends. For example, in the year ending June 25, 1999, Commonwealth Edison paid dividends of $2.14 per share, Monsanto paid $2.60, and Atlantic Richfield paid $2.85. High-growth companies, like those in the computer and biotechnology fields, finance most of their growth through retained earnings and pay little or no dividends to stockholders.

preferred stock

An equity security for which the dividend amount is set at the time the stock is issued.

Preferred Stock   Another form of equity is **preferred stock.** Unlike common stock, preferred stock usually has a dividend amount that is set at the time the stock is issued. These dividends must be paid before the company can pay any dividends to common stockholders. Also, if the firm goes bankrupt and sells its assets, preferred stockholders get their money back before common stockholders do. Preferred stock is described in greater detail in Chapter 22.

Like debt, preferred stock increases the firm's financial risk because it obligates the firm to make a fixed payment. But preferred stock is more flexible. The firm can miss a dividend payment without suffering the serious results of failing to pay back a debt.

Preferred stock is more expensive than debt financing, however, because preferred dividends are not tax-deductible. Also, because the claims of preferred stockholders on income and assets are second to those of debtholders, preferred stockholders require higher returns to compensate for the greater risk.

Venture Capital   As we learned in Chapter 6, *venture capital* is another source of equity capital. It is most often used by small and growing firms that aren't big enough to sell securities to the public. This type of financing is especially popular among high-tech companies that need large sums of money.

Venture capitalists invest in new businesses in return for part of the ownership, sometimes as much as 60 percent. They look for new businesses with high growth potential, and they expect a high investment return within 5 to 10 years. By getting in on the ground floor, venture capitalists buy stock at a very low price. They earn profits by selling the stock at a much higher price when the company goes public. Venture capitalists generally get a voice in management through a seat on the board of directors. For example, in June 1999 two-year-old Lara Technology, which develops communications systems and networking technologies to transmit voice over the Internet, raised almost $14 million from two venture capital firms. Representatives of the investing firms joined

Lara's board and are using their expertise and industry contacts to help the company expand.[6]

Getting venture capital is difficult, even though there are hundreds of private venture capital firms in this country. Most venture capitalists finance only about 1 to 5 percent of the companies that apply. In 1998, U.S. venture capital firms invested a record $14.3 billion in almost 3,000 companies, up 24 percent from 1997. Technology companies received the lion's share of the funds—almost $11 billion. Investments in Internet-related companies nearly tripled in just two years, reaching $3.5 billion in 1998.[7]

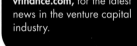

Browse the Venture Capital Resource Library, **www. vfinance.com,** for the latest news in the venture capital industry.

A new source of venture funding is large technology companies. For example, Oracle Corp., a major enterprise software developer, set up a $100 million venture capital fund for start-up companies developing Internet applications or services based on its software technology. Intel, Novell, and Adobe have formed similar funds.[8]

Some venture capitalists are moving away from financing brand-new firms. As a result, other sources of venture capital, including private foundations, states, and wealthy individuals (called *angel investors*), are emerging to help start-up firms find equity capital. Angel investors are motivated by the potential to earn a high return on their investment. Accountants, attorneys, business associates, financial consultants, bankers, and others may help the small firm find an angel.

c o n c ə p t   c h ə c k

- Compare the advantages and disadvantages of debt and equity to the issuer.
- Discuss the costs involved in issuing common stock.
- Briefly describe these sources of equity: retained earnings, preferred stock, venture capital.

CAPITALIZING ON TRENDS IN BUSINESS

>lg 8

The job of Microsoft's financial managers is complex as they manage the company's global manufacturing, licensing, and wholesale and retail distribution of more than 200 products, such as the software sold by the retailer in Hong Kong shown here.

Many of the key trends shaping financial management as we enter the new millennium echo those in other disciplines. For example, as we have seen from the Avon and Dell examples earlier in the chapter, technology is improving the efficiency with which financial managers run their operations. As in other areas, the increasing interdependence of the world's economies requires an international approach to finance. One different note, however, is the expanding role of the financial manager in risk management.

Finance Goes Global

Just as venturing overseas affects marketing, production, and general management practices, globalization brings additional complexity to financial management. Today's financial managers can make investments and raise financing both in the United States and overseas. They may have to compare the costs, risks, and benefits of relocating manufacturing facilities to another country versus expanding at home. And they must pay attention not only to the U.S. economy, but to economic developments in Japan, Russia, Germany, and other nations as well.

Take Karl Strauss Breweries, for example. The San Diego microbrewery tried for over a year to break into foreign markets. It was already exporting to Taiwan when the financial turmoil in Asia erupted. Not only did those shipments stop, but attempts to enter other Asian markets failed. Next Karl Strauss focused on several Russian cities—only to have the ruble collapse due to political and economic conditions in Russia just as the company was finalizing the deal. The ruble's devaluation pushed the price of Karl Strauss's product to more than double that of Russian beer. Rather than abandon plans to enter international markets, the brewery has continued to focus on a long-term strategy but now looks closer to home—Mexico and Canada.[9]

Managing foreign currency exposure and developing strategies to protect against increased foreign currency risk are now major activities for many financial managers. Fluctuating exchange rates affect the revenues, costs, and profits of businesses that operate in global markets. And because once-stable currencies can become extremely volatile, as happened in Asia in the fall of 1998, companies must track currency rates closely and change their strategies as necessary.

For everything you need to know about the euro, start at this Union Bank of Switzerland page **www.ubs.com/e/euro.html.**

The introduction of the euro, a common currency that will replace the currencies of the 11 European Union nations by 2002, should make global financial markets more efficient and improve access to European capital markets. It can also bring advantages to early adopters. Rapidly growing technology companies, for example, can bring their products to a unified European market more quickly and at lower cost. Other advantages include elimination of currency transaction costs, streamlined financial and accounting systems, simplified currency risk management, and reduced hedging costs.

Risk Management

risk management

The process of identifying and evaluating risks and selecting and managing techniques to adapt to risk exposures.

The 1998 turmoil in Asian and Russian financial markets proved that going global increases a company's risk, whether or not the company has operations in those regions. As a result, financial managers are spending more time on **risk management,** the process of identifying and evaluating risks and selecting and managing techniques to adapt to risk exposures. Companies face a wide range of risks, including:

- *Credit risk.* Exposure to loss as a result of default on a financial transaction or a reduction in a security's market value due to decline in the credit quality of the debt issuer.
- *Market risk.* Risk resulting from adverse movements in the level or volatility of market prices of securities, commodities, and currencies.
- *Operational risk.* The risk of unexpected losses arising from deficiencies in a firm's management information, support, and control systems and procedures.

A failure in a company's risk control procedures can lead to substantial financial losses. Major financial institutions like Daiwa and Sumitomo Corp. lost huge amounts of money because their control systems collapsed. A breakdown in risk control eventually costs the shareholders money. They may have to invest more capital to bail out the troubled firm. Otherwise their equity investment will decline in value when the company's problems become known to the public.[10]

Recently, some insurance companies have entered the risk management arena. They offer new types of policies to protect companies against disappointing financial results. Reliance Group, a New York insurer, introduced Enterprise Earnings Protection Insurance. This policy reimburses a company for any operating earnings shortfall that is due to forces beyond management's control, such as drought, floods, or the Asian economic crisis. Reliance is hoping that CFOs will buy its policies to prevent earnings surprises. Guaranteeing results is likely to be an expensive proposition, however. And predicting the volatility of a client's earnings is a new area for insurers.[11]

Learn how Reuters Risk Management Services, **risk.reuters.com,** helps companies with global operations identify, measure, and manage financial risk.

APPLYING THIS CHAPTER'S TOPICS

Whether you are a marketing manager, purchasing agent, or systems analyst, knowledge of finance will help you to do your job better. You'll be able to understand your company's financial statements, its financial condition, and management's investment and financing decisions. Financial information also provides feedback on how well you are doing and identifies problems. On a more practical note, you may be asked to prepare a budget for your department or unit. Employees who understand the financial decision-making process will be able to prepare proposals that address financial concerns. As a result, they will be more likely to get the resources they require to accomplish the firm's goals.

If you own a business, you must pay close attention to financial management. Without financial plans you may find yourself running out of cash. It's easy to get so caught up in growing sales that you neglect your billing and collection methods. In fact, managing accounts receivable is often one of the more challenging aspects of running a young company. But you can't rely on revenue increases to solve your cash flow problems. Good receivables practices start with credit policies. Be choosy when it comes to offering trade credit and check customers' credit references and payment history thoroughly. Set the initial credit limit fairly low until the customer establishes a prompt payment history. Here are some other ways to improve collections:

- Bill frequently, not just at the end of the month, so that money flows in throughout the month.
- Clearly state payment terms.
- Establish regular and frequent follow-up procedures. Some companies call to notify the customer that the bill has been sent and to make sure the customer is satisfied. Weekly calls are in order for late payments.
- Monitor results of outstanding receivables collection.
- Don't fill new orders from customers who are continually delinquent.[12]

You can also apply financial management techniques to your personal life, as the budget exercise in the Try It Now! box demonstrates.

Prepare a Personal Budget A personal budget is one of the most valuable tools for personal financial planning. It will help you evaluate your current financial situation, spending patterns, and goals.

- Using credit card receipts, check records, and other documents, record your income and expenses for the past 30 days. Based on this information, develop a personal budget for the next month. Follow the worksheet in Exhibit 21-5. Include scholarships or grants as other income sources.
- Track your actual income and expenses for one month. Write down *everything* you spend on a

daily basis, or you will forget little things (like snacks) that add up over the course of a month.
- At the end of the budget period, compare your budget to your actual results. How close were you to your budget estimates? In what categories did you overspend? Where did you underspend? Did creating the budget have any impact on how you allocated your money to different categories and how you spent your money?
- Optional: Use the results of your first month's budget to project next month's income and expenditures. And repeat the monitoring process.

SUMMARY OF LEARNING GOALS

>lg 1 **What roles do finance and the financial manager play in the firm's overall strategy?**

Finance involves managing the firm's money. The financial manager must decide how much money is needed and when, how best to use the available funds, and how to get the required financing. The financial manager's responsibilities include financial planning, investing (spending money), and financing (raising money). Maximizing the value of the firm is the main goal of the financial manager, whose decisions often have long-term effects.

>lg 2 **How does a firm develop its financial plans, including forecasts and budgets?**

Financial planning enables the firm to estimate the amount and timing of the financial resources it needs to meet its business goals. The planning process begins with forecasts based on the demand for the firm's products. Short-term forecasts project expected revenues and expenses for one year. They are the basis for cash budgets, which show the flow of cash into and out of the firm and are used to plan day-to-day operations. Long-term forecasts project revenues and expenses for 2 to 10 years. These strategic plans allow top management to analyze the impact of different options on the firm's profits.

>lg 3 **What types of short-term and long-term expenditures does a firm make?**

A firm invests in short-term expenses—supplies, inventory, and wages—to support current production, marketing, and sales activities. The financial manager manages the firm's investment in current assets so that the company has enough cash to pay its bills and support accounts receivable and inventory. Long-term expenditures (capital expenditures) are made for fixed assets such as land, buildings, and equipment. Because of the large outlays required for capital expenditures, financial managers carefully analyze proposed projects to determine which offer the best returns.

> e x h i b i t   2 1 - 5 <

Monthly Budget Worksheet

Name: _____

Month of _____

	Planned	Actual	Variance
Income			
Wages (take-home pay)	_____	_____	_____
Support from relatives	_____	_____	_____
Loans	_____	_____	_____
Withdrawals from savings	_____	_____	_____
Other _____	_____	_____	_____
Other _____	_____	_____	_____
Total Available Income	_____	_____	_____
Expenses			
Fixed Expenses			
Housing	_____	_____	_____
Automobile payment	_____	_____	_____
Insurance	_____	_____	_____
Loan repayment	_____	_____	_____
Savings for goals	_____	_____	_____
Tuition and fees	_____	_____	_____
Other _____	_____	_____	_____
Subtotal, Fixed Expenses	_____	_____	_____
Flexible Expenses			
Food	_____	_____	_____
Clothing	_____	_____	_____
Personal care	_____	_____	_____
Entertainment and recreation	_____	_____	_____
Transportation	_____	_____	_____
Telephone	_____	_____	_____
Utilities (electricity, gas, water)	_____	_____	_____
Cable TV	_____	_____	_____
Medical and dental	_____	_____	_____
Books, magazines, educational supplies	_____	_____	_____
Gifts	_____	_____	_____
Other _____	_____	_____	_____
Other _____	_____	_____	_____
Subtotal, Flexible Expenses	_____	_____	_____
Total Expenses	_____	_____	_____
Cash Surplus (Deficit)	_____	_____	_____

>lg 4 **What are the main sources and costs of unsecured and secured short-term financing?**

Short-term financing comes due within one year. The main sources of unsecured short-term financing are trade credit, bank loans, and commercial paper. Secured loans require a pledge of certain assets, such as accounts

>looking ahead

After years of shaky financial skies, Continental Airlines is flying high. Its solid financial condition has paid off in many areas. With improved access to the financial markets, the airline has been able to finance the acquisition of new aircraft and retire old ones, giving Continental one of the youngest fleets in the industry. Newer planes appeal to business travelers and allow Continental to offer higher quality service and comfort. Other airlines are now eager to form alliances with the revitalized Continental. Recently, Continental expanded its domestic and international route networks through a strategic partnership with Northwest and marketing alliances with Alaska, Air France, British Midland, Virgin, and other airlines.

Employees and passengers like the new Continental as well. In addition to 1998's record financial results, *Fortune* magazine named Continental one of its "100 Best Companies to Work for in America." Gordon Bethune, Continental's chairman and CEO, praised employees' efforts to focus on eliminating non-value-added costs.[13]

receivable or inventory, as security for the loan. Factoring, or selling accounts receivable outright at a discount, is another form of short-term financing.

>lg 5   How do the two primary sources of long-term financing compare?
Financial managers must choose the best mix of debt and equity for their firm. The main advantage of debt financing is the tax-deductibility of interest. But debt involves financial risk because it requires the payment of interest and principal on specified dates. Equity—common and preferred stock—is considered a permanent form of financing on which the firm may or may not pay dividends. Dividends are not tax-deductible.

>lg 6   What are the major types, features, and costs of long-term debt?
The main types of long-term debt are term loans, bonds, and mortgage loans. Term loans can be secured or unsecured and generally have 5- to 12-year maturities. Bonds usually have maturities of 10 to 30 years. Mortgage loans are secured by real estate. Long-term debt usually costs more than short-term financing because of the greater uncertainty that the borrower will be able to make the scheduled loan payments.

>lg 7   When and how do firms issue equity, and what are the costs?
The chief sources of equity financing are common stock, retained earnings, and preferred stock. The cost of selling stock includes issuing costs and potential dividend payments. Retained earnings are profits reinvested in the firm. For the issuing firm, preferred stock is more expensive than debt because its dividends are not tax-deductible and its claims are secondary to those of debtholders, but less expensive than common stock. Venture capital is often a source of equity financing for young companies.

>lg 8   What trends are affecting the field of financial management?
Globalization brings additional complexity to financial management. Financial managers must be prepared to invest and raise funds overseas and make transactions in multiple currencies. Financial managers are spending more time on risk management, identifying and evaluating risks and selecting techniques to control and reduce risk. Companies face a wide range of risks, including credit risk, market risk, and operational risk.

PREPARING FOR TOMORROW'S WORKPLACE

1. The head of your school's finance department has asked you to address a group of incoming business students about the importance of finance to their overall business education. Develop an outline with the key points you would cover in your speech.

KEY TERMS

accounts payable 630
accounts receivable 627
bonds 634
budgets 626
capital budgeting 628
capital budgets 626
capital expenditures 628
cash budgets 626
cash flows 623
cash management 626
commercial paper 627
common stock 634
dividends 635
factoring 631
financial management 622
financial risk 632
line of credit 630
long-term forecasts 626
marketable securities 627
mortgage loan 634
operating budgets 626
preferred stock 636
retained earnings 636
return 624
revolving credit agreement 630
risk 624
risk management 638
risk-return trade-off 624
secured loans 631
short-term forecasts 625
stock dividends 636
term loan 633
trade credit 630
unsecured loans 629

2. You are a financial analyst at General Foods Co. and have been asked to prepare forecasts and budgets for a new line of high-nutrition desserts. Why is it important for the finance department to prepare these plans for the product-development group? What factors would you consider in developing your projections? How would you assess their impact on the firm's profits?

3. You are the cash manager for a chain of sporting goods stores, and the CFO has asked you to recommend ways to increase cash. To date, the chain has always paid accounts payable within the credit period. The CFO wants to consider extending payments beyond the due date. Write a memo that discusses the pros, cons, and ethics of stretching accounts payable and also suggests other options to investigate.

4. "Simply put, dividends are out of style—and rightly so," claims Edward M. Kerschner, a securities analyst at Wall Street's PaineWebber. "Dividends are a terribly tax-inefficient way of delivering returns to investors," he says, because they are taxed twice, at the corporate and individual level. Companies in many industries that traditionally paid large dividends—telecommunications and utilities, for example—are allocating funds to acquisitions, investment, debt paydown, share buybacks, and other uses and raising dividends more slowly as they face intensified competition. Divide the class into two teams to debate Kerschner's statement that dividends no longer add value.

5. You are the CFO of Discovery Labs, a privately held, five-year-old biotechnology company. Discovery has an idea for a new drug that could be a big medical breakthrough. But the firm needs to raise $3 million to fund its development. Prepare a report for the board of trustees that discusses the types of long-term financing available to the firm, their pros and cons, and the key factors to consider in choosing a financing strategy.

WORKING THE NET

1. The Internet can help companies determine the best type of loan for their needs. GetSmart (**www.getsmart.com**) is an information service that offers advice on business as well as personal loans. Click on Business Finance Center and move through the various types of loans. Try the questionnaires in each area, using different answers, to see what is necessary to qualify for each financing option.

2. If factoring accounts receivable is still a mystery to you, the Time-Value Financial Services site, **www.tvfs.com,** will end your confusion. The company helps businesses with commercial accounts receivable meet their cash flow needs. Click on the "Factoring Accounts Receivable Invoices" link and use the information at the site to prepare a list of benefits of receivables factoring and briefly describe the process.

3. At the Tips and Guides section of the Lenders Interactive site, **www.lenders-interactive.com,** you'll find valuable suggestions to improve the quality of a personal or business loan application and avoid common mistakes. Which suggestions were the most surprising to you, and why?

4. Use the venture capital area of Finance Hub, **financehub.com/vc,** to link to three different venture capital firms. Compare the firms' investment strategies (industry specialization, age of companies in which they invest, etc.).

5. The International Finance and Commodities Institute (IFCI) Risk Watch site, **risk.ifci.ch/index.htm,** offers an excellent introduction to risk management concepts. After exploring the site, especially the Key Concepts page, develop a list of sources and types of financial risks. Give an example of each and briefly discuss the consequences of not controlling these risks. How can companies implement sound risk management procedures?

CREATIVE THINKING CASE

A Logical Financing Strategy

Many of today's young Internet-related companies try to grow as quickly as possible, seeking venture capital and other types of external funding before they show any profits. New Jersey-based Integration Logic, Inc., which develops marketing automation and e-commerce applications for Web sites, took a different approach. Started in 1998 by former bank executive Lance Miller and technology consultants Phil Underwood and Mohammed Kabir, the company chose to fund its operations from cash flow, not outside capital.

"My partners and I agree that there is a strong need for our products in the marketplace right now," says Miller. "We want to be able to satisfy that need, not get so distracted chasing after money." While executing their business plan, the management team focused on three business fundamentals: achieve and maintain profitability from day one, keep cash flow positive, and create value by building customer relationships and quality products.

Financing its growth through internally generated funds imposes strict financial discipline on Integration Logic. The company has to develop forecasts and budgets to estimate its financial needs. Although this strategy means that Integration Logic is growing more slowly than some other businesses, it is building a solid foundation for raising money in the future. Miller wants Integration Logic to prove it can achieve its goals before approaching outside investors, not simply have "a good story to tell."

Other entrepreneurs try to raise large sums of cash because the money is available. But Miller thinks this "whatever I can raise, I can use" philosophy is dangerous. "We get scared when we look at companies that have raised money and are burning through it in situations where their business fundamentals are still weak," he says.

This is exactly what happened to Fulcrum Direct, a children's clothing catalog retailer. CEO Scott Budoff had an ambitious business plan that called for rapid growth. He first raised money from family, friends, angel investors, banks, factoring companies, and other sources. He then decided to go public in 1997. He and his management team spent so much time arranging financing, however, that they neglected their main business. Then the market for small company stock offerings collapsed. The company could not raise the funds to finance the expansion plan and filed for bankruptcy in 1998.

Critical Thinking Questions

1. Evaluate Integration Logic's financing strategy. What other options could the company have used to finance its start-up? Discuss the advantages and disadvantages of each alternative.
2. "I come from the old school," says Lance Miller. "I focus on profitability and cash flow above all else." Based on this statement, what are some financial management techniques that Miller might promote at Integration Logic?
3. Describe the alternatives now available to Integration Logic to raise several million dollars to finance its growth. Which do you recommend, and why?

VIDEO CASE

Growth through Acquisitions

Scotsman Industries (**www.scotsman-ind.com**) is a leading international manufacturer and marketer of refrigerated display cases, food preparation and storage equipment, beverage systems, ice machines, and walk-in coolers and freezers. Its products are purchased mainly by supermarkets, restaurants, lodging and health care facilities, and convenience stores.

Scotsman's goals are to increase sales and earnings by 15–20 percent annually. Internal growth is expected to account for about 6–8 percent of this increase. The remainder is expected to come through acquisitions.

Growth through acquisitions has been an important element in Scotsman's success. The company's acquisition strategy is to seek leading companies that either strengthen existing product lines or venture into new, but related, areas. Originally, Scotsman was a manufacturer of ice machines for a variety of commercial applications. During the mid and late 1990s, Scotsman transformed itself from a company that was "highly dependent on one product line to a leading source of related, but diverse, product lines marketed to similar customer groups on an increasingly global basis."

One such acquisition was the Delfield Co. (**www.delfield.com**). Founded in 1949 by Paul DeLorenzo and Thomas Springfield, Delfield produced commercial foodservice equipment. Over the years, the company changed ownership several times. In May 1994, it was acquired by Scotsman Industries. Today, Delfield has manufacturing facilities in Mt. Pleasant, Michigan, and Covington, Tennessee. It has become a leading supplier of foodservice equipment, including commercial refrigerators, freezers, display cases, heated units, serving and dispensing systems, food preparation tables, fabricated counters, and ventilation systems.

The acquisition of Kysor Industrial Corp. in March 1997 enabled Scotsman Industries to enter the walk-in cooler and freezer market. The Kysor subsidiary designs, manufactures, and markets walk-in coolers, freezers, and environmental control systems for use in U.S. supermarkets and convenience stores. Additionally, industrial applications incorporate the Kysor environmental [control] systems to test products under a range of temperatures.

Other acquisitions have enabled Scotsman to expand its global business. Scotsman manufactures and markets beverage systems in Europe through its Whitlenge, Homark, and Hartek subsidiaries. Whitlenge and Homark, located in the United Kingdom, were acquired in April 1994. Hartek, located in Germany and Austria, was acquired in December 1995.

These acquisitions have helped fuel Scotsman's growth during the 1990s. Its sales and earnings have more than tripled over this period. The company intends to continue this pattern of growth through acquisitions. According to Richard Osborne, Scotsman's chairman, president, and CEO, "acquisitions will continue to be targeted and selective. The focus will be on complementary companies with strong fundamentals and competitive advantages that can improve the strategic positions of our current businesses."

Critical Thinking Questions

1. What are the financial management implications of a business strategy of growth through acquisitions?
2. Should a company finance acquisitions with debt or with equity? Explain your answer.
3. What does Richard Osborne mean when he says that future acquisitions will focus on complementary companies with strong fundamentals?

chapter twenty-two

Understanding Securities and Securities Markets

learning goals

>lg 1   What is the function of the securities markets?

>lg 2   How do common stock, preferred stock, and bonds differ as investments?

>lg 3   What other types of securities are available to investors?

>lg 4   Where can investors buy and sell securities,

>lg 5   How do investors open a brokerage account and make securities transactions?

>lg 6   Which sources of investment information are the most helpful to investors?

>lg 7   What can investors learn from stock, bond, and mutual fund quotations?

>lg 8   What are the current trends in the securities

The No-Frills Broker Dresses Up

Charles Schwab & Co. (**www.schwab.com**) moved into discount brokerage when the Securities and Exchange Commission outlawed fixed commissions in 1975. Founder Charles Schwab capitalized on experienced investors' dissatisfaction with traditional brokerage firms. These clients made their own investment decisions and didn't like paying high prices for advice they didn't want. At Schwab's no-frills brokerage, the emphasis was on executing trades—not pushing products.

By the early 1990s, Schwab & Co. was well established. As other discount brokerages opened, Schwab broadened its services to include TeleBroker, a 24-hour trading service available in English, Spanish, Mandarin, or Cantonese, and futures and commodities trading. Visionary CEO Charles Schwab then identified yet another important emerging trend. The soaring stock market was bringing novices who needed investment education and advice on financial planning to the company's offices. Schwab was happy to provide these and other additional services—and develop a new and loyal client base at the same time.

Because of new products like OneSource, a centralized mutual fund marketplace that offers funds from 120 fund families, Schwab is now one of the top three mutual fund distributors in the United States. As its services expanded, so did its performance. From 1991 to 1997, customer accounts tripled, customer assets increased tenfold, and profits increased 14 times.

The first no-frills broker was starting to look like its traditional competitors. But not for long. Co-CEOs Schwab and David Pottruck were among the first to recognize the next big trend: the Internet. Buoyed by Schwab's enthusiasm and love of technology, a group of talented information technology (IT) professionals developed a Web-based trading system in record time—in three months for less than $1 million, versus the 9 to 12 months and $2 million that outsourcers wanted.

e.Schwab debuted in March 1996 to instant success. By May the service had 10,000 customers—the goal for year-end 1996—and the company quickly expanded its IT infrastructure to meet customer demand.

Integrating Net and traditional brokerage operations was expensive for Schwab. Despite concerns that the lower prices for Internet trades—a flat fee of $29.95 for up to 1,000 shares—could cost Schwab $125 million in revenue, management decided to forge ahead. Soon productivity gains, lower costs, and increased

Critical Thinking Questions

As you read this chapter, consider the following questions as they relate to Charles Schwab & Co.:

- How has Schwab combined the best of traditional and online brokerages?

- If you were on the team developing Schwab's new online trading system, what would be your major concerns? How would you resolve them?

- As an investor, would Schwab's services appeal to you, and why?

volume compensated for the lower revenues and profits. The number of trades doubled without any increase in phone calls as customers switched to the Web. The Web now handles five times as many trades as call centers, for annual savings of $100 million.

Other Net trading companies offer commissions as low as $8 per trade, but Schwab is the number one Internet brokerage, with 30 percent of daily online trading volume—more than its next three competitors combined (E*Trade, Fidelity, Waterhouse Securities). Its success is based on service, not price. Its customers like Schwab's breadth of information and the ability to talk to service representatives—and will pay more for the service than at pure online brokerages. In just three years, the company went from no Net exposure to weekly trading volume of $4 billion—almost 60 percent of its total trading volume. By mid-1999 weekly volume had jumped to $10 billion, making Schwab one of the largest e-commerce businesses in the nation.[1]

BUSINESS IN THE 21ST CENTURY

Charles Schwab & Co. has capitalized on the forces that are reshaping the once-stodgy securities industry, from rising stock prices to new regulations and the power of the Internet. In addition to climbing to record levels, the securities markets are undergoing tremendous structural changes. Like other financial institutions, the securities industry is experiencing consolidation and technological change. Online trading companies and electronic stock exchanges are challenging the dominance of traditional stock brokerage firms and securities exchanges.

Today more people have a direct stake in the stock market than ever before. No longer is investing the province of the very wealthy. Over 40 percent of all American households own stocks, compared to 31 percent in 1989.

No doubt some of the attraction is due to the dramatic rise in stock prices during the 1990s. Between year-end 1994 and 1998, the total value of U.S. common stocks increased 25 percent each year. Although most investors are thrilled with the increasing value of their securities portfolios, they are also exposed to greater risk when the market falls.[2]

We would all like to make money in the securities markets. Before plunging in, however, it helps to understand the basics of securities markets and the securities traded there. This chapter begins with a brief discussion of the functions of securities markets and the professionals that sell securities—investment bankers and stockbrokers. A description of the different types of securities—common and preferred stocks, bonds, mutual funds, futures contracts, and options—follows. Next we'll examine the operation and regulation of securities exchanges and other markets. The chapter then describes the process of buying and selling securities and the popular sources of investment information. Finally, we'll look at some important trends affecting the securities markets today.

SECURITIES MARKETS

>lg 1

securities
Investment certificates issued by corporations or governments that represent either equity or debt.

Stocks, bonds, and other securities are traded in securities markets. These markets streamline the purchase and sales activities of investors by allowing transactions to be made quickly and at a fair price. They make the transfer of funds from lenders to borrowers much easier. **Securities**—investment certificates issued by corporations or governments—represent either equity (ownership in the issuer) or debt (a loan to the issuer).

Securities markets are busy places. On an average day, individual and institutional investors trade more than 1.8 billion shares of stock in over 10,000 companies. They also trade bonds, mutual funds, futures contracts, and options. *Individual investors* invest their own money to achieve their personal financial goals. Over 60 million individual investors (representing about 40 percent of U.S. households) hold about 64 percent of the more than $5 trillion total U.S. equities outstanding, either directly (54 percent) or through mutual funds (10 percent). We'll discuss how to set investment goals in Chapter 23.

institutional investors
Investment professionals who are paid to manage other people's money.

Institutional investors are investment professionals who are paid to manage other people's money. Most of these professional money managers work for financial institutions, such as banks, mutual funds, insurance companies, and pension funds. Institutional investors control very large sums of money, often buying stock in 10,000-share blocks. They aim to meet the investment goals of their clients. Institutional investors are a major force in the securities markets, accounting for about half of the dollar volume of equities traded.

primary market
The securities market where new securities are sold to the public.

secondary market
The securities market where already issued securities are traded among investors; includes the organized stock exchanges, the over-the-counter market, and the commodities exchanges.

Businesses and governments also take part in the securities markets. Corporations issue bonds and stocks to raise funds to finance their operations. They are also among the institutional investors that purchase corporate and government securities. Federal, state, and local governments sell securities to finance specific projects and cover budget deficits.

Types of Markets

Securities markets can be divided into primary and secondary markets. The **primary market** is where new securities are sold to the public, usually with the help of investment bankers. In the primary market, the issuer of the security gets the proceeds from the transaction. A security is sold in the primary market just once—when it is first issued by the corporation or government.

Later transactions take place in the **secondary market,** where "old" (already issued) securities are bought and sold, or traded, among investors. The issuers generally are not involved in these transactions. The vast majority of securities transactions take place in secondary markets, which include the organized stock exchanges, the over-the-counter securities market, and the commodities exchanges. You'll see *tombstones*, announcements of both primary and secondary stock and bond offerings, in *The Wall Street Journal* and other newspapers.

Most securities transactions take place in secondary markets such as on the trading floor of the New York Stock Exchange, shown here.

investment bankers
Firms that act as underwriters, buying securities from corporations and governments and reselling them to the public.

underwriting
The process of buying securities from corporations and governments and reselling them to the public; the main activity of investment bankers.

concept check

- How do securities markets help businesses and investors?
- Distinguish between primary and secondary securities markets.
- How does an investment banker work with companies to issue securities?

The Role of Investment Bankers and Stockbrokers

Two types of investment specialists play key roles in the functioning of the securities markets. **Investment bankers** help companies raise long-term financing. These firms act as intermediaries, buying securities from corporations and governments and reselling them to the public. This process, called **underwriting,** is the main activity of the investment banker, which acquires the security for an agreed-upon price and hopes to be able to resell it at a higher price to make a profit. Investment bankers advise clients on the pricing and structure of new securities offerings, as well as on mergers, acquisitions, and other types of financing. Well-known investment banking firms include Goldman, Sachs & Co., Merrill Lynch & Co., Morgan Stanley Dean Witter, First Boston, PaineWebber, and Salomon Smith Barney (a division of Citigroup).

A **stockbroker** is a person who is licensed to buy and sell securities on behalf of clients. Also called *account executives,* these investment professionals work for brokerage firms and execute the orders customers place for stocks, bonds, mutual funds, and other securities. We'll discuss the different types of brokers later in this chapter.

STOCK: EQUITY FINANCING

>lg 2

stockbroker
A person who is licensed to buy and sell securities on behalf of clients.

Chapter 21 discussed equity from a corporation's perspective, as a source of long-term funding. Here we'll examine equity from an investor's viewpoint. The two types of equity securities are common stock and preferred stock.

Common Stock

As discussed in Chapter 21, *common stock* is a security that represents an ownership interest in a corporation. A share of stock is issued for each unit of ownership. The stockholder (owner) gets a stock certificate to prove ownership. If you own a share of the common stock of General Electric Corp., you are a partial owner of GE. Your ownership interest isn't very big, because GE has about 3.3 billion shares of stock outstanding. But you are an owner just the same, and your ownership gives you certain rights.

As a stockholder, you have a right to the profits of the corporation. You would get them as dividends on your common stock. As discussed in Chapter 21, *dividends* are the part of the profits of a corporation that the firm distributes to stockholders. Dividends are paid only after all the other obligations of the firm—payments to suppliers, employees, bondholders, and other creditors, plus taxes and preferred stock dividends (discussed later)—have been met. Dividends can be paid in cash or stock (called *stock dividends*). Some firms, especially rapidly growing companies and those in high-technology industries, pay no dividends. Instead, they reinvest their profits in more buildings, equipment, and new products to earn greater future profits. As noted in Chapter 19, these reinvested profits are called *retained earnings.*

Common stockholders also have *voting rights.* They get one vote for each share of stock they own. They can vote on such issues as election of the board of directors, mergers, and selection of an independent auditor.

Potential Returns to Investors   Common stock offers two types of potential returns: dividends and stock-price increases. Dividends are declared annually or quarterly (four times a year) by the board of directors and are typically paid quarterly. For instance, in June 1999 Caterpillar, Inc.'s board announced that the company would raise its quarterly dividend rate to 32.5 cents a share, up from 30 cents in the previous quarter. Investors will receive an annual dividend of $1.30 for each share of stock they own. The increase signals to investors that the world's largest construction equipment maker is confident of its long-term prospects, even though 1999 profits could be lower than 1998 levels.[3]

An investor can also benefit by selling a stock when its price increases, or *appreciates,* above the original purchase price. Suppose you bought shares of America Online (AOL) in June 1998 at $26 and sold them for $115 in July 1999. The per-share profit of $89 ($115 sales price − $26 original price) represents a 342 percent *rate of return* ($89 profit ÷ $26 original price). Although Internet stocks like AOL and Yahoo! have posted exciting results, most stocks rarely provide such high returns. And common stockholders have no guarantee that they will get any return on their investment. Compaq Computer, a favorite of investors in 1998, peaked at about $51 in January 1999. Six months later it had slid to $21, losing ground to other computer manufacturers.

Advantages and Disadvantages of Common Stock　The returns from common-stock dividends and price appreciation can be quite attractive. Over the long term, common-stock investments have been better than most other types of investments. The historical average annual return on common stock since World War II has been about 12 percent. Another advantage is liquidity: many stocks are actively traded in securities markets and can be quickly bought and sold.

The major disadvantage is the risky nature of common-stock investments. Stockholders may not get any return at all. Stocks are subject to many risks related to the economy, the industry, and the company. These risks can hold down a stock's dividends and its price, making it hard to predict the stock's return.

Preferred Stock

Preferred stock is the second form of equity financing. As described in Chapter 21, preferred stock has advantages over common stock, specifically in the payment of dividends and the distribution of assets if the firm is liquidated. Preferred stockholders get their dividends before common stockholders do. Unlike common stock, preferred stock usually has a dividend amount that is set at the time the stock is issued. This dividend can be expressed in either dollar terms or as a percentage of the stock's par (stated) value. Investors buy preferred stock mainly for these dividend payments rather than for price appreciation. Because the dividends are fixed, the price of preferred stock generally does not change as much as the price of common stock.

Features of Preferred Stock　Preferred stock has features of both common stocks and bonds. Like common stock, it is a form of ownership. Dividends may not be paid on either type of stock if the company encounters financial hardships. But most preferred stock is *cumulative preferred stock.* Its owners must receive all unpaid dividends before any dividends can be paid to the holders of common stock. Suppose that a company with a $5-per-year preferred dividend missed its annual dividend payment in 1999. It must pay the preferred stockholders $10 ($5 in unpaid preferred dividends from 1999 plus the $5 preferred dividend for 2000) before it can pay any dividends to common stockholders.

Like bonds, preferred stock provides fixed income to investors, and their claim on income and assets comes before that of common stockholders (but after bondholders).

Advantages and Disadvantages of Preferred Stock   Investors like preferred stock because of the steady dividend income. Although companies are not legally obligated to pay preferred dividends, most have an excellent record of doing so. But the fixed dividend is also a disadvantage because it limits the cash paid to investors. Thus, preferred stock has less potential for price appreciation than common stock.

BONDS: DEBT FINANCING

interest

A fixed amount of money paid by the issuer of a bond to the bondholder on a regular schedule, typically every six months; stated as the *coupon rate.*

principal

The amount borrowed by the issuer of a bond; also called *par value.*

Bonds are long-term debt obligations (liabilities) of corporations and governments. A bond certificate is issued as proof of the obligation. The issuer of a bond must pay the buyer a fixed amount of money—called **interest,** stated as the *coupon rate*—on a regular schedule, typically every six months. The issuer must also pay the bondholder the amount borrowed—called the **principal,** or *par value*—at the bond's maturity date (due date). Bonds are usually issued in units of $1,000—for instance, $1,000, $5,000, or $10,000. The two sources of return on bond investments are interest income and gains from sale of the bonds.

Bonds do not have to be held to maturity. They can be bought and sold in the securities markets. Unlike common and preferred stockholders, who are owners, bondholders are creditors (lenders) of the issuer. In the event of liquidation, the bondholders' claim on the assets of the issuer comes before that of any stockholders.

Corporate Bonds

high-yield (junk) bonds

High-risk, high-return bonds.

secured bonds

Corporate bonds for which specific assets have been pledged as collateral.

mortgage bonds

Corporate bonds that are secured by property, such as land, equipment, or buildings.

debentures

Unsecured bonds that are backed only by the reputation of the issuer and its promise to pay the principal and interest when due.

convertible bonds

Corporate bonds that are issued with an option that allows the bondholder to convert them into common stock.

Corporate bonds, as the name implies, are issued by corporations. They usually have a par value of $1,000. They may be secured or unsecured, include special provisions for early retirement, or be convertible to common stock. Exhibit 22-1 summarizes the features of some popular types of corporate bonds.

High-yield, or **junk, bonds** are high-risk, high-return bonds that became popular during the 1980s, when they were widely used to finance mergers and takeovers. Today, they are used by companies whose credit characteristics would not otherwise allow them access to the debt markets. Because of their high risk, these bonds generally earn 3 percent or more above the returns on high-quality corporate bonds.

Secured versus Unsecured Bonds   Corporate bonds can be either secured or unsecured. **Secured bonds** have specific assets pledged as collateral, which the bondholder has a right to take if the bond issuer defaults. **Mortgage bonds** are secured by property, such as land, equipment, or buildings. **Debentures** are unsecured bonds. They are backed only by the reputation of the issuer and its promise to pay the principal and interest when due. In general, debentures have a lower risk of default than secured bonds and therefore have lower interest rates. Of course, a debenture issued by a financially shaky firm probably has greater default risk than a mortgage bond issued by a sound one.

Convertible Bonds   Corporate bonds may be issued with an option for the bondholder to convert them into common stock. **Convertible bonds** generally

> e x h i b i t   2 2 - 1 <

> e x h i b i t   2 2 - 1 <

Popular Types of Corporate Bonds

Bond Type	Characteristics
Collateral trust bonds	Secured by securities (stocks and bonds) owned by the issuer. Value of collateral is generally 25 to 35 percent higher than the bond's par value.
Convertible bonds	Unsecured bonds that can be exchanged for a specified number of shares of common stock.
Debenture	Unsecured bonds typically issued by creditworthy firms.
Equipment trust certificates	Used to finance "rolling stock"—airplanes, ships, trucks, railroad cars. Secured by the assets financed.
Floating-rate bonds	Bonds whose interest rate is adjusted periodically in response to changes in specified market interest rates. Popular when future inflation and interest rates are uncertain.
High-yield (junk) bonds	Bonds rated Ba or lower by Moody's or BB or lower by Standard & Poor's. High-risk bonds with high returns to investors. Frequently used to finance mergers and takeovers.
Mortgage bonds	Secured by property, such as land, equipment, or buildings.
Zero-coupon bonds	Issued with no coupon rate and sold at a large discount from par value. "Zeros" pay no interest prior to maturity. Investor's return comes from the gain in value (par value minus purchase price).

allow the bondholder to exchange each bond for a specified number of shares of common stock. For instance, a $1,000 par value convertible bond may be convertible into 40 shares of common stock—no matter what happens to the market price of the common stock. Because convertible bonds could be converted to stock when the price is very high, these bonds usually have a lower interest rate than nonconvertible bonds. In January 1999, Amazon.com issued $1.25 billion in convertible bonds, the largest U.S. convertible bond offering to date. The bonds had a 10-year maturity and a 4.75 percent interest rate. They were convertible to Amazon common stock at $156.05 per share, a 28 percent premium over the $122 share price at the time of issuance.[4]

U.S. Government Securities

The U.S. Treasury sells three major types of debt securities, commonly called "governments": Treasury bills, Treasury notes, and Treasury bonds. All three are viewed as risk-free because they are backed by the U.S. government. *Treasury bills* mature in less than a year and are issued with a minimum par value of $1,000. *Treasury notes* have maturities of 10 years or less, and *Treasury bonds* have maturities as long as 25 years or more. Both notes and bonds are sold in denominations of $1,000 and $5,000. The interest earned on government securities is subject to federal income tax but is free from state and local income taxes.

What is the current level of outstanding Treasury securities? Find out at the Bureau of the Public Debt site
www.publicdebt.treas.gov/

municipal bonds

Bonds issued by states, cities, counties, and other state and local government agencies.

Municipal Bonds

Municipal bonds are issued by states, cities, counties, and other state and local government agencies. These bonds typically have a par value of $5,000 and are

You'll find a minicourse on municipal bonds at

www.investinginbonds.com/ info/igmunis/what.htm

For the latest news about bond rating upgrades and downgrades, visit Moody's Investor Services at

www.moodys.com/

bond ratings

Letter grades assigned to bond issues to indicate their quality, or level of risk; assigned by rating agencies such as Moody's and Standard & Poor's.

c o n c ə p t c h ə c k

- Describe the common features of all bonds. What are the advantages and disadvantages of bonds for investors?
- What are corporate bonds? Discuss secured and unsecured types.
- What are bond ratings? Why are they important to both investors and issuers?

either general obligation or revenue bonds. *General obligation bonds* are backed by the full faith and credit (and taxing power) of the issuing government. *Revenue bonds*, on the other hand, are repaid only from income generated by the specific project being financed. Examples of revenue bond projects include toll highways and bridges, power plants, and parking structures. Because the issuer of revenue bonds has no legal obligation to back the bonds if the project's revenues are inadequate, they are considered more risky and therefore have higher interest rates than general obligation bonds.

Municipal bonds are attractive to investors because interest earned on them is exempt from federal income tax. For the same reason, the coupon interest rate for a municipal bond is lower than for a similar-quality corporate bond. In addition, interest earned on municipal bonds issued by governments within the taxpayer's home state is exempt from state income tax as well. In contrast, all interest earned on corporate bonds is fully taxable.

Bond Ratings

Bonds vary in quality, depending on the financial strength of the issuer. Because the claims of bondholders come before those of stockholders, bonds are generally considered less risky than stocks. But some bonds are in fact quite risky. Companies can *default*—fail to make scheduled principal or interest payments—on their bonds.

Investors can use **bond ratings,** letter grades assigned to bond issues, to evaluate their quality or level of risk. Ratings for corporate bonds are easy to find. The two largest and best-known rating agencies are Moody's and Standard & Poor's (S&P), whose publications are in most libraries and in stock brokerages. Exhibit 22-2 lists the letter grades assigned by Moody's and S&P. A bond's rating may change with events.

OTHER POPULAR SECURITIES

>lg 3

In addition to equity and debt, investors have several other types of securities available to them. The most popular are mutual funds, futures contracts, and options. Mutual funds appeal to a wide range of investors. Futures contracts and options are more complex investments for experienced investors.

Mutual Funds

mutual fund

A financial service company that pools investors' funds to buy a selection of securities that meet its stated investment goals.

Suppose that you have $1,000 to invest but don't know which stocks or bonds to buy, when to buy them, or when to sell them. By investing in a mutual fund, you can buy shares in a large, professionally managed *portfolio*, or group, of stocks and bonds. A **mutual fund** is a financial service company that pools its investors' funds to buy a selection of securities—marketable securities, stocks, bonds, or a combination of securities—that meet its stated investment goals.

Each mutual fund focuses on one of a wide variety of possible investment goals, such as growth or income. Many large financial service companies, like

> e x h i b i t   2 2 - 2 <

Moody's and Standard & Poor's Bond Ratings

Moody's Ratings	S & P Ratings	Description
Aaa	AAA	**Prime-quality investment bonds:** Highest rating assigned; indicates extremely strong capacity to pay.
Aa A	AA A	**High-grade investment bonds:** Also considered very safe bonds, although not quite as safe as Aaa/AAA issues; Aa/AA bonds are safer (have less risk of default) than single As.
Baa	BBB	**Medium-grade investment bonds:** Lowest of investment-grade issues; seen as lacking protection against adverse economic conditions.
Ba B	BB B	**Junk bonds:** Provide little protection against default; viewed as highly speculative.
Caa Ca C	CCC CC C D	**Poor-quality bonds:** Either in default or very close to it.

Fidelity Investments and Vanguard, sell a wide variety of mutual funds, each with a different investment goal. Investors can pick and choose funds that match their particular interests. Some specialized funds invest in a particular type of company or asset—in one industry such as health care or technology, a geographical region such as Asia, or an asset such as precious metals. To help investors find the right fund for their needs, many mutual fund companies are using the Internet to good advantage, as the Applying Technology box describes.

Mutual funds appeal to investors for three main reasons. First, they are a good way to hold a diversified, and thus less risky, portfolio. Investors with only $500 or $1,000 to invest cannot diversify much on their own. Buying shares in a mutual fund lets them own part of a portfolio that may contain 100 or more securities. Second, funds are professionally managed. And third, mutual funds may offer higher returns than individual investors could achieve on their own.

HOT links

How much is currently invested in mutual funds? The Investment Company Institute tracks these figures on a monthly basis at **www.ici.org/facts_figures/ current_statistics.html**

Futures Contracts

futures contracts

Agreements to buy or sell specified quantities of commodities or financial futures at an agreed-on price at a future date.

Futures contracts are agreements to buy or sell specified quantities of commodities (agricultural or mining products) or financial futures (financial instruments) at an agreed-on price at a future date. An investor can buy commodity futures contracts in cattle, pork bellies (large slabs of bacon), eggs, frozen orange juice concentrate, gasoline, heating oil, lumber, wheat, gold, and silver. Financial futures include Treasury securities and foreign currencies, such as the British pound or Japanese yen.

Futures contracts do not pay interest or dividends. The return depends solely on favorable price changes. These are very risky investments because the prices can vary a great deal.

part six Finance

> a p p l y i n g   t e c h n o l o g y <

MUTUALLY BENEFICIAL WEB SITES LURE INVESTORS

Internet technology has "raised the bar" for investment companies by giving the investing public more knowledge about investing. Companies with effective Internet strategies, like Charles Schwab, are reaping the benefits.

Those that are slow to catch on, however, are losing ground to their net-savvy peers. Mutual funds are among the laggards. Although most funds have Web sites, often they are poorly developed and function mainly as online sales brochures. Today's investors don't want advertising; they want information to help them analyze their investments. If they don't find what they need, they go elsewhere. In fact, many investors are shifting money out of smaller mutual funds and buying individual stocks instead.

Although a poor Web site is not the only reason for losing customers, mutual funds that understand the power of the Internet are taking customers away from their competitors. The two largest fund families, Fidelity and Vanguard, have comprehensive Web sites (**www.fidelity.com** and **www.vanguard.com**) and are among those whose assets have grown significantly. Investors find not only research but also tools to trade funds, analyze and track their portfolios, and transfer money between financial institutions. Financial planning assistance is another popular feature. Investors can even download data into financial software like Quicken. Information on a fund's holdings, however, is not as easy to find. Fidelity includes only the top 10

holdings of its funds, and Vanguard requires investors to download fund reports.

Not surprisingly, technology funds do an even better job of using the Internet to their advantage. Technology fund manager Firsthand Funds (**www.firsthand funds. com**) provides complete details on all the stocks in each of its funds, updated monthly. (Most companies list only the top 10 holdings.) Munder Funds' NetNet fund (**netnet.munder.com**), the largest Internet fund in the United States, has the most comprehensive of the fund family's Web sites. In addition to fund performance statistics and its holdings, the site lists the trades made during the month. That way investors can follow the fund's investment strategy. The site also educates visitors with a guide to investing in Internet-related stocks and other information about the Internet. In its first two years, the NetNet fund attracted almost $3 billion.

Critical Thinking Questions

1. Why do mutual fund sites that provide investors with detailed information about how their money is being invested attract more funds?
2. What type of information would you expect to find at an investment company's Web site? Would a lack of information cause you to invest elsewhere? Why or why not?

concept check

- Why do mutual funds appeal to investors? Discuss some of the investment goals pursued by mutual funds.
- What are futures contracts? Why are they risky investments?
- How do options differ from futures contracts?

Options

Options are contracts that entitle holders to buy or sell specified quantities of common stocks or other financial instruments at a set price during a specified time. As with futures contracts, investors must correctly guess future price movements in the underlying financial instrument to earn a positive return. Unlike futures contracts, the price paid for an option is the maximum amount that can be lost. But because options have very short maturities, it is easy to quickly lose a lot of money with them.

SECURITIES EXCHANGES

>lg 4   The two key types of securities exchanges are organized stock exchanges and the over-the-counter market. **Organized stock exchanges** are organizations on

options

Contracts that entitle holders to buy or sell specified quantities of common stocks or other financial instruments at a set price during a specified time.

organized stock exchanges

Organizations on whose premises securities are resold using an auction-style trading system.

whose premises securities are resold. They operate using an auction-style trading system. All other securities are traded in the over-the-counter market.

To make transactions in an organized stock exchange, an individual or firm must be a member and own a "seat" on that exchange. Owners of the limited number of seats must meet certain financial requirements and agree to observe a broad set of rules when trading securities.

U.S. Stock Exchanges

The oldest and most prestigious U.S. stock exchange is the *New York Stock Exchange (NYSE)*, which has existed since 1792. Often called the Big Board, it is located on Wall Street in downtown New York City. The NYSE, which lists the securities of about 3,110 corporations, handles most of the shares traded on organized stock exchanges in the United States. Major companies like IBM, Coca-Cola, AT&T, Procter & Gamble, Ford Motor Co., and Chevron list their shares on the NYSE. In 1998, 170 billion shares were traded on the NYSE, with a total dollar value of over $7 trillion. The NYSE is also popular with non-U.S. companies. About 400 foreign companies now list their securities on the NYSE.

How many shares traded hands today? Find out at the New York Stock Exchange site

www.nyse.com/public/market/2b/2bix.htm

Another national stock exchange, the American Stock Exchange (AMEX), lists the securities of about 770 corporations. With 1998 trading volume of just over 7 billion shares, it is dwarfed by the NYSE. Because the AMEX's rules are less strict than those of the NYSE, most firms traded on the AMEX are smaller and less well known than NYSE-listed corporations. Some firms move up to the NYSE once they qualify for listing there. Other companies choose to remain on the AMEX. Well-known companies listed on the AMEX include Audiovox, Hasbro, and Trans World Airlines. Companies cannot be listed on both exchanges at the same time.

In addition to the NYSE and AMEX, several regional exchanges list about 100 to 500 securities of firms located in their area. Regional exchange membership rules are much less strict than for the NYSE. The top regional exchanges are the Boston, Cincinnati, Chicago, and Pacific (in San Francisco) exchanges. An electronic network linking the NYSE and many of the regional exchanges allows brokers to make securities transactions at the best prices.

Global Trading and Foreign Exchanges

Improved communications and the elimination of many legal barriers are helping the securities markets go global. The number of securities listed on exchanges in more than one country is growing. Foreign securities are now traded in the United States. Likewise, foreign investors can easily buy U.S. securities.

Stock exchanges also exist in foreign countries. The London

Many U.S. and other firms outside of Japan list their stock on the Tokyo Stock Exchange, one of the world's largest foreign exchanges.

How do the world's stock exchanges compare? Find out at the London Stock Exchange site, **www. londonstockex.co.uk/stats/ stats_07.htm**—but remember that the monetary values are stated in pounds, not dollars!

and Tokyo Stock Exchanges rank behind the NYSE and Nasdaq (described below). Other important foreign stock exchanges include those in Toronto, Montreal, Buenos Aires, Zurich, Sydney, Paris, Frankfurt, Hong Kong, and Taiwan. The number of big U.S. corporations with listings on foreign exchanges is growing steadily, especially in Europe. For example, over 10 percent of the daily activity in NYSE-listed stocks is due to trades on the London Stock Exchange.

The Over-the-Counter Market

over-the-counter (OTC) market

A sophisticated telecommunications network that links dealers throughout the United States and enables them to trade securities.

National Association of Securities Dealers Automated Quotation (Nasdaq) system

The first electronic-based stock market and the fastest-growing part of the stock market.

Unlike the organized stock exchanges, the **over-the-counter (OTC) market** is not a specific institution with a trading floor. It is a sophisticated telecommunications network that links dealers throughout the United States. The **National Association of Securities Dealers Automated Quotation (Nasdaq) system,** the first electronic-based stock market, is the fastest-growing part of the stock market. It provides up-to-date bid and ask prices on about 5,125 of the most active OTC securities, with a 1998 market value totaling $2.6 trillion. It is the main reason for the popularity and growth of the OTC market. In 1998, 202 billion shares with a value of $5.8 trillion exchanged hands, gains of 23 percent and 28 percent, respectively, over the preceding year.

The securities of many well-known companies, some of which could be listed on the organized exchanges, trade on the OTC market. Examples include Apple Computer, Ben & Jerry's, Coors, Dell Computer, Intel, MCI Worldcom, Microsoft, Nordstrom Department Stores, and Starbucks. The stocks of most commercial banks and insurance companies also trade in this market, as do most government and corporate bonds. About 440 foreign companies also trade OTC.

What makes the Nasdaq different from an organized exchange? On the NYSE, one specialist handles all transactions in a particular stock, but on the Nasdaq system, a number of dealers handle ("make a market in") a security. For instance, about 40 dealers make a market in Apple Computer stock. Thus, dealers compete, improving investors' ability to get a good price.

Market Conditions: Bull Market or Bear Market?

bull markets

Markets in which securities prices are rising.

bear markets

Markets in which securities prices are falling.

Two terms that often appear in the financial press are "bull market" and "bear market." Securities prices rise in **bull markets.** These markets are normally associated with investor optimism, economic recovery, and government action to encourage economic growth. In contrast, prices go down in **bear markets.** Investor pessimism, economic slowdown, and government restraint are all possible causes. As a rule, investors earn better returns in bull markets; they earn low, and sometimes negative, returns in bear markets.

Bull and bear market conditions are hard to predict. Usually, they can't be identified until after they begin. Over the past 50 years, the stock market has generally been bullish, reflecting general economic growth and prosperity. Bull markets tend to last longer than bear markets. The bull market that started in 1982 lasted a full five years, and the bear market that preceded it lasted just over a year and a half. The longest bull market on record began in October 1990 and was still going strong in fall 1999.

Regulation of Securities Markets

The securities markets are regulated by both state and federal governments. The states were the first to pass laws aimed at preventing securities fraud. But most securities transactions occur across state lines, so federal securities laws are more effective. In addition to legislation, the industry has self-regulatory groups and measures.

Securities Legislation   The *Securities Act of 1933* was passed by Congress in response to the 1929 stock market crash and subsequent problems during the Great Depression. It protects investors by requiring full disclosure of information about new securities issues. The issuer must file a *registration statement* with the Securities and Exchange Commission (SEC), which must be approved by the SEC before the security can be sold.

The *Securities Exchange Act of 1934* formally gave the SEC power to control the organized securities exchanges. The act was amended in 1964 to give the SEC authority over the OTC market as well. The amendment included rules for operating the stock exchanges and granted the SEC control over all participants (exchange members, brokers, dealers) and the securities traded in these markets.

insider trading

The use of information that is not available to the general public to make profits on securities transactions.

The 1934 act also banned **insider trading,** the use of information that is not available to the general public to make profits on securities transactions. Because of lax enforcement, however, several big insider trading scandals occurred during the late 1980s. The *Insider Trading and Fraud Act of 1988* greatly increased the penalties for illegal insider trading and gave the SEC more power to investigate and prosecute claims of illegal actions. The meaning of insider was expanded beyond a company's directors, employees, and their relatives to include anyone who gets private information about a company.

Other important legislation includes the *Investment Company Act of 1940,* which gives the SEC the right to regulate the practices of investment companies (such as mutual funds), and the *Investment Advisers Act of 1940,* which requires investment advisers to disclose information about their background. The *Securities Investor Protection Corporation (SIPC)* was established in 1970 to protect customers if a brokerage firm fails by insuring each customer's account for up to $500,000.

circuit breakers

Measures that, under certain conditions, stop trading in the securities markets for a short cooling-off period to limit the amount the market can drop in one day.

Self-Regulation   The investment community also regulates itself, developing and enforcing ethical standards to reduce the potential for abuses in the financial marketplace. The National Association of Securities Dealers (NASD), the parent organization of the Nasdaq-Amex Market Group, oversees the nation's 5,600 brokerage firms and more than half a million registered brokers. It develops rules and regulations, provides a dispute resolution forum, and conducts regulatory reviews of member activities for the protection and benefit of investors.

In response to "Black Monday"—October 19, 1987, when the Dow Jones Industrial Average plunged 508 points and the trading activity severely overloaded the exchange's computers—the securities markets instituted corrective measures to prevent a repeat of the crisis. Now, under certain conditions, **circuit breakers** stop trading for a short cooling-off period to limit the amount the market can drop in one day. For instance, the NYSE circuit breakers stop trading for an hour if the Dow Jones Industrial Average drops 250 points and two hours if it falls another 150 points.

c o n c ə p t   c h ə c k

- Describe the organized stock exchanges. How does the OTC market differ from them? What role does each type of market play?
- What is insider trading, and how can it be harmful?
- Briefly describe the key provisions of the main federal laws designed to protect securities investors. How does the securities industry regulate itself?

HOW TO BUY AND SELL SECURITIES

>lg 5

Before investing in securities, investors must select a stock brokerage firm, select a stockbroker at that firm, and open an account. Investors should seek a broker who understands their investment goals and can help them pursue their objectives.

Investors can open two basic types of accounts at a brokerage firm: cash accounts and margin accounts. With a *cash account*, security purchases are paid for in full (cost of the securities plus commissions). In a *margin account*, the investor puts up only 50 percent of the cost of the securities. He or she borrows the balance from the broker and pays interest on the loan. The broker holds the securities as collateral for the loan.

Securities Transaction Basics

When investors decide to buy or sell securities, they place their order with their broker, who makes the transaction. For an organized exchange like the NYSE, the broker transmits the order to the exchange, where it is sent to the trading floor for execution. To make transactions in the Nasdaq/OTC market, the broker uses a computer to find out who deals in the security. She or he then contacts the dealer offering the best price and makes the transaction.

Stocks usually are bought and sold in blocks of 100 shares, called *round lots*. But sometimes an investor can't afford 100 shares of a stock. A purchase of less than 100 shares is called an *odd lot*. Because only round lots are traded on the exchanges, odd lots are grouped together to make up a round lot. An extra fee is charged for odd-lot transactions.

Investors can place three basic types of orders when buying or selling securities. A *market order* is an order to buy or sell a security immediately at the best price available. A *limit order* is an order to buy a security at a specified price (or lower) or to sell at a specified price (or higher). The trade is executed only if the requested limit is reached. With a *stop-loss order*, the stock is sold if the market price reaches or drops below a specified level. A stop-loss order limits an investor's loss in the event of rapid declines in stock prices.

Brokerage firms are paid commissions for executing clients' transactions. Although brokers can charge whatever they want, most firms have fixed commission schedules for small transactions. These commissions usually depend on the value of the transaction and the number of shares involved.

Online Investing

Although traditional brokerage firms still dominate the investment industry, more and more investors are using online brokerage firms for their securities transactions. Improvements in Internet technology make it possible for investors to research, analyze, and trade securities online. Since 1996, an estimated 7 million investors have opened online brokerage accounts. More than 100 online brokerage firms now account for about 14 percent of all trading activity and about 30 percent of individual investor trades, posing a major threat to established brokerage firms.

The Internet has also made a wealth of financial information, once available only to professionals, immediately accessible to individual investors. (We'll discuss online sources of investment information later in the chapter.) As a result, online brokerages are especially popular with "do-it-yourself" investors who choose their own stocks and don't want to pay a broker for advisory services they do not use. Many online firms charge extra for research and other services such as paper confirmations of trades. Lower transaction costs are a major benefit. Fees at online brokerages range from $8 to $20 to buy 200 shares of a $20 stock, compared to at least $116 at a traditional firm.

At first, full-service brokerage firms like Merrill Lynch resisted the move to the Internet. As many of their customers began shifting some or all of their trading to companies like Ameritrade, Charles Schwab, Datek, DLJDirect, and E*Trade Group, the full-service firms began adding some form of online trading services.

The increasing competition for investors will benefit consumers, whether they invest online or through human brokers. To build market share, both types of brokerage firms will need new products, services, and pricing options. Already, online brokerages are adding services such as research, access to initial public offerings for individual investors, and analytic tools for investment analysis and financial planning. They have also reduced the likelihood of system crashes by adding capacity to handle larger transaction volumes and installing "fault-tolerant" computer systems.

Traditional firms are looking for ways to increase their value-added services and retain their wealthiest customers. Prudential Securities, for example, introduced a program for some customers that separates the financial advisory and execution services. It charges a management fee based on account size and a flat per-trade transaction fee, whether executed through a broker or online.[5]

An as-yet unresolved issue is the regulation of online brokerages. Using an online brokerage is so easy and convenient that many investors, especially novices, do not properly consider the risks. Complaints to the SEC are on the rise. Some investors have sued online firms for allowing the investors to make unsuitable investments. The SEC is increasing its oversight of online brokerages, and the firms are looking at various ways to regulate themselves.

concept check

- Differentiate between cash and margin brokerage accounts.
- What are the three types of orders investors can place to trade securities?
- How are online brokerage firms changing the investment industry?

POPULAR SOURCES OF INVESTMENT INFORMATION

Good information is a key to successful investing. Knowledge of current market conditions and investment options should increase returns. Individual investors can now benefit from the type of information formerly available only to investment professionals. The following sections describe commonly used sources of investment information.

Economic and Financial Publications

Two of the best-known publications for economic and financial information are *The Wall Street Journal*, the weekday newspaper providing the most complete and up-to-date coverage of business and financial news, and *Barron's*, a weekly newspaper that carries detailed company analyses. Other excellent sources are magazines such as *Business Week, Kiplinger's Personal Finance, Forbes, Fortune, Smart Money, Worth*, and *Money*. Newspapers in most cities have sections with business news. Subscription advisory services also offer investment information and recommendations. Moody's, Standard & Poor's, Morningstar, and Value Line Investment Survey are among the best known. Each offers a wide range of services. Numerous investment newsletters also give subscribers market analyses and make specific buy and sell recommendations.

Online Information Resources

There has been a virtual explosion of online investment Web sites over the past five years. Invest-O-Rama, an Internet directory for investors, now links

> m a k i n g   e t h i c a l   c h o i c e s <

A STOCK ANALYST'S TALE

Sean Ryan, who is employed by Bear Stearns as a research analyst of bank stocks, knows all too well "what can happen to an analyst who rocks the boat too hard, regardless of his skill at picking stocks or sniffing out details about the companies he covers." Ryan issued his initial report on First Union, the nation's sixth largest bank, in mid-January of 1999. In the highly favorable report, Ryan described First Union – a fixed-income securities trading client of Bear Stearns – as "one of the best operating banks around." Two weeks later First Union announced that its earnings would not meet expectations. Embarrassed and angry, Ryan grew increasingly skeptical about First Union's prospects unless the bank's current management changed. Ryan began listing First Union as his leading takeover candidate.

Soon afterward, Ryan was ordered by his boss to avoid writing or saying anything negative about First Union or its top management. About the same time, First Union withdrew its trading business from Bear Stearns. Since then First Union and Bear Stearns have restored their trading relationship. As of late August 1999, Ryan has not issued any further reports on First Union. However, analysts employed by other securities firms have been openly critical of First Union's revenue and earnings performance—and they were not being reined in by their employers.

Critical Thinking Questions

1. Is it ethical for research analysts in the securities industry to be openly critical of a company that they have analyzed when that company also does business with their employer?
2. Did Bear Stearns' management act ethically in ordering Sean Ryan to avoid making any negative statements about First Union?

Start your online exploring at Invest-o-Rama, **www. investorama.com/**, which offers everything from articles to annual reports.

with more than 11,754 investment Web sites in 141 categories—up from just 200 sites in 1995. But do not confuse this volume of information with good information! "Buyer beware" is certainly appropriate advice when using investment information from the Internet. Standards for accuracy and integrity are lax, and conflict-of-interest policies are rare. That glowing report on a stock investment could be written by owners of the stock who will profit by pushing up the price.

Despite these cautions, the Internet has many valuable investment resources, such as those listed in Exhibit 22-3. Some offer current economic and business news, others allow you to track investment performance, and some provide databases of information that allow investors to screen (filter) vast amounts of information to make stock or mutual fund selections.

Security Price Quotations

>lg 7

The security price quotations in *The Wall Street Journal* and other financial media provide a wealth of current information. The quotations typically report the results of the previous day's trading activity. Stock brokerage firms have electronic quotation systems that give up-to-the-minute prices. Investors with a

> e x h i b i t   2 2 - 3 <

Online Sources of Investment Information

Worth Magazine's Favorite Investment Sites*

Briefing.com	www.briefing.com
FreeEdgar	www.freeedgar.com
Microsoft Investor	www.investor.com
Morningstar	www.morningstar.net
The Motley Fool	www.fool.com
Stock Detective	www.stockdetective.com
The Street.com	www.thestreet.com
The Wall Street Journal Interactive Edition	www.wsj.com
Yahoo! Finance	quote.yahoo.com

Investment Tracking Sites

INVESTools	www.investools.com
Quicken	www.quicken.com
Reuters MoneyNet	ww.moneynet.com
Thomson Investors Network	www.thomsoninvest.net
Yahoo! Finance	quote.yahoo.com

Stock and Mutual Fund Screening Sites

America Online Stock Screening	www.aol.com
TIP@Wallstreet '98 with ProSearch	www.wallstreetcity.com
MSN MoneyCentral Investor	moneycentral.msn.com
Mutual Funds—Fund Selection System	www.mfmag.com
NetScreen on Marketguide.com	www.marketguide.com
SmartMoney.com—Fund Finder	www.smartmoney.com
Standard & Poor's Personal Wealth	www.personalwealth.com
Stock-Screener On-Line	www.stockscreener.com
Wall Street City	www.wallstreetcity.com
Zacks Analyst Watch	www.zacks.com

*Leland Montgomery, "Dive Right In," *Worth* (Special Issue, 1998), pp. 22–31.

personal computer can subscribe to special services, such as Prodigy and Dow-Jones News/Retrieval, that also give current stock quotations, and now many of the sites listed in Exhibit 22-3 provide up-to-the-minute quotations.

Stock Quotations   Prices for NYSE, AMEX, and Nasdaq stocks are all quoted the same way: in sixteenths of a dollar, shown as fractions. (A change to decimal pricing, which is used in other global markets, is under consideration.) Exhibit 22-4 shows a portion of the July 2, 1999 stock quotations for NYSE-listed stocks, as they appeared in *The Wall Street Journal* on July 6, 1999. These quotations show not only the most recent price, but also the highest and lowest price paid for the stock during the previous 52 weeks, the annual dividend, the dividend yield, the price/earnings ratio, the day's trading volume, high and low prices for the day, and the change from the previous day's closing price. The

price/earnings (P/E) ratio
The current market price of a stock divided by its annual earnings per share.

price/earnings (P/E) ratio is calculated by dividing the current market price by annual earnings per share. A company's P/E ratio should be compared to those of other companies in the same industry.

To understand how to read stock quotations, follow the listing for the common stock of Hormel Food Corp. in Exhibit 22-4, highlighted in yellow. Over the previous 52 weeks, the stock traded at a high of 40⅝ ($40.625) and a low of 25¹¹⁄₁₆ ($25.6875). It paid annual dividends of $.66, a 1.7 percent dividend yield. (Note that these columns are blank for HollywdPk (Hollywood Park), a firm that doesn't pay a dividend.) On July 2, Hormel Food's P/E ratio was 21, and

> e x h i b i t 2 2 - 4 <

Listed Stock Quotations for July 2, 1999

Stock split, stock dividend, or cash dividend of 10% or more in past 52 weeks

Annual and quarterly reports available through the WSJ

Newly issued stocks within past 52 weeks

High and low prices for previous 52 weeks

52 Weeks											
Hi	Lo	Stock	Sym	Div	Yld %	PE	Vol 100s	Hi	Lo	Close	Net Chg
17⅛	8	HollywdPk	HPK		...	23	1150	16⁹⁄₁₆	16	16⁵⁄₁₆	− ⁵⁄₁₆
38⁷⁄₁₆	18	Holophane	HLP		...	21	663	38¼	38	38¹⁄₁₆	− ¹⁄₁₆
s 67¹⁵⁄₁₆	31⅝	HomeDepot	HD	.16f	.3	55	18721	64³⁄₁₆	63⅛	64	+ ⅜
29⅛	21³⁄₁₆ ♣	HomePropNY	HME	1.92	7.1	19	401	27¼	27⅛	27³⁄₁₆	− ¹⁄₁₆
10³⁄₁₆	4¹⁄₁₆	Home Base	HBI		...	12	1082	6⅜	6	6¹⁄₁₆	− ⁵⁄₁₆
15	7½	Homestake	HM	.10	1.2	dd	4098	8¼	8¹⁄₁₆	8³⁄₁₆	− ⅛
13¹⁵⁄₁₆	**2⅛**	**HmstdVlg**	**HSD**		...	...	570	2⁹⁄₁₆	2⅜	2⅜	− ⅛
32⅞	19¾	HonInd	HNI	.38	1.4	18	127	28¼	27⅝	27¹³⁄₁₆	− ¹⁄₁₆
94	51⁵⁄₁₆ ♣	HondaMotor	HMC	.19e	.2	...	142	87¼	86⅝	87⅛	+ ¾
125⅜	58⅝ ♣	Honeywell	HON	1.16	1.0	25	5355	116¾	115⅜	115⅜	− ¹⁵⁄₁₆
28¾	15⅞	HK Telcm	HKT	1.10e	4.1	...	947	27¹⁄₁₆	26⅝	27¹⁄₁₆	− ¹⁄₁₆
35¾	20¼ ♣	HoraceMn	HMN	.37	1.4	15	1102	27⅛	26¾	26⅞	− ¹⁄₁₆
40⅝	25¹¹⁄₁₆	HormelFood	HRL	.66	1.7	21	1107	39³⁄₁₆	38⁵⁄₁₆	38⅜	− ¾
34⁹⁄₁₆	23¹³⁄₁₆	HsptlyProp	HPT	2.72f	10.0	13	866	27½	27³⁄₁₆	27⁵⁄₁₆	...
n 26	24⅞	HsptlyProp	pfA	.51p	...	...	32	25⅜	25⅜	25⅜	− ¹⁄₁₆

Abbreviated company name

Symbol for the company

Annual dividends per share for past 12 months

Dividend yield (annual dividend as percentage of price per share)

Price/earnings ratio

$$\left(\frac{\text{market price}}{\text{annual earnings per share}} \right)$$

Volume of shares traded on given day, in hundreds

High and low prices for day's trading

Closing (final) price for day

Net change from previous day's closing price

110,700 shares (1,107 × 100) were traded. The stock traded at a high of 39³⁄₁₆ ($39.1875), a low of 38⁵⁄₁₆ ($38.3125), and closed at 38⅜ ($38.375). The closing (final) price was 75 cents, or ¾ of a point, below the previous day's closing price.

Preferred stocks are listed with common stocks. The letters *pf* or *pr* after the company's name identify a preferred stock, as in the "HsptlyProp pfA" listing in Exhibit 22-4. The exhibit also explains other symbols used in stock quotes.

Bond Quotations   Bond quotations are also included in the *Wall Street Journal* and other financial publications. Exhibit 22-5 shows quotations for NYSE bonds trading on July 2, 1999. The labels indicate how to interpret the quotations. The numbers after the issuer's name are the coupon (interest) rate and maturity. For the highlighted DukeEn (Duke Energy) issue, "7½ 25" means that this bond has a fixed annual interest rate of 7.5 percent and that it matures in the year 2025. Many companies have more than one issue of bonds outstanding. Notice that GMA has nine different bond series listed.

> e x h i b i t   2 2 - 5 <

Corporate Bond Quotations for July 2, 1999

Labels	Bonds	Cur Yld.	Vol.	Close		Net Chg.
Abbreviated company name, coupon interest rate, and maturity date	DukeEn 7½25	7.6	46	99–	⅞	
	GMA 9⅝00	9.4	50	102⁹⁄₁₆		...
	GMA 9⅜00	9.3	5	101	–	⅜
Current interest yield	GMA 7s02	6.9	40	101½	+	⅝
	GMA 6⅝02	6.6	6	100¼	–	¼
	GMA 5⅞03	6.1	6	97	–	½
	GMA 6⅛08	6.4	5	96	+	2
Number of bonds traded	GMA dc6s11	6.7	20	89⅛	–	¾
	GMA zr12	...	3	377		...
	GMA zr15	...	34	314⅛	+	1⅛
	GenesisH 9¾05	12.1	5	80½		...
Closing price for the day	GtNoR 2⅝10	3.9	3	66½	+	½
	Hallwd 7s00	7.5	30	93	–	½
	Hlthso 9½01	9.4	20	101⅛	–	1⅛
	Hexcel 7s03	cv	14	87		...
Net change in closing price since previous day	Hilton 5s06	cv	19	92	–	1

Means this is a deep discount bond

Means this is a zero-coupon issue

Means this is a convertible issue

> e x h i b i t   2 2 - 6 <

Mutual Fund Quotations for June 30, 1999

Fund Name	Objective	Minimum $ Invest.	Assets ($Mil)	Max. Sales Charge Initial	Max. Sales Charge Exit	Annual Exp As %	NAV $ 6/30	Second Quarter	Year-to-Date	One Year	Three Years†	Five Years†
HEARTLAND FUNDS ☎ 800-432-7856												
High Yield Muni Bond	HM	1K	102	No	No	0.76	10.19	−0.6	1.2	4.2-A	NS	NS
US Govt Secs	LG	1K	52	No	No	0.78	9.52	−1.5	−2.6	1.3-C	7.3-A	6.7-C
Large Cap Value	GI	1K	10	No	No	0.00	12.61	14.4	8.0	3.9-E	NS	NS
Mid Cap Value	MC	1K	22	No	No	1.25	11.27	11.4	−3.6	−18.6-E	NS	NS
Sht Dur Hi Yld Muni	HM	1K	164	No	No	0.62	9.87	0.2	1.7	3.0-B	NS	NS
Value	SC	1K	1,287	No	No	1.15	32.71	21.7	11.7	−4.8-D	9.1-C	13.8-D
Value Plus	EI	1K	170	No	No	1.24	14.73	18.7	9.1	−2.0-E	13.8-E	15.8-E
WI Tax Free	SS	1K	147	No	No	0.80	10.24	−1.4	0.1	2.7-A	6.1-B	6.6-B
HENLOPEN ☎ 800-922-0224												
Henlopen Fund	GR	10K	57	No	No	1.50	19.84	13.2	14.8	16.4-D	17.5-E	23.5-C
HENSSLER ☎ NA												
Equity	GR	NA	16	No	No	NA	12.17	NA	NA	NA	NA	NA
HERITAGE FUNDS ☎ 800-421-4184												
Aggr Growth;A	CP	1K	23	4.75	No	NA	20.76	16.7	14.8	NS	NS	NS
Aggr Growth;C †	CP	1K	11	No	1.00	NA	20.62	16.4	14.4	NS	NS	NS
Capital Apprec;A	CP	1K	163	4.75	No	1.41	28.53	10.8	14.0	26.0-B	32.3-A	26.2-B
Capital Apprec;B	CP	1K	18	No	5.00	2.01	27.75	10.6	13.6	25.2-B	NS	NS
Capital Apprec;C †	CP	1K	31	No	1.00	2.00	27.73	10.7	13.6	25.2-B	31.6-A	NS
Growth Equity;A	GR	1K	53	4.75	No	1.38	39.13	4.3	15.8	27.9-A	33.5-A	NS
Growth Equity;B	GR	1K	11	No	5.00	2.11	38.08	4.1	15.4	26.9-A	NS	NS
Growth Equity;C †	GR	1K	59	No	1.00	2.13	38.07	4.1	15.4	26.9-A	32.5-A	NS
High Yield;A	HC	1K	38	3.75	No	1.19	9.41	−1.0	0.6	−2.6-C	7.1-D	7.8-D
Income-Growth;A	EI	1K	68	4.75	No	1.29	16.40	6.9	7.4	5.6-E	15.4-E	17.6-D
Income-Growth;C †	EI	1K	30	No	1.00	2.04	16.20	6.7	7.0	4.9-E	14.5-E	NS
Int Mat Gov;A	IG	1K	12	3.75	No	0.92	9.18	−0.8	−1.7	3.4-A	5.7-D	5.6-E
Eagle Intl Eqty;Eagle †	IL	50K	32	No	No	2.60	28.66	3.2	4.0	4.7-C	10.0-C	NS
MidCap Growth;A	MC	1K	15	4.75	No	1.60	16.21	7.6	2.3	4.7-D	NS	NS
MidCap Growth;C †	MC	1K	10	No	1.00	2.35	16.01	7.4	1.8	3.9-D	NA	NS
Small Cap Stk;A	SC	1K	158	4.75	No	1.22	26.87	21.6	7.1	−8.5-D	9.3-C	17.6-B
Small Cap Stk;B †	SC	1K	11	No	5.00	1.98	26.01	21.4	6.7	−9.2-D	NA	NA
Small Cap Stk;C †	SC	1K	79	No	1.00	1.97	26.02	21.4	6.7	−9.2-D	8.5-D	NS
Value Equity;A	GI	1K	17	4.75	No	1.45	20.73	10.4	7.1	7.0-E	14.4-E	NS
Value Equity;C †	GI	1K	13	No	1.00	2.20	20.48	10.2	6.8	6.2-E	13.5-E	NS

Callout labels (left margin):
- Net asset value
- Investment objective
- Indicates additional sales charges to buy fund
- Fund name
- Minimum required investment
- Total value of assets in fund
- Total return data from Lipper Analytical Services: year-to-date, periodic return, performance rank

Callout labels (bottom):
- Annual expense ratio
- Means there is no sales charge; offer price is same as NAV
- Indicates redemption fee to sell fund

Bond prices are expressed as a percentage of the face value (principal). A closing price above 100 means the bond is selling at more than its face value (at a *premium*). A closing price below 100 is less than the face value (the bond is selling at a *discount*). The price of the DukeEn bond on July 2 is 99, or $990; it is trading at a discount. Treasury and other government bonds are also listed in the securities quotations pages. Their listings are similar to corporate bond listings.

Mutual Fund Quotations The mutual fund quotations shown in Exhibit 22-6 are the ones that appear the first of each month in *The Wall Street Journal.* Less comprehensive quotations that include net asset value, net change in NAV from the previous day, and year-to-date percent return appear daily in *The Wall Street Journal* and in most major newspapers. Mutual fund share prices are quoted in dollars and cents and trade at their NAV, or **net asset value,** the price at which each share of the mutual fund can be bought or sold. The exhibit explains other items in the quotes, such as fees, total assets, and annual expense ratio.

Market Averages and Indexes

"How's the market doing today?" This question is commonly asked by people interested in the securities market. An easy way to monitor general market conditions is to follow market averages and indexes, which provide a convenient way to gauge the general mood of the market by summarizing the price behavior of securities. **Market averages** use the arithmetic average price of groups of securities at a given point in time to track market movements. **Market indexes** measure the current price behavior of groups of securities relative to a base value set at an earlier point in time. The level of an average or index at any given time is less important than its behavior—its movement up and down over time.

The most widely used market average is the **Dow Jones Industrial Average (DJIA).** It measures the stock prices of 30 large, well-known NYSE corporations, listed in Exhibit 22-7. The companies in the DJIA are chosen for their total

net asset value (NAV)
The price at which each share of a mutual fund can be bought or sold.

market averages
Summarize the price behavior of securities based on the arithmetic average price of groups of securities at a given point in time; used to track market conditions.

market indexes
Measures of the current price behavior of groups of securities relative to a base value set at an earlier point in time; used to track market conditions.

Dow Jones Industrial Average (DJIA)
The most widely used market average; measures the stock prices of 30 large, well-known corporations that trade on the New York Stock Exchange.

> e x h i b i t   2 2 - 7 <
The Dow Jones Industrial Average Then and Now: The Original 12 and Current 30 Stocks

Original 12 Dow Jones Stocks	Today's 30 Dow Jones Stocks	
American Cotton Oil	Allied Signal	Home Depot
American Sugar Refining Co.	Aluminum Co. of America (ALCOA)	IBM
American Tobacco	American Express	Intel
Chicago Gas	AT&T	International Paper
Distilling & Cattle Feeding Co.	Boeing	Johnson & Johnson
General Electric Co.	Caterpillar	McDonald's
Laclede Gas Light Co.	Citigroup	Merck
National Lead	Coca-Cola	Microsoft
North American Co.	Walt Disney	Minnesota Mining
Tennessee Coal, Iron & Railroad Co.	DuPont	J.P. Morgan
U.S. Leather	Eastman Kodak	Phillip Morris
U.S. Rubber Co.	Exxon	Procter & Gamble
	General Electric	SDC Communications
	General Motors	United Technologies
	Hewlett Packard	Wal-Mart Stores

Standard & Poor's 500 stock index

An important market index that includes 400 industrial stocks, 20 transportation stocks, 40 public utility stocks, and 40 financial stocks; includes NYSE, AMEX, and Nasdaq companies.

concept check

- What are four popular sources of investment information? What information do they provide?
- What type of investment information can investors find on the Internet? What are the positive and the negative aspects of using Internet sources of investment information?
- What role do market averages and indexes play in the investment process? How do they differ? Distinguish between the Dow Jones Industrial Average and the Standard & Poor's 500 stock index.

market value and broad public ownership. It is calculated by adding the closing price of each of the 30 stocks and dividing by the DJIA divisor, a number that changes over time to adjust for events such as stock splits.

The DJIA changes daily. If the DJIA closes at 10,500 one day and at 10,620 the next, the typical stock in the index would have moved up by 1 percent [(10,620 − 10,500) ÷ 10,500]. The DJIA exceeded 11,000 for the first time in July 1999. There are three other Dow Jones averages: a 20-stock transportation average, a 15-stock utility average, and a composite average based on the stocks in all three averages. Dow Jones introduced its World Index in January 1993 to provide a way to measure international stock performance. It tracks 2,200 companies in 120 industry groups. Recently, Dow Jones added the Dow Jones Internet Index, composed of e-commerce and Internet service companies.

An important market index is the **Standard & Poor's 500 stock index.** The S&P 500 is broader than the DJIA. It includes 400 industrial stocks, 20 transportation stocks, 40 public utility stocks, and 40 financial stocks. In addition to NYSE-listed companies, the S&P 500 also includes a number of AMEX and Nasdaq stocks. Many market analysts prefer the S&P 500 index to the DJIA because of its broad base. It is calculated by dividing the sum of the closing market prices of the 500 stocks by the sum of the market values of those stocks in the base period and multiplying the result by 10. Like the DJIA, the S&P 500 is only meaningful when compared to index values at other time periods. The S&P MidCap 400 Index tracks stocks of medium-size companies. It is composed of about 66 percent NYSE companies, 31 percent Nasdaq companies, and 3 percent AMEX companies.

CAPITALIZING ON TRENDS IN BUSINESS

>lg 8

As described earlier in the chapter, advances in information technology have revolutionized the securities markets. Wall Street's brokerage firms, investment bankers, and stock exchanges—historically the core of the securities industry—are being challenged by the Nasdaq system, the emergence of online brokerage firms, and electronic exchanges. In addition, technology is empowering individual investors, who now have access to many of the same tools as institutional investors.

Market Competition Heats Up

Whereas the NYSE was once the undisputed leader among stock exchanges, the Nasdaq has successfully challenged its position. The largest electronic exchange in the world, Nasdaq captured 56 percent of total U.S. trading volume in 1998, compared to the NYSE's 42 percent—reversing their positions of five years earlier. The Nasdaq lists 5,125 companies versus 3,110 on the NYSE. The average Nasdaq share price increased from $25.16 to $31.30 in 1998, while the average NYSE share price fell from $42.68 to $41.80.

As a result, the competition between the two institutions is intense. Each promotes itself as the best place for a major corporation to list its securities. The NYSE touts its prestige, which in 1998 helped convince 68 Nasdaq and 17

AMEX companies to switch their listings to the NYSE. Even though it spent millions on new information technology and uses order-matching technology for almost half its trades, the NYSE still lags behind the Nasdaq and major foreign exchanges technologically, however.[6]

The Nasdaq, calling itself "The market for the next 100 years" due to its emphasis on technology, merged with the AMEX in early 1999 to create what it termed a "market of markets." They will operate as separate markets under the management of the Nasdaq-Amex Market Group, a new subsidiary of the National Association of Securities Dealers, Inc. (NASD). This merger could pressure the remaining regional exchanges to find partners.

HOT links

Visit the Web site for the first cooperative venture by major securities markets—Nasdaq and Hong Kong—at

porttracker.nasdaq-sehk.com/default.asp

Threatening both the NYSE and the Nasdaq is the emergence of other electronic exchanges called *electronic communications networks (ECNs)*. ECNs allow institutional traders and some individuals to make direct transactions, without using brokers, securities exchanges, or the Nasdaq, in what is called the *fourth market*. Because they deal mostly in Nasdaq stocks, ECNs are taking trading volume away from the Nasdaq. ECNs are most effective for high-volume, actively traded stocks. Money managers and institutions such as pension funds and mutual funds with large amounts of money to invest like ECNs because they cost less than other trading venues.[7]

Starting in April 1999, the SEC allowed ECNs to register as exchanges. Orders could bypass members of the NYSE entirely. Discount brokerage firm Datek Online was the first to petition the SEC to turn its ECN, Island, into a self-regulated stock exchange. Niphix Investments, the ECN described in the Focusing on Small Business box, specializes in helping small companies go public.

Rise of the Individual Investor

Stock ownership is no longer reserved for wealthy individuals and large institutions. People in a wide range of age groups and income levels are participating in the securities markets. In 1960, less than 20 percent of households owned stocks. By 1989, the figure had grown to 31 percent, and today it's over 40 percent. In addition, almost 40 percent of today's investors are under 35 years old.

Although institutional investors continue to be a force in the securities markets, individual investors are now making their own decisions rather than following the crowd. When the market dropped 540 points in October 1997, individuals continued to buy—even though institutional investors were selling. Several trends are responsible for the increasing influence of the individual investor:[8]

Contributing to the growing number of individual investors are discount brokerages and online trading firms as well as home computers, the Internet, and sophisticated financial software.

- The proliferation of mutual funds offers small investors the ability to acquire a diverse group of securities with a limited amount of money.

GOING DIRECT WITH NIPHIX

Companies that are too small to trade in the OTC market no longer have to wait to qualify for Wall Street to tap the equity markets. Electronic trading networks like Niphix Investments provide an alternate route to the capital markets.

Niphix—itself a small company—is the first Internet-based direct stock market. "We cater to companies that are too small for Nasdaq, but we hope they can grow at Niphix," says Nimish Ghandi, Niphix's founder. At Niphix, microcap companies (with a market capitalization—the value of their equity—under $50 million) find services designed for their needs. Niphix helps small companies market and sell their stock without using an underwriter. Such issues are called direct public offerings (DPOs). Niphix's goal is to be a starting point for high-growth companies that will eventually move up to the more established exchanges.

To be listed on Niphix, a company must agree to full disclosure, including quarterly and annual audited reports using GAAP accounting (generally accepted accounting principles). Standard & Poor's has agreed to cover all companies listed with Niphix.

Investors who want to buy and sell shares in Niphix-listed companies simply open a standard brokerage account with Niphix. Unlike similar trading systems, Niphix operates a matching system rather than acting as an intermediary. Buyers and sellers conduct their own online negotiations until they agree on a price. Then Niphix immediately executes the trade using its staff of registered brokers. Niphix also offers low transaction fees, ranging from $24 to $44.

Niphix is still young, and it is too soon to know if it will improve the liquidity of shares of companies going the DPO route. Thus far, the number of companies and investors using Niphix remains small. Tom Stewart-Gordon, editor of a DPO report, believes that investors who buy DPO shares focus on the company's products or philosophy rather than its liquidity. Supporters of exchanges like Niphix think that having a place to sell their securities will encourage more investors to consider DPOs.

Critical Thinking Questions

1. What advantages does Niphix offer a small company?
2. If you were a company owner planning to go public, would you consider Niphix? Justify your answer.
3. How does the availability of research reports for Niphix companies from a major firm like Standard & Poor's help both Niphix and the companies?

c o n c ə p t   c h ə c k

- Discuss the rivalry between the NYSE and the Nasdaq. If you were on the board of a major corporation, where would you want your stock to be traded, and why?
- How has technology increased competition among the securities exchanges?
- Summarize the reasons for the increasing influence of the individual investor.

- New products and services, such as discount brokerages and on-line trading, have reduced the cost of owning stocks directly.
- Technology—personal computers, sophisticated financial software, and the Internet—is bringing investing knowledge within the reach of millions of investors and making it easier and less costly for the average person to invest.
- The responsibility for managing retirement funds is shifting to individuals because fewer companies have pension plans that guarantee their employees a fixed retirement income.
- The dramatic rise of stock prices during the 1990s—average annual growth of 17 percent—has brought more people into the market.

APPLYING THIS CHAPTER'S TOPICS

After reading this chapter, you may be ready to join the millions of people who are putting their savings to work by investing in stocks and bonds. The basic introduction to the securities markets and various types of investments presented here is a good starting point. But you may be wondering whether this is the right time to invest and how to use the convenience of online investing to your advantage.

The Time Is Now

As the bull market continued and the Dow Jones Industrial Average reached ever higher levels, many investors wondered if they had waited too long and missed the boat. Was the market too high to buy stocks?

These investors were falling prey to some common mistakes of novice investors. For one thing, they got caught up in the mystique of the DJIA. Although it is the most publicized market indicator, it represents the activity of just 30 large industrial stocks. A milestone on the DJIA is just another number. The DJIA doesn't tell investors where the market is going or how long it will stay at a particular level. More than 8,000 companies trade on the NYSE and the Nasdaq, including small and mid-size firms whose movements are not reflected in the Dow.

Another mistake is trying to time the market. Although every investor dreams of buying a stock at its low point and selling it at its peak, predicting the market's ups and downs is impossible. In fact, studies prove that the returns of hypothetical investors who bought on the lowest day of each year were not much better than those who bought on the highest day.

The key is not so much *when* you invest as that you do indeed invest—and for the long term. It's more important to start investing and to let your investments grow. You don't want to be like the many investors who put off investing because they thought the market was too high in 1998—and watched it continue to climb throughout 1999.

The best time to buy equities is *now*. Financial advisers suggest investing small amounts over time. Start early and invest regularly, whether the market is up or down. Don't immediately panic if the market takes a nosedive. The highs and lows will average out over time, and you'll find yourself with long-term gains.[9]

Tips for Online Investing

Online investing can be quite appealing. The transaction costs are low, and you can do your research at any hour. However, online investing also carries risks. You don't have the safety net of a live broker suggesting that you rethink your trade. Before venturing into the world of online investing, you should follow some commonsense rules.

- *Do your homework.* Don't make investment decisions based only on what you find at a Web site, read on a bulletin board, or get from a chat room. It's easy to be taken in by someone hyping a stock. To avoid investment scams, do your own research. The company should be registered with the SEC. In addition to the sites listed in Exhibit 22-3, find the latest news articles on the company in major business publications or at their Web sites.

1. **Compare brokerages** Visit the sites of two on-line brokerages, such as Charles Schwab (**www. schwab.com**), E*Trade (**www.etrade.com**), Discover Brokerage (**www.discoverbrokerage.com**), Datek Online (**www.datek.com**), or any others you know. Compare them for ease of use, quality of information, and other criteria you select. To check out the firms, use a ratings service such as Gomez Advisors' Internet Broker Scorecard, **www.gomez.com**, and Motley Fool Brokerage Center, **www.fool.com**. Summarize your findings. Which firm would you prefer to use, and why?

2. **Track stock prices** Pick a portfolio of five companies in at least three different industries. Choose companies you know, read the financial press to find good candidates, or try one of the stock screening sites in Exhibit 22-3. Set up a table to track the stock prices. Record the end-of-month prices for the past six months and track the daily price movements for at least two weeks (longer is even better!). Also monitor economic and market trends and other events that affect market conditions. Share the performance of the portfolio with your classmates. Explain your basis for selecting each stock and analyze its price changes.

- *Pick the right online broker.* Know your investment needs and choose a brokerage firm that can help you meet them. A day trader, for example, wants low-cost, fast trades but doesn't care about research. A long-term investor wants a firm that offers timely information, research, and quick, reliable trades. The same online firm may not be good for both.

- *Use limit orders.* If you place a market order, the brokerage buys the stock for you—no matter what the price. With a limit order, you specify the highest price you will pay. This protects you in rapidly rising markets. For example, theGlobe.com announced its initial public offering (IPO) at $9. It reached a high of $90 during its first trading day. People who placed market orders thinking they would pay around $9 a share got a shock when their orders were executed at a much higher level. Some tried to cancel the orders but couldn't get through to their brokers. After situations like this, Charles Schwab now requires limit orders for online IPO purchases on the first day of trading.

- *Open accounts at two brokers.* This protects you if your online brokerage's computer system crashes or gives you an alternative if one brokerage is blocked with heavy trading volume.

- *Double-check orders for accuracy.* It's very easy to make typos or use the wrong stock symbol.[10]

Remember, if it sounds too good to be true, it probably is!

SUMMARY OF LEARNING GOALS

>lg 1   **What is the function of the securities markets?**
Securities markets allow stocks, bonds, and other securities to be bought and sold quickly and at a fair price. New issues are sold in the primary market. After

>looking ahead

at Charles Schwab & Co.

Charles Schwab & Co. continues to develop its online strategies. The company now bridges the online and traditional investing worlds. It offers investors other investing channels—an extensive network of branch offices and phone representatives—but "the Net is totally embedded in the center of our business," says co-CEO Pottruck. Schwab will face increasing competition as more companies enter the online market. Even venerable Merrill Lynch, one of the last holdouts, has announced plans to offer online services. With over 6 million active accounts, including 2.5 million online accounts, Schwab will be hard to catch, however. The company continues to upgrade its IT infrastructure to keep up with the phenomenal growth of online investing. By 2000, it expects that at least 80 percent of its trades will take place over the Web, at a rate of 4 million transactions an hour.

Because competition is just a click away, Schwab is strengthening customer relationships and building loyalty. It is forming partnerships to become a one-stop financial center for its customers, offering more information and choices. For example, Schwab teamed up with Excite and Intuit to share financial planning content. "Companies don't own the customer anymore, so trying to build walls around the customer is not going to work," says co-CEO Pottruck.[11]

that, securities are traded in the secondary market. Investment bankers specialize in issuing and selling new security issues. Stockbrokers are licensed professionals who buy and sell securities on behalf of their clients.

>lg 2 How do common stock, preferred stock, and bonds differ as investments?

Common and preferred stocks represent ownership—equity—in a corporation. Common stockholders have voting rights, but their claim on profits and assets ranks behind that of holders of other securities. Preferred stockholders receive a stated dividend. It must be paid before any dividends are distributed to common stockholders.

Bonds are a form of debt and may be secured or unsecured. Bondholders are creditors of the issuing organization, and their claims on income and assets rank ahead of those of preferred and common stockholders. The corporation or government entity that issues the bonds must pay interest and repay the principal at maturity.

Common stocks are more risky than preferred stocks and bonds. They offer the potential for increased value due to growth in the stock price and income through dividend payments. But neither dividends nor price increases are guaranteed. Preferred stocks are usually bought for their dividend income rather than price appreciation. Bonds provide a steady source of income and the potential for price appreciation.

>lg 3 What other types of securities are available to investors?

Mutual funds are financial service companies that pool the funds of many investors to buy a diversified portfolio of securities. Investors choose mutual funds because they offer a convenient way to diversify and are professionally managed. Futures contracts are agreements to buy or sell specified quantities of commodities or financial instruments at an agreed-on price at a future date. They are very risky investments because the price of the commodity or financial instrument may change drastically. Options are contracts that give the holder the right to buy or sell specified quantities of common stock or other financial instruments at a set price during a specified time. They, too, are high-risk investments.

>lg 4 Where can investors buy and sell securities, and how are these securities markets regulated?

Securities are resold on organized stock exchanges, like the New York Stock Exchange and regional stock exchanges, and in the over-the-counter market, a telecommunications network linking dealers throughout the United States.

KEY TERMS

bear markets 658
bond ratings 654
bull markets 658
circuit breakers 659
convertible bonds 652
debentures 652
Dow Jones Industrial Average (DJIA) 667
futures contracts 665
high-yield (junk) bonds 652
insider trading 659
institutional investors 649
interest 652
investment bankers 650
market averages 667
market indexes 667
mortgage bonds 652
municipal bonds 653
mutual fund 654
National Association of Securities Dealers Automated Quotation (Nasdaq) system 658
net asset value (NAV) 667
options 00
organized stock exchanges 657
over-the-counter (OTC) market 658
price/earnings (P/E) ratio 664
primary market 649
principal 652
secondary market 649
secured bonds 652
securities 649
Standard & Poor's 500 stock index 668
stockbroker 650
underwriting 650

The most actively traded securities are listed on the Nasdaq system, so dealers and brokers can perform trades quickly and efficiently.

The Securities Act of 1933 requires disclosure of important information regarding new securities issues. The Securities Act of 1934 and its 1964 amendment formally empowered the Securities and Exchange Commission and granted it broad powers to regulate the organized securities exchanges and the over-the-counter market. The Investment Company Act of 1940 places investment companies such as mutual funds under SEC control. The securities markets also have self-regulatory groups like the NASD and measures such as "circuit breakers" to halt trading if the Dow Jones Industrial Average drops rapidly.

>lg 5 **How do investors open a brokerage account and make securities transactions?**
Investors must first choose a brokerage firm and a stockbroker in that firm. Then they open a cash account or a margin account. In a cash account, all securities transactions are paid in full. Margin accounts allow investors to put up 50 percent of the price of the securities and borrow the rest from the broker. The investor gives an order to buy or sell securities to the broker, who sends it to the stock exchange to be carried out or, in the case of an over-the-counter stock, finds the dealer with the best price. Today more and more investors are using online brokerage firms for their security transactions.

>lg 6 **Which sources of investment information are the most helpful to investors?**
The most popular sources of investment information are economic and financial publications like *The Wall Street Journal, Barron's, Business Week, Fortune, Smart Money,* and *Money.* The newest sources of information include the numerous Internet sites. Other sources are subscription services and investment newsletters and security price quotations.

>lg 7 **What can investors learn from stock, bond, and mutual fund quotations?**
Stock quotations show the highest and lowest prices paid for the stock during the previous 52 weeks, the annual dividend, the dividend yield, the price/earnings ratio, the day's trading volume, the closing price, high and low prices for the day, and the change from the previous day's closing price. Bond quotations show the coupon interest rate, maturity date, current yield, trading volume, closing price, and change in closing price from the previous day. Mutual fund quotations provide the fund's net asset value, net change in NAV from the previous day, and year-to-date percent return.

>lg 8 **What are the current trends in the securities markets?**
The securities markets and investment industry are in the midst of considerable change. No longer does the New York Stock Exchange dominate equity market activity. The Nasdaq is challenging the Big Board, and the emergence of electronic exchanges could further alter the market positions of these two securities marketplaces. The individual investor is becoming a market force due to improved technology, the relative ease of online investing, and the move toward self-management of retirement funds.

PREPARING FOR TOMORROW'S WORKPLACE

1. You have just won $100,000 in your state lottery. In light of your personal situation (age, finances, family status, and so on), what types of securities would you choose, and why?
2. Now that you, as a lottery winner, have chosen some possible investments, you have to find a broker to execute the transactions. But should you use a

traditional full-service brokerage, a discount broker, or an online brokerage? Using the Internet and personal finance publications to gather information, compare the services of these types of firms. Summarize the pros and cons of each and decide which best meets your needs. Justify your choice.

3. Divide the class into two groups to debate direct ownership of securities versus mutual fund ownership. Afterwards summarize your discussions, including the advantages and disadvantages of each. For whom are mutual funds a good investment, and why?

4. About 5,000 companies have gone public during the bull market of the 1990s. However, a sizable percentage have failed, and many are trading below their offering prices despite substantial gains in the early days of their lives as public companies. Research the trends in the IPO marketplace from 1995 to 2000. Then select two IPO success stories and two failures. Prepare a report for the class on their performance. What lessons about the securities markets can you learn from their stories? Is it better to wait longer to go public or to use one of the alternative exchanges like Niphix to go public while the firm is still fairly small?

5. While having dinner at a Manhattan restaurant, you overhear two investment bankers at the next table. They are discussing the takeover of Bellamco Industries by Gildmart Corp., a deal that has not yet been announced. You have been thinking about buying Bellamco stock for a while, so the next day you buy 500 shares for $30 each. Two weeks later, Gildmart announces its acquisition of Bellamco at a price of $45 per share. Have you fairly earned a profit, or are you guilty of insider trading? What's wrong with insider trading?

WORKING THE NET

1. At the Vanguard Online University, **www.vanguard.com/educ/univ.html**, you'll find a course called "The Fundamentals of Mutual Funds." Use it to learn about the basics of mutual funds. Prepare a presentation for the class based on the materials.

2. Compare the listing requirements of the NYSE, Nasdaq, and AMEX using the information at their Web sites: **www.nyse.com/public/listed/3b/3bix.htm** and **www.nasdaq-amex.com/mktofmkts/listing_information.stm**. What types of companies qualify for listing on each exchange? Why do the Nasdaq and AMEX offer alternative listing standards?

3. You've been asked to address your investment club on socially responsible investing and how companies qualify as socially responsible. Research this topic at the Web sites of the Social Investment Forum, **www.socialinvest.org**, and Co-op America, **www.coopamerica.org**. Prepare a detailed outline of the key points you would include in the speech. How can your personal financial decisions have a positive impact on communities and the environment? Do you support socially responsible investing?

4. Become a pro at researching companies on the Web. Take the tutorial on Researching Companies Online at **home.sprintmail.com/~debflanagan/index.html**, and then go to BizInfo (**www.hbs.edu/applegate/bizinfo3/**) for a guide to conducting business research on the Internet. Put your newfound skills to use by researching the investment potential of a company of your choice.

5. Go to Niphix, **www.niphix.com**, and try the demonstration of the Niphix Trading System. How does the Niphix System compare to using an investment banker for an IPO and an organized exchange for secondary trading?

CREATIVE THINKING CASE

Nonstop Trading

For many do-it-yourself investors, the normal trading day—9:30 A.M. to 4:00 P.M. Eastern time for the NYSE and Nasdaq—is not long enough. Now that they can research companies online at all hours, they want to manage their portfolios when they get home from work or react to late-breaking news outside normal trading hours. West Coast investors, for whom regular trading ends at 1:00 P.M. Pacific time, have long been unhappy about losing afternoon trading hours. Day traders, who buy and sell stocks the same day to capture tiny differences in stock prices, also want longer hours.

In 1999, brokers rushed to respond to the demand for longer trading hours by tapping into the resources of electronic stock trading systems. Datek was one of the first, extending its trading day with a 4:00 P.M. to 5:15 P.M. Eastern time session. Discover Brokerage and Dreyfus Brokerage Services added a session from 6:00 P.M. to 8:00 P.M. Eastern time. E*Trade allowed individual investors to join major traders such as mutual fund managers and institutional investors and trade from 4:00 P.M. to 6:30 P.M. through Instinet, a major ECN. "What our customers want is access to opportunity and a level playing field with larger institutional investors," says Christos Cotsakos, chairman of E*Trade. "It's all part of democratizing personal investing."

Following suit, the NYSE and Nasdaq announced plans for longer hours as well. Starting in fall 1999, investors could trade 100 of the largest Nasdaq stocks during a 5:30 P.M. to 10:00 P.M. after-hours session. The NYSE delayed the introduction of after-hours trading for about 500 of its stocks until 2000. By limiting trading to major companies, these exchanges hope to generate sufficient demand to avoid sharp price swings.

Not everyone is in favor of after-hours trading sessions, however. Conditions in after-hours trading could be different from regular daytime trading sessions. Prices could be more volatile, increasing the risk for small investors. As Alan Davidson, president of the Independent Broker-Dealer Association, says, "It extends the stock market into a casino . . . and emphasizes short-term over long-term investment."

Critical Thinking Questions

1. What are some of the advantages and disadvantages of extended trading hours?
2. Do you think it's important to have a "resting period" to allow investors to reflect on the day's market activity?
3. Why are smaller online brokerages and ECNs in the forefront of the push toward longer trading hours, while the NYSE and Nasdaq are following a more conservative approach?

VIDEO CASE

The Edward Jones Co.: An Unusual Brokerage Niche

In 1922, Edward D. Jones Sr. founded a brokerage firm in St. Louis, Missouri. In 1943, he merged the firm with Whitaker & Co., a bond dealer that was founded in 1871. The Edward Jones Co. continued to grow. For years it was a typical Wall Street brokerage firm, dealing extensively with large institutional investors. Then in 1955, Edward D. Jones Jr. embarked on a new course for the brokerage firm.

The younger Jones "believed that individuals should have easy access to professional investment advice [and] that individual investors would be best served by someone who lived and worked in their community—someone who could become well-acquainted with their individual financial needs and goals." This belief in individualized service became the basis of the company's philosophy and "has helped [it] carve an unusual niche."

The company's one-on-one, personalized service appeals to investors in smaller communities as well as larger metropolitan areas. Today, the Edward Jones Co. (**www.edwardjones.com**) has more than 4,600 offices in small, medium, and large communities throughout all 50 states. The company also has more than 190 offices in Canada and more than 50 offices in the United Kingdom.

Edward Jones is the only major financial services firm that is exclusively aimed at smaller, individual investors and business owners. More specifically, the company targets retired investors, working investors, tax professionals and attorneys, and small business owners. Edward Jones leaves the "large, institutional investors to other firms."

The Edward Jones Co. provides investment services to its targeted clientele through a branch office network and a comprehensive IT system. Branch offices are located where people live and work rather than in "downtown office high-rises or major financial centers." Account representatives in the branch offices seek to promote long-term relationships with their customers. The representatives also strive to ensure that customers are comfortable with and confident about their investment decisions.

Through its IT system, the Edward Jones Co. provides customers with a variety of services to simplify management of their investments. These services include:

- Real-time pricing information and execution of investment transactions within seconds.
- The same financial information that is available in the financial centers.
- An extremely broad selection of high-quality investment alternatives.
- Research reports on the stocks of hundreds of companies.
- Easy-to-comprehend customer statements.
- Consolidated statements to simplify tax preparation.
- Historical pricing information to assist customers in addressing tax questions.
- Personalized reports to aid customers in planning for their financial goals.

The various features of Edward Jones's business philosophy and business practices combine to create a special approach for dealing with each of the firm's investment clients. From the company's perspective, this special approach can be summed up in four words: quality, relationships, involvement, and service.

Critical Thinking Questions

1. The Edward Jones Co. targets retired investors, working investors, tax professionals and attorneys, and small business owners and leaves the "large, institutional investors to other firms." In your opinion, is this a wise market segmentation strategy?
2. What value does Edward Jones's IT system provide for its customers?
3. How do you think the trend toward online investing will affect Edward Jones's strategy of providing one-on-one, personalized investment services?

chapter twenty-three

Managing Your Personal Finances

learning goals

>lg 1   What is the personal financial planning process, and how does it facilitate successful financial management?

>lg 2   How can cash flow planning and management of liquid assets help you meet your financial goals?

>lg 3   What are the advantages and disadvantages of using consumer credit?

>lg 4   What are the major types of taxes paid by individuals?

>lg 5   What is the most important principle in deciding what types of insurance to purchase?

>lg 6   What personal characteristics are important when making investment decisions?

>lg 7   What are the emerging trends in personal financial planning?

Appendix:

>lg 8   What is risk and how can it be managed? What makes a risk insurable?

>lg 9   What types of insurance coverage should businesses consider?

When Planning Pays Off

Lounging on the floor of their near-empty living room, Todd and Amy lift their plastic glasses in a toast. "To our first home!" Todd and Amy Murray of Austin, Texas, are among the 66 percent of U.S. households who own homes, which may make them appear normal. But the achievement of home ownership is anything but an everyday accomplishment for a couple in their mid-20s. Only 37 percent of households between the ages of 25 and 29 are home-owners.[1] Todd and Amy did not win the lottery or receive a large inheritance. They did not empty a trust fund, nor did they borrow the down payment from their parents. For Todd and Amy, purchasing their first home was the result of careful planning and financial sacrifice. Months before their wedding, Todd and Amy developed a spending plan for their wedding and honeymoon. And before they were married, they listed and prioritized their financial goals: short-term goals like suits for job interviews, long-term goals like retirement, and mid-term goals like the house they purchased this very afternoon.

"By knowing what we really wanted to accomplish with our money, we were able to manage our money instead of letting it manage us," says Todd. "I am the one who spends impulsively. Electronic equipment for myself, jewelry for Amy—you name it and I like it. But we figured out what we really wanted to achieve financially and how much we had to save to accomplish those goals within our time frame. Knowing the money was being set aside for important things—like this house—made it easier to forgo spending."

"It was hard sometimes," Amy chimes in. "I remember about three years ago when our best friends all went skiing over the holidays. It would have been so easy to just 'charge it,' but we needed to reduce our debt to qualify for a home mortgage loan. Many times we would have much rather gone out to eat than fix dinner at home. But thanks to our list of goals and a spending plan, look where we are today! In our very own home!"

Critical Thinking Questions

As you read this chapter, consider the following questions as they relate to Todd and Amy:

- How did the financial planning process help Todd and Amy purchase their first home?

- What investment instruments are appropriate for mid-term goals such as saving for a house? Will Todd and Amy want to reconsider their investment strategy now that they have purchased their house?

- Now that they have purchased a home, what new financial priorities do Todd and Amy face in the area of insurance?

BUSINESS IN THE 21ST CENTURY

Perhaps more than any recent generation, young adults like Todd and Amy are interested in financial planning and know that it is important to their future success. Many factors, both demographic and economic, have contributed to this interest in financial planning:

- As a result of having children later in life and increased longevity, more families (now called sandwich families) find themselves financially responsible for both their children and their aging parents at the very time in their lives when they hoped to retire.

- Divorce and remarriage are creating an increasing number of blended families.

- A significant number of single individuals are solely responsible for their own finances.

- Although unemployment is at a record low, large numbers of people have experienced job loss due to the corporate downsizing of the 1980s and 1990s.

- The average cost of raising a child to age 18 for a middle-income family is now $153,660; the cost of a college education averages $8,822 per year at a public university and $22,055 at a private one.[2]

- Employees are increasingly responsible for accumulating their own retirement funds.

Factors influencing the heightened interest in financial planning include higher costs in raising children and paying for their education, taking financial responsibility for aging parents, and planning for one's own retirement years.

- People have more financial products from which to choose and an overwhelming amount of financial information to help them make those choices.

This chapter will introduce you to the information and skills needed to meet the many challenges of managing your own finances. First, we'll show you how the personal financial planning process can help you meet your financial goals. Next we'll turn to managing your personal cash flow, and describe various types of savings instruments. Then we'll explain how to use consumer credit wisely. The focus next shifts to managing taxes and selecting insurance. Then we'll discuss how to set investment goals and develop an investment strategy. Finally, we'll consider emerging trends in personal finance.

FINANCIAL PLANNING AND CASH MANAGEMENT

>lg 1

personal financial planning
The process of managing one's personal finances to achieve financial goals.

Personal financial planning is the process of managing one's personal finances to achieve financial goals. The reason the process is so important in managing your finances is that it starts with your goals and then logically proceeds through information gathering, analysis of the data, and then the development, implementation, and monitoring of a financial plan designed to meet your goals. Exhibit 23-1 illustrates the personal financial planning process.

The Personal Financial Planning Process

6. **Monitor the plan.** You will need to review the performance of the savings/investment vehicles used in the plan, look at your goals to see if they have changed since you developed the plan, and remain up-to-date on the financial environment.

5. **Implement the plan.** Put the plan into action. You may need the help of experts to implement more complicated plans.

4. **Develop a plan.** Normally, there will be more than one way to meet your goals, so you must consider the various alternatives and decide on the best plan for you.

3. **Analyze the information.** Now it is time to analyze the data and revise your goals if necessary.

2. **Gather information.** Both objective and subjective information is necessary to make decisions.

1. **Establish financial goals.** These goals will provide the road map that helps guide your spending and saving decisions.

The Cash Flow Plan

cash management
The day-to-day handling of one's liquid assets.

liquid assets
Cash and other assets that can be converted into cash quickly at little or no cost, such as checking accounts.

cash flow plan
A cash management tool that includes a plan for managing income and expenses, including contributions to savings and investments needed to accomplish one's financial goals; often called a *budget*.

Cash management is generally defined as the day-to-day handling of one's liquid assets. **Liquid assets** include cash and other assets that can be converted to cash both quickly and at little or no cost, such as checking accounts and various savings instruments. A **cash flow plan** (often called a *budget*) is an important tool for cash management and includes a plan for managing income and expenses, including contributions to savings and investments needed to accomplish one's financial goals. The following steps will help you develop and utilize a cash flow plan:

- *Establish your goals and calculate how much you need to save to meet them.* For goals to be useful, you must identify each goal, estimate how much money it will take to accomplish the goal, and specify the time frame for the goal. It is also helpful to prioritize your goals because you will often have more goals than you have money.

- *Estimate your income and your expenses, including any contributions to savings.* Evaluate your monthly income and estimate your monthly expenditures. The monthly budget worksheet in Exhibit 21-5 in Chapter 21 illustrates one way to monitor your income and expenses. You can also create a spreadsheet that covers several months.

- *Track your actual income and expenses for a one-month period.* Write down all your income and expenses. Carry a pad of paper with you so you don't forget the numerous small expenditures you make. At the end of the month, total the income and expenses for each category and enter them on Exhibit 21-5 in the "actual" column.

- *Compare your planned and actual income and expenses.* Analyze each category that was either over or under your estimate in the "planned" column. For example, if you planned to spend $150 on clothing but actually spent $285, determine whether this was an unusual situation (you needed a suit for an unexpected interview) or a normal pattern of spending. If you

find that it was normal, decide whether you want to cut back your expenditures on clothes or increase your clothing budget for the next month. Of course, if you add $135 to the clothing category, you will need to reduce something else by that same amount.

- *Modify your estimates for the next month and repeat the process.* Depending on your analysis, you will want to make some changes in your original plan. You must be flexible as it may take several months before you are actually able to live within your cash flow plan. But within a short period of time, you will be in control of your spending and saving.

Your computer can simplify the personal financial planning process, as the Applying Technology box on p. 684 explains.

net worth statement
A summary of a person's financial situation on a given day; provides information about assets and liabilities.

The Net Worth Statement

While cash flow management will help you live within your means, a **net worth statement** provides information about your assets and liabilities. As Chapter 19 explained, *assets* are the things you own. They are valued at their current market value on a personal net worth statement. *Liabilities* are what you owe, and they are recorded at the amount you would have to pay if you paid off the entire debt immediately. A net worth statement is a snapshot of your financial situation on a given day whereas a cash flow statement reflects the flow of funds over a period of time. Exhibit 23-2 is an example of a net worth statement. Note that if you complete a net worth statement regularly, perhaps annually, you will be able to track your financial progress. It's like taking a picture of a baby at 3 months, 6 months, 9 months, and a year. Each picture captures a point in time, but the series of pictures shows change.

Checking Accounts

Checking accounts and savings accounts are the most common liquid assets held by consumers. A *check* is a written order, drawn on a depository institution by a depositor, ordering the depository institution to pay on demand a specific amount of money to the person or firm named on the check. You will probably find that a checking account is a necessity in managing your income and expenses. Several types of checking accounts are widely available to meet the diverse needs of consumers. These were described in Chapter 20.

To research interest rates for liquid assets, consumer credit, and home mortgages, check the Bank Rate Monitor site at
www.banxquote.com

Electronic Fund Transfers Regardless of the type of checking account you select, you will probably be offered *electronic fund transfer (EFT) services.* EFT allows you 24-hour access to cash through an *automated teller machine (ATM)* and *point-of-sale (POS)* transfers for retail purchases with a debit card. With an ATM you can withdraw cash, make deposits, or transfer funds between accounts using your ATM card and your personal identification number (PIN). You pay for goods and services with a POS transfer using your debit card. It works very much like a credit card with one important exception—the money for the purchase is transferred immediately (or very shortly) from your checking account to the vendor's account.

Net Worth Statement

Name ___Jay Martin_____

Date _2/3/98_   Date _2/3/99_   _Change_____

ASSETS			
Liquid assets			
Checking accounts	$ 1,230	$ 895	$ (335)
Savings/money market accounts	385	1,546	1,161
Money market mutual funds			
Certificates of deposit (6 months)			
Cash on hand	76	153	77
Other _____			
Other investment assets			
Certificates of deposit (>6 months)	500	1,000	500
Mutual funds		2,421	2,421
Stocks			
Bonds			
Other _____			
Personal assets			
Automobile	5,346	3,421	(1,925)
Furniture and appliances	3,460	8,000	4,540
Clothing	2,000	4,000	2,000
Other _____			
Other _____			
(1) Total assets	$ 12,997	$ 21,436	$ 8,439
LIABILITIES			
Bills past due			
Credit cards	$ 857	$ 472	$ 385
Auto loans	2,569		2,569
Appliance/furniture loans			
Mortgage loans			
Education loans	9,365	8,593	772
Other _____			
Other _____			
(2) Total liabilities	$ 12,791	$ 9,065	$ 3,726
NET WORTH (1 – 2)	$ 206	$ 12,371	$ 12,165

Using these cards requires good management skills. With both ATM and POS transactions, be sure to enter withdrawals in your check register or you will have checks bouncing all over town! Also guard your cards so that they will not be stolen and fraudulently used. This is especially important with POS (debit) cards because they can be used without a PIN. According to federal regulations, if your ATM or debit card is lost or stolen, you can be responsible for up to $50 if you report the loss within 2 business days, up to $500 if you report it between 3 and 60 days, and for an unlimited amount if you wait more than 60 days to report the loss. Also watch the ATM fees charged by your bank and by the institutions that own the machines you use. The average fee for withdrawing cash is currently $1.40, and these fees can really add up if you make several small withdrawals.[3] You can usually reduce or eliminate ATM fees by using your own bank's ATMs.

MANAGING YOUR PFP FROM YOUR PC

Technology has made huge contributions in many areas of personal financial planning (PFP). Software packages as well as online programs can help you select and track investments (as discussed in Chapter 22), file income taxes, and make numerous types of financial decisions. However, true financial management software is multidimensional—as broad-based as the individuals who use it and the decisions they want to make. Most experts agree that currently two software packages in particular do a great job in meeting these comprehensive financial needs. Microsoft's *Money* seems to be a slight favorite for computer or financial management beginners, and Intuit's *Quicken* is favored (again slightly) for more sophisticated users.

What do these programs do? Both *Money* and *Quicken* provide the ability to organize all of your assets and liabilities: your checkbook, savings accounts, brokerage accounts, credit cards, and loans. They also perform basic budgeting and record keeping (if you are brave enough to learn how you are really spending your money!). Both programs have debt-reduction managers that can suggest the smartest way to pay off debt and then tell you how much interest you will save and when you will be out of debt.

And there are reports galore! For Robert James, a senior at the University of Texas-Austin, it is the reports that make *Quicken* so useful. He generates pie charts that tell him the percentage of expenditures going to various budget categories and monthly reports that compare actual to projected expenditures by category. The newest versions of *Quicken* and *Money* also have alerts that will tell you when your stock reaches a certain price and will "nag" you when an expenditure cat-

egory has been exceeded—again! (The alerts can be turned off, however.)

Depending on your needs, there are basic and deluxe versions of both *Quicken* and *Money*. The deluxe versions come with tax, budget, and financial planning information; electronic bill paying; banking and online brokerage access; and links to the Web for investment tools and research. They also include calculators to assist with retirement planning, loan amortization, mortgage refinancing, and other common financial issues.

As with any software, these packages are limited by the information you input. According to Molly Johnson, a junior at Michigan State University, when she and her husband Toby ran their first month's reports, they found that 45 percent of their expenditures were in a category called ATM. "We were going to the ATM for cash very frequently and not keeping track of what we did with the cash," Molly says. "Before *Money* could help us get a better picture of our finances, we had to keep better records." Molly and Toby started writing more checks and keeping receipts for their cash expenditures. That way they could enter the expenditures into more meaningful categories and get a better idea of where their money was going.

Critical Thinking Questions

1. Would you use a software program to manage your personal finances, or do you think it's easier to use traditional methods for this job? What advantages does technology provide?
2. List several ways *Money* or *Quicken* could help you organize your finances.

Account Reconciliation   According to a recent survey, 42 percent of college students balance their checkbooks monthly, and you should be one of these students![4] This important task will uncover any mistakes you or the bank made as well as help you discover fraudulent debit card withdrawals. It can also help avoid overdrafts (bounced checks), which can be both expensive and embarrassing. Exhibit 23-3 lists the steps to follow in balancing your checkbook.

Savings Instruments

Checking accounts are excellent for money that you will need very soon, but savings instruments are more appropriate for accumulating money for short-term

> e x h i b i t   2 3 - 3 <

Seven Steps to a Balanced Checkbook

1. If you receive canceled checks, arrange them in numerical order.
2. Compare each check (or check entry on your bank statement) with the entry in your checkbook to make sure the dollar amounts agree. Place a checkmark next to each item compared. Repeat this same process for all other withdrawals (including ATM and cash withdrawals).
3. List and total all withdrawals that are still outstanding, that is, those deducted in your checkbook but not returned (or listed on your bank statement).
4. Repeat steps 2 and 3 for all of your deposits.
5. Subtract the total amount of checks outstanding from your bank statement, and add the total amount of deposits outstanding to this balance. This is your *adjusted bank balance.*
6. Subtract any bank service charges and add any interest earned to your checkbook balance. This is your *adjusted checkbook balance.*
7. Compare the adjusted bank balance with the adjusted checkbook balance. They should be the same. If not, check your subtraction and addition and then recheck the deposit and withdrawal amounts entered in your checkbook. If you cannot find an error, consult the bank to see if it made an error in your account.

c o n c ə p t   c h ə c k

- What are the five steps to follow when setting up and using a cash flow plan?
- What important management skills are required when using ATMs and making POS transfers?
- What type of savings instrument would be best for a student who currently has $250 to deposit in savings but wants to add $50 monthly to the account? Why?

goals (like a new television or holiday spending) and for unexpected expenses (emergencies and opportunities). Banks, thrift institutions, and credit unions offer a variety of savings instruments, as described in Chapter 20. Exhibit 23-4 summarizes the features of the most popular savings instruments.

Before selecting a savings vehicle, consider your goals and how you want to use the instrument. Regardless of the type of instrument you select, you should compare the interest rate you will receive with that paid by other institutions. Rates are always changing, but there are several excellent sources of information including financial institutions, magazines such as *Kiplinger's Personal Finance* and *Money,* and the Internet.

> e x h i b i t   2 3 - 4 <

Features of Popular Savings Instruments

Savings Instrument	Minimum Deposit	Interest Earned	Penalty for Early Withdrawal	Check-Writing Privileges	Federally Insured
Savings account	$5–$50	~2%	No	No	Yes
Certificate of deposit	$100 and higher	~5%	Yes, not appropriate for deposit and withdrawal activity	No	Yes
Money market deposit account	$500–$2,500	~3%	No	Yes, but limited	Yes
Money market mutual fund	$500–$2,000	~5%	No	Yes, but limited	No, but considered safe

USING CONSUMER CREDIT

>lg 3

Using credit to make purchases is really just the opposite of saving money to buy things. We have discussed how to set goals and then save using various types of instruments so that you have the funds to meet your future needs. But what if you want (or have) to make a purchase before you have accumulated the money? You might use a credit card or a loan to make the purchase and then pay interest to the lender for the privilege of borrowing the money. In this section, we will investigate the positive and negative aspects of using consumer credit, look at various types of credit, and learn how to build a positive credit rating.

The Pros and Cons of Using Credit

There are a number of very good reasons for using consumer credit:

- Convenience
- Immediate use of a good or service
- Bargain prices on sale merchandise
- Better service (because the seller doesn't have your money)
- Opportunity to establish a credit rating
- Convenient record keeping
- Payment for financial emergencies
- Perks such as rebates and frequent flyer miles

Although not as numerous, there are also important disadvantages to using consumer credit:

- It's easy to overspend.
- Most types of credit cost money in the form of interest charges.
- Merchandise may cost more.
- The legal commitment to repay debt reduces future discretionary income.

The ability to overspend, especially because credit cards are so convenient to use, can be the most devastating disadvantage. According to a recent report released by the Consumer Federation of America, 70 percent of college undergraduates at four-year institutions have at least one credit card. Although more than half of these students pay their credit cards off monthly, the average outstanding debt of students who do not pay their balances in full each month is $2,226. One-fifth of these students report having more than $10,000 of credit card debt.[5] The financial and psychological stress created by this debt forces some students to work more hours or to drop out of college altogether.

The secret of using credit to your advantage is your cash flow plan. Don't buy anything using credit that does not fit into your plan. Use your credit card to make the same purchases you would use cash for, and then pay the total bill at the end of the month. Use a credit card as a source of credit (meaning that you will not pay it off monthly) only when it is really necessary, and then revise your cash flow plan to repay the debt as quickly as possible.

If you currently have outstanding debt, use a form like Exhibit 23-5 to inventory your debt and develop a debt repayment strategy. For Becky Sampson, whose debt inventory is presented in this exhibit, an effective strategy might be to borrow from her personal line of credit (at 12 percent) to pay off her high-interest loans—the credit card balances (18 percent and 21 percent). But Becky must be careful not to run up her credit card balances again after paying them off.

open-end credit

Any type of credit where the borrower applies for the credit and then, if approved, is allowed to use it over and over again; for example, credit cards.

Debt Inventory

Name Becky Sampson	Date 6/10/99				
Type of Debt	**Creditor**	**Annual Rate of Interest**	**Current Monthly Payment**	**Latest Balance Due**	**Comments**
Auto Loans	1 University Federal				
	2 Credit Union	8%	$315	$6,893	Car will be
	3				repossessed if loan
					is not repaid
Education Loans	1				
	2				
Home Mortgage Loan					
Home Improvement Loan					
Other Installment Loans	1				
	2				
Single-Payment Loans	1				
	2				
Credit Cards	1 MasterCard	18%	$22	$716	$1,000 credit line
	2 Visa	21%	$40	$1,608	$2,000 credit line
	3				
	4				
	5				
	6				
	7				
Personal Line of Credit	First National Bank	12%	—	—	$3,500 credit line
Home Equity Credit Line					
Overdraft Protection Line					
Loan on Life Insurance					
Margin Loan from Broker					
Other Loans	1				
	2				
	3				
TOTALS			$377	$9,217	

Credit Cards

line of credit

For credit cards, the maximum amount a person can have outstanding on a card at any one time.

revolving credit cards

Credit cards that do not require full payment upon billing.

Credit cards are the most common type of open-end credit used today. **Open-end credit** includes any type of credit where you apply for the credit and then, if approved, are allowed to use it over and over again. Some credit cards have an annual fee and some do not. You will generally be given a **line of credit,** the maximum amount you can have outstanding at any one time. Some cards require you to pay the entire balance upon billing, but most require only that you make a minimum monthly payment. Those cards that do not require full payment upon billing are called **revolving credit cards.** All will send you a monthly bill, and if you don't pay the entire balance, you will

Open-end credit like revolving credit cards can be a convenient and inexpensive way to buy goods and services provided that the holders pay their balance in full each month when they receive their bill from the credit card issuer.

grace period

The period after a purchase is made on a credit card during which interest is not owed if the entire balance is paid on time.

principal

The total amount borrowed under a loan.

Use the loan calculators offered at **www. investorguide.com** to figure out the monthly payments on various types of loans.

be charged interest. Some (those that do not have a grace period) even charge interest if you do pay the entire bill monthly. The **grace period** gives you a period after making a purchase when you do not pay interest if you pay your total balance on time.

Depending on how they are used, credit cards can be either one of the least expensive ways to make purchases or an extremely expensive method of payment. According to RAM Research, 41 percent of credit card users paid their bills in full in 1997, up from only 29 percent in 1990.[6] These people are called convenience users of credit cards. If they select cards with no annual fee and with a grace period, they get free use of money for a period of time until the bill must be paid. On the other hand, credit card users who pay only the minimum monthly payment can incur high interest charges, as Exhibit 23-6 shows.

Credit card fraud is widespread, so it is important to protect your credit cards and to review your monthly statement carefully. Your card does not even have to be out of your possession for it to be used fraudulently. With just your card number, expiration date, and name, someone can counterfeit your card and make charges. Federal legislation limits your responsibility to the amount charged before you report the problem, up to a maximum of $50 per card. Even though your direct loss is rather low, the thief may tie up your total line of credit for months until the issue is resolved and may use one card to get other cards. And we all pay indirectly for fraudulent charges through higher interest rates and fees.

Loans

Loans differ from credit cards because loans are closed-end agreements. You borrow a specific amount of money, the **principal,** for a stated period of time and agree to pay off the debt either in installments or as a lump sum at the end of the term. Interest will be charged on the amount of the principal borrowed, and you may be required to secure the loan with something of value. An auto loan is an example of a secured, installment loan—you are expected to pay back the loan in equal monthly

> e x h i b i t   2 3 - 6 <

Minimum Payments Don't Pay

Making minimum payments on your credit cards can cost you a bundle over a number of years. Here's what would happen if you paid the minimum—or more—every month on a $2,705 card balance, with an 18.38 percent interest rate.

Payment	How Long to Pay Off	Interest Paid
2% of balance	27 years, 2 months	$11,047
4% of balance	8 years, 5 months	$ 2,707
8% of balance	2 years, 1 month	$ 594

CREDIT CARDS FOR THE MENTALLY DISABLED?

Managing one's personal finances can be challenging, even for someone who has basic financial management skills and can exercise some degree of self-restraint. Managing personal finances can easily and rapidly move from being a challenge to being a disaster for people who do not possess these skills or find it difficult to exercise self-restraint.

The approximately 887,000 mentally disabled adults living on their own are among those who are especially vulnerable to financial difficulties. Not only do they tend to have low incomes, but they often have no opportunity to learn how to manage money.

Many credit card companies now are offering cards to mentally disabled people. The practice raises a number of issues. On the one hand, if the companies do not offer cards, they are denying the mentally disabled the credit that is so essential to the American way of life. Indeed, some states prohibit lenders from discriminating against mentally disabled people in granting credit.

On the other hand, offering credit to those who do not know how to use it or who may not understand how interest is calculated or when late fees and other penalties are imposed can easily lead to financial disaster. Under these circumstances, the independent life that has been carefully constructed for the mentally disabled with the help of family and social workers can be severely shaken, if not destroyed.

Critical Thinking Questions

1. What ethical issues exist with regard to issuing credit cards to mentally disabled people?
2. Do businesses have a moral responsibility not to take advantage of customers who are vulnerable in some way?
3. Should mentally disabled people have the right to manage their own personal finances?

installments, and a lien is placed against the auto so that if you default on the debt, the car will be repossessed. In addition to auto loans, loans are often used to finance a college education, to fix up a home, and to purchase appliances.

Before you apply for a loan, shop around to get the best deal just as you would shop for a product you are purchasing. There are numerous sources of consumer loans. Banks and savings and loan associations offer relatively low interest rates to low-risk borrowers. Credit unions generally offer even lower interest rates, but you have to be a member of the credit union to get a loan there. Consumer finance companies specialize in borrowers who are higher risk, and captive finance companies (Ford Credit Corp. and GMAC) offer credit when you are making a specific type of purchase. A family member may charge the lowest interest rate, but if you decide to borrow money from Grandma, treat the transaction in a business-like manner. Draft a loan repayment agreement specifying the amount being borrowed, the interest rate to be paid (if any), and how the debt will be repaid. Both Grandma and you should sign the agreement and keep a copy. This will help avoid misunderstandings about the terms of the loan.

Three of the most important factors to consider when comparing loans are the dollar cost of credit (finance cost), the annual percentage rate of interest

HOT links

What rates is Ford Motor Credit offering on car loans, and how can you apply? Find out at
www.fordcredit.com

(APR), and the monthly payment. According to the federal Truth-in-Lending Law, lenders must calculate the APR in a standardized way, so, other things being equal, a loan with a lower APR will be less expensive.

But when the term of the loan varies, loans with the same APR will have different monthly payments and finance costs. As you can see from Exhibit 23-7, the longer the term of the loan, the lower the monthly payment—but the higher the finance cost. Selecting a shorter repayment term will save money.

In addition to these factors, check a loan for **prepayment penalties,** additional fees owed if you decide to repay the loan early, and **security requirements,** which allow the lender to take back the collateral if you do not repay the loan according to the terms of the agreement. Also beware of add-ons a lender may offer. For example, **credit life insurance** will repay the loan if you die while the loan is still outstanding. Although this sounds like a good idea, first consider whether you really need life insurance for this purpose. And if you do, find out what the coverage would cost from an insurance agent rather than the lender. The lender offers convenience, but that convenience generally comes at great cost. It is not uncommon to pay 10 times as much for credit life insurance compared to a term life policy purchased through an insurance agent!

Credit History and Credit Ratings

One of the reasons for using credit is to build a good credit rating, but this will be an advantage only if you maintain a clean credit history. Three national credit bureaus—Equifax (800-685-1111), Experian (888-397-3742), and TransUnion (800-888-4213)—collect credit information and make it available for a fee to retailers, banks, and other organizations that are subscribers and approved recipients. The credit bureaus do not evaluate the data, but they do report the following types of credit information for each lender: the date the account was opened; the highest amount of credit extended; the current outstanding balance; the number of times the account has been 30, 60, and 90+ days overdue; and the number of inquiries there have been for this account information. Negative account information can stay in the file for no more than 7 years, 10 years in the case of bankruptcy.

Lenders use information from your credit report as well as other information from your credit application to decide whether to grant credit and under what terms. The better "score" you receive, the more likely you are to be approved for a credit

prepayment penalties

Additional fees that may be owed if a loan is repaid early.

security requirements

Provisions that allow a lender to take back the collateral if a loan is not repaid according to the terms of the agreement.

credit life insurance

Insurance that will repay a loan if the borrower dies while the loan is still outstanding.

To find out how to order a copy of your credit report, visit Experian's Web site at **www.experian.com/ product/consumer/**

> e x h i b i t   2 3 - 7 <

Cost Comparisons of a $20,000, 8 Percent Loan

Number of Payments	Monthly Payment	Finance Cost
36	$627	$2,572
48	488	3,424
60	406	4,360

card or loan and to be offered lower rates of interest. Because the information in your credit bureau file is so important, you should check your file for accuracy periodically. If you will be applying for a loan or if you have been in a dispute with a creditor, request a copy of your credit report from all three major credit bureaus.

If you find inaccurate information in your credit file, report it to the credit bureau. The credit bureau must investigate your dispute within 30 days or remove the disputed item from your file. If the investigation does not resolve your dispute, you may add a brief statement to your file, which must be included in future reports. In addition, credit bureaus must prevent deleted information from reappearing in a credit report, and creditors will be liable if they neglect to correct errors.

concept check

- What are the advantages and disadvantages of consumer credit?
- How can an inventory of your debt help you make better decisions about debt repayment?
- What is a credit bureau, and what function does it perform in the granting of credit?

MANAGING TAXES

>lg 4

In 1998 the average American had to work 131 days to pay for federal, state, and local taxes. Taxes are the largest expenditure category in the average American family's budget, but they are paid incrementally as payroll deductions or as a small percentage of the purchase price of goods and services. Legally, we all have to pay taxes, but a little knowledge on the subject will help keep you from overpaying your taxes. In this section, we will briefly discuss the four types of taxes that are paid directly by individuals: income, Social Security and Medicare, sales, and property taxes.

Income Taxes

Income tax is the largest single tax expenditure for the average American. Because the tax code is very complex, lack of knowledge about federal income taxes is often the reason for the most common financial mistakes. The federal income tax is a **progressive tax,** meaning that the higher your taxable income, the higher the percentage of that income you pay in taxes. Taxpayers in the lowest tax bracket pay 15 percent of taxable income, and higher-income taxpayers pay at rates of 28, 31, 36, and 39.6 percent. As a result of the progressive structure and automatic deductions (the personal exemption and the standard deduction), people with low incomes may pay little or no federal income taxes.

progressive tax

An income tax that is structured so that the higher a person's taxable income, the higher the percentage of income paid in taxes.

Pay-As-You-Go System The federal government expects us to pay both federal income taxes and Social Security taxes (discussed later) as we earn income. This is accomplished through tax withholding by employers and by filing quarterly tax estimates on self-employment, investment, and other income that is not subject to withholding. When you start a new job, your employer will ask you to fill out a W-4 form on which you will report your **filing status** (similar to your marital status) and the number of **withholding allowances** you want to claim. The more withholding allowances claimed, the less your employer will withhold from each paycheck. However, the goal is to have the right amount withheld, so use the W-4 worksheet for guidance.

filing status

The status of a taxpayer as single, married, or some other situation on the income tax return.

withholding allowances

Amounts that are deducted from the income tax that would otherwise be withheld by a taxpayer's employer; vary according to the number of dependents and other criteria.

Minimum Filing Requirements The federal government does not require all income earners to file federal income tax returns. If your income is below the minimum filing requirement in a given year, you do not have to file. If you are entitled to a tax refund, however, you must file to receive the refund.

Taxpayers can claim **personal exemptions** that reduce the amount of income on which they pay taxes. You can take a personal exemption for yourself, your

personal exemptions

Deductions that reduce the amount of income on which income tax is paid. Each taxpayer is entitled to one exemption, but the exemption can be used only once.

standard deduction

An amount that most taxpayers can automatically deduct from their gross income in computing their income tax; not permitted if the taxpayer itemizes deductions.

earned income

Income that is earned from employment such as wages, tips, and self-employment income.

unearned income

Income that is not earned through employment such as interest, dividends, and other investment income.

spouse, and each of your dependents. If you are a taxpayer who is claimed as a dependent by someone else, however, you cannot claim the personal exemption. In 1999 an exemption was worth $2,750. The **standard deduction** is another amount that most taxpayers can automatically deduct from gross income. In 1999 the standard deduction for the two most common filing categories was $4,300 for single people and $7,200 for married couples filing jointly. If a taxpayer elects to *itemize deductions*, the standard deduction would not be permitted.

Filing a Federal Income Tax Return Individuals may use one of three basic forms when filing their income tax returns: the 1040EZ, the 1040A, and the 1040. The 1040EZ and the 1040A are limited to taxpayers with relatively simple finances. In addition, some taxpayers can use the TeleFile system to file their returns by punching in their data on touch-tone phones.

When completing a tax return, you start by listing your gross income. This includes **earned income** (wages, tips, and self-employment income) and **unearned**

Have a tax question? You'll probably find the answer at the IRS Web site:

www.irs.gov

income (interest, dividends, and other investment income). Students must include in gross income scholarship and grant proceeds to the extent that they exceed the direct cost of the education. After totaling your gross income from all sources, the next step is to subtract any legal deductions you are eligible to take: adjustments to gross income, itemized deductions, and tax credits. The adjustments of most interest to the typical young person are for interest paid on student loans, job-related moving expenses, and contributions to Individual Retirement Arrangements (IRAs). In addition, two relatively new tax credits, the HOPE Scholarship credit and the Lifetime Learning credit, provide credits for specified educational expenses.

The tax filing deadline is April 15 of the year following the calendar tax year (April 15, 2000 for the 1999 tax year). If the 15th falls on a weekend, the filing date is the next business day.

Tax Planning As long as your financial life is relatively simple, your biggest tax planning issues will probably be having the correct amount of money withheld and keeping the appropriate tax records. However, once you purchase a home, begin investing, and earn a larger income, tax planning becomes very important. At that point you will need to learn more about the federal income tax law and keep up with the frequent changes made to the law. Although there are numerous popular tax strategies, the two most important are being knowledgeable and maintaining good records.

Social Security and Medicare Taxes

Like income taxes, the Social Security and Medicare taxes are payroll taxes—the tax is deducted from each employee's paycheck. Social Security taxes, often seen on a payroll stub as FICA (Federal Insurance Contributions Act), are paid at a uniform rate on a specified amount of earned income (the wage base). Both the percentage and the wage base can change annually. In 1999 the combined social security and Medicare tax rate was 7.65 percent of the first $72,600 of earned income. In addition, an additional 1.45 percent Medicare tax (Hospital Insurance), is paid on all earned income above 72,600.

If your gross income were $500 for the pay period, $38.25 would be withheld for the Social Security and Medicare tax. Your employer would withhold that amount from your paycheck, match that amount with company funds, and send a total of $76.50 to the Internal Revenue Service (IRS). Self-employed people are responsible for paying both the employee's and the employer's share of this tax by making quarterly estimated payments. They are then allowed to deduct one-half of their Social Security tax as an adjustment to gross income on their federal income tax returns.

Sales and Property Taxes

Two additional types of taxes are sales taxes and property taxes. All but five states (Alaska, Delaware, Montana, New Hampshire, and Oregon) currently have sales taxes on purchased items and some services. In some states, some items are not taxed, most commonly food consumed in the home, prescription drugs, and services such as doctor's fees, haircuts, and laundry bills. Generally, the tax rates range from 4 to 7 percent for the state's share with an additional 1 to 2 percent added by some cities.

Some state and local governments impose a personal property tax on items such as automobiles, boats, and even intangible personal property, but the biggest single property tax for most individuals is on real estate, including a person's home. The property tax (real estate tax) is generally divided among the city, the county, the school system (which gets the largest portion), and in some cases the state government. The annual property tax (often paid in two installments) is calculated by multiplying the appraised (or assessed) value of the property by the tax rate. A house assessed at $100,000 could be taxed at 2 percent of assessed valuation, resulting in an annual tax of $2,000.

concept check

- What is a progressive tax? Explain why the federal income tax is progressive.
- What are the personal exemption and the standard deduction? How do these amounts differ for taxpayers who are dependents as compared to independent taxpayers?
- Briefly describe three other types of taxes besides the income tax.

SELECTING INSURANCE

>lg 5

Financial planning helps us meet our financial goals. With the many uncertainties in life, however, we could suffer major losses from a serious illness, an auto accident, or a fire. Assessing your financial risks and purchasing the appropriate insurance to protect against those risks is therefore an important part of a good financial plan. Insurance planning includes setting priorities for insurance needs and learning about the various types of insurance that are commonly needed by individuals—property and liability insurance, health and disability insurance, and life insurance. The appendix to this chapter covers additional aspects of managing risk and insurance.

Complete your own risk analysis by visiting the University of Illinois site for Developing a Personal Risk Management plan at **www.urbanext.uiuc.edu/risk/index2.html**

Prioritizing Insurance Needs

Before buying an insurance policy, it is important to identify, evaluate, and prioritize your insurance needs. Start by identifying the types of insurable risks you face. For example, if you own a car, you face the risk of being in an accident that is your fault, injuring the other driver and damaging his or her car. You also could damage your own car and hurt yourself. Some of the common insurable risks people face include:

- Property damage to items such as personal property, automobiles, homes, and boats.
- Liability losses due to negligent actions.
- Medical expenses due to illness or accidents.
- Loss of income due to disability or premature death.

Some things, such as a long-term illness, have devastating financial consequences while other events, such as losing your contact lens, are minor. The key to managing your insurance needs in a cost-effective way is to budget for those minor losses. For major losses you can purchase insurance to protect property, health, and life.

Property and Liability Insurance

Property insurance covers financial losses from damage to or destruction of the insured's assets as a result of specified perils, such as fire or theft. *Liability insurance* covers financial losses from injuries to others and damage to or destruction of others' property when the insured is considered to be the cause. It also covers the insured's legal defense fees. The two property and liability policies most often purchased by individuals are automobile insurance and home-owner's/renter's insurance. Nationwide, the average auto insurance premium was $691 in 1996, and the average homeowner's insurance premium was $418.[7]

Automobile Insurance Auto insurance covers financial losses from such perils as accidents, theft, fire, and liability lawsuits. The two main types of automobile insurance are liability coverage and physical damage coverage. **Automobile liability insurance** protects the insured from financial losses caused by automobile-related injuries to others and damage to their property. The maximum payment limits are set for each policy. A $50,000/$100,000/$25,000 policy, for instance, will pay up to $50,000 for each person injured in an accident but a total of no more than $100,000 per accident for personal injuries, no matter how many people are involved. In addition, it will pay a maximum of $25,000 for damage to other people's property.

All 50 states have financial responsibility laws that require drivers to show proof of the ability to pay the costs (up to a limit) of any accidents for which they are responsible. Most drivers buy automobile liability insurance to provide that proof of responsibility.

Automobile physical damage insurance covers damage to or loss of the policyholder's vehicle from collision, theft, fire, or other perils. It includes collision coverage for damage caused by colliding with another vehicle or object and **comprehensive (other-than-collision) coverage** for losses due to perils such as fire, floods, theft, and vandalism.

Automobile insurance rates generally depend on the driver's age, marital status, gender, area of residence, and driving record, as well as the characteristics of the automobile being insured. Young male drivers who live in cities and who have had more than one traffic ticket are charged the highest rates. This group historically has been involved in the most accidents.

Homeowner's/Renter's Insurance Homeowners and renters purchase this insurance to protect themselves against both property damage and liability losses. Originally, it covered only losses due to fires, but coverage has now been extended to include perils such as windstorms, lightning, hurricanes, vandalism, riots, frozen water pipes, and falling airplanes. Special federally subsidized coverage is also available for earthquakes and floods. Homeowners buy coverage for both their homes and their personal property (furniture, clothing, etc.); renter's insurance covers personal property but not the dwelling itself. A standard policy pays only the **actual cash value** (similar to market value) on personal property. **Replacement cost coverage** that provides enough money to replace lost and damaged personal property costs about 10 to 15 percent more.

Homeowners and renters also purchase liability coverage for protection against financial losses arising from their liability for the injury of others. For

---

automobile liability insurance

Insurance that protects the insured from financial losses caused by automobile-related injuries to others and damage to their property.

automobile physical damage insurance

Insurance that covers damage to or loss of the policyholder's vehicle from collision, theft, fire, or other perils; includes collision coverage and *comprehensive (other-than-collision) coverage*.

comprehensive (other-than-collision) coverage

Automobile insurance that covers damage to or loss of the policyholder's vehicle due to perils such as fire, floods, theft, and vandalism; part of *automobile physical damage insurance*.

actual cash value

The market value of personal property; the amount paid by standard homeowner's and renter's insurance policies.

replacement cost coverage

Homeowner's and renter's insurance that pays enough to replace lost and damaged personal property.

example, if you threw a small party where you served liquor and one of your inebriated guests was injured in a fall, you could be held legally liable for the subsequent medical expenses. The comprehensive personal liability coverage purchased as part of a homeowner's policy protects against a wide range of occurrences, both on and off your property. But it does not protect you when you are driving a motor vehicle, for slander or libel, or for professional malpractice.

Health Insurance

Health insurance is a very important component of financial stability. Average annual per capita medical expenses are nearly $5,700, and health-related expenses account for nearly 14 percent of gross domestic product (GDP). Furthermore, the Congressional Budget Office has projected that national health care spending will grow at an average annual rate of 6 percent from 1997 to 2008.[8]

Most families and individuals have health insurance coverage through group policies offered as part of employer fringe benefit plans. Group policies usually include comprehensive coverage at a low cost. If you leave your job for any reason, your group coverage will terminate, although a federal regulation, commonly called **COBRA,** allows most employees and their families to continue group health coverage at their own expense for up to 18 months. You should also be aware that coverage through a parent's policy normally ends at a certain age, usually around age 23 to 25.

There are two basic types of health insurance coverage with several variations and combinations of the two types. Traditional health insurance plans, commonly called **indemnity (fee-for-service) plans,** reimburse the insured for medical costs covered by the insurance policy. The policyholder selects the physician, hospital, and other health care providers, gets the required services, in many cases pays for the services, and then files for reimbursement from the health insurance company. The primary advantage of this type of plan is greater choice of health care providers.

The fastest-growing segment of the health insurance market is **managed care plans.** They became popular in the late 1980s as a way to control the spiraling cost of medical care. Unlike traditional health insurance plans, managed care plans generally pay only for services provided by doctors and hospitals that are part of the plan (or they pay a smaller portion of costs when the insured uses providers that are not part of the plan).

COBRA
A federal regulation that allows most former employees and their families to continue group health insurance coverage at their own expense for up to 18 months after leaving an employer.

indemnity (fee-for-service) plans
Health insurance plans that reimburse the insured for medical costs covered by the insurance policy. The policyholder selects the health care providers.

managed care plans
Health insurance plans that generally pay only for services provided by doctors and hospitals that are part of the plan.

major medical insurance
Health insurance that covers a wide range of medical costs with few exclusions and high maximum limits. The insured pays a deductible and a *coinsurance* portion.

coinsurance (participation)
A percentage of covered expenses that the holder of a major medical insurance policy must pay.

Managed care health insurance plans help control soaring medical costs by focusing on preventive care.

Major Medical Insurance **Major medical insurance** can be sold as a stand-alone product or combined with a managed care plan. It typically covers a wide range of medical costs with few exclusions, and it has high maximum limits ($250,000 to $1 million). The insured pays a deductible and then pays a portion called **coinsurance (participation),** typically 15 to 25 percent of covered expenses. Many policies include a limit on the total amount the insured must pay.

Managed Care Plans Unlike traditional health insurance, managed care plans cover preventive care. The insured typically pays a small copayment ($10 to $20) each time she or he needs care.

health maintenance organizations (HMOs)

Managed care organizations that provide comprehensive health care services for a fixed periodic payment.

preferred provider organizations (PPOs)

Networks of health care providers who enter into a contract to provide services at discounted prices; combine a major medical insurance plan with features of health maintenance organizations.

waiting period (elimination period)

In disability income insurance, the period between the onset of the disability and the time when insurance payments begin.

duration of benefits

In disability income insurance, the length of time the insurance payments will continue.

term life insurance

Life insurance that covers the insured's life for a fixed amount and a specific period and has no *cash value;* provides the maximum amount of life insurance for the lowest premium.

cash value

The dollar amount paid to the owner of a life insurance policy if the policy is canceled before the death of the insured.

whole life (straight life, cash value, continuous pay) insurance

Life insurance that covers the insured's entire life, as long as the premiums are paid; has a cash value that increases over the life of the policy.

There is generally no cost for hospitalization. The most common types of managed care plans are health maintenance organizations and preferred provider organizations.

Health maintenance organizations (HMOs) provide comprehensive health care services for a fixed periodic payment (the monthly premium). Patient care is managed by a *primary care physician (PCP),* also known as a gatekeeper. The PCP is responsible for decisions about the health care received and refers the patient to specialists when necessary. Except in an emergency, the HMO will not pay for care that is given by non-HMO providers.

To learn how to use managed care plans to your benefit, check out Snap Online's Managed Care Health Care Handbook at **home.snap.com/main/ channel/item/0,4,- 9088,00.html?dd.snap.e6**

Preferred provider organizations (PPOs) combine a major medical insurance plan with a network of health care providers who enter into a contract to provide services at discounted prices. You can use the preferred providers, or you can go to a physician who is not a preferred provider. However, your out-of-pocket costs (deductibles and coinsurance) will be lower if you receive care from preferred providers. In some plans, if you use the preferred providers, you pay only a small copayment (as with an HMO), thus reducing your paperwork as well as your out-of-pocket costs.

Disability Income Insurance

Disability income insurance replaces a portion of your earnings, typically 60 to 70 percent of your monthly income, if you are unable to work due to illness or an accident. There is generally a **waiting period (elimination period),** ranging from three months to a year after the onset of the disability before the insurance payments begin. The shorter the waiting period, the more expensive the premium. The policy will also have a stated **duration of benefits,** the length of time the insurance payments will continue. Under short-term policies, benefits are paid for periods ranging from 13 weeks to two years; under long-term policies payments continue for periods of five years up to the insured's lifetime. One of the most important points to consider is the policy's definition of disability. With some policies, you are considered disabled if you cannot perform the functions of your own occupation; with others, you are disabled only if you are unable to do any work.

Life Insurance

Life insurance provides a specific amount of money at the death of the insured person. The money is paid to the beneficiary that the policy owner has chosen or to the deceased's estate if there is no named beneficiary. The primary reason to purchase life insurance is to provide income for the surviving family members. In addition, some people use life insurance to save for the future. The most common types of life insurance are term life, whole life, and universal life insurance.

Term life insurance provides the maximum amount of life insurance coverage for the lowest premium. It covers the insured's life for a fixed amount and a specific period, typically 5 to 20 years. It has no **cash value** (the dollar amount paid to the policy owner if the policy is canceled before the death of the insured). When the term ends, protection stops, unless the policy is renewed or a new policy is purchased.

Whole life insurance (also called **straight life, cash value,** or **continuous pay insurance**) covers the insured's entire life, as long as the premiums are paid. In

concept check

- Distinguish between property and liability insurance coverage. Why should families and individuals have both?
- What are the primary differences between traditional indemnity health insurance and managed care health plans?
- What are the two main reasons for buying life insurance? Which types of policies meet each need?

universal life insurance

A combination of term life insurance and a tax-deferred savings plan. Part of the premium is invested in securities, so the cash value earns interest at current market rates.

investing

The process of committing money to various instruments in order to obtain future financial returns.

addition to death protection, it has a cash value that increases over the life of the policy. Whole life is much more expensive than term insurance, and the interest rate used to determine its cash value is low—usually 4 to 6 percent. But it does provide a way to save for the future.

Universal life insurance combines term life insurance with a tax-deferred savings plan. It was developed in the 1980s to help insurance companies compete with other financial institutions for investment funds. The portion of the premium that is not used to pay for the term life coverage, commissions, and other business expenses is invested in short- and medium-term securities. Thus, the cash value earns interest at current market rates.

MAKING INVESTMENT DECISIONS

>lg 6

People invest their money for all sorts of reasons. Some want to save for a new home, a great vacation, or their children's education. Still others invest to build up a nest egg that will supplement their retirement income. The Focusing on Small Business box on p. 699 describes the additional financial planning and goal-setting complications faced by self-employed people. **Investing** is the process of committing money to various instruments in order to obtain future financial returns. It is a long-term strategy, and as Chapter 22 described, the most common investments used by individuals are stocks, bonds, and mutual funds.

Investment Goals

Every investor should start with this question: "What do I want to achieve with my investment program?" Realistic investment goals are based on the investor's investment motives, financial resources, age, and family situation. Once set, the goals can be used to develop an investment strategy. Your investment goals should relate to the goals set in your financial plan, such as saving for your first home, education, and retirement or supplementing your income. Investment goals also play a role in determining how conservative or aggressive you want to be in making investment decisions.

Investors have different levels of tolerance for risk. How much uncertainty can you stand as to whether your investment will achieve the expected level of return? The more risk you are willing to take, the higher the potential return on an investment. The investment risk pyramid shown in Exhibit 23-8 depicts the relationship between risk and reward.

The most common investment goals are income, growth, and safety. Investors wishing to supplement their *income* will choose securities that provide a steady, reliable source of income from bond interest, stock dividends, or both. Good choices include low-risk securities such as U.S. Treasury issues, high-quality corporate bonds, preferred stock, and common stock of large, financially sound corporations that regularly pay dividends (called *income stocks*).

Another important investment goal is *growth,* or increasing the value of the investment. Many investors try to find securities that are expected to increase in price over time. Generally, they choose stocks with above-average rates of growth in earnings and price that are expected to continue. For instance, the earnings of so-called *growth stocks* might increase 15 to 20 percent or more at a time when the earnings of most common stocks are increasing only 5 to 6 percent.

Safety is yet another investment goal. Investors who opt for safety do not want to risk the funds they've invested. They generally choose government and high-quality corporate bonds, preferred stocks, and mutual funds. They avoid common stock because of its frequent price fluctuations.

Investment Risk Pyramid

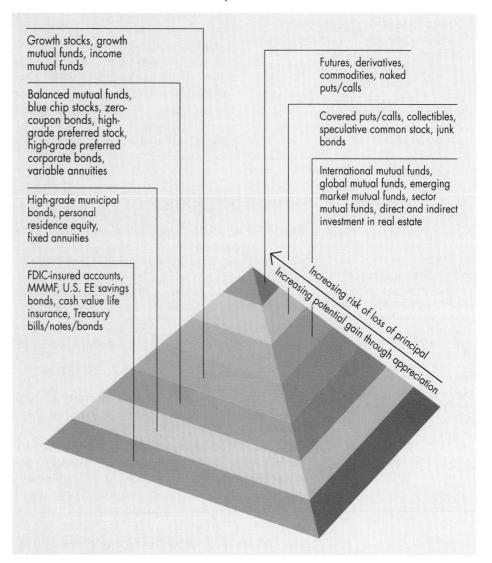

Growth stocks, growth mutual funds, income mutual funds

Balanced mutual funds, blue chip stocks, zero-coupon bonds, high-grade preferred stock, high-grade preferred corporate bonds, variable annuities

High-grade municipal bonds, personal residence equity, fixed annuities

FDIC-insured accounts, MMMF, U.S. EE savings bonds, cash value life insurance, Treasury bills/notes/bonds

Futures, derivatives, commodities, naked puts/calls

Covered puts/calls, collectibles, speculative common stock, junk bonds

International mutual funds, global mutual funds, emerging market mutual funds, sector mutual funds, direct and indirect investment in real estate

Increasing risk of loss of principal

Increasing potential gain through appreciation

Developing an Investment Strategy

emergency fund

Liquid assets that are available to meet emergencies.

Although much is written about various investment strategies, the secret to success is to start investing early. First, however, you should establish an adequate **emergency fund** (liquid assets that are available to meet emergencies), obtain necessary insurance, and reduce debt. Then diversify your investments and invest regularly.

Start Early In a recent survey, financial planning practitioners and educators identified "starting early so that returns can compound" as the most important element in a successful savings/investment program. Consider Jeff Stier, a 27-year-old attorney, who has already invested $32,000 for his retirement. With no additional contributions to this investment and assuming a 10 percent annual return, Jeff's $32,000 will grow to $1,196,939 by the time he is 65 years old! If Jeff had waited until age 45 to start saving for retirement, he would have had to invest $20,898 a year for the remaining 20 years (a total of $417,960) in order to accumulate $1,196,939.[9]

Start early and let your investments work for you. But do remember that a sound investment foundation is formed with an adequate amount of liquid as-

FINANCIAL PLANNING CHALLENGES OF THE SELF-EMPLOYED

"About two-thirds of us who are working are self-employed," write Thomas J. Stanley and William D. Danko in *The Millionaire Next Door.* "Interestingly, self-employed people make up less than 20 percent of the workers in America but account for two-thirds of the millionaires."

Despite the high concentration of self-employed people among the millionaire crowd, most self-employed people are not wealthy. In addition, self-employed people like David and Larissa Caramanidis face many complications in their personal finances that employees do not experience.

The Caramanidises are in their early 30s. Their son Johnathan is 7, and their second child is due in a few months. In many ways their financial goals are typical of young families: saving for retirement and for the down payment on their first home. They have already started contributing to the Texas Tomorrow Plan, a state-sponsored education plan, for Johnathan's college education.

David owns and operates the tennis pro shop for the Woodlands Athletic Club in the Houston area. He is considered an independent contractor to Woodlands and receives an annual retainer fee of $20,000. Woodlands also pays for one full-time employee for the pro shop, so David has hired Larissa as shop manager. This not only provides a steady income, but it also solves a major problem faced by the self-employed—the whole family is eligible for the club's group health insurance plan.

As is typical for small business owners, there is a very fine line between the finances of the business and David and Larissa's personal finances. Employees generally receive a regular paycheck, which makes planning relatively easy. The retainer and Larissa's regular salary from the club provide some stability in their income flow.

Since starting the business three months ago, David has been trying to figure out how much salary to pay himself from the shop's profits and how much to put back into the business. Since the business is so new, David and Larissa don't know how to predict its cash flow over a full year.

Being his own boss means that David also is responsible for all taxes associated with the business: his own self-employment and income taxes, Social Security tax withholding for his one full-time and seven part-time employees, and the sales taxes collected on products sold in the shop.

The Caramanidises think they can handle regular living expenses from the retainer and Larissa's salary, but they need David's self-employment income to save for retirement and a home. Because David is self-employed, he will use special retirement accounts (such as Keogh plans, and simplified employee pension plans, or SEPs) rather than investing through an employer-provided plan. Buying a home will also be more challenging because mortgage lenders look very closely at a self-employed person's income stability before approving the loan.

Self-employment has its perks, however. In addition to being potentially profitable, you can be your own boss. David can help Johnathan become a tennis prodigy (on work time). And he has turned his love for tennis into a business. But his tennis coach never taught him about operating a small business!

Critical Thinking Questions

1. In what personal financial planning areas does self-employment present unique challenges?
2. Where could David get the information he needs to learn more about meeting his tax obligations?
3. What should David and Larissa do to get a better grasp of the business cash flow? How will that help them achieve their personal financial goals, a secure retirement, and a home?

diversification

An investment strategy that involves investing in different asset classes, such as cash equivalents, stocks, bonds, and real estate, and combining securities with different patterns and amounts of return.

sets to meet emergencies. You also want to protect your assets with the needed insurance and reduce debt because generally the interest paid on debt is more than you can earn on investments.

Diversify Another important element of a successful investment strategy is **diversification.** It involves investing in different asset classes—cash equivalents,

portfolio
A collection of investments.

dividend reinvestment plan (DRIP)
A program in which dividends paid by a stock are automatically reinvested in that stock along with any additional contributions submitted by the stockholder.

c o n c ə p t   c h ə c k

- What is investment risk? What is the relationship between risk and return?
- What steps should be taken before starting an investment program? Why?
- Discuss three strategies that can be used to implement a successful investment plan.

stocks, bonds, real estate—and combining securities with different patterns and amounts of return. The resulting **portfolio,** or collection of investments, is more likely to meet investment goals than any one security is. A portfolio that includes preferred stocks paying high dividends and growth stocks paying modest dividends increases the potential of achieving both income and growth. Investing in 5 to 10 different companies in different industries is another way to diversify. Diversification is an important method of reducing risk, and it may also increase return.

Invest Regularly   Make investing for your goals part of your cash flow plan. Decide how much to invest, and then use your own willpower to purchase the investments each period (monthly, quarterly, or annually). Or, better yet, set up automatic transfers from your checking account to a mutual fund or to a stock **dividend reinvestment plan (DRIP)** so that a given amount is regularly invested in the investments of your choice.

Most mutual funds welcome monthly contributions of $50 or more through their automatic investment plans, and more and more stock can now be purchased regularly in small amounts. Originally, stock DRIPs were set up to automatically reinvest dividend income paid on the stock, but many companies have also added stock purchase plans that are available to investors who own as little as one share of the company stock.

CAPITALIZING ON TRENDS IN BUSINESS

>lg 7

One of the most important trends in personal finance is the move toward more employee responsibility for the choices made in employer fringe benefit plans. This is true both in the insurance area, with an increasing number of "cafeteria" benefit plans, and in the retirement area, where increasing numbers of employers offer self-directed defined contribution plans. Although this may be a positive trend given the great diversity and mobility of our workforce, it further emphasizes the need for all individuals to understand their financial needs and the best ways to achieve them.

Cafeteria Benefit Plans

In a typical cafeteria-style benefit plan, employees pick from a selection of benefits that might include two or three health insurance plans as well as life, disability, and dental insurance; child care assistance; educational assistance; and legal assistance. With the menu of benefits offered by the employer and a stipulated amount of "money" or "credits," employees are free to choose the benefits that best fit their needs. If the cost of covering an employee's needs exceeds the amount of money allotted by the employer, the difference can generally be deducted from the employee's paycheck.

With this type of plan, responsibility for meeting personal financial needs rests squarely on the employee's shoulders. If you select dental insurance rather than long-term disability insurance and then become disabled, you have made a devastating financial mistake. But since you know from our earlier discussion of insurance that you should always buy insurance first for the very large dollar losses, you would never select dental coverage over disability income insurance!

Self-Directed Retirement Accounts

Just as there is a trend to allow employees to select their own insurance benefits, employers are also moving to types of retirement plans—401(k) plans, SIMPLE plans, and others—that require the employee to decide how the money in these plans should be invested. Employers typically offer a range of mutual funds or similar type accounts from which the employee must choose. Some will be very safe investments such as money market funds and **guaranteed investment contracts (GICs).** GICs are insurance company products that are similar to bank certificates of deposit. Other options will be funds invested for income, growth, or a combination of income and growth.

guaranteed investment contracts (GICs)

Insurance company products that are similar to bank certificates of deposit.

If you have the opportunity to contribute to an employer retirement plan, it is generally a good idea to do so. Most plans shelter income from taxes, and many employers will match all or part of your contributions. For example, you may work for a company that matches 50 cents on the dollar for the first 7 percent of your salary that you contribute to your 401(k) plan. If you earn $40,000 annually and contribute $2,800, your employer will kick in an additional $1,400. That's a 50 percent return plus whatever the investment actually makes! Investing in an employer retirement plan also encourages regular investment, as funds are deducted from each paycheck and placed in your selected investment. As with other investment decisions, consider your goals when selecting specific investments for a self-directed retirement plan, but growth is typically the appropriate goal when younger employees invest for retirement.

concept check

- How do the emerging trends in employer fringe benefit plans place more responsibility on the individual?
- Explain the concept of a cafeteria benefit plan. How does an employee pay for selected benefits?
- Why is it important to participate in an employer-offered retirement plan?

APPLYING THIS CHAPTER'S TOPICS

As this chapter clearly demonstrates, you will be making financial planning decisions throughout your life. You can either make these decisions without information and knowledge, or you can start now to learn about the various areas of financial planning that you will face over the years. Lack of knowledge will cost you dearly in money, time, and missed opportunities. Financial knowledge will allow you to manage your resources to best meet your goals. You can make your money work for you by spending it in a way that gives you the most satisfaction for the dollar and investing it so you get the most return for the amount of risk taken.

Let's look specifically at some of the areas of financial planning discussed in this chapter. The cash management section described liquid assets such as money market accounts that could be used for an emergency fund. Financial experts often recommend that you keep two to six times your monthly expenditures in your emergency fund to cover not only unexpected emergencies but also investment opportunities.

You cannot know what will happen or how much it will cost, but you should know that unexpected expenses *will* happen! You might need a new set of tires or have an opportunity to go skiing over the holiday break. To structure your cash flow so that you can put aside money for these unexpected expenses, you need a spending plan and the discipline to follow it.

Then you must choose the best account for an emergency fund. Putting this money in a two-year certificate of deposit will be a mistake if your tires need

> t r y   i t   n o w ! <

1. **Choose a bank** Select three different financial institutions—one that you actually use for checking and/or savings and two others. Determine what checking and savings accounts are available that suit your needs, and find out how these accounts are structured (minimum ATM opening deposits, minimum required balances, fees, and other limitations). Look at the institution's complete list of fees, not just the cost of the checking account. Get a written copy of all account descriptions and fees if possible. Which one would be best for you given your needs? Be sure to discuss your needs as well as the characteristics of the institutions.

2. **Select a credit card** What's the best way to use credit cards wisely and to choose the best one? Compare three different credit cards. If you already have a credit card(s), use your own in addition to those offered through local banks or flyers you see on campus. Compare annual fees, APRs, methods of calculating finance costs, grace periods, and other terms. Get a written copy of the credit card terms if possible. Which one would be best for you given your needs and the way you intend to use a credit card? Be sure to discuss your needs as well as the characteristics of the cards.

replacing in 14 months, because you will pay a penalty for early withdrawal. You'll also want to look for the best interest rate. Putting the money in a money market deposit account at 3 percent rather than a money market mutual fund paying 5 percent will cost you $20 a year for each $1,000 in the account. You can probably find something fun to do with $20.

Not having enough insurance will cost you dearly if you suffer a loss. Lack of health insurance can put families on welfare. Lack of property insurance on your car may mean that you start taking the bus to work. And buying too much insurance or insurance from the wrong company can also be expensive. In the tax area, you can be assessed significant penalties if you don't pay what you legally owe in taxes. It will also cost you dearly if you don't take legitimate deductions that could save tax dollars. The key to making the best use of your money in all these cases is having the knowledge to make informed decisions.

Even in areas such as banking and credit, which are generally considered easier to understand than insurance and taxes, knowledge about how accounts are structured and the fees associated with their use is very important. Take the case of the student who wondered why his checking account cost him so much. With the help of his personal finance instructor, he discovered that he had made 23 ATM withdrawals from ATMs not owned by his bank—and each one had cost him $1. The monthly checking account fee was only $3, but the total cost that month was a whopping $26! By walking one more block to use his own bank's ATM, he could spend the $23 for something more enjoyable than this slight convenience.

at Todd and Amy Murray

Since purchasing their house, Todd and Amy Murray became parents, and Amy cut back to half-time employment. This has reduced their income and increased their expenditures, although Todd has been very successful in software development and has high hopes for his income potential.

Looking into the future, there are several issues Todd and Amy should consider. They need to accumulate liquid assets for an emergency fund, and they must evaluate their insurable risks to make sure their insurance coverage is adequate. These issues are particularly important now that Amy is not employed full-time. In addition to health, liability, and property insurance, life and disability income insurance on Todd will be critical to their financial security. They should also monitor their student loan debt and pay it off as quickly as possible. Fortunately, they have not amassed credit card debt, so they can focus on the student loans.

With the purchase of the house and then the arrival of the new baby, Todd and Amy's tax lives became more complex. They need to set up a good record-keeping system so that they can take advantage of the various tax breaks available to homeowners and parents. In addition, they need to plan for their future goals. A secure retirement, college education for their children, and a new car are among their most pressing concerns. A cash management plan that incorporates saving/investing for these goals is essential.

SUMMARY OF LEARNING GOALS

>lg 1　What is the personal financial planning process, and how does it facilitate successful financial management?
Financial planning is a six-step process that includes establishing financial goals, gathering financial and nonfinancial information, analyzing the information, developing a financial plan, implementing the plan, and monitoring the plan. The process starts with your own goals and provides a way to meet those goals.

>lg 2　How can cash flow planning and management of liquid assets help you meet your financial goals?
A cash flow plan is a plan for managing income and expenditures. It is based on financial goals and includes saving for those goals. Since money is being set aside to pay for the goals, you are more likely to actually achieve them. Liquid assets such as checking and savings-type accounts are important for day-to-day spending, to meet short-term goals, and for unexpected expenditures. Liquid assets can be held in safe, convenient accounts so that money will be readily available when needed.

>lg 3　What are the advantages and disadvantages of using consumer credit?
The benefits of consumer credit include convenience, purchasing an item sooner, taking advantage of bargains, better service, establishing a credit rating, convenient record keeping, meeting a financial emergency, and perks such as rebates and frequent flyer miles. Using consumer credit also has important disadvantages including the ease of overspending, the cost of credit (interest charges), the possibility that merchandise may cost more, and the reduction in future discretionary income due to the legal commitment to repay debt.

>lg 4　What are the major types of taxes paid by individuals?
The major taxes paid by individuals are income, Social Security, sales, and property taxes. Income and Social Security taxes are called payroll taxes because they are based on income and deducted from an employee's paycheck. Sales taxes are assessed on purchases made, and property taxes are based on the value of property owned, usually real estate.

KEY TERMS

actual cash value 694
automobile liability insurance 694
automobile physical damage insurance 694
cash flow plan 681
cash management 681
cash value 696
COBRA 695
coinsurance (participation) 695
comprehensive (other-than-collision) coverage 694
credit life insurance 690
diversification 699
dividend reinvestment plan (DRIP) 700
duration of benefits 696
earned income 692
emergency fund 698
filing status 691
financial planning 680
grace period 688
guaranteed investment contracts (GICs) 701
health maintenance organizations (HMOs) 696
indemnity (fee-for-service) plans 695
investing 697
line of credit 687
liquid assets 681
major medical insurance 695
managed care plans 695
net worth statement 682
open-end credit 686
personal exemptions 691
portfolio 700
preferred provider organizations (PPOs) 696

>lg 5   **What is the most important principle in deciding what types of insurance to purchase?**

The key to managing your insurance needs in the most cost-effective way is to budget for problems that represent a small financial loss. Set aside money in savings so that you can pay for the loss when it happens. Buy good insurance policies to cover major losses, those that would present a large financial loss if they occurred.

>lg 6   **What personal characteristics are important when making investment decisions?**

Investment decisions should be based on your goals and on your risk tolerance. Examples of investment goals include the desire for income from interest and dividends, the need for growth (capital gains), and the need for safety.

>lg 7   **What are the emerging trends in personal financial planning?**

Both in the insurance area, where an increasing number of cafeteria benefit plans are being offered, and in the retirement area, where increasing numbers of employers are offering self-directed defined contribution plans, the trend is toward more employee responsibility for the choices made in employer fringe benefit plans. Although this may be a positive trend given the great diversity and mobility of our workforce, it further emphasizes the importance of all individuals understanding their financial needs and the best ways to achieve them.

>lg 8   **What is risk, and how can it be managed?**

Risk is the chance for financial loss due to a peril. Both individuals and businesses need to protect themselves against several types of risks. Many of these—death, poor health, property damage—can be covered by insurance, which pays the insured up to a specified amount in the event of loss from a particular peril. Risk can be managed by avoiding situations known to be risky, by assuming the responsibility for losses due to certain types of risk (called self-insurance), by reducing it through taking safety measures, and by transferring it to an insurance company.

>lg 9   **What types of insurance coverage should businesses consider?**

Property insurance covers losses arising from damage to property owned by the insured person or business. Liability insurance covers losses due to injuries to others or their property determined to be caused by the insured. Other important coverages for businesses include business interruption, automobile, theft, fidelity and surety bonds, personal liability, professional liability, and product liability.

Businesses must also be knowledgeable about health and life insurance, which they typically offer employees as part of fringe benefits packages.

PREPARING FOR TOMORROW'S WORKPLACE

1. Use the six-step financial planning process to develop a financial plan for yourself for the next year. Start by listing your financial goals. Then gather the appropriate information needed to analyze your situation. Develop the plan and explain how it will be implemented.

2. College junior Andy Jung overused his credit cards last year. He currently has the following outstanding debt on three credit cards plus an auto loan and a student loan:

   - MasterCard—$984 outstanding debt, $40 minimum monthly payment, 18 percent interest rate, no annual fee, $25 late payment fee, 2 percent cash advance fee ($20 maximum), $1,000 line of credit.

prepayment
   penalties 690
principal 688
progressive tax
   691
replacement cost
   coverage 694
revolving credit
   cards 687
security
   requirements 690
standard deduction
   692
term life insurance
   696
unearned income
   692
universal life
   insurance 697
waiting period
   (elimination
   period) 696
whole life (straight
   life, cash value,
   continuous pay)
   insurance 696
withholding
   allowances 691

- Visa—$569 outstanding debt, $17 minimum monthly payment, 14 percent interest rate, $20 annual fee, $20 late payment fee, 1.5 percent cash advance fee ($20 maximum), $800 line of credit.
- Gold MasterCard—$388 outstanding debt, $12 minimum monthly payment, 13 percent interest rate, no annual fee, $25 late payment fee, 2 percent cash advance fee ($25 maximum), $1,000 line of credit.
- Auto loan—$3,490 outstanding balance, $257 monthly payment, 8 percent interest, 15 more payments.
- Student loan—$15,490 outstanding balance, deferred payments, 7.5 percent interest (unsubsidized).

Andy has $450 a month to use for debt repayment.

Divide into small groups and advise Andy on how best to pay off his debt obligations. Start by completing a debt inventory for Andy. Then write a one-to two-page memo with your recommendations on how to allocate the $450 and the rationale for your recommendations.

3. Use the steps detailed in this chapter to balance your most recent checking account statement. After completing this process, analyze your use of the checking account, EFT services, etc. Are you satisfied with the way you are handling this account? If not, what changes do you want to make in how you use it?

4. Kristi lost her wallet at the Barton Creek Square shopping center on Monday. She reported her ATM card and credit cards stolen on Monday evening. By then the following charges had been made: Dillard's, $550; Foley's, $450; Visa, $45. The thief had also used Kristi's ATM card to withdraw $350 from an ATM. How much of these losses is Kristi responsible for under federal regulations? If Kristi had waited until Thursday (rather than Monday evening) to report the missing cards, how much would she be responsible for under federal law?

5. Form a team of four or five classmates to evaluate employer fringe benefit plans. Gather written information on the insurance and retirement benefits offered by at least two employers. This information may be available directly from an employer, from your parents, or from senior classmates who are interviewing with companies. Read the information carefully and then write a brief summary evaluating each plan. Look specifically at the types of insurance offered, the type of retirement plan offered, and the investment choices available through the retirement plan.

WORKING THE NET

1. Explore Finance Center (**www.financecenter.com**), one of the highest-rated comprehensive financial planning Web Sites. It includes more than 100 online calculators to help with the number-crunching involved in personal finance decisions. Go to the auto section of this site and determine how much your monthly payment would be on a $20,000 car assuming an 8 percent loan with no rebate, no trade-in, a $3,000 down payment, and repayment over four years. Click on Graphs to see how the payment changes with different lengths of repayment. Click on Table to see the amortization table for this loan. Repeat the first exercise assuming a 10 percent loan, with everything else remaining the same. How do the monthly payments and the total amount of interest paid change? While at this site, check out one other application that interests you.

2. Go to Tax Cut (**www.taxcut.com**) for a variety of tax information (in addition to information about their tax preparation software). Click on the information

regarding Fringe Benefits to find out more about the tax implications of these important financial planning tools. Also find one other topic that is of interest to you.

3. Bankrate (**www.bankrate.com**) provides a wealth of data about interest rates and other financial planning information. Find the current average rates on standard, gold, and platinum credit cards. Then use the site to find the best rate for you. Fill in the required information based on your wants and needs in a credit card. Then check out auto loans by selecting your home state and the city nearest you. Compare the terms for new car loans with 36-month repayment terms versus those with 60-month repayment terms. Read one of the featured articles for the week. These change regularly, but typically provide useful information on a variety of financial planning topics.

4. Does financial planning interest you? Maybe it's a potential career! Explore the Certified Financial Planner Board's site at **www.cfp-board.org** to find out more about the Certified Financial Planner (CFP) license, the primary designation in the personal financial planning industry. Go to the General Information Booklet to learn about the certification requirements. Check out which educational institutions near you are Registered Programs with the CFP Board. Investigate the career opportunities for CFP practitioners.

5. At DowJones.com you'll find a whole section of information to assist in your personal investing. Go to **www.dowjones.com,** then click on Personal Finance and Get Going and read one of the featured articles. Select a company that you would like to know more about, perhaps one that produces a product you like or a company you might like to work for. Get the current stock quote for that company and see if there is any breaking news about the company.

CREATIVE THINKING CASE

The Young Financial Planner

You are a junior member of a small financial planning firm. Although you have a degree in financial planning, you are currently studying for the Certified Financial Planner (CFP) exam and accumulating the experience needed to be a CFP practitioner. Your newest clients are Becky and Ray Jackson, a couple in their early 30s who have three children (ages 2, 4, and 8). Both Becky and Ray are professionals, and they have a combined annual income of approximately $90,000; nevertheless, they are having trouble controlling their spending. Their only assets, other than personal property, are their home and some funds held in retirement accounts through their employers. They are not sure how those retirement funds are currently invested.

Critical Thinking Questions

1. In working with Becky and Ray to establish a financial plan, what is the first thing you would help them do? What types of information would you collect from Becky and Ray?

2. What would you recommend to help Becky and Ray control their spending?

3. What types of insurable risks would Becky and Ray likely be exposed to? What types of insurance are they likely to need?

4. What would you expect their investment goals to be for the money in their retirement funds? What specific types of investments would be appropriate to meet those goals?

VIDEO CASE

The Edward Jones Approach to Personal Finance

As the Video Case in Chapter 22 described, the Edward Jones Co. (**www. edwardjones.com**) is a brokerage firm that offers one-on-one personalized service to retired investors, working investors, tax professionals and attorneys, and small business owners. How does the company implement its strategy of one-on-one, personalized investment services? The answer lies in the following key elements:

- Customizing financial strategies and solutions to each client's needs and goals.
- Providing a Full Service Account (FSA) for simplifying customers' financial management needs.
- Focusing on customers who are interested in long-term, relatively high-quality, low-risk investments.

Edward Jones attempts to meet clients' investment needs with custom-tailored financial strategies and solutions. For instance, the company provides small business owners with a variety of financial services, including but not limited to retirement plan choices, cash flow management, and information on legislative issues. The company targets working investors with financial strategies and solutions that focus on managing personal finances, saving for retirement, and financing their children's college education. Retired investors and tax professionals and attorneys also are targeted with various financial services appropriate to their needs and goals.

Edward Jones's Full Service Account is designed to help clients simplify their financial lives. This cash and investment management account enables clients to coordinate their savings and investments into an organized portfolio. It can help clients to simplify record-keeping, increase their investment earnings, streamline transactions, achieve their financial goals, borrow money through an automatic line of credit, and acquire an appropriate money market account.

A third element of the company's strategy is its focus on customers who are interested in relatively high-quality, low-risk investments that are held for the long term. These investments include certificates of deposit; mutual funds; government, municipal, and corporate bonds; common stocks of companies with histories of sound management and solid growth; retirement plans and individual retirement arrangements (IRAs); and life insurance products, including annuities.

By successfully executing the three elements of its one-on-one, personalized service strategy, the Edward Jones Co. seeks to establish long-term relationships with the retired investors, working investors, tax professionals and attorneys, and small business owners that it serves.

Critical Thinking Questions

1. How can Edward Jones's strategy of one-on-one, personalized investment services assist customers in their personal financial planning?
2. How can Edward Jones help a customer develop an investment strategy?
3. Suppose that you are looking for investment management services. Would you be inclined to become a client of the Edward Jones Co.? Why or why not?

APPENDIX: MANAGING RISK AND INSURANCE

Overview

Every day, businesses and individuals are exposed to many different kinds of risk. Investors who buy stocks or speculate in commodities may earn a profit, but they also take the risk of losing all or part of their money. Illness is another type of risk, involving financial loss from not only the cost of medical care but also the loss of income.

Businesses, too, are exposed to many types of risk. Market risks, such as lower demand for a product or worsening economic conditions, can hurt a firm. Other risks involve customers, who could be injured on a company's premises or by a company's product. Like homes and cars owned by individuals, business property can be damaged or lost through fire, floods, and theft. Businesses must also protect themselves against losses from theft by dishonest employees. The loss of a key employee is another risk, especially for small firms.

It is impossible to avoid all risks, but individuals and businesses can minimize risks or buy protection—called insurance—against them. Although some risks are uninsurable, many others are insurable. Let's now look at basic risk concepts and the types of insurance available to cover them.

Risk Management

Every business faces risks like the ones listed above. **Risk management** involves analyzing the firm's operations, evaluating the potential risks, and figuring out how to minimize losses in a cost-efficient manner. In today's complex business environment, the concern for public and employee welfare and the potential for lawsuits have both increased. Risk management thus plays a vital role in the overall management of a business.

Types of Risk

Individuals and firms need to protect themselves against the economic effects of certain types of risk. In an insurance sense, **risk** (sometimes called *pure risk*) is the chance of financial loss due to a peril. Insurable risks include fire, theft, auto accident, injury or illness, a lawsuit, or death. **Speculative risk** is the chance of either loss or gain. Someone who buys stock in the hope of later selling it at a profit is taking a speculative risk and cannot be insured against it.

Strategies to Manage Risk

Risk is part of life. Nevertheless, people have four major ways to deal with it:

- **Risk avoidance.** Staying away from situations that can lead to loss. A person can avoid the risk of a serious injury by choosing not to go skydiving. Kinder-Care, a nationwide day-care chain, could avoid risk by not transporting children to and from school or taking them on field trips. Manufacturers who wish to avoid risks could produce only goods that have a proven track record. But these risk-avoidance strategies could stifle growth in the long run. Thus risk avoidance is not good for all risks.

- **Self-insurance.** The willingness to bear a risk without insurance, also called *risk assumption*. This offers a more practical way to handle many types of risks. Many large firms with warehouses or stores spread out over the United States—Sears or Kmart, for instance—may choose not to insure them. They assume that, even if disaster strikes one location, the others won't be harmed. The losses will probably be less than the insurance premiums for all the locations. Many companies self-insure because it is cheaper to assume some risks than to insure against them. Some choose to pay small claims themselves and insure only for catastrophic losses. Others "go naked," paying for all claims from company funds. This is clearly the most risky strategy. A big claim could cripple the firm or lead to bankruptcy.

- **Risk reduction.** Adopting techniques to prevent financial losses. For example, companies adopt safety measures to reduce accidents. Construction workers are required to wear hard hats and safety glasses. Airlines keep their aircraft in good condition and require thorough training programs for pilots and flight attendants. Hotels install smoke alarms, sprinkler systems, and firewalls to protect guests and minimize fire damage.

- **Risk transference.** Paying someone else to bear some or all of the risk of financial loss for certain risks that can't be avoided, assumed, or reduced to acceptable levels. The way to transfer risk is through **insurance.** Individuals and organizations can pay a fee (a *premium*) and get the promise of compensation for certain financial losses. The companies that take on the risks are called *insurance companies.*

Insurance Concepts

Companies purchase insurance to cover insurable risks. An **insurance policy** is the written agreement that defines what the insurance covers and the risks that the insurance company will bear for the insured party. It also outlines the policy's benefits (the maximum amount that it will pay in the event of a loss), and the premium (the cost to the insured for coverage). Any demand for payment for losses covered by the policy is a *claim.*

Before issuing a policy, an insurance company reviews the applications of those who want a policy and selects those that meet its standards. This **underwriting** process also determines the level of coverage and the premiums. Each company sets its own underwriting standards based on its experience. For instance, a life insurance company may decide not to accept an applicant who has had a heart attack within five years (or to charge a 50 to 75 percent higher premium). A property insurer may refuse to issue a policy on homes near brush-filled canyons, which present above-average fire hazards.

To get insurance, the applicant must have an **insurable interest**—the chance of suffering a loss if a particular peril occurs. In most cases, a person cannot insure the life of a friend, because the friend's death would not be considered a financial loss. But business partners can get life insurance on each other's lives because the death of one of them would have a financial impact on their firm.

Insurable Risks

Insurance companies are professional risk takers, but they won't provide coverage against all types of risk. Some risks are insurable, some are not. For instance, changes in political or economic conditions are not insurable. An **insurable risk** is one that an insurance company will cover. For a risk to be insurable, it must meet these criteria:

- *The loss must not be under the control of the insured.* The loss must be accidental—that is, unexpected and occurring by chance. Insurance companies do not cover losses purposely caused by the insured party. No insurance company will pay for the loss of a clothing store that the insured set on fire. Nor will most companies pay life insurance benefits for a suicide.

- *There must be many similar exposures to that peril.* Insurance companies study the rates of deaths, auto accidents, fires, floods, and many other perils. They know about how many of these perils will occur each year. The **law of large numbers** lets them predict the likelihood that the peril will occur and then calculate premiums.

  Suppose that an insurance company has 150 policies in Morton, Iowa. The company knows from past experience that these policyholders are likely to have twelve car accidents a year and that the average payment for a claim in Morton has been $1,000. The total claims for one year's car accidents in Morton would be $12,000 (12 accidents × $1,000). Thus the company would charge each policyholder a premium of at least $80 ($12,000 ÷ 150). Profits and administrative expenses would make the premium somewhat higher.

- *Losses must be financially measurable.* The dollar amount of potential losses must be known so the insurance company can figure the premiums. Life insurance is for a fixed amount specified at the time the policy is bought. Otherwise, the company and the *beneficiary* (the one who gets the funds) would have to agree on the value of the deceased's life at the time of death. Premiums have to be calculated before then, however.

- *The peril must not be likely to affect all the insured parties at the same time.* Insurance companies must spread out their risks by insuring many people and businesses in many locations. This strategy helps minimize the chance that a single calamity will wipe out the insurance company.

- *The potential loss must be significant.* Insurance companies cannot afford to insure trivial things for small amounts. Many policies have **deductibles,** amounts that the insured must pay before insurance benefits begin.

- *The company must have the right to set standards for insurance coverage.* Insurance companies can refuse to cover people with health problems like AIDS, cancer or heart trouble, a poor driving record, or a dangerous job or hobby. They can also charge higher premiums because of the higher risks they are covering.

Premium Costs

Insurance policies must be economical—relatively low in cost compared to the benefits—so people will want to buy them. Yet the premiums must also cover the risks that the insurance company faces. Insurance companies collect statistics on many perils. Then specially trained mathematicians called *actuaries* use the law of large numbers to develop actuarial tables. These tables show how likely each peril is. Actuarial tables are the basis for calculating premiums. For example, actuaries use a mortality table showing average life expectancy and the expected number of deaths per 1,000 people at given ages to set life insurance premiums.

Almost every homeowner buys insurance to cover the perils of fire, theft, vandalism, and other home-related risks. With such a large pool of policyholders, homeowners' policies are usually inexpensive. Annual premiums are about 0.5 percent (or less) of the value of the home. This low cost encourages people to buy policies and thereby helps spread the insurance companies' risk over many homes throughout the country.

When setting premiums, insurers also look at the risk characteristics of certain groups, to assess the probability of loss for those groups. For instance, smokers tend to die younger than nonsmokers do and thus pay higher life insurance premiums. Female drivers under the age of twenty-five have a lower rate of accidents than male drivers, so their car insurance premiums are lower.

Insurance Providers

Insurers can be either public or private. Public insurance coverage is offered by specialized government agencies. The federal government is in fact the largest single insurer in the United States. Private insurance coverage is provided by privately organized (nongovernment) companies.

Public Insurance   Government-sponsored insurance falls into two general categories: social insurance programs and other programs. Social insurance provides protection for problems beyond the scope of private insurers. These programs include:

- *Unemployment insurance.* Every state has an **unemployment insurance** program that pays laid-off workers weekly benefits while they seek new jobs.

Persons who terminate their employment voluntarily or are fired for cause are not eligible for unemployment insurance. These programs also provide job counseling and placement services. The benefits usually start a week after a person has lost a job and continue for twenty-six to thirty-nine weeks, depending on the state. The size of the weekly benefit depends on the workers' previous income and varies from state to state. Unemployment insurance is funded by payroll taxes levied on employers.

- *Workers' compensation.* Every state has laws requiring employers to fund **workers' compensation** insurance to cover the expenses of job-related injuries and diseases, including medical costs, rehabilitation, and job retraining if necessary. It also provides disability income benefits (salary and wage payments) for workers who can't perform their job. Employers can buy workers' compensation policies or self-insure. A company's premium is based on the amount of its payroll and the types of risks present in the workplace. For instance, a construction company would pay a higher premium for workers' compensation insurance than would a jewelry store.

- *Social Security.* **Social Security** insurance provides retirement, disability, death, and health insurance benefits. Social Security is funded by equal contributions from workers and employers. These benefits go mostly to people over sixty-five, although they are available to younger people who are disabled. More than 90 percent of all U.S. workers and their families are eligible to qualify for Social Security benefits.

- *Medicare.* A health insurance program for those over sixty-five, **Medicare** was added to Social Security in 1965 and has two parts: hospital insurance, financed through the Social Security tax, and medical insurance, financed through government contributions and monthly premiums paid by those who want this coverage. Because Medicare pays only part of the insured's medical expenses, many people buy *supplemental insurance* from private insurance companies.

Private Insurance Companies   Private insurance companies sell property and liability insurance, health insurance, and life insurance. Life and health insurance companies dominate the industry, accounting for about 70 percent of total assets. Regulation of private insurance companies is under the control of the states and thus varies from state to state.

There are two basic ownership structures for private insurance companies: stockholder and mutual. Just like other publicly owned corporations, *stock insurance companies* are profit-oriented companies owned by stockholders. The stockholders do not have to be policyholders, and the policyholders do not have to be stockholders. Their profits come from insurance premiums in excess of claim payments and operating expenses and from investments in securities and real estate. CIGNA Corporation is the largest stockholder-owned insurance company in the United States, with assets of about $114 billion. Other major stock insurance companies are Aetna, Allstate Insurance, Continental Insurance, Fireman's Fund Insurance, and Metropolitan Life. Of about 5,000 insurance companies in the United States, most are stock insurance companies.

The rest are **mutual insurance companies,** which are not-for-profit organizations owned by their policyholders and chartered by each state. Any excess income is returned to the policyholder-owners as dividends, used to reduce premiums, or retained to finance future operations. The policyholders elect the board of directors, who manage the company. Most of the large life insurance companies in the United States are mutuals, including John Hancock, New York Life, and Northwestern Mutual Life. State Farm, the largest auto insurer, is also a mutual insurance company.

>lg 9

Types of Insurance

In Chapter 23, we introduced several types of personal insurance coverage: property, liability, health, and life. Businesses also purchase insurance for these risks, but with some differences. Most companies offer group health and life insurance plans for their employees as a fringe benefit. Employers typically pay some of the health insurance premiums, and employees pay the rest. The cost is usually considerably less than for individual policies, although it pays to check before signing up. For example, companies may pay for the entire cost of life insurance equal to one or two times the employee's annual salary, with an option to purchase more under the group plan, but the premiums may be more expensive than buying an individual policy.

Businesses often insure the lives of key employees, such as top executives, salespeople, inventors, and researchers, whose death could seriously limit the income or value of a firm. To protect themselves, businesses buy **key-person life insurance,** a term insurance policy that names the company as beneficiary. In the case of a partnership, which is dissolved when a partner dies, key-person insurance is often bought for each partner, with the other partner named as the beneficiary, so that the surviving partner can buy the partnership interest from the estate of the deceased and continue operating.

Property and Liability Insurance

Over 3,500 companies offer property and liability policies. This type of insurance is important for businesses, which wish to protect against losses of property and lawsuits arising from harm to other people.

As we learned in Chapter 23, *property insurance* covers financial losses from damage to or destruction of the insured's assets as a result of specified perils, while *liability insurance* covers financial losses from injuries to others and damage to or destruction of others' property when the insured is considered to be the cause. It also covers the insured's legal defense fees up to the maximum amount stated in the policy. Automobile liability insurance is an example. It would pay for a fence damaged when the insured person lost control of his or her car. Commercial and product liability insurance also fall into this category.

Commercial liability insurance covers a variety of damage claims, including harm to the environment from pollution. In the case of product liability, if a defective furnace exploded and damaged a home, the manufacturer would be liable for the damages. If the manufacturer were insured, the insurance company would cover the losses or pay to dispute the claim in court.

Property and liability insurance is a broad category. Businesses buy many types of property and liability insurance. These protect against loss of property due to fire, theft, accidents, or employee dishonesty and financial losses arising from liability cases. Landlords and owners of business property buy building insurance, a type of property coverage, for protection against both property damage and liability losses. For instance, if a person broke an arm slipping on a wet floor in a hardware store, the business's insurance policy would cover any claim.

Property insurance policies usually include a coinsurance clause. **Coinsurance** requires the property owner to buy insurance coverage equal to a certain percentage of the property's value. To cut premium costs, policyholders often insure buildings for less than their full value, in the hope that a fire or other disaster will damage only part of the property. But insurers limit the payout if the property is underinsured. They use coinsurance clauses as an incentive for businesses to maintain full insurance on their buildings. For instance, some fire insurance policies have an 80 percent coinsurance clause. If the owner of a building valued at $400,000 buys a policy with coverage equal to at least $320,000 (80% × $400,000), he or she will collect the full amount

KEY TERMS

business
  interruption
  insurance 713
coinsurance 712
deductibles 710
insurable interest
  709
insurable risk 709
insurance 709
insurance policies
  709
key-person life
  insurance 712
law of large
  numbers 709
Medicare 711
mutual insurance
  companies 711
professional liability
  insurance 713
risk 708
risk avoidance 708
risk management
  708
risk reduction 709
risk transference
  709
self-insurance 708
Social Security
  711
speculative risk
  708
theft insurance 713
underwriting 709
unemployment
  insurance 710
workers'
  compensation
  711

of any partial loss. If the owner buys a policy for less coverage, the insurance company will pay for only part of the partial loss.

Special Types of Business Liability Insurance

Businesses also purchase several other types of insurance policies, depending on their particular needs:

- *Business interruption insurance.* This optional coverage is often offered with fire insurance. It protects business owners from losses occurring when the business must be closed temporarily after property damage. **Business interruption insurance** may cover such costs as rental of temporary facilities, wage and salary payments to employees, payments for leased equipment, fixed payments (for instance, rent and loans), and profits that would have been earned during the period. *Contingent business interruption insurance* covers losses to the insured in the event of property damage to a major supplier or customer.

- *Theft insurance.* Businesses also want to protect their property against financial losses due to crime. **Theft insurance** is the broadest coverage and protects businesses against losses from an act of stealing. Businesses can also buy more limited types of theft insurance.

- *Fidelity and surety bonds.* What if a firm has a dishonest employee? This situation is covered by a *fidelity bond,* an agreement that insures a company against theft committed by an employee who handles company money. If a restaurant manager is bonded for $50,000 and steals $60,000, the restaurant will recover all but $10,000 of the loss. Banks, loan companies, and retail businesses that employ cashiers typically buy fidelity bonds.

  A *surety bond,* also called a *performance bond,* is an agreement to reimburse a firm for nonperformance of acts specified in a contract. This form of insurance is most common in the construction industry. Contractors buy surety bonds to cover themselves in case the project they are working on is not completed by the specified date or does not meet specified standards. In practice, the insurance company often pays another contractor to finish the job or to redo shoddy work when the bonded contractor fails to perform.

- *Title insurance.* A title policy protects the buyer of real estate against losses caused by a defect in the title—that is, a claim against the property that prevents the transfer of ownership from seller to purchaser. It eliminates the need to search legal records to be sure that the seller was actually the owner of (had clear title to) the property.

- *Professional liability insurance.* This form of insurance covers financial losses (legal fees and court-awarded damages up to specific limits) resulting from alleged malpractice by professionals in fields like medicine, law, architecture, and dentistry. *Directors and officers insurance* is a type of **professional liability insurance** designed to protect top corporate management, who have also been the target of malpractice lawsuits. It pays for legal fees and court-awarded damages up to specific limits.

Careers in Finance

If you have an interest in the dollars and cents of running a business, like to follow the daily ups and downs of the securities markets, or have a knack for numbers, the world of finance may be for you. Because businesses and individuals need many different financial services, you can choose from a wide variety of positions.

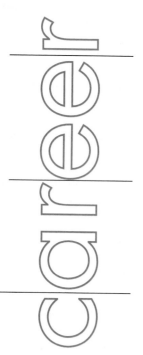

There are two basic career paths in finance:

- *Managerial finance.* Managing the finance function for manufacturers of consumer and commercial products or other businesses not directly involved in financial services.
- *Financial services.* Creating and selling financial products and services for companies that supply financial services such as banking, insurance, and securities firms.

With mergers and downsizing affecting many industries, the rate of job creation for financial positions has slowed somewhat. Business graduates can still find many interesting and challenging positions, however.

DREAM CAREER: FINANCIAL PLANNER

Today's financial world is more complex than ever. Americans constantly face new investment opportunities, changes in tax laws, and revised employee benefit plans. The variety of savings plans, securities, mutual funds, insurance policies, real estate investments, and other options confuses and frustrates many people. They are concerned with preserving or increasing their financial assets, protecting their families, and planning for their retirement, but often do not have the time to do all the research needed to make wise savings and investment decisions.

Enter the financial planner. She or he asks clients specific questions about their financial needs. The planner then advises them about budgeting, securities, insurance, real estate, taxes, and retirement and estate planning and prepares a comprehensive financial plan to meet their goals. The financial planner is paid a straight fee or a fee plus commission on the dollar amount handled. Although financial planning is a rather new field, it has grown fast. More and more people are seeking professional advice on managing their personal financial assets.

Financial planners should be good at dealing with people, communicating, and problem-solving. The two main credentials for financial planners are the Certified Financial Planner (CFP) and the Chartered Financial Consultant (ChFC). Each requires approximately two years of study and testing. The accounting and banking fields also have certification programs.

- *Places of employment.* Large securities or insurance companies such as Merrill Lynch or Prudential in medium-to-large cities throughout the United States; financial planners can also work independently in any area, although a population base of 50,000 or more is desirable.
- *Skills required.* A four-year degree is generally required, although it is possible to enroll in the CFP program without a bachelor's degree. Courses in financial planning topics plus three to five years' professional experience in personal financial planning or a related field such as banking or accounting is required to earn the CFP license. To establish an independent practice, a CPA (certified public accountant), CFP, or ChFC credential is helpful.
- *Employment outlook through 2006.* Excellent.
- *Salaries:* $18,000+ for an entry-level position with a large firm; planners with experience and a good reputation can earn $100,000+. The average gross earnings (fees, commissions, and/or salary) are $65,000 per year.

WHERE THE OPPORTUNITIES ARE

Corporate Financial Manager

There are many positions of financial responsibility in corporations of all types—manufacturing, trade, service, and financial institutions. The highest positions are financial manager, controller, vice-president of finance, and treasurer. Assistant managers and financial analysts work with financial managers.

Financial managers are concerned with raising and spending money for the firm's operations. They prepare financial plans to determine what funds will be required for payroll, raw materials purchases, other operating expenses, equipment purchases, loan payments, and so on. Financial managers work closely with the accounting department.

Most people starting out in managerial finance begin as financial analysts in the planning and budgeting area. Larger firms tend to have financial analysts who specialize in one area—forecasting, short- or long-term borrowing, or capital budgeting, for example. Smaller firms may assign the analyst several areas of responsibility.

Financial managers should have a good math aptitude, analytical ability, communications skills, computer skills, and the ability to work independently.

- *Places of employment.* Throughout the country.
- *Skills required.* A four-year degree in business, with an accounting or finance major preferred; many employers require an MBA for advancement.
- *Employment outlook through 2006.* Average.
- *Salaries.* $27,000 to $34,000 for entry-level financial analysts (higher for MBAs); $31,000 to $45,000 with up to three years' experience; $50,000 to $70,000+ for higher-level positions.

Credit Manager

Over the years, buying on credit has become a common method of doing business. Consumers use credit to pay for houses, cars, appliances, and travel, as well as for everyday purchases. Most business purchases are also made on credit.

Credit managers establish a firm's credit policies, decide whether to accept or reject credit applicants, and oversee the collection of accounts receivable. In extending credit, the credit manager or credit analyst analyzes detailed financial reports submitted by the applicant and reviews credit agency reports to determine the applicant's history in repaying debts. Credit managers usually start as credit analysts and advance as they gain experience.

- *Places of employment.* Throughout the country.
- *Skills required.* Generally, a four-year degree in accounting or finance, but sometimes a two-year degree is acceptable.
- *Employment outlook through 2006.* Average.
- *Salaries.* $23,000 to $36,000 for credit analysts; $26,000 to $46,000 for assistant credit managers; $33,000 to $68,000 for credit managers.

Stockbroker or Securities Account Executive

Stockbrokers and securities account executives handle orders for clients who wish to buy or sell securities. They also advise customers on financial matters and supply the latest stock and bond quotations and analyst reports. Stockbrokers are usually hired by brokerage firms, investment banks, mutual funds, and insurance companies. Job opportunities for brokers are also emerging in other financial institutions such as commercial banks.

In addition to knowledge of financial analysis and investments, successful account executives have good sales and interpersonal skills, self-confidence, and a high energy level. Most large brokerage firms offer a training program at the entry level that prepares the stockbroker to take a licensing examination.

- *Places of employment.* Opportunities are available in all medium-to-large cities.

- *Skills required.* Generally, a four-year degree, but a two-year degree may be acceptable at some smaller firms.
- *Employment outlook through 2006.* Above average.
- *Salaries.* $20,000 to $25,000 plus commissions for trainees; $50,000 to $200,000 for experienced brokers.

A

absolute advantage   The situation when a country can produce and sell a product at a lower cost than any other country or when it is the only country that can provide the product.

accounting   The process of collecting, recording, classifying, summarizing, reporting, and analyzing financial activities.

accounts payable   Purchase for which a firm has not yet paid.

accounts receivable   Sales for which a firm has not yet been paid.

acid-test (quick) ratio   The ratio of current assets excluding inventory to total current liabilities; used to measure a firm's liquidity.

acquisition   The purchase of a corporation by another corporation or by an investor group; the identity of the acquired company may be lost.

activity ratios   Ratios that measure how well a firm uses its assets; for example, inventory turnover.

actual cash value   The market value of personal property; the amount paid by standard homeowner's and renter's insurance policies.

administrative distribution system   A vertical marketing system in which a strong organization takes over as leader and sets policies for the distribution channel.

advertising agencies   Companies that help create ads and place them in the proper media.

advertising media   The channels through which advertising is carried to prospective customers; includes newspapers, magazines, radio, television, outdoor advertising, direct mail, and the Internet.

advertising   Any paid form of nonpersonal presentation by an identified sponsor.

advocacy advertising   Advertising that takes a stand on a social or economic issue; also called grassroots lobbying.

affirmative action programs   Programs established by organizations to expand job opportunities for women and minorities.

agency shop   A company where employees are not required to join the union but must pay it a fee to cover its expenses in representing them.

agents   Sales representatives of manufacturers and wholesalers.

American Federation of Labor (AFL)   A national labor organization made up of numerous craft unions; founded in 1881 by splinter groups from the Knights of Labor. In 1955, the AFL merged with the Congress of Industrial Organizations (CIO) to form the AFL-CIO.

angel investors   Individual investors or groups of experienced investors who provide funding for start-up businesses.

annual report   A yearly document that describes a firm's financial status and usually discusses the firm's activities during the past year and its prospects for the future.

antitrust regulation   Laws that prevent companies from entering into agreements to control trade through a monopoly.

appellate courts (courts of appeals)   The level of courts above the trial courts; the losing party in a civil case and the defendant in a criminal case may appeal the trial court's decision to an appellate court.

applications software   Software that is applied to a real-world task; used to perform a specific particular task or to solve a particular problem.

apprenticeship   A form of on-the-job training that combines specific job instruction with classroom instruction.

arbitration   The process of settling a labor-management dispute by having a third party-a single arbitrator or a panel—make a decision, which is binding on both the union and the employer.

assembly process   A production process in which the basic inputs are either combined to create the output or transformed into the output.

assets   Things of value owned by a firm.

audience selectivity   An advertising medium's ability to reach a precisely defined market.

auditing   The process of reviewing the records used to prepare financial statements and issuing a formal auditor's opinion indicating whether the statements have been prepared in accordance with accepted accounting rules.

authority   Legitimate power, granted by the organization and acknowledged by employees, that allows an individual to request action and expect compliance.

autocratic leaders   Directive leaders who prefer to make decisions and solve problems on their own with little input from subordinates.

automobile liability insurance   Insurance that protects the insured from financial losses caused by automobile-related injuries to others and damage to their property.

automobile physical damage insurance   In-surance that covers damage to or loss of the policyholder's vehicle from collision, theft, fire, or other perils; includes collision coverage and comprehensive (other-than-collision) coverage.

B

baby boomers   Americans born between 1946 and 1964.

backward integration   The acquisition of the production process by a wholesaler or retailer.

balance of payments   A summary of a country's international financial transactions showing the difference between the country's total payments to and its total receipts from other countries.

balance of trade   The difference between the value of a country's exports and the value of its imports during a certain time.

balance sheet   A financial statement that summarizes a firm's financial position at a specific point in time; reports the company's assets, liabilities, and owners' equity.

bank charter   An operating license issued to a bank by the federal government or a state government; required for a commercial bank to do business.

bankruptcy   The legal procedure by which individuals or businesses that cannot meet their financial obligations are relieved of their debt.

bargaining unit   The employees who are eligible to vote in a union certification election and who will be represented by the union if it is certified.

barriers to entry   Factors, such as technological or legal conditions, that prevent new firms from competing equally with a monopoly.

batch processing   A method of updating a database in which data are collected over some time period and processed together.

bear markets   Markets in which securities prices are falling.

benefit segmentation   The differentiation of markets based on what a product will do rather than on customer characteristics.

bill of material   A list of the components and the number of each required to make a given product.

board of directors   A group of people elected by the stockholders to handle the overall management of a corporation, such as setting corporate goals and policies, hiring corporate officers, and overseeing the firm's operations and finances.

bond ratings Letter grades assigned to bond issues to indicate their quality, or level of risk; assigned by rating agencies such as Moody's and Standard & Poor's.

bonds Long-term debt obligations (liabilities) of corporations and governments.

brainstorming A method of generating ideas in which group members suggest as many possibilities as they can without criticizing or evaluating any of the suggestions.

brand equity The value of company and brand names.

brand loyalty A consumer's preference for a particular brand.

brand A company's product identifier that distinguishes the company's products from those of its competitors.

breach of contract The failure by one party to a contract to fulfill the terms of the agreement without a legal excuse.

breakeven point The price at which a product's costs are covered, so additional sales result in profit.

breaking bulk The process of breaking large shipments of similar products into smaller, more usable lots.

brokers Go-betweens that bring buyers and sellers together.

browser Software that allows users to access the World Wide Web with a graphical point and click interface.

budgets Formal written forecasts of revenues and expenses that set spending limits based on operational forecasts; include cash budgets, capital budgets, and operating budgets.

bull markets Markets in which securities prices are rising.

bundling The strategy of grouping two or more related products together and pricing them as a single product.

business cycles Upward and downward changes in the level of economic activity.

business plan A formal written statement that describes in detail the idea for a new business and how it will be carried out; includes a general description of the company, the qualifications of the owner(s), a description of the product or service, an analysis of the market, and a financial plan.

business An organization that strives for a profit by providing goods and services desired by its customers.

business-to-business e-commerce Electronic commerce that involves transactions between companies.

business-to-consumer e-commerce Electronic commerce that involves transactions between businesses and the end user of the goods or services; also called e-tailing.

buyer behavior The actions people take in buying and using goods and services.

C

capital budgeting The process of analyzing long-term projects and selecting those that offer the best returns while maximizing the firm's value.

capital budgets Budgets that forecast a firm's outlays for fixed assets (plant and equipment), typically for a period of several years.

capital expenditures Investments in long-lived assets such as land, buildings, machinery, and equipment that are expected to product benefits over a period longer than a year.

capital products Large, expensive items with a long life span that are purchased by businesses for use in making other products or providing a service.

capital The inputs, such as tools, machinery, equipment, and buildings, used to produce goods and services and get them to the customer.

capitalism An economic system based on competition in the marketplace and private ownership of the factors of production (resources); also known as the private enterprise system.

cash and carry wholesaler A limited-service merchant wholesaler that does not offer credit or delivery services.

cash budgets Budgets that forecast a firm's cash inflows and outflows and help the firm plan for cash surpluses and shortages.

cash flow plan A cash management tool that provides a plan for managing income and expenses, including contributions to savings and investments needed to accomplish financial goals; also called a budget.

cash flows The inflow and outflow of cash for a firm.

cash management The day-to-day handling of one's liquid assets.

cash value The dollar amount paid to the owner of a life insurance policy if the policy is canceled before the death of the insured.

central processing unit (CPU) The central part of a computer system that performs all calculations, interprets program instructions, remembers information, and tells other parts of the computer what to do.

centralization The degree to which formal authority is concentrated in one area or level of an organization.

certified management accountant (CMA) A managerial accountant who has completed a professional certification program, including passing an examination.

certified public accountant (CPA) An accountant who has completed an approved bachelor's degree program, passed a test prepared by the American Institute of Certified Public Accountants, and met state requirements. Only a CPA can issue an auditor's opinion on financial statements.

chain of command The line of authority that extends from one level of an organization's hierarchy to the next, from top to bottom, and makes clear who reports to whom.

chief information officer (CIO) An executive with responsibility for managing all information resources in an organization.

circuit breakers Measures that, under certain circumstances, stop trading in the securities markets for a short cooling-off period to limit the amount the market can drop in one day.

circular flow The movement of inputs and outputs among households, businesses, and governments; a way of showing how the sectors of the economy interact.

closed shop A company where only union members can be hired; made illegal by the Taft-Hartley Act.

COBRA A federal regulation that allows most former employees and their families to continue group health insurance coverage at their own expense for up to 18 months after leaving an employer.

code of ethics A set of guidelines prepared by a firm to provide its employees with the knowledge of what the firm expects in terms of their responsibilities and behavior toward fellow employees, customers, and suppliers.

coercive power Power that is derived from an individual's ability to threaten negative outcomes.

cognitive dissonance The condition of having beliefs or knowledge that are internally inconsistent or that disagree with one's behavior.

coinsurance (participation) A percentage of covered expenses that the holder of a major medical insurance policy must pay.

collective bargaining The process of negotiating labor agreements that provide for compensation and working arrangements mutually acceptable to the union and to management.

command economy An economic system characterized by government ownership of virtually all resources and economic decision making by central government planning; also known as communism.

commercial banks Profit-oriented financial institutions that accept deposits, make business and consumer loans, invest in government and corporate securities, and provide other financial services.

commercial paper Unsecured short-term debt (an IOU) offered by large, financially strong corporations.

committee structure An organizational structure in which authority and responsibility are held by a group rather than an individual.

common stock A security that represents an ownership interest in a corporation.

comparative advertising Advertising that compares the company's product with competing, named products.

competitive advantage A set of unique features of a company and its products that are perceived by the target market as significant and superior to those of the competition; also called differential advantage.

component lifestyle A lifestyle made up of a complex set of interests and choices.

comprehensive (other-than-collision) coverage Automobile insurance that covers damage to or loss of the policyholder's vehicle due to perils such as fire, floods, theft, and vandalism; part of automobile physical damage insurance.

computer network A group of two or more computer systems linked together by communications channels to share data and information.

computer virus A computer program that copies itself into other software and can spread to other computer systems.

computer A machine that stores and manipulates symbols based on a set of instructions.

computer-aided design (CAD) The use of computers to design and test new products and modify existing ones.

computer-aided manufacturing (CAM) The use of computers to develop and control the production process.

computer-integrated manufacturing (CIM) The combination of computerized manufacturing processes such as robots and flexible manufacturing systems with other computerized systems that control design, inventory, production, and purchasing.

conceptual skills A manager's ability to view the organization as a whole, understand how the various parts are interdependent, and assess how the organization relates to its external environment.

conciliation A method of attempting to settle labor disputes in which a specialist from the Federal Mediation and Conciliation Service helps management and the union focus on the issues and acts as a go-between.

conglomerate merger A merger of companies in unrelated businesses; done to reduce risk.

conglomerate union A union that represents a wide variety of workers in various industries.

Congress of Industrial Organizations (CIO) A national labor organization made up of numerous industrial unions; founded in 1935. In 1955, the CIO merged with the American Federation of Labor (AFL) to form the AFL-CIO.

consensual leaders Leaders who encourage discussion about issues and then require that all parties involved agree to the final decision.

consultative leaders Leaders who confer with subordinates before making a decision, but who retain the final decision-making authority.

consumer fraud The practice of deceiving customers by such means as failing to honor warranties or other promises or selling goods or services that do not meet advertised claims.

consumer price index (CPI) An index of the prices of a market basket of goods and services purchased by typical urban consumers.

consumerism A social movement that seeks to increase the rights and powers of buyers vis-à-vis sellers.

contingency plans Plans that identify alternative courses of action for very unusual or crisis situations.

contingent workers Persons who prefer temporary employment, either part-time or full-time.

continuous improvement A commitment to constantly seek better ways of doing things so as to maintain and increase quality.

continuous process A production process that uses long production runs lasting days, weeks, or months without equipment shutdowns; generally used for high-volume, low-variety products with standardized parts.

contract manufacturing The practice in which a foreign firm manufactures private-label goods under a domestic firm's brand name.

contract An agreement that sets forth the relationship between parties regarding the performance of a specified action; creates a legal obligation and is enforceable in a court of law.

contractionary policy The use of monetary policy by the Fed to tighten the money supply by selling government securities or raising interest rates.

contractual distribution system A vertical marketing system in which a network of independent firms at different levels (manufacturer, wholesaler, retailer) coordinate their distribution activities through a written contract.

controlling The process of assessing the organization's progress toward accomplishing its goals; includes monitoring the implementation of a plan and correcting deviations from the plan.

convenience products Relatively inexpensive items that require little shopping effort and are purchased routinely without planning.

conventional ethics The second stage in the ethical development of individuals in which people move from an egocentric viewpoint to consider the expectations of an organization of society.

convertible bonds Corporate bonds that are issued with an option that allows the bondholder to convert them into common stock.

cooperatives Legal entities typically formed by people with similar interests, such as customers or suppliers, to reduce costs and gain economic power.

copyright A form of protection that gives the creator of intellectual property the exclusive right to use, produce, and sell the creation during the lifetime of the creator and for 50 years thereafter.

corporate campaign A union strategy in which a union disrupts a corporation's relations with its shareholders or investors as a means of attacking the company.

corporate culture The set of attitudes, values, and standards that distinguishes one organization from another.

corporate distribution system A vertical marketing system in which one firm owns the entire distribution channel.

corporate philanthropy The practice of charitable giving by corporations; includes contributing cash, donating equipment and products, and supporting the volunteer efforts of company employees.

corporation A legal entity that is chartered by the state in which it is formed and can own property, enter into contracts, sue and be sued, and engage in business operations under the terms of its charter.

corrective advertising An advertisement run to correct false impressions left by previous ads.

cost competitive advantage A firm's ability to produce a product or service at a lower cost than all other competitors in an industry while maintaining satisfactory profit margins.

cost of goods sold The total expense of buying or producing a firm's goods or services.

cost per thousand (CPM) Cost per thousand contacts is a term used in expressing advertising costs; refers to the cost of reaching 1,000 members of the target market.

cost-of-living adjustment (COLA) A provision in a labor contract that calls for wages to increase automatically as the cost of living rises (usually measured by the consumer price index).

cost-push inflation Inflation that occurs when increases in production costs push up the prices of final goods and services.

costs Expenses incurred in creating and selling goods and services.

countertrade A form of international trade in which part or all of the payment for goods or services is in the form of other goods and services.

craft union A union that represents skilled workers in a single craft or occupation such as bricklaying, carpentry, or plumbing.

credit life insurance Insurance that will repay a loan if the borrower dies while the loan is still outstanding.

credit unions Not-for-profit, member-owned financial cooperatives.

critical path method (CPM) A project management tool that enables a manager to determine the critical path of activities for a project-the activities that will cause the entire project to fall behind schedule if they are not completed on time.

critical path In a critical path method network, the longest path through the linked activities.

cross-functional teams Teams of employees who are from about the same level in the organizational hierarchy but from different functional areas; for example, task forces, organizational committees, and project teams.

crowding out The situation that occurs when government spending replaces spending by the private sector.

current assets Assets that can or will be converted to cash within the next 12 months.

current liabilities Short-term claims that are due within a year of the date of the balance sheet.

current ratio The ratio of total current assets to total current liabilities; used to measure a firm's liquidity.

customer departmentalization Departmentalization that is based on the primary type of customer served by the organizational unit.

customer satisfaction The customer's feeling that a product has met or exceeded expectations.

customer value The ratio of benefits to the sacrifice necessary to obtain those benefits, as determined by the customer; reflects the willingness of customers to actually buy a product.

customization The production of goods or services one at a time according to the specific needs or wants of individual customers.

cyclical unemployment Unemployment that occurs when a downturn in the business cycle reduces the demand for labor throughout the economy.

 D

data warehouse An information technology that combines many databases across a whole company into one central database that supports management decision making.

data The many facts that together describe a company's status.

database marketing The creation of a large computerized file of the profiles and purchase patterns of customers and potential customers; usually required for successful micromarketing.

database software Software that records, updates, and stores information.

dealer brands Brands that are owned by the wholesaler or retailer rather than the name of the manufacturer.

debentures Unsecured bonds that are backed only by the reputation of the issuer and its promise to pay the principal and interest when due.

debt ratios Ratios that measure the degree and effect of a firm's use of borrowed funds (debt) to finance its operations; for example, the debt-to-equity ratio.

debt A form of business financing consisting of borrowed funds that must be repaid with interest over a stated time period.

debt-to-equity ratio The ratio of total liabilities to owners' equity; measures the relationship between the amount of debt financing and the amount of equity financing.

decentralization The process of pushing decision-making authority down the organizational hierarchy.

decertification election An election in which workers vote, by secret ballot, on whether they want to continue to be represented by their union.

decision support system (DSS) An interactive, flexible, computerized information system that allows managers to make decisions quickly and accurately; used to conduct sales analyses, forecast sales, evaluate advertising, analyze product lines, and keep tabs on market trends and competitors' actions.

decisional roles A manager's activities as an entrepreneur, resource allocator, conflict resolver, or negotiator.

delegation of authority The assignment of some degree of authority and responsibility to persons lower in the chain of command.

demand curve A graph showing the quantity of a good or service that people are willing to buy at various prices.

demand deposits Money kept in checking accounts that can be withdrawn by depositors on demand.

demand The quantity of a good or service that people are willing to buy at various prices.

demand-pull inflation Inflation that occurs when the demand for goods and services is greater than the supply.

democratic leaders Leaders who solicit input from all members of the group and then allow the members to make the final decision through a vote.

demographic segmentation The differentiation of markets through the use of categories such as age, education, gender, income, and household size.

demography The study of people's vital statistics, such as their age, race and ethnicity, and location.

demotion The downgrading or reassignment of an employee to a position with less responsibility.

departmentalization The process of grouping jobs together so that similar or associated tasks and activities can be coordinated.

depreciation The allocation of an asset's original cost to the years in which it is expected to produce revenues.

deregulation The removal of rules and regulations governing business competition.

desktop publishing software Software that combines word processing, graphics, and page layout software and is used to create documents such as sales brochures, catalogs, advertisements, and newsletters.

detailing The physical stocking of merchandise at a retailer by the salesperson who delivers the merchandise.

devaluation A lowering of the value of a nation's currency relative to other currencies.

differential competitive advantage A firm's ability to provide a unique product or service that offers something of value to buyers besides simply a lower price.

direct foreign investment Active ownership of a foreign company or of manufacturing or marketing facilities in a foreign country.

discount rate The interest rate that the Federal Reserve charges its member banks.

distribution centers Warehouses that specialize in changing shipment sizes, rather than in storing goods.

distribution channel The series of marketing entities through which goods and services pass on their way from producers to end users.

distribution strategy The part of the marketing mix that involves deciding how many stores and which specific wholesalers and retailers will handle the product in a geographic area.

diversification An investment strategy that involves investing in different asset classes, such as cash equivalents, stocks, bonds, and real estate, and combining securities with different patterns and amounts of return.

diversity Employee differences in age, race and ethnicity, gender, educational background, and work experience.

dividend reinvestment plan (DRIP) A program in which dividends paid by a stock are automatically reinvested in that stock along with any additional contributions submitted by the stockholder.

dividends Payments to stockholders from a corporation's profits.

division of labor The process of dividing work into separate jobs and assigning tasks to workers.

double-entry bookkeeping A method of accounting in which each transaction is recorded as two entries so that two accounts or records are changed.

Dow Jones Industrial Average (DJIA) The most widely used market average; measures the stock prices of 30 large, well-known corporations that trade on the New York Stock Exchange.

dumping The practice of charging a lower price for a product in foreign markets than in the firm's home market.

duration of benefits In disability income insurance, the length of time the insurance payments will continue.

E

earned income Income that is earned from employment such as wages, tips, and self-employment income.

earnings per share (EPS) The ratio of net profit to the number of shares of common stock outstanding; measures the number of dollars earned by each share of stock.

economic growth An increase in a nation's output of goods and services.

economic system The combination of policies, laws, and choices made by a nation's government to establish the systems that determine what goods and services are produced and how they are allocated.

economics The study of how a society uses scarce resources to produce and distribute goods and services.

efficient consumer response (ECR) A method of managing inventory and streamlining the movement of products from supplier to distributor to retailer that relies on electronic data interchange.

electronic commerce (e-commerce) The process of selling a product or service via the Internet; also called electronic business (e-business).

electronic data interchange (EDI) Computer-to-computer exchange of information, including automatic shipping notifications, invoices, inventory data, and forecasts; used in efficient consumer response systems.

embargo A total ban on imports or exports of a product.

emergency fund Liquid assets that are available to meet emergencies.

employee orientation Training that prepares a new employee to perform on the job; includes information about job assignments, work rules, equipment, and performance expectations, as well as about company policies, salary and benefits, and parking.

empowerment The process of giving employees increased autonomy and discretion to make decisions, as well as control over the resources needed to implement those decisions.

enterprise resource planning (ERP) A computerized resource planning system that includes information about the firm's suppliers and customers as well as data generated internally.

entrepreneurs People with vision, drive, and creativity who are willing to take the risk of starting and managing a new business to make a profit or of greatly changing the scope and direction of an existing firm.

environmental scanning The process in which a firm continually collects and evaluates information about its external environment.

equilibrium The point at which quantity demanded equals quantity supplied.

equity theory A theory of motivation that holds that worker satisfaction is influenced by employees' perceptions about how fairly they are treated compared with their coworkers.

equity A form of business financing consisting of funds raised through the sale of stock in a business.

ethics A set of moral standards for judging whether something is right or wrong.

European Union (EU) An organization of 15 European nations (as of 1999) that works to foster political and economic integration in Europe; formerly called the European Community.

exchange controls Laws that require a company earning foreign exchange (foreign currency) from its exports to sell the foreign exchange to a control agency, such as a central bank.

exchange The process in which two parties give something of value to each other to satisfy their respective needs.

excise taxes Taxes that are imposed on specific items such as gasoline, alcoholic beverages, airline tickets, and guns.

exclusive distribution A distribution system in which a manufacturer selects only one or two dealers in an area to market its products.

executive information system (EIS) A management support system that is customized for an individual executive; provides specific information for strategic decisions.

expansionary policy The use of monetary policy by the Fed to increase the growth of the money supply.

expectancy theory A theory of motivation that holds that the probability of an individual acting in a particular way depends on that individual's belief that the act will have a particular outcome and on whether the individual values that outcome.

expense items Items, purchased by businesses, that are smaller and less expensive than capital products and usually have a life span of less than one year.

expenses The costs of generating revenues.

experiment A marketing research method in which the investigator changes one or more variables—price, packaging, design, shelf space, advertising theme, or advertising expenditures—while observing the effects of these changes on another variable (usually sales).

expert power Power that is derived from an individual's extensive knowledge in one or more areas.

expert system A management support system that uses artificial intelligence to enable computers to reason and learn to solve problems in much the same way humans do.

exporting The practice of selling domestically produced goods to buyers in another country.

exports Goods and services sold outside a firm's domestic market.

express contract A contract in which the terms are specified in either written or spoken words.

express warranty A written guarantee about a product, such as that it contains certain materials, will perform a certain way, or is otherwise fit for the purpose for which it was sold.

extranet A private computer network that uses Internet technology and a browser interface but is accessible only to authorized outsiders with a valid user name and password.

F

factoring A form of short-term financing in which a firm sells its accounts receivable to a factor.

factors of production The resources used to create goods and services.

federal budget deficit The condition that occurs when the federal government spends more for programs than it collects in taxes.

Federal Deposit Insurance Corporation (FDIC) An independent, quasi-public corporation backed by the full faith and credit of the U.S. government that insures deposits in commercial banks and thrift institutions for up to a ceiling of $100,000 per account.

Federal Reserve System (the Fed) The central banking system of the United States.

Federal Trade Commission (FTC) An agency of the U.S. government that works to prevent deception and misrepresentation in advertising.

filing status The status of a taxpayer as single, married, or some other status on the income tax return.

Financial Accounting Standards Board (FASB) The private organization that is responsible for establishing financial accounting standards in the United States.

financial accounting Accounting that focuses on preparing the financial reports used by outsiders such as lenders, suppliers, investors, and government agencies to assess the financial strength of a business.

financial intermediation The process in which financial institutions act as intermediaries between the suppliers and demanders of funds.

financial management The art and science of managing a firm's money so that it can meet its goals.

financial planning The process of managing one's personal finances to achieve financial goals; involves establishing financial goals, gathering information, analyzing the information, developing a plan, implementing the plan, and monitoring the plan.

financial risk The chance that a firm will be unable to make scheduled interest and principal payments on its debt.

fiscal policy The government's use of taxation and spending to affect the economy.

fixed assets Long-term assets used by a firm for more than a year, such as land, buildings, and machinery.

fixed costs Costs that do not vary with different levels of output; for example, rent.

fixed-cost contribution The selling price per unit (revenue) minus the variable costs per unit.

fixed-position layout A facility arrangement in which the product stays in one place and workers and machinery move to it as needed.

flexible manufacturing system (FMS) A system that combines automated workstations with computer-controlled transportation devices—automatic guided vehicles (AGVs)—that move materials between workstations and into and out of the system.

floating exchange rates A system in which prices of currencies move up and down based upon the demand for and supply of the various currencies.

focus group A group of 8 to 12 participants led by a moderator in an in-depth discussion on one particular topic or concept.

formal organization The order and design of relationships within a firm; consists of two or more people working together with a common objective and clarity of purpose.

forward integration The acquisition by a manufacturer of a marketing intermediary closer to the customer, such as a wholesaler or retailer.

four Ps Product, price, promotion, and place (distribution), which together make up the marketing mix.

franchise agreement A contract setting out the terms of a franchising arrangement, including the rules for running the franchise, the services provided by the franchisor, and the financial terms.

franchisee In a franchising arrangement, the individual or company that sells the goods or services of the franchisor in a certain geographic area.

franchising A form of business organization based on a business arrangement between a franchisor, which supplies the product concept, and the franchisee, who sells the goods or services of the franchisor in a certain geographic area.

franchisor In a franchising arrangement, the company that supplies the product concept to the franchisee.

free trade The policy of permitting the people of a country to buy and sell where they please without restrictions.

free-rein (laissez-faire) leadership A leadership style in which the leader turns over all authority and control to subordinates.

free-trade zone An area where the nations allow free, or almost free, trade among each other while imposing tariffs on goods of nations outside the zone.

frequency The number of times an individual is exposed to an advertising message.

frictional unemployment Short-term unemployment that is not related to the business cycle.

fringe benefits Indirect compensation such as pensions, health insurance, and vacations.

full employment The condition when all people who want to work and can work have jobs.

full warranty The manufacturer's guarantee to meet certain minimum standards, including repair or replacement of the product or refunding the customer if the product does not work.

full-service merchant wholesalers Wholesalers that provide many services for their clients, such as providing credit, offering promotional and technical advice, storing and delivering merchandise, or providing installation and repairs.

functional departmentalization Departmental-ization that is based on the primary functions performed within an organizational unit.

futures contracts Agreements to buy or sell specified quantities of commodities or financial future at an agreed-on price at a future date.

G

Gantt charts Bar graphs plotted on a time line that show the relationship between scheduled and actual production.

general partners Partners who have unlimited liability for all of the firm's business obligations and who control its operations.

general partnership A partnership in which all partners share in the management and profits. Each partner can act on behalf of the firm and has unlimited liability for all its business obligations.

generally accepted accounting principles (GAAP) The financial accounting standards followed by accountants in the United States in preparing financial statements.

Generation X Americans born between 1968 and 1979.

Generation Y Americans born after 1982.

generic products Products that carry no brand name, come in plain containers, and sell for much less than brand-name products.

geographic departmentalization Departmentaization that is based on the geographic segmentation of the organizational units.

geographic segmentation The differentiation of markets by region of the country, city or county size, market density, or climate.

give-backs Benefits given up by a union; also called concession bargaining.

global management skills A manager's ability to operate in diverse cultural environments.

global vision The ability to recognize and react to international business opportunities, be aware of threats from foreign competition, and effectively use international distribution networks to obtain raw materials and move finished products to customers.

goal-setting theory A theory of motivation based on the premise that an individual's intention to work toward a goal is a primary source of motivation.

goods Tangible items manufactured by businesses.

grace period The period after a purchase is made on a credit card during which interest is not owed if the entire balance is paid on time.

grievance A formal complaint, filed by an employee or by the union, charging that management has violated the contract.

gross domestic product (GDP) The total market value of all final goods and services produced within a nation's borders in a year.

gross profit The amount a company earns after paying to produce or buy its products but before deducting operating expenses; the differences between net sales and cost of goods sold.

gross sales The total dollar amount of a company's sales.

group cohesiveness The degree to which group members want to stay in the group and tend to resist outside influences.

guaranteed investment contracts (GICs) Insurance company products that are similar to bank certificates of deposit.

H

hardware The equipment associated with a computer system; includes the input system, the central processing unit with primary storage, secondary storage, and the output system.

Hawthorne effect The phenomenon that employees perform better when they feel singled out for attention or feel that management is concerned about their welfare.

health maintenance organizations (HMOs) Managed care organizations that provide comprehensive health care services for a fixed periodic payment.

high-yield (junk) bonds High-risk, high-return bonds.

horizontal merger A merger of companies at the same stage in the same industry; done to reduce costs, expand product offerings, or reduce competition.

host computer The central computer for a Web site that stores services and data used by other computers on the network.

human relations skills A manager's interpersonal skills that are used to accomplish goals through the use of human resources.

human resource (HR) planning Creating a strategy for meeting future human resource needs.

human resource management The process of hiring, developing, motivating, and evaluating employees to achieve organizational goals.

hygiene factors Extrinsic elements of the work environment that do not serve as a source of employee satisfaction or motivation.

hypertext A file or series of files within a Web page that links users to documents at the same or other Web sites.

I

implied contract A contract that depends on the acts and conduct of the parties to show agreement; the terms are not specified in writing or orally.

implied warranty An unwritten guarantee that a product is fit for the purpose for which it is sold.

import quota A limit on the quantity of a certain good that can be imported.

imports Goods and services that are bought from other countries.

income statement A financial statement that summarizes a firm's revenues and expenses and shows its total profit or loss over a period of time.

income taxes Taxes that are based on the income received by businesses and individuals.

indemnity (fee-for-service) plans Health insurance plans that reimburse the insured for medical costs covered by the insurance policy.

industrial distributors Independent wholesalers that buy related product lines from many manufacturers and sell them to industrial users.

industrial union A union that represents all of the workers in a particular industry, such as auto workers or steel workers.

inflation The situation in which the average of all prices of goods and services is rising.

informal organization The network of connections and channels of communication based on the informal relationships of individuals inside an organization.

information system (IS) The methods and equipment that provide information about all aspects of a firm's operations.

information technology (IT) The equipment and techniques used to manage and process information.

information A meaningful and useful summary of data.

informational roles A manager's activities as an information gatherer, an information disseminator, or a spokesperson for the company.

infrastructure The basic institutions and public facilities upon which an economy's development depends.

injunction A court order barring certain union activities.

insider trading The use of information that is not available to the general public to make profits on securities transactions.

institutional advertising Advertising that creates a positive picture of a company and its ideals, services, and roles in the community.

institutional investors Investment professionals who are paid to manage other people's money.

intangible assets Long-term assets with no physical existence such as patents, copyrights, trademarks, and goodwill.

integrated marketing communications (IMC) The coordination of all promotional activities—media advertising, sales promotion, personal selling, and public relations, as well as direct marketing and packaging—to produce a consistent, unified message.

intensive distribution A distribution system in which a manufacturer tries to sell its products wherever there are potential customers.

interest A fixed amount of money paid by the issuer of a bond to the bondholder on a regular schedule.

intermittent process A production process that uses short production runs to make batches of different products; generally used for low-volume, high-variety products.

International Monetary Fund (IMF) An international organization, founded in 1945, that promotes trade, makes short-term loans to member nations, and acts as a lender of last resort for troubled nations.

Internet service provider (ISP) A commercial service that connects companies and individuals to the Internet.

Internet A worldwide computer network that includes both commercial and public networks and offers various capabilities including e-mail, file transfer, online chat sessions, and news-groups.

interpersonal roles A manager's activities as a figurehead, company leader, or liaison.

intranet An internal corporate-wide area network that uses Internet technology to link employees in many locations and with different types of computers.

intrapreneurs Entrepreneurs who apply their creativity, vision, and risk taking within a large corporation, rather than starting a company of their own.

inventory management The determination of how much inventory a firm will keep on hand and the ordering, receiving, storing, and keeping track of inventory.

inventory turnover ratio The ratio of cost of goods sold to average inventory; measures the speed with which inventory moves through a firm and is turned into sales.

inventory The supply of goods that a firm holds for use in production or for sale to customers.

investing The process of committing money to various instruments in order to obtain future financial returns.

investment bankers Firms that act as underwriters, buying securities from corporation and governments and reselling them to the public.

ISO 14000 A set of technical standards designed by the International Organization for Standardization to help ensure clean production processes to protect the environment.

ISO 9000 A set of five technical standards of quality management that were created in the late 1980s by the International Organization for Standardization to provide a uniform way of determining whether manufacturing plants and service organizations have sound quality procedures.

J

job analysis A study of the tasks required to do a particular job well.

job description The tasks and responsibilities of a job.

job enlargement The horizontal expansion of a job by increasing the number and variety of tasks that a person performs.

job enrichment The vertical expansion of a job by increasing the employee's autonomy, responsibility, and decision-making authority.

job fair An event, typically one day, held at a convention center to bring together thousands of job seekers and hundreds of firms searching for employees.

job rotation The shifting of workers from one job to another; also called cross-training.

job sharing A scheduling option that allows two individuals to split the tasks, responsibilities, and work hours of one 40-hour-per-week job.

job shop A manufacturing firm that produces goods in response to customer orders.

job specification A list of the skills, knowledge, and abilities a person must have to fill a job.

joint venture An agreement in which a domestic firm buys part of a foreign firm or joins with a foreign firm to create a new entity.

judiciary The branch of government that is responsible for settling disputes by applying and interpreting points of law; consists of the court system.

justice What is considered fair according to the prevailing standards of society; in the twentieth century, an equitable distribution of the burdens and rewards that society has to offer.

just-in-time (JIT) A system in which materials arrive just when they are needed for production rather than being stored on site.

K

Knights of Labor The first important national labor organization in the United States; founded in 1869.

knowledge The combined talents and skills of the workforce.

L

labor union An organization that represents workers in dealing with management over disputes involving wages, hours, and working conditions.

Landrum-Griffin Act A statute enacted in 1959 to regulate the internal affairs of unions; contains a bill of rights for union members, rules for electing union officers, and safeguards to keep unions financially sound.

layoff A temporary separation of an employee from the organization; arranged by the employer, usually because business is slow.

leader pricing The strategy of pricing products below the normal markup or even below cost to attract customers to a store where they would not otherwise shop.

leadership style The relatively consistent way that individuals in leadership positions attempt to influence the behavior of others.

leadership The process of guiding and motivating others toward the achievement of organizational goals.

lean manufacturing Streamlining production by eliminating steps in the production process that do not add benefits that customers are willing to pay for.

legitimate power Power that is derived from an individual's position in an organization.

leveraged buyout (LBO) A corporate takeover financed by large amounts of borrowed money; can be done by outside investors or by a company's own management.

liabilities What a firm owes to its creditors; also called debts.

licensing The legal process whereby a firm agrees to allow another firm to use a manufacturing process, trademark, patent, trade secret, or other proprietary knowledge in exchange for the payment of a royalty.

limited liability company (LLC) A hybrid organization that offers the same liability protection as a corporation but may be taxed as either a partnership or a corporation.

limited partners Partners whose liability for the firm's business obligations is limited to the amount of their investment.

limited partnership A partnership with one or more general partners, who have unlimited liability, and one or more limited partners, whose liability is limited to the amount of their investment.

limited-service merchant wholesalers Whole-salers that typically carry a limited line of fast-moving merchandise and do not offer many services to their clients.

line extension A new flavor, size, or model using an existing brand name in an existing category.

line of credit For credit cards, the maximum amount a person can have outstanding on a card at any one time.

line organization An organizational structure with direct, clear lines of authority and communication flowing from the top managers downward.

line positions All positions in the organization directly concerned with producing goods and services and which are directly connected from top to bottom.

line-and-staff organization An organizational structure that includes both line and staff positions.

liquid assets Cash and other assets that can be converted to cash quickly at little or no cost, such as checking accounts.

liquidity ratios Ratios that measure a firm's ability to pay its short-term debts as they come due; for example, the current ratio, the acid-test (quick) ratio, and net working capital.

liquidity The speed with which an asset can be converted to cash.

local area network (LAN) A network that connects computers at one site, enabling the computer users to exchange data and share the use of hardware and software from a variety of computer manufacturers.

local union A branch or unit of a national union that represents workers at a specific plant or in a specific geographic area.

lockout An employer tactic in a labor dispute in which the employer refuses to allow workers to enter a plant or building to work, which means that the workers do not get paid.

logistics management The management of the physical distribution process.

long-term forecasts Projections of a firm's activities and the funding for those activities over a over a one-year period that is longer than a year, typically 2 to 10 years; also called strategic plans.

long-term liabilities Claims that come due more than one year after the date of the balance sheet.

loss leader A product priced below cost as part of a leader pricing strategy.

M

Maastricht Treaty A 1993 treaty concluded by the members of the European Community (now the European Union) that outlines plans for tightening bonds among the members and creating a single market; officially called the Treaty on European Union.

macroeconomics The subarea of economics that focuses on the economy as a whole by looking at aggregate data for large groups of people, companies, or products.

mainframe computers Large computers that have much greater storage capacity than PCs or minicomputers.

major medical insurance Health insurance that covers a wide range of medical costs with few exclusions and high maximum limits.

make-or-buy decision The determination by a firm of whether to make its own production materials or buy them from outside sources.

Malcolm Baldrige National Quality Award An award bestowed on U.S. companies whose goods and services offer world-class quality; established by Congress in 1987 and named for a former secretary of commerce.

managed care plans Health insurance plans that generally pay only for services provided by doctors and hospitals that are part of the plan.

management support system (MSS) A dynamic information system that helps managers make decisions by allowing them to analyze data, identify business trends, make forecasts, and model business strategies.

management The process of guiding the development, maintenance, and allocation of resources to attain organizational goals.

managerial accounting Accounting that provides financial information that managers inside the organization can use to evaluate and make decisions about current and future operations.

managerial hierarchy The levels of management within an organization; typically, includes top, middle, and supervisory management.

manufacturer brands Brands that are owned by national or regional manufacturers and widely distributed; also call national brands.

manufacturer A producer; an organization that converts raw materials to finished products.

manufacturers' representatives Salespeople who represent noncompeting manufacturers; function as independent agents rather than as salaried employees of the manufacturers.

manufacturing resource planning II (MRPII) A complex computerized system that integrates data from many departments to control the flow of resources and inventory.

market averages Summaries of the price behavior of securities based on the arithmetic average price of a group of securities at a given point in time; used to track market conditions.

market indexes Measures of the current price behavior of groups of securities relative to a base value set at an earlier point in time; used to track market conditions.

market segmentation The process of separating, identifying, and evaluating the layers of a market in order to design a marketing mix.

market structure The number of suppliers in a market.

marketable securities Short-term investments that are easily converted into cash; for example, Treasury bills, certificates of deposits, and commercial paper.

marketing concept Identifying consumer needs and then producing the goods or services that will satisfy them while making a profit for the organization.

marketing intermediaries Organizations that assist in moving goods and services from producers to end users.

marketing mix The blend of product offering, pricing, promotional methods, and distribution system that brings a specific group of consumers superior value.

marketing research The process of planning, collecting, and analyzing data relevant to a marketing decision.

marketing The process of discovering the needs and wants of potential buyers and customers and then providing goods and services that meet or exceed their expectations.

markup pricing A method of pricing in which a certain percentage (the markup) is added to the product's cost to arrive at the price.

Maslow's hierarchy of needs A theory of motivation developed by Abraham Maslow; holds that humans have five levels of needs and act to satisfy their unmet needs.

mass customization A flexible manufacturing technique in which mass-market goods and services are tailored to the unique needs of the individuals who buy them.

mass production The ability to manufacture many identical goods at once.

master brand A brand so dominant that consumers think of it immediately when a product category, use, attribute, or customer benefit is mentioned.

materials requirement planning (MRP) A computerized system of controlling the flow of resources and inventory. A master schedule is used to ensure that the materials, labor, and equipment needed for production are at the right places in the right amounts at the right times.

matrix structure (project management) An organizational structure that combines functional and product departmentalization by bringing together people from different functional areas of the organization to work on a special project.

mechanistic organization An organizational structure that is characterized by a relatively high degree of job specialization, rigid departmentalization, many layers of management, narrow spans of control, centralized decision making, and a long chain of command.

mediation A method of settling disputes in which the parties submit their case to an impartial third party but are not required to accept the mediator's decision.

mentoring A form of on-the-job training in which a senior manager or other experienced employee provides job- and career-related information to a protégé.

merchant wholesaler An institution that buys goods from manufacturers (takes ownership) and resells them to businesses, government agencies, other wholesalers, or retailers.

Mercosur A trade agreement among Argentina, Brazil, Paraguay, and Uruguay that eliminates most tariffs among the member nations.

merger The combination of two or more firms to form a new company, which often takes on a new corporate identity.

microcomputers Small computers that can fit on a desktop; also called personal computers (PCs) or desktop computers.

microeconomics The subarea of economics that focuses on individual parts of the economy such as households or firms.

middle management Managers who design and carry out tactical plans in specific areas of the company.

minicomputers Medium-sized computers that are too large for a desktop but small enough to fit in an office.

mission statement A formal document that states an organization's purpose and reason for existing and describes its basic philosophy.

mission An organization's purpose and reason for existing; its long-term goals.

mixed economies Economies that combine several economic systems.

modem The part of a computer system that translates data into a form that can be transmitted.

monetary policy A government's programs for controlling the amount of money circulating in the economy and interest rates.

money Anything that is acceptable as payment for goods and services.

monopolistic competition A market structure in which many firms offer products that are close substitutes and in which entry is relatively easy.

mortgage bonds Corporate bonds that are secured by property, such as real estate, equipment, or buildings.

mortgage loan A long-term loan that uses real estate as collateral.

motivating factors Intrinsic job elements that lead to worker satisfaction.

multiculturalism The condition when all major ethnic groups in an area, such as a city, county, or census tract, are about equally represented.

multinational corporations Corporations that move resources, goods, services, and skills across national boundaries without regard to the country in which their headquarters are located.

municipal bonds Bonds issued by states, cities, counties, and other state and local government agencies.

mutual fund An investment company that pools investors' funds to buy a selection of securities.

mutual-aid pact An agreement by companies in an industry to create a fund that can be used to help cover fixed costs of any member company whose workers go on strike.

N

National Advertising Division (NAD) A subdivision of the Council of Better Business Bureaus that investigates complaints about advertising from consumers and other advertisers.

National Advertising Review Board (NARB) A board that hears appeals from the decisions of the National Advertising Division (NAD) of the Council of Better Business Bureaus or resolves issues if the NAD is deadlocked.

National Association of Securities Dealers Auto-mated Quotation (Nasdaq) system The first electronic-based stock market and the largest over-the-counter market.

national debt The accumulated total of all of the federal government's annual budget deficits.

National Labor Relations Board (NLRB) An agency established by the Wagner Act of 1935 to enforce the act and investigate charges of employer and union wrongdoing and supervise elections for union representatives.

national union A union that consists of many local unions in a particular industry, skilled trade, or geographic area and thus represents workers throughout an entire country.

nationalism A sense of national consciousness that boosts the culture and interests of one country over those of all other countries.

net asset value (NAV) The price at which each share of a mutual fund can be bought or sold.

net loss The amount obtained by subtracting all of a firm's expenses from its revenues, when the expenses are more than the revenues.

net profit (net income) The amount obtained by subtracting all of a firm's expenses from its revenues, when the revenues are more than the expenses.

net profit margin The ratio of net profit to net sales; also called return on sales. It measures the percentage of each sales dollar remaining after all expenses have been deducted.

net sales The amount left after deducting sales discounts and returns and allowances from gross sales.

net working capital The amount obtained by subtracting total current liabilities from total current assets; used to measure a firm's liquidity.

net worth statement A summary of a person's financial situation on a given day; provides information about both assets and liabilities.

niche competitive advantage A firm's ability to target and effectively serve a single segment of the market within a limited geographic area.

nonprogrammed decisions Responses to infrequent, unforeseen, or very unusual problems and opportunities where the manager does not have a precedent to follow in decision making.

Norris-La Guardia Act A statute enacted in 1932 that barred the use of injunctions to prevent strikes and other union activities and made yellow-dog contracts unenforceable; also called the Anti-Injunction Act.

North American Free Trade Agreement (NAFTA) A 1993 agreement creating a free-trade zone including Canada, Mexico, and the United States.

not-for-profit organization An organization that exists to achieve some goal other than the usual business goal of profit.

O

observation research A marketing research method in which the investigator monitors respondents' actions without interacting directly with the respondents; for example, by using cash registers with scanners.

odd-even (psychological) pricing The strategy of setting a price at an odd number to connote a bargain and at an even number to suggest quality.

office automation system An information system that uses information technology tools such as word processing systems, e-mail systems, cellular phones, pagers and fax machines, to improve communications throughout an organization.

oligopoly A market structure in which a few firms produce most or all of the output and in which large capital requirements or other factors limit the number of firms.

online (real-time) processing A method of updating a database in which data are processed as they become available.

on-the-job training Training in which the employee learns the job by doing it with guidance from a supervisor or experienced coworker.

open market operations The purchase or sale of U.S. government bonds by the Federal Reserve to stimulate or slow down the economy.

open shop A company where employees do not have to join the union or pay dues or fees to the union.

open-end credit Any type of credit where the borrower applies for the credit and uses it over and over again; for example, credit cards.

operating budgets Budgets that combine sales forecasts with estimates of production costs and operating expenses in order to forecast a firm's profits.

operating expenses The expenses of running a business that are not directly related to producing or buying its products.

operating system A collection of programs that manages a computer system's activities and runs applications software.

operational planning The process of creating specific standards, methods, policies, and procedures that are used in specific functional areas of the organization.

operations management Management of the production process.

options Contracts that entitle the holder to buy or sell specified quantities of common stocks or other financial instruments at a set price during a specified time.

organic organization An organizational structure that is characterized by a relatively low degree of job specialization, loose departmentalization, few levels of management, wide spans of control, decentralized decision making, and a short chain of command.

organization chart A visual representation of the structured relationships among tasks and the people given the authority to do those tasks.

organized stock exchanges Organizations on whose premises securities are resold using an auction-style trading system.

organizing The process of coordinating and allocating a firm's resources in order to carry out its plans.

outsourcing The purchase of items or services from an outside source.

over-the-counter (OTC) market A sophisticated telecommunications network that links dealers throughout the United States and enables them to trade securities.

owners' equity The total amount of investment in the firm minus any liabilities; also called net worth.

P

participative leadership A leadership style in which the leader shares decision making with group members and encourages discussion of issues and alternatives; includes democratic, consensual, and consultative styles.

partnership An association of two or more persons who agree to operate a business together for profit.

patent A form of protection established by the government for inventors; gives an inventor the exclusive right to manufacture, use, and sell an invention for 17 years.

payroll taxes The employer's share of Social Security taxes and federal and state unemployment taxes.

penetration pricing The strategy of selling new products at low prices in the hope of achieving a large sales volume.

pension funds Large pools of money set aside by corporations, unions, and governments for later use in paying retirement benefits to their employees or members.

perfect (pure) competition A market structure in which a large number of small firms sell similar products, buyers and sellers have good information, and businesses can be easily opened or closed.

performance appraisal A comparison of actual performance with expected performance to assess an employee's contributions to the organization.

perpetual inventory A continuously updated list of inventory levels, orders, sales, and receipts.

personal exemptions Deductions that reduce the amount of income on which income tax is paid.

personal selling A face-to-face sales presentation to a prospective customer.

physical distribution (logistics) The movement of products from the producer to industrial users and consumers.

picketing Union members parade in front of the employer's plant carrying signs and trying to persuade nonstriking workers to stop working and customers and suppliers from doing business with the company.

planning The process of deciding what needs to be done to achieve organizational objectives.

portfolio A collection of investments.

postconventional ethics The third stage in the ethical development of individuals in which people adhere to the ethical standards of a mature adult and are less concerned about how others view their behavior than about how they will judge themselves in the long run.

power The ability to influence others to behave in a particular way.

preconventional ethics A stage in the ethical development of individuals in which people behave in a childlike manner and make ethical decisions in a calculating, self-centered, selfish way, based on the possibility of immediate punishment or reward.

preferential tariff A tariff that is lower for some nations than for others.

preferred provider organizations (PPOs) Networks of health care providers who enter into a contract to provide services at discounted prices; combine features of major medical insurance plans with features of health maintenance organizations.

preferred stock A security for which the dividend amount is set at the time the stock is issued.

prepayment penalties Additional fees that may be owed if a loan is repaid early.

prestige pricing The strategy of increasing the price of a product so that consumers will perceive it as being of higher quality, status, or value.

price skimming The strategy of introducing a product with a high initial price and lowering the price over time as the product moves through its life cycle.

price/earnings (P/E) ratio The current market price of a stock divided by its earnings per share.

pricing strategy The part of the marketing mix that involves establishing a price for the product based on the demand for the product and the cost of producing it.

primary data Information collected directly from the original source to solve a problem.

primary market The securities market where new securities are sold to the public.

principal The total amount borrowed through a loan.

principle of comparative advantage The concept that each country should specialize in the products that it can produce most readily and cheaply and trade those products for those that other countries can produce most readily and cheaply.

private accountants Accountants who are employed to serve one particular organization.

problem-solving teams Teams of employees from the same department or area of expertise and from the same level of the organizational hierarchy who meet regularly to share information and discuss ways to improve processes and procedures in specific functional areas.

process departmentalization Departmentalization that is based on the production process used by the organizational unit.

process layout A facility arrangement in which work flows according to the production process. All workers performing similar tasks are grouped together, and products pass from one workstation to another.

process manufacturing A production process in which the basic input is broken down into one or more outputs (products).

producer price index (PPI) An index of the prices paid by producers and wholesalers for various commodities such as raw materials, partially finished goods, and finished products.

product (assembly-line) layout A facility arrangement in which workstations or departments are arranged in a line with products moving along the line.

product advertising Advertising that features a specific good or service.

product departmentalization Departmentalization that is based on the goods or services produced or sold by the organizational unit.

product liability The responsibility of manufacturers and sellers for defects in the products they make and sell.

product life cycle The pattern of sales and profits over time for a product or product category; consists of an introductory stage, growth stage, maturity, and decline (and death).

product manager The person who develops and implements a complete strategy and marketing program for a specific product or brand.

product strategy The part of the marketing mix that involves choosing a brand name, packaging, colors, a warranty, accessories, and a service program for the product.

product In marketing, any good or service, along with its perceived attributes and benefits, that creates value for the customer.

production orientation An approach in which a firm works to lower production costs without a strong desire to satisfy the needs of customers.

production planning The aspect of operations management in which the firm considers the competitive environment and its own strategic goals in an effort to find the best production methods.

production process The way a good is made.

production The creation of products and services by turning inputs, such as natural resources, raw materials, human resources, and capital, into outputs.

productivity The amount of goods and services one worker can produce.

profit maximization A pricing objective that entails getting the largest possible profit from a product by producing the product as long as the revenue from selling it exceeds the cost of producing it.

profit The money left over after all expenses are paid.

profitability ratios Ratios that measure how well a firm is using its resources to generate profit and how efficiently it is being managed.

program evaluation and review technique (PERT) A project management tool that is similar to the CPM method but assigns three time estimates for each activity (optimistic, most probable, and pessimistic).

programmed instruction A form of computer-assisted off-the-job training.

progressive tax An income tax that is structured so that the higher a person's income, the higher the percentage of income owed in taxes.

promotion An upward move in an organization to a position with more authority, responsibility, and pay; or the attempt by marketers to inform, persuade, or remind consumers and industrial users to engage in the exchange process.

promotional mix The combination of advertising, personal selling, sales promotion, and public relations used to promote a product.

property taxes Taxes that are imposed on real and personal property based on the assessed value of the property.

prospecting The process of looking for sales prospects.

protected classes The specific groups who have legal protection against employment discrimination; include women, African Americans, Native Americans, and others.

protectionism The policy of protecting home industries from outside competition by establishing artificial barriers such as tariffs and quotas.

protective tariffs Tariffs that are imposed in order to make imports less attractive to buyers than domestic products are.

psychographic segmentation The differentiation of markets by personality or lifestyle.

public accountants Independent accountants who serve organizations and individuals on a fee basis. A wide range of services, including preparation of financial statements and tax returns, independent auditing, and management consulting.

public relations Any communication or activity designed to win goodwill or prestige for a company or person.

publicity Information about a company or product that appears in the news media and is not directly paid for by the company.

pull strategy A promotional strategy in which a manufacturer focuses on stimulating consumer demand for its product, rather than on trying to persuade wholesalers to carry the product.

purchasing power The value of what money can buy.

purchasing The process of buying production inputs from various sources; also called procurement.

pure monopoly A market structure in which a single firm accounts for all industry sales and in which there are barriers to entry.

push strategy A promotional strategy in which a manufacturer uses aggressive personal selling and trade advertising to convince a wholesaler or retailer to carry and sell its merchandise.

Q

qualifying questions Inquiries used by salespeople to separate prospects from those who do not have the potential to buy.

quality control The process of creating standards for quality and then measuring finished products and services against them.

quality of life The general level of human happiness based on such things as life expectancy, educational standards, health, sanitation, and leisure time.

quality Goods and services that offer customer value and satisfaction.

R

random access memory (RAM) The primary type of memory in a computer's central processing unit; an active, short-term memory that stores data and instructions for manipulating the data.

ratio analysis The calculation and interpretation of financial ratios taken from the firm's financial statements in order to assess a firm's condition and performance.

rational branding A tactic for advertising on the Internet that combines the emotional aspect of traditional brand marketing with a concrete service that is offered only online.

reach The number of different target consumers who are exposed to a commercial at least once during a specific period.

recession A decline in GDP that lasts for at least two consecutive quarters.

recruitment The attempt to find and attract qualified applicants in the external labor market.

reengineering The complete redesign of business structures and processes in order to improve operations.

referent power Power that is derived from an individual's personal charisma and the respect and/or admiration the individual inspires.

relationship management The practice of building, maintaining, and enhancing interactions with customers and other parties in order to develop long-term satisfaction through mutually beneficial partnerships.

relationship marketing A strategy that focuses on forging long-term partnerships with customers by offering value and providing customer satisfaction.

reminder advertising Advertising that is used to keep a product's name in the public's mind.

replacement cost coverage Homeowner's and renter's insurance that pays enough to replace lost and damaged personal property.

reserve requirement Requires banks that are members of the Federal Reserve System to hold some of their deposits in cash in their vaults or in an account at a district bank.

resignation A permanent separation of an employee from the organization, done voluntarily by the employee.

retailers Firms that sell goods to consumers and to industrial users for their own consumption.

retained earnings The amounts left over from profitable operations since the firm's beginning; equal to total profits minus all dividends paid to stockholders.

retirement The separation of an employee from the organization at the end of his or her career.

return on equity (ROE) The ratio of net profit to total owners' equity; measures the return that owners receive on their investment in the firm.

return The opportunity for profit.

revenues The dollar amount of a firm's sales plus any other income it received from sources such as interest, dividends, and rents.

revolving credit agreement A guaranteed line of credit whereby a bank agrees that a certain amount of funds will be available for a business to borrow over a given period.

revolving credit cards Credit cards that do not require full payment upon billing.

reward power Power that is derived from an individual's control over rewards.

right-to-work laws State laws that allow employees to work at a unionized company without having to join the union.

risk management The process of identifying and evaluating risks and selecting and managing techniques to adapt to risk exposure.

risk The potential to lose time and money or otherwise not be able to accomplish an organization's goals.

risk-return trade-off A basic principle in finance that holds that the higher the risk associated with an investment, the greater the return that is required.

robotics The technology involved in designing, constructing, and operating robots (computer-controlled machines that can perform tasks independently).

routing The aspect of production control that involves setting out the work flow-the sequence of machines and operations through which the product or service progresses from start to finish.

S

S corporation A hybrid entity that is organized like a corporation, with stockholders, directors, and officers, but taxed like a partnership, with income and losses flowing through to the stockholders and taxed as their personal income.

sales promotions Marketing events or sales efforts—not including advertising, personal selling, and public relations—that stimulate buying.

sales prospects The companies and people who are most likely to buy a seller's offerings.

sales taxes Taxes that are levied on goods when they are sold; calculated as a percentage of the price.

savings bond Government bonds of relatively small denominations.

scheduling The aspect of production control that involves specifying and controlling the time required for each step in the production process.

scientific management A system of management developed by Frederick W. Taylor and based on four principles: developing a scientific approach for each element of a job, scientifically selecting and training workers, encouraging cooperation between workers and managers, and dividing work and responsibility between management and workers according to who can better perform a particular task.

seasonal unemployment Unemployment that occurs during specific seasons in certain industries.

secondary data Information that has already been collected for a project other than the current one, but which may be used to solve the current problem.

secondary market The securities market where already issued securities are traded among investors; includes the organized stock exchanges and the over-the-counter market.

secondary storage The part of a computer that provides long-term storage for programs and data.

secured bonds Corporate bonds for which specific assets have been pledged as collateral.

secured loans Loans for which the borrower is required to pledge specific assets as collateral, or security.

securities Investment certificates issued by corporations or governments that represent either equity or debt.

security requirements Provisions that allow a lender to take back the collateral if a loan is not repaid according to the terms of the agreement.

selection interview An in-depth discussion of an applicant's work experience, skills and abilities, education, and career interests.

selection The process of determining which persons in the applicant pool possess the qualifications necessary to be successful on the job.

selective credit controls The power of the Federal Reserve to use credit rules to influence the terms of consumer credit and margin requirements.

selective distribution A distribution system in which a manufacturer selects a limited number of dealers in an area (but more than one or two) to market its products.

selective strike strategy A union strategy of conducting a strike at (shutting down) a critical plant that supplies parts to other plants.

self-managed work teams Highly autonomous teams of employees who manage themselves without any formal supervision.

separation The departure of an employee from the organization; can be a layoff, termination, resignation, or retirement.

servicemark A symbol, name, or design that identifies a service rather than a tangible object.

services Intangible offerings of businesses that can't be held, touched, or stored.

shop steward An elected union official who represents union members to management when workers have complaints.

shopping products Items that are bought after considerable planning, including brand-to-brand and store-to-store comparisons of price, suitability, and style.

short-term forecasts Projections of revenues, costs of goods, and operating expenses for a one-year period; also called operating plans.

sick-out A union strategy in which a group of employees claim they cannot work because of illness, thereby disrupting the company.

Small Business Administration (SBA) A government agency that helps people start and manage small businesses, helps small business owners win federal contracts, and speaks on behalf of small business.

Small Business Investment Company (SBIC) Privately owned and managed investment companies that are licensed by the Small Business Administration and provide long-term financing for small businesses.

small business A business that is independently owned, is owned by an individual or a small group of investors, is based locally, and is not a dominant company in its industry.

social investing The practice of limiting investments to securities of companies that behave in accordance with the investor's beliefs about ethical and social responsibility.

social marketing The application of marketing techniques to social issues and causes.

social responsibility The concern of businesses for the welfare of society as a whole.

socialism An economic system in which the basic industries are owned either by the government itself or by the private sector under strong government control.

software The set of instructions that directs a computer's activities.

sole proprietorship A business that is established, owned, operated, and often financed by one person.

span of control   The number of employees a manager directly supervises; also called span of management.

specialization   The degree to which tasks are subdivided into smaller jobs.

specialty products   Items for which consumers search long and hard and for which they refuse to accept substitutes.

spreadsheet software   Software that is used to prepare and analyze numerical data such as for financial statements, sales forecasts, and budgets.

staff positions   Positions in an organization held by individuals who provide the administrative and support services that line employees need to achieve the firm's goals.

stakeholders   Individuals or groups to whom a business has a responsibility; include employees, customers, the general public, and investors.

standard deduction   An amount that most taxpayers can automatically deduct from their gross income in computing their income tax; not permitted if the taxpayer itemizes deductions.

standard of living   A country's output of goods and services that people can buy with the money they have.

statement of cash flows   A financial statement that provides a summary of the money flowing into and out of a firm.

stock dividends   Payments to stockholders in the form of more stock; may replace or supplement cash dividends.

stockbroker   A person who is licensed to buy and sell securities on behalf of clients.

stockholders   The owners of a corporation, who hold shares of stock that provide certain rights; also known as shareholders.

stocklift (buyback)   The practice in which a company purchases all of a competitor's products from retailers and replaces the merchandise with its own products.

strategic alliance   A cooperative agreement between business firms; sometimes called a strategic partnership.

strategic giving   The practice of tying philanthropy closely to the corporate mission or goals and targeting donations to regions where a company operates.

strategic planning   The process of creating long-range (one to five years), broad goals for the organization and determining what resources will be needed to accomplish those goals.

strict liability   A concept in product-liability law under which a manufacturer or seller is liable for any personal injury or property damage caused by defective products or packaging even though all possible care was used to prevent such defects.

strike replacements   Nonunion employees hired to replace striking union members; also known as scabs.

structural unemployment   Unemployment that is caused by a mismatch between available jobs and the skills of available workers in an industry or region.

supercomputers   The most powerful computers. Only slightly larger than the typical microcomputer, they can perform many interrelated calculations quickly and are used to do complex computations to stimulate or predict difficult problems.

supervisory management   Managers who design and carry out operation plans for the ongoing daily activities of the firm.

supply chain management   The process of smoothing transitions along the supply chain so that the firm can satisfy its customers with quality products and services; focuses on developing tighter bonds with suppliers.

supply chain   The entire sequence of securing inputs, producing goods, and delivering goods to customers.

supply curve   A graph showing the quantity of a good or service that a business will make available at various prices.

supply   The quantity of a good or service that businesses will make available at various prices.

survey research   A marketing research method in which an interviewer interacts with respondents, either in person, by mail, a mall, or the Internet to obtain facts, opinions, and attitudes.

systems software   Software that controls the computer and provides program routines that enable applications programs to run on a particular computer.

T

tactical planning   The process of beginning to implement a strategic plan by addressing issues of coordination and allocating resources to different parts of the organization.

Taft-Hartley Act   A statute enacted in 1947 that defined unfair union practices, outlined the rules for dealing with strikes of major economic impact, broadened employer options for dealing with unions, and further defined the rights of employees as individuals.

target market   The specific group of consumers toward which a firm directs its marketing efforts.

target return on investment   A pricing objective where the price of a product is set so as to give the company the desired profitability in terms of return on its money.

tariff   A tax imposed on imported goods.

technical skills   A manager's specialized areas of knowledge and expertise, as well as the ability to apply that knowledge.

technology   The application of science and engineering skills and knowledge to solve production and organizational problems.

telecommuting   An arrangement in which employees work at home and are linked to the office by phone, fax, and computer.

term life insurance   Life insurance that covers the insured's life for a fixed amount and a specific period and has no cash value.

term loan   A business loan with a maturity of more than a year; can be secured or unsecured.

termination   A permanent separation of an employee from the organization, arranged by the employer.

Theory X   A management style that is based on a pessimistic view of human nature and assumes that the average person dislikes work, will avoid it if possible, prefers to be directed, avoids responsibility, and wants security above all.

Theory Y   A management style that is based on a relatively optimistic view of human nature; assumes that the average person wants to work, accepts responsibility, is willing to help solve problems, and can be self-directed and self-controlled.

thrift institutions   Depository institutions formed specifically to encourage household saving and to make home mortgage loans.

time deposits   Deposits at a bank or other financial institution that pay interest but cannot be withdrawn on demand.

top management   The highest level of managers; includes CEOs, presidents, and vice-presidents, who develop strategic plans and address long-range issues.

tort   A civil, or private, act that harms other people or their property.

total cost   The sum of the fixed costs and the variable costs.

total profit   Total revenue minus total cost.

total quality management (TQM)   The use of quality principles in all aspects of a company's production and operations.

total revenue   The selling price per unit times the number of units sold.

trade credit The extension of credit by the seller to the buyer between the time the buyer receives the goods or services and the time it pays for them.

trade deficit An unfavorable balance of trade that occurs when a country imports more than it exports.

trade surplus A favorable balance of trade that occurs when a country exports more than it imports.

trademark The legally exclusive design, name, or other identifying mark associated with a company's brand.

training and development Activities that provide learning situations in which an employee acquires additional knowledge or skills to increase job performance.

transaction processing system (TPS) An information system that handles the daily business operations of a firm. The system receives and organizes raw data from internal and external sources for storage in a database.

transfer A horizontal move in an organization to a position with about the same salary and at about the same organizational level.

transmission control protocol/Internet protocol (TCP/IP) A communications technology that allows different computer platforms to communicate with each other to transfer data.

trial courts The lowest level of courts, where most cases begin; also called courts of general jurisdiction.

U

underwriting The process of buying securities from corporations and governments and reselling them to the public; the main activity of investment bankers.

unearned income Income that is not earned through employment such as interest, dividends, and other investment income.

unemployment rate The percentage of the total labor force that is actively looking for work but is not actually working.

Uniform Commercial Code (UCC) A model set of rules that apply to commercial transactions between businesses and between businesses and individuals; has been adopted by all states except Louisiana, which uses only part of it.

union busting The process by which a company avoids unionization by moving to another region of the country or shifting operations offshore.

union certification election An election in which workers vote, by secret ballot, on whether they want to be represented by a union; conducted by the National Labor Relations Board.

union shop A company where nonunion workers can be hired but must then join the union.

universal life insurance A combination of term life insurance and a tax-deferred savings plan. Part of the premium is invested in securities, so the cash value earns interest at current market rates.

unsecured loans Short-term loans for which the borrower does not have to pledge specific assets as security.

unsought products Products that either are unknown to the potential buyer or are known but the buyer does not actively seek them.

Uruguay Round A 1994 agreement by 117 nations to lower trade barriers worldwide.

utilitarianism A philosophy that focuses on the consequences of an action to determine whether it is right or wrong; holds that an action that affects the majority adversely is morally wrong.

V

value pricing A pricing strategy in which the target market is offered a high-quality product at a fair price and with good service.

variable costs Costs that change with different levels of output; for example, wages and cost of raw materials.

variable pay A systems of paying employees in which a portion of an employee's pay is directly linked to an individual or organizational performance measure.

vendor-managed inventory A system of managing inventory in which the supplier manages the distributor's inventory, thereby reversing the traditional arrangement.

venture capital Financing obtained from investment firms that specialize in financing small, high-growth companies and receive an ownership interest and a voice in management in return for their money.

vertical marketing system An organized, formal distribution channel in which firms are aligned in a hierarchy from manufacturer to wholesaler to retailer.

vertical merger A merger of companies at different stages in the same industry; done to gain control over supplies of resources or to gain access to different markets.

vestibule training A form of off-the-job training in which trainees learn in a scaled-down version or simulated work environment.

virtual corporation A network of independent companies linked by information technology to share skills, costs, and access to one another's markets; allows the companies to come together quickly to exploit rapidly changing opportunities.

volume segmentation The differentiation of markets based on the amount of the product purchased.

W

Wagner Act A statute enacted in 1935 that established that employees have a right to organize and join labor unions and to engage in collective bargaining; also known as the National Labor Relations Act.

waiting period (elimination period) In disability income insurance, the period between the onset of the disability and the time when insurance payments begin.

warranty A guarantee of the quality of a good or service.

Web sites Locations on the World Wide Web consisting of a home page and, possibly, other pages with documents and files.

whole life (straight life, cash value, continuous pay) insurance Life insurance that covers the insured's entire life, as long as the premiums are paid; has a cash value that increases over the life of the policy.

wholesalers Firms that sell finished goods to retailers, manufacturers, and institutions.

wide area network (WAN) A network that connects computers at different sites via telecommunications media such as phone lines, satellites, and microwaves.

wildcat strike A strike by a group of union members or an entire local union without the approval of the national union while the contract is still in effect.

withholding allowances Amounts that are deducted from the income tax that would otherwise be withheld by a taxpayer's employer; vary according to the number of dependents and other criteria. The more allowances, the less tax withheld.

word processing software Software that is used to write, edit, and format letters and other documents.

work groups Groups of employees who share resources and coordinate efforts so as to help members better perform their individual duties and responsibilities.

work teams Groups of employees who not only coordinate their efforts, but also collaborate by pooling their knowledge, skills, abilities, and resources in a collective effort to attain a common goal.

World Bank An international bank that offers low-interest loans, as well as advice and information, to developing nations.

World Trade Organization (WTO) An organization established by the Uruguay Round in 1994 to oversee international trade, reduce trade barriers, and resolve disputes among member nations.

World Wide Web (WWW) A subsystem of the Internet that consists of an information retrieval system composed of Web sites.

Y

yellow-dog contracts Contracts in which employees agreed not to join a labor union as a condition of being hired.

CHAPTER 1 NOTES

1. Sandra Baker, "A Uniform Approach to Expansion," *Fort Worth Star Telegram—Tarrant Business* (June 15, 1998), p. 7.
2. John Daniels and Lee Radebaugh, *International Business*, 8th ed. (Reading, Mass.: Addison-Wesley, 1998), p. 153.
3. Jennifer Kushnell, "Minding Their Own Business," *Brandweek* (February 9, 1998), pp. 28–32.
4. Ibid.
5. Lester Thurow, "Changing the Nature of Capitalism," in *Rethinking the Future*, ed. Rowan Gibson (London: Nicholas Brealey, 1997), p. 228; also see Thomas Stewart, "Knowledge, the Appreciating Commodity," *Fortune* (October 12, 1998), pp. 199–200.
6. "GM to Build the Next Catera in Michigan," *San Diego Union Tribune* (June 20, 1998), p. NC-3.
7. "2 Dockers Away," *The Globe and Mail* (April 23, 1998), p. C9.
8. "Wives Earn More of Family Income, Stay Home Less," *Fort Worth Star Telegram* (September 30, 1998), p. A5.
9. "Retooling for Buying Power of '90s Women," *The Plain Dealer* (August 18, 1998), p. 3C.
10. Ibid.
11. Melinda Beck, "Next Population Bulge Shows Its Might," *Wall Street Journal* (February 3, 1997), pp. B1, B6.
12. J. Walker Smith, "Beyond Rocking the Ages," *American Demographics* (May 1998), pp. 45–50.
13. "Influx of Immigrants Benefits American Economy Overall," *Fort Worth Star Telegram* (May 18, 1997), p. A18.
14. "The Next Wave," *Business Week* (August 31, 1998), pp. 80–83.
15. "Two Steps Forward, One Step Back," *Business Week* (August 31, 1998), p. 116.
16. "It Was a Hit in Buenos Aires—So Why Not Boise?" *Business Week* (September 7, 1998), pp. 56–58.
17. Ibid.
18. "ISO 9000 Helps Firms Achieve Consistency," *USA Today* (May 27, 1998), p. 2B
19. Ibid.
20. "The ISO 14001: What It Means to Be Green," *The Times of London* (February 24, 1998), p. 2.
21. "The War for Talent," *Fast Company* (August 1998), pp. 104–108.
22. "Work Week," *Wall Street Journal* (July 21, 1998), p. A1.
23. Ibid.
24. Kushnell, "Minding Their Own Business," p. 32.

Making Ethical Choices source: Suein L. Hwang, "Tobacco Companies Enlist the Bar Owner to Push Their Goods," *Wall Street Journal* (April 21, 1999) pp. A1, A6.

Focusing on Small Business source: J. C. Conklin, "Don't Throw Out Those Old Sneakers, They're a gold Mine," *Wall Street Journal* (September 21, 1998), pp. A1, A20.

Applying Technology sources: "E-Gads," *Wall Street Journal* (September 17, 1998), p. A1, "The Click Here Economy," *Business Week* (June 22, 1998), pp. 122–128; and Howie Simon, "Net Profit: How the Internet and Intranets Will Affect Business," *Journal of Commerce* (July 29, 1998), p. 5c.

Creative Thinking Case source: Mark Maremont, "Aquarium Quandary: Do Visitors come to See Food, or for Seafood?" *Wall Street Journal* (September 30, 1998), p. B1.

Video Case source: Adapted from material contained in the following articles: Carpenter, K. "Let It Snowboard," *Sporting Goods Business* (December 15, 1998): p. 2; Carpenter, K. "The SGB Interview: Jake Burton," *Sporting Goods Business* (November 5, 1998): pp. 30–32; and Rosenberg, D., "All Aboard," *Newsweek* (February 9, 1998): pp. 72–77; and from material in the video: *A Case Study in the Business Environment: Burton Snowboards.*

CHAPTER 2 NOTES

1. Brandon Mitchener, "Can Daimler's Tiny Swatchmobile Sweep Europe?" *Wall Street Journal* (October 2, 1998), pp. B1, B4.
2. "U.S. Jobless Rate Plunges to 4.3 Percent, Lowest Since 1970," *New York Times Abstracts* (May 9, 1998), p. 1.
3. "Unemployment Held Down Despite Layoffs," *South China Morning Post* (June 6, 1998), p. 4.
4. "Editorial," *The Indianapolis News* (October 5, 1998), p. A10.
5. Dorothy Dowling, "Frequent Perks Keep Travelers Loyal," *American Demographics* (September 1998), pp. 32–36.
6. "Governor's Task Force Recommends High-Tech Tools in Employee Training and Education to Meet 21st Century Demands," *Business Week* (March 11, 1998), pp. 1–2.
7. Louis Tong, "Consumerism Sweeps the Mainland," *Marketing Management* (Winter 1998), pp. 32–36.
8. "The Amazing Mr. Kuok," *Forbes* (July 28, 1998), pp. 90–98.
9. Ibid.
10. "Revolution in Reverse," *Sydney Morning Herald* (September 27, 1997), p. 6.
11. "Russia's 'Peoples Capitalism' Benefitting Only the Elite; Big Tycoons Squeeze Out Small Business," *Washington Post* (December 28, 1997), p. AO1.

Making Ethical Choices sources: Adapted from P. Dodson, "Prices Show Dramatic Rise," *South Bend Tribune,* (March 20, 1999); pp. A1, A10; and B. Stanley, "Pump Prices Up; Supply Cuts Anticipated," *South Bend Tribune* (March 23, 1999); pp. A1, A8.

Focusing on Small Business source: Republished with permission of the *Wall Street Journal,* from "Microcredit Arrives in Africa, But Can It Match Asian Success," by Ken Wells, September 29, 1998, pp. A1, A15; permission conveyed through Copyright Clearance Center.

Creative Thinking Case source: Glen R. Simpson and John Simons, "A Little Internet Firm Got a Big Monopoly; Is That Such a Bad Thing?" *Wall Street Journal* (October 8, 1998), pp. A1, A6.

Video Case source: Adapted from material contained on the following Internet sites: "Awards & Sponsorships," **http://www.mercedescenter.com/black/information-awards.html**; "Meet Our Departments," **http://www.mercedescenter.com/black/information-departments.html**; and "Our History," **http://www.mercedescenter.com/black/information-history.html**.; and from material in the video: *A Case Study in Customer Value and Satisfaction: Mercedes-Benz.*

CHAPTER 3 NOTES

1. Lisa Shuckman, "How Does GM's Saturn Sell Cars in Japan? Very Slowly," *Wall Street Journal* (August 25, 1998), pp. B1, B4.
2. "Gillette Won't Meet Profit-Growth Goal While Emerging Markets Face Turmoil," *Wall Street Journal* (September 30, 1998), pp. A3, A8.
3. "Salty Snack Attack on Europe," *Financial Times* (February 2, 1998), p. 13.
4. Charles Lamb, Joe Hair, and Carl McDaniel, *Essentials of Marketing* (Cincinnati: South-Western Publishing Company 1999), p. 55.
5. "Secretary of Commerce William Daley Recognizes U.S. Companies for Excellence in Exporting," *U.S. Department of Commerce Press Release* (December 17, 1997).

6. Figure projected by authors from **www.gov/foreign-trade/Press-Release/current_press_release/exhl.txt** on October 12, 1998.
7. "U.S. to Face Brunt of Economic Crisis," *New York Times* (October 9, 1998), p. 8.
8. "Russian Devaluation a High Stakes Gamble," *The Financial Post* (August 18, 1998), p. 9.
9. "U.S., China Reach Trade Accord, Avoid Import Levies," *Fort Worth Star Telegram* (February 3, 1998), p. 5.
10. "United States Anti-Dumping Laws Hook Many Countries," *Miami Herald* (July 27, 1998), p. 3–19.
11. "World Bank Report: Focus on Acquiring Knowledge: Information Gaps Help Cause Crisis," *Bangkok Post* (October 13, 1998), p. A1.
12. "Ambassador: NAFTA Works, We Just Need to Tell People," *Orlando Sentinel* (October 2, 1998), p. A14.
13. See Kent Granzin, John Painter, Jeffrey Brazell, and Janeen Olsen, "Public Support for Free Trade Agreements," *Journal of Macromarketing* (Spring 1998), pp. 11–23.
14. Masuaki Kotabe and Maria de Arruda, "South America's Free Trade Gambit," *Marketing Management* (Spring 1998), pp. 38–46.
15. *Opportunities in Exporting* (Washington, D.C.: Small Business Administration Office of International Trade, 1998) p. 2.
16. "International Trading Partners Help Small Wisconsin Firms Grow," *Knight Ridder Tribune Business News* (March 23, 1998), p. 15.
17. "Trouble Underneath the Arches," *Australian Financial Review* (March 9, 1998), p. 14.
18. "E*Trade Signs Second International Joint Venture Agreement in Seven Days; U.K. Joint Venture Follows Entry into Japanese Market," *PR Newswire* (June 11, 1998).
19. "Kodak Quickly Develops Deal to Purchase State-Owned Firms," *Journal of Commerce* (October 1, 1998), pp. 1C–3C.
20. "Barter Grows as Trade Deals Hit Problems," *Financial Times* (September 17, 1998), p. O7.
21. "France Rejects Coca-Cola's Purchase of Orangina," *Wall Street Journal* (September 18, 1998), p. A3.
22. "The Stateless Corporation," *Business Week* (May 14, 1990), p. 99.
23. Hal Lancaster, "Global Managers Need Boundless Sensitivity, Rugged Constitutions," *Wall Street Journal* (October 13, 1998), p. B1.

Focusing on Small Business source: Michael White, "Small American Business Scrambles for Success in China," Associated Press Business News (online), September 10, 1998 at 17:53 EDT.

Making Ethical Choices source: C. Adams, "Trade Secrets; Steelmakers Complain about Foreign Steel; They Also Import It," *Wall Street Journal* (March 22, 1999): pp. A1 & A11.

Creative Thinking Case source: Gautam Naik, "Inventor's Adjustable Glasses Could Spark Global Correction," *Wall Street Journal* (October 14, 1998), pp. B1, B4.

Video Case source: Adapted from material contained on the following Internet sites: **www.autocite.com/**; **http://208.240.91.101/main/conference/or199/exh_99.htm**; and from material in the video: *Global Strategy: A Study of ETEC.*

CHAPTER 4 NOTES

1. Greg Jaffe, "Miami Airport's Lack of Luggage Carts Is Cause for Carrying On," *Wall Street Journal* (November 2, 1998), pp. A1, A22.
2. The section "Individual Rights" is from John Jackson, Roger Leroy Miller, and Shawn Miller, *Business and Society Today* (Cincinnati: International Thomson Publishing Company, 1997), pp. 92–93.
3. The concept of "Justice" is from John Jackson et al. pp. 89-90.
4. Milton Borden, "The Three R's of Ethics," *Management Review* (June 1998), pp. 59–61.
5. Marianne Moody Jennings, *Case Studies in Business Ethics*, 2d. ed. (St. Paul: West Publishing Company, 1996), pp. xx–xxiii.
6. Ibid.
7. L. S. Berger, "Train All Employees to Solve Ethical Dilemmas," *Life-Health Insurance Edition* (March 1, 1998), p. 70.
8. Jennings, *Case Studies*, p. 11.
9. Margaret Ann Cleek and Sherry Lynn Leonard, "Can Corporate Codes of Ethics Influence Behavior?" *Journal of Business Ethics* (April 1998), pp. 619–630.
10. "3 Out of 4 Say They Have Not Faced Ethical Dilemma at Work," *New York Times* (October 26, 1998), p. 10D.
11. Charles Lamb, Joe Hair, Carl McDaniel, *Essentials of Marketing* (Cincinnati: South-Western College Publishing Co., 1999), pp. 46–47.
12. "Pollution Fine Hits Cruise Line," *Orlando Sentinel* (September 17, 1998), p. B1.
13. "Louisiana-Pacific To Pay Pollution Fines," *Los Angeles Times* (May 28, 1998), p. D3.
14. "Effect of Tobacco Maker's $60 Million Effort Lingers On," *Advertising Age* (September 21, 1998), p. 18.
15. "Third Annual Lucent Technologies 'Global Days of Caring' Set," *PR Newswire* (September 24, 1998), pp. 1–4.
16. "IOMEGA Agrees to Improve Customer Support," *Business* (March 4, 1998), pp. 1–2.
17. Karen Krouse, "Computer School Hit With State Fraud Suit; Students Accuse of Unrealistic Claims," *Chicago Tribune* (March 11, 1998), p. 1.
18. Curt Weeden, "Corporate Social Investing," *Journal of Commerce* (September 23, 1998), p. 6A.
19. "Bittersweet Charity," *Industry Week* (September 7, 1998), pp. 16–20.
20. "The Only Way to Stay Ahead," *Industry Week* (August 17, 1998), pp. 98–102.
21. "Bittersweet," . . . . p. 19.
22. Ibid.
23. Karl Schoenberger, "Human Rights: The Firm Should Clarify Its Reentry Into the Nation and Set a Code of Conduct for Multinationals," *Los Angeles Times* (April 20, 1998), p. B5.

Applying Technology source: "Hey, You! Back to Work," *Seattle Times* (October 17, 1998), p. A15.

Focusing on Small Business source: Thomas Love, "Taking the Ethical Temperature of Entrepreneurs and Managers," *Nations Business* (September 1998), p. 12.

Making Ethical Choices sources: J. Versau, "At Costas, Profits Drive the Bottom Line, But Values Start at the Top, *The times* (December 25, 1997), pp. D1, D2; J. Versau, "Being Good for Goodness' Sake: Striking a Balance between Value-Free Management and Paying Heed to Ethics Is a Challenge to Businesses Worldwide," *The Times* (December 25, 1997), pp. D1, D5.

Creative Thinking Case source: Yumiko Ono, "Seeking Adventure, Girl Scouts Hike to the Mall," *Wall Street Journal* (August 17, 1998), pp. B1, B4.

Video Case source: Adapted from material contained on the following Internet sites: "Bank of Alma Mission," "CEO's Message," "History and Over-view," "and Products & Services," links at **www.firstbank-alma.com/ban.../**; and from material in the video: *Business Environment: A Study of Healthcare and Central Michigan Community Hospital.*

CHAPTER 5 NOTES

1. David D'Addio, "Job Search Ends Up Creating New Jobs," Pittsburgh

Post-Direct (July 15, 1998), downloaded from **www.post-gazette.com;** Carlye Adler, "Have Resumes, Will Travel," *Business Week, Enterprise* section (May 25, 1998), p. ENT 18; Robert E. Ford, President, Job-Direct, telephone interview, January 6, 1999; JobDirect Web site, **www. jobdirect.com.**

2. Carreen Maloney-Monro, "For Starters, Small Firms Don't Need Big Problems," *San Diego Union-Tribune* (April 19, 1998), Electric Library, Business Edition, downloaded from **business.elibrary.com;** and personal interview with Gail Cecil, January 1, 1999.

3. Jerry Useem, "Partners on the Edge," *Inc.* (August 1998), pp. 52–64.

4. Ibid.

5. "National Cooperative Bank Releases NCB Co-op 100," National Cooperative Bank press release (October 5, 1998), downloaded from**www.ncb.com;** and "The Coop Home Page—Coop Primer," downloaded January 13, 1999, from **www.ncba.org/primer.htm.**

6. Jane Seccombe, "Doing It Best Independent Store Holds Its Own," *Greensboro News & Record* (December 30, 1998), Electric Library, Business Edition, downloaded from **business.elibrary.com.**

7. Chieh Chieng, "Do You Want to Know a Secret?" *Entrepreneur* (January 1999), pp. 177–178.

8. Mark Hamstra, "Diedrich Coffee Inks Franchisee Deal with Taco Bell," *Nation's Restaurant News* (September 28, 1998), Electric Library, Business Edition, downloaded from **business.elibrary.com;** and Greg Hardesty, "Diedrich Inks Deal to Open on East Coast," *The Orange County Register* (September 17, 1998), Electric Library, Business Edition, downloaded from **business.elibrary.com.**

9. *Profile of Franchising*: vol. 1—*Fact Sheet,* press release from the IFA Educational Foundation (November 9, 1998).

10. Alf Nucifora, "Franchising Stays Hot as Millennium Approaches," *Jacksonville Business Journal* (June 26, 1998), Electric Library, Business Edition, downloaded from **business.elibrary.com.**

11. "Worldwide Refinishing Announces Expansion into Korea," Franchise Handbook Online NewsBytes, downloaded January 7, 1999, from **www.franchise1.com/articles/ newsbyte.html.**

12. Peter Coy, "Tremors from Cheap Oil," *Business Week* (December 12,

1998), pp. 34-37; and Sallie L. Grimes, "Appetite for Cost Cutting Keeps Mergers on Menu," *San Diego Union-Tribune* (January 1, 1999), p. C-3.

13. Ira Sager, "A New Cyber Order," *Business Week* (December 7, 1998, pp. 27–31.

14. Christopher Rhoads, "Low Key GE Capital Expands in Europe," *Wall Street Journal,* (September 17, 1998), p. A18; Bill Shepherd, "GE Capital's M&A Strategy," *Global Finance,* (November 1, 1998), Electric Library, Business Edition, downloaded from **www.business. elibrary.com.**

15. Julie Bennett, "Franchising: New Companies Take Offbeat Path to Profits," *Wall Street Journal* (December 13, 1998), p. B13 (special advertising section)

16. Ibid.

17. Echo Montgomery Garrett, "The Changing World of Franchising," (special advertising section), *Inc.* (November 1998), pp. 120–123.

18. Geoffrey Colvin, "The Year of the Mega-Merger," *Fortune* (January 11, 1999), pp. 62–64; and "So How Big Was It?" *Fortune* (January 11, 1999), pp. 65–71.

19. "So How Big Was It?" pp. 65–71.

20. "Mergers Weren't Job-Friendly," *San Diego Union-Tribune* (January 25, 1999), p. C–1.

21. Robert E. Ford, President, Job-Direct, telephone interview, January 13, 1999; "JobDirect Partners with Barnes and Noble College Bookstores to Launch JobDirect's Job-Drive for the 1998–99 Academic Year," press release downloaded from **www.jobdirect.com/pr-barnesnoble.html;** and JobDirect Web site, **www.jobdirect.com.**

Focusing on Small Business sources:
Carol Dannhauser, "How One Couple Parlayed Their Differences into a Thriving PR Company, *Business Week Online* (December 9, 1998), downloaded from **www.businessweek.com/smallbiz;** and Alison Bass, "Home Sweet Home Away from Home: Couples Find Work is a Labor of Love," *San Diego Union-Tribune* (January 2, 1999), pp. E-1, E-3.

Making Ethical Choices source:
Adapted from D. Morse, "Just Sell It: Where Gang Members Are Shoe Salesmen: A Novel Franchise," *Wall Street Journal* (February 19, 1999), pp. A1, A6.

Applying Technology sources:
"Franchising Meets the Internet," Intel E-Business Web site, downloaded January 5, 1999, from **www.intel.com/ businesscomputing/ebusiness/biz-biz/**

franchise.htm; Tricon Global Web site, **www.triconglobal.com;** and "Tricon's KFC Brands Itself," Intel E-Business Web site, downloaded January 5, 1999, from **www.intel.com/businesscomputing/ ebusiness/biz-biz/kfc.htm.**

Creative Thinking Case sources:
Richard Behar, "Franchises: Why Subway Is "The Biggest Problem in Franchising,." *Fortune* (March 16, 1998) p. 126; "Subway Sandwich Shops Inc.," *Hoover's Company Capsules* (December 1, 1998), downloaded from Electric Library, Business Edition, **business. elibrary.com;** Subway corporate Internet site, **www.Subway.com;** Dan Uhlinger, "Let the Sandwich Wars Begin: Rival Shops to Fight for Fast-Food Business," *Hartford Courant* (June 29, 1998), downloaded from Electric Library, Business Edition, **business.elibrary.com.**

Video Case source: Adapted from material contained on the following Internet site: "Second Chance Body Armor," **www.sruniforms.com/fsecond. html;** and from material in the video *Second Chance Body Armor: A Study of Entrepreneurship.*

CHAPTER 6 NOTES

1. Nick Charles and Tom Duffy, "Not Pulp Fiction: 'Juice Guys' Tom Scott and Tom First Built an Empire out of Fresh Fruit," *People* (November 10, 1997), downloaded from Electric Library, Business Edition, **business.elibrary.com;** Paul Tanklefsky, "Future Is Looking Sweet for Juice Guys," *Boston Herald* (November 9, 1998), downloaded from Electric Library Business Edition, **business.elibrary. com;** and "Two Men and a Bottle," *Inc. State of Small Business* (May 19, 1998), pp. 60–63.

2. Edith Updike, "A Green Thumb for Startups," *Business Week* (October 12, 1998), p. ENT 26.

3. Nora Caley, "Batter Up! Colorado Pines Recycled into Treebats," *Denver Rocky Mountain News* (March 1, 1998), downloaded from Electric Library, Business Edition, **business.elibrary.com.**

4. Robert D. Hof, "The Wild World of Amazon.com," *Business Week* (December 14, 1998), pp. 106–108.

5. Steve Hamm, "Jim Clark Is Off and Running Again," *Business Week* (October 12, 1998), pp. 64–69.

6. Marshall Goldsmith, "Retain Your Top Performers," *Executive Excellence* (November 1, 1997), downloaded from Electric Library Business Edition, **business.elibrary.com;** Jan

Norman, "Intrapreneurs Keep Creativity In-House," *Austin-American Statesman* (November 17, 1997), downloaded from Electric Library, Business Edition, **business. elibrary.com;** and Robert G. Stein and Gifford Pinchot, "Are You Innovative?" *Association Management* (February 1, 1998), downloaded from Electric Library, Business Edition, **business.elibrary.com.**

7. Steve Ginsberg, "Xerox Makes New Attempt to Duplicate Research Triumphs," *San Francisco Business Times* (March 28, 1997), downloaded from Electric Library, Business Edition, **business.elibrary.com;** and "Stimulating Creativity and Innovation," *Research-Technology Management* (March 1, 1997), downloaded from Electric Library, Business Edition, **business.elibrary.com.**

8. Gina M. Larson, "Once Is Not Enough," *Entrepreneurial Edge* (Winter 1998), downloaded from **www.edgeonline.com.**

9. Daile Tucker, "Are You an Entrepreneur?" *Home Business* (April 1998), downloaded from **www.homebusinessmag.com;** and "Do You Act Like an Entrepreneur?" *Entrepreneur Magazine's Small Business Square* (September 30, 1998), downloaded from **www. entrepreneurmag.com.**

10. "CEO's Notebook," *Inc.* (December 1998), p. 123.

11. Hamm, Jim Clark Is Off and Running Again."

12. Elaine W. Teague, "Designing Woman," *Entrepreneur* (January 1999), pp. 112–115.

13. Gina M. Larson, "Judy Estrin Spots Trends before They Emerge," *Entreprenuerial Edge* (Winter 1998), downloaded from **www.edgeonline.com.**

14. "Do You Act like an Entrepreneur?" *Entrepreneur Magazine's Small Business Square.*

15. Tom Richman, "The Eight Books to Read before You Start Your Business," *Inc. State of Small Business* (May 19, 1998), p. 114.

16. Robert McGarvey, "Words from the Wise," *Entrepreneur* (May 1997), pp. 152–155.

17. "Small Business: An Economic Powerhouse," National Federation of Independent Businesses (1998), downloaded from **www.nfibonline. com.**

18. "Small Business Answer Card, 1998," Office of Advocacy, Small Business Administration, downloaded from **www.sba.gov/ADVO.**

19. Michael Barrier, "Raking in the Blue Chips," *Nation's Business* (April 1, 1998), downloaded from **www.nbmag.com.**

20. All information for the SBA section is from the Small Business Administration Web site, **www.sba.gov/.**

21. Jerry Useem, "Ideas by the Gross," *Inc.* (February 1997), p. 50.

22. Don Debelak, "Where's the Big Idea?" *Business StartUps* (March 1998), downloaded from **www. entrepreneurmag.com.**

23. Carrie Mason-Draffen, "Business Plan Is a Tool No Company Should Be Without," *Newsday* (October 12, 1998), downloaded from Electric Library, Business Edition, **business.elibrary.com.**

24. Ibid.

25. "Inc. 500 Almanac," *Inc. 500* (October 20, 1998), p.18; and "Small Business: An Economic Powerhouse," National Federation of Independent Businesses (1998).

26. "Small Business Answer Card, 1998," Office of Advocacy, Small Business Administration.

27. Anne Zeiger, "The Many Virtues of 'Virtual Services,'" *Business Week Enterprise* (September 14, 1998), p. ENT 20.

28. Gary Andrew Poole, "Help Wanted: Desperately: Horizon Communications," *Business Week Enterprise* (May 25, 1998), p. ENT 8.

29. Marla Dickerson, "Women Are Geared for Growth," *Los Angeles Times* (October 7, 1998), p. C-1; "Inbox: Anybody Home? You Bet," *Business Week Enterprise* (December 7, 1998), pp. ENT 2–3; and "Two of Three New Businesses Formed in the Home," National Federation of Independent Business press release, July 23, 1997, downloaded from **www.nfib.org.**

30. John Grossman, "Meeting's at 9. I'll Be the One in Slippers," *Inc. State of Small Business* (May 19, 1998), pp. 47–48.

31. Debra Phillips et al., "Quick Guide for Women Entrepreneurs," *Entrepreneur* (January 1999), pp. 23–26.

32. "Women's World," *Entrepreneur* (January 1999), p. 24–25.

33. Cynthia E. Griffin, "Quick Guide for Minorities," *Entrepreneur* (February 1999), p. 24.

34. Lee Romney, "Latino Entrepreneurs Looking to Mexico," *Los Angeles Times* (September 30, 1998), downloaded from Electric Library Business Edition, **business.elibrary.com.**

35. Griffin, "Quick Guide for Minorities"; Gene Koretz, "Wanted: Black Entrepreneurs," *Business Week* (December 14, 1998), p. 26; and

Julianne Malveaux, "Banking on Us: The State of Black Wealth," *Essence* (October 1, 1998), p. 100.

36. Quentin Hardy, "Think Big," *Wall Street Journal Interactive Edition* (December 7, 1998), downloaded from **interactive.wsj.com.**

37. John J. O'Callaghan, "Ten Tips for Would-Be Entrepreneurs," downloaded from Home Business Magazine Web site, **www. homebusinessmag.com,** February 12, 1999; and Bob Weinstein, "What's the Big Idea?" *Entrepreneur* (February 1999), pp. 184A–184C.

38. Charles and Duffy, "Not Pulp Fiction: 'Juice Guys' Tom Scott and Tom First Built an Empire out of Fresh Fruit"; Gerry Khermouch, "Nantucket Resets 'Super' Nectars in Push for Broader Herbal Appeal," *BrandWeek* (March 22, 1999), p. 6; Jennie Leszkiewisz, "Drinking Is Their Life: Tom and Tom Return to Brown," *Brown Daily Herald* (October 23, 1997), downloaded from Electric Library, Business Edition, **business.elibrary. com,** and Tanklefsky, "Future Is Looking Sweet for Juice Guys."

Making Ethical Choices source: Adapted from: J.G. Auerbach, M. Maremont, and G. Putka, "Prying Eyes: With These Operators, Your Bank Account Is Now an Open Book," *Wall Street Journal* (November 5, 1998), pp. A1, A3.

Focusing on Small Business sources: Marc Ballon , MIT Springboard Sends Internet Company Aloft," *Inc.* (December 1998), pp. 23–25; Marc Ballon, "Spawning Start-Ups at San Diego State," *Inc.* (December 1998), p. 24; and Marc Ballon, "Texas Super Bowl," *Inc.* (March 1998), p. 39–41.

Applying Technology sources: "Cold Fusion and Pandesic Partner to Sell Snowboards Online," *Business Wire* (October 20, 1998) downloaded from Electric Library, Business Edition, **business.elibrary.com;** Cold Fusion Sports Incorporated Web site, **www. boardshop.com;** Quentin Hardy, "Think Big," *Wall Street Journal Interactive Edition* (December 7, 1998), downloaded from **interactive.wsj.com;** Tom Williams, telephone interview, February 24, 1999.

Creative Thinking Case sources: "For the Two Biggest Failures of All Time, Life Couldn't Be Better," *Inc.* (May 1, 1998), downloaded from Electric Library, Business Edition, **business. elibrary.com;** Gina M. Larson, "Once Is Not Enough," *Entrepreneurial Edge* (Winter 1998), downloaded from www.edgeonline.com; Susan Moran, "Life after Death," *Business 2.0* (January 1999), pp. 72–73; and "Onsale CEO Reports High Growth in Sales and Customer Registrations," *PR Newswire* (February 24, 1998), downloaded from Electric Library, Business Edition, **business.elibrary.com.**

Video Case source: Adapted from material contained on the following Internet sites: "Yahoo! Home Page," **http://www.yahoo.com/**; "Yahoo! – Company History," **http://www.docs. yahoo.com/info/misc/history.html**; "Yahoo! Introduces Expanded Suite of Services for Small Businesses," **http://www.yahoo.com/docs/pr/**; "Yahoo! Reports Fourth Quarter and 1998 Fiscal Year End Financial Results," **http://www.yahoo.com/docs/pr/**; and from material in the video: *Entrepreneurship and Innovation: A Study of Yahoo!*

CHAPTER 7 NOTES

1. Alex Taylor III, "Rally of the Dolls: It Worked for Toyota. Can It Work for Toys?" *Fortune* (January 11, 1999), p. 36.
2. Steve Hamm, "No Letup—And No Apologies," *Business Week,* (October 26, 1998), pp. 58–64.
3. Nina Munk, "Gap Gets It," *Fortune* (August 2, 1998), pp. 68–82.
4. Scott Wilson, "From Ice Storm to Fire Storm, Did Pepco Slip?" *Washington Post* (January 31, 1999) pp. A1, A6.
5. Leslie Walker, "Business at Cyberspeed," © 1999, *The Washington Post.* Reprinted with permission.
6. Peter Elkind, "A Merger Made in Hell," *Fortune* (November 9, 1998).
7. John Huey and Geoffery Colvin, "The Jack and Herb Show," *Fortune* (January 1, 1999), p. 163.
8. Tara Parker-Pope, "New CEO Preaches Rebellion for P&G's Cult," *Wall Street Journal* (January 11, 1998), p. B1.
9. Jeffrey Ball, "DaimlerChrysler's Renschler Holds Job of Melding Officieal Into Cohesive Team," *Wall Street Journal* (January 12, 1999).
10. Scott Thurm, "A Blitz of Fixes Helps Factories Prepare for 2000," *Wall Street Journal* (January 5, 1999).
11. Dana Fields, "Teamwork Powers Harley Bike Factory," *Fort Worth Star-Telegram* (June 16, 1998), Section C, p. 3.
12. Richard Pascale, "Grassroots Leadership—Royal Dutch Shell," Fast Company, (April 1998), p. 110.
13. "Humane Technology— PeopleSoft," Paul Roberts, *Fast Company* (April 1998), p. 122.

14. Anna Muoio, "Decisions, Decisions," *Fast Company* (October 1998), pp. 93–106.
15. Danielle Sessa, "For College Students, Web Offers a Lesson in Discounts," *Wall Street Journal* (January, 21, 1999), p. B7.

Focusing on Small Business source: Carol Hymowitz, "CEO's Set the Tone for How to Handle Questions of Ethics," *Wall Street Journal* (December 22, 1998).

Making Ethical Choices source: Adapted from R. Wartzman, "Trade Patterns: In the Wake of Nafta, a Family Firm Sees Business Go South," *Wall Street Journal* (February 23, 1999), pp. A1, A10.

Applying Technology source: J. William Gurley, "A Dell for Every Industry," *Fortune* (October 12, 1998), pp. 167–172.

Creative Thinking Case source: Leigh Buchanan, "The Smartest Little Company in America," *Inc.* (January 1999), pp. 43-54.

Video Case source: Adapted from material contained on the following Internet sites: **www.dhc.com; http**: and **//www.corporate-ir.com**; and from material in the video: *Planning and Implementing: A Study of Hudson's.*

CHAPTER 8 NOTES

1. Tara Parker-Pope, "P&G, in Effort to Give Sales a Boost, Plans to Revamp Corporate Structure," *Wall Street Journal* (September 2, 1998), pp. B1, B6.
2. Peter Galuszka, "P&G's Hottest New Product: P & G," *Business Week* (October 5, 1998), pp. 92–96.
3. Dana Fields, "Teamwork Powers Harley Bike Factory," *Fort Worth Star-Telegram* (June 16, 1998), Section C, p. 3.
4. Roy S. Johnson, "Home Depot Renovates," *Fortune* (November 23, 1998), pp. 201–219.
5. Carol Hymowitz, "More Top Executives Used to the Single Life, Are Cohabiting Now," *Wall Street Journal* (January 5, 1999), p. B1.
6. Roger O. Crockett, "Motorola: Slow and Steady Isn't Winning Any Races," *Business Week* (August 10, 1998), pp. 62–64.
7. Cathy Olofson, "Stairway to Information Heaven," *Fast Company* (April 1999), p. 68.
8. Gina Imperato, "He's Become BankAmerica's 'Mr. Project,'" *Fast Company* (June 1998; first appeared in *Fast Company* issue 15, p. 42).

9. John A. Byrne, "The Corporation of the Future," *Business Week* (August 31, 1998), pp. 102–106.
10. "How New Chief Forged One Company from Two While Boosting Profit," Carol Hymowitz, *Wall Street Journal,* February 2, 1999, p. B1.
11. Tara Parker-Pope, "New CEO Preaches Rebellion for P&G's 'Cult,'" *Wall Street Journal* (December 11, 1998), pp B1, B4.

Applying Technology source: Nellie Andreeva, "Do the Math–It is a Small World," *Business Week* (August 17, 1998), pp. 54–55.

Focusing on Small Business source: Cathy Olofson, "Stairway to Information Heaven," *Fast Company* (April 1999), p. 68.

Making Ethical Choices source: Adapted from L. Cohen, "U.S. Organizers of Olympics Control Damage," *Wall Street Journal* (March 22, 1999), pp. B1, B4; S. Fatsis, "Olympic Sponsors Study Their Options amid Scandal," *Wall Street Journal* (March 10, 1999), p. B2; S. Fatsis, "IOC Tries to Sell Reforms to Corporate Sponsors," *Wall Street Journal* (March 19, 1999), p. B2; S. Fatsis, "Olympic Scandal Is Result of Culture of Corruption, U.S. Panel Concludes," *Wall Street Journal* (March 22, 1999), p. A4.

Creative Thinking Case source: Lisa Chadderdon, "Monster World," *Fast Company* (January 1999), pp. 112–117.

Video Case source: Adapted from material contained on the following Internet sites: "About JIAN," **www. jian.com/ab_jian.asp;** and "Powerful Software to Build Your Business," **www.jian.com/prod.asp;** and from material in the video: *Organizational Design: A Study of JIAN.*

CHAPTER 9 NOTES

1. Joanne Lee-Young, "Starbucks' Expansion in China Is Slated," *Wall Street Journal* (October 5, 1998), p. A27c.
2. Ellen Joan Pollock, "Sir: Your Application for a Job Is Rejected; Sincerely, Hall 9000," *Wall Street Journal* (July 30, 1998), pp. A1, A12.
3. Eileen P. Gunn, "How Mirage Resorts Sifted 75,000 Applicants to Hire 9,600 in 24 Weeks," *Fortune* (October 12, 1998), p. 195.
4. "Work Week," *Wall Street Journal* (December 22, 1998), p. A1.
5. "Gore-Text," *Fast Company* (January 1999), p. 160.
6. "Study May Spur Job-Applicant Drug Screening," *Wall Street Journal* (November 28, 1998), pp. B1, B7.

7. "Companies Are Finding It Really Pays to Be Nice to Employees," *Wall Street Journal* (July 22, 1998), p. B1.

8. Joann S. Lubin, "New Hires Win Fast Raises in Accelerated Job Reviews," *Wall Street Journal* (October 6, 1998), pp. B1, B16.

9. "It's Not a Job, It's an Adventure," *Fast Company* (January 1999), pp. 52–54.

10. "Eight Years Later, Many Still Unaware of Disabilities Act," *Dallas Morning News* (September 26, 1998), p. 7C.

11. Sandra Baker, "Service Helps Employees Manage Challenges of Their Private Lives," *Fort Worth Star-Telegram Tarrant Business* (October 26, 1998), p. 17.

12. Patricia Sellers, "The 50 Most Powerful Women in American Business," *Fortune* (October 12, 1998), pp. 76–98.

13. Michael J. Flynn, "Crystal Vision," *Telecommute* (January 1999), pp. 14–19.

14. "Making Stay-at-Homes Feel Welcome," *Business Week* (October 12, 1998), pp. 155–156.

15. Sherry E. Sullivan, William A. Carden, and David F. Martin, "Careers in the Next Millennium: Directions for Future Research," *Human Resource Management Review* (Summer 1998), pp. 165–185.

16. "Saying Adios to the Office," *Business Week* (October 12, 1998), pp. 152–154.

Applying Technology source: Adapted from Jerry Useem, "The Matchmaker," *Inc.* (December 1998), pp. 71–83.

Focusing on Small Business source: Robert Reich, "The Company of the Future," *Fast Company* (November 1998), pp. 124–148.

Creative Thinking Case source: Christopher Cuggiano, "Worker, Rule Thyself," *Inc.* (February 1999), pp. 89–90.

Making Ethical Choices source: Adapted from: Siconolfi, M. "Lynched? Merrill Broker Protests Policies, Is Fired, Finds His Clients Divvied Up," *Wall Street Journal* (February 27, 1998): pp. A1, A8.

Video Case source: Adapted from material contained on the following Internet sites: **www.valassis.com:** and **www.pathfinder.com/fortune/;** and from material in the video: *Employee Recruitment and Selection: A Study of Valassis Communications, Inc.*

CHAPTER 10 NOTES

1. Charles Fishman, "Sanity Inc.," *Fast Company,* (January 1999), p. 85.

2. Timothy D. Schellhardt, "An Idyllic Workplace under a Tycoon's Thumb," *Wall Street Journal* (November 23, 1998), p. B1.

3. Shelly Branch, "The 100 Best Companies to Work for in America," *Fortune* (January 11, 1999), pp. 118-144.

4. Ibid.

5. Sherry Caudron, "The Only Way to Stay Ahead," *Industry Week* (August 17, 1998).

6. Steve Hamm, "Jim Clark Is Off and Running Again," *Business Week* (October 12, 1998), pp. 64–71.

7. De'Ann Weimer, "I Want to Lead with Love not Fear," *Business Week* (August 17, 1998), pp. 52–53

8. David A. Nadler and Edward E. Lawler III, "Motivation—A Diagnostic Approach," in William Hackman, Edward E. Lawler III, and Michael Porter (Eds.), *Perspectives on Behavior in Organizations* (New York, McGraw-Hill, 1977).

9. Bruce Tulgan, *FAST Feedback,* (HRD Press, 1998).

10. Gina Imperato, "How to Give Good Feedback," *Fast Company* (September 1998), pp. 144–156.

11. G. Fuchsberg, "Four-Day Workweek Has Become a Stretch for Some Employees," *Wall Street Journal* (August 2, 1994), pp. B1, B4.

12. Robert B. Reich, "The Company of the Future," *Fast Company* (November 1998), p. 124.

13. John R. Katzenbach and Douglas K. Smith, *The Wisdom of Teams: Creating the High-Performance Organization,* (Boston: Harvard Business School Press, 1993).

14. Ibid.

15. Shari Caudron, "The Only Way to Stay Ahead," *Industry Week* (August 17, 1998).

16. Shelly Branch, "The 100 Best Companies to Work for in America."

17. Ibid.

18. Ibid.

19. "Culture Watch," *Fortune* (November 9, 1998), p. 67.

Focusing on Small Business sources: Chuck Salter, "Insanity Inc.," *Fast Company* (January 1999), p. 106;

Evan Ramstad "High Rollers: How Trilogy Software Trains Its Raw Recruits to be Risk Takers," *Wall Street Journal* (September 21, 1998), p. B1.

Applying Technology source: Anthony M. Townsend, Samuel M. DeMarie, and Anthony R. Hendrickson, "Virtual Teams: Technology and the Workplace of the Future," *Academy of Management Executive,* 13 no. 3 (August 1998), p. 17(13).

Making Ethical Choices source: Adapted from: T. Appeal, "Missing the Boss: Not All Workers Find Idea of Empowerment as Neat as It Sounds," *Wall Street Journal* (September 8, 1997), pp. A1, A13; R.Y. Bergstrom, "Be Prepared to Be Involved," *Automotive Manufacturing & Production* (February 1997); pp. 66+.

Creative Thinking Case source: Almar Latour, "Detroit Meets a Worker Paradise," *Wall Street Journal* (March 3, 1999), pp. B1, B4.

Video Case source: Adapted from material contained on the following Internet sites: **http://www.valassis.com:** and **http://www.pathfinder.com/fortune/;** and from material in the video: *Motivating for Performance: A Study of Valassis Communications, Inc.*

CHAPTER 11 NOTES

1. Scott McCartney, "At American Airlines, Pilots Trace Grievances to Deals in Lean Years," *Wall Street Journal* (February 1, 1999), pp. A1, A10.

2. Ron Fournier, "Union Leaders to Raise Money to Help Democrats Retake House," *Fort Worth Star-Telegram* (February 18, 1999), p. 3A.

3. Court Cifford, "Simultaneous Conventions Approve Merger of UPIU, OCAW into 320,000 Member Group," *Daily Labor Report* (January 6, 1999), p. AA-1.

4. "SEIU Organizes More Than 60,000 Members; Adds Another 121,000 through Affiliation," *Daily Labor Report,* (December 30, 1998), p. A-3.

5. "NLRB Provides Web Access to Agency Forms," *Daily Labor Report,* (January 5, 1999), p. A-9.

6. Bebe Raupe, "Continental General Tire Says Talks with USW Have Deadlocked," *Daily Labor Report* (February 16, 1999), pp. A-10, A-11.

7. Michael Bologna and Brian Lockett, "Laborers, Justice Department Negotiate Oversight Agreement for Another Year," *Daily Labor Report* (January 8, 1999), p. AA-1.

8. Elizabeth Walpole-Hofmeister, "Teamsters, UAW Vie for Coors Workers; Await NLRB Ruling on Size of Bargaining Unit," *Daily Labor Report* (February 16, 1999), p. A-1.

9. "Agreement between USW, Magnetic Specialty Could End 22-Month Union Recognition Strike," *Daily Labor Report,* (January 8, 1999), pp. A-4, A-5.

10. Elizabeth Walpole-Hofmeister, "New Jersey UFCW Local Bargains 54-Month Master Pact with Area Chains," *Daily Labor Report* (January 7, 1999), p. A-7.

11. Ibid.
12. "Tentative Agreement Reached on Pact for 30,000 NYC Building Workers," *Daily Labor Report,* (January 7, 1999), pp. A-8, A-9.
13. "Airborne Express Contract for 3,500 Gains 90 Percent Approval from Teamsters," *Daily Labor Report,* (December 7, 1998), p. A-2.
14. "Arbitration Award Affirmed Despite Agency Finding of Improper Drug Test," *Daily Labor Report,* (January 8, 1999), p. A-3.
15. "Discipline for 28 Chicago Firefighters Rescinded by Arbitrator as Untimely," *Daily Labor Report,* (January 5, 1999), p. A-3.
16. Robert L. Simison, "GM Wins Chance to Restructure under Labor Truce," *Wall Street Journal* (August 10, 1998), p. B4.
17. Stefan Fatsis, "NBA, Players Reach Accord, Saving Season," *Wall Street Journal* (January 7, 1999), pp. A3, A12.
18. Keith Knass and Michael Matuszak, "An Antiunion Corporate Culture and Quality Improvement Programs," *Labor Studies Journal* 19 (Fall 1994), pp. 21–39.
19. "SEIU Organizes More Than 60,000 Members," p. A-3.
20. Michelle Amber, "SEIU Local Unions Representation Rights for Some 2,500 Las Vegas Hospital Workers," *Daily Labor Report* (December 10, 1998), pp. A-9, A-10.
21. Joyce E. Cutler, "CNA Wins Two Representation Elections, Lands Contracts with Income Increases," *Daily Labor Report* (December 22, 1998), p. A-2.
22. "United Steelworkers Represents 3,500 U. of Toronto Employees," *Daily Labor Report* (December 10, 1998), p. A-3.
23. "Job Cut Announcements in 1998 Largest in Decade, Challenger Reports," *Daily Labor Report,* (January 8, 1999), p. A-3.
24. Brian Lockett, "Skilled Worker Shortage, Training among Workforce Issues Facing Industry," *Daily Labor Report* (January 8, 1999), pp. C1, C2.
25. Andrew Backover, "Career Fair Set to Promote Jobs in Construction," *Fort Worth Star-Telegram* (February 26, 1999), p. 46.

Applying Technology sources: Douglas A. Blackman, "FedEx Pilots Trade Their Old Loyalties for a Tougher Union," *Wall Street Journal* (October 19, 1998), pp. A1, A10; Woody Baird, "FedEx Pilots Union Approves First Pact with Cargo Airline," *Fort Worth Star-Telegram* (February 5, 1999), p. 2C; Pam Ginsbach, "FedEx Pilots Union, Company Reach Tentative Pact with 17 Percent Pay Hike," *Daily Labor Report* (December 21, 1998), pp. AA-1, AA-2.

Making Ethical Choices source: Adapted from: Valbrun, M. "Hard Labor: To Reverse Declines, Unions Are Targeting Immigrant Workers," *The Wall Street Journal* (May 27, 1999): pp. A1 & A10.

Video Case source: Adapted from material contained on the following Internet sites: **http://www.cj.msu. edu~outreach/cp; http://www. mt-pleasant.org/comact/reports/ 98annrep.html; http://www.sagchip. com/observer/2percent.htm**; and from material in the video: *Mt. Pleasant Police: Look Behind the Badge.*

CHAPTER 12 NOTES

1. Cindy Eberting, "The Harley Mystique Comes to Kansas City," *Kansas City Star* (January 6, 1998); Randolph Heaster and Cindy Eberting, "Harley Celebrates Start of Production," *Kansas City Star* (January 7, 1998); Geeta Shjarma Jensen and Dyan Machan, "Is Hog Going Soft?" *Forbes* (March 10, 1997), p. 114; Rick Romell, "With $517.2 Million in Revenue, Harley Sets Another Record," *Milwaukee Journal Sentinel* (July 14, 1998); Stephen Roth, "New Harley Plant Spotlights Training and Empowerment," *Kansas City Business Journal* (January 9, 1998), all articles except Jensen/Machan were downloaded from Electric Library, Business Edition, **business.elibrary.com.**
2. "Golf-equipment Manufacturer Cuts Strokes off Its Process," *Industry Week* (September 21, 1998): downloaded from **www.industryweek. com.**
3. Charles W. Thurston, "Branded Offshore Manufacturing Finds a Home in Ireland and Singapore," *Chemical Market Reporter* (June 8, 1998), downloaded from Electric Library, Business Edition, **business. elibrary.com.**
4. Keith E. Gottschalk, "Bloomington OKs Tax Extension," *Peoria Journal Star* (December 15, 1998), downloaded from Electric Library, Business Edition, **business.elibrary. com.**
5. Louis Uchitelle, "Not Too Big, Not Too Small, Midsize Cities Proving to Be a Profitable Lure to Corporate America," *San Diego Union Tribune* (January 9, 1999), downloaded from Electric Library, Business Edition, **business.elibrary.com.**
6. "Cabot's Microelectronics Materials Division Opens New Slurry Manufacturing Facility in Geino, Japan, to Meet Increasing Customer Demand," company press release (January 10, 1999).
7. Emily R. Sendler and Gregory L. White, "Auto Makers Battle Y2K Bug in Vast Supplier Network," *Wall Street Journal* (November 30, 1998), p. B4.
8. "World Class Supplier Process," from AMD corporate Web page, **www.amd.com,** downloaded February 5, 1999.
9. "We're Not There Yet," downloaded from National Association of Purchasing Managers Web site, **www.napm.org,** February 12, 1999.
10. Kimberly Koster, "What's Cooking? *Quick Service Restaurant* (September/ October 1998), p. 47.
11. "Winnebago Revs Up Quality," *Providence Journal-Bulletin* (July 2, 1997), downloaded from Electric Library, Business Edition, **business. elibrary.com.**
12. Lawrence Gould, "What Makes Automotive CAD/CAM Systems So Special?" *Automotive Manufacturing & Production* (October 1, 1998), downloaded from Electric Library, Business Edition, **business.elibrary. com.**
13. Jon Van, "Automation Making Inroads at Hospitals: Robots Free Medical Personnel from Repetitive Tasks," *Cincinnati Enquirer* (September 13, 1998), downloaded from Electric Library, Business Edition, **business.elibrary.com.**
14. Glenn Hasek and Weld Royal, "Measuring Industry's Might," *Industry Week* (June 8, 1998), downloaded from Industry Week Web site, **www.industryweek.com.**
15. Peronet Despeignes, "Bulging Economy Outpaces Job Losses," *Detroit News* (December 20, 1998), downloaded from Electric Library, Business Edition, **business.elibrary.com.**
16. Bill Vlasic, "Imitation is Sincere Form of Productivity: Lean Manufacturing System Focuses on Team Production, *Detroit News* (December 21, 1998), p. F9.
17. Charles Gilbert, "Did Modules Fail Levi's or Did Levi's Fail Modules?" *Apparel Industry Magazine* (September 1, 1998), downloaded from Electric Library, Business Edition, **business.elibrary.com.**
18. Bruce Caldwell, "Harley Shifts into High Gear," *Information Week*

(November 30, 1998), downloaded from **www.informationweek.com.**

Focusing on Small Business sources: Jeffrey Zygmont, "Does Size Really Matter?" and "The Ties That Bind," *Inc. Technology No. 3* (September 15, 1998) downloaded from Electric Library, Business Edition, **business.elibrary.com.**

Making Ethical Choices source: Adapted from R. L. Simison, "Buyer's Market: General Motors Drives Some Hard Bargains with Asian Suppliers," *Wall Street Journal* (April 2, 1999), pp. A1, A6.

Applying Technology sources: Kimberly Koster, "What's Cooking?" "Speedy Delivery," and "Bringing 'Em Back," *Quick Service Restaurant* (September/ October 1998), pp. 46, 49, 53; Alan Liddle, "The Millennium: A Food-service Odyssey," *Nation's Restaurant News* (September 14, 1998), down-loaded from Electric Library, Business Edition, **business.elibrary.com.**

Creative Thinking Case sources: Marla Dickerson, "Tailored for Efficiency: Apparel Makers Respond to Need to Automate, " *Los Angeles Times* (April 8, 1998), downloaded from Electric Library, Business Edition, **business. elibrary.com;** Clay Parnell, "Supply Chain Management in the Soft Goods Industry," *Apparel Industry Magazine* (June 1, 1998), downloaded from Apparel Industry Magazine Online, **www.aimmagazine.com.**

Video Case source: Adapted from ma-terial contained on the following Internet site: The Vermont Teddy Bear Company!®" **www.vtbear.com;** and from material in the video *A Case Study in Manufacturing Operations: The Vermont Teddy Bear Company.*

CHAPTER 13 NOTES

1. Jennifer Lach, "Boomers on the Drawing Board," *American Demograph-ics* (November 1998), pp. 48–49.
2. "The New Chief Is Ordering Up Changes at McDonald's," *Wall Street Journal* (August 24, 1998), p. B1.
3. Leonard Goodstein and Howard Butz, "Customer Value: The Linch-pin of Organizational Change," *ASAP* (June 22, 1998), p. 22.
4. "NYSEG Highlighting Superior Customer Satisfaction," *PR Newswire* (October 6, 1998), p. 1.
5. Goodstein and Butz, "Customer Value," p. 24.
6. Kevin Clancy and Robert Shulman, "Marketing—Toss Fatal Flaws," *The Retailing Issues Letter* (November 1998), p. 4.

7. "Frequent Perks Keep Travelers Loyal," *American Demographics* (September 1998), pp. 32–35.
8. "As Children Become More Sophisticated, Marketers Think Older," *Wall Street Journal* (October 13, 1998), pp. A1, A6.
9. "Gillette's New Strategy Is to Sharpen Pitch to Women," *Wall Street Journal* (May 11, 1998), pp. B1, B16.
10. "Kraft's Miracle Whip Targets Core Consumers," *Advertising Age* (February 3, 1998), p. 12.
11. "Hard Core Shoppers," *American Demographics* (September 1998), p. 49.
12. "Rating Wars," *American Demograph-ics* (October 1998), pp. 31–33.
13. "The New Ratings Game," *Business Week* (April 27, 1998), pp. 73–75.
14. David Wolfe, "What Your Customers Can't Say," *American Demographics* (February 1998), pp. 24–29.
15. "A Potent New Tool for Selling—Database Marketing," *Business Week* (September 5, 1997), pp. 56–62.

Creative Thinking Case source: Don Schultz, "AAA Gets an 'F' in Build-ing Relationships with Customers," *Marketing News* (March 30, 1998), pp. 5–6.

Focusing on Small Business source: Louise Lee, "If You Also Want to Buy a Crock-Pot, This Isn't the Place," *Wall Street Journal* (August 26, 1997), pp. A1, A11.

Applying Technology source: Dick McCullough, "Web-Based Market Research Ushers In New Age," *Marketing News* (September 14, 1998), pp. 27–28.

Video Case source: Adapted from material contained on the following Internet site: **www.burke.com;** and from material in the video: *A Case Study in Decision Support Systems and Marketing Research: Burke Inc.*

Making Ethical Choices source: Adapted from: Friedland, J. "Sweet Solution: Mexican Mogul Offers Omnilife as the Answer to Poor Diet, Poverty," *Wall Street Journal* (March 2, 1999); pp. A1, A8.

CHAPTER 14 NOTES

1. Joseph Pereira, "Your Inner Skateboard: Grinding Shoes," *Wall Street Journal* (November 9, 1998), pp. B1, B4.
2. "Quaker Oats Raises Cereal Prices; Brand Loyalty May Give a Lift to Profit," *Washington Post* (May 23, 1998), p. D1.

3. "New Report Finds How Companies Treat Customers Is a Major Driver of Brand Loyalty and Impacts Future Sales," *PR Newswire* (November 10, 1998), pp. 1–4.
4. For Pepsi, a Battle to Capture Coke's Fountain Sales," *Wall Street Journal* (May 11, 1998), p. B1.
5. "New Products," *Ad Age International* (April 15, 1998), p. 18.
6. "Secrets of the New Brand Builders," *Fortune* (June 22, 1998), pp. 167–170.
7. The material on mass customization is from Erick Schonfeld, "The Customized, Digitized, Have-it-Your-Way Economy," *Fortune* (September 18, 1998), pp. 114–124.
8. Katharine Mieszkowski, "Wanna Buy? What Am I Bid?" *Fast Company* (November 1998), pp. 288–290.

Focusing on Small Business source: Dale Buss, "Making Your Mark through Branding," *Nation's Business* (October 1998), pp. 27–31.

Making Ethical Choices source: Adapted from R., Langreth, M., Waldholz, and S. D. Moore, "DNA Dreams: Big Drug Firms Discuss Linking up to Pursue Disease-Causing Genes," *Wall Street Journal* (March 4, 1999), pp. A1, A6.

Applying Technology source: George Anders, "Comparison Shopping Is the Web's Virtue—Unless You're a Seller," *Wall Street Journal* (July 23, 1998), pp. A1, A8.

Creative Thinking Case source: 1 "Makers of Herb-Dusted Chips Tout Mood-Altering Effects, But Some Are Skeptical," *Dallas Morning News* (September 27, 1998), p. 9A.

Video Case source: Adapted from material contained on the following Internet site: **http://www.bluejays.ca;** and from material in the video: *A Case Study in Pricing Concepts: The Toronto Blue Jays.*

CHAPTER 15 NOTES

1. Roy S. Johnson, "Home Depot Renovates," *Fortune* (November 23, 1998), pp. 200–205.
2. Eric Johnson, "Giving 'em What They Want; Effective Supply Chain Management," *Management Review* (November 1998), pp. 62–70.
3. Ibid.
4. "Value Retailers Go Dollar for Dollar," *Fortune* (July 6, 1998), pp. 164–166.
5. "Revamped Colors Send Eddie Bauer Down Wrong Path," *Advertising Age* (September 14, 1998), p. 30.

6. "Gadzooks! Claire's Stores Moves in on a Rival," *Wall Street Journal* (September 11, 1998), pp. B1, B4.

7. Charles Lamb, Joe Hair, and Carl McDaniel, *Essentials of Marketing* (Cincinnati: SouthWestern Publishing Co. 1999), pp. 291–292.

8. Ibid.

9. Yumiko Ono, "Where Are the Gloves? They Were Stock Lifted by a Rival Producer," *Wall Street Journal* (May 15, 1998), pp. A1, A10.

10. Ibid.

11. Lamb, Hair, and McDaniel *Essentials of Marketing*" p. 293.

Making Ethical Choices source:
Adapted from M. Maremont and R. Berner, "Store Markdowns: Leaning on Suppliers, Rite Aid Deducts Cash at Bill-Paying Time," *Wall Street Journal* (March 31, 1999), pp. A1, A6.

Focusing on Small Business source:
Heather Green and Seanna Browder, "Cyberspace Winners: How They Did It," *Business Week* (June 22, 1998), pp. 154–160.

Applying Technology source: Emily Nelson, "Why Wal-Mart Sings, Yes, We Have Bananas!" *Wall Street Journal* (October 6, 1998), pp. B1, B4.

Creative Thinking source: Richard Gibson, "Fame Proves Fleeting at Planet Hollywood As Fans Avoid Reruns," *Wall Street Journal* (October 7, 1998), pp. A1, A6.

Video Case source: Adapted from material contained on the following Internet site: **www.burton.com/main. asp**; and from material in the video: *A Case Study in Distribution Strategy: Burton Snowboards.*

CHAPTER 16 NOTES

1. "Dockers Relaxed-Fit Cool," *Fortune* (August 17, 1998), p. 32.

2. Pepsi Cola Puts Hopes, Dreams, $$, into Pepsi One," *Advertising Age* (October 5, 1998), p. 16.

3. "Total Measured Media Spending 1998," *Advertising Age* (November 9, 1998), p. 50.

4. "1998 Advertising-to-Sales Ratios," *Advertising Age* (June 29, 1998), p. 22.

5. "Price of NFL TV-Commercials Could Skyrocket 20 Percent Next Season," *Wall Street Journal* (January 15, 1998), p. B12.

6. Charles Lamb, Joe Hair, and Carl McDaniel, *Essentials of Marketing* (Cincinnati: South-Western Publishing Company, 1999), p. 363.

7. Mark Jarvis, "When I'm in the Selling Zone, Every Cell in My Body Is Working toward the Same Goal," *Fast Company* (November 1998), p. 106.

8. Letter to the authors from Suzanne Gornowicz, Valassis Communications Inc., dated September 4, 1998.

9. The material on digital VCRs is from J. William Gurley, "How the Web Will Warp Advertising," *Fortune* (November 9, 1998), pp. 119–120.

10. "Spam That You Might Not Delete," *Business Week* (June 15, 1998), pp. 115–118.

Making Ethical Choices source:
Adapted from S. Beatty, "Recasting the Gun as Sports Equipment: New Ads Stress Shooting's Safety and Popularity," *Wall Street Journal* (April 5, 1999), p. B1.

Applying Technology source: David Webster, "Will We Choke the Web With Ad Clutter?" *Advertising Age* (September 21, 1998).

Focusing on Small Business source:
"Floor Show," *Dallas Morning News* (September 4, 1998), p. 11D.

Creative thinking source: Scott McCartney, "We'll Be Landing In Kansas So the Crew Can Grab a Steak," *Wall Street Journal* (September 8, 1998), pp. A1, A18.

Video Case source: Adapted from material contained on the following Internet site: **http://www.redroof.com/ about_the_roof/**; and from material in the video: *A Case Study in Advertising Strategy: Red Roof Inns.*

CHAPTER 17 NOTES

1. Ann B. Graham, "All for One and One for All," *Executive Edge* (Special Gartner Group/Forbes Magazine supplement) (September 1998), pp. 24–28; "IBM Bolsters Business Intelligence Solutions with Exchange Applications' Software for Managing Marketing Campaigns," *Business Wire* (July 21, 1998); Carol Power, "Key-Corp Touts Payoff from Data Warehouse In Marketing Efforts," *American Banker* (March 12, 1999). The latter two articles were downloaded from Electric Library, Business Edition, **business.elibrary.com.**

2. Lawrence M. Fisher, "Big Mainframes Facing Fuzzy Future," *San Diego Union-Tribune ComputerLink* (June 9, 1998), p. 21.

3. "Delivering What the Customer Wants," S/390 Success Stories, IBM Web Site, **www.s390.ibm. customer/.**

4. Scott LaJoie, "Size Matters Again," and Carol Pickering, "Blue Mountain," *Forbes ASAP* (February 22, 1999), pp. 51–54.

5. LaJoie, "Size Matters Again."

6. "LANs of Opportunity," *Inc. Technology* 1998, No. 2 (June 16, 1998), p. 20.

7. "Let a LAN Leverage Productivity," *Inc.'s 301 Great Ideas for Using Technology,* downloaded May 5, 1999, from **www.inc.com/301/ideas.**

8. Emily Esterson, "Inner Beauties," *Inc. Technology 1998,* No. 4 (December 15, 1998), pp. 79–90.

9. "Largest Privately Held Department Store Chain Implements Micro-strategy Decision Support Tech," *M2 PressWIRE* (November 16, 1998), downloaded from Electric Library, Business Edition, **business.elibrary.com.**

10. Michael Menduno, "Software That Plays Hardball," *Hospitals & Health Networks* (May 20, 1998), downloaded from Electric Library, Business Edition, **business. elibrary.com.**

11. M. Bensaou and Michael Earl, "The Right Mind Set for Managing Iinformation Technology," *Harvard Business Review* (September 1, 1998), downloaded from Electric Library, Business Edition, **business. elibrary.com.**

12. Bronwyn Fryer, "No False Moves," *Inc. Technology 1998,* No. 4 (November 17, 1998), pp. 48–58.

13. Emily Esterson, "Bluebird's Unhappiness," *Inc. Technology 1998,* No. 1 (March 16, 1998), p. 20.

14. John Omicinski, "Internet Explosion Has Given Hackers Thousands of New Entry Points," Gannett News Service (February 27, 1998), downloaded from Electric Library, Business Edition, **business. elibrary.com.**

15. Marcia Stepanek, "Y2K Is Worse Than Anyone Thought," *Business Week* (December 14, 1998), pp. 38–40; Scott Thurm, "A Blitz of Fixes Helps Factories Prepare for 2000," *Wall Street Journal* (January 5, 1999), pp. B1, B6.

16. Denise Caruso, "Long Running Fight over Data Privacy Has Been Heating Up," *San Diego Union-Tribune ComputerLink* (March 9, 1999), p. 2; Michael Gardner, "Shopper Privacy Bill Goes to Assembly," *San Diego Union-Tribune* (April 27, 1999), pp. A3–A4.

17. Teena Massingill, "Privacy Lost," The San Diego Union-Tribune (April 4, 1999), pp. I3, I6.

18. Gary McWilliams, "Taming the Info Monster," *Business Week* (June 22,

1998), pp. 171–172; and "Surfing the Hype Curve," *Executive Edge* (September 1998), pp. 16-17.

19. Bruce Caldwell, "CEOs Turn to IT," *Information Week* (June 26, 1998), downloaded from Electric Library, Business Edition, **business.elibrary. com.**

20. Peter Burrows, "Beyond the PC," *Business Week* (March 8, 1999), pp. 79-88; "High-tech Rejuvenation," *PC Week Online* (March 1, 1999), downloaded from **www.zdnet.com/ pcweek/stories;** Stephen Wildstrom, "The Year of the Home Network?" *Business Week* (January 18, 1999), p. 22.

21. Aileen Crowley, "No Crying Wolf: The Shortage Is Real," *PC Week Online* (May 18, 1998), downloaded from **www.zdnet.com/pcweek/news;** "IT Skills Gap Research Program," Information Technology Association of America, downloaded from **www.itaa.org/workforce/.**

22. Teena Massingill, "Privacy Lost."

23. Graham, "All for One and One for All"; Power, "KeyCorp Touts Payoff."

Applying Technology sources: Frank Gibney, Jr., "Pepsi Gets Back in the Game," *Time* (April 26, 1999), downloaded from Electric Library, Business Edition, **business.elibrary.com;** Julia King and Thomas Hoffman, "The Next IT Generation," *Computerworld* (April 6, 1998), p. 1; Ian Springsteel, "Pepsi's Next Generation of Purchasing," *CFO* (December 1997), downloaded from **www.cfonet.com.**

Focusing on Small Business sources: Leigh Buchanan, "The Buying Game," *Inc. Tech 1998, No. 2* (June 16, 1998), p. 11; Emily Esterson, "Hail to the Chiefs," *Inc. Tech 1998, No. 2* (June 16, 1998), pp. 65–78; and Tim McCollum, "Computer Systems According to Plan," *Nation's Business* (August 1, 1998), downloaded from Electric Library, Business Edition, **business.elibrary.com.**

Video Case source: Adapted from material contained on the following Internet sites: "Archway (r) News," **www.archwaycookies.com;** "Archway Cookies: Solutions & Success Stories," **www.intermec.com/solutions/archway. htm;** and from material in the video *Management Information Systems: A Study of Archway Cookies.*

Making Ethical Choices source: Adapted from M. Maremont, "Extra! Extra! Internet Hoax, Get the Details," *Wall Street Journal* (April 8, 1999), pp. C1, C18; M., Maremont, and W. M. Bulkeley, "Who Did the Hoax? SEC Seeks Answers a Day after PairGain's Stock Rockets," *Wall Street Journal* (April 9, 1999), p. C22.

CHAPTER 18 NOTES

1. Paul Davidson, "Net Retailer eToys Faces Big Risks As Its Star Rises," *USA Today* (April 8,1999), p. 1B; Joshua Macht, "Toy Seller Plays Internet Hardball," *Inc.* (October 1998), p. 17; Patricia Sellers, "Behind the First E-Christmas," *Fortune* (February 1, 1999), pp. 71–73; "Patricia Seybold Names Top Ten Customers.com(R) 1998 Holiday E-Tailers," PR Newswire (January 13, 1999); Thom Weidlich, "Toys in the Bandwidth," *Direct* (October 1, 1998). The latter tow articles were downloaded from Electric Library, Business Edition, **business.elibrary.com.**

2. *The Emerging Digital Economy* (U.S. Department of Commerce, 1998), pp. 2–4, downloaded from **www.ecommerce.gov.**

3. America Online/Roper Starch Cyberstudy 1998, cited in *The Technology Primer,* vol. 5, Morgan Stanley Dean Witter (May 1999), p. 325.

4. "Internet Domain Survey, January 1999," Network Wizards, downloaded from **www.nw.com;** Bob Metcalfe, "Early Signs Appear of Slowing Internet Growth," *Infoworld* (May 10, 1999), downloaded from **www.infoworld.com.**

5. Information from NUA and Mediamark Research Spring 1999 CyberStats, cited in *NUA Internet Surveys* (May 17, 1999), downloaded from **www.nua.ie/surveys.**

6. Roger O. Crockett, "A Web That Looks like the World," *Business Week e.biz* (March 22, 1999), pp. EB 46–47; Thomas E. Weber, "The Big Question: Who Is on the Net?" *San Diego Union-Tribune ComputerLink* (May 8, 1998), p. 6.

7. Lori Ioannou, "Going Public with iVillage," *Your Company* (February 1, 1999).

8. "Booz Allen & Hamilton: 89 Percent of Corporates Have A Website," *NUA Internet Surveys* (June 8, 1999), downloaded from **www.nua.ie/surveys.**

9. J. William Gurley, "How the Net Is Changing Competition," *Fortune* (March 15, 1999), p. 168.

10. Peter H. Lewis, "Travel Transforms Technology," *San Diego Union-Tribune ComputerLink* (June 8, 1999), pp. 6–8.

11. Edward M. Kerchner, Thomas M. Doerflinger, and Michael Geraghty, "The Information Revolution Wars," *PaineWebber Portfolio Managers' Spotlight* (May 18, 1999), pp. 3–40.

12. "The Great Terrain Robbery," *Technology Trends: 1999 Software and Services Annual Report,* Deloitte & Touche LLP, pp. 14–15.

13. David Bank, "Buying Power," *The Wall Street Journal Interactive Edition* (December 7, 1998), downloaded from **interactive.wsj.com.**

14. Erick Schonfeld, "The Exchange Economy," *Fortune* (February 15, 1999), pp. 67–68.

15. *The Technology Primer,* vol. 5, Morgan Stanley Dean Witter (May 1999), p. 351.

16. George Anders, "Click and Buy," *The Wall Street Journal Interactive Edition* (December 7, 1998), downloaded from **interactive.wsj.com.**

17. John R. L. Rizza, "The Internet Gets Down to Business," *Entrepreneurial Edge Magazine* (Summer 1998), downloaded from **www.edgeonline.com.**

18. Annette Hamilton, "Five Lessons from the Holiday Shopping Season," *ZDNet Anchor Desk* (January 6, 1999), downloaded from **www. zdnet.com/anchordesk.com.**

19. James R. Hagerty, "Home Depot, Lowe's Test the Waters of Online Selling," *Wall Street Journal* (January 4, 1999), p. A15.

20. "Few E-Ventures Will Show Short-Term Profits," Giga Information Group survey, reported by *NUA Internet Surveys,* (January 11, 1999), downloaded from **www.nua.ie/ surveys.**

21. Mary Beth Grover, "Lost in Cyberspace," *Forbes* (March 8, 1999), pp. 124–128.

22. Ibid.

23. Maryann Jones Thompson, "Spotlight: The Economic Impact of E-commerce," *The Industry Standard* (April 26, 1999), downloaded from **www.thestandard.com/metrics/.**

24. Robert D. Hof, "The Click-Here Economy," *Business Week* (June 22, 1998), pp. 122–128.

25. Sandy Reed, "Can't Get No Satisfaction," *Infoworld* (May 24, 1999), p. 83.

26. Jesse Berst, "E-commerce Breakthrough: Finally, an Easy Way to Pay Online," *ZDNet Anchor Desk* (June 14, 1999), downloaded from **www.zdnet.com/anchordesk.**

27. Jan Norman, "E-commerce Is Fast Becoming the Internet's 800-pound Gorilla," *San Diego Union-Tribune* (May 10, 1999), p. C2.

28. Jane Asteroff and Maureen Fleming, "Four Ways to Increase

a Web Site's Strategic Value," *Executive Edge* (September 1998), pp. 6–7.

29. "Association of National Advertisers: Report Looks at Corporate Web Spending Effectiveness," *NUA Internet Surveys* (May 17, 1999), downloaded from **www.nua.ie/ surveys.**

30. James R. Hagerty, "Home Depot, Lowe's Test the Waters of Online Selling," *Wall Street Journal* (January 4, 1999), p. A15.

31. Heather Green, "Portals Are Mortal After All," *Business Week* (June 21, 1999), pp. 144–146; "Online E-commerce Players Go Offline to Raise Profile," *Reuters News Service* (November 24, 1998), downloaded from ZD News Net, **www.zdnet.com/zdnn.**

32. Steven Levy, "The New Digital Galaxy," *Business Week*

33. Robert D. Hof, "Now It's Your Web," *Business Week* (October 5, 1998), pp. 164–176.

34. Ibid.

35. Jon G. Auerbach, "To Get IBM Ad, Sites Must Post Privacy Policies," *Wall Street Journal* (March 31, 1999), pp. B1, B4; Margaret Kane, "Disney Joins Web Privacy Movement," *ZDNewsNet* (June 29, 1999), downloaded from **www.zdnet.com/zdnn.**

36. "Amazon Buys Stake in Homegrocer," *Reuters News Service* (May 18, 1999), downloaded from ZD News Net, **www.zdnet.com/zdnn.**

37. Eleena de Lisser, "For Many Firms, Web Is Still What You Catch Flies In," *Wall Street Journal* (August 17, 1999), p. B2.

38. Bruce Haring, "Untangling the Sticky Habits of Web Users," *USA Today* (April 14, 1999), p. 5D; and "What's the Secret of E-Commerce? Web Designers Offer a Few Hints," *Wall Street Journal Interactive Edition* (December 7, 1998), downloaded from **interactive.wsj.com.**

39. Adapted from Carolyn Lawrence, "Substance, Not Flash, Is the Key to Internet Success," *TRADEWinds* (Costa Mesa, CA: Deloitte & Touche LLP, Spring 1999), pp. 1–3.

40. Wes Conard, "Toys 'R' Us Plans Online Challenge," *Dallas Morning News* (June 9, 1999), p. 11D; Jeffrey Davis, "Mall-Rats," *Business 2.0* (January 1999), pp. 41–50; "No More Fun and Games for Toys 'R' Us," *The Industry Standard* (May 3, 1999); Martin Wolk, "NetTrends: Retailers Bet on Boom in Net Toy Sales," *Reuters Business Report* (June 15, 1999). The latter two

articles were downloaded from Electric Library, Business Edition, **business.elibrary.com.**

Creative Thinking Case sources: "Amazon Adds Grocery Biz to Shopping List," *Newsday* (May 19, 1999), p. A47; George Anders, "Co-Founder of Borders to Launch Online Megagrocer," *Wall Street Journal* (April 22, 1999), pp. B1, B4; Jane Hodges, "HomeGrocer," *Fortune* (July 5, 1999), p. 104; "Online Grocer Webvan Plans $1 Billion Expansion," *Newsbytes News Network* (July 9, 1999) and Therese Poletti, "Another Internet Grocer Debuts in Crowded Market," *Reuters Business Report* (June 2, 1999), both downloaded from Electric Library, Business Edition, **business.elibrary.com.**

Focusing on Small Business sources: "Delia's Launches E-Commerce Site; Finds Teens Ready to Buy On-Line," *PR Newswire* (May 21, 1998), downloaded from Electric Library, Business Edition, **business.elibrary.com;** Katia Hetter and James T. Madore, "Delia's Planning to Take Its Six Web Sites Public," *Newsday* (January 5, 1999), p. A40; David S. Murphy, "Delia's Next Big Step," *Fortune* (February 15, 1999), pp. 192C]-192H]; Ellen Neuborne, "'We Are Going to Own this Generation,'" *Business Week* (February 15, 1999), p. 88; and Jennifer Steinhauer, "Catalog Marketers Discover 'Echo Boomer' Teenagers," *Minneapolis Star Tribune* (August 7, 1997), p. 6E.

Making Ethical Choices source: Adapted from R. Sharpe "Stalking Claims: One Effect of a Law on Diet Supplements Is Leaner Regulation," *Wall Street Journal* (January 27, 1999), pp. A1, A5.

Video Case source: Adapted from material contained on the following Internet site: "Elderly Instruments Welcome," **http://www.elderly.com**; and from material in the video: *A Case Study in Internet Marketing: Elderly Instruments.*

CHAPTER 19 NOTES

1. Based on personal interview with Jared Wells, Wells Test Preparation Center, La Jolla, CA, April 8, 1999.

2. Karen M. Kroll, "Auditors: No Longer Shooting the Wounded?" *Industry Week* (April 20, 1998), downloaded from **www.industryweek. com**; Melody Petersen, "When Watchdog, Watched Become Business Partners," *Minneapolis Star Tribune* (July 26, 1998), downloaded from Electric Library Business Edition, **business.elibrary.com.**

3. Bernard Condon, "Gaps in GAAP," *Forbes* (January 25, 1999), pp. 76–80; S. L. Mintz, "Seeing Is Believing," *CFO* (February 1999), downloaded from **www.cfonet.com.**

4. Condon, "Gaps in GAAP."

5. This section is based on Nanette Byrnes and richard Melcher, "Earnings Hocus-Pocus," *Business Week* (October 5, 1998), pp. 134–142; Shawn Tully, "The Earnings Illusion," *Fortune* (April 26, 1999), pp. 206–210.

6. Telephone interview, Jared Wells, April 15, 1999.

Applying Technology sources: Russ Banham, "A New Beginning for Case," *CFO* (December 1997); Russ Banham, "Case Conquers All," *CFO* (January 1999), and "Best at the Basics," *CFO* (January 1999). All articles were downloaded from **www.cfonet.com.**

Focusing on Small Business source: Norm Brodsky and Bo Burlingham, "Forget Spreadsheets," *Inc.* (November 1997), pp. 27–28.

Creative Thinking Case source: Jill Andresky Fraser, "Straight Talk," *Inc.* (March 1990), p. 97.

Making Ethical Choices source: Adapted from E. Nelson, and J. S. Lublin, "Buy the Numbers? How Whistle-Blowers Set Off a Fraud Probe That Crushed Cendant," *Wall Street Journal* (August 13, 1998), pp. A1, A8.

Video Case source: Adapted from material contained on the following Internet sites: **www.charlevoix.org/ cvb/;** and **www.weathervane-chx.com/ main.htm;** from the promotional brochure, *Weathervane Terrace Hotel*; and from material in the video: *Accounting Information Systems: A Study of the Weathervane Terrace Inn and Suites.*

CHAPTER 20 NOTES

1. Bob Violino, "Banking on E-Business—Citigroup Is Dramatically Expanding Its Internet Presence in an Effort to Approach Its Target of 1 Billion Customers," Information Week (May 3, 1999), downloaded from Electric Library, Business Edition, **www.business.elibrary. com;** Joseph Nocera, "Banking Is Necessary—Banks Are Not," *Fortune,* (May 11, 1998), pp. 82–84; Kevin Maney, "Citigroup's Billion-Customer Plan Relies on High Tech," *USA Today,* (April 16, 1998), downloaded from **www.usatoday. com;** "Citigroup and Travelers Group to Merge, Creating Citigroup: The Global Leader in

Financial Services," press release (April 6, 1998), downloaded from **www.citi.com/citigroup/.**
2. Steven Butler, "Japan's Down, Citibank's Up," *U.S. News & World Report,* (September 7, 1998), pp. 34–38.
3. "Singapore's Little Bang," *The Economist,* (May 22, 1999), p. 86.
4. Jim Rohwer, "Asia's Meltdown: The Risks Are Rising," *Fortune,* (February 16, 1998), pp.84–90; Brian Bremmer, Pete Engardio, Dean Foust, Kerry Capell, and Bruce Einhorn, "What to Do about Asia," *Business Week,* (January 26, 1998), pp. 26–30; "Reality Hits Japan," *The Economist,* (November 29, 1997), pp. 15–16.
5. Joseph Weber, "Just Over the Horizon: North American Banks," *Business Week,* (February 23, 1998), pp. 100–102.
6. "Online Banking Booming, Says IDC," downloaded from **www. electronicbanker.com,** (June 2, 1999).
7. "Banking Technologies," downloaded from **www.electronicbanker. com,** (June 4, 1999).
8. "Top Banks Plan Online Billing Network," (Reuters), The Sheboygan Press, June 24, 1999, p. C5.
9. Robert Avery, Raphael Bostic, Paul Calem, and Glenn Canner, "Trends in Home Purchase Lending: Consolidation and the Community Reinvestment Act," Federal Reserve Bulletin, February 1999, pp. 81–85.
10. James Kraus, "Citigroup Said to Plan Opening 25 Branches in Poland," *American Banker* (April 22, 1999), downloaded from **www. americanbanker.com;** "Citigroup Strengthens Core Consumer Business with Three Acquisitions," press release (March 23, 1999), downloaded from **www.citi.com/ citigroup/pr/news.**

Applying Technology sources: Scott Woolley, "Virtual Banker," Forbes, June 15, 1998, pp. 127-128; "About NetBank" and "NetBank FAQ," **www.netbank.com/** and NetBank 1998 Annual Report, downloaded from **www.netbank.com/ annlrpt98.**

Focusing on Small Business sources: Sharon Nelton, "Sizing Up Megabanks," Nation's Business, November 1998, pp. 14–21; and **www.unitedbankofphila.com.**

Creative Thinking Case source: Joshua Macht, "Niche Bank Targets White-Collar Market, Inc., March 1999, pp. 23–24.

Making Ethical Choices source: Adapted from: R. Brooks, "How Banks Make the Most of Bounced Checks," *Wall Street Journal* (February 25, 1999), pp. B1, B8.

Video Case source: Adapted from material contained on the following Internet sites: **www.roney.com;** and **www.firstbank-alma.com;** and from material in the video *Financial Statement Analysis/Creditor and Investor Decisions: Firstbank and Roney & Co.*

CHAPTER 21 NOTES

1. Russ Banham, "Larry Kellner—Continental Airlines: Managing External Stakeholders," *CFO* (September 1998), downloaded from **www.cfonet.com;** "Continental Airlines, Inc.," *Hoover's Company Profiles* (May 1, 1999); "Continental Airlines Reports 15th Consecutive Profitable Quarter, Ends Year on High Note," *PR Newswire* (January 21, 1999). The latter two articles were downloaded from Electric Library, Business Edition, **business.elibrary.com.**
2. Mike Hofman, "CEO's Notebook: Speeding Up Government Collections," *Inc.* (December 1998), pp. 122–123.
3. Richard Gamble, "No More Dunning Days," *Treasury & Risk Management* (September 1998), downloaded from **www.cfonet.com.**
4. John F. Greer, Jr., "Commercial Paper Redux," *Treasury & Risk Management* (October 1998), downloaded from **www.cfonet.com.**
5. "eToys IPO Takes a Rocket Ride," *Bloomberg News* (May 20, 1999): Dawn Kawamoto, "eToys Prices IPO at $20 per Share," *CNET News.com* (May 19, 1999), both downloaded from CNET News.com, **www.news. com.**
6. "Lara Technology, Inc. Completes $13.8 Million Second Round Funding," *Business Wire* (June 24, 1999), downloaded from Electric Library, Business Edition, **business.elibrary.com.**
7. "1998 VC Investments Rise 24%," *Bloomberg News* (February 16, 1999), downloaded from CNET News.com, **www.news.com.**
8. Wylie Wong "Oracle Details Venture Capital Fund," CNET News.com (January 14, 1999), downloaded from *CNET News.com,* **www.news.com.**
9. Diane Lindquist, "Trouble Brewing," *San Diego Union-Tribune* (September 10, 1998), pp. C-1, C-3.

10. Information downloaded July 1, 1999, from the International Finance and Commodities Institute (IFCI) Risk Watch site, **risk.ifci.ch/ index.htm.**
11. Diane Brady, "Is Your Bottom Line Covered?" *Business Week* (February 8, 1999), pp. 85–86.
12. Jill Andresky Fraser, "Riding the Economic Roller Coaster," *Inc.* (December 1998), pp. 126–129.
13. "Continental Airlines Receives No. 1 Spot for Long Flights in Frequent Flyer Magazine/J.D. Power and Associates Study," *PR Newswire* (May 11, 1999); "Continental Airlines Reports 15th Consecutive Profitable Quarter, Ends Year on High Note," *PR Newswire* (January 21, 1999); "Continental Airlines Retires Its Last Boeing 747 and 737-200; Launches 777 Service between London and Houston," *PR Newswire* (March 2, 1999), all downloaded from Electric Library, Business Edition, **business.elibrary.com.**

Applying Technology sources: Cathy Lazere, "All Together Now," *CFO* (February 1998), downloaded from **www.cfonet.com;** Bethany McLean, "Not Your Mother's Avon," *Fortune* (May 24, 1999), p. 44.

Focusing on Small Business sources: Mary Addonizio, "Loanshop.com Measures Productivity in Terms of Leads and Sales," *Mainspring ProofPoint* (November 1998), downloaded from **www.mainspring.com/BaseAll/;** and Beth Lipton, "Net Investment Still Exceeds Return," *CNET News.com* (August 31, 1998), downloaded from **www.news.com.**

Creative Thinking Case source: "Capitalization Plan: Think Ahead," *Inc.* (April 1999), p. 120; Jill Andresky Fraser, "Capital Steps," *Inc.* (April 1999), pp. 119–120; and Susan Greco, "Raising Capital is Job One," *Inc.* (February 1999), p. 49.

Making Ethical Choices source: Adapted from: N. Templin, "Inn Trouble: Hurricane Georges Was Just One of the Blows That Battered Patriot," *Wall Street Journal* (March 4, 1999), pp. A1, A16.

Video Case source: Adapted from material contained on the following Internet sites: **www.delfield.com;** and **www.scotsman-ind.com;** and from material in the video *Capital Structure and Dividend Policy: Scotsman Industries.*

CHAPTER 22 NOTES

1. "The Charles Schwab Corporation," *Hoover's Company Profiles* (May 1,

1999); "Charles Schwab Debuts Web Site," *Newsday* (May 15, 1998), p. A73; Saroja Girishankar, "Schwab Makes the Trade," *InternetWeek* (May 25,1998), all downloaded from Electric Library, Business Edition, **business.elibrary.com;** Jeffrey Laderman, "Remaking Schwab," *Business Week* (May 25, 1998), pp. 122–123; and Erick Schoenfeld, "Schwab Puts It All Online," *Fortune* (December 7, 1998), pp. 94–100.

2. "Rising Tide Economics," *Research Reports,* American Institute for Economic Research (June 14, 1999), pp. 61–62.

3. "Caterpillar Inc. Raises Dividend," *Reuters* (June 9, 1999), downloaded from Electric Library, Business Edition, **business.elibrary.com.**

4. Gregory Zuckerman and George Anders, "Amazon.com Launches Convertible Bond Issue, as Internet Craze Enters New Financial Arena," *Wall Street Journal* (January 29, 1999) p. C17.

5. Mike McNamee, "Why Old-Line Firms Need New Online Tricks," *Business Week* (May 24, 1999), p. 100; Leah Nathans Spiro, "Who Needs a Broker?" *Business Week* (February 22, 1999), pp. 113–118.

6. Terzah Ewig, "How Electronic Networks Snag Trades," *Wall Street Journal* (March 1, 1999), pp. C1, C26.

7. "Rising Tide Economics."

8. Suze Orman, "Minding Your Money," *Self* (July 1999), p. 113.

9. Carolyn T. Geer, "A Crash Course for Online Investors," *Fortune* (May 24, 1999), p. 326–328; Geoffrey Smith, "Your Guide to Online Investing," *Business Week* (May 24, 1999), pp. 90–96.

10. Schoenfeld, "Schwab Puts It All Online"; "Schwab Ranks among Top 15 Companies Leading the Internet Economy," *PR Newswire* (June 24, 1999), downloaded from Electric Library, Business Edition, **business.elibrary.com.**

11. "The Charles Schwab Corporation," *Hoover's Company Profiles* (May 1, 1999); "Charles Schwab Debuts Web Site," *Newsday* (May 15, 1998), p. A73; Saroja Girishankar, "Schwab Makes the Trade," *InternetWeek* (May 25,1998), all downloaded from Electric Library, Business Edition, **business.elibrary.com;** Jeffrey Laderman, "Remaking Schwab," *Business Week* (May 25, 1998), pp. 122–123; and Erick Schoenfeld, "Schwab Puts It All Online," *Fortune* (December 7, 1998), pp. 94–100.

Applying Technology sources: Geoffrey Smith, "If Funds Are Smart, They'll Get Net-Friendly," *Business Week Online* (August 16, 1999), downloaded from **www.businessweek.com/ebiz**; Firsthand Funds Web site, **www.firsthands.com**; and Munder Funds Web sites, **www.munderfunds.com** and **netnet.munder.com**.

Making Ethical Choices source: Adapted from: Brooks, R. "Analyst's Silence on First Union Isn't Accidental," *The Wall Street Journal* (August 17, 1999): pp. C1 & C4.

Focusing on Small Business sources: "An Internet Stock Exchange? Not Quite Yet," *Investor Relations Business* (November 23, 1998);"Beacon Light Announces Entrance Into the Internet Stock Exchange," *Business Wire* (May 28, 1999); Kimberly Weisul, "New Web-Based Exchange Is Tailored to 'Nanocap' Companies," *Investor Relations Business* (September 28, 1998); all downloaded from Electric Library, Business Edition, **business.elibrary.com;** and Niphix Investments Web site, **www.niphix.com**.

Creative Thinking Case sources: "After-hours Trading Debuts in New Venue," *Washington Times* (August 26, 1999), p. B8; James Bernstein, "ETrade to Expand Trading, *Newsday* (August 18, 1999), p. A51; ileen Glanton, "Not All Take Stock in Extended Trading Days," *San Diego Union-Tribune* (June 5, 1999), pp. C-1, C-3; Greg Ip and Terzah Ewing, "NASD Prepares for Late Hours; Date Isn't Set," *Wall Street Journal* (May 28, 1999), pp. C1, C18.

Video Case source: Adapted from material contained on the following Internet site: **www.edwardjones.com**.

CHAPTER 23 NOTES

1. U.S. Census Bureau, **www.census.gov/hhes/www/housing/hvs/q199tab7.html** (May 25, 1999).

2. College Entrance Examination Board, **www.collegesure.com** (July 31, 1998); Mark Lino, "Expenditures on Children by Families, 1997," *Family Economics and Nutrition Review* vol. 11, no. 3 (1998).

3. Catherine Siskos, "ATM Fees Are Finally Starting to Level Off," *Kiplinger's Personal Finance Magazine* (December 1998), p. 30.

4. Cindy Hall and Quin Tian, "Rubber Checks 101," *USA Today* (September 15, 1998).

5. Kevin Harris, "Charging Away Their Future," *Austin American Statesman* (June 13, 1999), p. J2.

6. Genevieve Lynn, "Paying in Full," *USA Today* (March 27, 1998).

7. *The Fact Book.* (Insurance Information Institute, 1999), pp. 54–55.

8. *The Fact Book,* p. 56.

9. Peter Carbonara, "Super Saver," *Money* (May 1999), p. 73.

Source: This ethical dilemma is adapted from: Cahill, J.B. "Charged Up: Credit Cards Invade a New Market Niche: The Mentally Disabled," *The Wall Street Journal* (November 10, 1998): pp. A1 & A6.

Applying Technology sources: Robert James, personal interview, June 14, 1999. Molly Johnson, personal interview, June 14, 1999.

Making Ethical Choices source: J. B. Cahill, "Charged Up: Credit Cards Invade a New Market Niche: The Mentally Disabled," *Wall Street Journal* (November 10, 1998), pp. A1, A6.

Focusing on Small Business sources: Larissa Caramanidis, personal interview, June 21, 1999; Thomas J. Stanley and William D. Danko, *The Millionaire Next Door* (New York: Pocket Books, 1996), p. 8.

Video Case source: Adapted from material contained on the following Internet site: **www.edwardjones.com**.

A

Absolute advantage, 70
Accelerated commission schedule, 268
Access, unauthorized, 520
Accessories, 415
Accountants, 597
  role of, 585–86
Account executives, 650
Accounting, 623
  balance sheet in, 574–77
  basic procedures in, 571–74
  computers in, 573–74
  definition of, 568
  financial, 569
  and financial statement analysis,
    581–85
  income statement in, 577–79
  managerial, 569
  purpose of, 568–71
  statement of cash flows in, 579–81
Accounting cycle, 572–73
Accounting equation, 572
Accounting profession, 570–71
Account reconciliation, 684
Accounts payable, 577, 630
Accounts receivable, 575
  managing, 627–28
Acid-test ratio, 583
Acquisitions, 156
Active Corps of Executives (ACE), 180
Activity ratios, 584
Actual cash value, 694
Actual satisfaction, 426
Adams, Phyllis, 189
Administrative agencies, 126
Administrative distribution systems,
  449–50
Administrative law, 125
Advanced observation research methods, 401–2
Advancing technology, 276–77
Advantage, taking unfair, 104
Adverse impact, 274–75
Advertising
  advocacy, 475
  benefits from, 491–92
  broadcast, 487
  in building brand recognition, 474–
    80
  comparative, 474
  corrective, 480
  costs and market penetration, 477
  defined, 474
  e-mail, 492
  federal regulation of, 479–80
  institutional, 475
  product, 474
  in promotional mix, 473
  regulation of, 132
  reminder, 474–75
  self-regulation of, 479
  types of, 474–75
  on World Wide Web, 490
Advertising account manager, 497–98

Advertising agencies, 478–79
Advertising media
  choosing, 475–78
  definition of, 475
  strengths and weaknesses of, 476
Advertising media planner, 499
Advocacy advertising, 475
Affirmative action, 274–75
AFL-CIO, 318
African Americans and business owner-
  ship, 190–91
Age Discrimination Act (1967), 271,
  273
Agency shop, 326
Agents, 445–46, 453
Agile manufacturing, 368
Albo, Lazaro, 100, 120
Alcohol Labeling Legislation (1988),
  133
American Association of Home-Based
  Businesses, 193
American Federation of Labor,
  316–17
American Institute of Certified Public
  Accountants, 571
Americans for Tax Reform, 57
American Stock Exchange (AMEX),
  657, 668
  prices on, 663
Americans with Disabilities Act (1990),
  133, 273
Analytic systems, 513
Anderson, Kent, 492
Andersson, Claes, 311
Andreessen, Marc, 171
Angel investors, 184, 637
Annual percentage rate of interest
  (APR), 689–90
Annual report, 570
Antidumping laws, 74
Anti-Injunction Act, 320
Antitrust regulation, 131–34
Appellate courts, 126
Applications software, 508
Apprenticeship, 265
Arbitration, 127, 330–31
ARPAnet, 535
Arthur, W. Brian, 222
Assembly process, 350
Assets, 572, 575
  current, 575
  fixed, 575
  intangible, 575
Atmosphere, 459
Attributes, 412
  intangible, 412
  tangible, 412
Audience selectivity, 478
Auditing, 571
Auditor's opinion, 571
Authority, 234
  delegation of, 234
Authorization cards, 323
Autocratic leaders, 210–211
Automated teller machine (ATM), 682

Automation
  in nonmanufacturing operations, 366
  in productions and operations man-
    agement, 364–65
Automobile insurance, 694
  comprehensive, 694
  liability, 694
  physical damage, 694
Awareness, creating, 472

B

Babcock, Lewis, 110–11
Baby boomers, 9–10
Background check, 263–64
Backward integration, 449
Balance of payments, 68–69
Balance of trade, 68
Balance sheet, 574–77
Baldrige, Malcolm, National Quality
  Award, 18
Bank charter, 606
Bank deposits, insuring, 609–10
Banking
  international, 610–11
  online, 612
Banking Act (1933), 609
Bank Insurance Fund (BIF), 609
Bank loans, 630–31
Bankruptcy, 131
Bankruptcy Reform Act (1978), 131
Banks, 689
  commercial, 606
  consolidation of, 612–13
Bar codes, 505–6
Bar-code scanners, 434
Bargaining agenda, 325
Bargaining unit, 323–324
Barriers to entry, 50
Barriers to trade, 70–74
Barron's, 661, 674
Barter, 426
Batch processing, 514–15
Batcup, Felix, 20
Batson, Hayes, 183
Bear markets, 658
Behavior
  illegal and irresponsible, 110–11
  irresponsible but legal, 111
  legal and responsible, 111–12
Benefit rights, 330
Benefits
  cafeteria benefit plans, 700
  and labor relations, 329–30
  self-directed retirement accounts, 701
Benefit segmentation, 397
Benn, Edwin, 330–31
Bezos, Jeffrey P., 171, 172, 457
Bill of material, 356
BizInfo, 675
Black Monday, 659
Blair, Tony, 13
Blake, David, 467
Bleustein, Jeffrey, 345–46
Board of directors, 146–47

Bonds, 634
  debt financing, 652
    corporate bonds, 652–53
    futures contracts, 655
    municipal bonds, 653–54
    mutual funds, 654–55
    options, 656
    U.S. government securities, 653
  quotations, 665, 667, 674
  ratings of, 654
Bonus, 268, 299
Bookkeeping, 571
  double-entry, 572
Borders, Louis, 563
Borovoi, Konstantin, 57
Bounced checks, 604
Boyd, Ben, 552
Boylan, Jo Ann, 502
Bracken, Josh, 385
Bracken, Michael, 385
Brady Law (1998), 133
Brainstorming in generating new prod-
    ucts, 422–23
Brand equity, 416
  building, 415–19
Branding
  benefits of, 416–17
  rational, 490
Brand recognition
  building immediate, 432–34
  role of advertising in building, 474–
    80
Brands, 415
  building loyalty with repeat sales,
    417
  dealer, 419
  manufacturer, 418–19
  master, 416
  types of, 418–19
Breach of contract, 128–29
Breakeven analysis, 430
Breakeven point, 430
Breaking bulk, 448
Broadcast advertising, 487
Brodsky, Norm, 580
Brokerage firms, 609
Brokers, 445–46, 453
Brown, Herbert, 203
Browsers, 535–36
Bruns, Nicolaus, 462
Bruyn, Steven, 381
Bryant, Robin, 150
Budgeting, capital, 628
Budgets, 626, 681
Budoff, Scott, 644
Building relationships, 385–86
Bull markets, 658, 671
Bundling, 431–32
Burton, Jake, 24–25
Business. See also Small business
  capitalizing on trends in, 6–19, 52–
    55, 89–90, 116–18, 187–92
  classifying products, 414–15
  competitive trends among, 52–55
  cycles of, 39
  definition of, 2

developing plan, 181–83
financing, 183–84
legal environment of, 125–35
nature of, 2–3
recognizing unethical actions, 103–4
responsibilities to stakeholders, 112–
    16
starting your own, 180–85
taxation of, 134–35
Business information systems, 513–17
Business law, 125–26
Business organization
  choosing form of, 181
  cooperatives as, 150–51
  corporations as, 144–49
  joint ventures as, 151
  partnerships as, 141–44
  sole proprietorships as, 139–41
  types of, 139
Business-to-business e-commerce, 542,
    543–45
Business-to-business market, characteris-
    tics of, 394
Business-to-business purchase decision
    making, 393–94
Business-to-consumer e-commerce, 542,
    545–46
Business unionism, 317
Business Week, 661, 674
Buyback, 462
Buyer behavior, 392
  business-to-business purchase deci-
    sion making, 393–94
  characteristics of business-to-business
    market, 394
  influences on consumer decision mak-
    ing, 392–93
Buyer cooperatives, 150
Buy-national regulations, 73
Byrnes, Pat, 519

C

CAD/CAM systems, 364
Cafeteria benefit plans, 700
Capacity, 128
Capital, 3
  budgets, 626, 628
  expenditures, 628
  venture, 636–37
Capitalism, 11–12, 14, 36
Capital products, 414–15
Career Employment Opportunities
    Directory, 26
Career Mosiac, 20, 28
Career progression, 277
Carpenter, Jim, 158
Carreño, Guedea, 226
Cash, 575
Cash accounts, 660
Cash-and-carry wholesalers, 453, 454
Cash budgets, 626
Cash flow plan, 681–82
Cash flows, 623
Cash management, 626–27, 681
Cash value, 696

Cash value insurance, 696–97
Cassar, Ken, 563
Cassidy, Mike, 213
CD-ROM drives, 506
Cecil, Gail, 140
Celler-Kauver Act (1950), 131–32
Cellular phones, 517
Centralization of decision making,
    235–37
Central processing unit (CPU), 506
Cents-off-coupons, 485
Certification election for unions, 323
Certified management accountant
    (CMA), 571–74
Certified public accountant (CPA), 571
Chain of command, 234
Chalfa, Tace, 5
Chambers, John, 247, 544
Changing Times Annual Survey, 27
Channels, function of, in organizing
    and covering markets, 448–51
Chappell, Emma, 613
Chapter 7 (liquidation), 131
Chapter 11 (reorganization), 131
Charren, Peggy, 123
Chavez, Cesar, 333
Checkbook, steps to balanced, 685
Checking accounts, 682–84
Checks
  bounced, 604
  clearing of, 603–4
Chief financial officers (CFOs), 622
Chief information officers (CIOs), 502
Child Protection Act (1966), 133
Children's Television Act (1990), 133
Chung-Jen Tan, 222
Churchman, Michael, 627
Cigarette Labeling Act (1965), 133
Circuit breakers, 659
Circular flow, 37–38
Citizens for Tax Justice, 57
City manager, 377
Civil Aeronautics Board, 125
Civil Rights Act (1964), 273, 274
Clancy, Mo, 471, 492
Clark, Jim, 172, 175, 291–92
Clark, Martha Gross, 209
Classical era of management, 288
Classic entrepreneurs, 172
Clayton Act (1914), 131, 132
Clean Air Act, 277
Clients, 536
Closed shop, 325–26
Coaching, 265
COBRA, 695
Code of ethics, establishing formal,
    107
Coercive power, 209
Cognitive dissonance, 403–4
Cohen, Ben, 105–6
Cohen, Jeffrey, 546
Cohesiveness, group, 300
Coinsurance, 695
Collaboration, 301
Collaborative software systems, 303
Collateral, 631

Collateral trust bonds, 653
Collection policies, 627
Collective bargaining, 316, 318
  emergence of, 316–19
College recruiter, 379
Command economies, 12, 14
  entrepreneurial spirit in former, 56
Commerce, U.S. Department of, 187
Commercial banks, 606
Commercial finance companies, 609
Commercial paper, 627, 631
Commission, 268
Committees
  selling to, 481
  structure of, 239–40
Commodities, 3
Common law, 125
Common market, 77
Common stock, 634, 650–51, 697
  advantages and disadvantages of,
    651
    potential returns to investors, 650–51
  selling new issues of, 634–35
Communications, 15–17, 511
  face-to-face, 242
Communication Workers, 334
Comparative advantage, 70
Comparative advertising, 474
Competition in global marketplace, 90
Competitive advantage
  cost, 388
  creating, 387
  differential, 388–89
  niche, 389
Competitive status seniority, 330
Competitive workforce, creating, 55
Component lifestyles, 7
  growth of, 7–8
Component parts and materials, 415
Comprehensive insurance, 694
Compressed workweek, 298
Computer-aided design (CAD), 364
Computer-aided manufacturing (CAM),
  364
Computer hardware, 504–8
Computer-integrated manufacturing
  (CIM), 365
Computerized resource planning, 357–
  58
Computer literacy, 525
Computer networks, 507, 512–13
Computer programmer, 596–97
Computers, 505
  in accounting, 573–74
  components of, 505–6
  protecting, 518–23
  types of, 506–8
Computer software, 508–11
Computer viruses, 520–21
Conceptual skills, 219–20
Concession bargaining, 329–30
Conciliation, 321
Confiscation, 85
Conflict of interest, 104
Conglomerate merger, 157
Conglomerate union, 318

Congress of Industrial Organizations,
  317
Consensual leaders, 211
Consideration, 128
Consultative leaders, 211
Consumer credit
  cards, 687–88
  history and ratings, 690–91
  loans, 688–90
  pros and cons of using, 686
  rules, 603
Consumer durables, 413
Consumer Federation of America, 686
Consumer finance companies, 609,
  689
Consumer fraud, 113
Consumerism, 132
Consumer nondurables, 413
Consumer price index (CPI), 42
Consumer Product Safety Act (1972),
  127, 133
Consumer Products Safety Commission,
  127, 133
Consumer protection laws, 132
Consumers. See also Customers
  classifying products, 413–14
  and product boycott, 333
  in trying products, 472–73
Consumer sales promotion, 483
Continental General Tire, 321
Contingency plans, 207
Contingent workers, 260
Continuous improvement, 18
Continuous pay insurance, 696–97
Contractionary policy, 43
Contract law, 127–29
Contract manufacturing, 83
Contracts, 127–28
  breach of, 128–29
  requirements for, 128
  tying, 131
  yellow-dog, 320
Contractual distribution systems, 450
Control and feedback, 213–14
Controlling, 212–15
Convenience products, 414
Conventional ethics, 102
Convertible bonds, 652–53
Cooling-off period, 321
Co-op America, 675
Cooperatives, 150–51
Copyright, 129
Corigliano, Cosmo, 583
Corporate bonds, 652–53, 697
Corporate campaign, 333
Corporate culture, 212
Corporate distribution systems, 449
Corporate financial manager, 709
Corporate growth through mergers and
  acquisitions, 155–58
Corporate philanthropy, 115–16
  trends in, 116–17
Corporations, 144–49
  advantages of, 147–48
  definition of, 144
  disadvantages of, 148

  multinational, 87–89
  S, 148
  structure of, 146–47
  types of, 148–49
  virtual, 246–47
Corrective advertising, 480
Cost competitive advantage, 388
Cost-of-living adjustment (COLA),
  328
Cost per thousand (CPM), 477
Cost-push inflation, 41
Costs, 2
  fixed, 430
  of goods sold, 578
  total, 430
  variable, 430
Cotsakos, Christos, 676
Countertrade, 84
Couponing, 483
Coupon rate, 634, 652
Court system, 126
Craft union, 317
Credit, role of Federal Reserve System
  in setting rules on, 603
Credit cards, 601–2, 687–88
  for mentally disabled, 689
Credit life insurance, 690
Credit manager, 709
Credit policies, 627
Credit risk, 638
Credit terms, 627
Credit unions, 607
Crimes, 130
Critical path, 362
Critical Path Method (CPM), 362
Cross-border mergers, 159
Cross-functional team, 302–3
Cross-training, 297
Crowding out, 44, 45
Cullis, Gary, 213
Culture
  corporate, 212
  differences in, in global marketplace,
    85
Cumulative preferred stock, 651
Currencies, 601
  changing value of, 69–70
  role of Federal Reserve System in dis-
    tributing, 603
Current assets, 575
Current liabilities, 575, 577
Current ratio, 582–83
Currid, Cheryl, 518
Customer departmentalization, 232
Customers, 357. See also Consumers
  identifying target, 473
  keeping loyal, 473
  responsibility to, 113
Customer satisfaction, 383–84
  goal of, 347–48
Customer service on Internet, 554
Customer value, 18, 383
Customization, 349–50
Custom regulations, 73–74
Customs union, 77
Cutler, Alexander, 302

Cyber résumé, 28
Cyclical unemployment, 40

D

Dahl, Heather, 20
Daily News Record, 1
Danko, William D., 699
Data, 503
  analyzing, 401
  collecting, 400
Database management, 510, 514
Database manager, 597
Database marketing, 402–3
Databases, using, for micromarketing, 402–3
Data security issues, 520–21
Data warehouse, 516
Davidson, Alan, 676
Davis, Richard, 166–67
Dealer brands, 419
Debentures, 652, 653
Debit cards, 683
Debt financing, 633–34
Debt ratios, 584–85
Debts, 184, 572
Debt-to-equity ratio, 585
Decentralization, 236
Decertification election, 325
Decisional roles, 215
Decision making
  centralization of, 235–37
  developing skills in, 222
  gathering infomation on Web for, 398
  using information for, 503
Decision support systems (DSS), 402, 516
Decline stage, 425
Defamation, 130
Default, 654
Delegation, 230
  of authority, 234
DeLorenzo, Paul, 645
Demand, 46
  changes in, 48–49
  interaction of supply and, in determining prices, 47–49
  nature of, 46–47
Demand curve, 46
Demand deposits, 601
Demand forecast, 259
Demand-pull inflation, 41
Deming, W. Edwards, 363
Democratic leaders, 211
Demographic forces, 386
Demographics, 275–76
Demographic segmentation, 395–96
Demography, 8
  trends of, 8–11
Demotion, 270
Dennis, William J., 189
Departmentalization, 230, 231–32
  customer, 232
  functional, 232

geographic, 233
process, 232
product, 232
Departmental scheduling systems, 517
Depository financial institutions, 606–7
  services offered by, 607
Depreciation, 575
Deregulation of industries, 132–33
Desktop computers, 506
Desktop publishing, 510–11
Desktop videoconferencing systems (DVCS), 303
Detailing, 487
Devaluation, 69
Differential advantage, 472
Differential competitive advantage, 388–89
Digital VCRs, impact of, on television, 490–91
Direct distribution, 394
Direct investment, 83–84
Direct-response marketing, 456
Direct selling, 455–56
Disability income insurance, 696
Discount, 667
Discount rate, 603
Dispute, 334
Disputes, nonjudicial methods for settling, 126–27
Distribution
  intensive, 451
  role of, 444–45
  selective, 451
Distribution centers, 460
Distribution channels
  definition of, 445
  functions of, 447–48
  improving delivery through new, 462–63
  marketing intermediaries in, 445–47
  nature and functions of, 445–51
Distribution strategy, 390
Distribution traffic manager, 499
Diversification, 699–700
Diversity, 275
Dividend reinvestment plan (DRIP), 700
Dividends, 635–36, 650
Division of labor, 230–31
Divorce, 680
Doppelmayer, Arthur, 389
Double-entry bookkeeping, 572
Dow Jones Industrial Average (DJIA), 667–68, 671, 674
Dow Jones Internet Index, 668
Drayton, Terry, 563
Drexler, Mickey, 206–7
Drop shippers, 454
Drucker, Peter, 110
Dues checkoff, 327
Dumping, predators, 74
Durables, consumer, 413
Duration of benefits, 696
Durocher, Joe, 523

E

Earned income, 692
Earnings per share (ESP), 584
Eberle, Karl, 219
E-business, launching successful, 550–55
E-commerce, 456
  benefiting from, 548–49
  business models for, 542–43
  capitalizing on, 541–50
  profit in, 546–48
  roadblocks on, 549–50
Economic environment in global marketplace, 85–86
Economic forces, 386
Economics
  as circular flow, 37–38
  definition of, 36–37
  and financial publications, 661
  striving for growth, 39
Economic system, 36
Edenborg, Mats, 311
Edgar, Christopher, 557
Education and motivation, 304–5
Efficient consumer response (ECR), 458
Egan, Michael, 169
Ehrlich, Robert, 439
Electrical Workers, 334
Electronic bulletin boards, 517
Electronic commerce modeling language (ECML), 549–50
Electronic communications networks (ECNs), 669
Electronic data interchange (EDI), 360, 458
Electronic fund transfers, 682
Electronic stock exchanges, 648
Elimination period, 696
E-mail advertising, 492
E-mail systems, 517
Embargoes, 73
Emergency fund, 698
Emergency strike procedures, 321
Employee Retirement Income Security Act (1974), 273
Employees
  compensation and benefits for, 267–69
  empowerment of, 211–12, 299
  managers empowering, 220–21
  motivating, 287
  orientation, 265
  ownership and motivation, 305
  recruitment of, 260–62
  responsibilities to, 112–13
  selection of, 262–64
  training and development of, 264–66
Employee stock options (ESOPs), 299
Employer, strategies of, in labor-management relations, 333–34
Employment, full, 40
Employment testing, 262
Empowerment, employee, 211–12
Enterprise Earnings Protection Insurance, 639

Enterprise resource planning (ERP), 358, 364, 512
Entrepreneurial personality, 174
Entrepreneurs, 4–5, 171, 417
  characteristics of successful, 173–75
  ethics of, 109
  managerial ability and technical knowledge of, 174–75
  reasons for becoming, 173
  trends for, 187–92
  types of, 171–72
Environmental protection, 115
Environmental Protection Agency (EPA), 127
Environmental scanning, 386
Equal Credit Opportunity Act (1975), 133, 610
Equal Employment Opportunity Commission, 274
Equal Pay Act (1963), 273
Equilibrium, 48
Equipment trust certificates, 653
Equity, 184
Equity financing, 634–37
Equity theory, 295
Estrin, Judy, 174
Ethical development, stages of, 101–2
Ethical problems, resolving, in business, 104
Ethics
  conventional, 102
  definition of, 100
  individual business, 100–102
  organizational influence on, 102–7
  postconventional, 102
  preconventional, 101–2
Ethics training, 106
Ethnic markets, growing, 11
Euro, 80
European Union (EU), 78–80, 90
Evangelista, Patrick, 4
Even-numbered pricing, 432
Event sponsorship, 487
Exchange, 382
Exchange controls, 74
Excise taxes, 135
Exclusive dealing, 131
Executive information systems, 516
Expansionary policy, 43
Expectancy theory, 294–95
Expected satisfaction, 426
Expenditures, long-term, 628
Expense items, 415
Expenses, 578–79
  operating, 626
Experiment, 399
Expert power, 209
Expert systems, 516–17
Exporting, 81
Export management companies (EMCs), 187
Exports, 67–68
Export Working Capital Program, 81
Express contract, 127
Express warranties, 129
Express warranty, 420

Expropriation, 85
External environment, 386–87
Extranets, 544–45

F
Face-to-face communication, 242
Facility layout, 354
Facsimile (fax) systems, 517
Factoring, 631
Factors, 631
  of production, 3–6
Fair Credit Reporting Act (1971), 133
Fair Debt Collection Practice Act (1978), 133
Fair Labor Standards Act (1938), 272, 273, 274
Fair Packaging and Labeling Act (1968), 133
False impressions, giving or allowing, 103–4
Families, changing role of, 8
Family and Medical Leave Act (1993), 273–74
FAST Feedback (Tulgan), 296
Federal budget deficit, 45
Federal Communications Commission (FCC), 126, 127
Federal Deposit Insurance Corporation (FDIC), 606, 609
  enforcement by, 610
  role of, 610
Federal Insurance Contribution Act (FICA), 692
Federal mediation and conciliation services, 321
Federal regulation of advertising, 479–80
Federal Reserve System, 43, 602, 606
  check clearing, 603–4
  distributing currency, 603
  monetary policy, 602–3
  setting rules on credit, 603
Federal Savings and Loan Insurance Corporation (FSLIC), 609
Federal Trade Commission (FTC), 125, 126, 127, 132
  in regulating advertising, 479–80
Federal Trade Commssion Act (1914), 132
Federation of Organized Trades and Labor Unions, 316
Feedback and control, 213–14
Fee-for-service plans, 695
Filing status, 691
Filo, David, 198
Finance
  careers in, 708–10
  global, 637–38
  role of, 622–24
Finance companies, 609
Finance Hub, 643
Financial accounting, 569
Financial Accounting Standards Board (FASB), 570
Financial intermediation, 605

Financial management, 622
Financial manager
  goal of, 624
  responsibilities and activities of, 623–24
Financial planner, 708–9
Financial planning, 624–26, 680
  cash flow plan, 681–82
  checking accounts, 682–84
  net worth statement, 682
  for self-employed, 699
Financial reports, 569–70
Financial risk, 632–33
Financial services, 708
Financial Services Modernization Act, 613
Financial statements, 569
  analyzing, 581–85
Financing, 624
  debt, 633–34
  equity, 634–37
Firewall, 513
First, Tom, 169–70, 174, 179, 194
Fiscal policy, 43–45
Fisher, Alan, 198
Fixed assets, 575
Fixed-cost contribution, 430
Fixed costs, 430
Fixed-position layout, 354
Flammable Fabrics Act (1953), 133
Flat organizational structure, 237
Flexible manufacturing systems (FMS), 365
Flextime, 298
Floating exchange rates, 69
Floating-rate bonds, 653
Focus group, 422
Food, Drug, and Cosmetic Act (1938), 133
Food and Drug Administration (FDA), 127, 133
Forbes, 661
Forbes, Walter, 211
Ford, Henry, 349
Ford, Rob, 162
Ford, William, Jr., 234
Forecasts, 625–26
Formal organization, 230
Fortune, 30, 120, 661, 674
Forward integration, 449
Foundation for Enterprise Development, 310
4-40 Schedule, 298
401(k) plans, 701
Four Ps, 389
Fourth market, 669
Franchise agreement, 151
Franchisee, 151
Franchises, 450
  advantages of, 152–53
  disadvantages of, 153–54
  growth of, 154
  new twists for existing, 158–59
Franchising, 82, 151–55, 160–61
  definition of, 151
  international, 155

Franchisor, 151
Franklin, Burke, 252–53
Free market, competing in, 49–52
Free-rein leadership, 211
Free-Standing Insert, 283–84
Free-trade, 70
Free-trade zone, 77
Frequency, 477–78
Frictional unemployment, 40
Fringe benefits, 268–69
Front page of newspaper test, 105
Full employment, 40
Full-service merchant wholesalers, 453
Full warranty, 421
Functional departmentalization, 232
Funds, organizational use of, 626–28
Futures contracts, 655

G

Gainsharing plans, 299
Gallagher, Debbie, 181
Gantt, Henry, 361
Gantt charts, 361
Gates, Bill, 5, 171, 205, 209–10, 299
General Agreement on Tariffs and
    Trade (GATT) (1948), 76
Generally accepted accounting princi-
    ples (GAAP), 570, 585, 586–87
General obligation bonds, 654
General partners, 142
General partnership, 142
General public, responsibility to, 115–
    16
Generation X, 9
Generation Y, 8–9
Generic products, 419
Geographic departmentalization,
    232
Geographic or niche market, 418
Geographic segmentation, 396
Gerber, Michael, 175
GetSmart, 643
Ghandi, Nimish, 670
Give-backs, 329–30
Givens, Beth, 526
Glass ceiling, 276
Glass-Steagall Act (1933), 599, 613
Global business, importance of, to
    United States, 67
Global competition, 277
    trends in, 15–19
Global economics
    evolving systems in, 11–14
    trends in, 55–57
Global ethics, trends in, 118
Global finance, 637–38
Global management skills, 220
Global marketplace. *See also*
    International trade
    capitalizing on trends in, 89–90
    managing in, 221
    participating in, 80–84
    threats and opportunities in, 84–86
Global mergers, structuring, 247
Global trading and foreign exchanges,
    657–58

Global vision, 66
Goal-setting theory, 295–97
Goh Chok Tong, 611
Going public, 634
Goizueta, Roberto, 265
Gomez Advisors' Internet Broker
    Scorecard, 672
Gompers, Samuel, 316–17
Goodnight, James H., 287
Goods, 2
Goodwill, 575
    public relations in building, 486–87
Gore, W. L., 114
Government, 3
    actions in global marketplace, 90
Grace period, 688
Graphical user interface, 508
Graphics, 510
Grassroots leadership, 221
Grassroots lobbying, 475
Gray, Hudson, 323
Greenfield, Hank, 8
Grievance, 330
Grimes, Danner, 608
Gross, Bill, 180–81
Gross domestic product (GDP), 15, 39
Gross profits, 579, 580
Gross revenue, 426
Gross sales, 577
Group behavior, understanding, 300
Group cohesiveness, 300
Group norms, 244
Grove, Andrew, 212, 387
Growth-oriented entrepreneurs, 172
Growth stage, 424
Growth stocks, 697
Guaranteed investment contracts
    (GICs), 701

H

Hagel, John, III, 541
Hamm, Elle, 174
Hand, Learned, 125
Handheld computers, 506
Hardware, 505
Harper, Kathy, 178
Hassan, Fred, 247
Hawthorne effect, 290
Hawthorne studies, 289–90
Health insurance, 695–96
Health maintenance organizations
    (HMOs), 696
Herrera, George, 190
Herzberg, Frederick, 293
Hierarchy of needs, 290–92
Higgins, Chris, 242
Highsmith, Duncan, 225–26
High-yield bonds, 652, 653
Hillman, Sidney, 317
Hills, Eric, 183
Hirshon, Jonathan, 186
Home office, 188
Home Office Association of America,
    193
Homeowner's insurance, 694–95
HOPE Scholarship credit, 692

Horizontal merger, 157
Horton, Mark, 191
Hospitality Sales and Marketing
    Association International (HSMAI),
    496
Host computer, 536
Hotchkiss, John, 276
Hotel and motel management, 377
Hotel and Restaurant, 334
Hourly wages, 268
Hughes, Christine, 91
Human genome, 433
Human relations era, 289
Human relations skill, 219
Human resource development special-
    ist, 378–79
Human resource management
    definition of, 256
    job analysis and design, 258
    laws affecting, 271–75
    planning and forecasting, 259–60
    steps in, 256–57
Human resource planning, 257–58
    and forecasting, 259–60
Human rights, 101
Hunter, Billy, 334
Hutton, Amy, 586
Hygiene factors, 293
Hypertext, 535

I

Ibbotson, Stephen, 625
Ilaw, Marianne, 123
Image, creating, 459
Immigrant workers, organizing, 322
Immigration Reform and Control Act
    (1986), 273
Implied contract, 127–28
Implied warranties, 129
Implied warranty, 420
Import quotas, 73
Imports, 67–68
Incentives, local, 352
Income statement, 577–79
Income taxes, 134, 691
    filing federal income form, 692
    minimum filing requirements, 691–92
    planning, 692
Income taxes payable, 577
Incorporation process, 145–46
Indemnity plans, 695
Independent Bankers Association of
    America, 612–13
Independent Broker-Dealer Association,
    676
Individual business ethics, 100–102
Individual investors, 649
Individual Retirement Accounts (IRAs),
    692
Individual rights, 101
Industrial distributors, 446
Industrial production manager, 378
Industrial union, 317
Industries
    competitive trends among, 52–55
    deregulation of, 132–33

Infant-industry argument for tariffs, 72
Inflation, 41
    impact of, 42
    measurement of, 42
    types of, 41–42
Infomediaries, 541
Informal organization, 244
    functions of, 244
Information, 503
    deliberate damage to, 520
    hiding or divulging, 104
    protecting, 518–23
    providing, 473
    using 21st century, for decision making, 503
Informational roles, 215
Information broker, 178
Information management, 523
Information reporting systems, 516
Information Superhighway, 534
Information systems, 503
Information technology (IT), 503
    and managers, 221
    managing, 517–23
    searching for talent, 524
Infrastructure, 85–86
Initial public stock offering (IPO), 634
Initial screening, 262
Injunction, 320
Inman, Dave, 411
Inputs, 295
    converting, to outputs, 350
Insider trading, 659
Insider Trading and Fraud Act (1988), 659
Insourcing, 356
Installations, 415
Institutional advertising, 475
Institutional investors, 649
In-store retailing, 454–55
Insurance
    automobile, 694
    cash value, 696–97
    continuous pay, 696–97
    disability income, 696
    health, 695–96
    homeowner's, 694–95
    liability, 694
    life, 696–97
    prioritizing needs, 693–94
    property, 694
    renter's, 694–95
    straight life, 696–97
    term life, 696
    universal life, 697
    whole life, 696–97
Insurance companies, 608
Intangible assets, 575
Intangible attributes, 412
Integrated marketing communications, 489–90
Integrated software, 511
Integration
    backward, 449
    forward, 449
Intelligent agents, 541

IntelliMatch, 28
Intensive distribution, 451
Interest, 652
Intermittent process, 351
Internal Revenue Code, 125–26
Internal Revenue Service, 125
Internal supply forecast, 259
International Accounting Standards Committee, 570
International banking, 610–11
International Brotherhood of Teamsters, 316
International economic communities, 77–80
International Finance and Communities Institute, 643
International franchising, 155
International Herald Tribune, 92
International location considerations, 353
International Monetary Fund (IMF), 76–77
International trade. See also Global marketplace
    barriers to, 71–74
    fostering global, 74–77
    measuring, 67–70
    reasons for, 70
Internet, 16, 534, 535–36. See also World Wide Web (WWW)
    as advertising media, 476
    attractions on, 537–38
    business use of, 538
    competition on, 539
    customer service and order fulfillment on, 554
    definition of, 535
    direct connections to, 539–40
    functioning of, 536
    in helping consumers make better pricing decisions, 428
    impact of, 464, 534
    as information source, 685
    in jump-starting job search, 27–28
    marketing on, 552–54
    and market investments, 660–61
    merchandising, 551–52
    privacy policies on, 556
    regulation of, 134
    resources for small business exporting, 82
    retailing on, 456
    and shopping, 464
    site costs and design, 552
    users of, 537–38
    Web site operations and infrastructure, 554–55
Internet auctions, 435
    growth of, 434
Internet explosion, 191–92
Internet/Intranet systems, 303
Internet service providers (ISPs), 535
Interpersonal roles, 215
Intranets, 513
Intrapreneurs, 172
Introductory stage, 424

Inventory, 575, 628
    management of, 357
    vendor-managed, 444
Inventory turnover ratio, 584
Investment Advisers Act (1940), 659
Investment bankers, 650
Investment Company Act (1940), 659, 674
Investments, 624, 697–700
    achieving target return on, 427–28
    developing strategy for, 698–700
    goals, 697
    sources of information on, 661–68, 674
Invest-O-Rama, 661–62
Investors, responsibilities to, 116
Involuntary bankruptcy, 131
ISO 9000 standards, 18–19
ISO 14000 standards, 18–19
Ivester, Douglas, 265

J

Jager, Durk, 229, 248
James, Robert, 684
Japan, selling Saturn in, 65
Jarvis, Mack, 482
Jinks, Barry, 282
Job analysis, 258
Job dissatisfiers, 293
Job enlargement, 297
Job enrichment, 297
Job fair, 261
Job placement, 277
Job rotation, 265, 297
Jobs
    changes within organization, 269–70
    choosing right, 20–21
    description of, 258
    finding perfect, 26–33
    hopping, 20
    interview for, 28
    motivational design, 297
    protection argument for tariffs, 72–73
Job satisfiers, 293
Job security, 330
Jobs for New College Graduates, 27
Job sharing, 298
Job shop, 349
Job specification, 258
JobTrak, 28
Johnson, Paul, 612
Joint ventures, 83, 151
Josephson, Wayne, 553
Jospin, Lionel, 13
Journal, 572
Judiciary, 126
Junk bonds, 652, 653
Justice, 101
Just-in-time (JIT), 364

K

Kabir, Mohammed, 644
Kahn, Stephen, 557

Kaplan, Jerry, 197–98
Kellner, Larry, 621, 622
Kendall, Joe, 337
Kerschner, Edward M., 643
Kimble, Thomas, 117
Kiplinger's Personal Finance Magazine, 661, 685
Kleinman, Jerry, 182–83
Knights of Labor, 316
Knowledge, 5–6
  managing resources, 523
Knowledge assets, 586
Koch, Ed, 222
Koch, Jay, 512
Koogle, Tim, 199
Kryshtanovska, Olga, 57
Kuok, Robert, 56
Kutner, Harold, 356

L

Labor, 3
  shortages of skilled, 335
Labor-management conflict, managing, 331–34
Labor-Management Relations Act, 321
Labor-Management Reporting and Disclosure Act, 321–22
Labor movement, today, 318–19
Labor union, 316
Lagman, Randy, 269
Laissez-faire leadership, 211
Lambert, Debra, 523
Lambros, Alex, Jr., 272
Land, 3
Landrum-Griffin Act, 321–22
Laptop computers, 506
Lawrence, Tom, 372
Laws, 125
  bankruptcy, 131
  business, 125–26
  product-liability, 130–31
  to promote fair competition, 131–34
  sources of, 125
  tort, 130
Layoff, 270
Leader pricing, 431
Leadership, 209
  free-rein, 211
  laissez-faire, 211
  styles of, 210–11
Leading, 209–12
Lean manufacturing, 363–64
Ledgers, 572
Legal environment of business, 125–35
Legal environment of unions, 320–22
Legal rights, 101
Legitimate power, 209
Lenk, Edward "Toby," 533
Leveraged buyout (LBO), 158
Lewis, John L., 317
Liabilities, 572, 575, 577
Liability insurance, 694
Libel, 130
Licensing, 81–82
Liemandt, Joe, 271, 296

Life insurance, 696–97
Lifetime Learning credit, 692
Limited liability companies, 149
Limited liability partnerships (LLPs), 142
Limited partners, 142
Limited partnership, 142
Limited-service merchant wholesalers, 453
Limit orders, 660, 672
Line-and-staff organization, 239
Line extension, 421
Line of credit, 630, 687
Line organization, 239
Line positions, 239
Liquid assets, 681
Liquidity, 575
Liquidity ratios, 582–84
Litow, Stanley, 117
Loans, 688–90
Local area networks, 512
Local incentives, 352
Local union, 318–19
Location, choosing, 459
Lockout, 333
Logistics, 444
Logistics management, 444
Long-term expenditures, 628
Long-term financing, raising, 632–37
Long-term forecasts, 626
Long-term liabilities, 577
Long-term planning, 348
Long-term relationships, creating, 54
Lopker, Pamela, 222
Loss leader, 431
Lump-sum wage adjustments, 328
Lyons, David, 330

M

Maastricht Treaty, 78–79
Machinists, 334
Macroeconomics, 37, 38–42, 55
  achieving goals, 42–45
Magnuson-Moss Warranty Act (1975), 133
Magnuson-Moss Warranty-Federal Trade Commission Improvement Act (1975), 421
Mail Fraud Act (1872), 133
Mainframe computers, 507
Major medical insurance, 695
Make-or-buy decision, 356
Managed care plans, 695–96
Management
  controlling in, 213–15
  in global marketplace, 221
  leading in, 209–12
  organizing in, 208–9
  planning in, 204–8
  rights of, in labor relations, 327
  role of, 204
  roles in, 215–17
  skills in, 217–20
Management prerogatives, 327
Management pyramid, 232
Management-rights clause, 327

Management support, 513
Management support systems, 515–16
Management tool, product life cycle as, 425
Managerial ability of entrepreneur, 174–75
Managerial accounting, 569
Managerial decision making, 215–17
Managerial finance, 708
Managerial hierarchy, 232–34, 233
Managers
  of corporate training, 378
  in empowering employees, 220–21
  and information technology, 221
  in setting prices, 429–30
Mannes, Alexis, 35
Manufacturer brands, 418–19
Manufacturers, 444
Manufacturers' agents, 453
Manufacturers representatives, 453, 498
Manufacturing, 348
Manufacturing environment, 353
Manufacturing resource planning II (MRPII), 357, 358, 364
Maquiladora plants, 190
Marcus, Bernie, 443
Mardon, Rebecca, 590
Margaret, Julie, 181
Margin accounts, 660
Margin requirements, 603
Marketable securities, 575, 627
Market averages, 667–68
Market characteristics, 487
Market competition, 668–69
Market conditions, 658
Market coverage, intensity of, 450–51
Market density, 396
Market equilibrium, 48
Market expansion in global market-place, 89–90
Market indexes, 667–68
Marketing, 382
  on Internet, 552–54
Marketing communications, integrated, 489–90
Marketing concept, 382–83
  building relationships, 385–86
  customer satisfaction, 383–84
  customer value, 383
Marketing factors, 352
Marketing intermediaries in distribution channel, 445–47
Marketing mix, developing, 389–92
Marketing problem, defining, 399
Marketing research, 397
  in serving existing customers and finding new customers, 397–401
Marketing research surveys, 403
Marketing strategy, creating, 386–89
Market order, 660
Market penetration, advertising costs and, 477
Market researcher, 498
Market risk, 638
Markets, function of channels in organizing and covering, 448–51

Market segmentation, 394–97
    benefit, 397
    demographic, 395–96
    geographic, 396
    psychographic, 397
    volume, 397
Market structure, 49
Markup pricing, 429
Marshall, Colin, 383
Martin, Doug, 322
Maslow, Abraham, 290
Mass customization, 349–50, 434, 435
Mass production, 349
Master brand, 416
Material requirement planning (MRP), 357, 358, 364
Materials-handling system, setting up, 460
Matrix structure, 240–42
Maturity stage, 424
Maude, Dan, 261
Maximizing profits, 426–27
Mayo, Elton, 289
McConnell, Martin, 282–83
McCormack, John, 123–24, 618
McCracken, Jim, 592
McEvoy, Ron, 507
McGinn, Richard, 111
McGraw, Jean, 201
McGregor, Douglas, 292
McKay, Gene H., III, 530
McKinnel, Neil, 191
McVey, Michael, 172
Mechanistic organization, 237
Mediation, 127, 321
Medicaid, 269
Medicare, 269
Medium-term planning, 348
Menough, Scott, 158
Mentally disabled, credit cards for, 689
Mentoring, 265
Merchant wholesalers, 453
Mergers, 162
    definition of, 156
    motives behind, 156–57
    types of, 157–58
Metzger, Blaine, 574
Michaels, Ed, 19
Microcomputers, 506
Microeconomics, 37, 46–49
Microelectromechanical systems (MEMS), 14–15
Micromarketing, using databases for, 402–3
Middle management, 209
Millennium bug, 521–22
Miller, Lance, 644
Miller, Steve, 220
Millgram, Stanley, 245
Minicomputers, 506–7
Minimum payments, credit cards, 688
Minnesota Clerical Test, 262
Mission, 205
Mission statement, 206
Mitterrand, François, 13
Mixed economic systems, 13

Mixed economy, 14
Model Business Corporation Act, 145
Modem, 511
Modular production, 367
Monetary incentives, 299
Monetary policy, 42–43, 602–3
Money
    characteristics of, 600–601
    definition of, 600
    functions of, 601
    U.S. supply of, 601
Money magazine, 661, 674, 685
Monopolistic competition, 51–52
Moody's, 654, 661
Moore, Darla, 276
Moore, Howard, 519
Morgan, Carl, 426–27
Morgan, J. P., 112
Morningstar, 661
Morris, Chris, 411
Mortgage bonds, 652, 653
Mortgage loan, 634
Motivating factors, 293
Motivation
    contemporary views on, 294–97
    and education, 304–5
    and employee ownership, 305
    and training, 304–5
    using teams to enhance, 299–304
    and work-life benefits, 305
Motivational job design, 297
Motivation theory, evolution of, 288–94
Motivator-hygiene theory, 293–94
Mott, Randy, 458
Multiculturalism, 11
Multinational corporations, impact of, 87–89
Multipreneur, 172
Municipal bonds, 653–54
Murray, Carolyn, 263
Mutual-aid pact, 334
Mutual assent, 128
Mutual fund quotations, 667, 674
Mutual funds, 654–55
Myers-Briggs Type Indicator, 262–63

N

Nanotechnology, 15
Napoleonic Code, 125
Nasdaq-Amex Market Group, 659, 669
Nasser, Jacques, 234, 311
National Advertising Division (NAD), 479
National Advertising Review Board (NARB), 479
National Association of Securities Dealers, Inc. (NASD), 659, 669, 674
National Association of Securities Dealers Automated Quotation (NASDAQ) system, 658, 668
    prices for, 663

National banks, 606
National Center for Employee Ownership, 310
National Credit Union Share Insurance Fund, 610
National debt, 45
National Education Association, 318
National Environmental Policy Act (1970), 125
National Health and Human Service Employees Union, 319
Nationalism and global marketplace, 84–85
National Labor Relations Act, 320
National Labor Relations Board (NLRB), 125, 320, 323
National rollout, 423
National Science Foundation (NSF), 535
National unions, 319
Nations
    measuring trade between, 67–70
    reasons for, 70
Natural barriers to trade, 70
Negligence, 130
Nelson, Marilyn, 293
Net asset value, 667
Net loss, 579
Net profit, 579
Net profit margin, 584
Net sales, 577
Network administrator, 597
Net working capital, 584
Network service providers (NSPs), 536
Net worth, 572
Net worth statement, 682
Newell, Chris, 222
New products. See also Products
    development of, 421–23
    facilitating sales of, 418
    organizing effort, 421
    publicity for, 486–87
New York Stock Exchange (NYSE), 657, 668, 673
    prices for, 663
Niccollai, John, 325
Niche competitive advantage, 389
Niche markets, 158
Nielsen, Jakob, 559
Niphix Trading System, 675
Noble, Alex de, 183
Nondepository financial institutions, 608–9
Nondurables, consumer, 413
Nonjudicial methods for settling disputes, 126–27
Nonmanufacturing operations
    automation in, 366
    technology in, 366
Nonprogrammed decisions, 216–17
Nonstore retailing, 455
Nontariff barriers to trade, 73–74
Norms, group, 244
Norris-La Guardia Act, 320
North American Free Trade Agreement (NAFTA), 77–78, 90, 190

Notebook computers, 506
Notepad computers, 506
Notes payable, 577
Not-for-profit marketing, 391–92
Not-for-profit organizations, 3
Nussbaum, Paul, 632
Nutrition Labeling and Education Act (1990), 133

O

Observation research, 399
Occupational Outlook Handbook, 26–27
Occupational Safety and Health Act (1970), 272, 273
Occupational Safety and Health Administration (OSHA), 272, 274
Odd-even pricing, 432
Odd lot, 660
Office automation systems, 514, 517
Office of Federal Contract Compliance Programs (OFCCP), 274
Off-the-job training, 265–66
Oil, Chemical and Atomic Workers Union (OCAW), 319
Older consumers, 10
Oligopoly, 52
Olim, Jason, 556–57
Olsen, Ken, 504
Omidyar, Pierre M., 457
Online banking, 612
Online information resources, 661–62
Online investing, 660–61, 671–72
Online processing processes, 515
Online trading companies, 648
On-the-job training, 265
Open-book management, 310
Open-end credit, 687
Open market operations, 602
Open shop, 326
Operating budgets, 626
Operating expenses, 579, 626
Operating plans, 625
Operating system, 508
Operational planning, 206
Operational plans, 209
Operational risk, 638
Operations, improving, 348
Operations management, 345–69, 347
Operations managers, 348
Optical scanners, 505–6
Options, 656
Order fulfillment on Internet, 554
Ordinances, 125
Organic organization, 237
Organizational career management, 269–71
Organizational structures, 238
  committee, 239–40
  informal, 244
  line, 239
  line-and-staff, 239
  matrix, 240–42
  reengineering, 242–43
Organization chart, 231

Organization of Petroleum Exporting Countries (OPEC), 51
Organizations
  influences of, on ethical conduct, 102–7
  permitting abuse, 104
Organized stock exchanges, 656–57
Organizing, 208–9, 230
Osborne, Richard, 645
Outcomes, 295
Outputs, converting inputs to, 350
Outside consultants, using, 186
Outsourcing, 276, 356
Over-the-counter market, 658
Owners' equity, 572, 577

P

Pacheco, Javier, 190
Pacioli, Luca, 572
Package, functions of, 419–20
Packaging, importance of, in self-service economy, 419–21
Padget, Nat, 590
Pagers, 517
Painter, Doug, 475
Panic of 1907, 602
Paper, Allied-Industrial, Chemical and Energy International Union (PACE), 319
Park, John, 152
Parker, Steve, 496
Parker, Tom, 323
Participative leadership, 211
Partnerships, 141–44
  advantages of, 142
  definition of, 141
  disadvantages of, 142–43
  forming, 141
  general, 142
  limited, 142
Pate, John, 263
Patent, 129
Payne, Allison, 275
Payroll taxes, 134–35
Pember, Anne, 583
Penetration pricing, 431
Pension funds, 608–9
Pension Reform Act, 272
Pepper. John, 229
Perceived value, 425
Perfect competition, 50
Performance, using teams to enhance, 299–304
Performance appraisal, 266
Performance planning and evaluation, 266–67
Performance standards, 213
Perpetual inventory, 357
Personal behavior, committing improper, 104
Personal computers (PCs), 506
Personal exemptions, 691–92
Personal financial planning (PF), 684
Personal selling, 487
  importance of, 480–83
  in promotional mix, 473

Peterson's Business and Management Jobs, 27
Pfeffer, Jeffrey, 287
Physical distribution, 444, 460
  in increasing efficiency and customer satisfaction, 460–61
  and services, 462–63
Physical exams, 264
Picketing, 333
Piece-rate pay plans, 299
Piecework, 268
Piech, Ferdinand, 36
Pinchot, Gifford, 172
Pine, Joseph, 434
Planned economy, 36
Planning, 204–8
  operational, 206
  tactical, 206
Plant health and safety officer, 378
Platt, Lewis, 229, 524
Point-of-sale (POS) cards, 683
Point-of-sale (POS) transfers, 682
Political considerations in global marketplace, 84–85
Poppen, Sherman, 24
Population, geographic shift of, 10
Portals, 541
Porter, Jim, 305
Portfolio, 654, 700
Postconventional ethics, 102
Potok, Fred, 485
Pottruck, David, 647, 673
Power, 209
  coercive, 209
  expert, 209
  legitimate, 209
  referent, 209
  reward, 209
Preconventional ethics, 101–2
Predators dumping, 74
Preferential tariff, 77
Preferred provider organizations (PPOs), 696
Preferred stock, 636, 651–52
  advantages and disadvantages of, 652
  features, 651–52
Pregnancy Discrimination Act (1978), 273
Premiums, 608, 667
Preparedness argument for tariffs, 73
Prepayment penalties, 690
Press release, 486
Prestige pricing, 432
Price discrimination, 131
Price/earnings (P/E) ratio, 663–65
Prices
  interaction of supply and demand in determining, 47–49
  role of managers in setting, 429–30
  setting, 459
Price skimming, 431
Pricing
  leader, 431
  markup, 429
  objectives, 426

odd-even, 432
penetration, 431
prestige, 432
product, 430–32
of products, 425–29
psychological, 432
regulation of, 132
strategy, 390
value, 428–29
Primary care physician (PCP), 696
Primary data, 400
Primary market, 649
Primary storage, 506
Principal, 652, 688
Principle of comparative advantage, 71
The Principles of Scientific Management, 289
Printer, 506
Privacy concerns, 522–23
Privacy Rights Clearinghouse, 526
Private accountants, 571
Private enterprise system, 12
Private investment, crowding out, 45
Problem-solving teams, 301
Process departmentalization, 232
Process layout, 354
Process manufacturing, 350
Producer price index (PPI), 42
Producers' cooperatives, 454
Product advertising, 474
Product departmentalization, 232
Product identification, 416
Production, 347
improving, 348
Production and operations control, 360
improving, 363–66
routing, 360
scheduling, 360–63
Production control, 348
Production inputs, availability of, 352
Production orientation, 383
Production planning, 348
facility layout, 354
process, 349–51
resource planning, 354, 356–58
site selection, 351–53
supply chain management, 359–60
Production process, 349–51
Productions and operations management, automation in, 364–65
Production timing, 350–51
Productivity, 13
improvements in, 17–18
Product layout, 354
Product liability, 130–31
Product life cycle, 424
as management tool, 425
stages of, 424–25
Product manager, 499
role of, 424
Product offering, developing, 457–58
Products. See also New products
capital, 414–15
classifying business, 414–15
classifying consumer, 413–14
convenience, 414

creating, that deliver value, 421–24
definition of, 412–15
generic, 419
getting consumers to try, 472–73
nature of, 487
pricing, 430–32
pricing right, 425–29
shopping, 414
specialty, 414
strategy, 390
unsought, 413–14
Professional Association of Resume Writers, 28
Professional employer organization (PEO), 260
Professional salesperson, 480
Professional WebResume software, 27
Profit, 2
total, 430
Profitability ratios, 584
Profit maximization, 426
Profit sharing, 268
Profit-sharing plans, 299
Program Evaluation and Review Technique (PERT), 361, 362–63
Programmed instruction, 266
Progressive tax, 691
Project management approach, 240
Promotion, 269, 472
Promotional goals, 472–74
Promotional mix, 473–74
factors that affect, 487–89
Promotional strategy, 390, 459
Property insurance, 694
Property taxes, 134, 693
Prospecting, 481–83
Protected classes, 274
Protectionism, 70
Protective tariffs, 72
Psychographic segmentation, 397
Psychological pricing, 432
Public accountants, 571
Publicity, 486
Public relations, 390, 486–87
in promotional mix, 474
Public relations agent, 498–99
Pull strategy, 488–89
Purchase volume, 394
Purchasing, 356
Purchasing agents, selling to, 481
Purchasing manager, 377–78
Purchasing power, 41
Pure Food and Drug Act (1906), 133
Pure monopoly, 50–51
Push strategy, 488

Q

Qualifying questions, 482
Quality, 18
delivering, 52–53
of life, 2
Quality control, 363
Quality-control manager, 377
Questions, qualifying, 482
Quick ratio, 583

R

Rack jobbers, 454
Ragsdale, Jon, 1
Raiffa, Howard, 222
Rainbow, Roger, 222
Random access memory (RAM), 506
Ratio analysis, 581–82
Rational branding, 490
Rational purchase decisions, 394
Raw materials, 415
Rayden, Michael, 123
Reach, 477
Real-time processing processes, 515
Recession, 39
Recognition, 298–99
Recruitment, 260
Reed, John, 234, 615
Reengineering, 242–43
Reference check, 263–64
Referent power, 209
Regional Community Policing Institute, 342
Registration statement, 659
Relationship management, 54
Remarriage, 680
Reminder advertising, 474–75
Renschler, Andreas, 212
Renter's insurance, 694–95
Repeat sales, building, with brand loyalty, 417
Replacement cost coverage, 694
Researching Companies Online, 675
Reserve requirement, 603
Resignation, 270
Resource acquisition in global marketplace, 90
Resource planning, 354, 356–58
Restitution, 129
Résumé, cyber, 28
Retail business in cyberspace, 457
Retail buyer, 498
Retailers, 446
selling to, 481
Retailing
competitive world of, 454–59
components of successful strategy, 456–59
types of operations, 454–56
Retained earnings, 577, 636, 650
Retirement, 271
Return on equity (ROE), 584
Return on investment capital (ROIC), 219
Return on sales, 584
Returns, 624
and allowances, 577
Revenue, 2
total, 430
Revenue bonds, 654
Revolving credit agreement, 630–31
Revolving credit cards, 687
Reward power, 209
Richards, Stan, 240, 241
Ricks, Bob, 495
Right principle, 382
Right-to-work laws, 326
Rings of defense approach, 270

Rios, Danielle, 271
Risk, 2, 624
Risk management, 638–39
Risk-return trade-off, 624
Robinson-Patman Act (1936), 132
Robotics, 365
Rocca, Mike, 277
Rodgers, Jack, 629
Rodriguez, Arturo, 391
Rogers, Fran, 144
Romero, Elena, 1
Roney, William C., Sr., 618
Roosevelt, Franklin D., 609
Rosenthal, Norman, 439
Round lots, 660
Routing production, 360
Ruether, Walter, 317
Ryan, Sean, 662

S

Saarelainen, Jari, 311
Sabatino, Casper, 583
St. Laurent, Yves, 390
Salaries, 268
Salary Calculator, 30
Salazar, Elaine, 183
Sales
    gross, 577
    net, 577
Sales discounts, 577
Sales positions, 481
Sales promotion, 483–85, 487
    in promotional mix, 474
Sales prospects, 481
Sales taxes, 135, 693
Salzman, Barry, 91
Samaranch, Juan Antonio, 243
Satisfaction
    actual, 426
    expected, 426
Saving banks, 606
Savings and loan associations (S&Ls),
    606
Savings Association Insurance Fund
    (SAIF), 609
Savings bonds, 45
Savings instruments, 684–85
    characteristics of, 685
Scheduling, 360–63
Schulz, Carol, 282
Schutz, Jared, 171
Schwartz, Paula Mae, 144
Scientific management, 288–89
S corporation, 148
Scott, Tom, 169–70, 174, 179, 194
Screen Writers Guild, 319
Seasonal unemployment, 41
Secondary data, 400
Secondary market, 649
Secondary storage, 506
Secured bonds, 652
Secured short-term loans, 631
Securities, 649, 660
    marketable, 627
    market competition, 668–69
    online investing, 660–61, 671–72

rise of individual investor, 669–70
    transaction basics, 660
Securities Act (1933), 674
Securities and Exchange Commission
    (SEC), 125, 587, 659
Securities Exchange Act (1934), 659,
    674
Securities exchanges, 656–57
    global trading and foreign, 657–58
    market conditions, 658
    over-the-counter market, 658
    U.S. stock exchanges, 657
Securities Investor Protection
    Corporation (SIPC), 659
Securities legislation, 659
Securities markets, 649
    current trends in, 674
    regulation of, 659
    role of investment bankers and stock-
        brokers, 650
    types of, 649
Security breaches, 520
Security price quotations, 662–63
Security requirements, 690
Selection interview, 263
Selective credit controls, 603
Selective distribution, 451
Selective strike strategy, 332
Self-directed retirement accounts,
    701
Self-employed, financial planning for,
    699
Self-managed work teams, 301–2
Self-regulation, 659
Self-service economy, importance of
    packaging in, 419–21
Seller cooperatives, 150
Selling process, 481–83
Seniority, 330
Separations, 270–71
Servers, 536
Service capacity, managing, 462
Service Corps of Retired Executives
    (SCORE), 180
Service Employees International Union
    (SEIU), 319, 334
Servicemark, 130
Services, 2, 415
    and physical distribution, 462–63
Sherman Antitrust Act (1890), 125,
    131, 132
Shopping products, 414
Shop steward, 319
Short-term expenses, 626
Short-term financing, obtaining, 628–
    32
Short-term forecasts, 625
Short-term planning, 348
Sick-out, 332
Silver, Joshua, 94–95
Silverman, Henry, 211
SIMPLE plans, 701
Site design, trends in, 368
Site selection, 351–53
Skills inventory, 260
Skimming, price, 431
Slander, 130

Small business, 175–76. See also
        Business
    advantages of, 177–78
    buying, 184
    characteristics of, 176–77
    definition of, 176
    disadvantages of, 178–79
    hiring and retaining employees,
        186–87
    international operations, 187
    Internet resources for exporting, 82
    managing, 185–87
    risks of ownership, 184–85
Small Business Administration (SBA),
    81, 179
    financial assistance programs, 179–80
    management assistance programs,
        180
    Office of Minority Enterprise
        Development, 180
Small Business Investment Companies
    (SBICs), 179
Small Business Knowledge Base, 197
Smart car, 35–36
Smart Money, 661, 674
Smith, Fred, 329
Smoot, P. J., 33
Social change, 275
Social contract trends, 117–18
Social forces, 386
Social investing, 116
Social Investment Forum, 675
Socialism, 13, 14
Social marketing, 392
Social responsibility, 107–12
    trends in, 118
    understanding, 110–12
Social Security, 269
    and Medicare taxes, 692–93
Social Security Act (1935), 273
Social trends, 7–8
Software, 508–11
    applications, 508
    integrated, 511
    piracy of, 520
    systems, 508
Sole proprietorships, 139–41
    advantages of, 140
    definition of, 140
    disadvantages of, 140–41
Soliman, Peter, 35
Span of control, 234–35
Span of management, 235
Sparks, Steven, 583
Specialization, 230
Specialty products, 414
Spreadsheets, 509–10
Springfield, Thomas, 645
Staff positions, 239
Stairwell meetings, 241
Stakeholders
    definition of, 112
    responsibilities to, 112–16
Standard deduction, 692
Standard of living, 2
Standard & Poor's (S&P), 654, 661,
    668

Stanley, Thomas J., 699
State, County and Municipal Workers, 334–35
State banks, 606
Statement of cash flows, 579–81
Statutory law, 125
Steel industry and global competition, 75
Steffinski, Traci, 529
Stock, equity financing, 650
  common stock, 650–51
  preferred stock, 651–52
Stockbroker, 650
Stock dividends, 636, 650
Stockholders, 146
Stocklift, 462
Stocklifting, 462
Stock quotations, 663–65, 674
Stop-loss order, 660
Storage warehouse, 460
Stovall, Jim, 178
Straight life insurance, 696–97
Strategic alliance, 54
Strategic giving, 116
Strategic planning, 205
Strategic plans, 209, 626
Strauss, Karl, 638
Strict liability, 131
Strike replacements, 334
Structural building blocks, 230
  centralization of decision making, 235–37
  departmentalization, 231–32
  division of labor, 230–31
  managerial hierarchy, 232–34
  span of control, 234–35
Structural unemployment, 40
Structures, organizational, 238
Sullivan, Thomas, 618
Supercomputers, 507–8
Supervisory management, 209
Supplementary unemployment benefits, 329
Supplier communications, improving, 359–60
Supplies, 415
  changes in, 49
  interaction of demand and, in determining prices, 47–49
  nature of, 47
Supply chain, 359
Supply chain management, 359–60, 444
  strategies for, 359
Supply curve, 47
Survey research, 399
Sweeny, John, 318
Synergy, 301
Systems analyst, 596
Systems software, 508

T

Tactical plans, 206, 209
Taft-Hartley Act, 321
Tall organizational structure, 237

Tam, Sabrina, 508
Tangible attributes, 412
Tape drives, 506
Target market, 387, 456
Target return on investment, 427–28
Tariffs, 72
  arguments for and against, 72–73
  barriers, 72–73
  preferential, 77
Taxation, of business, 134–35
Taxes, 43
  excise, 135
  income, 134, 691
  payroll, 134–35
  property, 134, 693
  sales, 135, 693
  Social Security and Medicare, 692–93
Tax politics, 43
Taylor, Frederick, 288–89
Taylor, James, 255, 256
Teams
  building high-performance, 303–4
  cross-functional, 302–3
  in enhancing motivation and performance, 299–304
  problem-solving, 301
  self-managed work, 301–2
  virtual, 303
  work, 301
Teamsters Union, 318, 325
Technical knowledge of entrepreneur, 174–75
Technical skills, 217–18
Technological forces, 386
Technology, 14, 15–17
  change of, in global marketplace, 90
  in nonmanufacturing operations, 366
  planning, 518
  trends of, 13–15
Tedesco, Ralph, 383–84
Teich, Jonathan, 517
Telecommuting, 276–77, 298
Television, impact of digital VCRs on, 490–91
Temkin, Bruce, 550
Termination, 270
Term life insurance, 696
Term loan, 633–34
Test-marketing, 423
Textile Workers Union, 333
Theory X, 292
Theory Y, 292–93
Thompson, Richard, 19
Thompson, Todd, 502
Three-questions test, 105
Thrift institutions, 606–7
Thurow, Lester, 5–6
Thylefors, Bjorn, 96
Tilbury, Hal, 520
Time deposits, 601
Time management, 222
Time-Value Financial Services, 643
Tombstones, 649
Top management, 209
Tort, 130
Tort law, 130

Total cost, 430
Total profit, 430
Total quality management, 363
Total revenue, 430
Trade. See International trade
Trade credit, 630
Trade deficit, 68
Trademark, 130
Trademarks, 415, 575
Trade sales promotion, 483
Trade surplus, 68
Training and motivation, 304–5
Transaction processing systems, 513, 514–15
TransAtlantic Business Dialogue, 134
Transfer, 269
Transmission control protocol/Internet protocol (TCP/IP), 535, 536
Transportation decisions, making, 460–61
Treasury bills, 653
Treasury bonds, 602–3, 653
Treasury notes, 653
Trial balance, 572–73
Trial courts, 126
Triant, Deborah, 222
Truck wholesalers, 454
Truth-in-Lending Act (1968), 133
Truth-in-Lending Law, 690
Tulgan, Bruce, 296
Tying contracts, 131

U

Underwood, Phil, 644
Underwriting, 650
Unearned income, 692
Unemployment, 680
  compensation, 269
  cyclical, 40
  measuring, 40
  rate of, 40
  structural, 40
  types of, 40–41
Unethical actions, condoning, 104
Uniform Commercial Code (UCC), 126
Unions
  busting of, 334
  certification election for, 323
  emergence of, 316–19
  legal environment of, 320–22
  negotiating contracts, 325–30
  organizing and membership of, 334–35
  security of, 325–27
  strategies of, in labor-management relations, 332–33
Union shop, 326
United Auto Workers Union, 41, 318, 319, 325, 332, 334
United Farm Workers, 333
United Food and Commercial Workers (UFCW), 325, 334
United Mine Workers (UMW), 317
United Papermakers International Union (UPIC), 319

United States
    financial system in, 604–5
        credit unions, 607
        depository institutions, 606–7
        nondepository institutions, 608–9
    global vision of, 66
    government securities in, 653
    importance of global business to, 67
    stock exchanges in, 657
United States Treasury, 697
United Steelworkers of America, 318, 319, 334
United Steelworkers Union, 321
Unity of command principle, 234
Universal Commercial Code for Electronic Commerce, 134
Universal life insurance, 697
Unsecured bonds, 652
Unsecured short-term loans, 629–31
Unsought products, 413–14
Uruguay Round, 74–76
U.S. Patent Office, 129
U.S. Supreme Court, 126
USA Today International, 92
Use, increasing amount and frequency of, 473
Utilitarianism, 100–101

V

Value, 652
    adding, through warranties, 420–21
    creating products that deliver, 421–24
    delivering, 52–53
    perceived, 425
Value Line Investment Survey, 661
Value pricing, 428–29, 440–41
Vanguard Online University, 675
Variable costs, 430
Variable pay, 299
Vendor-managed inventory, 444
Venture capital, 184, 636–37
Vergara, Jorge, 391
Vergara, Pepe, 391
Vernon, Lillian, 175

Verrochi, Paul M., 174
Vertical marketing systems, 449–50
Vertical merger, 157
Vestibule training, 265–66
Vietnam Veterans Readjustment Act (1974), 273
Virtual corporation, 246–47
Virtual teams, 303
Voice mail systems, 517
Volume segmentation, 397
Voluntary bankruptcy, 131
Voluntary reduction in pay, 270
Voluntary time off, 270
Voting rights, 650

W

Wages, Robert, 319
Wages and labor-relations, 328–29
Wagner Act, 320
Waiting period, 696
Wait times, minimizing, 462
Wall Street Journal, 649, 661, 662, 667, 674
Warehouse location and type, choosing, 460
Warranties, 129
    adding value through, 420–21
    express, 420
    full, 421
    implied, 420
Watson, Thomas, 504
Web-based training, 285
Web browser, 513
Website designer, 595–96
Websites, 535
    costs and design, 552
    creating successful, 558–59
    operations and infrastructure, 554–55
Weill, Sandy, 234
Weill, Sanford, 615
Weinberg, Sandy, 188
Welch, Jack, 112, 211, 229
Wells, Jared, 567–68, 589
Wheeler-Lea Act (1938), 132
Whole life insurance, 696–97

Wholesalers, 446
    selling to, 481
    types of, 452–54
Wholesaler sales representative, 498
Wholesaling, 451–54
Wickham, Dave, 103
Wide area networks, 512–13
Wildcat strike, 332
Williams, Julie, 178
Williams, Tom, 191
Winfrey, Oprah, 491
Withholding allowances, 691
Women, changing role of working, 8
Women-owned businesses, 189–90
Wonderlic Personnel Test, 262
Woodbury, Edwina, 625
Word processing, 508–9, 517
Work cell design, 368
Worker's compensation, 269
Work groups, 301
Work-life benefits and motivation, 305
Work scheduling options, 298
Work teams, 301
World Trade Organization (WTO), 76, 90
World Wide Web (WWW), 535. *See also* Internet
    growth of advertising on, 490
Worm, 521
Worth magazine, 661

Y

Yang, Jerry, 198
Yellow-dog contracts, 320
Young, Sharon, 255
Young American Business Network, 20
Young Entrepreneurs Network, 20

Z

Zarate, Steve, 221
Zero-coupon bonds, 653
Zickle, Sally, 372
Zip drives, 506

A

ABC.com, 556
ABCNews.com, 556
Ace cooperatives, 150
Actuarial Consultants, Inc. (ACI), 519
ACT-UP, 117
Adaptive Eyecare Ltd., 95–96
Adobe Illustrator, 510, 637
Air Canada, 259
Air France, 642
AirTouch Communications, 159
Alamo Rent a Car, 170
Alaska Airlines, 642
Alertbox, 559
Alexander Doll Co., 203, 204, 223
Allegheny Ludlum, 421
AlliedSignal, 305, 352
Amazon.com., 2, 171, 172, 248, 433, 439, 455, 457, 492, 539, 542, 547, 556–57, 560
AMD, 359
American Airlines, 3, 263, 264, 266, 275, 315, 337, 386, 429, 473, 491–92, 556
American Automobile Association, 407
American Building Restoration Products, 81
American Cancer Society, 3
American Express, 106
American Fare, 455
American Information Systems, Inc. (AIS), 171
American International Group, 88
America Online (AOL), 157, 432, 433, 534, 537, 547, 586, 651
America's Employers, 29
America's Job Bank, 29
Ameritech, 157
Ameritrade, 661
Amoco, 157
Ampersand Art Supply, 183
Amway, 455
Andersen Worldwide, 571
Anderson Consulting, 16
Anheuser-Busch, 117
Anthro Corp., 358
Apple Computer, 109, 116, 658
Archway Cookies, 530–31
Artemis, 411, 436
Athlete's Foot, 152
Atlantic Richfield, 636
AT&T, 17, 80, 88, 117, 145, 274, 435, 474, 512, 609, 657
Audiovox, 657
Aussie, 432
AutoCITE, 96
AutoPARK, 97
Avado Brands, 279
Avon Products, 390, 455, 624–25, 637

B

Baan Co., 271
Bacon, R. S., Veneer Co., 592
Banana Boat, 429
Band-Aids, 416
Bang and Olufsen, 450
BankAmerica, 242, 611, 612
Bank Boston, 611
Bank of Alma, 123–24, 618
Bank of America, 265
Bank of Lakeview, 618
Bankrate, 705
Barnes & Noble, 546, 547, 552
BASF, 88
Beacon Application Services Corp., 261
Bechtel Group, 563
Beecham, 88
Belk, Inc., 516, 523
Bell Atlantic/GTE, 234
Bell Labs, 388
Ben & Jerry's, 105, 109, 206, 220, 658
Berkshire Hathaway, 88
Berne Apparel, 368
Best, 455
Bethlehem Steel, 288
BetzDearborn, 631
Bic, 415
Black & Decker, 203, 415
Bloomingdale's, 455
Bluebird Systems, 520
Blue Diamond, 150
Bluefly.com, 455
BMW, 7, 389, 434
Boeing Co., 16, 17, 52, 68, 84, 145, 260, 628, 632
Borden's, 420
Borders Books and Music, 548, 563
Boys and Girls Clubs of America, 115
Breck, 413
Brigham and Women's Hospital, 517
Brik Pak, 420
Bristol-Myers Squibb, 88, 112, 633
British Airways, 383
British Midland Airlines, 642
British Petroleum, 88, 157
British Telecom, 19
BT: Employee Screening Services, 263
Budweiser, 111
Bumblebee, 479
Burger King, 159, 366, 413
Burke Marketing Research, 407
Burlington Northern Railroad, 264
Burton Snowboards, 24–25, 468–69

C

Cabot Corp. Microelectronics, 353
Cacharel, 83
Cadaco, 10
Cadillac, 7
Calavo, 150
CAMI Automotive, 83
Campbell Soup, 106, 421, 449, 473
Camp Fire Boys and Girls, 111
Canteen, 455
Canyon Cafe, 279
Cape Cod Chips, 418
Capital Research Center, 117
Cardio Chips, 439
CareerBuilder Network, 29
Career Central, 261
Careerpath.com, 29
Carlson Co., 293
Carlson Travel Network, 293
Carnival Cruise Lines, 387, 390
Carrier, 459
Cartier, 389
Case Corp., 574
Catalog City, 543
Caterpillar, Inc., 277, 332, 389, 651
CD Now, Inc., 428, 455
Cendant Corp., 583, 586–87
Chamber of Commerce, 486
Champion, 415
Chapparal Steel, 388
Chase Manhattan, 611, 612
Chattahoochee National Bank, 617–18
Check Point Software Technologies, Inc., 222
Cheer, 89
Chemdex.com, 543
Chemlawn, 450
Chevrolet, 396, 416, 432
Chevron Corp., 523, 657
Children's Orchard, 513
China Mist Tea Co., 418
Chrysler Corp., 35, 65, 159, 212, 381, 473
Circle K, 455
Cisco Systems., 88, 246–47, 276, 542, 544
Citibank, 151, 610
Citicorp, 159, 599
Citigroup, 112, 145, 234, 586, 599–600, 601, 615, 650
City Snapshots, 30
Claire's, 456
ClarisWorks, 511
Cle Elum, 103
Clinique, 390
Clothestime, 455
Club Med, 9
CMP Media, 113
CNET Message Boards, 529
Coca-Cola, 6, 18, 56, 80, 85, 88, 112, 115, 118, 134, 206, 262, 265, 274, 389, 416, 418, 421, 432, 435, 451, 474, 657
Colby Care Nurses, Inc., 107
Cold Fusion Sports, 191
Colgate Palmolive, 491
Colorado Rules, 172
Colorado Wild Birds Unlimited, Inc., 158
Commonwealth Edison, 636
Company Blueprint, 30
Compaq Computer, 2, 257, 266, 386, 473, 651
CompareNet, 541
Computer Learning Centers, 113–14
Computer Renaissance, 158
Continental Airlines, 473, 621, 642
Control Data Corp., 270
Coopers, Price Waterhouse, 571

Coors, 658
Corel Draw, 510
Corning, Inc., 115, 421
Costas Foods, 112
Costco, 453, 546
Cover Girl, 390
Craftsman, 419
CSX Corp., 543, 548
CUC International, 210–11, 583
Cyberian Outpost, 557
Cyprus Amax Mineral Co., 13–14

D

Daimler-Benz Ag, 35, 58, 159, 212,
    381
DaimlerChrysler, 7, 18, 234, 381,
    384, 405, 429, 508
Daiwa, 638
Dana Corp., 113, 291
Dansk, 455
Datek Online, 661, 669, 672
DateOnline, 557
Datsun, 80
Dayton Hudson, 226–27, 454
DeBeers Consolidated Mines Ltd.,
    51
DejaNews, 103
Delfield Co., 645
Delia's, Inc., 557
Dell Computers, 219, 434, 464, 540,
    549, 586, 628, 637, 658
Del Monte, 420
Deloitte & Touche Tohmatsu
    International, 571
Denny's, 115
Deutsche Bank AG, 159
Diamond Walnut Cooperative, 333
Dickies, 3
Diedrich's, 159
Diehard, 419
Digital Equipment Corporation (DEC),
    257–58, 302, 504
Dillard, 458
Direct Hit Technologies, 183, 213
Discover Brokerage, 672, 676
Discovery Labs, 643
Disney, 206, 263, 556
Disneyland, 245
DLJDirect, 661
DNA Visual Solutions, 156
Dockers, 471, 472, 492
Doing It Best, 150
Dollar General, 456
Domino's pizza, 414
Don Pablos, 255, 256, 279
DoubleClick International, 91
Double Tree Hotels, 384
Dow Chemical, 87, 89, 421
DowJones, 706
Dreyfus Brokerage Services, 676
Drugstore.com, 556
Duke Energy, 665
DuPont, 19, 273, 388, 427
Duracell International, 66
Dustbusters, 422

E

Eastman Kodak, 19, 116, 117
Eaton Corp., 302
eBay, 248, 542
Eddie Bauer, 456
Edward Jones, 676–77, 706–7
Edwards, 325
Egghead Software, 134
Elderly Instruments, 564
Electronic Share Information (ESI), 83
Eli Lilly, 522
Embassy Suites, 384
Enforcement Technology, Inc., 96–97
Equifax, 526, 690
Erickson, 134
Ernst & Young, 571
ESPAN, 29
Esprit, 104
Estee Lauder, 390
eToys, 439, 455, 533–34, 539, 560
E*Trade Group, Inc., 428, 648, 661,
    672
Evans Products, 449
Excel, 510
Experian, 526, 690
Experience Online, 28
Expo Design Centers, 465
Exxon, 18, 87, 88, 112, 145, 157,
    234, 236, 633

F

Family.com, 556
Family Dollar, 456
Farmland Industries, 150
FAST, Inc., 366
Federal Express, 87, 90, 113, 265,
    277, 291, 329, 389, 487
Fel-pro, 114
Fiat, 73
Fidelity Investments, 648, 654–55,
    656
FileMaker Pro, 510
Financiero Atlas, 615
Firstbank Corp., 618
First Bank of West Branch, 618
First Boston, 650
Firsthand Funds, 656
First Union, 612, 662
Fisher Scientific, 333
Floorgraphics, 485
Flower Aviation, 494–95
Food Town, 325
Ford Credit, 689
Ford Motor, 7, 18, 35, 37, 65, 68,
    80, 112, 134, 145, 234, 236,
    311, 396, 422, 625, 657
Forrester Research, 542
Fort Howard Paper, 388
4Work, 29
Ben Franklin, 455
Freehand, 510
Freemarkets, 542
Fridgedoor.com, 542
Frito-Lay, 66

Frontier Hotel (Las Vegas), 333
Fruit-of-the-Loom, 82
Frullati Cafe and Bakery, 159
FTD florist association, 475
Fuji Xerox, 84, 89
Fulcrum Direct, 644
Fuller Brush, 455

G

Gallo, 431
Gap, Inc., 104, 206–7, 459, 546,
    586
GapKids, 207
Garden Escape, 557
Gatch, 459
Gateway, 464
Gatorade, 115
GE Capital Corp., 157
GE Capital Small Business Finance,
    609
General Electric Co., 2, 6, 19, 68, 80,
    84, 87, 88, 112, 117, 144, 145,
    157, 211, 220, 229, 236, 260,
    264, 427, 544, 650
General Motors, 7, 12, 17, 18, 37,
    65, 68, 80, 81, 83, 84, 87, 112,
    116, 145, 245, 271, 332, 356,
    357, 365, 384, 415, 474, 543–
    44, 622, 630
General Motors Foundation, 117
Gillette, 16, 66, 87, 206, 396, 431,
    449
Gingko Biloba Rings, 439
Glaxo Wellcome, 88
GMAC, 689
Go Corporation, 197–98
Goldman, Sachs & Co., 650
Gomez Advisors' Internet Broker
    Scorecard, 672
Goodyear, 134, 630
W. C. Gore and Associates, 263
Grand Union, 325
Greenpeace, 3
Grey Corp., 430
GrowBiz, 158
Gucci, 390, 414

H

Häagen-Dazs, 16–17
Hagberg Consulting Group, 174
Hallmark Cards, 398
Hanes, 449
Harley-Davidson, 219, 220, 231, 291,
    345–46, 356, 370, 416
Hartek, 645
Hasbro, 657
Hawthorne Western Electric, 289
Healtheon Corp., 292
Henri Bendel, 387
Herbalife, 391, 455
Hewlett-Packard, 87, 114, 117, 229,
    271, 302, 421, 524, 633
HFS, Inc., 210, 583
Highsmith, Inc., 225–26

Hilfiger, Tommy, clothing, 451, 540
Hllton Hotel Corp., 274, 523
Hoechst AG, 159
Homark, 645
Home Depot, 102, 151, 232, 385, 443–44, 465, 544, 546, 552
HOMEFAIR, 30
HomeGrocer, 563
Homegrocer.com, 556
Home Shopping Network, 455
Homestyle Corp., 508
Honda USA, 87, 88, 265, 413
Hood Furniture Co., 333
Hops, 279
Horizon Communications, 186
Hormel Food, 664–65
HotJobs.com, 29
Hot Pots, 139–40
Hot Shop, 201
HotWired, 559
Houston Astros, 270
Hudson's, 226, 227
Hunt's/Del Monte, 420
Hyatt Hotels, 392–93, 429
Hypermart USA, 455

I

IBM, 68, 80, 84, 88, 115–16, 116, 117, 144, 145, 222, 271, 277, 415, 421, 504, 556, 657
Idealab, 181
Inca Kola, 85
Independent Grocers Association (IGA), 419
Infoseek Corp., 556
Ingersoll-Rand Co., 334
Inglenook, 431
Integration Logic, Inc., 644
Intel, 88, 212, 359, 506, 522, 586, 637, 658
International Data Corp., 360, 629
International Olympic Committee, 243
International Paper, 33
Intuit, 537
Iomega Corp., 113
Iowa Plastics, 340–41
It's About Games, 158
iVillage, 537

J

J. Crew, 456
Jaguar, 450
Jamaican Tourism, 488–89
Jamba Juice, 151, 159
Jango, 428
Jantzen, 109, 460
Jeep, 415, 428
JIAN, 252–53
Jiffy Lube, 151
JobDirect, Inc., 137–38, 162, 165
Jody B Fashions, 373–74
Johnson & Johnson, 88, 416
Juno Online Services, 634

K

Kava Corn Chips, 439
Keep America Beautiful, 3
Kellogg's, 53, 80
Kenmore, 419
Kentucky Fried Chicken (KFC), 154, 156
Kerry Group, 57
KeyCorp, 501–2, 513, 523, 526
Kingston Technology, 114
Kinko's, 151
Kleenex, 415
Kmart, 454, 455, 459, 462, 485
Kodak, 51, 84, 416, 460, 477
Kool-Aid, 424
Korn Ferry, 261
KPMG International, 571
Kraft General Foods, 421, 474
Kroger, 265, 455
K-Tel, 455
Kysor Industrial Corp., 645

L

Labatt Brewing Company, 82
Lagasse Brothers, 451
Land O' Lakes, 150
Lands' End, 269, 456
Lane Bryant, 387
Lauder, Estée, 540
Lays, 413
L'eggs, 428
Lerner, 387
Lever, 472
Lexus, 7, 53, 383, 472
Limited, Inc., 387
Limited Too, 122–23
Liz Claiborne, 419
L.L. Bean, 455, 456
Longaberger, 456
Lord and Taylor, 459
Lotus, 510, 511
Lotus Institute, 222
Louisiana-Pacific Corp., 110–11
Lowe's Home Improvement Warehouse, 151, 462, 552
Lucent Technologies, 88, 111, 115, 285
Lufthansa, 259
Lurias, 455
L-Z Marketing, 372

M

Macintosh, 506
Macy's, 492, 540
Mail Boxes Etc., 159
Mardon Consulting Associates, 590
Marine Power, 545
Marion Merrell Dow, 489
Marlboro, 416
Marriott International, 105, 387, 431
Mars, 39, 394
Marshall Field's, 226, 227
Mary Kay Cosmetics, 455

N

Mattel, 434
May Co., 455
Maytag, 389, 451
Mazda, 90
MBE Business Express, 159
MBNA, 114
McCormick and Schmicks, 279
McDonald's, 2, 18, 82, 87, 105, 151, 154, 268, 273, 360, 366, 383, 389, 391, 435, 450
McDonnell Douglas, 52
McGraw-Hill, 434
McGraw's Shortbread, 201
MCI WorldCom, 265, 474, 512, 658
McKinsey Consulting, 19
McLane Co., 449
Men's Warehouse, 264
Mercantile Transport, Inc., 190
Mercedes-Benz, 62, 384
Merck, 88, 114
Mercosur, 78, 90
Merisel, 540
Merrill Lynch, 265, 272, 650, 661, 673
Miami Baggage Cart, 100
Miami International Airport, 99–100, 120
Microsoft Corp., 5, 12, 18, 88, 114, 144, 151, 205, 209–10, 263, 266, 277, 299, 416, 464, 509, 510, 511, 540, 556, 567, 586, 633, 658
Midvale, 288
Miller Brewing Company, 82, 268, 475
Minolta, 415
Miracle Restoration Kit, 8
Mitsubishi Motors, 85
Mobile One, 600
Mobil Oil, 157, 159, 234, 236
Money Store Commercial Lending, 609
Monsanto, 636
Monster Board, 29, 251–52, 284
Morgan Stanley Dean Witter, 650
Motley Fool Brokerage Center, 672
Moto Photo, 151
Motorola, 40, 236–37, 274, 508
Moving Calculator, 30
Mrs Smith's, 472
MultiMedia Solutions, 141
Munder Funds' NetNet fund, 656
Music Go Round, 158

N

Nantucket Nectars, Inc., 169–70, 179, 194
National Geographic Society, 276
National SemiConductor, 261
National Shooting Sports Foundation, 475
NationJob NetWork, 29
NationsBank, 262, 612
Nationwide Papers, 451
Navistar, 633
NBC, 537

Neiman-Marcus, 389, 414, 459
Nestlé, 89, 90
NetBank, 608
Netscape Communications, 157, 171, 172, 292
Network Solutions, Inc., 61
New York State Electric and Gas Corp., 383–84
Nicholson-Hardie Nursery & Garden Center, 385
Nielsen, A. C., 399, 401
Nike, 52, 90, 212, 416, 418, 419
Niphix Investments, 670
Nippon Telegraph & Telephone, 88
Nissan, 90
Nokia, 487
Norand Base Bakery, 530
Nordstrom, 658
Norfolk and Western Railway Co., 330
Novartis, 88
Novell, 637

O

Ocean Spray, 150
Office Depot, 546
Old Navy, 207
Olive Garden, 398
Omnilife, 391
Once Upon a Child, 158
1-800 Contacts, 183
1-800-Flowers, 492
OneSource, 647
Online Career Center, 29
OnSale, 542
Onsale, 198
Optimal Resolutions, Inc., 183
Oracle Corporation, 482–83, 637
Orangina, 85
Oscar Mayer, 421
Otis Elevator, 89

P

Pacific Telesis, 157
PageMaker, 511
PaineWebber, 643, 650
Palm Computing, 367
Palm Pilot, 432–33
Panasonic, 424
Pathmark, 325
Patriot American Hospitality, 632
PC Flowers and Gifts, 557
Peapod, 563
JC Penney, 10, 111, 236, 264, 454, 455
Pennzoil, 415
PeopleSoft, Inc., 221, 271
Pepperidge Farms, 414, 418
PepsiCo., 66, 84, 302, 414, 418, 420, 435, 449, 473, 474, 485, 503, 504, 544
Personality Puffs, 439
Pets.com, 556
Peugeot, 80
Pfizer, 88, 134

Pharmacia AB, 247
Pharmacia & Upjohn, 247
Philip Morris, 82, 88, 117, 145, 474
Philips Electronics, 19
Phillips Petroleum, 271
Phylway Construction, 190
Pizza Hut, 156, 396
Planet Hollywood, 464–68
Planned Parenthood, 117
Play It Again Sports, 158
Point Brewing Co., 418
Polaroid, 50–51, 419, 540
Porsche, 414
Potomac Electric Power Co. (Pepco), 207–8
Precision Tune Auto Care, 158–59
Preiss, Byron, Multimedia Co., 9
Preview Travel, 464, 557
Price Costco, 107, 108
Priceline.com, 435, 464
Procter & Gamble, 88, 89, 144, 212, 229, 230, 232, 236, 245, 248, 277, 416, 421, 427, 433, 444, 474, 657
Provant, 174
Prudential Securities, 661
Publix Super Markets, 102

Q

QAD, Inc., 222
Quaker Oats Co., 387, 417
QuickBooks, 567
Quicken, 656, 684
QVC, 455

R

Radio Shack, 455
Radisson Hotels, 293
Rainmaker Thinking, 296
Rainwater, Inc., 276
Ralston Purina Co., 420
RCA, 424
Redken, 390
Red Light's, 5
Red Roof Inns, 495–96
Reel.com, Inc., 428, 557
Relevant-Knowledge, 402
Reliance Group, 639
Reliance Systems, 372
Relocation Crime Lab, 30
Renault, 80
Reno Air, 315
Restrac, 262
Resumix, 262
ReTool, 158
Revco drugstores, 462
Rhone-Poulene SA, 159
Richards, Atwood, Co., 84
Richards Group, 240, 241
Rich's, 455
Ricoh, 109
Rite Aid, 450
Ritz Carlton, 113
RJR Nabisco Holdings Corp., 4

Roaman's, 387
Robs, 455
Rocket Electric Co., 66
Rocky Mountain Radar, 627
Rolex, 74
Rome Laboratory, 520
Ronco, 455
Roney & Co., 618
Royal Caribbean Cruise Lines, 110–11
Royal Dutch/Shell Group, 88, 220–21
Rudwear Collection, 174

S

Safeway, 455, 523
St. John's Wort Tortilla Chips, 439
Saks Fifth Avenue, 454, 455, 459
Salomon Brothers, 105
Salomon Smith Barney, 650
Sam's Club, 453
Santa Fe Southern Pacific Railroads, 274
SAP AG, 271
SAS Institute, Inc., 114, 259, 287, 307
Saturn, 65, 93, 123
SBC Communications, 157
Schaffner, Hart, and Marx, 449
Schwab, Charles, & Co., 7, 428, 473, 647–48, 656, 661, 672, 673
Schwartz Communications, 144
Schwinn, 419
Scotsman Industries, 644–45, 645
Sears, 274, 454, 540
Second Chance Body Armor, 166–67
Secure Computing, 91
Seiko, 421
Service Master, 87
Service Merchandise, 455
7-Eleven, 455
Seven Seas, 423
Shell International Ltd., 222
Sherwin-Williams, 449
Ship 'n Shore, 455
ShopperConnection, 557
Shopping.com, 543
Shop Rite, 325
Shuhei Toyoda, 36
Shurfine, 419
Siemens A.G., 87
Sierra Club, 3
Silicon Graphics, Inc., 172, 292
SMART Commercial Kitchen system, 366
Smarte Carte, Inc., 99–100
Smart Money, 661, 674
SmithKline, 88
Snap-on Tools, 274
Société Cease de Microelectronic et d'Horlogerie SA, 35
Softbank Corp., 83
Sony, 419, 421, 424, 432, 433, 451
Southwest Airlines, 105, 114, 260, 291
Spaulding Company, 82
Spectrum Signal Processing, Inc., 282–83

Sprint, 512
Starbucks, 90, 115, 260, 658
Stardot Consulting, 171
Stariye Petrishchi, financial crisis in, 70
Statistical Research Inc. (SRI), 401
Stearns, Bear, 662
Steelcase, 113
Stern, David, 333–34
Stevens, J. P., 333
Stick-Up, 422
Strauss, Karl, Breweries, 638
Strauss, Levi, and Company, 7, 17, 54,
    55, 83, 104, 106, 118, 434,
    455, 471, 472, 492, 540
Stryker, 421
Sumitomo Corp., 638
Sunkist, 150
SupplyBase, 543
Sure deodorant, 414
Suzuki, 83, 390

T

T. J. Maxx, 455
Taco Bell, 151, 156
Tandy, 264
Tanqueray, 115
Target, 429, 455, 459
Taurus, 422
Tax Cut, 705
Taylor California Cellars, 431
Taylor Made Golf, 349
TBM Consulting, 203
TDIndustries, 114, 264
Telecom, 134
Television Network (NTN), 178
Texaco, 102, 265
Texas Instruments, 105, 260–61
TGIFriday franchises, 293
Thai, 259
3M, 427
Tide, 89
Timberline boots, 451
Time Warner, 134
Toronto Blue Jays, 440–41
Tositos, 487
Toyota Motor, 36, 53, 65, 80, 85, 88,
    90, 115, 214, 239–40, 368, 429
Toys "R" Us, 455, 534, 546, 560
TransUnion, 526, 690
Trans World Airlines, 657
Travelers Group, 599

Travelocity, 464, 542
Travelodge, 54
TravelWeb, 464
Treebats, 172
Tricon Restaurants International, 156
Trilogy Software, Inc., 270, 271, 296
True Value, 150
Tupperware, 456
Turck, W. S., & Co., 123
Tylenol, 52

U

Unilever Group, 88, 491
United Airlines, 3, 259, 263, 386,
    413
United Bank of Philadelphia, 613
United Parcel Service (UPS), 260, 289,
    414
United States Olympic Committee
    (USOC), 243
United States Postal Service, 51, 264
United Way, 3, 486
Upjohn Co., 247
UPR, Inc., 270
Utz Potato Chip Co., 418

V

V-8 vegetable juice, 475
Valassis Communications, 283–84,
    312
Vanguard, 655, 656
Varig, 259
Vermont Teddy Bear, 374–75
Vernon, Lillian, 456
VF Corp., 243
Viacom, Inc., 428
Videoflicks Canado Ltd., 428
Virgin Airlines, 642
Virtual Vineyards, 557
Vittadini, Adrienne, 450
Vodaphone Group, 159
Volkswagen, 35, 36
Volvo, 311

W

Walgreen, 429
Wal-Mart, 18, 88, 134, 145, 260,
    385, 429, 444–45, 449, 454,
    455, 458, 546

Walt Disney Co., 9
Waterford, 451
Waterhouse Securities, 648
Wazzu Corp., 542
Weathervane Terrace Inn and Suites,
    593–94
Webber, Paine, 262
WebResume software, 27
Webvan, 562–63
Wells Fargo & Co., 434, 611, 612
Wells Lamont, 462
Wells Test Preparation Center, 567,
    589
Wendy's, 389, 422
Westinghouse, 80, 81, 449
Whirlpool, 413, 429, 432
Whitlenge, 645
Who's On First, 4
Wicks 'n' Sticks, 151
Williamson-Dickie, 1, 2, 21
Winn Dixie, 455
Wired Ventures, Inc., 428
Woolworths, 455
WordPerfect, 509
Work/Family Directions, 144
Workforce Solutions, 276
World Bank, 76–77
Wrigley, 109, 450
Wyndham Hotels, 632

X

Xerox, 87, 89, 271, 302
Xerox Technology Ventures (XTV),
    172–73

Y

Yahoo!, 198–99, 199, 432, 439,
    539, 552, 651

Z

Zales Jewelers, 74, 455
ZSHelp, 529
ZymeTX, 3

For permission to reproduce the photographs on the pages indicated, acknowledgment is made to the following: